South India

Paul Harding
Janine Eberle, Patrick Horton,
Amy Karafin, Simon Richmond

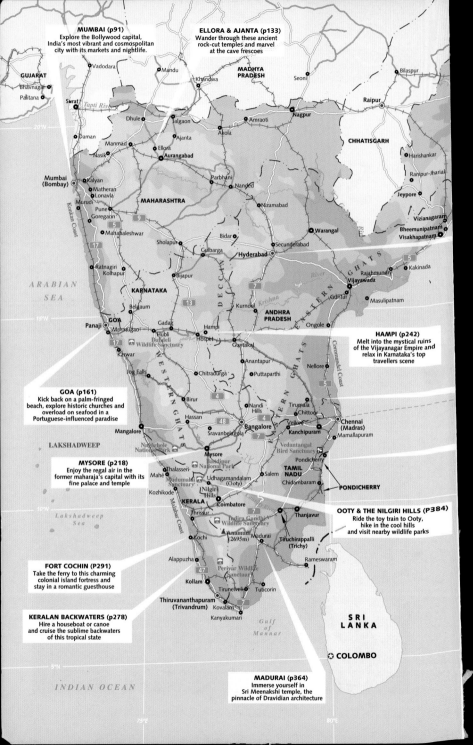

MUMBAI (p91)
Explore the Bollywood capital, India's most vibrant and cosmopolitan city with its markets and nightlife.

ELLORA & AJANTA (p133)
Wander through these ancient rock-cut temples and marvel at the cave frescoes

HAMPI (p242)
Melt into the mystical ruins of the Vijayanagar Empire and relax in Karnataka's top travellers scene

GOA (p161)
Kick back on a palm-fringed beach, explore historic churches and overload on seafood in a Portuguese-influenced paradise

MYSORE (p218)
Enjoy the regal air in the former maharaja's capital with its fine palace and temple

FORT COCHIN (P291)
Take the ferry to this charming colonial island fortress and stay in a romantic guesthouse

KERALAN BACKWATERS (p278)
Hire a houseboat or canoe and cruise the sublime backwaters of this tropical state

OOTY & THE NILGIRI HILLS (P384)
Ride the toy train to Ooty, hike in the cool hills and visit nearby wildlife parks

PONDICHERRY

MADURAI (p364)
Immerse yourself in Sri Meenakshi temple, the pinnacle of Dravidian architecture

GUJARAT
MADHYA PRADESH
CHHATISGARH
MAHARASHTRA
KARNATAKA
GOA
ANDHRA PRADESH
KERALA
TAMIL NADU
LAKSHADWEEP
SRI LANKA

ARABIAN SEA
Laksadweep Sea
INDIAN OCEAN
Gulf of Mannar
Konkan Coast
WESTERN GHATS
EASTERN GHATS
DECCAN
Malabar Coast
Coromandel Coast

Vadodara
Mandu
Khandwa
Seoni
Bilaspur
Raipur
Bhavnagar
Palitana
Surat
Tapti River
Dhule
Jalgaon
Amraoti
Nagpur
Daman
Manmad
Ajanta
Akola
Nasik
Ellora
Aurangabad
Harishankar
Mumbai (Bombay)
Kalyan
Matheran
Lonavla
Parbhani
Nanded
Nizamabad
Ranipur-Jharial
Jeypore
Murud
Pune
Goregaon
Mahabaleshwar
Bidar
Warangal
Vizianagaram
Bheemunipatnam
Visakhapatnam
Ratnagiri
Kolhapur
Sholapur
Gulbarga
Secunderabad
Bijapur
Hyderabad
Belgaum
Kurnool
Rajahmundry
Kakinada
Vijayawada
Panaji
Mormugao
Gadag
Hampi
Guntur
Masulipatnam
Hubli
Hospet
Dandeli Wildlife Sanctuary
Guntakal
Karwar
Anantapur
Ongole
Jog Falls
Chitradurga
Puttaparthi
Nellore
Birur
Nandi Hills
Tirumala
Chittoor
Hassan
Bangalore
Vellore
Chennai (Madras)
Mangalore
Sravanbelagola
Kanchipuram
Mamallapuram
Nagarhole National Park
Mysore
Vedantangal Bird Sanctuary
Bandipur National Park
Pondicherry
Thalasseri
Udhagamandalam (Ooty)
Salem
Mahé
Mudumalai Sanctuary
Nilgiri Hills
Chidambaram
Kozhikode
Coimbatore
Thrissur
Indira Gandhi Wildlife Sanctuary
Thanjavur
Anaimudi 2695m
Kochi
Madurai
Tiruchirappalli (Trichy)
Alappuzha
Periyar Wildlife Sanctuary
Rameswaram
Kollam
Tirunelveli
Tuticorin
Thiruvananthapuram (Trivandrum)
Kovalam
Kanyakumari
COLOMBO

20°N
15°N
10°N
5°N
75°E
80°E

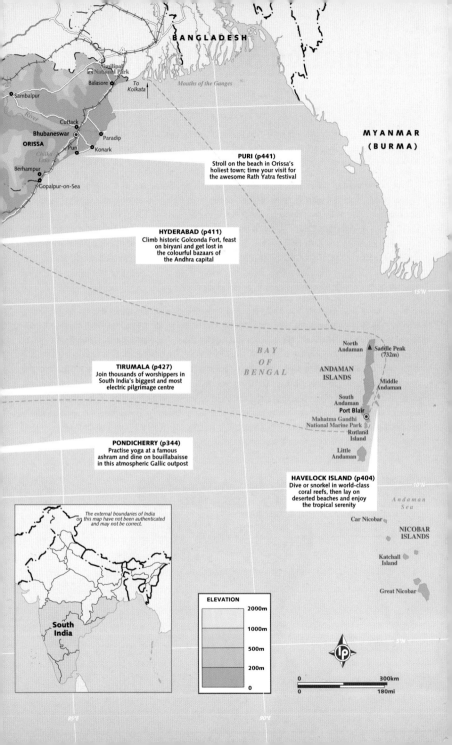

BANGLADESH

MYANMAR
(BURMA)

Mouths of the Ganges

Simlipal
National Park
Balasore
To
Kolkata

Sambalpur

Cuttack
Bhubaneswar
ORISSA
Paradip
Puri
Konark

Berhampur
Chilka
Lake

Gopalpur-on-Sea

PURI (p441)
Stroll on the beach in Orissa's
holiest town; time your visit for
the awesome Rath Yatra festival

HYDERABAD (p411)
Climb historic Golconda Fort, feast
on biryani and get lost in
the colourful bazaars of
the Andhra capital

15°N

BAY
OF
BENGAL

North
Andaman
Saddle Peak
(732m)

ANDAMAN
ISLANDS

Middle
Andaman

South
Andaman
Port Blair

Mahatma Gandhi
National Marine Park

Rutland
Island

TIRUMALA (p427)
Join thousands of worshippers in
South India's biggest and most
electric pilgrimage centre

Little
Andaman

PONDICHERRY (p344)
Practise yoga at a famous
ashram and dine on bouillabaisse
in this atmospheric Gallic outpost

HAVELOCK ISLAND (p404)
Dive or snorkel in world-class
coral reefs, then lay on
deserted beaches and enjoy
the tropical serenity

10°N

Andaman
Sea

Car Nicobar

NICOBAR
ISLANDS

Katchall
Island

Great Nicobar

The external boundaries of India
on this map have not been authenticated
and may not be correct.

South
India

5°N

ELEVATION
2000m
1000m
500m
200m
0

0   300km
0   180mi

85°E   90°E

Destination South India

Like a giant wedge driving into the Indian Ocean, peninsular South India is the Hindu heartland of the subcontinent, a vastly different place from the landlocked mountains and deserts of the north.

This is the 'softer' side of India, where thousands of kilometres of coastline wrap around fertile plains and the gentle hills of the Western and Eastern ghats (mountains), and the double-barrelled monsoon brings distinct wet and dry seasons. This is the India you're looking for if you're in search of the laid-back beaches and tropical backwaters of Goa and Kerala; the riotously carved, towering Hindu temples of Tamil Nadu and Karnataka; the upbeat, modern urban India of Bangalore and Mumbai (Bombay); the easily accessible hiking and wildlife watching in the hills and sanctuaries away from the coast; and the unfettered rural and tribal cultures of Andhra Pradesh and Orissa.

South India is an extraordinarily diverse region in terms of landscapes, peoples and cultures, which makes it a rewarding and fascinating destination for travellers. The major cities – Mumbai, Chennai (Madras), Bangalore and Hyderabad – are prosperous thanks to the IT revolution, but it's away from here that you'll discover the intricacies of a country brimming with colour and contradictions. Experience Indian hospitality on a long train trip, join the thronging pilgrims to holy sites you'd never heard of, get caught up in a noisy temple festival, or spend time practising yoga and meditation in a serene ashram. South India offers a gentle pace of travel, most sites are easily accessible and the beach is never very far away. India is too vast to explore in a single trip, so settle into the south and enjoy the journey.

PAUL BEINSSE

Beaches & Backwaters

Float along the lush, green backwaters (p278) of Kerala

KAREN TRIST

Go fishing the traditional way in Fort Cochin (p291), Kerala

NOBORU KOMINE

Experience beach culture on Palolem beach (p200), Goa

PAUL HARDING

Cities & Towns

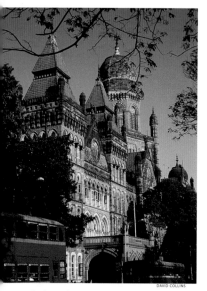

Soak up the inspiring remnants of British imperialism in Mumbai (p91)

Shop for your supper at the markets in Panaji (Panjim; p167), Goa

Live it up among the hustle and bustle of the MG Rd area of Bangalore (p215), Karnataka

Cook up a storm in Hyderabad (p411), Andhra Pradesh

Explore the winding streets of Pune
(p149), Maharashtra

Go vegetable shopping at Devaraja Market (p221),
Mysore, Karnataka

Historic Sites

Wander among awe-inspiring rock carvings at Viswakarma Cave (p134), Ellora, Maharashtra

View the magnificent Basilica of Bom Jesus in Old Goa (p177), Goa

Prepare for a journey to nirvana alongside the reclining Buddha at Ajanta (p135), Maharashtra

Admire the amazingly detailed Five Rathas (chariots) in Mamallapuram (Mahabalipuram; p331), Tamil Nadu

PAUL BIGLAND

Stroll through the ancient ruins of Hampi (p242), Karnataka

PAUL BIGLAND

Step back in time at the Maharaja's Palace (p220), Mysore, Karnataka

PAUL HARDING

Temples & Religious Sites

EDDIE GERALD

Meditate on life at Vaikunta Perumal Temple (p339), Kanchipuram, Tamil Nadu

Gaze upon divine sculptures at Sri Meenakshi Temple (p366), Madurai, Tamil Nadu

CRAIG PERSHOUSE

Worship among the intricate Dravidian carving at Sri Meenakshi Temple (p366), Madurai, Tamil Nadu

NOBORU KOMIE

Study intricately carved images of erotica on the Sun Temple (p447), Konark, Orissa

HIRA PUNJABI

Spy upon the 12th-century Jagannath Mandir (p443), Puri, Orissa

HIRA PUNJABI

Stroll through the stunning 1000-pillared hall at Devarajaswami Temple (p339), Kanchipuram, Tamil Nadu

EDDIE GERALD

Arts & Festivals

NOBORU KOMINE

Observe the beauty and ritual of Kathakali dance in Kochi (Cochin; p297), Kerala

Experience the chaotic fun of honouring Ganesh in the Ganesh Chaturthi festival (p96), Mumbai

KAREN TF

Soak up the atmosphere at the Thrissur Pooram festival (p303), Thrissur (Trichur), Kerala

PAUL BEINSS

Contents

Lonely Planet books provide independent advice. Lonely Planet does not accept advertising in guidebooks, nor do we accept payment in exchange for listing or endorsing any place or business. Lonely Planet writers do not accept discounts or payments in exchange for positive coverage of any sort.

लोनली प्लैनेट द्वारा प्रकाशित पुस्तकों में निष्पक्ष सूचना दी जाती है। लोनली प्लैनेट अपनी मार्गदर्शिकाओं में कोई विज्ञापन नहीं छापते। हम किसी व्यवसाय और किसी जगह का समर्थन करने या उनको अपनी सूची में सम्मिलित करने के लिए कोई धनराशि भी स्वीकार नहीं करते। लोनली प्लैनेट के सभी लेखक किसी स्थान के बारे में सकारात्मक सूचना देने के एवज में किसी तरह की छूट या रुपया-पैसा स्वीकार नहीं कर सकते।

லோன்லீ பிளானட் (Lonely Planet) வெளியீடுகள் சுதந்திரமான ஆலோசனைகளை வழங்குகின்றது. வழிகாட்டி நூல்களில் விளம்பரம் செய்வதை லோன்லீ பிளானட் ஏற்பதில்லை, அத்துடன் ஏதாவது ஒரு இடத்தை அல்லது ஒரு வியாபாரத்தை பட்டியல் படுத்துவதற்காக நாம் பணம் பெறுவதில்லை. லோன்லீ பிளானட் எழுத்தாளர்கள் எவ்வித திடமான ஆதரவுகளையும் வழங்குவதற்காக சலுகைகளையோ அல்லது பணம் கொடுப்பனவுகளையோ பெறுவதில்லை.

The Authors	16
Getting Started	19
Itineraries	24
Snapshot	32
History	34
The Culture	48
Environment	69
Food & Drink	80

Mumbai (Bombay) 91

History	92
Orientation	93
Information	93
Sights	98
Activities	105
Walking Tour	105
Courses	106
Tours	106
Sleeping	106
Eating	110
Drinking	112
Entertainment	113
Shopping	115
Getting There & Away	116
Getting Around	119
GREATER MUMBAI	120
Elephanta Island	120
Sanjay Gandhi National Park	121

Maharashtra 122

NORTHERN MAHARASHTRA	125
Nasik	125
Around Nasik	127
Aurangabad	128
Around Aurangabad	132
Ellora	133
Ajanta	135
Jalgaon	138
Lonar Meteorite Crater	139
Nagpur	139
Around Nagpur	141
Sevagram	141
Around Sevagram	141
SOUTHERN MAHARASHTRA	142
Konkan Coast	142
Matheran	144
Lonavla	146
Karla & Bhaja Caves	148
Pune	149
Around Pune	156
Mahabaleshwar	156
Around Mahabaleshwar	158
Kolhapur	159

Goa 161

NORTH GOA	167
Panaji (Panjim)	167
Old Goa	176
Torda	178
Mapusa	178
Fort Aguada & Candolim	179
Calangute & Baga	181
Anjuna	186
Vagator & Chapora	188
Chapora To Arambol	190
Arambol (Harmal)	191
Terekhol (Tiracol) Fort	193
SOUTH GOA	193
Margao (Madgaon)	193
Chandor	195
Loutolim	195
Bogmalo & Arossim	196
Colva & Benaulim	196
Benaulim To Palolem	199
Palolem & Around	200
CENTRAL GOA	202
Ponda & Around	202
Bondla Wildlife Sanctuary	202
Molem & Bhagwan Mahavir Wildlife Sanctuary	202
Dudhsagar Falls	203

Karnataka 204

SOUTHERN KARNATAKA	207
Bangalore	207
Around Bangalore	218
Mysore	218
Around Mysore	226
Bandipur National Park	227
Nagarhole National Park	228
Tibetan Settlements	228
Madikeri (Mercara)	229
Around Madikeri	231
Hassan	232
Belur & Halebid	233
Sravanabelagola	234
THE COAST	235
Mangalore	235
Around Mangalore	238
Jog Falls	239
Gokarna	240
CENTRAL KARNATAKA	242
Hampi	242
Hospet	247
Hubli	248
NORTHERN KARNATAKA	249
Badami	249
Around Badami	252
Bijapur	252
Bidar	256

Kerala 258

SOUTHERN KERALA	261
Thiruvananthapuram (Trivandrum)	261
Around Trivandrum	267
Kovalam	267
Around Kovalam	270
Varkala	272
Kollam (Quilon)	275
Around Kollam	277
Alappuzha (Alleppey)	277
Kottayam	282
Around Kottayam	284
THE WESTERN GHATS	284
Periyar Wildlife Sanctuary	284
Munnar	287
Around Munnar	289
Parambikulam Wildlife Sanctuary	290
CENTRAL KERALA	290
Kochi (Cochin)	290

Around Kochi	301
Thrissur (Trichur)	301
Around Thrissur	304
NORTHERN KERALA	304
Kozhikode (Calicut)	304
Wayanad Wildlife Sanctuary	306
Kannur (Cannanore)	307
Bekal	309
LAKSHADWEEP	309
Bangaram Island	310
Agatti Island	310
Kadmat Island	311
Minicoy Island	311

Tamil Nadu 312

CHENNAI (MADRAS)	316
History	316
Orientation	316
Information	316
Sights	320
Courses	323
Tours	323
Sleeping	323
Eating	325
Drinking	326
Entertainment	326
Shopping	327
Getting There & Away	327
Getting Around	330
NORTHERN TAMIL NADU	330
Chennai To Mamallapuram	330
Mamallapuram (Mahabalipuram)	331
Around Mamallapuram	337
Vedantangal Bird Sanctuary	337
Kanchipuram	337
Vellore	340
Tiruvannamalai	342
Gingee (Senji)	343
Pondicherry	344
Auroville	351
CENTRAL TAMIL NADU	352
Chidambaram	352
Kumbakonam	354
Around Kumbakonam	355
Cauvery Delta	356
Thanjavur (Tanjore)	356
Around Thanjavur	360
Tiruchirappalli (Trichy)	360
SOUTHERN TAMIL NADU	364

Madurai	364
Rameswaram	370
Kanyakumari (Cape Comorin)	372
THE WESTERN GHATS	375
Kodaikanal (Kodai)	375
Indira Gandhi (Annamalai) Wildlife Sanctuary	379
Coimbatore & Around	379
Coonoor	382
Kotagiri	384
Udhagamandalam (Ooty)	384
Mudumalai National Park	390

Andaman & Nicobar Islands 392

Port Blair	398
Around Port Blair & South Andaman	403
Havelock Island	404
Neil Island	406
Long Island	407
Middle Andaman	407
North Andaman	407
Little Andaman	408

Andhra Pradesh 409

Hyderabad & Secunderabad	411
Nagarjunakonda	422
Warangal	423
Around Warangal	424
Visakhapatnam	424
Around Visakhapatnam	425
Vijayawada	426
Tirumala & Tirupathi	427
Around Tirupathi	429
Puttaparthi	430
Lepakshi	431

Orissa 432

Bhubaneswar	435
SOUTHEASTERN ORISSA	441
Puri	441
Raghurajpur	446
Konark	447
Chilika Lake	449
Gopalpur-on-sea	450
WESTERN ORISSA	451
Taptapani	451
Jeypore	451

Around Jeypore 452
Jeypore To Sambalpur 453
Sambalpur 453
Around Sambalpur 453
NORTHEASTERN ORISSA 454
Similipal National Park 454
Jashipur 454
Baripada 455
Cuttack 455
Balasore 455
Chandipur 455
Bhitarkanika Wildlife Sanctuary 456

Lalitgiri, Udayagiri & Ratnagiri 456

Directory 457

Transport 487

Health 501

Language 509

Glossary 515

Behind the Scenes 523

World Time Zones 526

Index 531

Map Legend 540

Regional Map Contents

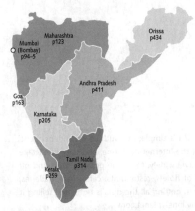

Maharashtra p123
Mumbai (Bombay) p94–5
Orissa p434
Andhra Pradesh p411
Goa p163
Karnataka p205
Tamil Nadu p314
Kerala p259
Andaman & Nicobar Islands p394

The Authors

PAUL HARDING

Coordinating Author, Tamil Nadu,
Andaman & Nicobar Islands

After almost losing his passport to a scam artist in Delhi on his first trip to India eight years ago, Paul has gotten the hang of subcontinental travel during six return visits. Over the past 15 years he has worked as a journalist, travel editor and writer, backpacked around most of Asia, travelled overland from Kathmandu to London and contributed to numerous Lonely Planet guides, including *India* and *Goa*. For this edition he researched Tamil Nadu and the Andaman Islands twice – returning after the Boxing Day tsunami for a second update.

THE COORDINATING AUTHOR'S FAVOURITE TRIP

I love most parts of South India (with particular fondness for Goa and the Andaman Islands – and not only for the beaches!), but if I had to choose one trip I'd combine the chaos of urban India and the beauty of South Indian temple architecture with the coast and the mountains. Starting in **Mumbai** (Bombay; p91), I'd head down to **Goa** (p161), shift across to **Hampi** (p242) for its wonderful temples set in a lunar landscape, go south to hi-tech **Bangalore** (p207) and **Mysore** (p218), head up into the hills to **Udhagamandalam** (Ooty; p384), toy train down and on to **Kochi** (Cochin; p290) in Kerala, take a backwater boat trip from **Alappuzha** (Aleppey; p277) and finally travel across to **Madurai** (p364) for the Sri Meenakshi temple.

LONELY PLANET AUTHORS

Why is our travel information the best in the world? It's simple: our authors are independent, dedicated travellers. They don't research using just the Internet or phone, and they don't take freebies in exchange for positive coverage. They travel widely, to all the popular spots and off the beaten track. They personally visit thousands of hotels, restaurants, cafés, bars, galleries, palaces, museums and more – and they take pride in getting all the details right, and telling it how it is. For more, see the authors section on www.lonelyplanet.com.

JANINE EBERLE   Kerala

Janine Eberle joined Lonely Planet in 2000 as an editor, and first visited Kerala a couple of years later, where she learned never to ask a leading question and how to decipher *Trains at a Glance*, and pondered the multiple meanings of the head wobble. Janine lives in Melbourne, Australia, where she's the Commissioning Editor for Lonely Planet's South and Central Asia books.
It's a lie about *Trains at a Glance*.

PATRICK HORTON   Orissa

Donning a disguise of kurta pyjama and chappals, Patrick Horton, free-lance travel writer and photographer, slipped around Orissa searching out the 'good oil' for this guide. When not on his annual visit to India, Patrick nurtures his peach trees, restores and rides classic motorcycles, and adds to his collection of old books.

AMY KARAFIN   Andhra Pradesh, Karnataka

Amy Karafin grew up on the US Jersey shore, where she developed a curiosity about the horizon that grew into a phobia of residence. Indian in several former lives, she headed straight there after studying for an extended trip that would turn out to be karmically ordained. She spent the next few years alternating between New York and faraway lands, until finally, fed up with the irony of being a travel editor in a Manhattan cubicle, she relinquished her MetroCard and her black skirts to make a living closer to the equator. She lives in Dakar, where she writes and translates in a little studio by the sea.

SIMON RICHMOND   Mumbai (Bombay), Goa, Maharashtra

This was travel writer and photographer Simon Richmond's third trip to India. He first visited in 1999 to research a series of adventures in southern India that took him from the backwaters of Kerala and through the temples of Tamil Nadu to the Andaman Islands. Entranced by the experience, he returned in 2000 at the tail end of an epic overland haul from Istanbul to Kathmandu for Lonely Planet, when he visited northern India. Apart from authoring many guidebooks for Lonely Planet, Simon works for several other publishers, and has his features published in newspapers and magazines around the world.

CONTRIBUTING AUTHOR

Dr Trish Batchelor Trish is a general practitioner and travel medicine specialist who works at the Ciwec Clinic in Kathmandu, Nepal, as well as being a medical advisor to the Travel Doctor New Zealand clinics. Trish teaches travel medicine through the University of Otago, and is interested in underwater and high-altitude medicine, and the impact of tourism on host countries. She has travelled extensively through Southeast and East Asia, and particularly loves high-altitude trekking in the Himalaya.

Getting Started

Vibrant, inspiring, frustrating, laid-back, confronting, thought provoking and frustrating in equal measure, colourful India is an exciting challenge for the traveller. But whatever your preconceptions, South India is a surprisingly easy region in which to travel. There are fewer touts and scam-artists than in the north, and plenty of beaches to head for if travel gets too much. Covering a large area and with a wealth of natural and historical attractions, deciding where to go and what to see will be one of your biggest and most difficult decisions (see Itineraries, p24). But getting around is easier than you might think. Trains and buses run frequently, you can generally communicate with somebody in English, and accommodation – from budget fleapits to luxury hotels – is plentiful.

See Climate Charts (p462) for more information.

India is also very cheap, so travellers can get by on a budget that suits their needs and bank balance, and you can pick up just about anything you need when you get there – clothing, toiletries, extra bags, sunglasses, you name it – for less than you would at home. The trick is to pack light. The hot climate will probably mean those jeans and jackets will remain folded at the bottom of your pack and never see the light of day.

Planning a trip is always half the fun, so before you head off, spread out those maps, flip through your guidebook, read up and surf the Internet. A little preparation works wonders. Get visas, insurance, vaccinations and book flights well in advance. Work out a rough itinerary – you don't want to miss that spectacular festival by three days or plan to be relaxing on a Goan beach in June – but factor in a certain amount of flexibility, too, as India has a wonderful way of throwing up surprises and guiding you off the beaten track.

WHEN TO GO

Except in the elevated hills of the Western Ghats, South India is hot year-round and can be roughly divided into two main seasons – dry and wet (monsoon). There are two monsoon periods – the northeast and southwest monsoons – with dates varying slightly across the region.

DON'T LEAVE HOME WITHOUT...

- Swiss army knife – essential multipurpose tool
- Torch – for power blackouts and unlit lanes at night
- Moneybelt – to keep passport, tickets, travellers cheques and cash safe
- Sunscreen and sunglasses – the sun can be a killer
- Visa and insurance – a valid visa with as much time to run as possible!
- Mobile phone – cheap and easy to hook up, and handy for staying in touch
- Padlock – useful for locking your pack, or rooms and lockers at hotels
- Swimsuit and towel – for all the good beaches in South India
- Debit or credit card – to access the widespread and convenient ATMs that accept foreign cards
- Sense of adventure and humour – for everything from haggling with a rickshaw driver or battling train queues, to discovering true Indian hospitality

MONSOON

The onset of the monsoon season brings mixed blessings. For locals, especially farmers, it means much-needed rain. For fishermen it's time to pack up the boats and nets, and wait out the stormy conditions. For travellers, it means a humid wet period when umbrellas are standard issue and clothes never seem to dry. However, many feel the monsoon brings out the beauty of rural South India, when paddy fields and forests turn an emerald green.

Kerala is the first place the southwest monsoon strikes in early June, drenching the state as it sweeps in eastward from the Arabian Sea. As it rises over the Western Ghats, it cools and soaks the windward slopes before dropping over the leeward side, parts of which receive only about a quarter of the rainfall dumped on the windward side. Within about 10 days the monsoon has usually travelled as far as northern Maharashtra, and by early July it has covered the entire country.

Karnataka's Western Ghats are among the wettest parts of South India, with Madikeri recording an annual average rainfall of 3250mm. In contrast, the stony Deccan region around Hyderabad receives about 700mm of rain each year.

A second soaking occurs in Tamil Nadu and Kerala in November and early December when the retreating monsoon (commonly referred to as the northeast or winter monsoon) blows in from the Bay of Bengal. The coasts of Andhra Pradesh, Orissa and Tamil Nadu are occasionally hit by cyclones during these months.

Being tropical, you won't find the large variations in temperature found in northern India.

In general, October to March is the best time to visit South India. It is relatively dry and cool, although in November and the beginning of December parts of Tamil Nadu and Kerala get a soaking as the northeast monsoon retreats across them. In the beach resorts of Goa some facilities (such as beach shacks) don't open until late October and, in the weeks immediately after the monsoon (ie in October), there can be strong rips, which can make swimming hazardous. Accommodation prices in popular tourist places, such as Goa, Kerala and the offshore islands, hit a peak around Christmas and New Year.

Temperatures start to rise rapidly in most places in late March, and by April South India sizzles. The peak travel season in the mountains is April to June, where the altitude provides welcome relief from the heat of the plains. Conversely, the Western Ghats can get misty and quite cold in winter (late December and January), and the nights are often cold regardless of the time of year.

The climate in the Andaman and Nicobar Islands is tropical, with temperatures averaging 29°C, but this is moderated by sea breezes. The islands receive about 3300mm of rain annually, most of it during the southwest monsoon (May to September), and during the cyclonic storms in October and November. Lakshadweep has similar tropical weather.

Apart from climate, you might want to consider the timing of festivals when planning your trip. Diwali, Dussehra and Ganesh Chaturthi are the three big Hindu festivals in October and November. Christmas is an interesting time to be in Goa thanks to its large Christian population and enduring Christmas traditions. See Festivals (p468) for more information.

COSTS & MONEY

India is cheap. At the budget end of the scale it can be one of the least expensive countries in the world for travel, but of course you can also stay in luxury hotels, hire a car and driver, fly between cities and ultimately spend a fortune. The beauty of India is that you'll get excellent value for money regardless of your budget. Costs can vary depending on the season – high-season prices for hotels can be 50% more, but usually only at popular tourist spots – and depend on if you're travelling solo or with a group. High season is November to February in most regions, with a specific peak season of mid-December to early January in coastal resorts. High season in the mountains (such as hill stations) is April to June.

Accommodation is the major expense, but this can range from a beach-side shack or rundown pilgrims' lodging for Rs 50 to 100 a night to business or luxury hotels in larger towns and resorts for Rs 1000 to 3000 a night. Clean, comfortable midrange accommodation costs around Rs 500 to 900 for a double room. Eating out can cost Rs 20 for an all-you-can-eat thali (traditional meal) or Rs 300 for a fine-dining splurge in a city hotel restaurant. You can eat well in a sit-down restaurant virtually anywhere for less than Rs 100. Alcohol is comparatively expensive – Rs 50 to 100 for a bottle of beer in a bar or restaurant. Transport costs are low: a 100km train trip costs Rs 35 in 2nd class and from Rs 158 in AC sleeper class. Buses are even cheaper. You can hire a car with driver for a full day for around Rs 800.

In recent years entry fees to many historical sites and even museums have been cranked up, with a higher charge for foreign tourists. Entry for foreigners to all World Heritage sites, which include Hampi, Ajanta and Ellora, and Konark's Sun Temple, is Rs 250 (US$5). Lesser-known sights and museums usually cost around Rs 10 (many are free), with additional charges for cameras and videos.

So how does this translate to a daily budget? Shoestring travellers staying in cheap hotels, eating at local restaurants and travelling by bus or 2nd-class train can get by on Rs 500 (US$12) per person per day for basic expenses. A more generous budget, allowing for occasional restaurant splurges, a few drinks and admission to sights, is US$20 to US$35. A budget of Rs 2500 to 3500 (US$50 to US$70) a day will allow for a good midrange hotel, restaurant meals, taxi rides and AC train travel. If you plan to stay in five-star hotels, count on at least US$100 per day. On top of this you can add shopping expenses, the odd domestic flight and extras, such as trekking tours and diving.

HOW MUCH?

100km train ride
Rs 35 to 542

Internet access (one hour)
Rs 15 to 50

Haircut/shave Rs 50/15

Newspaper Rs 3

Sarong Rs 50

TRAVEL LITERATURE

Reading other travellers' accounts of South India is a great way to get a feel for the region.

Chasing The Monsoon, by Alexander Frater, is an Englishman's story of his monsoon-chasing journey from Kovalam (Kerala) to one of the wettest places on earth, Cherrapunji in Meghalaya in the Northeastern Region. It offers a captivating window into the monsoon's significance and its impact on people.

Geoffrey Moorhouse's *Om: An Indian Pilgrimage* provides erudite observations into the lives of a vibrant potpourri of people in South India, from humble coir makers to royalty and holy men. This book pays particular attention to the ashrams of South India.

Take an architectural tour with Sarayu Ahuja in *Where the Streets Lead*. It covers several of South India's major settlements and cities, offering interesting insights into not just the structures, but the lives of the people who inhabit them.

Maximum City: Bombay Lost & Found, by Suketu Mehta, is an incisively researched and elegantly written epic, equal parts memoir, travelogue and journalism, which focuses on the vibrant city of Mumbai (Bombay) – riots, gang warfare, Bollywood, bar girls and all.

Third Class Ticket, by Heather Wood, is a funny and at times poignant account of a 15,000km journey across India by a group of poor Bengali villagers.

In *Divining the Deccan* Bill Aitken rides through the little-visited centre of South India on a motorbike, painting a fascinating picture of the south with some fine historical and cultural detail.

The Smile of Murugan, by Michael Wood, profoundly depicts the author's time in Tamil Nadu during the mid-1990s. Revolving around a pilgrimage in a bus, it offers compelling insights into this intriguing South Indian state.

William Sutcliffe's *Are You Experienced?* is an hilarious tale of a novice backpacker, who accompanies his best friend's girlfriend to India in an attempt to seduce her. Perceptively portrays the backpacker scene in India.

TOP FIVES

Great Reads

Nothing beats a good read, and there are plenty of novels set in the seething, spiritual mass of India. Explore the hustle and bustle of Mumbai (Bombay) city life in *Shantaram* or *Midnight's Children*, or head off the beaten track and delve into Indian culture and history with *White Mughals* or *A Fine Balance*. For additional recommended reading, see p21, p59 and the boxed text, p114.

- *Shantaram* by Gregory David Roberts
- *Midnight's Children* by Salman Rushdie
- *White Mughals* by William Dalrymple
- *A Suitable Boy* by Vikram Seth
- *A Fine Balance* by Rohinton Mistry

Favourite Festivals

South India has a phenomenal variety of major and minor festivals – for comprehensive details, see p468 and the Festivals In... boxed texts appearing at the start of regional chapters.

- Ganesh Chaturthi (especially in Mumbai and Pune), August/September (p96)
- Ellora Dance & Music Festival (Ellora), December (p124)
- Feast of St Francis Xavier (Old Goa), 3-10 December (p164)
- Rath Yatra (Orissa), June/July (p433)
- Nehru Trophy Snake Boat Race (Kerala), August (p260)

Top Journeys

- Toy train to Ooty (Udhagamandalam; p389) – the miniature steam train to Ooty passes through spectacular mountain scenery
- Backwater cruise from Alappuzha (Alleppey) to Kollam (Quilon; see the boxed text, p278) – cruising the Keralan backwaters is an unforgettable experience
- Mumbai to Goa by train (p116) – travel down the Konkan coast on India's newest stretch of rail line
- Island hopping in the Andamans (p396) – lounge on the ferry deck and hop from one pristine island to another in the Andamans
- Cycling in Goa – ride from Panaji to Old Goa along the Ribander Causeway (p178)

INTERNET RESOURCES

Best Indian Sites (www.bestindiansites.com) Lists the most popular Indian websites.

Deccan Herald (www.deccanherald.com) Major South Indian newspaper with coverage of recent events.

Hindu (www.the-hindu.com) Comprehensive newspaper website.

Incredible India (www.incredibleindia.org) The official government tourism site, with national travel-related information.

India Today (www.india-today.com) Coverage of recent events.

Indiavarta (www.indiavarta.com) South Indian news and lifestyle site with links to shopping and weather sites.

Lonely Planet (www.lonelyplanet.com) Apart from plenty of useful links there's the popular Thorn Tree, where you can swap information with fellow travellers to India.

Maps of India (www.mapsofindia.com) An awesome assortment of maps, including thematic offerings, such as those pinpointing India's wildlife sanctuaries, and even its major golf courses and cricket stadiums.

National Informatics Centre (www.nic.in) Portal for Indian government websites.

New Ind Press (www.newindpress.com) Online news site devoted to South India.

Online Newspapers (www.onlinenewspapers.com/india.htm) Provides links to India's major national and regional newspapers, enabling you to stay tuned to what's happening where.

South India (www.southindia.com) True to its name, this vast portal focuses on South India with links to everything from universities to train timetables and a state-by-state guide.

Times of India (www.timesofindia.com) Major newspaper website.

Itineraries

CLASSIC ROUTES

SOUTH INDIA EXPRESS
Three to Eight Weeks / Mumbai to Chennai

sFrom Mumbai (Bombay), this route covers some of the best sights in Maharashtra, Karnataka and Tamil Nadu, ending in Chennai (Madras).

Start in **Mumbai** (p91), then head northeast to **Aurangabad** (p128), to visit the rock-cut caves at **Ellora** (p133) and **Ajanta** (p135). Journey south to **Pune** (p149) and its famous Osho Meditation Resort. It's a long but easy trip to **Bijapur** (p252), with the Golgumbaz, then south to the former Vijayanagar capital of **Hampi** (p242). Continue on to **Bangalore** (p207), the IT hub. Worth a detour is the pilgrimage centre of **Sravanabelagola** (p234), and the temples of **Belur** (p233) and **Halebid** (p234). Next the former Maharaja's capital of **Mysore** (p218) and for a change of pace, head into the Western Ghats to **Udhagamandalam** (Ooty; p384), with a stop at **Mudumalai National Park** (p390). Take the toy train down to Mettupalayam and west to **Kochi** (Cochin; p290). From here you can travel to the **Periyar Wildlife Sanctuary** (p284). It's then an easy trip to **Madurai** (p364) and the Sri Meenakshi Temple. Take the train up to **Chennai** (p316), with sidetrips to **Pondicherry** (p344), with its French flavour, or the beach at **Mamallapuram** (Mahabalipuram; p331). From Chennai make a trip to **Tirumala** (p427), before finishing in Bangalore.

From Mumbai to Chennai and on to Bangalore, this route mostly steers away from the coast, but includes some of the best of South India's city life, temple towns and a journey into the mountains, where you can trek and look for wildlife. You'll need at least three weeks to cover the main stops, but to do this trip any justice, count on at least five weeks to cover the 3500km.

BEACHES & BACKWATERS   One to Three Months / Mumbai to Kovalam

For many travellers, South India is synonymous with the west-coast beaches and this stunning coastline can keep dedicated beachgoers occupied for months. Throw in the Keralan backwaters and you have a very cruisy tropical holiday.

Begin in **Mumbai** (p91) and spend an evening in the carnival atmosphere of Chowpatty Beach, then make a beeline for Goa, India's favourite beach state. After visiting the capital **Panaji** (Panjim; p167) and the ruined former Portuguese capital of **Old Goa** (p176), pick a beach that suits and settle in for some sun and sand. **Calangute** (p181) is the most developed beach, **Anjuna** (p186) and **Vagator** (p188) are still good for rave parties during December and January, while **Arambol** (p191) and **Palolem** (p200) are beautiful, relatively secluded beaches ideal for relaxing. Hit the rails southwards and get off at Karwar for **Gokarna** (p240), a dusty pilgrimage town leading to a string of secluded crescent beaches popular with the chilled-out, chillum-puffing crowd. A worthwhile detour from here is to **Jog Falls** (p239), India's highest waterfalls. Leaving Karnataka you enter the slender coastal state of Kerala. Pass through **Kozhikode** (Calicut; p304) and your next stop is the delightful island stronghold of Kochi's **Fort Cochin** (p291), reached from mainland Ernakulam. From there head to **Alappuzha** (Alleppey; p277), a great place to organise a serene houseboat journey through the backwaters of Kerala, or you can take the eight-hour cruise from Alappuzha to **Kollam** (Quilon; p275). From here it's a short trip south to **Varkala** (p272), a dramatic clifftop resort that remains idyllic and charming. Your last stop is further down the coast, near the tip of India. **Kovalam** (p267) is home to a small sweep of crescent beaches offering good places to unwind and meet other travellers.

South India's western coastline makes for a laid-back tropical holiday. Heading south from Mumbai, you're spoiled for choice with the beaches of Goa, **Karnataka and Kerala**. The sublime backwaters of Kerala make a scenic change of pace from the beach. This 1600km trip could be done in as little as three weeks, but to enjoy the slow pace of travel, allow six.

COAST TO COAST   Two to Three Months / Mumbai to Chennai

The southern tip of India offers everything from crowded cities and deserted beaches to the Hindu heartland with its riot of temples and festivals. With Mumbai and Chennai providing international gateways at opposite sides of the country, a popular route is to fly into one city and out of the other. For the first part of this route, see Beaches & Backwaters (p25), which takes you from Mumbai to Kovalam. From Kovalam or nearby **Thiruvananthapuram** (Trivandrum; p261), it's only about three hours to **Kanyakumari** (p372) in Tamil Nadu – India's 'Land's End' and a popular pilgrimage centre. From here take the train to **Madurai** (p364), one of Tamil Nadu's most popular temple towns thanks to the Sri Meenakshi temple.

From Madurai you can follow Tamil Nadu's temple route through **Tiruchirappalli** (Trichy; p360), with its superb Rock Fort Temple; **Thanjavur** (p356), famous for the World Heritage–listed Brihadishwara Temple, as well as Thanjavur Palace; and **Chidambaram** (p352), a dusty little town centred around the Nataraj Temple. From here take a bus to the French colonial enclave of **Pondicherry** (p344), famous for its ashram and its great French-inspired restaurants. A possible side trip from here is west to **Tiruvannamalai** (p342), an engaging town with a famous Shiva Temple and an ashram. From Pondicherry it's an easy trip up the coast to **Mamallapuram** (p331), popular with travellers for its laid-back beach, Shore Temple and ancient rock-cut monuments. Bird-watchers will enjoy a quick trip to the **Vedantangal Bird Sanctuary** (p337) about 50km west. From Mamallapuram it's only an hour north to **Chennai** (p316), where you can visit a film studio, stroll on Marina Beach and plan your next move.

Starting in Mumbai and finishing in Chennai (or vice versa), this route starts with the laid-back coastal route from Mumbai to Kovalam, then climbs up through Tamil Nadu, South India's Hindu heartland and the place to get acquainted with towering temples. Allow at least eight weeks for the 2400km trip.

ROADS LESS TRAVELLED

HEAD FOR THE HILLS   Three to Six Weeks / Mumbai to Munnar

A great way to get off the beaten track is to leave the coastal towns and go trekking in the national parks and hill country of the Western Ghats.

From Mumbai take the toy train up to **Matheran** (p144), a traffic-free hilltop retreat with walks and panoramic lookouts. Head back down via Lonavla and Pune before winding your way back up into the hills to **Mahabaleshwar** (p156), a hill station popular with Indian families and famous for its berry farms. From here it's a bit of a trek south to **Madikeri** (p229) in the Kodagu (Coorg) Hills, but worth it for the trekking and coffee plantations. Journey east to Mysore, and head back up into the hills again. Four adjoining national parks – **Bandipur** (p227) and **Nagarhole** (p228) in Karnataka, **Mudumalai** (p390) in Tamil Nadu and **Wayanad** (p306) in Kerala – form the Nilgiri Biosphere Reserve, and together they offer some of the best wildlife viewing, trekking and jungle camps in South India. From Mudumalai it's an easy trip to **Udhagamandalam** (Ooty; p384), a sprawling Raj-era hill station set amid beautiful hills and forests. If you still haven't had your fill of hiking and hill stations, head south from Coimbatore through the Palani Hills to **Kodaikanal** (p375), a much quainter and quieter town than Ooty. From Kodaikanal you can take a Kochi-bound bus to **Munnar** (p287), which boasts the world's highest tea plantations and dramatic mountain scenery. Another 70km south of here is the **Periyar Wildlife Sanctuary** (p284), a good place for wildlife watching, jungle trekking and lake cruises.

National parks, forests and cool hill stations make a welcome change from the coast and plains, especially when the heat gets too much. This 1500km route takes you to some of South India's best hill stations and finest wildlife-watching areas.

ACROSS THE DECCAN   Two to Six Weeks / Mumbai to Konark

The central and eastern parts of South India, including Andhra Pradesh and Orissa, are often overlooked by travellers. This route crosses the dry Deccan Plains and the Eastern Ghats from Mumbai to Bhubaneswar.

Starting in **Mumbai** (p91), journey by train to either **Pune** (p149) or the pilgrimage town of **Nasik** (p125). From either town it's an easy trip to **Aurangabad** (p128), the base for visiting the **Ellora** (p133) and **Ajanta** (p135) caves. It's a long trip across the interior to **Hyderabad** (p411), capital of Andhra Pradesh, and a fascinating blend of Muslim and Hindu cultures, colourful bazaars and the stunning Golconda Fort. Heading east you come to **Vijayawada** (p426), the heart of Andhran culture, with Hindu temples, rock-cut cave temples and a Buddhist site at nearby Amaravathi. From here the rail line runs up the coast into Orissa. Stop in at **Gopalpur-on-Sea** (p450), a peaceful village with an attractive beach and few crowds, then take a boat trip on **Chilika Lake** (p449), Asia's largest brackish lagoon and a haven for migratory birds. Next stop is **Bhubaneswar** (p435), Orissa's capital, but mainly a jumping-off point for the popular pilgrimage town **Puri** (p441) and the atmospheric Sun Temple at **Konark** (p447). If you still have time, head north for some wildlife watching at **Similipal National Park** (p454).

Not too many travellers set out to traverse east–west across the dry Deccan plains, but this interesting 2500km route takes you to some of the less-visited parts of South India, including Andhra Pradesh and Orissa, from the Arabian Sea to the Bay of Bengal. You could cover this comfortably in two or three weeks.

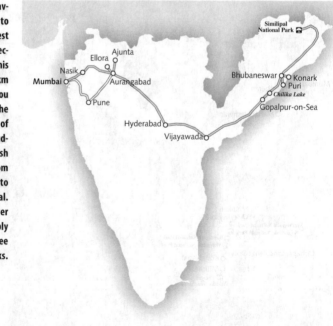

ISLAND HOPPING   Two to Four Weeks / Port Blair to Little Andaman

If you're after islands, deserted beaches, snorkelling and diving, the Andamans are hard to beat. The island chain, 1000km east of the mainland in the Bay of Bengal, can be reached by boat (three-day crossing) or air (two hours) from Chennai or Kolkata (Calcutta). From Chennai, you'll arrive by air or sea in the capital, **Port Blair** (p398), a busy town with little tropical charm, but some good museums and reminders of the colonial past. After a visit to **Ross Island** (p403) and the Cellular Jail, book a ferry to **Havelock Island** (p404), where you can stay in huts on the beach, and indulge in scuba diving, snorkelling or fishing. For a quieter alternative, stay on nearby **Neil Island** (p406). From Havelock there are ferries to **Rangat** (p407), with a possible stop at **Long Island** (p407). From Rangat a bus runs up through Middle Andaman to **Mayabunder** (p407), where you can take a boat to tiny **Avis Island** (p407). From Mayabunder, travel overland to **Diglipur** (p407) on North Andaman (or take an overnight ferry from Port Blair to Diglipur), a remote area where you can climb Saddle Peak or laze on deserted beaches. Back in Port Blair, hire a moped or catch a bus and head down to **Wandoor** (p403), the jumping-off point for the **Mahatma Gandhi Marine National Park** (p404) and Jolly Buoy and Red Skin Islands. Another possibility is to take a long ferry ride south to **Little Andaman** (p408), known for its surfing beaches and forests.

From Port Blair, fly or take the boat to Kolkata and head south to resume your journey in South India.

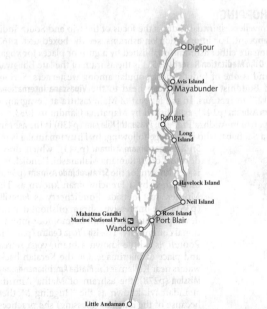

Travel in the beautiful Andaman Islands is a trip unto itself, so we've given them their own itinerary. If deserted beaches and turquoise waters aren't enough, superb diving and snorkelling should be! This route covers about 800km to 1000km of land and ferry travel. You'll need a minimum of two weeks and permit restrictions limit you to one month.

TAILORED TRIPS

TEMPLES & PILGRIMAGES

If there's one thing that will leave a mark on you during your trip in South India, it's likely to be the devotion to religion. There's a well-worn pilgrimage route through Tamil Nadu, which includes the temple towns of **Kanchipuram** (p337); **Tiruvannamalai** (p342); **Chidambaram** (p352); **Kumbakonam** (p354); **Thanjavur** (p356); **Tiruchirappalli** (Trichy; p360), with the Rock Fort Temple and Sri Ranganathaswamy Temple; **Madurai** (p364) for the Sri Meenakshi Temple; **Rameswaram** (p370), one of the four holiest Hindu pilgrimage places in India; and **Kanyakumari** (p372), where pilgrims flock not only for the Kumari Amman Temple, but also to see the sun rise and set at the tip of India.

In Andhra Pradesh, the Venkateshwara Temple at **Tirumala** (p427) receives as many as 100,000 pilgrims a day! In Karnataka, **Sravanabelagola** (p234) is a pilgrimage centre for Jains who come to honour the statue of Gomateshvara. **Gokarna** (p240), apart from being a chilled-out beach paradise, is one of South India's most sacred sites for Shaivites who come to worship at the Mahabaleshwara Temple. **Nasik** (p125) is Maharashtra's most holy pilgrimage town and host (every 12 years) to the massive Kumbh Mela. In Orissa, join the crowds at **Puri** (p441), one of the four holiest pilgrimage places in India.

ASHRAM HOPPING

For many travellers, spiritual India is the focus of the trip and South India doesn't disappoint. For information on ashrams, see the boxed text, p465. The following are either ashrams established by a guru or places for yoga.

In Pune, **Osho Meditation Resort** (p151) is the ashram of the late Bhagwan Rajneesh, and is one of India's most popular among westerners. Serious devotees of Buddhist meditation can head to the **Vipassana International Academy** (p127) in Igatpuri. In the far east of Maharashtra at Sevagram is the **Sevagram Ashram** (p141), established by Mahatma Gandhi in 1933.

At Puttaparthi in Andhra Pradesh, **Prasanthi Nilayam** (p430) is the ashram of Sri Sathya Sai Baba, who has a huge following. In Tiruvannamalai is the **Sri Ramanasramam Ashram** (p343), which draws devotees of Sri Ramana Maharashi. Pondicherry is well known for the **Sri Aurobindo Ashram** (p345), established by a Frenchwoman known as The Mother. Just outside Pondicherry is **Auroville** (p351), the impressive ashram offshoot that has developed into a large and harmonious international community. The **Isha Yoga Centre** (p379) in Poondi, is a little-known ashram, yoga retreat and place of pilgrimage. On the Keralan backwaters near Kollam is the **Matha Amrithanandamayi Mission** (p278), the ashram of Matha Amrithanandamayi, known as the 'Hugging Mother' because of the *darshan* (blessing) she practices, often hugging thousands in a session.

WORLD HERITAGE SITES

Of the 26 World Heritage Sites scattered throughout India, 10 are in South India and most represent ancient monuments or temples.

In Mumbai, the newest addition to the list is **Chhatrapati Shivaji Terminus** (p101) – better known as Victoria Terminus – the main railway station, and a riotous blend of architecture. **Elephanta Island** (p120), just out of Mumbai, boasts rock-cut cave temples dedicated to Shiva. The finest historical attractions in Maharashtra are the rock-cut cave temples at **Ellora** (p133) and the caves and frescoes at **Ajanta** (p135).

The churches and convents of Goa's former capital, **Old Goa** (p176), should not be missed. They include the Basilica Bom Jesus, Se Cathedral and the Church of St Francis Assisi. **Hampi** (p242) is a favourite as much for the atmosphere as for the stunning temples of the Vijayanagar Empire. Just north, the temples of **Pattadakal** (p252) are less well known, but the Virupaksha Temple is worth a look. At **Mamallapuram** (p331), the Shore Temple and Five Rathas are among a large group of monuments from the Pallava dynasty, while at **Thanjavur** (p356), the Brihadishwara Temple is the crowning glory. Finally you can't miss the Sun Temple at **Konark** (p447).

FOLLOWING THE FESTIVALS

The colour and exuberance of Indian festivals make for an unforgettable experience. The trick is to be in the right place at the right time. For details, see the Festivals boxed text in each regional chapter.

Ganesh Chaturthi (August/September; p96) is celebrated all over South India, but is best seen in Mumbai and Pune when the cities come alive. The **Ellora Dance & Music Festival** (December; p124) is a cultural event set against the stunning backdrop of the Kailasa Temple. Goa turns it on with India's best Christian festivals, the biggest being the **Feast of St Francis Xavier** (3-10 December; p164) in Old Goa.

Some of Karnataka's biggest bashes are in Bangalore, such as **Karaga** (March/April; p206), with a colourful procession at Dharmaraya Swamy Temple. One of the great **Dussehra** festivals (September/October; p206) is held in Mysore. Also worth a look is **Maha Mastakabhisheka** (p206) at Sravanabelagola in December 2005 to January 2006. This ceremony only happens once every 12 years. In Kerala, Thrissur is the festival hotspot with the elephant processions of **Thrissur Pooram** (April/May; p260). An exciting backwater event is the **Nehru Trophy Snake Boat Race** (2nd Saturday in August; p260) in Alappuzha (Alleppey).

The **Mamallapuram Dance Festival** (December-January; p315) in Tamil Nadu is a great cultural event and, there's also the **International Yoga Festival** (January; p315) in Pondicherry. The nine-day **Brahmotsavam Festival** (September/October; p410) is at Tirumala, and in Hyderabad, the **Deccan Festival** (February; p410) pays tribute to Deccan culture. **Rath Yatra** (June/July; p433) is best experienced in Puri, or plan to be in Konark to witness the temple rituals at the **Konark Festival** (1-5 December; p433).

Snapshot

Wherever you travel in South India, you'll never be short of conversation with locals. Whether chatting with your autorickshaw driver about the state of the roads, a young family on the train about their annual pilgrimage, or an IT professional about the burgeoning software industry, you'll find that Indians are friendly and generally well informed.

In 2004 the Congress Party steamed into power for the first time since 1988, winning the central government elections largely on the back of major support from South Indian voters, particularly in Andhra Pradesh and Tamil Nadu. The Congress Party campaign was led by controversial Italian-born Sonia Gandhi, but after victory she promptly stepped aside, neatly avoiding anticipated outrage that a foreign woman might become prime minister. Manmohan Singh – the first member of any religious minority community (Sikh) to hold India's highest-elected office – took over as prime minister. Although Congress had been biting at the Bharatiya Janata Party's (BJP) heels for a number of years, the result sent a message that the policies of the Hindu nationalist party were no longer working, especially for the rural poor who continued to suffer from droughts and poverty while the urban-based elite continued to prosper.

In 2004 in Kerala, the state with the highest literacy rate but also the highest unemployment, there was a backlash against the ruling Congress-led United Democratic Front, which failed to win a single seat in the Lokh Sabha. Meanwhile in Goa, the Manohar Parrikar–led BJP government was dismissed in 2005 – after a series of resignations whittled away its majority – and was replaced by the Congress Party, further damaging the BJP. With a high level of tourism and a lucrative mining industry, the tiny beach state is India's wealthiest – the per capita income here is almost twice the national average.

These are strange times for Tamil Nadu, long driven politically by Dravidian nationalist policies that espouse 'Tamil Nadu for Tamils' and a distaste for the Hindi language (you'll see a lot more Tamil films screened here than Bollywood blockbusters). The state's Chief Minister is Jayalalitha Jayaram, a former film star from a well-to-do Brahmin family, who first took over the All-India Anna Dravida Munnetra Kazhagam (AIADMK) party leadership in 1991. A series of corruption scandals – massive even by Indian political standards – forced her to resign as Chief Minister and brought down her government in 1996. But even after being convicted (the sentence was quashed at appeal, then suspended), she was back as head of the party, which went on to win the 2001 elections. Despite losing ground in the national polls in 2004, the AIADMK remains in power.

South India was hit hard by the 2004 tsunami that slammed into the coast of Tamil Nadu and the Andaman and Nicobar Islands. More than 15,000 people died and many more were injured or left homeless in the tragedy. Worst-affected areas were the Nicobar Islands, 1000km east of the Indian mainland in the Bay of Bengal – although the more northerly Andaman Islands were largely spared – and the central coast of Tamil Nadu, including the Nagapattinam and Cuddalore districts. Relief camps and temporary housing were quickly set up, and aid poured in to help villages with new housing and fishing boats. The tsunami had a severe affect on the fishing industry, as not only were fishermen grounded for several months, but the demand for seafood declined – many believed

FAST FACTS

Population: 1.2464 billion

GDP per capita: US$487

Inflation: 4.4%

Unemployment rate: 9.5%

Life expectancy: 64.37 years (women) and 62.92 years (men)

Proportion of India's foreign earnings to be earned by IT industry in 2008: 30%

Number of tourists annually: 2.38 million

Number of doctors/nurses per 100,000 people: 48/45 (compared with 164/500 in the UK)

Literacy: 48.3% (women) and 70.2% (men)

Number of Internet users per 1000 people: 15.9

Mobile-phone subscribers per 1000 people: 12

Proportion of population living on less than US$1 per day: 34.7%

the fish were contaminated from feeding on the flesh of victims. The salt farmers of Tamil Nadu also suffered when thousands of tonnes of stock salt was washed away from the salt pans.

In Tamil Nadu's Cauvery Delta district, farmers are also in crisis – first from severe droughts, then from floods following a lashing northeast monsoon in 2004 and 2005. Since 2002 a battle has raged over the waters of the Cauvery River after the Karnataka government, which controls the headwaters, refused to release its dams. Protests, strikes and tension followed until the Supreme Court ruled that Karnataka release some of its precious water. After three years of poor monsoons, the rains finally came and devastated crops. The flow-on effect to the economy has meant cottage industries in the region are suffering as no-one can afford to buy crafts or nonessentials.

Mumbai (Bombay) continues to stamp its authority as the economic, financial and industrial capital of South India, churning out Bollywood movies and software giants, but is also prone to communal violence. Two car bombs (one near the Gateway of India) in 2003 killed 52 people, reigniting fears that the city is a target for Islamic terrorism. In spite of a history of organised crime and underworld dons, the Congress government (which took over from the BJP–Shiv Sena alliance in 2004) has decided that dancing girls are corrupting its youth, and the city's 600 dancing-girl bars, where young girls (fully clothed) dance to Bollywood music for appreciative rupee-waving men, have been ordered to close. The decision has put some 75,000 girls out of work.

'You don't need to know the game, just the names...'

Nothing is guaranteed to get a conversation going in India faster than cricket. Indians are certifiably crazy about it. Even if you're not familiar with the intricacies of the sport, it helps to be armed with a small amount of cricket knowledge with which to impress your new Indian friends. You don't need to know the game, just the names – Indians are adoring of their star cricketers. Mumbai-born Sachin Tendulkar (the Little Master) is revered as some sort of god and is one of the world's greatest batsmen (by the time you read this he should hold the record for most Test centuries). Anil Kumble is a star spin bowler from Bangalore. Sourav Ganguly is the team captain, and Rahul Dravid and VVS Laxman are pin-up boys and star batsmen.

tory

e of Dravidian culture, southern India has had a long history
ting dynasties and empires, peppered with the arrival of traders
uerors arriving on sea routes. Evidence of human habitation in
southern India dates from Stone Age times; finds include hand axes in
Tamil Nadu and a worn limestone statue of a goddess that is between
25,000 and 15,000 years old from an excavation in the Vindhya Range.

India's first major civilisation flourished around 2500 BC in the Indus
River valley, much of which lies within present-day Pakistan. This civilisation, which continued for a thousand years and is known as the
Harappan culture, appears to have been the culmination of thousands
of years of settlement. The decline of the culture at the beginning of the
2nd millennium BC was thought by some to have been caused by an
Aryan invasion. Aryans were a white expansionist civilisation, probably
from Russia or Central Asia, who invaded northern Indian (including
present-day Pakistan) around 2000 to 1500 BC. Their language was the
precursor to most Indo-European languages. (As a side note, Hitler used
the name Aryan, which means noble, to describe his perfect race.) Recently, however, historians have suggested several alternatives, one theory
being that the decline was caused by the flooding of the Indus Valley.
Another possibility is that climatic changes led to decreased rainfall and
the subsequent failure of agriculture.

Suggestions that the contemporaneous rise in South India of settlements based on cattle herding and agriculture were the result of Harap-
pans moving south have been dismissed by scholars, and it seems more
likely that North and South India evolved quite independently of one
another at this time. Indeed, archaeologists working in various parts of
South India have discovered some significant differences between the
ancient cultures of the region, especially in agriculture.

INFLUENCES FROM THE NORTH

While the Indus civilisation may not have affected South India, the same
cannot be said for the Aryan invasion. Although the Aryan invasion
theory has come under attack in recent years, especially by nationalist
historians, most experts agree that the Aryan influx is a historical fact –
although whether it was a conquest or more of a gentle migration is not
known. The Aryans arrived in India between 2000 BC and 1500 BC,
and eventually controlled all of North India. The Ramayana (one of the
great Indo-Aryan epics, along with the Mahabharata) was written about
300 BC, and some consider it to be a literary allusion to the Aryan push
into India.

The Aryanisation of the south was a slow process, but it had a profound
effect on the social order of the region and the ethos of its inhabitants.
The northerners brought their literature (the four Vedas – a collection
of sacred Hindu hymns), their gods (Agni, Varuna, Shiva and Vishnu),
their language (Sanskrit) and a social structure that organised people into
castes, with Brahmins at the top.

A History of South India From Prehistoric Times to the Fall of Vijayanagar by Nilakanta Sastri is argu-ably the most compre-hensive (if heavy-going) history of this region; required reading if you're heading for Hampi.

India: A History by John Keay is a recent (2001) and highly readable study of India's history, going back to 3000 BC and concentrating on pre-European dynasties and cultures.

TIMELINE	25,000–15,000 BC	2000–1500 BC
	Evidence of Stone Age settlement in South India	Aryans invade North India and push towards the south; Dravidian culture takes root

Over the centuries other influences flowed from the north, including Buddhism and Jainism. Sravanabelagola in Karnataka, an important place of pilgrimage to this day, is where over 2000 years ago the northern ruler Chandragupta Maurya, who had embraced Jainism and renounced his kingdom, arrived with his guru. Jainism was then adopted by the trading community (its tenet of ahimsa, or nonviolence, precluded occupations tainted by the taking of life), who spread it through South India.

Emperor Ashoka, a successor of Chandragupta who ruled for 37 years from about 272 BC, was a major force behind Buddhism's inroads into the south. Once a campaigning king, his epiphany came in 260 BC when, shocked by the carnage and suffering caused by his campaign against the Kalingas in Orissa, he renounced violence and embraced Buddhism after a battle near Bhubaneswar turned into a massacre. He sent Buddhist missionaries far and wide, and his edicts (carved into rock and incised into specially erected pillars) have been found in Andhra Pradesh, Orissa and Karnataka. Stupas were also built in southern India under Ashoka's patronage, mostly along the coast of Orissa and Andhra Pradesh, although at least one was constructed as far south as Kanchipuram in Tamil Nadu.

The appeal of Jainism and Buddhism, which arose about the same time, was that they rejected the Vedas and condemned the caste system. Buddhism, however, gradually lost favour with its devotees, and was replaced with a new brand of Hinduism, which emphasised devotion to a personal god. This bhakti (devotional) cult developed in southern India about AD 500. Bhakti adherents opposed Jainism and Buddhism, and the cult certainly hastened the decline of both in South India. Bhakti was also anti-Vedic, rejecting the notion that priests were required as intermediaries between mortals and gods, and opposing the reliance on ritual with its requisite knowledge of Sanskrit.

Web India 123 (www.web india123.com/history) offers a historical overview of India.

MAURYAN EMPIRE & SOUTHERN KINGDOMS

Chandragupta Maurya was the first of a line of Mauryan kings to rule what was effectively the first Indian empire. The empire's capital was in present-day Patna in Bihar. Chandragupta's son, Bindusara, who came to the throne about 300 BC, extended the empire as far as Karnataka. However, he seems to have stopped there, possibly because the Mauryan empire was on cordial terms with the southern chieftains of the day.

The identity and customs of these chiefdoms have been gleaned from various sources, including archaeological remains and ancient Tamil literature. These literary records describe a land known as the 'abode of the Tamils', within which resided three major ruling families: the Pandyas (Madurai), the Cheras (Malabar Coast) and the Cholas (Thanjavur and the Cauvery Valley). The region described in classical Sangam literature (written between 300 BC and AD 200) was still relatively insulated from Sanskrit culture, but from 200 BC this was starting to change.

A degree of rivalry characterised relations between the main chiefdoms and the numerous minor chiefdoms, and there were occasional clashes with Sri Lankan rulers. Sangam literature indicates that Sanskrit traditions from the old Aryan kingdoms of the north were taking root in South India around 200 BC. Ultimately, the southern powers all suffered at the hands of the Kalabhras, about whom little is known except that they

320 BC	272–232 BC
Maurya dynasty founded in Bihar	Reign of Emperor Ashoka; Buddhism spread in South India

appeared to have come from somewhere north of the Tamil region, and that they were generally regarded as 'evil rulers'.

By around 180 BC the Mauryan empire, which had started to disintegrate soon after the death of Emperor Ashoka in 232 BC, had been overtaken by a series of rival kingdoms that were subjected to repeated invasions from northerners such as the Bactrian Greeks. Despite this apparent instability, the post-Ashokan era produced at least one line of royalty whose patronage of the arts and ability to maintain a relatively high degree of social cohesion have left an enduring legacy. This was the Satavahanas, who eventually controlled all of Maharashtra, Madhya Pradesh, Chhatisgarh, Karnataka and Andhra Pradesh. Under their rule, between 200 BC and AD 200, the arts blossomed, especially literature, sculpture and philosophy. Buddhism reached a peak in Maharashtra under the Satavahanas, although the greatest of the Buddhist cave temples at Ajanta (p135) and Ellora (p133) were built later by the Chaulukya and Rashtrakuta dynasties.

Most of all, the subcontinent enjoyed a period of considerable prosperity. South India may have lacked vast and fertile agricultural plains on the scale of North India, but it compensated by building valuable trade links via the Indian Ocean.

TRADE NETWORKS

India's trading links with the outside world go back a long way. There is evidence that trade between western Asian cultures, such as the Persians and Egyptians, and the west coast of India was taking place at least a thousand years before Christ. Indian teak and cedar were used by Babylonian builders as far back as the 7th century BC. But a major breakthrough came with the discovery of the monsoon winds, which enabled ships (such as Arab dhows) to travel between western Asia and India with relative ease. The extraordinary reach of the Roman empire during the period of the Pax Romana at the beginning of the Christian era assured the flow of goods between India, western Asia and Europe along two major routes: overland across Persia to North India, and by water (primarily from the Red Sea and the Persian Gulf) to South India.

An anonymous Greek document, the *Periplys Maris Erythraei*, written some time in the 1st century BC, describes various ports along the coast of India. Proof that Roman traders were active in South India has turned up over the years in the form of caches of gold coins, Roman pottery and glass. British archaeologist Sir Mortimer Wheeler, digging at Arikkamedu near Pondicherry, uncovered a Roman trading settlement as well as pieces of pottery that had been manufactured near Rome itself. At Rameswaram further south, pottery made in Tunisia when it was under Roman control has been uncovered. And at Iyyal in central Kerala in 1983, more than 200 gold coins minted in Rome in the 2nd century AD were discovered by workers excavating clay for bricks.

Goods exported from South India included ivory, precious stones, pearls, tortoiseshell, pepper and aromatic plants. Indian merchants used trade routes established by the Mauryan empire and natural corridors such as the Narmada and Ganges River valleys to move around India. Longer routes traversed vast tracts of Central Asia to link China with the

---

200 BC–AD200   **985**

Satavahana dynasty controls the Deccan, encouraging arts, literature and sculpture	Raja Raj ascends the throne of the Chola Kingdom, a powerful dynasty that established trade links in the south

Mediterranean. There is evidence Indian traders were also established in Red Sea ports, and after the decline of the Roman trade, they ventured in the other direction to Southeast Asia in search of spices and semi-precious stones.

THE FALL & RISE OF THE CHOLA EMPIRE

After the Kalabhras suppressed the Tamil chiefdoms, South India split into numerous warring kingdoms. The Cholas virtually disappeared and the Cheras on the west coast appear to have prospered through trading, although little is known about them. It was not until the late 6th century AD, when the Kalabhras were overthrown, that the political confusion in the region ended. For the next 300 years the history of South India was dominated by the fortunes of the Chalukyas of Badami, the Pallavas of Kanchi (Kanchipuram) and the Pandyas of Madurai.

The original game of chess was invented in India in the 6th century. Known as Shaturanga, it used 64 pieces in a battle of four armies.

The Chalukyas were a far-flung family. In addition to their base in Badami, they established themselves in Bijapur, Andhra Pradesh and near the Godavari Delta. The Godavari branch of the family is commonly referred to as the Eastern Chalukyas of Vengi. It's unclear from where the Pallavas originated, but it is thought they may have emigrated to Kanchi from Andhra Pradesh. After their successful rout of the Kalabhras, the Pallavas extended their territory as far south as the Cauvery River, and by the 7th century were at the height of their power, building monuments such as the Shore Temple and Arjuna's Penance at Mamallapuram (Mahabalipuram). They engaged in long-running conflicts with the Pandyas, who, in the 8th century, allied themselves with the Gangas of Mysore. This, combined with pressure from the Rashtrakutas (who were challenging the Eastern Chalukyas), had by the 9th century snuffed out any significant Pallava power in the south.

At the same time as the Pallava dynasty came to an end, a new Chola dynasty was establishing itself and laying the foundations for what was to become one of the most important empires on the subcontinent. From their base at Thanjavur (Tanjore), the Cholas spread north absorbing what was left of the Pallavas' territory, and made inroads into the south. But it wasn't until Raja Raja (985–1014) ascended the throne that the Chola kingdom really started to become a great empire. Raja Raja successfully waged war against the Pandyas in the south, the Gangas of Mysore and the Eastern Chalukyas. He also launched a series of naval campaigns that resulted in the capture of the Maldives, the Malabar Coast and northern Sri Lanka, which became a province of the Chola empire. These conquests gave the Cholas control over important ports and trading links between India, Southeast Asia, Arabia and East Africa. They were therefore in a position to grab a share of the huge profits involved in selling spices to Europe.

History & Society in South India by Noburu Karashima is an academic work focusing on the development of South Indian society during the Chola dynasty and the rule of the Vijayanagars.

Raja Raja's son, Rajendra (1014–44), continued to expand the Chola's territory, conquering the remainder of Sri Lanka, and campaigning up the east coast as far as Bengal and the Ganges River. Rajendra also launched a campaign in Southeast Asia against the Srivijaya kingdom (Sumatra), reinstating trade links that had been interrupted and sending trade missions as far as China. In addition to both its political and economic superiority, the Chola empire produced a brilliant legacy in

1336	1424
Powerful Vijayanagar empire founded at Hampi	Bahmani dynasty founded as rivals to Vijayanagar

the arts. Sculpture, most notably bronze sculpture (see p63), reached astonishing new heights of aesthetic and technical refinement.

Music, dance and literature flourished and developed a distinctly Tamil flavour, enduring in South India long after the Cholas had faded from the picture. Trade wasn't the only thing the Cholas brought to the shores of Southeast Asia; they also introduced their culture. That legacy lives on in Myanmar (Burma), Thailand, Bali and Cambodia in dance, religion and mythology.

The Wonder That Was India by AL Basham gives good descriptions of the Indian civilisations, origins of the caste system and social customs, and detailed information on Hinduism, Buddhism and other religions in India. It is also very informative about art and architecture.

But the Cholas, eventually weakened by constant campaigning, succumbed to expansionist pressure from the Hoysalas of Halebid and the Pandyas of Madurai, and by the 13th century were finally supplanted by the Pandyas. The Hoysalas were themselves eclipsed by the Vijayanagar empire, which arose in the 14th century. The Pandyas prospered and their achievements were much admired by Marco Polo when he visited in 1288 and 1293. But their glory was short-lived, as they were unable to resist the Muslim invasion from the north.

MUSLIM INVASION & THE VIJAYANAGAR EMPIRE

The Muslim rulers in Delhi campaigned in southern India from 1296, pushing aside a series of local rulers, including the Hoysalas and Pandyas, and by 1323 had reached Madurai in Tamil Nadu.

Muhammed Tughlaq, the sultan of Delhi, dreamed of conquering the whole of India, something not even Emperor Ashoka had managed. Earlier Muslim rulers had been happier looting temples than establishing empires. He rebuilt the fort of Daulatabad (p132) in Maharashtra to keep control of southern India, but eventually his ambition led him to overreach his forces. In 1334 he had to recall his army in order to put down rebellions elsewhere and as a result, local Muslim rulers in Madurai and Daulatabad declared their independence.

At the same time, the foundations of what was to become one of South India's greatest empires, Vijayanagar, were being laid by Hindu chiefs at Hampi.

Kamat's Potpourri (www .kamat.com) is an interesting 'personal' website covering India's history, politics, religion and culture with contemporary articles and links.

The Bahmanis, who were initially from Daulatabad, established their capital at Gulbarga in Karnataka, relocating to Bidar in the 15th century. Their kingdom eventually included Maharashtra and parts of northern Karnataka and Andhra Pradesh – and they took pains to protect it.

The Vijayanagar empire is generally said to have been founded by two chieftain brothers who, having been captured and taken to Delhi, where they converted to Islam, were sent back south to serve as governors for the sultanate. The brothers, however, had other ideas; they reconverted to Hinduism and around 1336 set about establishing a kingdom that was eventually to encompass southern Karnataka, Tamil Nadu and part of Kerala. Seven centuries later, the centre of this kingdom – the stunning ruins and temples of Hampi (p242) – is now one of South India's greatest tourist attractions.

Not unnaturally, ongoing rivalry characterised the relationship between the Vijayanagar and Bahmani empires until the 16th century when both went into decline. The Bahmani empire was torn apart by factional fighting and Vijayanagar's vibrant capital of Hampi was laid to waste in a six-month sacking by the combined forces of the Muslim sultanates of

Bidar, Bijapur, Berar, Ahmednagar and Golconda. Much of the conflict centred on control of fertile agricultural land and trading ports; at one stage the Bahmanis wrested control of the important port of Goa from their rivals (although in 1378 the Vijayanagars seized it back).

The Vijayanagar empire is notable for its prosperity, which was the result of a deliberate policy giving every encouragement to traders from afar, combined with the development of an efficient administrative system and access to important trading links, including west-coast ports. Its capital became quite cosmopolitan, with people from various parts of India as well as from abroad mingling in the bazaars.

Portuguese chronicler Domingo Paez arrived in Vijayanagar during the reign of one of its greatest kings, Krishnadevaraya (r 1509–29). It was during his rule that Vijayanagar enjoyed a period of unparalleled prosperity and power, even conquering the Gajapati rajas of Orissa.

Paez recorded the achievements of the Vijayanagars and described how they had constructed tanks and irrigated their fields. He also described how human and animal sacrifices were carried out to propitiate the gods after one of the tanks had burst repeatedly. He included detail about the fine houses that belonged to wealthy merchants, and the bazaars full of precious stones (rubies, diamonds, emeralds, pearls), textiles, including silk, 'and every other sort of thing there is on earth and that you may wish to buy'.

Like the Bahmanis, the Vijayanagar kings invested heavily in protecting their territory and trading links. Krishnadevaraya employed Portuguese and Muslim mercenaries to man the forts and protect his domains. He also fostered good relations with the Portuguese, upon whom he depended for access to trade goods, especially the Arab horses he needed for his cavalry.

The Career and Legend of Vasco da Gama by Sanjay Subrahmanyam is one of the best recent investigations of the person credited with 'discovering' the sea route to India.

THE PORTUGUESE ARRIVAL

By the time Krishnadevaraya ascended to the throne, the Portuguese were well on the way to establishing a firm foothold in Goa. It was only a few years since they had become the first Europeans to sail across the Indian Ocean from the east coast of Africa to India's shores.

On 20 May 1498 Vasco da Gama dropped anchor off the South Indian coast near the town of Calicut (Kozhikode). It had taken him 23 days to sail from the east coast of Africa, guided by a pilot named Ibn Masjid, sent by the ruler of Malindi in Gujarat.

The Portuguese sought a sea route between Europe and the East so they could trade directly in spices. They also hoped they might find Christians cut off from Europe by the Muslim dominance of the Middle East. The Portuguese were also searching for the legendary kingdom of Prester John, a powerful Christian ruler with whom they could unite against the Muslim rulers of the Middle East. However, in India they found spices and the Syrian Orthodox community, but not Prester John.

Vasco da Gama sought an audience with the ruler, the Zamorin of Calicut (Kozhikode), to explain himself, and seems to have been well received. The Portuguese engaged in a limited amount of trading, but became increasingly suspicious that Muslim traders were turning the ruler of Calicut against them. They resolved to leave Calicut, which they did in August.

Thousands were burned at the stake during the Goa Inquisition, which lasted more than 200 years. The judgment ceremony took place outside the Se Cathedral in Old Goa.

1510	1600
Portuguese capture Goa; Alfonso Albuquerque defeats Muslims in 1512	British East India Company formed

ENTER THE EUROPEANS & CHRISTIANITY

And so began a new era of European contact with the East. After Vasco da Gama came Francisco de Ameida and Afonso de Albuquerque, who established an eastern Portuguese empire that included Goa (first taken in 1510). Albuquerque waged a constant battle against the local Muslims in Goa, finally defeating them in 1512. But perhaps his greatest achievement was in playing off two deadly threats against each other – the Vijayanagars (for whom access to Goa's ports was extremely important) and the Bijapuris (who had split from the Bahmanis in the early 16th century and who controlled part of Goa).

The Bijapuris and Vijayanagars were sworn enemies, and Albuquerque skilfully exploited this antipathy by supplying Arab horses, which had to be constantly imported because they died in alarming numbers once on Indian soil. Both kingdoms bought horses from the Portuguese to top up their warring cavalries, thus keeping Portugal's Goan ports busy and profitable.

The Portuguese also introduced Catholicism, and the arrival of the Inquisition in 1560 marked the beginning of 200 years of religious suppression in the Portuguese-controlled areas on the west coast of India. Not long after the beginning of the Inquisition, events that occurred in Europe had major repercussions for European relations with India. In 1580 Spain annexed Portugal and, until it regained its independence in 1640, Portugal's interests were subservient to Spain's. After the defeat of the Spanish Armada in 1588, the sea route to the East lay open to the English and Dutch.

Today the Portuguese influence is most obvious in Goa, with its chalk-white Catholic churches dotting the countryside, Christian festivals and unique cuisine, although the Portuguese also had some influence in Kerala in towns such as Kochi (p290). By the mid-16th century, Old Goa (p176) had grown into a thriving city said to rival Lisbon in magnificence, and although only a ruined shadow of that time, its churches and buildings are still a stunning reminder of Portuguese rule. It wasn't until 1961 – 14 years after national Independence – that the Portuguese were finally forced out by the Indian military.

South Indian Customs by PV Jagadisa Ayyar seeks to explain a range of practices, from the smearing of cow dung outside the home to the formation of snake images beneath the banyan tree.

The Dutch got to India first but, unlike the Portuguese, were more interested in trade than in religion and empire. Indonesia was used as the main source of spices, and traded with South India primarily for pepper and cardamom. So the Dutch East India Company set up a string of trading posts (called factories), which allowed them to maintain a complicated trading structure all the way from the Persian Gulf to Japan. They set up trading posts at Surat in Gujarat and on the Coromandel Coast in South India, and entered into a treaty with the ruler of Calicut. In 1660 they captured the Portuguese forts at Kochi and Kodungallor.

The English also set up a trading venture, the East India Company, which in 1600 was granted a monopoly. Like the Dutch, the English were at this stage interested in trade, mainly in spices, and Indonesia was their main goal. But the Dutch proved too strong there and the English turned instead to India, setting up a trading post at Madras (now Chennai). The Danes traded off and on at Tranquebar (on the Coromandel Coast) from 1616, and the French acquired Pondicherry in 1674.

1627	1631
Birth of Shivaji, future Maratha king	The Taj Mahal is built at Agra as a memorial to Shah Jehan's wife, Mumtaz Mahal

MUGHALS VERSUS MARATHAS

Around this time the Delhi-based Mughals were making inroads into southern India, gaining Orissa and the sultanates of Ahmednagar, Bijapur and Golconda (including Hyderabad) before moving into Tamil Nadu. But it was here that Emperor Aurangzeb (r 1658–1707) came up against the Marathas, who, in a series of guerrillalike raids, captured Thanjavur and set up a capital at Gingee near Madras (now Chennai).

Although the Mughal empire gradually disintegrated following Aurangzeb's death, the Marathas went from strength to strength, and they set their sights on territory to the north. But their aspirations brought them into conflict with the rulers of Hyderabad (the Asaf Jahis), who had entrenched themselves when Hyderabad broke away from the declining Mughal rulers of Delhi in 1724. The Marathas discovered that the French were providing military support to the Hyderabadi rulers in return for trading concessions on the Coromandel Coast. However, by the 1750s Hyderabad had lost much of its power and became landlocked when much of its coast was lost to the British.

Down in the south, Travancore (part of Kerala) and Mysore were making a bid to consolidate their power by gaining control of important maritime regions, and access to trade links. Martanda Varma (r 1729–58) of Travancore created his own army and tried to keep the local Syrian Christian trading community onside by limiting the activities of European traders. Trade in many goods, with the exception of pepper, became a royal monopoly, especially under Martanda's son Rama Varma (r 1758–98).

Mysore started off as a landlocked kingdom, but in 1761 a cavalry officer, Hyder Ali, assumed power and set about acquiring coastal territory. Hyder Alis and his son Tipu Sultan eventually ruled over a kingdom that included southern Karnataka and northern Kerala. Tipu conducted trade

Vivekananda: A Biography by Swami Nikhilananda is an uplifting read if you're interested in the life of Swami Vivekananda, a philosopher, yogi and wandering ascetic, who was a powerful figure in the late 19th century.

SHIVAJI – MARATHA LEGEND

The name Chhatrapati Shivaji is revered in Maharashtra, with statues of the great warrior astride his horse gracing many towns, and street names and monuments being named (or renamed) in the case of Mumbai's Victoria Terminus, among others) after him. So who was this man and what did he do to achieve such adoration?

Shivaji was responsible for leading the powerful Maratha dynasty, a sovereign Hindu state that controlled the Deccan for almost two centuries, at a time when much of India was under Muslim control. A great warrior and charismatic leader, he has been likened to Alexander the Great. Shivaji was born to a prominent Maratha family at Shivneri in 1630. As a child he was sent to Pune with his mother, where he was given land and forts and groomed as a future leader. With a very small army, Shivaji took his first fort at the age of 20 and over the next three decades he continued to expand Maratha power around his base in Pune, holding out against the Muslim invaders from the north (the Mughal empire) and the south (the forces of Bijapur) and eventually controlling the Deccan. He was shrewd enough to play his enemies (among them Mughal emperor Aurangzeb) off against each other and, in a famous incident, he killed Bijapuri general Afzal Khan in a face-to-face encounter at Pratapgad Fort (p158).

In 1674 Shivaji was crowned *chhatrapati* (king) of the Marathas at Raigad Fort (p158). He died six years later and was succeeded by his son Sambhaji, but almost immediately the power he had built up began to wane.

1639	1673
Fort St George is constructed by the British at Madras (Chennai)	French establish colony at Pondicherry

directly with the Middle East through the west-coast ports he controlled. But Tipu was prevented from gaining access to ports on the eastern seaboard and the fertile hinterland by the British East India Company.

THE BRITISH TAKE HOLD

The British East India Company at this stage was supposedly interested only in trade, not conquest. But Mysore's rulers proved something of a vexation. In 1780 the Nizam of Hyderabad, Hyder Ali, and the Marathas joined forces to defeat the company's armies and take control of Karnataka. The Treaty of Mangalore, signed by Tipu Sultan in 1784, restored the parties to an uneasy truce. But meanwhile, within the company there was a growing body of opinion that only total control of India would really satisfy British trading interests. This was reinforced by fears of a renewed French bid for land in India following Napoleon's Egyptian expedition of 1798–99. It was the governor general of Bengal, Lord Wellesley, who launched a strike against Mysore, with the Nizam of Hyderabad as an ally (who was required to disband his French-trained troops and in return gained British protection). Tipu, who may have counted on support from the French, was killed when the British stormed the river-island fortress of Seringapatam (present-day Srirangapatnam, near Mysore) in 1799.

Wellesley restored the old ruling family, the Wodeyars, to half of Tipu's kingdom – the rest went to the Nizam of Hyderabad and the East India Company – and laid the foundations for the formation of the Madras Presidency. Thanjavur and Karnataka were also absorbed by the British, who, when the rulers of the day died, pensioned off their successors. By 1818 the Marathas, racked by internal strife, had collapsed.

By now most of India was under British influence. In the south the British controlled the Madras Presidency, which stretched from present-day Andhra Pradesh in the north to the tip of the subcontinent in the south, and from the east coast across to the western Malabar Coast. Coastal Orissa was ruled from Calcutta by the British until 1912, while much of the interior was ruled by a number of small princely states. Much of Maharashtra was part of the Bombay Presidency, but there were a dozen or so small princely states scattered around, including Kolhapur, Sawantwadi, Aundh and Janjira. The major princely states were Travancore, Hyderabad and Mysore, though all were closely watched by the Resident (the British de facto governor, who officially looked after areas under British control).

In the early days of British rule a fair degree of mixing was encouraged by the British rulers, and in the early 19th century British soldiers were encouraged to marry local women. The descendants of this group form the core of the small Anglo-Indian community. But after the 1857 Uprising (called the Mutiny by the British), the colonial rulers' attitudes hardened, and a doctrine of white superiority took hold. This then led to a backlash among the emerging urban Indian educated classes, which slowly coalesced into a nationalist movement. The British had created a class of English-speaking, well-educated Indians to help govern the country, but only grudgingly allowed them an actual say in politics. The Indian economy was also restricted, used as a captive market for British manufacturers. The British did leave a tangible legacy in the form of the railway system and other modern infrastructure, but the time was ripe for Indian independence.

Of the 545 seats in the Lok Sabha (the Lower House of India's bicameral parliament) 125 are reserved for Scheduled Castes.

In 1839 the British government offered to buy Goa from the Portuguese for half a million pounds.

1761	1799
Hyder Ali assumes power over Mysore kingdom	British finally defeat Tipu Sultan in Fourth Mysore War

ROAD TO INDEPENDENCE

Mohandas Gandhi, a lawyer born in Gujarat, led the nonviolent satyagraha (passive resistance) movement to force the British to leave India. He shed his British-educated past and adopted the lifestyle of a mystic, which greatly helped to popularise the independence movement with ordinary rural Indians. He was dubbed Mahatma, meaning 'Great Soul', by the

MAHATMA GANDHI

One of the great figures of the 20th century, Mohandas Karamchand Gandhi was born on 2 October 1869 in Porbandar, Gujarat, where his father was chief minister. After studying in London (1888–91), he worked as a barrister in South Africa, where the young Gandhi became politicised, railing against the discrimination he encountered. He soon became the spokesman for the Indian community and championed equality for all.

Gandhi returned to India in 1915 with the doctrine of ahimsa (nonviolence) central to his political plans, and committed to a simple and disciplined lifestyle. He set up the Sabarmati Ashram in Ahmedabad, which was innovative for its admission of Untouchables.

Within a year, Gandhi had won his first victory, defending farmers in Bihar from exploitation. This was when he first received the title 'Mahatma' (Great Soul) from an admirer. The passage of the discriminatory Rowlatt Acts through parliament in 1919 spurred him to further action and he organised a national protest. In the days that followed this hartal (strike), feelings ran high throughout the country. After the massacre of unarmed protesters in Amritsar, a deeply shocked Gandhi immediately called off the protest.

By 1920 Gandhi was a key figure in the Indian National Congress, and he coordinated a national campaign of noncooperation or satyagraha (passive resistance) to British rule, with the effect of raising nationalist feelings while earning the lasting enmity of the British. In early 1930 Gandhi captured the imagination of the country, and the world, when he led a march of several thousand followers from Ahmedabad to Dandi on the coast of Gujarat. On arrival, Gandhi ceremoniously made salt by evaporating sea water, thus publicly defying the much-hated salt tax; not for the first time, he was imprisoned. Released in 1931 to represent the Indian National Congress at the second Round Table Conference in London, he won over the hearts of the British people, but failed to gain any real concessions from the government.

Jailed again on his return to India, Gandhi immediately began a hunger strike, aimed at forcing his fellow Indians to accept the rights of the Untouchables. Gandhi's resoluteness and the widespread apprehension throughout the country forced an agreement, but not until Gandhi was on the verge of death.

Disillusioned with politics and convinced that the Congress leaders were ignoring his guidance, he resigned from his parliamentary seat in 1934 and devoted himself to rural education. He returned spectacularly to the fray in 1942 with the Quit India campaign, in which he urged the British to leave India immediately. His actions were deemed subversive and he and most of the Congress leadership were imprisoned.

In the frantic bargaining that followed the end of the war, Gandhi was largely excluded, and watched helplessly as plans were made to partition the country – a tragedy in his eyes. He toured the trouble spots, using his own influence to calm intercommunity tensions and promote peace.

Gandhi stood almost alone in urging tolerance and the preservation of a single India, and his work on behalf of members of all communities inevitably drew resentment from some Hindu hardliners. On his way to an evening prayer meeting on 30 January 1948, he was assassinated by a Hindu zealot.

1853	1869
First Indian railway opened from Bombay (Mumbai) to Thana	Mohandas 'Mahatma' Gandhi is born in Gujarat

The Gandhi autobiography, *The Story of My Experiments With Truth*, is essential reading if you're interested in the life, or more importantly the philosophies, of this influential Indian.

Bengali Nobel Prize–winner Rabindranath Tagore. Historical reminders of Gandhi's life and work can be found throughout South India: his ashram is at Sevagram (p141) in Maharashtra; the house where he stayed during many visits to Bombay (now Mumbai) and where he launched the Quit India campaign in 1942 is now a museum (Mani Bhavan; p103); and the former palace where he was imprisoned by the British for nearly two years is in Pune (p149), Maharashtra. There is also a fine museum devoted to Gandhi's life in Madurai (p367) and a memorial in Kanyakumari (p373) was used to store some of Gandhi's ashes before they were immersed in the sea.

You've probably seen *Gandhi*, starring Ben Kingsley, Candice Bergen, John Gielgud and 300,000 extras, before, but see it again because few movies capture the grand canvas that is India in tracing the nation's path to independence.

After 30 years of campaigns, demonstrations and frequent spells in prison, Gandhi succeeded in forcing the British to leave. WWII left the British financially unable to sustain a long fight against a determined independence movement. By the 1930s the independence movement had largely split along religious lines, with the Muslim League demanding a separate state called Pakistan. The Indian National Congress, led by Jawaharlal Nehru and his mentor Gandhi, argued long and hard for a united India, but to no avail. The partition of India in 1947 led to a devastating outbreak of religious violence, with Muslims migrating to Pakistan and Hindus to India. Nehru became the first prime minister and Gandhi was assassinated in Delhi in 1948 by a Hindu fanatic from Pune who believed he was responsible for dividing the sacred motherland. The repercussions of Partition are still felt today: Jammu and Kashmir, a Muslim-majority region whose former Hindu ruler chose to join his realm to India, has been a scene of conflict between India and Pakistan for more than 50 years.

CARVING UP THE SOUTH

While the chaos of Partition was largely felt in the north – mainly in Punjab and Bengal – the south faced problems of its own. Following Independence in 1947 the princely states and British provinces were dismantled and South India was reorganised into states along linguistic lines. Though most of the princely states acceded to India peacefully, an exception was that of the Nizam of Hyderabad. He wanted Hyderabad to join Muslim Pakistan, although only he and 10% of his subjects were Muslims. Following a time of violence between Hindus and Islamic fundamentalists, the Indian army moved in and forcibly took control of Hyderabad state in 1949.

The Remembered Village by MN Srinivas is an entertaining and revealing account of the author's field research during the late 1940s and early 1950s in a Karnataka village.

The Wodeyars in Mysore, who also ruled right up to Independence, were pensioned off. But they were so popular with their subjects that the maharaja became the first governor of the post-Independence state of Mysore. The opulent palace of the maharaja of Mysore (p218) is open to the public and it's possible to spend a night at the summer palace in Ooty (Udhagamandalam; p384). The boundaries of Mysore state were redrawn on linguistic grounds in 1956, and the extended Kannada-speaking state of Greater Mysore was established, becoming Karnataka in 1972.

Kerala, as it is today, was created in 1956 from Travancore, Cochin and Malabar (formerly part of the Madras Presidency). The maharajas in both Travancore and Cochin were especially attentive to the provision of basic services and education, and their legacy today is India's most literate state. Kerala also blazed a trail in post-Independence India by becoming the first state in the world to elect a communist government in 1957.

1877	1947
The Queen of England is proclaimed Empress of India in Delhi	Independence and Partition of India, creation of Pakistan and Bangladesh; Jawaharlal Nehru is India's first prime minister

Andhra Pradesh was declared a state in 1956, having been created by combining Andhra state (formerly part of the Madras Presidency) with parts of the Telugu-speaking areas of the old Nizam of Hyderabad's territory. In the last 20 years the government has alternated between the Congress Party and the Telugu Desam Party.

Tamil Nadu emerged from the old Madras Presidency, although until 1969 Tamil Nadu was known as Madras State. In 1956, in a nationwide reorganisation of states, it lost Malabar district and South Canara to the fledgling state of Kerala on the west coast. However, it also gained new areas in Trivandrum district, including Kanyakumari. In 1960 1049 sq km of land in Andhra Pradesh was exchanged for a similar amount of land in Salem and Chengalpattu districts.

The creation of Maharashtra was one of the most contested issues of the language-based demarcation of states in the 1950s, which Nehru opposed. After Independence western Maharashtra and Gujarat were joined to form Bombay state, but in 1960, after agitation by pro-Marathi supporters, the modern state of Maharashtra was created, separating from Gujarat while gaining parts of Hyderabad and Madhya Pradesh. Orissa was one of the first states to take form, having been separated from Bengal in 1912 and from Bihar in 1936. It was controlled by the British until Independence.

The French relinquished Pondicherry in 1954 – 140 years after claiming it from the British. It is a Union Territory (controlled by the government in Delhi), though a largely self-governing one, scattered across three states – Pondicherry and Karaikal (Tamil Nadu), Mahé (Kerala) and Yanam (Andhra Pradesh). Lakshadweep was granted Union Territory status in 1956, changing its name in 1973. Lakshadweep and Jammu and Kashmir remain the only Muslim-majority areas in India. The Andaman and Nicobar Islands were made a Union Territory in 1956 and were the first part of India to be free of British rule in 1943.

Throughout most of this carve-up, the tiny enclave of Goa was still under the rule of the Portuguese. Although a rumbling Independence movement had existed in Goa since the early 20th century, the Indian government was reluctant to intervene and take Goa by force, hoping the Portuguese would leave of their own volition. The Portuguese refused, so in December 1961 Indian troops crossed the border and liberated the state with surprisingly little resistance. It became a Union Territory of India, but after splitting from Daman and Diu (Gujarat) in 1987, it was officially recognised as the 25th state of the Indian Union.

MODERN INDIA

Despite the strife caused by Partition and an intractable conflict with Pakistan over disputed Kashmir, India went into the latter part of the 20th century as a surprisingly coherent democracy of 350 million people. Prime Minister Nehru tried to adopt a course of political nonalignment, maintaining relationships with the Commonwealth but also looking to the socialist ideas of the former USSR. Plans for economic development and reform were put in place, but with poor infrastructure and a minuscule share of world trade, it would be decades before India found its economic feet. When Nehru died in 1964, his daughter Indira Gandhi was elected to the top job in 1966. A popular but controversial leader, she declared a

The original design for the Indian flag featured a symbol for India's struggle for political and economic freedom. At the last minute it was changed to the Buddhist chakra modelled on the Ashoka pillar at Sarnath.

Tamil Nation (www.tamil nation.org) has everything you ever wanted to know about Tamil culture, politics and heritage.

Goa Freaks: My Hippie Years in Goa by Cleo Odzer is a mind-blowing account of the author's time as a drug-addled 'freak' in the 1970s. Gives a superb insight into the hedonistic early years of the South India hippie trail.

1948	1961
Mahatma Gandhi assassinated in New Delhi	India kicks Portuguese out of Goa

DEATH OF AN OUTLAW

On 18 October 2004, a moustachioed man named Veerapan was shot dead by police in an ambush near a remote forest village in Tamil Nadu. It was big news, with the media and government ministers rushing to congratulate the Special Task Force that had finally caught up with an outlaw who had evaded police for more than 30 years. Known as the 'forest brigand', Veerapan was a notorious elephant poacher, sandalwood smuggler and murderer. Feared by his enemies and seen by some as a modern-day Robin Hood, he led a gang and plied his illegal trade, eluding police task forces from three states. In 2000 he boldly kidnapped screen idol Rajkumar and held him hostage for three months; in 2002 he kidnapped Karnatakan politician H Nagappa, who was later found dead. Still no-one could flush him from his jungle stronghold. In the end, like a true outlaw, he went down with all guns blazing.

state of emergency (which became known as the Emergency) in 1975 and started economic reforms to boost the economy and control inflation. It proved to be her downfall as the government was bundled out of office in the 1977 elections in favour of the Janata People's Party (JPP). The JPP founder, Jaya Prakash Narayan, 'JP', was an ageing Gandhian socialist who died soon after the election but is widely credited with having safeguarded Indian democracy through his moral stature and courage to stand up to Congress' authoritarian and increasingly corrupt rule.

India: An Emerging Power by Stephen Philip Cohen is a thought-provoking study of India since Independence: its military power, influences of the Soviet Union and US, and where the world's second-most populous nation is heading.

The 1980 election brought Indira Gandhi back to power with a larger majority than ever before, but the new government grappled unsuccessfully with unrest in several areas, violent attacks on Dalits (the Scheduled Caste or Untouchables), numerous cases of police brutality and corruption, and upheavals in the northeast and Punjab. In 1984, following an ill-considered decision to send in the Indian army to flush out armed Sikh separatists (demanding a Sikh state to be called Khalistan) from Amritsar's Golden Temple, Indira Gandhi was assassinated by her Sikh bodyguards. Indira Gandhi's son, Rajiv, a former Indian Airlines pilot, became the next prime minister, with Congress winning in a landslide in 1984. However, after a brief golden reign, he was downed by corruption scandals, the inability to quell communal unrest, particularly in Punjab, and his intervention in the conflict in Sri Lanka. In 1991 he, too, was assassinated in Tamil Nadu by a supporter of the Liberation Tigers of Tamil Eelam (LTTE; a Sri Lankan armed separatist group). Over the years thousands of Tamil refugees have come from Sri Lanka to escape the war, most settling in Tamil Nadu.

Bombay & Mumbai: The City in Transition by Patel Sujata is a series of essays giving a sharp view of South India's powerhouse metropolis, its past, and political and economic future.

The 1992 destruction of the Babri Masjid by Hindu zealots in Ayodhya sparked communal violence and rioting across the country. In Bombay (renamed Mumbai in 1996), 800 people died in riots, and a series of flare-ups and bombings followed during the 1990s. Some blamed the city's underworld but the ruling Hindu nationalist party Shiv Sena was also accused of orchestrating the chaos – a view supported by a later state government report. Tamil Nadu also faced uneasy times in the new India. In 1998 a series of bombs killed 65 people in Coimbatore. They were blamed on Islamic terrorists and timed to coincide with the visit of BJP (Bharatiya Janata Party) minister LK Advani.

The fiercely independent and conservative Tamils have been led alternately by the DMK (Dravida Munnetra Kazhagam) and its offshoot the

1971	1984
Indira Gandhi becomes prime minister	Indira Gandhi assassinated; her son Rajiv Gandhi becomes prime minister

AIADMK (All-India Anna Dravida Munnetra Kazhagam) since 1957, both parties pushing strong Dravidian 'Tamil Nadu for Tamils' and anti-Hindi language policies, and for more independent powers. See Snapshot (p32) for news of Tamil Nadu's political circus.

Politically and culturally unique, and avoiding communal tensions, Kerala was led by the elected Community Party of India (CPI) from 1957 and again by the CPI-led Left Democratic from 1996. The Congress Party–led United Democratic Front took over in 2001. The state has India's highest literacy rate and, although the economy is mainly agricultural, a significant amount of money comes in from Keralans working abroad.

Of all the South Indian states, Goa has probably changed most since Independence, in the rampant development of both tourism and industry (mainly petrochemicals and mining). It's also had more shifts in power since 1987 than there are sunbeds on Calangute Beach, with ministers from Congress and BJP frequently crossing the floor (switching parties) or resigning. See p32 for the latest.

On a national level, central government elections were held in 2004 and the Congress Party swept to power, defeating the Hindu nationalist BJP. Although the campaign and party were led by controversial Italian-born Sonia Gandhi (widow of former prime minister Rajiv Gandhi), she stepped aside soon after victory, allowing Manmohan Singh to take the reins as prime minister (see p32).

At the dawn of the new millennium, South India appears more prosperous than ever, leading India's hi-tech push into the cyber age. Mumbai, Bangalore, Hyderabad and Chennai are at the centre of a software revolution (see the boxed text, below) and a burgeoning economy.

Bharatiya Janata Party (www.bjp.org) is the official website of the BJP, who held power from 1998 to 2004, while Indian National Congress (www.congress.org.in) is the official website for India's ruling Congress Party.

A SOFTWARE SUPERPOWER

India's burgeoning IT industry, born in the boom years of the 1990s and founded on India's highly skilled middle class and abundance of relatively inexpensive labour, has made India a major player in the world of technology.

The industry currently employs nearly 800,000 Indians, with that figure expected to rise to two million by 2008, with a further two million benefiting through indirect employment. When this is added to the trend towards large-scale outsourcing, whereby call centres attached to Western companies move offshore to India, the scale of the revolution in India's once-ramshackle economy starts to become apparent.

The IT boom has transformed cities like Hyderabad (p411), nicknamed 'Cyberabad' by many locals, and Bangalore (p207), known as India's 'Silicone Valley', into IT world leaders. Tamil Nadu, Karnataka and Andhra Pradesh now produce more than 50% of India's software exports, although the dominance of the current software-producing giants – Bangalore and Hyderabad – may soon be challenged by other growth centres such as Pune, Mumbai (Bombay), Kolkata (Calcutta) and Ahmedabad.

The industry does have its critics, particularly those who claim that India's IT growth is an entirely urban phenomenon with little discernible impact upon the lives of the vast majority of Indians. It is also true, however, that the IT-boom has been central to a resurgent national confidence and economic growth at stellar rates.

Whatever the rights and wrongs, IT promises to become one of the great success stories of Indian history.

1987	26 December 2004
Goa officially becomes India's 25th state in May	Tsunami hits the Andaman & Nicobar Islands and southeastern India, causing widespread destruction and claiming at least 16,000

The Culture

THE NATIONAL PSYCHE

In a country of more than a billion people it might seem difficult to pin down a single element that defines the national psyche. In India, however, that's comparatively easy to do: religion infuses everyday life for all. Whether it be the simple daily *puja* (prayer) at a household shrine, a pilgrimage to a holy site, buying garlands of flowers and other temple offerings from a street stall, a family outing to a Goan church or the fasting of Ramadan, an individual's faith (whether it be Hindu, Muslim, Christian or Buddhist) defines and guides daily life at home and work.

Along with religion, family is at the core of Indian society. For the vast majority of Indians the idea of being unmarried and without children by one's mid-30s (at the very latest) is inconceivable. Despite the growing number of nuclear families (predominantly in larger cities), the extended family remains a cornerstone in both urban and rural areas, with men – usually the breadwinners – generally considered the head of the household, and two or three generations of a family often living under one roof.

With religion and family being so highly revered, don't be surprised if you are constantly grilled about these subjects and receive curious (possibly disapproving) looks if you don't fit the mould. Apart from religion and marital status, frequently asked questions focus on age, profession and even income. Such questions aren't intended to offend, and it's also perfectly acceptable for you to ask the same questions in return.

India's most famous festival and the largest gathering of humankind on earth, the Kumbh Mela, was celebrated in Nasik, Maharashtra, in 2003. The Hindu pilgrimage will again be in Nasik in 2007.

TRADITIONAL DRESS

The sari is the traditional dress of women in South India. It is worn with a choli, a tight, short-sleeved blouse. If you've ever wondered how Indian women manage to keep their saris in position without any fastenings, here's how it's done:

1. With your left hand hold the inside end of the sari material.
2. Tuck the top border of the inner end of the sari into your petticoat, keeping the hem of the sari just above the floor.
3. Keeping the sari at the same height off the floor, wind the material around to the front.
4. Make sure the sari is still held firmly – tuck it in a little if necessary.
5. Fold most of the rest of the material into pleats, starting at the right.
6. Hold the pleats firmly, making sure the bottom hem is at floor level; tuck in the pleats, letting them fall straight.
7. Wind the remaining material around you and over your left shoulder.

This method of draping a sari is increasingly favoured; however, there are many other ways to do it. One researcher has documented more than 100, reflecting tribal and regional variations, and even caste differences within regions. In some areas saris were (and sometimes still are) traditionally worn in two pieces, the lower piece more closely resembling a sarong. An example is the *mundu* of Kerala.

The garment typically worn by men in South India is the dhoti, a simple piece of cloth knotted around the waist and pulled through between the legs. The lungi is also popular, particularly in Tamil Nadu. This is a coloured piece of material worn rather like a short sarong.

When it comes to everyday wear, young people in particular seem increasingly to favour the *salwar kameez*, a garment commonly associated with Punjab and North India. It comprises pyjamalike trousers over which is worn a loose, generally long-sleeved, collarless top.

National pride has always existed on the subcontinent, but has seen a surge in recent years as India attracts increasing international kudos in the fields of IT, literature, film and sport (chiefly cricket). In 21st-century India the juxtaposition of the time honoured and the New Age flies in the face of some common stereotypes about the country. In South Indian cities the explosion of the IT industry has created a young urban elite, where Western fashions and music are in vogue, American TV shows and movies are all the rage, and you'll see young couples chatting over an espresso or engrossed in conversation on their mobile phones.

LIFESTYLE

Although the lifestyle of a rice farmer in rural Karnataka bears little resemblance to that of a middle-class IT professional in Bangalore, certain cultural and caste traditions are shared by most Indians. An invitation to an average South Indian home will reveal that life revolves around the basic needs of faith, work, food and – even in many villages – TV!

Traditional Culture

BIRTH, DEATH & MARRIAGE

The birth of a child is an important occasion – though, unfortunately, among most Hindus it is still considered preferable to have a boy rather than a girl. Traditionally, mother and child are kept in seclusion for the first two weeks after the birth, and then a ritual bathing takes place. Four important ceremonies are performed by Hindu parents for their children: *jatakarma* (casting a horoscope), *nama karma* (name giving), *annaprasana* (giving the first solid food, usually rice) and *chaula* (shaving the head, usually when the child is about five years old).

Marriage is a highly auspicious event for Indians and a major cause for celebration. Although 'love marriages' have increased in recent years (mostly in urban centres), most Hindu marriages are arranged. Christian and Hindu communities follow similar processes to procure a suitable partner for a son or daughter. Discreet inquiries are made among friends and within the community. Desirable attributes in the potential partner include a good job, a good position in society, a respectable family, upstanding character and reasonable looks. In Hindu society horoscopes are drawn up to ensure the prospective couple is compatible, and sometimes the family deity is consulted.

In some Tamil communities, bride price (gifts given to the bride's family) used to be the convention, but these days dowries (though illegal) are usually required to be paid by the bride's family, and this can apply to both Hindu and Christian weddings. This custom can facilitate a Hindu match or hinder it: intercaste marriages become much more acceptable if there's a good dowry, but a high-caste girl whose family has no money can find it very difficult to secure a partner from the same background. Divorce is severely frowned upon in India, though it's gradually becoming more common. Hindus in particular consider divorce acceptable only under certain circumstances, such as when one of the partners is mentally ill or incapacitated, or if the wife is found to be infertile.

Funeral ceremonies in the Hindu community are similar for all castes. Children below the age of eight are buried, and all others are cremated. In preparation for the cremation, the body is washed, laid on a bier and covered with a shroud. The chief mourner (usually the eldest son) also bathes, and then friends or members of the family carry the body to the funeral pyre. The chief mourner lights the pyre and walks three times around it with a pot of water before standing at the head of the pyre.

Unveiling India, by Anees Jung, touches on her own experiences growing up in Hyderabad as a child in purdah and those of other women from both rural and urban backgrounds, and explores various issues that affect women all over India today.

Hindu Resources Online (www.hindu.org) has links to many Hindu-related sites covering culture, current affairs and religion.

On the third day after the cremation the chief mourner, accompanied by family and a few friends, collects the ashes, which are then consigned to water. Those with enough money will travel north to scatter the ashes on the sacred Ganges River.

The Caste System

Caste is the basic social structure of Hindu society. Living a righteous life and fulfilling your dharma (moral duty) augments your chances of being born into a higher caste and thus into better circumstances. Hindus are born into one of four varnas (castes): Brahmin (who were traditionally priests), Kshatriya (warriors), Vaishya (merchants) and Shudra (peasants). The Brahmins were said to have emerged from the mouth of Lord Brahma at the moment of creation, Kshatriyas were said to have come from his arms, Vaishyas from his thighs and Shudras from his feet. Castes are divided into thousands of *jati*, groups of 'families' or social communities into which individuals are born, which are sometimes but not always linked to occupation.

Traditional South Indian Brahmins live with probably the strictest and most detailed rules of lifestyle and behaviour of any Indian community. These include dietary laws (which dictate a strictly vegetarian regimen and no 'hot' foods, such as garlic or chilli), dress rules and social etiquette for every occasion. Some Brahmin groups immigrated to South India to escape oppression by Muslim rulers, who often targeted Brahmins to win the support of lower Hindu castes.

Beneath the four main castes are the Dalits (formerly known as Untouchables). Their lives were the most menial of all, and even today sweepers and latrine cleaners are invariably drawn from their ranks. Some Dalit leaders, such as Dr Ambedkar (see p140), have tried to change their status by adopting another faith; in his case it was Buddhism, and he brought many followers with him. Unfortunately, Muslims, Christians and Buddhists of Dalit origin still face discrimination, sometimes even from their co-religionists. At the very bottom of the social heap are the Denotified Tribes. They had been known as the Criminal Tribes until 1952, when a reforming law officially recognised 198 tribes and castes. Many are nomadic or seminomadic, forced by the wider community to eke out a living at the fringes.

Today the caste system, although weakened, still wields considerable power. While one of the main aims of the Indian Constitution is the abolition of the caste system, caste still appears in official life in everything from government jobs to primary-school enrolments. The relationship between caste and politics is quite potent; those seeking power may

Set in Kerala against the backdrop of caste conflict and India's struggle for independence, David Davidar's novel *The House of Blue Mangoes* spans three generations of a Christian family.

The word 'pariah' comes from the name of a Tamil Dalit group, the Paraiyars.

HOMOSEXUALITY IN INDIA

According to a 2004 report there are an estimated to be 50 million gay men in India (there are no available statistics regarding lesbians). Although the more liberal sections of certain cities (such as Mumbai (Bombay) and Bangalore) appear to be becoming more tolerant of homosexuality, gay life is still largely suppressed (see p470). Since marriage is so highly regarded in India, it's believed that most gay people stay in the closet or risk being disowned by their families and society. Nevertheless, freedom of expression in certain cities is growing. For instance, in 2003 Mumbai hosted the Larzish festival – India's first queer film festival – now held annually in November. This was quite a coup for the gay community considering the hullabaloo raised by religious zealots over Deepa Mehta's film *Fire* (with lesbian themes), which was famously banned by the ultra-conservative Shiv Sena party in 1998.

ADIVASIS – THE FIRST PEOPLE

At least 15 million people in South India belong to tribal communities. They are variously known as tribals, scheduled tribes or Adivasis (First People). As the name suggests, they predate both the Vedic Aryans and the Dravidians. A more traditional name is Girijan, which means 'Forest People'. For thousands of years they have lived more or less undisturbed in the hills and densely wooded regions that agriculturalists regard as unattractive. Many still speak tribal languages not understood by the politically dominant Hindus, and they follow customs foreign to both Hindus and Muslims. Major Adivasi communities in South India include the Kondhs and Santals of Orissa (see the boxed text, p452), the Lambanis and Halakkis of northern Karnataka, and the Todas of the Nilgiri Hills of Tamil Nadu (see the boxed text, p383).

Although there has obviously been some contact between the Adivasis and Hindu villagers on the plains, this has rarely led to friction since traditionally there has been little or no competition for resources and land. But this is changing. In the past 50 years the majority of Adivasis have been dispossessed of their ancestral land and turned into impoverished labourers.

In parts of South India, especially in Orissa, Andhra Pradesh and the Andaman and Nicobar Islands, exploitation, dispossession and widespread hunger have occurred with the connivance and even encouragement of officialdom. It's a record the government would prefer to forget and one it vehemently denies. Instead it points to the millions of rupees said to have been sunk into schemes to improve conditions for Adivasis. Although some of this money has got through, corruption has gobbled a substantial portion of it.

Yet the picture isn't all bleak. A policy of reserving government jobs for Adivasis is helping to create an educated, articulate elite. There has been some revival of tribal religions as a way of preserving their cultural identity. Adivasis are increasingly finding a voice in politics. The real threat is that with a change in traditional lifestyles from forest gathering or subsistence farming to more diverse activities, the Adivasis' cultures will wither away.

look to certain *jatis* as potential vote banks. In an effort to improve the position of the Dalits, the government reserves significant numbers of public-sector jobs, parliamentary seats and university places for them. Today these affirmative-action quotas account for up to 60% of sought-after government jobs (which usually translate into jobs for life). The situation varies from state to state, as different political leaders chase caste vote banks by promising to include them in reservations.

Contemporary Issues
AIDS IN INDIA

With some five million reported cases of HIV, India has the second-highest rate of HIV infection in the world. Mumbai has the highest rate of infection in the nation, while the coastal cities of Andhra Pradesh and Tamil Nadu also have high rates. In Mumbai an estimated 55% of sex workers are believed to be HIV positive. Health officials warn that unless there are dedicated educational programs and increased condom use throughout India, the number of HIV-positive people could swell to 31 million by 2010.

CHILD LABOUR

Despite national legislation prohibiting child labour, human-rights groups believe India currently has between 80 million and 115 million child labourers – the highest rate in the world. Poorly enforced laws, poverty and the lack of a social-security system are seen as major causes of the problem.

The majority of child labourers work in the agricultural industry, while others work as rag-pickers, household servants, carpet-weavers,

Everybody Loves a Good Drought, by Mumbai-based journalist Palagummi Sainath, is a collection of reports on the living conditions of the rural poor.

Chandni Bar, directed by Madhur Bhandarkar, offers a realistic and disturbing window into the lives of women who, driven by poverty and often family pressure, work as dancers/prostitutes in Mumbai's seedy bars.

brickmakers and even prostitutes. In Kanchipuram (Tamil Nadu), a large number of school-aged children work full time in the silk industry – see the boxed text, p339.

POVERTY

According to the Census of India (www.censusindia .net), India's population grew by 157 million between 1991 and 2001, which is more than the entire population of Russia.

Raising the living standards of India's poor has been high on government agendas since Independence. However, India still has one of the world's highest concentrations of poverty, with an estimated 350 million to 400 million Indians living below the poverty line – 75% of them in rural areas. An estimated 34.7% of the population survives on under US$1 per day.

The major causes of poverty include illiteracy and a population growth rate that substantially exceeds India's economic growth rate.

India's minimum daily wage is pegged at Rs 54.28 (about US$1.20), although this isn't always the case in reality. For instance, in one of the

---

DOS & DON'TS

Religious Etiquette

It pays to be respectful when visiting a temple, mosque or religious festival. Shorts and sleeveless tops aren't appropriate, nor is smoking or being physically affectionate with your partner. Keep in mind that Indians take gods seriously, even if at first glance a festival appears chaotic. You must remove your shoes before entering a non-Christian place of worship, and in Muslim shrines women should cover their hair with a scarf. Feet are seen to be particularly unclean, so you must avoid pointing your feet at other people or holy images. Non-Hindus are not permitted to enter Keralan temples or the inner sanctums of temples in other states (though it's amazing what a little baksheesh slipped to a temple priest can do).

In Hindu temples where you can approach the deity it's sensible to have the residing priest perform a *puja* (offering) for you; worshippers find it rather weird when foreigners turn up and treat a living temple as if it were a museum. A *puja* generally costs Rs 5 to 10; you put the money on a tray and then scoop some smoke from the tray's burning lamp to 'wash' it over your face. You might also be offered a small garland of flowers, which you should accept and hold onto until you leave the temple. This is only a very general description, and lots of temples have unique customs. If in doubt, ask what you should do, and you'll find that people are happy to help.

When visiting Buddhist shrines, you must walk around the various altars and statues in a clockwise direction.

Photographic Etiquette

You should be sensitive about taking photos of people, especially women – always ask first. Taking photos of funerals, religious ceremonies or of people bathing will almost certainly cause offence. Flash photography may be prohibited in certain areas of a shrine, or may not be permitted at all.

Other Travellers' Tips

To increase your chances of receiving an accurate response when seeking directions, avoid posing questions in a leading manner. For instance, it's best to ask 'Which way to the museum?' rather than pointing and asking 'Is this the way to the museum?'.

It's also worth noting that the commonly used sideways wobble of the head doesn't necessarily mean 'no'. It can translate to 'yes', 'maybe' or 'I have no idea'. Often it simply means 'I understand what you're saying'.

If you're invited to someone's home, remove your shoes before entering, avoid pointing your feet at anyone when sitting and wash your hands before eating.

Even at beach resorts, nudity is never acceptable; it's best to wear at least a swimsuit if you go swimming. Indian women prefer to take a dip fully clothed.

HIJRAS

India's most visible nonheterosexual group is the *hijras*, a caste of transvestites and eunuchs who dress in women's clothing. Some are gay, some are hermaphrodites and some were unfortunate enough to be kidnapped and castrated. Since it's traditionally unacceptable to live openly as a gay man, *hijras* get around this by becoming, in effect, a sort of third sex. They work mainly as uninvited entertainers at weddings and celebrations of the birth of male children, and as prostitutes.

Read more about *hijras* in *The Invisibles* by Zia Jaffrey and *Ardhanarishvara the Androgyne* by Dr Alka Pande.

---

lowest paid occupations, herd-keeping, the average daily wage is around Rs 40 to 45, and it's often even lower for women.

Poverty and prostitution are closely linked. A 2005 report indicated that India might have up to 10 million prostitutes, around 20% of them under the age of 18.

Poverty accounts for the escalating number of beggars, predominantly in the larger cities – it's certainly a confronting situation in big cities, such as Mumbai. Whether you give something or not is a matter of personal choice; however, your money can often be put to better long-term use if you donate it to a reputable charity. Alternatively, you could lend a hand by working as a volunteer at a charitable organisation (see p483).

POPULATION

India has a little over one billion people according to the 2001 census, but the majority of that population is concentrated in the north. Around 360 million live in South India. Although it may feel urbanised when you're in the crowded streets of Mumbai (Bombay) or Chennai (Madras), only about 12% of the population lives in the main cities (22 million in Mumbai and Chennai alone); the rest live in the hundreds of towns and rural villages. Maharashtra is by far the most populous South Indian state, with around 97 million people. Nationally, men outnumber women (933 females to 1000 males), so Kerala is unique in having substantially more women than men (1058 females to every 1000 males).

In South India a large proportion of the population is Dravidian. Over the millennia, however, invasion, trade and settlement have made the population as diverse as anywhere in the country. Jewish people settled in what is now Kerala about 2000 years ago. Invaders and traders from the north, such as Aryans, introduced their traditions in various parts of South India over the years. Christians from the Middle East also arrived on Kerala's coast in about AD 100. Arabian and Chinese people came to the Malabar and Coromandel Coasts as traders, and were followed by the Portuguese, the Danes, the French, the Dutch and the British.

RELIGION

South India has a diverse range of religions and religious sects. The vast majority are Hindu (around 82% of all Indians are Hindus), although, given the region's history, there's more mixing and melding than the census figures on religious affiliation would suggest. In Goa, Christians and Hindus often observe the same festivals, while in Vailankanni, in Tamil Nadu, the Church of Our Lady of Good Health attracts thousands of Hindus as well as Christian pilgrims at festival times, such as Christmas and Easter. Hyderabad has a large Muslim population, while Mumbai is home to a dwindling community of Parsis (Zoroastrians).

The Todas of South India: A New Look, by Anthony R Walker, is a comprehensive study of the Toda people of South India. Illustrated with drawings and some photography, it's an accessible read on one of the most documented Indian tribal groups.

For a tailored itinerary covering the key temples and pilgrimages of South India, see p30.

Communal conflict between religions has long been a bloody part of India's history, but tensions between religious groups, including Hindus and Muslims, is much less noticeable here than in the north. In Goa and Kerala the Christian population lives in relative harmony with the Hindu majority. An exception has been isolated cases of retribution against Christian missionaries seeking to convert Hindus.

Hinduism

Hinduism is the world's third-largest religion after Christianity and Islam, but uniquely it has no single founder, no church hierarchy and no central authority. The proliferation of deities in the Hindu pantheon (330 million according to some estimates) may be confusing, but they're all simply manifestations of the supreme being.

At the apex of all the millions of lesser gods and goddesses is the trinity of Brahma (the creator), Vishnu (the preserver) and Shiva (the destroyer). Of these three, Vishnu and Shiva are worshipped more prominently. Shiva is especially revered in South India, coupled with worship of the goddess Devi or Parvati (representing energy or *shakti*).

Hinduism's origins go back thousands of years, as early beliefs surrounding fertility and the power of natural forces combined with the need to placate them. The Aryan invaders enshrined their beliefs in the Veda scriptures, which were passed down from generation to generation until they were recorded in Sanskrit sometime between 1000 BC and 500 BC.

Hindus believe that earthly life is cyclical; you are born again and again (a process known as samsara), and the quality of these rebirths is dependent upon your karma (conduct or action) in previous lives. Living righteously will enhance your chances of being born into a higher caste and better circumstances. Alternatively, if you have accumulated too much bad karma, you may be reborn in animal form. It's only as a human that you can gain sufficient self-knowledge to escape the cycle of reincarnation and achieve moksha (liberation).

WORSHIP

Worship and ritual are paramount in Hinduism – in Hindu homes you'll often find a dedicated worship area. *Puja* is a focal point of worship and ranges from silent prayer to elaborate ceremonies. Devotees leave temples with a handful of *prasad* (temple-blessed food); other forms of worship include *aarti* (the auspicious lighting of lamps) and bhajans (devotional songs).

GODS & GODDESSES

Following are the most prominent deities in South India.

Vishnu

Vishnu preserves the cosmic order. He is considered a redeemer of humanity and a knowable god. Unlike Shiva, Vishnu takes on human form, and he is said to have appeared on earth in nine separate incarnations, the most well-known being Rama, Krishna and Buddha.

He is usually depicted with four arms, each holding a symbolic item: a lotus (whose petals are symbolic of the unfolding of the universe), a conch shell (as it can be blown like a trumpet, it symbolises the cosmic vibration from which all existence emanates), a discus, and a mace (a reward for conquering Indra, the god of battle).

Vishnu's most famous temple is the Venkateshwara Temple (p427) at Tirumala in southern Andhra Pradesh.

Travels Through Sacred India, by Roger Housden, is a very readable account of popular and classical traditions, and contains a gazetteer of sacred places and a summary of ashrams and retreats.

Autobiography of a Yogi, by Paramahansa Yogananda, is a timeless classic of Indian spiritual philosophy. Yogananda is a wonderful storyteller as he recounts his search for enlightenment.

Vishnu, preserver and sustainer

Shiva

Shiva is the agent of death and destruction, but without him growth and rebirth could not take place. At Chidambaram, in Tamil Nadu, he is worshipped as Nataraja, lord of the cosmic dance. Shiva is frequently represented as a lingam, a phallic symbol often set in a yoni, which is symbolic of the vulva and thus female energy. He is also shown with snakes draped around his neck and holding a trident, which is representative of the Trimurti (the Hindu triad of Brahma, Shiva and Vishnu). His guardian is the bull Nandi, whose statue can often be seen watching over the main shrine (and therefore over his master).

Shiva, creator and destroyer

Shiva's consort is Parvati; because of his generosity and reverence towards Parvati, Shiva is considered an ideal role model for a husband.

Lakshmi

Lakshmi is Vishnu's consort and the goddess of wealth. In Tamil Nadu the *kolams* (rice-flour patterns, see p66) that grace the thresholds of homes and temples aim to tempt Lakshmi, and hence prosperity, inside.

Murugan

One of Shiva's sons Murugan is a popular deity in South India, especially in Tamil Nadu. He is sometimes identified with another of Shiva's sons Skanda, who enjoys a strong following in North India. Murugan's main role is that of protector, and he is depicted as young and victorious. It is speculated that Murugan may have evolved from an earlier fertility god.

Ganesh

The chubby, gentle, wise, elephant-headed Ganesh is one of Hinduism's most popular deities. He is the remover of obstacles, the god whom worshippers first acknowledge when they visit a temple. He is also patron of learning; the broken tusk he holds is the one he used to write down parts of the Mahabharata.

Ganesh, remover of obstacles

How Ganesh came to have the head of an elephant is explained in various stories. Some say Ganesh was Shiva's son, and others say that Ganesh was created by the goddess Parvati to guard the door while she bathed. Regardless, the gist of it is that, when Shiva was refused entry to Parvati's quarters by Ganesh, he lopped off Ganesh's head. When Shiva realised he had killed Parvati's son he sent out attendants with orders to bring back the head of the first creature they encountered. That creature was an elephant. Ganesh was restored to life, and rewarded for his courage by being made lord of new beginnings and guardian of entrances. Hindus invariably smash a coconut – to symbolise the smashing of the undesirable forces inherent within oneself – when they offer a prayer to Ganesh. *Modhakam* (sweetened rice balls) are sometimes distributed to children in front of the deity, and it is thought that the *modhakam* represent wisdom and are one of the things Ganesh holds in his hands.

Parvati

As Shiva's consort, Parvati symbolises the power – shakti – embodied in Shiva. Parvati is capable of taking many forms. The goddess can be benign (this is how Parvati appears), terrifying (in the form of Durga or Kali) or both (as Devi).

Parvati, benign aspect of Devi

Ayyappan

Ayyappan is another of Shiva's sons who is identified with the role of protector. It is said that he was born from the union of Shiva and

From Here to Nirvana, by Anne Cushman and Jerry Jones, is a popular guide to India's many ashrams and gurus. It provides useful (though slightly dated) information that will help you figure out which place suits your needs and aspirations. It also provides tips on how to spot dodgy operators.

Vishnu, both male. Also Vishnu is said to have assumed female form (as Mohini) to give birth. Ayyappan is often depicted riding on a tiger and accompanied by leopards, symbols of his victory over dark forces. Dedicated to Ayyappan, the Sabarimala Temple in Kerala attracts huge numbers of male pilgrims, all hoping to receive a taste of the spiritual and temporal success that Ayyappan embodies. Today the Ayyappan cult has become something of a men's movement, with devotees required to avoid alcohol, drugs, cigarettes and general misbehaviour before making the pilgrimage.

Islam

Islam was introduced to South India from around the 7th century by Arab traders who settled in coastal Kerala and Karnataka. About 10% of South India's population is Muslim, although this figure is higher in parts of Andhra Pradesh, Karnataka and Kerala. Most are Sunni, although Iranian traders and adventurers also introduced the Shiite sect to the region. Although the Mughals, a Muslim dynasty whose Empire encompassed a large part of India from the 16th to 18th centuries, controlled northern India for two centuries, they never really gained a stronghold in the far south, which is one reason there are so many intact ancient Hindu temples in Tamil Nadu.

Islam as a religion was founded in Arabia by the Prophet Mohammed in the 7th century. Islam is monotheistic; Allah is unique and has no equal or partner. Everything is believed to have been created by Allah, and is deemed to have its own place and purpose within the universe. In the years after Mohammed's death a succession dispute split the movement, and the legacy today is the Sunnis and the Shiites. The Sunnis, the majority, emphasise the 'well-trodden' path or the orthodox way. They look to tradition, and the customs and views of the greater community. Shiites believe that only imams (exemplary leaders) are able to reveal the hidden and true meaning of the Quran. Most Muslims in India are Sunnis.

The Marriage of East and West, by Bede Griffiths, is the famous book by the equally famous monk who lived for many decades in Tamil Nadu. The author examines the essence of Eastern and Western thought in an attempt to forge a fresh approach to spirituality.

All Muslims, however, share a belief in the Five Pillars of Islam: the shahadah or declaration of faith, 'there is no god but Allah; Mohammed is his prophet'; prayer (ideally five times a day); the zakat (a tax), which today is usually a voluntary donation in the form of charity; fasting during the month of Ramadan; and the haj (the pilgrimage to Mecca – something every Muslim aspires to do at least once).

Christianity

India has about 25 million Christians, and around three-quarters of them live in South India. Christianity is said to have arrived in South India (specifically the Malabar Coast) with the apostle St Thomas in AD 52. However, scholars say that it's more likely Christianity arrived around the 4th century with a Syrian merchant (Thomas Cana) who set out for Kerala with 400 families to establish what later became a branch of the Nestorian church. Today the Christian community is fractured into a multitude of established churches and new evangelical sects.

Window on Goa, by Maurice Hall, is an authoritative labour of love featuring descriptions of Goa's churches, forts, villages and more.

The Nestorian church sect survives today; services are in Armenian, and the Patriarch of Baghdad is the sect's head. Thrissur (p301) is the church's centre. Other Eastern Orthodox sects include the Jacobites and the Syrian Orthodox churches.

Catholicism established a strong presence in South India in the wake of Vasco da Gama's visit in 1498. Catholic orders that have been active in the region include the Dominicans, Franciscans and Jesuits. The faith is most noticeable in Goa, not only in the basilicas and convents of Old Goa, but in the dozens of active whitewashed churches scattered through towns and villages. Protestantism arrived with the English, the Dutch and the Danish, and their legacy lives on today in the Church of South India (and the Church of North India in Orissa). The Mar Thoma Church in Kerala has an interesting combination of Orthodox and Protestant beliefs.

Evangelical Christian groups have made inroads both into the other Christian communities, and lower caste and tribal groups across South India. Congregations with names such as the Love Army and God's Family are sometimes quite aggressive in seeking converts, and in 'retaliation' many Christian communities have been targeted by Hindu fundamentalist groups, such as the Bajrang Dal (p433).

St Thomas the Apostle landed in Kerala in around AD 58, then lived for some time in a cave in present-day Chennai. A church now occupies the site.

Jainism

There are only about five million Jains in India, most of whom are city dwellers. South India's small community of Jain people is centred on coastal Karnataka; the 17m-high sculpture of Gomateshvara (one of the world's tallest monoliths) at Sravanabelagola is at one of Jainism's most important centres of pilgrimage. The Jain religion was founded about the same time as Buddhism (it evolved as a reformist movement against Brahminism) and is centred on the concept of ahimsa, or nonviolence.

Buddhism

Buddhism developed in India when it was embraced by Emperor Ashoka. It appears that Buddhist communities were quite influential in Andhra Pradesh between the 2nd and 5th centuries. Missionaries from Andhra helped establish monasteries and temples in countries such as Thailand. However, Buddhism's influence waned as Hinduism's waxed in South India, about 1000 years after it was first introduced. It underwent a sudden revival in the 1950s when the Dalit leader, Dr Ambedkar, converted to Buddhism at Nagpur and brought many Dalit followers with him (see p140). Today these Neo-Buddhists, as they are called, number about six million and are concentrated in Dr Ambedkar's home state of Maharashtra. There are several communities of Tibetan refugees in South India, who have established many new monasteries and convents since the 1960s. The Bylakuppe area of Karnataka is one of the more easily accessible Tibetan settlements.

Aghora: At the Left Hand of God, by Robert E Svoboda, is a positively bloodcurdling account of a Tantric holy man who practices necromancy – the practice of raising the spirits of the dead – as a way to enlightenment.

Judaism

South India has a very small population of Jews, who first settled in the region from the Middle East as far back as the 1st century. Jews became established at Kochi (Cochin), and their legacy continues in the still-standing synagogues and trading houses.

Zoroastrianism

Beginning in Persia, Zoroastrianism influenced the evolution of Judaism and Christianity. Zoroaster (also known as Zarathustra) was a priest about whom little is known, except that he lived in eastern Persia. Zoroastrianism has a dualistic nature whereby good and evil are locked in continuous battle, with good always triumphing. While the faith leans towards monotheism, it isn't fully monotheistic. Adherents believe that good and evil entities coexist, although Zoroastrians are enjoined to honour only the good. The religion was eclipsed in Persia by the rise of Islam in the 7th century, and its followers – many of whom openly resisted conversion – suffered persecution. In the 10th century some emigrated to India, where they became known as Parsis (Persians). These

A Handbook of Living Religions, edited by John R Hinnewls, provides a succinct and readable summary of all the religions in India, including Christianity and Judaism.

Parsis settled in Gujarat, becoming farmers and adopting the Gujarati language. When the British ruled India the Parsis moved into commerce and industry, forming a prosperous community in Mumbai (see p101). The Tatas are one example of a prominent Parsi family.

Local & Tribal Religions

For a comprehensive overview of the world's religions, including Hinduism, Buddhism, Islam and Jainism, check out www.religionfacts.com.

Village and tribal people in South India have their own belief systems, which are much less accessible or obvious than the temples, rituals and other outward manifestations of the mainstream religions. The village deity may be represented by a stone pillar in a field, a platform under a tree or an iron spear stuck in the ground under a tree.

Village deities are generally seen as less remote and more concerned with the immediate happiness and prosperity of the community; in most cases they are female. There are also many beliefs about ancestral spirits, especially of those who died violently.

WOMEN IN SOUTH INDIA

South Indian women have traditionally had rather more freedom than their northern sisters. This is especially so in Kerala. Unique in many ways, Kerala is the most literate state in India and is also famous for its tradition of matrilineal kinship. Exactly why the matrilineal family became established in this region is subject to conjecture, although one explanation is that it was in response to ongoing warfare in the 10th and 11th centuries. With the military men absent, women invariably took charge of the household. It has also been argued that the men would very likely form alliances wherever they found themselves, and that the children of these unions would become the responsibility of the mother's family. Whatever the reason, by the 14th century a matrilineal society was firmly established in many communities across Kerala, and it lasted pretty much unchallenged until the 20th century. In 1938 Kerala became the first state to recruit female police officers. These days you'll often see female police officers in Mumbai and Chennai.

Mumbai's Parsi (Zoro-astrian) community still use the Towers of Silence to dispose of their dead, but a scarcity of vultures has meant they have had to resort to chemical methods in recent years.

In other parts of South India, such as Tamil Nadu, women also had more freedom than was the norm elsewhere. Matriarchy was a long-standing tradition within Tamil communities, and the practice of marriage among cousins meant that young women did not have to move away and live among strangers. Dowry deaths and female infanticide were virtually unknown in South India until relatively recent times, but the imposition of consumerism on old customs and conventions, making dowries more expensive, has resulted in some instances.

Women in Modern India, by Geraldine Forbes, is a fascinating study of the achievements and struggles of Indian women from the reform movement to today, using many personal accounts.

Throughout India women are entitled to vote and own property, and they account for around 10% of parliamentarians. Although the professions are still very much male dominated, women are steadily making inroads. For village women it's much more difficult to get ahead, and an early marriage to a suitable provider (often arranged years beforehand) is regarded as essential. In low-income families girls can be regarded as a liability because at marriage a dowry must often be supplied, posing an immense financial burden. For the urban, middle-class woman, life is materially much more comfortable, but pressures still exist. She is far more likely to be given an education, but once married is still usually expected to 'fit in' with her in-laws and be a homemaker above all else. Like her village counterpart, if she fails to live up to expectations – even if it's just not being able to produce a grandson – the consequences can sometimes be dire, as demonstrated by the practice of 'bride burning', which is an illegal (naturally) form of domestic abuse where the husband inflicts pain, disfigurement or death on his wife because he's unhappy with her dowry. It may take the form of dowsing with fuel and setting alight or scalding with boiling water, and may be made to look like an accident or suicide. It's claimed that for every reported case some 250 go unreported, and that less than 10% of the reported cases are pursued through the legal system.

Although the constitution allows for divorcées (and widows) to re-marry, few do so, simply because they're generally considered outcasts from society. Even a woman's own family will often turn its back on her if she seeks divorce, and there's no social-security safety net. Not surprisingly, divorce rates in India are low, despite having risen from seven in 1000 in 1991 to 11 in 1000 in 2004. See p485 for information for women travellers in India.

ARTS
Literature

South India's main languages – Tamil, Kannada, Telugu, Malayalam and Marathi – each have a long literary history. Tamil is considered a case apart (some early works date from the 2nd century) because it evolved independently from the others, which all derive from Sanskrit.

In the 19th century South Indian literature began to reflect the influ-ence of European genres. Where once literature had been expressed primarily in verse, now it was widely available in prose. By the end of the 19th century South Indian writers were pioneering new forms; among them Subramania Bharati and VVS Aiyar, who are credited with trans-forming Tamil into a modern language.

Modern South Indian literature in English has been a wildly successful cultural export, with superstars such as Mumbai-born Salman Rushdie and Keralan writer Arundhati Roy, who won the 1997 Booker Prize for her novel *The God of Small Things*.

One of India's best-known writers, RK Narayan, from Mysore. Many of his stories centre on the fictitious South Indian town of Malgudi. His most well-known works include: *Swami and His Friends*, *The Financial Expert*, *The Guide*, *Waiting for the Mahatma* and *Malgudi Days*.

Family Matters and *A Fine Balance*, by Rohinton Mistry, are expertly crafted accounts of contemporary Indian society, both set in Mumbai. The plots have a touch of melodrama, but they're still an excellent read. Part memoir, part social investigation, part crime story and part travel book, *Maximum City: Bombay Lost and Found*, by Suketu Mehta, delves into the vibrant city of Mumbai.

A Matter of Time, by Shashi Deshpande, centres on the problems a middle-class family faces when the husband walks out. Deshpande, who hails from Bangalore, takes the reader back through several generations to demonstrate how family tradition affects contemporary behaviour.

Sharanpanjara (Cage of Arrows), by Karnatakan author Triveni, is hailed as one of the great novels in the Kannada language (now available in English). The story centres on an upper-class Mysore woman facing the stigma of mental illness.

The Revised Kama Sutra, by Richard Crasta, takes an irreverent look at growing up in Mangalore in the 1960s and 1970s. It's a book that leaves you with a lasting insight into the local life of Mangalore and other South Indian cities.

Nectar in a Sieve, by Kamala Markandaya, is a harrowing, though at times uplifting, account of a woman's life in rural South India, and the effect of industrialisation on traditional values and lifestyles.

May You Be the Mother of One Hundred Sons, by Elisabeth Bumiller, is worth getting hold of for an assessment of the po-sition of women in Indian society. It offers excellent insights into the plight of women, and rural women in particular, especially in relation to arranged marriages, dowry deaths, *sati* (ritual suicide) and female infanticide.

Many common English words are Indian in origin: shampoo, khaki, jungle, pyjamas, guru, yoga and juggernaut, to name a few.

The first part of Salman Rushdie's *The Moor's Last Sigh* is set in Kochi, Kerala. His *Midnight's Children* is a stunning fable of India from Independence until the disastrous Emergency of the mid-1970s.

Karma Cola, by Gita Mehta, amusingly and cynically describes the collision between India looking to the West for technology and modern methods, and the West descending upon India in search of wisdom and enlightenment.

India: From Midnight to the Millennium, by Kerala-born writer Shashi Tharoor, is both an account of modern India and a personal history, shot through with revealing anecdotes. The way he explains his attachment to Hinduism is particularly enlightening.

Cinema

Cinema is the quintessential form of escapism for Indians from all walks of life. The nation churns out more films than any other country – more than 800 films a year – and most come from South India.

Mumbai, or Bollywood, is the mainstay of India's dream factories, the studios that turn out formulaic but entertaining spectacles based on the old folk-theatre staples of drama, dance and comedy. Regional centres, such as Chennai and Hyderabad, compete for the vast film-going public, though in Chennai, only Tamil films are produced. It's possible to score a gig as an extra on a film at studios in Mumbai (see p104) or Chennai

About 800 films are produced annually in India – about twice the output of Hollywood.

GREAT EPICS – THE MAHABHARATA & RAMANYANA

The Mahabharata and the Ramayana are two great Hindu epics that have been told and retold over millennia, retaining their potency and popularity to the present day. In the 1980s they were serialised by Indian state TV; the Ramayana drew an estimated audience of 80 million.

Of the two, the Mahabharata's origins can be traced back the further. It is thought to have been composed sometime around the 1st millennium BC. Legend has it that the author of the Mahabharata was the sage Vyasa, who witnessed the events in the epic. Vyasa dictated the text to Ganesh, who wrote it all down using his broken tusk as a pen. The epic is thought to have been special to the Aryan rulers and their warriors, focusing as it does on the exploits of their favourite deity, Krishna.

By about 500 BC the Mahabharata had evolved into a far more complex creation with substantial additions, including the Bhagavad Gita (in which Krishna gives advice to Arjuna before a great battle). The Mahabharata is eight times longer than the Greek epics the Iliad and the Odyssey combined. The story centres on the struggle between the heroic Pandavas and their enemies the Kauravas. Overseeing events is Krishna (an incarnation of Vishnu), who has taken on human form. Krishna acts as charioteer for the Pandava hero Arjuna, who eventually triumphs in a great battle with the Kauravas.

The Ramayana was composed around the 3rd or 2nd centuries BC and is believed to be largely the work of one poet, Valmiki. Like the Mahabharata, it centres on conflict between gods and demons. Basically, the story goes that the childless king of Ayodhya called upon the gods to provide him with a son. His wife duly gave birth to a boy. But this child, named Rama, was in fact an incarnation of Vishnu, who had assumed human form to overthrow the demon king of Lanka, Ravana. The adult Rama, who won the hand of the princess Sita in a competition, was chosen by his father to inherit his kingdom. But at the last minute Rama's stepmother intervened and demanded her son take Rama's place. Rama, Sita and Rama's brother Lakshmana were sent into exile and went off to the forests, where Rama and Lakshmana battled demons and dark forces. During this time Ravana's sister tried to seduce Rama and his brother, but was rejected. In revenge, Ravana captured Sita and spirited her away to his palace in Lanka. Rama, assisted by an army of monkeys led by their loyal king, Hanuman, eventually found the palace, killed Ravana and rescued Sita. All returned victorious to Ayodhya, where Rama was crowned king.

(see p321) – if nothing else you'll get an interesting insight into the industry. If that fails, you can tour studios at Hyderabad (see p417) and Chennai (see p321).

Mumbai is the epicentre of the Hindi film industry, but along with Pune it also turns out Marathi-language films. The classic formula for a blockbuster is the masala (mixed) movie, which combines family-values moralising, outrageous violence and romantic sequences that test the country's strict censorship rules as far as possible. The chaste heroine who somehow finds herself drenched in a waterfall, her clothes clinging to her, is a cliché that still appears surprisingly often. While often dismissed as escapist rubbish, masala do movies tackle serious social issues, such as caste conflict, religious tensions, corruption and the economic divide. Sometimes it's hard to pick out the message among the abrupt jumps in plot, the hammy acting and the song-and-dance routines, but talented filmmakers have a long tradition of mixing current issues with good old-fashioned entertainment.

As well as the obvious Bollywood blockbusters, most states in South India have their own regional film industry. Tamil-language films from Tamil Nadu and Telugu films from Andhra Pradesh are the most numerous, but there are strong Malayalam films from Kerala and Kannada films from Karnataka.

Another Indian film form is the art or 'parallel' cinema, which adopts Indian 'reality' as its base. Made on infinitely smaller budgets than their commercial cousins, these films are the ones that win awards at international film festivals.

For the latest on the film industry, check out India Film (www.indiafilm .com), Bollywood World (www.bollywoodworld .com) or Tamil Cinema World (www.tamilcinema world.com).

Music

South India's form of classical music, called Carnatic, traces its origins to Vedic times, some 3000 years ago. There are two basic elements in Indian music, the *tala* and the raga. The *tala* is the rhythm and is characterised by the number of beats; the raga provides the melody. In Carnatic music both are used for composition and improvisation.

While it has many elements in common with its northern counterpart, Hindustani, Carnatic music differs in several important respects. This has been attributed to the fact that it has been less influenced by Islam. Song is more important in Carnatic music than in Hindustani music, and this affects even purely instrumental performances. Visitors may find that Carnatic music sounds a lot more passionate and less restrained than Hindustani.

One of the best-known Indian instruments is the sitar (a large stringed instrument) with which the soloist plays the raga. Other stringed instruments include the *sarod* (which is plucked) and the *sarangi* (which is played with a bow). Also popular is the tabla (twin drums), which provides the *tala*. The drone, which runs on two basic notes, is provided by the oboelike *shehnai* or the stringed *tampura* (also spelt *tambura*). The hand-pumped keyboard harmonium is used as a secondary melody instrument for vocal music.

Appreciating Carnatic Music, by Chitravina Ravi Kiran, is aimed at helping those more familiar with Western music get to grips with this South Indian art form. It's a compact little book with masses of useful information, including a question-and-answer section.

Architecture

From looming temple gateways adorned with a rainbow of delicately carved deities to whitewashed cubelike village houses, South India has a rich architectural heritage. Traditional buildings, such as temples often have a superb sense of placement within the local environment, whether perched on a boulder-strewn hill or standing by a large artificial reservoir, or tank.

The influence of British architecture is most obvious in cities like Chennai, Bangalore and Mumbai, which have many grand neoclassical structures. British bungalows with corrugated iron roofs and wide verandas are a feature of hill stations such as Udhagamandalam (Ooty). More memorable are the attempts to meld European and Indian architecture, such as in the great 19th-century public buildings of Mumbai and the Mysore Palace.

The History of Architecture in India: From the Dawn of Civilisation to the End of the Raj, by Christopher Tadgell, is an illustrated overview of the subject and includes most of the important sites in South India.

RELIGIOUS ARCHITECTURE

For Hindus the square is the perfect shape, and complex rules govern the location, design and building of each temple, based on numerology, astrology, astronomy and religious law. Essentially, a temple is a map of the universe. At the centre is an unadorned space, the *garbhagriha* (inner shrine), which is symbolic of the 'womb-cave' from which the universe emerged. This provides a residence for the deity to whom the temple is dedicated.

Above the shrine rises a superstructure known as a *vimana* in South India and a *sikhara* in North India. The *sikhara* is curvilinear and topped with a grooved disk, on which sits a pot-shaped finial, while the *vimana* is stepped, and the grooved disk is replaced with a solid dome. Some temples have a *mandapa* (temple forechamber) connected to the sanctum by vestibules. These *mandapas* may also contain *vimanas* or *sikharas*.

A *gopuram* is the soaring pyramidal gateway tower of a Dravidian temple. The towering *gopurams* of various South Indian temple complexes take ornamentation and monumentalism to new levels. A stunning example is Madurai's Sri Meenakshi Temple (p366).

Stupas, which characterise Buddhist places of worship, evolved from burial mounds. They served as repositories for relics of the Buddha and, later, other venerated souls. A relatively recent innovation is the addition of a chaitya (hall) leading up to the stupa itself.

India's Muslim invaders contributed their own architectural conventions, arched cloisters and domes among them. India's most spectacular Mughal monument is the Taj Mahal in Agra. One of the striking differences between Hinduism and Islam is religious imagery. While Islamic art eschews any hint of idolatry or portrayal of God, it has developed a rich heritage of calligraphic and decorative designs.

The basic elements of a typical mosque are the same worldwide. A large space or hall is dedicated to communal prayer. In the hall is a mihrab (niche), which marks the direction of Mecca. Outside the hall there's usually some sort of courtyard with places for devotees to wash their feet and hands before prayers. Minarets are placed at the cardinal points, and it's from here that the faithful are called to prayer. Most large towns and cities will have at least one mosque; the best examples of Muslim architecture in South India include Hyderabad's Mecca Masjid (p415) and Golconda Fort (p415), and Bijapur's Golgumbaz (p253).

Churches in India reflect the fashions and trends of typically European ecclesiastical architecture, with many also displaying Hindu decorative flourishes. The Portuguese, among others, made impressive attempts to replicate the great churches and cathedrals of their day.

FORTS & PALACES

A typical South Indian fort is situated on a hill or rocky outcrop, ringed by moated battlements. It usually has a town nestled at its base, which has grown up after the fortifications were built. Gingee (p343), in Tamil Nadu, is a good example. Vellore Fort (p340), in Tamil Nadu, is one of

India's best-known moated forts, while Bidar (p256) and Bijapur (p254) are home to great metropolitan forts.

Daulatabad (p132) in central Maharashtra is another magnificent fortress, with 5km of walls surrounding a hilltop fortress. The fortress is reached by passageways filled with ingenious defences, including spike-studded doors and false tunnels, which in times of war led either to a pit of boiling oil or to a crocodile-filled moat!

Few old palaces remain, as conquerors often targeted these for destruction. The remains of the royal complex at Vijayanagar, near Hampi (p242), indicate that local engineers weren't averse to using the sound structural techniques and fashions (such as domes and arches) of their Muslim enemies, the Bahmanis. Travancore's palace of the maharajas (p272), at Padmanabhapuram, which dates from the 18th century, has private apartments for the king, a zenana (women's quarters), rooms dedicated to public audiences, an armoury, a dance hall and temples. The Indo-Saracenic Maharaja's Palace (p220), in Mysore, is the best known and most opulent in South India. The interior is a kaleidoscope of stained glass, mirrors and mosaic floors.

Architecture and Art of Southern India, by George Michell, provides details on the Vijayanagar empire and its successors, encompassing a period of some 400 years. Other books by Michell include *The Hindu Temple* and *The Royal Palaces of India*.

Sculpture

Sculpture and religious architecture are closely related in South India, and it is difficult to consider them separately. Sculpture is invariably religious in nature and isn't generally an art form through which individuals express their own creativity.

The 7th-century relief Arjuna's Penance (p334), at Mamallapuram (Mahabalipuram), is one of the most striking examples of early sculpture. Its fresh, lively touch is also reflected in later 9th-century Chola shrine sculptures. The legacy and tradition of sculptors from the Pallava dynasty lives on in Mammallapuram, where hundreds of modern-day sculptors work with stone to produce freestanding sculptures of all shapes and sizes (see p334). Some mix the old with the new – such as a sculpture of Ganesh talking on a mobile phone.

Unlike in the north of India, a tradition of South Indian sculpture was able to develop without serious interruption from Muslim invasions. But curiously, despite a high level of technical skill, the 17th-century work appears to lack the life and quality of earlier examples. However, South India remains famous for its bronze sculptures, particularly those of the 9th and 10th centuries, created during the highly artistic Chola dynasty (p37). Artisans employed the lost-wax technique to make their pieces, which were usually of Hindu deities, such as Vishnu, Shiva and – in the south especially – Shiva in his adored form as Lord of the Dance, Nataraja. This technique, still in use in South India, involves carving a model out of wax then painting on a claylike mixture to form a mould. The wax is melted out, leaving a hollow mould into which molten bronze (or silver, copper, lead etc) is poured. Some of the most exuberant sculptural detail comes from the Hoysala period (see the boxed text, p234), and can be seen at the temples of Belur (p233) and Halebid (p234) in Karnataka.

Dance

Indian dance once enjoyed the patronage of kings. Accomplished artists were a matter of pride among royals; the quality of their respective dance troupes was at one stage the cause of intense competition between the maharajas of Mysore and Travancore. Between the 2nd and 8th centuries, trade between South India and Southeast Asia brought a cultural legacy that endures in the dance forms of Bali, Thailand, Cambodia and Myanmar (Burma). Today dance – classical, popular and folk – thrives on city stages, on the cinema screen and in villages throughout South India.

The classical dance forms of South India include Bharata Natyam (Tamil Nadu), Kuchipudi (Andhra Pradesh), Kathakali and Mohiniyattam (Kerala), Odissi (Orissa) and Yakshagana (Karnataka), as well as many others.

BHARATA NATYAM

Tamil Nadu's unique performing art is believed to be India's oldest continuing classical dance, remaining true to conventions laid down in ancient times. It was originally known as Dasi Attam, a temple art performed by young women called *devadasis*. After the 16th century, however, it fell into disrepute, largely because it became synonymous with prostitution. It was revived in the mid-19th century by four brothers from Thanjavur, credited with restoring the art's purity by returning to its ancient roots.

Excellence in Bharata Natyam requires not only talent but great dedication. It requires at least seven years of training to master the gestures and poses of the head, eyes, neck, hands and body – each and every movement is charged with meaning. The dancer must fully understand the symbolism of the stories behind the dance in order to infuse the performance with its own unique flavour, or *rasa* – something conveyed through particular emotions *(bhavas)*. The artist's skill in conveying the *rasa* is of more importance to the audience than the story's plot, which is usually well known anyway.

Bharata Natyam is sometimes performed by men, but it's more commonly a female solo performance. There are strict guidelines regarding every aspect of the art, right down to the attributes required to be an accomplished dancer. Some of these guidelines are listed in Mrinalini Sarabhai's *Understanding Bharata Natyam*:

> …the danseuse should possess a good figure, should be young, with round breasts, experienced, charming, well-versed in rhythm, skilled in the movements of the body and the intricacies of the steps…with large, well-shaped eyes, tastefully apparelled and bejewelled, endowed with a sparkling face, not too stout or too thin, not too tall or too short…

Delve into India's vibrant performing arts scene – especially Indian classical dance – at Art India (www.artindia.net).

The dance will normally be accompanied by a singer '…who should not shake his head while singing, nor show any unbecoming facial grimaces…', who chants the lines of the story, often using small cymbals for heightened emphasis in certain parts.

The song and performance of Bharata Natyam is invariably an intimate expression of a devotional love; the major theme of the art form is worship of God through pure devotion and love. A drummer and musicians on stringed instruments may also accompany the singer. A typical performance lasts about two hours.

FOLK DANCES

South India has many kinds of folk dance. These include the Puraviattams of Karnataka and Tamil Nadu, where dancers are dressed in horse costumes; the Koklikatai dance of Tamil Nadu, in which dancers move about on stilts that have bells attached; and the Kolyacha fishers' dance from the Konkan Coast. Goa's stylised Mando song and dance is a waltzlike blend of Indian rhythms and Portuguese melody accompanied by Konkani words.

Various forms of trance-dancing and dances of exorcism occur throughout the south, and almost all tribal peoples, including the Todas of Tamil Nadu, the Kondhs of Orissa and the Banjaras of Andhra Pradesh, retain their own unique dance traditions.

Legends of Goa, by Mario Cabral E Sa, is an illustrated compilation of Goan folktales that offers an insight into the state's colourful traditions and history.

KATHAKALI

One of South India's most renowned forms of classical dance-drama is Kathakali, a Keralan form of play, usually based on Hindu epics. See the boxed text (p298) in the Kerala chapter for more information.

KUCHIPUDI

Andhra Pradesh's dance-drama, Kuchipudi, originated in a small village from which it takes its name. Like Kathakali (above), its present-day form harks back to the 17th century, when it became the prerogative of Brahmin boys from this village. It often centres on the story of Satyambhama, wife of Lord Krishna. Though Kuchipudi was once a men-only dance, women are the main performers today.

MOHINIYATTAM

From Kerala comes the semiclassical form of dance known as Mohiniyattam, which is based on the story of Mohini, the mythical seductress (*mohini* means 'enchantress' and *attam* means 'dance'). Hindu mythology is full of Mohini-like characters – beautiful women, often in disguise, who captivate men. Known for its gentle poetic movements, the dance form is notable in that it mostly has female performers. Containing elements of Bharata Natyam and Kathakali, it combines songs in Malayalam with Carnatic music (p61). Though it was neglected for some time, there have been signs of a Mohiniyattam revival.

ODISSI

Orissa's classical dance form, Odissi, was traditionally performed by *devadasis* to honour Lord Jagannath, particularly in Puri's Jagannath Mandir (p443) and Konark's Sun Temple (p447). It's possible that Odissi is an even earlier dance form than Bharata Natyam, as sculptural forms of Odissi date from 200 BC. Odissi's sinuous, flowing movements, which incorporate poses similar to those found in Indian sculpture, contrast with the angular strength of Bharata Natyam. The *tribunga* pose, in which the dancer bends at the neck, the waist and the knee, is generally considered the most graceful. Museums throughout India exhibit sculptural figures demonstrating the *tribunga*.

THEYYAM

At Kannur, in Kerala, you can witness the fascinating ritual of Theyyam (see the boxed text, p308), an ancient dance form practised by tribal people and villagers in the north Malabar region. The headdresses, costumes, body painting and trancelike performances are extraordinary. The Parasinikadavu Temple (p308), near Kannur, stages Theyyam performances in the early morning, and from January to April there are Theyyam performances in villages throughout the region.

YAKSHAGANA

Unique to the Tulu-speaking region of Karnataka's south coast, Yakshagana has long served as a vehicle for moral tales and legends, usually centred on the cosmic struggle between good and evil. The focus in Yakshagana is less on the dance or movement aspect of performance, since (unlike Kathakali) the actors have vocal roles to play, both singing and speaking. As in Kathakali, the costumes and make-up are not only visually striking but are deeply symbolic of a particular character's essential traits.

Handicrafts

A vast range of handicrafts is produced in India. including ceramics, jewellery, leatherwork, metalwork, stone-carving, papier-mâché, woodwork and a dazzling array of textiles. For more information, see p476.

POTTERY

The potter's art is steeped in mythology. Although there are numerous stories that explain how potters came to be, they all share the notion that a talent for working with clay is a gift from the supreme being, Brahma. This gives potters a very special status; on occasion they act directly as intermediaries between the spiritual and the temporal worlds.

The Arts and Crafts of Tamil Nadu, by Nanitha Krishna, with photography by VK Rajamani, is a beautifully crafted volume that's much more than a coffeetable book. There is detailed information on a range of crafts, including textiles, bronzes, terracotta, woodcraft, stone-carving, basketry and painting.

The name for the potter caste, Kumbhar, is taken from *kumbha* (water pot), which is itself an essential component in a version of the story that explains how potters found their calling. The water pot is still an indispensable item in India. The narrow-necked, round-based design means that women can carry the water-filled pots on their heads with less risk of spillage. The shape is also symbolic of the womb and thus fertility.

Apart from water pots, potters create a variety of household items, including all manner of storage and cooking pots, dishes and *jhanvan* (thick, flat pieces of fired clay with one rough side used for cleaning the feet). The ephemeral nature of clay-made items means the potter never wants for work. Potters all over the state of Tamil Nadu are kept especially busy at their wheels thanks to such traditions as the Pongal harvest festival (see the boxed text, p315). On the day before the festival starts, clay household vessels are smashed and replaced with new ones.

Potters are also called upon to create votive offerings. These include the guardian horse figures (which can be huge creations) that stand sentry outside villages in Tamil Nadu, images of deities such as Ganesh (in Karnataka these are created for Ganesh's festival in July or August), and other animal effigies. Clay replicas of parts of the human body are sometimes commissioned by those seeking miraculous cures and are then placed before a shrine. Clay toys and beads are also among a potter's repertoire.

Glazing pottery is rare in South Indian states. One exception is Tamil Nadu, where a blue or green glaze is sometimes used.

TEXTILES

Textiles have always had a vital role in South Indian society and trade, and are still the region's biggest handicraft industry. India is famous for *khadi*

KOLAMS

Kolams, the striking and often intricate rice-flour designs (also called *rangoli*) that frequently adorn thresholds in South India, are both auspicious and symbolic. Traditionally drawn at sunrise, *kolams* are made of rice-flour paste, which may be eaten by small creatures – symbolising a reverence for all life. Deities are deemed to be attracted to a beautiful *kolam*, and they may also signal to sadhus that they can expect food at a particular house. Some believe that *kolams* protect against the evil eye.

MEHNDI

Mehndi is the traditional art of painting a woman's hands (and sometimes feet) with intricate henna designs for auspicious ceremonies such as marriage. If quality henna is used, the design can last up to three weeks.

If you're thinking about getting mehndi applied, allow at least a couple of hours for the design process and required drying time (during drying you can't use your hands).

It's wise to request the artist to do a 'test' spot on your arm before proceeding, as nowadays some dyes contain chemicals that can cause allergies or even permanent scarring.

(hand-spun silk and cottons) – Mahatma Gandhi's promotion of khadi and the symbol of the spinning wheel played an important part in the struggle for independence. Although chemical dye is widely used now, natural dyes made from plants, roots, bark and herbs are still in use.

The sari typifies Indian style, and exquisite ones brocaded with pure gold thread are still produced in the tiny village of Paithan (p131) in Maharashtra. Much time and effort are put into selecting the base fabric, style of embroidery, colour and thread for handmade saris. All sequined, beaded and salma (continuous spring thread) saris are handworked. The fabric is usually rayon, cotton, satin or silk.

Embroidered shawls have assumed a significant role in the culture of the Toda people from the Nilgiri Hills (see the boxed text, p383) in Tamil Nadu. Embroidered exclusively by women in distinctive red-and-black designs, the shawls are made of thick white cotton material.

Silk saris from Kanchi-puram (p337) in Tamil Nadu are among the most coveted in India, especially for weddings.

SPORT

Like many countries, India loves to follow sport, and Indians put their sporting heroes – especially cricketers – on a pedestal.

Cricket

Cricket is undoubtedly India's favourite sport, and showing even a slight interest in the game is usually a sure-fire way of striking up passionate conversations with locals. Indeed, cricket is more than a sport; it's a matter of national pride, and this is especially evident whenever India plays Pakistan. Matches between these two countries – which have had a rocky relationship since Independence – attract almost fanatical support, and all the players are under colossal pressure to do their country proud.

Today cricket is big business in India, attracting juicy sponsorship deals and celebrity status for its players, especially star batsman Sachin Tendulkar. The sport has not been without its dark side, though, with Indian cricketers among those embroiled in match-fixing scandals a few years back.

International cricket matches are played at several centres in South India, mainly during winter. These include Mumbai's Wankhede Stadium (p114), Bangalore's M Chinnaswamy Stadium (p216), Chennai's MA Chidambaram (Chepauk) Stadium and Nagpur's VCA Stadium (p139).

India's first recorded cricket match was in 1721. It won its first Test series in 1952 at Chennai against England.

In early 2005 India was ranked second in the world, after Australia, as a Test-playing nation.

Football (Soccer)

Football has a passionate following in Goa and Kerala. The local newspapers carry details of important matches, and tourist offices can assist with more information.

INDIA'S NEWEST YUPPIES

The recent IT boom and outsourcing of overseas industries to India has given birth to a new breed of Indian yuppie, particularly in major southern hubs such as Bangalore. According to a recent survey, these young professionals (many in their twenties and unmarried) are ditching traditional spending patterns (eg for household goods and retirement) and spending a sizeable chunk of their incomes on more hedonistic pursuits such as dining out at fancy restaurants and travelling to exotic destinations.

These 21st-century, latte-swilling yuppies are the product of international companies that establish offices in India to boost earnings by slashing personnel costs, taking advantage of India's substantially cheaper salaries. For instance, an Indian call-centre operator (there are currently over 160,000 international call-centre jobs in India) receives an average of around Rs 10,000 per month. This is at least several thousand rupees higher than that paid by the average Indian company, but a fraction of the cost of what the overseas-based company would pay back home. Meanwhile, promising young Indian managers who have worked with an international company for just a few years are often rewarded (and, from the company's perspective, hopefully deterred from being poached by other international companies) with incomes of around Rs 150,000 per month – up to 80% more than the national average income for a middle manager.

See also the boxed text, p47.

Horse Racing

One of the many legacies of the British rule is a fondness for horse racing in parts of South India. Mumbai's racing season runs from November to April, with meetings every Sunday and Thursday at the Mahalaxmi course (p115). Horse racing is also popular in Bangalore, Mysore and Hyderabad. The seasons usually run from May to July and from November to February. South India's highest race course is at Ooty in Tamil Nadu, where races are held from April to June (see p387).

Traditional Sports

Kambla (buffalo racing) is a local pastime in rural southern Karnataka during January and February. A pair of buffaloes and their handlers can cover about 120m in around 14 seconds.

Kerala is renowned for its ancient martial arts form, Kalarippayat (see the boxed text, p263); you can see it practiced at the *kalari* (training school) in Trivandrum and at some hotels around the state.

MEDIA

Despite often having allegiances to particular political parties, India's extensive print media enjoys widespread freedom of expression. There are several thousand daily and weekly publications in a range of vernaculars. Major English-language dailies and news magazines are listed on p461; the *Indian Express* is perhaps the most politically investigative, unafraid to challenge the establishment, while the *Hindu* is the most widely distributed in South India.

Indian TV was dominated by the notoriously dreary national (government-controlled) broadcaster Doordarshan until the introduction of satellite TV in the early 1990s, which revolutionised viewing habits by introducing several dozen channels. Satellite TV offers a variety of programming, from Indian and American soap operas to Hindi and English-language current affairs. There are also a number of Indian regional channels broadcasting in local dialects.

Environment

THE LAND

Long sweeping beaches, palm trees, rice paddies and fertile farmland typify tropical South India, but there's much more to the landscape. The most
prominent geographical feature is the range of mountains known as the
ghats (meaning steps), running down the spine of South India, while most
of Maharashtra and Andhra Pradesh sit on the dry Deccan plateau.

The Vindhya Range, which stretches nearly the entire width of peninsular India (roughly contiguous with the Tropic of Cancer), is the symbolic
division between north and south. South of the Vindhya Range lies the
Deccan plateau (Deccan comes from the Sanskrit word *dakshina*, meaning
south), a triangular-shaped mass of ancient rock that slopes gently towards
the Bay of Bengal. On its western and eastern borders, the Deccan plateau
is flanked by the Western and Eastern Ghats. These ranges provide travellers with a cool break from the heat of the plains, just as they did for the
British Raj who established hill stations at strategic locations. Pockets of
the ghats are now protected in forest reserves and national parks.

The Western Ghats (known in Goa and Maharashtra as the Sahyadris)
start to rise just north of Mumbai (Bombay) and run parallel to the coast,
gaining height as they go south until they reach the tip of the peninsula.
The headwaters of southern rivers, such as the Godavari and Cauvery, rise
in the peaks of the Western Ghats and drain into the Bay of Bengal.

The Eastern Ghats, a less dramatic chain of low, interrupted ranges,
sweep northeast in the direction of Chennai (Madras) before turning
northward, roughly parallel to the coast bordering the Bay of Bengal,
until they merge with the highlands of central Orissa.

At 2695m, Anamudi in Kerala is South India's highest peak. The Western Ghats have an average elevation of 915m, and are covered with tropical
and temperate evergreen forest and mixed deciduous forest. The western
coastal strip between Mumbai and Goa, known as the Konkan Coast, is
studded with river estuaries and sandy beaches. Further south, the Malabar Coast forms a sedimentary plain into which are etched the sublime
waterways and lagoons that characterise Kerala. The eastern coastline
(known as the Coromandel Coast where it tracks through Tamil Nadu) is
wider, drier and flatter, and attracts fewer travellers than the west coast.

WILDLIFE

Although South India is home to a diverse range of wildlife, unless you
spend some time trekking in the national parks or visiting one of its
sorry-looking zoos, you're unlikely to encounter much more than the odd
temple elephant or a bold macaque making off with your lunch. With a
bit of time and effort, you can easily discover jungle animals, a rich array
of birdlife and, by diving or snorkelling, marine life.

India is one of 12 'megadiversity' countries, which together make up 70%
of the world's biodiversity. South India has three recognised biogeographic
zones: the forested, wet and elevated Western Ghats, which run parallel to
the west coast from Mumbai to Kerala; the flat, dry Deccan plateau, and the
islands, including Andaman and Nicobar Islands and Lakshadweep.

Animals

Most people know that India is the natural home of the tiger and Indian
elephant, but the forests, jungles, coastline, waters and plains provide a

The Ministry of Environ-
ment & Forest (www
.envfor.nic.in) is the
official Government of
India website.

*This Fissured Land:
An Ecological History of
India,* by Madhav Gadgil
and Ramachandra Guha,
provides an excellent
overview of ecological
issues.

India's national animal
is the tiger, its national
bird is the peacock and
its national flower is
the lotus.

habitat for a vast range of species. The following are some of the more common animals in South India.

ENDANGERED SPECIES

In 1972 the Wildlife Protection Act was introduced to stem the abuse of wildlife, followed by other conservation-oriented legislation, including the Forest Conservation Act and the Environment Protection Act. There have been various other initiatives, such as Project Tiger (launched in 1973 to protect India's wildlife); however, most have had limited success. Ultimately, the escalating pressure from an ever-growing population hungry for land, and a constant demand for animal body parts (largely from the Chinese medicine market) are proving to be virtually insurmountable forces. Ill-equipped park rangers pose little opposition to the well-equipped, organised gangs of poachers, and if that isn't bad enough, there have been allegations of some park officials being in cahoots with the poachers.

India is the world's only country that's home to both lions and tigers. But throughout India many species are facing a perilous future and the tiger seems to personify the situation. With skins used as trophies and bones ground into virility potions, a whole tiger can easily fetch upwards of US$10,000 (often much higher). This has made poaching a lucrative business; in 2003 an estimated 35 tigers in India were killed by poachers.

The snow leopard is another endangered species; its fur and other body parts fetch high prices on the international market. A 2004 report claimed there were less than 1000 left in India.

The olive ridley turtle population on the coast of Orissa also faces problems – see the boxed text, p450. Other animals on the endangered list include barasinghas (swamp deer), tortoises, Indian elephants (believed to number less than 16,000) and Gangetic dolphins.

In the Andaman Islands, the once-common dugong has almost disappeared. It was hunted by mainland settlers for meat and oil, and has suffered from a loss of natural habitat (seagrass beds).

BIRDS

Birdlife is where South India comes into its own, and there are several wetlands and sanctuaries supporting a large percentage of the country's water birds. Many species, including herons, cranes, storks and even flamingos, can be spotted at sanctuaries, such as Vedangtal (p337), Calimere (p356) and Chilika Lake (p449), especially between November and January. In village ponds, you may see a surprising variety of birds, from the common sandpiper teetering on the mud to the Indian pond heron, or paddy bird surveying its domain. Waterways are particularly rich in birds; graceful white egrets and colourful kingfishers (including the striking stork-billed kingfisher, with its massive red bill) are common, as are smaller, drabber species, such as plovers, water hens and coots, which feed and nest among rank vegetation. Red-wattled and yellow-wattled lapwings can be readily recognised by the coloured, fleshy growths on their faces.

Birds of prey, such as harriers and buzzards, soar over open spaces looking for unwary birds and small mammals. Around rubbish dumps and carcasses, the black or pariah kite is a frequent visitor. Birds inhabiting forested areas are woodpeckers, barbets and malkohas, a colourful group of large, forest-dwelling cuckoos; specialities of the forest areas of South India are blue-faced and Sirkeer malkohas. Fruit-eaters include a number of pigeons (including the Nilgiri wood-pigeon and pompadour green-pigeon), doves, colourful parrots (including Malabar and plum-headed parakeets), minivets and various cuckoo-shrikes and mynahs.

When Project Tiger started in 1973 there were nine tiger reserves with a known population of 268 tigers. Today there are 27 reserves and some 1500 tigers.

India is home to 340 species of mammals, 80 types of rodents, 560 species of reptiles and amphibians, 200 types of fish, over 50,000 species of insects and at least 1200 species of birds.

Cheetal Walk: Living in the Wilderness, by ERC Davidar, describes the author's life among the elephants of the Nilgiri Hills and looks at how they can be saved from extinction.

THE INDIAN ELEPHANT

Revered in the popular Hindu god Ganesh and valued for its strength and stamina, the elephant appears in many guises in South India's land, art, history and culture.

Today Indian elephants are honoured as well as exploited: tamed elephants are used in religious ceremonies or in logging (though they have largely been replaced by heavy machinery), while farmers fear the destructive capabilities of their wild brethren. Indian elephants weigh up to five tonnes and live in family groups, usually led by the oldest females. At puberty, males leave to live solitary lives. Elephants live in forest or grassland habitats and have large appetites, eating for up to 18 hour per day and wolfing down some 200kg of food, mostly grass, leaves and small trees. While in search of food, elephants have been known to leave the forest and demolish farmers' entire crops, bringing them into unwanted human contact. Indeed, humans are the elephant's only enemy. Along with loss of habitat from urban development and logging, elephants face an ongoing threat from poachers. The tusk of the male elephant is valued for its ivory, and illegal poaching has had serious effects on the gender balance. A report from the Wildlife Protection Society of India noted that while there are around 20,000 elephants in India, there are only about 1000 male 'tuskers' of breeding age.

The cultural significance of the elephant can be seen at temples and during festivals, where they may be colourfully decorated and lead processions. In Hindu creation myths, the elephant is the upholder of the universe, the foundation of life, while the elephant-headed deity Ganesh is the remover of obstacles, a wise and kindly god. Many temples have their own elephant, which takes part in rituals or waits patiently at the entrance with its mahout (trainer), accepting offers or coins with its trunk. Some national parks (such as Mudumalai; p390) offer elephant safaris into the jungle as an alternative to a vehicle; for more information see p461. National parks and forest reserves are certainly your best chance of seeing an elephant in the wild, but it pays to be with an experienced guide or on a jeep safari – elephants kill around 40 people a year in South India.

Hornbills are bizarre forest-dwelling birds, with massive curved bills, similar to toucans. The largest is the great hornbill, sporting a massive bill and a horny growth on its head (called a casque); the Malabar grey hornbill is endemic to the Malabar region.

Good places to see birds include: Periyar Wildlife Sanctuary (p284) in Kerala (for great hornbills, Malabar grey hornbills, Malabar trogons and Malabar parakeets); Calimere Wildlife & Bird Sanctuary (p356) in Tamil Nadu (excellent for water birds), and the Andaman and Nicobar Islands (p392), where 13 unique species have evolved, as well as a further 86 distinct island forms, which can now be found elsewhere in South Asia.

A Pictorial Guide to the Birds of the Indian Subcontinent, by Salim Ali and S Dillon Ripley, is a good field reference to birds of South India.

FISH

The still-pristine luxuriant coral around the archipelagos of Lakshadweep, Andaman and Nicobar supports a diverse marine ecosystem that hosts a myriad of tropical fish, including butterfly fish, parrotfish, the very ugly porcupine fish and the light-blue surgeonfish. Along the Goan and Malabar coasts, mackerel and sardines are prevalent, though overfishing from mechanised trawlers is an increasing problem. Other marine life off the coast of South India includes moray eels, crabs and sea cucumbers. Migratory visitors include the sperm whale *(Physeter catodon)*.

INVERTEBRATES

South India has some spectacular butterflies and moths, including the Malabar banded swallowtail *(Papilio liomedon)* and the peacock hairstreak *(Thecla pavi)*.

In the Andaman and Nicobar Islands, you may come across the huge coconut (or robber) crab *(Birgus latro)*, a powerful crustacean easily able to climb coconut palms and rip apart the tough coconut husk.

The waters around the Andaman and Nicobar Islands contain more than 1200 species of tropical fish; on land, more than half of the mammals identified are unique to the islands.

Leeches are common in the forests, especially during and immediately after the monsoon.

MAMMALS

Indian Jungles (www .indianjungles.com) is an up-to-date website dedicated to Indian wildlife.

The nocturnal sloth bear *(Melursus ursinus)* has short legs and shaggy black or brown hair, with a touch of white on its chest. It lives in forested areas of the national parks, and in the Nilgiris.

The gaur *(Bos gaurus)*, a wild ox (sometimes referred to as the Indian bison), can be seen in major national parks in Karnataka, Goa and Kerala. Up to 2m high, it is born with light-coloured hair, which darkens as it ages. With its immense bulk and white legs, the gaur is easily recognised. It prefers the wet *sholas* (virgin forests) and bamboo thickets of the Western Ghats but, sadly, large herds are no longer a common sight.

The common dolphin *(Delphinus delphis)* is found off both coastlines of the Indian peninsula, and dugongs *(Dugong dugon)* have been observed off the Malabar Coast and the Andaman Islands.

Antelopes, Gazelles & Deer

You will see plenty of these browsers and grazers in national parks. Keep your eye out for the chowsingha *(Tetracerus quadricornis)*, as it is the only animal in the world with four horns. It prefers an open forest and grassland habitat, such as found in Bandipur National Park (p227) and Nagarhole National Park (p228). The nilgai *(Boselaphus tragocamelus)*, or blue cow, is the largest Asiatic antelope and it congregates in small herds, which can be observed in open forest in parks and reserves in Andhra Pradesh and Karnataka. As it lacks impressive horns it hasn't been a great target for hunters, and its association with the sacred cow has also helped protect it.

There are about 200 million cows in India.

Not so lucky is the blackbuck *(Antilope cervicapra)*, whose distinctive spiral horns and attractive dark coat make it a prime target for poachers. As the name suggests, dominant males develop dark, almost black, coats (usually dark brown in South India), while the 20 or so females and subordinate males in their herd are fawn in colour.

The slender chinkara, or Indian gazelle *(Gazella gazella)*, with its light-brown coat and white underbelly, prefers the drier foothills and plains. It can be seen in small herds in national parks and sanctuaries in Karnataka and Andhra Pradesh.

The little mouse deer *(Tragulus meminna)* only grows 30cm tall. Delicate and shy, its speckled olive-brown/grey coat provides excellent camouflage in the forest. The common sambar *(Cervus unicolor)*, the largest of the Indian deer, sheds its impressive horns at the end of April; new ones start growing a month later. The attractive chital, or spotted deer *(Axis axis)*, is common throughout India and can be seen in most of South India's national parks, particularly those with wet evergreen forests. The barking deer *(Muntiacus muntjak)* is a small deer that bears tushes (elongated canines) as well as small antlers, and its bark is said to sound much like that of a dog. It is a difficult animal to spot in its habitat, which is the thick forests of Tamil Nadu, Karnataka, Orissa and Andhra Pradesh.

Tigers & Leopards

The tiger *(Panthera tigris)* is the prize of wildlife watchers in India but, being a shy, solitary animal, it's a rare sight. India has the world's largest tiger population – estimated to be about 3500 – but most of the famous tiger reserves, such as Kanha, are in North India. Tigers prefer to live under the cover of tall grass or forest and can command vast areas of territory. The best places to try for a tiger sighting in South India are the

Periyar Wildlife Sanctuary (p284), Tadoba-Andhari Tiger Reserve (p139), Bandipur National Park (p227), Navagaon National Park (p139), Similipal National Park (p454) and Nagarhole National Park (p228).

The leopard *(Panthera pardus)* doesn't stick exclusively to heavy forest cover, but is possibly even harder to find. Leopards are golden brown with black rosettes, although in the Western Ghats they may be almost entirely black. You may be lucky and see one in the Sanjay Gandhi National Park (p121) near Mumbai or Periyar Wildlife Sanctuary (p284) in Kerala.

Project Tiger, a government-sponsored scheme to preserve the country's tiger population, started in 1973 with nine designated reserves. There are now 27 reserves throughout India, nine of which are in South India. They include Bandipur and Bhadra in Karnataka; Srisailam in Andhra Pradesh; Periyar in Kerala; Similipal in Orissa; Pench, Melghat and Tadoba-Andhari in Maharashtra; and Kalakad-Mundanthurai in Tamil Nadu.

Land of the Tiger by one of India's foremost wildlife experts, Valmik Thapar, is beautifully illustrated with plenty of interesting facts, figures and background.

Dog Family

The wild dog, or dhole *(Cuon alpinus)*, is found throughout India. This tawny predator hunts during the day in packs that have been known to bring down animals as large as a buffalo.

The Indian wolf *(Canis lupus linnaeus)* has suffered from habitat destruction and hunting, and is now rare in South India. Its coat is fawn with black stipples, and it is generally a much leaner looking animal than its European or North American cousins. For a chance to see the Indian wolf, head to its preferred habitat of dry open forest and scrubland of the Deccan plateau.

The Indian fox *(Vulpes bengalensis)* has a black-tipped tail and a greyish coloured coat, and because of its appetite for rodents can coexist much more comfortably with farming communities than other carnivores.

Primates

You can't miss these lively creatures all over South India, whether it's passing through signposted 'monkey zones' as you traverse the Western Ghats, or fending off overfriendly macaques at temples or while you wait to board a boat at Periyar.

The little pale-faced bonnet macaque *(Macaca radiata)* is so-named for the 'bonnet' of dark hair that covers its head. These macaques live in highly structured troops where claims on hierarchy are commonly and noisily contested. They are opportunistic feeders – barely a grub, berry or leaf escapes their alert eyes and nimble fingers – and they love to congregate at tourist spots where excited families throw scraps of rice and fruit their way. The crab-eating macaque *(Macaca fascicularis)*, found in the Nicobar Islands, looks rather like a rhesus or a bonnet macaque, but has a longer, thicker tail. In contrast, the lion-tailed macaque *(Macaca silenus)* has a thick mane of greyish hair that grows from its temples and cheeks.

Less shy is the common langur *(Presbytis entellus)* or Hanuman monkey, recognisable by its long limbs and black face. India's most hunted primate is the Nilgiri langur *(Presbytis johni)*, which inhabits the dense forests of the Western Ghats, including the *sholas* (virgin forests) the Nilgiri and Annamalai ranges. This vegetarian monkey is pursued by poachers for the supposed medicinal qualities of its flesh and viscera.

The peculiar-looking slender loris *(Loris tardigradus)* has a soft, woolly, brown/grey coat and huge, bushbaby eyes. Nocturnal, it comes down from the trees only to feed on insects, leaves, berries and lizards. Though not as obvious as it once was, there is still a trade in South India for live lorises – their eyes are believed by some to be a powerful medicine for human-eye diseases as well as a vital ingredient for love potions!

REPTILES & AMPHIBIANS

Of the 32 species of turtles and tortoises in India, you may see the hawks-bill, leatherback, loggerhead or endangered olive ridley species in the waters of South India. Turtles are protected, but it's possible to see them nesting in some areas, notably at Morjim (p190) in Goa and Bhitarkanika Wildlife Sanctuary (p456) in Orissa. You may see the Indian star tortoise *(Geochelone elegans)* waddling along the forest floor in Andhra Pradesh.

Three species of crocodiles are found in India, two of them in South India – the mugger, or marsh, crocodile *(Crocodylus palustris)* and the saltwater crocodile *(Crocodylus porosus)*. The latter lives in the Andaman and Nicobar Islands, while the mugger is extensively distributed in rivers and freshwater lakes in South India thanks to government breeding programs. If you don't see them in the wild, you certainly will at the Crocodile Bank (p331), a breeding farm in Tamil Nadu. India is also home to 155 species of lizards and to 244 species of snakes, such as the tiny Perrotet's shield-tail snake *(Plectrurus perroteti)*, found in the Western Ghats, and the fearsome 3m-long king cobra *(Ophiophagus hannah)*.

Plants

India boasts 15,000 species of plants and trees (of which 2200 are used in traditional medicines). A quarter of these are found in the Western Ghats.

Forest types include the tropical, wet and semievergreen forests of the Andaman and Nicobar Islands and Western Ghats; tropical, moist deciduous forests in the Andamans, southern Karnataka and Kerala; tropical thorn forest, found in much of the drier Deccan plateau; and montane and wet temperate forests in the higher parts of Tamil Nadu and Kerala. Along the coasts of Tamil Nadu and Kerala there are also mangroves.

Characteristic of the Nilgiri and Annamalai Hills in the Western Ghats, as well as the highlands of Orissa, are the patches of moist evergreen forest restricted to the valleys and steep, protected slopes. Known as *sholas,* these islands of dark green are surrounded by expansive grasslands covering the more exposed slopes. They provide essential shelter and food for animals, but their limited size and patchy distribution make *sholas* vulnerable to natural and human disturbances.

Teak, mahogany, rosewood and sandalwood are common in (and smuggled from) the Western Ghats. You will also see banyan figs; bamboo in the Western Ghats; coconut palms on the islands and along the coastal peninsula; Indian coral trees along the coasts, and mangroves in tiny pockets. India is home to 2000 species of orchid, about 10% of those found worldwide. The Nilgiris Range is one of the finest places to spot orchids, such as the Christmas Orchid *(Calanthe triplicata)*.

The Kurinji shrub, which only produces bright purple-blue coloured blossoms every 12 years, is unique to the hills of South India's Western Ghats. Unfortunately the next blossom is due in 2016!

NATIONAL PARKS & WILDLIFE SANCTUARIES

Around 4% of India's area is protected in national parks or forest reserves. In South India, most of the parks were established to protect wildlife from loss of habitat, so entry is often restricted or limited to tours. Some parks are remote, rarely visited and may require getting past a fair amount of Indian red tape to visit; however, there are plenty of parks in South India that fully reward the time and effort it takes to get there. Some of the best are the combined parks of Bandipur (p227), Nagarhole (p228), Wayanad (p306) and Mudumalai (p390), which form the Nilgiri Biosphere Reserve; Periyar Wildlife Sanctuary (p284) and Similipal National Park (p454).

While parks are generally accessible by public transport, many travellers prefer to use their own transport. However, private travel within the confines of most parks is not allowed and you may find you've gone to

---

VISITING NATIONAL PARKS

The words 'wildlife', 'national park', 'jungle', 'trekking' and 'safari' conjure up exciting ideas in travellers' minds, especially for people who have travelled in other parts of the world. In South India it can be quite different. Safari may mean a one-hour trip in a jeep through the forest and a little picnic by a river. A trek may mean just a short walk. It could also mean the 'real thing'. Whether you're visiting a park with a government or private operator, take care to ascertain exactly what the tour involves, and ensure that safety standards and environmental issues are respected.

Usually, but not always, entry to parks for a day visit (from 6am to 6pm) requires no permits. It is on the whole *not* permissible to walk or trek in the parks, or any forested area, without a guide. However, finding the right guide isn't easy. Many have little or no training, little knowledge and take no responsibility for looking after the environment. If you do find the right guide, however, you are assured of an experience that is educational and rewarding. The best way to find a good guide is to go through a company or accommodation facility close to the parks that employ guides, or seek advice from local hotels or tourist offices.

---

considerable expense only to be advised that you must use an organised tour bus. Often the best trekking or jeep safaris can be experienced outside park boundaries, such as near Mudumalai National Park, where private lodges are set up. For more information on wildlife safaris, see p461.

Most parks have limited accommodation facilities and may limit the length of stay to just a few nights. For government accommodation you'll need to book in advance. Some travellers prefer to stay in accommodation outside but close to the parks and make day visits. This is possible at some, but not all, parks; many are just too isolated.

At times, your wish to enter a park may simply be denied. The reasons (sometimes real, sometimes fictitious) may be due to circumstances completely outside forestry personnel control – an insurgency group may be using the park as refuge, there may be fires or insufficient water, or the park may have been booked by VIPs (or that Indian invention, VVIPs). In the last event, you have no chance!

ENVIRONMENTAL ISSUES

With a population of just over one billion people growing by 150 million people every decade, and an unrestrained rush to industrialise, India's ecology is stretched almost to breaking point. The population makes ever-increasing demands on dwindling resources. Considering the wide-scale damage India's ecology has already endured, conservation is perhaps a misnomer in this context, and 'damage limitation' is a more accurate description of what now takes place. It isn't all doom and gloom, however. Increasing literacy is helping the growth of community-based environmental groups, and unmistakable signs of ecological damage mean that everyone, from grassroots groups to the prime minister, is at least paying lip service to better environmental practices.

Travellers can help in a positive way when it comes to the environment. Being a responsible tourist means learning about a region before travelling, and being aware of the implications of your presence in that region. Encourage hotel management, particularly in tourist areas, to dispose of rubbish in an environmentally friendly manner.

If taking tours, such as trekking tours, ensure that the operator follows environmentally friendly practices, such as carrying rubbish out, not damaging forest habitat or wildlife, and not lighting fires. Many tour companies market themselves as 'eco-friendly' to cash in on the conservation bandwagon.

Rudyard Kipling's classic children's' tale *The Jungle Book* is set in the mystical Indian jungles with a cast of characters including wolves, tigers, panthers, bears and monkeys.

NATIONAL PARKS & WILDLIFE SANCTUARIES IN SOUTH INDIA

Park/Sanctuary	Page	Location	Features	Best time to visit
Bhitarkanika National Park	p456	northeast Orissa	estuarine mangrove forests: salt-water crocodiles, water monitor lizards, pythons, wild boars, chitals, herons & stork breeding sites	Oct–May
Bondla Wildlife Sanctuary	p202	eastern Goa	botanical garden, fenced deer, park & zoo: gaurs & sambars	Nov–Mar
Calimere Wildlife & Bird Sanctuary	p356	near Thanjavur, Tamil Nadu	coastal wetland: blackbucks, flamingos, waterfowls, dolphins, crocodiles & deer	Nov–Jan
Debrigarh Wildlife Sanctuary	p453	near Sambalpur, Orissa	dry deciduous forest: tigers, leopards, deer, boars, sloth bears & birdlife	Oct–May
Indira Gandhi Wildlife Sanctuary	p379	near Pollachi, Tamil Nadu	forested mountains: elephants, gaurs, tigers, panthers, boars, bears, deer, porcupines & civet cats	Nov–Dec
Mahatma Gandhi National Marine Park	p404	Andaman & Nicobar Islands	mangrove, rainforest & coral: diving & snorkelling	Nov–Apr
Molem & Bhagwan Mahavir Wildlife Sanctuary	p202	eastern Goa	tree-top viewing tower: gaurs, sambars, leopards, spotted deer & snakes	Nov–Mar
Navagaon National Park	p139	east of Nagpur, Maharashtra	hilly forest & bamboo groves around manmade lake: leopards, sloth bears, deer & migratory birds	Oct–Jun

Deforestation

About 7% to 8% of South India is forested today. One of the most dramatic examples of deforestation is in the Andaman and Nicobar Islands where forest cover has been slashed from 90% to a mere 20%. Although protected forest reserves have been established on most islands here, illegal and sanctioned logging continues.

Demand for fuel and building materials, natural fires and traditional slash-and-burn farming, destruction of forests for mining or farmland, and illegal smuggling of teak, rosewood and sandalwood have all contributed to this drastic deforestation.

Marine Environment

The marine life along the 3000km coastline of South India and around the outlying archipelagos is under constant threat from pollution, sewage and harmful fishing methods. Ports, dams and tourism (especially in Goa) all contribute to the degradation of South India's marine environment.

MANGROVES

About 2.5 million hectares of mangroves have been destroyed in India since 1900. Mangroves are home to migratory birds and marine life, and are the first defence against soil erosion. They also help protect the coast from natural disasters, such as tidal waves and cyclones. Destruction of the mangroves has been caused by cattle grazing, logging, water pollution, prawn

The Centre for Environment Education (www.ceeindia.org) is a website dedicated to environmental issues in India.

Park/Sanctuary	Page	Location	Features	Best time to visit
Nilgiri Biosphere Reserve	p227 p228 p306 p390	Bandipur Nagarhole Wayanad Mudumalai	forest: elephants, tigers, deer, gaurs, sambars, muntjacs, chevrotains, chitals, bonnet macaques, leopards, giant squirrels & birdlife	Mar-May
Periyar Wildlife Sanctuary	p284	Kumily, Kerala	highland deciduous forest & grasslands: langurs, elephants, gaurs, otters, wild dogs, tortoises, kingfishers & fishing owls	Nov-Apr
Ranganathittu Bird Sanctuary	p227	near Mysore, Karnataka	river & island: storks, ibis, egrets, spoonbills & cormorants	Mar-May
Sanjay Gandhi National Park	p121	near Mumbai, Maharashtra	scenic area: waterbirds & butterflies	Oct-Apr & Aug-Nov
Similipal National Park	p454	Balasore, Orissa	forest & waterfalls: tigers, leopards, elephants, crocodiles & birdlife	Nov-Jun
Tadoba-Andhari Tiger Reserve	p139	south of Nagpur, Maharashtra	deciduous forest, grasslands & wetlands: tigers, leopards, sloth bears, hyenas, wild boars, deer & antelopes	Feb-May
Vedantangal Bird Sanctuary	p337	near Chengalpattu, Tamil Nadu	lake & island: cormorants, egrets, herons, stork ibis, spoonbills, grebes & pelicans	Nov-Jan

farming and tidal changes caused by the erosion of surrounding land. Only recently have satellite images revealed the full extent of the damage that has been caused. On the coast of Tamil Nadu and in the Andaman Islands there have been calls to reintroduce mangroves around fishing villages as a protective barrier following the damage caused by the 2004 tsunami.

PRAWN FARMING

The international demand for prawns saw a plethora of prawn farms set up in South India, resulting in vast environmental damage to the coastline and birdlife as well as to farmland. Mangrove forests are cleared to build ponds to grow prawns, thus removing habitats for marine life as well as a crucial line of defence for coral reefs. About 25 million litres of precious fresh water are required to produce one tonne of prawns, and the cost of repairing the damage already exceeds the hundreds of millions of export dollars earned each year. Ironically, prawn production is affected by other environmental damage (eg 40% of prawn farms in Karnataka are affected by the erosion of, and chemicals in, the soil).

Fish Curry Rice, published by the Goa Foundation, is a comprehensive study of the Goan environment and the threats facing it.

CORAL REEFS

Three major coral reefs are located around the islands of Lakshadweep, Andaman and Nicobar, and the Gulf of Mannar (near Sri Lanka). Coral is a vital part of the fragile marine ecology, but is under constant threat from overfishing and bottom-of-the-sea trawling. Other factors contributing to the onslaught against the reefs are shipping, pollution, sewage, poaching, and excessive silt caused by deforestation and urban development on the land.

FISHERIES

India's seas have been overfished to such an extent that stocks are dwindling. Trawlers and factory fishing ships have largely replaced villagers in traditional log boats, and in some areas – the coast of Kerala for example – fishing communities are struggling to find other sources of income.

Mining

Throughout South India, many mining rights have been granted without regard for the environment, and with no requirement to undertake rehabilitation. A staggering 15% of Goa is being mined – nearly half the iron ore exported from India comes from Goa. When open-pit mines have been fully exploited they are often simply abandoned, scarring the hinterland. In Goa and other states of South India, heavy rains flush residues from open-cut mines into the rivers and sea. Some residues seep into the local water table, contaminating the drinking water.

Some licences for the mining of gold, silver, platinum and diamonds in Karnataka, and for gold and mica in the Nilgiris, have been granted under dubious circumstances with little regard for environmental impact.

Water

India's water table is sinking, and in states like Goa the situation is exacerbated by heavy development for tourism. For example, regulations that no bore holes be dug within 500m of the high water mark have been ignored to draw water for swimming pools. In rapidly growing Bangalore, the inability of the city's water board to keep up with demand has meant that thousands of bore wells have been drilled to supply water over the dry months – the water table has plummeted by 100m in 10 years as a result. Agriculture, which uses 85% of water, is expected to double its demand by 2025, while industry is similarly expected to double the amount it uses, and domestic use will triple. Water resources are becoming an increasingly hot political issue; Karnataka and Tamil Nadu have been engaged in a long-running dispute over the Cauvery River since Karnataka controls the headwaters. Fortunately, good monsoon rains in recent years have eased tensions; however, the 2004 tsunami caused water shortages in Tamil Nadu when wells and water sources became salinated.

Safe drinking water is becoming an increasingly valuable resource. Many South Indian urban neighbourhoods now rely on trucks to bring in fresh water during the dry months.

Pollution

India is the 10th most polluted country in the world, and the seventh-largest producer of air pollutants. The effects of pollution are staggering – it costs India at least 4.5% of its annual GDP (according to the World Bank), and 70% of available drinking water is contaminated by pollution.

While North India is most heavily affected by pollution, the south is by no means without its share of problems. It's hard to find a river or lake that has not been polluted with sewage, rubbish and chemical waste. Factories spew chemicals into the sea, rivers and air with little regulative control by understaffed, and often corrupt, local authorities.

Tanneries and textile factories are often the worst polluters. Some rivers, such as the Noyyal and the Bhavani, tributaries of the Cauvery, are

The World Wide Fund for Nature (WWF; www.wwfindia.org) is widely involved in environmental protection and wildlife conservation issues, and has offices throughout India.

Goa Foundation (www.goacom.com/goafoundation) is the leading environmental group in Goa.

now virtually unusable for drinking water and irrigation. Pesticides used for cash crops, such as cotton and tobacco, upset the ecology – only about 1% of pesticides (which are often those banned in developed countries) actually reach the pests; the rest seeps into the environment.

AIR POLLUTION

Air pollution is a serious problem in South India, with Mumbai among the world's 10 most polluted cities, and Chennai, Hyderabad and Bangalore not far behind. Just breathing the air in one of India's 23 cities with over a million inhabitants is said to be the equivalent of smoking 20 cigarettes a day. About 60% of vehicles are two-stroke vehicles, such as autorickshaws, which, though economical to run and despite attempts to control their emissions, spew out pollutants. There is little incentive to move away from diesel, which is subsidised and relatively cheap.

The government has rarely pressured manufacturers to improve emission controls – the classic Indian car, the Hindustan Ambassador, had the same engine design for 40 years – but recently the courts have tried to crackdown on urban air pollution. The Indian government has introduced a Pollution Under Control (PUC) certificate setting emission control standards for all new and private vehicles. Some would say the system is out of control, with many PUC certificates issued falsely, faked or ignored, while government vehicles (such as buses) seem to get around the law altogether. In 2004 the courts directed states to crackdown on the issue of PUCs in an effort to curb urban pollution. In Mumbai, autorickshaws have been banned from the central area for some years, but that seems to be a case of curbing congestion as much as pollution.

Another contributing factor is the number of vehicles in India – in 1951 there were 306,000 registered vehicles in India, in 1991 that figure had jumped to a staggering 21 million and that figure has since quadrupled to around 80 million. The long-neglected road system leaves cars, motorbikes, buses and trucks jammed in streets in ever-growing numbers.

Air pollution in many of India's urban hubs is purported to be around 2.3 times higher than the level recommended by the World Health Organisation. Surprisingly, Chennai ranks as the least polluted of India's major cities.

Plastic Waste

Almost everywhere in South India plastic bags and bottles clog drains, litter city streets and beaches, and even stunt grass growth in the parks. Of growing concern are the number of cows, elephants and other creatures that consume plastic waste, resulting in a slow and painful death. The anti-plastic lobby estimates that about 72% of the plastics used are discarded within a week; only 15% are recycled.

Fed up with ineffectual government policies to address the plastic problem, an increasing number of local initiatives are being pursued. For instance, in Kodaikanal shopping bags are now made from paper instead of plastic, Goa has imposed a number of 'plast-free' zones, including on its beaches, and Karnataka's state legislature is discussing a total ban.

Tourists can assist by not buying anything in plastic bags or bottles, and encouraging hotels and shops to use environmentally friendly alternatives. Shopkeepers almost invariably put your purchases in plastic bags, and without turning it into a crusade it does help to ask if they can use paper bags instead or none at all. Other ways to help include buying tea in terracotta cups at train stations, bringing your own canteen and purifying your water (see the boxed text, p507). Avoid using plastic water bottles (or reuse them if you can purify water) and definitely avoid the plastic soft-drink bottles now being marketed by Coca-Cola in place of the recyclable glass bottles.

Food & Drink

Traditional South Indian cuisine is as different from North Indian as the land and people. Although meals may at times appear simple – mounds of rice and side dishes of sambar (dhal with cubed vegetables and puree), spiced vegetables and curd served on a banana-leaf plate and eaten with the hands – within this simplicity hides a sensual array of flavours, spices, regional variations and customs that come as a surprise to many travellers. Add to this the regional variations across the states, the unique colonial-influenced cuisines of Goa, Kerala and Mumbai (Bombay), coastal seafood so fresh you might as well have caught it yourself, and plenty of fresh fruit and vegetables, and there's plenty to tingle those tastebuds.

Of course, North Indian dishes are widely available, especially in hotel restaurants, so you won't have to look far to find the familiar tandoori meat dishes, butter chicken, rogan josh (mutton curry), pilau and naan bread. Western tastes are also catered for. In cities like Mumbai, Bangalore and Chennai (Madras) there are American-style burger and pizza joints, and beach resorts accustomed to backpackers will serve everything from porridge and pancakes for breakfast, to fish and chips or pasta for dinner.

> Technically speaking, there is no such thing as an Indian 'curry' – the word, an anglicised derivative of the Tamil word *kari* (black pepper), was used by the British as a term for any dish, including spices.

STAPLES & SPECIALITIES

Rice

Without a doubt, rice is the staple grain in South India. It's served with virtually every meal, and is used to make anything and everything from *idlis* (spongy rice cakes) and dosas (rice-flour pancakes) to sweets and *puja* (temple offerings).

India is the second-largest producer and consumer of rice in the world (after China), and the majority of it is grown in the south. Long-grain white rice is the most common and is served boiled with any 'wet' dish, usually a thali in the south. In can be cooked up in a *pilao* (aromatic rice casserole) or in the spicy Muslim biryani, or flavoured with turmeric or saffron.

> On average, Indians eat almost 2kg of rice per person a week.

Spices

Spices are integral to any South Indian dish. Christopher Columbus was actually looking for the black pepper of Kerala's Malabar Coast when he stumbled upon America. The region still grows the be quality of the world's favourite spice, and it accompanies many dishes. Turmeric is the essence of most Indian curries, but coriander seeds are the most widely used spice, and lend flavour and body to just about every savoury dish. Most Indian 'wet' dishes – commonly known as curries in the West – begin with the crackle of cumin seeds in hot oil. Tamarind is sometimes known as the 'Indian date' and is a popular souring agent in the south. The green cardamom of Kerala's Western Ghats is regarded as the world's best, and you'll find it in savoury dishes, desserts and warming chai (tea). Saffron, the dried stigmas of crocus flowers grown in Kashmir, is so light it takes more than 1500 hand-plucked flowers to yield just 1g. Cinnamon, curry leaves, nutmeg and garlic are also widely used in cooking.

> Because of the prices it can fetch, saffron is frequently adulterated, usually with safflower – dubbed (no doubt by disgruntled tourists) as 'bastard saffron'.

A masala is a combination of spices (the word loosely means 'mixed'), the most popular being *garam* masala (hot mix), a blend of up to 15 spices used to flavour meat or stews.

Red chillies are another common ingredient used to give dishes a bit of fire. Often dried or pickled (in rural areas you may see chillies laid out to dry on the roadside), they are used as much for flavour as heat.

Fruit, Vegetables & Pulses

A visit to any Indian market will reveal a vast array of fresh fruit and vegetables, overflowing from hampers or stacked in neat pyramids and sold by weight. Naturally in a region of so many vegetarians, *sabzi* (vegetables) make up a large part of the diet, and they're served in a variety of ways. *Aloo* (potatoes), cauliflower, eggplant, spinach and carrots are some of the most commonly used veggies, but you'll rarely seen them simply boiled up plopped on your plate. They're more often used in sambar, cooked into sauces, stuffed into dosas, mashed into fritters or mixed with rice.

Pulses – lentils, beans and peas – are another important South Indian staple as they form the basis for dhal, the lentil-based stew served with every thali meal.

The Anger of Aubergines: Stories of Women and Food, by Bubul Sharma. It's an amusing and unique culinary analysis of social relationships, interspersed with mouth-watering recipes.

Dhal

Dhal is a word you'll hear a lot when you sit down to eat – along with rice it's a mainstay of the South Indian diet. Dhal refers to a wide range of pulse dishes, commonly made from lentils, but also from beans and chickpeas. The pulses are boiled or simmered until they dissolve, then mixed with spices tempered in hot oil or ghee and perhaps vegetables. The most common forms of dhal in South India are sambar and *tuvar* (yellow lentils).

Breads

Although breads are more commonly associated with North India, you'll certainly encounter them in the south, especially in restaurants serving North and South Indian cuisine. The simplest form of unleavened bread is the roti, or chapati, made with whole-wheat flour and cooked on a hotplate called a *tawa*. Naan bread, well known from Punjabi-style Indian restaurants around the world, is thicker and cooked in a tandoor oven. *Paratha* is a deep-fried, flaky bread often found in street stalls.

Dosas & Snacks

A classic of the south, the dosa is a thin crepelike mixture of fermented rice flour and dhal cooked on a griddle – the Indian pancake – usually served with a bowl of hot, orange sambar and another bowl of mild coconut *chatni* (chutney). The dosa is usually folded with a mixture of spiced vegetables and *chatni*. The ubiquitous masala dosa comes with a mix of spices, and is stuffed with potatoes cooked with onions and curry leaves. Don't miss it!

Breakfast in South India often consists of *idli* (spongy fermented rice cakes served with spicy sauce), *vadai* (deep-fried spiced doughnut) and *uttappams* (rice-flour and coconut milk pancakes) with pickles. These snacks can be eaten at any time of day as tiffin, an all-purpose Raj-era term for between-meal snacks.

Indian Food, A Historical Companion, by KT Achaya, is a terrific vehicle for understanding the geographical, historical and philosophical background of Indian food.

Meat & Fish

Although South Indian Hindus are largely vegetarian, fish is a staple food in coastal regions. South India is the 'fish basket' of the nation: in Goa and Kerala you can see fishermen on the beach hauling in the day's catch, which can include tuna, mackerel, kingfish, pomfret, shark, lobster and prawns. In Goa and Kerala, significant Christian populations mean you can find pork and even beef dishes. Chicken is available through the region in nonvegetarian restaurants. Goat is popular in Andhra Pradesh.

Dairy

Milk and milk products make a staggering contribution to Indian cuisine: *dahi* (curd) is served with most meals and is handy for countering heat; *paneer* (cheese) is a godsend for the vegetarian majority; popular lassi (yogurt drink) is just one in a host of nourishing sweet and savoury drinks; ghee (clarified butter) is the traditional and pure cooking medium (although not used nearly as much in India as in Indian restaurants abroad); and the best sweets are made with milk. About 60% of milk consumed in India is buffalo milk, a richer, high-protein version, which many prefer to cow's milk.

Indian Foods Co (www .indianfoodsco.com) is a busy website covering Indian cuisine, recipes and cookbook reviews.

Sweets

Indians have a mind-boggling range of *mithai* (sweets), most of them very sweet. The main categories are *barfi* (a milky fudgelike sweet), halwa (sweet that can be made with vegetables, cereals, lentils, nuts or fruit), *ladoos* (sweetmeats) and those made from *chhana* (unpressed *paneer*), such as *rasgulla* (literally, ball of juice; cooked briefly in syrup before being served chilled). There are also simple sweets like *jalebis* (orange-coloured whorls of fried batter dipped in syrup) that you will see all over the country.

Payasam (called *kheer* in the north) is one of India's favourite desserts. It's a rice pudding with a light, delicate flavour, and might be flavoured with cardamom, saffron, pistachios, flaked almonds, cashews or dried fruit. *Gulab jamun* are deep-fried balls of milk dough soaked in rose syrup. Kulfi is a firm-textured ice cream popular in Mumbai. It's made with reduced milk and flavoured with any number of nuts, fruits and berries.

In the hill areas of Maharashtra you'll find *chikki*, a rock-hard, ultra-sweet concoction of peanuts and *gur* sugar.

REGIONAL SPECIALITIES

If you think it's all thalis and dosas in South India, think again. One of the pleasures of travelling here is the variety of cuisine. Along with their own language, most states have a particular speciality worth seeking out.

Maharashtra

Maharashtra's capital, Mumbai, offers South India's most diverse dining scene – a melting pot of North and South Indian cuisines. Here you can

---

THE THALI EXPERIENCE

You'll soon discover in South India that the thali is the lunchtime meal of choice. Cheap, filling, nutritious and delicious, this is Indian food at its simple best. Whereas in North India the thali is usually served on a steel plate with indentations for the various side dishes (thali gets its name from the plate), in the south a typical thali is served on a flat steel plate covered with a fresh banana leaf. When the plate is put in front of you, pour some water on the leaf and spread it around with your right hand. Soon enough a waiter with a large pot of rice will come along and heap mounds of it onto your plate, followed by servings of dhal, sambar (dhal with cubed vegetables and puree), *rasam* (tamarind-flavoured vegetable broth), chutneys, pickles and curd (a cooling yogurtlike mixture).

Using the fingers of your right hand, start by mixing the various side dishes with the rice, kneading and scraping into mouth-sized balls, then scoop it into your mouth using your thumb to push the food in. It's considered bad form to stick your hand right into your mouth or to lick your fingers. If it's getting a bit messy, there should be a finger bowl of water on the table. Watching other diners will help get your thali technique right. The main thing to remember is not to use your left hand. Waiters will continue to fill your plate until you wave your hand over one or all of the offerings to indicate you've had enough.

Thalis are usually served in restaurants between 11am and 3pm, and cost from Rs 15 in simple places to Rs 100 or more for lavish spreads in better restaurants.

get a classic Gujarati thali, a tandoori feast, fresh seafood from the Konkan Coast or splash out in the fashionable new Euro-Indian fusion restaurants. A popular Mumbai dish is Bombay Duck – actually a tiny fish called *bombil*, sun dried and marinated in spices. Another speciality is *bhelpuri*, a crispy snack of puffed rice, fried vermicelli, peanuts and spices, best eaten at the stalls along Chowpatty Beach. Mumbai's Parsi (Zoroastrian) community adds another dimension to local cuisine with dishes such as *dhansaak*, which is chicken or mutton with a mild sauce of vegetables, coriander and dhal. This dish can be found in a number of city restaurants.

Maharashtrans enjoy simple veg fare, such as rice with *tuvar* dhal (yellow lentil dhal), while Marathi nonvegetarian food leans towards fish, fried or curried with the Marathi spice blend *kala* masala. Also worth trying is Kolhapuri mutton, originating from Kolhapur, and served in a fiery gravy of *garam* masala (hot spices), copra (dried coconut) and red chillies.

101 Kerala Delicacies, by G Padma Vijay, is a detailed recipe book of vegetarian and nonvegetarian dishes. It is especially useful for its meticulous glossary of 154 food items translated from English into Malayalam and Hindi.

Goa

Goa is famous for its fresh seafood – kingfish, snapper, pomfret, tuna, lobster and tiger prawns hauled in from the Sea – and the staple dish here is simply known as 'fish curry rice' – a dish of fish served in a spicy sauce over rice, which can be found in many restaurants for as little as Rs 20.

The Portuguese influence is also strong in Goan cooking. This is the place to sample pork dishes, such as *sorpotel* (pork and liver curry), pork vindaloo (pickled pork curry) and *chourisso* (a delicious Goan sausage). Other Goan specialities include chicken *cafrial* (pieces of chicken coated in a green masala paste) and *ambot tik* (a slightly sour but fiery curry dish), while the Portuguese influence in fish preparations can be seen in *caldeen* and *xacuti* (fish or chicken simmered in coconut milk and spices). *Balchão* is fish or prawns cooked in a dark red and tangy tomato sauce.

Goans also excel in desserts, the best known being *bebinca*, mouthwatering layers of coconut pancakes.

Karnataka

Although you can get any cuisine you'd care to think of in Bangalore, Karnataka cuisine is largely vegetarian, with simple rice, dhal and *rasam* making up the core diet, along with various masala rice dishes, vegetables, salads and dosas. The Mysore dosa is a treat, spicy and crisp, and stuffed with vegetables and chillies. The major exception to the veg diet is the Konkan coast of the state where Mangalorean seafood is a speciality. Even Brahmins in Mangalore eat fish. Promfret and ladyfish are some of the popular catches, often cooked in a spicy coconut sauce.

The Essential Goa Cookbook, by Maria Teresa Menezes, and *The Essential Kerala Cookbook*, by Vijayan Kannampilly, are excellent, in-depth books focussing on these culinary hotspots (available in India for Rs 295).

Kerala

Spice-rich Kerala has had many visitors to its shores over the centuries including Portuguese, British and Arab traders. The combination of those influences and a coastline reaping some of India's finest seafood makes Keralan cuisine some of the most satisfying. Keralan specialities feature fish cooked in coconut oil or simmered in coconut milk and spices, lending it a Southeast Asian quality. Other ingredients in sweet fish curries include cashew nuts and mangoes, while Malabar curries (fish or prawns) are made with coconut milk, tomatoes, ginger and spices cooked in a clay pot.

Kerala's Syrian Christian community also eats chicken, mutton and even beef – a popular dish is beef fry, beef slivers cooked with spices and onions. Other dishes include the combination of chicken coconut stew and *appam* (spongy rice pancake), or *meen,* a fish curry. Keralan Muslims from the north Malabar region also make a mean biryani.

Tamil Nadu & Pondicherry

Like Karnataka, Tamil Nadu epitomises South Indian cuisine, with veg meals based on rice, dhal and sambar, interspersed with *idlis* and masala dosas. Vegetarian cuisine rules, and in many small towns this may be all you'll find to eat. Chettinad cuisine is Tamil Nadu's main contribution to cooking with meat, consisting of chicken or mutton dishes in spicy gravy. You can find Chettinad restaurants in Chennai and most large towns.

Pondicherry offers an unusual French-Indian fusion, which can make a welcome change. Numerous restaurants here whip up *bouillabaisse* (fish and vegetable soup), baguettes, *coq au vin* (chicken in wine sauce) and crème caramel.

> Chettinad, the spicy meat-based cuisine of Tamil Nadu, comes from the Chettiars, a wealthy merchant community.

Andhra Pradesh

Andhra Pradesh is well known for its fiery cuisine and unique blend of Hindu and Muslim cultures. Don't miss a biryani in Hyderabad, an aromatic baked rice dish combined with vegetables, meat (often chicken), nuts and spices. Spicy kebabs wrapped in roti (thin bread cooked on a griddle) and *achhar gosht* (picklelike meat dish) are Hyderbadi favourites, while pickles and *chatnis* (combination of spices, dhal and chillies) are integral to Andhra cooking. Hyderabad is also the home of *kulcha*, a soft, round, unleavened bread. Andhra cuisine is made of lentil, vegetable and meat or fish dishes, usually flavoured with tamarind and frequently spiced up with red chillies from Guntoor. Dishes include *chapa pulusu,* a flaming red fish curry, or chicken curry in coconut sauce.

Orissa

Orissa offers a combination of flavours from South and East India, heavily influenced by the Bengalis. Fish – both fresh and saltwater – is a staple here, as well as prawns caught in the vast saltwater Chilika Lake. *Ambul* is a popular fish dish flavoured with mustard sauce and dried mangoes. Other flavours in Oriya cooking include tamarind, coconut and chillies.

DRINKS
Nonalcoholic Drinks
TEA & COFFEE

South India grows both tea and coffee – if you've travelled in North India you may be surprised to find that coffee is as popular down south as tea (chai) – and both are invariably prepared as a sort of stewed concoction with lots of milk and sugar (whether you like it or not!).

Tea is served as chai in the little shops, stalls or from mobile chai-wallahs, but it also comes in pots or more usually thermos containers in hotels, with the milk and sugar served separately. However, don't expect leaf tea; usually what you'll get are teabags. If you're invited to a home or somebody's workplace, you'll certainly be offered a small cup of coffee or chai.

OTHER DRINKS

Avoid water unless it comes out of a sealed bottle, or it has been boiled or purified (see p507).

Soft drinks (sodas) are a safe, if not exactly healthy, alternative to water, and they're usually cold. Coca-Cola and Pepsi are widely available, especially in cities, but sadly they've introduced plastic bottles (Rs 18) to add to the country's waste problem. If possible, buy the small recyclable glass bottles – they're cheaper (Rs 6), colder and more environmentally friendly, but you have to drink them at the shop or stall and leave the bottle. There are also many local brands with names like Thums Up, Limca, Gold Spot or Double Seven.

Coconut water is a popular drink in South India, and it's refreshing and healthy. Just about everywhere you'll see vendors standing by mounds of green coconuts, machete at the ready. One drinking coconut costs Rs 8 to 10.

In cities and towns particularly you'll come across sugar-cane juice and fruit-juice vendors. Be cautious if you decide to try fruit juice; it may have been mixed with ordinary (dodgy) water and the blenders generally look like they haven't been cleaned for a week. However, we've never had any problems drinking fruit juice, even from street stalls. Fresh juices, such as pineapple, orange, banana, papaya, watermelon or a combination, can be whipped up for around Rs 10. Finally, there's the lassi, a refreshing and delicious iced curd (yogurt) drink that comes in sweet and savoury varieties, or mixed with fruit. Again, you'll have to trust the water, and tell the vendor if you don't want ice.

India has more than 500 varieties of mangoes, and supplies 60% of the world with what is regarded as the king of fruit.

Alcoholic Drinks

India produces all sorts of beers, locally made spirits and a few wines, but you won't find the open drinking culture prevalent in the West. Apart from in Goa and Pondicherry, large cities and most tourist haunts, liquor is not always easy to get. There's a certain religious and cultural taboo that deems alcohol to be unsavoury and immoral, yet it's consumed clandestinely in vast quantities. As a result, alcohol abuse is a significant social problem in India. 'Permit rooms' are hotel or restaurant bars licensed to serve alcohol, but many restaurants in tourist areas will serve beer discreetly even if they don't have a licence.

BEER & WINE

Indian beer is certainly palatable when it's served cold (often it's not cold enough), though the added preservatives may give you a headache the following day (see the boxed text, below). The king of Indian beers is Kingfisher, which is often the only brand available, but you may also find Royal Challenge, United Breweries (UB), Eagle, King's (in Goa), Arlem, London Pilsener, Kalyani Black Label, Sandpiper and Fosters (which has a brewery in Maharashtra). Most beers contain around 5% alcohol volume, but there are strong beers (8%), such as Kingfisher Strong, Haywards 5000, Knockout and Charger. State taxes mean the price for a bottle varies widely. In Pondicherry you can by a bottle for only Rs 25 in a shop, but in Kerala or Tamil Nadu you'll pay around Rs 75. In a bar or restaurant expect to pay Rs 80 to 100, and in the bar of a five-star hotel you can pay upwards of Rs 150.

India is hardly synonymous with wine, and quality is not high, but that's slowly changing. The best wineries in the country are in Maharashtra; see the boxed text, p127. Chateau Indage, near Pune, makes some beaujolais-style dry whites and reds under the Riviera label, and a good sparkling wine (champagne) under its Marquise de Pompadour label.

TIP FOR BEER DRINKERS

Indian beer often contains the preservative glycerol, which can cause headaches. To avoid them, open the bottle and quickly tip it upside down, with the top immersed, into a full glass of water. An oily film (the glycerol) descends into the water – when this stops, remove the bottle and enjoy a glycerol-free beer.

Sula Wines, near Nasik, even has a tasting room at its vineyard. Wine from Grover Vineyards in Karnataka is also worth looking out for.

SPIRITS

Indian interpretations of Western alcoholic drinks are known as Indian Made Foreign Liquor (IMFL). They include imitations of Scotch, brandy, rum and gin under a plethora of different brand names. The taste varies from hospital disinfectant to passable imitation Scotch. A small bottle costs Rs 50 to 75 (Rs 35 in Pondicherry) from an alcohol shop and, mixed with a cold soft drink, they make a good alternative to beer.

A portal to websites about Indian wine, www .indianwine.com, has notes on manufacturers, information on growing regions and more.

LOCAL BREWS

Although you wouldn't go near some of the illicit village brews cooked up in India, there are a few regional specialities that deserve a mention.

In Kerala, Goa and parts of Tamil Nadu, toddy is a milky-white local brew made from the sap of the coconut palm. It's collected in pots attached to the tree by toddy-tappers and drunk either straight from the pot or distilled. In Goa, toddy is called *feni,* made either from coconut or – the more popular and potent version – from the fruit of the cashew tree. The fermented liquid is double-distilled to produce a knockout concoction that can be as much as 35% proof. Although usually drunk straight by locals, *feni* tastes better when mixed with a soft drink, such as Limca or Coke. Decorative *feni* bottles can be found in Goan shops and make a great gift or souvenir.

CELEBRATIONS

Bagpiper is India's largest-selling whisky, and the 14th most popular whisky in the world – even though it's only sold in India.

Although Hindu festivals have the sheen of religious reverence, they are also occasions for feasting and each festival has its own special dishes, which change in appearance according to the region. Sweets are considered the most luxurious of foods and almost every occasion is celebrated with a staggering range. *Karanjis* (crescent-shaped flour parcels stuffed with sweet *khoya,* or milk solids) and nuts are synonymous with Holi, the most boisterous Hindu festival. And Holi wouldn't be the same without *malpuas* (wheat pancakes dipped in syrup), *barfis* and *pedas* (multicoloured pieces of *khoya* and sugar). Pongal (Tamil for 'overflowing') is the major harvest festival of the south and is closely associated with the dish of the same name, made with the season's first rice, along with jaggery, nuts, raisins and spices. Diwali, the festival of lights, is the most widely celebrated national festival, and some regions have specific Diwali sweets; if you're in Mumbai, stuff your face with delicious *anarsa* (rice-flour cookies).

WHERE TO EAT & DRINK

Madhur Jaffrey is the West's foremost expert on Indian cookery; her books *Indian Cooking* and *A Taste of India* are bibles of subcontinental cuisine.

Apart from street food, the most basic place to dine in South India is a *dhaba* (wayside eatery) or 'meals' restaurant (confusingly often called a 'hotel'). Since most Indians eat their main meals at home, in villages or small rural towns, you may only find one or two simple veg restaurants, but in larger towns and cities there's plenty to choose from.

Restaurants

Restaurants in South India fall into five main categories: veg, nonvegetarian (often signposted as 'nonveg'), hotel restaurants, tourist restaurants, and restaurants specialising in regional or ethnic cuisine. The latter are really only found in major cities or tourist areas, such as Mumbai, Pune, Bangalore, Chennai, Hyderabad and Goa, where you can find versions of Italian, Chinese, Thai and even Mexican cuisine.

Veg restaurants (often called 'meals' restaurants) are simple places serving *idlis*, dosas and *vadai* for breakfast, and thalis for lunch and dinner. The food here is fresh, quick and cheap – you'll rarely spend more than Rs 30 on a meal. Nonveg restaurants have both a vegetarian menu and North Indian meat dishes, usually with chicken, mutton and fish, as well as Chinese dishes like fried rice and noodles.

Hotel restaurants are simply those attached to hotels (usually mid-range or top-end places) and in some towns these are the only genuine restaurants. They usually have veg and nonvegetarian sections, and an air-conditioned dining room. Five-star hotels in cities often put on lavish buffets for breakfast, lunch and dinner, which can be good value.

Other Options

In cities such as Mumbai, Bangalore and Chennai there's a trend towards trendy cafés where an espresso costs 20 times the price of a coffee from a street stall next door. For young middle-class Indians especially, these are cool (always air-conditioned) meeting places where you can get Western-style snacks, coffee and cakes. The main chains are Baristo and Café Coffee Day, but independent coffee shops are also starting to appear.

In coastal resorts, such as at Goa and Kerala, it's hard to beat the beach shacks for a fresh seafood meal and a cold beer as you watch the sun set over the Arabian Sea. The bamboo and palm thatch shacks are usually set up in late October and stay open until late March, when they're dismantled and put away in anticipation of the monsoon.

Street Food

Street food is part of everyday life in India, and the sights, smells and sounds of street cooking are a constant banquet for the senses. Throughout the day you'll see *thelas* (carts) and stalls with things being deep fried, griddled, steamed or otherwise cooked. The food is usually safe to eat, as long as it's cooked fresh in front of you. Any food that has been sitting around in the sun attracting flies is bad news. Fried food that is cold or soft and spongy is very suspect.

Good fast-food snacks include the Mumbai speciality *bhelpuri,* a riotous concoction of crisp thin rounds of dough mixed with puffed rice, fried lentils, lemon juice, chopped onions, herbs and *chatni;* samosas, deep-fried parcels of spiced vegetables; *vadai* (fried, spicy doughnuts); *poori* (deep-fried bread); *pao bhaja;* another Mumbai speciality of spiced vegetables with bread; biryani, a Hyderabadi speciality common throughout India; and *bhaja* (vegetable fritters). *Idlis* and dosas are also served at street stalls, with the thin dosa pancake cooked on a griddle right in front of you. For something more reminiscent of home, you'll see egg or omelette sandwiches available from street stalls, and cobs of corn roasting on braziers.

Locals gather to eat street food at all times of day – it's usually eaten as a between-meal snack rather than a replacement for a meal.

VEGETARIANS & VEGANS

Vegetarians will be in heaven in South India. Tamil Nadu and Karnataka are predominately vegetarian, but every town will have several veg restaurants. Indian restaurants are either pure veg (no eggs or meat), veg (no meat) or nonvegetarian (meat and veg dishes). You can bet that vegetables used in Indian cooking will be fresh and spiced up for flavour. Vegans will find that dairy products, such as butter, milk and curds, are used in many food preparations, so you'll need to be careful what you order and talk to the cashier, manager or head waiter about your needs.

Healthy South Indian Cooking, by Alamelu Vairavan and Patricia Marquardt, emphasises Chettinad cuisines, with almost 200 simple vegetarian recipes.

The website www.vegan .com has some useful information for vegans touring in India.

HABITS & CUSTOMS

South Indians generally eat an early breakfast, then have a thali for lunch and/or several tiffin (snacks), such as dosas, during the day. Dinner, usually large serves of rice, vegetables, curd and spicy side dishes, is eaten late. It's not unusual for dinner to start at 9pm or 10pm and any drinking (of alcohol) is always done before the meal.

Food is usually eaten with the fingers in South India, or more precisely the fingers of the right hand. The left hand is reserved for toilet duties, so is considered unclean, but it's still customary to wash your hands before every meal. Rice and side dishes are mixed together with the fingers and scooped into the mouth in small handfuls using your thumb to push it in. Avoid the temptation to lick your fingers – a finger bowl filled with warm water is usually placed on the table to wash your fingers at the end of the meal and serviettes should be on hand to dry them. In most restaurants, foreigners will at least be offered a fork (and perhaps a spoon). In North Indian restaurants it's customary to scoop the food up with the chapati or naan bread, and in restaurants serving Western food and fish dishes you'll almost certainly be given a knife and fork.

COOKING COURSES

You might find yourself so inspired by the food that you want to take home a little Indian kitchen know-how. More and more places – both guesthouses and restaurants – are offering informal cooking classes for a small fee; see the regional chapters of this book for details. If you want to base your entire trip around food, a number of India travel specialists offer cooking-based itineraries; see Tours (p498). **India on the Menu** (p172; www .indiaonthemenu.com; Panaji (Panjim), Goa) in Goa has five-day courses for £250.

EAT YOUR WORDS
Food Glossary

achhar	pickle
aloo tikka	mashed potato patty, often filled with vegetables
appam	rice pancake
arak	liquor distilled from coconut milk, potatoes or rice
baigan	eggplant; also known as *brinjal*
barfi	fudgelike sweet made from milk
besan	chickpea flour
betel	nut of the betel tree; chewed as a stimulant and digestive in *paan*; also called areca nut

from South India, by
Chandra Padmanabhan,
is an easy-to-read and
beautifully illustrated
book of fine recipes. The
suggested menus at the
back are great if you're
planning a vegetarian
banquet.

PAAN

An Indian meal should properly be finished with *paan* – the name given to the collection of spices and condiments chewed with betel nut. Found throughout eastern Asia, betel is a mildly intoxicating and addictive nut, but by itself it is quite inedible. After a meal you chew *paan* as a mild digestive.

Paan sellers have a whole collection of little trays, boxes and containers in which they mix either *sadha* (plain) or *mitha* (sweet) *paan*. The ingredients may include, apart from the betel nut itself, lime paste (the ash, not the fruit), the powder known as *catachu*, various spices and even a dash of opium in a pricey *paan*. The whole concoction is folded up in a piece of edible leaf, which you pop in your mouth and chew. When finished you spit the leftovers out and add another red blotch to the pavement. Over a long period of time, indulgence in *paan* will turn your teeth red-black and get you addicted to betel nut. Trying one occasionally shouldn't do you any harm.

DOS & DON'TS

Do...

- remove your shoes before entering the living area of a home
- wash your hands before eating
- bring a small gift (sweets or fruit) if invited to eat in an Indian home
- round up a bill in a restaurant – a few extra rupees won't hurt
- try as many new dishes as you can while in India

Don't...

- eat with or touch food with your left hand
- put your mouth directly to a shared drinking container (pour the liquid into your mouth)
- offer someone food (such as bread) that has come into contact with your mouth

bhajia	vegetable fritter
bhang lassi	blend of lassi and bhang (a derivative of marijuana)
bhelpuri	thin fried rounds of dough with rice, lentil, lemon juice, onion, herbs and *chatni*
biryani	fragrant steamed rice with meat or vegetables
bonda	mashed potato patty
chaat	snack
chai	tea
channa	spiced chickpeas
chapati	unleavened Indian bread
chatni	chutney
cheiku	small brown fruit that looks like a potato, but is sweet
dahi	curd
dhal	curried lentil dish; a staple food of India
dhal makhani	black lentils and red kidney beans with cream and butter
dhansaak	Parsi dish; meat, usually chicken, with curried lentils and rice
dosa	paper-thin lentil-flour pancake
falooda	rose-flavoured Muslim drink made with milk, cream, nuts and vermicelli
faluda	long chickpea-flour noodles
farsan	savoury nibbles
feni	Goan liquor distilled from coconut milk or cashews
ghee	clarified butter
gram	legumes
gulab jamun	deep-fried balls of dough soaked in rose-flavoured syrup
halwa	soft sweetmeat made with vegetables, cereals, lentils, nuts and fruit
idli	spongy, round, fermented rice cake
jaggery	hard, brown sugarlike sweetener made from palm sap
jalebi	circular deep-fried orange- or red-coloured squiggly sweet filled with sugar syrup
kheer	North Indian rice pudding
khichdi	heavy rice dish sometimes made with lentils, potatoes and peanut
korma	currylike braised dish
kulcha	charcoal-baked bread
kulfi	flavoured (often with pistachio) ice confection, very similar to ice cream
ladoo	sweetmeat ball made with gram flour and semolina; also *ladu*
lassi	refreshing yogurt and iced-water drink
masala dosa	large lentil-flour crepe (dosa) stuffed with potatoes cooked with onions and curry leaves

USEFUL WORDS

English	Tamil	Kannada	Konkani	Malayalam	Marathi	Telugu
butter	vennai	benne	masko	venna	lonee	wenna
coffee	kaappi	kaafi	kaafi	kaappi	kaafi	kaafee
egg	muttai	motte	tatee	muṭṭa	aanda	guḍḍu
fruit	pazham	hannu	phala	palam	phal	paṇḍu
ice	ais	ays	jell	ays	–	ays/mañchugaḍḍa
meat	maamisam	–	–	–	–	–
milk	paal	haalu	dudh	paala	dudh	paalu
rice	arisi	akki	tandul	ari	bhat/tandul (cooked/raw)	biyyam
sugar	sakkarai	sakkare	sakhar	panchasaara	sakhar	chakkera/pañcadaara
tea	teneer	tee	chay	caaya	chaha	ṭee/teneeru
vegetables	kaaykarikal	tarakaari	bhaji	pachakkaṛi	bhajee	kooragaayalu
water	neer	neeru	udhak	veḷḷam	paani	neeḷḷu

mattar paneer	peas and unfermented cheese in gravy
milk *badam*	invigorating morning drink made with saffron and almonds
misthi dhoi	Bengali sweet; curd sweetened with jaggery
mithai	Indian sweets
molee	Keralan dish; fish pieces poached in coconut milk and spices
momo	Tibetan fried or steamed dumpling stuffed with vegetables or meat
naan	flat bread
pakora	bite-sized piece of vegetable dipped in chickpea-flour batter and deep-fried
palak paneer	unfermented cheese in spinach gravy
paneer	cheese
paratha	bread made with ghee and cooked on a hotplate
pilau	rice cooked in stock and flavoured with spices; also *pulau*
puri	flat dough that puffs up when deep fried; also *poori*
raita	mildly spiced yogurt, often containing shredded or diced cucumber, carrot, tomato or pineapple; served chilled
rasam	dhal-based broth flavoured with tamarind
rasgulla	sweet little balls of cream cheese flavoured with rosewater
rogan josh	fiery lamb curry
saag	leafy greens
sabzi	vegetables
sambar	dhal with cubed vegetables and puree
samosa	deep fried pastry triangles filled with spiced vegetables or meat
sonf	aniseed seeds; used as a digestive; usually comes with the bill after a meal
thali	South Indian and Gujarati 'all-you-can-eat' meal; stainless steel or silver plate for meals
thukpa	hearty Tibetan noodle soup
tiffin	snack; also refers to meal container often made of stainless steel
tikka	spiced, often marinated, chunks of chicken, *paneer*, lamb etc
toddy	alcoholic drink, tapped from palm trees
toran	Keralan stir-fried green vegetables
tsampa	Tibetan staple of roast barley flour
vindaloo	Goan dish; fiery curry in a marinade of vinegar and garlic

Mumbai (Bombay)

Exciting and charismatic, Mumbai (Bombay) is India's past, present and future mixed into one dilapidated, overpopulated, irrepressibly vibrant whole. Like the slick, kaleidoscopic and crazy Hindi movies the city churns out with machine-gun rapidity, it's a city that, on the face of it, makes little sense but is still enormous fun.

Mumbai is the country's economic powerhouse, producing everything from software to petrochemicals, and yet it is also home to Asia's largest slums. It's a multicultural metropolis where everyone shares in and enjoys the packed schedule of festivals. At the same time religion divides Mumbai along suspicious and occasionally violent political lines. Making no excuses for theirs being a city of such extremes, Mumbaikers are in equal turns relaxed and vivacious. You might spend one languid day watching a casual cricket game on the *maidans* (open grassed areas) or admiring grand colonial and Art Deco architecture; the next you could be overloading your senses in Mumbai's teeming bazaars and dancing the night away beside Bollywood starlets and wannabes.

If you stay cocooned in the main tourist district of Colaba or stick around long enough only to organise transport elsewhere, you will only have seen a fraction of what Mumbai offers. Spend a few days wandering the city, soaking up its vital streetlife, and you'll discover that Mumbai draws you in like no other Indian metropolis.

HIGHLIGHTS

- Sail across the harbour to **Elephanta Island** (p120) to marvel at the triple-headed Shiva sculpture

- Explore the **bazaars** (p116): Crawford Market for food, Mangaldas Market for fabrics and Chor Bazaar for antiques and curios

- Indulge yourself in India's **dining capital** (p110) with everything from tasty snacks on the street to contemporary cuisine in high-class restaurants

- Survey Mumbai's incredible stock of colonial architecture from bombastic **Chhatrapati Shivaji Terminus** (the old Victoria Terminus; p101) to the stately **Bombay University** (p100) and **High Court** (p100)

- Spend an afternoon watching cricket on the **Oval or Azad Maidans** (p100) and the early evening soaking up the funfair atmosphere of **Chowpatty Beach** (p101)

Elephanta Island ★

Chowpatty Beach ★   Chor Bazaar ★

Mangaldas Market ★★ Crawford Market

Azaid Maidan ★★ Chhatrapati Shivaji Terminus

Oval Maidan ★★ High Court
★ Bombay University

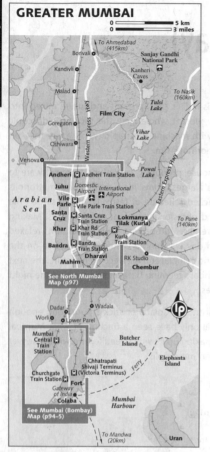

GREATER MUMBAI

0 ————— 5 km
0 ————— 3 miles

FAST FACTS

- Population: 16.4 million
- Area: 440 sq km
- Capital of: Maharashtra
- Main languages: Hindi, Marathi and Gujarati
- Telephone area code: ☎ 022
- When to go: October to February

HISTORY

The seven islands that now form Mumbai were first home to the Koli fisherfolk as far back as the 2nd century BC; Koli shanties still occupy parts of the city shoreline today. The islands were ruled by a succession of Hindu dynasties from the 6th century AD, invaded by Muslims in the 14th century and then ceded to Portugal by the sultan of Gujarat in 1534. It was the Portuguese who named the area Bom Bahai but they did little to develop the islands before they were included in Catherine of Braganza's dowry when she married England's Charles II in 1661. The British government took possession of the islands in 1665, but leased them three years later to the East India Company for the paltry annual rent of UK£10.

Then called Bombay, the area soon developed as a trading port and merchants were attracted from other parts of India by the British promise of religious freedom and land grants. Within 20 years the presidency of the East India Company was transferred to Bombay from Surat and it became the trading headquarters for the whole west coast of India.

Bombay's fort was built in the 1720s, and land reclamation projects began the process of joining the islands into a single land mass. Although Bombay grew steadily during the 18th century, it remained isolated from its hinterland until the British defeated the Marathas (the central Indian people who controlled much of India at various times) and annexed substantial portions of western India in 1818.

The fort walls were dismantled in 1864 and the city was rebuilt in grand colonial style. Trade boomed and money flooded into the city as Bombay took over as the principal supplier of cotton to Britain during the American Civil War.

Bombay played a formative role in the struggle for independence, hosting the first Indian National Congress in 1885 and the launch of the Quit India campaign in 1942 – Mahatma Gandhi lived here for many years. After Independence the city became capital of the Bombay presidency, but in 1960 this was divided on linguistic grounds into Maharashtra and Gujarat; Bombay then became the capital of Marathi-speaking Maharashtra.

The rise of the pro-Maratha regionalist movement, spearheaded by the Shiv Sena (Hindu Party; literally 'Shivaji's Army'), shattered the city's multicultural mould by actively discriminating against Muslims and non-Maharashtrans. The Shiv Sena won power in the city's municipal elections in 1985. Communalist tensions increased and the city's cosmopolitan self-image took a battering when nearly 800 people died in riots that followed the destruction of the Babri Masjid in Ayodhya in December 1992. They were followed by a dozen bombings on 12 March 1993, which killed more than 300 people and damaged the Bombay Stock Exchange and Air India Building.

In 1996 the city's name was officially changed to Mumbai, the original Marathi name derived from the goddess Mumba who was worshipped by the early Koli residents. The Shiv Sena's influence has since seen the names of many streets and public buildings changed from their colonial names. The airports, Victoria Terminus and Prince of Wales Museum have all been renamed after Chhatrapati Shivaji, the great Maratha leader, although the British names of these and many major streets are still in popular local use.

ORIENTATION

Mumbai is an island connected by bridges to the mainland. The principal part of the city is concentrated at the southern, claw-shaped end of the island known as South Mumbai.

The southernmost peninsula is Colaba, traditionally the travellers' nerve centre, and directly north of Colaba is the busy commercial area known as the Fort, where the old British fort once stood. It's bordered on the west by a series of interconnected, fenced grass areas known as maidans.

The island's eastern seaboard is dominated by the city's naval docks, which are off limits. Further north, across Mahim Creek are the suburbs of Greater Mumbai and the international and domestic airports (p116). Many of Mumbai's best restaurants and night spots can be found here, particularly in the upmarket suburbs of Bandra and Juhu.

Maps

Eicher City Map Mumbai (Rs 250) is the most comprehensive and up-to-date street atlas and is well worth picking up if you're going to be spending any lengthy time in town.

INFORMATION
Bookshops

For new and second-hand books check out the street vendors lining the footpaths around Flora Fountain, the maidans, and Mahatma Gandhi (MG) Rd.

Crossword (Map pp94–5; ☎ 23842001; Mohammed Bhai Mansion, NS Patkar Marg, Kemp's Corner; ⏰ 10am–9pm) Mumbai's biggest bookshop.

MUMBAI IN...

One Day

Kick off at the **Gateway of India** (p98), strolling south past the **Taj Mahal Palace & Tower** (p109) towards the colourful **Colaba Market** (p98). Grab a cab back to **Kala Ghoda** (p100) and explore the museums and art galleries here before tucking into lunch: try excellent seafood at **Mahesh Lunch Home** (p111).

Head next for **Chhatrapati Shivaji Terminus** (the old Victoria Terminus; p101) and then stroll back down Dr Dadabhai Naoroji Rd towards the Oval Maidan where the grand edifices of the **High Court** (p100) and **Bombay University** (p100) overlook many an impromptu cricket match. Relax over afternoon tea at the Oxford Bookstore's **Cha Bar** (p113).

Promenade in the early evening down **Marine Dr** (p101) towards **Chowpatty Beach** (p101), then return to Colaba for either a street-side barbecue at **Bade Miya** (p110) or a slap-up feast at **Indigo** (p111).

Three Days

Spend a day shopping in the traditional **bazaars** (p116) or upmarket boutiques around Colaba, Breach Candy and Kemp's Corner, where you can also drop by the **Mani Bhavan** (p103), Gandhi's old home, now a museum. Another day will slip easily by combining the ferry journey out to **Elephanta Island** (p120) with a visit to the inner-city enclave of **Kotachiwadi** (p102) where you should eat at **Anantashram** (p112).

MUMBAI (BOMBAY)

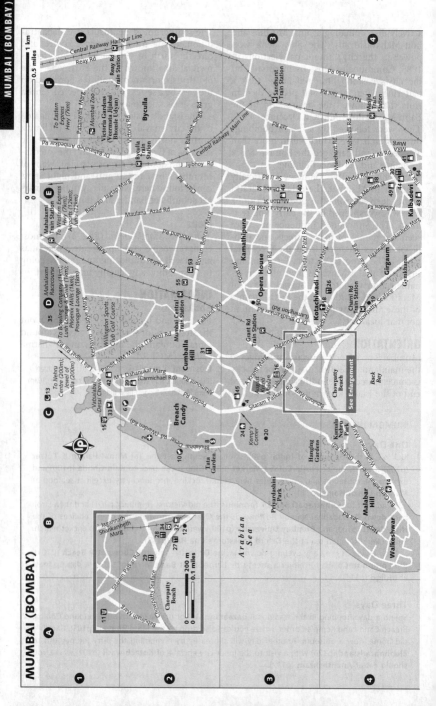

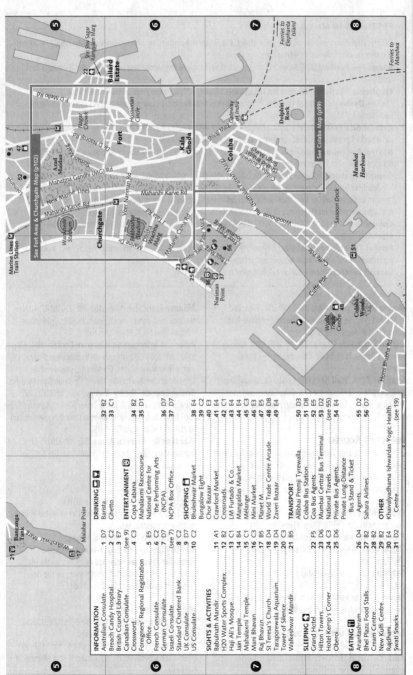

INFORMATION
Australian Consulate.................1 D7
Breach Candy Hospital.............2 C2
British Council Library..............3 E7
Canadian Consulate..............(see 9)
Crossword................................4 C3
Foreigners' Regional Registration
    Office...................................5 E5
French Consulate......................6 C2
German Consulate.....................7 D7
Israeli Consulate...................(see 7)
Standard Chartered Bank..........8 C2
UK Consulate............................9 D7
US Consulate...........................10 C2

SIGHTS & ACTIVITIES
Babulnath Mandir.....................11 A1
H2O Water Sports Complex......12 B2
Haji Ali's Mosque.....................13 C1
Jain Temple..............................14 B4
Mahalaxmi Temple...................15 C1
Mani Bhavan............................16 E3
Raj Bhavan...............................17 B5
St Teresa's Church....................18 D4
Taraporewala Aquarium...........19 D4
Tower of Silence.......................20 C3
Walkeshwar Mandir..................21 B5

SLEEPING
Grand Hotel.............................22 F5
Hilton Towers...........................23 D6
Hotel Kemp's Corner................24 C3
Oberoi.....................................25 D6

EATING
Arantashram.............................26 D4
Bhel Plaza Food Stalls...............27 B2
Cream Centre...........................28 B2
New Kulfi Centre......................29 B2
Rajdhani...................................30 E4
Swati Snacks.............................31 D2

DRINKING
Barista......................................32 B2
Ghetto......................................33 C1

ENTERTAINMENT
Copa Cabana...........................34 B2
Mahalaxmi Racecourse.............35 D1
National Centre for
    the Performing Arts
    (NCPA)..................................36 D7
NCPA Box Office.......................37 D7

SHOPPING
Bhuleshwar Market...................38 E4
Bungalow Eight.........................39 C2
Chor Bazaar..............................40 E3
Crawford Market.......................41 E4
Crossroads................................42 C1
LM Furtado & Co.......................43 E4
Mangaldas Market.....................44 E4
Melange...................................45 C3
Mini Market..............................46 E3
Planet M...................................47 E5
World Trade Centre Arcade........48 D8
Zaveri Bazaar............................49 E4

TRANSPORT
Alibhai Premji Tyrewalla.............50 D3
Colaba Bus Station....................51 D8
Goa Bus Agents........................52 E5
Mumbai Central Bus Terminal....53 D2
National Travels.....................(see 55)
Private Bus Agents....................54 E4
Private Long-Distance
    Bus Stand & Ticket
    Agents..................................55 D2
Sahara Airlines..........................56 D7

OTHER
Khaivalyadhama Ishwardas Yogic Health
    Centre................................(see 19)

See Fort Area & Churchgate Map (p102)

See Colaba Map (p99)

FESTIVALS IN MUMBAI

Practically every week of the year there's a festival happening somewhere in Mumbai. Read on for the best of these celebrations.

Banganga Festival (Jan) A classical music festival held early in the month over two days at the Banganga Tank (p103).

Elephanta Festival (Feb) Head out to Elephanta Island (p120) for more classical music and dance.

Indian Derby (Feb) Staged since 1942 this is India's richest and most popular horserace. It's run at Mahalaxmi Racecourse (p115).

Kala Ghoda Festival (Feb) Getting bigger and more sophisticated each year, this the two-week-long offering has a packed programme of arts performances and exhibitions.

Nariyal Poornima (Aug) Festivals in the tourist hub of Colaba kick off with this celebration of the start of the fishing season after the monsoon.

Ganesh Chaturthi (Aug/Sep) Mumbai's biggest annual festival – a 10-day event in celebration of the elephant-headed deity Ganesh – sweeps up the entire city. On the first, third, fifth, seventh and 10th days of the festival families and communities take their Ganesh statues to the seashore to drown them: the 10th day, which sees millions descending on Chowpatty Beach to submerge the largest statues, is particularly chaotic.

Colaba Festival (Oct) A small arts festival in Colaba that can merge with the general festivities of Diwali, depending on the year.

Prithvi Theatre Festival (Nov) A showcase of what's going on in contemporary Indian theatre; also includes performances by international troupes and artists.

Larzish Festival (Nov) A daring celebration of queer film making.

Magna Book Gallery (Map p102; ☎ 22671763; 2nd fl, Sassoon Bldg, 143 MG Rd, Kala Ghoda; ☼ 10am-9pm) Specialising in discounted books.

Oxford Bookstore (Map p102; ☎ 56339309; Apeejay House, 3 Dinsha Wachha Rd, Churchgate; ☼ 10am-10pm)

Shankar Book Stall (Map p99; Colaba Causeway) This stall, outside Café Mondegar on Colaba Causeway (also known as Shahid Bhagat Singh Marg) is also worth a browse for new books.

Internet Access

There are many Internet cafés across the city. Most charge Rs 30 to 40 per hour and almost all offer phone, fax, photocopying and printing services. Here are a few convenient places:

Cyber Online (Map p102; Jiji House, 17 Sukhadwala Rd, Fort; per hr Rs 30; ☼ 10.30am-11pm Mon-Sat)

Pick-up Communication Centre (Map p99; Shorab Manor, 6 Walton Rd, Colaba; per hr Rs 40; ☼ 7am-1am)

Satyam i-way Churchgate (Map p102; Prem Ct, J Tata Rd; per hr Rs 25; ☼ 9am-11pm); Colaba (Map p99; Colaba Causeway; per hr Rs 40; ☼ 8am-11pm) The entrance to the Colaba branch is on JA Allana Marg.

Libraries & Cultural Centres

Library books, newspapers, Internet access and cultural information and events are available at the following:

Alliance Française (Map p102; ☎ 22036187; 40 New Marine Lines; annual membership Rs 800; ☼ 9.30am-5.30pm Mon-Fri, 9.30am-1pm Sat)

American Information Resource Centre (AIRC; Map p102; ☎ 22624590; http://americanlibrary.in.library .net; 4 New Marine Lines, Churchgate; casual visit Rs 10, annual membership Rs 200; library ☼ noon-6pm Mon-Fri)

British Council Library (Map pp94-5; ☎ 22823560; www.bclindia.org; 1st fl, Mittal Tower A Wing, Barrister Rajni Patel Marg, Nariman Point; minimum monthly membership Rs 250; ☼ 10am-6pm Tue-Sat)

Max Mueller Bhavan (Map p102; ☎ 22027542; K Dubash Marg, Fort; library ☼ 11am-6pm Tue-Sat) For German books.

Media

English-language publications:

City Info Free monthly listings booklet available in many hotels and guesthouses.

Indian Express Has a Mumbai edition.

Mid-Day The main local English-language paper.

Time Out Mumbai Published every two weeks (Rs 25), this is the best round-up of what's going on the city.

Times of India Has a Mumbai edition.

Medical Services

Bombay Hospital (Map p102; ☎ 22067676; 12 New Marine Lines) Close to Fort and Colaba.

Breach Candy Hospital (Map pp94-5; ☎ 23671888; 60 Bhulabhai Desai Rd, Breach Candy) Best in Mumbai, if not India.

Money

ATMS

The number of 24-hour ATMs linked to international networks in Mumbai has exploded in recent years. Convenient ATMs include the following:

Bank of India (Map p99; Colaba Causeway, Colaba)

Citibank Fort (Map p102; 293 Dr Dadabhai Naoroji Rd); Nariman Point (Map p102; Air India Bldg, cnr Marine Dr & Madame Cama Rd)

HSBC Bank (Map p102; MG Rd, Fort) Also has a handy ATM at Chhatrapati Shivaji Terminus (CST; formerly Victoria Terminus), just outside the reservation hall.

ICICI Bank (Map p99; Colaba Causeway, Colaba)

Standard Chartered Bank (Map p102; MG Rd, Fort)

CURRENCY EXCHANGE

There's no shortage of foreign-exchange offices in Colaba that will change cash and travellers cheques, and there are 24-hour exchange bureaus at the domestic and international airports.

American Express (Amex; Map p99; ☎ 22048291; Shivaji Marg, Colaba; ☼ 9.30am-6.30pm Mon-Fri, 9.30am-2.30pm Sat) Next to the Regal Cinema, this is the best place to exchange cash and travellers cheques (1% commission on non-Amex cheques).

Standard Chartered Bank Breach Candy (Map pp94-5; Bhulabhai Desai Rd; ☼ currency exchange 24hr); Fort (Map p102; MG Rd; ☼ 9.30am-7pm Mon-Sat)

Thomas Cook (Map p102; ☎ 22048556; 324 Dr Dadabhai Naoroji Rd, Fort; ☼ 9.30am-6pm Mon-Fri, 9.30am-5pm Sat) Also provides swift foreign exchange.

Photography

Standard Supply Co (Map p102; ☎ 22612468; Image House, W Hirachand Marg, Fort; ☼ 10am-7pm Mon-Sat) Modern digital processing, print and slide film, video cartridges and camera accessories are available from this store opposite CST station, on the road also known as St Georges Rd.

Post

The **main post office** (Map p102; ☎ 22621671; ☼ 9am-8pm Mon-Sat, 10am-5pm Sun) is an imposing building behind CST station. **Poste restante** (☼ 9am-6pm Mon-Sat) is at Counter 3. Letters sent there should be addressed c/o Poste Restante, Mumbai GPO, Mumbai 400 001. You'll need to bring your passport to collect mail. There's an **EMS Speedpost parcel counter** (☼ 11am-1pm & 1.30-4pm Mon-Sat) to the left of the stamp counters. Regular parcels can be sent from the parcel office behind the main post office building. Directly opposite the post office is a group of parcel-wallahs who will stitch up your parcel for around Rs 30.

To send air-freight parcels out of India, try the following companies. A 10kg box to the UK or USA costs about Rs 5720.

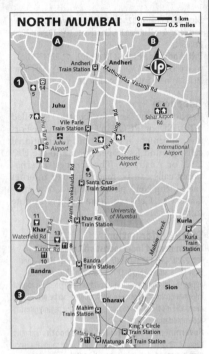

NORTH MUMBAI 0 — 1 km 0 — 0.5 miles

SLEEPING 🏠		
Hotel Airport International	1	B2
Hotel Columbus	2	A2
Hotel Sea Princess	3	A2
Hyatt Regency Mumbai	4	B1
Iskcon	5	A1
ITC Hotel Grand Maratha Sheraton & Towers	6	B1
JW Marriott	7	A1

EATING 🍴		
Culture Curry	......(see 9)	
Dosa Diner	8	A3
Goa Portuguesa	9	A3
Peshawri	......(see 6)	
Pot Pourri	10	A3

DRINKING 🍷		
Olive Bar & Kitchen	11	A2
Vie Lounge	12	A2
Zenzi	13	A2

ENTERTAINMENT 🎭		
Prithvi Theatre	14	A1

OTHER		
Yoga Institute	15	A2

Blue Dart (Map p102; ☎ 22828064; www.blue dart.com; Veer Nariman Rd, Churchgate; ✆ 10am-8.30pm Mon-Sat)
DHL Worldwide Express (Map p102; ☎ 22837183; www.dhl.com; 145A Marine Dr, Churchgate; ✆ 8am-8pm Mon-Sat) In the Sea Green South Hotel.

Telephone

Private phone and fax centres (labelled 'STD/ISD' or 'PCO') in Colaba and the Fort are convenient for STD and international calls (around Rs 25 per minute to the UK, USA or Australia). The cheapest international calls can be made through Internet cafés using Net2-phone, dialpad, or a similar service. Calls cost from Rs 5 per minute to the USA.

Tourist Information

Government of India tourist office (Map p102; ☎ 22207433; 123 Maharshi Karve Rd; ✆ 8.30am-6pm Mon-Fri, 8.30am-2pm Sat) This busy but efficient office opposite Churchgate train station cheerfully provides tourist information for the entire country. Guides can be organised here, and it's the place to find out about the paying guest accommodation scheme.
Government of India tourist office booths domestic airport (☎ 26156920; ✆ 7am-11pm); international airport (☎ 26829248; Arrival Hall 2A; ✆ 24hr)
Maharashtra Tourism Development Corporation (MTDC) booth (☎ 22841877; Apollo Bunder; ✆ 10am-5pm) Near the Gateway of India. Purchase tickets here for the MTDC bus tours of the city (p106).
Maharashtra Tourism Development Corporation (MTDC) reservation office (Map p102; ☎ 22026713; Madame Cama Rd, Nariman Point; ✆ 9.45am-5.30pm Mon-Sat) The head office of the MTDC gives information on travel in Maharashtra and can book MTDC hotels throughout the state.

Travel Agencies

American Express (Amex; Map p99; ☎ 22048291; Shivaji Marg, Colaba; ✆ 9.30am-6.30pm Mon-Fri, 9.30am-2.30pm Sat) Next to the Regal cinema; a reliable option.
Magnum International Travel & Tours (Map p99; ☎ 22840016; 10 Henry Rd, Colaba) Handy for those staying in Colaba.
Thomas Cook (Map p102; ☎ 22048556; 324 Dr Dadabhai Naoroji Rd, Fort; ✆ 9.30am-6pm Mon-Fri, 9.30am-5pm Sat) Another reliable option.
Transway International (☎ 26146854; transintl@ vsnl.com; ✆ 8am-8pm) A long-running agency which is good for travel information as well as bespoke tours (p106).

Visa Extensions

Foreigners' Regional Registration Office (Map pp94-5; ☎ 22620446; Annexe Bldg No 2, CID, 3rd fl, Sayed Badruddin Rd) Does not officially issue extensions on six-month tourist visas – even in emergencies they will direct you to Delhi (p482). However, travellers have managed to procure an emergency extension here after a lot of waiting and persuasion.

SIGHTS

The following are highlights of South Mumbai's tourist attractions and some places in North Mumbai, most notably Juhu Beach, an alternative accommodation base and home to several trendy bars and restaurants.

Colaba   Map p99

Occupying the city's southernmost peninsula, Colaba is undoubtedly Mumbai's travellers centre as well as one of the city's most happening districts. **Colaba Causeway** (Shahid Bhagat Singh Marg) is the busy commercial thoroughfare that runs the length of much of the promontory.

The causeway passes close to **Sassoon Dock**, a scene of intense and pungent activity at dawn (around 5am) when colourfully clad Koli fisherwomen sort the catch unloaded from fishing boats at the quay. The fish drying in the sun are *bombil*, the fish used in the dish Bombay duck. Photography at the dock is forbidden without permission from the **Mumbai Port Trust** (☎ 56565656; fax 22611011).

Even if you don't rise early enough for the unloading of the fish, there's still plenty of activity and colour during the daytime at **Colaba Market** (Lala Nigam St), a short walk northeast of the dock back towards where most of the tourist hotels are.

GATEWAY OF INDIA

This bold basalt arch of colonial triumph, derived from the Islamic styles of 16th-century Gujarat, is Mumbai's icon. Facing out to Mumbai Harbour at the tip of Apollo Bunder it was officially opened in 1924, but was redundant just 24 years later when the last British regiment ceremoniously departed India through its archway.

The gateway is a favourite gathering spot for locals and a great place to hang out if you can tolerate the associated beggars and touts. Giant-balloon sellers, photographers and the like give the area the hubbub of a bazaar. Nearby inside an often-closed area

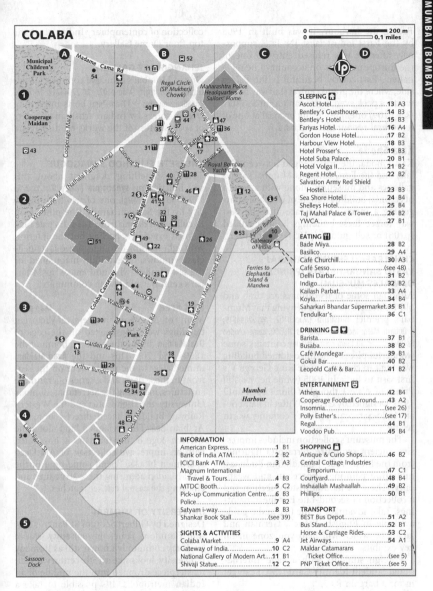

COLABA

0 ————— 200 m
0 ————— 0.1 miles

SLEEPING
Ascot Hotel.............................**13** A3
Bentley's Guesthouse................**14** B3
Bentley's Hotel.......................**15** B3
Fariyas Hotel.........................**16** A4
Gordon House Hotel..................**17** B2
Harbour View Hotel..................**18** B3
Hotel Prosser's.......................**19** B3
Hotel Suba Palace....................**20** B1
Hotel Volga II.........................**21** B2
Regent Hotel..........................**22** B2
Salvation Army Red Shield
Hostel.................................**23** B3
Sea Shore Hotel......................**24** B4
Shelleys Hotel.........................**25** B4
Taj Mahal Palace & Tower..........**26** B2
YWCA...................................**27** B1

EATING
Bade Miya..............................**28** B2
Basilico..................................**29** A4
Café Churchill.........................**30** A3
Café Sesso.......................(see 48)
Delhi Darbar...........................**31** B2
Indigo...................................**32** B2
Kailash Parbat.........................**33** A4
Koyla....................................**34** B4
Saharkari Bhandar Supermarket.**35** B1
Tendulkar's............................**36** C1

DRINKING
Barista..................................**37** B1
Busaba..................................**38** B2
Café Mondegar........................**39** B1
Gokul Bar..............................**40** B2
Leopold Café & Bar..................**41** B2

ENTERTAINMENT
Athena..................................**42** B4
Cooperage Football Ground.......**43** A2
Insomnia.........................(see 26)
Polly Esther's...................(see 17)
Regal....................................**44** B1
Voodoo Pub...........................**45** B4

INFORMATION
American Express.......................**1** B1
Bank of India ATM.....................**2** B2
ICICI Bank ATM.........................**3** A3
Magnum International
Travel & Tours......................**4** B3
MTDC Booth.............................**5** C2
Pick-up Communication Centre...**6** B3
Police......................................**7** B2
Satyam i-way............................**8** B3
Shankar Book Stall................(see 39)

SIGHTS & ACTIVITIES
Colaba Market...........................**9** A4
Gateway of India......................**10** C2
National Gallery of Modern Art....**11** B1
Shivaji Statue...........................**12** C2

SHOPPING
Antique & Curio Shops..............**46** B2
Central Cottage Industries
Emporium............................**47** C1
Courtyard..............................**48** B4
Inshaallah Mashaallah..............**49** B2
Phillips.................................**50** B1

TRANSPORT
BEST Bus Depot.......................**51** A2
Bus Stand..............................**52** B1
Horse & Carriage Rides.............**53** C2
Jet Airways.............................**54** A1
Maldar Catamarans
Ticket Office......................(see 5)
PNP Ticket Office..................(see 5)

of park are statues of the religious reformer Swami Vivekananda, and of the Maratha leader Chhatrapati Shivaji astride his horse. Boats depart from the gateway's wharfs for Elephanta Island and Mandwa.

You can ride in one of the horsedrawn gilded carriages that ply their trade along Apollo Bunder. Get them to go around the

Oval Maidan at night so you can admire the illuminated buildings – it should cost Rs 300 if you bargain hard. Kids are sure to love the ride.

TAJ MAHAL PALACE & TOWER
Another Mumbai institution is this majestic **hotel** (☎ 5665336; www.tajhotels.com; Apollo Bunder).

Facing the harbour, it was built in 1903 by the Parsi industrialist JN Tata, supposedly after he was refused entry to one of the European hotels on account of being 'a native'. Particularly beautiful is the Palace side, where the grand central stairway is well worth a peek even if you can't afford to stay (see p109) or enjoy a drink or meal at one of its several restaurants and bars.

Kala Ghoda

Kala Ghoda, the area wedged between Colaba and the Fort, contains Mumbai's main galleries and museums, along with a wealth of colonial buildings, some of which are now getting a much-needed face-lift. The best way to see these buildings is on a guided (p106) or self-guided (p105) walking tour.

CHHATRAPATI SHIVAJI MAHARAJ VASTU SANGRAHALAYA (PRINCE OF WALES MUSEUM)

Although some of its displays are drab and old-fashioned, there's no denying that Mumbai's premier **museum** (Map p102; ☎ 22844519; K Dubash Marg; Indian/foreigner Rs 10/300, camera/video Rs 30/200; ⏰ 10.15am-6pm Tue-Sun) contains some wonderful pieces. The huge domed building was built to commemorate King George V's first visit to India in 1905 (while he was still Prince of Wales), though it didn't open until 1923. Designed by George Wittet in flamboyant Indo-Saracenic style, it's certainly worth seeing.

The museum's collection includes impressive ancient sculpture, terracotta figurines from the Indus Valley, Gandharan Buddhas, miniature paintings, porcelain and weaponry. There's a natural-history section and a collection of second-rate European paintings. Take advantage of the free audio guide available in English, French, German and Japanese, which will help you zone in on key exhibits.

Foreign students with a valid International Student Identity Card (ISIC) can get in for a bargain Rs 6.

NATIONAL GALLERY OF MODERN ART

This **gallery** (Map p99; ☎ 22881969; MG Rd; admission Rs 5; ⏰ 11am-6pm Tue-Sun) in the Sir Cowasji Jehangir Public Hall is a bright, spacious and modern exhibition space showcasing a range of changing exhibitions by Indian and international artists. There's a small permanent collection of contemporary Indian art in the top-floor Dome Gallery.

JEHANGIR ART GALLERY

One of Mumbai's principal commercial galleries, **Jehangir** (Map p102; ☎ 22048212; 161B MG Rd; admission free; ⏰ 11am-7pm) hosts interesting weekly shows by Indian artists in a variety of spaces. Most of the works on display are for sale.

KNESSETH ELIYAHOD SYNAGOGUE

There's something poignant about this still functioning **synagogue** (Map p102; ☎ 2283 1502; Dr VB Gandhi Marg), one of two built in the city by the Sassoon family (the other is in Byculla) and dating from 1884. Its pale blue painted exterior is peeling but the interior, with light shafting through gorgeous stained-glass windows, is beautifully maintained for the few families who now make up Mumbai's centuries-old Jewish community.

Fort Area   Map p102

Many of Mumbai's impressive Victorian buildings were constructed on the edge of **Oval Maidan** during the building boom of the 1860s and '70s. This and the **Azad Maidan**, immediately to the north, were on the seafront in those days, and a series of grandiose structures, including the Secretariat, Bombay University, the High Court and the Western Railway Building, faced directly onto the Arabian Sea. The reclaimed land along the western edge of the maidans is now lined with an impressive collection of Art Deco apartment blocks. Spend some time in the Oval Maidan admiring these structures and enjoying the casual cricket matches.

UNIVERSITY OF MUMBAI

Designed by Gilbert Scott of St Pancras Station (London) fame, the **university** (Bhaurao Patil Marg), commonly known still as Bombay University, looks like a 15th-century Italian masterpiece dropped into the middle of an Indian metropolis. It's possible to take a peek inside both the exquisite **University Library** and **Convocation Hall** but the 80m-high **Rajabai Clock Tower**, decorated with detailed carvings, is off limits.

HIGH COURT

The neighbouring **High Court** (Eldon Rd) was obviously designed to dispel any doubts about the weightiness and authority of the justice dispensed inside. Local stone carvers, who often worked independently, presumably saw things differently: they carved a one-eyed monkey holding the scales of justice on one of its pillars. It's permitted (and highly recommended) to walk around inside and check out cases in progress – the vivid scenes here resemble something between those in books by Dickens and Rushdie!

ST THOMAS' CATHEDRAL
This charming **church** (Veer Nariman Rd) is the oldest English building standing in Mumbai. Construction began in 1672, but remained unfinished until 1718. The church has recently been restored (winning a Unesco World Heritage award in the process) and its airy, whitewashed interior is full of colonial memorials and ornately carved gravestones.

CHHATRAPATI SHIVAJI TERMINUS (VICTORIA TERMINUS)
The city's most exuberant Gothic building looks more like a lavishly decorated palace or cathedral than something as mundane as a transport depot – don't wait until you have to catch a train to see it. Designed by Frederick Stevens, it was completed in 1887, 34 years after the first train in India left this site on its way to nearby Thana. Carvings of peacocks, gargoyles, monkeys and lions are mixed up among the buttresses, domes, turrets, spires and stained-glass windows. Topping it all is a 4m-high statue of 'Progress'.

In 1998 the station was officially renamed Chhatrapati Shivaji Terminus (CST), but it's still better known locally as 'VT'.

Marine Drive & Chowpatty Beach   Map pp94–5
Built on land reclaimed from Back Bay in 1920, **Marine Dr** (Netaji Subhashchandra Bose Rd), running into Chowpatty Seaface and Walkeshwar Marg, sweeps along the shore of the Arabian Sea from Nariman Point past Chowpatty Beach to the foot of Malabar Hill. Lined with flaking Art Deco apartments and a series of gymkhanas where grand Hindu weddings are often held, this is one of Mumbai's most popular promenades and sunset-watching spots. The lights that twinkle along the promenade at night give it its nickname, 'the Queen's Necklace'.

The uninspiring **Taraporewala Aquarium** (☎ 22082061; Marine Dr; adult/child Rs 4/2; ☼ 10am-7pm Tue-Sat, 10am-8pm Sun) is near Chowpatty Beach. Kids might appreciate it but beware, half the tanks are empty and the other half murky; hardly surprising, as water is piped in from the bay!

Chowpatty Beach, scene of the riotous climax of the Ganesh Chaturthi festival (p96), remains a favourite evening spot for courting couples, families, political rallies and anyone out to enjoy what passes for fresh air. Eating *bhelpuri* (crisp fried thin rounds of dough mixed with puffed rice, fried lentils, lemon juice, chopped onions, herbs and chutney) at the collection of stalls on the edge of the

THE PARSI CONNECTION
Mumbai has a strong – but diminishing – Parsi community. The Parsis (descendants of Persian Zoroastrians who first migrated to India after persecution by the Muslims in the 7th century) settled in Bombay in the 17th and 18th centuries. They proved astute businesspeople, enjoyed a privileged relationship with the British colonial powers, and became a very powerful community in their own right while managing to remain aloof from politics.

With the departure of the British, the influence of the Parsis waned in Mumbai, although they continued to own land and established trusts and estates, or colonies, built around their temples, where many of the city's 60,000-plus Parsis still live.

Perhaps the most famous aspect of the Zoroastrian religion is its funerary methods. Parsis hold fire, earth and water sacred, so they do not cremate or bury their dead. Instead, the corpses are laid out within towers – known as Towers of Silence – to be picked clean by vultures. In Mumbai the Parsi Tower of Silence is on Malabar Hill (although it's strictly off limits to sightseers). But traditions are being eroded by a shortage of vultures around the city, due mainly to urban growth and pollution which has driven the birds away. This has meant that the Parsis have sometimes had to resort to artificially speeding up the natural decomposition of their dead with solar-powered heaters or chemical methods.

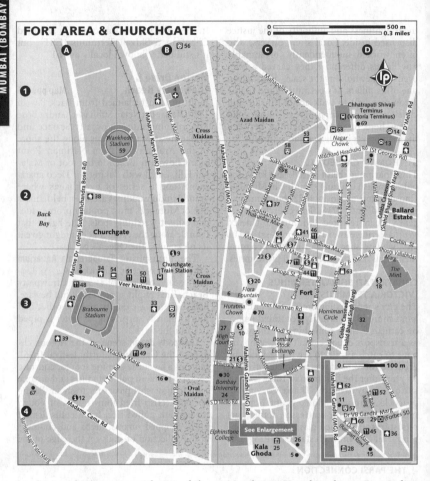

FORT AREA & CHURCHGATE

beach at night is an essential part of the Mumbai experience, as is getting a vigorous head rub from a *malish*-wallah (head masseur). Forget about visiting during the day for a sunbathe or a dip; the water is filthy.

A short walk northwest from the beach towards Kemp's Corner is the venerable **Babulnath Mandir** (Babulnath Marg), which along with Mahalaxmi Temple (p104) is one of the city's principal Hindu temples. There's always a lively throng of people on the stairs up towards the flower-bedecked lingam (phallic image of Shiva).

Kotachiwadi   Map pp94–5

A *wadi* (hamlet) that has miraculously survived amid the high-rise jumble of South

Mumbai is Kotachiwadi, an East Indian Christian enclave of some 30-odd elegant two-storey wooden mansions. A 10-minute or so walk northeast of Chowpatty, Kotachiwadi is a little difficult to find: aim for **St Teresa's Church** on the corner of Jagannath Shankarsheth Marg and RR Roy Marg (Charni Rd) then duck into the warren of streets directly opposite. Worth searching out here is the **Ferreira House** (☎ 23887292); call to see if the owner James Ferreira might be free to welcome you inside and give an introduction to the history of the area. Next door is the restaurant Anantashram (p112), a neighbourhood institution. Guided walks of the area are occasionally organised by Bombay Heritage Walks (p106).

INFORMATION
Alliance Française.................................1 B2
American Information Resource Centre.2 B2
ATM...(see 69)
Blue Dart...3 A3
Bombay Hospital..................................4 B1
Bombay Natural History Society...........5 C4
Bookstalls...6 C3
Citibank ATM..7 C2
Citibank ATM................................(see 67)
Cyber Online...8 C2
DHL Worldwide Express...................(see 42)
Government of India Tourist Office.......9 B3
HSBC Bank ATM..................................10 C3
Magna Book Gallery............................11 D4
Maharashtra Tourism Development
    Corporation (MTDC)
    Reservation Office......................12 A4
Main Post Office..................................13 D2
Main Post Office Parcel Counter..........14 D1
Max Mueller Bhavan...........................15 D4
Oxford Bookstore................................16 B4
Parcel-wallahs.....................................17 D2
Reserve Bank of India..........................18 D3
Satyam i-way.......................................19 B3
Standard Chartered Bank.....................20 C3
Standard Chartered Bank ATM.............21 C4
Standard Supply Co.......................(see 35)
Thomas Cook......................................22 C3
UTI Bank ATM.....................................23 C3

SIGHTS & ACTIVITIES
Asiatic Society of Bombay Library.......(see 32)
Bombay University..............................24 C4
Chhatrapati Shivaji Maharaj
    Vastu Sangrahalaya
    (Prince of Wales Museum)............25 C4

Concern India Foundation....................26 C4
High Court..27 C3
Jehangir Art Gallery............................28 D4
Knesseth Eliyahod Synagogue.............29 D4
Rajabai Clock Tower............................30 C4
St Thomas' Cathedral..........................31 C3
State Central Library......................(see 32)
Town Hall...32 D3

SLEEPING
Astoria Hotel......................................33 B3
Chateau Windsor Hotel.......................34 A3
Hotel City Palace................................35 D2
Hotel Lawrence...................................36 D4
Hotel Outram......................................37 C2
Intercontinental..................................38 A2
Marine Plaza.......................................39 A3
Railway Hotel......................................40 D2
Residency Hotel..................................41 C2
Sea Green Hotel..................................42 A3
Sea Green South Hotel....................(see 42)
West End Hotel...................................43 B1

EATING
210°C..(see 49)
Apoorva Restaurant & Bar...................44 C3
Chetana..45 D4
Ideal Corner..46 C2
Mahesh Lunch Home.......................(see 47)
Mocambo Café & Bar..........................47 C3
Pearl of the Orient.........................(see 3)
Pizzeria..48 A3
Relish...(see 49)
Samrat..49 B3
Suryodaya...50 B3
Tea Centre..51 B3
Trishna...52 D4

DRINKING
Barista...53 C1
Cha Bar..(see 16)
Mocha Bar...54 A3
Samovar Café..................................(see 28)

ENTERTAINMENT
Eros...55 B3
Metro...56 B1
Not Just Jazz By The Bay.................(see 48)
Red Light...57 D4
Sterling...58 C2
Wankhede Stadium.............................59 B2

SHOPPING
Bombay Paperie...................................60 C4
Bombay Store......................................61 C3
Fabindia..62 D4
Groove...(see 55)
Kashmir Government
    Arts Emporium............................63 D3
Khadi & Village
    Industries Emporium....................64 C2
Rhythm House.....................................65 D4
Uttar Pradesh
    Handicrafts Emporium..................66 D3

TRANSPORT
Air India..67 A4
Bus Stand...68 D1
Central Railways Reservation Centre....69 D1
Indian Airlines................................(see 67)
Western Railways
    Reservation Centre....................(see 9)

OTHER
Davar's College....................................70 C3

Malabar Hill   Map pp94–5

On the northern promontory of Back Bay is the expensive residential area of Malabar Hill. The colonial bungalows that peppered the hillside in the 18th century have now been replaced by the apartment blocks of Mumbai's nouveau riche.

The most interesting part of the promontory is at the southern end where you'll find the sacred precinct of **Banganga Tank**. Bathing pilgrims, picturesque old *dharamsalas* (pilgrim's rest houses), a dozen temples and scores of curious kids make this neighbourhood an oasis from the intrusive apartment blocks towering above. The **Banganga Festival**, a classical music festival organised by the MTDC, is held here in January.

The most significant temple in the area is the **Walkeshwar Mandir** (Sand Lord Temple), on the tank's western flank. In the Hindu epic, the Ramayana, Rama is said to have constructed a lingam of sand at the site while on his way to Lanka to rescue Sita. The original temple was possibly built 1000 years ago; the current unimpressive structure dates only from the 1950s.

At the end of the promontory is the off-limits **Raj Bhavan**, once the British governor's house and now home to the governor of Maharashtra.

On the way back towards Chowpatty along the main road climbing Malabar Hill you won't fail to miss the garish **Jain temple**, built in 1904 and dedicated to the first Jain *tirthankar* (teacher), Adinath.

The formal **Hanging Gardens** (Pherozeshah Mehta Gardens) on top of the hill are a pleasant but often crowded place for a stroll – they're popular with Mumbai's courting couples. The smaller **Kamala Nehru Park**, opposite, has good views of towards Marine Dr and the city; the best time to visit is in the evening when the city lights twinkle.

Kemp's Corner & Mahalaxmi   Map pp94–5

MANI BHAVAN

The building in which Mahatma Gandhi stayed during his visits to Bombay from 1917 to 1934 is now a small but engrossing **museum** (☎ 23805864; 19 Laburnum Rd; admission free; ⏰ 10am-6pm) that shouldn't be missed. Many important events in India's struggle for independence emanated from here. Gandhi's simple room remains untouched and there's a wonderful photographic record of his life, along with dioramas and

---

BOLLYWOOD EXTRAS

Although film studios are not officially open to volunteers, some travellers visiting Mumbai have been 'spotted' and subsequently asked to play a small role in a Bollywood film.

Mumbai is the epicentre of India's huge Hindi-language film industry. Many visitors to the city hope to get a glimpse of the action inside one of the top Bollywood film studios but there are presently no organised tours of any studios, and, in view of increased security fears, getting beyond the gates is unlikely to be possible for any reason...except one.

Studios are often looking for extras for background scenes and sometimes want Westerners to fill the bill. Getting a part, though, is a matter of luck. When extras are required the studios usually send scouts down to Colaba – often around the Gateway of India – to conscript travellers for the following day's shooting. You receive between Rs 500 and 1000 for a day's work, but it's clearly not something you do for the money. It can be a long, hot day standing around on the set, without promised food and water; others have described the behind-the-scenes peek as a fascinating experience. Before agreeing to be an extra, always ask for identification from the person who has approached you.

The following are some major Mumbai film studios, but remember, unless you've been invited (eg to play a role as an extra) official permission must be obtained before you can even set foot in one.

Film City (☎ 022-28401755; filmcityfilmcity@hotmail.com; Goregaon (East), Mumbai 400065)

Kamal Amrohi Studio (☎ 022-28371160; mahal_pictures@hotmail.com; Mahal Pictures Pty Ltd, 6 Jogeshwari Vikhroli Link Rd, Andheri (East), Mumbai 400093)

RK Studios (☎ 022-25203250; fax 25200234; Chembur-Sion, Mumbai 400071)

---

original documents such as letters he wrote to Adolf Hitler and US president Franklin D Roosevelt. Mani Bhavan is near August Kranti Maidan, from where the campaign to persuade the British to 'Quit India' was launched in 1942.

MAHALAXMI TEMPLE

This popular Hindu temple, one of Mumbai's busiest and most colourful, is dedicated to Mahalaxmi, the goddess of wealth. It's perched on a headland reached by the alleyways just off Bhulabhai Desai Marg (Warden Rd), and is the focus for Mumbai's **Navratri** (Festival of Nine Nights; the Hindu festival leading up to Dussehra) celebrations in September/October. After paying your respects to the goddess, climb down the steps towards the shore and snack on tasty *gota bhaji* (fried lentil balls) at the cliffside Laxmi Bhajiya House.

HAJI ALI'S MOSQUE

A short walk north from the Mahalaxmi Temple, at the end of a long causeway snaking into the Arabian Sea, is a whitewashed mosque. Best viewed from afar, the mosque contains the tomb of the Muslim saint Haji Ali and was built by devotees in the early 19th century. One version of Haji Ali's legend says he died while on a pilgrimage to Mecca and his casket miraculously floated back to Mumbai and landed at this spot.

The mosque becomes an island at high tide, but is accessible at other times via the concrete causeway lined with beggars and change (coin) vendors.

MAHALAXMI DHOBI GHAT

At Mumbai's dhobi ghat (place where clothes are washed) at Mahalaxmi, some 5000 men use rows of open-air troughs to beat the dirt out of the thousands of kilograms of soiled clothes brought from all over the city each day. The best view, and photo opportunity, is from the bridge across the railway tracks near Mahalaxmi train station (Map pp94–5), which can be reached from Churchgate station.

North Mumbai

NEHRU CENTRE & NEHRU PLANETARIUM

The most striking thing about this **cultural complex** (Off Map pp94-5; Dr Annie Besant Rd, Worli), which includes a decent **planetarium** (☎ 249 20510; adult/child Rs 25/15; ☾ English show 3pm Tue-Sun) and the serpentine but surprisingly interesting **Discovery of India** history exhibition (free), is the bold modern architecture of the buildings. The tower looks like a giant circular honeycomb, the planetarium a UFO. There's also a theatre here (p114) and the Jewel of India (p112) restaurant.

JUHU BEACH
The beach here is badly littered, and you'll get pestered by hawkers and beggars, but there's no denying Juhu's popularity with locals, who throng here to enjoy the sea breezes. There's a fun atmosphere around the food stalls, and kids (and ecofriendly adults) will be thrilled by the human-powered carnival rides.

ACTIVITIES
Swimming
Despite the heat don't be tempted by the lure of Back Bay, or even the open sea at Juhu; the water is filthy. If you want to swim and aren't staying at a luxury hotel, Fariyas Hotel (p108) in Colaba has a tiny terrace pool (Rs 300 for nonguests).

Water Sports
H20 Water Sports Complex (Map pp94-5; ☎ 236 77546; Marine Dr, Mafatlal Beach; ☼ 10am-10pm) on the southeast side of Chowpatty Beach rents out jet skis (Rs 180), speed boats (Rs 125 for a minimum of four people) and kayaks (Rs 400) by the hour. It's closed during the monsoon (May to September).

  Outbound Adventure (www.outboundadventure.com) run one-day rafting trips on the Ullas River near Karjat, 88km southeast of Mumbai, from the end of June to early September.

WALKING TOUR

Start	Gateway of India
Finish	Churchgate train station
Distance	2.5km
Duration	3hr minimum

Mumbai's distinctive mix of colonial and Art Deco architecture is one of its defining features. This walk takes you past many of the city's key buildings and is a great way to spend anything from a few hours to a whole day, depending on your pace. If you wish to explore further on foot then pick up *Fort Walks*, a guidebook available at all major bookstores.

  Starting from the **Gateway of India (1; p98)** walk up Shavaji Marg past the members-

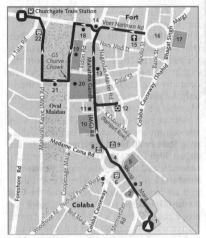

only colonial relic **Royal Bombay Yacht Club (2)** on one side and the Art Deco residential-commercial complex **Dhunraj Mahal (3)** on the other towards **Regal Circle (4**; SP Mukherji Chowk). Dodge the traffic to reach the car park in the middle of the circle for the best view of the surrounding buildings, including the **Old Sailors Home (5)**, which dates from 1876 and is now the Maharashtra Police HQ, the Art Deco **Regal Cinema (6)** and the old **Majestic Hotel (7)**, now the Sahakari Bhandar cooperative store.

  Continue up MG Rd, past the beautifully restored façade of the **Institute of Science (8)**. Opposite here is the **Chhatrapati Shivaji Maharaj Vastu Sangrahalaya (9**; Prince of Wales Museum; p100); step into the front gardens to admire this grand building. Back across the road is the 'Romanesque Transitional' **Elphinstone College (10)** and the charming **David Sassoon Library (11)**, a good place to escape the heat of the day lazing on planters chairs on the upper balcony.

  Cross back over to Forbes St to visit the **Knesseth Eliyahod Synagogue (12**; p100) before returning to MG Rd and continuing north along the left-hand side so you can admire the vertical Art Deco stylings of the **New India Assurance Company Building (13)**. In a traffic island ahead lies the pretty **Flora Fountain (14)**, named after the Roman goddess of abundance, and erected in 1869 in honour of Sir Bartle Frere, the governor of Bombay who was responsible for dismantling the fort and shaping much of modern Mumbai.

Turn east down Veer Nariman Rd walking towards **St Thomas' Cathedral (15; p101)**. Ahead of here lies the stately **Horniman Circle (16)**, an arcaded ring of buildings, laid out in the 1860s. The circle is overlooked from the east by the neoclassical **Town Hall (17)**, which contains the regally decorated members-only Asiatic Society of Bombay Library and Mumbai's State Central Library.

Retrace your steps back to Flora Fountain and continue west past the Venetian Gothic-style **State Public Works Department (18)** to the august **High Court (19; p100)** and the equally venerable and ornately decorated **University of Mumbai (20; p100)**. The façades of both buildings are best observed from within the **Oval Maidan (21)** entered at GS Churve Chowk opposite the university's Rajabai Clock Tower. Turn around to compare the colonial edifices with the row of Art Deco beauties lining Maharshi Karve (MK) Rd, culminating in the wedding cake tower of the **Eros Cinema (22)**. End your walk at Churchgate station.

COURSES
Yoga
Serious yoga classes are held at the **Kaivalyadhama Ishwardas Yogic Health Centre** (Map pp94-5; ☎ 22818417; www.kdham.com; 43 Marine Dr, Chowpatty; ☉ 6.30-10am & 3.30-7pm Mon-Sat). Fees are a minimum Rs 300, plus Rs 350 extra for a monthly

---

GO AHEAD & LAUGH

In 1995 Mumbai physician Dr Madan Kataria decided to prove the theory that laughter is the best medicine, a therapy for health and wellbeing as beneficial as yoga or meditation. He gathered a few people and encouraged them to laugh out loud – about anything or nothing. When the jokes wore thin he devised ways of encouraging people to laugh for laughter's sake, even developing laughing 'exercises'. The movement has grown nationwide into hundreds of 'laughter clubs' – there are more than 70 in Mumbai alone. If you want to join in the mirth, get up around 7am and head down to the Gateway of India, Marine Dr (opposite the Oberoi), or the Hanging Gardens, and find the club members – they'll be the ones laughing. Just be sure to join in. For information on club gatherings and contacts, check out www.laughteryoga.org.

---

membership, and you are expected to attend a one-hour class, six days a week for the whole month. You must undergo a routine physical examination before enrolling.

Also offering yoga courses is the **Yoga Institute** (Map p97; ☎ 26122185; www.yogainstitute.org; Prabhat Colony, Shri Yogendra Marg, Santa Cruz). Some classes are free, others start at Rs 200 for the month.

Language
Davar's College (Map p102; ☎ 22045072; davarcol@vsnl.in; 3rd fl, Jehangir Bldg, MG Rd, Fort) offers Hindi and Marathi language classes for beginners. A one-month course in basic grammar and conversation costs Rs 5000, with daily 45-minute classes (Monday to Friday).

TOURS
The best city tours are offered by **Bombay Heritage Walks** (☎ 23690992, 26835856; heritage walks@hotmail.com), which is run by two enthusiastic female architects. There's often a monthly Sunday walk (Rs 75) lasting no more than a couple of hours; otherwise private guided tours are Rs 500 per person.

Transway International (p98) runs a **Bombay By Night tour** (US$25) which includes an arts performance and drinks at the members-only Royal Bombay Yacht Club.

MTDC (p98) runs uninspiring AC **bus tours** of the city (Rs 225; Tuesday to Sunday) and one-hour open-deck bus tours of the city's illuminated heritage buildings at 7pm and 8.30pm on weekend evenings (Rs 70), departing from the Gateway of India. All can be booked at the MTDC booth at Apollo Bunder near the Gateway of India.

The Government of India tourist office (p98) can arrange **multilingual guides** (Rs 350/500 per half/full day) if you wish to explore Mumbai at your own pace. They cost an extra Rs 180 for a guide using a foreign language other than English.

Cruises on Mumbai Harbour are a good way to escape the city and offer the chance to see the Gateway of India as it was intended. Short ferry rides (one hour) cost Rs 30. If you want to do a cruise in luxury hire the **Taj Yacht** (Rs 12,000 per hour); contact the Taj Mahal Palace & Tower (p109) for details.

SLEEPING
Mumbai is India's most expensive city for accommodation and pressure for a room

can be intense during the Christmas season and Diwali. A budget place here is anything under Rs 1000 for a double, while midrange places are those with rooms for Rs 6500 or less.

Colaba has the best selection of budget and midrange hotels, and is a lively, well-placed area for the main sights. Fort is also convenient (close to CST and Churchgate stations). If you're in Mumbai on business or a stopover then chances are that the midrange and top-end hotels near the airports or at Juhu will suit you best.

To stay with a local family anywhere in the city, contact the Government of India tourist office (p98) for a list of homes participating in Mumbai's paying guest scheme. There's also a **hotel reservation desk** (☎ 56048772; ☺ 24hr) in the arrivals hall of the international airport which can book hotels for you and arrange transfers.

Hotel checkout time is usually noon. If you have a late flight out, ask about luggage storage in advance. Note that while all hotels add the 6% government tax to the bill for rooms over Rs 1200 some places hike this to as much as 20% with service charges – we note such higher taxes in the reviews; otherwise unless mentioned all room rates are quoted without tax.

Budget

Apart from Colaba and Fort there are some budget hotels in Vile Parle, a middle-class suburb adjoining the domestic airport, but they are pretty grotty and you'd be better off camping out at the airport for the night if needs be.

COLABA   Map p99

Bentley's Hotel (☎ 22841474; www.bentleyshotel.com; 17 Oliver Rd; d incl breakfast & tax Rs 770-1328; ✵) Bentley's is the most characterful of Colaba's budget hotels, with two main buildings on Oliver Rd and a less appealing but slightly cheaper guesthouse a block away on Henry Rd. Rooms have cable TV. The more expensive rooms are midrange standard – huge, spotless and good value, with colonial furniture and balconies. Rooms 31 and 21 overlooking a garden are among the best. AC costs around Rs 200 extra. Reservations are recommended and major credit cards are accepted.

Hotel Volga II (☎ 22885341; 1st fl, Rustam Manzil, Nawroji F Rd; s/d with shared bathroom Rs 300/450, d with private bathroom Rs 600, d with private bathroom, AC & TV Rs 800; ✵) Just around the corner from the travellers' haunt Leopold's (p113) the Volga II's tiny but clean rooms will do for a few nights. It's often full because of its central location.

Sea Shore Hotel (☎ 22874237; 4th fl, Kamal Mansion, 1 Arthur Bunder Rd; s/d with shared bathroom Rs 350/450, d with AC Rs 600; ✵) The best of the three budget places in this building has spartan, windowless rooms with TV, or better doubles with small harbour views. The singles are minuscule, but clean enough. All rooms have shared bathrooms.

Hotel Prosser's (☎ 22841715; 2 Henry Rd; d/tr Rs 400/600) This hotel's exterior is pretty decrepit and ramshackle, but the rooms are reasonably well kept. The shared bathrooms have hot water and sit-down flush toilets.

Salvation Army Red Shield Hostel (☎ 22841824; 30 Mereweather Rd; dm without/with full board Rs 135/205, d/tr with full board Rs 585/855) Easily the cheapest place to stay in Mumbai, if you take the dorm option, this hostel is reasonably clean but institutional. Dorm beds are leased on a first-come first-served basis and checkout time is 9am. Luggage storage is available at Rs 50 a day.

FORT AREA   Map p102

Hotel City Palace (☎ 22615515; www.hotelcitypalace .net; 121 City Tce, W Hirachand Marg; economy s/d from Rs 550/700, larger s/d Rs 875/1075; ✵) Rather cramped rooms but spotlessly clean and surprisingly quiet given its location directly opposite CST station. A good option if you're only in Mumbai for a night or two.

Hotel Lawrence (☎ 22843618; 3rd fl, ITTS House, 33 Sai Baba Marg; s/d/tr with shared bathroom incl breakfast & tax Rs 400/500/700) The basic but clean rooms here defy the disgusting, *paan*-stained walls in the stairwell. It's down the lane from TGI Fridays on K Dubash Marg.

Hotel Outram (☎ 22094937; Marzaban Rd; small s/d with shared bathroom Rs 350/450, s/d with AC from Rs 750/850; ✵) This plain but welcoming place is in a quiet location between CST station and the maidans. The rooms with private bathroom are passably clean but lacking sunlight.

Railway Hotel (☎ 22616705; www.hotelrailway.com; 249 P D'Mello Rd; s/d incl breakfast from Rs 825/1195, s/d with AC incl breakfast Rs 1195/1650; ✵) Convenient for CST, this reasonably tidy place offers grubbily carpeted rooms with TV and fridge.

Midrange

COLABA   **Map p99**

Gordon House Hotel (☎ 22871122; www.ghhotel.com; 5 Battery St; s/d Rs 5500/6000, ste Rs 10,000; 🌐 💻) Gordon House Hotel is a dazzlingly white, European-style boutique hotel with elegant rooms decorated in three styles: Mediterranean, Country and Scandinavian. It's a little kitsch, but fun with hi-tech touches such as CD player and flat-screen TV in all rooms. Rooms above its nightclub are noisy but available at a discount if you ask.

Fariyas Hotel (☎ 22042911; www.fariyas.com; 25, Off Arthur Bunder Rd; s/d from US$135/150; 🌐 💻 🏊) This comfortable and friendly hotel is close to the bustling Colaba market and trendy Courtyard designer boutique centre. The furnishings may be a bit old fashioned but the rooms are otherwise good. There's also a small swimming pool on the 1st-floor terrace, a gym, a restaurant and the Tavern & Beyond pub (a good option for a quiet drink).

Ascot Hotel (☎ 56385566; www.ascothotel.com; 38 Garden Rd; s/d incl breakfast & tax Rs 2650/2862; 🌐 💻) Easily the most appealing of the trio of midrange hotels along Garden Rd, the Ascot has recently been given a contemporary makeover. The design is colourful yet quite tasteful with spacious comfortable rooms. Internet access is free.

Shelleys Hotel (☎ 22840229; www.shelleyshotel.com; 30 PJ Ramchandani Marg; d incl tax from Rs 1622; 🌐) Overlooking the waters of Mumbai Harbour, Shelleys is a lovely small hotel with a slight touch of the Raj about it. All rooms have balconies and smart deep-blue upholstery.

Harbour View Hotel (☎ 22821089; www.viewhotels india.com; 4th fl, 25 PJ Ramchandani Marg; d incl breakfast Rs 2190-2475; 🌐 💻) A tastefully refurbished hotel with spotless doubles occupying the 3rd and 4th floors (above Strand Hotel); the more expensive rooms have those namesake harbour views. The breezy rooftop restaurant is a major bonus. A 20% tax is added to the room rates.

Regent Hotel (☎ 22871854; www.regenthotelcolaba.com; 8 Best Marg; s/d incl breakfast & tax Rs 2226/2332; 🌐 💻) This is quite a stylish hotel with plenty of marble surfaces and a vaguely Middle Eastern flavour thanks to the artwork. Rooms are comfortable with enclosed balconies. Internet access is free.

Hotel Suba Palace (☎ 22020636; www.hotelsuba palace.com; Battery St; s/d incl breakfast Rs 1660/2350; 🌐)

This standard issue yet comfortable, modern place is well located and gets positive reviews from travellers.

YWCA (☎ 22025053; www.ywcaic.info; 18 Madame Cama Rd; dm/s/d Rs 688/723/1360, d with AC Rs 1590; 🌐) The YWCA is a well-run place that accepts men and women. The spacious four-bed dorm rooms are a good deal especially as the rates for all rooms include buffet breakfast and dinner. Other rooms are small but tidy, and it's well located between Colaba and Fort.

FORT AREA

West End Hotel (Map p102; ☎ 22039121; www.westendhotelmumbai.com; 45 New Marine Lines; s/d Rs 2668/3132; 🌐) The retro feel of this old-fashioned place, popular with media types, is summed up by its grey velour-lined bar, Chez Nous, that looks like a set from an Austin Powers movie. The rooms are plain but spacious, with soft beds.

Residency Hotel (Map p102; ☎ 22625525; residencyhotel@vsnl.com; 26 Rustom Sidhwa Marg; s/d incl tax from Rs 1378/1484; 🌐 💻) This is one of the few comfortable options in the heart of the Fort. It has a marble-clad lobby and spotless rooms decorated with Indian-themed paintings.

Grand Hotel (Map pp94-5; ☎ 22618211; www.grandhotelbombay.com; 17 Shri Shiv Sagar Ramgulam Marg, Ballard Estate; s/d from Rs 1800/2100; 🌐 💻) The Grand fails to live up to its name, but it's not too bad with clean, dowdily furnished rooms and a relatively quiet location.

CHURCHGATE, MARINE DRIVE & KEMP'S CORNER

Astoria Hotel (Map p102; ☎ 56541234; astoria@hathway.com; Churchgate Reclamation, Churchgate; s/d incl breakfast Rs 1800/2200; 🌐 💻) This conveniently located, smartly renovated hotel has a sleek, modern lobby and restaurant where you can also access the Internet. The rooms don't quite live up to the lobby's promise, but they're spacious and clean.

Chateau Windsor Hotel (Map p102; ☎ 2204 4455; www.chateauwindsor.com; 5th fl, 86 Veer Nariman Rd, Churchgate; s/d with shared bathroom Rs 990/1290, s/d with private bathroom from Rs 1440/1890; 🌐) This place is looking a bit tired but the rooms are well maintained, and have cable TV and balconies. It's also in a decent location near Marine Dr.

Hotel Kemp's Corner (Map pp94-5; ☎ 23634646; fax 23634732; 131 August Kranti Marg; s/d from Rs 1100/1500;

Haji Ali's mosque (p104), Mumbai (Bombay)

ALAIN EVRARD

DAVID COLLINS

Imperialist architecture (p61),
Mumbai

Chowpatty Beach (p101), Mumbai

GREG ELMS

Detail of rock carving at Ajanta (p135),
Maharashtra

Bollywood poster on a wall in Pune (p149),
Maharashtra

Landscape near Matheran (p144), Maharashtra

⊠) It's worth forking out a bit more for the deluxe double rooms at this long-running, old-fashioned hotel. It's in a handy location for shopping at Kemp's Corner.

Sea Green Hotel (Map p102; ☎ 56336525; www.seagreenhotel.com; 145 Marine Dr; s/d Rs 1800/2200; ⊠) and **Sea Green South Hotel** (Map p102; ☎ 56336535; www.seagreensouth.com; 145A Marine Dr; s/d Rs 1800/2200; ⊠) are identical hotels (same rates) offering spacious but spartan AC rooms. Ask for a sea-view room as they are no more expensive than others. A 16% tax is added to room rates.

JUHU BEACH & AIRPORT AREA   Map p97
There are about half a dozen midrange hotels clustered on Nehru Rd Extension, close to the entrance to the domestic airport. The room rates are twice the price of equivalent rooms in the city and there's no compelling reason to stay in the Vile Parle area unless you're just filling in time between flight connections. At least Juhu has the beach.

Hotel Sea Princess (☎ 26611111; www.seaprincess.com; Juhu Tara Rd, Juhu; s/d incl breakfast Rs 6000/7000; ⊠ 🖳 🛋) At the very top end of the midrange, the Sea Princess is worth splashing out on. The sizeable rooms are pleasantly decorated, all with views of the beach and the rates include airport transfers.

Iskcon (☎ 26206860; guest.house.Bombay@pamho.net; 111 Hare Krishna Lane, Juhu; s/d incl tax Rs 1248/1584, s/d with AC incl tax Rs 1452/1971; ⊠) Part of the Hare Krishna complex, this is a garishly pink, efficiently run high-rise place set back from the beach. The plain rooms are large and spotless but have no TV or fridge. Also in the building is the good vegetarian buffet restaurant Govinda's.

Hotel Columbus (☎ 26182029; columbus@rediffmail.com; 344 Nanda Patkar Rd, Vile Parle; s/d from Rs 1650/2000; ⊠) The Columbus is one of the few midrange hotels in the airport neighbourhood that we'd happily spend more than a night at. Airport transfers are free but you'll need to call the hotel from the airport for the pick-up. It also has a modern, appealing restaurant.

Hotel Airport International (☎ 26182222; Nehru Rd, Vile Parle; s/d from Rs 1195/2400; ⊠) So close to the domestic airport you can see the runway from most of the rooms, this hotel is slowly being upgraded throughout. The older economy rooms are OK for one night.

SOMETHING SPECIAL

Taj Mahal Palace & Tower (Map p99; ☎ 56 653366; www.tajhotels.com; Apollo Bunder, Colaba; tower rooms s/d from US$230/255, palace rooms s/d from US$290/315; ⊠ 🖳 🛋) A Mumbai institution, this elegant, well-run hotel is practically a world unto itself with every conceivable facility, including a host of restaurants, many swish shops, a large outdoor swimming pool, a gymnasium, the nightclub Insomnia (p113) and even a resident fortune-teller! Although the rooms in the new tower are fine (and have great views), the plush heritage themed ones on the palace side of the complex are the ones to go for.

Top End
MARINE DRIVE
Intercontinental (Map p102; ☎ 56399999; www.intercontinental.com; 135 Marine Dr, Churchgate; d incl breakfast from US$315; ⊠ 🖳 🛋) You'll want to pay a little extra for the splendid sea views at this sophisticated boutique-style hotel. Nice touches include daily papers from a range of countries downloaded from the Internet. Discounts of up to 40% may be available on the rack rates which include airport pick-ups.

Marine Plaza (Map p102; ☎ 22851212; hotel marineplaza@vsnl.com; 29 Marine Dr, Nariman Point; d from US$250; ⊠ 🖳 🛋) Appealing boutique five-star hotel with Art Deco flourishes and stylish rooms. The rooftop swimming pool has a glass bottom that looks down on the foyer five floors below! The hotel also has a gym, two restaurants and the popular Boston-style Geoffrey's Bar.

Hilton Towers (Map pp94-5; ☎ 56324343; www.hilton.com; Marine Dr, Nariman Point; s/d from US$230/255 ⊠ 🖳 🛋) The Hilton Towers (once the Oberoi Towers) wins out over its neighbour both on price and the spiffy design of its restaurants, bars and pool area. Although managed separately, both hotels still share facilities so you can wander happily between the two.

Oberoi (Map pp94-5; ☎ 56325757; www.oberoi hotels.com; Marine Dr, Nariman Point; s/d from US$702/295; ⊠ 🖳 🛋) The Oberoi has an understated opulence, and cannot compete with the Taj Mahal Palace & Tower (above) on the heritage factor. Nor does it have the with-it style of the attached Hilton Towers (p109). It does have a spa, though, offering Ayuverdic and other styles of massage.

JUHU BEACH & AIRPORT AREA   Map p97
ITC Hotel Grand Maratha Sheraton & Towers (☎ 28 303030; www.welcomgroup.com; Sahar Airport Rd, Andheri; s/d incl breakfast & tax from US$210/235; 🅿 🖳 🕸) Easily the hotel in this area with the most luxurious Indian character, from the Jaipur-style lattice windows around the atrium to the silk pillows on the beds and the embalmed palms in the lobby. It's right outside the international airport and is also home to the celebrated restaurant Peshawri (p112).

JW Marriott (☎ 56933000; mail@jwmarriottmumbai .com; Juhu Tara Rd, Juhu; d incl breakfast & tax from US$169; 🅿 🖳 🕸) Smack in the middle of Juhu beach is this monumental luxury hotel sporting no less than three pools, one of them filled with heavily filtered sea water. The rooms are suitably plush. Its Enigma nightclub (closed for renovation at the time of research) is a popular party spot. Upgrade to the US$199 rooms and airport transfers are included.

Hyatt Regency Mumbai (☎ 56961234; www.mum bai.regency.hyatt.com; Sahar Airport Rd, Andheri; d incl tax from US$170; 🅿 🖳 🕸) Also just outside the international airport is this contemporary-style hotel that is in a more convenient location than its sister property, the Grand Hyatt in Santa Cruz, and has slightly more snazzily decorated rooms.

EATING

Mumbai is a gourmand's paradise. You could trace the cultural history of the metropolis by trawling through the variety of food available: from Parsi dhansaak (meat with curried lentils and rice), Gujarati thalis ('all-you-can-eat' meals) and Muslim kebabs to Goan vindaloo and Mangalorean seafood. And very few restaurants serve it, but if you find it on a menu, Bombay duck is actually *bombil* fish dried in the sun and deep-fried.

Don't miss Mumbai's famous *bhelpuri*; it's readily available at stalls on Chowpatty and Juhu beaches although you'd be safer sampling it in a restaurant such as Swati Snacks (p112). During the Islamic holy month of Ramadan, fantastic night food-markets line Mohammed Ali and Merchant Rds in Kalbadevi. Street food-stalls offering rice plates, samosas and *pav bhaji* (spiced vegetables

and bread) for around Rs 15 do a brisk trade around the city.

If you're self-catering try the **Colaba market** (Map p99; Lala Nigam St), with plenty of fresh fruit and vegetables, and there's the **Saharkari Bhandar Supermarket** (Map p99; cnr Colaba Causeway & Wodehouse Rd) at the north of Colaba Causeway. Just off Veer Nariman Rd next to Churchgate train station is **Suryodaya** (Map p102; E Rd; ⏰ 7.30am-8.30pm), another well-stocked supermarket.

If not otherwise mentioned in the reviews the restaurants will be open from noon to 3pm and 7pm to 11.30pm daily.

Colaba   Map p99
Bade Miya (☎ 22848038; Tulloch Rd; mains Rs 70; ⏰ 7pm-1am) A takeaway kebab cart with a phone number? Such is the citywide popularity of this place that it does fantastic business each night serving the likes of chicken tikka rolls, *boti kebab* (lamb kebab) and *paneer masala* (cheese and tomato curry). There are metal tables and chairs in the street if you want to eat here.

Café Churchill (103B Colaba Causeway; mains Rs 50-90; ⏰ 10.30am-11.30pm; 🕸) This tiny, packed place with booth seating does some of the best Western comfort food around. The specialities are tasty sandwiches, reasonable pasta meals and tempting desserts such as honey walnut tart.

Kailash Parbat (5 Sheela Mahal, 1st Pasta Lane, Colaba; mains Rs 50-80; ⏰ 8am-11pm) Nothing fancy, but a Mumbai legend nonetheless thanks to its inexpensive Sindhi-influenced pure-vegetarian snacks and its mouthwatering sweets.

Basilico (Sentinel House, Arthur Bunder Rd; mains Rs 145-285; ⏰ 7.30am-1.30am; 🕸) Enjoy creative salads, risottos and tagines among other dishes at this chic Euro-style bistro and deli. It also serves top-notch pastries and cakes.

Tendulkar's (☎ 22829934; Narang House, Shivaji Marg, Apollo Bunder; mains Rs 200-475; 🕸) Cricket superstar Sachin Tendulkar bowls up a kind of Hard Rock cricket café. The décor's an icy mix of neon, glass and booth seating, and the menu offers Indian and European dishes, including Tendulkar's mum's recipe for Bombay duck! Happy hour (25% off drinks) is 6.30pm to 8.30pm daily.

Café Sesso (Courtyard, SP Centre, 41/44 Minoo Desai Marg; mains Rs 165-200; ⏰ 11.30am-11.30pm; 🕸) This chic café and deli is the perfect spot to refuel by day while cruising the designer boutiques of the Courtyard complex. The sandwiches and salads are tasty and there are more substantial dishes if you're really hungry.

Koyla (☎ 56369999; Gulf Hotel, Arthur Bunder Rd; mains Rs 100-250; ☒ 8am-2.30pm Tue-Sun) An Arabia meets Café del Mar atmosphere engulfs this rooftop restaurant-bar where you can lounge on low sofas and puff on a hookah pipe (Rs 200) as you nibble the tasty food and sip cooling drinks.

Delhi Darbar (☎ 22020235; Colaba Causeway; mains Rs 80-165; ☒ 11.30am-12.30pm; ☒) This is one of South Mumbai's best Mughlai and tandoori restaurants. There's a slightly formal atmosphere, but the standard of food is excellent.

Kala Ghoda & Fort Area

Mahesh Lunch Home (Map p102; ☎ 22870938; 8B Cowasji Patel St, Fort; mains Rs 85-200; ☒) This is the place to try Mangalorean seafood. It's renowned for its ladyfish, pomfret, lobster and crabs, and its *rawas tikka* (marinated white salmon) and tandoori pomfret are superb.

Trishna (Map p102; ☎ 22614991; Sai Baba Marg, Kala Ghoda; mains Rs 300-500; ☒) Another local legend that deserves its strong reputation for seafood cooked in myriad ways. The prawns and lobsters will be bought to your table for inspection before you order.

Chetana (Map p102; 34 K Dubash Marg, Kala Ghoda; thali buffet Rs 170-190; ☒) Chetana is a venerable restaurant that's a popular lunch spot and a great place to deconstruct the mysteries of the North Indian vegetarian thali, which is offered as a lunch and dinner buffet, along with dessert. The street it is on is also known as Rampart Row.

Rajdhani (Map pp94-5; 361 Sheikh Memon St, Kalbadevi; ☒ noon-4pm, 7-10pm; ☒) This smart place, opposite Mangaldaas Market, is another good spot to refuel on a very tasty thali (Rs 125) while shopping in the Crawford Market area.

Apoorva Restaurant & Bar (Map p102; ☎ 228 70335; Noble Chambers, SA Brelvi Rd, Fort; mains Rs 60-380; ☒) The decorative décor is a bit dubious but there's no faulting the Mangalorean seafood, including fried prawn masala and the classic Bombay duck, at this venerable restaurant.

Mocambo Café & Bar (Map p102; 23A Sir P Mehta Rd, Fort; mains Rs 50-170; ☒ 9am-9.30pm Mon-Sat; ☒) Recently taken over by the same team in charge of Colaba's Café Churchill (opposite), this is a modern, convivial and con-

venient spot for breakfast, sandwiches, a main meal or a cold beer.

Ideal Corner (Map p102; 12 Gunbow St, Fort; mains Rs 40-60; ☒ 9am-6pm Mon-Fri) This spotless corner place on two levels is the classic Parsi café serving a different menu of Parsi dishes each day.

Churchgate   Map p102

Tea Centre (78 Veer Nariman Rd; mains Rs 60-130; set lunch Rs 185; ☒ 8am-11pm; ☒) A great place to try out some of India's premium teas, as well as sample some excellent light meals and snacks, this is a serene, colonial-meets-contemporary place. It's also fiercely air-conditioned.

Samrat (Prem Ct, J Tata Rd; mains Rs 60-150; ☒ noon-11pm; ☒) is a good traditional Indian vegetarian restaurant; **Relish** (Prem Ct, J Tata Rd; mains Rs 60-150; ☒ noon-11pm; ☒) is its funkier cousin with dishes ranging from fondue to Mexican. Both are run by the same company and share a corner building along with the outdoor café and bakery **210° C** (Prem Ct, J Tata Rd; pastries from Rs 10; ☒ noon-11pm), which serves a tempting range of vegan pies and cakes.

A couple of places at the Marine Dr end of Churchgate that are good for bay views as well as decent non-Indian food are the **Pizzeria** (Soona Mahal, 143 Marine Dr; pizzas Rs 110-350; ☒) and **Pearl of the Orient** (☎ 22041131; Ambassador Hotel, Veer Nariman Rd; mains Rs 300-600; ☒), which specialises in Asian dishes and is Mumbai's only revolving restaurant.

Chowpatty Beach
& Around   Map pp94-5

The stalls at Bhel Plaza on Chowpatty Beach open up in the evening and are the most atmospheric spots to snack on *bhelpuri*

(Rs 10), *panipuri* (deep-fried roti filled with dhal; Rs 15 to 20) and ice cream.

Swati Snacks (☎ 56608405; 248 Karai Estate, Tardeo Rd, Tardeo; mains Rs 20-50; ✹ 11.30am-11pm; ✖) Over four decades in the business and recently installed in a sleek contemporary-design space, Swati Snacks is all stainless steel and smooth wood. Try the *bhelpuri*, *panki chatni* (savoury pancake steamed in a banana leaf) and homemade ice cream in delectable flavours such as rose and ginger.

Anantashram (46 Kotachiwadi, Girgaum; ✹ 11am-1.30pm & 7-9pm Mon-Sat) This no-frills restaurant is as renowned for its Spartan décor and the surliness of its staff as for its supremely delicious cooking. Many a Mumbaiker will cross town to sample its chicken curry and fried fish.

Cream Centre (25B Chowpatty Seaface; mains Rs 50-80; ✹ 11am-11.30pm; ✖) Enjoy pure veg dishes and such hybrids as Indian Mexican cuisine at this iconic café-bar and ice-cream parlour that's been gracing Chowpatty for over 40 years.

New Kulfi Centre (cnr Chowpatty Seaface & Sardar V Patel Rd; kulfi Rs 20-30; ✹ 10am-1am) For kulfi, a pistachio-flavoured sweet similar to ice cream, try the New Kulfi, which has been in business since 1965.

Northern Mumbai   Map p97

North Mumbai's centres of gravity as far as trendy dining and drinking are concerned lie in Bandra West and Juhu. Also see the drinking reviews for a few more options (right).

Peshawri (☎ 28303030; ITC Hotel Grand Maratha Sheraton & Towers, Sahar Airport Rd; mains Rs 500-1150; ✹ 7.30-11.45pm; ✖) Make this Indian northwest frontier restaurant, conveniently located just outside the international airport, your first or last stop in Mumbai. You will not regret forking out for the sublime leg of spring lamb and amazing dhal Bukhara (a thick black dhal cooked for over a day!).

Goa Portuguesa (☎ 24440202; www.goaportuguesa.com; Kataria Rd, Mahim; dishes Rs 70-200; ✹ noon-4pm, 7pm-1am; ✖) As good as making a trip to Goa is a visit to this fun restaurant, which specialises in the fiery dishes of the former Portuguese colony. It's opposite Mahim Head post office.

Culture Curry (Kataria Rd; dishes Rs 70-200; ✹ noon-4pm, 7pm-1am) Alongside Goa Portuguesa and run by the same people, Culture Curry of-

fers all kinds of curries from around India. Guitar-strumming musicians and singers wander between the two connected spaces.

Dosa Diner (☎ 26404488; 187 Zainab Villa, Turner Rd, Bandra West; ✹ 11.30am-11.30pm; ✖) Family diner heaven, where kids and the young at heart will be enchanted by hat- and cat-shaped dosas (paper-thin lentil-flour pancakes) and other South Indian snacks. It also does excellent veg and nonveg thalis.

Pot Pourri (☎ 26414543; Carlton Ct, cnr of Turner & Pali Rds, Bandra West; mains Rs 100-180; ✹ 11am-midnight) Dishing up delicious Western-style cuisine – everything from Highland Scotch broth to its famed chicken stroganoff (Rs 160) – Pot Pourri has recently expanded around the entire corner of this busy junction. The daily specials are excellent and the reasonable prices put other places to shame.

Jewel of India (Off Map pp94-5; ☎ 24949435; Nehru Centre, Dr Annie Besant Rd, Worli; mains Rs 250-400; ✖) This smart restaurant serves up a fine Indian buffet (Rs 450) for lunch and an à la carte menu at night, which includes tandoori dishes and seafood. It has a decent wine list and there's a convivial clubby bar attached.

DRINKING

Mumbai has a relaxed attitude to alcohol and a vibrant nightlife that ranges from simple beer bars to glamorous Mumbai-elite clubs. A large bottle of beer in a bar or restaurant costs between Rs 80 and 120 – more in a nightclub or fashionable drinking spot.

Cafés

Mocha Bar (Map p102; 82 Veer Nariman Rd, Churchgate; ✹ 9am-1am daily; ✖) This is a mellow, Arabian-style coffee house with low cushioned seating, hookah pipes, exotic coffee varieties and world music playing – a great place to hang out for the afternoon.

Samovar Café (Map p102; Jehangir Art Gallery, 161B MG Rd, Kala Ghoda; ✹ 11am-7pm Mon-Sat) Overlooking the gardens of the Prince of Wales Museum this is a pleasant place to chill out over a beer, mango lassi (Rs 50) or light meal.

The Rs 5 chai-wallahs are still out there but otherwise Starbucks-style 'espresso-bars' have really taken off in Mumbai. Barista and Café Day vie for dominance across the city, often with branches practically next door to each other. **Barista** (Chowpatty Beach pp94-5; Chowpatty Seaface; Colaba Map p99;

Colaba Causeway; near CST Map p102; Marzaban Rd) is slightly more stylish with pristine orange- and cream-coloured surroundings.

Crossword, Magna Book Gallery and Oxford Bookstore (p93) all have good cafés within their premises, the best being the Oxford's slick **Cha Bar** (Map p102; Apeejay House, 3 Dinsha Wachha Rd, Churchgate; 🕑 10am-10pm), which serves an impressive range of teas and tasty snacks.

Bars

COLABA   Map p99
Leopold Café & Bar (cnr Colaba Causeway & Nawroji F Rd; 🕑 7.30am-11pm) A Mumbai institution dating back to 1871, Leopold's is the most popular travellers hang-out in the city. There's an extensive food menu but most people come here to drink and soak up the old-time atmosphere.

Busaba (☎ 22043779; 4 Mandlik Marg; 🕑 noon-3pm & 7pm-12.30am; 🍴) Red walls, framed post-cards and old photos give this restaurant-bar a bohemian feel. It's next to Indigo so gets the same trendy crowd, but the advantage is that the potent cocktails aren't quite as pricey.

Café Mondegar (Metro House, 5A Colaba Causeway; mains Rs 40-80; 🕑 8am-midnight) Colourful cartoons on the walls and a CD jukebox define this popular café-bar where a steady flow of travellers down draught beers (Rs 60).

Gokul Bar (Tulloch Rd; 🕑 11am-12.30am; 🍴) This classic, 100% male, Indian drinking den can get pretty lively and the beer is cheap (starting at Rs 45). There's an AC section upstairs where the real boozers hang out.

BREACH CANDY & LOWER PAREL
Ghetto (Map pp94-5; ☎ 23538418; 30 Bhulabhai Desai Marg, Mahalaxmi; 🕑 7pm-1.30am; 🍴) Mumbai's original rock-and-roll bar, covered with graffiti, is a friendly spot that can hop on a good night. A bonus is the international movies screened free every Monday at 7.30pm.

Lush Lounge & Grille (Off Map pp94-5; ☎ 566 3460; Phoenix Mills, 462 Senapati Bapat Marg, Lower Parel; 🕑 12.30pm-3.30pm & 7pm-1.30am; 🍴) Tucked away in an old fabric mill that's been converted into a shopping centre is this industrial-chic restaurant-bar, current darling of Mumbai's bright young things. There's a cover charge of Rs 500 to 1000 on Wednesday, Friday and Saturday. While at Phoenix Mills you might also want to check out **Provogue Lounge** (Off Map

pp94-5; 🕑 10pm-1.30am Tue-Sat; 🍴), a boutique by day, banging lounge bar by night.

BANDRA & JUHU
Vie Lounge (Map p97; ☎ 26604884; Juhu Tara Rd, Juhu; 🕑 7pm-1.30am; 🍴) About as close to Juhu Beach as you can get without sand spoiling your shoes, is this glamorous party spot (opposite Little Italy restaurant). Call before dragging all the way out here to check there isn't a private Bollywood bash on.

Zenzi (Map p97; ☎ 56430670; 183 Waterfield Rd, Bandra West; 🕑 10am-1.30am; 🍴) This ultracool black and burnt orange decorated place is bathed in soft lighting and has a choice of AC or non-AC dining and drinking areas. The eclectic menu is more finger food than bust-a-gut dining, so come for the drinks, the DJ and the beautiful people.

Olive Bar & Kitchen (Map p97; ☎ 26058228; Pali Hill Tourist Hotel, 14 Union Park, Khar; 🕑 8.30am-12.30pm; 🍴) Booking is essential for this hip but snooty Mediterranean-style restaurant and bar in the chichi Pali Hill area. The food is light and delicious, the DJ sounds soothing and the décor is pure Ibiza. There's an Arabian cushion and carpet chill zone tucked away in the back.

ENTERTAINMENT
The daily English-language tabloid *Mid-Day* incorporates the *List*, a guide to Mumbai entertainment. Newspapers have information on mainstream events and film screenings as does *Time Out Mumbai* (p96).

Nightclubs
The big nights in clubs are Wednesday, Friday and Saturday when there's usually a cover charge. Dress codes apply so don't rock up in shorts and sandals.

Insomnia (Map p99; ☎ 56653366; Taj Mahal Palace & Tower, Apollo Bunder, Colaba; 🕑 8pm-3am) For Bollywood star-spotting, ultrachic Insomnia is the place to be. It doesn't get going till after midnight and the minimum drinks spend is Rs 600 per person (Rs 1200 on Friday and Saturday nights), payable in advance on a prepaid card that you present at the bars.

Athena (Map p99; ☎ 22028699; 41/44 Minoo Desai Marg, Colaba; cover per couple Rs 1000; 🕑 8pm-1am daily) Depending on the night Athena also snares many of Mumbai's brash young things. Admission is free on midweek nights when it can be dead. Cocktails cost around Rs 250.

READING MUMBAI

Containing all the beauty and ugliness of the human condition is it any wonder that Mumbai has inspired a host of the best writers on the subcontinent as well as international scribes such as VS Naipaul and Pico Iyer. Leading the field are Booker Prize–winner Salman Rushdie (*Midnight's Children*, *The Moor's Last Sigh* and *The Ground Beneath Her Feet*) and Rohinton Mistry (*A Fine Balance* and *Family Matters*), who have both set many of their novels in the city.

Making a credible grab to be the ultimate chronicle of the modern city is Suketu Mehta's *Maximum City: Bombay Lost and Found*. This incisively researched and elegantly written epic – equal parts memoir, travelogue and journalism – covers such topics as Mumbai's riots, gang warfare, Bollywood and bar girls. Another doorstopper is Gregory David Robert's factional saga *Shantaram*, about the prison escapee's life on the run in Mumbai's slums and jails. Also well worth dipping into is the anthology *Bombay, Meri Jaan* edited by the talented Jerry Pinto and Naresh Fernandes.

Polly Esther's (Map p99; ☎ 22871122; Gordon House Hotel, 5 Battery St, Colaba; cover per couple Rs 600-1000; ☽ 8.30am-1am) Retro pop, rock and disco rule at the Gordon House Hotel's (p108) mirror-plated, groovy nightclub. It comes complete with a *Saturday Night Fever* illuminated dance floor and waiters in Afro wigs!

Red Light (Map p102; ☎ 56346249; 145 MG Rd, Fort; cover Rs 300; ☽ 7pm-midnight) Above the upmarket North Indian restaurant Khyber is this *über*-trendy bar. Wednesday's hip-hop session is the most happening.

Copa Cabana (Map pp94-5; ☎ 33680274; Darya Vihar, 39 Chowpatty Seaface; admission free; ☽ 7pm-12.30am) This buzzing, Latin-flavoured clubbar dishes up decent music, fine margaritas (Rs 200) and no elbow room. It sometimes hosts Gay Bombay parties (see p470).

Voodoo Pub (Map p99; ☎ 22841959; 2/5 Kamal Mansion, Arthur Bunder Rd, Colaba; cover charge after 8.30pm Rs 130; ☽ 7.30pm-1.30am) Famous for hosting Mumbai's only regular gay night (Saturday) this lacklustre bar is best avoided at any other time.

Cinema

Going to see a movie in India's film capital is practically mandatory; with well over 100 cinemas around the city there's no excuse not to. Try the following:

Eros (Map p102; ☎ 22822335; MK Rd, Churchgate; tickets Rs 35-80) For Bollywood blockbusters.

Metro (Map p102; ☎ 22030303; MG Rd, New Marine Lines, Fort; tickets Rs 35-80) Also good for Bollywood blockbusters.

Regal (Map p99; ☎ 22021017; Colaba Causeway, Colaba; tickets Rs 80-120) Art Deco cinema showing first-run English-language movies.

Sterling (Map p102; ☎ 22075187; Marzaban Rd, Fort; tickets Rs 60-87) First-run English-language movies.

Also check out the Ghetto (p113) on Monday nights for free international movies.

Music, Dance & Theatre

Not Just Jazz By the Bay (Map p102; ☎ 22851876; 143 Marine Dr; admission Rs 150; ☽ 6pm-2am) This is the best jazz club in South Mumbai, but, true to its name, there are also live pop, blues and rock performers here most nights of the week from 10pm.

National Centre for the Performing Arts (NCPA; Map pp94-5; ☎ 22833737; www.tata.com/ncpa; tickets Rs 40-280) At the tip of Nariman Point, this is the hub of Mumbai's music, theatre and dance scene. In any given week, it might host Marathi theatre, dance troupes from Bihar, ensembles from Europe and Indian classical music. It also contains the Tata Theatre (which occasionally has English-language plays) and the Experimental Theatre. Many performances are free. The **box office** (Map pp94-5; ☎ 22824567; ☽ bookings 9am-1.30pm & 4.30-6.30pm) is at the end of NCPA Marg.

Nehru Centre (Off Map pp94-5; ☎ 24933340; www.nehrucentremumbai.com; Dr Annie Besant Rd, Worli) performances of English-language plays.

Prithvi Theatre (Map p97; ☎ 26149546; www.prithvitheatre.org; Juhu Church Rd, Vile Parle) At Juhu Beach, this is a good place to see both English-language and Hindi theatre. It also hosts an annual international theatre festival.

Sport

CRICKET

The cricket season runs from October to April. Test matches and One Day Internationals are played a handful of times a year at **Wankhede Stadium** (Map p102; ☎ 22811795; mcacrick@vsnl.com; D Rd, Churchgate), just off Marine Dr. To buy tickets apply in writing well in advance. One-day match tickets start at Rs 150. For a test match you'll have to pay for the full five days – around Rs 500 for general admission or Rs 3000 for the members stand, replete with lunch and afternoon tea. For state matches tickets (Rs 25) are available at the gate.

HORSE RACING
Mumbai's horse-racing season runs from November to the end of April. Races are held on Sunday and Thursday afternoons (Saturday and Sunday towards the end of the season) at **Mahalaxmi Racecourse** (Map pp94-5; ☎ 23071401). Big races, such as the Indian Derby held in February, are major social occasions. Entry costs Rs 30 in the public enclosure.

FOOTBALL
The **Cooperage Football Ground** (Map p99; ☎ 220 24020; MK Rd, Colaba; tickets Rs 50) is home to the Mumbai Football Association and hosts national and state league soccer matches between November and February. Tickets are available at the gate.

TENPIN BOWLING
Kids may love a round of tenpin bowling at the **Bowling Company** (Off Map pp94-5; ☎ 24914000; www.thebowlingcompany.com; High St Phoenix, SB Marg, Lower Parel West; ☼ 11am-11pm).

SHOPPING
Mumbai is India's great marketplace, with some of the best shopping in the country. Colaba Causeway is lined with hawkers' stalls and shops selling better-quality garments, including genuine sporting apparel. Electronic gear, pirated CDs and DVDs, leather goods and mass-produced gizmos can be found at stalls on Dr Dadabhai Naoroji Rd between CST and Flora Fountain, and along MG Rd from Flora Fountain to Kala Ghoda.

Antiques & Curios
Small antique and curio shops line Merewether Rd behind the Taj Mahal Palace & Tower (see Map p99). Prices aren't cheap, but the quality is definitely a step up from government emporiums.

If you prefer Raj-era bric-a-brac, head to Chor Bazaar (Map pp94–5; p116); the main area of activity is Mutton St where you'll find a row of shops specialising in antiques (many ingenious reproductions, so beware) and miscellaneous junk.

Mini Market (Map pp94-5; ☎ 23472427; 33/31 Mutton St; ☼ 11am-8pm Sat-Thu) Sells original vintage Bollywood posters and other movie ephemera as well as many trinkets.

Phillips (Map p99; ☎ 22020564; www.phillipsanti ques.com; opposite Regal Cinema, Woodhouse Rd, Colaba; ☼ 10am-1.30pm & 2.30-7pm Mon-Sat) Long-running antique shop known for its quality prints, silver, brassware and glass lamps – all late Victorian.

Fashion
Snap up a bargain backpacking wardrobe at 'Fashion Street', the cheap stalls lining MG Rd between Cross and Azad maidans (Map p102). This is definitely a place to hone your bargaining skills.

Designer clobber can be bought at the boutiques at Kemp's Corner, between the flyover and the junction with Nepean Sea Rd. Pieces by Indian designers sell here for half the price of off-the-shelf gear back home. Check out **Mélange** (Map pp94-5; 33 Altamount Rd, Kemp's Corner; ☼ 10am-7pm), an Aladdin's cave of high fashion, with garments from some 70 designers across India.

Courtyard (Map p99; SP Centre, 41/44 Minoo Desai Marg; ☼ 11am-7.30pm) This collection of boutiques is Mumbai's fashion nexus, with appealing, keenly priced couture clothes, shoes and interior goods by top local designers such as Narendra Kumar and the Gaultier-goes-to-Bollywood look of Manish Arora.

Fabindia (Map p102; Jeroo Bldg, 137 MG Rd, Kala Ghoda; ☼ 10am-7.45pm Tue-Sun) All the vibrant colours of the country are represented in the top quality, keenly priced cotton and silk fashions, materials and homewares of this very modern Indian shop.

Khadi & Village Industries Emporium (Map p102; 286 Dr Dadabhai Naoroji Rd, Fort; ☼ 10.30am-6.30pm Mon-Sat) Time seems to have stopped somewhere in the 1940s at this place, where you can pick up ready-made traditional Indian clothing in homespun cotton and silk as well as material, shoes and handicrafts.

Crossroads (Map pp94-5; 28 Pandit MM Malviya Rd, Breach Candy; ☼ 10am-8pm) Mumbai's biggest shopping mall is full of glitzy, expensive international designer label shops and fast-food joints; it's nothing you've not seen at home already.

Handicrafts & Gifts

You can pick up handicrafts from various state government emporiums in the World Trade Centre Arcade (Map pp94–5) near Cuffe Parade. All the following places have fixed prices and accept credit cards.

Bombay Store (Map p102; Western India House, Sir P Mehta Rd, Fort; ☒ 10.30am-7.30pm Mon-Sat, 10.30am-6.30pm Sun) The place to browse if you're looking for souvenirs from around India. Although the prices are considerably higher than at the markets or Central Cottage Industries Emporium (below), the range and quality is impressive. It sells rugs, textiles, home furnishings, silverware, glassware, *pietra dura* (marble inlay work) and bric-a-brac.

Bombay Paperie (Map p102; 59 Bombay Samachar Marg, Fort; ☒ 10.30am-6pm Mon-Sat) Sells hand made cotton-based paper made in the village of Kagzipura near Aurangaba, crafted into charming cards, sculptures and lampshades.

Bungalow Eight (Map pp94-5; 8 Carmichael Rd, Vasant Vihar; ☒ 10.30am-7.30pm Mon-Fri, noon-7pm Sat) Check out the interior design goods, from beautifully embroidered slippers and pillows to buffalo-horn carved bowls and hand-painted photo albums at this upmarket boutique just east of Breach Candy.

Inshaallah Mashaallah (Map p99; Best Marg, Colaba; ☒ 11am-9pm) Helpful staff will guide you through the olfactory chaos offering a vast range of local perfumed oils and potions.

Central Cottage Industries Emporium (Map p99; Shivaji Marg, Colaba; ☒ 10am-7pm) This emporium has a wide selection of mass-produced trinkets, and is a convenient places to buy gifts.

Other government emporiums worth checking out include the following:

Kashmir Government Arts Emporium (Map p102; Sir P Mehta Rd, Fort; ☒ 10am-7pm Mon-Sat)

Uttar Pradesh Handicrafts Emporium (Map p102; Sir P Mehta Rd, Fort; ☒ 10.30am-7.30pm Mon-Sat)

Markets

You can buy just about anything in the dense bazaars north of the Fort (see Map pp94–5). The main areas are Crawford Market (fruit and veg), Mangaldas Market (silk and cloth), Zaveri Bazaar (jewellery), Bhuleshwar Market (fruit and veg) and Chor Bazaar (Mumbai's 'thieves' market', for antiques and furniture),

where Dhabu St is worth a peek for leather goods, and Mutton St specialises in antiques, reproductions and junk.

Colourful Crawford Market (officially called Mahatma Phule Market) is the last outpost of British Bombay before the tumult of the central bazaars begins. Bas-reliefs by Rudyard Kipling's father, Lockwood Kipling, adorn the Norman-Gothic exterior. The meat market is strictly for the brave; it's one of the few places you can expect to be accosted and asked to buy a bloody goat's head.

Music

Poor-quality pirated CDs and DVDs are available on the street for around Rs 200. If you want quality discs it's best to drop by one of the following:

Planet M (Map pp94-5; Dr Dadabhai Naoroji Rd, Fort; ☒ 11am-9pm Mon-Sat, noon-8pm Sun)

Groove (Map p102; 1st fl, Cambata Bldg, MK Rd, Churchgate; ☒ 11.30am-8.30pm Mon-Sat)

Rhythm House (Map p102; 40 K Dubash Marg, Fort; ☒ 10am-8.30pm Mon-Sat, 11am-8.30pm Sun) A good place to browse for older stuff including Hindi film songs and devotional music.

The best place in Mumbai for musical instruments – sitars, tablas, accordions and Indian-made and imported guitars – as well as a startling collection of plaster Christian icons, is **LM Furtado & Co** (Map pp94-5; ☎ 220 13163; 540-544 Kalbadevi Rd, Kalbadevi; ☒ 10am-8pm Mon-Sat). It also has a branch around the corner on Lokmanya Tilak Rd.

GETTING THERE & AWAY
Air
AIRPORTS

Mumbai is the main international gateway to South India. It also has the busiest network of domestic flights. The **international airport** (www.mumbaiairport.com), officially renamed Chhatrapati Shivaji but still known as Sahar, is about 4km away from the domestic airport, also called Chhatrapati Shivaji but known as Santa Cruz. There's a free shuttle bus between the airports if you have a connecting flight. They are north (30km and 26km respectively) of Nariman Point in downtown Mumbai.

The international airport has two arrivals halls which have foreign-exchange counters offering reasonable rates, a **Government of India tourist office booth** (☎ 26829248; Arrival Hall

2A), a **hotel reservation desk** (☎ 56048772) and a prepaid taxi booth – all open 24 hours.

The **domestic airport** has two terminals a couple of minutes' walk apart. Terminal A handles Indian Airlines flights, while terminal B caters to Air Deccan, Jet Airways and Sahara Airlines. Both terminals have foreign-exchange bureaus, ticketing counters and a restaurant-bar. The Government of India tourist office booth is in terminal B. Note that flights on domestic sectors of Air India routes depart from the international airport.

INTERNATIONAL AIRLINES

The free English-language publication *City Info* has a list of major international airline offices in Mumbai. Travel agencies are a better bet for booking international flights, and will reconfirm your flight for a small fee.

DOMESTIC AIRLINES

Domestic carriers servicing Mumbai include the following:

Air Deccan (☎ 9892577008; www.airdeccan.net; domestic airport)

Indian Airlines (Map p102; ☎ 22023031, 24hr reservations ☎ 1401; www.indian-airlines.nic.in; Air India Bldg, cnr Marine Dr & Madame Cama Rd, Nariman Point)

Jet Airways (Map p99; ☎ 22855788; www.jetairways.com; Amarchand Mansion, Madame Cama Rd)

Sahara Airlines (Map pp94-5; ☎ 22835671, 24hr tollfree ☎ 1600-115466; www.airsahara.net; 7 Tulsiani Chambers, Free Press Journal Marg, Nariman Point)

There are flights to more than 30 Indian cities from Mumbai. Major flights include the following:

Destination	Fare (US$)	Duration (hr)	Flights per day
Bangalore	150	1½	16
Chennai	170	1¾	13
Delhi	195	2	29
Goa	95	1	11
Hyderabad	130	1¼	9
Kochi	190	1¼	7
Kolkata	240	2¼	9

Bus

Numerous private operators and state governments run long-distance buses to and from Mumbai. Private operators provide faster service, more comfort and simpler booking procedures.

Private long-distance buses depart for all points from Dr Anadrao Nair Rd, near Mumbai Central train station (Map pp94–5). Fares for non-AC deluxe buses include the following:

Destination	Fare (Rs)	Duration (hr)
Ahmedabad	250	13
Aurangabad	200	10
Bangalore	450	24
Panaji (Goa)	250	14-18
Mahabaleshwar	200	7
Pune	150	7
Udaipur	400	16

There are also sleeper buses to Goa for Rs 350 to 450. Note that fares to popular destinations such as Goa are up to 75% higher during holiday periods such as Diwali and Christmas. To check on departure times and current prices, try **National Travels** (Map pp94-5; ☎ 23015652; Dr Anadrao Nair Rd; ⏰ 6am-10pm).

More convenient for Goa and southern destinations are the private buses that depart twice a day from MG Rd, just south of the Metro cinema. Some buses to South India depart from MRA Marg at the rear of Crawford Market. It's best to purchase tickets directly from agents – pavement stalls are clustered in either of these areas.

Long-distance state-run buses depart from Mumbai Central bus terminal (Map pp94–5) close to Mumbai Central train station. Buses service major towns in Maharashtra and neighbouring states. They're marginally cheaper and more frequent than the private services, but they're also decrepit, crowded, uncomfortable vehicles. Destinations include Pune (Rs 120, four hours), Aurangabad (Rs 181, eight to nine hours) and Mahabaleshwar (Rs 110, seven hours).

Train

Three train systems operate out of Mumbai, but the main two that are important for overseas visitors are Central Railways and Western Railways. See the boxed text (p118) for information on key services.

Central Railways (☎ 134), handling services to the east and south, plus a few trains to the north, operates mainly from Chhatrapati Shivaji Terminus (CST, formerly Victoria Terminus). The **reservation centre** (Map p102;

8am-8pm Mon-Sat, 8am-2pm Sun) is at the back of CST where the taxis gather. Tourist-quota tickets are available at Counter 52 on the 1st floor (from 8am to 3pm) but can only be bought during the 24 hours before the date of travel and must be paid in foreign currency or with rupees backed by an en-cashment certificate or ATM receipt. Indrail passes (p500) can be bought at Counter 7. You can buy tickets (but not tourist-quota tickets) with a Visa or MasterCard at the credit-card counters (10 and 11) up to 60 days in advance. There's rarely a queue here so this should definitely be your first port of call if you have a credit card. There's a Rs 30 fee.

A few Central Railways trains depart from Dadar (D), which is a few stations north of CST. Other leave from Church-gate or Lokmanya Tilak (T), 16km north of CST on the suburban main line. One these is the *Chennai Express*, the fastest train to Chennai. You can book tickets for all these trains at CST.

Western Railways (☎ 131) has services to the north (including Rajasthan and Delhi) from Mumbai Central (MC) train station (often still called Bombay Central). The easiest place to make bookings for Western Railways trains is at the crowded **reservation centre** (Map p102; 8am-8pm Mon-Sun) opposite Churchgate train station. The **foreign tourist-**

MAJOR TRAINS FROM MUMBAI

Destination	Train No & name	Fare (Rs)	Duration (hr)	Departure
Agra	2137 *Punjab Mail*	417/1118	21½	7.05pm CST
Ahmedabad	2901 *Gujarat Mail*	235/604	9	9.50pm MC
Aurangabad	1003 *Devagiri Exp*	178/471	7½	9.05pm CST
	7617 *Tapovan Exp*	110/369*	7½	6.10am CST
Bangalore	6529 *Udyan Exp*	381/1043	24½	7.55am CST
Bhopal	2137 *Punjab Mail*	330/872	14	7.05pm CST
Chennai	6011 *Chennai Exp*	389/1065	26½	2pm CST
Delhi	2951 *Rajdhani Exp*	1485/2210**	17	4.55pm MC
	9023 *Janata Exp*	245/1405	30	7.25am MC
	2137 *Punjab Mail*	449/1203	25¼	7.05pm CST
Goa	0111 *Konkan Kanya Exp*	293/796	12	10.50pm CST
0103 *Mandavi Exp*	293/796	11½	7.05am CST	
2051 *Shatabdi Exp*	197/675*	8	5.35am D	
Hyderabad	7001 *Hussainsagar Exp*	297/807	15	9.50pm CST
Indore	2961 *Avantika Exp*	325/861	15	7.05pm MC
Jaipur	2955 *Jaipur Exp*	389/1039	18	6.50pm MC
Kochi	6345 *Netravati Exp*	441/1211	32	11.45pm T
Kolkata	2859 *Gitanjali Exp*	517/1399	30	6am CST
	2809 *Howrah Mail*	517/1399	32	8.15pm CST
Pune	2123 *Deccan Queen*	83/270*	3½	5.10pm CST
1007 *Deccan Exp*	73/240*	4½	6.45am CST	
Varanasi	1093 *Mahanagari Exp*	429/1178	29	11.50pm CST
	1027 *Gorakhpur Exp*	461/1268	31	6.35am T

Abbreviations for train stations: CST – Chhatrapati Shivaji Terminus; MC – Mumbai Central; T – Lokmanya Tilak; D – Dadar
Note: Fares are for sleeper/3AC sleeper on overnight trips except for *2nd class/AC seat and **3AC/2AC.

quota counter (No 28; ⏰ 9.30am-4.30pm Mon-Fri, 9.30am-2pm Sat) is upstairs next to the Government of India tourist office, but the same rules apply as at CST station. The credit-card counter is No 20. There's a reservation centre adjacent to Mumbai Central train station, but it doesn't sell tourist-quota tickets.

GETTING AROUND
To/From the Airports
INTERNATIONAL
Taxis operate 24 hours a day from the airport and, although they'll add a night surcharge, the trip into South Mumbai is much quicker at night.

There's a prepaid-taxi booth at the international airport with set fares to various places. To Colaba, the Fort and Marine Dr the fare is Rs 350 during the day (Rs 440 for AC). There's a 25% surcharge between midnight and 5am and a charge of Rs 5 to 10 per bag. The journey takes about 45 minutes at night and 1½ to two hours during the day. To Juhu the day fare is Rs 130, to Chowpatty Rs 300 and to Mumbai Central train station Rs 260. You could try to negotiate a lower fare with a private taxi, but it's hardly worth the hassle. A tip of 5% to 10% is appreciated. Don't catch an autorickshaw from the airport to the city: they're prohibited from entering downtown Mumbai and can take you only as far as Mahim Creek.

The cheap alternative is to catch an autorickshaw (around Rs 25) to Andheri train station and catch a suburban train (Rs 9, 45 minutes) to Churchgate or CST. You can only do this if you arrive during the day and it's unlikely that you'll be up for this after a long-haul flight; don't attempt it during rush hours (particularly the morning rush into the city from around 7am to 10am), or if you're weighed down with luggage. At the very least, buy a 1st-class ticket (Rs 76).

Minibuses outside the arrival hall offer free shuttle services to the domestic airport and Juhu hotels. There's also a free Air India shuttle service between the international and domestic airports.

A taxi from the city centre (say CST station) to the international airport costs around Rs 300 with a bit of bargaining, plus extra for baggage; taxi drivers in Colaba ask for a fixed Rs 350. You'll pay about 30% more between midnight and 5am.

DOMESTIC
Taxis and autorickshaws queue up outside both domestic terminals. There's no prepaid-taxi counter, but the taxi queue outside is controlled by the police – make sure your driver uses the meter and conversion card. A taxi takes one to 1½ hours to reach the city centre and costs around Rs 300, plus extra for baggage.

If you don't have too much luggage, bus No 2 stops on nearby Nehru Rd, opposite the junction to Nanda Patkar Rd, and terminates at the Kala Ghoda bus stand, right near Colaba (Rs 13). It stops on the highway opposite the airport when heading out of the city.

A better alternative is to catch an autorickshaw between the airport and Vile Parle train station (Rs 15), and catch a suburban train between Vile Parle and Churchgate (Rs 9, 45 minutes). Don't attempt this during rush hour.

Boat
Both **PNP** (☎ 22885220) and **Maldar Catamarans** (☎ 22829695) run regular ferries to Mandwa (Rs 100 one-way), useful for access to Murud-Janjira and other parts of the Konkan coast (p142), avoiding the long bus trip out of Mumbai. Their ticket offices are beside the Gateway of India (Map p102); PNP's services are more frequent and run throughout the year.

Bus
Mumbai's single- and double-decker buses are good for travelling short distances in the city. Fares around South Mumbai cost around Rs 3 for a section so have some small change available and pay the conductor once you're aboard. The service is run by **BEST** (www.bestundertaking.com), which has its main depot in Colaba (the website has a useful search facility for bus routes across the city). Just jumping on a double-decker bus (such as No 103) is a good and inexpensive way to have a look around South Mumbai.

Route numbers and destinations on the front of buses are written in Marathi; English signs are on the side.

Following are some useful bus routes; all of these buses depart from the southern end of Colaba Causeway and pass Flora Fountain:

Destination	Bus no
Breach Candy	132, 133
Chowpatty	103, 106, 107, 123
Churchgate	70, 106, 123, 132
Haji Ali	83, 124, 132, 133
Hanging Gardens	103, 106
Mani Bhavan	123
Mohammed Ali Rd	1, 3, 21
Mumbai Central train station	124, 125
CST (VT) & Crawford Market	1, 3, 21, 103, 124

Car

Cars are generally hired for an eight-hour day and with a maximum of 80km travel allowed; additional charges rack up if you exceed these limits.

Agents at the Apollo Bunder ticket booths near the Gateway of India can arrange a non-AC Maruti with driver for a half-day of sightseeing for Rs 600 (going as far as Mahalaxmi and Malabar Hill). Regular taxi drivers in this area accept a similar price.

Motorcycle

Allibhai Premji Tyrewalla (Map pp94-5; ☎ 2309 9313; www.premjis.com; 205/207 Dr D Bhadkamkar Rd, Opera House; ⌚ 10am-7pm Mon-Sat) is the place to purchase a new or used motorcycle with a guaranteed buy-back option. Although you can work on as little as a two- to three-week period, which qualifies as 'rental', you must pay the full cost of the bike upfront. The company prefers to deal with longer-term schemes of two months or more, which work out cheaper anyway. A 350cc or 500cc Enfield costs Rs 30,000 to 50,000, with a buy-back price of around 50% after three months. A smaller bike (100cc to 180cc) starts at Rs 20,000. They can also arrange shipment of bikes overseas. Check the website for more information.

Taxi & Autorickshaw

Every second car on Mumbai's streets seems to be a black-and-yellow Premier taxi (India's version of a 1950s Fiat). They are the most convenient way to get around the city and in South Mumbai drivers almost always use the meter without prompting and give the correct change. Autorickshaws are confined to the suburbs north of Mahim Creek.

Taxi meters are out of date, so the fare is calculated using a conversion chart, which all drivers carry – ask to see it at the end of the journey. The rough conversion rate during the day is around 13 times the meter reading. The minimum fare is Rs 13 for the first 1.6km (flag fall) and Rs 7 per kilometre after this. It's about 25% more expensive between midnight and 6am.

Cool Cabs (☎ 28227006) operates correctly metered, blue AC taxis. They're about a third more expensive than regular cabs and can be booked by telephone.

If you're north of Mahim Creek and not heading into the city, it's best to catch autorickshaws. They're metered but also use a conversion chart. The fare is roughly 7.5 times the meter reading.

Train

Mumbai has an efficient but overcrowded suburban train network – it's virtually the only place in India where it's worth taking trains for travel within a city.

There are three main lines, making it easy to navigate. The most useful service operates from Churchgate heading north to stations such as Charni Rd (for Chowpatty Beach), Mumbai Central, Mahalaxmi (for the dhobi ghat; p104), Vile Parle (for the domestic airport), Andheri (for the international airport) and Borivali (for Sanjay Gandhi National Park). Other suburban lines operate from CST, servicing places such as Byculla (for Victoria Gardens), Dadar, and as far as Neral (for Matheran). Trains begin operating just after 4am and run until almost 1am. From Churchgate, 2nd/1st-class fares are Rs 5/49 to Mumbai Central, Rs 9/76 to Vile Parle or Andheri and Rs 11/102 to Borivali.

Avoid rush hours when trains are jam-packed, even in 1st class. Women should take advantage of the ladies-only carriages. Trains stop at suburban train stations for about 10 seconds so be ready – and watch your valuables.

GREATER MUMBAI

ELEPHANTA ISLAND

Rock-cut temples on **Elephanta Island** (Map p92; Indian/foreigner Rs 10/250; ⌚ caves 9am-5.30pm Tue-Sun), 9km northeast of the Gateway of India, are Mumbai's premier tourist attraction. Little is known about their origins, but they are thought to have been created between AD 450 and 750, when the island was known as Gharapuri (Place of Caves). The Portuguese renamed it Elephanta because of a large stone elephant near the shore. This statue collapsed in 1814 and the British moved and reassembled the remaining pieces at Victoria Gardens, where it stands today. There is one main cave with a number of large sculpted panels, all relating to Shiva. The most famous of the panels is the Trimurti, where the god is depicted as destroyer, preserver and creator. The enormous central bust of Shiva, its eyes closed in eternal contemplation, may be the most serene sight you witness in India.

There are also figures of Shiva dancing the Tandava, the marriage of Shiva and Parvati, Ravana shaking Kailasa, Shiva killing the demon Andhaka, and one in which Shiva appears as Ardhanari, uniting both sexes in one body.

Take advantage of the English-language guide service (free with deluxe boat tickets). Tours depart every hour on the half-hour from the ticket booth in front of the temple complex. If you prefer to explore independently, pick up Pramod Chandra's *A Guide to the Elephanta Caves* from the stalls lining the stairway. There's also a small **museum** on site, which has some informative pictorial panels on the origin of the caves and the history of Maharashtran rock-cut architecture.

Getting There & Away

Launches head to Elephanta Island from the Gateway of India. Small economy boats cost Rs 80 return and more spacious 'deluxe' launches cost Rs 100 return. There's not a great deal of difference between the boats, but if you depart on an economy boat you must return on one – if you have a deluxe ticket you can return on any boat, which means less waiting around. Tickets are sold at booths lining the southern end of Shivaji Marg at Apollo Bunder. Boats depart every half-hour from around 9am to 3pm Tuesday through Sunday. The voyage takes just over an hour and, though not particularly picturesque, does give an indication of the size of Mumbai Harbour. (The island you pass with the whitewashed fortresslike structure is **Butcher Island**. The building was originally a prison but is now used by the navy.)

The ferries dock at the end of a concrete pier, from where you can walk (about three minutes) or take the miniature train (Rs 8) to the stairway leading up to the caves. It's lined

with handicraft stalls and patrolled by pesky monkeys. Palanquins (Rs 150/250 one-way/return) are available for those who feel the need to be carried.

SANJAY GANDHI NATIONAL PARK

This 104 sq km **protected area** (Map p92; ☎ 288 60362; adult/child Rs 5/2; ☽ 7.30am-7pm Tue-Sun) of forested hills, on the city's northern fringe, has some interesting flora, birdlife and butterflies, a small population of wild leopards and a fenced area with captive tigers, including two white tigers. It's a great asset to have within the city limits – the only national park in India with a city postcode – but it's under serious threat from urban encroachment, and the public areas close to the entrance are littered and unkempt.

Just inside the main northern entrance is an **information centre** with a small exhibition on the park's wildlife. The best time to see birds is October to April and butterflies August to November.

For many visitors (mostly Indian families) the main attraction is the **lion and tiger safari**. These depart from the tiger orientation centre (a free display explaining the demise of the tiger), about 1km in from the main entrance. Tickets cost Rs 30 for a whirlwind 20-minute jaunt by bus through the two separate areas of the park housing the tigers and lions. Safari buses leave roughly every 20 minutes from 9am to 12.40pm and 2pm to 5.20pm daily except Monday.

Another major attraction in the park are the 109 **Kanheri Caves** (Indian/foreigner Rs 2/100; ☽ 9.30am-5.30pm Tue-Sun), which line the side of a rocky ravine 5km from the northern park entrance. They were used by Buddhist monks between the 2nd and 9th centuries as *viharas* (monasteries) and *chaityas* (temples), but don't compare to the caves at Ajanta (p136), Ellora (p133) or even Lonavla (p146).

For information on the park, contact Mumbai's main conservation organisation, the **Bombay Natural History Society** (Map p102; ☎ 22821811; www.bnhs.org; Colaba Causeway) in Kala Ghoda.

Getting There & Away

Take the train from Churchgate to Borivali train station (Rs 11, one hour). From there take an autorickshaw (Rs 10) or catch any bus to the park entrance. It's a further 10-minute walk from the entrance to the safari park.

Maharashtra

Sprawling Maharashtra, India's second most populous state, parks up against the Arabian Sea and juts deeply into the beating heart of India. Laying within its borders is a treasure house of architectural and artistic wonders, topped by the World Heritage–listed cave temples of Ellora and Ajanta. This is where most visitors head first, using the ramshackle city of Aurangabad as a base.

Other northern Maharashtrian cities such as Nasik, with its sacred bathing ghats and temples, and Nagpur, near to Gandhi's ashram at Sevagram, are magnets for the faithful and those in search of the spiritual side of India. In the southern section of the state is the lively go-ahead metropolis Pune, home of the infamous Osho Meditation Resort. Further south the old maharaja's palaces of Kolhapur are also well worth dropping by. Many of the seemingly ubiquitous forts built by legendary Maratha leader Chhatrapati Shivaji are also ripe for exploration; most are in ruins but their hilltop locations are spectacular.

Those same peaks of the Deccan plateau harbour a range of soothing cool-air hill resorts, such as Matheran and Mahabaleshwar, while down on the Konkan Coast lie practically uncombed stretches of sand where you can relax and warm up again. Many travellers opt to rush through the state, with stops in Pune and the caves, before hightailing it south to Goa. If you can spare some time, however, you'll find that Maharashtra is a fascinating state stacked with rewards.

HIGHLIGHTS

- Gape at the hand-carved brilliance of Kailasa Temple, the star beauty of the cave temples at **Ellora** (p133)

- Admire the fascinating Buddhist art in a series of rock-cut caves set in a stunning landscape at **Ajanta** (p135)

- Breathe in the serene wooded atmosphere of **Matheran** (p144), fabulously free of traffic and pollution

- Pilgrimage to **Nasik** (p125) and its ghats on the Godavari River, a dreamy place to watch Hindu ritual unfold

- Chill out at **Tarkarli** (p143), Maharashtra's most serene beach

- Eat, drink and make merry in **Pune** (p149), the state's go-ahead economic hub

★Ajanta
★Nasik ★Ellora
★Matheran
★Pune
★Tarkarli

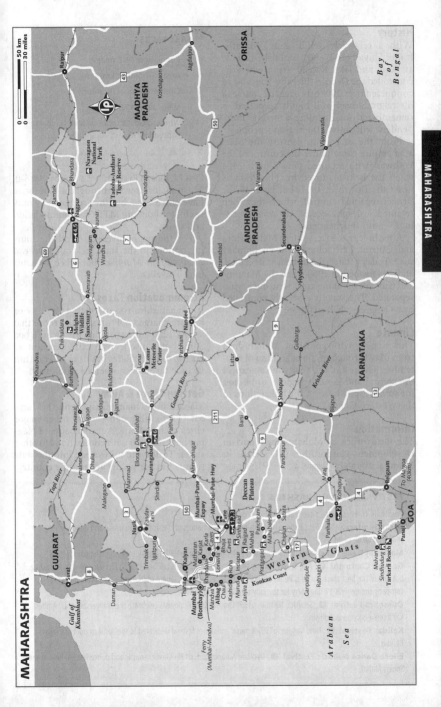

MAHARASHTRA

MAHARASHTRA

History

With a relatively small army, Maratha leader Shivaji (1627–80) established a base at Pune and later Raigad, from where he controlled the Deccan (literally 'south') and conquered over 300 forts over the course of his reign. Shivaji, still highly respected, is remembered for instilling a strong, independent will among the region's people.

From the early 18th century the Maratha empire came under the control of the Peshwas, who retained power until 1804 when the British moved in. The Peshwas upset the British in 1817, but by 1819 the British regained control, which they then retained – despite occasional small uprisings – until Independence.

After Independence, western Maharashtra and Gujarat were joined to form Bombay state. Today's state has Mumbai as its capital, and was formed in 1960 when the Marathi- and Gujarati-speaking areas were once again separated. The state is currently controlled by a Congress-NCP coalition.

Climate

The monsoon hits most of Maharashtra from May through to the beginning of September. The rest of the year you can expect the coastal and interior regions to be hot; for some respite head to the hill stations of the Western Ghats.

Information

The head office of Maharashtra Tourism Development Corporation (MTDC) is in Mumbai (Map p102; in Mumbai ☎ 22026713; Madame

Cama Rd, Nariman Point; ☺ 9.45am-5.30pm Mon-Sat). Most major towns throughout the state have offices, too, but they're generally only useful for booking MTDC accommodation and tours.

For thorough coverage of all the touring options in the state seek out *Weekend Breaks From Mumbai*, published by Outlook Traveller.

Accommodation Taxes

In Maharashtra rooms costing Rs 1199 or less are charged a 4% tax, while those that are Rs 1200 and up are hit with a 10% tax. Some hotels also levy an extra expenditure tax (up to 10%). Rates in this chapter do not include tax, unless otherwise indicated.

Getting There & Away

Maharashtra's main transport hub is Mumbai (p116), although several other major cities such as Pune, Aurangabad and Nagpur have airports with connections to other states. Trains and buses head into the state from all major points around the country.

FESTIVALS IN MAHARASHTRA

Festivals in this boxed text are marked on Map p123.

Sarai Gandarvar (❶; Feb; Pune, p149) Top-notch performances of classical Indian music and dance, where the shows go on all night.

Matharaj Naag Panchami (❷; Aug; Pune, p149, & Kolhapur, p159) A quirky snake-worshipping festival.

Ganesh Chaturthi (❸; Aug & Sep; Pune, p149) Ganesh Chaturthi is celebrated with fervour across Maharashtra, but one of the best places to be is Pune, 163km southeast of Mumbai, where special arts and cultural events accompany the general 11-day party for the jolly elephant-headed deity.

Dussehra Festival (❹; Sep/Oct; Nagpur, p139) Thousands of Buddhists celebrate the anniversary of Dr Ambedkar's conversion to Buddhism.

Kalidas Festival (❺; Nov; Nagpur, p139) A music and dance festival dedicated to the Sanskrit poet Mahakavi Kalidas.

Ellora Dance & Music Festival (❻; Dec/Jan; Aurangabad, p128) Classical music and dance festival held at the Soneri Mahal.

Getting Around
Because the state is so large you might want to consider taking a few internal flights (say Mumbai to Nagpur) to speed up your explorations. Otherwise there are plenty of trains and private long-distance buses, with rickety state transport buses connecting up the more remote places.

NORTHERN MAHARASHTRA

NASIK
☎ 0253 / pop 1.2 million / elev 565m
Standing on the Godavari, one of India's holiest rivers, Nasik (also known as Nashik) is peppered with hundreds of temples and bathing ghats. It's an absorbing, colourful town, increasingly an industrial and business centre, but also with many associations with the Hindu epic Ramayana. Lord Rama and his wife Sita were exiled here, and its where Lakshmana hacked off the nose (nasika) of Ravana's sister, giving the city its name.

Nasik is a common base for pilgrims visiting Trimbak (p127) or Shirdi, birthplace of the original Sai Baba and some 85km southeast of the city. It's also shaping up into the capital of one of India's major wine producing areas (see the boxed text, p127).

Orientation
Mahatma Gandhi Rd, better known as MG Rd, a couple of blocks north of the Old Central bus stand, is Nasik's commercial hub. The temple-strewn Godavari River flows through town just east of here.

Information
Internet cafés are common in town.
Cyber Café (8 Twin Centre, Vakil Wadi; per hr Rs 20; ☼ 10am-10pm Mon-Sat, 10am-3pm Sun) Near Hotel Panchavati.
HDFC Bank (MG Rd) 24-hour ATM.
Matrix Cyber Café (Meghdoot Shopping Centre; per hr Rs 20; ☼ 9am-11.30pm) Close to the Old Central bus stand.
MTDC tourist office (☎ 2570059; Paryatan Bhavan, Old Agra Rd; ☼ 10.30am-5.30pm Mon-Sat) About 700m south of the Old Central bus stand. Has a pretty useless city map (Rs 5).

MAHARASHTRA

NASIK

0 _____ 800 m
0 _____ 0.5 miles

Approximate Scale

INFORMATION
Cyber Café..................................1 B2
HDFC Bank................................2 B2
Matrix Cyber Café..............(see 14)
MTDC Tourist Office................3 B2
State Bank of India....................4 B2

SIGHTS & ACTIVITIES
Gumpha Panchivati.....................5 C2
Kala Rama..................................6 C2
Market......................................7 B2
Ramkund....................................8 B2
Sundur Narayan Temple.............9 B2

SLEEPING
Hotel Abhishek.........................10 B2
Hotel Panchavati Yatri..............11 B2
Hotel Samrat............................12 B2

EATING
Annapoorna Lunch Home..........13 B2
Dhaba...................................(see 11)
Tandoor...................................14 B2

TRANSPORT
Mahamarg Bus Stand................15 B3
New Central Bus Stand.............16 B2
Old Central Bus Stand..............17 B2
Railway Reservation Office.........18 A2

State Bank of India (☎ 2502436; Old Agra Rd; ☉ 10.30am-4pm Mon-Fri, 10.30am-1.30pm Sat) Less than 100m from the Old Central bus stand. Changes cash and travellers cheques and has an ATM.

Sights

RAMKUND

This holy **bathing tank**, 1.5km northeast of the town centre on the Godavari, is the focal point for Nasik's pilgrims. The Ramkund's waters, like those of the Ganges at Varanasi, are believed to provide *moksha* (liberation of the soul) to those whose ashes are immersed here. The lively scene is only enhanced by the colourful **market**, further down the riverside and best visited in the early morning.

TEMPLES

A short walk uphill east of the Ramkund, the **Kala Rama** (Panchavati Karanja; ☉ 6am-9pm), or Black Rama, is the city's holiest temple. Dating to 1794, the black-stone structure is in a stark 96-arch enclosure containing representations of Rama, Sita and Lakshmana. Nearby is the **Gumpha Panchivati** (☉ 6am-9pm), where it's fun to crawl into the cramped cave containing the deity Sita.

Among the many other temples, ones worth checking out include the picturesquely ramshackle **Sundar Narayan Temple** (☉ 6am-9pm), at the western end of Victoria Bridge; and the **Muktidham Temple** (Muktidham-Nasik Rd; ☉ 6am-9pm), near the train station about 7km southeast of the city. The latter is a modern, white marble structure; the 18 chapters of the Bhagavad Gita line its interior walls.

Tours

An all-day tour of Nasik, conducted in Marathi and including Trimbak and Pandav Leni, departs daily at 7.30am from the Old Central bus stand (Rs 80). If you want to see a few of Nasik's estimated 2000 temples, it's as good a way as any other.

Sleeping & Eating

Nasik has no shortage of hotels to house all those pilgrims. Don't bother searching for any fancy restaurants though – this is a town where the thali reigns supreme.

Hotel Abhishek (☎ 2514201; hotabhi_nsk@san charnet.in; Panchavati Karanja; s/d from Rs 210/280) A couple of minutes' walk uphill from the

Godavari, this is the best budget base for exploring the temples and markets of the old Panchavati area. Rooms are respectable with hot showers and TV.

Hotel Samrat (☎ 2577211; fax 2578211; Old Agra Rd; s/d from Rs 450/500, with AC from Rs 625/775; ☒) Close to the bus stands, this cordial place offers some decent rooms with balconies and all have cable TV. Its spick-and-span restaurant is open 24 hours and makes delectable Gujarati thalis (Rs 70).

Hotel Panchavati Yatri (☎ 2578782; fax 2572293; 430 Chandak Wadi; s/d Rs 540/740, with AC from Rs 750/850) Tucked behind its slightly fancier sister establishment Hotel Panchavati is this decent midrange option with freshly painted, spacious rooms. There's a gym in the basement and a good range of restaurants including Dhaba, serving excellent thalis (Rs 55).

Taj Residency (☎ 25604499; www.tajhotels.com; MIDC, Ambad; d from US$85; ☒ ☐ ☒) Nasik's most luxurious hotel is on the Mumbai Rd, close by Pandav Leni. Garden view rooms are worth shelling out the extra US$10 for and its restaurant offers about as fine dining as you get in Nasik.

Annapoorna Lunch Home (☎ 2576846; MG Rd; snacks & meals Rs 10-35; ☉ 6am-10.30pm) This place keeps its staff busy dishing out South Indian eats to a constant influx of locals. The no-surprises menu includes *masala dosas* (Rs 15) and thalis (Rs 20).

Tandoor (Megdoot Centre; dishes Rs 45-80) Opposite the Old Central bus stand, Tandoor is tucked away in a small lane off Shivaji Rd. Come night-time its dimly lit indoor tables – plus a few out front – are good spots for some finger-licking tandoori.

Getting There & Away

BUS

Nasik is a major player on the road-transport scene, with frequent state buses operating at nearly all hours from three different stands.

The **Old Central bus stand** (CBS; ☎ 2572854) is useful mainly for those going to Trimbak (Rs 15, 45 minutes). A block south the **New Central bus stand** (☎ 2572915), formerly the Mela bus stand, has services to Aurangabad (ordinary/semideluxe Rs 96/112, five hours) and Pune (ordinary/semideluxe Rs 99/125, 4½ hours). Head south on Old Agra Rd for 750m to reach **Mahamarg bus stand** (☎ 2582532), with services hourly to Mumbai (ordinary/

semideluxe Rs 90/110, 4½ hours) and twice-hourly to Shirdi (Rs 50, 2½ hours).

Many private bus agents are based near the CBS and most buses depart from Old Agra Rd. Destinations include Pune (with/without AC Rs 180/120, 4½ hours), Mumbai (with/without AC Rs 200/130, 4½ hours), Aurangabad (without AC Rs 130; 11.30pm only) and Ahmedabad (with/without AC Rs 450/300, 12 hours). Note that most of the Mumbai-bound buses terminate at Dadar.

TRAIN

The Nasik Rd train station is 8km southeast from the town centre, but a useful **railway reservation office** (☎ 134; ☼ 8am-8pm Mon-Sat, 8am-2pm Sun) is on the 1st floor of the Commissioner's Office, Canada Corner, 500m west of the CBS. The 7.02am *Panchavati Express* is the fastest train to Mumbai (Rs 55/191 in 2nd class/chair, four hours), and the 9.55am *Tapovan Express* is the only convenient direct train to Aurangabad (Rs 55/191 in 2nd class/chair, 3½ hours). Local buses leave frequently from Shalimar Circle, a few minutes' walk northeast of the CBS, to the train station (Rs 6). An autorickshaw costs about Rs 70.

AROUND NASIK
Pandav Leni

Providing an excellent view of the countryside and some vivid ancient carvings are the hillside caves of **Pandav Leni** (pronounced Pandu Lena; ☎ 0253-2380529; Indian/foreigner Rs 5/US$2; ☼ 8am-6pm), about 8km south of Nasik along the Mumbai road. A stiff 10-minute hike up a stone stairway brings you to the group of 24 Early Buddhist caves dating from around the 1st century BC to the 2nd century AD. All are *viharas* (monasteries) except for cave 18, which is a *chaitya* (temple).

At the base of the hill is the **Dadasaheb Phalke Memorial** (☎ 0253-2382857; admission Rs 10; ☼ 10am-9pm), a landscaped park dedicated to the pioneering Indian movie producer of the same name. Inside the park is the huge domed Buddhist prayer hall Buddha Vihar and a kids' water park (adult/child Rs 85/55) with a sound-and-light show every evening at 7.30pm.

Local buses (Rs 5) run past the caves from Shalimar Circle, near the CBS, in Nasik, but the easiest way there is by autorickshaw; a

return journey including waiting time costs around Rs 100.

Trimbak

From a spring high on a steep hill above Trimbak, 33km west of Nasik, the source of the Godavari River dribbles into the **Gangadwar bathing tank**, whose waters are reputed to wash away sins. From this tiny start the Godavari eventually flows down to the Bay of Bengal, right across India.

Trimbakeshwar Temple is one of India's most sacred, containing a *jyoti linga*, one of the 12 most important shrines of Shiva. It's open to Hindus only, but it's possible to see into the courtyard, and it's interesting to watch pilgrims going about their ritual business around the main tank. The walk up to the temples on **Brahmagiri Hill**, high above the town, makes for a great day hike. Continue on the road past the MTDC Resort for the four-hour return journey.

MTDC Resort (☎ 02594-233143; d Rs 250, tr ste Rs 800) is in a modern building housing spacious suites with creature comforts such as cable TV.

Regular buses run from the New CBS in Nasik to Trimbak (Rs 15, 45 minutes).

Igatpuri

About 44km south of Nasik on the rail line to Mumbai, the village of Igatpuri is home to the world's largest *vipassana* centre, **Vipassana International Academy** (☎ 02553-244076; www.vri.dhamma.org).

WINE COUNTRY

You'd be forgiven for breaking into a wry smile at the idea of Indian wine, but it's a fact that the fertile soils and relatively cooler climate of Nasik (at around 600m above sea level) has made it into one of India's top wine-producing regions. One winery welcoming visitors is **Sula Vineyards** (☎ 0253-2231663; www.sulawines.com; Govardhan, Gangapur-Savargaon Rd; ☼ 11am-4pm), 8km southwest of Nasik, not far from Pandav Leni. This pioneer of the Indian wine industry, producing decently drinkable drops since 1998, opened in 2005 an architect-designed tasting room; call it in advance if you're planning on dropping by to try out its whites and reds.

Residential courses in this strict form of Theravada Buddhist meditation are held over 10 days from January to October; advanced 45-day sessions are held in November and December. Courses are free (although donations are appreciated), and students – who are segregated by sex – must stay on site and observe a regime of 'noble silence'. Basic board and food are given; it's best to reserve ahead. *Vipassana* was first taught by Gautama Buddha in the 6th century BC, but was reintroduced to India by teacher SN Goenka in the 1960s.

Igatpuri is easy to reach by rail with several expresses from Mumbai (Rs 44/153 in 2nd class/chair, three hours) passing through daily. Trains and buses from Nasik take only an hour. The centre is a 15-minute walk from the train station.

AURANGABAD
☎ 0240 / pop 872,667 / elev 513m

Even though it's a fairly tatty place, Aurangabad is central Maharashtra's most visited city because it's a highly convenient base for the Ellora caves, and not terribly far from Ajanta either. Named after Aurangzeb, who established a capital here in 1653, it also has a few interesting sites of its own.

Silk fabrics are Aurangabad's traditional trade but the city has also become something of an industrial centre; most of Maharashtra's beer is supplied by several breweries based around the city, and the Bajaj-Kawasaki factory, India's biggest producer of two-wheel motorcycles, is located near here, too.

Orientation
The train station, cheap hotels and restaurants are clumped together in the south of the town. The **Maharashtra State Road Transport Corporation (MSRTC) bus stand** (Station Rd West) is 1.5km to the north. Northeast of the bus stand is the buzzing old town with its narrow streets and distinct Muslim quarter.

Information
BOOKSHOPS
Sharayu (☎ 2335220; 119-A Kailash Market, Station Rd East; ⏲ 10.30am-9.30pm) Aurangabad's best selection of English-language books.

INTERNET ACCESS
Internet cafés are all around Aurangabad. Try the following:

Café Internet (Shop No 12, Station Rd East; per hr Rs 30; ⏲ 9.30am-11pm)
Cyber-dhaba (Station Rd West; per hr Rs 20; ⏲ 8am-11pm) Also changes money.
Global Access (Konark Estate, Osmanpura; per hr Rs 20; ⏲ 9am-1am)

MONEY
ICICI has ATMs on Nirala Bazaar and Station Rd East.
Bank of Baroda (☎ 2337129; Pattan Darwaza Rd; ⏲ 10.30am-3pm Mon-Fri, 10.30am-12.45pm Sat) Near the Paithan Gate, it gives cash advances on Visa and MasterCard.
Trade Wings (☎ 2322677; Station Rd West; ⏲ 9am-7pm Mon-Sat, 9am-1pm Sun) Charges a Rs 50 fee.

POST
Main post office (☎ 2331420; Juna Bazaar; ⏲ 10am-6pm Mon-Sat) Poste restante can be collected from Counter 3.

TOURIST INFORMATION
Government of India tourist office (☎ 2331217; Krishna Vilas, Station Rd West; ⏲ 9am-6pm Mon-Fri, 9am-1.30pm Sat) Has a decent range of brochures and is helpful.
MTDC office (☎ 2331513; Station Rd East; ⏲ 10am-6pm Mon-Sat) Only notable for booking MTDC tours and accommodation.

TRAVEL AGENCIES
Classic Tours (☎ 2335598; classictours@vsnl.com; MTDC Holiday Resort, Station Rd East) Trusty place to book transport, tours and even accommodation.
Trade Wings (☎ 2322677; Station Rd West; ⏲ 9am-7pm Mon-Sat, 9am-1pm Sun) Also offers travel services.

Sights
BIBI-KA-MAQBARA
The so-called 'poor man's Taj Mahal', the **Bibi-ka-Maqbara** (☎ 2400620; Indian/foreigner Rs 5/US$2; ⏲ sunrise-10pm) was built in 1679 as a mausoleum for Aurangzeb's wife, Rabia-ud-Daurani. Though it's a modest imitation of the Taj in design and execution, the inevitable comparisons are unfortunate because it's still exceedingly impressive. The mood is particularly right at night when it's floodlit. Climbing the small hill behind the Bibi-ka-Maqbara affords a good view.

AURANGABAD CAVES
If it wasn't for nearby Ellora and Ajanta, these interesting **caves** (☎ 2400620; Indian/

foreigner Rs 5/US$2; ☺ sunrise-sunset), 2km north of the Bibi-ka-Maqbara, would see a lot more visitors. Carved out of the hillside in the 6th or 7th century AD, the 10 caves – consisting of two groups 1km apart – are all Buddhist.

All the caves in the Western Group are *viharas*, except for Cave 4, an older Early Buddhist *chaitya* with a ribbed roof. Cave

7's sculptures of scantily clad and bejewelled women are indicative of the rise of Tantric Buddhism during this period. You can hike up to the caves from the Bibi-ka-Maqbara or take an autorickshaw up to the Eastern Group, walk back down the road to the Western Group and then cut straight back across country to the Bibi-ka-Maqbara.

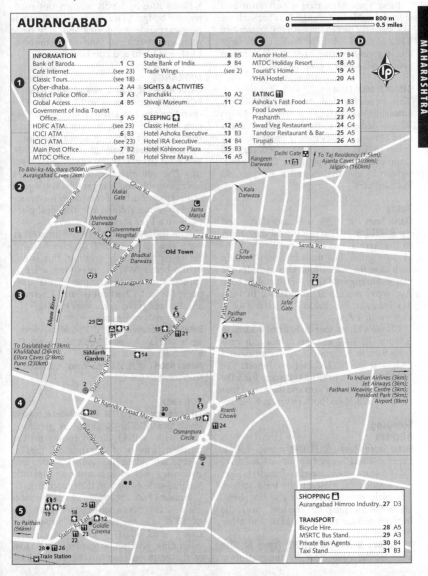

AURANGABAD

0 ————— 800 m
0 ————— 0.5 miles

MAHARASHTRA

INFORMATION
Bank of Baroda..........................1 C3
Café Internet........................(see 23)
Classic Tours.......................(see 18)
Cyber-dhaba.............................2 A4
District Police Office.................3 A3
Global Access...........................4 B5
Government of India Tourist
  Office......................................5 A5
HDFC ATM..........................(see 23)
ICICI ATM.................................6 B3
ICICI ATM.........................(see 23)
Main Post Office........................7 B2
MTDC Office.......................(see 18)

Sharayu..8 B5
State Bank of India....................9 B4
Trade Wings..........................(see 2)

SIGHTS & ACTIVITIES
Panchakki..................................10 A2
Shivaji Museum.........................11 C2

SLEEPING 🏠
Classic Hotel..............................12 A5
Hotel Ashoka Executive............13 B3
Hotel IRA Executive..................14 B4
Hotel Kohinoor Plaza................15 B3
Hotel Shree Maya.....................16 A5

Manor Hotel..............................17 B4
MTDC Holiday Resort................18 A5
Tourist's Home...........................19 A5
YHA Hostel.................................20 A4

EATING 🍴
Ashoka's Fast Food....................21 B3
Food Lovers................................22 A5
Prashanth...................................23 A5
Swad Veg Restaurant................24 C4
Tandoor Restaurant & Bar........25 A5
Tirupati......................................26 A5

SHOPPING 🛍
Aurangabad Himroo Industry..27 D3

TRANSPORT
Bicycle Hire...............................28 A5
MSRTC Bus Stand......................29 A3
Private Bus Agents....................30 B4
Taxi Stand..................................31 B3

PANCHAKKI

Panchakki (Water Wheel) takes its name from the mill which in its day was considered a marvel of engineering. Driven by water carried through earthen pipes from the river 6km away, it once ground grain for pilgrims. You can still see the humble machine at work.

Baba Shah Muzaffar, a Sufi saint and spiritual guide to Aurangzeb, is buried here. His **memorial garden** (admission Rs 5; ☼ 6am-8pm) has a series of fish-filled tanks, near a large shade-giving banyan tree. It's a pleasant spot to relax over a glass of chai.

SHIVAJI MUSEUM

This somewhat drab **museum** (☎ 2350166; Dr Ambedkar Rd; admission Rs 5; ☼ 10.30am-1.30pm & 3-6pm Tue-Sun), dedicated to the life of the Maratha hero Shivaji, focuses mostly on his military prowess. Exhibits include a 500-year-old chain-mail suit, a copy of the Quran handwritten by Aurangzeb and a 400-year-old Paithani sari.

Tours

Classic Tours (☎ 2335598; www.ajantaindia.com) and the **MSRTC** (☎ 2331513) run similar daily tours to the Ajanta and Ellora caves, which include a guide but no admission fees. In each case the Ellora tour also includes the major Aurangabad sites – Daulatabad Fort, Aurangzeb's tomb at Khuldabad, Bibi-ka-Maqbara and Panchakki – which is a lot to swallow in a day.

Classic's Ellora tour runs from 9.30am to 5.30pm (Rs 140) and the Ajanta tour runs from 8am to 5.30pm (Rs 200), starting and ending at the MTDC Holiday Resort. The MSRTC Ellora tour (Rs 84) departs from the MSRTC bus stand at 9am and the Ajanta tour (Rs 186) at 8.30am; both return at 5.30pm.

Sleeping

BUDGET

Hotel Shree Maya (☎ 2333093; shrimaya_agd@san charnet.in; Bharuka Complex; d with/without AC Rs 495/345; ✖) Presentable and traveller-friendly budget accommodation close by the train station. The plain rooms have TVs and hot showers in the morning, but the real plus is the outdoor terrace where breakfast and other meals are served.

Tourist's Home (☎ 2337212; Station Rd West; s/d Rs 150/200) Also close by the station is

this basic, friendly place with a convivial café. Its no-frills rooms come with bucket showers and squat toilets.

Hotel Ashoka Executive (☎ 5620136; Nehru Pl; s/d Rs 325/425, with AC 500/600; ✖) This is the best of several offerings opposite the bus stand, with smart, clean rooms.

YHA Hostel (☎ 2334892; Station Rd West; dm/d Rs 60/160) Run by kindly women this rock-bottom budget place set in quiet grounds offers separate-sex dorms and very basic rooms, most with mosquito nets on the beds. Curfew is 10pm and checkout is 9am.

MIDRANGE

Classic Hotel (☎ 5624313; www.aurangabadhotel.com; Railway Station Rd; s/d from Rs 800/1000; ✖ 🖳) This sparkling new hotel next to the Goldie Cinema has comfortable modern rooms and a restaurant that whips up a mean biryani.

Hotel Kohinoor Plaza (☎ 2358971; fax 5625774; Nirala Bazaar; s/d from Rs 495/790, with AC from Rs 890/940; ✖) The well-maintained Kohinoor Plaza has reasonably appealing rooms and a good central location, but its real draw is a breezy rooftop restaurant and bar, the ideal place to down a beer at night.

MTDC Holiday Resort (☎ 2331513; Station Rd East; 'Ajanta' d low/high season Rs 550/700, 'Ellora' tr Rs 550/750) Set in its own shady grounds, this is one of the better MTDC operations, offering spruce, spacious rooms, the 'Ajanta' ones being the best. Checkout is 9am. A restaurant, bar and travel agency are on site.

Other recommendations:

Hotel IRA Executive (☎ 2352161; hotelarts@satyam .net.in; Varad Ganesh Mandir Rd; s/d Rs 550/595, with AC from 850/895; ✖)

Manor Hotel (☎ 2333383; hotelmanor@rediffmail.com; Kranti Chowk; s/d from Rs 799/999)

TOP END

Taj Residency (☎ 2381106; www.tajhotels.com; Ajanta Rd; s/d from US$65/75; ✖ 🖳 🖳) A gleaming oasis with well-appointed rooms on the northern fringes of Aurangabad, the Taj sweeps around an immaculate garden and swimming pool. Most rooms have romantic Mughal-style swings on their balconies.

President Park (☎ 2486201; www.presidenthotels .com; R-7/2, Chikalthana, Airport Rd; s/d from Rs 1800/2300; ✖ 🖳 🖳) On the road to the airport this classy hotel boasts a giant semicircular swimming pool set in gardens that most of the plain but comfortable rooms look out on to. Nonguests can use the pool for Rs 175 per hour.

Eating

Tandoor Restaurant & Bar (☎ 2328481; Shyam Chambers, Station Rd East; mains Rs 60-200; ☯ 10am-4pm & 6.30-11pm; ✖) Offering fine tandoori dishes and flavourful North Indian and Chinese vegetarian options in a weirdly Pharonic atmosphere, this is one of Aurangabad's top restaurants.

Food Lovers (Station Rd East; dishes Rs 40-130; ☯ noon-11.30pm) This garden restaurant with palm trees, an earthen floor and candles flickering at night is a fine choice. The Punjabi and Chinese food is good, and the beer is cold.

Ashoka's Fast Food (Nirala Bazaar; dishes Rs 20-40; ☯ 8am-11pm) Offering both indoor seating and an outdoor terrace that is all the rage at night, Ashoka's serves tasty South Indian fare, as well as Chinese food, pizza and sandwiches. You can also binge on a kilo (!) of black forest cake (Rs 160).

Tirupati (Station Rd East; dishes Rs 25-40; ☯ 6am-11pm) The area near the train station has a gaggle of quick-eats options, including this one, which specialises in satisfying vegetarian fare. Its South Indian breakfasts (Rs 10 to 20) are a fine start to the day.

Prashanth (Siddharth Arcade, Station Rd East; dishes Rs 25-70) Prashanth, just next to Food Lovers, wins trophies from travellers for its delightful vegetarian-only dishes and patio setting. You won't be frowning at the special (Rs 50) either.

Swad Veg Restaurant (Kanchan Chamber, Station Rd East; dishes Rs 20-55; ☯ 11am-3pm & 7pm-11pm) Come here for great Gujarati thalis (Rs 60) and crispy mile-long dosas – all eaten under the benevolent gaze of swami Yogiraj Hansthirth. Look for an orange circular sign (in Marathi) pointing the way down to the entrance just below street level.

Shopping

Hand-woven Himroo material is an Aurangabad speciality. Made from cotton, silk and silver threads, it was developed as a cheaper alternative to Kam Khab, the more lavish brocades of silk and gold thread woven for royalty in the 14th century. Most Himroo shawls and saris you'll see today are mass-produced using power looms, but there are a couple of showrooms in the

city which still run traditional workshops, set up for onlooking tourists. Many of the designs are based on motifs in the Ajanta frescoes.

Tucked away in the old town near Jafar Gate, **Aurangabad Himroo Industry** (☎ 2337830; ☯ 10am-8pm) has a small workshop with hand-looms going. Another, **Paithani Weaving Centre** (☎ 2482811; 54 P1 Town Centre, Jalna Rd; ☯ 11am-8.30pm), is behind the Indian Airlines office.

The lustrous Paithani silk saris, named for their birthplace of Paithan, 56km south of Aurangabad, are made of silver- and gold-weave brocades and are woven in both places.

Himroo saris start at Rs 500 (cotton and silk blend). Paithani saris range from Rs 5000 to 300,000. Be warned that if you're escorted by an autorickshaw-wallah and make a purchase, the driver will likely get a piece of the pie, at your expense.

Getting There & Away

AIR

The airport is 10km east of town. En route you'll find the offices of **Indian Airlines** (☎ 2483392; Jalna Rd) and, almost opposite, **Jet Airways** (☎ 2441770; Jalna Rd). Indian Airlines has daily flights to Mumbai (US$85, 45 minutes) and Delhi (US$185, 3½ hours). Jet Airways flies daily to Mumbai (US$85, 45 minutes).

BUS

Local buses take off half-hourly to Ellora (Rs 15, 45 minutes) and hourly to Jalgaon (Rs 84, four hours) via Fardapur (Rs 60, two hours). The T-junction near Fardapur is the drop-off point for Ajanta (see p138 for more details).

MSRTC buses leave regularly from the **bus stand** (☎ 2331647; Station Rd West) to Pune (Rs 107, five hours) and Nasik (Rs 102, five hours). For longer-distance journeys, private luxury buses are more comfortable and better value for money. The private bus agents congregate around the corner where Dr Rajendra Prasad Marg becomes Court Rd, and a few sit closer to the bus stand on Station Rd West. Deluxe overnight bus destinations include Mumbai (Rs 180, with AC Rs 250, sleeper Rs 550, eight hours), Ahmedabad (Rs 300, 15 hours) and Nagpur (Rs 270, 12 hours).

TRAIN

On the southern edge of town is Aurangabad **train station** (☎ 131). It's not on a main line, but two direct trains daily (often heavily booked) run to/from Mumbai. The 2.45pm *Tapovan Express* (Rs 95/344 in 2nd class/chair, eight hours), coming from Mumbai, leaves at 6.10am, and the overnight 11.30pm *Devgiri Express* (Rs 148/666 in sleeper/2AC, nine hours).

To Hyderabad (Secunderabad), the *Manmad Express* departs daily at 7.20pm (Rs 218/980 in sleeper/2AC, 12 hours). To reach northern or eastern India by train, eg Delhi or Kolkata (Calcutta), bus up to Jalgaon and board one of the major trains from there.

Getting Around

Some autorickshaw-wallahs willingly use their outdated meters; some don't. Final fares are about 25% more than the meter reading, and drivers are required to carry conversion cards. The taxi stand is next to the bus stand; share jeeps also depart from here for destinations around Aurangabad, including Ellora and Daulatabad.

Hiring a bicycle from a stall near the train station (Rs 3 per hour) can make for a fun day's sightseeing around the city.

AROUND AURANGABAD
Daulatabad

Halfway (13km) between Aurangabad and the Ellora caves is the ruined but truly magnificent hilltop fortress of Daulatabad. The **fort** (☎ 2615700; Indian/foreigner Rs 5/US$2; ☼ 6am-6pm) is surrounded by 5km of sturdy walls, while the central bastion tops a 200m-high hill – originally known as Devagiri, the Hill of the Gods.

In the 14th century it was renamed Daulatabad, the City of Fortune, by sultan Mohammed Tughlaq, who came up with the crazy scheme of not only building himself a new capital here, but marching the entire population of Delhi 1100km south to populate it. Those who didn't die on the way here sloped back to Delhi a couple of years later when Daulatabad proved untenable as a capital.

Climb to the top for superb views over the surrounding countryside. It's a 45-minute ascent, but you'll want to allow more time to nose around. Along the way you'll pass through an ingenious series of defences, including multiple doorways with spike-studded doors to prevent elephant charges. A tower of victory, known as the **Chand Minar** (Tower of the Moon), built in 1435, soars 60m high.

Higher up is the blue-tiled **Chini Mahal**, where Abul Hasan Tana Shah, king of Golconda, died after being imprisoned for 12 years from 1687. Finally, you climb to a 6m **cannon**, cast from five different metals and engraved with Aurangzeb's name.

Part of the ascent to the top goes through a pitch-black spiralling tunnel – down which the fort's defenders hurled burning coals, arrows or even boiling water at invaders. (Allegedly the fort was once successfully conquered despite all these elaborate pre-

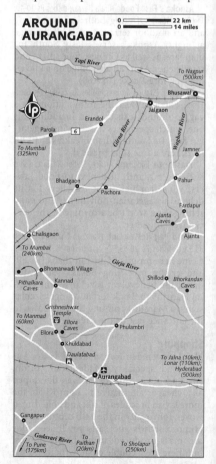

AROUND AURANGABAD

0 — 22 km
0 — 14 miles

cautions – by simply bribing the guard at the gate.) There may be a guide waiting near the tunnel to light the way with a flame for a small tip; best to take your own torch in case not.

If you take an organised tour from Aurangabad to Daulatabad and Ellora, you won't have time to climb to the summit.

Khuldabad

The walled town of Khuldabad, the Heavenly Abode, is just 3km from Ellora. It is the Karbala (Holy Shrine) of Deccan Muslims. A number of historical figures are buried here, including Aurangzeb, the last great Mughal emperor. His final resting place is an unfussy affair of bare earth in a courtyard of the **Alamgir Dargah** (☼ 7am-8pm) at the centre of the town.

Generally a quiet place, Khuldabad is swamped with millions of pilgrims every April when a robe said to have been worn by the Prophet Mohammed, and kept within the dargah (shrine), is shown to the public. The shrine across the road from the Alamgir Dargah contains hairs of the Prophet's beard and lumps of silver from a tree of solid silver, which miraculously grew at this site after a saint's death.

ELLORA
☎ 02437

World Heritage–listed **Ellora cave temples** (☎ 244440; Kailasa Temple Indian/foreigner Rs 10/US$5; ☼ sunrise-sunset Wed-Mon), about 30km from Aurangabad, are the pinnacle of Deccan rock-cut architecture.

Over five centuries, generations of monks (Buddhist, Hindu and Jain) carved monasteries, chapels and temples from a 2km-long escarpment and decorated them with a profusion of remarkably detailed sculptures. Because of the escarpment's gentle slope, in contrast with the sheer drop at Ajanta (p136), many of the caves have elaborate courtyards in front of the main shrines. The masterpiece is the astonishing Kailasa Temple (Cave 16). Dedicated to Shiva, it is the world's largest monolithic sculpture, hewn from the rock by 7000 labourers over a 150-year period.

Altogether Ellora has 34 rock-cut caves: 12 Buddhist (AD 600–800), 17 Hindu (AD 600–900) and five Jain (AD 800–1000). The site represents the renaissance of Hinduism

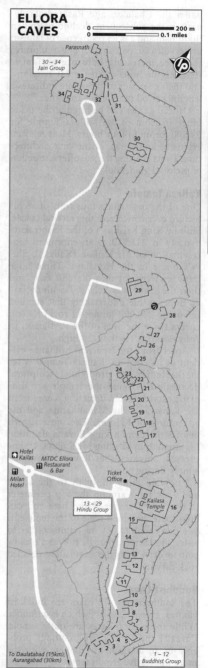

ELLORA CAVES

0 — 200 m
0 — 0.1 miles

Parasnath

30 – 34 Jain Group

33
34 32 31

30

29

28
27
26
25
24 23 22
21
20
19
18
17

Hotel Kailas
MTDC Ellora Restaurant & Bar
Milan Hotel

Ticket Office

13 – 29 Hindu Group

Kailasa Temple 16

15
14
13
12
11
10
9
8
7
6
1 2 3 4 5

To Daulatabad (15km); Aurangabad (30km)

1 – 12 Buddhist Group

MAHARASHTRA

under the Chalukya and Rashtrakuta dynasties, the subsequent decline of Indian Buddhism and a brief resurgence of Jainism under official patronage. The sculptures show the increasing influence of Tantric elements in India's three great religions, and their coexistence at one site indicates a lengthy period of religious tolerance.

Official guides can be hired at the ticket office in front of the Kailasa Temple for Rs 280 for up to four hours. Most relay an extensive knowledge of the cave architecture. Touts cruising the site offer a selection of pictorial guidebooks.

Kailasa Temple

One of the most audacious feats of architecture ever conceived, this **rock-cut temple**, built by King Krishna I of the Rashtrakuta dynasty in AD 760, is an enormous representation of Mt Kailasa (Kailash), Shiva's home in the Himalaya. Three huge trenches were cut into the cliff face, and then the shape was 'released' with tools – an unbelievable undertaking that entailed removing 200,000 tonnes of rock! Kailasa covers twice the area of the Parthenon in Athens and is 1½ times as high.

Apart from the technical brilliance evident in its creation, Kailasa Temple is remarkable for its prodigious sculptural decoration. Around the temple are dramatic carved panels, depicting scenes from the Ramayana, the Mahabharata and the adventures of Krishna. The most superb depicts the demon king Ravana flaunting his strength by shaking Mt Kailasa. Unimpressed, Shiva crushes Ravana's pride by simply flexing a toe.

You can climb the path to the south and walk right around the top perimeter of the 'cave' for free. From here you can appreciate the grand scale of the temple, if you don't wish to pay the admission fee to enter the temple, though it doesn't allow you to delve into the exquisitely detailed rock carving.

Buddhist Caves

The southernmost 12 caves are Buddhist *viharas*, except Cave 10, which is a *chaitya*. While the earliest caves are quite simple, Caves 11 and 12 are more ambitious, probably in an attempt to compete with the more impressive Hindu temples.

Cave 1, the simplest *vihara*, may have been a granary. **Cave 2** is notable for its ornate pillars and its imposing seated Buddha figure facing the setting sun, his huge feet firmly planted on the earth. **Cave 3** and **Cave 4** are unfinished; they're earlier and less well preserved.

Cave 5 is the largest *vihara* in this group, at 18m wide and 36m long; the rows of stone benches hint that it may have been an assembly hall.

Cave 6 is an ornate *vihara* with wonderful images of Tara, consort of the Bodhisattva Avalokiteshvara, and of the Buddhist goddess of learning, Mahamayuri, looking remarkably similar to Saraswati, her Hindu equivalent. **Cave 7** is an unadorned hall, but from here you can pass through a doorway to **Cave 8**, the first cave in which the sanctum is detached from the rear wall. **Cave 9** is notable for its wonderfully carved façade.

Cave 10, the Viswakarma (Carpenter's) Cave, is the only *chaitya* in the Buddhist group, and one of the finest in India. It takes its name from the ribs carved into the roof, in imitation of wooden beams; the balcony and upper gallery offer a closer view of the ceiling and a frieze depicting amorous couples. A small, decorative window gently illuminates an enormous figure of the teaching Buddha.

Cave 11, the Do Thal (Two Storey) Cave, is entered through its third, basement level, not discovered until 1876. Like Cave 12 it probably owes its size to competition with the more impressive Hindu caves of the same period.

Cave 12, the huge Tin Thal (Three Storey) Cave, is entered through a courtyard. The (locked) shrine on the top floor contains a large Buddha figure flanked by his seven previous incarnations. The walls are carved with relief pictures, like those in the Hindu caves.

Hindu Caves

Where calm and contemplation infuse the Buddhist caves, drama and dynamic energy characterise the Hindu group (Caves 13 to 29), in the middle of the escarpment. In terms of scale, creative vision and skill of execution, these caves are in a league of their own.

All these temples were cut from the top down so that it was never necessary to use scaffolding – the builders began with the roof and moved down to the floor.

Cave 13 is a simple cave, most likely a granary. **Cave 14**, the Ravana-ki-Khai, is a Buddhist *vihara* converted to a temple dedicated to Shiva sometime in the 7th century.

Cave 15, the Das Avatara (Ten Incarnations of Vishnu) Cave, is one of the finest at Ellora. The two-storey temple is reached through its courtyard by a long flight of steps. Traditional scenes depicted here include a mesmerising Shiva Nataraja, and Shiva emerging from a lingam (phallic image) while Vishnu and Brahma pay homage.

Caves 17 to **20** and numbers **22** to **28** are simple monasteries.

Cave 21, known as the Rameshvara, features interesting interpretations of the familiar Shaivite scenes depicted in the earlier temples. The figure of goddess Ganga, standing on her *makara* (crocodile), is particularly notable.

The large **Cave 29**, the Dumar Lena, is thought to be a transitional model between the simpler hollowed-out caves and the fully developed temples exemplified by the Kailasa. It has a serene outlook over the nearby waterfall.

Jain Caves

The five Jain caves may lack the artistic vigour and ambitious size of the best Hindu temples, but they are exceptionally detailed. The caves are 1km north of the last Hindu temple (Cave 29) at the end of the bitumen road.

Cave 30, the Chota Kailasa (Little Kailasa), is a poor imitation of the great Kailasa Temple and stands by itself some distance from the other Jain temples.

In contrast, **Cave 32**, the Indra Sabha (Assembly Hall of Indra), is the finest of the Jain temples. Its ground-floor plan is similar to that of the Kailasa, but the upstairs area is as ornate and richly decorated as the downstairs is plain. There are images of the Jain *tirthankars* (great teachers) Parasnath and Gomateshvara, the latter surrounded by wildlife. Inside the shrine is a seated figure of Mahavira, the last *tirthankar* and founder of the Jain religion.

Cave 31 is really a simple extension of Cave 32. **Cave 33**, the Jagannath Sabha, is similar in plan to 32 and has some particularly well-preserved sculptures. The final

temple, the small **Cave 34**, also has interesting sculptures. On the hilltop over the Jain temples, a 5m-high image of Parasnath looks down on Ellora.

Sleeping & Eating

Hotel Kailas (☎ 244543; www.hotelkailas.com; d Rs 300, cottages with/without AC Rs 1200/700) Ellora's only real hotel offers attractive, simply furnished stone-clad cottages, many with direct views to the caves. The budget annexe tucked away to the rear of the garden compound has two plain doubles with squat toilets.

Hotel Kailas's restaurant looks pretty but gets mixed reviews. Locals say **Milan Hotel** (dishes Rs 20-50), across the road, serves better food. Also reliable is the spotless **MTDC Ellora Restaurant & Bar** (dishes Rs 20-75; ☺ 9am-5pm), with a courtyard facing onto the caves.

Getting There & Away

Buses travel regularly between Aurangabad and Ellora (Rs 15); the last returns from Ellora at around 7pm. Share jeeps leave when they're full and drop off outside the bus stand in Aurangabad (Rs 11). A full-day autorickshaw/taxi tour to Ellora with stops en route costs around Rs 350/600.

AJANTA
☎ 02438

A World Heritage site, the **Buddhist caves of Ajanta** (☎ 244226; Indian/foreigner Rs 10/US$5; ☺ 9am-5.30pm Tue-Sun) – 105km northeast of Aurangabad, and about 60km south of Jalgaon – date from around 200 BC to AD 650, predating those at Ellora. As Ellora developed and Buddhism gradually waned, the glorious Ajanta caves were abandoned and forgotten until 1819, when a British hunting party stumbled upon them. Their isolation contributed to the fine state of preservation in which some of their remarkable paintings remain to this day.

Information

Flash photography is banned in the caves; a video-camera permit costs Rs 25. Many of the caves are too dark to see much without a torch, so its a good idea to bring your own if you really want to glimpse any detail. Avoid visiting on weekends or holidays when everybody and their second cousin turns up.

A cloakroom near the main ticket office is a safe place to leave gear (Rs 4 per bag for four hours), so you could even arrive in the morning from Jalgaon, check out the caves, and continue to Aurangabad in the evening, or vice versa. There's a short, steep climb to the first cave from the entrance; if you're not up to the hike, a chair carried by four bearers (Rs 400) can be hired at the foot of these steps.

Government of India tourist office guides can be hired by Cave 1 for Rs 280 for an approximately two-hour tour. They have extensive knowledge and can tell you complex stories behind the frescoes which really make them come alive.

The Caves

The 30 caves are cut into the steep face of a horseshoe-shaped rock gorge on the Waghore River. Apart from Caves 29 and 30, they are sequentially numbered from one end of the gorge to the other. They do not follow a chronological order; the oldest are mainly in the middle and the newer ones are close to each end. At busy times viewers are allotted 15 minutes within each cave.

Five of the caves are *chaityas* while the other 25 are *viharas*. Caves 8, 9, 10, 12, 13 and part of 15 are older Early Buddhist caves, while the others are Mahayana (dated from around the 5th century AD). In the simpler, more austere Early Buddhist school, the Buddha was never represented directly – his presence was always alluded to by a symbol such as the footprint or wheel of law.

Of special note are the Ajanta 'frescoes', which are technically not frescoes at all. A fresco is a painting done on a wet surface that absorbs the colour; the Ajanta paintings are more correctly tempera, since the artists used animal glue and vegetable gum mixed with the paint pigments to bind them to the dry surface.

Caves 3, 5, 8, 22 and 28 to 30 are closed and/or inaccessible; Cave 14 is sometimes closed.

Cave 1, a Mahayana *vihara*, is one of the latest to be excavated and is the most beautifully decorated of the Ajanta caves. A veranda at the front leads to a large congregation hall, with elaborate sculptures and narrative murals. Perspective in the paint-

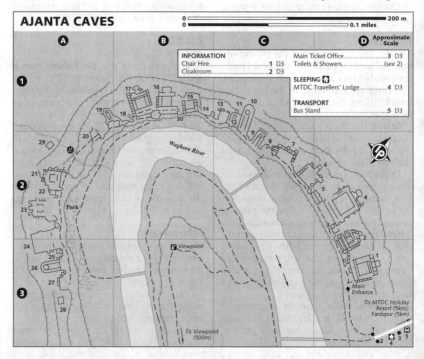

AJANTA CAVES

0 — 200 m
0 — 0.1 miles

Approximate Scale

| INFORMATION |
| Chair Hire..........................1 D3 |
| Cloakroom..........................2 D3 |

| Main Ticket Office.......................3 D3 |
| Toilets & Showers.....................(see 2) |

| SLEEPING |
| MTDC Travellers' Lodge...............4 D3 |

| TRANSPORT |
| Bus Stand.................................5 D3 |

Waghore River

Viewpoint

Main Entrance

To MTDC Holiday Resort (5km);
Fardapur (5km)

To Viewpoint (500m)

Park

ings, details of dress and daily life, and many of the facial expressions are all wonderfully executed. The colours in the paintings were created from local minerals, with the exception of the vibrant blue made from Central Asian lapis lazuli. Look up to the ceiling to see the carving of four deer sharing a common head.

Cave 2 is also a late Mahayana *vihara* with deliriously ornamented columns and capitals, and some fine paintings. The ceiling is decorated with geometric and floral patterns. Mural scenes include a number of jatakas and events surrounding the Buddha's birth, including his mother's dream of a six-tusked elephant, which heralded the Buddha's conception.

Cave 4 is the largest *vihara* at Ajanta and is supported by 28 pillars. Although never completed, the cave has some impressive sculptures, including scenes of people fleeing from the 'eight great dangers' to the protection of the Buddha's disciple Avalokiteshvara.

Caves 6 is the only two-storey *vihara* at Ajanta, but parts of the lower storey have collapsed. Inside is a seated Buddha figure and an intricately carved door to the shrine. Upstairs the hall is surrounded by cells with fine paintings on the doorways.

Cave 7 has an atypical design, with porches before the veranda, leading directly to the four cells and the elaborately sculptured shrine.

Cave 9 is one of the earliest *chaityas* at Ajanta. Although it dates from the Early Buddhist period, the two figures flanking the entrance door were probably later Mahayana additions. Columns run down both sides of the cave and around the 3m-high dagoba at the far end. The vaulted roof has traces of wooden ribs.

Cave 10 is thought to be the oldest cave (200 BC) and was the one first spotted by the British soldiers who rediscovered Ajanta. Similar in design to Cave 9, it is the largest *chaitya*. The façade has collapsed and the paintings inside have been damaged, in some cases by graffiti dating from soon after the rediscovery. The indentations in the floor near the left-hand wall were used for mixing paint pigments.

Cave 16, a *vihara*, contains some of Ajanta's finest paintings and is thought to have been the original entrance to the entire

WHEN WAS AJANTA'S GOLDEN AGE?

Theories on major archaeological sites continuously undergo review, and there's no exception with the Ajanta caves.

American professor Dr Walter M Spink (who has studied the caves for over 40 years) suggests that the splendour of the later Mahayana group may have been accomplished in less than 20 years – rather than over centuries as previously thought.

Scholars agree that the caves had two periods of patronage: an early group was crafted around the 1st and 2nd centuries BC and a second wave of work began centuries later. Spink pinpoints the Vakataka emperor Harisena as a reigning sponsor in the incredible renaissance of activity. Soon after his rise to the throne in AD 460 the caves began to realise their present forms, until Harisena's unexpected death in AD 477. The site was probably deserted in the AD 480s.

The silver lining to the tragedy is, according to Spink, that the sudden downfall of the eminent Vakataka empire at the pinnacle of the caves' energetic crafting is solely responsible for their phenomenally preserved state today.

If you're interested, Spink's book *Ajanta: A Brief History and Guide* (1994) can be bought from touts near the site. If you adopt Spink's theory, you may have to reconsider the caves of Ellora and Elephanta Island too, but that's a whole other cave – er, can – of worms.

complex. The best known of these paintings is the 'dying princess' – Sundari, wife of the Buddha's half-brother Nanda, who is said to have fainted at the news that her husband was renouncing the material life (and her) in order to become a monk. Carved figures appear to support the ceiling in imitation of wooden architectural details, and there's a statue of the Buddha seated on a lion throne teaching the Noble Eightfold Path.

Cave 17, with carved dwarfs supporting the pillars, has the best-preserved and most varied paintings at Ajanta. Famous images include a princess, surrounded by attendants, applying make-up, an amorous prince plying his lover with wine, and the Buddha returning from his enlightenment to his own home to beg from his wife and astonished son. A detailed panel tells of Prince Simhala's expedition to Sri Lanka. With his 500 companions he is shipwrecked on an island where ogresses appear as enchanting women, only to seize and devour their victims. Simhala escapes on a flying horse and returns to conquer the island.

Cave 19, a magnificent *chaitya*, has a remarkably detailed façade; its dominant feature is an impressive horseshoe-shaped window. Two fine standing Buddha figures flank the entrance. Inside is a three-tiered dagoba with a figure of the Buddha on the front. Outside the cave to the west sits a striking image of the Naga king with seven cobra hoods around his head. His wife, hooded by a single cobra, sits at his side.

Cave 24, if it had been finished, would be the largest *vihara* at Ajanta. You can see how the caves were constructed – long galleries were cut into the rock, and then the rock between them was broken through. Architecturally it is a fascinating study.

Caves 26, a largely ruined *chaitya*, contains some fine sculptures. On the left wall is a huge figure of the 'reclining Buddha', lying back in preparation for nirvana. Other scenes include a lengthy depiction of the Buddha's temptation by Mara.

Cave 27 is virtually a *vihara* connected to the Cave 26 *chaitya*.

Viewpoints

Two lookouts offer picture-perfect views of the whole horseshoe-shaped gorge from which the Ajanta caves were carved. The first is a short walk beyond the river, crossed via one of the concrete bridges below Caves 8 and 27. A further 20-minute uphill walk leads to the lookout from where the British party first saw the caves. It's also possible to take a taxi up to the latter viewpoint from Fardapur.

Sleeping & Eating

You're much better off using Jalgaon or Aurangabad as a base for a trip to Ajanta but if you'd prefer to stay close by there are a couple of MTDC hotels.

MTDC Holiday Resort (☎ 244230; Aurangabad-Jalgaon Rd; d with/without AC from Rs 850/750; 🔀) At Fardapur, 1km from the T-junction, this is the best option. The comfortable rooms have TVs and hot showers. The rates include a vegetarian meal, either lunch or dinner.

Only consider the **MTDC Travellers' Lodge** (☎ 244226; s/d with shared bathroom from Rs 225/300), near the main ticket office, if you're really stuck: the rooms are dismal. There's a restaurant here too but the food sure ain't gourmet. Our advice is to pack a picnic and enjoy it in the shady park below Caves 22 to 27.

Getting There & Away

Buses from Aurangabad (p131) or Jalgaon (opposite) will drop you off at the T-junction (where the Aurangabad–Jalgaon Rd meets the road to the caves), 4km down the hill from the caves. From here, after paying an 'amenities' fee (Rs 5), you must take one of the green-coloured Euro I buses (Rs 6, with AC Rs 10) the rest of the way to the caves. Buses return on a regular basis (half-hourly) to the T-junction from the caves.

During the day all MSRTC buses passing through Fardapur stop at the T-junction. After the caves close you can board buses to either Aurangabad or Jalgaon outside the MTDC Holiday Resort in Fardapur, 1km down the main road towards Jalgaon. Taxis are available in Fardapur; Rs 500 should get you to Jalgaon.

JALGAON

☎ 0257 / elev 208m

On the main railway line from Mumbai to the country's northeast, Jalgaon is a hub for trains in all directions and not a bad place to hole up for a night or two. It's a more practical overnight stop for the Ajanta caves, 60km to the south, than Aurangabad, and is a good base for visiting Ellora and Lonar.

Sleeping & Eating

Most of the hotels in Jalgaon have 24-hour checkout.

Hotel Plaza (☎ 2227354; hotelplaza_jal@yahoo.com; Station Rd; dm/s/d from Rs 150/150/220; 🔀 🖳) About 150m up from the station is one of the cleanest and most welcoming budget hotels in Maharashtra. White-tiled rooms have private bathrooms and TVs. The effusive owner is a mine of useful information.

Anjali Guest House (☎ 2225079; Khandesh Mill Complex, Station Rd; s/d from Rs 200/250) On the right past the autorickshaw stand, this guesthouse is another good place with comfy rooms, some with squat toilets. The vegetarian restaurant downstairs is reliable.

Hotel Galaxy (☎ 2223578; Jilha Rd; s/d from Rs 220/ 375, d with AC Rs 600; 🖭) Next to the bus stand, about 2km from the train station, this hotel has tidy, carpeted rooms with private bathrooms and TVs.

Silver Palace (mains Rs 30-60; 🕑 10.30am-11.30pm) Next door to Hotel Plaza is this top-class restaurant and bar, the largest in Jalgaon, serving a wide range of Indian and Chinese dishes.

Hotel Arya (☎ 2226803; Navi Peth; mains Rs 20-60) Opposite Kelkar Market and near the clock tower, this place is a seven-minute walk southeast of the train station. It serves flavourful Indian food that won't set your taste buds aflame, and is so popular you may have to queue for a table.

Getting There & Away

Several express trains between Mumbai and Delhi or Kolkata stop briefly at Jalgaon **train station** (☎ 131). Expresses to Mumbai (Rs 160/720 in sleeper/2AC, eight hours) are readily available. The *Sewagram Express*, leaving from Jalgaon at 10.14pm, goes to Nagpur (Rs 157/707 in sleeper/2AC, eight hours).

The first run from the **bus stand** (☎ 2229774) to Fardapur (Rs 29, 1½ hours) is at 6am, dropping you at the T-junction, 4km away from the Ajanta caves; buses depart every half hour thereafter. The same bus continues to Aurangabad (Rs 77, four hours).

Jalgaon's train station and bus stand are about 2km apart (Rs 10 by autorickshaw). Luxury bus offices on Railway Station Rd offer services to Aurangabad (Rs 120, 3½ hours), Mumbai (Rs 200, nine hours) and Nagpur (Rs 220, 10 hours).

LONAR METEORITE CRATER

Near the village of Lonar, on a flat plain about 165km east of Aurangabad, is a huge meteorite crater believed to be about 50,000 years old. The crater is 2km in diameter and 170m deep, with a shallow lake at the bottom. A plaque at the rim states that it is 'the only hypervelocity natural impact crater in basaltic rock in the world'. Scientists suspect that the meteorite is still embedded about 600m below the southeastern rim of the crater.

A peaceful and undeveloped spot, the crater lake's edge is home to several **Hindu temples** as well as wildlife, including langur

monkeys, peacocks, gazelles and an array of birds. The **Government Rest House**, which is the starting point for the trail down to the bottom, is about 15 minutes' walk from the bus stand.

MTDC Tourist Complex (☎ 07260-221602; d Rs 525), with standard non-AC rooms, has a prime location just across the road from the crater. You'll also find here the **Tarangan Restaurant** (meals Rs 30-80; 🕑 6am-11pm), serving decent Punjabi, South Indian and Chinese meals.

Getting There & Away

Four direct buses leave daily to Lonar from Aurangabad (Rs 70, five hours). The last bus back to Aurangabad departs at 5pm. Lonar can also be reached by bus from Fardapur with a change at Buldhana.

It's possible to visit Lonar on a day trip from Aurangabad or Jalgaon if you hire a car and driver. A full day there and back from either town will cost at least Rs 1800.

NAGPUR

☎ 0712 / pop 2.1 million / elev 305m

Nagpur, the geographic centre and orange-growing capital of India, is the jumping off point for a series of trips into the far eastern corner of Maharashtra. In addition to its proximity to Ramtek (p141) and the ashrams around Sevagram (p141), the clean, affluent city is a convenient stop for those heading to the isolated **Navagaon National Park**, 135km east, and **Tadoba-Andhari Tiger Reserve**, 150km south of Nagpur. The former has bears, wild dogs and rarely seen leopards, while the latter hosts gaurs, chitals, nilgais and seldom-spotted tigers.

The city itself, though, is not particularly worth hanging around in unless you happen to be visiting during the **Dussehra Festival** (September or October); see the boxed text, p140.

Information

Computrek (18 Central Ave; per hr Rs 20; 🕑 9am-9pm Mon-Sat) Central Ave has a few Internet centres, including this one.

MTDC office (☎ 2533325; Sanskrutik Bachat Bhavan, Sitabuldi; 🕑 10am-5.45pm Mon-Sat) In the compound opposite Hotel Hardeo.

State Bank of India (☎ 2531099; Kingsway) A two-minute walk west of the train station. Deals with foreign exchange.

Sleeping & Eating

The best area for budget and midrange hotels is Central Ave, a 15-minute walk east of the train station. Turn right as you leave the station concourse, then right again across the bridge over the train tracks into Central Ave. An autorickshaw to Central Ave from the bus stand costs around Rs 20.

Hotel Blue Diamond (☎ 2727461; fax 2727591; 113 Central Ave; s/d with shared bathroom from Rs 130/180, with private bathroom Rs 150/250, with AC Rs 450/550; ☒) The pick of the budget options, the Blue Diamond has clean, well-maintained rooms, including good-value AC ones.

Hotel Hardeo (☎ 2529115; hardeo_ngp@sancharnet.in; s/d Rs 1700/2200; ☒ ▯) Around 1km east of the train station, the Hardeo is a classy place to stay with big, clean rooms and welcoming staff. The rates include breakfast.

Hotel Skylark (☎ 2724654; fax 2726193; 119 Central Ave; s/d Rs 425/550, with AC Rs 725/825; meals Rs 50-120; ☒) The non-AC rooms at this friendly, well-run hotel are overpriced and worn, but the AC ones are not too bad and have cable TV. The convivial restaurant/bar at the Skylark serves a diverse range of North Indian food, and sometimes has live music performances.

Hotel Blue Moon (☎ 2726061; ktcbaja_ngp@sancharnet.in; Central Ave; s/d with TV from Rs 225/350) This is one of the first places you come to if walking from the train station. Rooms, which are plain but pleasant enough, can suffer noise from the road.

Krishnum (Central Ave; ☒) A highly popular place, and once you sample its thalis (Rs 30 to 60), great *upma* (spicy South Indian semolina pancake; Rs 12), pizzas (around Rs 40), and other South Indian snacks you'll understand why. There's also a wide choice of ice creams (Rs 12 to 20) and fresh juices as well as a bakery downstairs.

The dozens of *dhabas* (snack bars), food stalls and fruit stands opposite the train station rouse in the evening. Summer is the best time to sample the famed oranges – they're at their sweetest May to July.

Getting There & Away

AIR

Indian Airlines (☎ 2533962) has flights to Hyderabad (US$115, one hour, twice weekly), Mumbai (US$140, 1¼ hours, twice daily), Delhi (US$160, 1½ hours, daily) and Kolkata (US$175, 1½ hours, three weekly). **Jet Airways** (☎ 5617888) has flights to Mumbai (US$140, twice daily).

BUS

The main **MSRTC bus stand** (☎ 2726221) is 2km south of the train station and hotel area. Buses head regularly for Wardha (Rs 36, two hours) and Ramtek (Rs 22, 1½ hours). Two buses roar off daily to Jalgaon (Rs 208, 10 hours), and a semideluxe bus to Hyderabad (Rs 256, 12 hours) leaves at 6pm. Services also run to Jabalpur (Rs 117, seven hours) and Indore (Rs 251, 16 hours). Other Madhya Pradesh–

UNTOUCHABLE CHAMPION

One of the most highly respected humanitarians in Maharashtra's history was Dr Bhimrao Ramji Ambedkar, a low-caste Hindu who became Law Minister and Scheduled Castes leader. He was born into a Dalit household in the district of Ratnagiri in 1891. After graduating from Bombay's Elphinstone College he studied in Britain and the USA, but encountered only discrimination upon his return to India, where his workmates refused to hand him anything for fear of ritual pollution. Thus began a lifelong campaign for Dalit rights, in which he unrelentingly sought equality for the depressed classes. Ambedkar was also one of the key architects of the Indian constitution – a document that officially wiped out untouchability in India.

Despite his victories for the people, Dr Ambedkar lost faith that Hindu prejudice against Dalits would ever be eradicated, and on 14 October 1956 converted to Buddhism in Nagpur, an act that was repeated by an estimated three million low-caste Hindus. Along with vows embracing tenets of the Buddha, he stated, 'I shall believe in the equality of man'. He died only weeks later on 6 December 1956, leaving behind a newly revived Buddhism and greatly inspired masses.

Every year thousands commemorating Dr Ambedkar descend upon Diksha Bhoomi in Nagpur during the Hindu Dussehra Festival, which is when the momentous 1956 conversion incidentally occurred. For more information on Dr Ambedkar, Buddhism and the fight for Dalit parity, see www.ambedkar.org.

GREG ELMS

Market in Panaji (Panjim; p167), Goa

NEIL SETCHFIELD

Church of St Cajetan (p177), Old Goa, Goa

Benaulim beach (p197), Goa

GREG ELMS

Virupaksha Temple (p243), Hampi, Karnataka

KAREN

Devaraja Market (p221), Mysore, Karnataka

GREG ELMS

ANTONY GIBLIN

Hoysaleswara Temple (p234), Halebid, Karnataka

bound buses, including to Bhopal (Rs 201, 12 hours), operate from a separate stand about 500m south of the station.

TRAIN

Nagpur Junction **train station** (☎ 131), on the main Mumbai–Howrah line, is an impressive edifice in the centre of town. The overnight *Vidarbha Express* originates in Nagpur and departs for Mumbai CST (Rs 265/1193 in sleeper/2AC, 17 hours) at 5pm. The same train departs Mumbai at 9.40am for Nagpur. Heading north to Kolkata the *Mumbai Howrah Mail* departs from Nagpur at 11.15am and arrives at Howrah at 6.30am (Rs 325/1460 in sleeper/2AC, 1138km). Five Mumbai-bound expresses stop at Jalgaon (for Ajanta caves; Rs 157/707 in sleeper/2AC, seven hours). There are also connections between Nagar and Bangalore, Delhi and Hyderabad.

AROUND NAGPUR
Ramtek

About 40km northeast of Nagpur, Ramtek has a number of picturesque 600-year-old **temples** (☒ 6am-9pm) which sit contentedly atop the Hill of Rama, looking down upon the town. It is said in the epic Ramayana that Rama spent time here with Sita and Lakshmi.

On the road to the temples you'll pass **Ambala Tank**, lined with smaller temples. Further along, **Kalidas Memorial** (admission Rs 10; ☒ 8am-8.30pm) is dedicated to famous classical Sanskrit dramatist Kalidas (also spelled Kalidasa). Autorickshaws will cart you the 5km from the bus stand up to the main temples for Rs 25, but walking down via the 700 steps from the back of the temple and through the village is more fun.

Rajkamal Resort (☎ 07114-255620; d with/without AC Rs 700/400; ✿), on the hilltop, has overpriced but neat rooms with TVs. The hotel has a basic restaurant/bar.

Buses run half-hourly between Ramtek and the MSRTC bus stand in Nagpur (Rs 22, 1½ hours). The last bus back to Nagpur is at 8.30pm.

SEVAGRAM
☎ 07152

If you're even faintly interested in the life of Mahatma Gandhi, it's worth the trek into the heart of India to visit Sevagram, the Village of Service, where Gandhi established the **Sevagram Ashram** (☎ 284753; ☒ 6am-6pm) in 1933.

The peaceful and simple ashram encompasses 40 hectares of farmland, as well as residences and research centres, though the central complex itself is quite small. The original adobe huts of the ashram are well preserved, as are the Mahatma's personal effects, including his famous spinning wheel and spectacles.

Across the road from the ashram, the **Gandhi Picture Exhibition** (admission free; ☒ 10am-6pm Wed-Mon) follows the events in the Mahatma's life.

Daily nondenominational prayer services are held at 4.45am and at 6pm or 6.30pm beside the peepul tree planted by Gandhi in 1936. Ashramites follow a strict daily routine including half an hour of community spinning each day (starting at 2pm). Otherwise, life at Sevagram is extremely laidback. Homespun cloth *(khadi)* is for sale at the ashram, as are volumes of Gandhi's writings.

Lodging at the ashram, in **Yatri Nivas** (d Rs 80), across the road from the entry gate, is clean and takes care of the basics. Vegetarian meals (Rs 12) are served in the ashram's dining hall; after you'll wash up the stainless steel plates using water and ash.

Getting There & Away

The ashram can be reached from Wardha or Sevagram train stations, both on the Central Railway. There are around five express trains from Nagpur to Sevagram (Rs 33, one hour). Express MSRTC buses run more frequently between Nagpur and Wardha (Rs 40, two hours).

Local buses go regularly to the ashram from Wardha (Rs 5, 20 minutes), or an autorickshaw will cost Rs 40 for the 8km trip.

AROUND SEVAGRAM

Just 3km from Sevagram on the road to Nagpur at Paunar is **Brahmavidya Mandir Ashram** (☎ 07152-288388; ☒ 4am-noon & 2-8pm), the ashram of Gandhi's disciple Vinoba Bhave. This persistent soul walked through India asking rich landlords to hand over land for redistribution to the poor – he managed to persuade them to fork out a total of 1.6 million hectares.

MAHARASHTRA

With just 33 members, the inspiring ashram is run almost entirely by women. Dedicated to *swarajya* (rural self-sufficiency), it is operated on a social system of consensus with no central management. Basic accommodation and board (about Rs 75) in two rooms sharing a bathroom is available; call ahead to arrange. All are welcome, but men who want to stay more than seven days will need special permission from the community. The bus from Nagpur runs past the ashram; otherwise it's Rs 40 in an autorickshaw to Paunar from Wardha or Sevagram.

SOUTHERN MAHARASHTRA

KONKAN COAST

Maharashtra's Konkan Coast – the narrow strip between the Western Ghats and Arabian Sea – is an appealing region of deserted beaches, palm trees, abandoned forts and isolated fishing communities. Though it runs some distance from the coast, the Konkan Railway provides access to the region. Local buses can help connect the dots, so grin and bear the discomfort – beautiful strips of sand seldom trod by foreigners lie in wait.

Murud

☎ 02144 / pop 12,551
About 160km south of Mumbai, the sleepy fishing town of Murud is best visited for the commanding island fortress of **Janjira**, 5km south of the village. The fortress was built in 1140 by Siddi Jahor and became the 16th-century capital of the Siddis of Janjira, descendants of sailor-traders from the Horn of Africa. Although constructed on an island, its 12m-high walls seem to emerge straight from the sea. This made the fort utterly impregnable, even to the mighty Marathas – Shivaji tried to conquer it by sea and his son, Sambhaji, even attempted to tunnel to it. Even though the fort is in ruins and the interior is overgrown it remains a highly impressive place; walk along the outer walls and check out the 22 watchtowers, battlements and rusting remains of cannons to get a feel for this island stronghold.

The only way to reach Janjira is by local boat (Rs 12 return, 10 minutes) from Rajpuri Port, about 5km south of Murud. Boats depart from 7am to 6pm daily, but require a minimum of 20 passengers. On weekends and holidays you won't have to wait long. To get to Rajpuri from Murud, either take an autorickshaw (Rs 40) or hire a bicycle (Rs 4 per hour) from the small shop opposite the mid-road shrine on Darbar Rd, Murud's main beach road.

Back in Murud there's little to see other than the beach and the off-limits **Ahmedganj Palace**, estate of the Siddi Nawab of Murud – the bus into town passes this Gothic pile.

SLEEPING & EATING

Several accommodation options are strung out along Murud's beach road. Discounts are generally available when it's quiet.

Golden Swan Beach Resort (☎ 274078; www.goldenswan.com; Darbar Rd; d with/without AC from Rs 1800/1000; ✷) The first place you come to as the bus enters town, this resort is also the plushest. The AC rooms are clean, have TVs and are practically on the beach. The non-AC rooms are not as nice.

Mirage Holiday Homes (☎ 276744; opposite Kumar Talkies, Darbar Rd; d with/without AC Rs 1500/600; ✷) Simple but clean rooms are offered at this small place set back from the road behind a neat circular front garden.

The Nest Bamboo House (☎ 276144; Darbar Rd; d hut Rs 500) Hammocks sway between the palms at this rustic beachside place. The basic bamboo huts each have private bathrooms and bucket showers.

All the above serve food with the Golden Swan Beach Resort offering the best selection of dishes. Otherwise try **Patel Inn** (☎ 274153; ⊙ 11.30am-2pm & 8-10pm), serving simple veg, chicken or fish thalis (Rs 35 to 50).

GETTING THERE & AWAY

In Mumbai hop on one of the regular ferries (Rs 55, one hour) or hydrofoils (Rs 100, 45 minutes) from the Gateway of India in Colaba to Mandva. If you take the hydrofoil the ticket includes a free shuttle bus to Alibag (30 minutes), otherwise an autorickshaw will be about Rs 120. Rickety local buses from Alibag head down the coast to Murud (Rs 26, two hours). Alternatively, buses from Mumbai Central bus stand take almost six hours to Murud (Rs 120).

The nearest railhead on the Konkan Railway is Roha, reachable by bus (Rs 26, two hours).

Ganpatipule
☎ 02357

Ganpatipule, on the coast 375km south of Mumbai, has several kilometres of almost pristine beaches and waters begging you to take a swim. The pull for thousands of Hindu pilgrims, however, is the town's seaside **temple** (☎ 235223; ☼ 5am-9pm) with its Swayambhu Ganpati, or 'naturally formed' monolithic Ganesh (painted a lurid orange), allegedly discovered 1600 years ago.

There are several places to stay on the hillside above the beach, but the best place to bunk down is the **MTDC Resort** (☎ 235248; fax 235328; d with/without AC from Rs 1700/700; ✷), nicely ensconced among palms, beside the beach. Its **Tent Resort** (☎ 235348; 2-bed/4-bed tents Rs 300/400), set back from the beach, is a cheaper option but only open mid-October to the end of May. Rates rise by 30% outside the high season. The resort offers a variety of water sports, has a **Bank of Maharashtra** (☎ 235304), which can change travellers cheques but not currency, and the **Tarang Restaurant** (mains Rs 40-90), serving local specialities like Malvani fish curry (Rs 70).

GETTING THERE & AWAY
One MSRTC bus heads daily to Ganpatipule (Rs 250 in semideluxe, 10 hours) from Mumbai, leaving the state road transport terminal near Mumbai Central bus stand at 7.30pm. The bus heads back to Mumbai from Ganpatipule at 6.00am. Frequent ordinary buses rumble down to Ratnagiri (Rs 23, one hour). Autorickshaws to Ratnagiri cost Rs 250.

Ratnagiri
☎ 02352 / pop 70,335

Around 50km south of Ganpatipule, Ratnagiri is the largest town on the south coast and the main transport hub (it's on the Konkan rail line). The town itself is not hugely alluring; neither the former home of freedom fighter Lokmanya Tilak, now a small **museum** (Tilak Alley; admission free; ☼ 9am-7pm), nor the ruined **Thibaw Palace** (Thibaw Palace Rd), where the last Burmese king, Thibaw, was interned under the British from 1886 until his death in 1916 (a tale recounted

in Amitav Ghosh's *The Glass Palace*), are particularly worth going out of your way for. However, just outside the town centre the pretty **Bhatya Beach** is a pleasant spot to watch the sun sink.

There's an ATM opposite the old bus stand and you can access the Internet at **Royal Cyber Café** (Maruti Mandir; per hr Rs 15; ☼ 9am-10pm).

Hotel Landmark (☎ 220120; fax 220124; Thibaw Palace Rd; s/d Rs 495/695, d with AC Rs 995; ✷), 2km west of the bus stands, this hotel is the best option if you need a place to stay; its restaurant serves very good Indian food (mains Rs 60 to 90).

Hotel Kanchan (☎ 228250; P-55 Mirjole Block; s/d from Rs 300/400, with AC Rs 600/700; ✷ ✷) is the closest hotel to the train station (less than 2km) and has clean rooms with squat toilets, a restaurant and the bonus of a swimming pool.

GETTING THERE & AWAY
Ratnagiri **train station** (☎ 131) is 10km east of town; all express trains stop here, including the *Jan Shatabdi* south to Margao (Rs 103/322 in 2nd class/chair, three hours) in Goa and north to Mumbai (Rs 124/395, 5½ hours); both depart daily except Wednesday. In the town centre on Maruti Mandir go to the **old bus stand** (☎ 222340) to catch state buses to Kolhapur (Rs 66, four hours) and Ganpatipule (Rs 23, one hour). The **new bus stand** (☎ 227882), 1km further west, has two buses daily to both Malvan (Rs 100, five hours) and Panaji in Goa (Rs 122, seven hours).

Tarkarli & Malvan
☎ 02365

Two hundred kilometres south of Ratnagiri and within striking distance of Goa is Tarkarli, one of Maharashtra's loveliest beaches. Right beside it, shaded by pine trees, is the serene **MTDC Holiday Resort** (☎ 252390; d from Rs 850), offering simple but sturdy chalets and an excellent restaurant run by a local family who cook delicious Malvani fish dishes. Get up early and you may see turtles on the beach or a school of dolphins playing in the waters. Also inquire at the resort about backwater tours on their houseboat.

Malvani cuisine takes its name from the lively fishing town of Malvan, 8km north along the coast. Just 500m off the harbour is the low-slung **Sindhudurg Fort**. Dating from 1664 it's said that the great Chhatrapati Shivaji had a hand in building this island citadel; his hand- and footprints can be found in one of the turrets above the entrance. A village and several temples lie within the 3km of fort walls. If you're lucky enough to pitch up at the jetty and find a crowd of 12 people waiting to visit the island then it will be Rs 35 per person. Otherwise it's Rs 350 to hire a boat for the return journey.

GETTING THERE & AWAY

The closest train station is Kudal, 38km west of the coast. Reasonably frequent buses (Rs 15, one hour) run between here and Malvan **bus stand** (☎ 252034). Otherwise an autorickshaw from Kudal to Malvan or Tarkali is Rs 250. Malvan has several buses daily to Panaji, Goa (Rs 69, five hours) and a couple of services to Ratnagiri (Rs 86, six hours). An autorickshaw between Malvan and Tarkarli costs Rs 50.

MATHERAN

☎ 02148 / pop 5139 / elev 803m

Easily the most gorgeous of Maharashtra's hill stations, Matheran (Jungle Topped) rests atop the Sahyadris Mountains amid a shady Jambol forest. Walking tracks lead to breathtaking lookouts that drop sheer to the plains.

Hugh Malet, Collector for the Thane district, 'discovered' Matheran in 1850 while climbing the path known as Shivaji's Ladder; thereafter it quickly became a popular hill station. The place owes its tranquillity to a ban on motor vehicles (and bicycles), making it an ideal place to rest the ears and lungs. The monkey-populated trails are clean and, furthermore, the town council is eco-minded, having banned plastic bags from the town and being conscious of clearing other rubbish, too.

From mid-June to early October the monsoon-mudded village practically hibernates. Otherwise weekends generally see Matheran clogged with day-trippers, while during the true high season – the peak holiday periods of May to June, Diwali and Christmas – it is packed to the gills and hotel prices get ludicrous.

Getting to Matheran is half the fun; from Neral Junction a narrow-gauge toy train (mini train) chugs up a 21km route to the heart of the village. It's a scenic two-hour ascent around the steep slopes. A carnival ride to many on board, it's especially riotous if there's a school group present, bound to erupt as the train moseys through 'One Kiss Tunnel'.

Information

Entry to Matheran costs Rs 25 (Rs 15 for children), which you pay on arrival at the train station or the car park. Beware of porters or touts trying to drag you into a particular hotel – they're mainly eager for a commission.

There's no tourist office, but some hotels have a basic map of Matheran. **Vishwa's Photo Studio** (☎ 230354), on Mahatma Gandhi (MG) RD, sells useful miniguides (Rs 25). **Union Bank of India** (☎ 230282; MG Rd; ☼ 10am-2pm Mon-Fri, 10am-noon Sat) changes travellers cheques only.

Walks & Views

You can walk to most of Matheran's viewpoints in a matter of hours, and it's a place suited to stress-free ambling. **Panorama Point** is the most dramatic place to glimpse the sunrise, while **Porcupine Point** (also known as Sunset Point) is the most popular (read: packed) as the sun drops. **Louisa Point** and **Little Chouk Point** also have stunning views, and if you're visiting **Echo Point**, be sure to give it a yell. You can reach the valley below One Tree Hill down the path known as **Shivaji's Ladder**, allegedly trod upon by the Maratha leader himself.

Horses can be hired from people along MG Rd – you will certainly be approached – for rides to lookout points for about Rs 100 per hour. Most of these creatures are well behaved and healthy; some even work on the side as racehorses!

Sleeping & Eating

A few budget places sit near the train station, but most of the midrange and upscale 'resort' accommodation is between 10 and 20 minutes' walk away. Checkout times vary wildly in Matheran – they can be as early as 7am. Unless otherwise stated, rates quoted here are outside the high season, when they can be anything from 30% to 200% more.

Lord's Central Hotel (☎ 230228; www.matheran .com; MG Rd; s/d Rs 800/1600, valley-view s/d Rs 1200/2400;

🖳 🖫) A charming heritage place whose owners bend over backwards to make you feel at home. It has a well-placed pool, small library, bar, dining room and a giant chess board. Rates include three fabulous meals. Nonguests can dine here, too; a four-course lunch or dinner is Rs 350.

Hope Hall Hotel (☎ 230253; MG Rd; s/d Rs 190/250, 5-person room Rs 375) This garden-set lodge, run by a very welcoming family, is a lovely place to rest your heels for a while. Large, cheery rooms have mosaic-tiled floors and private bathrooms with bucket hot water. Check-out is 24 hours.

Pramod Lodge (☎ 230302; Kotwal Nagar; d with TV Rs 150) Off Main Bazaar, this no-frills hotel has tidy, well-priced doubles and wonderful valley views from its wraparound balcony. It's a pale-yellow building – you may need to ask a local to point the way.

MTDC Resort (☎ 230277; d with TV Rs 600) Next to Dasturi car park, 2.5km northeast of the train station, this place has a peaceful, wooded location, but the rooms don't square up to their price tag. Still, it's a handy option if you arrive by car.

SOMETHING SPECIAL

Verandah in the Forest (☎ 30296; www .neemranahotels.com; d from Rs 2500) Completely without modern distractions, old Barr House, set amid the woods close by Charlotte Lake, is a gem of a hotel. The late-19th-century aura of the house has been retained with period furniture including an elegant dining table seating 20 and spacious, comfortable bedrooms. Rates include breakfast. A set Indian lunch is Rs 275 and Continental dinner Rs 325, for which outside guests can also book. Or you could just drop by for afternoon tea (Rs 35).

Hotel Kumar Plaza (☎ 230329; MG Rd; mains Rs 40-110) The restaurant at this hotel serves up kebabs (Rs 85) galore and other tasty fare, made better with its appealing open-air patio seating.

Khan's Parkview Restaurant (☎ 230240; MG Rd; mains Rs 35-80) This eatery, in Khan's Hotel, is a popular place that makes great parathas to accompany its Punjabi and Mughlai dishes.

MAHARASHTRA

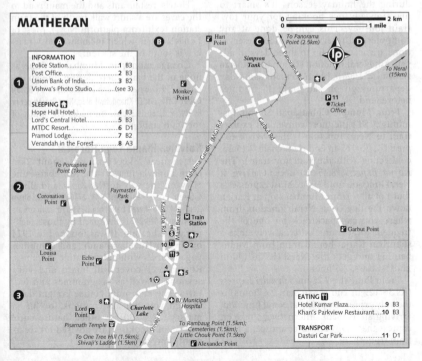

MATHERAN

0 —————— 2 km
0 —————— 1 mile

INFORMATION
Police Station.....................1 B3
Post Office.........................2 B3
Union Bank of India.............3 B2
Vishwa's Photo Studio..........(see 3)

SLEEPING 🏠
Hope Hall Hotel....................4 B3
Lord's Central Hotel..............5 B3
MTDC Resort.......................6 D1
Pramod Lodge......................7 B2
Verandah in the Forest..........8 A3

Hari Point
Simpson Tank
Monkey Point

To Panorama Point (2.5km)
To Neral (15km)

6
P 11 Ticket Office

To Porcupine Point (1km)

Coronation Point
Paymaster Park

Louisa Point
Echo Point

Garbut Point

Train Station
7
10
2
9
4
1
5

Lord Point
Charlotte Lake
B/ Municipal Hospital

To Rambaug Point (1.5km);
Cemeteries (1.5km);
Little Chouk Point (1.5km)

Pisarnath Temple

To One Tree Hill (1.5km);
Shivaji's Ladder (1.5km)

Alexander Point

EATING 🍴
Hotel Kumar Plaza...................9 B3
Khan's Parkview Restaurant....10 B3

TRANSPORT
Dasturi Car Park....................11 D1

Matheran is famed for its locally produced honey and for *chikki*, a rock-hard
workout for the jaws, made of *gur* (unre-
fined sugar made from cane juice) and nuts.
Find it at the '*chikki* marts' and shops on
MG Rd.

Getting There & Away

TAXI

From Neral to Matheran taxis cost around
Rs 250 and take 20 to 30 minutes. A seat
in a shared taxi is Rs 50, but you may have
to twiddle your thumbs waiting for it to
fill up. Taxis stop at the Dasturi car park,
2.5km from Matheran's bazaar area and
train station.

TRAIN

The toy train (Rs 39/225 in 2nd/1st class,
two hours) departs from Neral Junction
train station at 9am, 10.45am and 5pm
weekdays; in the opposite direction it
leaves Matheran at 5.45am, 1.20pm and
4pm. During the monsoon season (June to
September) there *may* be one train daily,
but it's very unreliable. At weekends and
during the holiday seasons it's smart to
make an advance booking for your toy-
train journey. This can be done at any
computerised reservation office. Reservations are accepted up to three days in advance at Neral Junction station or **Matheran
station** (☎ 230264), but tickets for same-day
departures go on sale only 45 minutes
beforehand.

From Mumbai Chhatrapati Shivaji Terminus (CST) the most convenient express
train to Neral Junction is the *Deccan Express* (Rs 35/165 in 2nd class/chair, 7.15am,
connecting with the 9am toy train). The
Koyna Express (8.45am) doesn't arrive at
Neral Junction until 10.45. Most expresses –
but not all – from Mumbai stop at Karjat,
down the line from Neral Junction, from
where you can backtrack on one of the
frequent local trains. Alternatively, take a
suburban Karjat-bound train from Mumbai CST and get off at Neral (Rs 20/140 in
2nd/1st class, 2½ hours).

From Pune the 7.20am *Sahyadri Express*
(Rs 36/129 in 2nd class/chair, 2½ hours) is
the only express stopping at Neral Junction,
arriving at 10.15am. Alternatively, take an
express that stops at Karjat and get a local
train from there.

Getting Around

Matheran is one of the few places left in
India where you'll find hand-pulled rickshaws; they charge Rs 160 to haul you up
from the Dasturi car park to the town.
Apart from the rickshaws the only other
transport options are your own feet, or a
horse. It takes 30 minutes to walk up to
Matheran from the car park (porters are
available for Rs 60 or more, depending on
baggage), or you can hire a horse (Rs 80).

LONAVLA

☎ 02114 / pop 55,650 / elev 625m

Lonavla and nearby twin Khandala, 106km
southeast of Mumbai, are hill resorts catering to weekenders and conference groups.
The surrounding landscape is attractive, but
the towns themselves aren't exceptional –
unless you're head over heels for *chikki*, the
rock-hard nut brittle sweet; every second
shop seems to be a *chikki* mart! However,
Lonavla is a convenient base from which
to visit the Karla and Bhaja Caves and to
undertake paragliding or holistic medicine
courses.

Hotels, restaurants and the main road to
the caves are a short walk north of the train
station (exit from platform No 1). Most of
Lonavla town, which includes a busy market, is south of the station.

Change money in Mumbai or Pune as
none of the banks here deal in foreign exchange. Internet access is available at **Balaji
Cyber Café** (1st fl, Khandelwal Bldg, New Bazaar; per hr
Rs 20; ⌚ 12.30-10.30pm), immediately south of
the train station.

Kaivalyadhama Yoga Hospital

Set in neatly kept grounds about 2km
from Lonavla just off the Mumbai–Pune
Hwy on the way to the Karla and Bhaja
Caves, this **ashram** (☎ 273039; www.kdham
.com; s/d with shared bathroom US$12/20, with private
bathroom US$20/24) is favoured by those seek-
ing yogic healing. It was founded in 1924
by Swami Kuvalayanandji and combines
yoga courses with naturopathic therapies.
Room rates cover full board and yoga
sessions as well as programmes and lectures. The minimum course is eight days,
though you can always book for just a
massage (Rs 200) or other 'nature cure'
treatment. Bookings are advised for treatments and stays.

Activities

Mumbai-based **Nirvana Adventures** (☎ 022-26053724; www.nirvanaadventures.com) offers paragliding courses, or tandem flights if you don't have the time or inclination to take a course, at Kamshet, 25km from Lonavla.

Sleeping & Eating

Most of Lonavla's hotels and restaurants are teeming with action on weekends and empty during the week. All hotels listed here have a 10am checkout time.

Hotel Chandralok (☎ 272294; fax 272921; Shivaji Rd; d with/without AC from Rs 1275/390; 🟦) Set back from the traffic, this is a friendly place with reasonably comfortable rooms. They'll negotiate over rates out of busy periods. The res-

taurant does superb Gujarati thalis (Rs 75) for lunch and dinner.

Hotel Lonavla (☎ 272914; Mumbai-Pune Hwy; d with/without AC Rs 895/595; 🟦) This place faces the noisy highway, but its spacious rooms with TVs are good value. All rooms have geysers.

Kumar Resort (☎ 273091; kumarini@hotmail.com; Mumbai-Pune Hwy; d/t Rs 2490/3490; 🟦 🟦 🟦) As well as sizable, reasonably well furnished rooms, the rates at this place include the in-house amusement park (bumper cars, anyone?). It also has a bar and restaurant with toothsome tandoori dishes (Rs 50 to 70). Just to enter the park costs Rs 175.

Hotel Rama Krishna (☎ 273600; Mumbai-Pune Hwy; dishes Rs 45-120; ⏱ 7am-midnight) The restaurant at

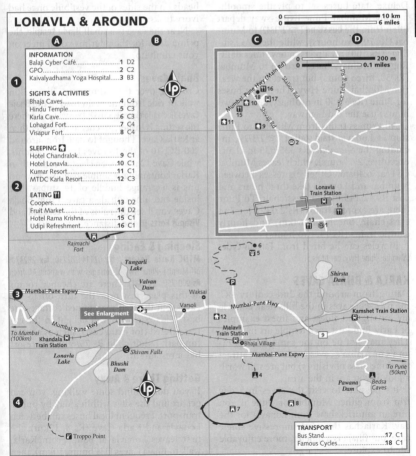

LONAVLA & AROUND

0 ———— 10 km
0 ———— 6 miles

INFORMATION
Balaji Cyber Café..............................1 D2
GPO...2 C2
Kaivalyadhama Yoga Hospital.........3 B3

SIGHTS & ACTIVITIES
Bhaja Caves....................................4 C4
Hindu Temple..................................5 C3
Karla Cave.......................................6 C4
Lohagad Fort....................................7 C4
Visapur Fort....................................8 C4

SLEEPING 🛏
Hotel Chandralok.............................9 C1
Hotel Lonavla.................................10 C1
Kumar Resort.................................11 C1
MTDC Karla Resort.........................12 C3

EATING 🍴
Coopers..13 D2
Fruit Market...................................14 D2
Hotel Rama Krishna........................15 C1
Udipi Refreshment..........................16 C1

0 ———— 200 m
0 ———— 0.1 miles

Lonavla Train Station

Rajmachi Fort

Tungarli Lake

Valvan Dam

Waksai

Varsoli

Shirsta Dam

Mumbai-Pune Expwy

Mumbai-Pune Hwy

Kamshet Train Station

See Enlargment

Mumbai-Pune Hwy

Malavli Train Station

Bhaja Village

To Mumbai (100km)

Khandala Train Station

Lonavla Lake

Bhushi Dam

Shivam Falls

Mumbai-Pune Expwy

To Pune (50km)

Pawana Dam

Bedsa Caves

Troppo Point

TRANSPORT
Bus Stand.......................................17 C1
Famous Cycles................................18 C1

MAHARASHTRA

this hotel has a particularly pleasant open-air patio on which to enjoy its Punjabi fare.

Udipi Refreshment (Mumbai-Pune Hwy; breakfast Rs 12-25, mains Rs 25-50; ☉ 5.30am-midnight) This is a no-frills, pure-vegetarian joint serving quick and tasty South and North Indian fuel food.

The bazaar, south of the train station, holds a fine fruit market. If you've got a sweet tooth, search out **Coopers** (☎ 272564; Jaychand Chowk; ☉ 11am-1pm & 3-5pm, closed Wed), on the southern side of the railway tracks. It's been in business for over 50 years and is justly renowned for its gooey chocolate fudges.

Getting There & Away

Deluxe state buses set to ply the smooth-moving Mumbai–Pune Expressway depart often from the **bus stand** (☎ 273842) to Mumbai (Rs 70, two hours), while their AC siblings (Rs 100) rev up just a few times daily. Rugged ordinary buses also go to Mumbai (Rs 50, three hours) but travel on the wearier Mumbai–Pune Hwy. The many buses for Pune (Rs 35/50 in ordinary/deluxe, two hours) use the old highway.

All express trains from Mumbai to Pune stop at Lonavla **train station** (☎ 273725), including the *Shatabdi* (Rs 335/635 in chair/executive, 2½ hours), which leaves Mumbai CST at 6.40am. Other expresses between Mumbai and Lonavla take three hours and cost Rs 42/145 in 2nd class/chair. To Pune there are express trains (Rs 27/122 for 2nd class/chair, one hour, 64km) and hourly shuttle trains (Rs 14, two hours).

Bicycles can be hired from **Famous Cycles** (Mumbai-Pune Hwy; per hr Rs 5).

KARLA & BHAJA CAVES

Dating from around the 2nd century BC, the rock-cut caves in the hills near Lonavla are among the oldest and finest examples of Early Buddhist rock temple art in India. They may not be on the same scale as El-lora's or Ajanta's caves (and so don't attract the same mass of visitors) but are still worth a look if you are in the area.

It's possible to visit the caves in a day trip from either Mumbai or Pune if you hire an autorickshaw from Lonavla for the day. Karla has the most impressive single cave, but Bhaja is a quieter, more enjoyable site to explore.

Karla Cave

A 20-minute climb via stone steps from the car park brings you to the impressive **Karla Cave** (☎ 02114-282115; Indian/foreigner Rs 5/US$2; ☉ 9am-5pm), the largest Early Buddhist *chaitya* in India. Completed in 80 BC, the *chaitya* is around 40m long and 15m high, and was carved by monks and artisans from the rock in imitation of more familiar wooden architecture.

A semicircular 'sun window' filters light in towards the cave's representation of the Buddha – a dagoba, or stupa, protected by a carved wooden umbrella. The cave's roof is ribbed with teak beams said to be original. The 37 pillars forming the aisles are topped by kneeling elephants. The carved elephant heads on the sides of the vestibule once had ivory tusks.

Near the cave is a small **Hindu temple**, the prime draw for the pilgrims you'll meet on your climb up.

Bhaja Caves

Crossing over the expressway, it's a 3km walk or ride from the main road to the **Bhaja Caves** (Indian/foreigner Rs 5/US$2; ☉ 8am-6pm), where the setting is lusher, greener and quieter than at Karla Cave. Thought to date from around 200 BC, 10 of the 18 caves here are *viharas*, while Cave 12 is an open *chaitya*, earlier than Karla, containing a simple dagoba. Beyond this is a strange huddle of 14 stupas, five inside and nine outside a cave. From Bhaja Caves you'll see the ruins of the **Lohagad** and **Visapur Forts** in the distance.

Sleeping & Eating

MTDC Karla Resort (☎ 02114-282230; fax 282370; off Mumbai-Pune Hwy; d cottages with/without AC from Rs 900/750; ☒ ☒) There are cheaper rooms at this place just near the turn-off to the caves, but the well-maintained cottages are best. Kids especially will delight in the extras offered (for extra cost), such as a water fun park (adult/child Rs 75/60). The resort has a restaurant.

Getting There & Away

If you don't mind some walking, you can get around the sites within a day by public transport. Frequent local buses run between Lonavla and Karla Cave (Rs 8, 12km); the first leaves Lonavla at 6am. From Karla, walk to Bhaja Caves (1½ hours, 10km), then follow your feet back to Malavli train station (one hour, 3km) to catch a local train to Lonavla. You can trim some walking time by taking an autorickshaw from Karla to Bhaja village (around Rs 60). The last bus from Karla to Lonavla leaves at 7pm.

Autorickshaws are plentiful, but they drive a hard bargain. The price should include waiting time at the sites (about three hours all up), and a return trip from Lonavla to the Karla and Bhaja Caves will cost Rs 350.

PUNE

☎ 020 / pop 3.8 million / elev 457m

A place where old and new India increasingly interweave without a second thought, Pune (pronounced Poona) is a thriving centre of academia and business as well as a historic centre and home to famous Osho Meditation Resort, better known as the ashram of Bhagwan Rajneesh.

The great Maratha leader Shivaji would be astonished to see how his city has changed in 500 years. He was raised here after the city was granted to his grandfather in 1599. Later, after the Brahmin Peshwa family had a go at power, it fell to the British in 1817 and became their alternative capital during the monsoon. Many maharajas had palaces here, too, taking advantage of its cooler climate.

Despite the pollution and clogged traffic that typically go with Indian cities, Pune is an interesting place to tour by day and a fun spot to party by night. It's well worth a day or two.

Orientation

The city is at the confluence of the Mutha and Mula Rivers. Mahatma Gandhi (MG) Rd, about 1km south of Pune train station, is the main street and is lined with banks, restaurants and shops. Southwest of here, the streets narrow and take on the atmosphere of a traditional bazaar town. Northeast of the train station, Koregaon Park, home of the Osho ashram, has shady streets and a Western flavour.

Information
BOOKSHOPS

Crossword (Sohrab Hall, 1st fl, RBM Rd; ☽ 10.30am-9pm) Offers the most diverse collection of books and magazines as well as a small café.

Manneys Booksellers (7 Moledina Rd; ☽ 9.30am-1.30pm & 4-8pm Mon-Sat)

INTERNET ACCESS

Internet centres are scattered around the city, try:

Computology Systems (326 Ashok Vijay Complex, Bootie St; per hr Rs 10; ☽ 9.30am-9.30pm Mon-Sat, 11am-8pm Sun) The cheapest place in town, just off MG Rd.

Cyber-Net (1B Gera Sterling, North Main Rd, Koregaon Park; per hr Rs 30; ☽ 8am-11.30pm)

Dishnet Hub Internet Centre (Sadhu Vaswani Rd; per hr Rs 30)

MAP

The *TTK Discover India* series map of Pune (Rs 50) is the best map around. You can find it at the bookshops listed on the left or at the bookstand on platform 1 of the train station.

MONEY

Citibank has 24-hour ATMs at its main branch on East St and at the branches on Bund Garden Rd and North Main Rd. ICICI Bank has an ATM at the Pune train station and another on Koregaon Rd. Southwest of Koregaon Park there is a HSBC ATM, near the Air India office on Mangaldas Rd. On MG Rd you'll find a UTI Bank ATM.

American Express (☎ 26055337; MG Rd; ☽ 9.30am-6.30pm Mon-Fri, 9.30am-2.30pm Sat) Next to Hotel Aurora Towers.

Thomas Cook (☎ 26346171; 2418 G Thimmaya Rd; ☽ 9.30am-6pm Mon-Sat)

POST

Main post office (☎ 26349441; Sadhu Vaswani; ☽ 10am-6pm Mon-Sat) The parcel office closes at 4pm.

TOURIST INFORMATION

MTDC tourist office (☎ 26126867; I Block, Central Bldg; ☽ 10am-5.30pm Mon-Sat) Buried in a government complex south of the train station and not of great help other than to book MTDC accommodation. It also has a small desk at the **train station** (☽ 9am-7pm Mon-Sat, 9am-3pm Sun).

TRAVEL AGENCIES

Rokshan Travels (☎ 26136304; rokshantravels@ hotmail.com; 1st fl, 19 Kumar Pavilion, East St; ☽ 10am-6pm) Small, friendly and professional outfit. Staff can arrange bus and train journeys and domestic and international flights, as well as taxis.

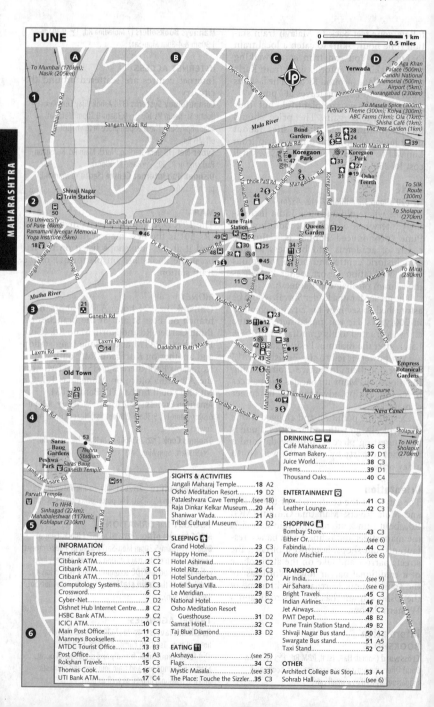

PUNE

| | 0 ———————————— 1 km |
| | 0 ———————————— 0.5 miles |

To Mumbai (170km);
Nasik (205km)

Deccan College Rd

Yerwada

To Aga Khan
Palace (500m);
Gandhi National
Memorial (500m);
Airport (5km);
Aurangabad (230km)

Ahmednagar Rd

To Masala Spice (300m);
Arthur's Theme (300m); Kolya (300m);
ABC Farms (1km); Ola (1km);
Shisha Café (1km);
The Jazz Garden (1km)

Sangam Wadi Rd

Mula River

Bund
Gardens

North Main Rd

Koregaon
Park

Boat Club Rd

Koregaon
Park

Shivaji Nagar
Train Station

Dhole Patil Rd

Osho
Teerth

To Silk
Route
(300m)

To University
of Pune (4km);
Ramamani Iyengar Memorial
Yoga Institute (5km)

Raibahadur Motilal (RBM) Rd

Pune Train
Station

Queens
Garden

To Sholapur
(270km)

Dr B Ambedkar Rd

Sasson Rd

Mutha River

Ganesh Rd

Biramji Rd

To Mirai
(280km)

Laxmi Rd

Laxmi Rd

Dadabhat Butti Marg

Moledina Rd

Sachapir St

Empress
Botanical
Gardens

Old Town

Sanas Rd

Jawaharlal Nehru Rd

S Dorabji Padmali Rd

Racecourse

Nava Canal

Saras
Baug
Gardens

Peshwa
Park

Nehru
Stadium

Saras Baug
Ganesh Temple

Sholapur Rd

To NH9;
Sholapur
(270km)

Parvati Temple

To NH4;
Sinhagad (22km);
Mahabaleshwar (117km);
Kohlapur (230km)

SIGHTS & ACTIVITIES
Jangali Maharaj Temple...........18 A2
Osho Meditation Resort...........19 D2
Pataleshvara Cave Temple......(see 18)
Raja Dinkar Kelkar Museum....20 A4
Shaniwar Wada.........................21 A3
Tribal Cultural Museum.............22 D2

SLEEPING
Grand Hotel..............................23 C3
Happy Home.............................24 D1
Hotel Ashirwad.........................25 C2
Hotel Ritz.................................26 C3
Hotel Sunderban......................27 D2
Hotel Surya Villa.......................28 D1
Le Meridian..............................29 B2
National Hotel...........................30 C2
Osho Meditation Resort
Guesthouse..........................31 D2
Samrat Hotel............................32 C2
Taj Blue Diamond....................33 D2

EATING
Akshaya..................................(see 25)
Flags.......................................34 C2
Mystic Masala.........................(see 33)
The Place: Touche the Sizzler...35 C3

DRINKING
Café Mahanaaz......................36 C3
German Bakery........................37 D1
Juice World.............................38 C3
Prems......................................39 D1
Thousand Oaks........................40 C4

ENTERTAINMENT
Inox..41 C3
Leather Lounge.......................42 C3

SHOPPING
Bombay Store.........................43 C3
Either Or................................(see 6)
Fabindia.................................44 C2
More Mischief........................(see 6)

TRANSPORT
Air India.................................(see 9)
Air Sahara..............................(see 6)
Bright Travels.........................45 C3
Indian Airlines........................46 B2
Jet Airways.............................47 C2
PMT Depot.............................48 B2
Pune Train Station Stand.........49 B2
Shivaji Nagar Bus stand...........50 A2
Swargate Bus stand................51 A5
Taxi Stand..............................52 C2

OTHER
Architect College Bus Stop......53 A4
Sohrab Hall...........................(see 6)

INFORMATION
American Express......................1 C3
Citibank ATM............................2 C2
Citibank ATM............................3 C4
Citibank ATM............................4 D1
Computology Systems..............5 C3
Crossword.................................6 C2
Cyber-Net.................................7 D2
Dishnet Hub Internet Centre....8 C3
HSBC Bank ATM.......................9 C2
ICICI ATM...............................10 C1
Main Post Office.....................11 C3
Manneys Booksellers...............12 C3
MTDC Tourist Office................13 B3
Post Office..............................14 A3
Rokshan Travels......................15 C3
Thomas Cook..........................16 C4
UTI Bank ATM........................17 C4

MAHARASHTRA

Sights & Activities

OSHO MEDITATION RESORT

The Bhagwan Rajneesh's famous **ashram** (☎ 24019999; www.osho.com; 17 Koregaon Park) is in a leafy northern suburb of Pune. Since the Bhagwan's death in 1990, it has continued to draw in manifold *sanyasins* (seekers), many of them Westerners. Facilities include a swimming pool, sauna, 'zennis' (Zen tennis) and basketball courts, a massage and beauty parlour, a bookshop, an Internet café and a boutique guesthouse (p153). The main centre for meditation and the nightly white-robed spiritual dance is the Osho Auditorium (a 'cough-free and sneeze-free zone'!). The Osho Samadhi, where the guru's ashes are kept, is also open for silent or music-accompanied meditation.

The commune is big business. Its 'Multiversity' runs a plethora of courses in meditation as well as New Age techniques. If you wish to take part in any of the courses, or even just to visit for the day to meditate you'll have to pay Rs 1150 (Rs 830 if you're under 25). This covers registration, a mandatory on-the-spot HIV test (sterile needles are used), introductory sessions and your first day's meditation pass (five days for under 25s). You'll also need two robes (one maroon and one white, from Rs 300 per robe). Meditation is then Rs 300 per day (or R1250 for five days), and you can come

and go as you please. If you want to contribute further, there's the resort's 'Work-as-Meditation' programme.

The curious can watch a video presentation at the visitor centre and take a 10-minute silent tour of the facilities (Rs 10) between 9.45am and 11.30am and 2pm and 3.30pm daily. Even if you decide not to enter the resort, it's worth checking out the placid five-hectare **Osho Teerth** gardens (admission free; to public ⏱ 6-9am & 3-6pm) behind the commune; the gardens are accessible all day for those with a meditation pass.

RAJA DINKAR KELKAR MUSEUM

This quirky **museum** (☎ 24482101; www.rajakelkar museum.com; 1377-78 Natu Baug, Bajirao Rd; admission foreigner Rs 150; ⏱ 9.30am-6pm) is one of Pune's true delights. The exhibits are the personal collection of Sri Dinkar Gangadhar (also known as Kaka Kelkar), who died in 1990. Among the 17,000 or so artworks and curios he collected over 70 years are Peshwa and other miniatures, a surreal collection of musical instruments, ornately carved doors and windows, hookah pipes and a superb collection of betel-nut cutters, adorned brass foot-scrubbers and carved wooden noodle-makers. There are plans to build a much larger home for the museum on the outskirts of Pune which would certainly enable its vast collection to be better displayed.

THE ARMANI OF ASHRAMS

Old-timers say that it ain't what it used to be. Looking at the sleek Osho Meditation Resort today it's clear to see it has moved with the times, offering everything spiritually bereft first-worlders could wish for. One wonders if Bhagwan Shree Rajneesh (1931–90), or Osho as he preferred to be called, would recognise the place.

Osho was one of India's most flamboyant 'export gurus', and undoubtedly the most controversial. He followed no particular religion or philosophy and outraged many Indians (and others) with his advocacy of sex as a path to enlightenment, earning him the epithet 'sex guru'. In 1981 Rajneesh took his curious blend of Californian pop psychology and Indian mysticism to the USA, where he set up an agricultural commune and ashram in Oregon. There, his ashram's notoriety as well as its fleet of Rolls Royces grew like weeds. Eventually, with rumours and local paranoia about the ashram's activities running amok, the Bhagwan was charged with immigration fraud, fined US$400,000 and deported to India in 1985. By 1987 he was back at the Pune ashram, where thousands of foreigners soon flocked for his nightly discourses and meditation courses.

They still come in droves. The unveiling of the capacious Osho Auditorium in 2002 also marked the alteration of the centre's name from 'Osho Commune International' to 'Osho Meditation Resort'. Prices for the 'resort' privileges are continually on the rise. Still, the ashram's popularity speaks for itself; many do find their seeking satisfied (in whatever form that may take), and Osho's grounds – whether they be ashram or resort, spiritual or indulgent – are indeed soothing, immaculate and experienced uniquely by every entering seeker.

SHANIWAR WADA

The ruins of this fortresslike **palace** (☎ 243 35597; Shivaji Rd; admission US$2; ⊙ 8am-6.30pm) stand in the old part of the city. Built in 1732, the palace of the Peshwa rulers burnt down in 1828, but the massive walls remain, as do the sturdy palace doors with their angry enemy-repelling spikes. Today there's a dull two-hectare garden inside; you might prefer to return in the evening for the hour-long **sound and light show** (Rs 25; ⊙ 8.15pm Thu-Tue) that is held here.

PATALESHVARA CAVE TEMPLE

Across the river is the curious rock-cut **Pataleshvara Cave Temple** (☎ 25535941; Jangali Maharaj Rd; ⊙ 6am-9.30pm), a small, unfinished 8th-century temple similar in style to the grander Elephanta Island one. It's an active temple, with people coming here for worship or simply to relax in the gardens. In front of the excavation is a circular Nandi *mandapa* (pillared pavilion). Adjacent is the Jangali Maharaj (Lord of the Jungle) **temple** (⊙ 6am-10pm), dedicated to a Hindu ascetic who died here in 1818.

TRIBAL CULTURAL MUSEUM

About 1.5km east of the Pune train station, this is an excellent **museum** (☎ 26362071; 28 Queens Garden, Richardson Rd; admission foreigner Rs 10; ⊙ 10am-6pm) which documents the cultures of Maharashtran Adivasi communities, particularly the inhabitants of the Sahyadri and Gondwana regions. It displays a vibrant collection of papier-mâché festival masks, Warli paintings and other absorbing relics.

GANDHI NATIONAL MEMORIAL

Across the Mula River in Yerwada is the grand **Aga Khan Palace**, set in 6.5 hectares of gardens, where you'll also find this fine **memorial** (☎ 26680250; Ahmednagar Rd; admission Indian/foreigner Rs 5/100; ⊙ 9am-5.45pm) to Gandhi. After the Mahatma delivered his momentous Quit India resolution in Bombay in 1942, the British interned him and other leaders of India's Independence movement here for nearly two years. Both Kasturba Gandhi, the Mahatma's wife, and Mahadoebhai Desai, his secretary for 35 years, died while imprisoned here. Their ashes are kept in memorial *samadhis* (shrines) in the gardens.

Photos and paintings exhibit moments in Gandhi's extraordinary career, but most moving are the simple details (such as a pair of sandals and a thermos) and narrative on the personal tragedies that the Mahatma underwent during this period.

GARDENS

At the **Empress Botanical Gardens** (admission Rs 5; ⊙ 6.30am-7pm) cosy couples on park benches enjoy the spots of shade from fine tropical trees. In the evening, dozens of food stalls and kiddie carnival rides are set up outside **Peshwa Park** (admission Rs 2; ⊙ 9.30am-5.30pm). Other good places to relax are **Saras Baug Gardens**, next to Peshwa Park, and **Bund Gardens**, on the banks of the Mula River.

RAMAMANI IYENGAR MEMORIAL YOGA INSTITUTE

To attended classes at this famous **institute** (☎ 25656134; www.bksiyengar.com; 1107 B/1 Hare Krishna Mandir Rd, Model Colony), around 7km northwest of the train station, you need to have been practising yoga for at least five years.

Tours

Good bus tours of Pune leave the **Pune Municipal Transport depot** (PMT; Sasson Rd; bookings ⊙ 8am-noon & 3-6pm), near the train station, at 9am daily, returning around 4.30pm (Rs 91). Covering all of Pune's major sights plus several others such as the snake park on the city's southern outskirts, they are ideal if you're in a hurry.

Sleeping

There's no shortage of accommodation in Pune with many cheap hotels clustered around the railway station. In Koregaon Park, convenient for the Osho Meditation Resort, many family homes rent out to both short- and long-term guests. Rooms with shared bathrooms start at Rs 150, while rooms with private bathrooms are at least Rs 250. Quality varies widely, so check out a few before deciding. For longer-term stays you can negotiate a room in one of these places from Rs 3000 to 10,000 per month.

BUDGET

National Hotel (☎ 26125054; 14 Sasson Rd; d/tr Rs 350/400, s/d/tr cottages Rs 300/350/400) Opposite the train station is this Bahai-run, old colonial mansion with verandas and high ceilings set in a pleasing garden. The rooms are lofty and the cottages have little porches.

Hotel Surya Villa (☎ 26124501; www.hotelsurya villa.com; 294/1 Koregaon Park; s/d Rs 700/800, d with AC Rs 1000; 🔀) One of the better budget hotel options in the Koregaon Park area, the Surya Villa offers clean, spacious rooms with TVs, and has a café.

Grand Hotel (☎ 26360728; MG Rd; s with shared bathroom Rs 200, d with private bathroom Rs 450) You wouldn't want to linger long in one of the Grand's single 'cabins' (beds separated by partition walls), and the double rooms are bare. The hotel's ambience, however, is amicable and it has its own beer and juice bars, patio and restaurant.

Also recommended:
Happy Home (☎ 26122933; 294 Koregaon Park; s/d Rs 300/400)

MIDRANGE
All hotels listed have a noon checkout and accept credit cards.

Samrat Hotel (☎ 26137964; thesamrathotel@vsnl .net; 17 Wilson Garden; s/d Rs 900/1100, with AC Rs 1100/1300; 🔀) This hotel, with spotless, agreeable rooms, is superb value. Service is professional and complimentary airport pick-up is offered.

Hotel Ashirwad (☎ 26128585; hotelash@vsnl.com; 16 Sadhu Vaswani Rd; s/d from Rs 1600/1950; dishes Rs 40-70; 🔀) An appealing modern hotel across the road from the station and with rooms so clean they're gleaming. The rates include breakfast and its restaurant, Akshaya, is a worthy choice serving Punjabi, Mughlai and Chinese vegetarian fare.

Hotel Sunderban (☎ 26124949; www.tghotels .com; 19 Koregaon Park; d with shared bathroom from Rs 700, with private bathroom with/without AC from Rs 1300/1000) Next to the Osho Resort is this well-kept heritage property set in gardens with a wide variety of clean rooms; the more modern studios (Rs 2900) come with their own fully equipped kitchens. Rates are slashed by 30% between 1 May and 30 September. It also has a branch of the stylish Barista espresso bar.

Hotel Ritz (☎ 26122995; fax 26136191; 6 Sadhu Vaswani Path; d with/without AC Rs 1550/1250; 🔀) The exterior of this heritage hotel, complete with three geese in a tiny pond, is more appealing than the somewhat worn rooms. All rooms have TVs and the cheaper ones are at the back next to the garden restaurant, which serves good Gujarati thalis (Rs 120).

If your visit to Pune is to attend the Osho Meditation Resort (p151), its stylish **guesthouse** (s/d Rs 1600/1800; 🔀) is worth considering.

TOP END
Taj Blue Diamond (☎ 4025555; bluediamond.pune@ tajhotels.com; 11 Koragaon Rd; d from US$140; 🔀 💻 📞) An elegant, top-class business hotel with all the trimmings from courteous staff in saris to pleasantly decorated rooms and a stylish selection of restaurants.

Le Meridien (☎ 26050505; www.lemeridien -pune.com; RBM Rd; d from US$150; 🔀 💻 📞) This sumptuous and grandiose hotel designed in Mughal and Rajput styles offers compact, comfortable rooms. Assets include three restaurants, two bars, a nightclub, gym and a small rooftop pool (open to nonguests for Rs 350 per day).

Eating
Pune has some outstanding place to eat. Unless otherwise mentioned the following are open noon to 3pm and 7pm to 11pm daily.

RESTAURANTS
Flags (☎ 26141617; G2 Metropole, Bund Garden Rd; mains Rs 75-200; 🔀) With possibly Pune's longest menu, running the global gamut from cauliflower Mongolian to *yakisoba* (fried Japanese-style noodles), the highly popular Flags has something to please practically everyone, all wrapped up in a comfy contemporary interior.

> **SOMETHING SPECIAL**
>
> **Mystic Masala** (☎ 4025555; Taj Blue Diamond, 11 Koregaon Rd; mains Rs 35-650; ⏰ 7-11.30pm; 🔀) The cheesy warrior waxworks are the only odd note amid the warm contemporary design of this exemplary Indian restaurant. It specialises in local Peshwa cuisine, which in dishes such as *kothimbir wadi* (crispy disks of deep fried lentils), *komdi saar* (chicken, coriander and lemon soup) and *bharleli wangi* (stuffed brinjals) have subtle, delicate flavours. Live Indian classical music every night and professional service make this one of Pune's top dining experiences.

Silk Route (☎ 26135793; 357/1 Pringle Corner, Cosmos Bank Lane, Koregaon Park; mains Rs 140-500; 🍴) One of the best options from among the several oriental cuisine restaurants in town. The purple draped décor looks particularly fetching in the garden patio at night but, if it's too hot, there's an AC section and a chic bar too.

Shisha Café (☎ 26818885; ABC Farms, Koregaon Park; mains Rs 100-180; 🕙 10.30am-1.30pm) One of the most appealing dining options at the ABC Farms compound is this jazz café/bar raised above the ground and sheltered by a soaring *atap* (a type of thatching) roof. It specialises in Iranian food which is good and goes well with the hookah pipes (Rs 125).

The Place: Touche the Sizzler (☎ 26134632; 7 Moledina Rd; mains Rs 120-200; 🍴) As its name suggests this long-running place specialises in sizzlers, but it also offers Indian, tandoori, seafood and Continental dishes.

At the eastern end of North Main Rd in Koregaon Park are clustered some particularly good pickings:

Arthur's Theme (☎ 26132710; 🍴) A stylish place offering French cuisine.

Kolya (☎ 309074896; 🍴) Hyderabadi dishes complimented with an extraordinary glitzy interior.

Masala Spice (☎ 26136293; 🕙 11am-11pm; 🍴) A colourful place serving Southeast Asian food.

Drinking & Entertainment
Pune has a handful of lively pubs and clubs that bustle with the college crowd and some foreigners. Goa-style parties and raves occasionally blast off outside of Pune. Ask around Koregaon Park for the latest.

CAFES
Café Mahanaaz (Sterling Centre, 12 MG Rd; meals Rs 15-25) This no-nonsense café and bakery popular with locals. It's good for breakfast – if you've forgotten what real toast tastes like, this is the place.

Juice World (2436/B East Street Camp; 🕙 8am-1am) As well as delicious fresh fruit juices and shakes this casual café with outdoor seating serves inexpensive snacks such as pizza and *pav bhaji* (spiced vegetables and bread) for around Rs 30.

Prems (North Main Rd, Koregaon Park; mains Rs 40-180; 🕙 8.30am-11.30pm) In a leafy courtyard tucked away from the main road, Prems is a relaxing place to hang out over a drink or light meal. It also serves beer and wine.

German Bakery (North Main Rd, Koregaon Park; dishes Rs 50-80, cakes Rs 10-25; 🕙 6am-11.30pm) Part and parcel of the Koregaon Park scene, this long-running café makes good coffee, great cakes and healthy food. Fruits and vegetables are sterilised, and water used for beverages is purified.

BARS & CLUBS
Leather Lounge (☎ 24012001; 2nd fl, Amba Complex, 320 MG Rd; 🕙 7.30pm-1.30am) There's a great vibe at this medium-sized bar/club, one of Pune's best places to party. It gets packed out with a lively, smartly dressed crowd Wednesday, Friday and Saturday nights when you have to buy Rs 500 of drinks vouchers as entry.

Ola (☎ 30921906; 35/36 ABC Farms, Koregaon Park; 🕙 noon-5pm & 7pm-1am) At the entrance to ABC Farms is this stylish, vaguely Mediterranean bar that gets going late in the evenings. There's a Rs 300 cover charge on Wednesday, Friday and Saturday. Also on the ABC Farms plot check out the **Jazz Garden** (☎ 26817412; closed Mon) for live music on most Wednesday and Saturday nights starting at 9pm.

Thousand Oaks (☎ 26343194; thousandoaks@vsnl.com; 2417 East St; admission Fri & Sat Rs 200) This cosy pub-style bar, with DJ-driven music ranging from hard rock to techno, has an outdoor terrace on which to cool down.

Inox (☎ 26050101; Queen's Garden Rd; adult Rs 130) is a state-of-the-art four-screen multiplex showing both Hindi- and English-language films.

Shopping
Pune has some good shopping options, particularly for modern Indian clothing: try **Either Or** (24/25 Sohrab Hall, 21 Sasson Rd; 🕙 10.30am-8pm, closed Thu), **Fabindia** (Sakar 10, Sasson Rd; 🕙 10am-7.45pm) or **More Mischief** (34/35 Sohrab Hall, 21 Sasson Rd; 🕙 10am-9pm, closed Mon).

The **Bombay Store** (322 MG Rd; 🕙 10.30am-8.30pm Mon-Sat, 11am-8pm Sun) is best for general souvenirs.

Getting There & Away
AIR
Airline offices in Pune include:
Air India (☎ 26128190; Hermes Kunj, 4 Mangaldas Rd)
Air Sahara (☎ 26059003; 131 Sohrab Hall, 21 Sasson Rd)
Indian Airlines (☎ 140 or 141; 39 Dr B Ambedkar Rd)
Jet Airways (☎ 26137181; 243 Century Arcade, Narangi Bung Rd)

Indian Airlines flies twice daily to Delhi (US$230, two hours) and daily to Bangalore (US$155, 2½ hours), Goa (US$90 45 minutes) and Mumbai (US$80, 30 minutes). Jet Airways flies twice daily to Mumbai (US$60, 30 minutes), and daily to Bangalore (US$155, 1½ hours), Chennai (US$192, 2½ hours), Delhi (US$231, two hours) and Kolkata US$285, 2½ hours). Air Sahara flies twice daily to Delhi (US$231, two hours) and daily to Bangalore (US$155, 1½ hours), Hyderabad (US$136, one hour) and Kolkata (US$285, 2½ hours).

BUS
Pune has three bus stands: **Pune train station stand** (☎ 26126218), for Mumbai and points south and west, including Goa, Belgaum, Kolhapur, Mahabaleshwar and Lonavla; **Shivaji Nagar bus stand** (☎ 25536970), for points north and northeast, including Ahmednagar, Aurangabad, Ahmedabad and Nasik; and **Swargate bus stand** (☎ 24441591), for Sinhagad, Bangalore and Mangalore. Deluxe buses shuttle from the train station bus stand to Dadar (Mumbai) every 15 minutes (Rs 125, four hours).

Even the better MSRTC buses (semideluxe and deluxe) are sometimes just a smidgen cheaper than private buses. Plenty of private deluxe buses head to most centres, including Panjim in Goa (Rs 250 for ordinary class, Rs 350 in sleeper, 12 hours), Nasik (Rs 180, five hours) and Aurangabad (Rs 120, six hours). Make sure you know where the bus will drop you off (going to Mumbai, for instance, some private buses get no further than Borivali). Try **Bright Travels** (☎ 26050878; Connaught Rd); its buses

depart from the service station near the roundabout.

For Mumbai and Kolhapur, the train is the wisest option.

TAXI
Long-distance shared taxis (four passengers) link up Pune with Dadar in Mumbai round the clock. They leave from the **taxi stand** (☎ 24114040) in front of Pune train station (Rs 255 per seat, AC Rs 315, three hours). A similar service runs from Shivaji Nagar train station to Nasik (Rs 250, four hours) and Aurangabad (Rs 250, four hours).

TRAIN
Pune is an important rail hub with connections to many parts of the state. The swarming **computerised booking hall** (☎ 131) is in the building to the left of the station as you face the entrance.

The *Deccan Queen*, *Sinhagad Express* and *Pragati Express* are fast commuter trains to Mumbai, taking three to four hours.

Getting Around
The airport is 8km northeast of the city. An autorickshaw there costs about Rs 50, a taxi is Rs 150.

City buses gather at the PMT depot across from Pune train station, but journeys are slower than Sunday. Useful buses include No 4 to Swargate, No 5 to Shivaji Nagar bus terminal, and No 159 to Koregoan Park.

Autorickshaws are everywhere here and, if you're lucky, the drivers will use their meters and conversion cards without much strife. Rates are Rs 7 for the first kilometre and Rs 5 per kilometre thereafter (or around

MAHARASHTRA

MAJOR TRAINS FROM PUNE

Destination	Train No & Name	Fare (Rs)	Duration (hr)	Departure
Bangalore	6529 *Udyan Exp*	345/1528	21½	11.30am
Chennai	6011 *Chennai Exp*	345/1528	22½	6.00pm
Delhi	1077 *Jhelum Exp*	437/1900	27¾	5.35pm
Hyderabad	7031 Hyderabad Exp	250/1050	13½	4.40pm
Mumbai CST	2124 *Deccan Queen*	56/280	3½	7.15am
	2028 *Shatabdi*	83/270	3	6.00pm

Shatabdi fares are chair/AC; express fares are 2nd class/chair for day trains, sleeper/2AC sleeper for overnight trains; *Deccan Queen* fares are 2nd class/chair. To calculate 1st class and other fares see p499.

five times the rate shown on the outdated meters). After dark, chances are you'll have to negotiate a fare. A ride from the Pune train station to Koregaon Park costs about Rs 20.

AROUND PUNE
Sinhagad

Scene of a victory by Shivaji's forces over those of Bijapur in 1670, Sinhagad (Lion Fort), 24km southwest of Pune, is a possible day out. The ruined fort stands on top of a steep hill cluttered with telecommunications towers and tourist stalls; the real attractions are the sweeping views and the chance for a healthy workout on the hike up from the bus stop in Sinhagad village.

If you don't want to walk, jeeps (Rs 25) are usually around to cart you to within a short stroll of the summit. The Pune city bus No 50 runs frequently to Sinhagad village from 7am until evening, leaving from either Swargate (platform 12) or the Architect College bus stop opposite Nehru Stadium (Rs 12, 45 minutes).

MAHABALESHWAR
☎ 02168 / pop 12,736 / elev 1372m

The terraced hills of Mahabaleshwar provide pleasant walks and panoramic look-

---

BERRY DELICIOUS

Mahabaleshwar and its smaller twin Panchgani, 19km east, are ripe with some of India's finest strawberries, as well as raspberries, mulberries and gooseberries.

Along the road between the two hill stations stretches some 5km of strawberry fields producing varieties such as Australian and Sweet Chandler. Planting begins after the monsoon and fruits are harvested from late November to June with the best crops coming around February. You can visit the farms and buy direct, or get them from the vendors who sit cross-legged in Mahabaleshwar's bazaar presiding over neat pyramids of berries. The vast industry also dips into fruit drinks, sweets, fudge and jam. Free factory tours are offered at **Mapro Gardens** (☎ 02168-240112; ☑ 10am-1pm & 2pm-6.30pm Wed-Mon), between Mahabaleshwar and Panchgani, as well as chance to sample the many mouthwatering products.

---

outs. Founded in 1828 by Sir John 'Boy' Malcolm, it was the summer capital of the Bombay presidency during the days of the Raj. Few vestiges of these times remain and given the tatty, commercialised centre of town today it's difficult to image how grand Mahabaleshwar once was.

The hill station virtually shuts up shop during the monsoon (from late June to mid-September), when an unbelievable 6m of rain falls. Buildings are clad with *kulum* grass to stave off damage from the torrential downpours. After things calm down, the reward is abundantly green landscapes.

Mahabaleshwar's charms are no secret, and the town and trails are brimful of people during the peak periods of summer school holidays (April to June), Christmas and Diwali. To get a larger lungful of that fresh mountain air, come anytime but then.

Orientation

Most of the action is in the main bazaar (Main Rd, also called Dr Sabane Rd) – a 200m strip of ice-cream and *chikki* parlours, video games, flashing lights and tacky stalls. The bus stand is at the western end. An Rs 10 entry fee is due on arrival.

Information

Mahabaleshwar has no Internet facilities.
Bank of Maharashtra (☎ 260290; Main Rd) Changes cash and travellers cheques.
MTDC tourist office (☎ 260318; Bombay Point Rd) At the MTDC Resort south of town, has crude maps but helpful staff whom you can allegedly call upon 24 hours.
State Bank of India (Masjid St) Has a 24-hour ATM.

Sights & Activities

Faded traces of the Raj persist in the dilapidated buildings and various preserved 19th-century lodges and colonial homes dotted around Mahabaleshwar. Look out for them on the way to the various viewpoints which are the town's main attraction. Fine views can be savoured from **Wilson's Point** (also known as Sunrise Point), a quiet lookout within walking distance of town, as well as **Elphinstone**, **Babington**, **Kate's** and **Lodwick Points**. The latter is dedicated to Peter Lodwick, the first European to set foot in Mahabaleshwar in 1824.

The sunset views at **Bombay Point** are stunning; you won't be the only one who thinks so. The spell-binding **Arthur's Seat**, 9km from

Mahabaleshwar, looks out over a sheer drop of 600m to the Konkan coastal strip. Attractive waterfalls around Mahabaleshwar include **Chinaman's**, **Dhobi's** and **Lingmala Falls**. The boathouse on **Venna Lake** (Temple Rd; boathouse 8am-8pm) rents out rowboats (Rs 160 per hour) and pedal boats (Rs 200 per hour).

The village of Old Mahabaleshwar has two ancient temples. The **Panchganga Mandir** (7am-9pm) is said to contain the springs of five rivers, including the sacred Krishna River which issues from the mouth of a sculpted cow suckling a calf. The **Mahabaleshwar Mandir** (6am-9pm) has a naturally formed lingam.

Tours

The MSRTC conducts sightseeing tours, with wheels provided by semideluxe buses. The Mahabaleshwar round (Rs 45, 4½ hours) takes in nine points plus Old Mahabaleshwar; it leaves the bus stand at 2.30pm. Alternatively, taxi drivers will fall over themselves to get you on their three-hour, 12-point tour of Mahabaleshwar's

sights for a fixed Rs 280. This amounts to a ride out to Arthur's Seat and back with a stop at Old Mahabaleshwar along the way – if the weather's good, it's well worth it. Tours are also available to the lookout points south of town (Rs 280, 2½ hours), Panchgani (Rs 300, three hours) and Pratapgad Fort (Rs 450, three hours).

Sleeping & Eating

Hotel prices are all about supply and demand in Mahabaleshwar – rates soar during peak holiday times; at other times the budget and midrange hotels can be good value. Most of the budget places are around the main bazaar near the bus stand, but dozens of resort-style lodges (most offering full board) are scattered around the village.

New Hill Retreat (☎ 261361; fax 261363; 187 School Mohalla, Murray Peth Rd; d low/high season Rs 500/1100) A short walk from the heart of the main bazaar, this is a smart choice, boasting spotless modern rooms and eager-to-please staff. Meals are included in the high season. Its exterior has a touch of European villa.

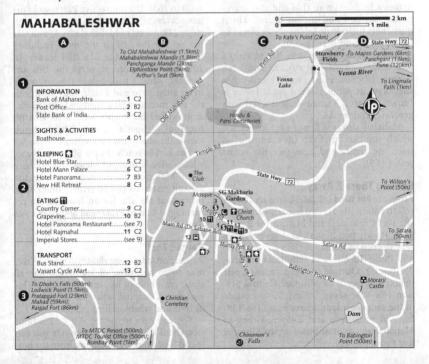

MAHABALESHWAR

INFORMATION
Bank of Maharashtra...................**1** C2
Post Office...............................**2** B2
State Bank of India.....................**3** C2

SIGHTS & ACTIVITIES
Boathouse.................................**4** D1

SLEEPING
Hotel Blue Star..........................**5** C2
Hotel Mann Palace......................**6** C3
Hotel Panorama.........................**7** B3
New Hill Retreat.........................**8** C3

EATING
Country Corner..........................**9** C2
Grapevine................................**10** B2
Hotel Panorama Restaurant......(see 7)
Hotel Rajmahal.........................**11** C2
Imperial Stores.......................(see 9)

TRANSPORT
Bus Stand................................**12** B2
Vasant Cycle Mart.....................**13** C2

Hotel Panorama (☎ 260404; fax 261234; 28 MG Rd; r low/high season from Rs 850/1200; meals R60-100; 🍴 🍷) The best upmarket option, this is a friendly place with comfortable rooms and all the mod cons. The pool comes with its own waterfall and paddleboats. Its pure-veg restaurant is one of the best in town and certainly has the quirkiest interior design.

MTDC Resort (☎ 260318; fax 260300; d low/high season from Rs 325/650) A couple of kilometres southwest of the town centre in a quiet location not far from Bombay Point, this is one of the better budget options particularly in high season.

Hotel Mann Palace (☎ 261778; d from Rs 500), next door to New Hill Retreat, is a respectable place, and **Hotel Blue Star** (☎ 260678; 114 Main Rd; d/tr Rs 250/350) is also worth considering (although its high season prices are insane).

Hotel Rajmahal (80 Main Rd; meals Rs 25-60) This is a buzzing, pure-vegetarian pad frequented by locals for its satisfying thalis (Rs 40) and other South Indian and Punjabi eats.

Grapevine (Masjid Rd; dishes Rs 80-140) A stylish outfit with hip music and friendly staff that makes a healthy go at Thai and also serves pastas, seafood and Indian dishes. Thirst quenchers include nonalcoholic coolers (Rs 70) and icy-cold beer (Rs 60).

Country Corner (Imperial Stores; Main Rd; snacks & dishes Rs 40-95) churns out chicken and lamb burgers (Rs 50), pizza (Rs 95) and other snacks on its petite, relaxed patio. Inside is Imperial Stores, a small shop stocked with groceries and books.

Mahabaleshwar is famous for its berries, which you can buy fresh (in season) or as juice, ice cream and jams (see the boxed text, p156).

Getting There & Away

From the **bus stand** (☎ 260254) frequent buses roll to Satara (Rs 31, two hours), Panchgani (Rs 10, 30 minutes) and Mahad (for Raigad Fort; Rs 31, two hours), and several daily services run to Kolhapur (Rs 94, five hours) and Pune (Rs 69/94 in semideluxe/deluxe, 3½ hours). Outside of the monsoon, one deluxe bus heads to Mumbai Central Station (Rs 178, seven hours). Also outside of the monsoon semideluxe buses (Rs 139) leave at 9am, 1pm and 2.45pm. Going to Mahabaleshwar, state buses depart Mumbai five times per day.

Private agents in the bazaar book luxury buses to destinations within Maharashtra or to Goa (Rs 375/425 in seat/sleeper, 12 hours via Surul). They all quote similar prices and times, but inquire where they intend to drop you off. None of the luxury buses to Mumbai (Rs 180/250 in low/high season, 6½ hours) go into the city – the furthest you'll get is Borivali. Private buses to Pune (Rs 150) will bid you adieu at Swargate.

Getting Around

Heaps of taxis and Maruti vans hang around near the bus stand to take you around the main viewpoints or to Panchgani. For trips around town, the minimum charge is Rs 30 (for up to 2km).

The light traffic makes cycling a sensible option, though take care along the narrow lanes with their blind corners if you ride to the viewpoints. Bikes can be hired from **Vasant Cycle Mart** (Main Rd; 🕑 8am-9pm) for Rs 10 an hour.

AROUND MAHABALESHWAR
Pratapgad Fort

Built in 1656, the impressive Pratapgad Fort (admission free; 🕑 7am-7pm) dominates a high ridge 24km west of Mahabaleshwar and was the setting for one of the most enduring legends involving the Maratha leader. In 1659 Shivaji agreed to meet the Bijapuri general, Afzal Khan, below the fort walls in an attempt to end a stalemate. However, the two men arrived armed and Shivaji disembowelled his enemy with a set of iron *waghnakh* (tiger's claws). Khan's tomb marks the site of the encounter.

The fort is reached by a 500-step climb, which affords brilliant views. To get here from Mahabaleshwar, you can take the 9.30am state bus (Rs 50 return, one hour). It waits at the site for an hour before returning. A taxi to Pratapgad and back costs Rs 450.

Raigad Fort

Raigad Fort (Indian/foreigner Rs 5/US$5; 🕑 8am-5.30pm), over 80km northwest of Mahabaleshwar, all alone on a hilltop, has stunning views. This was Shivaji's capital, where he was crowned in 1648 and where he died in 1680.

You can hike to the top – it's a 2½-hour steep haul covering 1460 steps. Or you can spend four minutes ascending from the bottom of the hill via a smooth, scenic **ropeway** (☎ 02145-274831; ☼ 8.30am-6.30pm). The return ticket (Rs 110) includes a guide and entry into a small museum. From the drop-off at the southern end of the fort, a little trolley (Rs 10) will cart you over a small hill or you can walk.

Raigad is best reached from Mahad (Rs 13, 45 minutes).

KOLHAPUR
☎ 0231 / pop 485,183 / elev 550m
Kolhapur was once the capital of an important Maratha state, but it's more famous these days for producing some of India's finest wrestlers and trendiest leather chappals (sandals). There's a small-town charm to the place, particularly the old quarter around the Mahalaxmi Temple, and the maharaja's 'new' palace is certainly worth seeing if you've a day to spare.

In August the **Matharaj Naag Panchami**, a snake-worshipping festival, is held here and in Pune.

Orientation
The old town around the Mahalaxmi Temple is around 3km southwest of the bus and train stations, while the 'new' palace is a similar distance to north. Rankala Lake, a popular spot for evening strolls and the location of the Hotel Shalini Palace, is 5km southwest of the stations.

Information
Ajab (Bhausinghji Rd; ☼ 9am-8.30pm Sun-Fri) A small selection of English-language novels and a Marathi map of the town (Rs 20).
Internet Zone (Kedar Complex, Station Rd; per hr Rs 20; ☼ 8am-midnight) Internet access.
MTDC tourist office (☎ 2652935; Assembly Rd; ☼ 10am-5.45pm Mon-Sat) On the way to the maharaja's palace, opposite the Collector's Office.
State Bank of India (☎ 2660735; Udyamnagar) A Rs 15 autorickshaw ride southwest of the train station near Hutatma Park. Deals in foreign exchange.
UTI Bank (Station Rd) Has a 24-hour ATM just west of Hotel International.

Sights
SHREE CHHATRAPATI SHAHU MUSEUM
The maharaja's 'new' palace, completed in 1881, houses this extraordinary **museum** (☎ 2538060; admission Rs 24; ☼ 9.15am-12.30pm & 2.15-6pm), one of the most bizarre collections

of memorabilia in the country. The building, worthy of a visit in its own right, was designed by 'Mad' Charles Mant, the British architect who fashioned the Indo-Saracenic style of colonial architecture, and is a cross between a Victorian train station and the Addams Family mansion.

The palace contains a mind-boggling array of the old maharaja's possessions, including many reminders of his passion for killing wild animals. One particularly eerie room resembles a macabre natural history exhibition with stuffed heads and/or bodies of a variety of animals, including oddities like a pangolin, oryx, gnu and dik-dik!

Other Mant-designed buildings in Kolhapur include the attractive old **Town Hall**, which now houses a dull museum.

OLD TOWN
Dominating the old town, the lively and colourful **Mahalaxmi Temple** (☼ 5am-10.30pm) is dedicated to the goddess Amba Bai. Of particular interest is the carved ceiling of the columned *mandapa*.

Nearby in the grounds of the Old Palace (the former home of the maharaja's family), the **Bhavani Mandap** (Shivaji Rd; ☼ 6am-8pm) is dedicated to the goddess Bhavani.

Kolhapur is famed for the calibre of its wrestlers and at the **Motibag Thalim**, a courtyard beside the entrance to the Bhavani Mandap, you can watch young athletes train (☼ 7-8.30am & 4-6pm Fri-Wed) in a muddy pit.

Professional matches are held in the **Kasbagh Maidan**, a red-earth arena in a natural sunken stadium a short walk south of Motibag Thalim, where you can experience a big match during the season (June to December). Events are announced in local papers, so ask around if you're here then.

CHANDRAKANT MANDARE MUSEUM
One of the most pleasant surprises of Kolhapur is this small, well-maintained **gallery** (☎ 2525256; Rajarampuri, 7th Lane; admission Rs 3; ☼ 10.30am-1pm & 1.30-5.30pm Tue-Sun). Dedicated to actor and artist Chandrakant Mandare (1913–2001), it houses stills of his movies as well as his fine paintings and sketches.

Sleeping & Eating
The main hotel and restaurant area is around the square opposite the bus stand,

MAHARASHTRA

10 to 15 minutes' walk east of the centre of town and the train station.

Hotel Sony Lodging (☎ 2658585; Mahalaxmi Chambers; s with shared bathroom Rs 150, s/d with private bathroom Rs 225/275) This is one of the best of a handful of budget options on the square. Its cheaper singles are closet-sized but tidy. All rooms have TVs, and hot water in the morning. Checkout is 24 hours.

Hotel Tourist (☎ 2650421; kpr_tourist@sancharnet .in; Station Rd; s/d/tr Rs 340/425/500, s/d with AC from Rs 600/650; ✢) A few minutes' walk east of the bus stand is this well-managed hotel offering cheerful rooms with TVs and phones. It also has a reasonable restaurant and bar.

Hotel International (☎ 2536641; fax 2536644; 517 A1 Shivaji Park; s/d from Rs 450/550, with AC Rs 800/850; meals Rs 55-100; ✢) A good-value hotel, with comfy rooms and a positive ambience. The friendly staff provide spot-on room service. Its Harvest Garden Bar & Restaurant has an excellent, varied pure-vegetarian menu and a garden setting. The veg sizzler (Rs 85) is delightful.

Hotel Panchshil (☎ 2537517; hotelpanchshil@ hotmail.com; 517 A2 Shivaji Park; s/d Rs 700/775, with AC Rs 900/975; ✢ 💻) Big, plainly decorated and clean rooms are on offer at this professionally run hotel.

Hotel Shalini Palace (☎ 2630401; fax 2630407; Rankala Lake; standard s/d Rs 1250/1400, top ste Rs 3000; meals Rs 60-120; ✢) Close by Rankala Lake, this hotel is in the maharaja's old summer palace, built in the 1930s. Huge rooms, with marble balconies and four-poster beds, hint at regal glamour, but the overall atmosphere is somewhat soulless. However, the hotel's Darbar Restaurant is a splendid place to dine. Indian mains can be accompanied by a bottle of Indian red (Rs 450) if you wish.

Surabhi (Hotel Sayhadri Bldg; snacks & mains Rs 10-25) This eatery is one of those clustered around the bus stand, and almost moves it's so busy. The crowds come for its thalis (Rs 25), Kolhapuri snacks such as *misal* (a spicy snack not unlike *bhelpuri*; Rs 10) and lassi (Rs 10).

There's a well-stocked supermarket, **Shetkari Bazaar** (☎ 2530055; ✢ 8.30am-8.30pm Sun-Fri), across from the Old Palace.

Getting There & Around

Rickshaws are abundant in Kolhapur, most drivers using their outdated meters; multiply the meter reading by four to figure the fare owed.

From the **bus stand** (☎ 2650620) services head regularly to Pune (Rs 128 semideluxe, 5½ hours), Mahabaleshwar (Rs 88, five hours) and Ratnagiri (Rs 61, four hours), as well as to Belgaum (Rs 45, 2½ hours) and Bijapur (Rs 84, four hours). For popular longer hauls your body will be happier on a deluxe private bus. Most of the private bus agents are on the western side of the square at Mahalaxmi Chambers, just across from the bus stand. AC overnight services head to Mumbai (Rs 250/450 in seat/sleeper, nine hours) and Aurangabad (Rs 270, 10 hours), and non-AC overnights to Panaji (Rs 150, 5½ hours) and Bangalore (seat/sleeper Rs 300/450, 14 hours).

The **train station** (☎ 2654389) is 10 minutes' walk west of the bus stand towards the centre of town. Three daily expresses, including the 10.50pm *Sahyadri Express*, zoom to Mumbai (Rs 164/734 in sleeper/2AC, 13 hours) via Pune (Rs 104/477, eight hours). The *Rani Chennamma Express* embarks daily for Bangalore (Rs 239/1072, 17¼ hours).

Goa

It's easy to see why Goa is so appealing to travellers. The sun-kissed, palm-fringed beaches of the former Portuguese enclave are justly famous, as is Goa's renowned party scene. But apart from this, Goa has a character quite distinct from the rest of India. Roman Catholicism remains a major religion, skirts far outnumber saris, and Goans display an easy-going tropical indulgence, humour and civility. Whitewashed churches, paddy fields, coconut-palm groves and crumbling forts guarding rocky capes make up the Goan landscape. Markets are lively, colourful affairs and there are feasts and festivities throughout the year.

Goa splits into three general districts: north, south and central Goa. North Goa has the state capital of Panaji (Panjim), the former capital of Old Goa with its fascinating churches and cathedrals, the market town of Mapusa and a string of beaches running right up the coast to Maharashtra. This is where the party crowd settles. With generally less tourist development, south Goa has more of a laid-back feel than the north. The beaches include travellers' centres such as Colva and Benaulim, a sprinkling of upmarket resorts and the picture-perfect Palolem. Central Goa takes in the inland town of Ponda, which is surrounded by spice plantations, as well the Dudhsagar Falls and several of Goa's wildlife sanctuaries.

The Portuguese influence lingers on, notably in the state's unique architectural heritage. In recent years, Goans have taken to restoring decaying mansions. Explore Goa – preferably on a motorbike or moped – to discover these grand houses nestling amid the lush foliage of the countryside. It's proof that Goa offers so much more than sand, sea and partying – although that is reason enough alone to visit this supremely laid-back state.

HIGHLIGHTS

- Wander the picturesque lanes of the old Portuguese quarter of **Panaji** (Panjim; p167)
- Explore the magnificent cathedrals of **Old Goa** (p176), the fallen city that once rivalled Lisbon
- Haggle for souvenirs at the colourful Wednesday flea market and then watch the sunset at **Anjuna** (p186)
- Imagine the rich colonial life in the grand mansions of **Chandor** (p195) or at the architecture museum in **Torda** (p178)
- Relax under coconut palms at **Palolem** (p200), Goa's most idyllic beach
- Hire a moped or motorbike and explore Goa at your own pace (p167)

History

In the 3rd century BC Goa formed part of the Mauryan empire. Later it was ruled by the Satavahanas of Kolhapur and eventually passed to the Chalukyas of Badami from AD 580 to 750.

Goa fell to the Muslims for the first time in 1312, but the invaders were forced out in 1370 by Harihara I of the Vijayanagar empire, whose capital was at Hampi. During the next 100 years Goa's harbours were important landing places for ships carrying Arabian horses to Hampi for the Vijayanagar cavalry.

Blessed as it is by natural harbours and wide rivers, Goa was the ideal base for the seafaring Portuguese, who arrived in 1510 aiming to control the spice route from the East; Jesuit missionaries led by St Francis Xavier arrived in 1542. For a while, Portuguese control was limited to a small area around Old Goa, but by the middle of the 16th century it had expanded to include the provinces of Bardez and Salcete.

The Marathas (the central Indian people who controlled much of India at various times) almost vanquished the Portuguese in the late 18th century and there was a brief occupation by the British during the Napoleonic Wars in Europe. However, it was not until 1961, when the Indian army marched into Goa, that Portuguese rule finally ended on the subcontinent.

Today, Goa has India's highest per-capita income, with farming, fishing, tourism and iron-ore mining forming the basis of its economy.

Climate

The monsoon hits Goa between June and the end of September; many places close up shop during this time. From late October to February the climate is near perfect, the humidity rising from March to the start of the monsoon.

Information

The **Goa Tourism Development Corporation** (GTDC; www.goa-tourism.com), commonly known as Goa Tourism, has branches in Panaji (p171), Margao (p193) and at Dabolim Airport (Goa's airport, 29km south of Panaji). You can also pick up information on the state from the Government of India tourist office in Panaji (p171).

FAST FACTS

- Population: 1.34 million
- Area: 3701 sq km
- Capital: Panaji (Panjim)
- Main languages: Konkani, Marathi, English and Hindi
- Telephone area code: ☎ 0832
- When to go: October to March

ACCOMMODATION

Accommodation prices in Goa are based on high, middle (shoulder) and low seasons. The high season is mid-December to late January, the middle periods are October to mid-December and February to June, and the low season is July to September (the monsoon season). Unless otherwise stated, prices quoted in this chapter are high-season rates. There's a fourth season, when some hotel prices rise again, sometimes to ludicrous heights, over the peak Christmas period from around 22 December to 3 January.

Few places have 24-hour checkout – most are noon checkout but many are 9am or 10am, so check first before sleeping in.

Activities

Water sports such as **parasailing**, **jet-skiing** and **windsurfing** are available on the beaches at Candolim (p180), Calangute and Baga (p183) and Colva (p197). You can try **paragliding** at Arambol (p191) and Anjuna (p187). Although the waters off Goa aren't crystal clear, there are three **scuba-diving** outfits offering boat dives and PADI (Professional Association of Diving Instructors) courses: the very professional Barracuda Diving is based at the Goa Marriott Resort in Miramar (p174); Goa Diving is in Bogmalo (p196); and Goa Dive Center is in Baga (p183).

Boat trips to spot dolphins, go fishing or cruise the backwaters are also available from most beaches, including Arambol (p191) and Palolem (p200) – the boat owners will probably find you. An interesting day trip is to visit one of the **spice plantations** near Ponda (p202), where you get a tour and lunch for around Rs 300. You can go by yourself but most tour operators offer

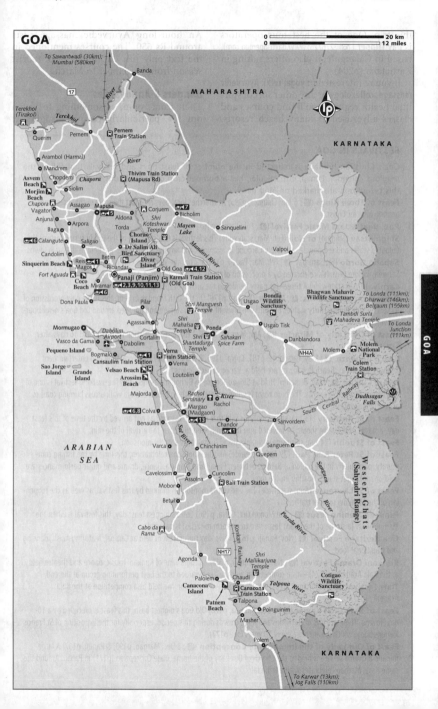

GOA

Scale: 0 — 20 km / 0 — 12 miles

To Sawantwadi (30km); Mumbai (580km)

MAHARASHTRA

KARNATAKA

Terekhol (Tirakol)
Terekhol
Querim
Pernem
Banda
17
Arambol (Harmal)
Mandrem
Chopdem
Asvem Beach
Morjim Beach
Chapora Vagator
Siolim
Chapora
Thivim Train Station (Mapusa Rd)
Pernem Train Station
River
River
Anjuna
Baga
Assagao
Mapusa
Corjuem
Bicholim
7
Calangute
6
Arpora
Aldona
Torda
Shri Koteshwar Temple
Chorao Island
Mayem Lake
Sanquelim
Candolim
Saligao
Betim
Dr Salim Ali Bird Sanctuary
Mandovi River
Valpoi
Sinquerim Beach
Reis Magos
1
Ribandar
Divar Island
Old Goa
4,12
Fort Aguada
Coco Beach
6
Panaji (Panjim)
2,3,9,10,11,13
Karmali Train Station (Old Goa)
Bhagwan Mahavir Wildlife Sanctuary
Miramar
Bondla Wildlife Sanctuary
To Londa (111km); Dharwar (146km); Belgaum (155km)
Dona Paula
Pilar
Agassaim
Shri Manguesh Temple
Usgao
Tambdi Surla Mahadeva Temple
To Londa Junction (111km)
Mormugao
Dabolim Airport
Cortalim
Shri Mahalsa Temple
Ponda
Usgao Tisk
NH4A
Molem
Molem National Park
Vasco da Gama
Dabolim
Shri Shantadurga Temple
Sahakari Spice Farm
Danblandora
Colem Train Station
Pequeno Island
Bogmalo
Cansaulim Train Station
1
Verna Train Station
Verna
Sao Jorge Island
Grande Island
Velsao Beach
Arossim Beach
Loutolim
South Central Railway
Dudhsagar Falls
Majorda
Rachol Seminary
Rachol
Zuari River
Colva
6,8
Margao (Madgaon)
13
Chandor
1
Sanvordem
Benaulim
Sal River
ARABIAN SEA
Varca
Chinchinim
Sanguem
Quepem
Western Ghats (Sahyadri Range)
Cavelossim
Assolna
Cuncolim
Bali Train Station
Sanguem River
Mobor
Betul
Parede River
Cabo da Rama
NH17
Shri Mallikarjuna Temple
Konkan Railway
Agonda
Talpona River
Cotigao Wildlife Sanctuary
Palolem
Chaudi
Canacona Island
Canacona Train Station
Patnem Beach
Talpona
Poinguinim
Masher
Polem

KARNATAKA

To Karwar (13km); Jog Falls (110km)

GOA

this trip. One of the best tour operators is **Day Tripper** (☎ 2276726; www.daytrippergoa.com), based in Calangute; it also offers rafting in Karnataka (p204).

If you're interested in **yoga**, **reiki**, **Ayurvedic massage**, **reflexology** or any other sort of spiritual health regime, you'll find courses and classes advertised at many beach resorts.

An hour-long Ayurvedic massage costs around Rs 650. The courses mentioned in the text only run during the peak tourist season from November to March.

Dangers & Annoyances

Theft from rooms is something to watch out for, particularly on party nights at

---

FESTIVALS IN GOA

Goa's Christian heritage is reflected in the number of feast days and festivals that follow the religious calendar. Panaji, in particular, has a bumper crop of nonreligious festivals. Festivals in this boxed text are marked on Map p163.

Feast of Three Kings (❶ ; 6 Jan; Chandor, p195) At churches local boys re-enact the story of the three kings bearing gifts for Christ.

Pop, Beat & Jazz Music Festival (❷ ; Feb; Panaji, p167)

Shigmotsav (Shigmo) of Holi (Feb/Mar; statewide) This festival is Goa's version of the Hindu spring festival Holi. Coloured water and red powder are thrown around at everyone and anyone and parades are held in the main towns.

Sabado Gordo (Fat Saturday; ❸ ; Feb/Mar; Panaji, p167) Part of the statewide Carnival, this festival is held on the Saturday before Lent. It's celebrated by a procession of floats and raucous street partying.

Carnival (Mar; statewide) A three-day party heralding the arrival of spring.

Procession of All Saints (❹ ; Mar/Apr; Old Goa, p176) On the fifth Monday in Lent, this is the only procession of its sort outside Rome. Thirty statues of saints are brought out from storage and paraded around Old Goa's neighbouring villages.

Feast of Our Lady of Miracles (❺ ; Apr; Mapusa, p178) A Hindu and Christian feast day held 16 days after Easter.

Beach Bonanza (❻ ; May; Calangute, p181, Colva, p196, & Miramar, p172) Several food and entertainment festivals, known as 'Beach Bonanzas', are held at various beach towns.

Igitun Chalne (❼ ; May; Bicholim) Held at Sirigao Temple in Bicholim province, this fire-walking festival is one of Goa's most distinctive events. The high point is when devotees of the goddess Lairaya walk across burning coals to prove their devotion.

Feast of St Anthony (13 Jun; statewide) It is said that if the monsoon has not arrived by the time of this feast day, a statue of the saint should be lowered into the family well to hasten the arrival of the rain.

Feast of St John (24 Jun; statewide) A thanksgiving for the arrival of the monsoon.

Feast of St Peter & St Paul (29 Jun; statewide) Another monsoon celebration, this time by the fishing community, particularly in the region of Bardez, between Panaji and Mapusa. Dance, drama and music performances are held on makeshift stages floating on the river.

Feast of St Lawrence (Aug; statewide) The end of the monsoon is marked by this festival, as well as the reopening of the Mandovi to river traffic.

Fama de Menino Jesus (❽ ; 2nd Mon in Oct; Colva, p196) Colva's biggest feast day, this festival is when the Menino Jesus (a statue of the infant Jesus said to perform miracles) is paraded.

Goa Heritage Festival (❾ ; Nov; Panaji, p167) A two-day cultural event held at Campal, featuring music, dancing and traditional food.

Konkani Drama Festival (❿ ; Nov/Dec; Panaji, p167) A programme of Konkani music, dance and theatre held at the Kala Academy (p174)– it's a competition, with prizes awarded to the best performing group at the end.

Tiatr Festival (⓫ ; Nov; Panaji, p167) Another drama-arts programme held as a competition at the Kala Academy (p174).

Feast of St Francis Xavier (⓬ ; 3 Dec; Old Goa, p176) Old Goa's biggest bash, this feast is preceded by a 10-day Novena. There are lots of festivities and huge crowds during this period, especially for the Exposition of St Francis Xavier's body, which is held once every 10 years (see p177).

Feast of Our Lady of the Immaculate Conception (⓭ ; 8 Dec; Margao, p193, & Panaji, p167) A large fair and a church service is held at the Church of Our Lady of the Immaculate Conception (p171) in Panaji. Around the same time, Margao celebrates with a large fair.

places such as Anjuna and Vagator, or if you're renting a flimsy beach shack at Palolem. Many guesthouses and hotels provide safe deposit boxes.

Muggings have been reported in Goa, particularly in quiet, unlit lanes away from the beach. Avoid walking alone at night unless there are plenty of people around.

Women should be aware that it is not safe to wander about alone after dark; in the past there have been reports of rape in the area, so take appropriate precautions. Also, on the more popular beaches such as Calangute, Anjuna and Vagator there could be a degree of ogling from local men regardless of how skimpy (or not) your bathing costume is. Going topless is taboo everywhere and will certainly get you unwanted attention.

DRUGS

Acid, ecstasy, cocaine and hash – the drugs of choice for many party goers – are illegal (though still very much available) and any attempt to purchase or carry them is fraught with danger. Fort Aguada prison houses some foreigners serving lengthy sentences for drug offences, because for some time now authorities have been taking a hard line on the parties and even have an Anti-Narcotics Cell set up to deal with offenders.

Possession of even a small amount of *charas* (hashish) can mean 10 years in prison. Cases of corrupt policemen approaching hapless tourists and threatening to 'plant' drugs on them, or simply demanding a relatively large *baksheesh* (bribe) on the spot are becoming less common than in the past, but the possibility of such occurences does remain.

Food & Drink

Goans are passionate about their food and there are several local specialities, including the ubiquitous fish curry and the popular pork vindaloo. Other pork specialities include the *chourisso* (Goan sausage) and *sorpotel* (a vinegary stew made from pig liver, heart and kidneys). *Xacutí* is a spicy chicken or meat dish incorporating coconut milk and flesh. *Cafrial* and *balchao* are methods of cooking meat in a spicy sauce. *Recheiado* is fish, such as mackerel of pomfret, stuffed with a spicy red sauce. *Sanna* are rice 'cupcakes' soaked in coconut or palm toddy before cooking. *Dodol*, traditionally eaten at Christmas, and *bebinca* are special sweets, the latter made from layers of sweet pancake.

Commercially produced alcohol, including wine, is readily available and inexpensive; try Goa's own firewater feni, made from the distilled cashew apple juice. It's very strong, both in taste and effect, and is best mixed with a soft drink (soda) such as Limca.

Entertainment

Goa has long been renowned among Western visitors as a party place where all-night, open-air raves dominated the scene in places such as Anjuna and Vagator. A central government ban on loud music in open spaces between 10pm and 6am was aimed partly at curbing Goa's intrusive party scene, but with a tourist industry to nurture (and a bit of *baksheesh*) the authorities have tended to turn a blind eye to parties during the peak Christmas–New Year period. Rave parties are organised at open-air locations such as Disco Valley at Vagator and Bamboo Forest in Anjuna,

---

GREEN GOA

Increased tourism, overuse of water and mining are all posing a threat to the environment in Goa. As a traveller, you can help by responsibly disposing of litter, conserving water when showering and frequenting the few restaurants that have installed water filters. Discarded plastic bottles are a major problem, prompting authorities to declare some beaches and historical sites such as Old Goa as 'Plastic Free Zones' where the sale and use of the bottles are banned.

The **Goa Foundation** (☎ 2263306; www.goacom.com/goafoundation) in Mapusa is the state's main environmental pressure group and has been responsible for a number of conservation projects since its inauguration in 1986. It also produces numerous conservation publications, such as the excellent *Fish Curry & Rice*, which is available from the Other India Bookstore (p178) in Mapusa, other Goan bookstores and on the website.

and occasionally at Arambol, but they are not advertised so you'll have to ask around to find out what's on and be prepared to ride around aimlessly on a motorcycle looking for the right place. More permanent nightclubs have also become established in the Candolim-Calangute-Baga area over the years.

Getting There & Away

AIR

Goa's airport, Dabolim, is 29km south of Panaji, on the coast near Vasco da Gama. Most of India's domestic airlines operate services here, and several direct charter companies fly into Goa from the UK and Europe. Be aware that it's illegal to fly into India on a scheduled flight and out on a charter flight. If you book an international flight from Goa, it will involve a domestic flight to Mumbai (Bombay), or another international airport, and a connection there; there are numerous flights between Goa and Mumbai. Details of major domestic flights from Goa are listed in the boxed text (below).

Note: Indian Airlines has a daily flight from Pune to Goa (US$90, 45 minutes), but not Goa to Pune.

BUS

Long-distance interstate buses operate to/from Panaji, Margao, Mapusa and Calangute, and you can pick up some buses from Chaudi near Palolem. See those sections for more information.

TRAIN

The **Konkan Railway** (www.konkanrailway.com) connects Goa with Mumbai and Mangalore. The main Konkan Railway station in Goa is Madgaon in Margao, but expresses and passenger trains stop at most other stations along the line. Note that these trains often run late.

There are two daily expresses between Margao's Madgaon train station and Mumbai's Chhatrapati Shivaji Terminus (CST; the old Victoria Terminus), plus two between Madgaon and Lokmanya Tilak and one between Madgaon and Dadar (both in northern Mumbai). From Mumbai CST the overnight *Konkan Kanya Express* departs at 10.50pm (sleeper/3AC Rs 293/796, 12 hours) and the *Mandavi Express* departs at 7.05am. The fastest train (in theory) is the *Shatabdi Express*, which departs from Dadar at 5.35am daily except Wednesday (2nd class/AC seat Rs 179/675, eight hours). From Margao to Mumbai, the *Konkan Kanya Express* leaves at 6pm, the *Mandavi Express* at 10.10am and the *Shatabdi Express* at 2.10pm.

There are 12 direct trains between Margao and Mangalore (sleeper/3AC Rs 217/553, 4½ hours), most stopping at Mangalore's Kankanadi station.

The South Central Railway operates from Vasco da Gama via Margao and Londa, and runs to Pune, Delhi and Bangalore. The *Nizamuddin–Goa Express* goes to Delhi (sleeper/3AC Rs 531/1438, 41 hours).

The Delhi–Goa (Margao) *Rajdhani Express* (3AC/2AC/1st class Rs 1985/2915/5430,

DOMESTIC FLIGHTS FROM GOA

Destination	Airline code	Price (US$)	Duration (hr)	Frequency
Bangalore	IC	115	1½	daily
	9W	118	1½	daily
	DN	60	1½	daily
Chennai	IC	150	3	twice weekly
Kochi	IC	135	1	twice weekly
Delhi	IC	250	2½	daily
	S2	250	2½	2 daily
Mumbai	IC	95	1	daily
	S2	100	1	daily
	9W	100	1	4 daily
	DN	78	1	daily

IC – Indian Airlines; S2 – Sahara Airlines; 9W – Jet Airways; DN – Air Deccan

25½ hours) leaves Delhi Nizamuddin station Sunday and Tuesday. It also goes from Delhi to Goa every Wednesday and Friday, leaving Margao at 11.30am.

Bookings can be made at Madgaon (p195) and Vasco da Gama stations, or at the train reservation office at Panaji's Kadamba bus stand (p175). Other useful stations on the Konkan route are Pernem for Arambol, Thivim for Mapusa and the northern beaches, Karmali (Old Goa) for Panaji and Canacona for Palolem.

Getting Around

BICYCLE

There are plenty of places to hire bicycles in the major towns and beach resorts, although you will usually only find gearless Indian bikes. Better-quality mountain bikes can be found at Colva and Calangute. Bicycles cost around Rs 40 for a full day.

BOAT

Passenger/vehicle ferries cross the state's many rivers. Foot passengers ride for free, and motorcycles cost Rs 4. The main ferries of interest to travellers are Panaji–Betim for the back road to Candolim and Calangute, Querim–Terekhol for Terekhol Fort, Old Goa–Divar Island, Ribandar–Chorao for Dr Salim Ali Bird Sanctuary, and Cavelossim–Assolna on the coastal ride from Benaulim to Palolem.

BUS

The state-run Kadamba bus company is the main operator of public buses, although there are also private companies running more comfortable buses to Mumbai, Hampi, Bangalore and several other interstate destinations. Local buses are cheap, services are frequent and they run to just about everywhere, eventually. Express buses run between Panaji and Mapusa, and Panaji and Margao (see p175 for more details).

CAR

Self-drive car rental is not worth the trouble, especially since it's more expensive than a chauffeur-driven car. The main self-drive rental company is **Fulari** (☎ 9822141435; baba car@rediffmail.com), based in Panaji. Rates start at Rs 800 per day for a Maruti Alto or Zen, dropping to Rs 600 per day if you hire for the week.

MOTORCYCLE

Goa is one of the few places in India where hiring a motorcycle or scooter is cheap and easy, and the relatively short distances make travel a breeze, although India is no place to learn to ride a motorcycle, or even a scooter. Bikes available include old Enfields, more modern Yamaha 100s and the gearless Kinetic Honda scooters. Rental prices vary according to season, length of rental and quality of the bike. In the peak Christmas season, you're looking at paying up to Rs 300 per day for a scooter, Rs 400 for the small bikes and Rs 500 for an Enfield. Outside this time, when there's a glut of idle bikes, especially at the northern beach resorts, you should only pay Rs 100 per day for a scooter, Rs 200 for the small bikes and Rs 350 for an Enfield if you hire for a week or more. In most cases you don't need to provide a deposit, but you'll probably be asked for your passport details (don't hand over the passport itself) and the name of your hotel. Guesthouses, hotels and places where taxi drivers congregate are good places to rent a bike, but you'll get plenty of offers on the street at beach resorts.

TAXI

Perhaps the biggest threat to your sanity at Goa's beach resorts is the taxi men. You can't walk a few metres without being asked if you want one (a taxi, that is). If you do, always negotiate the fare before getting in; for a full day's sightseeing, depending on the distance, you're looking at anything from Rs 800 to 1000.

Motorcycles are a licensed form of taxi in Goa. They are cheap, easy to find, backpacks are no problem and they can be identified by a yellow front mudguard.

NORTH GOA

PANAJI (PANJIM)
pop 98,915

Most travellers bypass Panaji (also known as Panjim) on their way to the beaches, but this is a grave mistake. With the narrow winding streets of its old Portuguese quarter, and its fine location at the mouth of the broad Mandovi River, Panaji is one of India's smallest and most pleasant state capitals. It officially became the capital of

Goa in 1843 when Old Goa was finally abandoned. Well worth a couple of days' exploration it is the perfect base for touring nearby Old Goa (p176) and central Goa (p202).

Information
BOOKSHOPS
Hotel Mandovi (☎ 2426270; Dayanand Bandodkar Marg; ☺ 9am-9pm) Small, well-stocked bookshop in hotel lobby.

Pauline Book & Media Centre (☎ 2231158; Rani Pramila Arcade; ☺ 10am-7pm Mon-Wed, Fri & Sat, 9am-1pm Thu) Specialising in self-help, spiritual and religious titles. Down a laneway off 18th June Rd.

Singbal's Book House (☎ 2425747; Church Sq; ☺ 9.30am-1pm & 3.30-7.30pm Mon-Sat)

INTERNET ACCESS
There are plenty of Internet cafés. Try the following:

Cozy Nook Travels (18th June Rd; per hr Rs 35; ☺ 8am-9pm)

Log In (1st fl, Durga Chambers, 18th June Rd; per hr Rs 30; ☺ 9am-11pm)

Shruti Communications (31st January Rd; per hr Rs 35; ☺ 9am-11pm Mon-Sat)

THE BEACH FILES

Goa's biggest attraction is its beaches. The beaches themselves, the associated villages and resorts that have grown up around them, and the people who are drawn to them are all quite different in character. Some have changed beyond recognition in the past 10 years, others are just being discovered and a few pockets remain unspoiled. Here's a brief rundown of Goa's main beaches from north to south.

Arambol (Harmal; p191)
The most northerly of Goa's developed beaches, Arambol has an attractive rocky headland and a chilled-out, but increasingly busy, scene with music bars and some good restaurants; it attracts backpackers and some of the old Anjuna crowd looking for a quieter time. Because it's a cheaper place to stay, the season kicks of a little earlier than in and around Anjuna.

Mandrem (p191)
The next beach south is clean but uninspiring, with a small knot of bamboo huts between the road and the beach, and good midrange accommodation among the coconut groves near Mandrem Creek.

Morjim & Asvem (p190)
Stretching down to the Chapora River, the beaches here are nothing special in themselves, but travellers have drifted here to escape the scene further south. There are bamboo and palm-thatch huts, an upmarket tent camp and a few beach shacks but essentially it's a quiet place to do nothing.

Vagator (p188)
There are three small, picturesque beaches at Vagator backed by a rocky headland. It's the centre of the night-time party scene, popular with European and Israeli ravers.

Anjuna (p186)
There's a good stretch of beach near the flea market, and plenty of accommodation strung out over a wide area. Anjuna retains its popularity with the party crowd but its days as the place to 'see and be seen' are virtually over. Market day (Wednesday), however, should not be missed.

Calangute & Baga (p181)
The long stretch of crowded beach here is overloaded with beach shacks and sun beds, backed by midrange concrete-block hotels. This is package-tourism central, though many travellers

MEDICAL SERVICES
Goa Medical College Hospital (☎ 2458725; Bambolin) Situated 9km south of Panaji on National Hwy 17.

MONEY
American Express (Amex; ☎ 2432645; 14 Alcon Chambers, Dayanand Bandodkar Marg; ⏰ 9.30am-6.30pm)
Centurion (MG Rd) Has a 24-hour ATM accepting international cards (MasterCard, Cirrus, Maestro, Visa). There's another branch on Dr Atmaram Borkar Rd.
HDFC (18th June Rd) There's another branch nearby.
Thomas Cook (☎ 2221312; Dayanand Bandodkar Marg; ⏰ 9.30am-6pm Mon-Sat year-round, 10am-5pm Sun Oct-Mar) Changes all brands of travellers cheques commission-free and gives cash advances on Visa and MasterCard.
UTI Bank (ground fl, Cardozo Bldg) Located next to Paulo Travels, it has an ATM near the bus stand.

POST
Main post office (MG Rd; ⏰ 9.30am-5.30pm Mon-Fri, 9am-5pm Sat) Has a Speedpost parcel service and reliable poste restante (⏰ 9.30am to 4pm).

TELEPHONE
There are also plenty of private STD/ISD offices around town.

---

still prefer the upbeat atmosphere here to that further north. It's also possible to find quiet accommodation in local houses set back from the beach.

Candolim & Sinquerim (p179)
A continuation of Calangute, Candolim is a mix of upmarket resorts, package hotels, beach shacks and some good restaurants, culminating in the sprawling Taj complex at Sinquerim.

Miramar (p172)
Miramar, Panaji's town beach, is no place for swimming but it's a popular spot from which to watch the sunset.

Bogmalo (p196)
A small, sheltered beach just 4km south of Dabolim Airport, Bogmalo has a feeling of exclusivity and can be used as a base for diving.

Majorda & Velsao
Blighted by a petrochemical plant in the distance, these beaches north of Colva (p196) have a few upmarket resort hotels but little tourist activity.

Colva & Benaulim (p196)
The beach here is similar to Calangute but it's much quieter and still has a noticeable fishing industry. There's a mix of package tourists, Indian tourists and backpackers, but no party scene. Benaulim village is quieter still and a good place to stay long-term.

Varca & Cavelossim (p199)
Five-star luxury resorts here front relatively empty, undeveloped beaches.

Agonda (p200)
North of Palolem, Agonda is an average-looking beach but a good place to chill out – it mostly attracts laid-back travellers doing as little as possible.

Palolem & Patnem (p200)
Palolem is still the most idyllic beach in the state, but it's fast filling up with travellers as well as the many businesses set up to service them. Accommodation is mostly in the string of bamboo huts fronting the beach. Patnem, a short distance south, is much quieter and has some decent surf.

GOA

PANAJI (PANJIM)

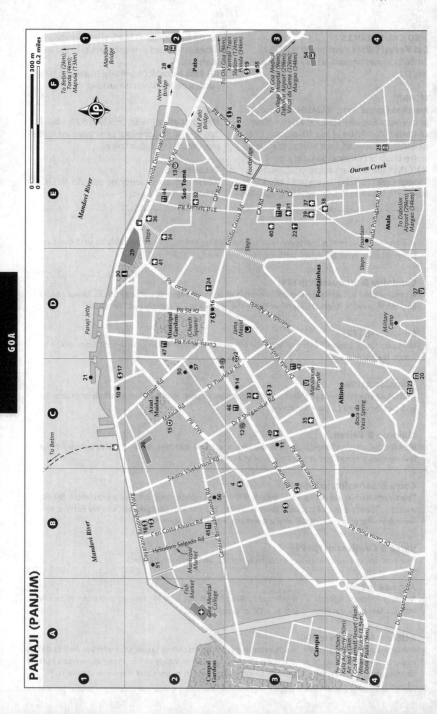

INFORMATION		
American Express	1	B2
Central Telegraph Office	2	D3
Centurion Bank	3	C1
Centurion Bank ATM	4	B2
Cozy Nook Travel	5	C2
Foreigners Registration Office	(see 15)	
Goa Tourism Development Corporation (GTDC) Office	6	F3
Goa Tourism Development Corporation (GTDC) Tourist Information Counter	(see 54)	
Government of India Tourist Office	7	D2
HDFC Bank ATM	8	B3
HDFC Bank ATM	9	B3
Hotel Mandovi	10	C1
ICICI ATM	(see 3)	
Log In	11	C3
Junta House (Forest/Parks Office)	12	C3
Main Post Office	13	D2
Pauline Book & Media Centre	14	C3
Police Headquarters	15	C2
Shruti Communications	16	D2
Singbal's Book House	17	C1
State Bank of India	18	B2
Thomas Cook	19	F3
UTI Bank ATM		

SIGHTS & ACTIVITIES		
Bishop's Palace	20	C4
Casino Goa	21	C1
Chapel of St Sebastian	22	E3
Chief Minister's Residence	23	C4
Church of Our Lady of the Immaculate Conception	24	D2
Gitanjali Gallery	(see 39)	
Goa State Museum	25	E4
Institute Menezes Braganza	26	C2
Maruti Temple	27	D4
Panaji Central Library	(see 26)	
Public Observatory	(see 11)	
River Cruises	(see 28)	
Santa Monica Jetty	28	F2

Secretariat Building	29	D2
Statue of Abbé Faria	30	D1

SLEEPING 🛏		
Afonso Guest House	31	E3
Comfort Guest House	32	C2
Hotel Nova Goa	33	C3
Mandovi White House	34	B2
MayFair Hotel	35	C3
Panaji Residency	36	E2
Panjim Inn	37	E3
Panjim Peoples	38	E3
Panjim Pousada	39	E3
Park Lane Lodge	40	E3
Republica Hotel	41	D2

EATING 🍴		
A Ferradura	42	E3
Goenchin	43	C3
Hotel Venite	44	E2
New Café Hema	45	B2

Riorico	(see 10)	
Sher-E-Punjab	46	C3
Sher-E-Punjab	47	D2
Viva Panjim	48	E3

DRINKING 🍸		
Aces Pub	49	C3

TRANSPORT		
Daud M Aga Cycle Store	50	C2
Indian Airlines	51	B2
Interstate Private Bus Stand	52	F2
Jet Airways	53	F3
Kadamba Bus Stand	54	F3
Paulo Travels	(see 55)	
Private Bus Agents	55	B2
Sahara Airlines	56	B2

OTHER		
Cine Nacional	57	C2

Central telegraph office (Dr Atmaram Borkar Rd; ☻ 24hr)

TOURIST INFORMATION

Goa Tourism Development Corporation office (GTDC; ☎ 2224132; www.goa-tourism.com; Dr Alvaro Costa Rd; ☻ 9.30am-5.45pm Mon-Fri) Commonly known as Goa Tourism, GTDC is just south of the Old Pato Bridge. There's not a lot of information to be gleaned here, but you can pick up maps of Goa and Panaji and book local tours.

Goa Tourism Development Corporation tourist information counter (☎ 2438520; Kadamba bus stand) Keeps unreliable hours.

Government of India tourist office (☎ 2223412; in diatourismgoa@sancharnet.in; Communidade Bldg, Church Sq; ☻ 9.30am-6pm Mon-Fri, 10am-1pm Sat) This office is far more helpful. Staff here are bright and enthusiastic, and qualified guides can be arranged (from Rs 350/500 per half-/full day depending on the size of the group).

Sights & Activities

Panaji is a city to savour on leisurely strolls, the best being in the atmospheric Sao Tomé, Fontainhas and Altino areas (see p172). The warren of narrow streets, lined with tiled and painted buildings, shuttered windows and tiny overhanging balconies, is a pleasure to wander through. Alternatively, take a walk beside the Mandovi River, where a promenade was newly laid for the 35th International Film Festival India, held in 2004.

CHURCH OF OUR LADY OF THE IMMACULATE CONCEPTION

Panaji's main **church**, standing above the square in the town centre, was originally consecrated in 1541. Panaji was the first port of call for voyages from Lisbon, so Portuguese sailors would visit this strikingly whitewashed church to give thanks for a safe crossing before continuing to Old Goa. Mass is held here daily in English, Konkani and Portuguese.

GOA STATE MUSEUM

An eclectic collection of items awaits visitors to this large, roomy **museum** (☎ 2458006; www.goamuseum.nic.in; admission free; ☻ 9.30am-5.30pm Mon-Fri), in a rather forlorn area southwest of the Kadamba bus stand. As well as Christian art, Hindu and Jain sculpture and bronzes, and paintings from all over India, exhibits include an elaborately carved table used in the Goa Inquisition, and an antique pair of huge rotary lottery machines.

GOA

SECRETARIAT BUILDING

Dating from the 16th century, this handsome **colonial building** on one of Panjim's most traffic-prone streets was originally the palace of the Muslim ruler Adil Shah before becoming the viceroy's official residence in 1759. Now it's government offices. Immediately to the west, the bizarre **statue** of a man apparently about to strangle a woman is of Abbé Faria, a famous Goan hypnotist, and his assistant.

INSTITUTE MENEZES BRAGANZA

On the west side of the Azad Maidan, the institute houses **Panaji Central Library** (Malaca Rd; 🕑 9.30am-1pm & 2-5.30pm Mon-Fri) and is worth popping into to see the pretty *azulejos* (blue-and-white-painted tile murals) in the entrance hall.

PUBLIC OBSERVATORY

You can study the stars at the **observatory** (Swami Vivekanand Rd; 🕑 7-9pm Nov-May) on the rooftop of the Junta House.

MIRAMAR

The closest beach to Panaji is at **Miramar**, 3km southwest of the city along Dayanand Bandodkar Marg. It's far from the cream of Goa's beaches but is a pleasant enough place for a sunset stroll and a good place to aim for on a short bike ride out the city. On the way you'll pass the Goa Marriot Resort (p174), where you'll also find **Barracuda Diving** (☎ 2463333, ex 6807; www.barracudadiving.com), one of the state's most professional diving operations.

Walking Tour

> Start & Finish: Church of Our Lady of Immaculate Conception
> Distance: 4.5km
> Duration: 1hr

From the **Church of Our Lady of Immaculate Conception** (1; p171) walk east up the hill along Emidio Gracia Rd (Corte de Oiterio). At the four-way junction, where you'll see fruit-seller barrows, turn right into 31st January Rd. After about 150m, turn right to view the tiny but picturesque **Chapel of St Sebastian (2)**. Built in the 1880s, its most striking feature is

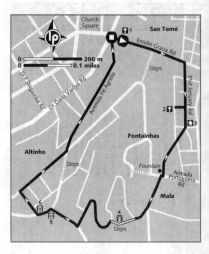

a crucifix that originally stood in the Palace of the Inquisition in Old Goa. Returning to 31st January Rd, continue on to the heritage hotel **Panjim Inn (3**; opposite), which recently took over and restored the old schoolhouse opposite, now the Panjim Peoples hotel.

Take the right fork of the road and continue south past the small fountain (not working) from which Fontainhas gets its name. Keep walking in the same direction until you see the steps off to the right leading uphill to the ornate, salmon-pink **Maruti Temple (4)**, dedicated to the monkey god Hanuman. The temple's veranda provides fine views towards the Mandovi River. Nip behind the temple and follow the road up into the Altinho district.

When you reach a junction with a red 'stop and proceed' sign, turn right and continue around to the **Bishop's Palace (5)**, residence of the Archbishop of Goa. This grand white mansion, with a silver painted Jesus statue outside, lords it over the much-humbler **chief minister's residence (6)** across the road. At the next junction, turn right and head downhill back towards where you started at Church Sq.

Courses

India on the Menu (www.indiaonthemenu.com; £250) is a recommended five-day Indian cookery course offered by London-based **On The Go Tours** (www.onthegotours.com). The programme is based in Betim, just across the river from

Panjim, and covers North and South Indian cuisines, Goan cuisine and a market tour. On the final day you can choose to be taught how to cook your favourite Indian dishes by the course tutor. Each of the cooking sessions lasts half a day (including lunch).

Cruises & Tours

GTDC operates entertaining hour-long **cruises** (Rs 100; ☺ sunset cruise 6pm, sundown cruise 7.15pm) along the Mandovi River aboard the *Santa Monica*. They include a live band performing Goan folk songs and dances. On full-moon nights there is a two-hour cruise at 8.30pm (Rs 150). Cruises depart from the Santa Monica jetty next to the huge Mandovi bridge and tickets can be purchased here. A couple of private operators, **Emerald Cruises** (☎ 2431192) and **Royal Cruises** (☎ 2435599), have virtually identical trips from Santa Monica jetty around 7.15pm (Rs 100), as well as open-sea 'dolphin cruises' (from mid-October to the end of April only; Rs 500) from 10am to 1pm and backwater cruises (Rs 1000, including lunch and drinks) from 10am to 4.30pm. Their boats are bigger and rowdier (for the boozy Indian party crowd) than the *Santa Monica*.

GTDC also offers a **Goa By Night bus tour** (Rs 140; ☺ 6.30pm), which leaves from the same spot, and includes a river cruise. It also offers day-long bus tours (non-AC/AC Rs 120/150), which depart at 9.30am daily. The day-long North Goa tour visits Mapusa, Mayem Lake, Vagator, Anjuna, Calangute and Fort Aguada. The South Goa tour takes in Miramar, Dona Paula, Colva, Margao, Shri Shantadurga Temple, Shri Manguesh Temple, Ancestral Goa (in Loutolim) and Old Goa. There's also a bus tour taking in Old Goa, Dudhsagar Falls and Molem National Park on Wednesday and Sunday only (non-AC/AC Rs 500/600).

Sleeping
BUDGET
Afonso Guest House (☎ 2222359; d Rs 350) On the same street as the Chapel of St Sebastian, this is a friendly, family-run place with four rooms and a pleasant rooftop terrace. Spotless doubles with hot water are a bit above budget range, but worth it. Rates zoom to Rs 800 during the peak Christmas–New Year period.

Comfort Guest House (☎ 5642250; 31st January Rd; d with shared/private bathroom incl tax Rs 240/340) This is a good-value little guesthouse in Sao Tomé. Rooms are clean and have cable TV. There's no increase in room rates over Christmas but there's a 50% discount in the off season.

Park Lane Lodge (☎ 2227154; pklaldg@sancharnet.in; s with shared bathroom Rs 185, d with private bathroom Rs 300) This rambling 1930s Portuguese house near the Chapel of St Sebastian has a bit of character and just six small, simply furnished rooms. Checkout is 8am and prices more than double at Christmas.

Republica Hotel (☎ 2224630; Jose Falcao Rd; s/d Rs 200/350) The Republica is an interesting old place with good views from the balcony over to the river and the Secretariat building. Some of the rooms are bright, with stained-glass windows, but avoid the dingy rooms at the back with no views.

Also recommended is the ramshackle **Mandovi White House** (☎ 2223928; d from Rs 250) behind the Panaji Residency.

MIDRANGE
Panjim Inn (☎ 2226523; www.panjiminn.com; 31st January Rd; s/d from Rs 990/1350; ✖) By far the most charming place to stay in Panaji, the Panjim Inn is a beautiful 300-year-old mansion with a large 1st-floor veranda, decent restaurant and leafy courtyard. All rooms have four-poster beds and colonial furniture, and the staff are exceedingly helpful.

Panjim Pousada (☎ 2435628; 31st January Rd; s/d from Rs 1035/1305; ✖) Across from Panjim Inn and under the same management, this is also a comfortable, well-furnished place in an old Hindu house. There's an art gallery around the bright central courtyard.

Mayfair Hotel (☎ 2223317; mayfair@goatelecom.com; Dr Dada Vaidya Rd; s/d from Rs 450/550, d with AC from Rs 700; ✖) This is one of Panaji's more colourful hotels, with mosaic-tile murals in the lobby. Standard rooms are small but clean, and have touches of character, such as Goan oyster-shell windows.

Hotel Nova Goa (☎ 2226231; www.hotelnovagoa.com; Dr Atmaram Borkar Rd; s/d from Rs 1500/2150; ✖ ▯ ▮) At the upper end of this range is this modern and well-kept business hotel. Simply furnished rooms have tiled floors and TVs, and there's a small pool to splash in.

Panaji Residency (☎ 2227103; MG Rd; d without/with AC from Rs 600/750; ✖) Run by the GTDC, this is an unremarkable place on a busy road, but it's popular with travellers. You'll pay slightly more for river-view rooms.

TOP END

Goa Marriott Resort (☎ 2463333; www.marriott .com; Miramar; d garden-view/bay-view from US$180/190; ⊠ 🖥 🔁) Panaji's luxury choice – a relaxed hotel with spacious, soothingly decorated rooms – is at Miramar, some 3km from the town centre. The swimming pool with bar overlooking the Mandovi River is a delight, as is the top-class fish restaurant and the trendy new Waterfront Terrace & Bar. There's also an excellent health club, and squash and tennis courts.

Panjim Peoples (☎ 2221122; www.panjiminn.com; 31st January Rd; d low/peak season from Rs 3000/5400; ⊠) The latest venture by the Panjim Inn is yet another top-class conversion of a heritage building. The bright rooms are furnished in the usual immaculate style with antique rosewood beds as well as TV, fridge, phone and charmingly mosaic-tiled bathrooms.

Eating

Riorico (☎ 2224405; Hotel Mandovi, Dayanand Bandodkar Marg; mains Rs 60-600; ☷ 12.30-2.30pm & 7.30-11pm; ⊠) Like dining in a Wedgewood box, this restaurant's atmosphere can be a bit stilted but the food, including Goan specialities such as the soup *caldo verde* (Rs 50) and stuffed pomfret Alfonso (pomfret stuffed with a piquant mixture of herbs and spices, Rs 350), is excellent.

A Ferradura (Horseshoe; ☎ 2431788; Ourem Rd; mains Rs 65-130; ☷ noon-2.30pm & 7-10.30pm Mon-Sat; ⊠) Intimate and informal, this modern restaurant serves a good range of Goan, Indian and Portuguese dishes such as *feijoada* (pork and bean stew) and *balchão de comavão* (prawns in a tangy coconut sauce).

Viva Panjim (☎ 2422405; 178 31st January Rd; mains Rs 50-160; ☷ 8am-3.30pm & 7-10.30pm Mon-Sat) The genial owner of this small, family-run restaurant on a quiet lane is likely to fill you in on her life story as you dine on lovingly prepared Goan, tandoori and Continental dishes. There are a couple of outdoor tables and the chicken *xacuti* is delicious.

Hotel Venite (☎ 2425537; 31st January Rd; mains Rs 65-110; ☷ 9am-3pm & 7-10pm Mon-Sat) Although the food could be better this is one of the most character-laden restaurants in Goa. With four tiny balconies hanging over the

street and rustic, colourful décor, it's a fine place to enjoy a meal or drink. Goan sausages and tiger prawns are among the specialities.

New Café Hema (General Bernado Guedes Rd; mains Rs 20-30; ☷ 6am-7.30pm Mon-Sat, to 12.30pm Sun) This is a cheap, clean place near the municipal market serving a very good fish curry and rice (Rs 20) and cheap veg snacks for under Rs 10. Entrance is at the rear and up some stairs.

Sher-E-Punjab Cunha-Rivara Rd (☎ 2227975; 1st fl, Hotel Aroma mains Rs 60-150; ☷ 11.30am-3.30pm & 7-11pm; ⊠); 18th June Rd (☎ 222 7204; ☷ 10.30am-midnight) Serving arguably the best tandoori in town, the Cunha-Rivara Rd branch has the widest range of dishes. The second branch is more informal.

Goenchin (☎ 2227614; ground fl, Mandovi Apartments; mains Rs 100-250; ☷ 11.30am-3.30pm & 7-11pm; ⊠) For excellent Chinese food try this place off Dr Dada Vaidya Rd.

Drinking

There's a new **café** (31st January Rd; ☷ 9am-9pm) beneath the Panjim Peoples (left) that's a convivial place to head for a drink while exploring the Fontainhas district.

Panaji has a fair smattering of darkened bars full of hard-core feni drinkers, and a few pubs frequented by young Goans rather than foreign tourists. Apart from Hotel Venite (left), try **Aces Pub** (Swami Vivekanand Rd; ☷ 7-11pm), opposite Junta House. It's a tiny, two-tier place that's like a little cocktail bar.

Entertainment

Kala Academy (☎ 2223280; www.kalaacademy.org; Dayanand Bandodkar Marg) The recently renovated Kala Academy, on the west side of the city at Campal, is Goa's premier cultural centre. There's a cultural programme of dance, theatre, music and art exhibitions throughout the year. Many performances are in Konkani, but there are occasional English-language productions.

INOX (☎ 2420999; tickets Rs 50-120) This new multiplex cinema, which shows English-language and Indian films, is near the Kala Academy.

Casino Goa (☎ 2234044; ☷ sunset cruise 5.30-6.30pm Rs 500, dinner cruise from 7pm Rs 2500-3000) Aboard a small luxury ship, the MV *Caravela*, moored at the Panaji jetty, opposite

Hotel Mandovi, is India's only live gaming casino – it can make for a fun night out. Drinks are free on all cruises and the dinner cruise includes an impressive buffet meal. On the sunset cruise you can gamble if you pay Rs 200 extra; if you stay on the boat after 7pm you can continue drinking for free but all snacks are chargeable. On the most expensive dinner cruise, Rs 2300 is given back as gaming chips. There are blackjack and poker tables, as well as roulette and slot machines. If you decide that you don't want to gamble there's an outdoor swimming pool in season. There's a smart dress code, so no shorts, singlets or flip-flops please.

Getting There & Away
AIR
Airlines with offices in Panaji include the following:
Air India (☎ 2431100) Near Bal Bhavan, Campal.
Indian Airlines (☎ 2237821; ground fl, Dempo Bldg, Dayanand Bandodkar Marg) On the road out to Miramar.
Jet Airways (☎ 2438792; shop 7-9, Sesa Ghor, Patto Plaza, Dr Alvaro Costa Rd) Near GTDC.
Sahara Airlines (☎ 2230237; General Bernado Guedes Rd)

Air Deccan (☎ 9890477008, airport 2542380) only has an office at the airport. A prepaid taxi from the airport to Panaji is Rs 380.

BUS
State-run bus services operate out of Panaji's **Kadamba bus stand** (☎ 2438034). Fares vary depend on the type of bus and include the following:

Destination	Fare (Rs)	Duration (hr)
Bangalore	360	14
Hospet	135	9
Mangalore	150-180	10
Mumbai	600	12-15
Mysore	225	17
Pune	200-225	12

There are also services to Londa (Rs 45, three hours), where you can get a daily direct train connection to Mysore and Bangalore, as well as services to Hubli (Rs 70, six hours) and Belgaum (Rs 60, five hours).

Many private operators have offices outside the entrance to the bus stand, with

luxury and AC buses to Mumbai, Bangalore, Hampi and other destinations. Most private interstate buses arrive and depart from a separate bus stand next to the Mandovi Bridge. **Paulo Travels** (☎ 2438531; www .paulotravels.com; 8am-9.30pm), just north of the bus stand, has nightly sleeper coaches to Hampi (Rs 450, 10 hours), Mumbai (Rs 375, 14 to 18 hours) and Bangalore (Rs 400, 14 hours), though these prices fluctuate – they rise from mid-December. Ordinary non-AC buses cost Rs 275 to Mumbai and Rs 350 to Hampi. Luxury buses can also be booked through agents in Margao, Mapusa and the beach resorts, but they still depart from Panaji.

For journeys within Goa, popular routes from Panaji depart from the Kadamba bus stand and include the following:
Calangute Frequent services throughout the day and evening (Rs 7, 45 minutes).
Mapusa Frequent buses run to Mapusa and there's a separate ticket booth at the Kadamba bus stand for express services (Rs 7, 25 minutes).
Margao Direct express buses run frequently to Margao (Rs 16, one hour). Change at Margao for the beaches of the south.
Old Goa Direct buses to Old Goa leave constantly (Rs 5, 25 minutes).

TRAIN
The train is a better bet than the bus for getting to/from Mumbai and Mangalore, but it can be difficult getting a seat into Goa around Christmas. The nearest train station to Panaji is Karmali, 12km to the east near Old Goa. There's a very busy **reservation office** (8am-8pm Mon-Sat) upstairs at Panaji's Kadamba bus stand.

Getting Around
Getting taxi and autorickshaw drivers to use their meters is impossible. Agree on the fare before heading off. Short trips around Panaji cost Rs 50; to Old Goa they cost one way/return Rs 150/250, but these prices are a matter of negotiation.

It's easy enough to rent a motorcycle or scooter in Panaji, though if you intend to spend most of your time at the beach resorts it's more convenient and usually cheaper to hire one there. There are no hire shops as such – ask at your guesthouse or head to the cluster of bikes opposite the main post office on MG Rd. Bicycles can be hired from **Daud M Aga Cycle Store** (☎ 2222670; per day Rs 40; ☷ 8am-8pm Mon-Sat, to noon Sun), opposite Cine Nacional.

OLD GOA

Just 9km east of Panaji, the former Portuguese capital of Old Goa is a highlight of any visit to Goa. Half a dozen imposing churches and cathedrals (among the largest in Asia) are all that remain of the city that was once said to rival Lisbon in magnificence.

Even before the arrival of the Portuguese, Old Goa was a thriving and prosperous city, and was the second capital of the Adil Shahi dynasty of Bijapur. At that time, it was a fortress surrounded by walls, towers and a moat, and contained temples, mosques and the large palace of Adil Shah. Today, none of these structures remain except for a fragment of the palace gateway.

The city's decline was accelerated by the Inquisition and a devastating epidemic that struck in 1635. In 1843 the capital shifted to Panaji.

Old Goa can get crowded on weekends and in the 10 days leading up to the Feast of St Francis Xavier on 3 December. The Archaeological Survey of India publishes the useful guide *Old Goa* (Rs 10), available from the archaeological museum (opposite).

Sights

SE CATHEDRAL

Construction of **Se Cathedral**, the largest church in Old Goa, began in 1562 during the reign of King Dom Sebastião (1557–68). Although the cathedral was completed by 1619, the altars were not finished until 1652. The cathedral was built for the Dominicans and paid for by the sale of crown property.

The building's style is Portuguese-Gothic with a Tuscan exterior and Corinthian interior. The remaining tower houses a famous bell, one of the largest in Goa, often called the Golden Bell because of its rich sound. The main altar is dedicated to St Catherine of Alexandria, and paintings on either side of it depict scenes from her life and martyrdom.

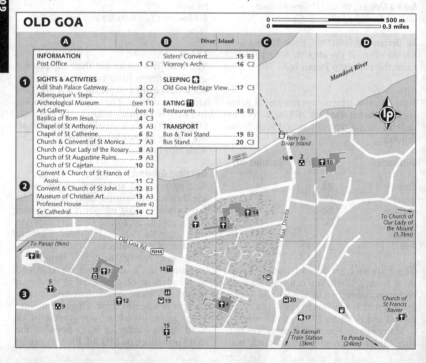

OLD GOA

0 — 500 m
0 — 0.3 miles

INFORMATION	
Post Office	1 C3

SIGHTS & ACTIVITIES	
Adil Shah Palace Gateway	2 C2
Alberqueque's Steps	3 C2
Archeological Museum	(see 11)
Art Gallery	(see 4)
Basilica of Bom Jesus	4 C3
Chapel of St Anthony	5 A3
Chapel of St Catherine	6 B2
Church & Convent of St Monica	7 A3
Church of Our Lady of the Rosary	8 A3
Church of St Augustine Ruins	9 A3
Church of St Cajetan	10 D2
Convent & Church of St Francis of Assisi	11 C2
Convent & Church of St John	12 B3
Museum of Christian Art	13 A3
Professed House	(see 4)
Se Cathedral	14 C2

Sisters' Convent	15 B3
Viceroy's Arch	16 C2

SLEEPING	
Old Goa Heritage View	17 C3

EATING	
Restaurants	18 B3

TRANSPORT	
Bus & Taxi Stand	19 B3
Bus Stand	20 C3

Divar Island

Mandovi River

Ferry to Divar Island

Rua Direita

To Church of Our Lady of the Mount (1.7km)

To Panaji (9km)

Old Goa Rd

NH4

To Karmali Train Station (3km)

To Ponda (24km)

Church of St Francis Xavier

CONVENT & CHURCH OF
ST FRANCIS OF ASSISI

One of the most interesting buildings in Old Goa, the **church** interior contains gilded and carved woodwork, a stunning *reredos* (ornamented screen behind the altar), old murals depicting scenes from the life of St Francis and a floor made of carved gravestones – complete with family coats of arms dating back to the early 16th century. The church was built by eight Franciscan friars who arrived here in 1517 and constructed a small chapel consisting of three altars and a choir. This was later pulled down and the present building was constructed on the same spot in 1661.

A convent behind this church is now the **archaeological museum** (admission Rs 5; 10am-5pm Sat-Thu). It houses portraits of the Portuguese viceroys, sculpture fragments from Hindu temple sites, and stone Vetal images from the animist cult that flourished in this part of India centuries ago.

BASILICA OF BOM JESUS

The **Basilica of Bom Jesus** is famous throughout the Roman Catholic world. It contains the tomb and mortal remains of St Francis Xavier who, in 1541, was given the task of spreading Christianity among the subjects of the Portuguese colonies in the East.

A former pupil of St Ignatius Loyola, the founder of the Jesuit order, St Francis Xavier embarked on missionary voyages that became legendary and, considering the state of transport at the time, were nothing short of miraculous.

Apart from the richly gilded altars, the interior of the church is remarkable for its simplicity. This is the only church that is not plastered on the outside (although it was originally). Construction began in 1594 and was completed in 1605. The focus of the church is the three-tiered marble tomb of St Francis, which took 10 years to build and was completed in 1698. The remains of the body are housed in a silver casket, which at one time was covered in jewels.

The **Professed House**, next door to the basilica, is a two-storey laterite building covered with lime plaster. It was completed in 1585, despite much opposition to the Jesuits from the local Portuguese. There is a modern **art gallery** attached to the basilica; even if the art isn't to your taste it's worth popping your head in to look through a small window down on the tomb of St Francis Xavier.

CHURCH OF ST CAJETAN

Modelled on the original design of St Peter's in Rome, this **church** was built by Italian friars of the Order of Theatines, who were sent

---

THE INCORRUPT BODY OF ST FRANCIS XAVIER

Goa's patron saint, Francis Xavier, spent 10 years as a tireless missionary in Asia but it was his death on 3 December 1552 that gave rise to his greatest influence on the region.

He died on the island of Sancian, off the coast of China. A servant is said to have emptied four sacks of quicklime into his coffin to consume his flesh in case the order came to return the remains to Goa. Two months later the body was still in perfect condition – refusing to rot despite the quicklime. The following year it was returned to Goa, where the people were declaring the preservation a miracle.

The church was slower to acknowledge it, requiring a medical examination to establish that the body had not been embalmed. This was performed in 1556 by the viceroy's physician, who declared that all internal organs were still intact and that no preservative agents had been used. He noticed a small wound in the chest and asked two Jesuits to put their fingers into it. He noted, 'When they withdrew them, they were covered with blood which I smelt and found to be absolutely untainted'.

It was not until 1622 that canonisation took place, but by then holy-relic hunters had started work on the 'incorrupt body'. In 1614 the right arm was removed and divided between Jesuits in Japan and Rome, and by 1636 parts of one shoulder blade and all the internal organs had been scattered through Southeast Asia. By the end of the 17th century the body was in an advanced state of desiccation, and the miracle appeared to be over. The Jesuits decided to enclose the corpse in a glass coffin out of view, and it was not until the mid-19th century that the current cycle of 10-yearly expositions began, the latest one being in 2004.

by Pope Urban III to preach Christianity in the kingdom of Golconda (near Hyderabad). The friars were not permitted to work in Golconda, so settled at Old Goa in 1640. The construction of the church began in 1655.

CHURCH OF ST AUGUSTINE (RUINS)

The **church** was constructed in 1602 by Augustinian friars and abandoned in 1835 due to the repressive policies of the Portuguese government, which resulted in the eviction of many religious orders from Goa. It fell into neglect and the vault collapsed in 1842. In 1931, the façade and half the tower also fell down. All that is really left is the enormous 46m tower that served as a belfry and formed part of the façade.

CHURCH & CONVENT OF ST MONICA

This huge, three-storey **laterite building** was completed in 1627, only to burn down nine years later. Reconstruction started the following year, and it's from this time that the buildings date. Once known as the Royal Monastery, due to the royal patronage that it enjoyed, the building is now used by the Mater Dei Institute as a nunnery. It was inaugurated in 1964.

Within the convent, the excellent **Museum of Christian Art** (adult/child Rs 10/free; ⏰ 9.30am-5pm) contains statuary, paintings and sculptures transferred here from the Rachol Seminary. Many of the works of Goan Christian art during the Portuguese era were produced by local Hindu artists.

OTHER HISTORIC SITES

Other monuments of interest in Old Goa are the **Viceroy's Arch**, **Gate of Adil Shah's Palace**, **Chapel of St Anthony**, **Chapel of St Catherine**, **Alburqueque's Steps**, the **Convent and Church of St John**, **Sister's Convent** and the **Church of Our Lady of the Rosary**. For a wonderful view of the city head to the hill-top **Church of Our Lady of the Mount**, 1.7km east of the Se Cathedral.

Sleeping & Eating

Most people visit Old Goa as a day trip, but there is one hotel, the GTDC **Old Goa Heritage View** (☎ 2285013; s/d Rs 225/400, d with AC Rs 500; 🗙), which has simple rooms with TV and geysers.

Outside the basilica are two restaurants geared primarily to local tourists, where you can get full meals and cold drinks,

including beer. They're raised up from the road and are a good spot to relax and take in the scene. You can also get cheap snacks (less than Rs 120) from the food stalls that line the road just north of the Old Goa Heritage View.

Getting There & Away

Frequent buses to Old Goa leave the Kadamba bus stand at Panaji (Rs 5, 25 minutes) and stop on the east side of the main roundabout. The trip out to Old Goa makes a pleasant bicycle ride as the flat road follows the Mandovi River (via Ribandar) most of the way. It takes about 45 minutes from Panaji.

TORDA

Just 5km north of Panaji, off the main road to Mapusa, is the village of Torda, where you'll find, on a traffic island, the **Houses of Goa Museum** (☎ 2410711; www.archgoa.org; admission Rs 25; 🗙 10am-7.30pm Tue-Sun). This extraordinary shiplike building, made from laterite stone, houses a small but illuminating collection of materials explaining the unique design and intricacies of Goa's traditional architecture (see p196). A slide show is held at 7pm. Inquire also about guided walks through the mangroves surrounding the village. The easiest way here is by autorickshaw from Panaji (around Rs 70).

MAPUSA

pop 40,100

Mapusa (pronounced 'Mapsa') is the main population centre in the northern *talukas* (districts) of Goa and the main town for supplies if you are staying at Anjuna or Vagator. There's not much to see in Mapusa, though the **Friday market** (🗙 8am-6.30pm) is a raucous affair that attracts vendors and shoppers from all over Goa (and interstate). Unlike the Anjuna market it's a local event where people shop for cheap clothing and produce, but you can also find a few souvenirs and textiles here.

Information

Other India Bookstore (☎ 2263306; www.goacom .com/oib; Mapusa Clinic Rd; 🗙 9am-5pm Mon-Fri, to 1pm Sat) stocks mainly books published in India, including books on Goa or by Goan authors. There's Internet access at **Cyber Zone** (per hr Rs 25; 🗙 9.30am-2pm & 2.30-6.30pm

Mon-Sat), around the corner from the Hotel Satyaheera.

Sleeping & Eating
Accommodation at the nearby beaches of Anjuna, Vagator and Calangute is far preferable to what's on offer in Mapusa.

Hotel Satyaheera (☎ 2262849; satya@goatelecom .com; d without/with AC from Rs 390/550, mains Rs 30-100; ☯ restaurant 11am-11pm; ☢) Near the Maruti Temple on the northern roundabout, this is Mapusa's most upmarket choice with decent, clean rooms. The hotel's rooftop Ruchira Restaurant is also one of Mapusa's best, serving Indian and Continental dishes.

Hotel Vilena (☎ 2263115; Feira Baixa Rd; d with shared/ private bathroom Rs 250/300, mains Rs 20-60; ☯ restaurant 9am-11pm) A clean place that will do for a night. There's the decent rooftop Tequila Restaurant, serving Goan, Indian and Continental food.

Vrundavan (dishes Rs 10-30; ☯ 7am-10pm Wed-Mon; ☢) Near the Municipal Gardens, this is a simple place offering good, cheap veg thalis (all-you-can-eat meals) and pizzas.

Pub (Market Rd; ☯ 10am-11pm Mon-Sat; ☢) The ideal place to escape the chaos of the Friday market for a cold beer or snack. The 1st-floor balcony gives a perfect view of the street below.

Bertsy Bar & Restaurant (Market Rd; ☯ 9am-11pm; ☢) Near the Pub, this is another friendly little pub serving cheap Goan food.

Getting There & Away
If you're coming by bus from Mumbai, Mapusa is the jumping-off point for the northern beaches. Private operators opposite the taxi and autorickshaw stand have buses to Mumbai (Rs 200/300 normal/ sleeper, 14 hours) and Bangalore (Rs 300/ 400, 15 hours). From the Kadamba bus stand there are state-run buses to Pune (Rs 230, 15 hours) and Belgaum (Rs 47, five hours).

There are frequent local express buses to Panaji (Rs 7, 25 minutes), and buses every 30 minutes to Calangute and Anjuna (both Rs 6). Other buses go to Chapora, Candolim and Arambol (Rs 10). A motorcycle taxi to Anjuna or Calangute costs Rs 50, an autorickshaw Rs 70.

Thivim, about 12km northeast of town, is the nearest train station on the Konkan Railway. Local buses meet trains (Rs 5); an autorickshaw costs around Rs 80.

FORT AGUADA & CANDOLIM
pop 8600

The beaches of Candolim and Sinquerim (below Fort Aguada) are popular with charter and upmarket tourists. The pace is a little less frenetic than at Calangute and Baga up the coast. Independent travellers are rare here, most of the hotels being favoured by package-tour operations. The clean beach's most notable feature is the grounded tanker, the *River Princess*, which has been rusting away 500m offshore for several years; there is little sign that it will be moving any time soon.

Internet access is available at **Online World** (per hr Rs 30; ☯ 9am-11pm).

Sights & Activities
Guarding the mouth of the Mandovi River, **Fort Aguada** was built by the Portuguese in 1612. It's worth visiting the moated ruins on the hill for the views, which are particularly good from the **old lighthouse**. Nearby is the **new lighthouse** (☯ 4-5.30pm). It's a pleasant ride along a hilly, sealed road to the fort, or you can walk via a steep 2km uphill path past Marbella Guest House. Beneath the fort, facing the Mandovi, is the **Aguada Jail**. Most of the inmates here (including Westerners) are in on drug charges. Needless to say, it's not really much of tourist destination.

Sinquerim Beach is a small curve of sand dominated by the five-star Taj Holiday Village complex. **Thunderwave** (☎ 2479779), on

---

EL SHADDAI

Lounging around on Goa's beaches, it's easy to forget that the state shares most of India's social problems. **El Shaddai** (☎ 226650; www.elshaddaigoa.com; 2nd fl, St Anthony Apartments, Mapusa Clinic Rd, Mapusa) is a charitable trust that has established five homes – three in Assagao, between Vagator and Mapusa, and two in Saligao – where local children live and receive schooling. It also runs a night shelter in Panaji.

You can visit the homes and the children daily between 4pm and 6pm. Donations of spare clothing or cash are welcome.

GOA

the beach outside the Taj Holiday Village, offer a range of water sports, including parasailing (Rs 700 to 1500) and jet-skiing (Rs 900 for 15 minutes), and also hires out a catamaran (Rs 2000 per hour).

There are various boat cruises on offer in the region. The best value are **John's Boat Tours** (☎ 2497450, bookings at Elephant Shop ☎ 2275850), found further up behind Candolim Beach. The half-day dolphin trip (Rs 750, with a no dolphin, no pay guarantee) includes lunch and beers on the boat. Their popular full-day 'Crocodile Dundee' river trip (Rs 995) includes lunch at a spice plantation and free drinks. It also offers an overnight backwater trip on a Kerala-style houseboat (Rs 4000 full board).

Sleeping
BUDGET
Villa Ludovici Tourist Home (☎ 2479684; Fort Aguada Rd; d incl breakfast Rs 500) This traditional, family-owned Goan house defies Candolim's upmarket trend with its four old-fashioned, homely rooms, each with private bathroom.

Tropicano Beach Resort (☎ 2277732; 835B Camotim Vaddo; d Rs 450) Another excellent choice offering clean, pleasant doubles (with private bathroom) based around a shady garden. The doors of this traditional laterite Portuguese house feature Goan glazing made from sea shells.

D'Mello's (☎ 2275050; dmellos_seaview_home@ hotmail.com; d Rs 250-600) At the Calangute end of Candolim is this very friendly family home with a garden, rooms with sea views and a restaurant shack on the beach.

Other inexpensive options include the following:
Moonlight Bar & Restaurant (☎ 2279249; santanatheresa@yahoo.com; d from Rs 250)
Ave Maria (☎ 2276074; s/d incl tax Rs 450/700; 🔲) Cute place with a tiny pool.

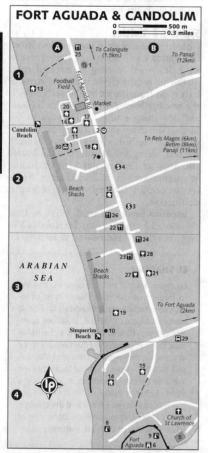

FORT AGUADA & CANDOLIM

0 — 500 m
0 — 0.3 miles

To Calangute (1.5km)
To Panaji (12km)
Fort Aguada Rd
Football Field
Market
Candolim Beach
To Reis Magos (6km); Betim (8km); Panaji (11km)
Beach Shacks
ARABIAN SEA
Beach Shacks
To Fort Aguada (2km)
Sinquerim Beach
Church of St Lawrence
Fort Aguada

INFORMATION		
Online World	1	A1
Post Office	2	A2
State Bank of India	3	B2
UTI Bank ATM	4	B2

SIGHTS & ACTIVITIES		
Aguada Jail	5	B4
Fort Aguada	6	B4
John's Boat Tours (Elephant Shop)	7	A2
New Lighthouse	8	B4
Old Lighhouse	9	B4
Thunderwave	10	B3

SLEEPING		
Aguada Hermitage	(see 14)	
Ave Maria	11	A2
Casa Sea-Shell	12	B2
D'Mello's	13	A1
Fort Aguada Beach Resort	14	B4
Marbella Guest House	15	B4
Moonlight Bar & Restaurant	16	A1
Pretty Petal Guest House	17	A1
Sea Shell Inn	18	A2
Taj Holiday Village	19	B3
Tropicano Beach Resort	20	A1
Villa Ludovici Tourist Home	21	B3

EATING		
Cinnabar	22	B2
Santa Lucia	23	B3
Stone House	24	B3
Viva Goa	25	A1
Xavier's	26	B2

DRINKING		
10 Downing St.	27	B3
Congo	28	B3

TRANSPORT		
Sinquerim Bus Stop	29	B3
Taxi Stand	30	A2

MIDRANGE

Marbella Guest House (☎ 2479551; marbella_goa@ yahoo.com; d/ste incl tax from Rs 1250/1700; ✂) One of the finest guesthouses in the area, this beautifully restored Portuguese villa is hidden down a quiet lane behind the Fort Aguada Beach Resort. There are three rooms and three suites, each charmingly decorated in a different style (such as Rajasthani and Mughal).

Sea Shell Inn (☎ 2276131; seashellgoa@hotmail .com; Fort Aguada Rd; d incl breakfast Rs 850) On the main road, this place has clean, comfortable rooms in an old colonial house.

Casa Sea-Shell (☎ 2479879; d Rs 950; ✂) Just up the road from the Sea Shell Inn, this is the Sea Shell's more modern sister hotel. It has a good restaurant.

Pretty Petal Guest House (☎ 2276184; Fort Aguada Rd; s/d from Rs 400/600; ✂) This is a lovely two-storey villa with a large garden and spacious rooms. The larger rooms (Rs 800) have balcony, fridge and AC.

TOP END

The **Taj Group** (☎ 5645858; www.tajhotels.com) operates a complex of three luxury hotels beside Sinquerim Beach. The hotels are justifiably popular and facilities include an award-winning spa and tennis courts. The hotels:

Aguada Hermitage (1-/2-bedroom villas from US$280; ✂ 💻 ✂) Above Fort Aguada Beach Resort, this top-of-the-range place has northern views.

Fort Aguada Beach Resort (s & d from US$195; ✂ 💻 ✂) Within the outer walls of the old fort.

Taj Holiday Village (d from US$155, cottages from US$190; ✂ 💻 ✂) Child friendly; beach-side location.

Eating

Stone House (☎ 2479909; Fort Aguada Rd; mains Rs 90-150; ✂ 11am-3pm & 6pm-midnight) A foot-tapping blues soundtrack puts you at ease at this mellow place, with tables laid out in a garden. The menu includes good grilled steaks and fiery fish curries.

Cinnabar (Acorn Arcade, 283 Fort Aguada Rd; mains Rs 40-120; ✂ 8am-midnight) On the corner of a classy shopping arcade is this smart café-bar serving decent coffee, grilled sandwiches and salads.

Xavier's (☎ 2479489; mains Rs 60-200; ✂ 8am-11pm) Just off Fort Aguada Rd and part of a small hotel, this convivial restaurant has an award-winning chef at the helm and is

known for its Saturday-evening barbecues and Sunday-lunch roasts.

Santa Lucia (Fort Aguada Rd; mains Rs 80-140; ✂ 6.30-11pm; ✂) This Italian place (with a Swiss chef) is one of the best restaurants in Candolim for food and ambience. Pasta dishes are predominant, and there's a pasta buffet.

Inexpensive restaurants include the busy **Viva Goa** (mains Rs 40-100; ✂ 11am-midnight), offering seafood and tandoori dishes. Down on the beach are dozens of beach shacks serving the obligatory Western breakfasts, seafood and cold drinks

Drinking

Congo (☎ 5644226; Fort Aguada Rd; ✂ noon-1am) Slump on four-poster beds in a garden lit by fairy lights and enjoy cocktails and Thai nibbles as trance music beats in the background at Candolim's hippest party bar. Over the peak Christmas–New Year period there's a Rs 1000 entrance fee.

10 Downing St (☎ 5649504; Fort Aguada Rd; ✂ 10.30am-4am) This stylish, minimalist bar has DJs playing pop, house and hip-hop till late and can get busy on weekends in the high season.

Getting There & Away

Buses run from Panaji (Rs 7, 45 minutes), Mapusa (Rs 6) or Betim to Sinquerim via the Calangute–Candolim road. There are frequent buses between Sinquerim and Calangute (Rs 3). A prepaid taxi from Daoblim Airport to Candolim costs Rs 550.

CALANGUTE & BAGA

pop 15,800

Calangute was the first beach to attract hippies travelling overland in the '60s, then the first to secure the rampant package and charter-tourist market in the '90s. It's India's answer to the Costa del Sol and, in high season at least, its centre is an overhyped, overpriced, overcrowded strip of mayhem.

Unsurprisingly, the long sandy beach can get crowded with sun beds, deck chairs and slowly burning bodies. There is, however, plenty going on, lots of good places to stay and eat, and outside the Christmas–New Year season heavy competition drives prices down.

Up near the mouth of the river, Baga is popular with backpackers and handy for

GOA

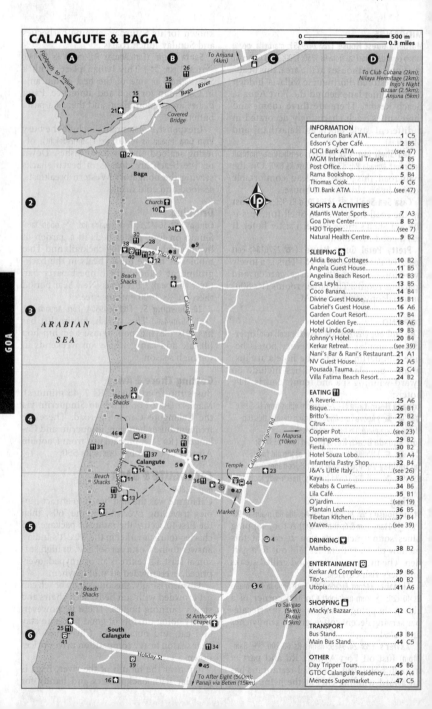

CALANGUTE & BAGA

0 ———— 500 m
0 ———— 0.3 miles

To Anjuna (4km)

To Club Cubana (2km); Nilaya Hermitage (2km); Ingo's Night Bazaar (2.5km); Anjuna (5km)

Baga River

Covered Bridge

Baga

Church

Tito's Rd

Beach Shacks

ARABIAN SEA

GOA

Calangute-Baga Rd

To Mapusa (10km)

Beach Shacks

Golden Beach Rd

Calangute

Church

Temple

Calangute-Anjuna Rd

Market

Beach Shacks

South Calangute

Holiday St

St Anthony's Chapel

To Saligao (5km); Panaji (15km)

To After Eight (500m); Panaji via Betim (15km)

INFORMATION
Centurion Bank ATM.............................1 C5
Edson's Cyber Café..............................2 B5
ICICI Bank ATM............................(see 47)
MGM International Travels....................3 B5
Post Office..4 C5
Rama Bookshop...................................5 B4
Thomas Cook.......................................6 C6
UTI Bank ATM..............................(see 47)

SIGHTS & ACTIVITIES
Atlantis Water Sports...........................7 A3
Goa Dive Center..................................8 B2
H2O Tripper.................................(see 7)
Natural Health Centre..........................9 B2

SLEEPING
Alidia Beach Cottages........................10 B2
Angela Guest House...........................11 B5
Angelina Beach Resort........................12 B3
Casa Leyla...13 B5
Coco Banana......................................14 B4
Divine Guest House............................15 B1
Gabriel's Guest House........................16 A6
Garden Court Resort..........................17 B4
Hotel Golden Eye...............................18 A6
Hotel Linda Goa.................................19 B3
Johnny's Hotel...................................20 B4
Kerkar Retreat.............................(see 39)
Nani's Bar & Rani's Restaurant...........21 A1
NV Guest House.................................22 A5
Pousada Tauma.................................23 C4
Villa Fatima Beach Resort...................24 B2

EATING
A Reverie..25 A6
Bisque...26 B1
Britto's..27 B2
Citrus..28 B2
Copper Pot..................................(see 23)
Domingoes..29 B2
Fiesta..30 B2
Hotel Souza Lobo..............................31 A4
Infanteria Pastry Shop........................32 B4
J&A's Little Italy...........................(see 26)
Kaya...33 A5
Kebabs & Curries...............................34 B6
Lila Café..35 B1
O'jardim.....................................(see 19)
Plantain Leaf.....................................36 B5
Tibetan Kitchen.................................37 B4
Waves..(see 39)

DRINKING
Mambo...38 B2

ENTERTAINMENT
Kerkar Art Complex............................39 B6
Tito's..40 B2
Utopia...41 A6

SHOPPING
Macky's Bazaar..................................42 C1

TRANSPORT
Bus Stand..43 B4
Main Bus Stand..................................44 C5

OTHER
Day Tripper Tours...............................45 B6
GTDC Calangute Residency.................46 A4
Menezes Supermarket.........................47 C5

those wanting to commute to the nightlife at Anjuna and Vagator, or be on hand for the parties at Tito's (p185), Goa's top club.

Orientation & Information

Most services cluster around the main market and bus stand, from where a road leads down to the beach.

Rama Bookshop (☽ 9am-9pm), at the roundabout at the start of the Calangute–Baga Rd, has a wide range of books in many languages and offers book exchange. **MGM International Travels** (☎ 2276249; ☽ 9.30am-6.30pm Mon-Sat) is a reputable travel agency nearby.

There are many currency-exchange offices scattered around that will change cash or travellers cheques, and most give cash advances on Visa and MasterCard. There are 24-hour ATMs accepting foreign cards at the ICICI and UTI banks in the market, and Centurion Bank, about 100m south on the main road.

There are plenty of Internet cafés and many hotels offer Internet access for guests. The standard charge is Rs 30 an hour. In the market area try Edson's Cyber Café; in Baga try the Internet café at Angelina Beach Resort (p184).

Sights & Activities

Water sports, including parasailing (Rs 700 to 1500), and jet-skiing (Rs 900 per 15 minutes), and boat trips are offered about halfway along the beach between Calangute and Baga by **Altantis Water Sports** (☎ 9890047272) and **H2O Tripper** (☎ 2277907).

The **Natural Health Centre** (☎ 2409275; ☽ 9.30am-6pm) has several branches in Goa, including one at the Biera Mar Resort in Calangute offering a range of Ayurvedic treatments, including massage (Rs 650 for one hour), reflexology, aromatherapy, acupressure and yoga. There's also a range of herbal medicines on offer and a free consultation by a Keralan doctor.

Diving trips and courses are offered by the German-run **Goa Dive Center** (☎ 9822157094; goadivecenter@rediffmail.com; Tito's Rd, Baga; ☽ 10am-1pm & 4-9pm).

There are two Saturday-night markets in the Baga area that are alternatives to the Anjuna Market; for details see the boxed text, p187.

If you're after something a little more laid-back, the **Kerkar Art Complex** (☎ 2276017;

www.subodhkerkar.com; ☽ 10am-11pm) showcases the colourful paintings and sculptures of local artist Dr Subodh Kerkar; here you'll also find a good restaurant (p184), a hotel (p184) and an open-air auditorium where classical Indian music concerts are held (p185).

Tours

Day Tripper (☎ 2276726; www.daytrippergoa.com; ☽ 9am-6pm end Oct-end April), with its head office in south Calangute, is one of Goa's best tour agencies. It runs a wide variety of trips around Goa, including to Dudhsagar Falls (p203), and also interstate to Hampi and the Kali River (for rafting) in Karnataka.

GTDC tours (see p173) can be booked at the **Calangute Residency** (☎ 2276024) beside the beach.

Sleeping

It's a solid line of hotels for about 3km along the main Calangute–Baga road and along lanes between the road and the beach, but few places actually have sea views.

CALANGUTE
Budget

South Calangute is generally quieter and more rustic than further north. In central Calangute there are several good places down a laneway called 'Golden Beach Rd', which runs parallel to the beach.

Coco Banana (☎ 2279068; www.cocobananagoa .com; d Rs 450-650, mid-Dec–mid-Jan Rs 900) Walter and Marina, a very helpful Goan-Swiss couple, run a tight ship and keep spotless, secure rooms set around a quiet courtyard. Coco Banana is often full, in which case you may want to stay at the couple's other property, Casa Leyla.

Casa Leyla (☎ 2279068; d Rs 450-600, during Christmas Rs 1500) Owned by the same people as Coco Banana, this two-storey apartment-style place has immaculate rooms in a peaceful area near the beach.

Garden Court Resort (☎ 2276054; mataraul@net cracker.com; budget r Rs 300-350, large r Rs 500-800; ✲) In the thick of things at the roundabout at the start of the Calangute–Baga road is this lovely old place run by a traveller-friendly family. Some rooms have AC and one has a kitchenette.

NV Guest House (☎ 2279749; budget r Rs 150-200, 1st fl r Rs 400) Just south of central Calangute, this simple place enjoys an excellent location close to the beach and is run by a friendly family.

Gabriel's Guest House (☎ 2279486; d Rs 300-600; 🛇) Halfway down a laneway to the beach, Gabriel's is a pleasant family home with spotless rooms (one with AC) with balconies. The Goan and Italian food served at the terrace restaurant here is superb.

Johnny's Hotel (☎ 2277458; johnnys_hotel@yahoo .com; s/d from Rs 250/300, d during Christmas Rs 800) Johnny's is close to the beach, down one of the first lanes you come to as you head north from the roundabout at the start of the Calangute–Baga road. There's a variety of clean rooms in this long-running guesthouse, along with rooftop Hatha yoga, massage and reiki sessions.

Angela Guest House (Golden Beach Rd; Rs 150) One of the cheapest places, Angela's offers basic doubles in a family home.

Midrange & Top End

Kerkar Retreat (☎ 2276017; www.subodhkerkar.com; d Rs 1500) This delightful boutique guesthouse, attached to the Kerkar Art Complex, offers five designer-decorated rooms, a small library, private terrace and common kitchen. An Ayurvedic masseur is on hand, too.

Hotel Golden Eye (☎ 2276187; d without/with AC Rs 650/800, deluxe d Rs 2000; 🛇) A Mediterranean-style place right on the beach at the end of Holiday St; the deluxe rooms are nicely designed but pricey.

Pousada Tauma (☎ 2279061; www.pousada-tauma .com; ste Rs 11,500; 🛇 💻 🌊) Built of laterite stone, Pousada Tauma offers a range of well-designed spacious suites decorated in eclectic themes. The excellent Goan cooking at the restaurant, Copper Pot, is worth a visit alone. It also runs Ayurvedic treatment courses.

BAGA
Budget

Angelina Beach Resort (☎ 2279145; angelinabeach resort@rediffmail.com; d without/with AC Rs 500/650; 🛇 💻) A good family-run place, with large, clean rooms. It's set a little back from the lane to Tito's so is reasonably peaceful.

Divine Guest House (☎ 2279546; divinehome@ satyam.net.in; d Rs 400-500) Across the Baga River in a quiet location, this friendly place has spotless, nicely painted rooms (some with fridges).

Nani's Bar & Rani's Restaurant (☎ 2276313; r Rs 250-600) Also located across the Baga River, this is a big old Portuguese house with a range of rustically simple rooms. There's a lovely garden and meals are served on the veranda.

Villa Fatima Beach Resort (☎ 2277418; fatimavi@ sancharnet.in; d without/with AC from Rs 300/500; 🛇) Set back from the Calangute–Baga road, this place is well run and popular among backpackers. There's a restaurant and TV area in an enclosed courtyard, and easy beach access from the back.

Midrange & Top End

Alidia Beach Cottages (☎ 2276835; alidia@rediffmail .com; cottages Rs 500-800, ste Rs 1200; 🛇) Set back behind the whitewashed church, this convivial place has beautifully kept rooms and cottages fronting onto the beach. There are two stylish AC suites.

Hotel Linda Goa (☎ 2276066; www.hotellindagoa .com; d without/with AC Rs 550/850; 🛇 🌊) This is one of a number of package-tour hotels along the main road that are reasonably priced outside the peak season. It has a pool, a bar and the recommended garden restaurant O'jardim.

Nilaya Hermitage (☎ 2276793; www.nilayahermit age.com; d incl breakfast & dinner US$280; 🛇 💻 🌊) The Nilaya Hermitage's relatively remote hill-side location in Arpora (about 4km northeast of Calangute), cleverly designed suites and fancy facilities have made it a hit with Goa's A-list travellers. Rates include Dabolim Airport transfers.

Eating

Calangute and Baga boast some of the best dining in Goa. There are literally hundreds of small restaurants, and the endless string of bamboo beach shacks is a great place to watch the sun go down with a cold beer and a plate of seafood.

CALANGUTE

After Eight (☎ 2279757; 1/274B Gaura Vaddo; mains Rs 195-260; ☻ 6.30-11pm) This candle-lit garden restaurant and cocktail bar is one of Candolim's best, with a broad, innovative European menu and a welcoming host. The chocolate mousse is divine and there's a quality wine list.

Waves (☎ 2276017; mains Rs 60-130; ☻ 10am-2.30pm & 6.30-11pm) Attached to the Kerkar Art

Complex, this relaxed restaurant-bar has an appealing menu embracing traditional Goan dishes as well as Western ones such as brandy pepper steak.

Kaya (Golden Beach Rd; mains Rs 50-150; ☑ 9am-9pm) This very cute café, run by Japanese expat Sachiko and her Indian family, offers tasty Japanese specials such as fried chicken and *okonomiyaki* (a kind of spicy pancake).

A Reverie (☎ 3114661; Holiday St; mains Rs 200-300; ☑ 6pm-midnight) Another contender in the contemporary décor stakes, the alfresco A Reverie serves up fine seafood and Western dishes to the style set.

Kebabs & Curries (☎ 2275931; mains Rs 75-130; ☑ 6-11pm; ⊠) In south Calangute and set back from the main road, this is one of the few quality North Indian restaurants in the area.

Hotel Souza Lobo (☎ 2276463; most mains Rs 50-140) This place, facing the main beach, has long been a favourite for quality seafood and is hard to beat. Tiger prawns cost Rs 490.

Other recommended places:

Infanteria Pastry Shop (Rs 50-100; ☑ 7am-midnight) Near the roundabout in central Calangute.

Tibetan Kitchen (mains Rs 70-110; ☑ 6-10.30pm) Tucked off the main beach road.

Plaintain Leaf (mains Rs 50-100; ☑ 7.30am-11pm) The best Indian vegetarian restaurant around.

BAGA

Lila Café (☎ 2279843; mains Rs 60-180; ☑ 8.30am-6.30pm) One of the best spots in Goa for breakfast (Rs 20 to 100), and not a bad place for lunch either, is this German bakery and hyper-relaxed café in a peaceful garden across the Baga River.

Bisque (☎ 2282364; mains Rs 115-285, pizza from Rs 155; ☑ 7-11pm) Enjoy excellent French-inspired food, as well as some classic Italian dishes, at this classy but casual restaurant with an alfresco dining area beside the Baga River.

J&A's Little Italy (☎ 2282364; mains Rs 115-285; pizza from Rs 155; ☑ 7-11pm) Next door to Bisque and run by the same people, this long-established restaurant enjoys a good reputation for its authentic Italian food.

Citrus (Tito's Rd; mains Rs 50-140; ☑ 6-11pm; ⊠) Near Tito's, this modern Euro-style vegetarian restaurant has an innovative menu featuring *mezzes*, pasta salads, risotto and rich desserts.

Domingoes (Tito's Rd; mains Rs 80-100; ☑ 6.30-11pm) This simple palm-thatch place specialises in excellent homemade pasta and some of the best beef steaks in Calangute (Rs 135).

Britto's (mains Rs 50-150; ☑ 8am-midnight) One of Baga's longest-running restaurants spills onto the beach. There's good Goan and Continental foods, appealing cakes and desserts, and live music Monday and Thursday nights.

Drinking & Entertainment

Tito's (☎ 2275028; www.titosgoa.com; Tito's Rd; club cover charge Rs 300; ☑ 6pm-3am) Where India's bright young things gather to see and be seen, Tito's has long been the centre of night-time activity along this beach belt. Apart from the club, there's a stylish terraced garden bar, and the lively bar Mambo, closer to the beach.

Club Cubana (☎ 2279799; www.clubcubana.net; women/men Rs 399/499; ☑ 9pm-4am Fri-Sun; ⊠) Competing with Tito's for the late-night drinking crowd, this stylish club's cover charge includes unlimited drinks. It has a spectacular hilltop location – bring your cossie because there's even a swimming pool.

Utopia (☎ 2282901; cover charge Rs 250; ☑ 11am-3am) If you're looking for a more intimate but stylish venue in which to party, this new club near the beach in south Calangute, with pool tables, is a good choice.

Kerkar Art Complex (☎ 2276017; www.subodh kerkar.com; ☑ 10am-11pm) Hosts open-air performances of Indian classical music and dance at 6.45pm on Tuesday (Rs 300).

Getting There & Away

There are frequent buses to Panaji (Rs 7, 45 minutes) and Mapusa (Rs 6) from the

GOA

bus stand opposite the main market. Some services also stop at the bus stop near the temple. A taxi from Calangute or Baga to Panaji costs Rs 150 to 200 and takes about 30 minutes. A prepaid taxi from Dabolim Airport to Calangute will set you back Rs 530.

ANJUNA

Famous throughout Goa for its Wednesday flea market (opposite), Anjuna is still a popular meeting point for backpackers, European ravers, long-term hippies and increasingly midrange tourist taking advantage of comfy new hotels. It's quite a spread-out village and still very rural compared with Calangute and Baga.

Orientation & Information

There are three distinct areas: the main crossroads and bus stand, where paths lead down to the beach; the back part of the village, where you'll find the post office and convenience stores; and the flea market area a couple of kilometres to the south.

Internet access is available at a number of places, including the Manali Guest House (opposite) and Villa Anjuna (opposite), both Rs 40 per hour. There's also an Internet café on the beach near White Negro.

The **Bank of Baroda** (🕑 9.30am-1.30pm) gives cash advances on Visa and MasterCard. There are no ATMs; the closest are in Baga.

Travel agencies where you can make onward travel bookings, get flights confirmed

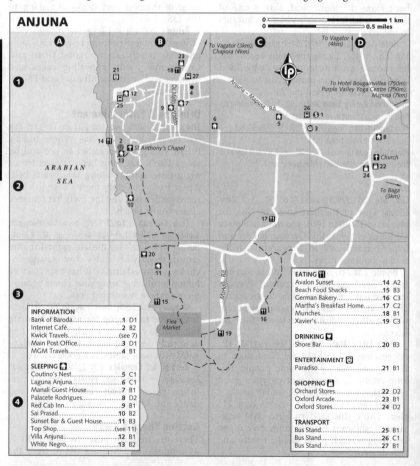

ANJUNA

0 — 1 km
0 — 0.5 miles

ARABIAN SEA

To Vagator (3km); Chapora (4km)
To Vagator (4km)
Anjuna–Mapusa Rd
To Hotel Bougainvillea (750m); Purple Valley Yoga Centre (750m); Mapusa (7km)
St Anthony's Chapel
Church
To Baga (3km)
Market Rd
Flea Market

INFORMATION
Bank of Baroda................................1 D1
Internet Café....................................2 B2
Kwick Travels...............................(see 7)
Main Post Office.............................3 D1
MGM Travels...................................4 B1

SLEEPING 🛏
Coutino's Nest.................................5 C1
Laguna Anjuna................................6 C1
Manali Guest House........................7 B1
Palacete Rodrigues.........................8 D2
Red Cab Inn....................................9 B1
Sai Prasad.....................................10 B2
Sunset Bar & Guest House.............11 B3
Top Shop....................................(see 11)
Villa Anjuna..................................12 B1
White Negro..................................13 B2

EATING 🍴
Avalon Sunset................................14 A2
Beach Food Shacks........................15 B3
German Bakery...............................16 C3
Martha's Breakfast Home...............17 C2
Munches..18 B1
Xavier's..19 C3

DRINKING 🍷
Shore Bar.......................................20 B3

ENTERTAINMENT 🎭
Paradiso...21 B1

SHOPPING 🛍
Orchard Stores...............................22 D2
Oxford Arcade................................23 B1
Oxford Stores.................................24 D2

TRANSPORT
Bus Stand......................................25 B1
Bus Stand......................................26 C1
Bus Stand......................................27 B1

and change foreign currency include **MGM Travels** (☎ 2274317; Anjuna-Mapusa road; ☺ 9.30am-6pm Mon-Sat) and **Kwick Travels** (☎ 2273477; Manali Guest House; ☺ 9am-9pm).

Activities
The long-established **Purple Valley Yoga Centre** (www.yogagoa.com; Hotel Bougainvillea) offers a variety of drop-in classes in Asthanga, hatha and pranayama yoga, as well as meditation, from November to April. It also runs longer residential courses at its retreat in Assagao, 3km east towards Margao.

Paragliding takes off the headland at the southern end of the beach, but usually only on market day.

Sleeping
Many restaurants and family homes have a few rooms out the back, so ask around and look out for 'To Let' signs on houses – there are plenty along the back lanes leading to the flea market. If you arrive before about 15 December you should easily be able to find a place for long-term rent.

BUDGET
Manali Guest House (☎ 2274421; manalionline@siffy .com; r with shared bathroom Rs 100-150; 🖳) This central place has simple, good-value rooms (often full), a bookshop and a travel agency.

White Negro (☎ 2273326; dsouzawhitenegro@ rediffmail.com; d Rs 500, at Christmas Rs 800) White Negro offers some of the tidiest budget rooms (with TV, safe lockers and hot water) in Anjuna. It also has a good garden restaurant.

Sai Prasad (☎ 2274232; d Rs 350-500; 🖳) Right on the beach this is a relaxed place with simple rooms, hot showers, hammocks and a good restaurant.

Coutino's Nest (☎ 2274386; shaldon_555@yahoo .co.in; d with shared/private bathroom Rs 200/350; 🏵) This is a clean home with six rooms on the road into Anjuna. It's run by a friendly family and there's a pleasant rooftop terrace. There's also one AC room for Rs 1000.

Midway down the beach are several decent options including the following:
Sunset Bar & Guesthouse (☎ 2273917; d Rs 200-300)
Top Shop (☎ 2274484; d Rs 250-400)

MIDRANGE & TOP END
Villa Anjuna (☎ 2273443; www.anjunavilla.com; d Rs 500-750, with AC Rs 1040; 🏵 🖳 🍴) In a prime location on the main road to the beach is this friendly hotel with comfortable rooms arranged around a pool (open to nonguests for Rs 100). It also has a decent café.

Hotel Bougainvillea (☎ 273271; granpas@hotmail .com; d/ste incl breakfast & tax from Rs 950/1950; 🏵 🖳 🍴) Also known as Granpa's Inn, this upmarket option is a relaxing place with an old-fashioned resort-style feel and very comfortable rooms. There's a garden and the Purple Valley Yoga Centre (left).

THE GOA MARKET EXPERIENCE

The ever-expanding Wednesday flea market at Anjuna is not just a place to browse for souvenirs – it's an essential part of the Goa experience! The famous market is a wonderful blend of Tibetan and Kashmiri traders, colourful Gujarati and Lamani tribal women, blissed-out 1960s-style hippies (they're still in there somewhere!) and travellers from all over the world. Whatever you need, from a used paperback novel to a tattoo, massage or haircut, you'll find it here – along with an endless jumble of stalls selling jewellery, carvings, T-shirts, sarongs, chillums and spices. Bargain hard to get a reasonable deal as the traders are wise to unsavvy tourists and start high with their prices.

There's lots of good Indian and Western food available, as well as a couple of bars, and when it all gets too much you can wander down to the beach. The best time to visit is early morning (it starts about 8am) or late afternoon (from about 4pm); the latter is good if you plan to stay on for the sunset and party at the Shore Bar (p188).

Anjuna's market can be a bit overwhelming. For something more relaxing try one of the Saturday-night markets near Baga (p181), where the emphasis is as much on entertainment and food stalls as it is on the usual collection of handicraft, jewellery and clothing stalls. **Ingo's Night Bazaar**, on Arpora Hill, halfway between Baga and Anjuna, is well organised and has a good mix of Indian and Western stalls. **Macky's Bazaar**, on the Baga River, is a smaller Goan-run affair. Both run from around 6pm to midnight.

Red Cab Inn (☎ 2274427; redcabinn@rediffmail.com; De Mello Vaddo; d Rs 400-700) The most appealing aspect of this quiet place is the unusual design of some of its rooms and cottages – the split-level rooms are good for families and if you're looking for a starry, romantic night, try the domed room studded with blue lights!

Palacete Rodrigues (☎ 2273358; r Rs 550-850; ❌) This somewhat gloomy, family-run colonial house built around a courtyard offers spacious doubles furnished with antiques. The AC suite (Rs 850) is a bargain.

Laguna Anjuna (☎ 2273248; www.lagunaanjuna .com; ste from US$125; ❌ ▢ ▣) Interestingly designed laterite stone cottages make up the comfy accommodation at this well-run place set in a quiet location.

Inland, also check out the rooms (Rs 600) and villas (Rs 1000) at Martha's Breakfast Home (below).

Eating

Anjuna has a few beach shacks at the southern end (near the flea-market site), a handful of restaurants overlooking the beach along the path from the bus stand, and some refreshingly different places back in the village.

Martha's Breakfast Home (breakfast Rs 50-100; ❌ 7.30am-3pm) This is a great place to start the day, with delicious pancakes, omelettes, fresh bread and various juices, served in a pleasant, shady garden or on the veranda. There are also rooms to rent.

German Bakery (Rs 30-100; ❌ 7am-11pm) Further along the road to the flea market, this place serves herbal teas and espresso coffee as well as fresh breads. It's a great place to relax.

Xavier's (mains Rs 150-350; ❌ 7-11pm) Hidden away behind the flea-market area, Xavier's is one of the best places for seafood in Anjuna.

Munche's (❌ 24hr) This place, widely known as Munchies Corner, is a laid-back café and juice bar that attracts plenty of party goers in the small hours.

There are quite a few places along the dirt path from the bus stand to the beach. **Avalon Sunset** (mains Rs 50-150; ❌ 7am-11pm), a good choice for watching the sun go down, serves decent tandoori and seafood dishes.

The retail needs of the expat community are served by Oxford Stores and Orchard Stores, opposite each other back in the village, and the Oxford Arcade, closer to the beach. Here you can get everything from a loaf of bread to such 'exotic' goodies as Vegemite and imported cheese.

Drinking & Entertainment

Shore Bar (❌ 7.30am-midnight) Still a popular spot to sink a few beers and watch the sun go down. On market day there's usually a party here from sunset.

Paradiso (women/men free/Rs 200; ❌ 10pm-4am Wed, Fri & Sat) Behind the walled entrance, Goa's biggest club, a temple to trance music, tumbles down to the beach in an impressive series of dance floors and bar terraces. Top DJs, including Goa Gil, perform here in season.

Getting There & Away

There are buses every hour or so from Mapusa to Anjuna (Rs 6). They park at the end of the road to the beach and continue on to Vagator and Chapora. Some go up to Arambol. The two other bus stops inland from the beach are drop-off points. Plenty of motorcycle taxis gather at the central crossroads and you can also hire scooters and motorcycles easily from here.

VAGATOR & CHAPORA

Although Vagator's beaches are small and rocky (Chapora has no beach), this is one of the prettiest and most interesting parts of North Goa's coastline. It's also long been the hot location for the outdoor rave parties that made the Goa party scene famous. Much of the inhabited area nestles under a canopy of dense coconut palms, and the village of Chapora is dominated by a rocky hill, on top of which sits a ruined Portuguese fort.

Secluded, sandy coves are found all the way around the northern side of this rocky outcrop, though Vagator's main beaches face west towards the Arabian Sea.

Information

There are STD/ISD phone places in the main street of Chapora. **Soniya Travels** (☎ 2273344; Chapora; ❌ 9am-11pm) is a good agency for transport bookings, foreign exchange and Internet access (Rs 50 per hour).

In Vagator, the **Rainbow Bookshop** (❌ 9am-2am), opposite Primrose Café, stocks a good

VAGATOR & CHAPORA

0 ————————— 500 m
0 ————————— 0.3 miles

Ⓐ　　　　　　　**Ⓑ**

❶

INFORMATION	
Jaws.....................................1	B5
Mira Cybercafé...................(see 16)	
Rainbow Bookshop...........................2	B6
Soniya Travels...................................3	B5

SLEEPING 🛏	
Bean Me Up Soya Station.................4	B6
Bethany Inn.......................................5	B6
Dolrina Guest House.........................6	A5
Helinda Restaurant............................7	B5
Jackie's Daynite.................................8	B6
Jolly Jolly Lester...............................9	A5
Jolly Jolly Roma...............................10	A6
Julie Jolly..11	B6
Leoney Resort..................................12	A6
Shertor Villa....................................13	B5

❷

EATING 🍴	
Alcove Restaurant............................14	A6
Le Bluebird.......................................15	A6
Marakesh...(see 16)	
Potala..16	A6
Scarlet Cold Drinks...........................17	B5
Sunrise Restaurant............................18	B5

DRINKING 🍸	
Nine Bar...19	A6
Paulo's Antique Bar.........................20	B5
Primrose Café...................................21	B6
Tin Tin Bar & Restaurant..................22	A5

❸

ENTERTAINMENT 🎭	
Hill Top Motels...............................23	B6

TRANSPORT	
Main Bus Stand...............................24	B6
Mapusa Bus Stand..........................25	B6

❹

Chapora River

Harbour

Chapora Fort

To Siolim (6km);
Arambol (13km)

❺ *Vagator Beach*

ARABIAN *Disco* *Valley*
SEA

Little *Vagator* *Beach*

Chapora

To Mapusa (10km)

Temple

Vagator

Church

To Petrol Station (300m)

❻

Ozran Beach *Spaghetti Beach*

To Anjuna (2km)

---

range of secondhand and new books. Internet access is available at several places; check out Jaws, Mira Cybercafé and Bethany Inn (below), all open from around 9am to midnight daily and charging Rs 50 per hour.

Sights

On the rocky headland separating Vagator from Chapora sits a ruined Portuguese **fort** dating from 1617. It's worth climbing up here (access is easiest from the Vagator side) for the coastal views.

Sleeping

If you're planning to stay long-term it's possible to find a basic room (with shared bathroom) in a private house for around Rs 50 per night; ask around at the budget hotels for recommendations.

VAGATOR

Dolrina Guest House (☎ 2274896; dolrina@hotmail .com; d with shared/private bathroom Rs 270/500) This family-run place has a good range of simple rooms and there's a garden and café at the back.

Jolly Jolly Lester (☎ 2273620; www.hoteljollygoa .com; s/d Rs 300/400, d with AC Rs 800; 🏊) Apart from this pleasant place, the same family runs **Jolly Jolly Roma** (s/d Rs 300/400, d with AC Rs 800; 🏊), along the path leading to Little Vagator, with stylish, angular rooms, and its original guesthouse **Julie Jolly** (s/d Rs 300/400, d with AC Rs 800; 🏊), near the Primrose Café. There's not much in the way of facilities at any of the trio, but they're clean and well-run places.

Bethany Inn (☎ 2273731; www.bethanyinn.com; d from Rs 400, 2-bedroom ste Rs 600; 💻) Has a good range of spacious, clean doubles and a negotiable pricing policy depending on how busy the season is.

Jackie's Daynite (☎ 2274320; melfordmele@yahoo .co.in; Ozran Beach Rd; r Rs 200-250, during Christmas Rs 650) Has some immaculate, good-value rooms set back in a small garden, and an established bar and restaurant.

Bean Me Up Soya Station (☎ 2273479; d with shared/private bathroom Rs 350/550) Check out the fun, themed, budget rooms at this renowned tofu restaurant (p190). It's a good place for families as it has a kids' play space.

Leoney Resort (☎ 2273634; fax 2274914; Ozran Beach Rd; d/cottages Rs 1500/2000; 🏊) The pick of Vagator's upmarket options, this family-run,

GOA

resort-style place is an oasis of rooms and airy cottages around an inviting pool.

CHAPORA

Shertor Villa (☎ 2274335; d with shared/private bathroom Rs 150/300) This place has about 20 basic rooms (there are reductions for long stays); only three have private bathrooms. If there's nobody here, check over the road at the Noble Nest restaurant.

Helinda Restaurant (☎ 2274345; s/d with shared bathroom Rs 150/200, d with private bathroom Rs 250-300) Clean and relaxed, Helinda has some of the best rooms in Chapora, which means it's often full.

Eating

VAGATOR

The area's best eating places are situated in Vagator.

Bean Me Up Soya Station (☎ 2273479; main Rs 120-150; ⏰ noon-11pm) On the road towards the Anjuna petrol station, this is the place to come for hearty vegetarian cuisine, including locally made tofu and tempeh. It has a juice bar, and live music twice a month. It also offers budget accommodation (p189).

Le Bluebird (☎ 2273695; mains Rs 100-280; ⏰ 9.30am-2pm & 7.30-11pm) This French-run alfresco place is one of the best restaurants around. On the menu are dishes such as ratatouille (Rs 100) and bouillabaisse (Rs 70). There's a good breakfast menu and a range of vegetarian dishes, plus imported (and decent Indian) wine by the bottle or glass.

Alcove Restaurant (mains Rs 65-120; ⏰ 8am-11pm) With the perfect sunset-viewing location, and handy for Nine Bar across the way, the Alcove offers the usual pick'n'mix range of world cuisines.

Also worth seeking out:

Potala (Rs 50-80; ⏰ noon-midnight) For Tibetan food such as *momos* (dumplings), *thukpa* (noodle soup, Rs 40) and herbal tea.

Marakesh (mains Rs 100-150; ⏰ noon-midnight) Goa's only Moroccan restaurant with couscous, kofta and Middle Eastern music.

CHAPORA

There are several small restaurants along the main street of Chapora, including **Sunrise Restaurant** (mains Rs 40-70; ⏰ 7-11am), which does a decent breakfast and is fine for a light lunch, and **Scarlet Cold Drinks** (juices Rs 20), the place for fresh juices, shakes and muesli.

Drinking & Entertainment

Vagator is the centre of Goa's party scene – as well as several established bars and clubs, impromptu raves are still organised (over Christmas–New Year) at places such as 'Disco Valley' and 'Spaghetti Beach'. The evening usually starts at the open-air Nine Bar, overlooking Little Vagator Beach, where trance and house music plays to a packed floor until 10pm. Depending on restrictions, the party then moves up to Primrose Café, towards the back of Vagator village, where music continues till 2am or 3am under a canopy of psychedelically painted trees.

Hill Top Motels is another venue that often has outdoor parties past the 10pm music restrictions.

You could try to catch the occasional live acoustic music, or you could just have a game of pool at **Tin Tin Bar & Restaurant** (⏰ 9am-midnight) in Vagator. **Paulo's Antique Bar** (⏰ 8.30am-midnight) in Chapora is tiny, but has a friendly atmosphere and cheap, ice-cold beer (Rs 20 for a small King's).

Getting There & Away

Fairly frequent buses run to both Chapora and Vagator from Mapusa (Rs 6) throughout the day. Many of these go via Anjuna. The bus stand is near the road junction in Chapora village. Most people hire a motorcycle to get around; enquire at hotels and restaurants.

CHAPORA TO ARAMBOL

The Siolim Bridge across the Chapora River provides an easy link to the string of relatively deserted beaches running up to the backpackers' centre of Arambol.

Public buses in this region of Goa are few and far between; to fully explore it you'd be advise to rent your own transport, preferably a scooter or motorbike.

Morjim & Asvem

Crossing the bridge to Chopdem, you can head east to **Morjim Beach**, an exposed strip of sand that has a handful of beach shacks at the southern car park and several places to stay at its northern end. Rare olive ridley turtles nest at the southern end of Morjim Beach from September to February, so this is a protected area.

Montego Bay (☎ 2244222; www.montegobaygoa .com; tents with shared/private bathroom Rs 800/1200, cabins with shared/private bathroom Rs 1200/3500) is an imaginative low-impact, beachside development offering luxury tents or rustic cabins, as well as a beach house that sleeps four from Rs 2000 per day. The restaurant, where you can relax in sunken lounge pits or a hammock, is excellent.

At the northern end of the beach, **Britto's** (☎ 2244245; d Rs 250) and **Goan Café** (☎ 2246394; anthonylobo2015@yahoo.co.uk; d Rs 300) are peaceful places to stay, the former with simple rooms, the latter with bamboo huts. Both serve good food.

Asvem Beach, a kilometre or so north of Morjim, is claimed to be where the first of Goa's bamboo beach huts was built in the mid-1990s. **Gopal's** (☎ 2247030; gopal@ingoa.com; r & huts Rs 200-250), one of those original places, is worth checking out if you're looking for a quiet beach-side pad.

Mandrem

Mandrem is a peaceful area with a broad beach and some good places to stay among the coconut groves. There are several groups of bamboo huts along the beach, all with semi-open-air restaurants and bars facing the Arabian Sea. One of the best is **Dunes Holiday Village** (☎ 2297219; www.dunesgoa .com; huts/cottages Rs 400/600), a laid-back place with a choice of thatched huts, tree houses and stone cottages. Hatha yoga and massage sessions are on offer here.

SOMETHING SPECIAL

Siolim House (☎ 2272138; www.siolimhouse .com; standard/superior d incl breakfast, dinner & tax Rs 2900/3850; 🖭) If you're looking for a classy, tranquil hotel in which to relax and unwind, there are few better places to do so than at this superbly restored colonial mansion in the small village of Siolim. The seven large rooms, some with reproduction antique furnishings, are spread around the two-storey house and in the tasteful extension around a shady courtyard where meals are served. Rates include Dabolim Airport transfers.

On the bank of the Mandrem River, **River Cat Villa** (☎ 2297928; d Rs 680-1500) is an arty Portuguese house with a distinctly bohemian air. The more expensive rooms are spacious and well furnished – the cheapest have a shared bathroom. This is one of the best guesthouses north of Calangute and there's a good restaurant serving Continental dishes, too.

ARAMBOL (HARMAL)

Travellers have been drifting to Arambol for years, attracted by the remote location and prominent headland with beautiful, rocky bays. A mushrooming industry of facilities and accommodation has appeared to service these visitors, and in the high season the beach and the road leading down to it is pretty crowded. This said, Arambol is still a lot quieter than anything south of Vagator, and generally attracts budget travellers looking to chill out for a while.

The main beach is good for swimming, but over the headland are several more attractive bays. At low tide, if you continue past the headland and keep walking you'll come to the near-deserted **Querim Beach**. You can also walk south along the beach to Mandrem (about one hour).

Information

Arambol village has travel agencies (handling foreign exchange), Internet cafés, motorbike hire and other services. Most of this is concentrated on the road leading to the northern end of the beach.

Activities

Arambol Paragliding (☎ 2292525; uwe@sify.com; Relax Inn) charges Rs 1200 for a tandem flight and also offers certified courses (four to five days; Rs 8500).

Also, from November to March it's possible to take **boat trips** to go fishing and dolphin spotting – operators will find you as you hang out on the beach.

Courses

About 2km south of Arambol is the **Himalayan Iyengar Yoga Centre** (www.hiyogacentre.com; 5-day course Rs 1800), which runs hatha yoga courses on the beach between late November and February. This is the winter centre of the Dharamsala school.

GOA

Sleeping

The prime accommodation is the jumble of cliff-side **chalets** (d Rs 200-400) on the next bay to the north of the main beach. Some are basic rooms, but many now have private bathrooms and running water, and the sea views and sheltered location are superb. Outside peak season you can certainly negotiate cheaper rates, especially for long stays. **Om Ganesh** (☎ 2297675) and **Sunny Guest House** (☎ 2297602) are two of the main places.

Residensea (☎ 2292413; pkresidensea_37@hotmail.com; huts Rs 150-250) At the north end of the beach, this is a group of simple, lockable bamboo huts arranged in a horseshoe around a restaurant.

Ave Maria Guest House (☎ 2297674; avemaria_goa@hotmail.com; dm Rs 30, d with shared/private bathroom Rs 150/300; 🖳) In a quiet area of coconut palms back from the beach is this solid old home run by a friendly family. There's a good rooftop restaurant, where you can also choose to sleep on a mattress at night. There's free filter water.

Priya Guest House (☎ 2292661; d with shared/private bathroom Rs 100/150) Next door, this guesthouse is popular with travellers for its cheap, clean rooms and friendly café.

Eating

There's a string of shacks lining the main beach, serving seafood and beer and offering similar menus and prices. Otherwise most places to eat (and drink) are on the busy lane leading down to the beach and all are open from breakfast until around 11pm. As well as the following, try Double Dutch, a bohemian-style garden café famed for its apple pie.

Fellini (mains Rs 60-135) This is Arambol's top restaurant, specialising in Italian food. There's a good range of pizzas, calzones and pasta, as well as focaccia sandwiches (Rs 40 to 75).

Rice Bowl (mains Rs 25-60) Maybe they should have called this place Noodle Bowl because it does pretty decent noodle dishes as well as other traveller favourites. It's got a prime position overlooking the beach, too.

Oasis On the Rocks (mains Rs 60-250) Along the path leading around the headland, this is a simple café with another great location.

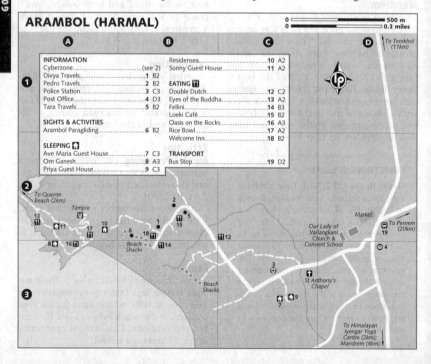

ARAMBOL (HARMAL)

0 ——————— 500 m
0 ——————— 0.3 miles

INFORMATION	
Cyberzone	(see 2)
Divya Travels	1 B2
Pedro Travels	2 B2
Police Station	3 C3
Post Office	4 D3
Tara Travels	5 B2

SIGHTS & ACTIVITIES	
Arambol Paragliding	6 B2

SLEEPING 🛏	
Ave Maria Guest House	7 C3
Om Ganesh	8 A3
Priya Guest House	9 C3

Residensea	10 A2
Sunny Guest House	11 A2

EATING 🍴	
Double Dutch	12 C2
Eyes of the Buddha	13 A2
Fellini	14 B3
Loeki Café	15 B2
Oasis on the Rocks	16 A3
Rice Bowl	17 A2
Welcome Inn	18 B2

TRANSPORT	
Bus Stop	19 D2

To Terekhol (11km)

To Querim Beach (2km)

Temple

Market

To Pernem (20km)

Our Lady of Vailangkani Church & Convent School

Beach Shacks

Beach Shacks

St Anthony's Chapel

To Himalayan Iyengar Yoga Centre (2km); Mandrem (4km)

It's best for a romantic candle-lit seafood meal at night.

Eyes of the Buddha (mains Rs 30-120; 🕑 7am-11pm) Further round, among the chalets, this place also has a good seafront location and the usual extensive menu. The breakfast fruit salad with curd (Rs 40) is spectacular.

Loeki Café (mains Rs 25-80) This relaxed place has a big breakfast menu, as well as Goan, Chinese and Continental dishes. It's also a good place for a drink – there's a jam session here on Sunday and Thursday.

Welcome Inn (mains Rs 50; 🕑 8.30am-11pm) A bakery and juice bar near the beach.

Getting There & Away
Buses from Mapusa stop on the main road at Arambol (Rs 10), where there's a church, a school and a few shops. From here, follow the road about 1.5km through the village to get to the main road down to the beach.

TEREKHOL (TIRACOL) FORT
At Terekhol (Tiracol), on the north bank of the river of the same name, is a small Portuguese **fort** (admission free; 🕑 11am-5pm) with a tiny chapel within its walls. Much of the structure is now the stylish **Fort Tiracol Heritage Hotel** (☎ 02366-227631; nilaya@sancharnet.in; d/suite incl breakfast & dinner Rs 3850/5480). It's an atmospheric place to stay with just five rooms and two suites, decorated in a sort of Mediterranean-meets-medieval style, with no phone or TV to distract from the impressive views. A speedboat is on hand (Rs 1500 per hour) to whisk you off to secluded beaches.

A trip to the fort makes a good outing on a motorcycle. The winding 11km road from Arambol passes through villages and rice paddies and rises up to provide good views over the countryside and Terekhol River. You can also stop for a swim on near-deserted **Querim Beach**.

There are occasional buses from Mapusa to Querim (Rs 12, 1¾ hours), on the south bank of the river, opposite Terekhol, and also between Arambol and Querim (Rs 7, 30 minutes), but without your own transport you'll have to walk a couple of kilometres to reach the fort. The ferry between Querim and Terekhol runs every hour in each direction from 6.15am to 9.45pm. The trip takes five minutes, is free for pedestrians and Rs 4 for car or motorbike.

SOUTH GOA

MARGAO (MADGAON)
pop 94,400

The capital of Salcete province, Margao (also known as Madgaon) is the main population centre of South Goa and is probably the busiest town in the state – the traffic, fumes and noise in the town centre make Panaji look positively comatose.

Information
Visa or MasterCard cash advances are available at the Bank of Baroda. HDFC Bank has a 24-hour ATM accepting international cards on the ground floor of the Caro Centre; Centurion Bank has an ATM just off Luis Miranda Rd; and UTI Bank has an ATM near the roundabout just south of the main bus stand.

Cyberlink (Caro Centre, Abade Faria Rd; per hr Rs 24; 🕑 8.30am-7pm Mon-Sat) Internet access.

GTDC tourist office (☎ 2715204; Margao Residency; 🕑 10am-5.30pm Mon-Sat) At the south end of the Municipal Gardens.

Hindnet (Valaulikar Rd; per hr Rs 20; 🕑 8.30am-11pm) Internet access, just east of the municipal gardens.

Main post office (🕑 9am-1.30pm & 2-4pm) On the north side of the municipal gardens.

Poste restante (🕑 8.30-10.30am & 3-4.30pm) One hundred metres from the post office.

Sights
Long-term visitors will want to visit Margao for its markets – the **covered market** in the centre is one of the best in Goa, and there's a fish and produce market in a vast complex near the Kadamba bus stand. The richly decorated **Church of the Holy Spirit** is also worth a quick look.

Sleeping
With the beaches of Colva and Benaulim less than 10km away there's no pressing reason to stay in Margao.

Hotel La Flor (☎ 2731402; laflor@sancharnet.in; Erasmo Carvalho St; s/d Rs 430/530, s/d with AC Rs 570/650; 🔀) This is Margao's best choice. It's clean, efficiently run and in a quiet but central location. Rooms come with TVs.

Margao Residency (☎ 2715528; Luis Miranda Rd; s/d Rs 475/550, d with AC Rs 700; 🔀) The GTDC's hotel also has decent but plain rooms with TV and hot water.

Eating

Banjara (☎ 2714837; D'Souza Chambers, Valaulikar Rd; mains Rs 60-125; ☽ noon-3pm & 7-11pm; ✖) This is Margao's best Indian restaurant. Open for lunch and dinner, it specialises in North Indian dishes and seafood. The subterranean dining room is intimate and the service good.

Tato (Apna Bazaar Complex, Varde Valualikar Rd; thalis Rs 24; ☽ 7am-10pm Mon-Sat; ✖) Down a small street east of the municipal gardens is this lively vegetarian restaurant with thalis (Rs 27 if eaten in the AC section).

Longuinhos (Luis Miranda Rd; mains Rs 55-80; ☽ 8.15am-10.45pm; ✖) This has long been Margao's classic colonial hang-out, with a languid, old-fashioned atmosphere. The food's not great but it's still a good place to sit and relax over a drink or light meal.

Marliz Cafeteria (Padre Miranda Rd; ☽ 7.30am-7.30pm Mon-Sat; ✖) This is a modern, open-fronted café looking out at the municipal gardens. It's a great spot for coffee and cake.

Getting There & Away

BUS

All local buses operate from the busy Kadamba bus stand 2km north of the town centre, but many also stop at the old bus stand opposite the municipal gardens. Catch buses to Colva and Benaulim from Kadamba or from the bus stop on the east side of the municipal gardens.

There are hourly buses to Colva from around 7am to 7pm (Rs 6, 20 minutes). Some go via Benaulim. Buses to Panaji run every 15 minutes (Rs 12/16 ordinary/

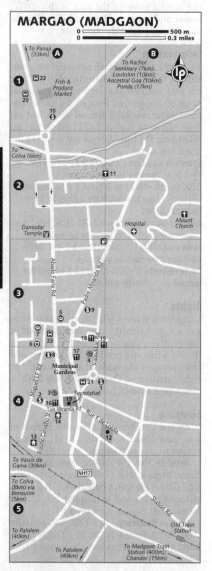

MARGAO (MADGAON)

INFORMATION
Bank of Baroda...1 A4
Centurion Bank ATM..2 A4
Cyberlink...3 A4
Goa Tourism Development Corporation (GTDC) Tourist
   Office..(see 14)
HDFC Bank ATM..(see 3)
Hindnet...4 A4
Main Post Office...5 A3
Police Station..6 A3
Poste Restante..7 A3
State Bank of India..8 A4
UTI Bank ATM...9 A3
UTI Bank ATM...10 A1

SIGHTS & ACTIVITIES
Church of the Holy Spirit...................................11 A2
Covered Market...12 B4

SLEEPING 🏠
Hotel La Flor...13 A4
Margao Residency...14 A4

EATING 🍴
Banjara..15 A3
Longuinhos..16 A4
Marliz Cafeteria...17 A4
Tato...18 A3

TRANSPORT
Advance Reservation Office.................................19 A4
Bus Stand..20 A1
Buses to Colva & Palolem....................................21 A4
Kadamba Bus Stand...22 A1
Old Bus Stand..23 A3
Petrol Station...(see 23)

express, one hour). There are around eight buses a day direct to Palolem (Rs 12, one hour) and many others heading south to Karwar (Rs 30), stopping in nearby Chaudi. There are also local buses to Vasco de Gama (for the airport), Ponda, Chandor and Rachol.

There is one public bus daily to Mumbai (Rs 510, 14 hours), Bangalore (Rs 345, 14 hours) and Pune (Rs 250, 10 hours). Head to the advance reservation office in the Secretariat building for bookings. There are also buses to Hubli (Rs 65, six hours), Belgaum (Rs 60, five hours) and Mangalore (Rs 146, 10 hours). A better option for most interstate trips is on a long-distance private bus. There are private booking offices clustered near the Margao Residency on Luis Miranda Rd. Private buses to Mumbai, Pune, Bangalore (all Rs 300) and Hampi (Rs 300/450 normal/sleeper) depart from a stand opposite the Kadamba bus stand.

TAXI
To get to Colva or Benaulim, taxis (around Rs 80), autorickshaws (Rs 60) and motorcycle taxis (Rs 40, backpacks fine) gather around the municipal gardens and at the Kadamba bus stand.

TRAIN
Margao's train station, Madgaon, is about 1.5km southeast of the town centre; vehicle access is via the road south of the train line but if you're walking there you can cross the tracks at the footbridge past the old station. There's a **reservation hall** (☎ 2721841) on the 2nd floor of the main building, a **tourist information counter** (☎ 2702298) and retiring rooms. See p166 for details of trains running from Margao to Mumbai.

Taxis between the train and bus stations cost Rs 40. There's a prepaid taxi booth out front (Rs 150 to Colva, Rs 500 to Panaji), as well as autorickshaws and motorcycle taxis.

CHANDOR
About 15km east of Margao, the village of Chandor is home to a couple of superb colonial mansions affording a peek at the opulent lifestyle of the colonial Goan landowners.

Braganza House takes up one complete side of Chandor's village square and dates back

to the 17th century. It's now divided into east and west wings, which stretch outwards from a common front entrance. Ongoing restoration is gradually returning the house to its former glory; wandering through the ballrooms with their Italian marble floors, Belgian glass chandeliers and carved rosewood furniture, it's not hard to imagine the sort of parties that were thrown here.

The most impressive side of the house is the **west wing** (☎ 2784201; ☼ 10am-5pm) belonging to the Menezes Braganza family. It's crammed with beautiful furniture and Chinese porcelain. The two large rooms behind the entrance halls contain Dr Menezes Braganza's extensive library.

The **east wing** (☎ 2784227; ☼ 10am-5pm) is owned by the Braganza Pereira family, and includes a small family chapel containing a carefully hidden relic of St Francis Xavier – a fingernail. The clutter of bric-a-brac collected by the family over the years gives the house an air of faded glory.

Both homes are open daily, but you may want to call ahead to ensure the owners will be there. The respective families give you guided tours of their homes, and though there is no official entry fee, the owners rely on contributions for maintenance and restoration – Rs 50 to 100 is reasonable.

A kilometre east past the church is the **Fernandes House** (☎ 2784245; ☼ 10am-5pm Mon-Sat). It's nowhere near as grand as the Braganza House, but is much older and has an interesting history. The original Hindu house here dates back more than 500 years, while the Portuguese section was built by the Fernandes family in 1821. A feature is the secret basement hideaway with an escape tunnel to the river – the Hindu occupants used it to flee attackers.

The best way to reach Chandor is by taxi from Margao (around Rs 120 round trip) or by motorcycle. It's also possible to stay over in a house owned by John Coutinho of Ciaran's Camp in Palolem (p201) for Rs 1500 per night.

LOUTOLIM
Another attractive village boasting some grand mansions is Loutolim, 10km northeast of Margao and nestled in pleasant countryside. The only mansion open to the public is the 250-year-old **Casa Arajao Alvarez** (admission Rs 100; ☼ 9am-6.30pm).

GOA

Also in the village, and set up purely for tourists, **Ancestral Goa** (☎ 2777034; admission Rs 20; ❧ 9am-6.30pm) is a re-creation of Goan village life under the Portuguese a century ago. The gardens feature a 14m-long laterite stone statue of Sant Mirabai, a Rajput princess and historical figure.

Loutolim is best visited by motorcycle or taxi (around Rs 100 round trip) from Margao.

BOGMALO & AROSSIM

The small village of **Bogmalo**, 4km from the airport, has a pleasant, sandy cove dominated by the ugly five-star Bogmalo Beach Resort. There's little here apart from the reasonably exclusive beach and watersports facilities. **Goa Diving** (☎ 2555117; www .goadiving.com), a reputable dive school, offers PADI courses. Guided dives start at Rs 1430, courses at Rs 15,000.

Regular buses run between Bogmalo and Vasco da Gama (Rs 5), from where you can pick up buses to Margao and Panaji.

William's Inn (☎ 2538004; d from Rs 500) is a friendly, family-run place with spacious, clean rooms. It's a little difficult to find; look for the yellow-painted, two-storey house set back from the beach.

The best place to stay in Bogmalo is **Coconut Creek** (☎ 2538800; joets@sancharnet.in; cottages without/with AC incl breakfast Rs 3250/3750;

🅺 🖵 🅡), a very stylish resort set back from the beach in the coconut groves. There's a shady pool surrounded by 10 double-storey laterite stone cottages and a good restaurant serving Italian and Goan cuisine. It also runs the beach-side **Joets Guest House** (d incl breakfast Rs 900), decorated to the same high standards and with a restaurant-bar offering fresh seafood and live music in the evenings.

Around the headland, beyond the eyesore petrochemical plant, is **Arossim** village and beach. Here you'll find the stylish **Park Hyatt Goa Resort & Spa** (☎ 2721234; www.goa.park .hyatt.com; d low/high season US$90/320; 🅺 🖵 🅡). This hermitic resort, set in 45 acres, offers spacious rooms, all with sunken baths and some with garden showers. The smart décor could be anywhere tropical other than Goa. The huge, sculptured pool is a plus though, as is the characterful Miranda bar, with original paintings by famed Goan artist Marvin Miranda. The spa offers Ayurvedic massage and other treatments.

COLVA & BENAULIM
pop 10,200

Some years ago, **Colva** went from being a peaceful little fishing village where locals pulled their catch in by hand each morning, to a hippy hang-out for travellers who had forsaken the obligatory sex, drugs and rock and roll of Calangute for the soothing tranquillity of this paradise. Package tourism changed the face of Colva village, but the scale of development here is nowhere near that of Calangute – and you can still see the fish being brought ashore in the morning.

Colva is popular with Indian tourists and a middle-aged European crowd, while **Benaulim**, 2km south, is still a very peaceful village with most of the accommodation in family guesthouses. It's a good place to rent long-term if you're after a relaxing Goan experience.

Colva and Benaulim are both easy to cycle around as there's little traffic on the back lanes. Bikes can be hired near the bus stand in Colva and on the beach in Benaulim. With fewer people than the northern beaches and quiet back lanes, occasional robberies do occur in Benaulim. Avoid walking from the beach alone at night.

THE TRADITIONAL GOAN HOUSE

Apart from its stock of churches, Goa's distinctive architectural heritage includes the beautiful traditional houses of colonial days. Although many are in sad disrepair, there's a pleasing trend for these houses to be restored and opened up to the public, either as hotels, such as Siolim House (p191), boutiques or museums, as in Chandor (p195) and Loutolim (p195).

Distinctive features of these houses to look out for are the wide, shady verandas, including the *tubalcao* (the porch where people would sit) and oyster shells used instead of glass in the ornate wooden window frames. If you're keen to discover more, a visit to the Houses of Goa Museum in Torda (p178) is recommended. You can buy the lavish photo book *Houses of Goa* here, and elsewhere in Goa.

Information

There are branches of the Bank of Baroda both in Colva (next to the church, on Colva Beach Rd) and Benaulim, near the intersection of Colva and Vasvaddo Beach Rds. You'll find several travel agencies in both Colva and Benaulim that will change cash and travellers cheques and give cash advances on Visa and MasterCard. There's a Centurion Bank ATM accepting foreign cards on the main road in Colva, near Gatsby's.

GK Tourist Centre (☎ 2770476; per hr Rs 20; 🕑 9am-10pm) In Benaulim. Has Internet access and changes cash and travellers cheques.

Hello Mae Communication (Colva Beach Rd; per hr Rs 40; 🕑 8am-10pm) Internet access.

Ida Online (Colva Beach Rd; 🕑 10am-1am) Internet access. Above Baskin Robbins.

Meeting Point Travel (☎ 2788626; Colva Beach Rd; 🕑 9am-10pm) Changes cash and travellers cheques.

Activities

Water sports have arrived at Colva, with parasailing and jet-skiing available in the high season – check with **Chris Watersports** (☎ 9822142110) on Colva Beach.

Pele's Dolphin Dream (☎ 2763522; Rs 300) organises two-hour dolphin trips. Dominick's (p199) offers full-day boat trips to Palolem beach on Sundays for Rs 950, including a buffet lunch and a drink. The boat trip there takes 2½ hours and there's a good chance of seeing dolphins; the return trip is by bus.

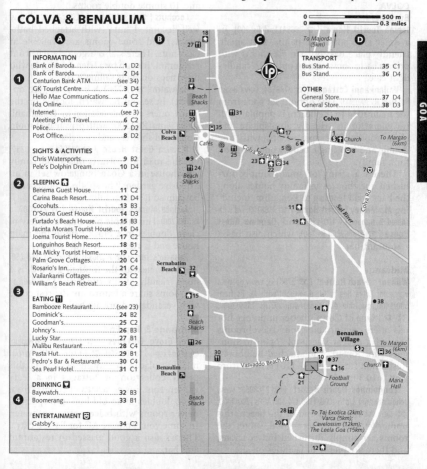

COLVA & BENAULIM

INFORMATION	
Bank of Baroda	1 D2
Bank of Baroda	2 D4
Centurion Bank ATM	(see 34)
GK Tourist Centre	3 D4
Hello Mae Communications	4 C2
Ida Online	5 C2
Internet	(see 3)
Meeting Point Travel	6 C2
Police	7 D2
Post Office	8 D2

SIGHTS & ACTIVITIES	
Chris Watersports	9 B2
Pele's Dolphin Dream	10 D4

SLEEPING	
Benema Guest House	11 C2
Carina Beach Resort	12 D4
Cocohuts	13 B3
D'Souza Guest House	14 D3
Furtado's Beach House	15 B3
Jacinta Moraes Tourist House	16 D4
Joema Tourist Home	17 C2
Longuinhos Beach Resort	18 B1
Ma Micky Tourist Home	19 C2
Palm Grove Cottages	20 C4
Rosario's Inn	21 C4
Vailankanni Cottages	22 C2
William's Beach Retreat	23 C2

EATING	
Bambooze Restaurant	(see 23)
Dominick's	24 B2
Goodman's	25 C4
Johncy's	26 B3
Lucky Star	27 B1
Malibu Restaurant	28 C4
Pasta Hut	29 B1
Pedro's Bar & Restaurant	30 C4
Sea Pearl Hotel	31 C1

DRINKING	
Baywatch	32 B3
Boomerang	33 B1

ENTERTAINMENT	
Gatsby's	34 C2

TRANSPORT	
Bus Stand	35 C1
Bus Stand	36 D4

OTHER	
General Store	37 D4
General Store	38 D3

0   500 m
0   0.3 miles

To Majorda (5km)

Beach Shacks

Colva Beach

Cafes

Colva Beach Rd

Colva

Church

To Margao (6km)

Beach Shacks

Sal River

Colva Rd

Sernabatim Beach

Beach Shacks

Benaulim Village

To Margao (6km)

Church

Maria Hall

Benaulim Beach

Vasvaddo Beach Rd

Football Ground

Beach Shacks

To Taj Exotica (2km); Varca (5km); Cavelossim (12km); The Leela Goa (15km)

GOA

If you're not planning to stay at any of the northern beaches, it's worth making the day trip to the Wednesday flea market at Anjuna. Minibus trips are advertised at the beach bars and cost about Rs 75. Tackling this trip by public bus involves three or four changes.

Sleeping

It's easy to rent houses long-term in Colva and Benaulim, particularly if you arrive early in the season (before December), and Benaulim is probably the best place in Goa for a long-term stay – just ask around in the restaurants and shops. Most houses are a 20-minute walk back from the beach.

COLVA
Budget
Joema Tourist Home (☎ 2888411; d Rs 200) In a quiet area amid the palms, this small, friendly place has four simple rooms with private bathrooms, and an open-air 'candle-light café'.

Vailankanni Cottages (☎ 2788584; Colva Beach Rd; r/apt Rs 300/800) This option, set back from the main road to the beach, is popular with travellers for its friendly atmosphere and clean rooms. The apartments, with one double and two single beds, would be good for a family.

There's a string of small, simply furnished guesthouses in family homes along the back road leading to Benaulim, including **Ma Mickey Tourist Home** (☎ 2788190; s/d with shared bathroom Rs 100/150) and **Benema Guest House** (☎ 2788698; d Rs 150), which also has a restaurant-bar.

Midrange
William's Beach Retreat (☎ 2788153; www.goagetaway.com; Colva Beach Rd; d without/with AC Rs from 500/1000, poolside d without/with AC Rs 1500/2000; 🛇 🖭) One of Colva's better midrange hotels offers comfortable ground-level rooms around a decent-size pool (open to non-guests for Rs 50). The attached Bambooze Restaurant (mains Rs 50-110) is open from 8am to10.30pm.

Longuinhos Beach Resort (☎ 2788068; www.longuinhos.net; s/d Rs 1000/1100, s/d with AC Rs 1200/1400; 🛇 🖭) At the north end of the beach, this upmarket place is very good value; the rooms are simply furnished but spacious, and there are plenty of facilities on site.

BENAULIM
Less than 2km south of Colva, Benaulim is much more peaceful and rustic, with numerous guesthouses and small hotels spread over a wide area.

Budget
There are several good budget places on the beach at Sernabatim, between Benaulim and Colva, including Furtado's Beach House, Cocohuts and Baywatch. Most other places are scattered around the village of Benaulim, about 1km from the beach, where accommodation is generally cheaper.

Furtado's Beach House (☎ 2770396; d without/with AC from Rs 350/600; 🛇) This place has a prime beach-front location, a restaurant and 10 simple double rooms.

Cocohuts (☎ 2780787; huts Rs 150, r Rs 250) A few well-decorated huts (with attached bathrooms) and some rooms are available at Cocohuts. There's also a good beach-front restaurant. It's run by a friendly couple who offer trips on their sailing boat.

Baywatch (☎ 2772795) A bar-disco (see opposite). In season Baywatch, located on the beach, offers accommodation in 'Rajasthani' safari tents (Rs 1500), with private bathroom (toilet and shower) and electricity.

D'Souza Guest House (☎ 2770583; d Rs 350) On the road to Colva is this small family guesthouse in a Goan bungalow set in an extensive garden. The spotless rooms are a bargain so it's often full.

Jacinta Moraes Tourist House (☎ 2770187; d Rs 100-200) This simple place has a variety of clean doubles in a block behind the main house and is run by a friendly family.

Rosario's Inn (☎ 2770636; d from Rs 150-250) Rosario's, next to the football ground, is a huge, friendly, family-run place. The cheapest rooms share a bathroom, the rest come with veranda and private bathroom.

Midrange & Top End
Palm Grove Cottages (☎ 2770059; www.palmgrovegoa.com; d Rs 500-900; 🛇) One of the most relaxing places to stay in Benaulim, this pretty collection of cottages in a leafy garden contains a variety of rooms, from basic doubles in an old house to spacious newer rooms with balcony and hot water. In some you can have AC for Rs 150 extra. There's also a good glassed-in restaurant and bar.

Carina Beach Resort (☎ 2770413; carinabeachresort@
yahoo.com; s/d without AC Rs 550/750, s/d with AC Rs 900/
1800; ❄ 🖳) Set in a peaceful compound
with a big pool, the Carina offers spotless,
simple rooms and friendly management.
It also has Ayurvedic massage during the
season.

Taj Exotica (☎ 2771234; www.tajhotels.com; d from
US$270; ❄ 🖳 🖳) One of Goa's most stylish
resorts, with an appealing contemporary
design to the rooms (which include DVD
players) and public areas. As with all resorts
down the coast, Dabolim Airport transfers
are included in the rates.

Eating

COLVA

The most popular places to eat (and drink)
are the open-sided wooden shacks lining
the beach either side of where the road
ends. Seafood is, of course, the staple of the
menu and the best stuff is brought in daily
from the Margao market. These restaurants
are a good place to watch the sunset with
a cold beer, and they also serve breakfast.
Among the beach shacks, Dominick's has
been around a long time and is consistently good.

Sea Pearl Hotel (☎ 2780176; mains Rs 50-150; ☯ 8am-
2pm & 6-11pm) This place is highly recommended for good-value seafood dishes and
Western dishes; the kitchen is spotlessly
clean and the menu impressive with lots of
daily specials.

Lucky Star (mains Rs 50-200; ☯ 7am-11pm) This
is a very popular open-air restaurant beside
the beach, with live entertainment twice
a week and a reputation for great steaks
(Rs 130 to 220). There are simply decorated
rooms here, too (Rs 300).

Goodman's (mains Rs 65-125; ☯ 8am-midnight)
On the road to the beach, Goodman's is
the place if you are craving a cooked breakfast. The English breakfast (Rs 90) includes
baked beans and sausages. It also has a
lengthy menu of Goan, Indian and Continental dishes, and a good bar.

Pasta Hut (mains Rs 60-90; ☯ 7am-11pm) In front
of the Hotel Colmar, and with beach views,
is this good place for Italian food and a
range of other dishes.

BENAULIM

Most of the hotels and guesthouses have
their own restaurants, but Benaulim village has fewer eating options than Colva.
The beach shacks here are spread across a
wider area than at Colva, but they serve the
same fare. Johncy's, at the end of the main
road from Benaulim village, is a perennial
favourite and a popular meeting place.

Pedro's Bar & Restaurant (mains Rs 60-120;
☯ 8am-midnight) Beside the beach, this airy
place has an extensive menu, including traditional Goan dishes and steak sizzlers.

Malibu Restaurant (mains Rs 60-100; ☯ 8.30am-
11pm) With a pleasant alfresco setting, this
place, a short walk back from the beach,
serves decent Indian and Continental food.
It's a good spot for breakfast, too.

Drinking & Entertainment

Compared to the northern beaches, Colva
and Benaulim (even more so) are very quiet
at night, with most people content to eat
out and enjoy a few drinks near the beach.

The only nightclub in the area is **Gats-
by's** (☎ 2789745; Colva Beach Rd; cover charge Rs 250;
☯ 7pm-3am), on the main road into Colva.
It's a small, dark club playing a wide range
of dance music. Lucky Star (left) and nearby,
beachside **Boomerang** (☯ 24hr) are among the
most popular bars in Colva.

Baywatch (☎ 2772795), over on Sernabatim
Beach, is a little isolated but has a good bar
and an enclosed disco with occasional party
nights. In season it also has accommodation (opposite).

Getting There & Away

Buses run from Colva to Margao roughly
every 30 minutes (Rs 7, 20 minutes) from
7.30am to about 7pm, departing from the
parking area at the end of the beach road.
Buses from Margao to Benaulim are also
frequent (Rs 5, 15 minutes); some continue
south to Varca and Cavelossim. Buses stop
at the crossroads known as Maria Hall.

BENAULIM TO PALOLEM

Immediately south of Benaulim are the upmarket beach resorts of **Varca** and **Cavelossim**. Boasting an uninterrupted, 10km-plus
strip of pristine sand, this is where you'll
find a cluster of five-star resorts, all luxurious, self-contained bubbles with pools,
extensive private grounds and practically
every whim catered for. One of the best
is the **Leela Goa** (☎ 2871234; www.ghmhotels.com;
d/ste from US$290/450; ❄ 🖳 🖳) at Mobor, 3km

GOA

south of Cavelossim, which, apart from an appealing Jaipur-ish lobby, sports a golf course, spa and casino.

Even if your budget doesn't run to such luxury it's possible to access the beaches, and the coastal road makes a more interesting and enjoyable route towards Palolem than the faster national highway from Margao. To cross the Sal River estuary, take the ferry from Cavelossim to Assolna – turn left at the sign saying 'Village Panchayat Cavelossim' before you get to Mobor, then continue on for 2km to the river. From there you can ride on to the fishing village of **Betul**.

The road from Betul to Agonda winds over hills and is a little rough in places. You can detour to the old Portuguese fort of **Cabo da Rama**, which has a small church within the fort walls, but not a lot else to see other than the views from the ruined ramparts.

Back on the main road there's a turn-off to the small village of **Agonda**, which has an empty 2km stretch of sand and a few places to stay. This beach is popular with travellers wanting to escape the resort scenes. Heading south along the beach road you'll find **Dersy Beach Resort** (☎ 2647503; huts Rs 200, d Rs 200-250), with spotless doubles with private bathrooms, and a few rooms with a shared bathroom for Rs 200. Across the road, on the beach side, it has simple palm-thatched huts.

Dunhill Resort (☎ 2647328; d Rs 250-300) is an established place with 12 clean, cottage-style rooms with private bathroom. There's also a shady bar and restaurant.

Sunset Bar (☎ 2647381; r Rs 500, cottages Rs 250-300), at the southern end of the beach, has a great outlook, simple accommodation and a small open-air restaurant – a great spot for sunset drinks.

At the even quieter north end of the beach, **Forget Me Not** (☎ 2647611; cottages Rs 200, r with private bathroom Rs 400) is a lovely place consisting of a series of novel mud-brick cottages and a bamboo bar facing the beach.

PALOLEM & AROUND

Palolem is the most southerly of Goa's developed beaches and arguably the state's most idyllic – the argument being whether the addition of wall-to-wall beach huts – a kind of 'bamboo Calangute' – has spoiled it.

There's no denying the sweeping crescent of white sand fringed by a shady rim of coconut palms is a postcard picture. The beach is hemmed in at either end by rocky crags and there's a small island (Green Island) off the northern tip that you can walk across to at low tide.

Many travellers, especially backpackers, have found that Palolem's mix of lazy beach-side life and large numbers of fellow travellers is perfect.

Further north along the coast, and reachable by boat, is pretty **Butterfly Beach**. Around the southern headland from Palolem Beach is a small, rocky cove called **Colomb Bay**, with a couple of basic places to stay, and beyond that is another fine stretch of sand, **Patnem Beach**, with a handful of beach huts and something approaching surf.

Information

Palolem has some pretty good restaurants. It also has motorcycle hire and foreign exchange through several travel agencies, including **Rainbow Travel** (☎ 2643912; ◷ 9am-11pm). **Bliss Travels** (☎ 2643456; ◷ 9am-midnight), near the main entrance to the beach, is a good travel agent with Internet access at Rs 40 per hour.

Sights & Activities

About 9km southeast of Palolem, and a good day trip, is the **Cotigao Wildlife Sanctuary** (☎ 2229701; admission Rs 5; ◷ 7am-5.30pm). It has two tree-top watchtowers, but the animals (including gaur, sambar, leopards, spotted deer and snakes) manage to remain well hidden. Cotigao is best visited early in the morning. There's a **cottage** (d Rs 200) at the park entrance.

Boat tours to see dolphins or to visit tiny Butterfly Beach are easy to arrange – just about everyone in Palolem owns an outrigger fishing boat or knows someone who does! A one-hour trip costs around Rs 150 per person. Three-hour **mountain bike tours** (Rs 300) out to Patnem and Rajbag run on demand; ask at Ciaran's Camp (opposite).

Sleeping

Along the edge of the beach at Palolem are palm-thatch or bamboo huts grouped together in about 30 little 'villages', usually with a beach-shack restaurant at the front. The most basic huts with sandy floor cost

Rs 100 a double (Rs 150 in peak season). Sturdier huts with hard floor, or huts on stilts, cost from Rs 150, rising to Rs 300 over the Christmas period. There's little to choose between many of the camps – just wander along the beach until you find something that suits your budget and taste.

Ciaran's Camp (☎ 2643477; johnciaran@hotmail .com; huts & d Rs 1000-2000; ☒) Every year John Coutinhou keeps improving his camp; it's now about as luxurious as you can expect for Palolem, with excellent huts with private bathrooms, one of the best restaurants and bars on the beach and a stylish boutique. Rooms in the house have AC and TV. John also offers accommodation at his family home in Chandor (p195).

PALOLEM

0 ———— 400 m
0 ———— 0.2 miles

INFORMATION
Bliss Travels.................................1 A3
Rainbow Travel...........................2 A3

SLEEPING
Bhakti Kutir................................3 B4
Ciaran's Camp.............................4 A3
Cozy Nook..................................5 A3
Oceanic Hotel.............................6 B4
Palolem Beach Resort................7 A3
Palolem Guest House.................8 B4

EATING
Casa Fiesta.................................9 A3
Hotel Jackson...........................10 B3
Magic Italy................................11 A3
Mamoo's Café............................12 A3
Smugglers' Inn..........................13 A3

TRANSPORT
Bus Stand.................................14 A3

Beach Huts
To Green Island (50m); Butterfly Beach (2km)
Beach Huts
ARABIAN SEA

To Canacona Train Staion (3km); Chaudi Train Station (3km); Cotigao Wildlife Sanctuary (9km); Margao (40km)

Mosque

To Patnem (2km); Home (2km); Intercontinental The Grand Resort (3.5km); Rajbag (3.5km)

Cozy Nook (☎ 2643550; huts & tree houses Rs 300-600) This is an excellent place in a great location at the far north end of the beach. The owners create a very friendly atmosphere and the huts – some with private bathroom – are better than most. The owner, Aggy, also runs trips out to secluded Butterfly Beach.

Palolem Guest House (☎ 2644880; palolemguest house@hotmail.com; d from Rs 600) A short walk from the beach is this smartly renovated house with modern rooms, all equipped with TV and phones. It also has a garden bar and restaurant.

Palolem Beach Resort (☎ 2643054; sunila@ goa telecom.com; tents Rs 350, d with private bathroom Rs 600) Offering freshly painted concrete cottages and tents (only available from late October to the end of April) set in neat gardens beside the beach, this is more upmarket than most places but still low-key.

Bhakti Kutir (☎ 2643472; www.bhaktikutir.com; huts Rs 675-1500, stone house Rs 2500; ☒) This 'eco-friendly' place, ensconced in a coconut grove between Palolem and Patnem beaches, is well designed and very peaceful. The predominantly vegetarian restaurant is excellent. Yoga and meditation workshops are held here, as well as the occasional musical performance.

Oceanic Hotel (☎ 2643059; oceanicpalolem@rediff .com; s/d Rs 400/800; ☒) On the road to Patnem, this British-run place is a fine choice if you want some creature comforts. There are six bright, comfortable rooms, a good restaurant and the only swimming pool in Palolem.

Home (☎ 2643916; homeispatnem@yahoo.com; d Rs 400-700) The best place to stay on Patnem Beach, Home is a far cry from the flimsy beach huts around it. It offers eight spotless rooms of varying sizes, all with private bathrooms, and a decent Euro-style restaurant.

Intercontinental The Grand Resort (☎ 2644777; goa@interconti.com; d incl breakfast from US$200; ☒ ☐ ☒) A little further down the coast at Rajbag is Goa's largest resort, with a sprinkling of colonial Portuguese style and a golf course, spa and six restaurants. Rates include Dabolim Airport transfers. Nonguests can use the pool for Rs 500 per day.

Eating & Drinking

Apart from the beach shacks, Palolem has plenty to offer in the way of restaurants and bars.

Magic Italy (mains Rs 120-160; ⏱ 5pm-midnight) Run by an Italian couple, this is one of the best places for authentic wood-fired pizzas and pasta in Goa. There's free filtered water and wine by the glass.

Smugglers' Inn (mains Rs 120-160; ⏱ 9am-11pm) With a Sunday roast (Rs 170), steaks and fish and chips, this is an unashamedly British place, but very stylishly done. The bar area is comfy and there's a nook where you can watch all the latest DVDs (Rs 50 per DVD).

Casa Fiesta (mains Rs 50-130; ⏱ 8am-11.30pm) This lively place with a garden setting does a good job of Mexican food – nachos, fajitas and burritos – and decent margaritas and cocktails.

Other recommendations:

Hotel Jackson (mains Rs 50-100; ⏱ 8.30am-11pm) A simple place with a good reputation for seafood.

Mamoo's Café (mains Rs 70-90; ⏱ 6.30am-midnight) Does reasonable Indian, Continental and Italian, including highly rated lasagne (in six varieties).

Getting There & Away

There are hourly buses to Margao (Rs 16, one hour) from the bus stand on the main road down to the beach. There are also regular buses to Chaudi (Rs 4), the nearest town, from where you can get frequent buses to Margao or south to Karwar and Mangalore. The closest train station is Canacona.

CENTRAL GOA

PONDA & AROUND

The busy inland town of Ponda, 29km southeast of Panaji, is of little interest to travellers, but there are a number of unique Hindu temples in the surrounding area, and several spice plantations that make for an interesting day of sightseeing.

The Hindu temples were rebuilt from originals destroyed by the Portuguese and their lamp towers are a distinctive Goan feature. The Shiva temple of **Shri Manguesh** at Priol-Ponda Taluka, 5km northwest of Ponda, is one of the best. This tiny 18th-century hill-top temple, with its white tower, is a local landmark. Close by is **Shri Mahalsa**, a Vishnu temple.

Among the other temples, the most interesting is the **Shri Shantadurga Temple**, 1km

southwest of the town centre. Dedicated to Shantadurga, the goddess of peace, this temple sports an unusual, almost pagoda-like structure with a roof made from long slabs of stone.

One of the best spice plantations to visit is **Sahakari Spice Farm** (☎ 2312394; www .sahakarifarms.com; ⏱ 8am-6pm). You can go on a very informative and entertaining 40-minute tour of the spice plantation, learning, among other things, how to pollinate vanilla and how feni is made from distilled cashew apple juice. You can also tuck into a splendid buffet lunch (Rs 300). Kids will be entertained by the elephant that you can feed, help wash and ride. The farm is about 1km east of Ponda along the NH4A road.

There are regular buses to Ponda from Panaji (Rs 8, 45 minutes), but to visit the temples and spice plantation you're better off with your own transport.

BONDLA WILDLIFE SANCTUARY

Up in the lush foothills of the Western Ghats, 52km from Panaji, lies **Bondla** (admission Rs 5, motorcycle/car Rs 10/50, camera/video Rs 25/100; ⏱ 9am-5pm Fri-Wed), the smallest of the Goan wildlife sanctuaries (8 sq km) and the easiest to reach.

For the benefit of tourists expecting to see some animals, there's a botanical garden, a fenced deer park (Rs 10) and a depressing zoo. Fauna in the wild here includes gaur and sambar, but unless you're prepared to spend a few days and put in the time on an observation platform, you're unlikely to see much.

There's **chalet accommodation** (☎ 2229701; dm/s/d Rs 50/200/300) at the park entrance.

Getting to Bondla is easiest if you have your own transport. By public transport there are buses from Ponda to Usgao village (Rs 5), from where you'll need to take a taxi (Rs 150) the remaining 5km to the park entrance.

MOLEM & BHAGWAN MAHAVIR WILDLIFE SANCTUARY

The forlorn village of **Molem** is the gateway to the much more rewarding Bhagwan Mahavir Wildlife Sanctuary. The largest of Goa's protected wildlife areas covers 240 sq km, incorporating the 107-sq-km Molem National Park; there's an observation platform a few kilometres into the park from where you may be fortunate enough to view animals such as jungle cats, deer and Malayan giant squirrels. Accommodation is available at Molem in the GTDC **Dhudhsagar Resort** (☎ 2612238; d without/with AC Rs 450/600; ❄).

The sanctuary is 53km east of Panaji, or 54km from Margao, with its main entrance on the NH4A. To reach here by public transport take any bus to Ponda, then change to a bus to Belgaum or Londa, getting off in Molem.

DUDHSAGAR FALLS

On the eastern border with Karnataka, Dudhsagar Falls (603m) are Goa's most impressive waterfalls – and the second highest in India, after Jog Falls. However, reaching them is expensive and time-consuming, and they are really only at their best during the monsoon – when they're inaccessible – and immediately after. To get here take an infrequent local train or taxi to Colem station, then a jeep for Rs 1800 (up to five people). The simpler option is to go on a full-day tour from Panaji (p173) or Calangute (p183).

Karnataka

The many dynasties that successively ruled Karnataka have ensured that you won't travel more than a few hours without stumbling on a pocket of architectural gems. In the north, impressive relics of India's Islamic past sit elegantly in their grassy fields, glorious and defiant even in old age. Further south in Hampi, the awesome ruins of the ancient city of Vijayanagar inspire and confuse: temples, monolithic sculptures and surreal boulder formations are so beautiful and so abundant that they defy all logic. Superbly crafted temples dating from the 6th century onwards blossom across the state like exquisite wildflowers, while enormous Jain sculptures of Gomateshvara look on from all over the south.

Paying no mind to all this brilliance are Karnataka's elephants: they meander through the lush mountains of Kodagu, get along just fine with the tigers and panthers in the south's national parks, and wear jewels, bells, pompoms and silks as they transport Mysore's flower-bedecked patron goddess through the archways of the palace. The hundreds of species of birds floating through Karnataka's skies don't seem to notice, either; the rose-ringed parakeets of Bidar simply call its majestic royal tombs 'home'.

To see it all, take lots of walks – treks through the Western Ghats, tiptoed walks through bird sanctuaries and pensive circumambulations through temple sanctums. Your pace will likely quicken in boomtown Bangalore, where ingenuity and style make up for the lack of parakeets and where you'll be reminded, once again, of India's refusal to be pinned down.

HIGHLIGHTS

- Wander mesmerised through **Mysore's** (p218) palaces, and the silks and sandalwood gods of its bazaars
- Listen to elephants cracking bamboo trees in the distance as you trek through the lush woods of the **Kodagu region** (p229)
- Have a drink in a chichi lounge among the beautiful people of **Bangalore** (p215)
- Get lost in the crowd of sculpted gods, dancers and elephants of the Hoysala temples of **Belur** (p233) and **Halebid** (p234)
- Experience the time warp of **Hampi** (p242), where the awesome ruins of the Vijayanagar capital breathe alongside boulders that defy gravity
- Climb around the ancient caves and temples of **Badami** (p249), set in a stunning red cliff
- Feel waves splash on to a secluded beach at **Gokarna** (p240) and then hike over the hill to a placid holy village

★ Badami

Hampi ★

★ Gokarna

Halebid

Belur ★

Bangalore ★

Kodagu
Region
★

★ Mysore

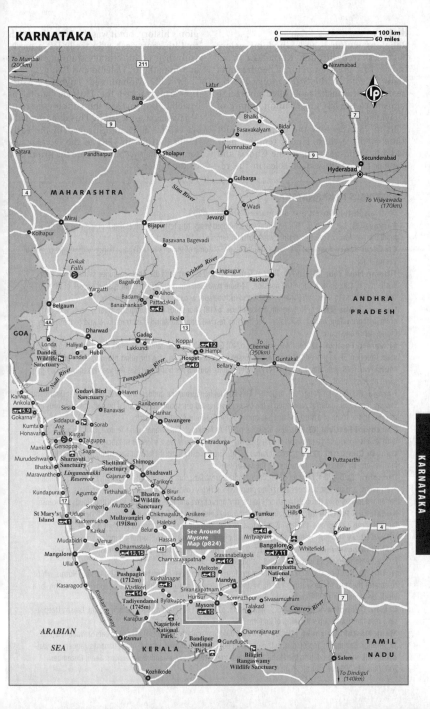

KARNATAKA

0 ____ 100 km
0 ____ 60 miles

To Mumbai (200km)

211

Nizamabad

7

Barsi

Latur

Bhalki

Bidar

Basavakalyam

9

Homnabad

Pandharpur

Sholapur

Secunderabad

9

Hyderabad

MAHARASHTRA

Sina River

Gulbarga

To Vijayawada (170km)

Miraj

Wadi

Kolhapur

Bijapur

Jevargi

4

Basavana Bagevadi

Krishna River

Gokak Falls

Lingsugur

Raichur

ANDHRA PRADESH

Yargatti

Bagalkot

Belgaum

Badami

Aihole

Banashankari

Pattadakal 2

Ilkal

4A

Dharwad

Gadag

13

GOA

Londa

Haliyal

Gajendragad

Koppal

Hampi 12

To Chennai (350km)

Dandeli Wildlife Sanctuary

Dandeli

Hubli

Lakkundi

Hospet 6

Guntakal

Kali Nadi River

Tungabhadra River

Bellary

Karwar

Gudavi Bird Sanctuary

Haveri

Ankola 5,9

Sirsi

Banavasi

Ranibennur

Gokarna

Kumta

Siddapur

Sorab

Harihar

Honavar

Jog Falls

Kargal

Davangere

7

Puttaparthi

Mankī

Gersoppa

Sagar

Talguppa

Chitradurga

Murudeshwar

Sharavati Sanctuary

Shettihalli Sanctuary

Shimoga

4

Bhatkal

Linganamakki Reservoir

Gajanur

Bhadravati

Sira

Maravanthe

Tankere

Nandi Hills

Kundapura

Agumbe

Tirthahalli

Bhadra Wildlife Sanctuary

Birur

Kadur

Kolar

4

St Mary's Island

Udupi

Sringeri

Muttodi

Chikmagalur

Arsikere

Tumkur

Kudremukh

Mullayangiri (1918m)

Halebid

Nrityagram

Whitefield

Karkal

Belur

Hassan

See Around Mysore Map (p824)

Bangalore 17,11

Mudabidri

Venur

Dharmastala 13,15

48

Sravanabelagola 16

Bannerghatta National Park

Mangalore

Channarayapatna

Melkote

Ullal

Pushpagiri (1712m)

Kushalnagar 3

8

Mandya

Madikeri 14

Srirangapatnam

Hunsur

Kasaragod

Bylakuppe

Somnathpur

Sivasamudram

Tadiyendamol (1745m)

Mysore 10

Talakad

Cauvery River

7

Karapur

Nagarhole National Park

Chamrajanagar

ARABIAN SEA

Kannur

Bandipur National Park

Gundlupet

TAMIL NADU

KERALA

Biligiri Rangaswamy Wildlife Sanctuary

Salem

Kozhikode

To Dindigul (140km)

KARNATAKA

History

Religions, cultures and kingdoms galore have sashayed through Karnataka, from India's first great emperor, Chandragupta Maurya, who in the 3rd century BC retreated to Sravanabelagola after embracing Jainism, to the last great Hindu empire of Vijayanagar.

In the 6th century the Chalukyas built some of the earliest Hindu temples near Badami. Dynasties such as the Cholas and Gangas played important roles in the region's history, but it was the Hoysalas (11th to 14th centuries), who really left a mark, with their architecturally stunning temples at Somnathpur, Halebid and Belur.

In 1327 Mohammed Tughlaq's Muslim army sacked the Hoysala capital at Halebid, but in 1346 the Hindu empire of Vijayanagar annexed it. This dynasty, with its capital at Hampi, peaked in the early 1550s, but fell in 1565 to the Deccan sultanates. Bijapur then became the prime city of the region.

FESTIVALS IN KARNATAKA

Festivals in this boxed text are marked on Map p205.

Paryaya (❶; Jan; Udupi, p238) Held in even-numbered years, this festival involves much procession and ritual to mark the handover of swamis at the town's Krishna Temple.

Classical dance festival (❷; Jan; Pattadakal, p252) Some of Indian's best classical dance without the crowds of Vasantahabba.

Tibetan New Year (❸; Jan/Feb; Tibetan Settlements, p228) Lamas in the Tibetan refugee settlements, near Kushalnagar, take shifts leading the nonstop, 24-hour *pujas* (offerings or prayers) that span the week of Tibetan New Year celebrations in January/February, which also include special dances and a fire ceremony.

Vasantahabba (❹; Feb; Nrityagram dance village, p218) Thousands descend on the modest gardens of Nrityagram, a dance village outside Bangalore, for this free festival featuring world-class traditional and contemporary Indian dance and music.

Shivaratri Festival (❺; Feb/Mar; Gokarna, p240) Gokarna's two gargantuan chariots barrel down the town's main street on 'Shiva power' (as bananas are tossed at them for luck) during the mind-blowing Shivaratri Festival.

Muharram (❻; Feb/Mar; Hospet, p247) Hospet's Shiite Muslim festival showcases fire walkers to the accompaniment of mass hoopla (see p248).

Karaga (❼; Mar/Apr; Bangalore, opposite) This festival honouring the goddess Draupadi, is held in at Dharmaraya Swamy Temple. A colourful procession is led by a cross-dressed priest and accompanied by half-naked swordsmen; the visit to the tomb of a Muslim saint has come to signify Hindu-Muslim solidarity.

Vairamudi Festival (❽; Mar/Apr; Melkote, p227) At Melkote's Cheluvanarayana Temple, Lord Vishnu is adorned with jewels – including a diamond-studded crown – belonging to Mysore's former maharajas.

Ganesh Chaturthi (❾; Aug/Sep; Gokarna, p240) The Ganesh Chaturthi festival is particularly moving here, as families quietly march their Ganeshes to the sea at sunset.

Dussehra (❿; Sep/Oct; Mysore, p218) One of India's great Dussehra festivals. The maharaja's palace is illuminated every night, and the last day sees a dazzling procession of richly costumed elephants, liveried retainers, cavalry and garlanded idols gliding through the streets to the rhythms of jazz and brass bands amid wafting clouds of incense.

Kadalekayi Parishe (⓫; Nov; Bangalore, opposite) Celebrates the first groundnut crop of the year, and farmers come from all over the region to Bangalore's Bull Temple seeking blessings for their harvests.

Vijaya Utsav (⓬; Nov; Hampi, p242) Traditional music and dance among Hampi's temples.

Manjunatheshwara (⓭; Nov; Dharmastala, p239) The Jain pilgrimage town of Dharmastala has a lively festival season beginning with Diwali and including this three-day event.

Huthri (⓮; Nov/Dec; Madikeri, p229) The many festivals of Madikeri's Kodavas (see p229) include Huthri, which celebrates the start of the season's rice harvests with ceremony, music, traditional dances and much feasting for a week, beginning on a full-moon night.

Laksha Deepotsava (⓯; Nov/Dec; Dharmastala, p239) Part of Dharmastala's festival season, Laksha Deepotsava sees the town lit up with lakhs of lanterns.

Maha Mastakabhisheka (⓰; Dec 2005/Jan 2006; Sravanabelagola, p234) Every 12 years Sravanabelagola's 17.5m-high Bahubali is anointed with thousands of pots of coconut milk, yogurt, ghee, bananas, jaggery, sandalwood, milk and saffron during the Maha Mastakabhisheka ceremony, attended by millions. See it December 2005/January 2006 or wait till 2018.

MYSORE

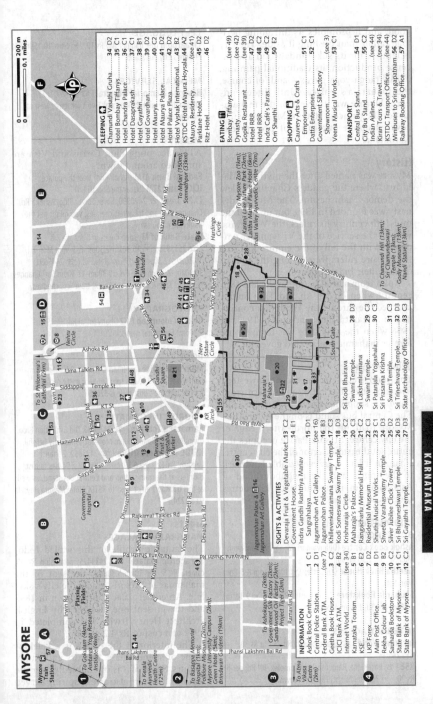

0   200 m
0   0.1 miles

SLEEPING 🏠
Chamundi Vasathi Gruha......34 D2
Hotel Bombay Tiffanys.........35 C1
Hotel Chandra Palace...........36 C1
Hotel Dasaprakash................37 C1
Hotel Gayathri.......................38 B1
Hotel Govardhan...................39 D2
Hotel Maurya.........................40 C2
Hotel Maurya Palace.............41 D2
Hotel Palace Plaza.................42 D2
Hotel Vyshak International.....43 B2
KSTDC Hotel Mayura Hoysala..44 A2
Maurya Residency...................45 D2
Parklane Hotel........................46 D2
Ritz Hotel...............................

EATING 🍴
Bombay Tiffanys..............(see 49)
Dynasty.............................(see 42)
Gopika Restaurant............(see 39)
Hotel RRR............................47 D2
Hotel RRR............................48 C2
Indra Café's Paras................49 C2
Om Shanthi..........................50 E2

SHOPPING 🛍
Cauvery Arts & Crafts
  Emporium............................51 C1
Datta Enterprises...................52 C1
Government Silk Factory
  Showroom........................(see 3)
Veena Musical Works............53 C1

TRANSPORT
Central Bus Stand..................54 D1
City Bus Stand........................55 C2
Indian Airlines.....................(see 44)
Kiran Tours & Travel............(see 34)
KSTDC Transport Office......(see 44)
Minibuses to Srirangapatnam..56 D2
Railway Booking Office...........57 A1

SIGHTS & ACTIVITIES
Devaraja Fruit & Vegetable Market..13 C2
Government House.................14 E1
Indira Gandhi Rashtriya Manav
  Sangrahalaya....................15 D1
Jaganmohan Art Gallery......(see 16)
Jaganmohan Palace................16 B3
Khillevenkataramana Swamy Temple..17 C3
Kodi Someswara Swamy Temple..18 D3
Krishnaraja Circle...................19 C2
Maharaja's Palace...................20 C3
Rangacharlu Memorial Hall....21 C2
Residential Museum...............22 C3
Shruthi Musical Works............23 C1
Shweta Varahaswamy Temple..24 D3
Silver Jubilee Clock Tower.......25 D2
Sri Bhuvaneshwari Temple......26 C3
Sri Gayathri Temple................27 D3
Sri Kodi Bhairava
  Swami Temple....................28 D3
Sri Lakshmiramana
  Swami Temple....................29 C3
Sri Patanjala Yogashala..........30 C3
Sri Prasanna Krishna
  Swami Temple....................31 C3
Sri Trineshwara Temple..........32 D3
State Archaeology Office.........33 C3

INFORMATION
Ashok Book Centre..................1 C1
Central Police Station...............2 D1
Federal Bank ATM...............(see 7)
Geetha Book House.................3 C2
ICICI Bank ATM......................4 B2
Internet World.....................(see 34)
Karnataka Tourism...................5 B1
KSE...6 E2
LKP Forex................................7 D2
Main Post Office......................8 D1
Rekha Colour Lab....................9 B2
Sauharda Bookstore...............10 C2
State Bank of Mysore..............11 C1
State Bank of Mysore..............12 C2

good, and it promotes its intriguing heritage rather than pushing it aside. The city is famous for its silk, sandalwood and incense production, its traditional painting, its Ashtanga yoga gurus – and, of course, the maharaja's palace. Until Independence, Mysore was the seat of the maharajas for the princely state of Mysore, which covered about one-third of present-day Karnataka.

History

Mysore was named after the mythical Mahisuru, where the goddess Chamundi slew the demon Mahishasura. The Mysore dynasty was founded in 1399, but up until the mid-16th century its rulers, the Wodeyars, were in the service of the Vijayanagar emperor. With the fall of the empire in 1565, the Mysore rulers were among the first to declare their independence.

Apart from a brief period in the late 18th century when Hyder Ali and Tipu Sultan usurped the throne, the Wodeyars continued to rule until Independence in 1947. In 1956 when the new state was formed, the former maharaja was elected governor.

Orientation

The train station is on the northwestern fringe of the city centre, about 1km from the main shopping street, Sayyaji Rao Rd. The Central bus stand is on the Bangalore–Mysore road, on the northeastern edge of the city centre. Mysore Palace occupies the entire southeastern sector of the city centre. Chamundi Hill is an ever-visible landmark to the south, and the neighbourhood of Ashokapuram is a couple of kilometres southwest of town.

Information

BOOKSHOPS
Ashok Book Centre (Dhanvanthri Rd; 9.30am-9pm Mon-Sat, till 2.30pm Sun)
Geetha Book House (KR Circle; 10am-1pm & 5-8pm Mon-Sat)
Sauharda Bookstore (Hanumantha Rao St; 9.30am-1.30pm & 4.30-8.30pm Mon-Sat)

INTERNET ACCESS
Internet World (☎ Chandragupta Rd; per hr Rs 30; 24hr)
KSE (☎ basement, Ramansashree Complex, BN Rd; per hr Rs 20; 7am-midnight) Fastest in town.

LEFT LUGGAGE
Cloakroom (per bag per day Rs 10; 6am-10.15pm) At Mysore's City bus stand.

MEDICAL SERVICES
Basappa Memorial Hospital (☎ 2512401; 22/B Vinoba Rd, Jayalakshmipuram) Two kilometres west of the city.

MONEY
ATMs accepting Plus, Cirrus and Visa are sprinkled around town.
Federal Bank ATM (Ashoka Rd) Near the palace.
ICICI Bank ATM (Narayana Shastri Rd)
LKP Forex (☎ 2420090; Silver Tower Bldg, Ashoka Rd) Changes cash and travellers cheques; you might get the bank rate if you ask.
State Bank of Mysore Cnr Irwin & Ashoka Rds (☎ 2538956; 10.30am-2.30pm & 3-4pm Mon-Fri, 10.30am-12.30pm Sat); Sayyaji Rao Rd (☎ 2445691; 10.30am-2.30pm Mon-Fri, 10.30am-12.30pm Sat) Changes cash and American Express (Amex) travellers cheques.

PHOTOGRAPHY
Rekha Colour Lab (142 Dhanvanthri Rd; 9am-9.30pm) For digital needs.

POST
Main post office (cnr Irwin & Ashoka Rds; 10am-6pm Mon-Sat, 10.30am-1pm Sun) For poste restante service (Mysore's post code is 570001).

TOURIST INFORMATION
Karnataka Tourism (☎ 2422096; Old Exhibition Bldg, Irwin Rd; 10am-5.30pm Mon-Sat) Unusually helpful.
KSTDC Transport Office (☎ 2423652; 2 Jhansi Lakshmi Bai Rd; 6.30am-8.30pm) KSTDC has tourist counters at the train station and Central bus stand, as well as this transport office next to KSTDC Hotel Mayura Hoysala (see p224).

Sights

MAHARAJA'S PALACE
The fantastic profile of this walled Indo-Saracenic **palace** (☎ 2434425; admission Rs 20, camera Rs 5; 10am-5.30pm), the seat of the maharajas of Mysore, graces the city's skyline. An earlier palace burnt down in 1897 and the present one, designed by English architect Henry Irwin, was completed in 1912 at a cost of Rs 4.2 million.

The interior of the palace is a kaleidoscope of stained glass, mirrors and gaudy colours. Some of it is undoubtedly over the top, but there are also awe-inspiring carved wooden doors and mosaic floors, as well as a series of historically interesting paintings depicting life in Mysore during the Edwardian Raj. The palace has a set of Hindu temples within its grounds, including the Shweta Varahaswamy Temple with its **gopuram** (Dravidian gateway tower), which influenced the style of the later Sri Chamundeswari Temple on Chamundi Hill.

The **main rooms** of the palace are open to the public and are often crowded. The entry fee is paid at the southern gate of the grounds, but you need to retain your ticket to enter the palace building itself. Cameras must be deposited at the entrance gate – you can only take photos of the outside of the buildings. Some books on historical sites are sold near the exit of the main rooms, though the state archaeology office, in the southwest part of the grounds, has a more complete collection.

Incorporating some of the palace's living quarters and personal effects belonging to the maharaja's family, the **Residential Museum** (admission Rs 20; ☉ 10.30am-5.30pm) is rather dull next to the palace's lustre.

On Sunday night and during Dussehra, a carnival atmosphere takes over the palace and 97,000 light bulbs illuminate the building from 7pm to 8pm.

CHAMUNDI HILL
Overlooking Mysore from the 1062m summit of Chamundi Hill, the **Sri Chamundeswari Temple** (☎ 2590027; ☉ 7.30am-2pm, 3.30-6pm, 7.30-9pm), dominated by a towering seven-storey 40m-high *gopuram* (gateway tower), makes a fine half-day excursion. Pilgrims are supposed to climb the 1000-plus steps to the top; those not needing a karmic boost will

find descending easier. A road goes to the top; bus No 201 departs from the City bus stand in Mysore for the summit every 40 minutes (Rs 6, 30 minutes). A taxi will cost about Rs 200.

Near the car park, the **Godly Museum** (admission free; ☉ 7.30am-6pm) is worth a stop for a glimpse of what awaits this 'vicious world'. The statue in the car park is of the demon Mahishasura, who was one of the goddess Chamundi's victims. The goddess was the family deity of the maharajas.

A path that starts near the stalls behind the statue will lead you down the hill, a 45-minute descent taking in 1000 steps and re-energising views. One-third of the way down is the famous 5m-high **Nandi** (Shiva's bull vehicle), carved out of solid rock in 1659. It's one of the largest in India and is visited by hordes of pilgrims offering *prasad* (food offering used in religious ceremonies) to the priest in attendance. The garlanded statue has a flaky black coating of coconut-husk charcoal mixed with ghee.

You may have rubbery legs by the time you reach the bottom of the hill and it's still about 2km back to Mysore's centre. Fortunately, there are usually autorickshaws nearby, charging Rs 30 or so for the trip back to town.

DEVARAJA FRUIT & VEGETABLE MARKET
The Devaraja Market, stretching along the western side of Sayyaji Rao Rd, south of Dhanvanthri Rd, is one of the most colourful in India and provides riveting subject material for photographers. The first stalls set up just after sunrise, when the first truckloads of fruits and vegetables arrive.

KARNATAKA

SANDALWOOD (SP)OILS
It's not unusual to end a day in the Mysore streets and markets wearing a pungent rainbow of scents – sandalwood, jasmine, lotus etc – in jumbled-together patches on your skin. Market vendors sell scented oils for roughly Rs 50 per 5ml – a seeming bargain, particularly when they claim them to be pure or '100% natural'. However, these 'bargains' are well known locally to be mixed with other substances (coconut or almond base oils, or even alcohol). They are worthwhile purchases if you're in it just for the smell, but they are by no means up to the standards set by aromatherapists and should never be used therapeutically.

For the real deal in sandalwood oil, go to the government-run sandalwood oil factory (see p225), where you're more likely to pay Rs 300 for 5ml – still, it's the price you pay for purity. Only sandalwood oil is manufactured in Mysore; other scents that you'll see around come from elsewhere in India or abroad.

The buzzing activity takes all shapes and forms throughout the day.

JAGANMOHAN PALACE & ART GALLERY
The Jaganmohan Palace, just west of Mysore Palace, houses the **Jayachamarajendra Art Gallery** (☎ 2423693; Jaganmohan Palace Rd; adult/child Rs 15/8; ⏰ 8.30am-5pm), which has a collection of kitsch objects and memorabilia from the Wodeyars, including weird and wonderful musical machines, rare instruments, Japanese art and paintings by Raja Ravi Varma. Built in 1861, the palace served as a royal auditorium.

INDIRA GANDHI RASHTRIYA MANAV SANGRAHALAYA
Indira Gandhi Rashtriya Manav Sangrahalaya (National Museum of Mankind; ☎ 2448231; Wellington House, Irwin Rd; admission free; ⏰ 10am-5.30pm Tue-Sat), an organisation headquartered in Bhopal, strives to preserve and promote traditional Indian arts and culture. This branch functions primarily as a cultural centre and exhibition space showcasing arts from rural India. Monthly demonstrations and lectures are open to the public, as are workshops, which are usually two-week courses in a traditional art form. The museum has excellent rotating exhibitions; recent shows included one on India's sacred groves and another on folk and tribal wall painting and floor decorations.

FOLKLORE MUSEUM
This small **museum** (☎ 2414548; Manasa Gangotri, Jayalakshmipuram; admission free; ⏰ 10am-1.30pm & 2.15-5.30pm Mon-Sat, closed alternate Sat) is in the Mysore University Campus, west of the city centre. It has some pieces with panache, including carved wooden figures from Karnatakan villages, decorative masks and ceremonial headdresses, and some spectacular *thogalu bombeeata* (leather shadow puppets). A display of wooden puppets includes one of a 10-headed demon Ravana. It's in the building behind the university canteen.

MYSORE ZOO
Mysore's **zoo** (☎ 2520302; www.mysorezoo.org; Indiranagar; adult/child Rs 20/10, camera Rs 10; ⏰ 8.30am-5.30pm Wed-Mon) is one of the best kept in India. It's set in parched but pretty gardens on the eastern edge of the city centre. Still, the animals live in depressing cages or – the luckier ones – in a grassy open-air enclosure. The four white tigers and nine Bengal tigers get to take turns stretching in an enclosure. A range of primates, elephants, bears, birds and rhinos also live here.

OTHER SIGHTS
Mysore is an architectural vaudeville of fine buildings and monuments. Dating from 1805, **Government House** (Irwin Rd), formerly the British Residency, is a 'Tuscan Doric' building set in 20 hectares of **gardens** (⏰ 5am-9pm).

In front of the north gate of Maharaja Palace in the New Statue Circle is the 1920 **statue** of Maharaja Chamarajendar Wodeyar, facing the 1927 **Silver Jubilee Clock Tower**. Nearby is the imposing town hall, the **Rangacharlu Memorial Hall** built in 1884. The next circle west is the 1950s **Krishnaraja Circle**, better known as KR Circle, graced by a statue of Maharaja Krishnaraja Wodeyar.

Towering **St Philomena's Cathedral** (☎ 2563 148; St Philomena St; ⏰ 8am-8pm, English mass 7am), built between 1933 and 1941 in neo-Gothic style, is one of the largest in India.

Activities
BIRD-WATCHING
Karanji Lake Nature Park (admission Rs 10, camera/video Rs 10/25; ⏰ 8.30am-5.30pm), along the recently resuscitated Karanji Lake, is home to a surprisingly large number of bird species, including great and little cormorant, purple and grey heron, various egret, black ibis, rose-ringed parakeet, green bee-eater and painted stork, as well as several kinds of butterfly. The aviary here is sad but fascinating; its enormous great pied hornbill is a sight to see. The park is just past the Mysore Zoo.

AYURVEDA
The very classy **Indus Valley Ayurvedic Centre** (☎ 2473437; www.ayurindus.com; Lalithadripura; per person per day from US$55), 7km east of Mysore, is set on 16 hectares of gardens at the foot of Chamundi Hill. Its academic approach to the science of Ayurveda is based strictly on the Vedas, and they offer training programmes for those interested in learning the technique. Rates include accommodation, food and treatments. The **Kerala Ayurvedic Health Centre** (☎ 5269111; www.keralaayurhealth.com; Jhansi

Lakshmi Bai Cross Rd) is more of a clinic than a spa, and it offers four-hour sessions for around US$20. Training courses are also given.

Courses

YOGA

K Pattabhi Jois, instructor at the **Ashtanga Yoga Research Institute** (AYRI; ☎ 2516756; www .ayri.org; 3rd Stage, 235 8th Cross, Gokulam), is famous in Ashtanga circles the world over. At the **Sri Patanjala Yogashala** (Yoga Research Institute; Sri Bramatantra Swatantra Parakala Mutt, Jaganmohan Palace Circle; ⏱ 6-8am & 5-7pm), BNS Iyengar, another Ashtanga practitioner (but not to be confused with BKS Iyengar, famed exponent of Iyengar yoga), is also well respected. Courses in yoga, Sanskrit and meditation are offered by the 'backbending expert', Yogacharya Venkatesh, at **Atma Vikasa Centre** (☎ 2341978; www.atmavikasa.com; Bharathi Mahila Samaja, Kuvempunagar Double Rd). Most courses require at least a month's commitment, and you'll need to book far in advance for AYRI and the Atma Vikasa Centre; call or write to the centres for details.

MUSIC

The folks at **Shruthi Musical Works** (☎ 2529551; 1189 3rd Cross, Irwin Rd; ⏱ 10.30am-9pm Mon-Sat, 10.30am-2pm Sun) get good reviews for their tabla instruction (Rs 200 per hour).

Tours

The KSTDC's Mysore city tour takes in city sights plus Chamundi Hill, the Keshava Temple at Somnathpur, Srirangapatnam and Brindavan gardens. It starts daily at 7.30am, ends at 8.30pm and costs Rs 160 – it's comprehensive but may leave you breathless.

The KSTDC also runs a Belur, Halebid and Sravanabelagola tour every Tuesday, Wednesday, Friday and Sunday (daily in the high season) at 7.30am, ending at 9pm (Rs 280). Buses leave from the KSTDC Hotel Mayura Hoysala, and you spend far more time in the bus (nine whopping hours) than on the ground. Book these at the KSTDC Transport Office (see p220) or at travel agencies around town.

Sleeping

Rooms fill up – and prices rise – during Dussehra (see p206), so book ahead if you're arriving in September or October.

BUDGET

Mysore has bunches of good budget hotels. All have hot water, at least in the morning, and 24-hour checkout.

Hotel Dasaprakash (☎ 2442444; hoteldasaprakash@ sancharnet.in; Gandhi Square; s/d from Rs 180/365; meals Rs 15 to 50; 🏢) The Dasaprakash has efficient service and lots of old-school charm, with antique wooden furniture in some rooms. The hotel has an ice-cream parlour, travel agency and, for emergencies, an astropalmist on call. Its restaurant gets kudos from travellers.

Hotel Maurya (☎ 2426677; Hanumantha Rao St; s/d/tr Rs 125/225/325) The good-value Maurya has shiny, well-kept rooms and smiling staff in a great location among Mysore's winding alleys.

Parklane Hotel (☎ 2434340; fax 2428424; 2720 Sri Harsha Rd; s/d/tr Rs 125/149/199) The eight rooms tucked away in the Parklane restaurant are basic but sweet, and Indian classical music wafts up from the dining room. Reservations are not accepted.

Hotel Govardhan (☎ 2434118; www.hotelgovard han.com; Sri Harsha Rd; s/d from Rs 150/230; 🏢) Set back from the road in the Palace District, the Govardhan is a bit institutional but clean and friendly.

Hotel Gayathri (☎ 2425654; Dhanvanthri Rd; s/d/tr from Rs 125/225/350) Not to be confused with New Gayathri Bhavan nearby, this Gayathri has new bathrooms, clean sheets and a 1940s train station vibe. It's all good except for the street noise and the tiny singles.

Chamundi Vasathi Gruha (☎ 5266162; Chandragupta Rd; s/d Rs 120/180) In the same building as Internet World, this family-run place has frequent water cuts but redeems itself with colonial charm and pumpkin-coloured walls.

MIDRANGE

Most of the hotels listed below have 24-hour hot water and checkout at noon.

Ritz Hotel (☎ 2422668; hotelritz@rediffmail.com; BN Rd; d/q Rs 400/640) The old-fashioned Ritz has four exceedingly charming rooms that open up on to a homy lounge and dining area shaded by reed blinds. There's a good restaurant and bar downstairs.

Hotel Maurya Palace (☎ 2435912; www.sangroup ofhotels.com; Sri Harsha Rd; r from Rs 500; 🏢) The staff is inordinately helpful, the tidy, newish rooms have bright white seersucker sheets and fluffy towels, and its nonveg restaurant, Jewel Rock, is beloved by carnivores. It, along with its sister property next door, **Maurya Residency** (☎ 2523375; r from Rs 665; 🔀), are the best of the Sri Harsha Rd hotel gang.

Hotel Vyshak International (☎ 2421777; fax 242-8111; Seebaiah Rd; d from Rs 500; 🔀) This hotel is spotless, efficiently run and very welcoming; the rooms are almost cosy.

Hotel Palace Plaza (☎ 2430034; www.hotelpalace plaza.com; Sri Harsha Rd; s/d from Rs 575/675; 🔀 🖳) The rooms here are a tad small, but they're modern, tastefully decorated and accompanied by thoughtful touches (eg a complementary sewing kit).

KSTDC Hotel Mayura Hoysala (☎ 2425349; 2 Jhansi Lakshmi Bai Rd; s/d Rs 500/650; 🔀) Mysore's KSTDC hotel is on a busy street, so its gardens do more than whisper. The huge rooms were being renovated at the time of writing, however, and it's convenient for the train station.

In the colourful lanes east of Sayyaji Rao Rd are the dapper **Hotel Bombay Tiffanys** (☎ 2435255; bombaytiffanys@yahoo.co.in; Sayyaji Rao Rd Cross; r from Rs 390; ☎) and **Hotel Chandra Palace** (☎ 2421333; chandrapalace@yahoo.com; KT St; r from Rs 350; 🔀), both with smart, tidy rooms. What they lack in character they more than make up for in value.

TOP END

Green Hotel (☎ 2512536; www.greenhotelindia.com; 2270 Vinoba Rd, Jayalakshmipuram; garden s/d from Rs 1250/1650, palace from Rs 2250/2500) Housed in a century-old palace once used as a country retreat for Wodeyar princesses, the Green Hotel has won awards for ecological awareness and donates all profits to charity. The palace's elegant atmosphere is impressively intact, with a library, chess sets, croquet lawn and bar, and the guest rooms are imaginatively themed. The garden wing has fresh (but themeless) modern rooms. The hotel is 5km west of town.

Lalitha Mahal Palace Hotel (☎ 2470470; www .lalithamahalpalace.com; s/d/ste from US$60/70/230; 🔀 🖳) Some 7km east of the city centre, this former maharaja's palace is now Mysore's most regal lodging option. Rooms in the newer wing are fine, but it's the suites, in the palace wing, that will transport you to never-never land, with canopied beds, period furniture and lots of froufrou. The

elevator is similarly precious, with carpeting and a tapestry-upholstered ottoman.

Eating

Bombay Tiffanys (Sayyaji Rao Rd; sweets Rs 2-40; 🕒 7.30am-10pm) No sweet shop has a better name, and none does better sweets. Be sure to try the local delicacy, the 'Mysore pak'.

Hotel RRR (Gandhi Square; mains Rs 35-72; 🕒 noon-4pm & 7-11pm) Andhra-style veg thalis (Rs 32) that are bigger, spicier and yummier than you've ever had before – and they're served on banana leaves. Some meaty options are available, too. The restaurant has a second branch on Sri Harsha Rd.

Gopika Restaurant (Hotel Govardhan, Sri Harsha Rd; mains Rs 10-40; 🕒 6.30am-10pm) Gopika serves up pure-veg goodness to a continual stream of locals and Indian tourists; 'meals' (Rs 22) are reliably delish.

Parklane Hotel (Sri Harsha Rd; mains Rs 35-100; 🕒 10.30am-3.30pm & 6.30-11.30pm) The garden courtyard here, candlelit at night, has the best ambience in town and has long been a travellers' favourite. Chinese, Continental and Indian dinners are served to the accompaniment of live music.

Om Shanthi (Hotel Siddharta, Guest House Rd; mains Rs 40-80; 🕒 noon-3pm & 8-10pm; 🔀) One of the best vegetarian spots this side of the Cauvery. Its Special South Indian Thali (Rs 75) is really quite special.

Mylari (Nazarbad Main Rd; snacks Rs 6-22; 🕒 6.30am-noon & 3-8.30pm Thu-Tue) You know if it can get away with serving only dosas, they must be good. Two brothers run two Mylari dosa houses; you want the one further from town, near the police station.

Indra Café's Paras (1740 Sayyaji Rao Rd; mains Rs 30-60; 🕒 7.30am-10pm) A popular South (Rs 30) and North (Rs 60) Indian thali joint, with *chaat* (snack) central (Rs 8 to 20) downstairs.

Dynasty (Hotel Palace Plaza, Sri Harsha Rd; mains Rs 40-85; 🕒 noon-3pm & 7-11pm) Joan Collins isn't here, but it's still worth a visit for the Keralan fish curry (Rs 65) and the atmospheric roof-top dining area, which has views of Chamundi Hill.

Lalitha Mahal Palace Hotel (☎ 2470470; mains Rs 200-350; 🕒 11.30am-3pm & 7-10pm) The city's grandest dining experience in the hotel of the same name (see left), complete with baby-blue Wedgwood-style décor in the dining hall.

Shopping

Mysore is famous for its carved sandalwood, inlay work, silk saris and wooden toys. Souvenir and handicraft shops are dotted around Jaganmohan Palace and Dhanvanthri Rd, while silk shops line Devaraj Urs Rd.

Cauvery Arts & Crafts Emporium (Sayyaji Rao Rd; ☺ 10am-7.30pm) The whole spread of Mysore's goods is here. It's expensive but relaxed.

Government Silk Factory (☎ 2481803; Mananthody Rd, Ashokapuram; ☺ 7-10.45am & 11.30am-3pm Mon-Sat) You can see weavers at work here, and an on-site shop sells silks, as does the factory showroom (☺ 9.30am-6.30pm) on KR Circle.

Sandalwood oil factory (☎ 2483531; Ashokapuram; ☺ 9am-1pm & 2-5pm Mon-Sat) Mysore is one of India's major incense-manufacturing centres, and scores of little family-owned *agarbathi* (incense) factories around town export their products globally. The incense is made with thin bamboo slivers, dyed red or green at one end, onto which a sandalwood putty base is rolled. The sticks are then dipped into piles of powdered perfume and laid out to harden in the shade. You can purchase incense sticks and oil at this factory, about 2km southeast of Maharaja's Palace, off Mananthody Rd.

Datta Enterprises (KR Hospital Rd; ☺ 10am-9pm) Get custom-made Ganesh stickers here.

Shruthi Musical Works (see p223) and **Veena Musical Works** (Irwin Rd; 10am-8.30pm Mon-Sat, 10am-1.30pm Sun) both sell a variety of traditional musical instruments.

Getting There & Away

AIR

There are no flights to Mysore, but **Indian Airlines** (☎ 2421846; Jhansi Lakshmi Bai Rd; 10am-1.30pm & 2.15-5pm) has an office next to KSTDC Hotel Mayura Hoysala.

BUS

The **Central bus stand** (☎ 2520853) handles all KSRTC long-distance buses. The **City bus stand** (KR Circle), is for city, Srirangapatnam and Chamundi Hill buses. See the table, right, for long-distance destinations. For Belur, Halebid or Sravanabelagola, the usual gateway is Hassan. There's one bus to Sravanabelagola, otherwise you can transfer at Channarayapatna. For Hampi, the best transfer point is Hospet.

Private long-distance buses go to Hubli, Bijapur, Mangalore, Ooty and Ernakulum. Book with **Kiran Tours & Travel** (☎ 5559404; 21/2 Chandragupta Rd).

KSRTC bus services from Mysore include the following:

Destination	Fare (Rs)	Duration (hr)	Departures
Bandipur	35 (O)	2	hourly
Bangalore	56 (O)/ 102 (R)	3	every 15min
Channarayapatna	35 (O)	2	hourly
Chennai	350 (R)	8	3 daily
Ernakulum	440 (R)	10	5 daily
Gokarna	240 (O)	12	1 daily
Hassan	48 (O)	3	every 45min
Hospet	160 (O)	8	4 daily
Mangalore	130 (O)/ 180 (D)	7	hourly
Nagarhole	55 (O)	3	4 daily
Ooty	65 (O)/ 110 (D)	5	hourly
Sravanabelagola	40 (O)	2½	1 daily

(O) Ordinary, (D) semideluxe, (R) Rajahamsa

TRAIN

At the **railway booking office** (☎ 131; ☺ 8am-8pm Mon-Sat, 8am-2pm Sun), you can reserve a seat on one of six daily expresses to Bangalore (Rs 61/198 in 2nd/chair, three hours), or on the high-speed *Shatabdi* (Rs 275/550 in chair/executive, two hours), departing at 2.20pm daily except Tuesday. The *Shatabdi* continues to Chennai (Rs 690/1315, seven hours). Several passenger trains also go daily to Bangalore (Rs 28, 3½ hours), stopping at Srirangapatnam (Rs 9).

Two passenger and three express trains go daily to Arsikere and Hassan. One express sets off to Mumbai on Thursday at 6.20am (Rs 369/1009/1583 in sleeper/3AC/2AC).

Getting Around

Agencies at hotels and around town rent out cars from Rs 5 per kilometre, with a minimum of 250km per day, plus Rs 125 for the driver.

Autorickshaw drivers are usually content to use the meter. Flag fall is Rs 10, and Rs 5 per kilometre is charged thereafter. Taxis are pricier and meterless, so fares must be negotiated.

KARNATAKA

AROUND MYSORE

Somnathpur

☎ 08227

The **Keshava Temple** (☎ 270059; Indian/foreigner Rs 5/US$2; ☒ 9am-5.30pm) stands at the edge of the tranquil village of Somnathpur, approximately 33km east of Mysore. Built in 1268 in the heyday of the Hoysala kings, it's an astonishingly beautiful building. It's also complete, unlike the larger Hoysala temples at Belur and Halebid. For a rundown on Hoysala architecture, see the boxed text, p234.

The walls of this star-shaped temple are covered with superb stone sculptures depicting various scenes from the Ramayana, Mahabharata and Bhagavad Gita, and the life and times of the Hoysala kings. No two friezes are alike.

On a tree in the temple grounds there's a red post box where you can drop your stamped mail to get it postmarked with a temple image.

Somnathpur is a few kilometres south of Bannur and 10km north of Tirumakudal Narsipur. Take one of the half-hourly buses from

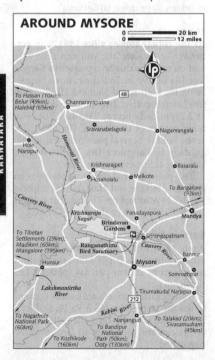

AROUND MYSORE

Mysore to either village (Rs 12, 30 minutes) and change there.

Srirangapatnam

☎ 08236

On the Bangalore road 16km from Mysore stand the ruins of Hyder Ali and Tipu Sultan's capital, from where they ruled much of southern India during the 18th century. In 1799 the British conquered them with the help of disgruntled local leaders. Tipu's defeat marked the real kick-off for British territorial expansion in southern India.

SIGHTS

Srirangapatnam was constructed on a long island in the Cauvery River. Little is left of it since the British came through like a whirlwind, but ramparts, battlements and some of the gates still stand.

A **fort** holds the dungeon where Tipu held British officers captive, a mosque and the handsome **Sri Ranganathaswamy Temple** (☎ 252273; ☒ 7.30am-1pm & 4-8pm).

Set in ornamental gardens 1km east of the fort is Tipu's summer palace, the **Daria Daulat Bagh**. Its highly decorated interior now houses a **museum** (☎ 252023; Indian/foreigner Rs 5/US$2; ☒ 9am-5pm) containing a motley collection of family memorabilia and paintings depicting Tipu's campaigns against the British.

About 2km further east is the impressive onion-domed **Gumbaz** (☎ 252007; ☒ 8am-8pm) of Tipu and his father, Hyder Ali.

Head 500m east of Gumbaz for the river banks. A short coracle ride runs for Rs 25 per person. Don't swim in the waters here if you don't like crocodiles.

SLEEPING & EATING

KSTDC Hotel Mayura River View (☎ 252114; cottages Rs 600), a few kilometres from the bus stand and train station, has pleasing rooms with TV, geyser and patio terrace. The **restaurant** (mains Rs 35-80) offers simple Indian mains, plus booze.

GETTING THERE & AWAY

From Mysore, bus Nos 313 and 316 go hourly to Srirangapatnam (Rs 10), or you can catch one of the private minibuses (Rs 8) that depart across the road from the clock tower. Mysore–Bangalore passenger trains also stop here (Rs 9).

The stand for private buses heading to Brindavan gardens (Rs 10, 30 minutes) is just across from the main bus stand.

GETTING AROUND
The points of interest are a little spread out, but walking isn't out of the question. All the sites are signposted, so finding your way around isn't too perplexing. For a quicker look round, tongas (horse carriages) cost about Rs 100 for three hours, and an auto-rickshaw is about Rs 150.

Ranganathittu Bird Sanctuary
This **sanctuary** (Indian/foreigner Rs 10/60, camera/video Rs 20/100; ☉ 8.30am-6pm) is on one of three islands in the Cauvery River, 3km upstream from Srirangapatnam. It's a good shady place to watch stork, ibis, egret, spoonbill and cormorant.

To see the most birdlife, try to get here in the early morning or late afternoon. Short **boat rides** (per person Rs 25) allow a closer peek into your feathered friends' personal lives. It's open all year, but the best time to visit is April to July.

Brindavan Gardens
These ornamental **gardens** (☎ 08236-290019; adult/child Rs 10/5, camera Rs 25; ☉ 10am-10pm), laid out below the immense waters of Krishnaraja Sagar, are a popular picnic spot, and crowds flock here each night to see the illuminated fountains – alight from 7pm to 8pm (till 9pm Sundays) to the accompaniment of film tunes.

Hotel Mayura Cauvery (☎ 08236-257252; s/d Rs 200/350) has clean, basic rooms with partial views of the garden. It also has an on-site restaurant.

The gardens are 19km northwest of Mysore. One of the KSTDC tours stops here, and buses Nos 301, 304, 305, 306 and 365 depart from Mysore's City bus stand hourly (Rs 7, 45 minutes).

Mandya District
Several stunning Hoysala temples colour the Mandya district, north and east of Mysore. The **Cheluvanarayana Temple** (☎ 08236-298739; Raja St; ☉ 8am-1pm & 5-8pm), at Melkote, about 50km north of Mysore, was built in the 12th century and later came under the patronage of the Mysore maharajas and even Tipu Sultan. The interesting **Yoganarasimha Temple**, up on a hill overlooking Melkote, offers fine views of the surrounding hills and valleys.

North of Melkote is Nagamangala, which was a prominent town even in the days of the Hoysalas. Its **Saumyakeshava Temple** (☉ 8am-6pm), off the Bangalore–Mysore Rd, was built in the 12th century and later added to by the Vijayanagar kings.

Approximately 20km west of Melkote, near Krishnarajpet, is the village of Hosaholalu. Here you'll find the **Lakshminarayana Temple** (☉ 8am-noon & 5-8pm), a superb example of 13th-century Hoysala temple architecture that rivals the temples at Belur and Halebid in artistry.

Basaralu village, 25km north of Mandya, is home to the exquisite 12th-century **Mallikarjuna Temple** (☉ 8am-8pm), executed in early Hoysala style. It's adorned with intriguing sculptures, including a 16-armed Shiva dancing on Andhakasura's head, and Ravana lifting Mt Kailash. There's also an exquisitely carved Nandi.

Getting to these towns involves navigating the web of local buses; you'll have to ask around to find the right ones, unless you can read the Kannada timetables. Mysore is your best base for all of these towns, except Basaralu, for which Mandya might be a better place to stay. Mandya has some modest accommodation.

Sivasamudram
About 60km southeast of Mysore, near the twin waterfalls of Barachukki and Gaganachukki, is **Georgia Sunshine Village** (☎ 08231-247646; www.georgiasunshine.com; Malavalli; d incl meals from Rs 2200; 🖳), which travellers can't stop talking about. Accommodation is in bungalows (the open-air bathrooms have small gardens), the comfy veranda is perfect for nature-watching (one reader counted 60 bird species in one morning), and the homemade food is some of the best around.

Frequent buses run from Mysore (Rs 22, one hour) and Bangalore (Rs 45, three hours) to Malavalli, which is 14km away (autorickshaw Rs 80).

BANDIPUR NATIONAL PARK
elev 780–1455m
About 80km south of Mysore on the Ooty road, the **Bandipur National Park** (Indian/foreigner Rs 50/150, camera Rs 50) covers 880 sq km and is

part of the Nilgiri Biosphere Reserve, which includes the sanctuaries of Nagarhole, Mudumalai in Tamil Nadu and Wayanad in Kerala. It was once the Mysore maharajas' private wildlife reserve.

Bandipur is noted for herds of gaur (Indian bison), chital (spotted deer), elephants, sambar, panthers, sloth bears and langur. More than 80 tigers reportedly roam here, but they're rarely seen. The vegetation is a hodgepodge of deciduous and evergreen forest and scrubland. The best time to see wildlife is March to April, but November to February is the most temperate.

Brief **elephant rides** (per person Rs 50, minimum 4 people) are available. Private cars – with the exception of resort vehicles – are not allowed to tour the park so you're stuck with the Forest Department's diesel-minibus **safari** (per person Rs 25; ☼ 6-8am & 4-5pm). The wildlife seen will be limited, as a bus lumbering through the forest doesn't exactly entice creatures out into the open. On Sundays tourists can outnumber the spotted deer.

Sleeping & Eating

Forest Department bungalows (r Rs 500) These basic bungalows have mosquito nets, and at night the grounds are shared with sleeping chital. Meals are available with advance notice. Reservations should be made at least two weeks in advance with **Project Tiger** (☎ 0821-2480901; fdptrm@sancharnet.in; Aranya Bhavan, Ashokapuram) in Mysore.

Bandipur Safari Lodge (Mysore-Ooty Rd; s/d US$65/100) Very comfy cottages here, 3km outside the park, have balcony and all the mod cons. Rates include three meals, jeep safari, an elephant ride and all park fees. Book with **Jungle Lodges & Resorts** (Map p210; ☎ 080-25597021; www.junglelodges.com; 2nd fl, Shrungar Shopping Complex, MG Rd) in Bangalore.

Tusker Trails (s/d US$90/150; ⌘) This high-end resort on the eastern edge of the park near Mangala village has six two-room cottages, a peaceful atmosphere and a pool. Rates here are likewise all-inclusive, with two daily safaris. Bookings should be made in advance at the company's Bangalore **office** (☎ 080-23618024; rajsafaris_9@yahoo.co.in; Bangalore Palace).

Getting There & Away
Buses between Mysore (2½ hours) and Ooty (three hours) will drop you at Bandipur National Park or Bandipur Safari Lodge.

NAGARHOLE NATIONAL PARK
elev 800-850m

This 643 sq km wildlife sanctuary (Rajiv Gandhi National Park; Indian/foreigner Rs 50/150, camera Rs 50) is in an isolated pocket of the Kodagu region, 93km southwest of Mysore. There are around 40 tigers as well as leopards and elephants in Nagarhole (nag-ar-hole-eh), but you're more likely to see gaur, muntjac (barking deer), wild dogs, bonnet macaques and common langur. The lush forest is more attractive than Bandipur's scrubby vegetation, and animal sightings are more common.

As with Bandipur, the only way to get around is on the bus **tour** (per person Rs 25; ☼ 6-8am & 4-5pm); the best time to view wildlife is the hot months (April to May), but the winter air (November to February) is kinder.

Sleeping & Eating

Forest Department rooms (Rs 1500) In the park, these rooms are overpriced but come with mosquito nets. Food and beer can be arranged. You should book at least two weeks in advance with **Project Tiger** (☎ 0821-2480901; fdptrm@sancharnet.in; Aranya Bhavan, Ashokapuram) in Mysore.

Jungle Inn (☎ 08222-246022; s/d first night US$95/150, additional nights US$85/140) Jungle Inn's welcoming atmosphere, evening camp fires and cosy rooms gets much applause from travellers. Rates include full board (your dinner's vegetables are grown on the site), taxes and safaris in the park. The resort is 35km from park reception on the Hunsur road. Book ahead.

Kabini River Lodge (Mysore-Mananthavadi Rd, Karapur; s/d US$130/220) Elephant lovers love this former maharaja's hunting lodge on the southern fringe of the park. Rates include full board and wildlife safaris. Book through **Jungle Lodges & Resorts** (Map p210; ☎ 080-25597021; www.junglelodges.com; 2nd fl, Shrungar Shopping Complex, MG Rd) in Bangalore.

Getting There & Away
Direct buses to Nagarhole depart Mysore twice daily and can drop you at Jungle Inn. Jungle Lodges & Resorts can arrange private transport to Kabini River Lodge.

TIBETAN SETTLEMENTS
Some of the kindest people on earth live in the many Tibetan refugee settlements

in the rolling hills near Madikeri. The **Namdroling Monastery** (☎ 08223-254921; www.palyul .org), about 5km from Kushalnagar, is home to the jaw-droppingly spectacular **Golden Temple** (Padmasambhava Buddhist Vihara; ⊙ 7am-8pm), which is dazzlingly presided over by an 18m-high gold-plated Buddha. The temple is in particularly good form when school is in session and it rings out with the gongs, drums and chanting of hundreds of young novices. You're welcome to sit and meditate on it all; look for the small blue 'guest' cushions lying around. The monastery also recently opened the **Zangdogpalri Temple**, a similarly spectacular affair, next door.

About 2km from Namdroling, Sera village is the site of the **Sera Jhe** and **Sera Mey** monasteries, which house about 5000 monks between them. The **Sera Jhe Health Care Committee Guest House** (☎ 08223-258672; r Rs 125) has clean, simple accommodation and a restaurant with basic meals like *thukpa* (Tibetan noodle soup; Rs 10). The atmosphere in the villages is heart-warmingly welcoming.

Hotel Choice (mains Rs 20-40; ⊙ 7am-11pm), near the Golden Temple, is quite good, with Indian, Chindian and some Keralan specialities. It's a popular monk hangout.

The settlements are most easily reached from Kushalnagar, where shared autorickshaws (per person Rs 10; Rs 30 if alone) ply the route to Sera. Buses run frequently to Kushalnagar from Madikeri (Rs 12, one hour) and Hassan (Rs 32, four hours); most buses on the Mysore–Madikeri route stop at Kushalnagar.

Contact Namdroling Monastery if you're interested in visiting the settlements for more than a few days.

MADIKERI (MERCARA)
☎ 08272 / pop 32,286 / elev 1525m

The market town of Madikeri is the naturally cool capital of the Kodagu (Coorg) region, a green mountainous expanse in southwest Karnataka. A good base for treks, the town straddles forested hills whose roads ramble through flowering vines, cardamom plantations, bamboo trees (nibbled by elephants) and coffee estates. In March and April, fragrant white blossoms illuminate the hills of deep-green coffee plants.

Kodagu was a state in its own right until 1956, and local politicians are pushing for statehood to be restored, or at least for more local autonomy.

Orientation
Madikeri is spread out along a series of ridges. The bus stand as well as most of the hotels and restaurants are compactly huddled in the centre.

KARNATAKA

THE KODAVAS

Most people in Kodagu, known as Kodavas, are not tribal, but are possibly descendants of migrating Persians and Kurds – no-one's exactly sure. The word 'Kodava' apparently comes from the local words for 'Blessed by Mother Cauvery'.

Some of the more interesting Kodava customs include refusal to recognise any head of religion; worship of unique deities, including the Cauvery River as godmother; and unique homes called *lyns*. Wedding ceremonies (which rarely involve dowries) include complex dances, mock fighting with sticks, and such symbolic exploits as chopping off a banana leaf with a sword. These are often held at Madikeri's Kodava Samaja building.

In addition to the lively November/December Huthri festival (see p206), the Kodavas fête Keil podu, which celebrates the end of rice-planting season in September and pays homage to the Kodavas' warrior tradition (Kodagu is the only place in India where citizens are allowed to own guns): men show off their weapons and marksmanship while invoking the gods' blessings. Other festivals include October's Tula Sankramana, when the goddess Cauvery appears in the form of a gush of water at the river's source; various ceremonies (usually in December) at the sacred temples in Madikeri (Omkareshwara) and Bhagamandala; and the irregularly held Yerava demon festivals, called *pandalatas*, with their unusual singing and dancing.

The Kodavas have distinctive traditional costumes for special occasions: the men wear sashes, daggers, black gowns, colourful turbans and plenty of jewellery, while the women wear bright scarves and saris draped with even more complexity than normal.

Information

Canara Bank (☎ 229302; Main Rd, Gandhi Chowk;
🕓 10.30am-2.30pm Mon-Fri) Changes cash and travellers
cheques and gives credit card advances.
Corp Bank (College Rd) Has a 24-hour ATM.
Digital Planet (College Rd; 🕓 8am-8pm) Digital
developing and burning.
Internet Paradise (Bus Stand Rd; per hr Rs 30;
🕓 9am-9pm)
Tourist Office (☎ 228580; 🕓 10am-5.30pm Mon-Sat)
Beside the first roundabout on the Mysore road.

Sights

On the way to **Abbi Falls**, a nice 7km hike
from the town centre, visit the quietly beautiful **Raja's Tombs**, better known as Gaddige.
An autorickshaw will cost about Rs 150
return. Madikeri's **fort**, now the municipal
headquarters, was built in 1812 by Raja Lin-
garajendra II. Cows graze around the old
church here, home to a small **museum** (admission free; 🕓 10am-5.30pm Tue-Sun) that's poorly
labelled, dusty and fascinating. The austere
Omkareshwara Temple (🕓 6.30am-noon & 5-8pm),
just below the fort, is an interesting blend
of Keralan and Islamic architectural styles;
reach it via the steps descending past the
police station. The view from **Raja's Seat** (MG
Rd; 🕓 5.30am-7.30pm) is extraordinary, and the
gardens are home to a tiny Kodava-style
temple.

Activities

TREKKING

The Kodagu region has some awesome
trekking routes; the best season is October to March. Facilities are limited, but
guides will arrange food, transport and accommodation in local houses, schools or
camping grounds. Most treks last two to
three days, but longer treks are possible;
the most popular treks are to the peaks
of Tadiyendamol (1745m) and Pushpagiri
(1712m), and to smaller Kotebetta. A guide
is essential for navigating the labyrinth of
forest tracks.

Recommended trek organiser Raja Shekar
runs **Friends Tours & Travels** (☎ 225672; v_trak@
rediffmail.com; College Rd; 10am-2pm & 4.30-8pm Mon-
Sat, 6-7.30pm Sun); if he's away trekking, contact Rao Ganesh at **Sri Ganesh Automobile**
(☎ 229102; Hill Rd), just up from the private
bus stand. They arrange one- to 10-day
treks for Rs 400 per person per day (more
if you're solo) including guide, accommo-

dation and food. Short walks take only a
day or two to prepare. For long treks, trips
on obscure routes or big groups, give them
a week's notice. **Coorg Tourist Travel Agency**
(☎ 225817; Udaya Raja Seat Rd; 🕓 9am-5pm) also
organises treks, and **Mr Muktar** (☎ 229152) at
Hotel Chitra leads half-day treks for Rs 250
per person.

AYURVEDA

One-hour sessions at the tiny **Shri Akhila Ravi
Ayurshala Ayurvedic clinic** (☎ 594288; Powerhouse
Rd; 🕓 9am-6pm) cost Rs 175; a normal course
runs seven days.

Bharath Ayurveda Clinic (☎ 08276-271063; Bypass
Rd, near Chythra Arts; 🕓 10am-4pm Mon-Sat) is run by
the highly recommended Dr Abdul Rahi-
man, who comes from the traditional guru
system but unfortunately doesn't speak
English; bring a Kannada (or Malayalam)
speaker. The clinic is about an hour outside
Madikeri in Kushalnagar (the transit point
for the Tibetan Settlements; see p228). Sessions cost Rs 300.

Sleeping

Many hotels reduce their rates in the off
season (January to March and June to September); all of those listed below have hot
water, at least in the morning, and 24-hour
checkout.

Hilltown Hotel (☎ 223801; www.madikeri.com/
hilltown; Daswal Rd; s/d Rs 250/500; mains Rs 30-60)
Down the lane running past Hotel Chitra,
the Hilltown is a classy little place with
small but smart singles and roomier doubles, all with constant hot water. It also has
a good restaurant.

Hotel Cauvery (☎ 225492; School Rd; s/d/tr
Rs 200/400/500) Madikeri's granddaddy budget
hotel, right near the bus stand, is spotless
and has some character. The staff is helpful,
and the amiable owner can arrange treks up
to Tadiyendamol.

Dawn (☎ 223388; outdoorindia@sancharnet.in;
Powerhouse Rd; dm Rs 125) The Dawn is worth
visiting for eccentric eco-warrior Anoop
Chinnappa, who can organise treks (and
meals). The rooms, in Anoop's family
home 1km from the bus stand, are basic but
have personality.

Shanthi Estate (☎ 223690; vgopal31@yahoo.co.in;
r Rs 300-800) A good choice if you can't make
it out to the hills: it's a stunning 2½km walk
to town and the plantation is lush.

Hotel Rajdarshan (☎ 229142; hrdraj@sancharnet .in; 116/2 MG Rd; s/d from Rs 750/850; mains Rs 50 to 75) On the way up to Raja's Seat, this modern place aspires to elegance and has the most accommodating rooms in town. Its restaurant is fairly polished.

Capitol Village Resort (☎ 225492; fax 229455; Chettali-Siddapur Rd; s/d/tr Rs 600/850/950) About 8km from Madikeri is this charming lodge nestled among coffee, cardamom and pepper plantations. Attractive, woodsy rooms have balconies, and the food (meals Rs 75 to 175) is delicious. Call ahead or book at Hotel Cauvery (opposite).

Eating

East End Hotel (GT Circle; mains Rs 30-100; ☺ 7am-10:30pm) Some veg dishes are available among the mutton offerings, but the very special *masala dosas* (Rs 15) are the real reason to come.

Udupi Hotel Vegland (Chickpet, Main Rd; meals Rs 15-20; ☺ 7am-9pm) This standard pure veg joint near the fort is a friendly local place with cheap, reliable thalis.

Popular Guru Prasad (Main Rd; meals Rs 20; ☺ 6.30am-10pm) The popular Popular Guru Prasad serves perfectly steamed *idlis* (rice dumpling, Rs 2.50 each) and other veggie options.

Hotel Capitol (School Rd; meals 15-40; ☺ 6am-11pm) The front room has your standard veggie goodies, but the nonveg room-cum-drinking den to the rear serves bacon-and-eggs breakfasts and the local speciality, *pandhi* (pork curry; Rs 40) – from porkers raised on the owner's estate.

Hotel Mayura Valley View (MG Rd; meals Rs 30-85; ☺ 6.30am-10.30pm) This recently renovated KSTDC bar/restaurant next to Raja's Seat has great views; try happy hour on the terrace.

Getting There & Away

Five deluxe buses a day depart from the KSRTC **bus stand** (☎ 229134) for Bangalore (Rs 152, seven hours), stopping in Mysore (Rs 70, 3½ hours) on the way. Deluxe buses also go to Mangalore (Rs 80, four hours, three daily), and frequent ordinary buses head to Hassan (Rs 42, three hours) and Shimoga (Rs 102, eight hours).

The private bus stand is mainly for local buses, and there's a theoretical daily morning bus to Nagarhole (Rs 74, 3½ hours),

which may or may not run. The scenery along nearby roads is worth taking random local buses for.

AROUND MADIKERI
☎ 08272

Staying at the remote guesthouses and resorts in the **Kodagu Hills** is a great way to immerse yourself in the area's lush beauty. Owners can arrange plantation tours and recommend local hiking routes, and the hills are a hot spot for bird-watching.

Honey Valley Estate (☎ 238339; www.momentum.freeserve.co.uk/honeyvalley; Kakkabe; s/d with shared bathroom Rs 150/200, with private bathroom Rs 700/900), 35km from Madikeri near the village of Kakkabe, is in the middle of a forest, so it doesn't get much more peaceful. The owners' friendliness, environmental mindfulness (they have a hydroelectric generator) and amazing food (with organic veggies from the farm) have won enthusiastic applause from travellers. The estate is only accessible by jeep or by walking; call in advance to arrange transport.

Palace Estate (☎ 238446; Yavakapudi; s/d Rs 300/ 400), at Yavakapudi, a Rs 100 jeep ride from Kakkabe, has a name for good hospitality and home cooking (meals Rs 60 to 125). You can book with them, or through Hotel Cauvery (opposite) in Madikeri.

Alath-Cad Estate Bungalow (☎ 08274-252190, 9845445519; fax 252589; www.alathcadcoorg.com; Ammathi; r Rs incl breakfast 1650-1900) is on a 26-hectare coffee plantation about 28km from

---

SOMETHING SPECIAL

Rainforest Retreat (☎ /fax 265636; www .rainforestours.com; per person Rs 1000-1500) Cottages on this organic plantation are forest-chic, while the main house, held up by tree trunks, resonates with the blues and the good vibes of its brainy owners. Sujata (the botanist) gives eye-opening nature walks, while Anurag (the molecular biologist) will teach you about biopesticides. The trekking is excellent – or you can just lie in a hammock and watch the birds. All proceeds go to the couple's NGO, which promotes environmental awareness and research into sustainable agriculture. Rainforest Retreat is 10km from Madikeri near Gallibedu; call to arrange transport.

KARNATAKA

Madikeri, 1.5km from the town of Ammathi. Its rooms have solar-heated water. Try to book at least a week in advance.

Orange County Resort (☎ 08274-258481; Siddapur; d cottages Rs 6500, with private pool Rs 10,500; ⊠ ⊠) On a 120-hectare plantation 32km south of Madikeri, the soothing mock-Tudor cottages here come with all the mod cons. Guided treks, boating and Ayurvedic massages are among the offerings (for extra cost), and room rates include taxes and all meals. Book through **Trails** (☎ 080-25325302; www.trailsindia.com) in Bangalore.

HASSAN
☎ 08172 / pop 117,386

With a good range of hotels, a railhead and other conveniences, Hassan is a handy base for exploring Belur (38km), Halebid (33km) and Sravanabelagola (48km).

Information
Banks here are not equipped with foreign-exchange facilities, although the Southern Star hotel will change dollars at a bad rate. ATMs are popping up around Hassan; the

one at Corp Bank, next to Hotel Sri Krishna, accepts Visa and Plus cards.

Other services:

Cyber Park (☎ Harsha Mahal Rd; per hr Rs 30)

Tourist office (☎ 268862; AVK College Rd; ◌ 10am-5.30pm Mon-Fri & alternate Sat) One of Karnataka's more helpful offices.

Sleeping
Sumukh Yatri Nivas (☎ 262366; Racecourse Rd; s/d Rs 150/250) Still under construction at the time of writing, this looks like it will be a good option, with wrought-iron furniture and big, sunny rooms, some with balconies.

Vaishnavi Lodging (☎ 263885; Harsha Mahal Rd; s/d Rs 140/200) Cheap and tidy, and the sheets are clean, though they've seen better days.

Hotel Sri Krishna (☎ 263240; fax 233904; BM Rd; s/d from Rs 250/395; ⊠) The best deal in town, on the Bangalore–Mangalore (BM) road, has super-clean, very agreeable rooms. Attached is a quality pure-veg eatery (mains Rs 30 to 60).

Hotel Suvarna Regency (☎ 266774; fax 63822; BM Rd; s/d from Rs 275/400; ⊠ ⊠) Slightly up-market, the Suvarna has snazzy rooms with real furniture, like in a house. Guests and nonguests can use the pool at the Suvarna Resort out back for Rs 30 per hour.

Southern Star (☎ 251816; www.ushashriramhotels .com; BM Rd; s/d from Rs 995/1195; ⊡ ⊠) The most comfortable place in town is almost cosy, and the amenities and service make up for the street noise.

Hotel Hassan Ashhok (☎ 268731; hsnashok@yahoo .com; BM Rd; s/d from Rs 700/1000; ⊠) Neatly presented rooms, attentive service, bars and restaurants but lacking personality.

Eating
Hotel GRR (Bus Stand Rd; meals Rs 15-35; ◌ 11am-11pm) The friendly GRR dishes out top-of-the-line, all-you-can-eat, Andhra-style thalis (Rs 15) on banana leaves, plus non-veg mains.

Hotel Sanman (Municipal Office Rd; meals Rs 15; ◌ 6am-10pm) This busy local joint does great dosas.

Karwar Restaurant (BM Rd; mains Rs 40-100; ◌ 6am-11pm; ⊠) The most posh option in town, in the Southern Star hotel (above) serves a range of cuisines; the grilled chicken gets good reviews.

Suvarna Gate (BM Rd; mains Rs 35-100; ◌ noon-3.30pm & 6.30-11.30pm) The terrace dining room has some ambience, and the Chinese and North Indian dishes (and the piña coladas) are not bad.

Getting There & Away

BUS

If you're planning to visit Belur and Halebid on the same day from Hassan, go to Halebid first as there are more buses from Belur to Hassan and they run until much later.

Buses to Halebid (Rs 12, one hour, every half hour) start running at 6am, with the last bus back leaving Halebid at 7.30pm. Frequent buses go between Hassan and Belur (Rs 15, 1½ hours); the first leaves Hassan at 6am, and the last bus from Belur is at 10pm.

To get to Sravanabelagola, you must take one of the many buses to Channarayapatna (Rs 15, 45 minutes) and change there.

Buses rumble off frequently to Mysore (Rs 45, three hours) as well as Bangalore (Rs 65/110 in ordinary/deluxe, four hours). Buses to Mangalore (Rs 76/102 in ordinary/ deluxe, four hours) leave every 30 minutes.

TAXI

Taxi drivers hang out on AVK College Rd, north of the bus stand. A tour of Belur and Halebid will run you about Rs 600 for the day. A return taxi to Sravanabelagola will cost the same. Firmly set the price before departure.

TRAIN

The well-organised **train station** (☎ 268222) is about 2km east of town (Rs 10 by auto-rickshaw); it has a cloak room (Rs 10) and retiring rooms (Rs 100). Three passenger trains head to Mysore daily (Rs 23 in 2d class, three hours); the one at 2.20pm is a 'fast passenger' train (two hours). For Bangalore, take one of the four daily trains to Arsikere (Rs 12, one hour) and change there. Rail services to Mangalore have not run for several years while the line is being converted to broad gauge. When the work is completed, one or two trains will ply the four-hour trip daily.

BELUR & HALEBID

☎ 08177 / elev 968m

The Hoysala temples at Halebid (also known as Halebeed or Halebidu) and Belur, along with the one at Somnathpur, near Mysore,

are the apex of one of the most artistically exuberant periods of Hindu cultural development. Their sculptural decoration rivals that of Khajuraho (Madhya Pradesh) and Konark (Orissa).

Base yourself at Belur, which is more atmospheric than Halebid, if you're staying longer than an afternoon.

Belur

The **Channekeshava Temple** (Temple Rd; ☼ sunrise-sunset) is the only one at the three major Hoysala sites still in daily use – try to be there for the ceremonies at 9am, 3pm and 7.30pm. Begun in 1116 to commemorate the Hoysalas' victory over the Cholas at Talakad, work continued on it for over a century. Although its exterior lower friezes are not as extensively sculpted as those of the other Hoysala temples, the work higher up is unsurpassed in detail and artistry. Particularly intriguing are the angled bracket figures depicting women in ritual dancing poses. Note that the front of the temple is reserved for dancers and characters from the Kama Sutra; the back is strictly for gods. Plentiful decorative work also lines the internal supporting pillars (no two of which are identical) and lintels. Allegedly, every major Hindu deity is represented here.

The temple grounds are worth a wander, with their smaller, aging temples and 14th-century seven-storey *gopuram*, which has some sensual sculptures explicitly portraying the après-temple activities of dancing girls.

Guides can be hired for Rs 100 and help to bring some of the sculptural detail to life.

The other, lesser, Hoysala temples at Belur are the **Chennigaraya** and the **Viranarayana** temples.

Belur has several accommodation options:

KSTDC Hotel Mayura Velapuri (☎ 222209; Temple Rd; r Rs 300; mains Rs 25-100) The recently renovated rooms here are big and airy and have constant hot water. The hotel, on the way to the temple, has a bar-restaurant and an irrelevant tourist office.

Vishnu Regency (☎ 223490; fax 230310; Kempegowda Rd; s/d/tr Rs 300/500/600; 🖵) Marble-floored rooms have comfy beds but frequent water cuts. The restaurant serves North Indian and Chinese (mains Rs 20 to 65). From the bus stand, walk up Temple Rd and turn left at the statue.

Vishnu Krupa (☎ 222263; Main Rd; s/d from Rs 75/150) Close to the bus stand, this place has dreary singles and OK doubles. It also has quirky, affable staff and a clean veg restaurant, Vishnu Refreshments.

Shankar Hotel (Temple Rd; meals Rs 20; 7am-9.30pm) Near the statue is this cheerful place serving especially good South Indian thalis with endless refills.

Halebid

Construction began on the **Hoysaleswara Temple** (sunrise-sunset) at Halebid around 1121. Despite more than 80 years of labour it was never completed, but it's still the most outstanding example of Hoysala art in India. The entire outside and some of the interior is covered with riots of Hindu deities, sages, stylised animals and friezes depicting the life of the Hoysala rulers.

The temple is set in large well-tended gardens, and a small **museum** (admission Rs 2; 10am-5pm Sat-Thu) houses a collection of sculptures.

Halebid also has a smaller temple known as **Kedareswara** and a little-visited enclosure containing three **Jain** temples, which also have fine carvings. These are peacefully tout-free.

KSTDC Mayura Shantala (☎ 273224; d/q with shared bathroom Rs 200/275), Halebid's only place to stay, has four rooms, a tourist office and a restaurant. There are also a couple of rustic eateries along the main road.

Getting There & Away

Belur and Halebid are only 16km apart. Buses shuttle between the two towns every 30 minutes or so from 6.30am to 7pm (Rs 8, 30 minutes). See p233 for details of buses to/from Hassan. Belur has frequent direct services to Mysore (Rs 60, 4½ hours), Bangalore (Rs 80, five hours), Dharmastala (Rs 35, three hours) and Arsikere (for Bangalore trains; Rs 24, 2½ hours). You must pass through Hassan to get to Sravanabelagola.

To get to Hampi, catch a bus for Kadur (Rs 14, one hour), where you'll find a bus to Shimoga. Buses leave Shimoga frequently for Hospet, the nearest station to Hampi.

SRAVANABELAGOLA
☎ 08176

Sravanabelagola, which means the Monk of the White Pond, is one of the oldest and most important Jain pilgrimage centres in India, and the site of the 17.5m-high naked statue of Gomateshvara (Bahubali), a Jain deity. Said to be the world's tallest monolithic statue, it overlooks the sedate town of Sravanabelagola from the bald rock of Vindhyagiri Hill. Its simplicity and serenity is in complete contrast to the complexity and energy of the sculptural work at the Belur and Halebid temples.

Sravanabelagola has a long pedigree, going back to the 3rd century BC when Chandragupta Maurya came here with his guru, Bhagwan Bhadrabahu Swami, after renouncing his kingdom. Bhadrabahu's disciples spread his teachings all over the

---

HOYSALA ARCHITECTURE

The Hoysalas, who ruled this part of the Deccan between the 11th and 13th centuries, originated in the hill tribes of the Western Ghats and were, for a long time, feudatories of the Chalukyas. They didn't become fully independent until about 1190, though they first rose to prominence under their leader Tinayaditya (1047–78), who took advantage of the waning power of the Gangas and Rashtrakutas. Under Bittiga (1110–52), later named Vishnuvardhana, they began to take off on a course of their own; it was during his reign that the distinctive temples at Belur and Halebid were built.

Typically, these temples are squat, star-shaped structures set on a platform. They are more human in scale than the soaring temples found elsewhere in India, but what they lack in size they make up for in sheer intricacy.

It's quickly apparent from a study of these sculptures that the arts of music and dance were highly regarded during the Hoysala period. It also seems that these were times of a relatively high degree of sexual freedom and prominent female participation in public affairs.

The Hoysalas converted to Jainism in the 10th century, but took up Hinduism in the 11th century. This is why images of Shaivite, Vaishnavite and Jain sects co-exist in their temples.

region, firmly planting Jainism in southern soils. The religion found powerful patrons in the Gangas, who ruled southern Karnataka between the 4th and 10th centuries, the zenith of Jainism's influence.

Information

The helpful **tourist office** (☎ 257254; ☒ 10am-5.30pm) is at the foot of Vindhyagiri Hill. Though there are no entry fees to the sites in Sravanabelagola, donations are encouraged.

Those who cannot walk up the stairs at Vindhyagiri Hill can hire a *dholi* (portable chair) with bearers, from 7am to 12.30pm and 3pm to 5.30pm, for Rs 130.

Sights

GOMATESHVARA STATUE

The statue of **Gomateshvara** (Bahubali; ☒ 6am-6.30pm) was created during the reign of the Ganga king, Rachamalla. It was commissioned by a military commander in the service of Rachamalla and carved out of granite by the sculptor Aristenemi in AD 981. Bahubali's father was the great Emperor Vrishabhadeva, who became the first Jain *tirthankar* (revered Jain teacher), Adinath. Bahubali and his brother Bharatha competed fiercely for the right to succeed their father but, on the point of victory, Bahubali realised the futility of the struggle and renounced his kingdom. He withdrew from the material world and entered the forest, where he meditated in complete stillness until he attained enlightenment. The statue has vines curling around his legs and an anthill at his feet, signs of his utter detachment. The gallery around his statue has many smaller images of Jain *tirthankars*.

Standing atop Vindhyagiri Hill, the statue is reached via 614 rock-cut steps. You must leave your shoes at the foot of the hill, which is a problem in summer, when the steps are too hot to trot upon. You're not supposed to wear socks.

TEMPLES

In addition to the Bahubali statue, there are several interesting Jain temples in the town and on Chandragiri Hill, the smaller of the two hills between which Sravanabelagola is nestled.

The **Chandragupta Basti** (Chandragupta Community; ☒ 6am-6pm), on Chandragiri Hill, is believed to have been built by Emperor Ashoka. The

Hoysala-style **Bhandari Basti** (Bhandari Community), in the southeast corner of town, is Sravanabelagola's largest temple. Nearby, **Chandranatha Basti** (Chandranatha Community) has well-preserved paintings that look like a 650-year-old comic strip of Jain stories.

Sleeping & Eating

Nearly all of Sravanabelagola's accommodation is run by the local Jain organisation, SDJMI, whose **central accommodation office** (☎ 257258) handles bookings for its 15 guesthouses. The office is behind the Vidyananda Nilaya Dharamsala, past the post office and before the bus stand on the way into town. Most foreigners find themselves bunked at the simple and well-maintained **Yathri Nivas** (d/tr Rs 175/300).

Hotel Raghu (☎ 257238; s/d/tr Rs 75/150/200; mains Rs 20-40) Sravanabelagola's only privately owned hotel is a little dingy, but it's straightforward and just at the foot of Vindhyagiri Hill. It also has a busy vegetarian restaurant.

Chai shops and no-frills eateries dot the street leading to the foot of Vindhyagiri Hill.

Getting There & Away

No buses go direct to Hassan or Belur – you must go to Channarayapatna (Rs 7, 20 minutes) and catch an onward connection there. Four direct buses a day run to Bangalore (Rs 54, 3½ hours) but only the 8am Mysore bus is direct (Rs 34, 2½ hours). Nearly all long-distance buses leave before 3pm; if you miss these, catch a local bus to Channarayapatna, 10km northwest, which is on the main Bangalore–Mangalore road and has lots of connections.

THE COAST

MANGALORE

☎ 0824 / pop 398,745

Once upon a time Mangalore was the major port of Hyder Ali's kingdom. Today it's a bustling and hassle-free city where you'll see everything from burkhas to blue jeans. The significant Catholic community dates back to the arrival of the Portuguese in 1526, while the large, mixed university population gives the city an air of progressiveness.

Mangalore is a centre for coffee and cashew nut export, but is perhaps most famous for the production of terracotta roof tiles. It's a good place to stop for amenities, a trip to the beach and some interesting local sites. Mangaloreans, along with those in the surrounding district, speak Tulu and have a reputation for being quick to smile.

Orientation

Mangalore is hilly with winding, disorienting streets. Luckily, all the hotels and restaurants, the bus stand and the train station are in or around the frenzied city centre and are easy to find. Less handily, the KSRTC long-distance bus stand is 3km to the north.

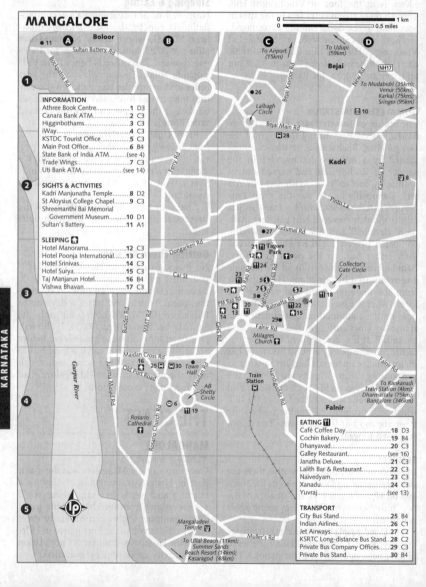

MANGALORE

0 —————— 1 km
0 —————— 0.5 miles

INFORMATION
Athree Book Centre	**1** D3
Canara Bank ATM	**2** C3
Higginbothams	**3** C3
iWay	**4** C3
KSTDC Tourist Office	**5** C3
Main Post Office	**6** B4
State Bank of India ATM	(see 4)
Trade Wings	**7** C3
Uti Bank ATM	(see 14)

SIGHTS & ACTIVITIES
Kadri Manjunatha Temple	**8** D2
St Aloysius College Chapel	**9** C3
Shreemanthi Bai Memorial Government Museum	**10** D1
Sultan's Battery	**11** A1

SLEEPING ☐
Hotel Manorama	**12** C3
Hotel Poonja International	**13** C3
Hotel Srinivas	**14** C3
Hotel Surya	**15** C3
Taj Manjarun Hotel	**16** B4
Vishwa Bhavan	**17** C3

EATING ☐
Café Coffee Day	**18** D3
Cochin Bakery	**19** B4
Dhanyavad	**20** C3
Galley Restaurant	(see 16)
Janatha Deluxe	**21** C3
Lalith Bar & Restaurant	**22** C3
Naivedyam	**23** C3
Xanadu	**24** C3
Yuvraj	(see 13)

TRANSPORT
City Bus Stand	**25** B4
Indian Airlines	**26** C1
Jet Airways	**27** C2
KSRTC Long-distance Bus Stand	**28** C2
Private Bus Company Offices	**29** C3
Private Bus Stand	**30** B4

KARNATAKA

Information

ATMs are everywhere, and several banks in town also have foreign-exchange facilities.

Athree Book Centre (Balmatta Rd; ☺ 8.30am-1pm & 2.30-8pm Mon-Sat)

Higginbothams (Lighthouse Hill Rd; ☺ 9.30am-1.30pm & 3.30-7.30pm Mon-Sat) Bookshop.

iWay (Crystal Arc Bldg, Balmatta Rd; per hr Rs 25; ☺ 7.30am-11pm) Speedy AC Web access.

KSTDC tourist office (☎ 2442926; Lighthouse Hill Rd; ☺ 10am-5pm Mon-Sat) Next to Hotel Indraprastha and mostly useless.

State Bank of India ATM (Balmatta Rd)

Trade Wings (☎ 2427225; Lighthouse Hill Rd; ☺ 9.30am-5.30pm Mon-Sat) The best place to change travellers cheques (and a good travel agency, too).

Uti Bank ATM (GHS Rd)

Sights

Peaceful **Sultan's Battery** (Sultan Battery Rd), a stone watchtower 4km from the centre on the headland of the old port, is the main remnant of Mangalore's past; bus No 16 will get you there. Take bus No 19 to **Shreemanthi Bai Memorial Government Museum** (☎ 2211106; admission Rs 2; ☺ 9am-5pm Tue-Sun), which has a motley collection that's worth a browse; check out the leather shadow puppets.

The town has some attractive temples, including the Keralan-style **Kadri Manjunatha Temple** (Kadri; ☺ 6am-1pm & 4-8pm), whose little Lokeshwara statue is supposedly one of the best bronzes in India. *Puja* at the temple is at 8am, noon and 8pm; take bus No 3, 4 or 6. The painted ceiling frescoes of **St Aloysius College Chapel** (Lighthouse Hill; ☺ 8.30am-6pm Mon-Sat, 10am-12pm & 2-6pm Sun) are stunning.

Serene **Ullal Beach**, 12km south of Mangalore, is best enjoyed at Summer Sands Beach Resort (see right), which costs Rs 25 to enter and Rs 60 to use the pool. An autorickshaw costs Rs 120 return, or catch bus No 44A, 44C or 44D from the City bus stand.

Sleeping

Mangalore has a range of good-value sleeping options, all with hot water. Except for the Summer Sands, all hotels listed here have 24-hour checkout.

Hotel Manorama (☎ 2440306; KS Rao Rd; s/d from Rs 230/330; ☒) This is a charmer: spotless and spacious, with 1940s-style coat racks.

Hotel Surya (☎ 2425736; Balmatta Rd; s/d/tr from Rs 175/225/275; ☒) Set back from the road near Lalith Restaurant, Hotel Surya has simple but fresh rooms; the best are on the third floor.

Hotel Poonja International (☎ 244071; www.hotel poonjainternational.com; KS Rao Rd; s/d from Rs 450/600; ☒) Gleaming lobby, professional staff and comfortable rooms make this place seem more expensive than it is.

Taj Manjarun Hotel (☎ 2420420; www.tajhotels .com; Old Port Rd; s/d from US$55/65; ☒ ☒) Away from the bustle of town, the Taj has cushy rooms, a good restaurant, bar and 24-hour coffee shop, and a pool (open to nonguests for Rs 150 per day).

Summer Sands Beach Resort (☎ 2467690; www .summer-sands.com; bungalow s/d from Rs 750/850; mains Rs 30-150; ☒ ☒) Amid leafy grounds on Ullal Beach, Summer Sands' funky bungalows are ideal for a quiet retreat. The restaurant has lots of fresh fish as well as the hum of the ocean nearby.

Other possibilities:

Hotel Srinivas (☎ 2440061; www.hotelsrinivas.com; GHS Rd; s/d from Rs 275/375; ☒) Quiet, blue-carpeted rooms.

Vishwa Bhavan (☎ 2440822; KS Rao Rd; d Rs 100) Basic doubles that are often booked.

Eating

Mangalorean-style food, famed throughout India, can be savoured at its most elegant in top-end hotel restaurants, which serve local specialities such as the seasonal ladyfish. Basic places around town fry up tasty fish as well, and the vegetarian fare also tends to be delish.

Janatha Deluxe (Hotel Shaan Plaza, KS Rao Rd; mains Rs 20-45; ☺ 6.30am-10.30pm) This local favourite serves good thalis (Rs 22) and a range of North and South Indian veg dishes.

Dhanyavad (cnr KS Rao & Lighthouse Hill Rds; mains Rs 15-30; ☺ 11am-10.30pm; ☒) Dhanyavad is a bustling vegetarian restaurant serving great thalis (Rs 15) and snacks.

Lalith Bar & Restaurant (Balmatta Rd; mains Rs 30-100; ☺ 9am-3pm & 5.30-11pm) The Lalith has an extensive selection, including some lip-smacking seafood (prawns, crab, kingfish) and cocktails, in its cool, dark interior.

Naivedyam (KS Rao Rd; mains Rs 45-70; ☺ 6.30am-11pm; ☒) In Hotel Mangalore International, Naivedyam serves exquisite veg dishes, including interesting takes on paneer.

Galley Restaurant (Taj Manjarun Hotel, Old Port Rd; mains Rs 100-300; ☺ 7.30-11.30pm; ☒) The place to try those local delicacies in high style. There's live music here Wednesday to Saturday.

Mangalore has lots of bakeries and sweets shops. **Cochin Bakery** (AB Shetty Circle; ☽ 9.15am-9pm Mon-Fri, 9.15am-1.30pm Sat) has paneer puffs and pineapple lardy cake in addition to the usual baked goods. Bangalorean Mangaloreans get wired at **Café Coffee Day** (Balmatta Rd; ☽ 10am-10pm).

Other spots for local specialities:

Xanadu (Woodside Hotel, KS Rao Rd; mains Rs 45-125; ☽ 10.30am-3pm & 7-11.30pm; ✖) Good seafood, kitschy décor.

Yuvraj (Hotel Poonja International, KS Rao Rd; mains Rs 60-135; ☽ 11.30am-3.30pm & 7-11.30pm; ✖)

Getting There & Away

AIR

About 3.5km out of town, **Indian Airlines** (☎ 2451048; Hathill Rd) flies daily to Mumbai (US$135, 1¼ hours). **Jet Airways** (☎ 2441181; Ram Bhavan Complex, KS Rao Rd) has two daily flights to Mumbai (US$135) and one to Bangalore (US$95, one hour). **Air Deccan** (☎ 9845777008) also flies daily to Bangalore (Rs 2180); book by phone or at Trade Wings (see p237).

BUS

The **KSRTC long-distance bus stand** (☎ 2211243) is 3km north of the city centre; an autorickshaw there costs about Rs 20. It's quite orderly, with bus services to:

Destination	Fare (Rs)	Duration (hr)	Frequency
Bangalore	209	9	several daily
Chennai	398	16	1 daily
Hassan	110	4½	several daily
Hospet	172	12	1 daily
Kasaragod	25	1¼	every 30min
Kochi	322 in deluxe	9	1 daily
Madikeri	83	4½	several daily
Mumbai	442	22	1 daily
Mysore	153	8	several daily
Panaji	144/196 in regular/deluxe	9	3 daily

Private buses heading to other destinations (including Udupi, Sringeri, Mudabidri and Jog Falls) operate from the bus stand opposite the City bus stand.

Several private bus companies have their offices near Falnir Rd.

TRAIN

The main **train station** (☎ 2423137) is south of the city centre. The 2.40pm *Matsyagandha Express* stops at Margao (Rs 217/843 in sleeper/2AC, five hours) in Goa, and continues to Mumbai (Rs 393/1631 in sleeper/2AC, 16 hours). The 5.50pm *Malabar Express* heads to Thiruvananthapuram (Rs 261/1096 in sleeper/2AC, 15½ hours). Express trains to Chennai (Rs 338/1384 in sleeper/2AC, 17 hours) depart at 12.30pm and 4pm.

Several Konkan Railway trains (to Mumbai, Margao, Ernakulam or Thiruvananthapuram) use **Kankanadi train station** (☎ 2437824), 5km east of the city.

Getting Around

TO/FROM THE AIRPORT

To get to the airport, located about 22km away, take bus No 47B or 47C from the City bus stand or a taxi (Rs 300). Indian Airlines has a free airport shuttle for its passengers.

BUS & AUTORICKSHAW

The City bus stand is opposite the State Bank of India, close to the Taj Manjarun Hotel. Plenty of autorickshaws are about. Flag fall is Rs 9 and Rs 5 per kilometre thereafter. For late-night travel, add on 50%. An autorickshaw to Kankanadi station costs around Rs 30, or take bus No 9 or 11B.

AROUND MANGALORE

The area around Mangalore is dotted with Jain temples, statues and Hindu temples.

Udupi

The Vaishnavite pilgrimage town of Udupi (Udipi), 58km north of Mangalore, is visited by many for its **Krishna Temple** (☎ 0820-2520598; Car St), which has round-the-clock *darshan* (viewing of a deity). The morning (4am) and evening (7pm) ceremonies, for which the temple elephants sometimes make an appearance, are lively affairs. The **tourist office** (☎ 0820-2529718; Krishna Bldg, Car St; ☽ 10am-1.30pm & 2.30pm-5.30pm Mon-Sat) is a good source of advice on Udupi and the surrounding area.

Sringeri

The southern seat of the orthodox Hindu hierarchy is in Sringeri, an unspoilt small

town nestled among the lush hills of
Chikmagalur, about 100km northeast of
Mangalore. The interesting **Vidyashankar
Temple** (☎ 08265-250123; ☺ 6am-2pm & 5-9pm)
has zodiac pillars and a huge paved **courtyard** (☺ 5am-10pm). The Tunga River flows
past the temple complex, and hundreds of
fish gather at the ghats to be hand-fed by
pilgrims. Pilgrim **accommodation** (r Rs 25-75)
is available through the temple's reception centre.

Dharmastala

Dharmastala, 75km east of Mangalore,
has a number of Jain temples, including
the lively **Manjunatha Temple** (☎ 0862-2228493;
☺ 6am-1pm & 5-9pm). There's also an interesting **museum** (admission Rs 2) and a 14m-high
statue of Bahubali. Dharmastala is big on festivals; see p206.

Venur

The tucked-away, glowing green Venur,
about 50km northeast of Mangalore, has
eight temples. An 11m-high **statue of Bahubali** (☺ sunrise-sunset), dating to 1604, stands
serenely on the southern bank of the Gu-
rupur River.

Mudabidri

Mudabidri, 35km northeast of Mangalore
has 18 temples, the oldest of which is the
15th-century **Chandranatha Temple** (☺ 6am-
1pm & 5-8.30pm).

Karkal

Another 20km north of Mudabidri, at
Karkal, are several important **temples**. A
13m-high **statue of Gomateshvara** (Bahubali),
second in height only to the massive monolith at Sravanabelagola, stands on a tranquil
hillock on the outskirts of the town.

JOG FALLS
☎ 08186 / pop 12,570

Jog Falls are the highest waterfalls in India,
but they're not that exciting: the Linganamakki Dam further up the Sharavati River
limits the water flow. The longest of the
four falls is the Raja, which drops 293m.

The lush, spectacular countryside here,
though, is perfect for gentle hiking. The
bottom of the falls is accessible via the 1200-
plus steps that start close to the bus stand;
beware of leeches during the wet season.

The friendly **tourist office** (☎ 244747; ☺ 10am-
5pm Mon-Sat) is located close to the bus
stand.

Jog Falls has two inspection bungalows,
usually reserved for VIPs. The **British Bungalow** (r Rs 60) sits atop the falls about 3km from
the bus stand. Reserve with the **Siddapur
Public Works Department** (☎ 08389-322103). The
PW Guesthouse (per person Rs 250), across from
the KSTDC hotel, is pretty fancy; book
with the **Shimoga PWD** (☎ 08186-344333).

The **KSTDC Hotel Mayura Gerusoppa** (☎ 244747;
s/d Rs 200/300), about 150m from the car park,
has enormous, musty rooms.

Stalls near the bus stand serve omelettes,
thalis, noodles and rice dishes, plus hot and
cold drinks. KSTDC's mediocre **restaurant**
(meals Rs 20-40) is just next door.

Jog Falls has buses roughly every hour
to Shimoga (Rs 45, three hours) and to
Sagar (Rs 12, one hour), two a day to Siddapur (Rs 10, one hour) and three daily
to Karwar via Kumta (Rs 38, three hours),
where you can change for Gokarna (Rs 12,
45 minutes). There are two painfully slow
daily buses to/from Mangalore (Rs 112, ten
hours); you may be better off going via
Shimoga.

BUFFALO SURFING

Kambala, the Canarese sport of buffalo racing, first became popular in the early part
of the 20th century, when farmers would
race their buffaloes home after a day in
the fields. Today the best of the races
have hit the big time, with thousands of
spectators attending. The valuable racing
buffaloes are pampered and prepared like
thoroughbreds – a good animal can cost
more than Rs 300,000.

The events are held in the Dakshina
Kannada region between November and
March, when the paddy fields are nice and
wet. Parallel tracks (120m long) are laid
out, and the fastest pairs of buffaloes can
cover the distance through water and mud
in around 14 seconds. There are two versions: in one, the man runs alongside the
buffalo; in the other, he rides on a board
fixed to a ploughshare, literally surfing his
way down the track behind the beasts. And
if you don't think these lumbering beasts
can really move, look out!

The nearest train station is at Talguppa, between Sagar and Jog Falls. There's only one train daily, at 6pm, to Shimoga (Rs 28, three hours), on a romantically slow and scenic narrow-gauge line.

GOKARNA
☎ 08386

Gokarna (Cow's Ear), 50km south of Karwar, attracts a potpourri of Hindu pilgrims, Sanskrit scholars, hippies and beach-lovers. For Hindus, Gokarna is one of the most sacred sites in South India, and the atmosphere is colourful and devout. It's a sleepy, charming town with wooden houses on the main street and attractive traditional houses in nearby alleys. Some locals feel the foreign influx has tarnished the holy atmosphere, while others are happy with the extra income it has generated. Modesty is probably your best policy here: keep shoulders and knees covered and take your parties to the beach.

Information
Pai STD Shop (Main St; ☼ 9am-9pm) Changes cash and travellers cheques and gives advances on Visa.

Shema Internet (Car Rd; per hr Rs 40; ☼ 7.30am-midnight)
Sub post office (1st fl, cnr Car & Main Sts)
Swastik Laundry (☼ 8.30am-1pm & 4-9pm)

Sights
TEMPLES
Foreigners are not allowed inside Gokarna's temples, but you'll certainly bear witness to religious rituals around town. At the western end of Car St is the **Mahabaleshwara Temple**, home to a revered lingam (phallic image of Shiva). Nearby is the **Ganapati Temple**, which honours the role Ganesh played in rescuing the lingam. At the other end of the street is the **Venkataraman Temple**, and 100m south of this is **Koorti Teertha**, the large temple tank, where locals, pilgrims and immaculately dressed Brahmins perform their ablutions next to dhobi-wallahs on the ghats.

BEACHES
Travellers have been drifting into Gokarna for some time now, lured by stories of beaches that rival anything Goa has to offer. Gokarna village has its own beach, but the

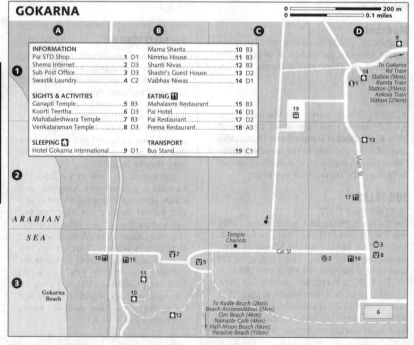

GOKARNA

0 ——— 200 m
0 ——— 0.1 miles

INFORMATION	
Pai STD Shop........................1 D1	
Shema Internet.....................2 D3	
Sub Post Office.....................3 D3	
Swastik Laundry....................4 C2	

SIGHTS & ACTIVITIES	
Ganapti Temple.....................5 B3	
Koorti Teertha.......................6 D3	
Mahabaleshwara Temple........7 B3	
Venkataraman Temple............8 D3	

SLEEPING	
Hotel Gokarna International......9 D1	

Mama Shanta......................10 B3	
Nimmu House......................11 B3	
Shanti Nivas.......................12 B3	
Shastri's Guest House...........13 D2	
Vaibhav Niwas....................14 D1	

EATING	
Mahalaxmi Restaurant..........15 B3	
Pai Hotel...........................16 D3	
Pai Restaurant....................17 D2	
Prema Restaurant................18 A3	

TRANSPORT	
Bus Stand..........................19 C1	

To Gokarna Rd Train Station (9km); Kumta Train Station (25km); Ankola Train Station (25km)

ARABIAN SEA

Gokarna Beach

Car St

Temple Chariots

Main St

To Kudle Beach (2km); Beach Accomodation (2km); Om Beach (4km); Namaste Café (4km); Half-Moon Beach (6km); Paradise Beach (10km)

KARNATAKA

best sands are via a footpath that begins on the southern side of the Ganapati Temple and heads southward (if you reach the bathing tank – or find yourself clawing up rocks – you're on the wrong path).

Twenty minutes on the path will bring you to the top of a barren headland with expansive sea views. On the southern side is **Kudle Beach** (kood-lee), the first in a series of four perfect beaches, backed by the foothills of the Western Ghats. Several shops on Kudle Beach sell basic snacks, drinks and offer basic accommodation.

At the southern end of Kudle a track climbs over the next headland, and a further 20-minute walk brings you to **Om Beach**, with a handful of chai shops and shacks. A dusty road provides vehicle access to Om (Rs 200 in an autorickshaw), but it's generally deserted except on holidays and some weekends, when day-trippers come by the car load. By the time you arrive, however, the new mega resort may have disrupted Om's *shanthi*. To the south, the more isolated **Half-Moon Beach** and **Paradise Beach** are a 30-minute and one-hour walk, respectively.

Depending on the crowds, boats run from Gokarna Beach (look for the fishermen) to Kudle (Rs 100) and Om (Rs 200).

Don't walk between the beaches and Gokarna after dark, and don't walk alone at any time – it's easy to get lost and muggings have occurred. For a wee fee, most lodges will safely stow valuables and baggage.

Sleeping

The choice here is between a rudimentary shack on the beach or a basic but more comfortable room in town. The advantages of being on the beach are obvious and, since it's a fair hike from town, you're pretty much left to your own devices.

BEACHES

December to January is high season on the beaches. Most places provide at least a bedroll, but you'll want to bring your own sleeping sheet or sleeping bag. Padlocks are provided and huts are secure. Communal washing and toilet facilities are simple.

Spanish Place (☎ 257311; huts Rs 70, d Rs 250; ☐) This chilled spot in the middle stretch of Kudle Beach has palm-thatch huts, and two lovely garden rooms with private shower but common 'toilet' (ie the bushes).

Namaste (☎ 257141; huts Rs 50, s with shared bathroom Rs 100, deluxe hut with private bathroom Rs 300; ☐) Namaste, on Om, is where the action's at during the high season. It's spotless and has a spacious restaurant/hangout that some travellers can muster no reason to leave.

Om Beach Resort (www.ombeachresort.com; s/d from US$55/60; ☒) Many Om Beach regulars aren't too happy about the new high-end Om Beach Resort, which will likely have opened by the time you arrive. As far as resorts go, though, you couldn't find a better location. Accommodation is in cottages set back from the beach, and the focus is on Ayurvedic treatments (from US$130 per week). Book online or with **Jungle Lodges & Resorts** (Map p210; ☎ 080-25597021; www.junglelodges.com; 2nd fl, Shrungar Shopping Complex, MG Rd) in Bangalore.

Both Kudle and Om Beaches have several other options in the form of huts and rooms – shop around. Huts and basic restaurants open up on Half-Moon and Paradise Beaches in the high season.

GOKARNA

Most guesthouses in town offer discounts in the low season.

Shastri's Guest House (☎ 256220; dr_murti@ rediffmail.com Main St; r Rs 125-150) Shastri's has claustrophobic singles, but the doubles out back are big and sunny; some have balconies and palm-tree views, and all have a comforting 1950s hospital vibe.

Vaibhav Nivas (☎ 256714; off Main St; r with shared bathroom Rs 80, s/d/tr with private bathroom from Rs 75/100/200) This cosy, recently renovated place is bustling in the high season and placid in the off months. It has snug rooms and a Western restaurant.

Nimmu House (☎ 256730; nimmuhouse@sancharnet .in; r with shared/private bathroom from Rs 90/200; ☐) Simple rooms set in relaxed green grounds near the beach.

Hotel Gokarna International (☎ 256622; hotel gokarn@yahoo.com; Main St; s/d/tr from Rs 195/230/300; ☒) It has more class than character, but it's well organised and modern and all rooms have balcony and TV.

Several kind-hearted families around town have begun to rent out rooms. Our favourites:

Mama Shanta (☎ 256213; r with shared/private bathroom Rs 100/150; ☼ Oct-May) Tender loving care, just past Nimmu House.

Shanti Nivas (☎ 256983; s/d with shared bathroom Rs 80/120) Cosy, colourful rooms tucked away in the woods near the beach; bear right off the Kudle Beach path.

Eating

The chai shops on all of the beaches rustle up basic snacks and meals.

Prema Restaurant (meals Rs 20-60; 8am-9pm) Beachfront Prema has excellent *masala dosa* (Rs 10) and thalis Rs 30) along with traveller treats: coffee milkshakes and yogurt with muesli and honey.

Mahalaxmi Restaurant (meals Rs 30-70; 8am-10pm) Its menu was heavily inspired by Prema, but the spaghetti and tomato sauce – and the location, near the beach – are quite good.

Pai Restaurant (Main St; mains Rs 20-40; 6.30am-9.30pm) Halfway along Main St, Pai is a friendly place with inspired vegetarian 'meals' (Rs 20).

Pai Hotel (Car St; mains Rs 15-30; 6am-9.30pm) Around the corner on Car St, Pai Hotel is unrelated to the other Pai but also happens to churn out tasty thalis (Rs 15).

Namaste Café (meals Rs 30-80; 7am-11pm) Om Beach's 'It' café serves OK Western standbys – pizzas and burgers – and some Israeli specials.

Getting There & Away

BUS

From Gokarna's **bus stand** (☎ 256233), one bus daily heads to Margao (Rs 50, four hours) or you can go to Karwar (Rs 22, 1½ hours, three daily), which has connections to Goa. Direct buses run to Hubli (Rs 56, four hours, five daily), and a daily 6.45am bus goes direct to Mangalore (Rs 95, six hours), continuing on to Mysore (Rs 120, 14 hours). If you miss this, get an hourly local bus to Kumta, 25km south, then one of the frequent Mangalore buses from there. Daily deluxe buses set off to Hospet for Hampi (Rs 120, 10 hours) at 7am and 2.30pm and to Bangalore (Rs 298, 12 hours) at 7pm.

TRAIN

The Konkan Railway is the best way to reach Goa and Mangalore, among other destinations, though only two slow passenger trains stop at **Gokarna Rd train station** (☎ 279487), 9km from town. A 10.45am train heads to Margao (Rs 24, two hours); another leaves at 6.30pm (Rs 55, 1½ hours). For Mangalore (Rs 45, five hours), trains depart from Gokarna Rd at 4pm and 1.45am. Trains head to Kochi (Rs 281 in sleeper, 15 hours) on Saturday, Sunday and Tuesday; you must buy a sleeper ticket and upgrade, if you like, upon boarding. Many of the hotels and small travel agencies on Main St can book tickets.

Autorickshaws charge Rs 100 to take you out to the station, but buses go hourly (Rs 6) and to meet arriving passenger trains.

Several express trains stop at Ankola and Kumta stations, both about 25km from Gokarna and accessible by local bus.

CENTRAL KARNATAKA

HAMPI

☎ 08394 / elev 467m

The fascinating ruins of Vijayanagar, near the village of Hampi, are set in a strange and sublime boulder-strewn landscape that resonates with a magical air. Once the capital of one of the largest Hindu empires in Indian history, Vijayanagar was founded by Telugu princes in 1336 and hit the peak of its power in the 16th century. With a population of about 500,000, the empire controlled the regional spice trade and cotton industry, and the city, surrounded by seven lines of fortification, covered an area of 43 sq km. Vijayanagar's busy bazaars were centres of international commerce brimming with precious stones and merchants from faraway lands. The empire came to a sudden end in 1565 when the city was ransacked by a confederacy of Deccan sultanates.

The region is much less dramatic these days – in fact, time seems to stand still in the bubble of Hampi, and you can spend a surprisingly large amount of time just boulder-watching. It's a thriving centre for travellers, the kind of place to connect and reconnect with people, and visitors tend to stay a while. It is, however, possible to see the main sites in a day or two – by bicycle, moped or, if you start early, on foot – but this goes against the laid-back grain of Hampi. Signposting in some parts of the site is inadequate, but you can't really get lost.

Orientation

Hampi Bazaar and the village of Kamalapuram to the south are the two main points of entry to the ruins. The KSTDC hotel and the museum are in Kamalapuram. The main travellers' scene is Hampi Bazaar, a village crammed with budget lodges, shops and restaurants, all dominated by the Virupaksha Temple. The ruins themselves can be divided into two main areas: the Sacred Centre, around Hampi Bazaar; and the Royal Centre, to the south around Kamalapuram.

Information

Aspiration Stores (Map p245; ⏲ 10am-1pm & 4-8pm) For books on the area, including *Hampi*, by John M Fritz and George Michell, which is a good architectural study.

Canara Bank (Map p245; ☎ 241243; ⏲ 11am-2pm Mon-Tue & Thu-Sat) Changes travellers cheques and gives cash advances on credit cards. The numerous authorised moneychangers around offer slightly worse rates.

Sree Rama Cyber Café (Map p245; per hr Rs 60; ⏲ 7am-11pm)

Tourist Office (Map p245; ☎ 241339; ⏲ 10am-5.30pm Sat-Thu) Can arrange guides for Rs 500 per day.

Dangers & Annoyances

Hampi is a safe place, generally free of any aggression. That said, don't wander around the ruins at sunrise or sunset, particularly on the climb up Matanga Hill, and don't wander alone, as muggings and violence have been on the rise in recent years.

Foreigners should register at the **police station** (Map p245) inside the Virupaksha Temple upon arrival. This is a simple process, involving logging your details in a book – it's as routine as a hotel check-in. The station, which is just inside the temple entrance on the right, has a photo gallery of crooks.

Sights

HAMPI BAZAAR & VIRUPAKSHA TEMPLE

Now that locals are occupying the ancient buildings lining the main street, **Hampi Bazaar** (Map p245) is once more a bustling village. The **Virupaksha Temple** (Map p245; ☎ 2441241; admission Rs 2; ⏲ sunrise-sunset), at the western end, is one of the city's oldest structures. The main *gopuram*, almost 50m high, was built in 1442, with a smaller one added in 1510. The main shrine is dedicated to Virupaksha, a form of Shiva.

If Lakshmi, the temple elephant, and her attendant are around, you can get a smooch (blessing) from her for a Rs 1 coin. The adorable Lakshmi gets her morning bath at 7.30am, just down the way by the river ghats.

To the south, overlooking Virupaksha Temple, **Hemakuta Hill** (Map p245) has a scattering of early ruins including Jain temples and a monolithic sculpture of Narasimha (Vishnu in his man-lion incarnation). It's worth the short walk up for the view over the bazaar.

VITTALA TEMPLE

From the eastern end of Hampi Bazaar a track, navigable only on foot, leads left to the **Vittala Temple** (Map p244; Indian/foreigner Rs 10/US$5; ⏲ 8am-6pm), about 2km away. The undisputed highlight of the Hampi ruins, the 16th-century Vittala Temple is a World Heritage site. It's in a good state of preservation, though purists may gasp at the cement-block columns erected to keep the main structure from collapsing.

Work likely started on the temple during the reign of Krishnadevaraya (1509–29) and, despite the fact that it was never finished or consecrated, the temple's incredible sculptural work is the pinnacle of Vijayanagar art. The outer 'musical' pillars reverberate when tapped, although this is discouraged to avoid further damage. There's an ornate stone chariot in the temple courtyard containing an image of Garuda. Its wheels were once capable of turning.

Keep your temple entry ticket for same-day admission into the Zenana Enclosure and Elephant Stables in the Royal Centre (see below).

SULE BAZAAR & ACHYUTARAYA TEMPLE

Halfway along the path from Hampi Bazaar to the Vittala Temple, a track to the right leads to deserted **Sule Bazaar** (Map p244), which gives you some idea of what Hampi Bazaar might have looked like if it hadn't been repopulated. At the southern end of this area is the **Achyutaraya Temple** (Map p244). Its isolated location at the foot of Matanga Hill makes it quietly atmospheric.

ROYAL CENTRE   Map p244

This area of Hampi is quite different from the area around Hampi Bazaar, since most of the rounded boulders that once littered the site have been used to create a mind-boggling proliferation of beautiful stone

KARNATAKA

walls. It's a 2km walk on a track from the Achyutaraya Temple, but most people get to it from the Hampi Bazaar–Kamalapuram road. This area is easily explored by bicycle since a decent dirt road runs through its heart.

Within various enclosures here are the rest of Hampi's major attractions, including the **Lotus Mahal** and the **Elephant Stables** (Indian/foreigner Rs 10/US$5; ☽ 8am-6pm). The former is a delicately designed pavilion in a walled compound known as the **Zenana Enclosure**. It's an amazing synthesis of Hindu and Islamic styles and gets its name from the lotus bud carved in the centre of the domed and vaulted ceiling. The Elephant Stables

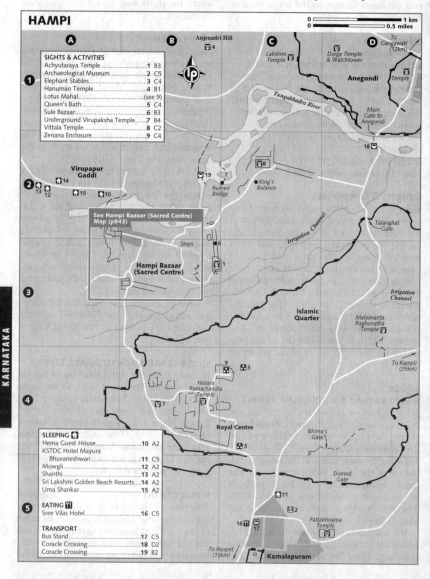

HAMPI

0 ——— 1 km
0 ——— 0.5 miles

SIGHTS & ACTIVITIES
Achyutaraya Temple..................1 B3
Archaeological Museum.............2 C5
Elephant Stables........................3 C4
Hanuman Temple.......................4 B1
Lotus Mahal..........................(see 9)
Queen's Bath.............................5 C4
Sule Bazaar...............................6 B3
Underground Virupaksha Temple......7 B4
Vittala Temple...........................8 C2
Zenana Enclosure......................9 C4

Anjenadri Hill
4

To Gangawati (12km)

Lakshmi Temple

Durga Temple & Watchtower

Anegondi

Temple

Tungabhadra River

Main Gate to Anegondi

18

Virupapur Gaddi
14
13 12   15   10

See Hampi Bazaar (Sacred Centre)
Map (p843)

Steps

Hampi Bazaar
(Sacred Centre)

19
Ruined Bridge

8
King's Balance

Irrigation Channel

Talarighat Gate

6
1

Irrigation Channel

Islamic Quarter

Malyavanta Raghunatha Temple

To Kampli (25km)

9
3
Hazara Ramachandra Temple

7

Royal Centre

5

Bhima's Gate

Domed Gate

SLEEPING
Hema Guest House.....................10 A2
KSTDC Hotel Mayura
   Bhuvaneshwari........................11 C5
Mowgli......................................12 A2
Shanthi......................................13 A2
Sri Lakshmi Golden Beach Resorts....14 A2
Uma Shankar.............................15 A2

EATING
Sree Vilas Hotel.........................16 C5

TRANSPORT
Bus Stand..................................17 C5
Coracle Crossing........................18 D2
Coracle Crossing........................19 B2

11
2
16   17
Pattabhirama Temple

To Hospet (13km)   Kamalapuram

KARNATAKA

is a grand building with domed chambers, where the state elephants once resided. Your entry ticket to the Zenana Enclosure and stables is valid for same-day admission to the Vittala Temple.

Further south, you'll find various temples and elaborate waterworks, including the **Underground Virupaksha Temple** and the impressive **Queen's Bath**, which is deceptively plain on the outside.

ARCHAEOLOGICAL MUSEUM

The **archaeological museum** (Map p244; ☎ 241561; Kamalapuram; admission Rs 5; ☯ 10am-5pm Sat-Thu) has well-displayed collections of sculptures from local ruins, Neolithic tools, 16th-century weaponry and a large floor model of the Vijayanagar ruins.

ANEGONDI

North of the river is the ruined fortified stronghold of **Anegondi** (Map p244); much of the old defensive wall is intact. The unruffled area, amid paddy fields, makes for a good afternoon's ambling. There are numerous small temples worth a visit, including the whitewashed **Hanuman Temple** (Map p244; ☯ sunrise-sunset), which is perched on top of a prominent rocky hill. The climb is a fine undertaking, but not in the prime heat of the day. Fittingly, lots of cheeky monkeys roam about, so don't walk up wearing bananas.

To get to Anegondi take a coracle (small boat made of waterproof hides) across the river (Rs 20) and follow the dusty road north.

Sleeping

Listed rates are for the high season, but prices shoot up by 50% or more during the manic fortnight around New Year's Day, and drop just as dramatically in the low season (from April to September). Checkout is usually around 10am. Aside from the KSTDC hotel, rooms are quaint but basic; if you want a cushy abode, stay in Hospet (see p247).

HAMPI BAZAAR   Map p245

Dozens of cute, basic lodges freckle the alleys leading off the main road.

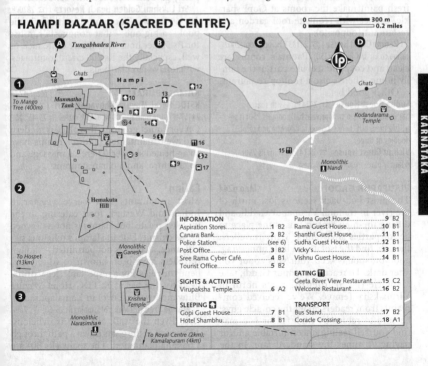

HAMPI BAZAAR (SACRED CENTRE)

0 — 300 m
0 — 0.2 miles

Tungabhadra River

To Mango Tree (400m)

Hampi

Ghats

Manmatha Tank

Kodandarama Temple

Hemakuta Hill

Monolithic Nandi

To Hospet (13km)

Monolithic Ganesh

Krishna Temple

Monolithic Narasimha

To Royal Centre (2km); Kamalapuram (4km)

INFORMATION	
Aspiration Stores	1 B2
Canara Bank	2 B2
Police Station	(see 6)
Post Office	3 B2
Sree Rama Cyber Café	4 B1
Tourist Office	5 B2

SIGHTS & ACTIVITIES	
Virupaksha Temple	6 A2

SLEEPING	
Gopi Guest House	7 B1
Hotel Shambhu	8 B1
Padma Guest House	9 B2
Rama Guest House	10 B1
Shanthi Guest House	11 B1
Sudha Guest House	12 B1
Vicky's	13 B1
Vishnu Guest House	14 B1

EATING	
Geeta River View Restaurant	15 C2
Welcome Restaurant	16 B2

TRANSPORT	
Bus Stand	17 B2
Coracle Crossing	18 A1

KARNATAKA

Rama Guest House (☎ 241962; s Rs 250, d Rs 300-350) The kind owners here are very proud of their four ultra-clean doubles, recently redone with cheerful, garish floor tiles and new bathrooms. Its restaurant does excellent food.

Shanthi Guest House (☎ 241568; s/d with shared bathroom Rs 100/150) The Shanthi is a Hampi tradition, with a peaceful courtyard, bike rental (Rs 30), morning bakery delivery and a small shop that runs on the honour system.

Vicky's (☎ 241694; vikkyhampi@yahoo.co.in; r Rs 300; ▢) The swing chair on the front porch is as comfy as Vicky's seven brightly painted rooms. The rooftop restaurant (see opposite) has better views than most.

Hotel Shambhu (☎ 241383; angadiparamesh1@ hotmail.com; r Rs 300) The rooms at this little guesthouse are small but sweet. Plus, they have lavender walls and are named after deities. The hallway has plants and an opalescent chandelier, and the rooftop restaurant isn't bad.

Gopi Guest House (☎ 241695; gopiguesthouse93@ yahoo.co.in; d Rs 200-250) Shiny new tiles and fresh paint make the rooms at Gopi sparkle. Comes with requisite roof garden and restaurant (opposite).

Padma Guest House (☎ 241331; hampipadma2002@ yahoo.co.in; s/d Rs 200/350) Padma's rooms are clean and cosy and feel like part of the family home. There's also a rooftop restaurant.

Other good bets:

Sudha Guest House (☎ 241451; s with shared bathroom Rs 150, d with private bathroom Rs 250) It's a little tired, but there's a good family vibe and some doubles fit three.

Vishnu Guest House (☎ 241415; r from Rs 250) A family place exuding friendliness.

VIRUPAPUR GADDI   **Map p244**
The most laid-back scene is just north of the river in tranquil Virupapur Gaddi, and during the high season this is the place to be for parties after hours. Many travellers, though, find the isolation a little unnerving, and you should keep your wits about you after dark. To reach Virupapur Gaddi, take a coracle (Rs 5) from the ghats north of Virupaksha Temple. We've received complaints from readers about the coracle guys: be sure to return by nightfall or you may find yourself feeling uncomfortable and/or paying 20 times the standard fare. In the monsoon season, when the river is running high, boats may not be able to cross.

The telephone code here is ☎ 08533.

Shanthi (☎ 287038; r with shared bathroom Rs 100, bungalows with private bathroom Rs 250) Shanthi's bungalows have paddy-field, river and sunset views and front porches with couch swings, while the restaurant, which does exceptional thalis (Rs 30) and pizzas (Rs 70 to 85), is in a quasi-treehouse.

Mowgli (☎ 287033; mowgli96@hotmail.com; r with shared bathroom Rs 100, bungalows with private bathroom Rs 250-300) Lush, shady gardens shelter hammocks and thatch-roof bungalows, some with sunset views.

Hema Guest House (☎ 387074; chemahome@yahoo .com; dm/bungalows Rs 50/300) The Hema compound is highly advanced. Its little houses are shiny and new, with maximum-security screening, and the restaurant is in a beautiful wooden belvedere with the best views in town.

Uma Shankar (☎ 287067; r Rs 150-350) This place is a little jewel run by a friendly, hard-working woman. The rooms, set amid pretty gardens, were recently renovated.

Sri Lakshmi Golden Beach Resorts (☎ 287008; d Rs 150-350; ▨) The important thing is the pool – a big one – that nonguests can use for Rs 50 per hour. Rooms are quite nice, as well, especially the Rs 200 circular cottages, which have circular beds.

KAMALAPURAM   **Map p244**
KSTDC Hotel Mayura Bhuvaneshwari (☎ 08394-241574; s/d/tr from Rs 300/400/450; mains Rs 25-45; ▨) On very quiet grounds, this place is modern and well maintained, and all rooms have solar-heated shower. There's a massage and yoga centre, and a bar-restaurant.

Eating
Most restaurants here serve vegetarian Indian and Western food catering to the traveller palate, but Hampi is not renowned for its cuisine. Due to Hampi's religious significance, alcohol is not permitted – though travellers have been known to (discreetly) bend the rules. For a respectable, legal drink, head for the bar at KSTDC Hotel Mayura Bhuvaneshwari (above) in Kamalapuram.

Mango Tree (Off Map p245; mains Rs 25-60; ☽ 7am-10pm) Even the walk out here is delicious: 400m west of the ghats down a path through a banana plantation. The thalis (Rs 30) are a treat, and the straw mats outside are ideal spots to laze with a book while a swing hangs contentedly from the eponymous mango tree.

Geeta River View Restaurant (Map p245; mains Rs 25-45; 🕑 7am-10pm) This quiet outdoor spot on the river has great food; try the *pakodas* (rice-flour fritters, Rs 20) or the subtle cashew veg curry (Rs 35). The restaurant's at the start of the path leading to Vittala Temple.

Welcome Restaurant (Map p245; mains Rs 20-45; 🕑 7am-11pm) Along with offering all the usual suspects, the humble little Welcome makes a worthy attempt at *kim chi* (Korean relish, Rs 10)! The woman who runs the place is an old soul.

Several of Hampi's lodges have good rooftop joints:

Gopi Guest House (Map p245; mains Rs 25-40; 🕑 6.30am-11pm) Serving espresso with milk (Rs 50) and 'Japanese' food – tomato don (Rs 30), for example – among lots of plants.

Vicky's (Map p245; mains Rs 20-45; 🕑 6.30am-10.30pm) Really good food, amazing views, purple tables and a family atmosphere.

Kamalapuram has a few simple eateries, such as **Sree Vilas Hotel** (Map p244; meals Rs 16; 🕑 5am-8.30pm), opposite the bus stand.

Getting There & Away
While some buses from Goa and Bangalore will drop you in Hampi Bazaar, you have to go to Hospet to catch most buses out. The first bus from Hospet (Rs 5, 30 minutes, half hourly) is at 6.30am; the last one back leaves Hampi Bazaar at 8.30pm. An auto-rickshaw costs Rs 80.

KSRTC has a daily Rajahamsa bus service between Hampi and Bangalore (Rs 204, nine hours) leaving Hampi at 8pm. The overnight sleeper bus to/from Goa (Rs 400), which runs during the high season, is a popular option – but don't expect a deep sleep. Solo travellers have to share a bunk. Numerous travel agents in Hampi Bazaar are eager to book onward bus, train and plane tickets or arrange a car and driver. See p248 for bus and train information to Hospet.

Getting Around
Once you've seen the Vittala and Achyu-taraya Temples and Sule Bazaar, exploring the rest of the ruins by cycle is the thing to do. There are key monuments haphazardly

signposted along the road from Hampi Bazaar to Kamalapuram. Bicycles cost Rs 30 to 40 per day in Hampi Bazaar. Mopeds can be hired for around Rs 200 plus petrol. You can take your bicycle (extra Rs 5), or motorbike (extra Rs 10), across the river on a coracle.

Walking is the only way to see all the nooks and crannies, but expect to cover at least 7km just to see the major ruins. Autorickshaws and taxis are available for sightseeing, and will drop you as close to each of the major ruins as they can. A five-hour autorickshaw tour costs Rs 250.

Organised tours depart from Hospet; see below for details.

HOSPET
☎ 08394 / pop 163,284
Hospet is an active regional centre with none of Hampi's atmosphere, but you'll certainly swing through here to make transport connections. It has some good hotels, but otherwise there's no reason to linger.

Information
College Rd has a few Internet joints with sluggish connections for Rs 40 per hour. The cloakroom at Hospet's bus stand holds bags for Rs 10 per day.

Andhra Bank (☎ 228249; off College Rd; 🕑 10.30am-4.30pm Mon-Fri, 10.30am-1.30pm Sat) Cash advances on Visa and MasterCard with a 1% commission. It's next to Hanuman Temple.

Hotel Malligi (☎ 228101; Jabunatha Rd) Changes travellers cheques.

KSTDC tourist office (☎ 228537; Shanbhag Circle; 🕑 7.30am-8.30pm)

State Bank of India (☎ 228576; Station Rd; 🕑 10.30am-4pm Mon-Fri) Changes currency; the ATM here sometimes accepts MasterCard.

Tours
KSTDC's Hampi tour (Rs 110) runs daily in the high season and on demand the rest of the year; it departs from the tourist office at 9.30am and returns at 5.30pm. It's in the lap of the gods whether you get an informative guide or one who rushes through the ruins. Book ahead in high season, but just show up other times as the tours won't run with fewer than 10 people.

Sleeping & Eating
Hotel Priyadarshini (☎ 228838; priyainnhampi@india.com; Station Rd; s/d from Rs 300/450; mains Rs 35-70 🕃)

Between the bus and train stations is this classy place with fresh, tidy rooms, all with balcony. Its nonveg restaurant, among trees and with sugarcane views, is worth a visit.

Hotel Malligi (☎ 228101; malligihome@hotmail .com; Jabunatha Rd; r Rs 200-2250; ✖ ▢ ▨) Rooms vary widely in the Malligi compound, from OK cheaper old-wing rooms to styly modern rooms in the new wing. It has Internet facilities, various restaurants and a pool (Rs 25 for nonguests).

Waves (mains Rs 45-80; ❍ 6am-11pm) The delicious veg and nonveg offerings at Hotel Malligi's multicuisine restaurant make it a great place to feast.

Udupi Sri Krishna Bhavan (meals Rs 15-40; ❍ 6am-11pm) Opposite the bus stand, this clean, no-nonsense spot dishes out North and South Indian fare.

Getting There & Away
BUS
Hospet's **bus stand** (☎ 228802) is unusually chaotic. Buses to Hampi depart from bay No 10 every half-hour (Rs 5, 30 minutes). Several express buses run to Bangalore (Rs 123/197 in ordinary/deluxe, nine hours) in morning and evening batches, and three overnight buses head to Panaji via Margao in Goa (Rs 150, 11 hours). Two buses a day go to Badami (Rs 75, six hours), or catch one of the many buses to Gadag (Rs 42, 2½ hours) and transfer. There are frequent buses to Hubli (Rs 58, 4½ hours) and Bijapur (Rs 90, six hours), four overnight services to Hyderabad (Rs 160/229 in ordinary/deluxe,

---

HOSPET ON FIRE

Hospet comes alive during the Shiite Muslim festival Muharram (February or March), which commemorates the martyrdom of Mohammed's grandson, Imam Hussain, in . Fire walkers walk barefoot across the red-hot embers of a fire that's been burning all day and night. Virtually the whole town turns out to watch or take part and the excitement reaches fever pitch around midnight. The daytime preliminaries appear to be a bewildering hybrid of Muslim and Hindu ritual, and those who are scheduled to do the fire walking must be physically restrained from losing control just before the event. For other festivals in Karnataka, see p206.

---

10 hours) and one direct bus, at 9am, to Gokarna (Rs 150, 10 hours). For Mangalore or Hassan, take one of the many morning buses to Shimoga and change there.

TRAIN
Hospet's **train station** (☎ 228360) is a 20-minute walk or Rs 10 autorickshaw ride from the centre of town. The daily *Hampi Express* heads to Hubli at 7.45am (Rs 47 in 2nd class, 3½ hours) and Bangalore at 8pm (Rs 212/881 in sleeper/2AC, 10 hours), or go to Guntakal (Rs 42, 2½ hours) and catch a Bangalore-bound express there. Every Tuesday, Friday and Saturday, an 8.45am express heads to Vasco da Gama in Goa (Rs 169/690 in sleeper/2AC, 9½ hours).

To get to Badami, catch a Hubli train to Gadag and change there.

HUBLI
☎ 0836 / pop 786,018
Hubli is a logical and sometimes necessary stop-off point for voyagers plying the rail routes from Mumbai to Bangalore, Goa and northern Karnataka. Several hotels and restaurants sit close to the train station; others surround the old bus stand (Lamington Rd), a 15-minute walk from the train station. Long-distance buses usually stop here before heading to the new bus stand 2km away, where there are no dazzling amenities.

Ing Vysya Bank, next to Sagar Palace, has an ATM.

Sleeping & Eating
Hotel Ajanta (☎ 2362216; Jayachamaraj Nagar; s/d from Rs 115/150) The Ajanta's a large place near the train station with a range of basic and functional rooms.

Hotel Samrat Ashok (☎ 2362380; Lamington Rd; s/d from Rs 350/400; ✖) The pick of the midrange standbys along Lamington Rd, about 500m from the train station.

Sagar Palace (Jayachamaraj Nagar; mains Rs 30-60; ❍ 11am-3.30pm & 7-11.30pm) Near the Samrat Ashok, this classy eatery serves up good veg dishes, as well as spiked desserts.

Plenty of late-night food stalls sizzle around the old bus stand and train station.

Getting There & Away
BUS
Long-distance buses depart from the new **bus stand** (☎ 2221085). Numerous morning buses

run to Bangalore (Rs 220 deluxe, nine hours), Hospet (Rs 57, four hours) and Mangalore (Rs 145, 10 hours). Buses also head to Mumbai (Rs 282, 14 hours, 10 daily), Mysore (Rs 220/300 in ordinary/deluxe, 10 hours, eight daily), Bijapur (Rs 92, six hours, six daily) and Gokarna (Rs 85, four hours, four daily).

KSRTC and Goa's Kadamba Transport Corporation have buses to Panaji (Rs 82, six hours), as well as Vasco da Gama and Margao.

Private companies operate deluxe buses from just opposite the old bus stand, 2km away.

TRAIN
From the train station, which has a **reservation office** (☎ 2325720; ⏰ 8am-8pm), three expresses head to Hospet (Rs 47, 3½ hours). Around six expresses run daily to Bangalore (Rs 258/1085 in sleeper/2AC, eight hours), but there's only one direct train to Mumbai (Rs 289/1223 in sleeper/2AC, 17 hours). Trains run on Tuesday, Friday, Saturday and Sunday to Vasco de Gama (via Margao; Rs 134/542 in sleeper/2AC, seven hours).

NORTHERN KARNATAKA

BADAMI
☎ 08357 / pop 25,851 / elev 177m

Set in beautiful countryside at the foot of a red sandstone ridge, the charming village of Badami was once the capital of the Chalukya empire, which covered much of the central Deccan between the 4th and 8th centuries. At its height the empire was enormous, stretching from Kanchipuram in Tamil Nadu to the Narmada River in Gujarat. The earliest Chalukya capital was in nearby Aihole, after which the site was moved to Badami, with a secondary capital in nearby Pattadakal. The result of this relocation is that the whole area around Badami is dripping with temples, and there are over 150 in the three main centres alone.

The sculptural legacy left by the Chalukya artisans includes some of the earliest and finest examples of Dravidian temples and rock-cut caves, as well as the earliest free-standing temple in India. Aihole was a sort of trial ground for new temple architecture,

which was further developed at Pattadakal, now a World Heritage site. The forms and sculptural work at these sites inspired later South Indian Hindu empires that rose and fell before the arrival of the Muslims.

Aihole has one hotel, but most people base themselves in Badami.

History
Badami was the Chalukyan capital from about AD 540 to 757. The surrounding hills are dotted with temples, fortifications, carvings and inscriptions dating not just from the Chalukyan period, but also from other times when the site was occupied as a fortress. After it fell to the Rashtrakutas, Badami was occupied successively by the Chalukyas of Kalyan (a separate branch of the Western Chalukyas), the Kalachuryas, the Yadavas of Devagiri, the Vijayanagar empire, the Adil Shahi kings of Bijapur, and the Marathas.

Orientation & Information
Station Rd, Badami's main street, has several hotels and restaurants; Badami village is between this road and the hilltop caves. The **tourist office** (☎ 220414; Ramdurg Rd; ⏰ 10am-5.30pm), in the KSTDC Hotel Mayura Chalukya, has neither maps nor tours on offer.

Mookambika Deluxe hotel changes currency for guests, but at a lousy rate; bring enough cash with you.

Sights
CAVES
Badami is best known for its beautiful **cave temples** (Indian/foreigner Rs 5/US$2; ⏰ sunrise-sunset). Nonpushy guides ask Rs 100 for a tour of the caves, or Rs 200 for the whole site.

Cave One
This cave, just above the entrance to the complex, is dedicated to Shiva. It's the oldest of the four, probably carved during the 6th century. On the cliff wall to the right of the porch is a captivating image of Nataraja striking 81 dance poses (one for every combination of his 18 arms). He holds, among other things, a snake, a musical instrument and a *trishula* (trident).

On the right of the porch area is a huge figure of Ardhanarishvara. The right half of the figure shows features of Shiva, such as matted hair and a third eye, while the left half of the image has aspects of Parvati. On

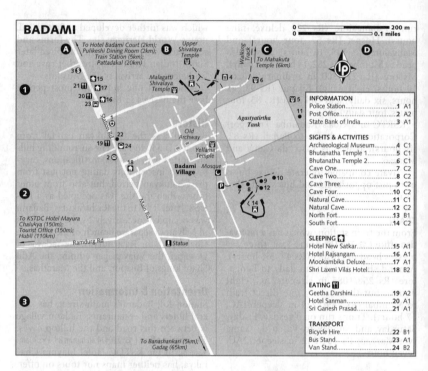

INFORMATION
Police Station....................................1 A1
Post Office..2 A2
State Bank of India..........................3 A1

SIGHTS & ACTIVITIES
Archaeological Museum..............4 C1
Bhutanatha Temple 1....................5 C1
Bhutanatha Temple 2....................6 C1
Cave One...7 C2
Cave Two...8 C2
Cave Three..9 C2
Cave Four..10 C2
Natural Cave....................................11 C1
Natural Cave....................................12 C2
North Fort.......................................13 B1
South Fort.......................................14 C2

SLEEPING
Hotel New Satkar............................15 A1
Hotel Rajsangam............................16 A1
Mookambika Deluxe.....................17 A1
Shri Laxmi Vilas Hotel.................18 B2

EATING
Geetha Darshini...............................19 A2
Hotel Sanman.................................20 A1
Sri Ganesh Prasad........................21 A1

TRANSPORT
Bicycle Hire.....................................22 B1
Bus Stand...23 A1
Van Stand..24 B2

the opposite wall is a large image of Hari-hara: the right half represents Shiva and the left half Vishnu.

Cave Two

Dedicated to Vishnu, this cave is simpler in design. As with caves one and three, the front edge of the platform is decorated with images of pot-bellied dwarfs in various poses. Four pillars support the veranda. The top of each pillar is carved with a bracket in the shape of a *yali*, or mythical lion creature. On the left wall of the porch is the bull-headed figure of Varaha, an incarnation of Vishnu and the emblem of the Cha-lukya empire. To his left is Naga, the snake couple. On the right wall is a large sculpture of Trivikrama, another incarnation of Vishnu, booting out a demon, while he holds various weapons in his eight hands. The ceiling panels contain images of Vishnu riding Garuda, *gandharva* (demigod) couples, swastikas and 16 fish arranged in a wheel (yet another incarnation of Vishnu).

Between the second and third caves are two sets of steps to the right. The first leads

to a **natural cave**. The eastern wall of this cave contains a small image of Padmapani (an incarnation of the Buddha). The second set of steps – sadly, barred by a gate – leads to the hilltop **South Fort**.

Cave Three

This cave, carved under the orders of Man-galesha, the brother of King Kirtivarma, in AD 578, contains some sculptural high-lights.

On the left-hand wall is a large carving of Vishnu, to whom the cave is dedicated, sitting on the coils of the snake. Nearby is an image of Varaha with four hands. The pillars have carved brackets in the shape of *yalis* and the sides of the pillars are also carved. The ceiling panels contain images including Indra riding an elephant, Shiva on a bull and Brahma on a swan.

Cave Four

Dedicated to Jainism, Cave Four is the smallest of the set and was carved from the 7th to 8th century. The pillars, with their roaring *yalis*, are of a similar design to the other caves. The right wall of the cave has an image of Suparshvanatha (the seventh Jain *tirthankar*, or teacher), surrounded by 24 Jain *tirthankars*. The sanctum contains an image of Adinath, the first Jain *tirthankar*.

OTHER ATTRACTIONS

The caves overlook the 5th-century **Agastyatirtha Tank** and the waterside **Bhutanatha temples**. On the other side of the tank is an **archaeological museum** (☎ 220157; admission Rs 2; ☼ 10am-5pm Sat-Thu), which houses superb examples of local sculpture, including a remarkable Lajja-Gauri image of a fertility cult that flourished in the area. The stairway just behind the museum climbs through a dramatic sandstone chasm and fortified gateways to reach the various temples and ruins of the **north fort**. The fort has expansive views and overlooks the rooftops of Badami.

It's worth exploring Badami's **laneways**, where you'll find old houses with brightly painted, carved wooden doorways, the occasional Chalukyan ruin and, of course, flocks of curious children.

Sleeping

Badami has a good range of hotels, many of which offer discounts in the low season.

Hotel New Satkar (☎ 220417; Station Rd; s/d from Rs 250/330; 🆒) Rooms here are bright in beiges and creams; the best are on the first floor. It's a friendly, professional place that's been recently renovated.

Mookambika Deluxe (☎ 220067; mukambika2@ sify.com; Station Rd; s/d from Rs 300/350; 🆒) The staff at Badami's de facto tourist office are friendly and helpful and can arrange taxis and guides. Rooms are mildly interesting, with kelly green walls.

Shri Laxmi Vilas Hotel (☎ 220077; Station Rd; r Rs 150) Some of the small, plain rooms have a balcony; all have constant hot water and a sort of raggedy charm.

Hotel Badami Court (☎ 220230; rafiqmht@blr .vsnl.net.in; Station Rd; s/d from Rs 1000/1300; 🆒 🆒) Classy Badami Court sits in pastoral countryside 2km from the town centre. Tiptop rooms have gleaming bathtubs, and rates include taxes and breakfast. Nonguests can use the pool for Rs 80.

Other possibilities:

Hotel Rajsangam (☎ 221603; Station Rd; r Rs 3000; 🆒) Under construction at the time of writing, the Rajsangam is looking luxe.

KSTDC Hotel Mayura Chalukya (☎ 220046; Ramdurg Rd; d/tr Rs 350/500) Nice but out of the way.

Eating

Geetha Darshini (Station Rd; snacks Rs 2-10; ☼ 6.30am-9pm) This unassuming little joint is single-handedly redefining *idlis* (South Indian rice dumpling) and masala rice; the sambar is the best you've ever had.

Sri Ganesh Prasad (Station Rd; meals Rs 15) Next to Hotel Anand Deluxe, this is a cheap and cheery standby for excellent South Indian thalis (Rs 15) and *masala dosas* (Rs 9).

Hotel Sanman (Station Rd; mains Rs 30-50) Popular with travellers and locals, nonveg Hotel Sanman has cold beers and curtained booths.

Pulikeshi Dining Room (mains Rs 55-125; ☼ 6am-11pm) This silver-service restaurant in Hotel Badami Court is a local celebrity, with Continental and Indian dishes that people rave about.

Getting There & Away

Buses shuffle off from Badami to Bijapur (Rs 60, 4½ hours, seven daily), Hubli (Rs 41, three hours, seven daily) and Bangalore (Rs 200/265 in ordinary/deluxe, 12 hours, five daily). Two buses go direct to Hospet (Rs 75, six hours), or you can catch any of the buses to Gadag (Rs 32, two hours) and go from there. Note that this route is particularly hard on the bum.

Work is ongoing on the Badami–Bijapur line, so trains only run to Gadag (Rs 15, two hours, three daily), where you can get a connecting train to Hospet or Hubli. They're all 2nd-class passenger trains – but still more comfortable than the buses.

Getting Around

Badami's **train station** (☎ 220040) is 5km from town. Tongas (Rs 30), taxis (Rs 55), autorickshaws (Rs 30) and shared vans or large autorickshaws (Rs 3) ply the route. You can hire bicycles in Badami for Rs 5 per hour.

Exploring the surrounding area by local bus is easy, since they're moderately frequent and usually run on time. You can visit both Aihole and Pattadakal in a day from Badami if you get moving early: it's best to start with the morning bus to Aihole (Rs 12, 1½ hours). Frequent buses then run between Aihole and Pattadakal (Rs 5, 30 minutes), and from Pattadakal to Badami

KARNATAKA

(Rs 8, one hour). The last bus from Pattadakal to Badami is at 8pm. It's a good idea to take food and water with you.

Taxis cost around Rs 600 for a day trip to Pattadakal, Aihole and Mahakuta. Badami's hotels can arrange taxis; alternatively, go to the taxi stand in front of the post office.

AROUND BADAMI
Pattadakal
This riverside village 20km from Badami was the second capital of the Badami Chalukyas; most of its **temples** (☎ 08357-243118; Indian/foreigner Rs 10/US$5; ☺ 6am-6pm) were built during the 7th and 8th centuries, but the earliest remains date from the 3rd and 4th centuries and the latest structure, a Jain temple, dates from the Rashtrakuta period (9th century). The group of temples is a World Heritage site.

Pattadakal, like Aihole, was a significant site in the development of South Indian temple architecture. In particular, two main types of temple towers were tried out here: curvilinear towers top the Kadasiddivisvesvara, Jambulinga and Galaganatha temples, while the Mallikarjuna, Sangamesvara and Virupaksha temples have a square roof and receding tiers.

The main **Virupaksha Temple** is a huge structure. The massive columns are covered with intricate carvings depicting episodes from the Ramayana and Mahabharata; they show battle scenes, lovers and decorative motifs. Around the roof of the inner hall are sculptures of elephants' and lions' heads. To the east, and facing the temple, is a pavilion containing a massive Nandi. The **Mallikarjuna Temple**, next to the Virupaksha Temple, is almost identical in design but slightly more worn. About 500m south of the main enclosure is the **Papanatha Temple**.

Aihole
The Chalukyan regional capital between the 4th and 6th centuries, Aihole (*ay*-ho-leh) teems with temples. Here you can see Hindu architecture in its embryonic stage, from the earliest simple shrines, such as those in the Kontigudi Group and the most ancient Lad Khan Temple, to the later and more complex buildings, such as the Meguti Temple.

In the centre of the village is a fenced enclosure with the most impressive building in Aihole, the **Durga Temple** (Indian/foreigner

Rs 5/US$2; ☺ 8am-6pm), which dates from the 7th century. It's notable for its semicircular apse, which was copied from Buddhist architecture, and for the remains of the curvilinear *sikhara* (Hindu temple spire). Even more striking than the formal layout are the outstanding intricate carvings crowding the colonnaded passageway around the sanctuary. The small **museum** (admission Rs 2; ☺ 10am-5pm Sat-Thu) behind the Durga temple contains further examples of the Chalukyan sculptors' work.

To the south of the Durga temple are several other collections of buildings including some of the earliest structures in Aihole – the Gandar, Ladkhan, Kontigudi and Hucchapaya groups, which are of the pavilion type with slightly sloping roofs. About 600m to the southeast, up a series of steps on a low hilltop, is the Jain **Meguti Temple**. Watch out for snakes!

KSTDC Tourist Home (☎ 08351-284541; Amingad Rd; r Rs 200-300), 1km from the village centre, is a sensible base if you want to see some of the area's 125-plus temples. Food is available by arrangement.

Mahakuta Temple
About 10km east of Badami, this **temple** (☎ 08357-240021; ☺ 10am-6pm) is easily visited en route to Aihole. Mahakuta was made sacred by the presence of the sage Agastya, who lived here, and the temple is still active as a pilgrimage site. Within the walled courtyard are two main temples on either side of an old tank. The first of these, nearest the entrance, is still in use, but the other one is now a deserted bat dwelling. A number of small Shiva shrines are arranged around the outside of the courtyard. Swimming is allowed in the tank, but women should be aware that even fully dressed (a must!) they will attract endless attention.

BIJAPUR
☎ 08352 / pop 245,946 / elev 593m
Ruins and still-intact gems of 15th- to 17th-century Muslim architecture embellish old, dusty Bijapur like so many tatters of faded sultans' finery. It's a fascinating place to explore, blessed by a wealth of mosques, mausoleums, palaces and fortifications whose austere grace is in complete contrast to the sculptural extravagance of the Chalukyan and Hoysala temples further south.

KARNATAKA

Bijapur was the capital of the Adil Shahi kings (1489–1686), and was one of the splinter states formed when the Bahmani Muslim kingdom broke up in 1482. The town has a strong Muslim character but is also a centre for the Lingayat brand of Shaivism, which emphasises a single personalised god. The **Lingayat Siddeshwara Festival** runs for eight days in January/February.

Orientation

The two main attractions, the Golgumbaz and the Ibrahim Rouza, are at opposite ends of the town. Between them runs Station Rd (also known as Mahatma Gandhi Rd, or MG Rd), along which you'll find most of the major hotels and restaurants. The bus stand is a five-minute walk from Station Rd; the train station is 2km east of the centre.

Information

Canara Bank (☎ 250163; Azad Rd; 🕑 10.30am-4pm Mon-Fri, 10.30am-1pm Sat) Changes travellers cheques; bring a photocopy of your passport and prepare to wait forever.

Net Mania (Bagalkot Rd; per hr Rs 40; 🕑 9.30am-11.30pm) Slow Internet access.

Tourist office (☎ 250359; Station Rd; 🕑 10am-5.30pm Mon-Sat) Not much on offer. It's behind KSTDC Hotel Mayura Adil Shahi Annexe.

Dangers & Annoyances

Bijapur has some air-quality issues. Keep a hankie on you for those breezy rickshaw rides.

Sights

GOLGUMBAZ

Bijapur's largest monument, in size and reputation, is the 1659 **Golgumbaz** (Indian/foreigner Rs 5/US$2; 🕑 6am-6pm). It's a mammoth, ill-proportioned but oddly beautiful building, containing an immense hall with octagonal seven-storey towers at each of its corners and capped by an enormous dome, 38m in diameter, said to be the world's second largest after St Peter's Basilica in Rome.

Around the base of the dome is the psychedelic 'whispering gallery'; the acoustics are such that if you whisper into the wall a person on the opposite side of the gallery can

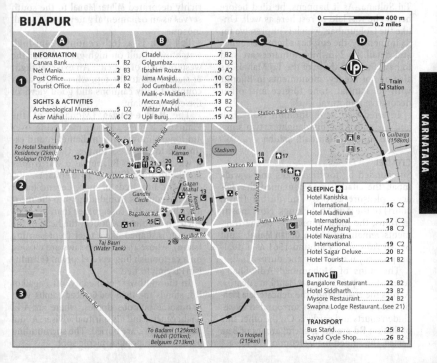

BIJAPUR

INFORMATION	
Canara Bank	1 B2
Net Mania	2 B3
Post Office	3 B2
Tourist Office	4 B2

SIGHTS & ACTIVITIES	
Archaeological Museum	5 D2
Asar Mahal	6 C2

Citadel	7 B2
Golgumbaz	8 D2
Ibrahim Rouza	9 A2
Jama Masjid	10 C2
Jod Gumbad	11 B2
Malik-e-Maidan	12 A2
Mecca Masjid	13 B2
Mihtar Mahal	14 C2
Upli Buruj	15 A2

SLEEPING 🛏	
Hotel Kanishka International	16 C2
Hotel Madhuvan International	17 C2
Hotel Megharaj	18 C2
Hotel Navaratna International	19 C2
Hotel Sagar Deluxe	20 B2
Hotel Tourist	21 B2

EATING 🍴	
Bangalore Restaurant	22 B2
Hotel Siddharth	23 B2
Mysore Restaurant	24 B2
Swapna Lodge Restaurant	(see 21)

TRANSPORT	
Bus Stand	25 B2
Sayad Cycle Shop	26 B2

To Hotel Shashinag Residency (2km); Sholapur (101km)

Market

Azad Rd

Nehru Rd

Bara Kaman

Station Back Rd

Stadium

Station Rd

Mahatma Gandhi Rd (MG Rd)

Gagan Mahal

Gandhi Circle

Bagalkot Rd

Anand Mahal Rd

Citadel

Munishvara Rd

Jama Masjid Rd

Taj Bauri (Water Tank)

Bagalkot Rd

Bypass Rd

Hubli Rd

To Badami (125km); Hubli (201km); Belgaum (213km)

To Hospet (215km)

To Gulbarga (158km)

Train Station

0   400 m
0   0.2 miles

KARNATAKA

hear you clearly, and any sound made is said to be repeated 10 times over. Unfortunately people like to test this out with their shouting so come in the early morning, before any school groups arrive. Access to the gallery is via a narrow staircase in the southeastern tower; the tough climb is tempered by the view of Bijapur from the top.

The Golgumbaz is the mausoleum of Mohammed Adil Shah (1626–56), his two wives, his mistress (Rambha), one of his daughters and a grandson. Their caskets stand on a raised platform in the centre of the hall, though their actual graves are in the crypt, accessible by a flight of steps under the western doorway.

The gardens house an **archaeological museum** (☉ 10am-5pm Sat-Thu).

IBRAHIM ROUZA

The magnificent **Ibrahim Rouza** (Indian/foreigner Rs 5/US$2, video Rs 25; ☉ 6am-6pm) is considered one of the most finely proportioned Islamic monuments in India. It was built at the height of Bijapur's prosperity by Ibrahim Adil Shah II (r 1580–1626) for his queen, Taj Sultana. As it happens, he died before her, so he was laid to rest here as well. Unlike the Golgumbaz, which is impressive for its immensity, the emphasis here is elegance and detail. Its 24m-high minarets are said to have inspired those of the Taj Mahal. It's also one of the few monuments in Bijapur with substantial stone filigree and other decorative sculptural work.

Interred here with Ibrahim Adil Shah and his queen are his daughter, two sons, and his mother, Haji Badi Sahiba.

CITADEL

Surrounded by fortified walls and a wide moat, the citadel once contained the palaces, pleasure gardens and durbar (royal court) of the Adil Shahi kings. Now mostly in ruins, the most impressive of the fragments remaining is the **Gagan Mahal**, built by Ali Adil Shah I around 1561 as a dual-purpose royal residency and durbar hall.

The ruins of Mohammed Adil Shah's seven-storey palace, the **Sat Manzil**, are nearby. Across the road stands the delicate **Jala Manzil**, once a water pavilion surrounded by secluded courts and gardens. On the other side of Station Rd are the graceful arches of **Bara Kaman**, the ruined mausoleum of Ali Roza.

JAMA MASJID

The finely proportioned **Jama Masjid** (Jama Masjid Rd; ☉ 9am-5.30pm) has graceful arches, a fine dome and a vast inner courtyard with room for 2250 worshippers. Spaces for them are marked out in black on the mosque's floor. It was constructed by Ali Adil Shah I (r 1557–80), who was also responsible for erecting the fortified city walls and the Gagan Mahal.

OTHER MONUMENTS

On the eastern side of the citadel is the tiny, walled **Mecca Masjid**, thought to have been built in the early 17th century. Some speculate that this mosque, with its high surrounding walls and cloistered feel, may have been for women. The **Asar Mahal**, to the east of the citadel, was built by Mohammed Adil Shah in about 1646 to serve as a Hall of Justice. The building once housed two hairs from the Prophet's beard. The rooms on the upper storey are decorated with frescoes and the front is graced with a square tank. A sign states that it's 'out of bounds' for women. The stained but richly decorated **Mihtar Mahal** to the south serves as an ornamental gateway to a small mosque.

Upli Buruj is a 16th-century, 24m-high watchtower built on high ground near the western walls of the city. An external flight of stairs leads to the top, where there are a couple of hefty cannons and good views of the city and plains.

The **Malik-e-Maidan** (Monarch of the Plains) is a huge cannon measuring over 4m long, almost 1.5m in diameter, and estimated to weigh 55 tonnes. Cast in 1549, it was brought to Bijapur as a war trophy thanks to the effort of 10 elephants, 400 oxen and hundreds of men. Legend has it that the gunners would jump into the moat after lighting the fuse, rather than be deafened. In a whimsical touch, the head of the cannon is shaped like a tiger (representing Islam), whose razor-sharp jaws are closing on a cartoonish bug-eyed elephant (Hinduism) trying to flee.

In the southwest of the city, off Bagalkot Rd, stands the twin **Jod Gumbad** tombs with handsome bulbous domes, where an Adil Shahi general and his spiritual adviser, Abdul Razzaq Qadiri, are buried. The surrounding gardens are a popular picnic spot.

Sleeping

Except for the Shashinag, Bijapur's hotels all have 24-hour checkout, and all have hot water.

Hotel Tourist (☎ 250655; MG Rd; s/d from Rs 80/150, deluxe Rs 150/250) The deluxe rooms here are quite nice; they're extremely clean and were recently spruced up, with fresh paint and new plastic chairs. The ordinary doubles are rough around the edges but OK.

Hotel Megharaj (☎ 254458; Station Rd; r from Rs 150; ☒) The Megharaj is also making efforts to keep things nice, and it's a little out of the downtown jumble.

Hotel Sagar Deluxe (☎ 259234; Barakaman Rd; s/d from Rs 175/200; ☒) The bathrooms here are falling down, but it'll do in a pinch.

Hotel Navaratna International (☎ 222771; fax 222772; Station Rd; r from Rs 300; ☒) The Navaratna is fresh and bright, with pastel-colour ceiling squares. It's all very colourful and new, but those shiny hallway tiles make the place echo like the Golgumbaz.

Hotel Kanishka International (☎ 223788; kanishka-bjp@rediffmail.com; Station Rd; s/d from Rs 400/450; ☒) This semiupscale place isn't perfect, but rooms are spacious, the beds are big and comfy and the floors are made of marble. Rates include tax.

Hotel Shashinag Residency (☎ 260344; shashinag _bijapur@yahoo.com; Sholapur Bypass Rd; s/d incl breakfast from US$20/30; ☒ ☒) Aspiring to greatness on a mammoth expanse of grass 3km from downtown, the Shashinag has a pool (Rs 30 per hour for nonguests), playground and gym. Rooms are polished, if unoriginal.

Hotel Madhuvan International (☎ 255571; fax 256201; Station Rd; r from Rs 950; ☒) You can tell it used to be elegant, with its pink walls and placid hallways, but then let itself go. It's still one of the nicer places in town, just overpriced. The restaurant (right) is good too.

Eating

Bangalore Restaurant (MG Rd; meals Rs 17; ☺ 6am-10pm) The modest little Bangalore does outrageously good South Indian veg thalis. It's next to Jayashree Talkies.

Mysore Restaurant (New Market; meals Rs 20; ☺ 7am-10.30pm) This place is always hopping with crowds who come in for good-value South Indian veg goods.

Hotel Siddharth (New Market; mains Rs 15-65; ☺ 8am-11pm) Hotel Siddharth, with curtained booths and rooftop seating, has a huge selection of vegetarian and meaty dishes, plus booze.

Swapna Lodge Restaurant (MG Rd; mains Rs 30-100; ☺ 9am-11pm) On the 2nd floor of the building next to Hotel Tourist, Swapna Lodge has good grub, cold beer and a 1970s lounge feel. Its open-air terrace is perfect for evening dining.

Hotel Madhuvan International (mains Rs 25-50; ☺ 6am-11pm) Dine on quality Indian, Chinese and Continental standards out in the garden or in air-con relief.

Getting There & Away

BUS

From the **bus stand** (☎ 251344) buses run direct to Badami (Rs 60, 4½ hours, seven daily) and Bidar (Rs 110, eight hours, four daily). Buses head every half-hour to Belgaum (Rs 84, six hours), Gulbarga (Rs 68, four hours), Hubli (Rs 92, six hours) and Sholapur (Rs 50, two hours). Eight evening buses go to Bangalore (Rs 292 deluxe, 12 hours) via Hospet, and a few buses a day go to Hyderabad (Rs 232 deluxe, 10 hours) and Pune (Rs 170, eight hours).

The plentiful private bus agencies near the bus stand run services to Bangalore (Rs 240) and Mumbai (Rs 295), as well as to Hubli, Mangalore and other destinations.

TRAIN

The line between Bijapur and Sholapur is now broad gauge, but conversion work is still under way on the route to Gadag – and it may take some time. For now, four trains a day run only to Sholapur (Rs 22, 2½ hours), which has connections to Mumbai, Hyderabad and Bangalore. An express to Bangalore (Rs 310/550 in sleeper/3AC, 12 hours, three weekly) also passes through **Bijapur station** (☎ 241120), as do 'fast passenger' trains to Mumbai (Rs 71/151 in chair/sleeper, 12 hours, three weekly) and Hyderabad (Rs 123 in sleeper, 15½ hours, daily).

Getting Around

Autorickshaws are oddly expensive in Bijapur; some haggling and Rs 20 should get you between the train station and the town centre. Between the Golgumbaz and Ibrahim Rouza autorickshaws cost about Rs 25. Tonga drivers are eager for business but charge around the same. Autorickshaw drivers ask for Rs 200 for four hours around town.

Sayad Cycle Shop (🕓 8am-8pm) near the bus stand rents out bicycles for Rs 3 an hour.

BIDAR

☎ 08482 / pop 172,298 / elev 664m

Generally nobody goes to Bidar, and it's not clear why. The old walled town has a magnificent 15th-century **fort** with the evocative ruins of **palaces** – the Rangin Mahal, Takht Mahal and Tarkash Mahal. It also has a triple moat hewn out of solid red rock, 5.5km of defensive wall, intricate battlements and a fairy-tale entrance on a roadway that twists in an elaborate chicane through three gateways. It's all well preserved and sprawls lazily across rolling hills that are mostly deserted except for boys playing cricket, and you can wander around peacefully for hours.

Bidar passed through a number of empires before becoming the capital of the Bahmani kingdom from 1428. It later became the capital of the Barid Shahi dynasty. The huge domed **tombs** of the Bahmani

---

BIDRI: THE ART OF BIDAR

Around the 14th century the Persian craftsmen of Bidar came up with an art form known as *bidriware*, by damascening (moulding together metals) to create imaginative blends of blackened zinc, copper, lead and tin. These are then embossed, and overlaid or inlaid with pure silver. In both design and decoration, the artefacts are heavily influenced by the typically Islamic decorative motifs and features of the time. Finely crafted pieces such as hookahs, goblets, boxes for *paan* (a mixture of betel nut and leaves for chewing) and bangles are exquisitely embellished with interwoven creepers and flowing floral patterns, and occasionally framed by strict geometric lines. The effect of the delicate silver filigree against the ebony-toned background is striking.

These days artists still tap away at their craft in the back streets of Bidar, as well as in Hyderabad. Shops selling *bidri*ware are congregated on and around Chowbara Rd, near Basveshwar Circle.

---

kings, located in Ashtur, 2km east of Bidar, have a desolate, moody beauty that strikes a strange harmony with the sunny hills around them. These impressive mausoleums were built to house the remains of the sultans – their graves are still regularly draped with fresh satin and flowers – and are arranged in a long line along the edge of the road.

In town, the **Khwaja Mahmud Gawan Madrasa**, a college built in 1492, has a few colourful remains of typical Islamic mosaics.

Cycling is a fun way to tour around; rent a bike at **Diamond Cycle Taxi** (Basveshwar Circle; 🕓 7am-10pm) for Rs 2 per hour.

Dangers & Annoyances

Foreigner-watching seems to be an unusually popular pastime in northern Karnataka, and especially Bidar. It's generally harmless curiosity, though travellers on their own – particularly women – may find it unsettling. Sunglasses help, and in Bidar, it gets better outside the town centre.

Sleeping & Eating

Krishna Regency (☎ 221991; Udgir Rd; s/d/tr from Rs 225/275/500; 🕃) The best place to stay in town is right near the new bus stand. It's a friendly, efficiently run hotel with red carpets and a glass elevator, but some rooms are dark.

Hotel Mayura (☎ 228142; Udgir Rd; r from Rs 150; mains Rs 22-80) The cheaper rooms here are a good deal, and the hotel, which has quite a decent nonveg restaurant, is quietly set back from the road, across from the new bus stand.

Hotel Kailash (☎ 227727; Pawar Complex; s/d from Rs 130/145) Near the old bus stand, the Kailash is aging, but it's clean and has lots of heart.

Jyothi Udupi (meals Rs 20-45; 🕓 6am-11pm) This place opposite the new bus stand has 21 kinds of dosas, filling South Indian thalis (Rs 20) and an ice-cream sundae named 'Beauty Ripples'.

Kamat Hotel (meals Rs 23-50; 🕓 9am-10pm; 🕃) A pure-veg place serving a wide selection of North Indian and Chinese favourites.

Getting There & Away

From the new **bus stand** (☎ 228508), frequent bus services run to Gulbarga (Rs 44, three hours). Gulbarga has good express-train connections to both Mumbai and Bangalore. Several buses also run to Hyderabad (Rs 61/85 in ordinary/deluxe, four hours), Bijapur (Rs 110, eight hours) and Banga-lore (Rs 398 in deluxe; 12 hours). No buses go direct to Badami – you must change at Gulbarga.

Kerala

In this narrow, fertile strip on the southwest coast, India shows its gentle and relaxed side. Kerala's backwaters have become an India 'must do' – taking a boat trip on this intricate system of rivers, canals, lakes and lagoons, you'll adjust to travel at floating pace, drifting in perfect silence by villages, paddy fields and coconut groves. Kerala's beautiful beaches fit the swaying-palm-tree ideal, and inland, along the Western Ghats, wildlife sanctuaries sit side by side with coffee and spice plantations and the aroma of cardamom and cinnamon sits in the air. The hill stations offer unrivalled serenity and stunning tea-plantation views.

The state's sheltered location (the Ghats, with their dense forests and long ridges, have deterred many mainland invaders) has allowed distinctive customs, arts and festivals to thrive. The most renowned art form, *kathakali* – an astonishing blend of dance, pantomime and religious play – is but one of a bamboozling array of performing arts and religious rituals. Attending a local *theyyam* – a holy dance performed as a sacred offering, where costumed dancers often go into a trancelike state – is an experience you won't quickly forget.

Kerala's long coastline has encouraged maritime contact with the outside world for centuries, and reminders of the colonial past are everywhere: Syrian Christian churches; a strong Muslim presence; Dutch and Portuguese heritage homes; Raj-era game lodges; and even a 16th-century synagogue in Kochi. All over the state, you'll feast on a distinctive and delicious cuisine, be pampered by clinics and resorts practicing Ayurvedic treatment and massage, and be welcomed by a deeply hospitable people. Come here with an open-ended itinerary and your plans to see the rest of India may be in serious trouble.

HIGHLIGHTS

- Hire a houseboat and experience the floating life of Kerala's **backwaters** (p278)
- Go elephant spotting in **Wayanad** (p306) or **Periyar Wildlife Sanctuary** (p284)
- Escape the mainland bustle and spend a few days admiring the colonial architecture and eating at the fabulous restaurants of **Fort Cochin** (p291)
- Explore the tea and spice plantations and soak up the mountain air in the lush hills around **Munnar** (p287)
- Hunt out a *theyyam* in one of the villages around **Kannur** (p307) and get a glimpse of the state's rich and intriguing spiritual culture
- Kick back for a few days, meet other travellers and dine on fresh seafood in **Varkala** (p272)
- Leave your modesty at home, lie back and submit to an **Ayurvedic massage** (p271) – you'll be glad you did

Wayanad Wildlife Sanctuary

Kannur ★

Munnar ★

Fort Cochin ★

Periyar ★ Wildlife Sanctuary

Backwaters ★

Varkala ★

KERALA

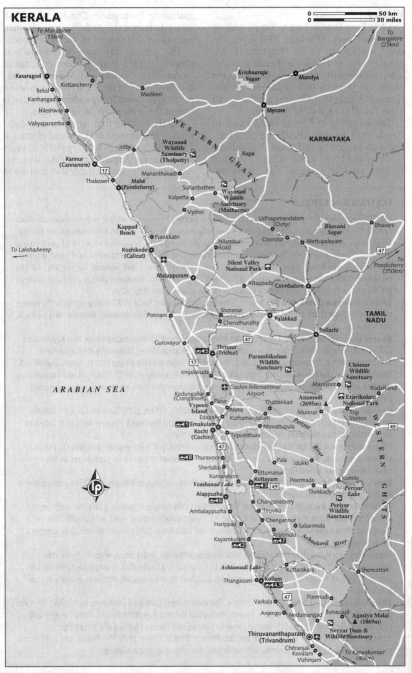

KERALA

0 —————— 50 km
0 —————— 30 miles

To Mangalore (15km)

To Bangalore (25km)

Kasaragod
Bekal
Kottancherry
Kanhangad
Madikeri
Nileshwar
Valiyaparamba

Krishnaraja Sagar

Mandya

Mysore

KARNATAKA

Iritty
Kannur (Cannanore)
17
Wayanad Wildlife Sanctuary (Tholpetty)
Mananthavadi
Nagu

W E S T E R N

Thalasseri
Mahé (Pondicherry)
Sultanbatheri
Kalpetta
Wayanad Wildlife Sanctuary (Muthanga)
Vythiri
Udhagamandalam (Ooty)
Bhavani Sagar
Bhavani

G H A T S

Kappad Beach
Purakkatri
Nilambur Road
Coonoor
Mettupalayam
47

To Lakshadweep
Kozhikode (Calicut)
To Pondicherry (350km)

Silent Valley National Park
Attappadi
Coimbatore

Malappuram

TAMIL NADU

Ponnani
Shoranur
Cheruthuruthy
Palakkad
Pollachi

Guruvayur
47
Thrissur (Trichur)
Parambikulam Wildlife Sanctuary
Chinnar Wildlife Sanctuary
Marayoor
Kodaikanal

17
Irinjalakuda
Anamudi (2695m)
Eravikulam National Park

A R A B I A N S E A
Kodungallur (Cranganore)
Cochin International Airport
Thattekkad
Munnar
Top Station
Periyar River

Vypeen Island
Parur
Aluva
Edapally
Kothamangalam
Ernakulam
Muvattupula

W E S T E R N

Kochi (Cochin)
1
Tripunithura
47
Pala
Idukki
49

8 Thuravoor
Shertallai
Ettumanur
Peermade
Kumily

Kumarakom
Kottayam
Periyar Lake

Vembanad Lake
Thekkady
Periyar Wildlife Sanctuary

Alappuzha
6
Changanassery
Tiruvilla

G H A T S

Ambalappuzha
Chengannur
Sabarimala
Harippad
Aranmula
Achankovil River

Kayamkulam
2
7

Ashtamudi Lake
Kottarakara
Shencottah

Thangasseri
Kollam
4 9

Varkala
47
Ponmudi

Anjengo
Bonacaud
Agastya Malai (1869m)
Nedumangad

Thiruvananthapuram (Trivandrum)
Neyyar Dam & Wildlife Sanctuary

Chitranjali
Kovalam
To Kanyakumari (40km)
Vizhinjam

KERALA

History

Traders have been sailing to Kerala seeking spices and ivory for at least 3000 years. The coast was known to the Phoenicians, Romans, Arabs and Chinese. Kerala was also a trans-shipment point for spices from the Moluccas (eastern Indonesia), and it was through Kerala that Chinese products and ideas found their way to the West.

The kingdom of Cheras ruled much of Kerala until the early Middle Ages, competing with kingdoms and small fiefdoms for territory and trade. Vasco da Gama's arrival in 1498 heralded an era of European colonialism as Portuguese, Dutch and English interests fought the Arab traders, and then each other, for control of the spice trade.

The present-day state of Kerala was created in 1956 from the former states of Travancore, Cochin and Malabar. A tradition of concern for the arts and education resulted in a post-Independence state that is one of the most progressive in India.

Kerala had the first freely elected communist government in the world, elected in 1957 and holding power regularly in years since. The participatory political system has resulted in a more equitable distribution of

FESTIVALS IN KERALA

Keralan festivals are astonishing, not only in the way they're celebrated but in their sheer number. Across the state, on any one night (but especially during festival season from November to mid-May), there are literally hundreds of temple festivals being held, featuring an array of performing arts and rituals, music and the odd elephant procession. Some of the biggest and most interesting festivals are listed here, but there are many, many more – ask around for details. All the temple festivals following take place in the temple grounds or in nearby paddy fields, so tourists are free to watch. Festivals in this boxed text are marked on Map p259.

Ernakulathappan Utsavam (❶; Jan/Feb; Shiva Temple, Ernakulam, Kochi, p290) Hugely significant for natives of Kochi, the climax of this eight-day festival brings a procession of 15 splendidly decorated elephants, ecstatic music and fireworks.

Bharni Utsavam (❷; Feb/Mar; Chettikulangara Bhaghavathy Temple, Chettikulangara village, near Kayamkulam, p277) This one-day festival is dedicated to one of the popular Keralan goddesses, Bhagavathy. It's famous for its *kootiattam* ritual and the spectacular procession to the temple of larger-than-life effigies (heroes, horses, chariots etc).

Thirunakkara Utsavam (❸; Mar; Thirunakkara Shiva Temple, Kottayam, p282) There's all-night *kathakali* on the third and fourth nights of this 10-day festival; on the last two nights there are processions of caparisoned elephants.

Pooram Festival (❹; Apr; Asraman Shree Krishna Swami Temple, Kollam, p275) There are full-night *kathakali* performances on the first nine nights of this 10-day festival; on the last day there's a procession of 40 ornamented elephants in Asraman Maidan to the accompaniment of temple music.

Thrissur Pooram (❺; Apr/May; Vadakkumnatha Temple, Thrissur, p301) The elephant procession to end all elephant processions. Thrissur is Kerala's festival hot spot; see the boxed text, p303, for more details on this and other festivals in and around Thrissur.

Nehru Trophy Snake Boat Race (❻; 2nd Sat in Aug; Punnamadakalyal, Alleppey, p277) The most popular of Kerala's boat races; see the boxed text, p277.

Aranmula Boat Race (❼; Aug/Sep; near Shree Parthasarathy Temple, Aranmula, p284) This water regatta re-creates a ritualistic journey in honour of Krishna. It's a spectacularly exciting event, with crowds cheering as the rowers shout along with the songs of the boatman, and has a lower profile among tourists than Alleppey's Nehru Trophy.

Onam (Aug/Sep; statewide) Kerala's biggest cultural celebration is the 10-day Onam, when the entire state celebrates the golden age of mythical King Mahabali. This is primarily a family affair, when people travel from all over the state back to their home village. The emphasis is on feasting and decorating the home, in anticipation of the king's visit.

Thiru Utsavam (❽; Oct/Nov; Mahadeva temple, Thuravoor village, 23km from Ernakulam, Kochi p290) There are a variety of ritual performances and music concerts throughout the nine days of this festival. There's an elephant procession on the eighth day and the festival comes to a climax with the ritual bathing of a Shiva effigy.

Ashtamudi Craft & Art Festival (❾; Dec/Jan; Asraman Maidan, Kollam, p275) This festival, held every second year, features folk art from all over India, with workshops, demonstrations and exhibitions.

FAST FACTS

■ Population: 31.8 million

■ Area: 38,864 sq km

■ Capital: Thiruvananthapuram (Trivandrum)

■ Main language: Malayalam

■ When to go: October to March

---

land and income, low infant mortality and a 91% literacy rate – the highest in India. Many Malayalis (speakers of Malayalam) work in the Middle East, and remittances play a significant part in the economy.

Information
ACCOMMODATION
Parts of Kerala – particularly the beach-side towns and backwater hubs – have a distinct high season around October to March. This is less pronounced in the major cities, the Western Ghats and the north, though many places will give significant discounts during the monsoon (around May to August). Within the high season there will sometimes be a peak season, around mid-December to mid-January, when prices will be higher again. Prices throughout this chapter are for high season; outside these times prices will drop significantly – by anything up to 50% to 75% in the beach towns.

Generally, quoted prices for homestays or guesthouses will include tax, while hotel and resort prices won't. Tax is 7.5%, 10% or 15% depending on cost of room.

All places, even budget rooms, have private bathroom unless otherwise stated.

MONEY
There are plenty of ATMs all over Kerala that accept foreign cards. Although there is some inconsistency from town to town, generally Federal Bank ATMs accept Visa, and State Bank of India ATMs accept MasterCard and Cirrus- and Maestro-linked cards. HDFC and ICICI ATMs accept all foreign cards.

TOURIST OFFICES
Kerala Tourism (☎ 0471-2321132; www.keralatourism .org) is a government tourism promotion body with information offices – usually called DTPC or Tourist Facilitation Centres – in

most major towns. Be aware there are numerous offices with official-sounding names that are actually private tour companies.

SOUTHERN KERALA

THIRUVANANTHAPURAM (TRIVANDRUM)
☎ 0471 / pop 889,191
Built over seven hills, Thiruvananthapuram (City of the Sacred Serpent) retains some of old Kerala's ambience, with its pagoda-shaped buildings, red-tiled roofs and narrow, winding lanes – as soon as you get off hectic MG Rd, things get much more sedate. While familiar problems such as air pollution are appearing, this is still one of India's more pleasant cities, and there's a plethora of cultural diversions to distract you from the fumes.

Orientation
MG Rd, centre of most of the action, runs about 4km north–south from the museums and zoo to Sri Padmanabhaswamy Temple. The Kerala State Road Transport Corporation (KSRTC) bus stand, train station and many budget hotels are close together, while the municipal bus stand is near the temple.

Information
BOOKSHOPS & LIBRARIES
Alliance Française (☎ 2320666; aftinfo@afindia.org; Forest Office Lane, Vazhuthacaud; ❨❩ 9am-1pm & 2-6pm Mon-Sat) Library and cultural events.

Bharath Book Emporium (☎ 2339586; MG Rd; ❨❩ 9.30am-7.30pm Mon-Sat, 3-7.30pm Sun) Fascinating collection of books on religion, astrology, the occult and spirituality. Opposite Ayurveda College.

British Library (☎ 2330716; bl.trivandrum@in .britishcouncil.org; YMCA Rd; ❨❩ 11am-7pm Mon-Sat) Officially open only to members (Rs 650), but the library does welcome visitors. It has British newspapers and magazines.

DC Books (☎ 2453379; Statue Rd; ❨❩ 9.30am-7.30pm Mon-Sat, 3-7.30pm Sun) This ultra-literate state has a fittingly superb bookshop chain, and this branch has a typically excellent selection of fiction in English and nonfiction about India.

Modern Book Centre (☎ 2331826; Gandhari Amman Kovil Rd; ❨❩ 9.30am-1.30pm & 2.30-8.30pm Mon-Sat) Has an outstanding collection of English-language books, including literature, philosophy, history and Keralan culture.

KERALA

THIRUVANANTHAPURAM (TRIVANDRUM)

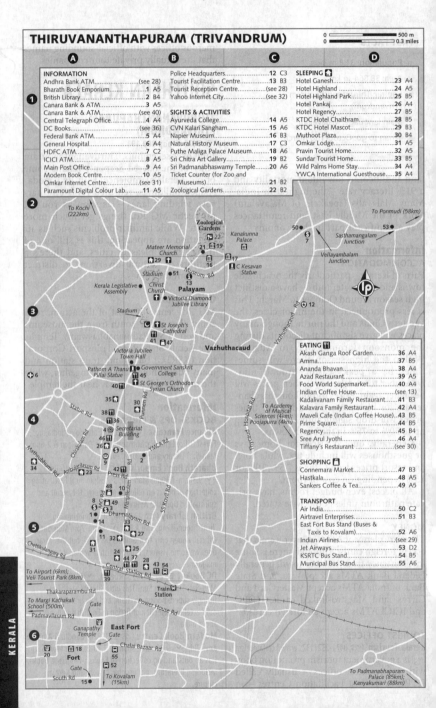

A **B** **C** **D**

INFORMATION
Andhra Bank ATM.........................(see 28)
Bharath Book Emporium........................1 A5
British Library....................................2 B4
Canara Bank & ATM...........................3 A5
Canara Bank & ATM......................(see 40)
Central Telegraph Office.......................4 A4
DC Books.....................................(see 36)
Federal Bank ATM................................5 A4
General Hospital.................................6 A4
HDFC ATM...7 C2
ICICI ATM..8 A5
Main Post Office.................................9 A4
Modern Book Centre.........................10 A5
Omkar Internet Centre...................(see 31)
Paramount Digital Colour Lab..........11 A5

Police Headquarters..........................12 C3
Tourist Facilitation Centre.................13 B3
Tourist Reception Centre................(see 28)
Yahoo Internet City.........................(see 32)

SIGHTS & ACTIVITIES
Ayurveda College...............................14 A5
CVN Kalari Sangham.........................15 A6
Napier Museum.................................16 B3
Natural History Museum...................17 C3
Puthe Maliga Palace Museum...........18 A5
Sri Chitra Art Gallery.........................19 B2
Sri Padmanabhaswamy Temple.........20 A6
Ticket Counter (for Zoo and
  Museums)....................................21 B2
Zoological Gardens...........................22 B2

SLEEPING
Hotel Ganesh....................................23 A4
Hotel Highland.................................24 A5
Hotel Highland Park.........................25 B5
Hotel Pankaj....................................26 A4
Hotel Regency..................................27 B5
KTDC Hotel Chaithram......................28 B5
KTDC Hotel Mascot..........................29 B3
Muthoot Plaza..................................30 B4
Omkar Lodge....................................31 A5
Pravin Tourist Home..........................32 A5
Sundar Tourist Home.........................33 B5
Wild Palms Home Stay......................34 A4
YWCA International Guesthouse........35 A4

EATING
Akash Ganga Roof Garden................36 A4
Amma...37 B5
Ananda Bhavan.................................38 A4
Azad Restaurant................................39 A5
Food World Supermarket..................40 A4
Indian Coffee House.....................(see 13)
Kadalivanam Family Restaurant........41 B3
Kalavara Family Restaurant...............42 A4
Maveli Cafe (Indian Coffee House)..43 B5
Prime Square....................................44 B5
Regency..45 B4
Sree Arul Jyothi................................46 A4
Tiffany's Restaurant.....................(see 30)

SHOPPING
Connemara Market...........................47 B3
Hastkala..48 A5
Sankers Coffee & Tea........................49 A5

TRANSPORT
Air India...50 C2
Airtravel Enterprises..........................51 B3
East Fort Bus Stand (Buses &
  Taxis to Kovalam)..........................52 A6
Indian Airlines..............................(see 29)
Jet Airways.......................................53 D2
KSRTC Bus Stand..............................54 B5
Municipal Bus Stand.........................55 A6

To Kochi
(222km)

To Ponmudi (58km)

Zoological
Gardens

Kanakunna
Palace

Sasthamangalam
Junction

Mateer Memorial
Church

Vellayambalam
Junction

Museum Rd

C Kesavan
Statue

Stadium

Kerala Legislative
Assembly

Christ
Church

Palayam

Victoria Diamond
Jubilee Library

Stadium

St Joseph's
Cathedral

Vazhuthacaud

Victoria Jubilee
Town Hall

Pathom A Thanu
Pillai Statue

Government Sanskrit
College

St George's Orthodox
Syrian Church

To Academy
of Magical
Sciences (4km);
Poojapura (4km)

Thycaud Hospital Rd

Secretariat
Building

YMCA Rd

Statue Rd

Chalukari Rd

Mathrubhumi Rd

Ambujavilasam Rd

Press Rd

Panmen Rd

SS Kovil Rd

Manjalikulam Rd

MG Rd

Dharmalayam Rd

Chettikulangara Rd

To Airport (6km);
Veli Tourist Park (8km)

Central Station Rd

Thakaraparambu Rd

To Margi Kathakali
School (500m);

Padmavilasam Rd

Train
Station

Power House Rd

Ganapathy
Temple

East Fort

Chalai Bazaar Rd

Fort

Gate

South Rd

To Kovalam
(15km)

To Padmanabhapuram
Palace (85km);
Kanyakumari (88km)

0 ___ 500 m
0 ___ 0.3 miles

Trains that go up the coast as far as Mangalore in Karnataka include the daily *Parasuram Express* (16 hours, departs 6.10am) and *Malabar Express* (departs 6.20pm).

There are frequent trains to Varkala (Rs 25/160 in 2nd/chair class, 45 minutes), Kollam (Rs 29/160, 1¼ hours) and Ernakulam (Rs 130/330 in sleeper/3AC, five hours); and daily services to Calicut (Rs 190/500 in sleeper/3AC, 10 hours) and Kanyakumari (Rs 121/210 in sleeper/3AC, two hours).

Getting Around

The airport is 6km from the city and 15km from Kovalam; take local bus No 14 from the East Fort bus stand (Rs 5). Prepaid taxi vouchers from the airport cost Rs 165 to the city and Rs 250 to Kovalam.

Autorickshaws are your best transport around the city. Standard rates are Rs 8 flag fall, then Rs 4.50 per kilometre, but all rules go out the window at night – 50% over the meter is fair, but you may have trouble getting drivers to use the meter at all – agree on a fare beforehand.

AROUND TRIVANDRUM
Ponmudi & the Cardamom Hills

The small hill resort of Ponmudi, 61km northeast of Trivandrum, is a scenic drive through tea estates and tiny villages, yet the destination itself is a dull, though picturesque, picnic spot for Indian families. If you want to stay overnight, there's a **KTDC Guest House** (☎ 0472-2890230; d/cottage Rs 430/550) 1.5km from Ponmudi with basic, clean and bright rooms. Its restaurant and beer parlour is popular with car loads of young men. There are seven daily buses from the KSRTC bus stand in Trivandrum to Ponmudi (Rs 24, 2½ hours); the last bus back is at 6pm. A taxi will cost about Rs 1100 for a day trip.

Sivananda Yoga Vedanta Dhanwantari Ashram

Near Neyyar Dam (watch for the turn-off on the road to Ponmudi), this **ashram** (☎ /fax 0471-2273093; www.sivananda.org/ndam), established in 1978, is renowned for its hatha yoga courses. Courses run for a minimum of two weeks and cost Rs 600 per day for accommodation in a double room (or Rs 450 per day for dormitory accommodation). There's an exacting schedule (6am to 10pm) of yoga

practice, meditation and chanting; students rave about the food (included in the rates). Prior bookings by email are required. Month-long yoga teacher training and Ayurvedic massage courses are also available. There are frequent buses to Neyyar Dam from Trivandrum (Rs 14, 1½ hours); a taxi one way costs around Rs 400.

KOVALAM
☎ 0471

Kerala's most popular beach-side resort, Kovalam is the scene of chaotic beachfront development, relatively high prices, desperate souvenir sellers and a dramatic high-season influx of charter groups. Nevertheless, it retains a certain charm, with good beaches, a lush and peaceful palm-and-paddy setting, decent restaurants and a plethora of places to stay in all price ranges (except ultra-budget in high season). Kovalam can be a good place to kick back for a few days, especially if you're here during the quieter times.

Orientation

Kovalam consists of two coves (Lighthouse Beach and Hawah Beach) separated from less-populated beaches north and south by rocky headlands. The town proper is at Kovalam Junction, about 1.5km from the beaches.

Information

There's a helpful **tourist facilitation centre** (☎ 2480085; ☻ 10am-5pm Mon-Sat) inside the entrance to the Kovalam Beach Resort. The **post office** (☻ 10am-5pm) is next door to the tourist centre.

Just about every shop and hotel wants to change your money, but ask around for the best rate. There are Federal Bank and ICICI ATMs at Kovalam Junction.

There are places all along the beach offering STD/ISD facilities, and plenty of small, slow, expensive Internet places charging Rs 50 to 60 per hour. **Top Shop Cyber Cafe** (per hr Rs 30; ☻ 9.30am-midnight), off the beach up a steep hill, is the only serious Internet joint.

United Books (NUP Beach Rd; ☻ 9am-8pm) has a kooky collection of books on Kerala, Indian spirituality and English-language trashlit. There's a rent/buy/exchange **bookshop** (☻ 7am-11pm) with a good range of books underneath the German Bakery.

Dangers & Annoyances

Women are likely to grow tired of the parade of male Indian day-trippers who stroll along the beach in the hope of glimpsing female flesh. Theft does occur, both from hotels and the beach. Lock the doors and windows and watch your possessions at the beach.

There are strong rips at both ends of Lighthouse Beach which carry away several swimmers every year. Swim only between the flags, in the area patrolled by lifeguards.

Kovalam has frequent blackouts and the footpaths further back behind Lighthouse Beach are unlit, so carry a torch (flashlight) after dark.

Sleeping

Although Kovalam is packed with hotels, decent budget digs are getting harder to find. Not listed here are many places that are block-booked by charter groups for the entire high-season period. In the off season, you should be able to get these relatively luxurious rooms for a song – shop around. Most places have only double rooms, but will cut the price considerably if you're on your own, especially out of season. Prices given here are for double occupancy unless otherwise stated.

There are plenty of appealing beach-front places with ocean views, but many of the smaller places tucked away in the labyrinth of paths behind the beach are more charm-

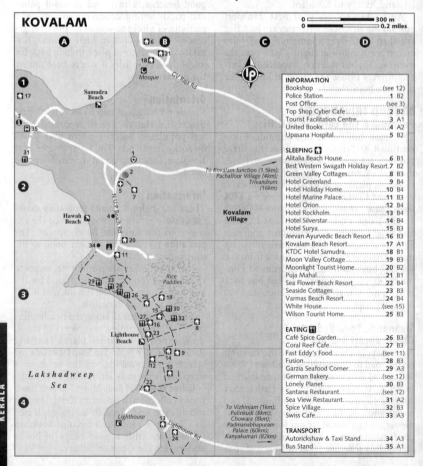

KOVALAM

0 _____ 300 m
0 _____ 0.2 miles

INFORMATION
Bookshop ....(see 12)
Police Station...1 B2
Post Office...(see 3)
Top Shop Cyber Cafe.............................2 B2
Tourist Facilitation Centre....................3 A1
United Books..4 A2
Upasana Hospital....................................5 B2

SLEEPING
Alitalia Beach House...............................6 B1
Best Western Swagath Holiday Resort.7 B2
Green Valley Cottages.............................8 B3
Hotel Greenland.......................................9 B4
Hotel Holiday Home..............................10 B4
Hotel Marine Palace.............................11 B3
Hotel Orion..12 B4
Hotel Rockholm.....................................13 B4
Hotel Silverstar......................................14 B4
Hotel Surya..15 B4
Jeevan Ayurvedic Beach Resort.........16 B3
Kovalam Beach Resort..........................17 A1
KTDC Hotel Samudra............................18 B1
Moon Valley Cottage............................19 B3
Moonlight Tourist Home.......................20 B2
Puja Mahal...21 B1
Sea Flower Beach Resort.......................22 B4
Seaside Cottages....................................23 B3
Varmas Beach Resort............................24 B4
White House.....................................(see 15)
Wilson Tourist Home.............................25 B3

EATING
Café Spice Garden.................................26 B3
Coral Reef Cafe.....................................27 B3
Fast Eddy's Food..............................(see 11)
Fusion..28 B3
Garzia Seafood Corner..........................29 A3
German Bakery.................................(see 12)
Lonely Planet..30 B3
Santana Restaurant.........................(see 12)
Sea View Restaurant.............................31 A2
Spice Village...32 A3
Swiss Cafe...33 A3

TRANSPORT
Autorickshaw & Taxi Stand..................34 A3
Bus Stand...35 A1

Mosque
CV Raja Rd
Samudra Beach
N-U-P Beach Rd
Hawah Beach
Rice Paddies
Lighthouse Beach
Lakshadweep Sea
Lighthouse
Kovalam Village

To Kovalam Junction (1.5km);
Pachalloor Village (4km);
Trivandrum (16km)

To Vizhinjam (1km);
Pulinkudi (8km);
Chowara (8km);
Padmanabhapuram
Palace (60km);
Kanyakumari (82km)

Lighthouse Rd

KERALA

ing and have great views of the lush, over-grown rice paddies. Remember that 'resort' is more a creative flourish than an accurate description in this part of India.

BUDGET

Hotel Silverstar (☎ 2482983; Info@hotel-silverstar .com; d Rs 350-600) In the heart of the village, this place has very clean rooms over three storeys – the higher you go, the more you pay. Balconies are spacious, mosquito nets are provided and there's a roof terrace up in the coconut tops.

Green Valley Cottages (☎ 2480636; indira _ravi@ hotmail.com; s/d Rs 400/500) These very simple, quite small rooms are in a wonderfully peaceful spot in a coconut grove next to the paddy fields.

Hotel Greenland (☎ 2487442; hotelgreenlandin@ yahoo.com; d Rs 350-500) This is a welcoming place with big, clean rooms and a personal, friendly touch. Good food is provided on request.

Moon Valley Cottage (☎ 9847049643; sknairkovalam@ yahoo.com; d from Rs 350, upstairs apt per week Rs 5000) This friendly place deep in the paddy fields offers good, clean rooms with patios.

Hotel Surya (☎ 2481012; kovsurya@yahoo.co.in; d downstairs/upstairs Rs 350/550, with AC Rs 1200; 🔾) The downstairs rooms here are small but clean; upstairs rooms have TV and fridge and share a big balcony.

White House (☎ 2483388; whitehousekovalam@ walla.com; d Rs 400) These are very simple, but clean, bright, good-value rooms in a central location.

Hotel Holiday Home (☎ 24863821; d Rs 250) Set back in a quiet spot in the maze of paths behind the beach, this is a good, cheap option popular with long-term travellers. The rooms aren't spotless, and a bit dark, but there's a nice garden and a laid-back vibe.

Seaside Cottages (☎ 2481937; d Rs 350) This low-rise place has eight small, clean ground-floor rooms that open directly on to the main beach-side promenade.

MIDRANGE

Hotel Rockholm (☎ 2480306; rockholm@techpark.net; Lighthouse Rd; s/d Rs 1110/1250, with AC Rs 1350/1500; 🔾 🖳) Overlooking crashing waves and set on a secluded beach, this place has touch of faded glamour, all red velour and dark wood. AC rooms are slightly bigger and have romantic window seats.

Varmas Beach Resort (☎ 2480478; varmabeach@ hotmail.com; Lighthouse Rd; d Rs 1500, with AC Rs 2500; 🔾) This is the best-looking place in Kovalam, with a cool, Kerala-style façade and small, simple rooms with superb views.

Sea Flower Beach Resort (☎ 2480554; visitindia@ eth.net; d downstairs/upstairs Rs 600/1000) The rooms here are a bit dingy but clean and with a direct view to the ocean; upstairs rooms are better value.

Wilson Tourist Home (☎ 9847363831; d Rs 750, with AC Rs 1200; 🔾) This place has large, clean court-yard rooms set around a lovely garden, with swing chairs on the balconies and Keralan dark-wood touches. Breakfast included.

Moonlight Tourist Home (☎ 2480375; d Rs 1300, with AC Rs 1500; 🔾 🖳) This popular, friendly place has character and the best balconies in town (downstairs rooms without balconies are cheaper). Rooms are clean and nicely furnished; some have four-poster beds.

Hotel Marine Palace (☎ 2481428; www.hotelmarine palace.com; d from Rs 1750, with AC from Rs 2000; 🔾) Dowdy but clean and comfortable rooms; only the more expensive ones have sea views.

Hotel Orion (☎ 2480999; orionbeachresort@hotmail .com; d downstairs/upstairs Rs 500/1000) All of the small, clean rooms face Lighthouse Beach; upstairs rooms have big balconies with views towards the lighthouse.

Jeevan Ayurvedic Beach Resort (☎ 2480662; jeevanresort@eth.net; d Rs 1200-2000; 🔾) The basic, cheaper rooms here aren't great value; the more expensive rooms are brand new with bathtub and balcony.

TOP END

Kovalam Beach Resort (☎ 2480101; reservations@ kovalamhotel.com; s/d from Rs 5000/6500, ste from Rs 9000; 🔾 🖳) This hotel is superbly located on the headland north of Hawah Beach, and is set in extensive grounds. There are three swimming pools, an Ayurvedic centre and all the luxury you'd expect for the price, though the standard rooms aren't huge. Le Meridian was in the process of taking over the resort while we were there; check www .lemeridienkovalam.com for developments.

Best Western Swagath Holiday Resort (☎ 248 1148; swagathresort@asianetindia.com; r Rs 1400-3600, with AC Rs 1800-4000, ste with AC Rs 5600; 🔾 🖳 🖳) This place is set in perfectly cultivated gardens looking over the coconut palms towards the lighthouse. The rooms are big and well furnished, but with a whiff of the chain hotel about them. Bottom-of-the-range 'row houses' are a cheap way to do pool-side luxury in the high season.

Eating

Open-air restaurants line the beach area and are scattered through the coconut palms behind it. At night they display their catch out front, and you select the method of preparation. Always check the prices before you order; fish typically costs around Rs 150, depending on variety and portion size; tiger prawns can push the price beyond Rs 400. Menus and prices are pretty indistinguishable, so it's more about which ambience takes your fancy.

Fusion (mains Rs 140-350) Has the funkiest interior design on the strip, and an inventive menu. The 'fusion' dishes – where the standard Indian and Continental choices collide to form new taste sensations – are particularly good.

German Bakery (mains around Rs 80-150) This rooftop bakery has a great range of breakfasts, decent coffee, fresh pastries, quiches, south German dishes and a varied selection of main courses, including stir-fried tofu (Rs 100) and seafood pizza (Rs 110).

Café Spice Garden (mains Rs 80-450) This tribal-themed place has a jungle feel, excellent service and a wide-ranging menu. It does seafood particularly well, and there are refreshingly different options such as pasta with crab and lemon sauce (Rs 200).

Swiss Cafe (mains Rs 120-370) There's not much Swiss about this breezy upstairs joint, but the Western breakfasts are great (eggs Rs 15 to 50) and the coffee might just be the best on the beach.

Lonely Planet (mains from Rs 40) This cheekily named vegetarian restaurant, nicely situated by a water-lily pond, serves excellent South and North Indian meals – the Kerala traditional thali (Rs 125) is a standout. Keralan cookery classes (Rs 250) are held from 1pm to 3pm and 6pm to 8pm Friday to Wednesday during high season.

Spice Village (dishes Rs 40-200) A romantic little oasis on the same lily pond, this place calls itself 'traditional Keralan', but can't resist including the same chow mein and pasta dishes as everywhere else. Nevertheless, it does some excellent Keralan seafood specialities such as fish pollichathu (mari-nated fish wrapped in a banana leaf and grilled or steamed, Rs 125).

Fast Eddy's Food (dishes Rs 20-40, thalis Rs 40-50) This no-frills vegetarian shack does good North and South Indian food.

Long-term visitors rate Santana Restaurant, Garzia Seafood Corner and Sea View Restaurant as good for seafood, and give Coral Reef Cafe the nod for the best chop suey on the beach.

Entertainment

During high season, a shortened version of kathakali is performed most nights – inquire about locations and times from the tourist facilitation centre (p267). Usually make-up starts at around 5pm, the performance itself at around 6.30pm. On weekends, cultural programmes involving music and dance are sometimes performed on the beach – look out for signs.

Western videos are shown twice a night in a few restaurants. There are no bars or nightclubs as such, but beer is available in most of the restaurants (around Rs 75) and some serve cocktails (Rs 80 to 100); they also provide an endless soundtrack of reggae, trance and classic rock.

Getting There & Away

BUS

There are local buses between Trivandrum and Kovalam every 20 minutes between 5.30am and 9.30pm (Rs 7, 30 minutes). From Kovalam, the buses start and finish at the entrance to the Kovalam Beach Resort. Buses also run to Kollam (Rs 41, 2½ hours) and Alleppey (Rs 75, four hours).

TAXI & AUTORICKSHAW

A taxi between Trivandrum and Kovalam Beach costs Rs 200 to 250. Autorickshaws should be Rs 100 to 125, depending on the season. Prepaid taxis from Trivandrum airport to Lighthouse Beach cost Rs 325.

AROUND KOVALAM

Samudra Beach

Samudra Beach (Map p268), about 4km north of Kovalam, has several resorts competing for space with local fishing villages. Although much more peaceful, the steep and rough beach is not as good for swimming as the beaches further south. There are a few restaurant shacks near the beach.

Alitalia Beach House (☎ 2480042; s/d Rs 500/1000) is tucked away behind the Uday Samudra, and is a charming little place with four eight-sided rooms with mosquito nets set around a lone coconut tree.

KTDC Hotel Samudra (☎ 2480089; samudra@md3.vsnl.net.in; s/d Rs 3000/3400; ❂ ❂) has cool, simple rooms with garden balconies in a peaceful, luxurious setting, a two-minute walk from Samudra Beach.

The new **Puja Mahal** (☎ 2481245; r Rs 1800-2000) was being set up when we were there; it could be worth a look.

Pulinkudi & Chowara

Around 8km south of Kovalam are some interesting alternatives to Kovalam's crowded beaches.

Bethsaida Hermitage (☎ 2267554; www.bethsaida-c.org; Pulinkudi; s Rs 1000-1500, d Rs 3000-3500) is a resort with a difference: this is a charitable organisation that helps support the orphanage nearby, as well as giving training and

employment to the orphaned children. But it's also a luxurious beach-side escape with a variety of different cottages, from rainbow-painted half-ovals scattered down a hillside, to spacious, cool Keralan-style huts.

Surya Samudra Beach Garden (☎ 2480413; suryasamudra@vsnl.com; Pulinkudi; r €120-240; ❂) is a beautiful small resort with individual cottages, many of which are constructed from transplanted traditional Keralan houses, with spectacular carved ceilings and open-air bathrooms. There are private beaches, an infinity pool and Ayurvedic treatments are offered. Occupancy for singles is 10% less.

For those serious about Ayurvedic treatment, **Dr Franklin's Panchakarma Institute** (☎ 248 0870; www.dr-franklin.com; Chowara; s/d from €63/114; ❂) is a less expensive alternative to the flashier resorts. Rates include treatments and Ayurvedic vegetarian meals. Accommodation is clean and comfortable but not resort style (though sea-view rooms are available). Treatment options include

---

AYURVEDA

With its roots in Sanskrit, the word Ayurveda is derived from *ayu* (life) and *veda* (knowledge); it is the knowledge or science of life. The principles of Ayurvedic medicine were first documented in the Vedas some 2000 years ago, but it is reputed to have been practised for centuries prior to its documentation.

Ayurveda sees the world as having an intrinsic order. Illness is a departure from this, a loss of balance or equilibrium. Fundamental to Ayurveda philosophy is the belief that we all possess three *doshas* (humours): *vata* (wind or air); *pitta* (fire); and *kapha* (water/earth). Together these are known as the *tridoshas* and disease is the result of imbalance among them. Each individual may express various aspects of each, but usually one type predominates. If there is deficiency or excess of any *dosha*, disease can result – an excess of *vata* may result in dizziness and debility; an increase in *pitta* may lead to fever, inflammation and infection. *Kapha* is essential for hydration and lubrication; a deficiency here could produce painful limbs and influenza-type illness.

Ayurveda treatment aims to restore the balance, and hence good health, principally through two methods: *panchakarama* (internal purification) and massage. The herbs used for both grow in abundance in Kerala's moist climate, and every town and village in Kerala has its Ayurvedic pharmacy where the medicinal plants, fresh and dried, are sold. Each *dosha* is identified with particular foods, and diet is crucial to Ayurvedic treatment.

Ayurvedic practice in Kerala places special emphasis on massage, which is claimed to be particularly beneficial for those suffering chronic ailments such as arthritis and rheumatism. The type of oil used in massage differs according to the ailment being treated, but ranges from castor and neem to mustard and camphor. To these are added various powdered herbs, nuts and bark.

Having an occasional Ayurvedic massage, something offered at tourist resorts all over Kerala, is relaxing, but reaping any long-term benefits necessitates rather more dedication – usually a 15-day or longer commitment, which will generally involve an Ayurvedic diet, exercises and a range of treatments as well as regular massages.

If you want to learn more, pick up a copy of *Ayurveda: Life, Health & Longevity* by Dr Robert E Svoboda, or check out www.ayur.com.

KERALA

packages for spine problems and slimming, as well as general rejuvenation and stress relief (see the website for more details).

Padmanabhapuram Palace

Padmanabhapuram Palace (admission Rs 10, camera/video Rs 25/1200; ⊙ 9am-5pm Tue-Sun) is regarded as the finest surviving example of traditional Keralan architecture, and shouldn't be missed. It was once the seat of the rulers of Travancore, a princely state taking in parts of Tamil Nadu as well as Kerala. The palace, a tiny enclave of Keralan territory in Tamil Nadu, is superbly constructed of teak and granite, the oldest parts dating from 1550. The architecture is exquisite, with rosewood ceilings carved in floral patterns, windows laid with jewel-coloured mica and floors finished to a high polish with a special compound of crushed shells, coconuts, egg whites and local plant juices. Chinese traders sold tea and bought spices here for centuries and their legacy is evident in intricately carved rosewood chairs, screens and ceilings, as well as the large Chinese pickle jars.

Good English-speaking guides wait inside the gate and are essential for getting the most from your visit. Rates are negotiable; count on Rs 50 to 100 depending on the group size.

Padmanabhapuram is around 60km southeast of Kovalam. Catch a local bus from Kovalam (or Trivandrum) to Kanyakumari and get off at Thuckalay, from where it is a short rickshaw ride or 15-minute walk. Alternatively, take one of the tours organised by the KTDC (see p264) or organise your own taxi (about Rs 900 return).

VARKALA

☎ 0470 / pop 42,273

With its dramatic cliff-top setting and perfect beaches, Varkala is an idyllic beach town with a more laid-back feel than Kovalam, and without its high-season charter-group scene. Although inappropriate developments already mar the area, and new hotels are springing up like coconut palms, an Arabian Sea sunset viewed from the cliff top over a fresh fish dinner is a small piece of heaven, and Papanasham Beach is relatively free of hawkers and gawkers.

Orientation & Information

The town and the train station are about 2km from the beach. There's a **police aid post** (⊙ Nov-Feb) at the helipad.

There's a State Bank of India ATM in Varkala town, between the town proper and the train station. The **Bureau de Change** (☎ 2606623; Temple Junction; ⊙ 8am-9pm) cashes travellers cheques, does credit-card cash advances and is very helpful for bus and train times. The **post office** (⊙ 10am-2pm Mon-Sat) is just north of Temple Junction.

There are plenty of Internet places along the cliff top but they're uniformly slow and expensive. Your best bet is at Varkala town, between the centre of the town proper and the train station – look for a sign on the 1st floor saying '**Internet café'** (per hr Rs 35; ⊙ 8am-6pm).

Dangers & Annoyances

There are very strong currents; even experienced swimmers have been swept away. This is one of the most dangerous beaches in Kerala, so be careful and swim between the flags or ask the lifeguards for the best place to swim.

Varkala is, unfortunately, gaining a reputation as a groping hot spot. Women travellers should be careful about wandering alone in isolated areas and after dark. Be sure to dress sensitively, especially if you're going into Varkala town.

Sights & Activities

Varkala is a temple town and the **Janardhana Temple** is on Beach Rd. Non-Hindus may not enter but may be invited into the temple grounds where there is a huge banyan tree and shrines to Ayyappan, Hanuman and other Hindu deities.

Sivagiri Mutt (☎ 2602221) is the headquarters of the Sree Narayana Dharma Sanghom Trust, the ashram devoted to Sree Narayana Guru (1855–1928), Kerala's most popular guru. This is a popular pilgrimage site, and the swami is happy to talk to visitors. If you're serious about studying meditation and philosophy here, it's possible to stay (rooms Rs 100 to 200). There's also a **bookstall** (⊙ 8am-1pm & 2-5pm) selling spiritual texts.

There are numerous centres for **Ayurveda**, **yoga** and **massage**; signs are posted along the cliff top. A recommended place for

Ayurvedic beauty treatments is **Dayana** (☎ 2609464; manicure & pedicure Rs 200, facials Rs 400-800; ☼ 9am-7pm); women only. Readers also have good things to say about **Dr Manoj** (☎ 2601237; drtmanoj@hotmail.com; Hill Top Resort) and **Dr Sathyanandhan** (☎ 2602950; smayur veda@hotmail.com), near Seaview. Single massage treatments cost between Rs 400 and 800, depending on the type.

Eden Garden (☎ 2603910; www.eden-garden.net), a popular Ayurvedic resort, offers single treatments and packages; massages cost €12 to €14; see p274 for accommodation details.

Sleeping

Most places to stay are along the cliff; some open only for the tourist onslaught in November. The quietest places are either inland or at the northern end of the cliff; although the guesthouse reach is spreading inexorably both north and south of the main cliff area. The accommodation scene is similar to Kovalam's (see p268): decent budget places are thin on the ground in high season; outside of the season you'll get great bargains.

The commission racket here is alive and well, so make sure that your rickshaw takes you to the place you've asked for, especially if you're arriving at night.

BUDGET

Along the cliff top and amid the coconut palms inland, accommodation is provided by small hotels and families. Some places haven't yet acquired names, so just look for signs advertising rooms. **Parvathy Bhavan** (☎ 2602596; d Rs 300-400) is a cheap option, but very basic.

Bamboo Village (☎ 2610732; huts Rs 300-500, r Rs 400) There's a short lull in the cliff top carnival here, and these simple but cute bamboo huts, run by a friendly local family, look directly on to the ocean. The front huts are new and bigger; there are also newly built, small, bright rooms behind the huts.

Kerala Bamboo House (☎ 9895270993; huts Rs 500) For a slightly more upmarket bamboo-hut experience, this place has brand-new huts with a charming interior of antique wood and painted bamboo, set well apart from each other. Recommended.

VARKALA

```
0 ————————— 100 m
0 ————————— 0.1 miles
```

Approximate Scale

INFORMATION
Bureau de Change................................**1** D3	
Police Aid Post (Nov-Feb)................**2** B2	
Post Office...**3** D3	

To Kollam (24km)

To Black Beach (20m)

SIGHTS & ACTIVITIES
Dayana...**4** B3	
Dr Manoj (Hill Top Resort)..............**5** A2	
Dr Sathyanandhan............................**6** B2	
Janardhana Temple...........................**7** D3	

SLEEPING
Bamboo Village.................................**8** A1	
Clafouti House...................................**9** A2	
Eden Garden....................................**10** C3	
Evergreen Beach Resort...................**11** A1	
Hill Palace.......................................**12** A2	
Jicky's Rooms..................................**13** B2	
Kerala Bamboo House......................**14** A2	

EATING
Amantha...(see 19)	
Cafe del Mar....................................**21** B2	
Caffe Italiano...................................**22** A2	
Clafouti..**23** A2	
Dolphin Bay Restaurant...................**24** A2	
Gnosh..(see 24)	
Kerala Coffee House........................**25** B2	
No 1 Beach Restaurant....................**26** C3	
Oottupura Vegetarian Restaurant....**27** B2	
Sunset...**28** B2	
Tibet Kitchen...................................(see 5)	

Parvathy Bhavan..............................**15** B2	
Red House.......................................**16** B2	
Sea Pearl Chalets............................**17** C3	
Taj Garden Retreat..........................**18** C3	
Taj Mahal Beach Resort...................**19** A2	
Thiruvambadi Beach Resort.............**20** A1	

TRANSPORT
Autorickshaw Stand.........................**29** B2	
Autorickshaw Stand.........................**30** D3	

Durga Temple

Cliffs

Papanasham Beach

Spring

Helipad

To Varkala Town (2km); Hotel Suprabhatham (2km); Train Station (2km); Sivagiri Mutt (3km); Thiruvananthapuram (42km)

Tank

Temple Junction

Devaswom Building

Lakshadweep Sea

Beach Rd

To Villa Jacaranda (200m)

KERALA

Jicky's Rooms (☎ 2606994; jickys2002@yahoo .co.in; s Rs 200-250, d Rs 200-700) Under the coconut palms behind Oottupura Restaurant, Jicky's Rooms is rated highly by readers. The smaller, cheaper downstairs rooms are good value; the upstairs rooms with balconies are cool and spacious.

Taj Mahal Beach Resort (☎ 2605215; tourists _varkala@hotmail.com; cottages Rs 250, r downstairs/upstairs Rs 400/500) This popular, slightly shambolic operation has great-value rooms and was very much the focus of the backpacker scene at the time of our visit. The accommodation is recommended, but we have had some negative reports about the travel agency here.

MIDRANGE

Evergreen Beach Resort (☎ 2603257; www.ever greenskm.com; d Rs 500, with AC Rs 1000, cottage Rs 1000, with AC Rs 1500; ⊠) This lovely, great-value place is a quick walk to Black Beach; all rooms have balcony and sea views and are set in peaceful gardens.

Eden Garden (☎ 2603910; www.eden-garden .net; d Rs 800) Delightfully situated overlooking paddy fields, this place has a few small, clean, well decorated double rooms set around a lush pond, and is a recommended Ayurvedic resort (see p273). Book ahead.

Red House (☎ 2603324; theredhouse@123india .com; r with breakfast Rs 800) Set in a tranquil spot well back from the cliff-top crowds, this relaxed place has good cottages with mosquito nets.

Sea Pearl Chalets (☎ 2605875; seapearlvarkala@ hotmail.com; d Rs 1100) The rooms here are concrete wigwams on the headland south of Beach Rd. They're a little cramped, but the views across the cliffs are perhaps the best in Varkala.

Clafouti House (☎ 2601414; d Rs 800) This place has an intimate, homy atmosphere, with bright, clean double rooms and the wafting smell of French pastries.

Thiruvambadi Beach Resort (☎ 2601028; d Rs 800-1200) This beautifully furnished place is at the very northern end of the cliff, only metres from Black Beach. The rooms are smallish and comfortable; the sea-facing ones at the front have big balconies.

Hill Palace (☎ 2610142; hillpalace@rediffmail.com; d Rs 1100) A new place that has bright, clean rooms with some chintzy personal touches; all have balconies facing the ocean. Perhaps a little overpriced in high season, but big discounts out of season.

TOP END

Villa Jacaranda (☎ 2610296; www.villa-jacaranda .biz; d Rs 2500) This romantic retreat has four huge, bright, beautiful rooms with balconies, individually decorated with a real sense of style. Front rooms have sea views; the roof-terrace room is especially good. A real find.

Taj Garden Retreat (☎ 2603000; retreat.varkala@ tajhotels.com; s US$100-115, d US$125-135, ste US$135-160; ⊠ ▯ ⊠) Luxury, '80s-style: this opulent but slightly dated resort has spacious rooms, an Ayurvedic centre, bar and health club.

Eating

Many of the cliff-top places are seasonal, opening only from November to February.

Kerala Coffee House (breakfast/mains around Rs 35/80) This is the most atmospheric place on the cliff top, with colourful lighting, a bamboo theme and tree-house dining. It does cocktails, too (Rs 65 to 70).

Hotel Suprabhatham (Varkala Town; meals Rs 18; ⏰ 6.30am-9.30pm) If you want to escape the cliff-top multicuisine scene, this is the locals' choice for cheap, delicious veg food.

No 1 Beach Restaurant (fish dishes around Rs 100) This place, at the southern end of the beach, is rated by long-term visitors for its fish and tandoori specials.

Oottupura Vegetarian Restaurant (mains from Rs 30) This is a popular place with a good range of dishes; great for breakfast *puttu* (wheat and coconut flour with milk, bananas and honey; Rs 35).

Gnosh, Dolphin Bay Restaurant, Caffe Italiano, Tibet Kitchen, Café del Mar and Sunset all offer similar standards (shaky tables and chairs), food (fresh fish on display at night; around Rs 100) and service (very slow). **Amantha** (thalis Rs 30) is a tiny, family-run hut, and **Clafouti** (mains around Rs 40) serves delicious French pastries and good coffee.

You can get an opulent buffet lunch at the restaurant at the Taj Garden Retreat (above) for Rs 300, including use of the pool.

Entertainment

Kathakali performances are organised during December and January; look out for signs advertising location and times.

Although most of the places along the cliff aren't licensed, most will serve beer (around Rs 70), usually in a discreet teapot and with a watchful eye for patrolling police.

Getting There & Away

There are frequent trains to Trivandrum (Rs 25/125 in 2nd/chair class, 40 minutes to one hour) and Kollam (Rs 31/125, 35 minutes), and three a day to Alleppey (Rs 35/125, two hours). It's easy to get to Kollam in time for the morning backwater boat to Alleppey (see the boxed text, p278). From Temple Junction, four daily buses go to/from Trivandrum (Rs 35, 1½ hours) and one goes to Kollam at 11.20am (Rs 25, one hour).

Getting Around

An autorickshaw trip between the train station and the beach is Rs 40, a taxi is about Rs 50. Many places along the cliff top hire out 350cc Enfield Bullets (Rs 300 per day) and Kinetic motor scooters (Rs 200 per day).

KOLLAM (QUILON)

☎ 0474 / pop 379,975

Kollam is the southern gateway to the backwaters, but is not as popular a hub as Alleppey, which gives it a more relaxed feel, and the waterways here are nowhere near as crowded as Alleppey's are becoming (see the boxed text, p278). Surrounded by co-conut palms and cashew plantations on the edge of Ashtamudi Lake, central Kollam is a bustling Keralan market town, but away from the busy main streets, village Kerala reappears with old wooden houses whose red-tiled roofs overhang winding alleys.

Information

There are a couple of ATMs in town.

Cyber Zone (☎ 2766566; ⏰ 9.30am-9.30pm) The fastest of the numerous Internet cafés at the Bishop Jerome Nagar Complex, all of which charge around Rs 20 an hour.

DTPC information centre (☎ 2745625; contact@ dtpckollam.com; ⏰ 7am-7pm) Very helpful; near the KSRTC bus stand.

Post office (☎ 2746607; ⏰ 10am-7.30pm Mon-Sat)

UAE Exchange (☎ 2751240; Bishop Jerome Nagar Complex; ⏰ 9.30am-5.30pm Mon-Sat, to 1pm Sun)

Sights

Stop for a look at the extraordinary **Shrine of Our Lady of Velamkanni** in town, where Christian iconography meets Hindu exuberance. Take a stroll down Main Rd, the commercial hub; the next street south has **Mukkada Bazaar**, with spice warehouses and metal merchants – a fun place to wander in the late afternoon.

Activities

Janakanthi Panchakarma Centre (☎ 2763014; Vaidyasala Nagar, Asraman North; s without/with AC Rs 225/320, d Rs 300) is an Ayurvedic resort, about 5km from Kollam town, which has an idyllic position on the shore of Ashtamudi Lake. Most people stay at the centre for a seven- to 21-day treatment package (seven-day packages start from around Rs 15,000), but you can just visit for a rejuvenation massage and herbal steam bath (Rs 500); a return boat trip from the jetty in Kollam should cost around Rs 250.

Tours

Canoe-boat tours (per person Rs 300; ⏰ 9am & 2pm) through the canals of Munroe Island and across Ashtamudi Lake are organised by the DTPC. These excellent tours (with knowledgeable guides) give you the chance to observe daily life in this isolated village area, and to see *kettuvallam* (rice barge) construction, toddy tapping, coir-making (coconut fibre) and coconut-oil processing, prawn and fish farming, and to do some bird-watching and perhaps a quick spice-garden tour.

Sleeping

BUDGET

The DTPC office keeps a list of **homestays** (Rs 150-200) in and around Kollam.

Government Guest House (☎ 2743620; d Rs 220) This Raj relic, 3km north of the centre on Ashtamudi Lake, has immense rooms with high ceilings and wooden floors. They're a bargain, but it's a pity that the place has fallen into such disrepair. Getting a rickshaw back into town can be difficult.

The cheapest places in town are pilgrim lodges near Sri Uma Maheshwara Temple: **Lekshmi Tourist Home** (☎ 2741067; Main Rd; s/d Rs 100/180) The pick of the lodges – very basic, musty rooms, some with small balconies and clean bathrooms. **Sri Uma Maheswara Tourist Home** (☎ 2743712; Main Rd; s/d Rs 85/160) Basic, grimy rooms; the ones in front are noisy to boot. At the time of writing it was planning to change its name to 'Aravind Guest House'.

KERALA

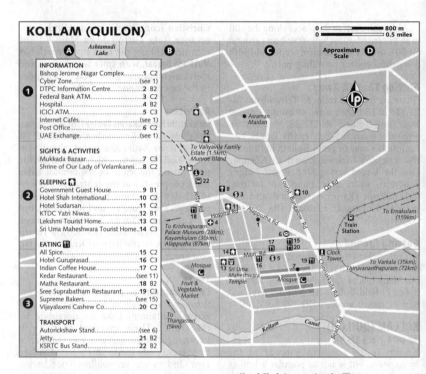

KOLLAM (QUILON)

0 — 800 m
0 — 0.5 miles

Approximate Scale

INFORMATION
Bishop Jerome Nagar Complex...........1 C2
Cyber Zone..(see 1)
DTPC Information Centre................2 B2
Federal Bank ATM.............................3 C2
Hospital...4 B2
ICICI ATM..5 C3
Internet Cafés...................................(see 1)
Post Office...6 C2
UAE Exchange...................................(see 1)

SIGHTS & ACTIVITIES
Mukkada Bazaar.................................7 C3
Shrine of Our Lady of Velamkanni.....8 C2

SLEEPING
Government Guest House....................9 B1
Hotel Shah International..................10 C2
Hotel Sudarsan................................11 C2
KTDC Yatri Niwas............................12 B1
Lekshmi Tourist Home......................13 C3
Sri Uma Maheshwara Tourist Home...14 C3

EATING
All Spice...15 C2
Hotel Guruprasad.............................16 C3
Indian Coffee House........................17 C3
Kedar Restaurant............................(see 11)
Matha Restaurant.............................18 B2
Sree Suprabatham Restaurant.........19 C3
Supreme Bakers..............................(see 6)
Vijayalaxmi Cashew Co....................20 C2

TRANSPORT
Autorickshaw Stand.........................(see 6)
Jetty...21 B2
KSRTC Bus Stand..............................22 B2

MIDRANGE

Hotel Sudarsan (☎ 2744322; www.hotelsudarsan.com; s/d US$8/10, with AC from US$15/20 incl taxes; ✱) Welcoming but overpriced. All non-AC rooms are in the front wing on Alleppey Rd, and are very noisy though spacious. The executive rooms at the back (US$30/35) are smaller and quieter.

KTDC Yatri Nivas (☎ 2745538; s Rs 275-330, d Rs 330-500, s/d with AC Rs 600/750; ✱) Though the rooms are run-down and slightly dysfunctional, they're clean and all have balconies overlooking the lake – spectacular in the mornings. The short taxi-boat ride across the lake to the town (Rs 20) is more fun than an autorickshaw.

Valiyavila Family Estate (☎ 3097979; valiyavila1@ rediffmail.com; s/d Rs 1300/1500, deluxe s/d with AC Rs 2300/2500; ✱) On a breezy peninsula marked by a startlingly ugly sculpture – the 'Goddess of Light' – this is an idiosyncratic, homy family house with big rooms that have balconies over the water (one of which looks directly on to the goddess' extraordinarily pert bosoms). It's a short boat ride from the main boat jetty (it'll send a boat to pick you up).

Hotel Shah International (☎ 2742362; s Rs 210, d Rs 310-350, d with AC from Rs 750; ✱) Slightly shabby and institutional, but rooms are big and renovations were under way at the time of our visit. Executive rooms (Rs 1200), huge and bright with AC and bathtub, are good value.

Eating

Matha Restaurant (biryani Rs 22; ☯ 6am-11pm) This speciality here is biryani – you'll find the place packed with local workers at lunch time tucking into delicious chicken and mutton varieties.

All Spice (mains Rs 30-100; ☯ noon-10pm) Desperate for a Western fast-food fix? Burgers (Rs 45 to 60), pizza (Rs 50 to 90), hot dogs (Rs 35) and ice-cream desserts are served here in a disconcertingly shiny cafeteria-style atmosphere, upstairs from Supreme Bakers.

Hotel Guruprasad (meals Rs 15-17; ☯ 7am-10pm) This bright and charmingly decorated place is good for breakfast (Rs 2 to 11), and has popular daily specials.

Sree Suprabatham Restaurant (meals Rs 18; ☯ 6am-10pm) This veg restaurant is very popular with local families. There's an impres-

KERALA

sive spread of breakfast dishes, especially dosas (from Rs 12).

Kedar Restaurant (mains Rs 40-100; ⏱ 7am-3pm & 7-11pm) The restaurant at Hotel Sudarsan does good Indian food; the tangy fish Malibari (Rs 65) is excellent.

Vijayalaxmi Cashew Co (⏱ 9.30am-8pm) Kollam is a cashew-growing centre and this is one of the biggest exporters. Quality nuts in a variety of flavours are around Rs 200 for 500g.

Supreme Bakers (⏱ 9am-8pm) Opposite the post office, Supreme has a great selection of Indian and Western cakes and sweets.

Indian Coffee House (Main Rd; ⏱ 8am-9pm) is reliably good for breakfast and coffee.

Getting There & Away
BOAT
See the boxed text, p278, for information on cruises to Alleppey. There are public ferry services across Ashtamudi Lake to Guhanandapuram (one hour) and Perumon (two hours), leaving from the jetty. Fares are around Rs 6 return.

BUS
Kollam is situated on the well-serviced Trivandrum–Kollam–Alleppey–Ernakulam bus route, with superfast/superexpress buses going every 10 or 20 minutes to Trivandrum (Rs 37/45, 1½ hours), Alleppey (Rs 40/50, two hours) and Kochi (Rs 70/85, 3½ hours). Buses depart from the KSRTC Bus Stand.

TRAIN
There are frequent trains to Ernakulam (Rs 72/110 in 2nd/chair class, 3½ hours, 10 daily) and Trivandrum (Rs 39/162, 1½ hours, nine daily), and two daily trains to Alleppey (Rs 47/168).

Getting Around
Most autorickshaw trips, including from the town to the other side of the lake, should cost around Rs 10, but they'll try for more at night. There's a prepaid stand near Supreme Bakers.

AROUND KOLLAM
Krishnapuram Palace Museum
Two kilometres south of Kayamkulam (between Kollam and Alleppey), this fully restored **palace** (admission Rs 10; ⏱ 10am-1pm & 2-5pm Tue-Sun) is a fine example of Keralan architecture. Now a museum, the two-storey palace

houses paintings and antique furniture and sculptures. Its renowned 3m-high mural depicts the Gajendra Moksha, or liberation of Gajendra, the chief of the elephants, as told in the Mahabharata.

Buses (Rs 26) leave Kollam every few minutes for Kayamkulam. Get off at the bus stand near the temple gate, 2km before Kayamkulam. From the bus stand it's an obvious 600m walk to the palace.

ALAPPUZHA (ALLEPPEY)
☎ 0477 / pop 282,727
This pleasant market town is built on canals and surrounded by coconut trees. It's a walking town, with some good old trading houses along the canals, and lovely, shaded paths along which you can stroll through leisurely village life. And, of course, this is the major centre from which to explore the backwaters (see the boxed text, p278). There's also a plentiful supply of great guesthouses here, which means that you can settle in and enjoy, rather than get yourself into an arrive-houseboat-depart frenzy.

NEHRU TROPHY SNAKE BOAT RACE

This famous regatta on Vembanad Lake in Alleppey takes place on the second Saturday of August each year, with scores of long, low-slung *chundan vallams* (snake boats) competing. Each boat is over 30m long with a raised prow like the head of a snake, and is crewed by up to 100 rowers singing in unison and shaded by gleaming silk umbrellas. Watched avidly by thousands of cheering spectators, the annual event celebrates the seafaring and martial traditions of ancient Kerala with floats and performing arts.

Tickets, available from numerous ticket stands, entitle you to seats on bamboo terraces, which are erected for the races. Ticket prices range from Rs 75 to 500 for the best seats in the Tourist Pavilion, which offers views of the finishing point and separates you from gatherings of rowdy men. Take food, drink and an umbrella.

At the time of writing there was talk of tourist boat races being held every month in high season; inquire at the ATDC.

KERALA

THE BACKWATERS

The highlight of a trip to Kerala is travelling through the 900km network of waterways that fringe the coast and wind far inland. The boats cross shallow, palm-fringed lakes studded with cantilevered Chinese fishing nets, and travel along narrow, shady canals where coir (coconut fibre), copra (dried coconut meat) and cashews are loaded on to boats. Along the way are small villages with mosques, churches, temples and schools, and villagers going about their daily chores, and tiny settlements where people live on narrow spits of reclaimed land only a few metres wide

Kerala Tourism (www.keralatourism.org) produces the *Backwater Map*, a detailed map of the region. More information is available on Kerala Tourism's website. The very helpful DTPC information centre in Kollam (see p275) provides a price list of its tours, which is a good way to get an idea of costs.

Tourist Cruises

The popular cruise between Kollam and Alleppey (adult/student Rs 300/250) departs at 10.30am and arrives at 6.30pm, operating daily from August to March and every second day at other times. Many hotels in Kollam and Alleppey take bookings for one or other of these services; some offer cheaper rates but you'll end up paying the difference on board.

Generally, there are two stops: a 1pm lunch stop (be aware that you'll pay extra for every element over the standard meal!) and a brief afternoon chai stop. The crew has an ice box full of fruit, soft drinks and beer to sell. Bring sunscreen and a hat.

It's a scenic and leisurely way to get between the two towns, but as a backwater experience the cruise is not the best – the boat travels along the 'major highways' of the canal system, and you won't see much of the close-up village life that makes the backwaters so magical. Some travellers have reported becoming bored with the eight-hour trip.

Another option is to take the trip halfway (Rs 150) and get off at the **Matha Amrithanandamayi Mission** (☎ 0476-2896278; www.amritapuri.org; Amrithapuri), the ashram of Matha Amrithanandamayi. One of India's very few female gurus, Amrithanandamayi is known as Amma (Mother) and is also called 'The Hugging Mother' because of the *darshan* (blessing) she practices, often hugging thousands of people in all-night sessions. Amma travels for around eight months of the year (so you might be out of luck if you're after a cuddle), but the ashram runs official tours at 5pm each day, and you may be able to get someone to show you around when you arrive off the boat. It's a huge ashram, with around 2000 people living here permanently – monks and nuns, students, Indian families and Westerners. There's food available (even a café!), Ayurvedic treatments, yoga and meditation.

Visitors should dress conservatively and there is a strict code of behaviour. You can stay at the ashram for Rs 150 per day (including simple vegetarian meals) and pick up an onward or return cruise a day or two later. Alternatively, you can take a (free) ferry to the other side of the canal anytime. From here a rickshaw will take you the 10km to Karunagappally (around Rs 80) and you can take one of the frequent buses from there to Alleppey (Rs 27, 1½ hours).

The DTPC in Alleppey also runs some sightseeing tours on tourist boats during the high season (see p280).

Houseboats

Renting a houseboat designed like a *kettuvallam* (rice barge) could be one of your most expensive experiences in India, but it's worth every rupee. Drifting through quiet canals lined with coconut palms, eating deliciously authentic Keralan food, meeting local villagers and sleeping on the water under a galaxy of stars – it's a world away from the clamour of India.

Houseboats cater for groups (up to eight bunks) or couples (one or two double bedrooms). Food (and an on-board chef to cook it!) is generally included in the quoted cost. Houseboats can be chartered through the DTPC in Kollam or Alleppey, or one of the multitude of private operators.

This is the biggest business in Kerala, and some operators are unscrupulous. The boats come in a range of qualities, from veritable rust buckets to floating palaces – your safest bet is to lay eyes on the boat you'll be travelling in before agreeing on a price and make sure that everything (eg food) has been included in the price you've agreed on.

Travel-agency reps will be trying to sell you a boat as soon as you set foot in Kerala, and most of the bad experiences we hear about are from people who booked their trip outside the backwater hub towns. Given the size of the fleet of boats for rent (250 and counting in Alleppey, only a handful in Kollam), it's probably safer to wait until you hit Alleppey or Kollam to organise your trip (even if it means waiting for a day or two). Your choice is greater in Alleppey, but it's also the more popular base and you're quite likely to get caught in something approaching backwater gridlock there in high season.

It's possible to travel between Alleppey and Kollam, or Alleppey and Kochi, by houseboat over 24 hours but only on larger boats that have an outboard motor, which not only cost more but aren't as environmentally friendly, nor as peaceful. Those that are propelled by punting with two long bamboo poles obviously don't allow you to cover as much distance (no more than 15km in 24 hours, usually a round trip from Alleppey), but are cheaper and a wonderfully relaxing way to travel.

Prices are hugely variable. For a punting boat for two people for 24 hours you should expect to pay anything from Rs 3000; for a motorboat, anything from Rs 6000. Shop around: outside the high season you should be able to negotiate a bargain; in peak season you'll definitely have to pay more.

Village Tours & Canoe Boats

Village tours usually involve small groups of five to six people, a knowledgeable guide and an open canoe or covered *kettuvallam*. The tours (from Kochi, Kollam or Alleppey) last from 2½ to six hours and cost around Rs 300 to 550 per person. You visit villages to watch coir making, boat building, toddy tapping and fish farming, and on the longer trips a traditional Keralan lunch is provided. The Munroe Island trip from Kollam (see p275) is an excellent tour of this type; the Tourist Desk in Ernakulam also runs recommended tours (see p293).

In Alleppey, rented canoe boats offer a nonguided laze through the canals on a small, covered canoe for up to four people (Rs 600 for four hours) – the ultimate way to spend a relaxing afternoon.

Public Ferries

Most passengers on the eight-hour Kollam–Alleppey cruise will be Western travellers. If you want the local experience, or a shorter trip, there are State Water Transport boats between Alleppey and Kottayam (Rs 10, 2½ hours, five boats daily from 7.30am to 5.30pm). The trip crosses Vembanad Lake and has a more varied landscape than the Alleppey cruise.

Environmental Issues

Environmental problems such as pollution, land reclamation and industrial and agricultural development seriously threaten the backwaters and the communities that live on their banks. It's estimated that the backwaters are only at one-third of their mid-19th-century levels. Many migratory birds no longer visit the backwaters. Another very obvious problem is the unhindered spread of water hyacinth (African moss or Nile cabbage), which clogs many stretches of the canals.

The Keralan authorities have introduced an ecofriendly accreditation system for houseboat operators. Among the categories an operator must fulfil before being issued with the 'Green Palm Certificate' are the installation of solar panels and sanitary tanks for the disposal of waste, as well as trying to minimise the use of outboard motors. Although the system is still new, ask operators whether they have the requisite certification. Seriously consider choosing a punting, rather than motorised, boat.

KERALA

Orientation

The bus stand and boat jetty are close to each other; the hotels are spread far and wide. The train station is 4km southwest of the town centre. The beach is about 2km from the city centre; it's a nice, shaded walk, but there's no shelter at the beach itself and swimming is dangerous.

Information

There are a few ATMs around town, including Federal and State Banks facing each other across YMCA Rd.

Danys Bookshop (Hotel Royale Park; 10am-8.30pm) Has a small but good selection of books about India and some English fiction.

DTPC Tourist Reception Centre (☎ 2253308) Very helpful.

Mailbox (☎ 2339994; Boat Jetty Rd; 8.30am-11.30pm)

National Cyber Park (☎ 2238688; YMCA Compound; 10am-10pm Mon-Sat)

UAE Exchange (☎ 2264408; cnr Cullan & Mullackal Rds; 9.30am-6pm Mon-Sat, to 1pm Sun) Changes cash and travellers cheques.

Tours

The many travel agencies around town offer canoe boat tours to the backwaters; see the boxed text, p278.

The DTPC runs a number of boat tours during high season (November to March):

Alleppey–Kumarakom & Alleppey–Kottayam (per person Rs 150; 10am) Two hours each way, with an hour to explore either destination.

Explore Kuttanad (per person Rs 150; 10am) A round trip of the backwaters around Alleppey.

Round the Venice (per person Rs 100; 9am & 2.30pm) A sightseeing tour around Alleppey town.

Sleeping

Recent years have seen a welcome explosion in guesthouse and 'heritage home' accommodation in Alleppey, which is better value and a much nicer experience than the deeply uninspiring hotels.

BUDGET

Komala Hotel (☎ 2243631; s/d/tr from Rs 172/279/322, s/d/tr with AC Rs 495/605/792 incl tax; 🕮) This conveniently located hotel has cheap, drab, musty rooms. The ambitiously named 'elegant' doubles (Rs 500) are a more spacious version.

Brothers Tourist Home (☎ 2251653; s/d from Rs 130/250) This place has clean but spartan rooms, some of which are a bit noisy. The more expensive 'deluxe' rooms have better (read: tackier) furniture and are otherwise poor value.

Hotel Raiban (☎ 2251930; s/d Rs 160/225, d with AC Rs 800; 🕮) Almost across the road from Brothers Tourist Home, with basic rooms in an institutional setting. Brothers' ordinary rooms are slightly better than these, but both places have a similarly odd take on 'deluxe'.

Government Guest House (☎ 2246502; d Rs 220) North of town, and by far the best place for the price; in theory you need to organise ahead to stay here, but it might be worth just showing up and trying your luck.

MIDRANGE & TOP END

Gowri Residence (☎ 2236371; www.gowriresidence.com; d from Rs 400, with AC Rs 900; 🕮) A great, friendly heritage home, near Uduppi Sree Krishna Temple, with a selection of spacious and comfortable rooms with mosquito nets. The owners will pick you up and drop you off in town anytime, there are free bicycles and the travel desk is reliable. Decent food is served in gazebos in the front garden.

Sona (☎ 2235211; www.sonahome.com; d Rs 700) This heritage home has five cool and spacious rooms with high rosewood ceilings, four-poster beds with nets and private sit-outs overlooking a well-kept garden. The family here is a pioneer of the homestay scene, and manages to be knowledgeable and charming without being overbearing.

Cherukara Nest (☎ 2251509; lakes_lagoon@satyam.net.in; d Rs 550-750, with AC Rs 1000; 🕮) This is a gracious, century-old family home, with four spacious doubles that have plenty of character, lovely furnishings and mosquito nets. Breakfast included.

Johnson's The Nest (☎ 2245825; johnsongilbert lk1@hotmail.com; d Rs 400) This place, near Convent Sq, has big, bright, breezy rooms with mosquito nets and balconies.

Anamika (☎ 242044; www.anamikahome.com; Boat Jetty Rd; d with breakfast Rs 1500) An elegant old Syrian Christian home located out of town towards the beach, this homestay has four big, cool rooms and a sense of peaceful grandeur.

Palmy Lake Resorts (☎ 2235938; palmyresorts@yahoo.com; Punnamada Rd East; cottages Rs 750) This small homestay is about 2km out of town (pick-up and drop-off provided), right on

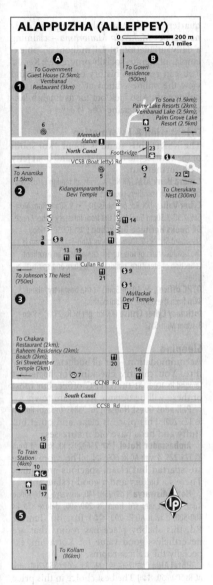

ALAPPUZHA (ALLEPPEY)

INFORMATION
Bank of India..1 B3
Canara Bank...2 B2
Danys Bookshop...3 A2
DTPC Tourist Reception Centre....................4 B2
Federal Bank ATM.....................................(see 3)
Mailbox...5 A2
National Cyber Park.......................................6 A1
Post Office..7 A4
State Bank ATM..8 A2
UAE Exchange...9 B3

SLEEPING
Brothers Tourist Home................................10 A5
Hotel Raiban..11 A5
Komala Hotel..12 B1

EATING
Green's Restaurant......................................13 A3
Hot Kitchen...(see 14)
Hotel Aryas...14 B2
Hotel Aryas...15 A4
Hotel Naalukettu...16 B4
Indian Coffee House....................................17 A5
Indian Coffee House....................................18 B2
Kream Korner...19 A3
Kream Korner...20 B4
New Green's Vegetarian Restaurant.......(see 3)
Sree Durga Bhavan Udipi Hotel..................21 A3

TRANSPORT
Bus Stand..22 B2
Jetty...23 B2

stylish cottages with sitouts, outdoor showers and loads of peace and quiet.

Raheem Residency (☎ 2230767; www.raheemresidency.com; Beach Rd; s/d from €90/110; ❄ ⚘) The only top-end place worth considering, this is a romantic, architecturally acclaimed refurbishment of an 1860s building. All rooms have bathtubs and beautiful antique furniture. The common areas are airy and comfortable, and there's a thoughtfully stocked library.

Eating

Kream Korner (Mullackal Rd; dishes Rs 40-100; ⦿ 9am-10pm) Calling itself an 'art café', this place has a relaxed atmosphere and is popular with Indian and foreign families. There's a multicuisine menu with tandoori choices (half-chicken Rs 100) and a range of ice-cream desserts. There's also a branch on Cullan Rd.

Hotel Naalukettu (dishes around Rs 30; ⦿ 6am-10pm) A great range of Keralan fish specialities, and biryanis (Rs 18 to 20) and fish meals (Rs 24) at lunch time.

Green's Restaurant (Cullan Rd; dishes Rs 25-45; ⦿ 8am-10.30pm) Popular with locals and travellers alike, this place does good lunch-time fish curry and North Indian meals (Rs 25 to 30), as well as a great range of veg and nonveg dishes. There's a vegetarian branch called New Green's Vegetarian Restaurant (YMCA Rd).

the backwaters. Accommodation is in spacious bamboo-weave huts or cottages. It's a lovely peaceful place with charming personal service. Meals provided on request.

Palm Grove Lake Resort (☎ 2235004; Punnamada; cottages d/tr Rs 950/1200) On Punnamada Lake, close to the starting point of the Nehru Cup race, this is an upmarket option, with

KERALA

Vembanad Restaurant (☎ 2243752; mains Rs 40-150; ☷ 6am-10.30pm) You can dine pool side at the restaurant at the Alleppey Prince Hotel; there's a small selection of good dinner dishes and live music from 7.30pm to 9.30pm.

Chakara Restaurant (☎ 2230767; 3 courses €10; ☷ 12.30-2.30pm & 7-10.30pm) The restaurant at Raheem Residency is the best in town, with an imaginative menu that combines elements of traditional Keralan and European cuisine. Grovers Estate wine is available at Rs 990 per bottle.

There are plenty of good places around for cheap vegetarian meals and South Indian breakfasts, including **Hot Kitchen** (Mullackal Rd), **Sree Durga Bhavan Udipi Hotel** (Cullan Rd) and two branches of **Hotel Aryas** (Mullackal Rd & YMCA Rd). There are also a few bakeries and restaurants near the boat jetty that serve good cheap food, and two branches of the **Indian Coffee House** (Mullackal Rd & YMCA Rd).

Getting There & Away
BOAT
Ferries run to Kottayam from the jetty on VCSB (Boat Jetty) Rd; see p278.

BUS
Services run frequently on the Trivandrum–Kollam–Alleppey–Ernakulam route, with buses to Trivandrum (Rs 74, 3½ hours, every 20 minutes) also stopping at Kollam and Kochi (Rs 30, 1½ hours). Buses to Kottayam (Rs 22, 1¼ hours, every 30 minutes) are considerably faster than the ferry.

TRAIN
The train station is about 4km southwest of the town centre. There are frequent trains to Ernakulam (Rs 24/158 in 2nd class/3AC, 1½ hours).

KOTTAYAM
☎ 0481 / pop 172,867
Kottayam's town centre is a rather ugly mess of concrete buildings and traffic, but it makes a pleasant enough stopover between Alleppey and the Western Ghats. When the Portuguese began forcing Keralan Christians to switch allegiance to Catholicism in the 14th century, the Orthodox churches moved inland to Kottayam, and the city is now a place of churches and seminaries.

Kottayam district was the first in India to achieve total literacy, and today it's the head-quarters of the Malayalam-language daily newspaper *Malayala Manorama* – claiming a daily circulation of 1.1 million, it's an exemplar of literate, socially progressive Kerala. You can read the history of the paper and view the online edition at www.manorama online.com. Also look out for its English-language news magazine *The Week*.

Orientation & Information
The KSRTC bus stand is about 1km south of the centre; the train station and boat jetty a bit further out.

Canara Bank ATM (KK Rd) Accepts all foreign cards; you can also cash travellers cheques here.

Cyber Valley (KK Rd; per hr Rs 20; ☷ 9.30am-8pm Mon-Sat, 2.30-7.30pm Sun) Upstairs from Intimacy Cyber Cruise.

DC Books Heritage Bookshop (☎ 300501; Good Shepherd St; ☷ 9.30am-7.30pm Mon-Sat) Kottayam is the headquarters of this superb chain, with an excellent collection of literature, philosophy, culture and spirituality titles.

DTPC office (☷ 10am-5pm) At the boat jetty, about 3km from the centre, at Kodimatha.

Intimacy Cyber Cruise (KK Rd; per hr Rs 25; ☷ 9am-8.30pm Mon-Sat)

Sleeping
Accommodation – for all budgets – is pretty dire. You can try checking for **homestays** (around Rs 1000) at the DTPC office, but most of these will be outside Kottayam town.

Paikados Guest House (☎ 2584340; Sastri Rd; s/d Rs 125/200) This place is clean and quiet but stuffy and beds have old mattresses.

Ambassador Hotel (☎ 2563293; KK Rd; s/d from Rs 175/225, d with AC Rs 600; ☒) The rooms here are spartan but clean, spacious and quiet. There's a bakery and a good restaurant.

Hotel Aiswarya (☎ 2581440; aiswarya_Int@yahoo .com; Azad Lane; s/d from Rs 200/300, deluxe s/d Rs 400/500, d with AC Rs 700; ☒) Just off Temple Rd, this shabby place has rooms that are nevertheless good value for Kottayam, especially the deluxe rooms.

Hotel Aida (☎ 2568391; MC Rd; s/d Rs 350/700, with AC Rs 500/850; ☒) The best choice in this price range, with comfortable but dark and dowdy rooms.

Windsor Castle (☎ 2363637; www.thewindsor castle.net; s/d Rs 1950/2300, cottages Rs 3700; ☒ ☒) This grandiose carbuncle of a building has the best rooms in Kottayam – minimally furnished, spacious and with bathtub – but they're still overpriced. It also has more

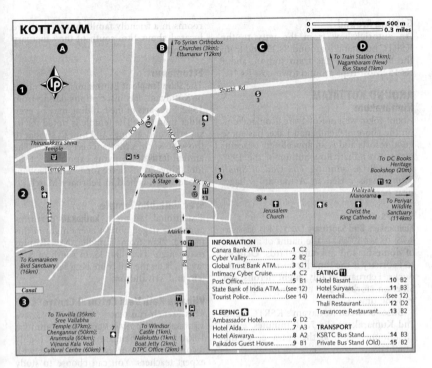

KOTTAYAM

Thirunakkara Shiva Temple

INFORMATION	
Canara Bank ATM...............1	C2
Cyber Valley......................2	B2
Global Trust Bank ATM........3	C1
Intimacy Cyber Cruise........4	C2
Post Office.......................5	B1
State Bank of India ATM....(see 12)	
Tourist Police...................(see 14)	

SLEEPING 🏠	
Ambassador Hotel...............6	D2
Hotel Aida........................7	A3
Hotel Aiswarya...................8	A2
Paikados Guest House..........9	B1

EATING 🍽	
Hotel Basant......................10	B2
Hotel Suryaas.....................11	B3
Meenachil......................(see 12)	
Thali Restaurant.................12	D2
Travancore Restaurant..........13	B2

TRANSPORT	
KSRTC Bus Stand...............14	B3
Private Bus Stand (Old).....15	B2

luxurious cottages set in lake-side grounds, with sitouts over the lake. There are two good restaurants, and nonguests can use the pool (Rs 150).

Eating

Travancore Restaurant (dishes around Rs 50; ⏰ noon-9pm) This clean and bright place, off KK Rd, does a great range of fish, chicken and mutton dishes, including fish thalis at lunch (Rs 30).

Thali Restaurant (KK Rd; thalis Rs 40-50; ⏰ 8am-8.30pm) This South Indian veg place, part of an upmarket restaurant complex at the Homestead Hotel, does a variety of lunch-time thalis.

Meenachil (KK Rd; ⏰ noon-3pm & 6-10pm) Upstairs from the Thali Restaurant, Meenachil does nonveg, Chinese and tandoori dishes.

Nalekattu (dishes Rs 60-125; ⏰ 7-11pm) The traditional Keralan restaurant at the Windsor Castle is set in an open-walled pavilion and serves delicious Keralan specialities such as *chemeen* mango curry (prawns with raw mango, chilli and coconut, Rs 125) and *tharavu* (duck in rich coconut gravy, Rs 110).

There are some good places along TB Rd, including **Hotel Suryaas** (dishes Rs 20-35; ⏰ 9am-10pm), with North and South Indian and Chinese veg cuisine; and the popular **Hotel Basant** (nonveg meals Rs 20; ⏰ 8.30am-9pm), which does good lunch-time biryanis (Rs 40 to 45).

Getting There & Away

BOAT
Ferries run to Alleppey; see p278.

BUS
The KSRTC bus stand has numerous buses to Trivandrum (Rs 70, four hours, every 20 minutes) and Kochi (Rs 33, two hours, every 30 minutes). There are also buses to Kumily for Periyar Wildlife Sanctuary (Rs 52, four hours, every 30 minutes) and Munnar (Rs 80, 5½ hours, five daily).

TRAIN
Kottayam is well served by express trains running between Trivandrum (Rs 51/221 2nd class/3AC, three hours, five daily) and Ernakulam (Rs 27/188, 1½ hours, six daily).

KERALA

Getting Around

An autorickshaw from the jetty to the KSRTC bus stand is around Rs 25, and from the bus stand to the train station, about Rs 15. Most trips around town cost Rs 10.

AROUND KOTTAYAM
Kumarakom

About 16km west of Kottayam, Kumarakom, on the shore of Vembanad Lake, has some good resorts and is an appealingly peaceful place. Arundhati Roy, author of the 1997 Booker Prize–winning *The God of Small Things*, was raised in Aymanam village, near here.

SIGHTS

Kumarakom Bird Sanctuary (☎ 2525864; admission Rs 45; ⏰ 6am-5.30pm) is the haunt of a variety of domestic and migratory birds. October to February is the time for cormorants and ducks; February to July, night herons and Siberian storks. Early morning is the best viewing time.

Buses between Kottayam's KSRTC stand and Kumarakom (Rs 7, 30 minutes, every 15 minutes) stop at the entrance to the sanctuary.

SLEEPING & EATING

Coconut Lagoon (☎ 2524491; coconutlagoon@cghearth .com; cottages US$160-190; 🍴 🛪) This sprawling resort has beautiful cottages constructed from *tharawads*. There's a great range of activities offered, including cooking classes, traditional music classes and village walks. This place can only be reached by boat, from the private jetty just north of the sanctuary entrance – ring ahead to organise pick-up.

Taj Garden Retreat (☎ 2524377; retreat.kumara kom@tajhotels.com; s/d US$150/160, cottage s/d US$190/200, villa US$320; 🍴 🛪) The height of secluded luxury, this excellent resort has rooms in a lovingly restored colonial house, cottages on a lagoon in extensive grounds and luxury villas on the lake.

Both of the resorts have restaurants and Ayurveda centres, and can organise various opportunities for boating and birdwatching. If your budget doesn't stretch to such indulgence, there's also **Lakshmi Hotel** (☎ 2523313; www.lakshmiresorts.com; s/d Rs 2000/2300), which has decent but not luxurious rooms, or **Mooleppura Guest House** (☎ 2525980; r without/ with AC Rs 600/1000; 🛪), which has small, basic

rooms in a friendly family home. Both are located about 1km south of the sanctuary entrance.

Ettumanur

The **Shiva Temple** at Ettumanur, 12km north of Kottayam, has inscriptions dating from 1542, but parts of the building may be even older than this. The temple is noted for its superb woodcarvings and murals similar to those at Kochi's Mattancherry Palace. The annual **festival**, involving exposition of the idol (Shiva in his fierce form) and elephant processions, is held in February/March.

Sree Vallabha Temple

Traditional, all-night **kathakali** performances are staged almost every night at this temple, 2km from Tiruvilla. Non-Hindus may watch. Tiruvilla, 35km south of Kottayam, is on the rail route between Ernakulam and Trivandrum.

Vijnana Kala Vedi Cultural Centre

This French-run **centre** (☎ 0468-2214483; www .vijnanakalavedi.org; Tarayil Mukku) at Aranmula, 10km from Chengannur, offers highly recommended courses in Indian arts with expert teachers. You can choose to study two from a range of 15 subjects, including Ayurveda, *kathakali* or *kathakali* make-up, *mohiniattam* and *bharatanatyam* (classical dances), Carnatic or percussive music, mural painting, Keralan cooking, languages (Malayalam, Sanskrit and Hindi) and *kalarippayat*. Classes are generally individual and are held for a minimum of three hours per day, Monday to Friday.

Fees, which include lessons, accommodation in the village and all meals, are US$200/630 per week/month – less for longer stays. You can volunteer to teach English to children in the village schools, which will entitle you to a discount on your fees. Short stays of one to three nights are also possible (US$30 per night).

THE WESTERN GHATS

PERIYAR WILDLIFE SANCTUARY
☎ 04869

Periyar (www.periyartigerreserve.org; admission Indian/ foreigner Rs 12/150; ⏰ 6am-6pm), South India's most popular wildlife sanctuary, encompasses 777 sq km, with a 26-sq-km artificial lake created by the British in 1895. It's home to bison, sambar, wild boar, langur, 900 to 1000 elephants and 35 to 40 tigers. This is an established tourist spot, and can sometimes feel like Kovalam-in-the-Ghats, but the mountain scenery on the road up, the lake cruise and a jungle walk make for an enjoyable visit. Bring warm and waterproof clothing.

Orientation

Kumily, 4km from the sanctuary, is a small strip of hotels, spice shops and Kashmiri emporiums. Thekkady is the centre inside the park with the KTDC hotels and boat jetty. When people refer to the sanctuary, they tend to use Kumily, Thekkady and Periyar interchangeably.

Information

DC Books (☎ 222548; ⏱ 9.30am-9.30pm) Has a small but quality selection of fiction and books about India.

DTPC office (bus stand; ⏱ 7.30am-6.30pm)

Internet centre (per hr Rs 40; ⏱ 9.30am-9.30pm) Near Lourdes Church.

IR Communications (per hr Rs 50; ⏱ 7am-11pm) Next to Spice Village.

Project Tiger office (☎ 322027; ⏱ 10am-5pm Mon-Sat) If you want to delve deeper, there's a Project Tiger inside the park, where innovative efforts to conserve both the natural environment and the local tribal people are underway.

State Bank of Travancore (⏱ 10am-3.30pm Mon-Fri, to 12.30pm Sat) Changes travellers cheques and currency; the ATM accepts foreign cards.

Wildlife Information Centre (☎ 322028) Above the boat jetty in Thekkady.

Wildlife interpretation centre (⏱ 7.30am-7.30pm) This excellent centre at Spice Village (see p287) is open to nonguests. The resident naturalist shows slides between 7.30pm and 9.30pm and answers questions about the park.

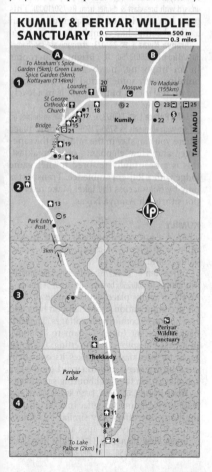

KUMILY & PERIYAR WILDLIFE SANCTUARY

INFORMATION	
DC Books..	1 A1
DTPC Office...	(see 23)
Internet Centre.....................................	2 B1
IR Communications.............................	(see 19)
Kumily Central Hospital......................	3 A1
Post Office...	4 B1
Post Office...	5 A2
Project Tiger Office.............................	6 A3
State Bank of Travancore ATM...........	7 B1
Wildlife Information Centre................	8 B4
Wildlife Interpretation Centre...........	(see 19)

SIGHTS & ACTIVITIES	
Ecotourism Centre...............................	9 A2
Mayura Ayurvedic Centre...................	(see 13)
Ticket Office...	10 B4

SLEEPING	
Aranya Nivas..	11 B4
Coffee Inn...	12 A2
Gangothri Resort.................................	13 A2
Green View Homestay.........................	14 A2
Michael's Inn..	15 A1
Periyar House.......................................	16 A3
Prime Castle...	17 A1
Rolex Tourist Home.............................	18 A1
Rose Cottage.......................................	(see 14)
Spice Village..	19 A2
White House...	(see 12)

EATING	
Hotel Lakeshore..................................	20 A1

ENTERTAINMENT	
Mudra..	21 A1

TRANSPORT	
Bicycle Hire Shacks.............................	22 B1
Bus Stand...	23 B1
Jetty...	24 B4
Tamil Nadu Bus Station......................	25 B1

KERALA

Sights & Activities

VISITING THE PARK

Two-hour **KTDC boat trips** (lower/upper deck Rs 45/100; ☾ 7am, 9.30am, 11.30am, 2pm & 4pm) on the lake are the usual way of touring the sanctuary. Although the boat trip itself is pleasant enough, any wildlife you'll see will be quite distant. The smaller, more decrepit **Forest Department boats** (per person Rs 15; ☾ 9.30am, 11.30am, 2pm & 4pm) offer a chance to get a bit closer to the animals, and are driven by sanctuary workers who may offer some commentary. Entry to the park doesn't guarantee a place on the boat; get to the **ticket office** (☾ 6.30am-5.30pm) just after the preceding trip leaves, in order to buy tickets for the next (reservations can't be made in advance). The first and last departures offer the best wildlife-spotting prospects.

Guided three-hour **jungle walks** (per person Rs 100; ☾ 7am, 10.30am & 2pm) cover 4km or 5km and are a better way to experience the park close up, accompanied by a trained tribal guide. Note that leeches are common after rain.

A range of more adventurous possibilities for exploring the park can be arranged by staff at the **Ecotourism Centre** (☎ 224571; ☾ 8am-6pm). The two-/three-day 'tiger trail' **treks** (per person Rs 3000/5000), full-day **hikes** (per person Rs 750), three-hour **night treks** (per person Rs 500) and full-day **bamboo rafting** (per person Rs 1000) on the lake are some of the options; see www.periyartigerreserve.org for more information on what's available.

SPICE GARDENS & PLANTATIONS

Spice tours are organised by almost every spice shop and homestay (around Rs 400/600 by autorickshaw/taxi, two to three hours), and are really interesting if you get a knowledgeable guide. Spice gardens are small domestic gardens, whereas plantations are bigger commercial affairs where you may also see harvesting and processing. If you want to see a tea factory in operation (worth it for the smell alone), do it here – tea-factory visits are not permitted in Munnar.

If you'd rather do it independently, you can visit two excellent spice gardens just 5km from Kumily: **Green Land Spice Garden** (☎ 223948; ☾ 7am-7pm) and the organic **Abraham's Spice Garden** (☎ 222919; ☾ 6.30am-7.30pm). There is no set fee at these places, but a tip is appropriate.

AYURVEDA

Mayura Ayurvedic Centre (☎ 223556; massage Rs 300-500; ☾ 8am-9pm) is recommended for massage and other treatments.

Sleeping & Eating

INSIDE THE SANCTUARY

The Ecotourism Centre (see left) can arrange accommodation in a **forest cottage** (d with meals Rs 2000).

The KTDC has three hotels in the park. It's a good idea to make reservations (at any KTDC office), particularly for weekends. Note that there's effectively a curfew at these places – guests are not permitted to leave their hotels after 6pm.

Periyar House (☎ 222026; periyar@sancharnet .in; s/d with breakfast & dinner from Rs 750/1000) This place has a variety of uninspiring rooms in a school camp–like complex.

Aranya Nivas (☎ 222023; aranyanivas@sancharnet .in; s/d from Rs 2250/3750; ☒) Bright, clean rooms in an imposing, newly renovated stone building with some period touches. There are no real views, but the pool is in a lovely forest setting.

Lake Palace (☎ 222023; aranyanivas@sancharnet.in; s/d ste with all meals Rs 5750/7250) The only place where you can stay in the midst of the sanctuary and view elephants over breakfast, this is a beautifully restored former game lodge with a Raj-era ambience. Transport is only by boat across the lake. Make reservations through Aranya Nivas.

KUMILY

There's a growing homestay scene in Kumily, with plenty of cheap, or just great-value, rooms on offer.

Coffee Inn (☎ 222763; coffeeinn@sancharnet.in; huts/cottages Rs 200/250; breakfast Rs 20-60) This is a lovely, friendly place with a range of simple accommodation, from bamboo huts and tree houses to comfortable cottages. The laid-back restaurant (open 7.30am to 7.30pm), in a peaceful spice garden setting, is a great place for breakfast – it bakes its own delicious brown bread, and you may be joined by monkeys from the neighbouring sanctuary.

White House (☎ 222987; huts/r Rs 250/300, cottages Rs 350-400) Next door to Coffee Inn, this charming homestay offers very similar accommodation in a variety of shapes and sizes.

Green View Homestay (☎ 211015; www.suresh greenview.com; s Rs 150, d Rs 200-600) This homy place has clean, bright rooms, a lush garden and friendly hosts; food is available as well as Keralan cooking demonstrations. Rose Cottage, next door, is also good.

Rolex Tourist Home (☎ 222081; s Rs 150-400, d Rs 250-600) This is the best budget-hotel choice, with small, clean, characterless rooms – you're much better off in a homestay.

Gangothri Resort (☎ 222299; d/tr Rs 700/1000) This new place has seven clean, cool, bright rooms with views across to the sanctuary's hills.

Prime Castle (☎ 223469; d Rs 850-1200) These are immaculate, spacious rooms with balconies and attentive service. The budget annexe (per person Rs 75) has small, dark, cheap rooms.

Michael's Inn (☎ 222355; michaelsinn@sify.com; r without/with AC Rs 1200/1600; 🐾) This is a friendly, well-run place with chintzy but clean and comfortable rooms, some of which are a bit small.

Spice Village (☎ 222314; spicevillage@cghearth .com; cottage s US$135-180, d US$145-180; breakfast/ lunch/dinner Rs 300/500/500; 🐾) This place has attractive, spacious cottages in beautifully kept grounds. All the facilities (including the Raj-style bar with billiard table) are open to nonguests. The restaurant (open 7.30am to 9.30am, 12.30pm to 2.30pm and 7.30pm to 9.30pm) does lavish buffets, and if you come for dinner you can also attend a Keralan cooking demonstration.

There are plenty of good cheap veg restaurants in the bazaar area, especially between the bus stand and Lourdes Church. **Hotel Lakeshore** (dishes around Rs 40; 🕙 7am-10pm), a gaudily decorated 1st-floor place, is a local favourite for veg and nonveg dishes – the *malai kofta* (Rs 35) is a winner.

Entertainment

Mudra (☎ 211059; admission Rs 125; shows 🕙 4.30pm & 7pm) *Kathakali* shows twice a day; make-up starts 30 minutes before the show begins.

Getting There & Away

Buses originating or terminating at Periyar start and finish at Aranya Nivas, but they also stop at the Kumily bus stand, at the eastern edge of town.

Eight buses daily operate between Kochi and Kumily (Rs 84, six hours) and buses leave every 30 minutes for Kottayam (Rs 52, four hours). There are two direct buses daily to Trivandrum (Rs 107, eight

hours). One afternoon bus goes to Munnar (Rs 50, 4½ hours).

Tamil Nadu buses leave every 30 minutes to Madurai (Rs 38, four hours) from the bus stand just over the border.

Getting Around

Kumily is about 4km from Periyar Lake; you can catch the bus (almost as rare as the tigers), take an autorickshaw (Rs 30) or set off on foot; it's a pleasant, shady walk into the park. **Bicycle hire** (per hr Rs 4; 🕙 6.30am-8pm) is available from a couple of shacks near the bus stand.

MUNNAR

☎ 04865 / elev 1524m

Once known as the High Range of Travancore, Munnar is the commercial centre of some of the world's highest tea-growing estates. Set amid dramatic mountain scenery, the craggy peaks, manicured tea estates and crisp mountain air make this former hill station an ideal retreat. The centre of the town is noisy and grubby, but the surrounds are delightful.

Information

There are ATMs near the bridge, south of the bazaar.

DTPC Tourist Information Office (☎ 531516; 🕙 10am-6pm) Helpful.

Ramm Communications (per hr Rs 50; 🕙 8am-10pm) Cramped and slow Internet access, but there's not much choice.

State Bank of Travancore (☎ 230274; 🕙 10am-3.30pm Mon-Sat, to noon Sun) Changes travellers cheques.

Sights & Activities

The main reason to be in Munnar is to explore the hills around it (see p288 for tour options). All the travel agencies and autorickshaw drivers, as well as most passers-by, want to organise a day of sightseeing for you – shop around. The DTPC can organise half-day, full-day and two- to four-day **treks** around Munnar.

Tata Tea Museum (☎ 230561; adult/child Rs 50/25; 🕙 10am-4pm) is as close as you'll get to a working tea factory around Munnar. It's a slightly sanitised and deserted version of the real thing, but it still shows the basic process. There's a guide, and tea tasting is available. A collection of old bits and pieces from the colonial era is also kept here.

KERALA

The stone **Christ Church** (1910), now administered by the Church of South India, has fine stained glass. Inside, brass plaques honour the memory of tea planters.

Tours

The DTPC runs a couple of fairly rushed full-day tours to points around Munnar:

Chinnar Wildlife Tour (per person Rs 300; ☺ 9am-7pm) Chinnar Wildlife Sanctuary (opposite).

Tea Valley tour (per person Rs 250; ☺ 10am-6pm) Echo Point, Top Station and Rajamalai (for Eravikulam National Park), among other places.

Sleeping

Good-value accommodation is hard to find here; the few homestays are your best bet. Ask at the DTPC for newly opened ones.

Krishna Lodge (☎ 230669; s with shared bathroom Rs 100, d with private bathroom Rs 250) Dark and basic rooms in the noisy bazaar.

JJ Cottage (☎ 230104; d Rs 400-500) This homestay has seven very clean, bright rooms with TV and geyser hot water – they're all different, so look at a few.

Westend Cottages (☎ 230954; d with shared bathroom Rs 250, with private bathroom Rs 350-400) There are a few bright, clean doubles in this friendly family home, not far from the bazaar.

Zina Cottages (☎ 230349; d incl tax Rs 500) This place has four nicely furnished, homy rooms with tea-estate views all around.

Sree Narayana Tourist Home (☎ 230212; snan nex@rediffmail.com; s/d from Rs 500/550) These are bright, ugly rooms, some cleaner than others. The more expensive rooms in the annexe at the other end of town are newer but still dowdy.

Royal Retreat (☎ 230240; royalretreat@sify.com; s Rs 850-1650, d Rs 950-1950) This is a comfortable, well-run place with a range of cosy rooms; good value by Munnar's standards.

Edassery Eastend (☎ 230451; info@edasserygroup .com; cottages Rs 1650-2200) Blandly comfortable, spacious rooms, though still overpriced. Single occupancy is 10% less.

There are some good top-end accommodation options in plantations in the hills around Munnar, where the mountain serenity is unbeatable.

Olive Brook (☎ 230588; www.olivebrookmunnar .com; Pothamedu; s Rs 1875-2250, d Rs 2500-3000) Set on 10 acres of cardamom estate, this is a small homestay with spacious and simple rooms. Breakfast and dinner are included.

Activities include cookery classes and hiking through the plantation.

Windermere Estate (☎ 230512; www.windermere munnar.com; Pothamedu; r/cottages with breakfast & dinner Rs 6000/8500) This place manages to be both luxurious and cosy, especially the homy 'farmhouse' rooms. The new cottages are slicker, with spectacular views.

Eating

Early morning food stalls in the bazaar serve breakfast snacks; there are also a few good cheap meals places here, as well as south of town, opposite the sports ground.

Rapsy Restaurant (dishes around Rs 25; ☺ 6.30am-9.30pm) This place is packed at lunch time, with locals eating the beef fry (Rs 14) with Rapsy's famous *parotta*. The biryani (Rs 25 to 40) is good, too.

Hotel Saravan Bhavan (dishes Rs 15-50; ☺ 7am-9.30pm) A popular place for great-value, pure-veg banana-leaf meals (Rs 17), juices and ice creams.

Royal Retreat (dishes Rs 50-100; ☺ noon-3pm & 7.30-9.30pm) The restaurant at this hotel has a cosy, genteel ambience and good multicuisine dishes. The other midrange and top-end hotels also have decent restaurants.

Getting There & Away

Some of the roads around Munnar are in poor condition and may be seriously affected by monsoon rains, so bus times may vary. The main **KSRTC station** (AM Rd) is south of the town, but all buses stop at the stand in the bazaar.

There are around 10 buses a day to Kochi (Rs 70, 4½ hours), mostly in the morning, and a few daily services to Kottayam (Rs 76, five hours), Kumily (Rs 60, five hours) and Trivandrum (Rs 146, nine hours). Tamil Nadu buses to Coimbatore (Rs 80, six hours, two daily) and Madurai (Rs 80, six hours, one daily) leave from the bus stand outside the post office.

Getting Around

Raja Cycles (per hr Rs 8; ☺ 8.30am-7.30pm) hires out bicycles. **Gokulam Bike Hire** (☎ 9447237165; per day Rs 150-250; ☺ 7.30am-7pm) has a couple of motorbikes for rent.

Autorickshaws ply the hills around Munnar with bone-shuddering efficiency; they charge from Rs 150 to nearby places up to Rs 650 for a full day's sightseeing.

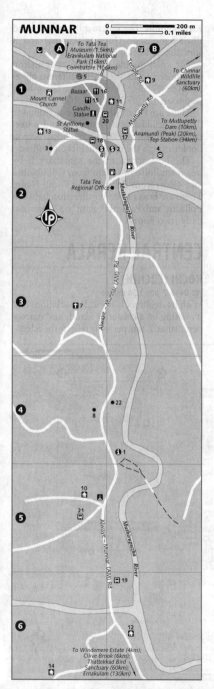

MUNNAR   0 ————— 200 m   0 ————— 0.1 miles

INFORMATION		
DTPC Tourist Information Office	1	B4
Federal Bank ATM	2	B2
Forest Information Centre	3	A2
Post Office	4	B2
Ramm Communications	5	A1
State Bank of Travancore ATM	6	A2

SIGHTS & ACTIVITIES		
Christ Church	7	A3
Sports Ground	8	A4

SLEEPING		
Edassery Eastend	9	B1
JJ Cottage	10	A5
Krishna Lodge	11	B1
Royal Retreat	12	B6
Westend Cottages	13	A1
Zina Cottages	14	A6

EATING		
Hotel Saravan Bhavan	15	A1
Rapsy Restaurant	16	A1

TRANSPORT		
Buses to Kumily & Tamil Nadu	(see 4)	
Buses to Top Station	17	B1
Gokulam Bike Hire	(see 21)	
Jeep & Rickshaw Stand	(see 17)	
KSRTC Bus Stand	18	A2
KSRTC Bus Stand	19	B6
Private Buses to Kumily	20	A1
Private Buses to Tamil Nadu	21	A5
Raja Cycles	22	B4

AROUND MUNNAR

Eravikulam National Park (Indian/foreigner Rs 10/50; 7am-6pm Sep-May), 16km from Munnar, is home to the rare, but almost tame, Nilgiri tahr (a type of mountain goat). From Munnar, an autorickshaw/taxi costs Rs 150/250 return.

Chinnar Wildlife Sanctuary (7am-6pm), about 10km past Marayoor and 60km northeast of Munnar, is home to deer, leopards, elephants and the endangered grizzled giant squirrel. Trekking and tree-house or hut stays within the sanctuary are available; for details contact the **Forest Information Centre** (231 587; enpmunnar@sify.com; 8am-7pm) in Munnar. There is also accommodation in Marayoor.

Top Station, on Kerala's border with Tamil Nadu, has spectacular views over the Western Ghats. From Munnar, four daily buses (Rs 35, from 7.30am) make the steep 32km climb in around an hour; the last bus back from Top Station is at 5pm. Taxis (Rs 700) and rickshaws (Rs 400) can also be hired from along the main street in Munnar for the return trip.

Thattekkad Bird Sanctuary (Indian/foreigner Rs 5/25; 6.30am-7pm Oct-Apr) is a 25-sq-km park, and home to over 270 species, including Malabar grey hornbills, parakeets and rarer species such as the Sri Lankan frogmouth and rose-billed roller, and is an important research

KERALA

area. There's an inspection bungalow and **watchtowers** (r Rs 900) in the sanctuary which you can stay in; contact the **assistant wildlife warden** (☎ 0485-2588302) at Kothamangalam. Otherwise, **Hornbill Camp** (☎ 0484-2310324; www .thehornbillcamp.com; d with full board US$45) has basic but comfortable 'cottage tents' right in the forest, with private bathrooms and sitouts.

Thattekkad is on the Ernakulam–Munnar road. Take a direct bus from Ernakulam to Kothamangalam, or a more frequent bus to Muvattupula, and change there for Kothamangalam – a further 8km. From Kothamangalam, take the Thattekkad bus for the final 15km (30 minutes).

PARAMBIKULAM WILDLIFE SANCTUARY

Parambikulam Wildlife Sanctuary (⏲ 7am-6pm), 135km from Palakkad, stretches around the Parambikulam, Thunakadavu and Peruvaripallam Dams, and covers an area of 285 sq km. It's home to elephants, bison, gaur, sloth bears, wild boars, sambar, chital, crocodiles, tigers, panthers and some of the largest teak trees in Asia. There's also an elephant camp at Kozhikamthi. The sanctuary is best avoided during monsoon (June to August) and it sometimes closes in March and April.

For entry to the sanctuary, permission is required from the **divisional forests officer** (☎ 04253-877233) at Thunakadavu. Three-hour jeep tours (Rs 700) are available.

There are Forest Rest Houses at Thunakadavu, Thellikkal and Anappady and a **treetop hut** (per person Rs 300-360) at Thunakadavu; book through the divisional forests officer.

The best access to the sanctuary is by bus from Pollachi (40km from Coimbatore and 49km from Palakkad) in Tamil Nadu. There are buses in either direction between Pollachi and Parambikulam via Anamalai daily (two hours).

CENTRAL KERALA

KOCHI (COCHIN)

☎ 0484 / pop 1.36 million

With its wealth of historical associations and its setting on a cluster of islands and narrow peninsulas, Kochi perfectly reflects the eclecti-

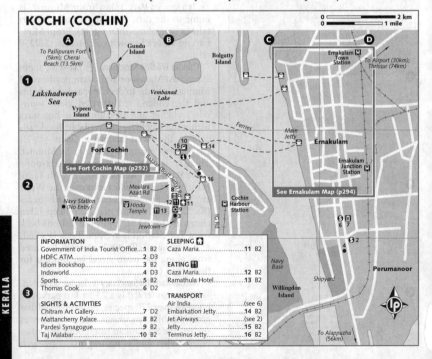

KOCHI (COCHIN)

0 — 2 km
0 — 1 mile

To Pallipuram Fort (5km); Cherai Beach (13.5km)

Gundu Island

Bolgatty Island

Emakulam Town Station

To Airport (30km); Thrissur (74km)

Lakshadweep Sea

Vembanad Lake

Vypeen Island

Ferries

Main Jetty

Ernakulam

Fort Cochin

See Fort Cochin Map (p292)

Moulara Azad Rd

Navy Station (No Entry)

Hindu Temple

Mattancherry

Jewtown

Ernakulam Junction Station

Cochin Harbour Station

See Ernakulam Map (p294)

IG Rd

Navy Base

Shipyard

Willingdon Island

Perumanoor

To Alappuzha (56km)

INFORMATION			SLEEPING		
Government of India Tourist Office	1	B2	Caza Maria	11	B2
HDFC ATM	2	D3			
Idiom Bookshop	3	B2	EATING		
Indoworld	4	D3	Caza Maria	12	B2
Sports	5	B2	Ramathula Hotel	13	B2
Thomas Cook	6	D2			
			TRANSPORT		
SIGHTS & ACTIVITIES			Air India	(see 6)	
Chitram Art Gallery	7	D2	Embarkation Jetty	14	B2
Mattancherry Palace	8	B2	Jet Airways	(see 2)	
Pardesi Synagogue	9	B2	Jetty	15	B2
Taj Malabar	10	B2	Terminus Jetty	16	B2

KERALA

train station to Fort Cochin should cost around Rs 200.

Vasco Tourist Information Centre (Map p292; ☎ 2216215; vascoinformations@yahoo.co.uk; Bastion St, Fort Cochin) hires out bicycles/motorscooters for Rs 40/200 per day.

AROUND KOCHI
Tripunithura

Hill Palace Museum (☎ 0484-2781113; admission Rs 11; ☻ 9am-12.30pm & 2-4.30pm Tue-Sun) at Tripunithura, 12km southeast of Ernakulam en route to Kottayam, was formerly the residence of the Kochi royal family and is an impressive, 49-building palace complex. It now houses the collections of the royal families, as well as 19th-century oil paintings, old coins, sculptures and paintings and temple models. From Cochi, catch the bus to Tripunithura from MG Rd or Shanmgham Rd, behind the Tourist Reception Centre; a rickshaw should cost around Rs 125 return.

Parur & Chennamangalam

About 35km north of Kochi, Parur encapsulates the cultural and religious mosaic of this region. There's a dusty **synagogue**, built around the same time as its famous counterpart in Mattancherry. Nearby is an **agraharam** (place of Brahmins), a small street of closely packed houses that was settled by Tamil Brahmins. Parur also boasts a Syrian Orthodox church, a Krishna temple and a temple dedicated to the goddess Mookambika.

About 4km from Parur is Chennamangalam, with the oldest **synagogue** in Kerala – it's slowly disintegrating. There's a **Jesuit church** and the ruins of a Jesuit college. The Jesuits first arrived in Chennamangalam in 1577 and, soon after their arrival, the first book in Tamil (the written language then used in this part of Kerala) was printed here. You can walk to the **Hindu temple** on the hill overlooking the Periyar River. On the way you'll pass a 16th-century **mosque** as well as Muslim and Jewish **burial grounds**.

Whereas Parur is compact and locals can point you in the right direction, Chennamangalam is best visited with a guide. **Indo World** (Map p290; ☎ 0484-2370127; mail@indoworld tours.com; Heera House, MG Rd, Ernakulam; ☻ 8am-8pm Mon-Sat, to 2.30pm Sun) can organise tours

(around Rs 500 plus guide). It also has an **office** (Map p292; Princess St) in Fort Cochin.

For Parur, catch a bus from the KSRTC bus stand in Kochi (Rs 13, one hour, every 10 minutes). From Parur catch a bus or autorickshaw to Chennamangalam.

THRISSUR (TRICHUR)
☎ 0487 / pop 330,067

Thrissur has long been regarded as Kerala's cultural capital, and it makes good on those claims with the state's most vibrant temple festival scene and a number of schools and institutions that nurture its performing arts. It is a busy, bustling place, home to a community of Nestorian Christians, whose denomination dates back to the 3rd century AD. The main reasons to come here are to visit the Sri Krishna Temple at Guruvayur and the performing arts school, Kerala Kalamandalam (see p304). If you're here during festival season (November to mid-May) Thrissur should be your base for encountering some of Kerala's spiritual celebrations.

Orientation & Information

Thrissur radiates from the Vadakkunathan Kshetram Temple, with the encircling roads named after the four directions.

There's HDFC, UTI and ICICI ATMs in town, accepting all foreign cards.

DTPC office (☎ 2320800; Palace Rd; ☻ 10am-5pm Mon-Sat)

UAE Money Exchange (☎ 2445668; TB Rd; ☻ 9am-6.30pm Mon-Sat, 9.30am-1pm Sun) Next to the Casino Hotel.

Many places in Thrissur offer Internet but connections are painfully slow. Try these places:

Classix Internet Café (Kuruppam Rd; per hr Rs 20; ☻ 9am-9pm Mon-Sat)

Paragon Web Inc (2nd fl, High Rd; per hr Rs 20; ☻ 8am-10.30pm)

Sights & Activities

Right in the centre of Thrissur, the Hindu-only **Vadakkunathan Kshetram Temple** is famed for its artwork. There are a number of interesting churches, including the large **Our Lady of Lourdes Cathedral**, **Puttanpalli (New) Church** and the **Chaldean (Nestorian) Church**.

The **Archaeological Museum** (admission Rs 6; ☻ 9am-5.15pm Tue-Sun), not to be confused with the decrepit State Museum, is also worth a visit. It contains temple models,

KERALA

stone reliefs, Gandharan pieces and reproductions of some of the Mattancherry murals. At the time of writing the museum was set to move into Sakthan Thampuran Palace; check with the DTPC.

Sleeping

Ramanilayam Government Guest House (☎ 233 2016; cnr Palace & Museum Rds; s/d Rs 165/220; ✗) This is the best-value place in town, if you can get in. Huge rooms, with balconies, are painted a particularly calming shade of green, and it's set in big grounds. Ring ahead, or just show up and try sweet-talking them.

Hotel Plaza Tower (☎ 446838; Marar Rd; s/d Rs 150/250, with AC Rs 450/550; ✗) This place has clean rooms, a bit scuffed but cheap.

Hotel Elite International (☎ 2421033; Chembottil Lane; s/d from Rs 240/340, with AC Rs 450/560; ✗ 💻) The decent rooms here have balcony, though some are a bit noisy. Those on the 8th floor (east side) have great views towards the churches.

Hotel Luciya Palace (☎ 2424731; luciyapalace@hotmail.com; s/d Rs 450/575, s/d with AC Rs 675/775; ✗) Considerably more splendid from the outside than it is on the the inside, this hotel off Marar Rd has comfortable rooms. Some of the non-AC rooms are nicer than those with AC.

Siddhartha Regency (☎ 2424773; cnr TB & Veliyannur Rds; s/d Rs 750/900; ✗ 🖥) This place has smallish, pleasant rooms, far from the centre of town but handy for transport.

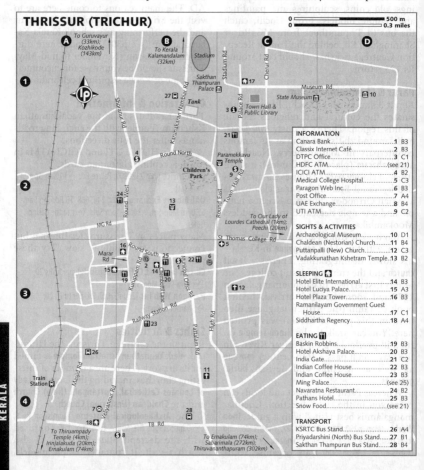

THRISSUR (TRICHUR)

INFORMATION	
Canara Bank	**1** B3
Classix Internet Café	**2** B3
DTPC Office	**3** C1
HDFC ATM	(see 21)
ICICI ATM	**4** B2
Medical College Hospital	**5** C3
Paragon Web Inc	**6** B3
Post Office	**7** A4
UAE Exchange	**8** B4
UTI ATM	**9** C2

SIGHTS & ACTIVITIES	
Archaeological Museum	**10** D1
Chaldean (Nestorian) Church	**11** B4
Puttanpalli (New) Church	**12** C3
Vadakkunathan Kshetram Temple	**13** B2

SLEEPING 🏠	
Hotel Elite International	**14** B3
Hotel Luciya Palace	**15** A3
Hotel Plaza Tower	**16** B3
Ramanilayam Government Guest House	**17** C1
Siddhartha Regency	**18** A4

EATING 🍴	
Baskin Robbins	**19** B3
Hotel Akshaya Palace	**20** B3
India Gate	**21** C2
Indian Coffee House	**22** B3
Indian Coffee House	**23** B3
Ming Palace	(see 25)
Navaratna Restaurant	**24** B2
Pathans Hotel	**25** B3
Snow Food	(see 21)

TRANSPORT	
KSRTC Bus Stand	**26** A4
Priyadarshini (North) Bus Stand	**27** B1
Sakthan Thampuran Bus Stand	**28** B4

Eating

Pathans Hotel (Round South; dishes start from Rs 20; ☺ 6.30am-9.30pm) An atmospheric place, popular with families for its lunch meal (Rs 25). There's a sweets counter downstairs.

Ming Palace (dishes Rs 40-75; ☺ 11am-10pm) In the same building as Pathans Hotel is this dark, plush Chinese restaurant good for noodles and daily specials.

Hotel Akshaya Palace (Chembottil Lane; dishes Rs 13-50; ☺ 6am-midnight) A good selection of fish dishes, and great biryanis at lunch (Rs 20 to 50).

Navaratna Restaurant (Round West; dishes Rs 27-46 ☺ 10am-11pm) An upmarket, North Indian veg place with excellent lunch-time meals (Rs 56).

India Gate (Palace Rd; dishes around Rs 25; ☺ 8.30am-10pm) In the same building as the HDFC Bank, this is a bright, pure-veg place serving an unbeatable range of dosas, including jam, cheese and cashew versions.

Snow Food (☺ 9am-10pm) Also in the same building as India Gate is this place, selling pastries, cakes and ice cream.

There are branches of the **Indian Coffee House** (☺ 7.30am-9.30pm) at Round South and Railway Station Rd, and a **Baskin Robbins** (☺ 10am-10pm) near Hotel Luciya Palace.

Getting There & Away

BUS

There are three bus stands in Thrissur; the KSRTC and Sakthan Thampuran stands in the south and the Priyadarshini (also referred to as North) stand in the north.

KSRTC buses leave around every 30 minutes for Trivandrum (Rs 140, 7½ hours), Kochi (Rs 38, two hours), Calicut (Rs 59, 3½ hours), Palakkad (Rs 30, 1½ hours) and Kottayam (Rs 64, four hours). Hourly buses go to Coimbatore (Rs 55, three hours). There are also buses to Ponnani and Prumpavoor (for connections to Munnar).

The large, private Sakthan Thampuran stand has buses bound for Guruvayur (Rs 16, one hour) and Irinjalakuda. The smaller, private Priyadarshini stand has many buses bound for Shoranur and Palakkad, and Pollachi and Coimbatore. There are also buses from here to Cheruthuruthy (1½ hours, every 10 minutes).

TRAIN

Services run regularly to Ernakulam (Rs 32/158 in 2nd class/3AC, two hours) and Calicut (Rs 73/215, four hours). There are also trains running to Palakkad (Rs 55/180) via Shoranur.

THRISSUR FESTIVALS

In a state where festivals are a way of life, Thrissur is the standout district for temple celebrations. Below are a few of the major events; ask at the DTPC for details of what's on during your visit.

Thypooya Maholsavam (Jan/Feb; Sree Maheswara Temple, Koorkancherry village, 2km from Thrissur) On the final day of this seven-day event, a spectacular *kavadiyattam* procession is held, where hundreds of dancers carry tall, ornate structures (called *kavadis*) on their shoulders – an amazing sight, even from a distance.

Elephant Race (Feb/Mar; Sri Krishna Temple, Guruvayur) The beginning of this10-day temple festival is marked by the racing of around 30 elephants. The winner is qualified to carry Thidampu, an image of the deity, during the rest of the festival. Non-Hindus aren't allowed inside the temple itself, but can view the race outside.

Peruvanum Pooram (Mar/Apr; Peruvanum Mahadeva Temple, Peruvanum village, 12km from Thrissur) The one-day festival of this majestic temple features processions from surrounding villages of sumptuously decorated elephants accompanied by scores of drummers – the traditional temple percussion music is a highlight.

Arattupuzha Pooram (Mar/Apr; Arattupuzha Temple, Arattupuzha village, 14km from Thrissur) On the sixth day of this seven-day festival, 61 gaily caparisoned elephants gather in the temple grounds, accompanied by temple music.

Uthralikavu Pooram (Mar/Apr; Sree Rudhira Mahakali Kavu, Parthipara village, near Vadakencherry town, 20km from Thrissur) One of the most famous festivals of central Kerala, the climax of this eight-day festival comes when around 20 elephants circle the shrine, accompanied by thousands of chanting devotees.

Thrissur Pooram (Apr/May; Vadakkunathan Kshetram Temple, Thrissur town) In Kerala's biggest and best-known temple festival, colourful processions of decorated elephants make their way from neighbouring temples, each team trying to outdo the other with the finest and most splendidly caparisoned elephants, the biggest number of drummers and the best fireworks. This festival draws thousands of devotees and spectators, and can result in crowds of rowdy and drunken men later in the day – it's best to go early in the morning. The eighth day is the grand finale.

KERALA

AROUND THRISSUR

The Hindu-only **Sri Krishna Temple** at Guruvayur, 33km northwest of Thrissur, is
perhaps the most famous in Kerala and a
popular pilgrim destination. The temple is
believed to date from the 16th century and
is renowned for its healing powers. Weddings and important family ceremonies are
often held here. The temple's elephants (63
at last count) are kept at an old Zamorin
palace, Punnathur Kota. See p303 for details of this temple's famous festival.

Kerala Kalamandalam (☎ 04884-262418; www.kala
mandalam.com), 32km northeast of Thrissur
at Cheruthuruthy, has made a significant
contribution to the renaissance of the traditional art of Kerala. Students undergo intensive training in *kathakali, mohiniattam,
kootiattam*, percussion, voice and violin.
Many of the performers in Kochi trained
here. Structured **visits** (per person incl lunch
US$20; ☉ 9.30am-1pm) are available, including a
tour around the theatre and classes, featuring
Kalamandalam students as guides. Individually tailored, introductory courses are offered
at just one subject at a time (between six and
12 months; around Rs 1000 per month, plus
Rs 1000 for accommodation).

**Natana Kairali Research & Performing Centre
for Traditional Arts** (☎ 0480-2825559; venuji@satyam
.net.in), 20km south of Thrissur near Irinjalakuda, offers training in traditional
arts, including rare forms of puppetry and
dance. The centre hosts a 12-day festival in
January. Short appreciation courses (usually
about one month) are available to foreigners. For details of performances or enrolments, telephone or write to the Director,
Natana Kairali Research & Performing Centre for Traditional Arts, Ammannu Thakyar,
Mathom, Irinjalakuda, Thrissur District.

NORTHERN KERALA

KOZHIKODE (CALICUT)

☎ 0495 / pop 880,168
Calicut is a thriving, prosperous town – a
showcase of the fruits of Keralan labour in
the Middle East. There are few imprints of
Calicut's long history – it was a significant
port for trade and commerce, becoming the
capital of the powerful Zamorin dynasty in
the 10th century, and the quality cotton,
calico, is believed to have originated here –

but it's a pleasant-enough place to break the
journey; and it's the jumping-off point for
Wayanad Wildlife Sanctuary.

Information

There's a HDFC ATM next to Hotel Malabar Palace, and a State Bank of India ATM
opposite Ansari Park.

Cat's Net (Mavoor Rd; per hr Rs 30; ☉ 9.30-1am)
KTDC Tourist Reception (☎ 2722391; Malabar Man-
sion, SM Rd) Offers rudimentary tourist information.
Net Ride (Bank Rd; per hr Rs 20; ☉ 9am-10pm Mon-Sat)
UAE Exchange (☎ 2723164; Mavoor Rd; ☉ 9.30am-
6pm Mon-Sat, to 1.30pm Sun) Opposite the new bus stand.

Sights

Mananchira Sq was the former courtyard of
the Zamorins. Of the city's religious buildings, the **Tali Temple** (Hindus only), the **Kut-
tichira Mosque** and the **Church of South India**
are all worth a visit. Calicut's **beach**, north
of the Beach Hotel, is a pleasant place to
stroll in the late afternoon. Although there
is a network of lakes and lagoons nearby,
there has been, as yet, no development of
backwater tourism here.

Sleeping

NCK Tourist Home (☎ 2723530; Mavoor Rd; s/d Rs 125/
170) These small, dank rooms are nothing
more than habitable, but have clean bathrooms and are good value if you're doing
it cheap.

Hotel Maharani (☎ 2723101; maharani@eth.net; Taluk
Rd; d without/with AC from Rs 300/600; 🛞) The rooms
here, attractively set around a pleasant courtyard, are spartan and a bit worn – not as
grand as the exterior suggests. But they're
clean and comfortable and, because the hotel
is slightly off the beaten track, quiet.

Hyson Heritage (☎ 2766726; hysonclt@satyam.net
.in; Bank Rd; s/d from Rs 350/500, with AC from Rs 800/950;
🛞) The standard non-AC rooms here are
good value – tidy, spacious and comfortable. Deluxe AC rooms are huge, with bad
paintings and bathtub.

Beach Hotel (☎ /fax 2365363; info@beachheritage
.com; r without/with AC Rs 1200/1400; 🛞) Built in
1890 to house the Malabar British Club, this
is now a charming 10-room hotel. Beach-
facing rooms have bathtubs and sitouts; all
the rooms are tastefully furnished and have
plenty of character. This is by far the nicest
place to stay in Calicut, but it's a bit out of
the way. There's a small, homy restaurant.

Hotel Malabar Palace (☎ 2721511; mpalace@san charnet.in; GH Rd; s/d with breakfast from Rs 950/1200; ❄) This place is a bit overpriced, but a reasonably good choice in a central location. Rooms are very comfortable, though some of the bathrooms are a bit on the nose. It'll make you pay in advance.

Eating

Dawn Restaurant (dishes Rs 60-150; ❄ 7am-11pm; ❄) The restaurant at the Hotel Malabar does multicuisine with class, and serves inventive Indian dishes, tandoori (including meat, fish and mushrooms) and a good range of Keralan specials and interesting desserts. Excellent food; truly awful, loud muzak.

Hotel Sagar (Mavoor Rd; dishes from Rs 20; ❄ 6-2am) This is a stylish and breezy veg and nonveg place with biryanis (including fish; Rs 56) and meals at lunch time.

There are some good cheap places:

Indian Coffee House (Mavoor Rd; ❄ 6am-10.30pm) Great for breakfast; there's also a branch on GH Rd.

Marvell (Marvoor Rd; ❄ 9am-10pm) A sweet tooth's delight: sweets, cakes, pastries and good bread.

Sopanam (Marvoor Rd; ❄ 6am-10pm) A clean and bright veg place with biryanis and meals at lunch.

Tom 'n' Jerry (sundaes Rs 30-50; ❄ 10am-9pm) Outside Hotel Malabar; ice creams and cakes.

Woodlands (1st fl, GH Rd; dishes Rs 20-50; ❄ 8am-10pm) A glossy veg restaurant in the easily spotted White Lines building.

Getting There & Away

AIR

Jet Airways (☎ 2740518; 29 Mavoor Rd) flies daily to Mumbai (US$160) – as does **Indian Airlines** (☎ 2766243; Eroth Centre, Bank Rd) for the same price. It also has daily flights to Chennai (US$105), Delhi (US$325) and Coimbatore (US$50).

BUS

The **KSRTC bus stand** (Mavoor Rd) has regular buses to Bangalore (via Mysore; Rs 144, eight hours, 10 daily), Mangalore (Rs 118, seven hours, four daily) and to Ooty (5½ hours, four daily). There are also frequent buses to Thrissur (Rs 52, 3½ hours), Trivandrum (going via Alleppey and Ernakulam; Rs 200, 10 hours, eight daily) and Kottayam (Rs 80, seven hours, 13 daily).

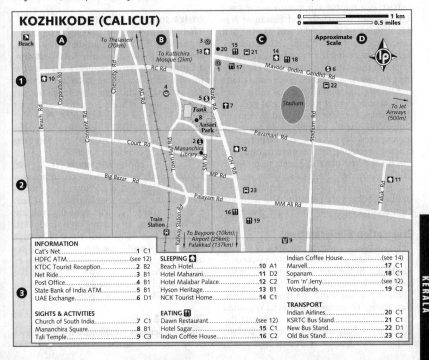

KOZHIKODE (CALICUT)

INFORMATION	
Cat's Net	1 C1
HDFC ATM	(see 12)
KTDC Tourist Reception	2 B2
Net Ride	3 B1
Post Office	4 B1
State Bank of India ATM	5 B1
UAE Exchange	6 D1

SIGHTS & ACTIVITIES	
Church of South India	7 C1
Mananchira Square	8 B1
Tali Temple	9 C3

SLEEPING	
Beach Hotel	10 A1
Hotel Maharani	11 D2
Hotel Malabar Palace	12 C2
Hyson Heritage	13 B1
NCK Tourist Home	14 C1

EATING	
Dawn Restaurant	(see 12)
Hotel Sagar	15 C1
Indian Coffee House	16 C1

Indian Coffee House	(see 14)
Marvell	17 C1
Sopanam	18 C1
Tom 'n' Jerry	(see 12)
Woodlands	19 C2

TRANSPORT	
Indian Airlines	20 C1
KSRTC Bus Stand	21 C1
New Bus Stand	22 D1
Old Bus Stand	23 C2

KERALA

There's also the new bus stand, further east along Mavoor Rd, for long-distance private buses, and the old bus stand, for local buses.

TRAIN

The train station is south of Mananchira Sq, about 2km from the new bus stand. There are trains to Mangalore (Rs 130/335 in 2nd class/3AC, five hours), Ernakulam (Rs 121/306, five hours) and Trivandrum (Rs 190/505, 11 hours).

Heading southeast, there are trains to Coimbatore (Rs 121/296), via Palakkad. These trains then head north to the centres of Bangalore, Chennai and Delhi.

Getting Around

There's no shortage of autorickshaws in Calicut, and the drivers will use their meters. It's about Rs 10 from the station to the KSRTC bus stand or most hotels.

WAYANAD WILDLIFE SANCTUARY

☎ 04936

Wayanad Wildlife Sanctuary, in Wayanad district, is a remote rainforest reserve contiguous with Nagarhole and Bandipur National Parks in Karnataka and Mudumalai Sanctuary in Tamil Nadu. Acclaimed by Keralans as having the most beautiful landscapes in the state, Wayanad is an enchanting patchwork of paddies, spice plantations and forest. You won't see many other travellers around, and it makes a great break in the journey between Kochi and Mysore or Bangalore. There's enough to do to justify staying a few days, even if your activity is restricted to soaking up the forest tranquillity, and it's the best place in Kerala to do some wildlife spotting – elephants, bison, sambar and spotted deer, peacocks, elephants and langur monkeys are plentiful, and there are even reports of leopard and tiger spotting.

Orientation & Information

The sanctuary, covering an area of 345 sq km, consists of two separate pockets – Muthanga in the east of the district, on the border with Bandipur and Mudamalai, and Tholpetty in the north, on the border with Nagarhole. Three major towns in Wayanad district make good bases for exploring the sanctuary – Kalpetta in the south, Sultanbatheri (also known as Sultan Battery) in

the east and Mananthavadi in the northwest.

The extremely helpful **DTPC office** (☎ 202 134; www.wayanadtourism.org; Kalpetta; ☼ 10am-5pm) can help organise permits and trekking.

Sights & Activities
VISITING THE SANCTUARY

Entry to both parts of the **sanctuary** (admission Rs 25, camera/video Rs 10/100; ☼ 7am-5pm) is only permitted with a guide; you can organise this through the DTPC office, with your hotel, or at the park's entrance offices. The **wildlife warden** (☎ 220454) at Sultanbatheri may also have information about **trekking** possibilities in the sanctuary.

At Tholpetty, five-hour **treks** (2/4 people Rs 670/720) are available. Early morning 2½-hour **jeep tours** (Rs 500 incl guide) are a great way to spot wildlife; afternoon tours are also available.

At Muthanga, two-hour **jeep tours** (Rs 375 incl guide) are offered. At the time of writing there were no organised trekking possibilities, but inquire at the DTPC or entrance office about the possibility of guided walks.

OTHER SIGHTS & ACTIVITIES

There are some great **trekking** possibilities around the district, including **Chembra Peak**, at 2100m the tallest summit; **Pakshipathalam**, a formation of large boulders deep in the forest; and a number of **waterfalls**. Permits are necessary, and available from the divisional forest officers for either South or North Wayanad – ask at the DTPC office for details. The DTPC can organise trekking guides (per day Rs 550) and camping equipment (per person Rs 200).

The 13th-century **Jain temple** (☼ 8am-noon & 2-6pm), near Sultanbatheri, has impressive stone carvings and is an important monument to the region's strong historical Jain presence. Close by, near Ambalavayal, are the **Edakal Caves**, with petroglyphs thought to date back over 3000 years. **Wayanad Heritage Museum** (Ambalavayal; admission Rs 5; ☼ 9am-5pm) exhibits headgear, weapons, pottery and other artefacts that shed light on the way of life of Wayanad's significant Adivasi population (around 17% of the total population).

Sleeping & Eating

There's a **seramby** (wooden hut; d Rs 600) at Tholpetty near the sanctuary entrance; it has

private bathroom but you'll have to bring
your own food. Contact the wildlife warden
(see opposite) at Sultanbatheri for details.

PPS Tourist Home (☎ 203431; Kalpetta; s/d Rs 150/
225, deluxe d Rs 400-500; 🐱) This friendly place
is in the middle of Kalpetta town; rooms
are clean, good-sized and perfectly comfortable. The deluxe rooms are much better
value; AC rooms have no windows!

Haritagiri Ecotel (☎ 203145; www.hotelharitagiri
.com; Kalpetta; s/d from Rs 350/690; 🐱 🖥) Although
it's unclear what's 'eco' about it, the simple
and fairly small rooms in this sterile complex are decent value. There are a few good,
reasonably priced restaurants here.

Pachyderm Palace (☎ 0484-2371761; touristdesk@
satyam.net.in; r per person with meals Rs 1000) This
bungalow is perched just outside the gate
of Tholpetty Wildlife Sanctuary – handy
for early morning treks and tours, and ad
hoc wildlife spotting. Rooms are simple and
clean, some bigger than others, and there's
a peaceful sitout where delicious Keralan
food is served. Make reservations through
the Tourist Desk in Ernakulam (see p291).

Stream Valley Cottages (☎ 202394; www.stream
valleycottages.com; Vythiri; d Rs 2500) These huge
modern cottages are set by a small stream
among the hills, about 3.5km off the main
road to Vythiri. Fully self-contained, with

kitchen (fridge and cooking facilities),
separate living area and balcony, they're
very peaceful, with only five cottages in
all. Traditional Keralan food is available
on request.

Tranquil (☎ 220244; www.tranquilresort.com;
Kuppamudi Estate, Kolagapara; s/d US$140/245, deluxe d
US$350 incl meals; 🐱) This luxury homestay is
in the middle of a private working plantation: 400 acres of pepper, coffee, vanilla
and cardamom surround it. The plantation house is delightful, with sweeping
verandas filled with plants and comfortable furniture, and there are lush gardens
and plenty of room to laze. The owners
are excellent hosts and will provide details
of walks around the plantation and local
sightseeing.

Getting There & Around

Buses from Calicut to Mysore and Bangalore pass through Kalpetta and Sultanbatheri (Rs 30 to 40, three hours), and there
are also a few morning services from Kannur (Rs 40 to 75). One bus per day passes
through Sultanbatheri on the way to Ooty,
at 1am. There are plenty of autorickshaws
for trips around the district, and the DTPC
can arrange car hire (from around Rs 1000
per day).

KANNUR (CANNANORE)

☎ 0497 / pop 498,175

Kannur's days of glory were under the
Kolathiri rajas, and its importance as a
spice-trading port was mentioned by the
Venetian traveller Marco Polo. From the
15th century, various colonial powers, including the Portuguese, Dutch and British,
exerted their influence. These days it's a
pleasant, unexciting coastal town, but there
are some decent beaches around and it's
the best place to come if you want to hunt
down a *theyyam* performance (see p308).

Information

The **DTPC** (🕙 10am-5pm Mon-Sat), opposite the
KSRTC bus stand, and the **information counter** (🕙 8am-7pm) at the railway station can
supply maps of Kannur. There are Federal Bank and State Bank of India ATMs
adjacent to the bus stand, and an HDFC
ATM about 50m from it, along with a **UAE
Exchange** (☎ 2708818; Mahatma Mandir Junction;
🕙 9.30am-5.30pm Mon-Sat, to 1.30pm Sun).

KERALA

THEYYAM

Kerala's most popular ritualistic art form, *theyyam* is believed to predate Hinduism and to have developed from folk dances performed in conjunction with harvest celebrations. *Theyyam* is performed as an offering to the deities, and to ward off poverty and illness. It is an intensely local ritual, usually performed in *kavus* (sacred groves), which are abundant throughout northern Kerala (there are estimated to be around 800 in Kannur district), and often celebrating stories of local heroes.

Theyyam refers to both the form or shape of the deity or hero portrayed, and to the ritual. There are around 450 different *theyyam*s, each with its own form and story of origin. Each *theyyam* has a distinct costume – face paint, bracelets, breastplates, skirts, garlands and especially headdresses are exuberant, intricately crafted and sometimes huge (one *theyyam*'s headdress measures 6m or 7m tall). The make-up and costume of some *theyyam*s, the popular goddess Muchilott Bhagavathy for example, serves to almost completely obscure the dancer's human form.

The performer prepares for the ritual with a period of abstinence, fasting and meditation, which extends into the long (sometimes eight-hour) make-up and costume session. During the performance, the performer loses his physical identity and speaks, moves and blesses the devotees as if he was the deity. There is frenzied dancing and wild drumming, and a surreal, otherworldly atmosphere is created; the kind of atmosphere in which a deity indeed might, if it so desired, manifest itself in human form. The ritual usually starts by midnight and will often go until noon the next day.

Theyyam is a religious rite, not taught in schools but passed down from generation to generation. Although certain castes may only perform certain *theyyam*s, all performers are from the lower castes (women do not perform *theyyam*). *Kavus*, however, are open to all, and Muslim characters appear in *theyyam* stories.

The *theyyam* season is October to May, during which time there will be an annual ritual at each *kavu*. *Theyyam*s are also often held to bring good fortune to important events such as marriages and house-warmings. See below for details on how to find one.

Sights

Kannur is the best place to see the ritual dance **theyyam** (see the boxed text, above); there should be a *theyyam* on somewhere reasonably close by every night of the year. To find it, ask at Costa Malabari (see the boxed text, p307), or try the **Kerala Folklore Academy** (☎ 2778090), near Chirakkal Pond, Valapattanam. Regular *theyyam*s are held at the **Parasinikadavu Temple**, 18km northeast of Kannur. These are usually from 4am to 9am, October to February; ask around to confirm details.

The Portuguese built **St Angelo Fort** (admission free; ☼ 9am-6pm) in 1505 on the promontory northwest of town. It's a peaceful place, and the tourist police here are happy to give you a guided tour; there's a good view of Kannur town and the ocean from the top. The fort is a Rs 15 rickshaw ride from town.

At the **Kanhirode Weavers Co-operative** (☎ 285 1259; ☼ 9am-5.30pm), 20km northeast of Kannur, you'll be given an interesting tour of the factory, where around 400 members turn out high-quality furnishing fabrics, saris, dhotis and fine silks. The co-op, on the Kannur–Mysore road, is easily reached by bus (or rickshaw, Rs 200) from Kannur. Ask to get off at Kudukkimotta.

Sleeping & Eating

Government Guest House (☎ 2706426; d Rs 220) Ostensibly only for government officials (but it will let visitors in if there's room), this is great value – huge, bright rooms, all with balcony, in a sprawling complex by the ocean. Phone ahead.

Centaur Tourist Home (☎ 2768270; MA Rd; s/d Rs 120/220) Has basic, spacious, clean rooms, across the road from the train station. There are plenty of similar lodges in this area.

Malabar Residency (☎ 2765456; Thavakkara Rd; s/d from Rs 900/1100; ☒) This is a three-star place 500m east of the train station with reasonable rooms, some with balcony. It has a 24-hour coffee shop and multicuisine restaurant.

Getting There & Away

There are frequent daily buses to Mysore (Rs 92, eight hours) and a few to Mangalore

(Rs 65 to 80, four hours). Most departures to Calicut (Rs 44, 2½ hours) leave in the evening. There's one bus daily to Ooty (via Wayanad; Rs 100, nine hours).

There are several daily trains to Mangalore (Rs 98/251 in 2nd class sleeper/3AC, three hours) Ernakulam (Rs 149/386, seven hours) and Calicut (Rs 35/218, 1¾ hours).

BEKAL

☎ 0467

Bekal, in Kerala's far north, has palm-fringed beaches and a rocky headland topped by the huge **Bekal Fort**, built between 1645 and 1660. **Kappil Beach**, 2km north of Bekal, has fine sand and calm water, but swimmers should beware shifting sand bars. Much of the prime beach-front land at Bekal has been parcelled off to resort groups; if all goes according to plan, this part of the Keralan coast will look very different in five years' time. For now, it's a wonderfully unspoiled stretch of coastline, but with very little choice in accommodation. Also note that this is a strongly Muslim area, with 12 mosques strung along the coastline – keep local sensibilities in mind, especially when you're at the beach.

Sleeping & Eating

Near Bekal and the beaches, most accommodation is in basic budget rooms. You won't get any closer to the beach than 2km; the budget places are all on the highway between Kanhangad and Kasaragod. During Ramadan you'll have some trouble getting a meal during the day.

Rajee's Inn (☎ 2237625; s/d Rs 100/175; 🗙) About 2km from Kappil Beach and 3km from Bekal, this is the pick of the bunch, with scuffed, cleanish rooms that have balconies. The AC rooms are very musty and not great value.

Eeyem Lodge (☎ 2236343; s/d Rs 75/100) A few doors north of Rajee's, the rooms here are small and a bit grotty. There's a restaurant.

Fortland Tourist Home (☎ 2236600; s/d from Rs 65 /100, deluxe d Rs 250; 🗙) A few kilometres further north, at Udma village, this place has clean, bright, comfortable rooms – go for the bigger deluxe rooms. The attached restaurant is decent.

Gitanjali Heritage (☎ 2234159; www.gitanjali heritage.com; s/d with meals US$45/65) Deep in the villages inland, about 5km from Bekal and

8km from Kappil Beach (about a Rs 60 auto-rickshaw ride), this is an intimate homestay in a tranquil heritage home. Rooms are a bit higgledy-piggledy, of all shapes and sizes, and filled with ancestral furniture.

Getting There & Around

The train station for Bekal Fort is Kotikulam in the village of Palakunnu, 3km from Bekal, and trains stop there regularly; Kanhangad, 13km south, is the major stop. There are many buses to/from Kasaragod, the nearest town of any size, and it's not too hard to find an autorickshaw or a bus at Bekal Junction to take you to/from Palakunnu and Udma.

LAKSHADWEEP

pop 60,595

The palm-covered islands of Lakshadweep, 300km west of Kerala, add up to only 32 sq km, scattered around 4200 sq km of lagoon waters. The archipelago's pristine lagoons, unspoiled coral reefs and average November to March temperatures of 24° to 34°C make it a diver's dream. Only 11 of the 36 islands are inhabited, and the population is 93% Sunni Muslim. Fishing and coir production are the main economic activities. A caste system divides the islanders between Koya (land owners), Malmi (sailors) and Melachery (farmers).

Information

Sports (Society for the Promotion of Recreational Tourism & Sports; Map p290; ☎ 0484-2668387; www.lakshad weeptourism.com; IG Rd, Willingdon Island; ☼ 10am-5pm Mon-Sat, closed 2nd Sat of the month) is the main tourism organisation.

Permits

While several islands have opened to visitors in recent years, foreigners are limited to staying in pricey resorts. A special permit is required to visit Lakshadweep; it's organised by tour operators, the two hotels or Sports; the cost of obtaining permits (one month's notice) is usually included in the rates quoted in this section. Foreigners and Indians can stay on Bangaram, Agatti and Kadmat, and Indians can make day visits to Kalpeni, Minicoy and Kavaratti.

Accommodation prices listed include meals and all water sports (except diving costs) and

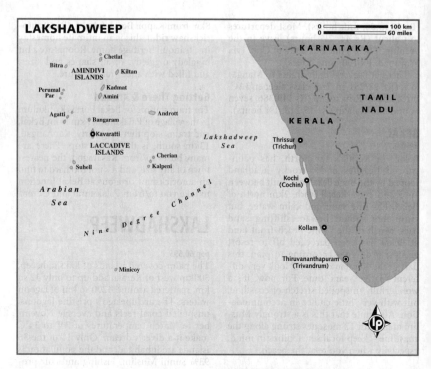

LAKSHADWEEP

are for the high season, around October to April (though within these months, there's a peak period from December to January when prices are even higher).

Getting There & Away

If you're travelling to Bangaram or Agatti, Indian Airlines has daily 9.15am flights Monday to Saturday from Kochi to Agatti Island (US$160 each way, 1¼ hours). The plane is a tiny Dornier 228 propeller aircraft and passengers are restricted to 10kg of luggage. The 1½-hour transfer by boat from Agatti to Bangaram costs an extra US$30 return or, during monsoon, US$100 by helicopter (check if transfers are included in your package). A boat trip to Agatti from Kochi is US$40 one way (16 to 20 hours).

For Kadmat, there are 18 boat departures from Kochi between 5 October and 5 May (US$75 return, including food, 18 hours one way) – allow a stay of three to five days plus travelling time. There are no cabins with beds, just push-back seats in an AC cabin. Contact Sports (see p309) in Kochi for details.

BANGARAM ISLAND

The 128-acre island is fringed with pure sand, and the sight of the moon slipping beneath the lagoon horizon is very nearly worth the expense. Activities include diving, snorkelling, deep-sea fishing and sailing.

Bangaram Island Resort (www.cghearth.com; s/d with full board Oct-Apr US$255/265, 4-person deluxe cottages with meals US$495) is run by the **CGH Earth group** (☎ 0484-2668421; bangaramisland@cghearth.com), and is administered from its hotel in Kochi. Shop around before you leave home – some operators can secure a better deal.

AGATTI ISLAND

The village on this 2.7-sq-km island has several mosques, which you can visit if dressed modestly. There's no alcohol on the island. Snorkelling and boat trips to nearby islands can be arranged.

Agatti Island Beach Resort (☎ 0484-2362232; www.agattiislandresorts.com; tw per person for 3 nights US$305-345, with AC US$430-470;) offers a range of packages. The resort has 10 simple, low-rise beach cottages, designed to be comfortably cool without AC, and a restaurant for 20.

KADMAT ISLAND

Kadmat Beach Resort (☎ 0484-2668387; laksports _2004@vsnl.net; s/d for Indians Rs 2000/3000, with AC Rs 2500/4000, s/d for foreigners US$75/125, with AC US$100/175; ❄) is administered by Sports (see p309).

MINICOY ISLAND

Indians wishing to stay on remote Minicoy can rent **cottages** (s/d Rs 2000/3000, with AC Rs 2500/4000; ❄). Boat transport from Kochi (Rs 3500 to 6000 return) must be added to the prices.

DIVING

The best time to dive in Lakshadweep is between October and mid-May. During the monsoon, diving is still possible in the lagoons or outside the reefs, but the weather can severely limit these opportunities.

Lacadives diving school runs dive centres on Bangaram and Kadmat Islands. Costs can vary, but a 'resort course' package for a beginner, consisting of a lesson followed by lagoon and boat dives, costs around US$100, and a PADI open-water course costs US$365. Experienced divers pay US$35 per dive, or packages are available for US$200/380/555 for six/12/18 dives. Information is available through the hotels or directly through **Lacadives** (☎ 0484-2206766; www.lacadives.com) in Ernakulam; its website has details about accommodation packages. The diving school on Agatti island is run by **Goa Diving** (☎ 0832-255517).

From Kadmat Island, dives range from 9m to 20m in depth and some of the better sites include **Garden of Eden**, **the Wall**, **Cross Currents** and **Sting Ray City**. Around Bangaram, good spots include the 32m-deep wreck of the **Princess Royale**, **Manta Point**, **Shark Point** and **the Wall**. Because of weight restrictions on aircraft, most divers rely on equipment provided on the islands. For a guide to environmentally friendly diving, see the boxed text, p460.

Tamil Nadu

While the beaches and backwaters of Kerala and Goa stir the romantic, sun-loving ideals of many travellers, Tamil Nadu – the Land of the Tamils – is the true heartland of South India. Dominating the southern tip of the country, this diverse state is often referred to as the cradle of Dravidian civilisation, an ancient culture distinguished by unique customs. The cultural icons are everywhere – colossal temples with their towering, riotously rainbow-coloured *gopurams* (gateway towers), intricate rock carvings, evocative music and complex classical dance. Pilgrims pour into the ancient sites of Kanchipuram, Chidambaram, Kumbakonam, Tiruchirappalli (Trichy), Thanjavur (Tanjore), Madurai, Kanyakumari and Rameswaram – far outnumbering tourists. This is a place where you'll often feel swept away by the religious and cultural fervour – joining worshippers for *puja* (offerings or prayers) in ancient temples or drawn into the colour, noise and chaos of one of the many temple festivals.

Although the eastern coastline fronting the Bay of Bengal has a few resorts and sleepy fishing villages, Tamil Nadu is not a beach state for travellers. Only Mamallapuram, just south of Chennai, attracts chilled-out tourists. The 2004 tsunami swept along this coastline, but rehabilitation was swift and tourist areas are no longer affected.

The mountains, or Western Ghats, that rise up in the northwest of the state, are a big attraction for their cool climate, easy-going colonial hill stations, treks and wildlife. The famous mountain towns of Ooty – reached by miniature train – and Kodaikanal should not be missed.

HIGHLIGHTS

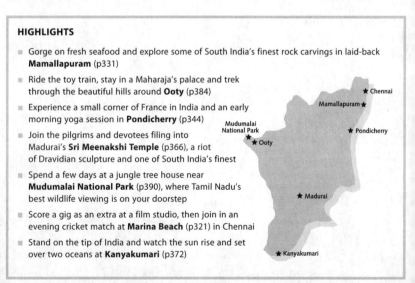

- Gorge on fresh seafood and explore some of South India's finest rock carvings in laid-back **Mamallapuram** (p331)

- Ride the toy train, stay in a Maharaja's palace and trek through the beautiful hills around **Ooty** (p384)

- Experience a small corner of France in India and an early morning yoga session in **Pondicherry** (p344)

- Join the pilgrims and devotees filing into Madurai's **Sri Meenakshi Temple** (p366), a riot of Dravidian sculpture and one of South India's finest

- Spend a few days at a jungle tree house near **Mudumalai National Park** (p390), where Tamil Nadu's best wildlife viewing is on your doorstep

- Score a gig as an extra at a film studio, then join in an evening cricket match at **Marina Beach** (p321) in Chennai

- Stand on the tip of India and watch the sun rise and set over two oceans at **Kanyakumari** (p372)

Chennai

Mamallapuram

Mudumalai National Park

Pondicherry

Ooty

Madurai

Kanyakumari

History

There is speculation that the first Dravidians were part of early Indus civilisations and that they came south to the area around 1500 BC. By 300 BC the region was controlled by three major dynasties – the Cholas in the east, the Pandyas in the central area and the Cheras in the west. This was the classical period of Tamil literature – the Sangam Age – that continued until around AD 300.

The domains of these three dynasties changed many times over the centuries. The Pallava dynasty became influential, particularly in the 7th and 8th centuries, when it constructed many of the monuments at Mamallapuram. Although all of these dynasties were engaged in continual skirmishes, their steady patronage of the arts served to consolidate and expand Dravidian civilisation.

In 1640 the British negotiated the use of Madraspatnam (now Chennai) as a trading post. Subsequent interest by the French, Dutch and Danes led to continual conflict and, finally, almost total domination by the British, when the region became known as the Madras Presidency. Small pocketed areas, including Pondicherry and Karaikal, remained under French control.

FAST FACTS

- Population: 62.1 million
- Area: 130,058 sq km
- Capital: Chennai (Madras)
- Main language: Tamil
- When to go: November to March

Many Tamils played a significant part in India's struggle for Independence, which was finally won in 1947. In 1956 the Madras Presidency was disbanded and Tamil Nadu was established – an autonomous state based on linguistic lines.

Information

The state tourism body is **Tamil Nadu Tourism** (www.tamilnadutourism.org) with tourist offices of varying uselessness in most cities and large towns around the state. It also runs a fairly average chain of hotels. Pondicherry has its own tourism department (www.tourisminpondicherry.com and www.pondy.com) and many towns have their own websites.

ACCOMMODATION

Accommodation over Rs 200 in Tamil Nadu (but not Pondicherry) is subject to a government 'luxury' tax – 10% on rooms up to Rs 1000 and 12.5% and rooms more than Rs 1000. There's often an additional 'service tax' at upmarket hotels. Prices throughout this chapter do not include tax, unless stated otherwise. There are few surprises with hotels in Tamil Nadu – the exceptions are Pondicherry, which has some lovely heritage hotels, and Ooty and Kodaikanal with everything from forest lodges to Raj-era mansions.

DANGERS & ANNOYANCES

Ambling through temples is clearly a highlight of Tamil Nadu. Dealing with temple touts is not. These self-appointed guides demand big bucks in exchange for very little. They often work as a front for nearby craft shops. Although they're widespread, Kanchipuram, Trichy and Madurai seem to be their breeding grounds. Don't be fooled by those who claim Lonely Planet backing or who flash pseudo-government-approved cards. A fair rate for a knowledgeable guide

---

TOP FIVE TEMPLES

Tamil Nadu is nirvana for anyone wanting to explore South Indian temple culture and architecture. Many are important places of pilgrimage for Hindus, where daily *puja* rituals and colourful festivals will leave a deep impression on even the most temple-weary traveller. Others stand out for the stunning architecture, soaring *gopurams* (gateway towers) and intricately carved, pillared *mandapams* (pavilions in front of a temple). There are so many that it pays to be selective, but the choice is subjective. Here's our top five.

- Sri Meenakshi Temple, Madurai (p366)
- Arunachaleswar Temple, Tiruvannamalai (p342)
- Brihadishwara Temple, Thanjavur (p357)
- Rock Fort Temple, Trichy (p360)
- Nataraja Temple, Chidambaram (p352)

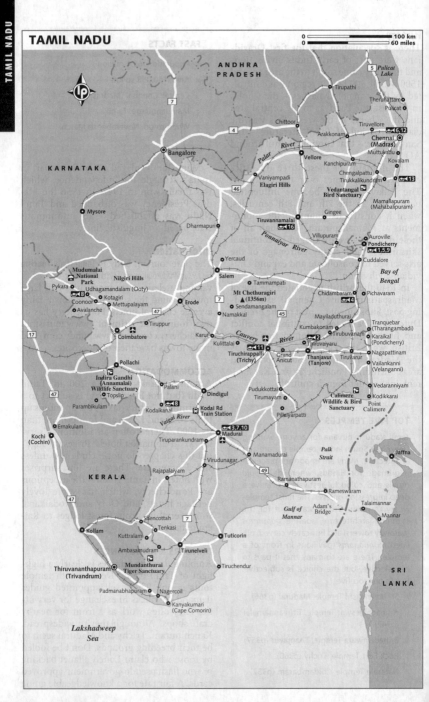

TAMIL NADU

is around Rs 60 per hour. Genuine guides exist and can greatly enhance your experience, but you'll need to search them out. As always, shop around, get recommendations from other travellers, question the knowledge of anyone offering guide services and agree on a price before you set out.

PERMITS

As well as for the areas listed below, permits are required for trekking in some areas of the Nilgiri Hills around Mudumalai National Park (see p390).

Conservator of Forests (Map pp318-19; ☎ 24321139; 8th fl, Panangal Bldg, Saidapet) The Conservator of Forests issues permits for all areas other than the Vedantangal Bird Sanctuary, but will only do so for researchers.

Wildlife Warden's Office (Map pp318-19; ☎ 24321471; 4th fl, DMS office, 259 Anna Salai, Teynampet) Issues permits for accommodation at Vedantangal Bird Sanctuary.

FESTIVALS IN TAMIL NADU

Many of Tamil Nadu's most colourful festivals revolve around temples – there's something going on somewhere in the state all year round.

International Yoga Festival (**1**; 4-7 Jan; Pondicherry, p344) Pondicherry's ashrams and yoga culture is put on show with workshops, classes and music and dance events. Held throughout the city, the event attracts yoga masters from all over India.

Pongal (mid-Jan; statewide). As the rice boils over the new clay pots, this festival symbolises the prosperity and abundance a fruitful harvest brings. For many, the celebrations begin with temple rituals, followed by family gatherings. Later it's the animals, especially cows, which are honoured for their contribution to the harvest.

Music festival (**2**; Jan; Thiruvaiyaru, p360) Held near Thanjavur, this music festival is held in honour of the saint and composer Thyagaraja.

Teppam Float Festival (**3**; Jan/Feb; Madurai, p364) A popular event held on the full moon of the Tamil month of Thai, when statues of deities are floated on the huge Mariamman Teppakkulam Tank.

Natyanjali Dance Festival (**4**; Feb/Mar; Chidambaram, p352) The five day festival attracts performers from all over the country to the Nataraja Temple to celebrate Nataraja (Shiva) – the Lord of Dance.

Masimagam Festival (**5**; mid-Mar; Pondicherry, p344) Statues from 64 temples are paraded through the streets before being immersed in the sea.

Arubathimoovar Festival (**6**; Mar/Apr; Chennai, p316) A colourful one-day festival when bronze statues of the 63 saints of Shiva are paraded through the streets of Mylapore.

Chithrai Festival (**7**; Apr/May; Madurai, p364) The main event on Madurai's busy festival calendar is this 14-day event that celebrates the marriage of Meenakshi to Sundareshwara (Shiva). The deities are wheeled around the Sri Meenakshi Temple in massive chariots that form part of long, colourful processions.

Summer festivals (**8**; May; Ooty, p384, & Kodaikanal, p375) Tamil Nadu's hill stations both hold similar festivals which feature boat races on the lake, horse racing (in Ooty), flower shows and music.

Bastille Day (**9**; July 14; Pondicherry, p344) Street parades and a bit of French pomp and ceremony are all part of the fun at this celebration.

Avanimoolam (**10**; Aug/Sep; Madurai, p364) Marks the coronation of Sundareshwar, when temple chariots are exuberantly hauled around the city.

Karthikai Deepam Festival (Nov/Dec; statewide) Held during full moon, Tamil Nadu's 'festival of lights' is celebrated throughout the state, with earthenware lamps and firecrackers, but best place to see it is Tiruvannamalai (see p342), where the legend began.

Vaikunta Ekadasi (**11**; Paradise Festival; mid-Dec; Tiruchirappalli, p360) This 21-day festival brings the Sri Ranganathaswamy Temple to life when the celebrated Vaishnavaite text, Tiruvaimozhi, is recited before an image of Vishnu.

Festival of Carnatic Music & Dance (**12**; mid-Dec–mid-Jan; Chennai, p316) One of the largest of its type in the world, this festival is a celebration of Tamil music and dance.

Mamallapuram Dance Festival (**13**; Christmas-late Jan; Mamallapuram, p331) A four-week dance festival showcasing dances from all over India, with many performances on an open-air stage against the imposing backdrop of Arjuna's Penance. Dances include the *bharata natyam* (Tamil Nadu), *kuchipudi* (Andhra Pradesh) tribal dance, *kathakali* (Kerala drama), puppet shows and classical music. Performances are held only from Friday to Sunday.

TAMIL NADU

CHENNAI (MADRAS)

☎ 044 / pop 6.4 million

If South India is, as some suggest, a different country, Chennai is its undisputed capital. Apart from when the monsoon rains are washing the streets away, the city still often called Madras (it was officially renamed Chennai in 1997) can be as hot as a bowl of chilli and as oppressive and polluted as any part of the subcontinent. Chennai lacks the cosmopolitan, prosperous air of Mumbai or the historical highlights of Delhi – instead it's an earthy, working-class conglomeration of districts expanding at an exponential rate. Culturally, the city has a long tradition of attracting and nurturing the region's finest thinkers, artists and artisans with its many esteemed educational institutes and a strong, sometimes volatile, tradition of journalism and publishing.

What started as a scattering of villages 500 years ago is now India's fourth-largest city and an international gateway. It is a deeply conservative city – the lungi is very much in fashion here, alcohol is frowned upon and *idlis* (rice dumplings) are all the rage for breakfast. But Chennai is an economic powerhouse and the quiet achiever in the IT industry, despite having to compete for talent with its close neighbour, Bangalore. This is also the centre for Tamil filmmaking.

With only a handful of tourist sights, Chennai doesn't demand too much of your time, but a couple of days spent hanging around a film studio, poking around the markets of George Town or Theagaraya Nagar and strolling along Marina Beach at sunset will give a rewarding insight into South Indian city life.

HISTORY

For over 2000 years the Chennai area has attracted seafarers, spice traders and cloth merchants. The Portuguese arrived in the 16th century, followed by the Dutch. In 1639, the British East India Company established a settlement in the fishing village of Madraspatnam.

Fort St George took 15 years to build and was completed in 1653. George Town grew in the area around the fort and was granted municipal charter in 1688 by James II, thus making it the oldest municipality in India today.

In the 18th and 19th centuries, French and British traders competed for supremacy in India. A key player in the British campaign was Robert Clive (Clive of India). Recruiting an army of around 2000 sepoys (locally engaged troops), he launched a series of military expeditions which developed into the Carnatic Wars. In 1756 the French withdrew to Pondicherry, leaving the relieved British to develop Fort St George.

In the 19th century, the city became the seat of the Madras presidency, one of the four divisions of British Imperial India. After Independence, it continued to grow into what is now a significant southern gateway.

ORIENTATION

Bordered to the east by the Bay of Bengal, Chennai is a combination of small districts with no real centre. Located in the north, near the harbour, is George Town, a jumble of narrow streets, bazaars and the court buildings.

To the southeast of George Town, Anna Salai is a major central thoroughfare, and just north are the two main train stations; Egmore, the departure point for most destinations in Tamil Nadu and a budget hotel district, and Central, for interstate trains. Southeast of Egmore, the Triplicane area has more budget hotels and the long Marina Beach.

INFORMATION
Bookshops

Bookpoint (Map p322; 160 Anna Salai) Spacious and well stocked with English-language titles.

Giggles bookshop (Map p322; Binny Rd; ⏰ 9am-8pm) In the Taj Connemara Hotel complex, this tiny shop has mountains of books.

Higginbothams (Map p322; 814 Anna Salai; ⏰ 8am-8pm) Huge bookshop chain with Chennai's best range of English-language books.

Landmark Books (Map pp318-19; 3 MG Rd; ⏰ 9am-9pm Mon-Fri, noon-9pm Sat & Sun) In Apex Plaza, this bookshop has an excellent selection. There's another branch in Spencer Plaza.

Cultural Centres

Alliance Française de Madras (Map pp318-19; ☎ 28279803; www.af-madras.org; 40 College Rd,

Tea plantations, Munnar (p287), Kerala

LINDSAY BROWN

CHRIS BEALL

Dancer at Thrissur Pooram festival (p303), Thrissur
(Trichur), Kerala

PETER PTSCHELINZEW

Periyar Lake, Periyar Wildlife Sanctuary (p284), Kerala

Ramoji Film City (p417), Hyderabad, Andhra Pradesh

Mudumalai National Park (p390), Tamil Nadu

Sri Meenakshi Temple complex
(p366), Madurai, Tamil Nadu

Nungambakkam; 9am-1pm & 2-7pm Mon-Sat) The French cultural centre has a library (closed Wed morning) and hosts film and theatre nights.

American Information Resource Center (Map pp318-19; ☎ 28112000; americanlibrary.in.library.net; Gemini Circle, Anna Salai; 11am-5pm Mon-Sat) Attached to the USA consulate, this centre also has a library.

British Council Library (Map p322; ☎ 52052600; 737 Anna Salai; 11am-7pm Mon-Sat)

Indian Council for Cultural Relations (Map p322; ICCR; ☎ 28274519; 201 Awai Shanmughan Salai) Cultural programmes and visits from international artists.

Internet Access

Internet cafés are plentiful all over Chennai, with charges from Rs 15 to 30 per hour. A particularly good chain to look out for is i-way. Useful Internet locations for travellers include the following:

Dishnet The Hub (Map pp318-19; 2nd fl, Apex Plaza, MG Rd, Nungambakkam; per hr Rs 25; 6am-midnight) Quick and efficient. There's another branch in Central Station.

Emerald Internet (Map p322; Triplicane High Rd; per hr Rs 15; 8am-midnight) Triplicane's best Internet café has fast connections and cheap international net-phone calls.

Gee Gee Net (Map p322; 20 Vallabha Agraharam; per hr Rs 20; 6am-1am) Near Broadlands Lodge in Triplicane, this cramped place offer Internet access for Rs 50 per day as well as hourly rates.

Internet Zone (Map p322; 1 Kennet Lane, Egmore; per hr Rs 25; 5.30am-11.30pm) Cramped AC place handy for Egmore area.

Left Luggage

There are left-luggage counters at Egmore and Central Stations, and at the international and domestic airport terminals (Rs 5 to 10 per 24 hours).

Medical Services

Apollo Hospital (Map p322; ☎ 28293333; 21 Greams Lane; 24hr) Also has 24-hour pharmacy.

St Isabel's Hospital (Map pp318-19; ☎ 24991081; 18 Oliver Rd, Mylapore; 24hr)

Money

ATMs are widespread in Chennai. The main banks with 24-hour ATMs accepting international cards (Cirrus, Maestro, Visa and MasterCard) are ICICI, HDFC, HSBC, Citibank, UTI and some State Bank of India.

American Express (Map p322; ☎ 28523638; G17 Spencer Plaza, Anna Salai; 9.30am-6.30pm Mon-Fri, 9.30am-2.30pm Sat)

HDFC (Map p322; Triplicane High Rd) ATM.

ICICI (Off map pp318-19; Anna International Airport) ATM.

State Bank of India (Map pp318-19; Rajaji Salai, George Town; 10am-4pm Mon-Fri, 10am-1pm Sat)

Thomas Cook Egmore (Map p322; ☎ 28553276; 45 Montieth Rd; 9.30am-6pm Mon-Sat); George Town (Map pp318-19; ☎ 25342374; 20 Rajaji Salai; 9.30am-6pm Mon-Sat); Nungambakkam (Map pp318-19; ☎ /fax 28274941; Eldorado Bldg, 112 MG Rd; 9.30am-1pm & 2-6.30pm Mon-Fri, 9.30am-noon Sat)

UTI (Map p322; Police Commissioners Rd, Egmore & Dr Radhakrishnan Salai) ATM.

Post

Anna Salai post office (Map p322; Anna Salai; 8am-8.30pm Mon-Sat, 10am-5pm Sun, poste restante 10am-6pm Mon-Sat) Best for parcels and poste restante.

Main post office (Map pp318-19; Rajaji Salai; 8am-8.30pm Mon-Sat, 10am-5pm Sun) In George Town

Post office (Map p322; Kennet Lane, Egmore)

Tourist Information

The free fortnightly *CityInfo* guide, available from the tourist office and some hotels, has useful information on eating out, nightlife and what's on. On the Internet, check out **Chennai Best** (www.chennaibest.com) and **Chennai Online** (www.chennaionline.com).

Indian Tourism Development Corporation (ITDC; Map p322; ☎ 28460285; 29 Victoria Crescent; 5.30am-7pm Mon-Sat) ITDC tour bookings.

Indiatourism (Map p322; ☎ 28460285; indtour@vsnl .com; 154 Anna Salai; 9am-6pm Mon-Fri, 9am-1pm Sat) The Government of India tourist office is a good place for maps and impartial information. Also has counters at the domestic and international airports.

Tamil Nadu Tourism Complex (Map p322; ☎ 25383333; www.tamilnadutourism.org; 2 Wallajah Rd, Triplicane; 10am-5.45pm Mon-Fri) Branches of state tourist offices from all over: Tamil Nadu (☎ 25368358), Andamans, Kerala and Karnataka. They mostly sell tours and book accommodation, but can offer advice.

Travel Agencies

Madura Travel Service (Map p322; ☎ 28192970; www.maduratravel.com; Impala Complex, Kennet Lane, Egmore; 24hr)

SP Travels and Tours (Map p322; ☎ 28533622; sptours@eth.net; 44 Wellington Plaza, 90 Anna Salai)

Visa Extensions

Foreigners' Regional Registration Office (FRRO; Map pp318-19; ☎ 28275444; 26 Haddows Rd, Nungambakkam; 10am-1pm & 2-5pm Mon-Fri) Visa extensions are only granted here for genuine emergencies.

www.lonelyplanet.com

TAMIL NADU

CHENNAI (MADRAS)

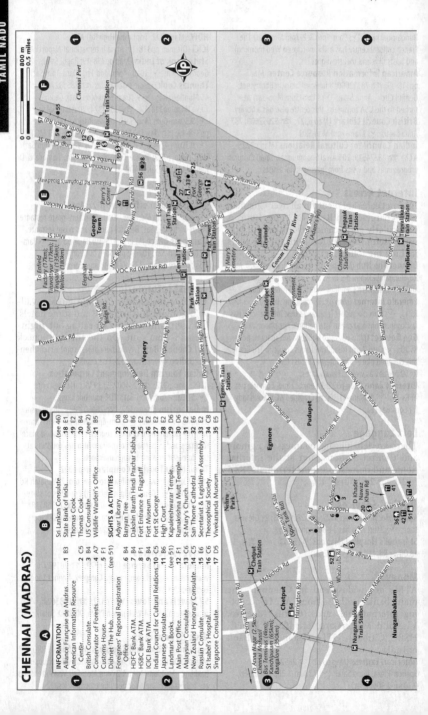

INFORMATION	
Alliance Française de Madras..........	1 B3
American Information Resource	
Center......................................	2 C5
British Consulate............................	3 B4
Conservator of Forests...................	4 A7
Customs House..............................	5 F1
Dishnet The Hub.......................(see 51)	
Foreigners' Regional Registration	
Office...	6 B4
HDFC Bank ATM.............................	7 B4
HSBC Bank ATM.............................	8 F1
ICICI Bank ATM..............................	9 B4
Indian Council for Cultural Relations..10	C5
Japanese Consulate........................	11 B6
Landmark Books.......................(see 51)	
Main Post Office............................	12 F1
Malaysian Consulate.......................	13 C6
New Zealand Honorary Consulate.....	14 C5
Russian Consulate..........................	15 E6
St Isabel's Hospital........................	16 C6
Singapore Consulate......................	17 D5

Sri Lankan Consulate.......................	18 B3
State Bank of India.........................	19 E1
Thomas Cook................................	20 B4
Thomas Cook..........................(see 2)	
US Consulate.................................	21 B5
Wildlife Warden's Office.................	

SIGHTS & ACTIVITIES	
Adyar Library.................................	22 D8
Banyan Tree..................................	23 D8
Dakshin Barath Hindi Prachar Sabha..24	B6
Fort Entrance & Flagstaff................	25 E2
Fort Museum.................................	26 E2
Fort St George..............................	27 E2
High Court....................................	28 E2
Kapaleeshwarar Temple..................	29 D6
Ramakrishna Mutt Temple...............	30 D6
St Mary's Church...........................	31 E2
San Thome Cathedral.....................	32 E6
Secretariat & Legislative Assembly...	33 E2
Theosophical Society......................	34 C8
Vivekananda Museum......................	35 D5

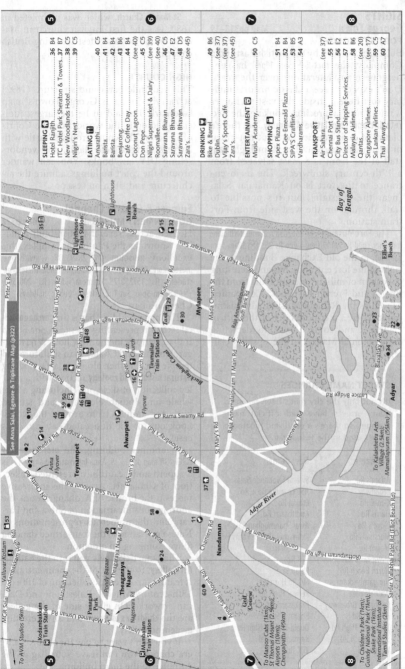

SLEEPING	
Hotel Ranjith	**36** B4
ITC Hotel Park Sheraton & Towers	**37** B7
New Woodlands Hotel	**38** C5
Nilgiri's Nest	**39** C5

EATING	
Amarathi	**40** C5
Barista	**41** B4
Barista	**42** B4
Benjarong	**43** B6
Café Coffee Day	**44** B4
Coconut Lagoon	(see 40)
Don Pepe	(see 39)
Nilgiri Supermarket & Dairy	**45** C5
Roomallee	(see 40)
Saravana Bhavan	**46** C5
Saravana Bhavan	**47** E2
Saravana Bhavan	**48** D5
Zara's	(see 45)

DRINKING	
Bike & Barrel	**49** B6
Dublin	(see 37)
Vijay's Sports Café	(see 37)
Zara's	(see 45)

ENTERTAINMENT	
Music Academy	**50** C5

SHOPPING	
Apex Plaza	**51** B4
Gee Gee Emerald Plaza	**52** B4
SIPA'S Craftlink	**53** B5
Vardharams	**54** A3

TRANSPORT	
Air Sahara	(see 37)
Chennai Port Trust	**55** F1
City Bus Stand	**56** E2
Director of Shipping Services	**57** F1
Malaysia Airlines	**58** B6
Qantas	(see 20)
Singapore Airlines	(see 17)
Sri Lankan Airlines	**59** C5
Thai Airways	**60** A7

TAMIL NADU

SIGHTS
George Town   Map pp318–19
FORT ST GEORGE
Built around 1653 by the British East India Company, the **fort** (🕙 5am-10pm) has undergone many alterations over the years. Don't expect to see a classic historic military fort here – inside the vast perimeter walls is now a precinct housing the **Secretariat and Legislative Assembly**, so there's plenty of daily activity here but not much of historical interest. The 46m-high **flagstaff** at the front is a mast salvaged from a 17th-century shipwreck. The main entrance to the fort is on Kamarajar Salai (near the flagstaff), but it's possible to walk through on the west side from Fort train station.

The **Fort Museum** (☎ 25670389; admission Indian/foreigner/child Rs 2/100/free, video Rs 25; 🕙 10am-5pm Sat-Thu), in the old Exchange Building to the right of the fort entrance, has an interesting collection of military memorabilia from the British and French East India Companies, as well as the Raj and Muslim administrations. There's a scale model of the fort in Gallery 2 and some fine prints depicting early colonial Madras in the upstairs Gallery 10.

STREET NAME CHANGES

It's not only the city that's been renamed; many streets have had official name changes, so there's a confusing mixture of names used in the vernacular.

Old name	New name
Adam's Rd	Swami Sivananda Salai
Broadway	NSC Chandra Bose Rd
C-in-C Rd	Ethiraj Rd
Harris Rd	Audithanar Rd
Lloyd's Rd	Awai Shanmughan Salai
Marshalls Rd	Rukmani Lakshmi Pathy Rd
Mount Rd	Anna Salai
Mowbray's Rd	TTK Rd
North Beach Rd	Rajaji Salai
Nungambakkam	MG Rd High Rd
Poonamallee	Periyar High Rd
Popham's Broadway	Prakasam Rd
Pycroft's Rd	Bharathi Salai
Triplicane High Rd	Quaid-Milleth High Rd
South Beach Rd	Kamarajar Salai
Waltax Rd	VOC Rd

St Mary's Church, which was completed in 1680, was the first English church in Madras, and is India's oldest surviving British church.

HIGH COURT
This red Indo-Saracenic structure (1892) at Parry's Corner is George Town's main landmark. It's said to be the largest judicial building in the world after the Courts of London. The court grounds bustle with lawyers, judges, defendants, and vendors selling DIY law books. You can wander around the court buildings, admire the architecture and sit in on sessions.

Egmore & Central Chennai
GOVERNMENT MUSEUM   Map p322
Housed across several British-built buildings known as the Pantheon Complex, this excellent **museum** (☎ 28193238; www.chennaimuseum.org; 486 Pantheon Rd; admission Indian/foreigner/student Rs 15/250/75, camera/video Rs 200/500; 🕙 9.30am-5pm Sat-Thu, closed public holidays) is Chennai's best.

The main building has a fine **archaeological section** representing all the major South Indian periods including Chola, Vijayanagar, Hoysala and Chalukya in sculpture and temple art. Further along, is a fascinating **natural history and zoology** section with a motley collection of skeletons (including a blue whale and Indian elephant) and stuffed birds and animals from around the world. Look out for the desiccated cat in a glass case!

In another building, the **bronze gallery ICICI** (Off map pp318-19; Anna International Airport) has a superb and beautifully presented collection of Chola art. Among the impressive pieces is the bronze of Ardhanariswara, the androgynous incarnation of Shiva and Parvati, and the numerous representations of Natesa or Nataraja, the four-armed dancing Shiva stomping on a demon.

The same ticket gets you into the **National Art Gallery**, to the left of the main entrance. It features an excellent collection of 10th- to 18th-century Mughal, Rajasthani and Deccan artworks. On either side of the gallery are the **children's museum** and an interesting **modern art gallery**.

If you don't want to pay the absurd camera charges you can leave your bag at the entrance to the main building.

VIVEKANANDA MUSEUM   Map pp318–19
This **museum** (☎ 28446188; Kamarajr Salai; admission adult/child Rs 2/1; ☻ 10am-12.30pm, 3-7pm Thu-Tue) is fascinating not only for the displays on the famous 'wandering monk', but also for the building in which it is housed. The semicircular seafront structure was formerly known as the Ice House and was once used to store massive ice blocks transported by ship from North America. Swami Vivekananda stayed here in 1897 on his return from the US and preached his ascetic philosophy to adoring crowds. The museum now houses a collection of photographs and memorabilia from the swami's life, a gallery of modern Indian art and the 'meditation room' where Vivekananda stayed.

South Chennai   Map pp318–19
Chennai's most active temple, the ancient Shiva **Kapaleeshwarar Temple** (Kutchery Rd, Mylapore; ☻ 4am-noon & 4-8pm) is constructed in the Dravidian style and displays the architectural elements – rainbow-coloured *gopurams, mandapams* and a huge tank – found in the famous temple cities of Tamil Nadu.

The tranquil, leafy grounds of the **Ramakrishna Mutt Temple** (RK Mutt Rd; ☻ 4.30-11.45am & 3-9pm) are a world away from the chaos outside. Orange-clad monks glide around and there's a reverential feel here. The temple itself is a handsome shrine open to followers of any religion for meditation.

Built in 1504, then rebuilt in neo-Gothic style in 1893, **San Thome Cathedral** is a soaring Roman Catholic church between Kapaleeshwarar Temple and Marina Beach. It is said to house the remains of St Thomas the Apostle (Doubting Thomas).

An early morning or evening stroll along the 13km sandy stretch of **Marina Beach** is a highlight of Chennai. Away from the pollution of the city streets you'll pass pavement cricket matches, kids flying kites, fortune tellers, fish markets and young couples enjoying the sea breeze. The beach was the scene of devastation after the 2004 tsunami, when fishing shanties lining the foreshore were inundated. Don't swim here – strong rips make it dangerous. About 2km further south in Besant Nagar, **Elliot's Beach** is a more affluent place, popular with young couples.

Situated on a green wedge between the Adyar River and the coast, the 250 acres of the **Theosophical Society** (Adyar Bridge Rd; ☻ gates 9.30am-12.30pm & 2-4pm Mon-Sat) provides a peaceful retreat from the city. The grounds contain a huge variety of native and introduced trees, including a 400-year-old **banyan tree** that was once thought to be the largest in the world (the mother trunk has since decayed). There's a church, mosque, Buddhist shrine and Hindu temple on the grounds. The **Adyar Library** (☻ 9am-5pm) here contains a huge collection of books on religion and philosophy. To become a member of the Theosophical Society you need to join in your home country, but if you're interested in the philosophy you can call into the public relations office and chat with the director.

Further south in Adyar are three adjacent **wildlife parks** that make an easy though not terribly inspiring diversion from the city. **Guindy National Park** (☎ 22301328; admission adult/child Rs 2/1; ☻ 9am-5.30pm Wed-Mon) is indeed a small national park within the city and while it contains some varied wildlife, it's a scraggy place and you're unlikely to see much. There's also a **snake park** and **children's park** nearby.

Other Areas
FILM STUDIOS
Chennai's film industry rivals that of Bollywood (Mumbai) for output, though almost all films are in Tamil. **AVM Studios** (Off map

---

WORKERS IN THE SHADOWS

They leave their slum dwellings at around 5am to begin work in the city by 6am. They scurry swiftly and silently across the city streets, keeping to the shadows and working mostly in pairs. They are the wastepickers – mostly women, sometimes children. They spend up to 10 hours a day rummaging through piles of domestic and industrial waste and separating it into bags of metal, plastic, paper, cloth and other recyclable items. Usually they sell their bundles to middlemen who then sell to the recycling companies. For this dangerous and dirty work they earn around Rs 45 a day. With assistance from NGOs, some waste-pickers have formed cooperatives, bypassing the middlemen and boosting their earning potential.

pp318-19; ☎ 24836700; 38 Arcot Rd, Vadapalani; admission free; ⏰ 9am-6pm, closed 2nd Sun) is the only one routinely open to the public. You don't exactly get a tour – they just give you a pass and you wander around the sets, so you'll probably see some filming being done at any given time. You might see movie scenes, commercials being filmed, dance sequences or actors swanning around fixing their hair. Don't expect Warner Bros or MGM – the studio is pretty small scale and the sets a bit feeble – but this is one of the most entertaining outings in Chennai.

Extras are occasionally needed – call the studio or simply hang about looking sexy and wait to be spotted. Buses 17M (from

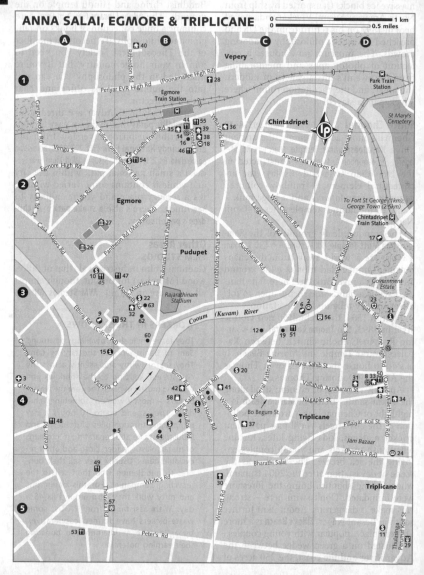

Anna Salai) and 17E (from Egmore Station) make the 10km trip.

ENFIELD FACTORY

Motorcycle fans should get a kick out of visiting the famous **Enfield factory** (Off map pp318-19; ☎ 25733310; www.royalenfield.com; Tiruvottiyur), located 17km north of Chennai, to tour the production line of bikes that have been made in India since 1955. Tours run only on Saturday morning, and at a cost of Rs 50 for a half-hour, you'd have to be very keen. You need to register for a tour on the website.

COURSES
Language

Dakshin Barath Hindi Prachar Sabha (Map pp938-9; ☎ 24341824; 12 Thanikachalam St, Theagaraya Nagar) Hindi courses in all levels.

International Institute of Tamil Studies (Map pp938-9; ☎ 22350992; Central Polytechnic Campus, Adyar) Courses in the state language of Tamil Nadu.

Yoga

Ice House (Map pp938-9; Vivekananda Museum; ☎ 28446188; Kamarajr Salai; ☷ 7-8.30am; Rs 500) Weekly yoga classes run by Sri Ramakrishna Mutt.

TOURS

Tamil Nadu Tourist Development Corporation (TTDC) and ITDC both conduct tours of Chennai and surrounds, with day trips going as far as Pondicherry and Tirupathi.

For information on where to book, see p317. Prices given here don't include entry fees.

City Sightseeing Tour (Rs 110, with AC bus Rs 160; ☷ 8am-1pm & 1.30pm-6.30pm) Half-day city tour.
Kanchipuram & Mamallapuram (Full-day tour Rs 295, with AC Rs 420) Includes breakfast, lunch and a visit to a crocodile farm.

SLEEPING

Chennai has plenty of accommodation, though there's a yawning gap between basic budget places and the flashy top-end hotels. Good places fill up in peak season (December to February), so call ahead. Egmore, on and around Kennet Lane, is good for budget accommodation and all the touts and chaos that goes with it. The location opposite Egmore train station is perfect for a quick exit. Longer-term visitors tend to prefer the slightly less chaotic Triplicane – there's a cluster of good budget and midrange places around Triplicane High Rd. The top hotels are scattered around Anna Salai, Dr Radhakrishnan Salai and MG Rd, south and west of the centre.

Budget
EGMORE   **Map p322**

Hotel Impala Continental (☎ 28191423; 12 Gandhi Irwin Rd; s/d Rs 220/372 incl tax) Entered through a large courtyard (with parking), Impala is one of the better value budget places in this area with clean, spacious double rooms.

INFORMATION	
American Express	(see 58)
AmEx ATM	**1** B4
Anna Salai Post Office	**2** C3
Apollo Hospital	**3** A4
Bookpoint	**4** B4
British Council Library	**5** B4
Canadian Honorary Consulate	**6** C3
Emerald Internet	**7** D3
Gee Gee Net	**8** D4
German Consulate	**9** A3
Giggles Bookshop	(see 42)
HDFC Bank ATM	**10** A3
HDFC Bank ATM	**11** D5
Higginbothams	**12** C3
Indiatourism	**13** B4
Internet Zone	**14** B2
ITDC	**15** A4
Madura Travel Service	**16** B2
Maldives Honorary Consulate	**17** D2
Post Office	**18** B2
SP Travels & Tours	**19** C3
State Bank of India	**20** C4
Tamil Nadu	
Tourist Complex	**21** D3
Thomas Cook	**22** B3
Triplicane Police Station	**23** D3
Triplicane Post Office	**24** D4
UTI Bank ATM	**25** B2

SIGHTS & ACTIVITIES	
National Art Gallery	**26** A3
Government Museum	**27** A2
St Andrew's Church	**28** B1
Sri Parthasarathy Temple	**29** D5
Wesley Church	**30** C5

SLEEPING 🛏	
Broadlands Lodge	**31** D4
Hotel Ambassador Pallava	**32** B3
Hotel Comfort	**33** D4
Hotel Himalaya	**34** D4
Hotel Impala Continental	**35** B1
Hotel New Park Plaza	**36** C1
Hotel Orchid Inn	**37** C4
Hotel Regent	**38** B2
New Victoria Hotel	**39** B1
Salvation Army Red Shield Guest House	**40** B1
Sarovara Deluxe Rooms	**41** C4
Taj Connemara	**42** B4
Thaj Regency	**43** D4

EATING 🍴	
Bhoopathy Cafe	**44** B1
Café Coffee Day	**45** A3
Ceylon Restaurant	**46** B2
Clay Oven & Cake Walk	**47** B3
Foodworld	(see 58)
Gallopin' Gooseberry	**48** A4

Gyan Vaishnav Punjabi Dhaba	**49** A5
Maharaja Restaurant	**50** D4
Only Veg	**51** C3
Ponnusamy Hotel	**52** B3
Royal Everest Restaurant	(see 34)
Saravanaas	**53** A5
Saravanaas	(see 56)
Udipi Home Mathsya	**54** B2
Vasanta Bhavan	**55** B1

ENTERTAINMENT 🎭	
Devi Cinema Complex	**56** D3
Sathyam Cinema	**57** A5

SHOPPING 🛍	
Spencer Plaza	**58** B4
Victoria Technical Institute	**59** B4

TRANSPORT	
Air France	(see 63)
Air India	**60** B3
American Airlines	(see 63)
British Airways	**61** B4
Cathay Pacific Airways	(see 42)
Gulf Air	**62** B3
Indian Airlines	(see 60)
Jet Airways	**63** B3
KLM	(see 42)
Lufthansa	**64** B4

Salvation Army Red Shield Guest House (☎ 2532 1821; 15 Ritherdon Rd; dm Rs 50, s/d Rs 200/250) In a quiet spot north of Egmore Station, this is a popular cheap option (dorm). It's clean enough, with cold running water only.

Hotel Regent (☎ 28253347; 11 Kennet Lane; s/d Rs 200/300) This standard budget hotel has a veg restaurant and quiet rooms set around a central courtyard.

TRIPLICANE   Map p322

Broadlands Lodge (☎ 28545573; broadlandshotel@ yahoo.com; 18 Vallabha Agraharam St; s with shared bathroom Rs 150-170, d Rs 200, s with private bathroom Rs 200, d Rs 250-400) A long-time travellers' hangout, Broadlands Lodge is a decaying old colonial-style place with bags of charm and friendly management. Simple rooms are set around a leafy central courtyard – the large upper storey rooms at the back are easily the best (check No 43 and 44). The shared bathrooms are dank and bucket hot water is available.

Thaj Regency (☎ 28529524; 300 Triplicane High Rd; s/d from Rs 195/250, d with AC Rs 495; ☒) The price here is unbeatable for basic but decent rooms with satellite TV and running hot water – the iron-frame beds are rock hard but what's new?

Hotel Comfort (☎ 28587661; hotel_comfort@yahoo .com; 22 Vallabha Agraharam; s/d from Rs 250/350; with AC Rs 500/600; ☒) This multistorey hotel is almost midrange standard and great value. Rooms are a bit cramped but are clean, with TV and hot water. It also has Triplicane's only rooftop bar and an AC restaurant. Credit cards accepted.

Midrange
EGMORE   Map p322
New Victoria Hotel (☎ 28193638; www.newvictoria hotel.com; 3 Kennet Lane; s/d from Rs 975/1250; ☒) This is a reasonably smart hotel has spacious rooms, though there appears to be no difference between the standard and deluxe rooms. Rates include breakfast; there's also a good multicuisine restaurant and the Tropicana Bar.

Hotel New Park Plaza (☎ 52148333; parkplaza@ eth.net; 29 Whannels Rd; s/d from Rs 900/1100; ☒) Imaginatively billed as a 'three-star hotel at a no-star rate', this is no-frills for the price but it's clean and rooms are apparently noise-proof. There's a bar and a rooftop restaurant with good views of the chaotic Egmore streets.

TRIPLICANE   Map p322
Hotel Himalaya (☎ 28547522; 91 Triplicane High Rd; s/d/tr Rs 350/399/550, s/d with AC Rs 550/799; ☒ 🖥) This is a great budget/midrange choice with plain but comfortable rooms, friendly staff and a travel desk. Rooms on three floors all have satellite TV (set-top box is Rs 75 extra) and hot and cold water.

Hotel Orchid Inn (☎ 28522555; orchidinn@vsnl .net; 19 Woods Rd; s/d Rs 550/650, with AC Rs 750/975; ☒) A short walk from Anna Salai, this is a comfortable, modern hotel with a more intimate feel than many Chennai midrange places. Spacious rooms have Western-style bathrooms and satellite TV.

Sarovara Deluxe Rooms (☎ 28552755; www.saro vararooms.com; 3 Woods Rd; s/d Rs 375/450, with AC Rs 600/ 700; ☒) Near Anna Salai and Spencer Plaza, this hotel has clean, basic rooms with TV.

MYLAPORE &
NUNGAMBAKKAM   Map pp318–19
Nilgiri's Nest (☎ 28115111; fax 8111719; nilgiri@hotels chennai.com; 105 Dr Radhakrishnan Salai; s Rs 1350-2100, d Rs 1800-2950) Nilgiri's is a relatively small, intimate place with spotless (though overpriced) rooms, a good restaurant (rates include breakfast) and a handy location close to many restaurants and the music academy.

Hotel Ranjith (☎ 28270521; hotelranjith@yahoo .com; 9 MG Rd; s/d Rs 850/1050, with AC Rs 1275/1525; ☒) A neat, comfortable hotel with numerous restaurants, including an excellent rooftop barbecue restaurant, and a bar.

New Woodlands Hotel (☎ 28113111; www.new woodlands.com; 72-75 Dr Radhakrishnan Salai; s Rs 450, s/d with AC Rs 600/900, cottages from Rs 1450; ☒ 🖥) A sprawling complex with 170 rooms and a certain eccentric character – it's a popular venue for weddings, so there's a good chance of seeing all the colour and noise of a Hindu marriage. It's a bit austere and some travellers find it run down, but it's well located.

Top End
All the following hotels have central AC, multicuisine restaurants, bar and accept major credit cards.

Hotel Ambassador Pallava (Map p322; ☎ 2855 4476; www.ambassadorindia.com; 53 Montieth Rd; s/d from US$65/75; ☒ 🖥 🍴) A very swanky lobby complete with old horse-drawn carriage gives way to spacious but slightly fading rooms. There's a pool, good bar and games room – in all, a cheaper alternative to the five-stars. Checkout is noon.

Taj Connemara (Map p322; ☎ 28520123; www .tajhotels.com; Binny Rd; s US$165-225, d US$180-240; ✗ ⌨ ⌨) This Chennai institution from the Raj era still retains some of its regal charm, along with the modern comforts of a five-star – shopping arcade, business centre, 24-hour coffee shop and health centre.

ITC Hotel Park Sheraton & Towers (Map pp318-19; ☎ 24994101; www.welcomgroup.com; 132 TTK Rd, Alwarpet; s/d from Rs 7000/8000; ✗ ⌨ ⌨) The plush Sheraton is the most luxurious of Chennai's top-end hotels, with its own shopping centre, health club, business centre and beautifully furnished rooms.

EATING

It's easy to find South Indian vegetarian cuisine in Chennai – *idli* and dosas (paper-thin lentil-flour pancakes) for breakfast, thali meals served on a banana leaf for lunch – but there are also an increasing number of more sophisticated restaurants, especially around Cathedral Rd.

For reliable, quality vegetarian meals try the Saravanaas/Saravana Bhavan chain. These range from clean, inexpensive self-service restaurants to more upmarket ones; open 7am to 11.30pm.

Some of the best restaurants in Chennai are in the upmarket hotels – most of the five-star places have three or four plush restaurants to choose from and put on spectacular lunch-time buffets ranging from Rs 200 to 600 plus taxes. This may seem a bit steep, but you can stuff your face and the atmosphere is less formal than an evening meal.

Restaurants

EGMORE   Map p322
Bhoopathy Café (33 Gandhi Irwin Rd; meals Rs 30-50; ✆ 9am-10pm) Bhoopathy offers cheap and cheerful standard veg fare, and is popular with locals and tourists alike.

Ceylon Restaurant (12 Kennet Lane; dishes 30-50; ✆ 8am-11pm) This place has a few good Sri Lankan speciality dishes on its menu.

Ponnusamy Hotel (Wellington Estate, 24 Ethiraj Rd; dishes Rs 40-60) This well-known place serves meat and fish curry, biryani and Chettinad dishes. Unusual dishes include pigeon and rabbit.

Clay Oven & Cake Walk (10 Monteith Rd; mains Rs 25-70; ✆ 10am-10pm) Modern, Western-style café with pastel shades and wrought-iron furniture serving up burgers, sandwiches and pizzas. The cake shop at the front has a mouth-watering array of sweet stuff such as apple pie and black forest cake.

TRIPLICANE   Map p322
Maharaja Restaurant (207 Triplicane High Rd; dishes Rs 16-40; ✆ 6am-11pm) Maharaja is a fabulous veg restaurant popular with travellers and locals alike. The lunch-time thalis (Rs 20 to 50) are a highlight and breakfast starts early.

Hotel Comfort (☎ 28587661; 22 Vallabha Agraharam; dishes Rs 20-100; ✆ 11am-11pm) This rooftop restaurant here has a typical menu of Indian and Chinese dishes but the open-air section is pleasant in the evenings and you can get a cold beer here.

ANNA SALAI AREA   Map p322
Saravanaas (48 Anna Salai) Located in the Devi Cinema Complex forecourt, this is a great place for a quick meal.

Saravanaas (293 Peter's Rd) This upmarket branch of Saravanaas has three floors of quality veg cuisine – on the 2nd and 3rd floors you can dine in style with fine dinner sets and silver cutlery.

Gyan Vaishnav Punjabi Dhaba (260 Anna Salai; dishes Rs 35-80; ✆ 11.30am-3pm & 7-11pm) With excellent North Indian food, good-value thalis and a clean, comfortable dining area, this is a busy little restaurant where you may have to wait for a seat in the evenings.

Gallopin' Gooseberry (11 Greams Rd; dishes Rs 60-125; ✆ 10am-10pm) This American diner-style place does fab burgers including Cajun, mushroom and barbecue (most around Rs 80) and Italian-style pasta, as well as steaks and sandwiches. The attached fruit shop offers an exotic range of juices and shakes (Rs 15 to 70).

MYLAPORE   Map pp318–19
The Mylapore area, especially Cathedral Rd and TTK Rd, has a plethora of fine independent restaurants, so it's a good place to head if you're looking for a night out. Across the road from the Music Academy is a small knot of interesting places specialising in regional cuisines.

Coconut Lagoon (☎ 28116416; cnr Cathedral & TTK Rds; mains Rs 65-90; ✆ 11am-3pm & 7-11pm) Excellent

Goan, Keralan and Karnatakan fare with particular attention to the west-coast seafood delicacies. Try the pomfret *recheiado* or Goan sausage.

Roomallee (cnr Cathedral & TTK Rds; mains Rs 45-80; 6-11pm) Open-air restaurant specialising in Hyderabadi barbecue dishes.

Amarathi (cnr Cathedral & TTK Rds; mains Rs 50-90; 11am-3pm & 7-11pm) To round off the South Indian culinary experience, Amarathi serves exciting Andhra dishes on banana leaf plates. The décor includes murals of rural India.

Don Pepe (☎ 28110413; 73 Cathedral Rd; 12.30-2.45pm & 7.30-11.45pm) An authentic Mexican place with burritos, tacos and tortillas.

Zara's (☎ 28111462; 74 Cathedral Rd; tapas Rs 55-195; 1-3pm & 6.30-11pm) An ultra-cool tapas bar with a genuine Spanish flavour, it has everything from octopus and olives to tortilla, washed down with sangria. See also right.

Benjarong (☎ 24322640; 146 TTK Rd; mains Rs 130-400; 11am-3pm & 7-11pm) From the finely crafted furniture and calming ambience to the attentive service and superbly presented food, this bone fide Thai restaurant is worth the splurge. Most mains on the extensive menu (such as green curry) are around Rs 200 and there's an excellent four-course set menu at lunch (Rs 158 to 250).

Quick Eats

Street stalls around the city cook up samosas, vadai (deep-fried spicy donut), omelettes and biryani for Rs 5 to 10. European-style cafés are becoming trendy places for young Chennaites to hang out over coffee and muffins. Around the city there are several branches of **Café Coffee Day** (Map pp318-19; MG Rd; coffee Rs 16-40, snacks Rs 30; 10am-11pm) and the hipper **Barista** (Map pp318-19; MG Rd; D Khader Nawaz Khan Rd), which both do good espresso coffee, sundaes, smoothies and snacks such as samosas, sandwiches and muffins. A spotlessly clean place offering tasty snacks and juices is **Only Veg** (Map p322; 82 Anna Salai; dishes Rs 15-20).

Self-Catering

Nilgiri Supermarket & Dairy (Map pp318-19; Dr Radhakrishnan Salai; 9.30am-8pm) Next to Nilgiri's Nest, this is a good place to buy dairy products, boxed tea, coffee and other edibles.

Foodworld (Map p322; Spencer Plaza, Anna Salai; 10am-8.30pm) This modern, well-stocked

supermarket wouldn't look out of place on a London high street.

If you're after fruit and vegetables or spices, head south along Ellis St to the junction of Bharathi Salai where you'll find the colourful Jam Bazaar (Map p322).

DRINKING

Chennai's nightlife scene is on the move but don't expect anything like Bangalore or Mumbai. Bars and nightclubs are restricted here – by law – to hotels (usually top-end places). The exceptions are the seedy backrooms you'll occasionally find behind the ubiquitous 'wine shops', where local men consume litres of cheap Indian rum and brandy. Some midrange hotels have darkened AC bars (or 'permit rooms') where you can get a reasonably cold beer for Rs 75 to 100. Good ones include the rooftop bar at Hotel Comfort in Triplicane, or Tropicana Bar at New Victoria Hotel in Egmore.

Zara's (Map pp318-19; ☎ 28111462; 74 Cathedral Rd; 1-3pm & 6.30-11pm) If you're wondering where the cool people are in Chennai on a Friday or Saturday, they're probably at this Spanish tapas and cocktail bar. Sangria is Rs 150 and tailored cocktails and margaritas are Rs 150 to 325. Dig deep in your wallet and your luggage – no shorts or sandals allowed!

Bike & Barrel (Map pp318-19; Sir Thyagaraya Nagar Rd; 11am-11pm) At the plush Residency Towers Hotel, this pub has walls full of memorabilia, barrels for tables and a Norton motorcycle hanging from the ceiling. Better vibe than most bars; beer is Rs 120 and food is available.

Dublin (Map pp318-19; 132 TTK Rd; 5pm-3am) At the Park Sheraton, Dublin is an Irish pub/nightclub. Entrance is Rs 750 per couple after 10pm. In the same hotel is Vijay's Sports Café, a bar showing international sports.

ENTERTAINMENT
Classical Music & Dance

Music Academy (Map pp318-19; ☎ 28115619; cnr TTK Rd & Dr Radhakrishnan Salai) This is Chennai's most popular public venue for Carnatic classical music and *bharata natyam* dance. Check newspapers for events. Expect to pay Rs 200 for a good seat, although there are many free performances.

Kalakshetra Arts Village (Off map pp318-19 ☎ 2491 1169; Dr Muthulakshmi Rd, Tiruvanmiyu; 10am-6pm)

Founded in 1936, this organisation is committed reviving classical dance and music. See one of the regular performances, or a class (9am to 11.15am Monday to Friday).

Cinema
There are over 100 cinemas in Chennai, a reflection of the vibrant film industry here. Most cinemas screen Tamil films. **Devi Cinema Complex** (Map p322; ☎ 28593589; 48 Anna Salai) and **Sathyam Cinema** (Map p322; ☎ 28512425; 8 Thiruvika Rd) often show English-language films, as well as Tamil films and Hindi Bollywood blockbusters. Tickets cost Rs 50 to 80. Check local papers for details.

SHOPPING
Like any big Indian city you can get just about anything in Chennai, from a silk sari to the latest digital camera. Modern new plazas are springing up while traditional stores are extending services. Ready-made or tailored clothing, crafts from all corners of India, contemporary artworks, genuine antiques, jewellery, musical instruments and quality fabrics are readily available.

For conventional souvenirs at fixed prices, head to the government emporiums along Anna Salai. These are usually open 10am to 6pm Monday to Friday and 10am to 1pm Saturday. Most of the finest Kanchipuram silks turn up in Chennai, so it's well worth seeing what's on offer around town.

The Theagaraya Nagar district (known locally as T Nagar) is a great place to shop, especially at the street-side Pondy Bazaar and the bustling markets around Panagal Park.

TRADITIONAL TRADERS
George Town, the area that grew around the Fort, retains much of its original flavour. This is the wholesale centre of Chennai. Many backstreets, bordered by NSC Bose Rd, Krishna Koil St, Mint St and Rajaji Salai, are entirely given over to selling one particular type of merchandise as they have done for hundreds of years – paper goods in Anderson St, fireworks in Badrian St and so on. Even if you're not in the market for any of these things, wandering the mazelike streets of this part of town is a great way to see another aspect of Indian life flowing seamlessly from the past into the present.

Victoria Technical Institute (Map p322; 765 Anna Salai) This place is worth visiting; the revenue from certain items supports various development groups.

SIPA'S Craftlink (Map pp318-19; 70 Kodambakkam High Rd, Nungambakkam; ⏰ 9am-8pm Mon-Sat) This is South India's first fair-trade craft shop, and an excellent place to shop if you want to support local artisans.

Vardharams (Map pp318-19; 88 Harrington Rd, Chetput) A good selection of Kanchipuram silk and some of the best prices in Chennai.

The best of the modern shopping plazas include **Spencer Plaza** (Map p322; Anna Salai), and **Gee Gee Emerald Plaza** (Map pp318-19; MG Rd), with a range of shops selling clothing, books, music, fabrics and children's gear.

GETTING THERE & AWAY
Air
Anna International Airport (☎ 22560551) in Tirisulam, 16km southwest of the centre, is efficient and not too busy, making Chennai a good entry or exit point. The newer **Kamaraj domestic terminal** (☎ 22560512) is next door in the same building.

DOMESTIC AIRLINES
Air Deccan has the cheapest fares to Bangalore, Coimbatore, Madurai and Hyderabad. Domestic airlines servicing Chennai include the following:
Air Deccan (☎ 30978596, airport 22560505; www.airdeccan.com; 32 92nd St, 18th Ave; ⏰ 9am-5pm Mon-Sat)
Air Sahara (Map pp318-19; ☎ 52110202, airport 22560771; airsahara@vsnl.net; ITC Hotel Park Sheraton & Towers, TTK Rd)
Indian Airlines (Map p322; ☎ 28555201, airport 22560771; www.indian-airlines.nic.in; 19 Rukmani Lakshmi Pathy Rd, Egmore; ⏰ 8am-8pm Mon-Sat)
Jet Airways (Map p322; ☎ 28414141, airport 22561818; www.jetairways.com; 41/43 Montieth Rd, Egmore; ⏰ 9am-8pm Mon-Sat, 9am-7pm Sun)

INTERNATIONAL AIRLINES
International airlines with offices in Chennai include these:
Air France (Map p322; ☎ 28554961; Thapar House, 43-44 Montieth Rd, Egmore)
Air India (Map p322; ☎ 28554477; 9 Rukmani Lakshmi Pathy Rd, Egmore)
American Airlines (Map p322; ☎ 28592564; Thapar House, 43-44 Montieth Rd, Egmore)
British Airways (Map p322; ☎ 52068181; 8th fl, Raheja Towers, 177 Anna Salai)

DOMESTIC FLIGHTS FROM CHENNAI

Destination	Airline	Fare (Rs/US$)	Duration (hr)	Frequency
Bangalore	IC	2655/75	¾	9 weekly
	9W	3235/75	1	5 daily
	DN	1800	1	1 daily
Delhi	IC	10,740/270	2½	4 daily
	9W	10,735/270	2½	4 daily
Goa	IC	5410/150	3	2 weekly
	9W	6440/180	3	1 daily
Hyderabad	IC	4635/115	1	3 daily
	9W	4635/115	1½	1 daily
	DN	2575	1½	2 daily
Kochi (Cochin)	IC	4625/130	1	8 weekly
	9W	4980/130	1	1 daily
Kolkata	IC	9275/230	2	2 daily
	9W	9350/230	2	1 daily
Madurai	IC	3655/100	1	2 daily
	9W	3655/100	1½	2 daily
	DN	2100	1½	1 daily
Mumbai (Bombay)	IC	5825/170	2	4 daily
	9W	5825/170	2	6 daily
Port Blair	IC	8550/205	2	1 daily
	9W	8545/205	2	1 daily
Thiruvananthapuram (Trivandrum)	IC	4710/115	1½	11 weekly

Note: Fares are one-way only. Rs fares apply to Indian travellers only, except with Air Deccan.
Airline codes: IC = Indian Airlines, 9W = Jet Airways, DN = Air Deccan

Cathay Pacific Airways (Map p322; ☎ 52140941; Taj Connemara, Binny Rd)
Gulf Air (Map p322; ☎ 28554417; 52 Montieth Rd, Egmore)
KLM (Map p322; ☎ 28524427; Taj Connemara, Binny Rd)
Lufthansa (Map p322; ☎ 28525095; 167 Anna Salai)
Malaysia Airlines (Map pp318-19; ☎ 52199999; Karumuttu Centre, 498 Anna Salai)
Qantas (Map pp318-19; ☎ 28278680; G3, Eldorado Bldg, 112 MG Rd)
Singapore Airlines (Map pp318-19; ☎ 28470170; West Minster, 108 Dr Radhakrishnan Salai)
Sri Lankan Airlines (Map pp318-19; ☎ 28111536; 76 Cathedral Rd)
Thai Airways International (Map pp318-19; ☎ 52171100; 31 Haddows Rd)

Boat

Passenger ships sail from Chennai to the Andaman Islands roughly twice a month. The harbour is in George Town north of the Fort. Contact the **Chennai Port Trust** (Map pp318-19; ☎ 25362501; Rajaji Salai) or the **Director of Shipping Services** (Map pp318-19; ☎ 25226873; www.shipindia. com) for information. See the Andaman & Nicobar Islands chapter, p398 for details of boat travel to and from these islands.

Bus

Most government bus services for Tamil Nadu and interstate operate from the vast **Chennai Mofussil Bus Terminus** (CMBT; general enquiries ☎ 24794705; Jawarhal Nehru Salai, Koyambedu), 7km west of town. Also known locally as the Koyambedu Bus Stand, it is claimed to be the largest bus station in Asia and is a bit of a revelation. The terminal looks more like an airport terminal than an Indian bus station and the platforms are well organised, with destinations listed in English at each end. Bus Nos 18B, 15B, 15C or 27B takes 40 minutes to make the trip from Anna Salai or Parry's Corner. An autorickshaw charges around Rs 100 for the same ride. Following is more information on buses from Chennai:

Destination	Fare (Rs)	Duration (hr)	Frequency
Bangalore	150	8	43 daily
Chidambaram	77	7	6 daily
Kodaikanal	203	14	1 daily
Madurai	144-176	10	41 daily
Mamallapuram	22	2	40 daily
Mysore	209	11	2 daily
Ooty	228	14	1 daily
Pondicherry	55	4	37 daily
Thanjavur	130	9	24 daily
Tiruchirappalli	105-145	8	53 daily
Tirupathi	58	4	18 daily

Private bus companies with offices opposite Egmore train station run superdeluxe video buses daily to Bangalore, Coimbatore, Madurai, Trichy and elsewhere. Prices for these services are slightly higher than for state buses.

Train

Interstate trains and those heading west generally depart from Central Station, while trains heading south depart from Egmore. You can make reservations on the 1st floor of the **Train Reservation Complex** (🕙 8am-2pm & 2.15-8pm Mon-Sat, 8am-2pm Sun), the large building on the west side of Central Station. For reservations and general inquiries call ☎ 131/2 (operator assistance), ☎ 1361 (English). The Foreign Assistance Tourist Cell, in the reservation complex, deals with Indrail Pass and tourist-quota bookings, and there's a less busy credit-card booking counter on the 2nd floor.

At Egmore, the **booking office** (☎ 135) keeps the same hours as the office at Central Station. The table, below, lists some of the services from Chennai. For Goa there's only one direct train a week – the *Chennai–Vasco Express* on Friday.

MAJOR TRAINS FROM CHENNAI

Destination	Train No & name	Fare (Rs)	Duration (hr)	Departure
Bangalore	2007 *Bangalore Shatabdi* *	505/990	5	6am CC
	6222 *Kaveri Express*	142/399/638	8	9.30pm CC
	6523 *Bangalore Exp*	89/311	7	1pm CC
Delhi	2615 *Grand Trunk Exp*	477/1340/2144	35½	4.30pm CC
	2621 *Tamil Nadu Exp*	2144/1340/477	34	10pm CC
Hyderabad	2759 *Charminar Exp*	257/722/1155	15	6.10pm CC
	7053 *Hyderabad Exp*	257/722/1155	14	4.45pm CC
Kochi	6041 *Alleppey Exp*	236/663/1060	12½	8.30pm CC
Kolkata	2842 *Coromandel Exp*	409/1149/1838	28	9.05am CC
	6004 *Howrah Mail*	409/1149/1838	32½	10.30pm CC
Madurai	2637 *Pandyan Exp*	182/510/816	9	9.30pm CE
	Vaigai Exp	114/397	8	12.25pm CE
Mettupalayam	2671 *Nilgiri Exp*	192/540/864	9½	8.30pm CC
Mumbai	6012 *Mumbai Exp*	345/969/1550	26	11.45am CC
	6010 *Mumbai Mail*	345/969/1550	29	11pm CC
Mysore	2007 *Mysore Shatabdi* *	645/1255	7	6am CC
	6222 *Kaveri Exp*	185/519/830	11	9.30pm CC
Thiruvananthapuram	2623 *Trivandrum Mail*	284/798/1277	16	7.30pm CC
Tiruchirappalli	2605 *Pallavan Exp*	85/297	5½	3.30pm CE
	6177 *Rock Fort Exp*	136/382/611	9	10.30pm CE
Tirupathi	6057 *Saptagiri Exp*	46/160	3	6.25am CC
	6053 *Tirupathi Exp*	46/160	3	1.50pm CC

CC = Chennai Central, CE = Chennai Egmore
Daily except Tuesday; AC chair only; fare includes meals and drinks
* Monday and Saturday only
Shatabdi fares are chair/executive; Express and Mail fares are 2nd/chair car for day trains, sleeper/3AC/2AC for overnight trains.

GETTING AROUND

To/From the Airport

The domestic and international terminals are 16km south of the city centre. The cheapest way to reach them is by suburban train from Egmore to Tirusulam, 500m across the road from the terminals. The trains run from 4.15am until 11.45pm (Rs 7/ 85 in 2nd/1st class, 40 minutes). Avoid them during peak hours.

The easiest way is an autorickshaw, which costs about Rs 150/250 for a day/ night trip.

At the prepaid taxi kiosk inside the international airport, you can buy a ticket into Chennai for Rs 210 (to Egmore) or Rs 230 to Anna Salai or Triplicane. There's another prepaid kiosk in the baggage collection area inside the domestic terminal.

Autorickshaw

Autorickshaws are tough to bargain with in Chennai and because it's not an easily walkable city, you're somewhat at their mercy. Still, they're the quickest way of cutting through Chennai's traffic. Officially, it's Rs 7 for the first kilometre, then Rs 3½ per kilometre, but let us know if you find a driver willing to use the meter! From Egmore to George Town, Triplicane or Anna Salai should cost no more than Rs 25. There's a prepaid booth outside Central Station. Prices are at least 25% higher after 10pm.

New arrivals will find drivers sidling up to them offering Rs 20 'sightseeing' rides for one hour to anywhere in the city. This means you'll be ferried to two or three private craft emporiums and asked to 'just look' for 10 minutes so the driver can reap a healthy commission. If you just want to get somewhere don't fall for it – the emporiums give you an uncomfortable hard sell and are unhappy if you walk out without buying.

Bus

The bus system in Chennai is typically confusing though less overburdened than other large Indian cities. However, it can be useful for a cheap ride between direct routes. The main city bus stand is at Parry's Corner, but buses pick up throughout the city. To T Nagar take Bus No 10 or 11, to the Mossufil bus station take bus No 15B or 17. Fares are between Rs 4 and 10.

Car & Taxi

Although most taxi drivers will happily set off on a long trip for the right price, for an extended hire it's wise to organise a driver through a reputable travel agent or large hotel – you might pay a little more but the driver should be reliable and you'll have a point of contact should something go wrong. Rates vary but a general rule is travel within the city is Rs 800 per day (eight hours) and travel beyond city limits costs Rs 5 per kilometre (Rs 7 with AC) with a minimum of 250km per day.

The government-approved **Manjoo Cabs** (☎ 23813083; manjoocabs@yahoo.com; 1 Subramaniya-swamy Koil West St, Saidapet) is a cooperative of enterprising drivers, who have worked to save for and purchase their own cars.

Train

The suburban train is a good way to get between Egmore and Central Stations (Rs 5), Egmore and Fort (Rs 5), Nungambakkam (Rs 5), to Guindy (Rs 7), St Thomas Mount (Rs 7) or the airport (Tirusulam; Rs 8). There are some relatively uncrowded ladies' compartments.

The MRTS (Mass Rapid Transport System) runs south from Beach station. All tickets are Rs 5, no matter how far or for how long you travel, and there are roughly four trains an hour from 7am to 9pm. Stations currently include Beach, Fort, Park Town, Chintadripet, Chepauk, Lighthouse and Luz.

NORTHERN TAMIL NADU

CHENNAI TO MAMALLAPURAM

Chennai's urban sprawl continues a fair way south before opening up on the East Coast Rd to Mamallapuram. Along this stretch, known as the Coromandel Coast, are several small beach resorts, recreation areas and wonderful artists' communities. At the time of research, tsunami-ravaged fishing villages were slowly being rebuilt along this stretch of coast.

In the village of Injambalkkam, 18km south of Chennai, **Cholamandal Artists' Village** (☎ 044-24490092; cholamandalartvillage.com; admission free; ☺ 9.30am-6.30pm) was set up in 1966 as a place for artists and sculptors to live, work and exhibit. The group of traditional thatch-roofed buildings includes galleries and studios where you can sometimes see artists at work or just browse the fine contemporary paintings and sculptures, many of which are for sale.

At Muttukadu, 12km south of Cholamandal, is **Dakshinachitra** (☎ 04114-272603; www .dakshinachitra.org; admission Indian student/adult Rs 25/50, foreign student/adult Rs 70/175; ☼ 10am-6pm Wed-Mon), a remarkable cultural centre and arts complex displaying traditional arts and crafts from Tamil Nadu, Kerala, Karnataka and Andhra Pradesh. Established by the Madras Crafts Association, the village includes traditional homes, buildings and workshops, such as weavers' houses, potters' sheds and merchants' homes from the respective states. Static arts and craft displays are complemented by weekend demonstrations of pottery, basket weaving, puppet making and palm-leaf decoration. Regular guided tours are included in the admission price and there's a short orientation film shown in the reception area.

To reach these places, take any bus heading south to Mamallapuram (Nos 188 or 118; Rs 22, one hour) and ask to be let off. A taxi for a full day costs about Rs 800 and an autorickshaw can be bargained down to about Rs 450.

The **Crocodile Bank** (☎ 04114-242511; admission adult/child Rs 20/10, camera/video Ts 10/75; ☼ 8am-5.30pm Tue-Sun), 40km south of Chennai, is a breeding farm for crocodile, alligator and turtle, and there's an adjacent **snake farm** (Rs 5/3) where antivenom is produced. There are hundreds of reptiles here, including the Indian mug-ger and gharial crocodiles and the saltwater crocs of the Andaman and Nicobar Islands. Late afternoon is feeding time (Rs 20).

About 5km north of Mamallapuram in the village of Salavankuppam, the **Tiger Cave** is a rock-cut shrine, possibly dating from the 7th century. It's dedicated to Durga and has a small *mandapam* featuring a crown of carved *yali* (mythical lion creature) heads.

MAMALLAPURAM (MAHABALIPURAM)

☎ 04114 / pop 12,049

Less than two hours by bus from Chennai, Mamallapuram is Tamil Nadu's only true travellers enclave – a coastal village where you can happily hang out for days, eating good seafood, wandering among ancient rock carvings and generally chilling out. But it's much more than that. Famous for its Shore Temple and once the second capital and seaport of the Pallava kings of Kanchipuram, Mamallapuram is listed as a World Heritage site and is a renowned centre for stone carving. You'll see and hear the daily tapping of hammer and chisel as the artisans chip away at exquisite sculptures, many of which are exported around the world.

With a reasonably good beach, an excellent combination of cheap accommodation, fish restaurants, handicraft shops, spectacular stone carvings dotted around the town and Tamil Nadu's most highly regarded dance festival (see p315), it's easy to see why travellers make a beeline here from Chennai and hang around for a while. Although beachfront restaurants and the local fishing community were affected by the 2004 tsunami, things are back to normal here.

THE ROCK CARVINGS OF MAMALLAPURAM

The images carved into the rocks around Mamallapuram are like no other in Tamil Nadu. So much religious stonework in the state is alive with complex depictions of gods and goddesses, and images of ordinary folk are conspicuous because of their absence. Yet the splendid carvings at Mamallapuram are distinctive for the simplicity of their folk-art origins. The sculptures show scenes of everyday life – women milking buffaloes, pompous city dignitaries, young girls primping and posing on street corners or swinging their hips in artful come-ons.

Most of the temples and rock carvings here were completed during the reigns of Narasimha Varman I (AD 630–68) and Narasimha Varman II (AD 700–28). But this is not an art form consigned to history. Approximately 200 sculptors line the streets and chisel their stone from dawn to dusk. Indeed Mamallapuram's historical reputation for skilled carvers remains sufficiently intact – the town's craftsmen are frequently commissioned to create sculptures for new temples around the world.

TAMIL NADU

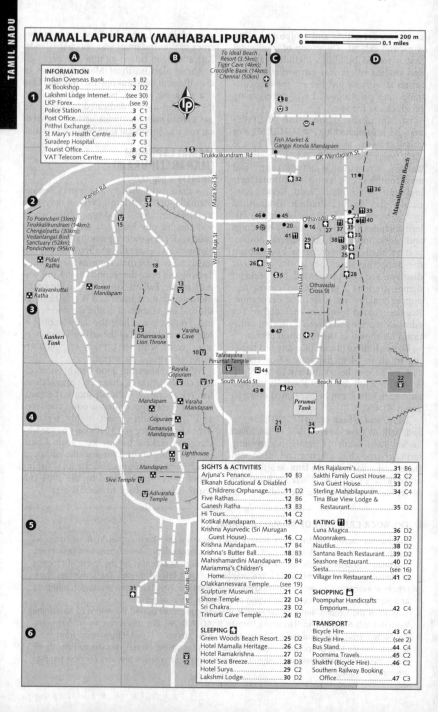

MAMALLAPURAM (MAHABALIPURAM)

0 _____ 200 m
0 _____ 0.1 miles

To Ideal Beach
Resort (3.5km);
Tiger Cave (4km);
Crocodile Bank (14km);
Chennai (50km)

INFORMATION
Indian Overseas Bank...............1 B2
JK Bookshop...........................2 D2
Lakshmi Lodge Internet........(see 30)
LKP Forex.............................(see 9)
Police Station.........................3 C1
Post Office............................4 C1
Prithvi Exchange.....................5 C3
St Mary's Health Centre.............6 C1
Suradeep Hospital...................7 C3
Tourist Office.........................8 C1
VAT Telecom Centre.................9 C2

Tirukkalikundram Rd

Fish Market &
Gangai Konda Mandapam

GK Mandapam St

To Pooncheri (3km);
Tirukkalikundram (14km);
Chengalpattu (30km);
Vedantangal Bird
Sanctuary (52km);
Pondicherry (95km)

Koneri Rd

Pidari
Ratha

Koneri
Mandapam

Valayankuttai
Ratha

Kanheri
Tank

Dharmaraja
Lion Throne

Varaha
Cave

Talasayana
Perumal Temple

Rayala
Gopuram

South Mada St

Beach Rd

Mandapam

Varaha
Mandapam

Gopuram

Ramanuja
Mandapam

Lighthouse

Mandapam

Siva Temple

Adivaraha
Temple

Perumal
Tank

Mamallapuram Beach

Othavadai St

Othavadai
Cross St

Thirukula St

West Raja St

Mada Koil St

East Raja St

Five Rathas Rd

SIGHTS & ACTIVITIES
Arjuna's Penance..................10 B3
Elkanah Educational & Disabled
   Childrens Orphanage.........11 D2
Five Rathas........................12 B6
Ganesh Ratha......................13 B3
Hi Tours............................14 C2
Kotikal Mandapam................15 A2
Krishna Ayurvedic (Sri Murugan
   Guest House)...................16 C2
Krishna Mandapam................17 B4
Krishna's Butter Ball.............18 B3
Mahishamardini Mandapam.....19 B4
Mariamma's Children's
   Home.............................20 C2
Olakkannesvara Temple......(see 19)
Sculpture Museum.................21 C4
Shore Temple......................22 D4
Sri Chakra.........................23 D2
Trimurti Cave Temple............24 B2

SLEEPING
Green Woods Beach Resort.....25 D2
Hotel Mamalla Heritage.........26 C3
Hotel Ramakrishna................27 D2
Hotel Sea Breeze..................28 D3
Hotel Surya........................29 C2
Lakshmi Lodge.....................30 D2

Mrs Rajalaxmi's....................31 B6
Sakthi Family Guest House......32 C2
Siva Guest House.................33 D2
Sterling Mahabilapuram.........34 C4
Tina Blue View Lodge &
   Restaurant.......................35 D2

EATING
Luna Magica.......................36 D2
Moonrakers........................37 D2
Nautilus............................38 D2
Santana Beach Restaurant......39 D2
Seashore Restaurant.............40 D2
Siesta...........................(see 16)
Village Inn Restaurant...........41 C2

SHOPPING
Poompuhar Handicrafts
   Emporium........................42 C4

TRANSPORT
Bicycle Hire.......................43 C4
Bicycle Hire.....................(see 2)
Bus Stand..........................44 C4
Poornima Travels.................45 C2
Shakthi (Bicycle Hire)...........46 C2
Southern Railway Booking
   Office.............................47 C3

Orientation & Information

Mamallapuram village is tiny and laid-back, with most of the action on East Raja St, Othavadai St and Othavadai Cross St, which runs parallel to the beach. Even the surrounding sites of interest can be explored on foot or by bicycle.

BOOKSHOP

JK Bookshop (☎ 246005; 13B Othavadai St; ☺ 8.30am-9pm) A small bookshop where you can buy or swap (Rs 50) books in several languages, including English, French and German. Half the proceeds go towards village schools established by the owner.

INTERNET ACCESS

You'll find Internet everywhere.
Lakshmi Lodge Internet (Othavadai Cross St; per hr Rs 30; ☺ 9am-10pm).
VAT Telecom Centre (East Raja St; ☺ 24hr)

MEDICAL SERVICES

St Mary's Health Centre (☎ 232334; ☺ 9am-12.30pm & 4.30-6.30pm) Near the tourist office.
Suradeep Hospital (☎ 242390; 15 Thirukula St; ☺ 24hr) Recommended by travellers.

MONEY

The best places to change cash or travellers cheques are the private exchange offices on East Raja St. Other suggestions:
LKP Forex (East Raja St; ☺ 9.30am-6.30pm Mon-Sat).
Prithvi Exchange (☎ 243265; East Raja St; ☺ 9.30am-7pm Mon-Sat)

POST

Post office (☺ 8am-4pm Mon-Fri) Down a small lane just east of the tourist office.

TOURIST INFORMATION

Tourist office (☎ 242232, East Raja St; ☺ 10am-5.45pm Mon-Fri) Staff can provide you with a map, bus timetables and a bit of aimless conversation.

Sights

You can easily spend a full day exploring the temples, *mandapams* and rock carvings around Mamallapuram. A bicycle is a good way to get around. Apart from the Shore Temple and Five Rathas, admission is free to these sites.

SHORE TEMPLE

Standing alone and majestic facing the Bay of Bengal (but enclosed by a steel fence),

this small but romantic **temple** (combined ticket with Five Rathas Indian/foreigner Rs 10/250, video Rs 25; ☺ 6.30am-6pm), weathered by the wind and sea, represents the final phase of Pallava art. Originally constructed around the middle of the 7th century, it was later rebuilt by Narasimha Varman II (also known as Rajasimha). The temple's two main spires contain shrines for Shiva. Facing east and west the original linga captured the sunrise and sunset. A third and earlier shrine is dedicated to the reclining Vishnu. A remarkable amount of temple carving remains, especially inside the shrines. The temple, which is World Heritage listed, is now protected from further erosion by a huge rock wall. Like many of Mamallapuram's sights, it's spectacularly floodlit at night.

FIVE RATHAS

A fine example of Pallava architecture is the **Five Rathas** (Five Rathas Rd; combined ticket with Shore Temple Indian/foreigner Rs 10/250, video Rs 25; ☺ 6.30am-6pm), rock-cut temples resembling chariots. Just 300m from the sea, they were hidden in the sand until they were excavated by the British 200 years ago.

The Five Rathas derive their names from the champions of the Mahabharata; the Pandavas and their collective wife, Draupadi.

The first *ratha* (a rock-cut Dravidian temple resembling a chariot), **Draupadi Ratha**, on the left after you enter the gate, is dedicated to the goddess Durga. Within, the goddess stands on a lotus, her devotees on their knees in worship. Outside, the huge sculpted lion stands proud in front of her temple.

Behind the goddess shrine, a huge Nandi (Shiva's bull vehicle) heralds the next chariot, the **Arjuna Ratha**, dedicated to Shiva. Numerous deities, including Indra, the rain god, are depicted on the outer walls.

The next temple chariot, **Bhima Ratha**, honours Vishnu. Within its walls a large sculpture of this deity lies in repose.

The outside walls of **Dharmaraja Ratha**, the tallest of the chariots, portray many deities, including the sun god, Surya, and the rain god, Indra. The final *ratha*, **Nakula-Sahadeva Ratha** is dedicated to Indra. The fine sculptured elephant standing next to the temple represents his mount. As you enter the gate, approaching from the north, you see its back first, hence its name **gajaprishthakara** (elephant's backside). The life-sized image is regarded as one of the most perfectly sculptured elephants in India.

ARJUNA'S PENANCE

This **relief carving** (West Raja St) on the face of a huge rock depicts animals, deities and other semidivine creatures as well as fables from the Hindu Panchatantra books. The panel (30m x 12m) is divided by a huge perpendicular fissure that's skilfully encompassed into the sculpture. Originally, water, representing the Ganges, flowed down the fissure.

Varying accounts relate the meaning of the relief, but whatever the carving depicts, it's one of the most convincing and unpretentious rock carvings in India. The main relief shows Shiva standing with a wizened Arjuna, balanced on one leg in a state of penance. Touts here are more persistent than elsewhere in Mamallapuram, but a guide (around Rs 30) can be useful to help explain the reliefs.

GANESH RATHA & AROUND

This *ratha* is northwest of Arjuna's Penance. Once a Shiva temple, it became a shrine to Ganesh (the elephant-headed god) after the original lingam was removed. Just north of the *ratha* is huge boulder known as **Krishna's Butter Ball**. Immoveable, but apparently balancing precariously, it's a favourite photo opportunity.

Nearby, the **Trimurti Cave Temple** honours the Hindu trinity – Brahma, Vishnu and Shiva – with a separate section dedicated to each deity.

MANDAPAMS

Many *mandapams*, featuring fine internal sculptures, are scattered over the main hill. The **Kotikal Mandapam**, southwest of the Trimurti Cave Temple, is dedicated to Durga. One of the earliest rock-cut temples, predating the penance relief, is the **Krishna Mandapam**. Its carvings of a pastoral scene show Krishna lifting up the mythical Govardhana mountain to protect his kinsfolk from the wrath of Indra, the rain god.

Mahishamardini Mandapam and **Olakkannesvara Temple** are just a few metres southwest of the lighthouse. Scenes from the Puranas (Sanskrit stories dating from the 5th cen-

tury AD) are depicted on the *mandapam* with the sculpture of the goddess Durga considered one of the finest.

Above the *mandapam* are the remains of the 8th-century Olakkannesvara Temple, and spectacular views of Mamallapuram. Photography is forbidden here for 'security reasons' – there's a nuclear power station a few kilometres south.

SCULPTURE MUSEUM

This **museum** (East Raja St; admission adult/child Rs 2/1, camera Rs 10; 9am-5.30pm) contains over 3000 sculptures by local artisans who work with stone, wood, metal and even cement. Some fine paintings are also on display and the front courtyard is littered with sculptures.

Activities
BEACH

The village is only about 200m from the wide beach, north of the Shore Temple, where local fishers pull in their boats. The beach is cleaner further north, or to the south of the Shore Temple, and you can take long unimpeded walks. At high tide you need to walk over the rocks in front of the Shore Temple. It's not a great place for swimming – there are dangerous rips and all too often lives are lost. It's possible to go fishing in one of the outrigger boat; negotiate a price with a local boat owner.

VISITING ORPHANAGES

Although there are orphanages all over India, in Mamallapuram their existence is soon made obvious because of representatives actively and aggressively seeking donations from travellers. Clearly the orphanages benefit from a donation of rupees or even old clothes, but it makes sense to pay a visit first and interact with the children. Most places welcome visitors (on weekends or after 4pm) and the children are ecstatic to meet foreigners. **Mariamma's Children's Home** (242079; Othavadai St) is in the town centre and is recommended. **Elkanah Educational & Disabled Children's Orphanage** (243474; Fisherman's Colony) encourages visitors.

Courses

There are numerous places offering massage, reiki, yoga and Ayurvedic practices. Sessions cost around Rs 350 for 30 to 45 minutes. **Krishna** (Siesta; Othavadai St), is recommended by both male and female travellers, as is **Kamaraj Ayurvedic** (☎ 242115; full body Rs 300, face & neck Rs 150), which can be contacted through Moonrakers restaurant.

Sri Chakra (Othavadai St; massage per hr Rs 300; ☺ 8am-9pm) offers Ayurvedic massage as well as yoga sessions (Rs 150) at 7am.

There are many other operators in town with similar rates and timings. As always, and especially for such an intimate service, ask fellow travellers, question the masseur carefully and if you have any misgivings, don't proceed.

Tours

To tour Mamallapuram on two wheels, **Hi! Tours** (☎ 243260; www.hi-tours.com; 123 East Raja St) runs bicycle tours (Rs 200; minimum four people) to local villages and sights, including the Tiger Cave and Tirukazhukundram Shiva Temple. The tours run from 8am to 2pm and include guide and lunch. Hi! Tours also runs day trips to Kanchipuram and Vedantangal Bird Sanctuary.

Sleeping

If you don't mind roughing it, you can stay in basic home accommodation with families in the backstreets near the Five Rathas and elsewhere around the village. Rooms and facilities are simple but travellers' reports are positive. The usual cost is around Rs 50 per day, or Rs 300 per week. If a tout takes you to any hotel, you'll pay more.

Mamallapuram is full of traveller accommodation. The main budget and midrange places are on Othavadai and Othavadai Cross St, and more upmarket hotels are north of town on the road to Chennai.

BUDGET

Mrs Rajalaxmi's (☎ 242460; r Rs 50) This is one of several cheap family-run places near the Five Rathas. It's friendly and homely but pretty basic; rooms have fans and electricity, and there's a communal squat toilet.

Sakthi Family Guest House (☎ 242577; 6 East Raja St; d Rs 60-150) This rambling old house in the town centre is owned by the affable Mrs Chandra Palani, headmistress of the local primary school. Rooms outside the house are basic but clean and guests are treated like part of the furniture. There's no sign but it's hidden down a lane behind the town hall building.

Siva Guest House (☎ 243234; sivaguesthouse@ hotmail.com; 2 Othavadai Cross St; d Rs 150-250; with AC Rs 600; 🖭) Deservedly popular with travellers, Siva gets consistently good reports. Rooms are spotless and each has a small veranda.

Hotel Ramakrishna (☎ 242331; 8 Othavadai St; s/d/tr Rs 100/150/250) This is a large place on three floors around a central parking area, with a good rooftop restaurant and bakery. Rooms are simple but clean and great value.

Tina Blue View Lodge & Restaurant (☎ 242319; 34 Othavadai St; r Rs 150-300) Run by the friendly Xavier, Tina Blue is one of Mamallapuram's originals so it looks a bit old hat, but it's set in a leafy garden with chairs and tables on the porch outside the rooms. There's a music/games room and a lovely bamboo and thatched restaurant on stilts.

Green Woods Beach Resort (☎ 243243; green woods_resort@yahoo.com; 7 Othavadai Cross St; d Rs 200-300, with AC Rs 550; 🖭) Although not flash, Green Woods is homely, with a leafy garden and some pleasant rooftop rooms.

Lakshmi Lodge (☎ 442463; d 250-350, with AC Rs 600; 🖭 🖳 🖭) At the end of Othavadai Cross St and with beach access, Lakshmi Lodge is a long-standing backpacker place. With a tanklike swimming pool and a half-decent rooftop restaurant, it's maintaining a standard but the owners can be a little overbearing.

MIDRANGE & TOP END

A string of midrange and top-end hotels are scattered for several kilometres along the road north to Chennai. Each is positioned on its own narrow strip of land between the road and the beach. All offer a range of facilities that usually include a swimming pool, bar, restaurant(s) and credit-card facilities.

Hotel Sea Breeze (☎ 243035; seabreezehotel@ hotmail.com; 11 Othavadai Cross St; s/d from Rs 300/490, d with AC Rs 850-975; 🖭 🖭) The biggest draw here is the shady garden and lovely pool which give the air of a more upmarket resort. Rooms are pretty standard but bright and spacious.

Hotel Mamalla Heritage (☎ 242060; 104 East Raja St; s/d 700/800, deluxe Rs 800/900; 🖭) This standard midrange place has spacious, comfortable rooms, all with phone, TV and minibar, and there's a quality veg restaurant.

Hotel Surya (☎ 242292; Thirukula St; cottages from Rs 350, d Rs 350-550, d with AC from Rs 750; 🖭) If you're interested in sculpture and temple architecture, Surya is a great place to stay. The owner is an artist and sculptor and the pleasant landscaped garden is crowded with sculptures, including a Buddhist *torana* (gateway). The rooms are simple but some have balconies overlooking the garden or a central pond.

Sterling Mahabilapuram (☎ 242287; Shore Temple Rd; d Rs 2000; 🍴 🖳) In a quiet location near the Shore Temple and set in sprawling, shady grounds, this is a pleasant but overpriced place. Facilities include a bar, restaurant, children's play area and large old-fashioned rooms.

Ideal Beach Resort (☎ 242240; www.idealresort .com; s/d Rs 1400/1700, cottages from Rs 2000/2200; 🍴 🖳 🖳) With a landscaped tropical garden setting and comfortable rooms or cottages, this is the best of the beachfront resorts. The design is small and secluded enough to have an intimate atmosphere and there's a lovely open-air pool-side restaurant serving Indian, Sri Lankan and seafood dishes. It's about 3.5km north of town.

Eating & Drinking

One of the pleasures of Mamallapuram is eating out. Palm-thatched beachside restaurants serve fresh seafood to the gentle sounds of the ocean and most places serve beer (whether they're allowed to or not!). Most will show you a selection of fresh fish, prawn, crab and squid from the day's catch before you order. Ask the price, as most seafood varies by weight or availability – king prawns and lobster can turn out to cost more than you expected, but some travellers find it's possible to do a little gentle bargaining. Mamallapuram's restaurants are neatly clustered around Othavadai St and the beach, and all have extensive breakfast menus, veg dishes, Continental and Chinese.

If the beachside ambience and the strains of Bob Marley are what you're after, **Seashore Restaurant** (⏰ 7.30am-10.30pm), **Santana Beach Restaurant** (⏰ 6.30am-10pm), and **Luna Magica** (mains Rs 60-140; ⏰ 7.30am-11pm) are all recommended for fresh seafood. Other meals are about Rs 30 to 50. They are also great places for breakfast.

Moonrakers (Othavadai St; mains Rs 40-150; ⏰ 7am-11pm) Run by three friendly brothers, Moonrakers has long been popular – the food is good and there's a big menu of seafood,

beef and chicken dishes plus breakfast fare such as pancakes and muffins. It's also a busy late night hang-out where you can get a beer and meet other travellers. Chinese lamps, wagon wheels and wooden carvings decorate the place.

Nautilus (Othavadai Cross St; mains Rs 35-105) This excellent French-run eatery is popular for its espresso coffee and European dishes such as ratatouille, stuffed tomatoes or steak and chips, along with the usual seafood and Indian fare.

Village Inn Restaurant (☎ 242151; Thirukula St; mains Rs 45-85, beer Rs 75; ⏰ 8am-11pm) Tucked away off the main strip, this intimate restaurant shows a bit of class with glass-top tables, cane furniture and Indian classical music playing in the background. There's inexpensive seafood, steaks (order in advance) and even Scotch eggs.

Siesta (Othavadai St; dishes Rs 25-60; ⏰ 9am-11pm) On the shady rooftop of Sri Murugan Guest House, this tapas restaurant offers Spanish omelette, *patatas bravas* (fried potatoes in a spicy sauce), garlic mushrooms and paella prepared by a Spanish chef. There's also seafood, pasta and baguettes.

Shopping

Mamallapuram has revived the ancient crafts of the Pallava sculptors, and the town wakes each day to the sound of chisels on granite. Sculptures are exported around the world but fitting one in your backpack is probably asking a bit much. You can browse hassle-free and buy from the fixed-price government-run **Poompuhar Handicrafts Emporium** (☎ 242224; South Mada Rd; ⏰ 10am-7pm Thu-Tue) or from the craft shops that line the main roads (prices negotiable). Sculptures range from Rs 300 (for a small piece to fit in your baggage) to Rs 400,000 for a massive Ganesh that needs to be lifted with a mobile crane.

Getting There & Away

Mamallapuram's small but busy bus stand is on the corner of East Raja and South Mada Sts. The most direct service to/from Chennai (Rs 22, two hours, 30 daily) is on bus Nos 188 and 118. The express (ECR) buses are fastest. To Chennai airport take bus No 108B (Rs 22, two hours, four daily).

To Pondicherry (Rs 35, two hours, nine daily) take bus No 188 or 188A. To Kanchipuram (Rs 20, two hours, 11 daily) via Ti-rukkalikundram and Chengalpattu (Chin-gleput) take bus Nos 212A or 212H.

To get to Madurai catch a bus to Chen-galpattu (Rs 9, one hour, 33 daily) and then a train from there.

Taxis are available from the bus station. Long-distance trips require plenty of bar-gaining. It's about Rs 600 to Chennai or the airport.

You can make train reservations at the **Southern Railway Booking Office** (East Raja St).

Getting Around

The easiest way to get around is on foot, though on a hot day it's quite a hike around all the monuments. You can hire bicycles from several places, including the bicycle shop near the bus station or **Shakthi** (137 East Raja St; 8am-8pm), for around Rs 5/30 per hour/day. **Hi! Tours** (123 East Raja St) also hires bikes for Rs 30 a day. You can hire mo-peds or motorcycles from **Poornima Travels** (242463; Othavadai St) and several other shops or restaurants around town. Costs are Rs 150 to 200 per day.

Sharing an autorickshaw or taxi is a good way to see local sights or nearby attractions but this is a tourist town, so bargain hard.

AROUND MAMALLAPURAM

About 14km west of Mamallapuram, Ti-rukkalikundram is a pilgrimage centre with the hilltop **Vedagirishvara Temple** (admission Rs 2; 8.30am-1pm & 5-7pm) dedicated to Shiva. It's often called the Eagle Temple; according to legend two eagles come here each day at noon from Varanasi. They often don't turn up on time.

In theory you must ascend the 550 steps to the hilltop bare-footed. Once there, the temple contains two beautiful shrines and there are views of the larger Bhaktavatsale-shavra Temple, rocky hills and rice paddies. It shouldn't matter too much if you visit the temple when it's closed – the custodian will let you in (for a small donation), and you can avoid the pressure from temple priests for constant *puja* and larger dona-tions. You can get here by bus or bicycle from Mamallapuram.

VEDANTANGAL BIRD SANCTUARY

Located about 52km from Mamallapuram, this **sanctuary** (admission Rs 5; 6am-6pm) is one

of the best bird-watching places in South India and an important breeding ground for waterbirds – cormorant, egret, heron, ibis, spoon-bill, stork, grebe and pelican – that migrate here from October to March. At the height of the breeding season (De-cember and January) there can be up to 30,000 birds. The best viewing times are early morning and late afternoon. Accom-modation is available at the **Forest Depart-ment Resthouse** (d Rs 300, with AC Rs 400), 500m before the sanctuary. Book with the **Wildlife Warden** (044-8413947; 4th fl, DMS Office, Teynampet) in Chennai.

To get to Vedantangal take a bus from Chengalpattu to the Vedantangal bus sta-tion, then walk the remaining 1km south. Often the buses will take you there. An al-ternative is to get a bus from any of the major centres to Madurantakam, the closest town of any size, and then hire transport for the last 8km, or make a day trip by taxi from Mamallapuram.

KANCHIPURAM

04112 / pop 188,349

Famous throughout India for its silk saris, the temple town of Kanchipuram is also a treasure-trove of Hindu temples and art from the Pallava, Chola and Pandyan dynasties. But for all its fame and histori-cal significance, Kanchipuram is one of Tamil Nadu's less endearing places – a busy, dusty town with few good accom-modation or eating options. Many travel-lers make a day trip here from Chennai or Mamallapuram, which isn't a bad idea. Its attraction for pilgrims and tourists has led to a culture of harassment at some temples and silk shops. Have plenty of small change handy at temples to meet demands for 'small considerations' from caretakers, shoe minders, guides and as-sorted priests.

Orientation & Information

The city is on the main Chennai–Bangalore road, 76km southwest of Chennai.

There's no tourist office. For information online check out www.hellokanchipuram .com. On Kamaraja St there's a small clus-ter of cheap Internet cafés. None of Kan-chipuram's banks will touch travellers cheques. Some hotels (and silk shops) ac-cept foreign cash and credit cards.

Dishnet DSL (81C Kamaraja St; per hr Rs 25; ⊙ 9am-10.30pm) Internet access.

ICICI Bank ATM (Gandhi Rd) Near the main State Bank of India branch.

Net Spot (☎ 235 375; 81B Kamaraja St; per hr Rs 10; ⊙ 8.30am-10.30pm) Internet access.

State Bank of India ATM (Hospital Rd) Accepts international cards. Near the bus stand.

Sights

All the temples are open from 6am to 12.30pm and 4pm to 8.30pm. Shoes can be left free of charge outside the temple gates, although you'll usually be accosted by someone willing to 'look after' them for a small charge.

KAILASANATHA TEMPLE

Dedicated to Shiva, Kailasanatha temple is the oldest temple in Kanchipuram and for many it is also the most beautiful. Reflecting the freshness of early Dravidian architecture, it was built by the Pallava king, Rayasimha, in the late 7th century, though its front was added later by his son, King Varman III.

The remaining fragments of 8th-century murals are a visible reminder of how magnificent the original temple must have looked. There are 58 small shrines honouring Shiva and Parvati and their sons, Ganesh and Murugan.

Non-Hindus are allowed into the inner sanctum here, where there is a prismatic lingam – the largest in town and third-largest in Asia. The guide and priest here are generous with information and this is the most pleasant temple to visit.

SRI EKAMBARANATHAR TEMPLE

This temple is dedicated to Shiva and is one of the largest in Kanchipuram, covering 12 hectares. Its 59m-high *gopuram* and massive outer stone wall were constructed in 1509 by Krishnadevaraya of the Vijayanagar empire, though construction was originally started by the Pallavas, with later Chola extensions. The temple's name is said to derive from Eka Amra Nathar – Lord of the Mango Tree – and there is an old mango tree, with four branches representing the four Vedas (sacred Hindu texts).

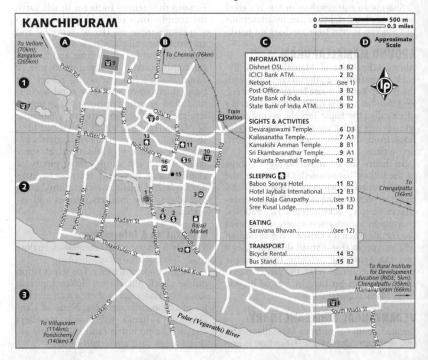

KANCHIPURAM

0   500 m
0   0.3 miles

Approximate Scale

To Vellore (70km); Bangalore (265km)

To Chennai (76km)

Train Station

INFORMATION	
Dishnet DSL..............................	**1** B2
ICICI Bank ATM.......................	**2** B2
Netspot...............................	(see 1)
Post Office...........................	**3** B2
State Bank of India.................	**4** B2
State Bank of India ATM..........	**5** B2

SIGHTS & ACTIVITIES	
Devarajaswami Temple.............	**6** D3
Kailasanatha Temple...............	**7** A1
Kamakshi Amman Temple.........	**8** B1
Sri Ekambaranathar Temple......	**9** A1
Vaikunta Perumal Temple........	**10** B2

SLEEPING 🏠	
Baboo Soorya Hotel.................	**11** B2
Hotel Jaybala International.......	**12** B3
Hotel Raja Ganapathy.............	(see 13)
Sree Kusal Lodge....................	**13** B2

EATING	
Saravana Bhavan....................	(see 12)

TRANSPORT	
Bicycle Rental........................	**14** B2
Bus Stand.............................	**15** B2

To Chengalpattu (36km)

Rajaji Market

To Rural Institute for Development Education (RIDE; 5km); Chengalpattu (35km); Mamallapuram (66km)

Palar (Vegavathi) River

To Villupuram (114km); Pondicherry (140km)

South Mada St

Non-Hindus cannot enter the sanctum. This temple is one of the worst for hustlers; if you wish to support the temple, get an official receipt for your donation.

KAMAKSHI AMMAN TEMPLE

This imposing temple is dedicated to the goddess Parvati in her guise as Kamakshi, who accedes to all requests. To the right of the temple's entrance is the marriage hall, which has wonderful ornate pillars, and directly ahead is the main shrine topped with gold. Each February/March carriages housing statues of deities are hauled through the streets in a colourful procession. The goddess' birthday is in October/November.

DEVARAJASWAMI TEMPLE

Dedicated to Vishnu, this enormous **monument** (admission Rs 2, camera/video Rs 5/100) was built by the Vijayanagars and is among the most impressive of Kanchipuram's temples. It has a beautifully sculptured '1000-pillared' hall (only 96 of the original 100 remain) as well as a marriage hall commemorating the wedding of Vishnu and Lakshmi. One of the temple's most notable features is a huge chain carved from a single piece of stone which can be seen at each corner of the *mandapam*. The annual temple festival is in May.

Every 40 years the waters of the temple tank are drained, revealing a huge statue of Vishnu. You may like to hang around for the next viewing – in 2019.

VAIKUNTA PERUMAL TEMPLE

Dedicated to Vishnu, this temple was built shortly after the Kailasanatha Temple. The cloisters inside the outer wall consist of

---

CHILD LABOUR AND THE SILK INDUSTRY

The sari is synonymous with Indian style, and a brocade bridal sari from Kanchipuram is among the most coveted of garments. The more expensive ones are shot through with gold and silver and can fetch up to Rs 25,000 for a wedding garment weighing around 1.5kg.

About 80% of Kanchipuram's population depend on hand weaving for a living, and most of the work is done in private homes as part of a larger cooperative. Such a diffuse operation is notoriously difficult to police. Despite national legislation prohibiting child labour, it is estimated that some 4000 school-aged children in Kanchipuram still work full time in the industry, though the situation has improved markedly in the past five years.

Owners of silk looms pay poor families a significant sum of money to buy the children's labour. The opportunity to receive an amount of money that most families could never otherwise dream about is a powerful lure. The payment is in the form of a loan, which families must later repay. When they are unable to pay, silk loom owners offer further loans at high interest rates, thereby perpetuating the cycle of indebtedness and culture of child labour, which is a foundation of this lucrative industry.

One organisation which is challenging the system is the **Rural Institute for Development Education** (RIDE; ☎ 268393, fax 268223; www.charityfocus.org/india/host/RIDE; 46 Periyar Nagar, Little Kanchipuram 631503), a secular, nongovernmental organisation. This impressive agency operates in over 200 villages in the Kanchipuram district by taking the children away from the looms and placing them into one of 11 special RIDE transition schools for six to 12 months, before facilitating their entry into the government education system.

There are many ways that travellers can assist the institute in its work. Volunteers are welcomed in training teachers, counselling and helping staff write proposals for funding and project development. Qualified teachers can also, with considerable advance notice, assist with teaching in the schools. Volunteers should be prepared to commit for at least two weeks, preferably one month.

If you're just passing through, RIDE offers a 24-hour programme that includes accommodation, and visits to: a local village to see the silk-weaving industry at work and meet its participants; a RIDE school; and silk-weaving factories and silk stores which support child-free labour. The cost is Rs 1300/2400 for a single/double; there are abridged half-day programmes for Rs 800/1300.

The RIDE office is near Patapay James College, about 5km east of Kanchipuram. It's a Rs 40 rickshaw ride or Rs 2 by bus. Call ahead for directions.

lion pillars and are representative of the first phase in the architectural evolution of the grand 1000-pillared halls. The main shrine, on three levels, contains images of Vishnu in standing, sitting and reclining positions.

Sleeping & Eating

Kanchipuram is not endowed with great hotels – the cheap pilgrims' lodges are pretty dire. Unless you're on a tight budget, head for one of the better-value midrange places. Most hotels and lodges are clustered in the noisy town centre, a few minutes' walk from the bus station.

Sree Kusal Lodge (☎ 223342; 68C Nellukkara St; s/d/tr from Rs 100/150/280, d with AC from Rs 400; ✖) A noisy, drab hotel with simple, marble-floor rooms and grotty bathrooms. It's acceptable for the cheapest rooms, but if you want AC or the so-called 'deluxe', pay the extra for Baboo Soorya.

Baboo Soorya Hotel (☎ /fax 222555; www.hotelbaboosoorya.com; 85 East Raja St; s/d Rs 325/375, s/d with AC Rs 450/550; ✖) Very smart three-storey hotel with marble walls and a glass elevator. Rooms are clean with TV. There's also a good veg restaurant and a bar.

Hotel Jaybala International (☎ 224348; 504 Gandhi Rd; s/d Rs 300/350, with AC 450/545; ✖) Set back from the main street in a small complex, this hotel has pleasant, spacious rooms of varying quality. All have TV, phone and hot water.

Eating out is hardly an adventure in Kanchipuram.

Saravana Bhavan (504 Gandhi Rd; dishes Rs 10-31; ⏲ 6am-10pm) At Hotel Jaybala International, this quality veg chain has an AC section, good South Indian meals and a spotless environment – signs warn: 'Don't comb here'.

Hotel Raja Ganapathy (meals Rs 6-15; ⏲ 8am-10pm) Next to Sree Kusal Lodge, this place offers cheap and good South Indian veg dishes.

Getting There & Away

The busy bus stand is in the centre of town. Bus No 76B, 76C and 79 run to Chennai (Rs 22.50, 1½-two hours) every 10 minutes from about 5am to 10pm. Take bus No 212A to Mamallapuram (Rs 20, two hours, nine daily).

There are direct buses to Trichy (Rs 90, seven hours, five daily) and Bangalore

(No 666; Rs 100, six hours) at 12.25pm and 7.15pm.

Frequent regional buses run to Vellore (Rs 20, 1½ hours, every 15 mins) and Tiruvannamalai (Rs 32, three hours, 22 daily). Pondicherry buses (Rs 30, three hours, 12 daily) operate from the south side of the bus stand.

From Chennai, take one of the suburban trains from Beach, Fort or Egmore stations direct to Kanchipuram (Rs 18, two hours).

Getting Around

Bicycles can be hired for Rs 3/40 per hour/day) from stalls around the bus station. An autorickshaw for a half-day tour of the five main temples (around Rs 150) will inevitably involve a stop at a silk shop. There are also cyclerickshaws.

VELLORE

☎ 0416 / pop 388,211

Vellore, 145km west of Chennai, is a dusty bazaar town with little to detain travellers other than its well-preserved Vijayanagar Fort and temple. The city is also famed for its Christian Medical College Hospital – a leader in research and health care, recognised as one of the finest hospitals in South India. The hospital attracts international medical students as well as patients from all over India, giving this unassuming town a cosmopolitan feel.

Information

There are Internet cafés along Ida Scudder Rd in front of the hospital.

Centurion Bank ATM (Jayalakshmi Complex, Katpadi Rd) A 24-hour ATM.

Dishnet DSL (Ida Scudder Rd; per hr Rs 20; ⏲ 9am-11pm) Internet access.

New Cyber Zone (Jayalakshmi Complex, Katpadi Rd; per hr Rs 20; ⏲ 9am-10pm) Internet access.

State Bank of India (102 Ida Scudder Rd; ⏲ 10am-4pm Mon-Fri, 10am-2pm Sat) Money can be exchanged here.

Tourist office (⏲ 10am-5.45pm Mon-Fri) Inside the fort complex, to the right of the main gate.

Sights

The solid walls and dry moat of **Vellore Fort** dominate the west side of town. It was built in the 16th century and passed briefly into the hands of the Marathas in 1676 and the Mughals in 1708. The British occupied the fort in 1760 following the fall of Sriranga-patnam and the death of Tipu Sultan. These days it houses various public and private offices, parade grounds, a university, church and a police recruiting school.

At the west side of the fort complex, the small **government museum** (admission free; 9am-5pm Sat-Thu) contains sculptures dating back to Pallava and Chola times. Interesting exhibits include the 'hero stones' dating from the 8th century and depicting the stories of war heroes in battle.

The **Jalakanteshwara Temple** (6am-1pm & 3-8pm), a gem of late Vijayanagar architecture, was built about 1566. During the invasions by the Adil Shahis of Bijapur, the Marathas and the Carnatic nawabs, the temple was occupied by a garrison and temple rituals ceased. However, it's once again a popular place of worship.

Sleeping & Eating

Vellore's cheap hotels are concentrated along the roads south of and parallel to the hospital, but there are some good midrange hotels scattered further afield.

Nagha International Lodge (2226731; 13/A KVS Chetty St; s/d/tr from Rs 85/145/199, d/tr with AC Rs 420/540 incl tax;) Down a very narrow lane in the town centre, this is a dingy place with impersonal service and squat toilets, but it's a step up from the cheap lodges around it.

Hotel Aavanaa Inn (2215073; 14 Arcot Rd; s/d Rs 390/490, with AC Rs 650/750;) At the eastern

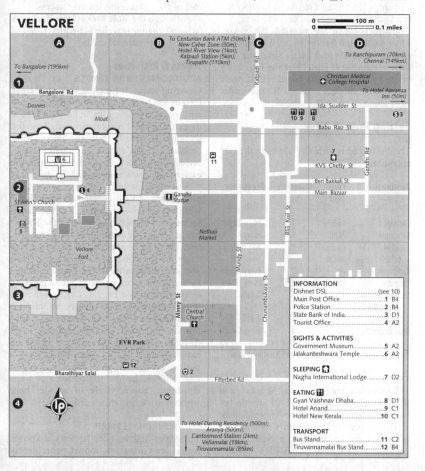

VELLORE

0 —— 100 m
0 —— 0.1 miles

To Centurion Bank ATM (50m);
New Cyber Zone (50m);
Hotel River View (1km);
Katpadi Station (5km);
Tirupathi (110km)

To Bangalore (195km)

Bangalore Rd

Douves

Moat

To Kanchipuram (70km);
Chennai (145km)

Christian Medical
College Hospital

To Hotel Aavanaa
Inn (50m)

Ida Scudder St

Babu Rao St

KVS Chetty St

Beri Bakkali St

Main Bazaar

St John's Church

Vellore
Fort

Gandhi
Statue

Nethaji
Market

EVR Park

Central
Church

Bharathiyar Salai

Filterbed Rd

To Hotel Darling Residency (500m);
Aranya (500m);
Cantonment Station (2km);
Vellamalai (18km);
Tiruvannamalai (85km)

INFORMATION
Dishnet DSL.............................(see 10)
Main Post Office.............................1 B4
Police Station.................................2 B4
State Bank of India........................3 D1
Tourist Office.................................4 A2

SIGHTS & ACTIVITIES
Government Museum.....................5 A2
Jalakanteshwara Temple..............6 A2

SLEEPING
Nagha International Lodge............7 D2

EATING
Gyan Vaishnav Dhaba...................8 D1
Hotel Anand...................................9 C1
Hotel New Kerala.........................10 C1

TRANSPORT
Bus Stand......................................11 C2
Tiruvannamalai Bus Stand...........12 B4

end of Ida Scudder Rd, about 1km from the bus stand, this is the smartest address in central Vellore – a new hotel with good-value rooms and a decent rooftop restaurant.

Hotel River View (☎ 2225251; New Katpadi Rd; s/d Rs 370/470, s/d with AC Rs 600/700; ✖) About 1.5km north of the town centre, this hotel benefits from a relatively quiet location but the 'view' is more of a putrid stream. Rooms are spacious and clean, there's a pleasant garden, three restaurants and a bar.

Cheap veg restaurants line Ida Scudder St, including Hotel New Kerala, Hotel Anand and Gyan Vaishnav Dhaba (thalis Rs 20).

Shikar (New Katpadi Rd; mains Rs 45-90; ✖ 3pm-midnight) Pleasant garden barbecue restaurant at Hotel River View. Pepper steak (Rs 60), fish and chips (Rs 85) and roast chicken (Rs 80) typify the menu and you get cold beer.

Aranya (11/8 Officers Line; mains Rs 40-150; ✖ noon-3.30pm & 6.30-11pm) Recommended by visiting medical students and locals alike, the top-floor restaurant at Hotel Darling Residency offers a great view and a broad multicuisine menu, including ace sundaes. It's just under 1km south of the fort entrance.

Getting There & Away

BUS
The bus stand is virtually opposite the fort entrance.

Destination	Fare (Rs)	Duration (hr)	Frequency
Chennai	46-60	3	every 10min
Bangalore (N444, N555 or 660)	74/85 standard/ deluxe	5	every half-hour
Kanchipuram	20	2	every 15min
Tirupathi	40	2½	every 30min
Mamallapuram (direct; No 157)	35	4	5 daily
Trichy (direct)	99	7	4 daily
Tiruvannamalai*	24	2	every 5min

*buses leave from a separate stand on Bharathiyar Salai

TRAIN
Vellore's main train station is 5km north at Katpadi. Buses (No 192, Rs 2) shuttle between the station and Vellore. There are least six daily express trains to/from Chennai Central (Rs 42/67 in 2nd/sleeper class), which continue to Bangalore (Rs 65/104).

TIRUVANNAMALAI
☎ 04175 / pop 130,301

The small, unassuming town of Tiruvannamalai, 85km south of Vellore, is something of a hidden gem in a region overwhelmed by significant temples. Flanked by Arunachala Hill, this is an important Shaivite town where Shiva is revered as Arunachaleswar, an aspect of fire. At each full moon the hill swells with thousands of pilgrims who circumnavigate the base of the mountain, but at any time you'll see gatherings of Shaivite priests, sadhus and devotees gathered around the temple.

The main post office is just off the road to Gingee; **Rose Computer Point** (55 Kattabomman St; per hr Rs 30; ✖ 8.30am-10pm), about three blocks east of the temple, has Internet access.

Although the **State Bank of India** (Kosamadam St) won't change travellers cheques, its ATM accepts international cards.

Sights & Activities

ARUNACHALESWAR TEMPLE
Covering some 10 hectares, this vast **temple** (✖ 6am-1pm & 5.30-10pm) is one of the largest, and most captivating, in India. Although it dates from the 11th century, much of the structure is actually from the 17th to 19th centuries. It has four large unpainted *gopurams,* one at each cardinal point, with the eastern one rising to 66m with 13 storeys.

The main (eastern) entrance to the temple is reached by a covered walkway lined with trinket sellers, merchants, half-naked sadhus and orange-clad priests – the atmosphere here in the evenings is noisy and electric. You may be approached to donate rice cakes for the poor. At Rs 50 for 10, which you can then hand to the grateful recipients, it's a lot more rewarding than handing a few rupees to a beggar. Once inside the temple, there's a 1000-pillared *mandapam* on the right and the large Sivaganga (tank) on the left, then another gateway leads through a central courtyard containing the main shrine, a Shiva lingam where *puja* is performed daily at 8am, 10am, 6pm, 8pm and 9.30pm. Unlike the temples of Kanchipuram, you're likely to wander here without attracting much attention.

MT ARUNACHALESWAR
This 800m-high boulder-strewn hill, known locally as Girivalam, looms prominently

over the town. On full moon and festival days thousands of pilgrims circumnavigate the 14km base of the mountain. If you're not quite that devoted, an autorickshaw will take you around, stopping at small temples and shrines along the way, for around Rs 120. More interesting for the superb view of the Arunachaleswar Temple is to climb part or all the way up the hill (about four hours return). There's a path that leads up through village homes near the northwest corner of the temple, passing two caves, **Virupaksha** and **Skandasramam**. Sri Ramana Maharshi lived and meditated in these caves for more than 20 years from 1899 to 1922, after which he and his growing band of spiritual followers established the Sri Ramanasramam Ashram.

SRI RAMANASRAMAM ASHRAM
This tranquil **ashram** (☎ /fax 2222491; office ⏰ 8am-11am & 2-5pm), 2km southwest of Tiru-vannamalai, draws devotees of Sri Ramana Maharishi, a guru who died in 1950 after nearly 50 years in contemplation. It's a very relaxed place where visitors are able to meditate or take part in *puja* at the guru's samadhi (shrine) or use the library and bookshop. Day visits are permitted and *devotees only* may stay at the ashram by applying in writing at least three months in advance to the President, Sri Ramanas-ramam, PO Tiruvannamalai.

Sleeping & Eating
There are several cheap lodges around the temple and a few guesthouses out on the road to the ashram. Festival time (November/ December) prices can rise by a staggering 1000%.

Park Hotel (☎ 2222471; 26 Kosamadam St; s/d Rs 70/ 130) Almost opposite the State Bank of India about two blocks northeast of the temple, this is a very basic lodge. Downstairs is a reasonable veg restaurant.

Hotel Ganesh (☎ 2226701; 111A Big St; s/d Rs 125/ 245, with AC Rs 495/645; 🖭) On the busy bazaar road running along the north side of the temple, Ganesh is a little haven of peace and excellent value. Although the rooms are a bit pokey, they are clean, have TV and the hotel's inner courtyard is very pleasant.

Trishul Hotel (☎ 2222219; 6 Kanakaraya Mudali St; s/d from Rs 450/495, with AC Rs 650/700; 🖭) Only a five-minute walk east of the temple, this is another good choice – a nondescript but comfortable hotel with helpful staff, a res-taurant and spacious rooms with TV.

Saravana Bhavan (111A Big St; ⏰ 6am-11pm, lunch 11.30am-3.30pm) Behind the Hotel Ganesh is a branch of this veg restaurant chain.

Getting There & Away
Buses leave for Chennai every half-hour (Rs 62, 3½ hours) and Vellore (Rs 23, two hours). There are at least three daily buses to Pondicherry (Rs 31, three hours), other-wise head to Villapuram and change there. A taxi to Pondicherry (via Gingee) costs around Rs 800.

Only local passenger trains currently use Tiruvannamalai train station – two trains a day pass through between Vellore and Villapuram (where you can change for Pondicherry).

GINGEE (SENJI)
☎ 04145
The twin ruined forts of **Rajagiri** and **Kris-hnagiri** (King & Queen Fort; admission Indian/foreigner

---

THE LINGAM OF FIRE
Legend has it that Shiva appeared as a column of fire on Arunachala Hill in Tiruvannamalai, creating the original symbol of the lingam. Each November/December full moon, the Karthikai Deepam Festival, one of India's oldest festivals, celebrates this legend throughout India but the festival is particularly significant at Tiruvannamalai. Here, a huge fire, lit from a 30m wick immersed in 2000L of ghee, blazes from the top of Arunachala Hill for days. In homes, lamps honour Shiva and his fiery lingam. The fire symbolises Shiva's light, which eradicates darkness and evil.

At festival time up to half a million people come to Tiruvannamalai. In honour of Shiva, they scale the mountain or circumnavigate its base (14km). On the upward path, steps quickly give way to jagged and unstable rocks. There's no shade and the sun is relentless. And the journey must be undertaken in bare feet – a mark of respect to the deity. None of this deters the thousands of pilgrims who quietly and joyfully make their way to the top and the abode of their deity.

Rs 5/100; ☼ 9am-5.30pm) are easily spotted crowning the hilltops as you pass through the rural countryside near Gingee (*shin-gee*), 37km east of Tiruvannamalai. Constructed mainly in the 16th century by the Vijayanagars (though some structures date from the 13th century), the fort has been occupied by various armies, including the forces of Adil Shah from Bijapur and the Marathas, who assumed control from 1677. In 1698 the Mughals took over. Then came the French, who remained until the British defeated them at Pondicherry.

Nowadays the fort is delightfully free of human activity – except for the odd picnicker, you may find you've got the place to yourself. A walk around will take half a day, especially if you cross the road and make the steep ascent to the top of Krishnagiri. Buildings within the main fort (on the south side of the road) include a granary, a Shiva temple, a mosque and the most prominent – the restored audience hall. The fort siren at 4.45pm warns stragglers the gates are about to be locked.

It's easy to day trip to Gingee from Pondicherry (67km) or Tiruvannamalai (37km), but there are a couple of places to stay.

Buses leave every 30 minutes from Tiruvannamalai (Rs 11.50, one hour). Ask to be let off at 'the fort', 2km before Gingee; an autorickshaw from town to the fort costs about Rs 25 one way.

PONDICHERRY
☎ 0413 / pop 220,749

With a seafront promenade, wide boulevards, enduring pockets of French culture and architecture, and a popular ashram, charming Pondicherry is unlike anywhere else in South India. That's hardly surprising – the former French colony was settled in the early 18th century as a colonial enclave and it manages to retain a mildly Gallic air superimposed on a typical Indian background.

The French relinquished their control of the Union Territory of 'Pondy' some 50 years ago, but reminders of the colonial days remain; the Tricolour flutters over the grand French consulate, there's a *hôtel de ville* (town hall), and local police wear red *kepis* (caps) and belts. Don't expect a subcontinental Paris though – this is still India, with all the autorickshaws, choked streets, bazaars and Hindu temples of any city.

A big draw in Pondicherry is its alluring restaurants – many serving an approximation of French cuisine – and some superb hotels that make use of the town's French architectural heritage. Without the crippling taxes of Tamil Nadu, beer is relatively cheap and accommodation good value.

Many travellers come here to study yoga or meditation at the Sri Aurobindo Ashram, so there's always a large contingent of foreigners in Pondy. In any case, this easygoing coastal city is firmly on the travellers itinerary and you may find yourself staying here longer than you'd intended.

Orientation
Pondy is split from north to south by a partially covered canal. The more 'French' part of town is on the east side (towards the sea) and the more typically Indian part to the west. With its grid design, navigating the town is easy, but there are still some eccentricities with street names. Many have one name at one end and another at the other end while others use the French 'rue' instead of 'street'. See the table, below, for more information.

Information
BOOKSHOPS
Focus Books (☎ 2345513; 204 Mission St; ☼ 9.30am-1.30pm & 3.30-9pm Mon-Sat) Excellent selection of books and postcards.
French Bookshop (☎ 2338062; Suffren St; ☼ 9am-12.30pm & 3.30-7.30pm) This small shop next to the Alliance Française has many French titles.
Higginbothams (☎ 2333836; 34 Ambour Salai; ☼ 9am-1pm & 3.30-7.30pm Mon-Sat)

CULTURAL CENTRES
Alliance Française (☎ 2338146; afpondy@satyam.net .in; 58 Suffren St; ☼ 9am-noon & 3-6pm Mon-Sat) The

RENAMED STREETS

Street name	Alternative name
Mission St	Cathedral St
Ambour Salai	HM Kasim St
AH Madam St	Kosakadai St
Beach Rd	Goubert Ave
La Bahabhur St	Bussy St
Gingee Salai	NC Bose St

French cultural centre has a library, computer centre, art gallery, and conducts French language classes. Films are shown on Sunday at 6pm. The monthly newsletter, Le Petit Journal, details forthcoming events.

INTERNET ACCESS
Coffee.Com (236 Mission St; 10am-1am Sat-Thu, 10am-12.30pm & 1.30pm-1am Fri; per 30min Rs 20) Hip Internet café with high-speed connections and great coffee.
Cyberzone (La Lal Bahadur St; per hr Rs 20; 8am-midnight) Part of the i-way chain this has fast connections and cheap Internet phone calls.
Net Info Kiosk (Nehru St; per hr Rs 25; 9am-10pm)
Sify i-way Nehru St (per hr 25; 24hr) St Louis St (7.30am-11pm; per hr Rs 25)

MEDICAL SERVICES
New Medical Centre (343434; 470 MG Rd; 24hr)

MONEY
Canara Bank (Gingy St; 10am-2pm & 2.30-3.30pm Mon-Fri, 10am-12.30pm Sat) The foreign exchange branch here changes cash and travellers cheques, issues cash advances on Visa and MasterCard, and there's an ATM.
ICICI Bank (Mission St, C Koil St & AH Madam St) Its ATMs accepts international cards.
LKP Forex (2224008; 2A Labourdonnais St; 9.30am-7.30pm Mon-Fri, 9.30am-6.30pm Sat) Best place to change a wide range of currencies and travellers cheques plus money transfers.
UTI Bank ATM (SV Patel Salai) Accepts international cards.

POST
Main post office (Rangapillai St; 9am-7pm Mon-Sat & 10am-5pm Sun) Post restante is available 10am-5pm Mon-Sat.

TOURIST INFORMATION
Pondicherry Tourist Office (2339497; www .tourisminpondicherry.com; 40 Goubert Ave; 9am-5pm Mon-Sat) Enthusiastic staff and touch-screen computers.

Sights & Activities
The best way to see its slightly tattered heritage buildings and the broad streets of the French quarter (bounded roughly by NSC Bose Street, SV Patel Rd and Goubert Ave) is to take Pondy's **heritage walk**. Start at the north end of Goubert Ave, the sea-front promenade, and wander south, past the French consulate and the **Gandhi Statue**. Turn right at the town hall on Rue Mahe

Labourdonnais, past the shady Bharathi Park. From there it's a matter of wandering south through Rue Dumas, Rue Romain Rolland and Rue Suffren.

SRI AUROBINDO ASHRAM
Founded in 1926 by Sri Aurobindo and a Frenchwoman known as The Mother, this **ashram** (cnr rue de la Marine & Manakula Vinayagar Koil St) propounds spiritual tenets that represent a synthesis of yoga and modern science. After Aurobindo's death spiritual authority passed to The Mother, who died in 1973 aged 97. These days, the ashram underwrites many cultural and educational activities in Pondicherry.

A constant flow of visitors file through the **main ashram building** (admission free; 8am-noon & 2-6pm Mon-Sat), which has the flower-festooned samadhi (a tomb venerated as a shrine) of Aurobindo and The Mother in the central courtyard, where devotees gather and meditate. Opposite the main building, in the educational centre, you can sometimes catch a film, slide show, play or lecture. For information on the ashram, call first at the **Information Centre** (2339648; bureaucentral@sriaurobindoashram.org; 3 Rangapillai St)

PONDICHERRY MUSEUM
This **museum** (St Louis St; admission adult/child Rs 2/1; 9.40am-1pm & 2-5.20pm Tue-Sun), housed in an interesting old colonial building, features a well-presented collection, including sculptures from the Pallava and Chola dynasties, fine bronzes, coins and an archaeological display. There's a striking collection of French colonial paraphernalia which includes a 19th century *pousse pousse* (like a rickshaw except the passenger would be pushed along), a horse-drawn carriage, colonial furniture, an antique grandfather clock and a bed slept in by a peripatetic Dupleix, the colony's most famous governor.

CHURCHES & TEMPLES
Pondy has several churches built by French missionaries which contribute greatly to the city's Mediterranean flair. The **Church of Our Lady of the Immaculate Conception** (Mission St) was completed in 1791. Its medieval architecture is in the style of many of the Jesuit constructions of that time. The **Sacred Heart Church** (Subbayah Salai) is an impressive sight with its Gothic architecture, stained glass

TAMIL NADU

and striking brown and white colours. The mellow pink-and-cream **Notre Dame de Anges** (Dumas St), built in 1858, looks sublime in the late afternoon light. The smooth limestone interior was made using eggshells in the plaster.

Although Pondy is not often associated with temples, the Hindu faith is celebrated here with as much vigour as anywhere – there are said to be more than 150 temples in the Pondicherry area and you'll often stumble across the entrance to an almost-hidden temple while wandering the central streets, particularly west of the canal. One of the most vibrant in the city is **Sri Manakula Vinayagar Temple** (Manakula Vinayagar

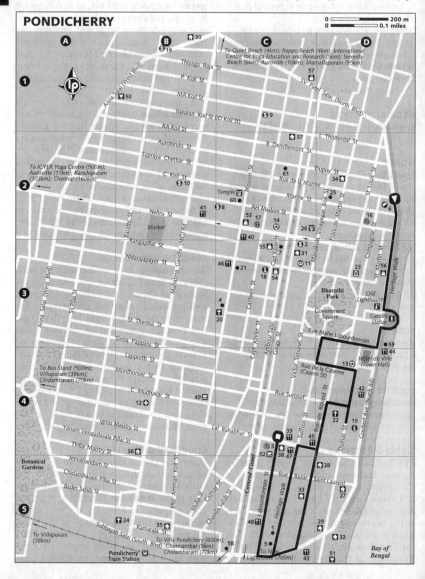

Koil St; ☯ 5.45am-12.30pm & 4-9.30pm), dedicated to Ganesh. Renovations have furnished its sanctum with Rajasthan marble and its *vimana* (a tower over the sanctum) with a gold roof. This small but bustling temple, tucked away down a backstreet just south of the Sri Aurobindo ashram, also contains more than 40 skilfully painted friezes.

BOTANICAL GARDENS
Established by the French in 1826, the **botanical gardens** (admission free; ☯ 6am-6pm) form a green oasis on the southwest side of the city. It makes a pleasant break to meander down the many pathways and enjoy the extensive variety of plants.

BEACHES
The long stretch of city 'beach' is virtually devoid of sand, but there are a few decent swimming beaches to the north and south of the centre. Quiet, Reppo and Serenity beaches are all north of the centre within 8km of Pondy. Chunnambar, 8km south, has Paradise Beach, some resort accommodation, water sports and backwater boat cruises. The tourist office has details.

Courses
Jayalakshmi Fine Arts Academy (Mission St; ☎ 234 2036; goodsin@md4.vsnl.net.in; ☯ 9.30am-1.30pm & 3.30-8.30pm Mon-Sat, 7am-12.30pm Sun) An established place with individual classes in *bharathanatiyam* (dance), singing, *veena* (stringed instrument), tabla and a range of other musical instruments. Tuition fees

start at Rs 150 per hour. There's also a once-off registration fee (Rs 300). Classes are held at 10am and 11am from Monday to Friday.

YOGA & AYURVEDA
International Centre for Yoga Education & Research (www.icyer.com; 16A Mettu Street, Chinnamudaliarchavady, Kottukuppam) Also known as the Ananda Ashram, established by Swami Gitananda, this renowned centre conducts yoga teacher-training courses and 10-day summer courses. Its city location is Yoganjali Natyalayam (25 II Cross Iyyana Nagar), near the bus stand.
Prana Ayurvedic Massage (☎ 2331214; 101 Canteen St) Ayurvedic massage (Rs 400 an hour), steam bath (Rs 150) and yoga classes (Rs 150 an hour). Inquire at Satsanga Restaurant.
Sri Aurobindo Ashram (☎ 23396483; bureaucentral@ sriaurobindoashram.org; Rangapillai St) Many ashramites come to Aurobindo to study or practice yoga.

Tours
The Pondy tourist office runs half-day sightseeing tours (Rs 80, 2pm to 6pm) that take you to the museum, the water sports complex at Chunnambar, Auroville and the ashram. Full-day tours (Rs 100, 9.30am to 6pm) run if there are more than six people. They cover the same area plus the botanical gardens, paper factory, sacred Heart Church and a couple of Hindu temples. Guided walking tours (Rs 200 to 500) are also available.

Another option is the full-day 'eco-friendly' tour of local villages (adult/child Rs 150/100).

INFORMATION		
Alliance Française	1	C5
Canara Bank	2	C3
Cyberzone	3	C4
Focus Books	4	C3
French Bookshop	5	C5
French Consulate	6	D2
Higginbothams	7	C3
ICICI Bank	8	C2
ICICI Bank	9	C1
ICICI Bank	10	B2
LKP Forex	(see 52)	
Main Post Office	11	C3
Net Info Kiosk	(see 53)	
New Medical Centre	12	B4
Police HQ	13	D4
Police Station & Police Museum	14	C2
Pondicherry Tourist Office	15	D4
Sify i-way	16	D2
Sify i-way	17	C2
Sri Aurobindo Information Centre	18	C3
UTI Bank ATM	19	B1

SIGHTS & ACTIVITIES		
Church of Our Lady of the Immaculate		
Conception	20	C3
Jayalakshmi Fine Arts Academy	21	C3

Notre Dame des Agnes	22	D4
Pondicherry Museum	23	D3
Sacred Heart Church	24	B5
Sri Aurobindo Ashram	25	D2
Sri Manakula Vinayagar Temple	26	C2

SLEEPING 🛏		
Ajantha Beach Guest House	27	D5
Hotel de l'Orient	28	D5
Hotel de Pondicherry	29	D5
Hotel Surguru	30	B1
International Guest House	31	C3
Park Guest House	32	D5
Patricia Coloniale Heritage		
Guest House	33	C5
Patricia Guest House 2	34	D2
Patricia Guest House 3	35	B5
Ram Guest House	36	B4
Surya Swastika Guest House	37	C2
Villa Helena	38	C4

EATING 🍴		
Au Feude Bois	39	C4
Bhuvanesh Traders	40	C2
Hotel Aristo	41	B2
La Coromandale	42	D4
La Terrasse	43	C5

Le Café	44	D4
Madam Santhe	45	C4
Nilgiri Supermarket	46	C3
Rendezvous	47	C4
Satsanga	48	C5

DRINKING 🍸 🍷		
Coffee.Com	49	B4
Moon & Rock Bar	50	B1
Seagulls Restaurant	51	D5
Space Coffee & Arts	52	C4

SHOPPING 🛍		
Casablanca	53	C2
Cottage Natural	54	C3
La Boutique d'Auroville	(see 14)	
Mementos	55	C3
Splendour	56	D3
Sri Aurobindo Handmade Paper		
Factory	57	C1

TRANSPORT		
Bicycle Hire	58	C5
Bicycle Hire	59	D3
SDP Bike Hire	60	C2
Vijay Arya		
Moped Rental	61	C2

Sleeping

Pondicherry has some of South India's best accommodation in the midrange and top end bracket – charming old colonial houses and gorgeously decorated guesthouses. At the budget end there's ashram accommodation and typical Indian lodges. The most pleasant part of town is east of the canal, but accommodation is scattered far and wide.

BUDGET

If you've come to Pondy to sample ashram life, the best budget places are the guesthouses run by the Sri Aurobindo Ashram. They're well maintained, well located and you'll be around like-minded souls. However, the accommodation is set up for ashram devotees, so you should respect their rules There's a 10.30pm curfew, and smoking and alcohol are banned. For information and reservations, contact the **Information Centre** (☎ 2339648; bureaucentral@sria urobindoashram.org; 3 Rangapillai St).

Park Guest House (☎ 2334412; Goubert Ave; s/d Rs 300/400, with AC Rs 500/600; ✍) This is the most sought-after ashram address in town thanks to its wonderful seafront position. All front rooms point to the sea and have their own porch or balcony, there's a large lawn area for morning yoga or meditation.

International Guest House (☎ 2336699; Gingy St; old wing s/d from Rs 100/250, with AC Rs 450; ✍) The most central of the ashram guesthouses, this large, ordered place fronts the canal in the city centre.

Surya Swastika Guest House (☎ 2343092; 11 Iswaran Koil St; s/d with shared bathroom Rs 70/110, s/d with private bathroom Rs 80/120) This small old-style guesthouse has simple rooms that are worth the price.

Ajantha Beach Guest House (☎ 2338898; 1 Bazar St Laurent St; d Rs 450, with AC Rs 700; ✍) The location is the main selling point for this new place – right on the beachfront promenade. The handful of rooms are plain but comfortable, with TV and hot water.

MIDRANGE & TOP END

Hotel Surguru (☎ 2339022; www.hotelsurguru.com; 104 SV Patel Salai; s/d Rs 430/570, with AC Rs 660/830; ste Rs 1050; ✍) If you're content in a business-type hotel, Surguru is the best value in Pondy. It's a large, modern hotel with bright, spacious rooms all with satellite TV. There's good veg restaurant and credit cards are accepted.

Villa Helena (☎ 2227075; villahelena@satyam.net .in; 22 Lal Bahabhur St; d Rs 1500-2500) This is a superb colonial home with a touch of class at reasonable prices. The five rooms are immaculate and individually designed. The courtyard is elegant and tranquil. If it's full, ask about its other properties.

Ram Guest House (☎ 2220072; ramguest@hotmail .com; 546 MG Rd; s/d Rs 350/500, d with AC Rs 700) This central heritage guest house has smallish rooms (just one single room) but a touch of old-world charm and a balcony overlooking the street.

Villa Pondicherry (☎ 2356253; villapondichery@alta vista.net; 23 Dr Ambedkar Salai; d with shared/private bathroom from Rs 550/650, with AC Rs 750; ✍) This ageing but charming colonial family residence is about 1km south of the train station next to St Francis Xavier Church. The five rooms and central lounge certainly have character but some may find it a little too earthy. It's not well signposted – look for the red door and small brass plaque under the veranda.

Patricia Coloniale Heritage Guest House (☎ 22 24720; colonialeheritage@rediffmail.com; 54 Romain Roland St; d Rs 1800-3000) For an intimate, peaceful stay, Patricia's is hard to beat. The delightful colonial home is run by a friendly family and the six rooms all have exotic but original character with stained glass window panes, traditional Indian furniture and a lovely central garden. The most expensive room has a private garden. There is no sign outside, so look for number 54 on the gate. If Patricia Guest House is full, ask the owners about their other properties – **Patricia 2** (cnr Dupuy & Francois Martin Sts) and **Patricia 3** (4 Ramaraja St), both of which have three similarly charming rooms (around Rs 1500 to 2000).

Hotel del'Orient (☎ 2343067; orient1804@neemrana hotels.com; 17 Romain Roland St; d Rs 2000-3750) This grand 200-year-old French colonial building has been tastefully renovated and furnished, though some travellers find it a little stuffy and the rooms cramped for this price. The 14 rooms around a small garden courtyard restaurant are all individually designed and while some are a bit on the cosy side (such as the attic room), others are spacious. They're furnished with four-poster beds, antique furniture, Jaipur *dhurries* (rugs) and fine etchings.

Buddha statue (p416), Hyderabad, Andhra Pradesh

Golconda Fort (p415), Hyderabad, Andhra Pradesh

Buffet at Indian wedding banquet (p49), Hyderabad, Andhra Pradesh

JANE SWEENEY

Local boys, Orissa (p432)

Carved wheel, Sun Temple (p447), Konark, Orissa

HIRA PUNJABI

Sun Temple (p447), Konark, Orissa

HIRA P

Hotel de Pondicherry (☎ 2227409; 38 Dumas St; s Rs 1350, d Rs 1600-2450; 🔀) Yet another heritage home, this newly renovated place has 10 lovely colonial-style rooms. It's more old-world than luxurious but it will certainly suit romantics.

Eating

If you've been on the road in Tamil Nadu for a while you'll find Pondicherry's restaurant scene a revelation. There are several French-Indian places, some good open-air restaurants, beer is relatively cheap and you can sample a glass of wine (Indian and imported). At the other end of the scale, you can eat cheaply at the ashram.

Satsanga (☎ 2225867; 30-32 Labourdonnais St; 🕙 8am-11pm; mains Rs 75-280) In the covered backyard of a rambling colonial house, Satsanga serves up tasty French and Italian food and is a good place for a casual lunch or dinner. It's also great for breakfast (Rs 25 to 50) – freshly baked bread, crepes, omelettes and yogurt and muesli are the perfect way to start the day and you can read the morning paper in low-slung chairs under the balcony.

Madam Santhe (☎ 2224920; 10 Lal Bahabhur St; most mains around Rs 45-200; 🕙 noon-3pm & 7-10.30pm Thu-Tue) Santhe is another of Pondy's pleasant Mediterranean-style restaurants with a rooftop dining area and eager service. French-inspired seafood is a speciality with dishes including butter squid with garlic and herbs (Rs 85), fish Provençale (Rs 110) and stuffed crab (Rs 100), plus a great range of salads, home-made pasta and steaks. There's no wine, but cold beer is Rs 75.

Au Feude Bois (☎ 2341821; 28 Lal Bahadur St; pizzas Rs 80-125; 🕙 11am-2pm & 6-10.30pm) With a wood-fired pizza and bakery oven, this new place is well worth a visit for Italian-style pizzas, fresh bread or crepes. There's a small rooftop courtyard as well as a rustic dining room.

Hotel Aristo (Nehru St; mains Rs 40-90; 🕙 9.30am-10.30pm Sat-Thu) The rooftop restaurant at Aristo is a great place for a cheap, tasty meal and is usually crowded in the evenings. Dishes include walnut chicken with brown rice (delicious but made with cashews!) for Rs 79 and grilled prawns (Rs 69). A small Kingfisher is Rs 30.

La Coromandale (☎ 2227232; 30 Goubert Ave; mains Rs 25-35; 🕙 7am-10.30pm) As the saying goes,

the simple things in life are often the best. Tasty South Indian thalis, rice, noodles, cold drinks and a relaxed atmosphere for meeting and chatting are the attractions of this open-fronted restaurant, situated on the promenade.

Coffee.Com (☎ 5201245; 236 Mission St; 🕙 10am-1am Sat-Thu, 10am-12.30pm & 1.30pm-1am Fri) This online café and meeting spot serves up great baguettes (Rs 50 to 70), pasta dishes (Rs 130 to 180), good coffee, pastries and milkshakes.

La Terrasse (5 Subbayah Salai; mains Rs 30-125, pizzas Rs 70-175; 🕙 8.30am-10pm Thu-Tue) This simple semi-open-air place near the southern end of the promenade is best known for the pizzas (spicy or Italian-style). No alcohol is served.

QUICK EATS
Le Café (Goubert Ave; snacks Rs 12-40) This slightly down-at-heel snack bar and ice-cream place is on the waterfront promenade. Popular with families for popcorn, ice cream (including kulfi) and sweets.

Bhuvanesh Traders (Mission St; 🕙 7am-10pm) This place is recommended by travellers for their fresh juices and cold lassis.

SELF-CATERING
Nilgiri Supermarket (cnr Mission & Rangapallai Sts; 🕙 9.30am-9pm) A well-stocked, modern place for grocery shopping in air-conditioned comfort. Credit cards are accepted.

SOMETHING SPECIAL
Rendezvous (☎ 2330238; 30 Suffren St; 🕙 10am-3.30pm & 6.30-11.30pm Wed-Mon; mains Rs 100-275) The bamboo and thatch rooftop section of Rendezvous is one of the more ambient places in Pondy, while the downstairs dining room is straight out of rural France, with wicker chairs and gingham tablecloths. The menu is naturally French, with *bouillabaisse* (seafood soup; Rs 60), grilled prawns (Rs 250), quiches (Rs 100 to 175) and coq au vin (Rs 210), along with burgers, pizzas, Indian and Chinese. For dessert try crème caramel or the intriguing pepper ice cream (Rs 60). Wash it all down with Indian house wine (Rs 80 a glass) or French wine (Rs 220 a glass or Rs 800 to 1500 a bottle).

Drinking & Entertainment

With low taxes on alcohol, Pondy has a reputation for cheap booze. The reality is you'll really only find cheap beer (Rs 25 to 30) in wine shops or the darkened bars attached to them. While you can get a Kingfisher for Rs 50, the better restaurants charge up to Rs 100. There are a few exceptions and the greatest concentration of bars can be found along Anna Salai West Blvd).

Seagulls Restaurant (19 Dumas St; 11.30am-11.30pm) Although this is a restaurant, the waiters generally look bewildered if you order food and then return to report that your chosen dish is unavailable. However, the location, with a balcony overlooking the sea and views north along the promenade, makes it great for a beer (cheap at Rs 50) on a warm evening.

Coffee.Com (5201245; www.coffeedotcom.net; 236 Mission St; 10am-1am Sat-Thu, 10am-12.30pm & 1.30pm-1am Fri) Pondy's cosmopolitan vibe is typified by this hip little Internet hangout. It's a meeting place where you can go online, read magazines, drink espresso coffee and there's a widescreen TV and a selection of DVDs (Rs 100 per hour).

Space Coffee & Arts (333734; 2 Labourdonnais St; 6pm-midnight) Space is a funky little semi-open air café for coffee or beer (Rs 75) in the evening, but it's also a gallery and performing arts venue with traditional dance and Tamil arts. Check the noticeboard to see what's going on.

Moon & Rock Bar (Anna Salai; 10am-11pm) One of the more salubrious places around.

Shopping

Shopping in Pondicherry, especially on Nehru St, Mission St and MG Rd, is a strange blend of Indian bazaar-meets-Western-style opulence, with sari and textile stalls competing for space with modern, neon-lit speciality shops.

Sri Aurobindo Handmade Paper Factory (233 4763; 50 SV Patel Salai; 8.30am-noon & 1.30-5pm Mon-Sat) Fine hand-made paper is sold at this paper factory.

La Boutique d'Auroville (Nehru St; 9.30am-1pm & 3.30-8pm Mon-Sat) It's fun browsing through the crafts such as jewellery, batiks, *kalamkari* (similar to batik) drawings, carpets and woodcarvings here.

You'll find a range of crafts at **Cottage Natural** (Rangapillai St; 9.30am-1pm & 3.30-8pm Mon-Sat),

while **Splendour** (16 Goubert Ave; 9.30am-1pm & 4-8.30pm Thu-Tue) has a good range of carvings, leathergoods and pottery.

For a modern take on Indian souvenirs and fashions, check out the excellent **Casablanca** (165 Mission St; 9am-10pm Mon-Sat & 9am-9pm Sun) or **Mementos** (2 Capt Xavier St; 9.30am-1.30pm & 3.30-8.30pm Mon-Sat).

Getting There & Away

BUS

The bus stand is 500m west of town. State buses include the following:

Destination	Fare (Rs)	Duration (hr)	Frequency
Bangalore	105	8	6 daily
Chennai	54	3½	83 daily
Chidambaram	23	1½	50 daily
Coimbatore	150	9	6 daily
Kanchipuram	40	3	5 daily
Karaikal	43	3½	15 daily
Kumbakonam	33	4	6 daily
Mamallapuram	33	2	5 daily
Nagapattinam	48	4	4 daily
Tirupathi	83	6	9 daily
Tiruvannamalai	25	3½	9 daily
Trichy	70	5	4 daily

TAXI

From Pondicherry to Chennai taxis cost Rs 1400 and to Chennai airport it's Rs 1300.

TRAIN

Four passenger trains depart to Villupuram daily (Rs 9, one hour, 38km), from where you can connect to other services. The computerised booking service at the station covers all of the trains on the southern railway.

Getting Around

One of the best ways to get around is by walking. Large three-wheelers shuttle between the bus stand and Gingy St for Rs 5, but they're hopelessly overcrowded. Cycle and autorickshaws are plentiful – an autorickshaw across town costs about Rs 25.

Since the streets are broad and flat, the most popular transport is pedal power. Bicycle hire shops line many of the streets, especially MG Rd and Mission St. You'll also find hire shops in Subbayah Salai and Goubert Ave. The usual rental is Rs 5 per hour, or Rs 20 per day, but some places ask Rs 70.

Mopeds or motorbikes are useful for getting out to the beaches or to Auroville and can be rented from a number of shops and street stalls. The going rate is Rs 100 a day for a gearless scooter and Rs 125 for a motorbike. You need to show some ID (such as a driving licence) and leave a Rs 500 deposit. **SDP** (☎ 2334101; Mission St) and **Vijay Arya** (23 Aurobindo St) hire bikes.

AUROVILLE
☎ 0413

Just over the border from Pondicherry in Tamil Nadu is the international community of Auroville – a project in 'human unity' that has ballooned to encompass more than 80 rural settlements spread over 20km, and about 1700 residents (two-thirds of whom are foreigners, representing around 35 different nationalities).

Auroville is not a tourist attraction, and casual visitors may find it a bit bewildering and unwelcoming. But if you're at all interested in the philosophy it's worth the ride out to see the visitors centre and find out how it all works, and with a bit of rigmarole (and a return visit), you can check out the space-age meditation centre.

Information

The **visitors centre** (☎ 2622239; www.auroville.org; ☿ 9am-5.30pm) is usually the first stop for anyone visiting Auroville. This centre has a permanent photographic exhibition of the community's activities and the usually helpful staff will answer queries, particularly if you show an interest in the philosophy, rather than a desire to make a beeline for a peek at the Matrimandir. A video is shown at 10.30am, 11.30am, 2.30pm, 3pm and 3.30pm. Also in this modern complex is a bookshop, café, and **Boutique d'Auroville** (☿ 9am-1pm & 2-5.30pm Mon-Sat), which sells Aurovillian handicrafts.

Matrimandir

This bizarre structure looks like a cross between a giant golden golf ball and a NASA space project. Designed to be the spiritual and physical centre of Auroville, the Matrimandir contains a meditation chamber lined with white marble and housing a solid crystal (reputedly the largest in the world) 70cm in diameter. Rays from the sun are beamed into this crystal from a tracking mirror in the roof. On cloudy days, solar lamps do the job. But if you're thinking of a day trip to see this engineering marvel, think again. The inner chamber of the Matramandir is open to casual visitors *only* between 2.30pm and 5.30pm on Sunday. Even then, you first have to get a pass to visit only the gardens and **amphitheatre** (☿ 10am-12.30pm & 2-4.30pm Mon-Sat, 10am-1pm Sun). To get this pass (free), go to the visitors centre between 9.45am and noon and 1.45pm and 4pm Monday to Friday and between 9.45am and 12.30pm Sunday. Once that's done, you can make an advance booking for a Sunday visit. Got it? Of course, Aurovillians with a guest card can visit the chamber daily between 5pm and 6pm.

Sleeping & Eating

People with a serious interest in the aims of Auroville can stay with any one of the 40

AUROVILLE: THE INTERNATIONAL VISION

Auroville is the brainchild of The Mother, 'an experiment in international living where people could live in peace and progressive harmony above all creeds, politics and nationalities'. Designed by French architect Roger Anger, its opening ceremony on 28 February 1968 was attended by the president of India and representatives of 124 countries, who poured the soil of their lands into an urn to symbolise universal oneness.

The geographical layout of Auroville was seen as a reflection of this striving for unity. At the community's centre stands the Matrimandir which The Mother called the soul of Auroville. Four zones – cultural, international, industrial and residential – were to radiate out from the Matrimandir to cover an area of 25 sq km, although as yet only 10 sq km has thus far been realised.

In the words of The Mother, the founding vision of Auroville is that 'There should be somewhere upon Earth a place that no nation could claim as its sole property, a place where all human beings of goodwill, sincere in their aspiration, could live freely as citizens of the world...'.

community groups here. A stay of no shorter than a week is preferred and although work isn't obligatory, it's very much appreciated. Accommodation is not offered in exchange for work; rooms range from Rs 150 to 1000. On top of this, guests are required to contribute Rs 60 per day for the 'maintenance and development' of Auroville.

There are more than 40 guesthouses in Auroville. The best way to find what you're looking for is to stop at the visitors centre in Auroville. To make the arrangements before arriving, check out the website or contact the **Auroville Guest Service** (☎ 2622704; avguests@auroville.org.in).

Although there are stores and small roadside eateries in Auroville, most people gather at the Solar Kitchen, which dishes out more than 400 meals daily from its buffet.

Getting There & Away
The best way to enter Auroville is from the coast road, at the village of Periyar Mudaliarchavadi, near the turn-off to Repos Beach. Ask around as it's not well signposted. A return autorickshaw ride is about Rs 150, but a better option is to hire a moped or bicycle. It's about 12km from Pondy to the visitors centre.

CENTRAL TAMIL NADU

CHIDAMBARAM
☎ 04144 / pop 58,740
Chidambaram's great temple complex of Nataraja, the dancing Shiva, is a Dravidian architectural highlight and one of the holiest Shiva sites in South India. Since it's the only thing worth seeing here, Chidambaram can be visited as a day trip from Pondy or as a stopover between Pondicherry and Kumbakonam or Trichy.

Of the many festivals, the two largest are the 10-day chariot festivals, which are celebrated in April/May and December/January. In February/March the five-day *natyanjali* Dance Festival attracts performers from all over the country to celebrate Nataraja – the Lord of Dances.

Orientation & Information
The small town is developed around the Nataraja Temple with streets named after

the cardinal points. This is an easy town for walking, as most accommodation is close to the temple. The bus stand is a five-minute walk to the southeast and the train station about 1km further south. None of the banks provide foreign exchange.

Hotel Saradharam (19 VGP St; per hr Rs 30; ⊙ 11.30am-10pm) Best place for Internet access.

ICICI Bank ATM In front of Hotel Saradharam, almost opposite the bus stand.

Post office (North Car St; ⊙ 10am-3pm Mon-Sat) Second branch on South Car St.

Tourist office (☎ 238739; Railway Feeder Rd; ⊙ 9am-5pm Mon-Fri) Next to Vandayar Gateway Inn. You may be able to pick up a brochure but the office is frequently deserted.

Sights
NATARAJA TEMPLE
Chidambaram's star attraction, this Shiva temple draws a regular stream of pilgrims and visitors. The region was a Chola capital from 907 to 1310 and the Nataraja Temple was erected during the later time of the administration. The high-walled 22-hectare complex has four towering *gopurams* with finely sculptured icons depicting Hindu myths. The **temple** (courtyard & shrines ⊙ 6am-12.30pm & 4-10.30pm) is renowned for its prime examples of Chola artistry and has since been patronised by numerous dynasties. The main temple entrance is at the east *gopuram*, off East Car St. The narrow street leading to the entrance is lined with the usual stalls and you can safely leave shoes (by donation) at a stall to the left of the entrance.

In the northeast of the complex, to the right as you enter, is the 1000-pillared **Raja Sabha** (King's Hall), open only on festival days, and to the left of that is the **Sivaganga** (Temple Tank) – guides will explain the stories from paintings and sculptures that surround the tank. In the southeast of the complex is an impressive statue of the elephant god, Ganesh.

Directly opposite the main (east) entrance, a large statue of Nandi (Shiva's escort) looks towards the hall leading to the inner sanctum. Although non-Hindus are officially not allowed inside the gold-roofed inner sanctum itself, it's possible to walk down the corridor and observe rituals such as the fire ceremony (usually held before the afternoon and evening closing), where worshippers light goblets of fire and bells clang. The afternoon *puja* at around 5pm is also worth seeing.

Brahmin priests will usually take you in for a fee and guide you around the temple complex. Since the Brahmins work as a co-operative to fund the temple you may wish to support this magnificent building by way of donation, but don't be intimidated by priests who try to pressure you into excessive amounts.

Sleeping & Eating

Most of Chidambaram's cheap lodges are clustered around the temple.

Star Lodging (☎ 222743; 101-102 South Car St; s/d Rs 60/80) This is an old budget traveller's standby – rooms are bare and have squat toilets only but it's a friendly place and you can't beat the price. There's a reasonable veg restaurant downstairs.

Mansoor Lodge (☎ 221072; 91 East Car St; s/d/tr Rs 80/150/200, d with TV Rs 200) This lodge is close to the temple and has clean, good-value rooms. The owners are eager to please.

Vandayar Gateway Inn (☎ 238056; vgl_cdm@sanchar.net; Railway Feeder Rd; d Rs 199-250, with AC Rs 550; 🖭) Although it has a bit of a forlorn feel, this is a spotless, excellent-value hotel close to the train station. The deluxe rooms have TV, there are two good restaurants, a bar and helpful staff.

Hotel Akshaya (☎ 220192; akshayahotel@hotmail.com; 17-18 East Car St; s/d Rs 199/250, with AC from Rs 499/600, ste Rs 850; 🖭) Close to the temple, this is another place that makes the mid-range grade with the budget price tag – the cheaper rooms are plain with peeling paint but still worth it.

Hotel Saradharam (☎ 221336; fax 222656; hsrcdm@vsnl.com; 19 VGP St; d with/without AC Rs 600/375; 🖭 🖵) This is the top hotel in town and is conveniently across from the bus stand, but it's starting to look its age.

Predictably, the best places to eat are in hotels. **Anuupallavi** (19 VGP St; mains Rs 25-70; 🕙 9am-10pm) is an excellent AC multicuisine restaurant in Hotel Saradharam with a range of Indian and Chinese dishes. In the same hotel is a veg restaurant, **Pallava**, and the **Pizza Shop** (dishes Rs 40-100; 🕙 4-10pm) which dishes up good Western-style pizzas and burgers.

Near the temple entrance, **Udipi Sri Vishna Vilas** (thalis Rs 20; 🕙 5.30-6.30am, noon-2.30pm & 3.30-9.30pm) is busy, clean place for tasty South Indian veg food and thalis.

Getting There & Away

The bus stand is very central – within walking distance to the temple and accommodation. There are buses to/from Chennai (Rs 66, seven hours), Pondicherry (Rs 21,

---

CHIDAMBARAM

0   300 m
0   0.2 miles

A   **B**

INFORMATION
Hospital...1 B5
ICICI Bank ATM........................(see 11)
Internet Café............................(see 11)
Police Station..................................2 A4
Post Office......................................3 A4
Post Office......................................4 A5
State Bank of India..........................5 A4
Tourist Office..................................6 B5

SIGHTS & ACTIVITIES
Main Temple Entrance......................7 A4
Nataraja Temple.............................8 A4
Tillai Kali Amman Temple.................9 A3

SLEEPING 🏠
Hotel Akshaya...............................10 A4
Hotel Saradharam..........................11 B5
Mansoor Lodge..............................12 A4
Star Lodging..................................13 A5
Vandayar Gateway Inn...................14 B5

EATING 🍴
Anuupallavi................................(see 11)
Pallava.......................................(see 11)
The Pizza Shop...........................(see 11)
Udipi Sri Vishnas Vilas...................15 A4

TRANSPORT
Bus Stand....................................16 B5

To Cuddalore (50km);
Pondicherry (71km);
Chennai (232km)

North Main Rd

North Car St

West Car St   East Car St

South Car St

VOC St

To Pichavaram (15km)

Pillaiyar Koil St

To Vaitheeswarankoil (25km); Kumbakonam (69km)

Khan Sahib Canal

Railway Feeder Rd

Train Station

TAMIL NADU

two hours) and Kumbakonam (Rs 22, 2½ hours) every half-hour. Bus No 157 (deluxe Rs 97, five daily) is the quickest to Chennai. There are also direct buses to Madurai (Rs 80, eight hours, five daily).

Chidambaram is on a metre gauge rail line rather than a main line but the train is useful for getting to Kumbakonam, where you can change trains for Thanjavur or Trichy. There's one daily express train to Kumbakonam (Rs 31/49 in 2nd/sleeper class, two hours) and several passenger trains. The **train station** (☎ 238759) is a 20-minute walk southeast of the temple (Rs 25 by cycle rickshaw).

KUMBAKONAM
☎ 0435 / pop 160,827
Kumbakonam is a busy, dusty commercial centre, nestled along the Cauvery River some 37km northeast of Thanjavur. Dozens of temples are scattered around the town and this is a good base to visit the superb Chola temples nearby, or to head east to the coastal towns of the Cauvery Delta.

There's no tourist office in Kumbakonam. The best place to exchange travellers cheques is at the **UAE Exchange** (☎ 2423212; 134 Kamaraj Rd) near the train station. You'll find an **ICICI Bank ATM** (TSR Big St) northwest of town.

The best place for Internet access is **Ashok Net Cafe** (☎ 2433054; 24 Ayikulam Rd; per hr Rs 20; ♡ 9am-10.30pm).

Sights
Dozens of colourfully painted *gopurams* point skyward from Kumbakonam's 18 temples, most dedicated to Shiva or Vishnu, but only the most dedicated temple-goer would tackle visiting more than a few. All temples are open from 6am to noon and 4pm to 10pm.

The largest Vishnu temple in Kumbakonam, with a 50m-high east gate, is **Sarangapani Temple**, just off Ayikulam Rd. The temple shrine, in the form of a chariot, was the work of the Cholas during the 12th century.

Kumbeshwara Temple, about 200m west and entered via a nine-storey *gopuram,* is the largest Shiva temple. It contains a lingam

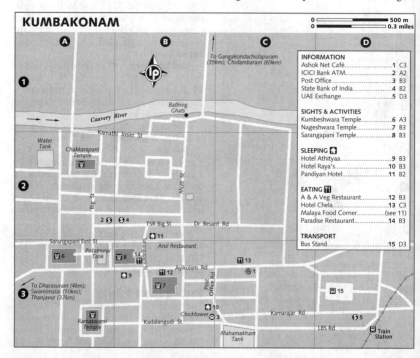

KUMBAKONAM

INFORMATION	
Ashok Net Café	1 C3
ICICI Bank ATM	2 A2
Post Office	3 B3
State Bank of India	4 B2
UAE Exchange	5 D3

SIGHTS & ACTIVITIES	
Kumbeshwara Temple	6 A3
Nageshwara Temple	7 B3
Sarangapani Temple	8 B3

SLEEPING	
Hotel Athityaa	9 B3
Hotel Raya's	10 B3
Pandiyan Hotel	11 B2

EATING	
A & A Veg Restaurant	12 B3
Hotel Chela	13 C3
Malaya Food Corner	(see 11)
Paradise Restaurant	14 B3

TRANSPORT	
Bus Stand	15 D3

0 — 500 m
0 — 0.3 miles

To Gangakondacholapuram (35km); Chidambaram (69km)

Bathing Ghats

Cauvery River

Kamathi Josier St

Water Tank

Chakkarapani Temple

Big St

Muth St

TSR Big St   Dr Besant Rd

Arul Restaurant

Sarangapani East St

Potamurai Tank

Ayikulam Rd

Post Office Rd

To Dharasuram (4km); Swamimalai (10km); Thanjavur (37km)

Ramaswami Temple

Clocktower

Kadalangudi St

Mahamakham Tank

Kamarajar Rd

LBS Rd

Train Station

said to have been made by Shiva himself when he mixed the nectar of immortality with sand.

The 12th century **Nageshwara Temple**, from the Chola dynasty, is also dedicated to Shiva in the guise of Nagaraja, the serpent king. It is said that on three days of the year (in April or May) the sun's rays fall on the lingam. The main shrine here is in the form of a chariot.

The huge **Mahamakhan Tank**, 600m southeast of Nageshwara Temple, is the most sacred in Kumbakonam. Current belief is that every 12 years, the waters of the Ganges flow into the tank and at this time a festival is held. The next festival is not until 2016.

Sleeping

Kumbakonam's hotels are nothing to write home about but there are plenty to choose from, especially along Ayikulum Rd and the busy bazaar, TSR Big St.

Pandiyan Hotel (☎ 2430397; 52 Sarangapani East St; s/d Rs 110/170) This budget hotel is popular though rooms are standard issue with mildewed walls.

Hotel Athityaa (☎ 2421794; 48 Ayikulum Rd; s/d Rs 395/420, with AC 575/600; ✗) Hotel Athityaa has a good central location opposite Sarangapani Temple and the rooms, some with balcony and all with TV, are as good as anywhere else for this price. There is a restaurant and bar at the front.

Hotel Raya's (☎ 2422545; 18 Post Office Rd; d/tr from Rs 500/650, with AC Rs 700/850; ✗) With Hindi music blaring in the lobby and pictures of deities hanging everywhere, Raya's gets you in the mood for some temple hopping. Its rooms are not luxurious but it's clean and comfortable and it's the best of the midrange places.

Eating

Malaya Food Corner (Sarangapani East St; mains Rs 20-55; ☽ noon-4pm & 6.30-11.30pm) This is a rustic but atmospheric restaurant next to Hotel Pandiyan. The dirt floor and cane furniture give it a 'village' feel and the food, such as fish curry or butter chicken (both Rs 25) is good and cheap.

A&A Veg Restaurant (Ayikulam Rd; ☽ 7am-11pm) and **Paradise Restaurant** (26 Sarangapani St; ☽ 6am-11pm) are two bright, clean restaurants which serve up veg food such as palm-leaf thalis (Rs 15).

Hotel Chela (9 Ayikulam Rd; mains Rs 30-80; ☽ noon-10pm) This hotel has a good North Indian restaurant serving tandoori chicken (Rs 70).

Getting There & Away

The bus stand and train station are about 2km east of the town centre.

SETC has buses (No 303) that leave every half-hour for Chennai (Rs 118, seven hours).

To Thanjavur buses go every 10 minutes (Rs 14.50, 1½ hours), some continuing on to Madurai (Rs 65, five hours, eight daily). Heading north there are buses every 20 minutes to Chidambaram (Rs 31, 2½ hours) and Pondicherry (Rs 40, 4½ hours). There's one bus at 7pm to Coimbatore (Rs 110, 10 hours).

For the Cauvery Delta area there are buses every half-hour to Karaikal (Rs 16, two hours), via Tranquebar and then on to Nagapattinam.

The overnight *Rock Fort Express* is the only major train to/from Chennai (Rs 130/365 in sleeper/3AC), going via Thanjavur and Trichy. The *Cholan Express* goes as far as Tambaram. Passenger trains run to Chidambaram (Rs 31, two hours) and Thanjavur.

AROUND KUMBAKONAM

Not far from Kumbakonam are two superb Chola temples at Dharasuram and Gangakondacholapuram. Few visitors go to these temples, so you can appreciate their beauty in peace. Both can be visited as a day trip from Kumbakonam.

Dharasuram

Only 4km west of Kumbakonam in the village of Dharasuram, the **Airatesvara Temple**, constructed by Raja Raja II (1146–63), is a superb example of 12th-century Chola architecture.

The temple is fronted by columns with unique miniature sculptures. In the 14th century, the row of large statues around the temple was replaced with brick and concrete statues similar to those found at the Thanjavur Temple. Many were removed to the art gallery in the raja's palace at Thanjavur, but they have since been returned to Dharasuram. The remarkable sculptures depict, among other things, Shiva as Kankala-murti – the mendicant. Stories from the epics are also depicted.

At the main shrine, a huge decorated lingam stands, the natural light illuminating it from sunrise to sunset.

You can get to Dharasuram by bus (Rs 5) or autorickshaw (Rs 50 return including waiting time).

Gangakondacholapuram

This **Brihadishwara Temple** (⊙ 6am-noon & 4-8pm), 35km north of Kumbakonam, was built by the Chola emperor Rajendra I (1012–44) in the style of the Brihadishwara Temple at Thanjavur, built by his father. Later additions were made in the 15th century by the Nayaks. The ornate tower is almost 55m high and is said to weigh 80 tonnes. Within the recesses of the temple walls stand many beautiful statues, including those of Ganesh, Nataraja and Harihara.

Next to the temple there's a small **museum** (free admission; ⊙ 9am-5pm Sat-Thu), which exhibits the excavated remains of the palace that once existed nearby.

Buses go from Kumbakonam bus stand to the temple every half-hour (Rs 11, 1½ hours); early morning is the best time to visit.

CAUVERY DELTA

The Cauvery River rises in the Western Ghats and flows eastwards before emptying out in the Bay of Bengal. The delta here is a fertile farming area and there are a number of coastal towns of minor interest along here. At the southern tip, the Calimere Wildlife & Bird Sanctuary is a haven for twitchers. The Nagapattinam district here was the worst affected part of Tamil Nadu when the 2004 tsunami struck, with up to 7000 lives lost and thousands more left homeless.

Tranquebar (Tharangambadi)

About 80km south of Chidambaram, Tranquebar was a Danish post, established 1620. The seafront **Danesborg Fort** (admission Indian/foreigner Rs 5/50; ⊙ 10am-1pm & 2-5.45pm Sat-Thu) was occupied by the British in 1801. It houses a small but fascinating **museum** on aspects of Danish history here. To get there take a bus from Chidambaram (Rs 28, 2½ hours). There's no accommodation here but there's plenty of places at Karaikal, 12km south.

Vailankanni (Velanganni)

☎ 04365 / pop 10,104

Vailankanni is the site of the Roman Catholic Basilica of Our Lady of Good Health. Thousands of Christian pilgrims file through the impressive white neo-Gothic structure, which was elevated to the status of basilica in 1962 during the Pope's visit. The annual nine-day festival culminates on 8 September, the celebration of Mary's birth. Tragically, hundreds of thousands of pilgrims were here when the tsunami struck on the morning after Christmas 2004. At least 2000 people were believed killed and 120 shops leading down to the beach were washed away. The church itself was untouched.

Just off the main road to the basilica, **Thiruvalluvar Guest House** (☎ 2263708; d Rs 150-250, with AC Rs 550; ✷) is a good budget choice with a range of clean rooms in a relatively quiet location. **Hotel Sea Gate** (☎ 2263910; Main Rd; d Rs 395, with AC 700, cottages Rs 1300, with AC Rs 900; ✷) is a modern, comfortable hotel on the road to the basilica and a good midrange choice. Their rooms have TV and hot water.

Calimere Wildlife & Bird Sanctuary

This 333 sq km sanctuary, also known locally as **Kodikkarai** (admission Rs 5; ⊙ 6am-6pm) is 90km southeast of Thanjavur. Noted for its vast flocks of migratory waterfowl, Calimere's tidal mud flats are home to teals, shovellers, curlews, gulls, terns, plovers, sandpipers, shanks and herons from November to January. In February/March, koels, mynas and barbets come here for the wild berries. To get the most from your visit, you'll need a bicycle and binoculars.

The easiest way to get to Calimere is by bus (Rs 6, every hour) or taxi from Vedaranniyam, 12km away and the nearest town linked by frequent buses to Nagapattinam or Thanjavur.

THANJAVUR (TANJORE)

☎ 04362 / pop 215,725

Dominated by the superb World Heritage-listed Brihadishwara Temple, and a sprawling Maratha Palace complex, Thanjavur is an easy-going town and well worth a detour off the Chennai–Madurai route.

The town is famous also for its distinctive art style, which is usually a combination of raised and painted surfaces. Krishna is the most popular deity depicted, and in the

Thanjavur school his skin is white, rather than the traditional blue-black. Thanjavur is set on a fertile delta and the accompanying harvests make the town a great place to be during Pongal (harvest) celebrations in January (see p315).

Thanjavur was the ancient capital of the Chola kings, whose origins go back to the beginning of the Christian era. The Cholas' era of empire building was in AD 850 and 1270; at the height of their power, they controlled most of the Indian peninsula.

Information

BBC Net (MKM Rd; per hr Rs 20; 9.30am-9.30pm) Internet access. In the basement of the Nallaiyah Shopping Complex.

ICICI Bank ATM (South Main Rd) About 500m west of East Main Rd.

Main post office (9am-7pm Mon-Sat, 10am-4pm Sun) Near the train station.

Raja Netcafé (☎ 2378175; 30 Gandhiji Rd; per hr Rs 25; 9am-11pm) Internet access.

Tourist office (☎ 230984; 10am-5.45pm Mon-Fri) In the Hotel Tamil Nadu complex.

VKC Forex (Golden Plaza; Gandhiji Rd; 9am-9pm) The best place to change cash and travellers cheques.

Sights

BRIHADISHWARA TEMPLE & FORT

Built by Raja Raja in 1010, the magnificent **Brihadishwara Temple** (6am-1pm & 3-8pm) is the crowning glory of Chola temple architecture and the highlight of Thanjavur. Known

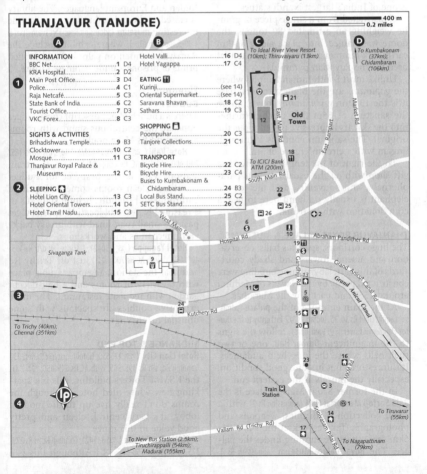

THANJAVUR (TANJORE)

0 — 400 m
0 — 0.2 miles

INFORMATION	
BBC Net	1 D4
KRA Hospital	2 D2
Main Post Office	3 D4
Police	4 C1
Raja Netcafé	5 C3
State Bank of India	6 C2
Tourist Office	7 D3
VKC Forex	8 C3

SIGHTS & ACTIVITIES	
Brihadishwara Temple	9 B3
Clocktower	10 C2
Mosque	11 C3
Thanjavur Royal Palace & Museums	12 C1

SLEEPING	
Hotel Lion City	13 C3
Hotel Oriental Towers	14 D4
Hotel Tamil Nadu	15 C3
Hotel Valli	16 D4
Hotel Yagappa	17 C4

EATING	
Kurinji	(see 14)
Oriental Supermarket	(see 14)
Saravana Bhavan	18 C2
Sathars	19 C3

SHOPPING	
Poompuhar	20 C3
Tanjore Collections	21 C1

TRANSPORT	
Bicycle Hire	22 C2
Bicycle Hire	23 C4
Buses to Kumbakonam & Chidambaram	24 B3
Local Bus Stand	25 C2
SETC Bus Stand	26 C2

To Ideal River View Resort (10km); Thiruvaiyaru (13km)

To Kumbakonam (37km); Chidambaram (106km)

Old Town

East Main Rd

East Rampart St

Market Rd

To ICICI Bank ATM (200m)

South Main Rd

West Main St

Hospital Rd

Abraham Pandither Rd

Grand Anicut Canal Rd

Grand Anicut Canal

Gandhiji Rd

Sivaganga Tank

Kutchery Rd

To Trichy (40km); Chennai (351km)

Train Station

To Tiruvarur (55km)

To New Bus Station (2.5km); Tiruchirappalli (54km); Madurai (155km)

Vallam Rd (Trichy Rd)

To Nagapattinam (79km)

Srinivasam Pillai Rd

locally as the 'Big Temple', this fascinating monument is one of only a handful in India with World Heritage listing and is worth a couple of visits – preferably early morning and late afternoon, when the setting sun bathes the sandstone tower and walls in a warm, golden-brown glow.

Set in spacious, well-tended grounds, the temple has several pillared halls and shrines and 250 linga enshrined along the outer walls. Inscriptions record the names of dancers, musicians and poets – a reminder of the significance of this area to the development of the arts. A huge covered statue of the bull, Nandi – 6m long by 3m high – faces the inner sanctum. Created from a single piece of rock, it weighs 25 tonnes and is one of India's largest Nandi statues.

Constructed from a single piece of granite weighing an estimated 80 tonnes, the dome was hauled into place along a 4km earthwork ramp in a manner similar to that used for the Egyptian pyramids.

Unlike most South Indian temples where the *gopurams* are the highest towers, here it is the 13-storey *vimanam* (tower) above the sanctum at 66m that reaches further into the sky. Its impressive gilded top is the original. The sanctum contains a 4m-high lingam with a circumference of 7m.

To the right of the temple entrance is a gift shop with all the usual religious paraphernalia and souvenirs, and the temple elephant is usually on hand here to take a coin donation with its trunk.

THANJAVUR ROYAL PALACE & MUSEUMS

The huge corridors, spacious halls, observation and arsenal towers and shady courtyards of this vast, labyrinthine building were constructed partly by the Nayaks of Madurai around 1550 and partly by the Marathas.

At the main entrance of the **palace** (admission adult/child Rs 50/25, Indian Rs 5/2 incl entry to the Durbar Hall & bell tower; 9am-6pm), follow the signs to the magnificent **Durbar Hall**, one of two such halls where the king held audiences. It's unrestored but in quite good condition, especially the murals at the eastern end.

In the former Sadar Mahal Palace is the **Raja Serfoji Memorial Hall** (admission Rs 2) with a small collection of thrones, weapons and photographs. Take a peek at the start of a 6km secret passage running under the palace. The **Royal Palace Museum** (admission Rs 1,

camera/video Rs 30/200; 9am-6pm) shows off an eclectic collection of regal memorabilia, most of it dating from the early 19th century when Serfoji II ruled.

The **Art Gallery** (admission Rs 15, camera/video Rs 30/200; 9am-1pm & 3-6pm), next door to the Royal Palace Museum, has a superb collection of Chola bronze statues from the 9th to 18th centuries. Nearby, the **Bell Tower** is worth the climb for the views right across Thanjavur and over the palace itself. The spiral stone staircase is narrow and slippery – watch your head!

The **Saraswati Mahal Library** is between the gallery and the palace museum. Established around 1700, its collection includes over 30,000 palm-leaf and paper manuscripts in Indian and European languages. The library is closed to the public but you can visit the interesting **museum** (admission free; 10am-1pm & 1.30-5.30pm Thu-Tue), where exhibits include the Ramayana written on palm leaf and explicit prints of prisoners under Chinese torture.

Sleeping
BUDGET
There's a bunch of nondescript cheap lodges opposite the central bus stand with rooms for around Rs 150 a double.

Hotel Valli (231580; 2948 MKM Rd; s/d from Rs 185/240-400, d with AC Rs 600;) Near the train station, Valli is the best bet for budget travellers. Clean rooms come with private bathroom and friendly, helpful staff. It's in a reasonably peaceful location once you get past the small road lined with greasy backyard mechanics and workshops.

Hotel Yagappa (230421; 1 Trichy Rd; d/tr Rs 195-400/460, d with AC Rs 700;) Just off Trichy Rd and near the station, Yagappa is a big place with a variety of rooms and a half-decent garden with requisite restaurant. The more expensive doubles are spacious with some unusual furnishings.

MIDRANGE & TOP END
Hotel Lion City (275650; hotellioncity@eth.net; 130 Gandhiji Rd; s/d Rs 395/545, with AC Rs 545/650;) In the KSMM Towers building, this is a sparkling new white-tiled hotel. Although the rooms don't really live up to the modern lobby, it's very central, clean and pretty good value in this range.

Hotel Tamil Nadu (331421; Gandhiji Rd; d Rs 275-375, with AC Rs 550-625;) Although this is a former raja's guesthouse, set in a quiet, leafy courtyard, that's where the royal treatment ends. Some of the rooms look like they haven't been cleaned since the Raj era and the staff give the impression they want to be somewhere else.

Hotel Oriental Towers (☎ 230850; www.hotelorientaltowers.com; 2889 Srinivasam Pillai Rd; s/d from Rs 1100/1300; ❄ 🖳 🖺) With a business centre, gym, sauna, spa, massage and 4th-floor swimming pool (Rs 100 for nonguests), this is an excellent-value business hotel around the corner from the train station. Rooms are small but comfortable, service is willing and there a couple of good restaurants and a bar.

Ideal River View Resort (☎ 250533; www.idealresort.com; s/d Rs 1500/2000, deluxe cottages Rs 2500/3000; ❄ 🖳 🖺) Although 10km northwest of the city, this tranquil resort is by far the best place to stay near Thanjavur. Set in beautiful gardens beside the Vennar River, the resort has immaculate, brightly furnished cottages with roomy balconies. The newer deluxe cottages overlook the river. There's a superb open-air restaurant, Ayurvedic centre and yoga classes. A free shuttle runs into Thanjavur at 10am (returning at 4.30pm) and you can call ahead for a free pick-up.

Eating

There are plenty of simple veg restaurants near the local bus stand and along Gandhiji Rd.

Sathars (☎ 331041; 167 Gandhiji Rd; mains Rs 35-85; ❄ noon-11pm) Good service and quality food make this place popular. Downstairs is a veg restaurant with lunchtime thalis, upstairs is an AC section with great value nonveg food – whole tandoori chicken for Rs 85 or prawn masala Rs 50.

The upmarket hotels all have good restaurants. **Kurinji** (Hotel Oriental Towers, 2889 Srinivasam Pillai Rd; mains Rs 30-90; ❄ 6pm-midnight) allows you to dine out under the stars in its lovely garden restaurant.

There are also good veg and multicuisine restaurants inside the hotel, and a bar. There's a branch of the excellent veg chain **Saravana Bhavan** (Gandhiji Rd; dishes Rs 10-30; ❄ 8am-10pm) near the palace. For self-caterers the excellent **Oriental Supermarket** (❄ 9am-9pm) at the Hotel Oriental Towers complex stocks a bit of everything.

Shopping

Thanjavur is a good place to shop for handicrafts and arts – autorickshaw drivers will have no hesitation in herding you to an emporium (for their commission) – especially around the palace area. Numerous places sell everything from quality crafts and readymade clothes to inexpensive kitsch, especially along Gandhiji Rd. One good place is **Tanjore Collections** (105 East Main St; ❄ 9am-6pm Mon-Sat), opposite the entrance to the palace. For fixed prices and hassle-free shopping, **Poompuhar** (❄ 10am-8pm Mon-Sat; Gandhiji Rd) is good for leatherwork, carvings, jewellery and other crafts.

Getting There & Away

BUS

The city bus stands are for local and SETC buses. SETC has a computerised **reservation office** (☎ 230950; ❄ 7.30am-9.30pm). There are regular buses to Chennai (Rs 105 to 135, eight hours, 20 daily). Other buses include Tirupathi (Rs 147, 11 hours, one daily), Ooty (Rs 125, 10 hours; one daily) and Pondicherry (Rs 60, six hours, one daily).

The new bus station, 2.5km south of the centre, services local areas and destinations south, such as Trichy (Rs 20, 1½ hours, every five minutes) and Madurai (Rs 50, four hours, every 15 minutes). For Kumbakonam (Rs 15, one hour) and Chidambaram (Rs 50, four hours), buses arrive and depart every 30 minutes from another bus stand just south of Brihadishwara Temple.

Bus No 74 shuttles between Thanjavur's three bus stations (Rs 3.50) regularly throughout the day.

TRAIN

The **train station** (☎ 2430052) is conveniently central at the south end of Gandhiji Rd. Thanjavur is off the main Chennai–Madurai line, so there's only one express train direct to Chennai – the overnight *Rock Fort Express* (Rs 151/425 in sleeper/3AC, 9½ hours) departing at 8.30pm. For more frequent trains north or south, including to Madurai, take a passenger train to Trichy (Rs 12, 1½ hours, eight daily) and change there. There's one daily express (6.50am) and a couple of passenger trains to Kumbakonam (Rs 10, one hour).

The *Thanjavur–Mysore Express* leaves daily at 7.15pm for Bangalore (Rs 176/493 in sleeper/3AC, 11 hours) and Mysore (Rs 213/598, 14½ hours).

Getting Around

Thanjavur's main attractions are close enough to walk between, but it can make for a long tiring day. Autorickshaws will take you on a tour of the temple and palace for around Rs 50 but most of them just want to get you into the emporiums. Bicycles can be hired from stalls opposite the train station and local bus stand for Rs 3 per hour.

AROUND THANJAVUR

About 13km north of Thanjavur, Thiruvaiyaru hosts the January international music festival in honour of the saint and composer, Thyagaraja. The saint's birthplace is at Tiruvarur, 55km east of Thanjavur. The Thyagararajaswami Temple here boasts the largest temple chariot in Tamil Nadu. The chariot is hauled through the streets during the 10-day car festival in April/May. Regular buses run from Thanjavur to Thiruvaiyaru for Rs 4.

TIRUCHIRAPPALLI (TRICHY)

☎ 0431 / pop 847,131

Tiruchirappalli, universally known as Trichy, is a sprawling but extremely satisfying city with two extraordinary temples – one perched high above the town on a rocky mount. Many travellers find Trichy and its temples more enjoyable than the clamour of the more renowned Madurai.

Trichy's long history dates back to before the Christian era when it was a Chola citadel. During the 1st millennium AD, both the Pallavas and Pandyas took power many times before the Cholas regained control in the 10th century. When the Chola empire finally decayed, Trichy came into the realm of the Vijayanagar emperors of Hampi until their defeat in 1565 by the forces of the Deccan sultans. The town and its most famous landmark, the Rock Fort Temple, were built by the Nayaks of Madurai.

Orientation

Trichy's places of interest are scattered over a large area from north to south, but for travellers it's conveniently split into three distinct areas: the Trichy Junction, or Cantonment, area in the south has most of the hotels and restaurants, the bus and train stations, tourist office and main post office, all conveniently within walking distance of each other. This is where you'll arrive and most likely stay. The Rock Fort Temple and main bazaar area is 2.5km north of here; and the other important temples are a further 3km to 5km north again, across the Cauvery River. Fortunately, the whole lot is connected by an excellent bus service.

Information

INTERNET ACCESS

G-Net (Map p362; per hr Rs 20; ☽ 9.30am-9.30pm)
Sify i-way (Map p362; Williams Rd; per hr Rs 30, ☽ 8am-11pm)

MEDICAL SERVICES

Seahorse Hospital (Map p362; ☎ 2462660; Royal Rd) A large hospital in the Cantonment.

MONEY

Delight Forex (Map p362; ☽ 9.30am-5.30pm Mon-Sat)
ICICI ATM (Map p362; Junction Rd) In front of the train station.
ICICI Bank ATM (Map p361; West Blvd Rd)
IDBI Bank (Map p362; Dindigul Rd)
UAE Exchange (Map p362; ☎ 401613; No 1 City Tower; Royal Rd; ☽ 9.30am-6pm) A good place to change travellers cheques or cash.
UTI Bank (Map p362; VOC Rd)
UTI Bank ATM (Map p361; Chinna Bazaar) In the bazaar area near the Rock Fort Temple entrance.

TOURIST INFORMATION

Tourist Office (Map p362; ☎ 2460136; 1 Williams Rd; ☽ 10am-5.45pm Mon-Fri) Has helpful and willing staff.

Sights

ROCK FORT TEMPLE

The spectacular **Rock Fort Temple** (Map p361; admission Rs 1, camera/video Rs 10/50; ☽ 6am-8pm) is perched 83m high on a massive rocky outcrop. Here, it's not so much the temple itself as the setting and joining the pilgrimage to the top that makes it special. This smooth rock was first hewn by the Pallavas who cut small cave temples into the southern face, but it was the Nayaks who later made use of its naturally fortified position. There are two main temples: **Sri Thayumanaswamy Temple**, dedicated to Shiva, halfway to the top, and **Vinayaka Temple**, at the summit, which is dedicated to Ganesh. It's a stiff climb to the top up the 437 stone-cut steps, but worth

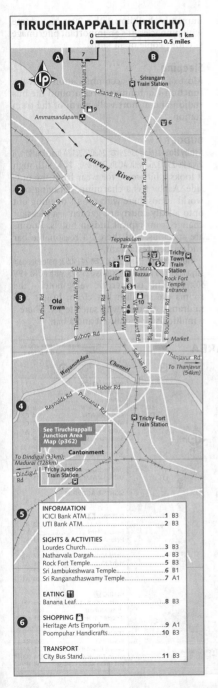

TIRUCHIRAPPALLI (TRICHY)

0 ————— 1 km
0 ————— 0.5 miles

INFORMATION
ICICI Bank ATM...................................1 B3
UTI Bank ATM....................................2 B3

SIGHTS & ACTIVITIES
Lourdes Church..................................3 B3
Natharvala Dargah.............................4 B3
Rock Fort Temple...............................5 B3
Sri Jambukeshwara Temple................6 B1
Sri Ranganathaswamy Temple............7 A1

EATING 🍴
Banana Leaf.......................................8 B3

SHOPPING 🛍
Heritage Arts Emporium......................9 A1
Poompuhar Handicrafts....................10 B3

TRANSPORT
City Bus Stand.................................11 B3

the effort – the view from the top is wonderful. Non-Hindus are not allowed into either temple, but occasionally – for a small fee – temple priests waive this regulation, particularly at the summit temple.

SRI RANGANATHASWAMY TEMPLE

The superb **temple complex** (Map p361; camera/video Rs 50/150; ⏰ 6am-1pm & 3-9pm) at Srirangam, about 3km north of the Rock Fort, is dedicated to Vishnu. Although mentioned in *sangam* poetry by an early academy of Tamil poets, temple inscriptions date its existence from the 10th century. With the Vijayanagar victory the temple was restored to the structure that exists today. Many dynasties have had a hand in its construction, including the Cheras, Pandyas, Cholas, Hoysalas, Vijayanagars and Nayaks – and work continues. The largest *gopuram*, the main entrance, was completed in 1987, and now measures 73m.

At 60 hectares, the Srirangam complex with its seven concentric walled sections and 21 *gopurams* is possibly the largest in India. Non-Hindus may go to the sixth wall but are not allowed into the gold-topped sanctum. Inside the fourth wall is a bookshop where you can buy a ticket (Rs 10) and have a guide unlock the gate to allow you to climb the wall for a panoramic view of sorts of the entire complex. Guides and priests ask high fees to show you around this temple – at least Rs 200 an hour. About half that is reasonable, but agree on a fee beforehand. Avoid guides wanting to take you shopping.

A **Temple Chariot Festival** where statues of the deities are paraded aboard a fine chariot is held here each January, but the most important festival is the 21-day **Vaikunta Ekadasi** (Paradise Festival) in mid-December, when the celebrated Vaishnavaite text, Tiruvaimozhi, is recited before an image of Vishnu.

Bus No 1 from Trichy Junction or Rock Fort stop right outside this temple.

SRI JAMBUKESHWARA TEMPLE

Much smaller and often overlooked, the nearby **Sri Jambukeshwara Temple** (Map p361; camera/video Rs 20/150; ⏰ 6am-1pm & 3-9pm) is an oasis of calm and serenity after the clamour of Sri Ranganathaswamy Temple. It is dedicated to Shiva and Parvati, and was built around the same time as Sri Ranganathaswamy. Being one of the five temples honouring the elements – in this case, water – the temple is built around a partly immersed Shiva lingam. Non-Hindus may not enter the sanctum, but beyond the second wall is an interesting chamber lined with linga and statues of gods.

If you're taking bus No 1, ask for 'Tiruvanakoil'; the temple is about 100m east of the main road.

Other Sights

Completed in 1896, the soaring, bone-white **Lourdes Church** (Map p361) is opposite the Teppakulam Tank in the bazaar area. Modelled on the neo-Gothic Basilica in Lourdes, France, it was renovated in January 1998. An annual procession, the Feast of Our Lady of Lourdes, is held on 11 February for people of all faiths. Built in 1812, **St John's Church** (Map p362) in the junction area has louvred side doors that open to turn the church into an airy pavilion. The **Natharvala Dargah** (Map p361), the tomb of the popular Muslim saint, Nath-her, is an impressive building with a 20m-high dome with pinnacles. It's an important pilgrimage site for people of all faiths.

Sleeping

Most of Trichy's accommodation is in the Junction-Cantonment area around the bus station and a short walk north of the train station.

BUDGET

Ashby Hotel (Map p362; ☎ 2460652; 17A Junction Rd; s/d from Rs 250/325, with AC Rs 700/850; 🕸) Although it looks a bit worse for wear from the outside, Ashby has a charming, decaying old-world atmosphere with rooms opening out onto a leafy courtyard garden – a pleasant change from typical Indian hotels. Rooms are spacious, and there's a reasonable bar and garden restaurant.

Hotel Mega (Map p362; ☎ 2414092; hotelmeega@satyamnet.in; 3 Rockins Rd; s/d Rs 225/325, with AC Rs 450/500; 🕸) This is a terrific value hotel – the rooms are smallish but clean, bright and midrange standard with satellite TV. There's a multicuisine restaurant and a bar.

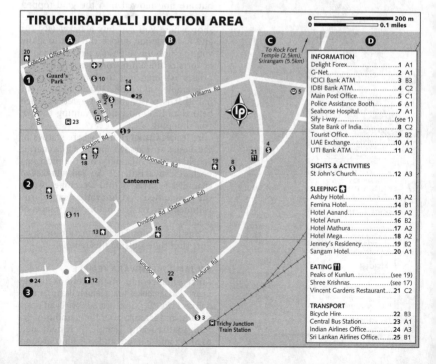

TIRUCHIRAPPALLI JUNCTION AREA

0 — 200 m
0 — 0.1 miles

To Rock Fort Temple (2.5km); Srirangam (5.5km)

INFORMATION	
Delight Forex	1 A1
G-Net	2 A1
ICICI Bank ATM	3 B3
IDBI Bank ATM	4 C2
Main Post Office	5 C1
Police Assistance Booth	6 A1
Seahorse Hospital	7 A1
Sify i-way	(see 1)
State Bank of India	8 C2
Tourist Office	9 B2
UAE Exchange	10 A1
UTI Bank ATM	11 A2

SIGHTS & ACTIVITIES	
St John's Church	12 A3

SLEEPING	
Ashby Hotel	13 A2
Femina Hotel	14 B1
Hotel Aanand	15 A2
Hotel Arun	16 B2
Hotel Mathura	17 A2
Hotel Mega	18 A2
Jenney's Residency	19 B2
Sangam Hotel	20 A1

EATING	
Peaks of Kunlun	(see 19)
Shree Krishnas	(see 17)
Vincent Gardens Restaurant	21 C2

TRANSPORT	
Bicycle Hire	22 B3
Central Bus Station	23 A1
Indian Airlines Office	24 A3
Sri Lankan Airlines Office	25 B1

Collector's Office Rd
Guard's Park
VOC Rd
Royal Rd
Williams Rd
Rockins Rd
McDonald's Rd
Cantonment
Dindigul Rd (State Bank Rd)
Junction Rd
Madurai Rd
Trichy Junction Train Station

Hotel Aanand (Map p362; ☎ 2415545; hotelaanand@ hotmail.com; 1 VOC Rd; s/d Rs 190/320, d with AC Rs 500; ✖) Clean, simple rooms and a good open-air restaurant make this a popular choice.

Hotel Arun (Map p362; ☎ 2415021; 24 Dindigul Rd; s/d Rs 175/195, with AC Rs 400/450; ✖) Set back from the road, this hotel is quiet, friendly and value for money. Fairly clean rooms have TV and phone.

MIDRANGE & TOP END

Hotel Mathura (Map p362; ☎ 2414737; www.hotel mathura.com; 1 Rockins Rd; s/d Rs 260/360, with AC Rs 495/595; ✖) Right next door to Hotel Mega, Mathura is another good choice. The rooms are clean and comfortable with thick foam mattresses – a rarity in an Indian hotel! – TV and phone. There's a popular restaurant at the front and credit cards are accepted.

Femina Hotel (Map p362; ☎ 2414501; try_femina@ sanchar.net.in; 109 Williams Rd; s/d from Rs 350/550, with AC Rs 800/1300; ✖ 🏊) Femina is one of those Indian business hotels that manages to give top-end quality yet be affordable even if you're on a budget – and the staff don't look at travellers as if they've just crawled out of a swamp. All rooms have TV and phone, there's a gym, a small shopping arcade, a 24-hour coffee shop and a couple of very good restaurants. Nonguests can use the pool or gym for Rs 75 per hour.

Jenneys Residency (Map p362; ☎ 2414414; jenneys@ satyam.net.in; 3/14 McDonald's Rd; s/d US$30/40, deluxe US$45/55, ste US$75; ✖ 🏊) Jenneys is enormous, semiluxurious and in a relatively quiet location. The best rooms are on the top floors but all are well appointed. Hotel facilities include shops, a health club and a bizarre Wild West theme bar.

Sangam Hotel (Map p362; ☎ 2414700; fax 2415 779; www.hotelsangam.com; Collector's Office Rd; s/d US$90/125; ✖ 🏊) This option has all the facilities of a four-star hotel, including restaurants, a bar, pool and shopping arcade. The rooms are comfortable and better value if they're offering them at a discounted rate, as they seem to on a regular basis.

Eating

All of the upmarket hotels have their share of good restaurants and most have bars.

Shree Krishnas (Map p362; Rockins Rd; ⌚ 8am-10pm) The restaurant in front of Hotel Mathura has a popular veg section serving top-notch thalis (Rs 20) – it's always packed at lunchtime – and a small AC nonveg section. There's a little veranda and snack bar at the front from where you can watch the bustle of the bus stand across the road.

Vincent Gardens Restaurant (Map p362; Dindigul Rd; mains Rs 30-70; ⌚ 12.30-10pm) Vincent Gardens has a pleasant outdoor setting and a limited veg and nonveg menu, but it does the few dishes well. Take mosquito repellent in the evening. There's a good bakery next door.

Banana Leaf (Map p361; ☎ 271101; West Blvd Rd; mains Rs 20-75; ⌚ 11am-midnight) One of the few good choices close to the Rock Fort Temple, this is an intimate little place with a big menu of inexpensive Indian and Chinese dishes – tandoori chicken (Rs 67), crab masala (Rs 45) and the intriguing rabbit masala (Rs 70). It's rustic rather than gourmet, but the food and service are fine.

The Peaks of Kunlun (Map p362; ☎ 2414414; Jenny's Residency, 3/14 McDonald's Rd; meals Rs 60-150) This place has a varied menu, including Indian, Chinese and Continental dishes and beer is served.

Shopping

Trichy's best shopping is in the bazaar area south of the Rock Fort Temple. Wandering along Big Bazaar Rd and Chinnar Bazaar in the evening is an assault on the sense – it's constantly packed with people and lit up like Times Square on New Years Eve.

For crafts and gifts check out **Poompuhar Handicrafts** (Map p361; West Blvd Rd; ⌚ 9am-8pm) or **Heritage Arts Emporium** (Map p361; ☎ 2432299; 5 Amma Mandapam Rd, Srirangam).

Getting There & Away

Trichy is virtually in the geographical centre of Tamil Nadu and it's well-connected by air, bus and train.

AIR

As well as domestic flights, Trichy's airport has flights to Sri Lanka, Kuwait and Sharjah. **Indian Airlines** (Map p362; ☎ 2341063; 4A Dindigul Rd) flies four days a week to Chennai (US$90), daily to Thiruvananthapuram (Trivandrum, US$115) and daily except Friday to Kozhikode (Calicut, US$95).

Sri Lankan Airlines (Map p362; ☎ 2462381; ⌚ 9am-5.30pm Mon-Sat, 9am-1pm Sun), at Femina Hotel, flies daily to Colombo (Rs 3800).

TAMIL NADU

BUS

Most buses use the central bus station on Rockins Rd. If you're travelling to Kodaikanal, a good option is to take one of the frequent buses to Dindigul (Rs 25, two hours) and change there.

Destination	Fare (Rs)	Duration (hr)	Frequency
Chennai	110-142	7	every 5min
Bangalore	150	8	3 daily
Thanjavur	15	1½	every 5min
Madurai	35	3	every 10min
Tirupathi	144	9	5 daily
Pondicherry	70	5	3 daily
Chidambaram	51	3½s	hourly
Coimbatore	73	7	every 30min
Kodaikanal	62	6	3 daily
Ooty	100	8	1 daily

TRAIN

Trichy is on the main Chennai–Madurai line so there are lots of rail options in either direction. Of the nine daily expresses to Chennai, the quickest is the *Vaigai Express* (Rs 85/297 in 2nd/chair class, 5½ hours) departing Trichy at 9.10am and the *Pallavan Express,* which leaves at 6.30am. The best overnight train is the *Rock Fort Express* (Rs 136/382, 7½ hours) at 9.40pm. For Madurai the best train is the *Guruvaya Express* (Rs 47/75 in 2nd class/sleeper; three hours), which leaves at 1pm. For Rameswaram, only passenger trains (6.40am and 9.30pm) operate and they take a tortuous 12 to 15 hours.

The *Mysore Express* goes daily to Bangalore (Rs 160/450 in sleeper/3AC, 11½ hours) and Mysore (Rs 200/562, 15 hours).

Getting Around

TO/FROM THE AIRPORT

The 7km ride into town is Rs 1250 by taxi and Rs 60 by autorickshaw. Otherwise, take a No 7, 59, 58 or 63 bus to the airport (30 minutes).

BICYCLE

Trichy lends itself to cycling as it's flat – it's a reasonably easy ride from Trichy Junction to the Rock Fort Temple, but a long haul to Srirangam and back. There are a couple of places on Junction Rd where you can hire bicycles for Rs 5 per hour.

BUS

Trichy's local bus service is mercifully efficient and easy to use. The No 1 (A or B) bus from the main bus stand on Rockins Rd flies every few minutes via the Rock Fort Temple, Sri Jambukeshwara Temple and main entrance to Sri Ranganathaswamy Temple (Rs 4). To see them all, get off in that order (ask the conductor or driver where the stops are), as it runs in a one-way circuit.

SOUTHERN TAMIL NADU

MADURAI

☎ 0452 / pop 1.19 million

Famous for the awe-inspiring Sri Meenakshi Temple complex, Madurai is an animated city packed with pilgrims, beggars, businesspeople, bullock carts and underemployed rickshaw drivers. It's one of South India's oldest cities and has been a centre of learning and pilgrimage for centuries.

Madurai's landmark temple in the heart of the old town is a riotously baroque example of Dravidian architecture with *gopurams* covered from top to bottom in a breathtaking profusion of multicoloured images of gods, goddesses, animals and mythical figures. The temple seethes with activity from dawn to dusk, its many shrines attracting pilgrims and tourists from all over the world; 10,000 visitors may come here on any one day. Madurai is on virtually every traveller's Tamil Nadu itinerary – it has excellent transport links and some good midrange accommodation – but the old part of the city is squalid, even by Indian standards, and touts can be oppressive.

History

Tamil and Greek documents record the existence of Madurai from the 4th century BC. It was popular for trade, especially in spices, and was also the site of the *sangam* – the academy of Tamil poets. Over the centuries Madurai has come under the jurisdiction of the Cholas, the Pandyas, the Muslim invaders, the Hindu Vijayanagar kings, and the Nayaks, who ruled until 1781. During the reign of Tirumalai Nayak (1623–55), the bulk of the Sri Meenakshi Temple was built, and Madurai became the cultural centre of the Tamil people, playing an important role in the development of the Tamil language.

MADURAI

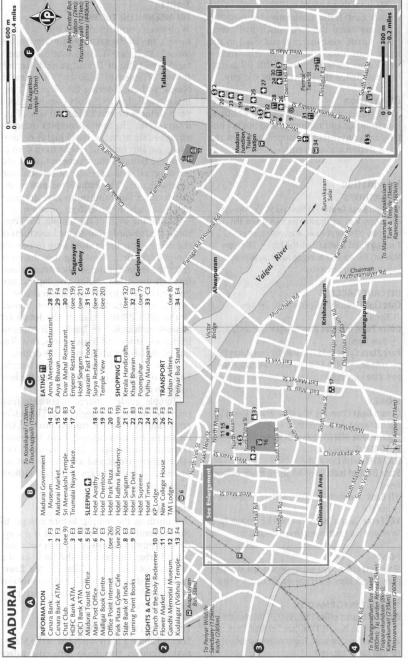

INFORMATION

Canara Bank	1 F3
Canara Bank ATM	2 F3
Chat Club	(see 9)
HDFC Bank ATM	3 E3
ICICI Bank ATM	4 B3
Madurai Tourist Office	5 E4
Main Post Office	6 B2
Malligai Book Centre	7 E3
Office Point Internet	(see 26)
Park Plaza Cyber Cafe	(see 20)
State Bank of India	8 E3
Turning Point Books	9 E3

SIGHTS & ACTIVITIES

Church of the Holy Redeemer	10 E3
Flower Market	11 C3
Gandhi Memorial Museum	12 E2
Kudalalgar (Vishnu) Temple	13 F4

SLEEPING

Madurai Government Museum	14 E2
Madurai Market	15 C3
Sri Meenakshi Temple	16 B3
Tirumalai Nayak Palace	17 C4
Hotel Aarithy	18 E4
Hotel Chentoor	19 F3
Hotel Park Plaza	20 F3
Hotel Rathna Residency	(see 19)
Hotel Sangam	21 E1
Hotel Sree Devi	22 B3
Hotel Supreme	23 E3
Hotel Times	24 E4
KP Lodge	25 E3
New College House	26 F3
TM Lodge	27 F3

EATING

Anna Meenakshi Restaurant	28 F3
Arya Bhavan	29 F4
Divar Mahal Restaurant	30 F3
Emperor Restaurant	(see 19)
Hotel Sangam	(see 21)
Jayaram Fast Foods	31 E4
Surya Restaurant	(see 23)
Temple View	(see 20)

SHOPPING

Kerala Handicrafts	(see 32)
Khadi Bhavan	32 E3
Poompuhar	(see 7)
Puthu Mandapam	33 C3

TRANSPORT

Indian Airlines	(see 8)
Periyar Bus Stand	34 E4

Madurai then passed into the hands of the British East India Company. In 1840 the company razed the fort, which had previously surrounded the city, and filled in the moat. Four broad streets – the Veli streets – were constructed on top of this fill and to this day define the limits of the old city.

Orientation
Most places, including the main post office, tourist office and midrange and budget hotels, are conveniently wedged between the train station and the temple.

Information
BOOKSHOPS
Malligai Book Centre (11 West Veli St; 🕑 9am-2pm & 4.30-9pm Mon-Sat) Opposite the train station, this place has a good selection of books, maps and cassettes.
Turning Point Books (Town Hall Rd; 🕑 10am-9pm Mon-Sat) This 4th-floor bookshop has many titles in English, including paperbacks.

INTERNET ACCESS
Chat Club (Town Hall Rd; per hr Rs 25; 🕑 9am-11.30pm)
Office Point Internet (New College House; per hr Rs 25; 🕑 9am-10pm)
Park Plaza Cyber Café (114 West Perumal Maistry St; per hr Rs 30; 🕑 24hr) Adjoining Hotel Park Plaza, this is part of the i-way chain.

MONEY
Canara Bank (Town Hall Rd & West Perumal Maistry St) Also has foreign exchange desks.
Canara Bank ATM (West Perumal Maistry St)
HDFC ATM (West Veli St)
ICICI ATM (North Chitrai St)
State Bank of India (West Veli St) Has foreign exchange desks
UTI Bank (Madurai Junction station) Has a conveniently located ATM.
VKC Forex (Zulaiha Towers, Town Hall Rd; 🕑 9am-7pm) An efficient place to change travellers cheques.

POST
Main post office (West Veli St; 🕑 9am-5pm Mon-Sat, parcel office 9.30am-7pm) Poste restante counter is No 8.

TOURIST INFORMATION
Madurai tourist office (☎ 2334757; 180 West Veli St; 🕑 10am-5pm Mon-Fri, 11am-1pm Sat) Helpful staff, as well as brochures and maps. Tourist counters are also at the train station and airport.

Sights
SRI MEENAKSHI TEMPLE
With its colourful, intricately carved temple towers, the **Sri Meenakshi Temple** (admission free, camera Rs 30; 🕑 6am-12.30pm & 4-9pm) is a spectacular pastiche of Dravidian architecture. It was designed in 1560 by Vishwanatha Nayak and built during the reign of Tirumalai Nayak, but its history goes back 2000 years to the time when Madurai was a Pandyan capital. The temple complex occupies an area of six hectares. Its 12 highly decorative *gopurams* range in height from 45m to 50m (the tallest is the southern tower) and are adorned with carvings of celestial and animal figures. The **Puthu Mandapam** in the east forms a long and impressive entrance hall that leads to the eastern *gopuram*.

Within the walls of the temple, long corridors lead towards gold-topped sanctums of the deities. It is the custom here to honour the goddess first. Most pilgrims therefore enter the temple at the southeastern corner, through the Ashta Shakti Mandapam, and proceed directly to the Meenakshi shrine.

Also within the temple complex, housed in the 1000 Pillared Hall, is the **Temple Art Museum** (admission Rs 1; 🕑 7am-7pm). It contains friezes and stone and brass images, as well as one of the best exhibits on Hindu deities.

Allow plenty of time to see this temple. Early mornings or late evenings are the best times to avoid crowds.

'Temple guides' charge negotiable fees, rarely below Rs 200. Haggle hard. The guides are usually a front for emporiums and tailor shops that miraculously have 'free' towers with temple views. These rooftops can offer superb views and are worth visiting, provided you don't expect to exit without persistent invitations to buy.

MADURAI MARKET
Just north of the temple, before you get to North Avani St, this daily market is a labyrinth of bustling laneways strewn with aromatic herbs. Adjacent, on the 1st floor of a nondescript cement building, is the **flower market**. Vendors dexterously heap mountains of marigolds and jasmine onto scales for the temple flower sellers here.

TIRUMALAI NAYAK PALACE
Located about 1.5km southeast of the Meenakshi Temple, this Indo-Saracenic **palace**

(Indian/foreigner Rs 5/50; ◷ 9am-1pm & 2-5pm) was built in 1636 by the ruler whose name it bears. Today, only the entrance gate, main hall and dance hall (Natakasala) remain but it is well worth visiting to see these. The rectangular courtyard, which measures 75m x 52m, is known as the Swargavilasa or Celestial Pavilion and it gives clues to the original grandeur of the building, regarded as one of the finest secular buildings in South India.

There's a daily **sound-and-light show** (Rs 10) which can be fun; the mosquitoes and people carrying on conversations throughout come at no extra cost. The English version is at 6.45pm and it's in Tamil at 8pm.

The palace is a 20-minute walk from the Meenakshi Temple.

MUSEUMS

Housed in the old palace of the Rani Mangammal is the excellent **Gandhi Memorial Museum** (admission free, camera/video Rs 10/50; ◷ 10am-1pm & 2-5.45pm), set in spacious and relaxing grounds. It contains an impressive and detailed historical account of India's struggle for Independence from 1757 to 1947 in a maze of rooms. Included in the exhibition is the blood-stained loincloth that Gandhi was supposedly wearing at the time he was assassinated.

The **Madurai Government Museum** (admission free; ◷ 9.30am-5.30pm Sat-Thu) is next door in the same grounds. Inside is a collection of archaeological finds, sculpture, bronzes, costumes and paintings.

MARIAMMAN TEPPAKKULAM TANK

This tank, 5km east of the old city, covers an area almost equal to that of the Meenakshi Temple and is the site of the popular **Teppam (Float) Festival**, held in January/February. When it's empty (most of the year) it becomes a cricket ground for local kids. The tank was built by Tirumalai Nayak in 1646 and is connected to the Vaigai River by underground channels.

Tours

The tourist office can organise half-day (five-hour) sightseeing tours that include the Tirumalai Nayak Palace and Gandhi Museum, and finish at the Sri Meenakshi Temple. Tours start at 7am and 3pm and cost Rs 125 per person.

Sleeping

Most of Madurai's accommodation is concentrated in the area between the train station and the Sri Meenakshi temple. There are loads of places but the choice at the true budget end is pretty dire – many places popular with pilgrims are little more than flophouses with stained walls and dank bathrooms. There are plenty of good hotels in the midrange bracket and if you don't need AC, and they're excellent value.

BUDGET

Town Hall Rd, running east from the train station, has a knot of cheap and not very cheerful hotels.

Hotel Sree Devi (☎ 2347431; 20 West Avani St; d from Rs 180, d/tr with AC Rs 400/600, rooftop room Rs 400) The pride and joy here is the cosy rooftop room, which has possibly the best views of the temple. Even if you go for something a bit cheaper, the location is right in the thick of things and the rooms are simple but clean.

KP Lodge (☎ 2340532; 29 West Perumal Maistry St; s/d 100/150) This small lodge is cleaner than most and reasonably quiet. Rooms are a decent size and come with TV.

New College House (☎ 2342971; 2 Town Hall Rd; s/d from Rs 185/250, with AC Rs 480/640; ⌘) This is a huge complex virtually opposite the train station. The 250 rooms are varied – from minuscule to spacious – so check out a few. The cheaper rooms are tired and old and street noise penetrates.

TM Lodge (☎ 2341651; tmlodge@maduraionline .com; 50 West Perumal Maistry St; s/d Rs 200/320, d with AC & TV Rs 550; ⌘) This is one of the brighter budget places in this area. Efficiently run with clean linen and reasonably well-kept rooms. The upper rooms are definitely lighter and airier.

Hotel Times (☎ 342651; 15-16 Town Hall Rd; s/d Rs 150/263, d with AC from Rs 350; ⌘) Hotel Times is another slightly dark budget place, but it's reasonably clean and trying hard not to be too depressing. Avoid the windowless rooms.

Hotel Aarathy (☎ 2331571; 9 Perumal Koil West Mada St; s/d/tr Rs 195/330/450, with AC Rs 495/550/650; ⌘) This is a step up from the real cheapies and the management is accustomed to travellers. It's a big, slightly soulless place with endless corridors and reasonable rooms with TV and hot water. Each morning the resident elephant from the Kudalagar Temple across the road pays a visit.

MIDRANGE & TOP END

Madurai's best value accommodation is in the midrange hotels along West Perumal Maistry St, near the train station. Rooms without AC are a bargain and worth making that step up from the budget joints. Most have rooftop restaurants with temple and sunset views.

Hotel Chentoor (☎ 2350490; hotelchentoor@tamilnadu.com; 106 West Perumal Maistry St; s/d Rs 420/460, with AC from Rs 750/850; 🔀) Chentoor is one of the first high-rise hotels you come to walking north along West Perumal Maistry St. The standard rooms are smallish but clean and comfortable with TV.

Hotel Rathna Residency (☎ 5370441; 109 West Perumai Maistry St; s/d Rs 450/500, with AC Rs 750/850) Near Hotel Chentoor, this is another stylish and excellent-value place with a rooftop restaurant and all the trimmings of hotels twice the price in any other city.

Hotel Supreme (☎ 2343151; www.supremehotels.com; 110 West Perumal Maistry St; s/d from Rs 450/480, with AC from Rs 810/880, ste Rs 1800; 🔀) This is another large, well-presented hotel with very comfortable rooms equipped with TV and large windows. Many of the deluxe/superdeluxe rooms (from Rs 980) have balconies and great views of the Sri Meenakshi Temple. It also has one of the city's best rooftop restaurants and a bar decked out like a spaceship!

Hotel Park Plaza (☎ 3011111; www.hotelparkplaza.net; 114 West Perumal Maistry St; s/d Rs 995/1350, ste Rs 1600; 🔀) The Plaza is slightly more upmarket than its neighbours (all rooms have central AC) but the rooms are standard midrange, comfortable and simply furnished. The front rooms have temple views from the 3rd floor up. There's a good rooftop restaurant and the inappropriately named Sky High Bar – on the 1st floor.

Hotel Sangam (☎ 2537531; www.hotelsangam.com; Alargakoil Rd; s/d US$90/125; 🔀 🏊) Not far from the bus stand, recently renovated Hotel Sangam is all class, with cool marble, huge modern rooms and a quality restaurant.

Taj Garden Retreat (☎ 2371636; retreat.madurai@tajhotels.com; 40 TPK Rd; s/d US$120/135; 🔀 🖳 🏊) This colonial-style Taj Group hotel is one of the fanciest in Madurai. Located 5km west of the city in Pasumalai, it's either peaceful or inconvenient, depending on your view. There's a pool, Ayurvedic centre, business centre and fine restaurant and bar

Eating

Along West Perumal Maistry St, the rooftop restaurants of a string of hotels offer breezy dining and temple views.

Surya Restaurant (110 West Perumal Maistry St; mains Rs 30-70; 🕑 6am-11pm) The rooftop restaurant of Hotel Supreme offers a superb view over the city, Indian, Chinese and Continental veg food, spectacular lunchtime thalis and cold beer.

Emperor Restaurant (☎ 2350490; 106 West Perumal Maistry St; mains Rs 30-80; 🕑 6am-midnight) The rooftop restaurant at the Hotel Chentoor appears to be an afterthought, but the food, views and service are all good and nonveg food is served.

Temple View (☎ 3011111; 114 West Perumal Maistry St; mains Rs 55-140; 8am-10pm) The rooftop restaurant at the Hotel Park Plaza serves veg and nonveg dishes, including North Indian, Chinese and Continental, with the same view as the Surya. Butter chicken masala is Rs 80 and the tandoori chicken (Rs 110 for half) is especially succulent.

Divar Mahal Restaurant (☎ 2342700; 21 Town Hall Rd; mains Rs 30-80; 11am-11pm) One of the better multicuisine restaurants not attached to a hotel, Divar Mahal is clean and bright. Roast leg of lamb (Rs 80), makes an interesting change, half tandoori chicken is Rs 80 and prawn masala is Rs 75.

Jayaram Fast Foods (Dindigul Rd; mains Rs 25-75; 🕑 10am-10pm) With a busy bakery downstairs and a spotless AC restaurant upstairs, this makes a pleasant change from thali places. The menu includes soups, spring rolls, pizzas and burgers, as well as North Indian dishes.

Hotel Sangam (☎ 2537531; www.hotelsangam.com; Alargakoil Rd; mains Rs 40-150; 🕑 11am-3pm & 7pm-11pm) For an intimate night out, fine dining and an escape to the other side of the river, the lovely restaurant at Sangam has a pond with a fountain, and is worth the trip. The multicuisine menu offers Indian, Chinese and Continental, including seafood.

Among the cheap and cheerful South Indian veg restaurants in the old town are **Arya Bhavan** (cnr West Masi St & Dindigul Rd), and **Anna Meenakshi Restaurant** (West Perumal Maistry St) a large, bright place good for thalis (Rs 30).

Shopping

Madurai, a textile centre from way back, teems with cloth stalls and tailors' shops. A great place for getting cottons and printed fabrics is Puthu Mandapam, the pillared former entrance hall at the eastern side of Sri Meenakshi Temple. Here you'll find rows of tailors, all busily treadling away and capable of whipping up a good replica of whatever you're wearing in an hour or two. Quality, designs and prices vary greatly depending on the material and complexity of the design, but you can have a shirt made up for Rs 100.

If you want garments made, have your designs ready. It's also important to know a little about materials, quality and quantity required. As always, take your time, look around carefully and bargain hard.

The fixed-price government shops are conveniently located together in West Veli St, including Poompuhar, Khadi Bhavan and Kerala Handicrafts. Every tout, driver, 'temple guide' and tailor's brother will lead you to the Kashmiri shops in North Chitrai St, initially offering to show you the temple view from the rooftop – the views are good, but there's the inevitable sales pitch and pressure to buy and anyone who takes you to a shop receives a commission.

Getting There & Away

AIR

Air Deccan (☎ 9894477008) has a daily flight to Chennai and offers the cheapest fares – Rs 2100, though Internet and special fares are even cheaper. **Indian Airlines** (☎ 2341234; West Veli St; airport ☎ 2690771; ☼ 10am-5pm Mon-Sat) has one flight daily to Chennai (US$100) and Mumbai (US$220). **Jet Airways** (☎ 526969) also flies twice daily to Chennai for the same price.

BUS

Most long distance buses arrive and depart from the **central bus station** (☎ 2580680; Melur Rd), 6km northeast of the old city. It appears chaotic but is actually a well-organised 24-hour operation. Local buses shuttle into the city every few minutes for Rs 2. Autorickshaw drivers charge Rs 50.

Private bus companies offer superdeluxe coaches with video services to Chennai and Bangalore (Rs 220 to 300) but the state bus companies have similar services so don't be ripped off by paying more through travel agencies – they may sell you a ticket at an inflated price and you'll end up on a state bus anyway. The following are prices for government buses.

Destination	Fare (Rs)	Duration (hr)	Frequency
Bangalore	152	12	6 daily
Chennai	144-186	10	every 20min
Chidambaram	110	8	3 daily
Coimbatore	66	5	every 15min
Kanyakumari	76	6	hourly
Kodaikanal	36	4	10 daily
Mysore	150	16	2 (via Ooty)
Palani	30	3	every half-hour
Pondicherry	105	8	2 daily
Rameswaram	49	4	every half-hour
Tirupathi	180	5½	6 daily
Trichy	38	3	every 10min

The Arapalaym bus stand, west of the train station has hourly buses to Kumili (Rs 40, 4½ hours) for the Periyar Wildlife Sanctuary, as well as some services to Kodaikanal and Palani.

Private minibuses also run daily to Kodaikanal (Rs 150), Rameswaram (Rs 120) and Kanyakumari (Rs 200). These are basically package trips for Indian pilgrims and sightseers making a day trip, but if there are seats available you can get a one-way drop (prices listed are for drop only). The only real advantage is that these buses leave from the city centre – travel agents can be found opposite the train station – and they pick up from hotels around town.

TRAIN

Madurai Junction is on the main Chennai–Kanyakumari line. There are at least nine daily trains to Chennai, including the overnight *Pearl City Express* (Rs 182/510 in sleeper/3AC, 10 hours) at 10.30pm and the *Vaigai Express* (Rs 114/397 in 2nd/chair class, eight hours). Chennai trains stop at Trichy (Rs 47/75 in 2nd/sleeper, three hours). To Kanyakumari there are three daily services; the best is *Kanyakumari Express* (Rs 107/300 in sleeper/3AC, six hours) at 7.15am.

Other services include Madurai to Coimbatore (Rs 62/98 in 2nd/sleeper class, 6½ hours) and Bangalore (Rs 179/502 in sleeper/3AC), as well as Trivandrum and Mumbai.

TAMIL NADU

Getting Around

The airport is 12km south of town and a taxi charges an extortionate Rs 200 to the town centre. Autorickshaws ask around Rs 100. Alternatively, bus No 10A from the central bus station goes to the airport but don't rely on it being on schedule.

The Periyar bus stand in the old city is still in use for city travel – buses regular shuttle from here to the new bus stand. Central Madurai is small enough to get around on foot.

RAMESWARAM

☎ 04573 / pop 38,035

Rameswaram is one of the most significant pilgrimage centres in South India for both Shaivites and Vaishnavaites. It was here that Rama (an incarnation of Vishnu and hero of the Ramayana) offered thanks to Shiva. At the town's core is the Ramanathaswamy Temple, one of the most important temples in South India.

Rameswaram is located on an island in the Gulf of Mannar, and is connected to the mainland at Mandapam by one of India's great engineering wonders, the Indira Gandhi bridge, which was opened by Rajiv Gandhi in 1988. The town was once an important ferry port with passenger services to and from Sri Lanka, but the service ceased when things got ugly in Sri Lanka and at the time of writing show no signs of resuming.

Apart from the regular influx of pilgrims, Rameswaram is a sleepy fishing village with a pleasantly laid-back atmosphere and the pungent smell of drying fish hanging in the air – a highlight is taking a stroll down to the harbour in the early morning to see the fishing boats come in and the catch being sorted. It's not a tourist town though, and accommodation and eating options are pretty basic.

Orientation & Information

Most hotels and restaurants are clustered around the Ramanathaswamy Temple. The bus stand, 2km to the west, is connected by shuttle bus to the town centre.

The **tourist office** (☎ 221371; ◷ 10am-5.45pm Mon-Fri) is at the bus stand.

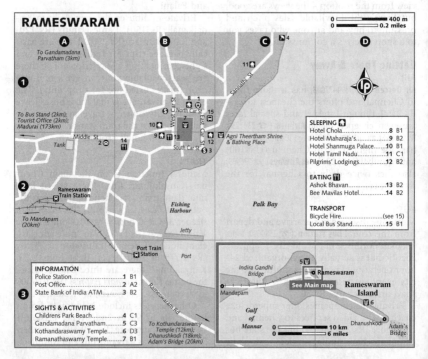

RAMESWARAM

0 — 400 m
0 — 0.2 miles

To Gandamadana
Parvatham (3km)

Sannathi St

To Bus Stand (2km);
Tourist Office (2km);
Madurai (173km)

West Car St
North Car St
East Car St
South Car St

Middle St

Tank

Agni Theertham Shrine
& Bathing Place

Rameswaram
Train Station

To Mandapam
(20km)

Fishing
Harbour

Jetty

Palk Bay

Port Train
Station

Port

SLEEPING
Hotel Chola..............................8 B1
Hotel Maharaja's.......................9 B2
Hotel Shanmuga Palace............10 B1
Hotel Tamil Nadu.....................11 C1
Pilgrims' Lodgings...................12 B2

EATING
Ashok Bhavan..........................13 B2
Bee Mavilas Hotel....................14 B2

TRANSPORT
Bicycle Hire.........................(see 15)
Local Bus Stand......................15 B1

INFORMATION
Police Station...........................1 B1
Post Office................................2 A2
State Bank of India ATM...........3 B2

SIGHTS & ACTIVITIES
Childrens Park Beach.................4 C1
Gandamadana Parvatham..........5 C3
Kothandaraswamy Temple.........6 D3
Ramanathaswamy Temple.........7 B1

Indira Gandhi
Bridge

Rameswaram

See Main map

Rameswaram
Island

Mandapam

To Kothandaraswamy
Temple (12km);
Dhanushkodi (18km);
Adam's Bridge (20km)

Gulf
of
Mannar

Dhanushkodi   Adam's
Bridge

0 — 10 km
0 — 6 miles

You can't change money here but the **State Bank of India** (East Car St) has an ATM accepting international cards.

Sights

RAMANATHASWAMY TEMPLE

A fine example of late Dravidian architecture, this **temple** (camera Rs 25; ☺ 4am-1pm & 3-8.30pm) is most renowned for its four magnificent corridors lined with elaborately sculpted pillars. Construction began in the 12th century AD. Later additions included a 53m-high *gopuram*. The 22 *theerthams* (tanks) within the complex are believed by devotees to have particular powers and you will often see ritual bathings taking place. Pilgrims are expected to bathe in, and drink from the waters in each *theertham*. The number of *theerthams* is said to correspond with the number of arrows in Rama's quiver, which he used to generate water on the island. Only Hindus may enter the inner sanctum (which is adorned with paintings depicting the origins of Rameswaram).

Even when the temple is closed, it is possible to take a peaceful amble through the extensive corridors.

DHANUSHKODI & ADAM'S BRIDGE

About 18km southeast of town, **Dhanushkodi** is a long, windswept surf beach and sandpit with an end-of-the-world feel. Other than the beach and some straggling fishing shanties, there's not much here, but it's a pleasant walk to the end of the peninsula where you can gaze out at **Adam's Bridge**, the chain of reefs, sandbanks and islets that almost connect Sri Lanka with India. Legend says that these are the stepping stones created and used by Rama to follow Ravana, in his bid to rescue Sita in the epic Ramayana. Buses (Rs 5, hourly) from the local bus stand on East Car St stop about 4km before the beach so you have to walk the rest of the way. Otherwise, an autorickshaw (45 minutes one way) from Rameswaram costs Rs 200 return.

About 6km before Dhanushkodi, the **Kothandaraswamy Temple** is the only structure to survive the 1964 cyclone that destroyed the village. Legend has it that Rama, overcome with guilt at having killed Ravana (a Brahmin), performed a *puja* on this spot and thereafter the temple was built. It is also believed that Vibhishana, brother of Sita's kidnapper Ravana, surrendered to Rama here.

GANDAMADANA PARVATHAM

This **temple**, 3km northwest of Rameswaram, is a shrine reputedly containing Rama's footprints. The two-storey *mandapam* is on a small hill – the highest point on the island – with good views over the town. Pilgrims visit at sunrise and sunset. To get there it's an easy and interesting cycle ride through village backstreets.

Activities

Touts hang around Hotel Tamil Nadu offering one-hour **snorkelling trips** from the Children's Park Beach. This amounts to a short paddle out in a canoe to a virtually nonexistent reef, but it's worthwhile just to go for a swim and you might see some fish. The boatmen ask Rs 300, but the going rate is no more than Rs 100 per person. Bargain hard.

Festivals & Events

Car Festival (Feb/Mar) During the festival, a huge decorated chariot with idols of the deities installed is hauled through the streets in a pulsating parade.
Thiru Kalyana (Jul/Aug) This festival celebrates the celestial marriage of Shiva and Parvati.

Sleeping & Eating

Hotels, mainly geared towards pilgrims, are often completely booked out during festivals. Don't come here expecting anything resembling luxury – there are no upmarket hotels and at the budget end the choices are a bit grim. Near the temple loud music blasts out from 4.30am.

The cheapest places to stay in Rameswaram are the pilgrim's lodgings run by the temple, where basic double rooms are Rs 100 to 200. There's an accommodation booking office (East Car St) opposite the main temple entrance.

Hotel Chola (☎ 221307; North Car St; d/tr Rs 170/ 250) This is a basic budget place with grim bathrooms but it's cheap enough.

Hotel Maharaja's (☎ 221271; 7 Middle St; s/d/tr Rs 194/294/367, d/tr with AC Rs 519/825 inc tax; 🖳) Near the temple's west entrance, this is one of Rameswaram's better choices and is certainly reasonably priced. Rooms are simple but most have TV and open out onto a common balcony (some have private balconies) – the upper floors have good temple views.

Hotel Shanmuga Palace (☎ 222945; 10/98 Middle St; d Rs 350, with AC Rs 600; 🖳) Opposite

Maharaja's this is one of the newer places in town, modern, clean with 30 smallish but comfortable rooms with TV.

Hotel Tamil Nadu (☎ 221277; Sannathi St; dm Rs 80, d/tr from Rs 300/450, d with AC Rs 700; ❄) The breezy oceanfront location close to the town beach is the main reason to choose this hotel. The rooms are worn and typical of a government hotel, but it's extremely popular with pilgrims so you may not get a room anyway. The **restaurant** (mains Rs 10-75; ⏰ 7.30am-10am, 12.30-3pm & 7.30pm-9.30pm) has all the atmosphere of a school canteen but it's very popular for its lunchtime thalis (Rs 30) and is one of the few places in town serving a range of nonveg food such as butter chicken (Rs 60), rice and noodles. There's also a **bar** (⏰ 6am-10pm).

Fine dining is nonexistent in Rameswaram, but there are a number of inexpensive vegetarian restaurants along West Car St that serve thalis (Rs 10 to 15), such as Ashok Bhavan or Ganesh Mess.

For a town so dependent on fishing, you'd think there would be some good fish restaurants. Not so, but **Bee Mavilas Hotel** (mains Rs 15-30; ⏰ noon-4pm) is a basic, local place that does serve fish fries, curries and decent biryanis.

Getting There & Away
BUS
Buses run to Madurai every 10 minutes (Rs 49, four hours). There are SETC buses to Chennai (Rs 228, 12 hours, one daily), Kanyakumari (Rs 108, 10 hours, two daily) and Trichy (Rs 82, seven hours). Bus No 1 runs between the bus stand and the temple on a semiregular basis.

There are also private buses and minibuses from the town centre to Chennai (Rs 400) and Madurai (Rs 125).

TRAIN
Rameswaram is on a metre-gauge line so there are limited services. Two daily express trains go as far as Tambaram (just outside Chennai) via Chidambaram at 12.45pm and 3.10pm – both bypass Madurai and Trichy, but there are four daily passenger (2nd class only) trains direct to Trichy.

Getting Around
Town buses (Rs 1) travel between the temple and the bus stand from early morning

until late at night. Cycling is a good way to get around with many stalls renting old rattlers for Rs 5 per hour – there's one opposite the temple entrance on East Car St and near the local bus stand.

KANYAKUMARI (CAPE COMORIN)
☎ 04652 / pop 19,678
Kanyakumari is the 'Land's End' of the Indian subcontinent, where the Bay of Bengal meets the Indian Ocean and the Arabian Sea. Chaitrapurnima (Tamil for the April full-moon day) is the best time to experience sunset and moonrise over the ocean simultaneously.

Kanyakumari has great spiritual significance for Hindus. It's dedicated to the goddess Devi Kanya, an incarnation of Parvati. Pilgrims come here to visit the temple and bathe in the sacred waters.

Kanyakumari is essentially a pilgrimage town – a place where people fulfil their spiritual duties – and the beaches are ordinary, but it has a certain relaxed charm and there's enough to keep you occupied for a day or two.

Orientation & Information
The main temple is right on the point of Kanyakumari and leading north from it is a small bazaar lined with restaurants, stalls and souvenir shops.

Janaki Forex (2 Saravana Complex; ⏰ 9.30am-6pm) Right outside the temple. You can change cash and travellers cheques pain-free here.

Post office (Main Rd; ⏰ 8am-6pm Mon-Fri) 300m north of the tourist office.

State Bank of India ATM (Main Rd) Accepts international cards.

Tourist office (☎ 246276; Main Rd; ⏰ 8am-6pm Mon-Fri) This useful office is near the temple and has maps and brochures.

World Net Cyber Cafe (South Car St; per hr Rs 50; ⏰ 9am-10pm) Internet access.

Sights & Activities
KUMARI AMMAN TEMPLE
According to legend, Devi (the goddess) single-handedly conquered demons and secured freedom for the world. At this **temple** (⏰ 4.30-11.45am & 5.30-8.30pm) pilgrims give her thanks for the safety and liberty she attained for them.

In May/June there is a **Car Festival** where an idol of the deity is taken in procession.

Unusually, men must remove their shirts, and everyone their shoes (as always). Cameras are forbidden but can be kept safely outside the temple until you return.

GANDHI MEMORIAL

This striking **memorial** (admission by donation; ☼ 7am-12.30pm & 3-7pm) resembling an Orissan temple and with elements of Hindu, Islamic and Christian architecture in its design, was used to store some of the Mahatma's ashes until they were immersed in the sea. Each year, on Gandhi's birthday (2 October), the sun's rays fall on the memorial stone where his ashes were safely kept. Guides may ask for an excessive donation, but Rs 10 is enough.

VIVEKANANDA EXHIBITION & VIVEKANANDAPURAM

In the quirky, purpose-built terracotta building, this **exhibition** (Main Rd; admission Rs 5; ☼ 8am-noon & 4-8pm) details the life and extensive journey across India made by the Indian philosopher Swami Vivekananda (the 'Wandering Monk'), who developed a synthesis between the tenets of Hinduism and concepts of social justice. Although the photographs and storyboards are labelled in English, there's a lot to digest in one visit.

A more interesting pictorial exhibition can be found at **Vivekanandapuram** (☎ 247012; admission free; ☼ 9am-1pm & 5-9pm), a spiritual mission and ashram 3km north of town. The exhibition of prints, sketches and pictures

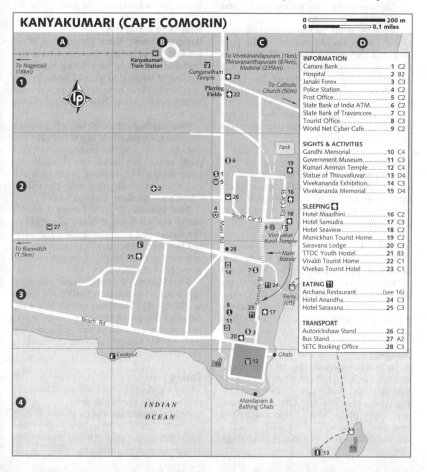

KANYAKUMARI (CAPE COMORIN)

0 —————— 200 m
0 —————— 0.1 miles

To Nagercoil (18km)

Kanyakumari Train Station

Gunganatham Temple

Playing Fields

To Vivekanandapuram (1km); Thiruvananthapuram (87km); Madurai (235km)

To Catholic Church (50m)

Tank

East Car St

South Car St

Main Rd

To Baywatch (1.5km)

Beach Rd

Lookout

Vinayakar Kovil Temple

Main Bazaar

Samuthi St

Ferry Jetty

Ghats

Mandapam & Bathing Ghats

INDIAN OCEAN

INFORMATION
Canara Bank.............................1 C2
Hospital....................................2 B2
Janaki Forex.............................3 C3
Police Station...........................4 C2
Post Office................................5 C2
State Bank of India ATM...........6 C2
State Bank of Travancore..........7 C3
Tourist Office............................8 C3
World Net Cyber Cafe...............9 C2

SIGHTS & ACTIVITIES
Gandhi Memorial....................10 C4
Government Museum...............11 C3
Kumari Amman Temple...........12 C4
Statue of Thiruvalluvar...........13 D4
Vivekananda Exhibition...........14 C3
Vivekananda Memorial............15 D4

SLEEPING
Hotel Maadhini......................16 C2
Hotel Samudra.......................17 C3
Hotel Seaview........................18 C2
Manickhan Tourist Home........19 C2
Saravana Lodge......................20 C3
TTDC Youth Hostel................21 B3
Vivaldi Tourist Home..............22 C1
Vivekas Tourist Hotel.............23 C1

EATING
Archana Restaurant...............(see 16)
Hotel Anandha......................24 C3
Hotel Saravana......................25 C3

TRANSPORT
Autorickshaw Stand...............26 C2
Bus Stand..............................27 A2
SETC Booking Office..............28 C3

covers not only the life of Vivekananda but a snapshot of Indian philosophy, religion, leaders and thinkers.

VIVEKANANDA MEMORIAL

This **memorial** (admission Rs 10; ☼ 7am-5pm daily) is located on a rocky island about 400m off-shore. Swami Vivekananda meditated here in 1892 before setting out to become one of India's most important religious crusaders. The *mandapam*, which was built here in Vivekananda's memory in 1970, reflects architectural styles from all over India. Regardless of the number of pilgrims filing through the memorial, it remains a very peaceful and reverent place. From the island there's a fine view back over the fishing harbour and to distant mountains and wind turbines.

The huge **statue** on the smaller island is not of Vivekananda but of Tamil poet Thiruvalluvar. India's 'Statue of Liberty' was the work of more than 5000 sculptors. It was erected in 2000 and honours the poet's 133-chapter work *Thirukkural* – hence its height of exactly 133 feet.

The ferry shuttles between the port and the islands every 30 minutes (last ferry is at 4pm) and costs Rs 20.

GOVERNMENT MUSEUM

This **museum** (Main Rd; ☼ 9.30am-5.30pm Sat-Thu; admission Indian/foreigner Rs 5/100) houses a mildly interesting display of archaeological finds and temple artefacts, but the admission is a bit steep.

BAYWATCH

Tired of temples? This impressive new **amusement park** (☎ 246563; Kovalam Rd; Rs 200; ☼ 10am-7pm) is a great way to spend the day, especially if you've got kids in tow. The entry ticket gives unlimited access to a wave pool with water slides and a host of rides.

Sleeping

Some hotels, especially the midrange places around the bazaar, have seasonal rates, so you may find that prices double here during April, May and late October to January. Many places also charge more for a 'sea view' or 'rock view' – neither of which are worth the extra. Few places offer single rates.

BUDGET

Saravana Lodge (☎ 246007; Sannathi St; d Rs 150-200) This is a fairly new place right outside the temple entrance. All rooms have private bathroom with squat toilet but it's very clean and good value.

Vivekas Tourist Hotel (☎ 246192; Main Rd; d/tr/q from Rs 195/295/395) Rooms here are simple but very spacious and reasonably clean.

Vivaldi Tourist Home (☎ 246972; Main Rd; d/tr Rs 200/250) This is a basic budget place close to the train station. Smallish rooms have private bathroom. The aroma from the bakery next door is a bonus.

TTDC Youth Hostel (☎ 246257; dm Rs 50) This hostel is part of Hotel Tamil Nadu. The dormitories and common bathrooms are pretty dire but you can't beat the price.

Midrange & Top End

Manickhan Tourist Home (☎ 246387; d Rs 350, with AC Rs 750; 🆒) Many of the rooms at this friendly hotel here were being renovated at time of writing so should be in tip-top condition. Most have balconies – rooms on the northern side have good views over the town.

Hotel Maadhini (☎ 246787; East Car St; d on ground fl/sea view Rs 400/600, with AC from Rs 1100; 🆒) The non-AC rooms at this midrange hotel are good value, airy and clean although the place itself is a bit soulless. Many have balconies that virtually hang over the village. There's an excellent restaurant here.

Hotel Samudra (☎ 246162; Sannathi St; d Rs 470, with sea view Rs 670, with AC Rs 970; 🆒) Right in the bazaar and near the temple, this hotel is a bit faded these days but the rooms and service are fine. Forget it in peak season when rates double.

Hotel Seaview (☎ 247841; seaview@sancharnet.in; East Car St; d without/with AC Rs 900/1450, with sea view Rs 1250/2050; 🆒) The flashy marble lobby signals that this is one of the top places to stay in town. Rooms are neat and well-furnished with TV but you pay a lot for the excellent sea views.

Eating

There are plenty of fruit stalls and basic veg restaurants in the bazaar area.

Archana Restaurant (East Car St; mains Rs 25-95; ☼ 7am-10.30pm) This restaurant at the Hotel Maadhini is one of the more atmospheric places to eat in town, especially in the evening when the garden section is open. There's a good menu including tandoori chicken, seafood and Chinese, and you can watch chapatis being made before your eyes.

Hotel Sea View (East Car St; mains Rs 30-150; ☺ 7am-11pm) This upmarket hotel also has an excellent AC multicuisine restaurant specialising in fresh local seafood.

Hotel Saravana is a busy little place with thalis (Rs 20) and good dosas. **Hotel Anandha** is another good veg place with an ocean view.

Getting There & Away

BUS

The surprisingly sedate bus stand is a 10-minute walk west of the centre along Kovalam Rd but there's a handy **SETC booking office** (☺ 7am-9pm) on Main Rd.

SETC buses run to Madurai (Rs 76, six hours, eight daily), Chennai (Rs 280, 16 hours, six daily), Rameswaram (Rs 108, nine hours, two daily), Bangalore (Rs 333, 15 hours, one daily) and Kodaikanal (Rs 132, 10 hours, one daily). KSTC has buses to Thiruvananthapuram (Trivandrum; Rs 31, three hours, six to seven daily) and there's one afternoon bus direct to Kovalam (Rs 40, 3½ hours).

Travel agencies around town advertise private buses to Madurai, Rameswaram, Kodaikanal and Trivandrum, but these are generally package tours. If there's a spare seat you may be able to negotiate a one-way ride.

TRAIN

The train station is about 1km north of the bazaar and temple. The daily *Chennai Egmore Express* departs for Chennai at 5.15pm (Rs 246/692/1106 in sleeper/2AC/3AC class, 13 hours; 738km) and the 6.35am *Tiruchchirappali–Howrah Express* departs on Tuesday, Friday and Saturday. The same trains stop at Madurai and Trichy.

To Thiruvananthapuram (Trivandrum) there are two daily express trains (Rs 33/183 in 2nd/3AC class, two hours, 87km).

For the real long-haulers or train buffs, the weekly *Himsagar Express* runs all the way to Jammu Tawi (in Jammu & Kashmir), a distance of 3734km, in 66 hours – the longest single train ride in India.

THE WESTERN GHATS

The Western Ghats stretch like a mountainous spine about 1400km from the north of Mumbai, across Maharashtra, Goa, Karnataka and Kerala, before petering out at the southernmost tip of Tamil Nadu. The hills (average elevation 915m) are covered with evergreen and deciduous forest, and are the source of all major rivers in South India. They also form a diverse biological and ecological haven with 27% of all India's flowering plants, 60% of all medicinal plants and an incredible array of endemic wildlife. For travellers these mountain areas mean opportunities to trek and see wildlife, and to hang out in Tamil Nadu's cool hill stations – Ooty and Kodaikanal. The ghats are home to a number of tribal groups but their traditional lifestyle is fast being eroded.

KODAIKANAL (KODAI)

☎ 04542 / pop 32,931 / elev 2100m

Kodaikanal, better known as Kodai, is a stunningly situated; easy-going hill station on the southern crest of the Palani knolls, about 120km northwest of Madurai. It's surrounded by wooded slopes, waterfalls and precipitous rocky outcrops and the winding journey up and down is breathtaking.

Kodai is the only hill station in India set up by Americans. American missionaries established a school for European children here in the 1840s, the legacy of which is the Kodaikanal International School – one of the country's most prestigious private schools.

The Kurinji shrub, unique to the Western Ghats, is found in Kodaikanal. This shrub has light, purple-blue-coloured blossoms and flowers every 12 years.

Kodaikanal provides an escape from the heat and haze of the plains and the opportunity to hike in the quiet *sholas* (forests). It's a much smaller and more relaxed place than Ooty. April to June (the main season) or August to October are the best times to visit. The mild temperatures here range from 11°C to 20°C in summer and 8°C to 17°C in winter. Given the mountainous environment, heavy rain can occur at any time.

Orientation & Information

For a hill station, Kodai is remarkably compact and the central town area can easily be

TAMIL NADU

explored on foot. There are a few Internet cafés, and a State Bank of India ATM near the Carlton Hotel.

Alpha Net (PT Rd; per hr Rs 40; 🕘 9am-10pm) The most reliable Internet centre.

Indian Bank (Anna Salai; 🕘 10am-2pm & 2.30pm-3.30pm Mon-Fri, 10am-12.30pm Sat) Has a foreign exchange desk.

Tourist office (☎ 41675; Anna Salai; 🕘 10am-5.45pm) Not particularly helpful, though it can put you in touch with trekking guides.

Sights & Activities
PARKS & WATERFALLS
Near the start of Coaker's Walk is **Bryant Park**, landscaped and stocked by the British

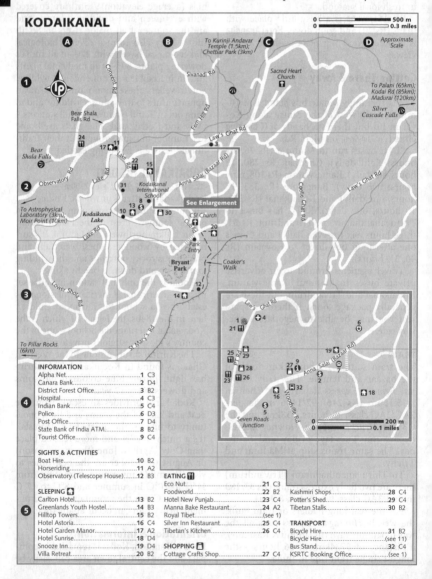

KODAIKANAL

INFORMATION
Alpha Net	1 C3
Canara Bank	2 D4
District Forest Office	3 B2
Hospital	4 C3
Indian Bank	5 C4
Police	6 D3
Post Office	7 D4
State Bank of India ATM	8 B2
Tourist Office	9 C4

SIGHTS & ACTIVITIES
Boat Hire	10 B2
Horseriding	11 A2
Observatory (Telescope House)	12 B3

SLEEPING 🏠
Carlton Hotel	13 B2
Greenlands Youth Hostel	14 B3
Hilltop Towers	15 B2
Hotel Astoria	16 C4
Hotel Garden Manor	17 A2
Hotel Sunrise	18 D4
Snooze Inn	19 D4
Villa Retreat	20 B2

EATING 🍴
Eco Nut	21 C3
Foodworld	22 B2
Hotel New Punjab	23 C4
Manna Bake Restaurant	24 A2
Royal Tibet	(see 1)
Silver Inn Restaurant	25 C4
Tibetan's Kitchen	26 C4

SHOPPING 🛍
Cottage Crafts Shop	27 C4
Kashmiri Shops	28 C4
Potter's Shed	29 C4
Tibetan Stalls	30 B2

TRANSPORT
Bicycle Hire	31 B2
Bicycle Hire	(see 11)
Bus Stand	32 C4
KSRTC Booking Office	(see 1)

officer after whom it is named. At **Chettiar Park**, about 3km uphill from town and 1.5km past the Kurinji Andavar Temple, you may be able to see some Kurinji flowers. There are numerous waterfalls – the main one, **Silver Cascade**, is on the road up to Kodai.

WALKING
The valley views along paved **Coaker's Walk** (admission Rs 2, camera Rs 5; ⓥ 7am-7pm) are superb when the mist clears. There's an **observatory** (admission Rs 3) with telescope about halfway along. You can start from either end, near Greenlands Youth Hostel or Villa Retreat, and the stroll takes all of five minutes.

The views from **Pillar Rocks**, a 7km hike (one way beginning near Bryant Park), are also excellent. Greenlands Youth Hostel and Villa Retreat can organise guided walks, and guides can also be arranged through the tourist office (Rs 50 to 70 per hour).

HORSE RIDING
At the bicycle hire area by the lake you'll be accosted by guides renting horses for high prices. The rate is around Rs 130 per hour unaccompanied or Rs 200 with a guide but you can take a short ride for Rs 25. Some of these horses should be retired.

BOATING
The lake at Kodai is beautifully landscaped and it appears to be *de rigueur* for Indian families to get out on a boat. Both the Kodaikanal Boat and Rowing Club and Tamil Nadu Tourist Development Corporation hire similar boats for similar prices: Rs 20 to 40 for a two-seater pedal boat to Rs 125 (including boatman) for a Kashmiri *shikara* (covered gondola-like boat) for 30 minutes.

Sleeping
Hotel prices jump by up to 300% during high season (from 1 April to 30 June). Prices listed here are off-season rates.

Most hotels in Kodai have a 9am or 10am checkout time in the high season but for the rest of the year it's usually 24 hours.

BUDGET
Greenlands Youth Hostel (☎ 240899; dm Rs 55, d from Rs 200-600) Near the southern end of Coaker's Walk, this is the number one choice for budget travellers, as much for the fine views as the cheap rooms. There's a crowded

dormitory and a range of rooms from very basic doubles on the edge of the valley to more spacious rooms with fireplace and TV. The location is peaceful and treks can be arranged here.

Hotel Sunrise (☎ 241358; d Rs 150) This is a down-at-heel but friendly enough place. The view from the front (though not from most of the simple rooms) is excellent.

Snooze Inn (☎ 40837; Anna Salai; d Rs 250-425) Snooze Inn is well run and good value. Rooms are plain but clean and all have TV.

MIDRANGE & TOP END
Villa Retreat (☎ /fax 240940; www.villaretreat.com; Club Rd, Coaker's Walk; d Rs 690, deluxe cottages Rs 1150) At the start of Coaker's Walk, the terrace garden of this lovely stone-built family hotel offers awesome valley views. The best rooms are the cottages with panoramic views but even the cheaper rooms are good value. Most rooms have fireplaces, TV and nice furnishings.

Hotel Astoria (☎ 240524; astoria1@eth.com; Anna Salai Rd; d from Rs 400, ste Rs 500) Right in the centre of town and next to the bus stand, Astoria is very good value. Small but comfortable rooms come with TV, phone and hot water. The downstairs restaurant is one of the busiest in town.

Hilltop Towers (☎ 240413; httowers@sancharnet.in; Club Rd; d/ste from Rs 550/725) Near the Kodaikanal International School, Hilltop is a neat if slightly nondescript hotel. Rooms have teak floors and satellite TV. Staff are welcoming.

Hotel Garden Manor (☎ 240461; www.sealord hotels.com; Lake Rd; d/ste Rs 1300/1900) The name says it all – a beautiful terraced garden overlooking the lake gives this hotel a special charm. You can observe the serene vista from the veranda of your room or sit in the small gazebo. Rooms are spacious with TV, hot water and phone. There's a good restaurant but it's pleasant to eat out on the lawn.

Carlton Hotel (☎ 240056; carlton@krahejah; Lake Rd; d Rs 4800, cottage Rs 8000, ste Rs 9000) Kodai's most prestigious hotel overlooks the lake and manages to blend colonial style with five-star luxury, and a price tag to match. Rooms are bright, spacious and some have private patios or balconies with lake views. Leather chairs huddle around a central stone fireplace in the main lounge which adjoins an excellent bar, billiard room and restaurant. There's also a children's playground, gym, sauna, massage and private boathouse.

Eating

PT Rd is the best place for cheap restaurants and it's here that most of the travellers and students from the international school congregate. There's a whole range of different cuisines available, including the Tibetan influence.

Silver Inn Restaurant (☎ 241374; PT Rd; mains Rs 30-100; ☯ 8.30am-9pm) This country-style, family-run restaurant is a great place for breakfast (full English breakfast is Rs 90) and the broad lunch and dinner menu ranges from pizzas, huge sizzler plates, home-made fettuccine and lasagne to Indian and Chinese dishes.

Hotel New Punjab (PT Rd; mains Rs 30-100; ☯ 11am-11pm) For North Indian and tandoori dishes this is the best value place in Kodai. Succulent tandoori chicken is Rs 100.

Tibetan's Kitchen (PT Rd; mains Rs 25-70; ☯ noon-10pm) This intimate subterranean place has a cute atmosphere and good momos (Rs 40-45), lemon chicken and hot lemon tea with honey.

Royal Tibet (PT Rd; ☯ noon-4pm & 5.30-10pm) This place serves tasty noodle soups and other Himalayan fare.

Hotel Astoria (☎ 240524; Anna Salai Rd; mains Rs 20-50, thalis Rs 30-50; ☯ 9am-9pm) The veg restaurant here is always packed at lunchtime for its excellent all-you-can-eat thalis.

Manna Bake Restaurant (☎ 243766; Bear Shola Falls Rd; dishes Rs 20-50; ☯ 9.30am-5pm & 6.30-7pm Mon-Sat) This tiny family-run bakery and café is worth seeking out for simple home-cooked Western vegetarian food (sandwiches, pizza and soup) and homely atmosphere. The brown bread is legendary and many a cold and hungry traveller has gorged on the home-made apple crumble and custard (Rs 35). For dinner you need to order by 3pm. It's a 15-minute walk from town near Bear Shola Falls (turn right off Observatory Rd near the entrance to Hotel Clifton).

Silver Oak Restaurant (☎ 240056; Lake Rd; breakfast buffet Rs 220, lunch buffet Rs 330, dinner buffet Rs 330) The restaurant at the Carlton Hotel puts on a lavish buffet for breakfast (8am to 11am), lunch (1pm to 3pm) and dinner (7.30pm to 10.30pm). It's a good way to fill up on decent food, but you might feel a bit out of place in shorts and sandals. After eating you can relax in the atmospheric bar or sit by the roaring fire in the coffee lounge.

SELF-CATERING

Food World (Lake Rd; ☯ 9am-7.30pm) This well-stocked supermarket near the lake is a good place to pick up supplies for trekking.

Eco Nut (☎ 243296; PT Rd; www.eco-nut.com; ☯ 10am-5pm) This interesting shop is run by an ecological farmer and sells a wide range of locally produced organic health food – whole wheat bread, cheese, coffee, essential oils, herbs and herb remedies.

Shopping

The many handicraft stores stock excellent craftwork.

Cottage Crafts Shop (Anna Salai), run by the voluntary organisation Corsock, (Coordinating Council for Social Concerns in Kodai), sells goods crafted by development groups and uses the commission charged to help the needy.

On PT Rd you'll find Kashmiri shops, as well as the **Potter's Shed** (☯ 9am-8pm Thu-Tue, 9am-5pm Wed) with fine ceramics; proceeds go to help disadvantaged children.

The road leading south to the lake is sometimes lined with stalls run by Tibetans selling warm clothing, shawls and other fabrics – good, cheap stuff to keep you warm on chilly nights.

Getting There & Away

Don't expect a bus to be leaving from Kodaikanal in the next five minutes. Tickets for private buses can be booked at travel agents near the bus stand. Following are details of bus departures from Kodaikanal:

Destination	Fare (Rs)	Duration (hr)	Frequency
Madurai*	34	3½	2 daily
Trichy*	57	5	2 daily
Palani*	20	2	2 daily
Chennai*	203	11	1 daily
Coimbatore*	96	5	1 daily
Bangalore	283	11	1 daily
Ooty∧	250	8	1 daily
Madurai∧	150	3	2 daily
Chennai∧	400	11	1 daily
Bangalore∧	450	11	1 daily
Kochi∧	400	8	1 daily

*State transport buses
KSRTC bus
∧Private buses

Getting Around

The central part of Kodaikanal is compact and very easy to get around on foot. There are no autorickshaws (believe it or not) but plenty of taxis willing to take you to various sightseeing points. Charges are fixed and relatively high – the minimum charge is Rs 60, and sightseeing tours cost from Rs 300 for two hours to Rs 700 for six hours.

If you're fit enough to tackle the hills, mountain bikes can be hired from several places around the lake, including the **bicycle stall** (per hr/day Rs 10/70 ; 😊 8am-6pm) near Hotel Garden Manor. Check that the brakes work before attempting any steep descents.

INDIRA GANDHI (ANNAMALAI) WILDLIFE SANCTUARY

One of three wildlife sanctuaries in the Western Ghats along the Tamil Nadu-Kerala border, this park covers almost 1000 sq km of mostly teak forest and evergreen jungle and is home to elephant, gaur, tiger, panther, spotted deer, wild boar, bear, porcupine and civet cat. The Nilgiri tahr, commonly known as the ibex, may also be spotted. Since less than 10% of the park is open to visitors and access is limited to tours or guided treks, advance planning is necessary to make the most of a visit here.

The **park** (admission Rs 20, camera/video Rs 10/50 ; 😊 6am-6pm) has a reception centre (where trekking guides can be arranged) and several lodges at the village of Topslip, about 35km southwest of Pollachi. Day visitors can head straight to Topslip.

The infrequent buses make accessibility difficult. If you come by private vehicle you cannot use it in the park and you'll be restricted to the tours that run from 8am to 1pm and 3pm to 5pm. These tours take one hour, cover about 14km and cost Rs 50 per person.

Sleeping & Eating

Forest accommodation is available near Topslip and is usually limited to one night only; definite maximum of three nights. All accommodation *must* be booked in advance in Pollachi at the **Wildlife Warden's Office** (☎ 04259-2225356; Meenkarai Rd; 😊 9am-5pm Mon-Fri).

Ambuli Illam (r per person Rs 50), 2km from the reception centre, is the best. There's a canteen here, which is about the only place in the park where you'll get a decent meal.

Should you get stuck in Pollachi (a likely occurrence given the erratic hours of the Wildlife Warden's Office), try **Sakthi Hotels** (☎ 04259-223050; Coimbatore Rd; d Rs 290, with AC Rs 600; 😢).

Getting There & Away

The sanctuary is between Palani and Coimbatore. Regular buses from both places stop at the nearest large town, Pollachi, which is also on the Coimbatore to Dindigul train line. From Pollachi, buses leave the bus stand for Topslip at 6am and 3pm and return at 8am and 6pm. A taxi from Pollachi to the sanctuary costs around Rs 600 one way.

COIMBATORE & AROUND

☎ 0422 / pop 1.45 million

Although a large business and industrial city, for travellers Coimbatore is mainly a transport junction – a convenient stop if you're heading to the hill stations of Ooty or Kodaikanal. Sometimes known as the Manchester of India for its textile industry, Coimbatore is a surprisingly easy-going place with plenty of accommodation and eating options.

Information

Email facilities are available throughout the city, especially around the bus stands, and there are 24-hour ATMs dotted around the city.

American Express Foreign Exchange (Avanashi Rd; 😊 9.30am-6.30pm Mon-Fri, 9.30am-2.30pm Sat) You can change money and travellers cheques here.

Blazenet (Nehru St; per hr Rs 20; 😊 9am-12.30pm) Internet access.

HDFC Bank (Avanashi Rd) 24-hour ATM.

HSBC (Racecourse Rd) 24-hour ATM, next to the Hotel Surya International.

Main post office (Railway Feeder Rd; 😊 10am-8pm Mon-Fri, 10am-2pm Sun) A few hundred metres northwest of the railway station. It can be reached via a footbridge from the platforms.

Travel Gate (Geetha Hall Rd; per hr Rs 25; 😊 9am-10pm) Internet access.

Tourist office (😊 10am-5.45pm) Small office inside the train station.

Sights

ISHA YOGA CENTER

This **ashram** (☎ 0422-2615345; www.ishafoundation .org; 😊 6am-8pm), located in Poondi, 30km west of Coimbatore, is also a yoga retreat and place of pilgrimage. The centrepiece is a multireligious temple housing the Dhyanalingam, which is said to be unique in that it embodies all seven chakras of spiritual energy. Visitors are welcome to the temple to meditate, or to take part in one- to two-week Isha yoga courses, for which you should register in advance. Accommodation is available. The ashram was founded by spiritual leader and yogi Sadhguru Jaggi Vasudev and is home to an order of Bhramhacharya monks and devotees.

Sleeping

Low-budget accommodation is generally in the bus stand area and down a lane directly opposite the train station, while more up-market places are along Avanashi Rd.

Hotel Ruby Palace (☎ 2300271; Geetha Hall Rd; s/d Rs 100/150) Down a small but bustling lane opposite the train station, this is a basic but friendly little hotel with good value rooms. There are several other similar places along this street.

Hotel Blue Star (☎ 2230635; 369A Nehru St; s/d Rs 250/440; d with AC Rs 750) This place has simple, clean rooms with TV and bathroom. Management is friendly and it's convenient for the bus stands. There's a bar and restaurant.

Hotel Vaidurya (☎ 5392777; ratnaalakshmi@vsnl .net; 73 Geetha Hall Rd; s/d from Rs 250/450, deluxe Rs 380/600, with AC Rs 600/710; 🖳) Shining among the budget hotels opposite the train station, Vaidurya is a smart midrange place with small but pleasant rooms. The deluxe rooms are also good value.

Nilgiri's Nest (☎ 2214309; nilgiris@md3.vsnl.net .in; 739A Avanashi Rd; s/d from Rs 1100/1350; 🖳) This intimate, well-run hotel has comfortable rooms, an excellent restaurant and supermarket.

The Residency (☎ 2201234; www.theresidency.com; 1076 Avanashi Rd; s/d from Rs 2500/2800; 🖳 💻 🖳) This is Coimbatore's finest hotel and it has all the trimmings, along with friendly staff and immaculate rooms. There's a well-equipped health club, two excellent restaurants, a coffee shop and a bookstore in the lobby.

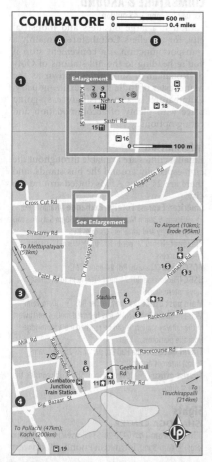

COIMBATORE

INFORMATION
American Express Foreign Exchange............................**1** B3
Blazenet...**2** A1
Centurion Bank ATM...**3** B3
HDFC Bank ATM...**4** B3
HSBC Bank ATM...**5** B3
Internet Cafés..**6** B1
Main Post Office..**7** A4
State Bank of India...**8** A4
Travel Gate...(see 11)

SLEEPING 🛏
Hotel Blue Star..**9** A1
Hotel Ruby Palace..**10** B4
Hotel Vaidurya...**11** A4
Nilgiri's Nest..**12** B3
The Residency..**13** B3

EATING 🍴
Annalakshmi...(see 5)
Gayathri Bhavan..**14** A1
Malabar...**15** A1

TRANSPORT
Central Bus Station..**16** B2
Jet Airways..**17** B3
Thiruvalluvar Bus Station.......................................**18** B1
Town Bus Stand...**19** B1
Ukkadam Bus Stand..**20** A4

Eating

There are numerous places around the train station that serve thalis for around Rs 25. Another good place for inexpensive restaurants is along Sastri Rd and Nehru St just north of the central bus station. Avanshi Rd is Coimbatore's trendy area with several high quality restaurants.

Annalakshmi (☎ 2212142; 106 Racecourse Rd; meals Rs 30-70, set meals Rs 150; ☿ 6am-11pm) This is the top veg restaurant in town. It's run by devotees of Swami Shatanand Saraswati, who established an educational trust, Shivanjali, for underprivileged children. Full meals are available for lunch and dinner but it's popular for coffee and snacks all day.

Gayathiri Bhavan (Nehru St; mains Rs 25-60; ☿ 6am-11pm) This is a very popular veg restaurant with an interesting menu, an AC dining hall and an inviting outdoor seating area where you may have to wait for a table. The 'kebab corner' features marinated diced cottage cheese, capsicum, onion and vegetable kebabs, and there's a great range of juices, ice creams and shakes.

Malabar (Sastri Rd; mains Rs 50-100; ☿ noon-11pm) This restaurant in the KK Residency Hotel near the bus stand specialises in Keralan and North Indian food. The Malabar chicken roast (Rs 100) is a spicy treat and there are seafood choices such as tandoori pomfret.

Getting There & Away
AIR

The airport is 10km east of town. **Indian Airlines** (☎ 2399821; 1604 Trichy Rd) flies daily between Coimbatore and Mumbai (US$160), Delhi (US$325) and Kozhikode (US$50) and three times a week to Chennai (US$100) and Bangalore (US$65).

Jet Airways (☎ 2212034) flies daily to Bangalore (US$75), Chennai (US$100) and Mumbai (US$160) **Air Deccan** (☎ 2599885) offers the cheapest flights to Bangalore (Rs 1400) and Chennai (Rs 2255).

BUS

There are three bus stands in the city centre: From the **Central Bus Station** (☎ 2431521) services depart to nearby northern destinations such as Ooty (Rs 31, 3½ hours, every 30 minutes) and Mettupayalam (Rs 10.50, one hour, every 10 minutes).

From Thiruvallur bus station (☎ 25249690) you can catch state and interstate buses to Bangalore (Rs 105, nine hours, 10 daily), Mysore (Rs 60, five hours, four daily) and Chennai (Rs 194, 11½ hours, seven daily). The Town Bus Station is for local buses within the city.

There's another bus station at Ukkadam, south of the city, and buses depart from here for nearby southern destinations including Pallani (Rs 22, three hours, every 20 minutes), Pollachi (Rs 8, one hour, every five minutes) and Madurai (Rs 66, five hours, every 30 minutes).

TRAIN

Coimbatore Junction is on the main line between Chennai and Ernakalum (Kerala). For Ooty, catch the daily *Nilgiri Express*; it connects with the miniature railway in time for the toy train departure at 7.10am. The whole trip to Ooty takes about seven hours.

Getting Around

For the airport take bus No 20 from the town bus stand or bus Nos 90 from the

MAJOR TRAINS FROM COIMBATORE

Destination	Train No & name	Fare (Rs)	Duration (hr)	Departure
Bangalore	*Kanyakumari–Bangalore Exp*	148/416 (sleeper/3AC)	9	10.35pm daily
Chennai	*Kovai Exp*	116/404 (2nd/chair class)	7½	1.40pm daily
	Cheran Exp	116/404 (2nd/chair class)	8½	10pm daily
Kochi	*Sabari Exp*	93/261 (sleeper/3AC)	5	8.50am daily
Madurai	*Coimbatore–Madurai Exp*	60/102 (2nd/sleeper class)	6	10.45pm daily
Ooty (via Mettupalayam)	*Nilgiri Exp*	22/35 (2nd/sleeper class)	7	5.15am daily
Pollachi		24	1½	5 daily

train station (Rs 4). Many buses ply between the train station and the town bus stand (Rs 1.50).

Autorickshaw drivers charge Rs 30 between the bus and train stations.

COONOOR

☎ 0423 / pop 50,079 / elev 1850m

Coonoor is the first of the three **Nilgiri hill stations** – Ooty, Kotagiri and Coonoor (see map p382) – that you come to when leaving behind the southern plains.

Although smaller than Ooty, Coonoor doesn't come across as being any less busy than that city, especially the area around the bus stand and the market – a bustling, choking mess without any of the charm of Ooty, and the tenacious touts here can be overwhelming. It's only after climbing up out of the busy market area and looking down at the sea of rusting rooftops that you'll get a sense of what hill stations were originally all about: a measure of peace and some beautiful scenery. Most accommodation is in Upper Coonoor, 1km to 2km up the hill from the town centre.

Sights & Activities

In Upper Coonoor the 12-hectare **Sim's Park** (admission adult/child Rs 5/2; camera/video Rs 25/250; ☼ 8.30am-6pm) is a peaceful oasis of manicured lawns and over 1000 plant species, including magnolia, tree ferns and camellia. Buses heading to Kotagiri can drop you here.

There are several popular viewpoints around Coonoor. **Dolphin's Nose** viewpoint, about 10km from town, exposes a vast panorama, which encompasses **Catherine Falls**. On the way you can stop off at **Lamb's Rock**. The site is named after the British captain who created a short path to this favourite picnic spot. The easiest way to see these sights is on a taxi tour for around Rs 200.

Sleeping & Eating

YWCA Wyoming Guesthouse (☎ 2234426; s/d Rs 200/400) This ramshackle guesthouse in Upper Coonoor is a budget favourite. Although ageing and draughty, the 150-year-old colonial house has character with wooden terraces and good views over Coonoor. To get there, take a town bus to Bedford; then it's a five-minute walk.

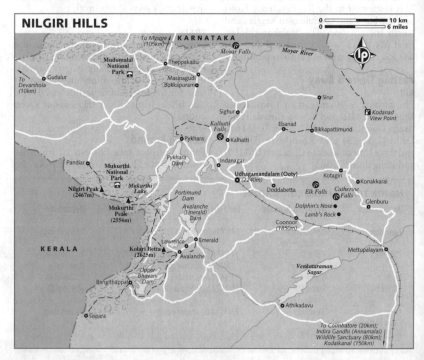

NILGIRI HILLS

Vivek Tourist Home (☎ 2230658; Figure of Eight Rd; dm Rs 70, s/d from Rs 150/190, s/d deluxe Rs 400/500) Near the YWCA, this is big place with a wide range of rooms – including a monster dormitory. It's clean, well run and has a bar and restaurant.

Taj Garden Retreat (☎ 2230021; retreat.coonoor@ tajhotels.com; Church Rd; s/d from US$60/70) On the hilltop beside the All Saints Church, this fine hotel has beautiful gardens and comfortable colonial rooms with polished floorboards, bathtubs and open fireplaces. It's

worth paying a few dollars extra for the 'superior' rooms, which have a separate sitting room. The hotel also has an excellent multicuisine restaurant and a bar, and for the more health conscious, a gym and an Ayurvedic and yoga centre.

Quality Restaurant (Mount Rd; mains Rs 20-70, lunchtime buffet Rs 50; ⏱ 8am-10pm) Near the Bedford Circle, this restaurant offers veg and nonveg Indian and Chinese dishes and puts on an excellent value lunchtime buffet between 12.30pm and 3pm.

HILL TRIBES OF THE NILGIRI

For centuries, the Nilgiris have been home to hill tribes. While retaining integrity in customs, dress, principal occupation and language, the tribes were interdependent economically, socially and culturally.

The Toda tribe lived on the western plateau in the area now called Ooty. Their social, economic and spiritual system centred on the buffalo. The produce derived from the buffalo (mainly milk and ghee) was integral to their diet and it was used as currency – in exchange for grain, tools, pots and even medical services. Most importantly, the dairy produce provided offerings to the gods as well as fuel for the funeral pyre. It was only at the ritual for human death that the strictly vegetarian Toda killed a buffalo. They killed not for food but to provide company for the deceased. Other traditional customs that continue today include the division of labour; men care for the buffaloes and women embroider shawls used for ritual, as well as practical purposes. Today, only about 1500 Toda remain.

The Badaga migrated to the Nilgiri Hills in the wake of Muslim invasions in the north, and are thus not officially a tribal people. With knowledge of the world outside the hills, they became effective representatives for the hill tribes. Their agricultural produce, particularly grain, added a further dimension to the hill diet, and they traded this for buffalo products from the Toda.

The Kotas lived in the Kotagiri area and were considered by other tribes to be lower in status. Artisans of leather goods and pots, the Kotas were also musicians. The Kotas still undertake ceremonies in which the gods are beseeched for rains and bountiful harvests.

The Kurumbas inhabited the thick forests of the south. They gathered bamboo, honey and materials for housing, some of which they supplied to other tribes. They also engaged in a little agriculture, and at sowing and harvest times they employed the Badaga to perform rituals entreating the gods for abundant yields. Kurumba witchcraft was respected and sought after by the other tribes.

The Irulus, also from the southern slopes, produced tools and gathered honey and other forest products that they converted into brooms and incense. They are devotees of Vishnu and often performed special rituals for other tribes.

British settlement in the Ooty area from the early 19th century has a significant impact on tribal life. Some tribes adapted quickly, especially the Badaga. Being cultivators, they continued their traditional pursuits in untraditional ways; they cultivated the cash crops (tea and coffee) of the new settlers, but they were no longer able to provide the grains that were essential to the economy of the other tribes. Eventually, tribal systems, especially economic and cultural ones, began to collapse. Displaced tribes have been 'granted' land by the Indian government. But the cultivation of land is anathema to the Toda, who see themselves as caretakers of the soil – for them, to dig into the land is to desecrate it.

Today many tribal people have assimilated to the point of invisibility. Some have fallen into destructive patterns associated with displacement and alienation. Others remain straddled across two cultures, maintaining vestiges of their traditions while embracing customs and beliefs of the dominant culture.

Getting There & Away

Coonoor is on the miniature train line between Mettupalayam (28km) and Ooty (18km) – see p389. Buses to Ooty (Rs 6.50, one hour) and Kotagiri (Rs 8, one hour) leave roughly every 15 minutes.

KOTAGIRI

☎ 0423 / pop 29,184

Kotagiri (Line of Houses of the Kotas) is a quiet village 28km east of Ooty. The oldest of the three Nilgiri hill stations, the village itself is dusty and uninspiring but the surrounding area of tea estates, tribal Kota settlements and rolling hills is a world away from the overdevelopment of Ooty.

From Kotagiri you can visit **Catherine Falls**, 8km away near the Mettupalayam road (the last 3km is by foot only), **Elk Falls** (6km) and **Kodanad Viewpoint** (22km), where there's a panoramic view over the Coimbatore Plains and the Mysore Plateau. Buses and taxis (Rs 600 return to Ooty) will take you there.

The best place to stay in Kotagiri, and a good reason to overnight there, this **Misty Heights Guesthouse** (☎ 04266-279353; www.misty heightsindia.com; cottages Rs 2500-4000), a peaceful, family-run forest homestay. There are just two cottages – a one and two bedroom, each with separate lounge or sun room, in a beautiful, natural setting. Call ahead for booking and directions.

Getting There & Away

Buses stop at the edge of town, about 1km from the centre. Buses to Ooty depart hourly (Rs 15, two hours), crossing one of Tamil Nadu's highest passes. Buses to Mettupalayam leave every 30 minutes and to Coonoor every 15 minutes.

UDHAGAMANDALAM (OOTY)

☎ 0423 / pop 93,921 / elev 2240m

Ooty is South India's most famous hill station, established by the British in the early 19th century as the summer headquarters of the Madras (now Chennai) government.

Until about 20 years ago, Ooty resembled an unlikely combination of southern England and Australia: single-storey stone cottages, bijou-fenced flower gardens, leafy winding lanes and tall eucalyptus stands. Times have changed and, if not for the climate and the rolling hills, Ooty's centre resembles any overburdened provincial Indian town.

But Ooty has an undeniable charm and the hills and forest around it are sensational for trekking. Life here is relaxed and just a few kilometres out of town you are in the peace of the hills with superb views.

The journey up to Ooty on the miniature train is romantic and the scenery stunning – try to get a seat on the left-hand side where you get the best views across the mountains.

From April to June Ooty is a welcome relief from the hot plains and in the colder months – October to March – it's crisp, clear and surprisingly cool. You'll need warm clothing – which you can buy very cheaply here – as the overnight temperature occasionally drops to 0°C.

Orientation & Information

Ooty is sprawls over a large area among rolling hills and valleys. Between the lake and the racecourse are the train station and bus station. From either of these it's a 10-minute walk to the bazaar area and 20 minutes to Ooty's real centre, Charing Cross.

BOOKSHOPS & LIBRARY

Higginbothams Commercial Rd (☎ 2443736; 🕑 9.30am-1pm & 3.30-7.30pm Thu-Tue); Commissioner's Rd (☎ 2442546; 🕑 9am-1pm & 2-5.30pm Mon-Sat)

Nilgiri Library (Bank Rd; 🕑 9.30am-1pm & 2.30-6pm Sat-Thu, reading room 9.30am-6pm daily; temporary membership from Rs 50) Quaint little haven in a lovely 1867 building with a good collection of over 40,000 books, including rare titles on the Nilgiris and hill tribes.

INTERNET ACCESS

Cyber World (Church Hill Rd; per hr Rs 30; 🕑 10am-9pm)

Cyber Zone (Commercial Rd; per hr Rs 20; 🕑 10am-10pm)

Global Net (Commercial Rd; per hr Rs 25; 🕑 8.30am-11pm)

MONEY

SBI ATM (Commercial Rd) A convenient ATM.

State Bank of India (Bank Rd; 🕑 10am-4pm Mon-Fri, 10am-2pm Sat) Change travellers cheques and has an ATM.

UTI Bank ATM (Ettines Rd) Accepts foreign cards.

PERMITS

There are two forest departments in Ooty that issue permits to enter the surrounding restricted forest areas, although such permits are usually issued to serious researchers and local guides only.

District Forest Officer (DFO; ☎ 2444083; 🕑 9am-6pm Mon-Sat) Next door to the WWO.

www.lonelyplanet.com   THE WESTERN GHATS •• Udhagamandalam (Ooty)   **385**

TAMIL NADU

UDHAGAMANDALAM (OOTY)

```
0 ———— 500 m
0 ———— 0.3 miles
```

INFORMATION

Charing Cross Post Office	1 C2
Cyber World	(see 32)
Cyber Zone	2 C4
District Forest Office (DFO)	3 B2
Global Net	4 B2
Higginbothams	5 A1
Higginbothams	(see 10)
Main Post Office	6 A1
NHRA Tourist Information Centre	7 C2
Nilgiri Library	8 A2
Police Station	9 A2
State Bank of India ATM	10 B2
State Bank of India	11 A2
Tourist Office	12 B2
UTI Bank ATM	13 C4
Wildlife Warden Office (WWO)	(see 3)

SIGHTS & ACTIVITIES

Boathouse (Boat & Horse Hire)	14 A5
Centenary Rose Park	15 C5
Jolly World	16 B5
St Stephen's Church	17 A1
Thread Garden	18 A4

SLEEPING

Fernhills Palace	19 A5
Hotel Khems	20 C2
King's Cliff	21 A3
Nilgiri Woodlands Hotel	22 B5
Reflections Guest House	23 B5
Savoy Hotel	24 B4
Sullivan Court	25 C4
TTDC Youth Hostel	26 B1
Willow Hill	27 B3
YWCA Anandagiri	28 C5

EATING

Chandan Restaurant	29 B2
Hot Breads	30 C2
Hotel Sanjay	31 C1
Kings	32 C1
Shinkow's Chinese Restaurant	33 A2
Sidewalk Café	(see 29)

SHOPPING

Kairali	34 B2
Khadi Gramodyog Bhavan	35 B2
Poompuhar	36 B2
Tibetan Market	37 C4

TRANSPORT

Bus Stand	38 B5
Classic Rentals	39 C2
Tourist Taxi Stand	40 B5
Tourist Taxi Stand	41 B2

To Mudumalai Wildlife Sanctuary (67km); Mysore (160km)

To Doddabetta (9km); Masinagudi (25km); Kotagiri (29km)

To Tribal Research Centre; Museum (11km); Avalanche (28km)

To Coonoor (18km); Mettupalayam (46km); Coimbatore (90km)

See Enlargement

Wildlife Warden Office (WWO; ☎ 2444098; ☺ 10am-5.45pm Mon-Sat) Manages Mudumalai National Park, including accommodation (see p390).

POST
Charing Cross post office (Ettines Rd; ☺ 9.30am-5.30pm Mon-Fri)
Main post office (Havelock Rd; ☺ 9am-5pm Mon-Sat) Next to the court buildings diagonally opposite St Stephen's Church.

TOURIST INFORMATION
NHRA tourist information centre (☎ 2450665; Coonoor Rd; ☺ 10am-7pm) Near Charing Cross, this private agency offers advice but lists only accommodation places that are members of the group.
Tourist office (☎ 2443977; ☺ 10am-5.45pm Mon-Sat) Maps and brochures and daily tours.

Sights
BOTANICAL GARDENS
Established in 1848, these beautifully maintained **gardens** (admission child/adult Rs 3/10, camera/video Rs 30/100; ☺ 8am-6.30pm) include numerous mature species as well as Italian and Japanese sections. There is also a fossilised tree trunk believed to be around 20 million years old.

ST STEPHEN'S CHURCH
Built in 1829, **St Stephen's Church** (Church Hill Rd; ☺ 10am-1pm & 3-5pm Mon-Sat, services 8am & 11am Sun) is the oldest in the Nilgiris. Its huge wooden beams came from the palace of Tipu Sultan in Srirangapatnam and were hauled the 120km by a team of elephants. The attached cemetery contains the graves of many an Ooty pioneer, including John Sullivan, the founder of Ooty.

TRIBAL RESEARCH CENTRE
Under the auspices of the Tribal Research Centre (TRC), this small but interesting **museum** (admission free; ☺ 10am-5pm Mon-Fri, closed holidays) has many exhibits, including models of homes of the various hill tribes. If you're lucky and have a Toda researcher guide you through the museum, you'll have a memorable experience. The museum is just beyond M Palada, 11km from Ooty on the way to Emerald. Catch an Emerald bus (several daily) to the TRC stop just after M Palada, or any of the frequent buses heading in the direction of M Palada and get off there.

THREAD GARDEN
The signs scream 'first time in world' and 'miracle', but for all the over-the-top enthusiasm, the **Thread Garden** (North Lake Rd; ☎ 2445145; www.threadgarden.com; admission Rs 10, camera/video Rs 15/30; ☺ 8.30am-7.30pm) is a unique exhibition. Over 150 species of flowers and plants from around the world have been meticulously recreated using coloured thread. At first glance the flowers look real but each one has been hand-embroidered without using a needle. The technique was perfected by Keralan artist Anthony Joseph and the work on display is said to have taken 12 years to complete.

CENTENARY ROSE PARK
With its terraced lawns and it's colourful flower beds, this **rose garden** (Selbourne Rd; admission adult/child Rs 10/5, camera/video Rs 30/50; ☺ 9am-6.30pm) is a pleasant place for a stroll. There are good views over Ooty from the hilltop location.

Activities
TREKKING
To appreciate the natural beauty of Ooty and its surrounds, walking is the way to go and a day hike will take you to some fine viewpoints, through evergreen forest and grassland and possibly to a Toda village. If you want to get off the beaten track it's best to get a reliable guide with good local knowledge. For more trekking options, consider the resorts near Mudumalai National Park (see p391).
Camtrek (☎ 2451809; camtrekindia@rediffmail.com; day hikes Rs 400) Run by long-time local and experienced guide Mike Dawson, these treks have been recommended by travellers and range from an easy day hike to more demanding jungle treks or jeep safaris (minimum Rs 2500). Visits to a Toda village, campfire singalongs and lunch are included.
Ooty Tourist Guides Association (☎ 24444449; half-/full-day trek Rs 200/350) This association has a number of local guides who can usually be found by asking at the tourist office or bus stand. One such guide is the affable Seni (seniappan@yahoo.com). Walks are mainly in the hills and forest near the town area, but overnight treks staying in a local village can also be arranged.
Reflections Guest House (☎ 2443834; North Lake Rd; day hikes Rs 300) Reflections has two experienced guides for day trips into the hills.
YWCA (☎ 2442218, Ettines Rd) The guides organised by the YWCA have been recommended by travellers.

HORSE RIDING

Alone or with a guide, you can hire horses outside the boathouse on the north side of the lake. The rides mostly consist of a short amble along bitumen. Prices are set, from Rs 50 for a short ride to Rs 150 for an hour, which takes you part way around the lake. The horses at the boathouse looked a lot better cared for than the mangy ponies hanging around the bus stand.

For more serious riding, book at Fernhills Palace (see p388). Each morning a pony man arrives with sturdy animals for a three-hour trek through rolling hills and into a Toda village.

BOATING

Rowboats can be rented from the **boathouse** (9am-5.30pm; admission Rs 5, camera/video Rs 10/100) by the lake. Prices start from Rs 60 for a two-seater pedal boat (30 minutes) and up to Rs 250 for a 15-seater motor boat (20 minutes).

HORSE RACING

Ooty's racecourse dominates the lower part of the hill station between Charing Cross and the lake. The horse racing season runs from mid-April to June and on race days the whole town is a hive of activity. Outside the season, the 2.4km racecourse is little more than an overgrown paddock. If you're in town for a race it's an entertaining event not to be missed.

JOLLY WORLD

Jolly World (admission Rs 5; 9am-7.30pm) is an amusement park between the lake and the bus stand with stalls, sideshows, rides and all the good stuff to keep kids occupied. For grown-up kids there's a **go-kart track** (Rs 60). It's busy on weekends when families invade Ooty.

Tours

The tourist office organises trips to Mudumalai National Park via the Pykhara Dam (Rs 200) starting at 9.30am and returning at 7pm, with just a quick spin through the park. Trips to Coonoor and surrounds are Rs 125 and take eight hours.

An alternative is to hire a taxi for the day. The rates are set at Rs 450 for a four-hour trip around Ooty, or Rs 1100 for a full day.

Sleeping

Ooty has some of Tamil Nadu's best accommodation if you're prepared to pay for it. It's a sellers' market in the busy high season (1 April to 15 June) when many hotel prices double. Prices listed here are for the low season when most places are good value. Checkout time is often 9am. In town you'll be close to all amenities, noise and pollution, but peace, tranquillity and some wonderful upmarket hotels can be found just a few kilometres away. Some guesthouses have open fires, either in rooms or in a common lounge, but there's generally a small charge for firewood and cleaning.

BUDGET

Reflections Guest House (2443834; North Lake Rd; d from Rs 250-300) This delightful, family-run place overlooks the lake in a peaceful location between the bus stand and the boathouse. Rooms are simple and clean with private bathroom and hot water in the morning – the ones above the main house have good lake views. Home-cooked meals (order in advance) are good, there's a lounge with TV and an open fire, and you can organise trekking from here.

YWCA Anandagiri (2442218; Ettines Rd; dm Rs 99-110, s/d from Rs 276/414, deluxe Rs 792, bungalow Rs 678, incl tax) The YWCA has many things going for it, not least the good location overlooking the racecourse – walking distance to the centre and bus stand. It's set in spacious grounds with a main building, a group of separate cottages and a small chapel. There's a large, colonial-style lounge, library and dining room with fireplace, and most rooms are spacious and clean. It's an efficiently run place and you can organise hiking here.

TTDC Youth Hostel (2443665; Church Hill Rd; dm/d Rs 70/250, 8-bed r Rs 645) The cramped 20-bed dorm gives this place an army camp atmosphere. There's also a bar and restaurant here.

MIDRANGE

Hotel Khems (2444188; www.hotelkhems.com; Shoreham Palace Rd; d Rs 475-675, ste Rs 900) In a quiet but central location, this is a modern, comfortable and well-appointed hotel with friendly staff and a striking faux stone design.

Willow Hill (☎ 2444037; www.thewillowhill.com; 58/1 Havelock Rd; d Rs 900-1600) Sitting high above the town with large windows providing some of the best views in Ooty. The rooms, all with wooden floors, are spacious and comfortable in the style of an alpine chalet, with the most expensive room offering those wonderful views and a private garden. Willow Hill is definitely not as stylish as other places in this area, but it's friendly and affordable and there's a reasonable restaurant.

Nilgiri Woodlands Hotel (☎ 2442451; Racecourse Rd; d/cottage/ste low Rs 660/825/1045, incl tax) This Raj-era hotel is looking a bit the worse for wear in places but its manicured gardens offer great views of Ooty across the racecourse and the gabled roof and red-tiled cottages are a reminder of old Ooty.

TOP END

King's Cliff (☎ 2452888; www.kingscliff-ooty.com; Havelock Rd; d Rs 975-1675) High above Ooty on Strawberry Hill, King's Cliff is a delightful new hotel in a colonial mansion with wood panelling, antique furnishings and brilliant views over Ooty. With only nine rooms it's an intimate retreat and all have individual character – the deluxe rooms have a private covered porch with superb views. There's

---

SOMETHING SPECIAL

Fernhills Palace (South Lake Rd; ☎ 2442555; regency@sancharnet.in; ste Rs 3500-12,000; 🛋) If you want to live like a king, stay in a palace. The former summer residence of the Maharaja of Mysore reopened as a hotel in 2004 after extensive restoration, and this is the place to experience right royal treatment. Walking through the lobby you enter the original high-ceilinged ballroom, now a regal lounge with antique furniture, oriental rugs and teak wood panelling. The 19 individual rooms retain Raj-era charm but with modern touches such as spa baths and TV. Some of the suite rooms are big enough to host a game of cricket, the beds are so comfortable you'll never want to get up, and the furniture, floor coverings and fireplaces are all class. Relax with a cigar and brandy in the Fox Hunt Bar, dine in style in the restaurant, and make use of the health club, horse riding, golf and trekking facilities.

---

also a fine restaurant, and staff can organise trekking, mountain-biking and other activities.

Savoy Hotel (☎ 2444142; savoy.ooty@tajhotels.com; 77 Sylks Rd; s/d from US$65/75, ste from US$105/115) The Savoy is one of Ooty's oldest hotels, with parts of it dating back to 1829. Cottages are arranged around a beautiful garden of flowerbeds, manicured lawns and clipped hedges. Quaint rooms have large bathrooms, polished floors, log fires and bay windows. Modern facilities include a 24-hour bar, excellent multicuisine dining room, an Ayurvedic centre, gym and tennis courts.

Sullivan Court (☎ 2441416; wgsull@md5.vsnl.net.in; Selbourne Rd; standard s/d Rs 1150/2000, deluxe s/d Rs 1195/2200) Ooty's most modern hotel, Sullivan Court boasts a stunning lobby with glass elevator, plush rooms, a good restaurant, children's play area, and gym – it's excellent value if you're after contemporary comfort rather than old-fashioned style.

Eating

Sidewalk Café (Commercial Rd; dishes Rs 40-60, pizzas Rs 45-125; ☯ 11am-11pm) This cross between an American diner and an Italian café is something you're more likely to find in Mumbai than the mountains but it's a welcome change from South Indian food and very popular. In bright, modern décor, efficient staff wheel out wood-fired veg pizzas, burgers, sandwiches (try the chilli cheese or mushroom toast), soups, salads and awesome desserts and smoothies.

Most of the hotels have their own restaurants and some of the upmarket places are great for a splurge, with lavish meals and atmospheric dining rooms.

Hotel Sanjay (☎ 2443160; Charing Cross; mains Rs 35-85; ☯ 7am-9.30pm) This is a basic but bustling place with generous servings of veg and nonveg fare and a bar on the first floor.

Shinkow's Chinese Restaurant (☎ 2442811; 38/83 Commissioner's Rd; mains Rs 50-150; ☯ noon-3.45pm & 6-9.45pm) Shinkow's is a bit of an Ooty institution and the simple menu of chicken, pork, beef, fish, noodles and rice dishes is usually pretty good.

Chandan Restaurant (mains Rs 50-75, thalis Rs 50-70; ☯ noon-3pm & 7-11pm) At Hotel Nahar, Chandan serves up delicious veg dishes in elegant surroundings. Thalis are served at lunch-time or choose from a big range of biryanis and Chinese dishes.

Sullivan Court (lunch buffet Rs 300 per person; ⊗ noon-4pm) The restaurant at the Sullivan Court puts together a wonderful Sunday lunch buffet.

Both the **Savoy Hotel** (mains from around Rs 140; ⊗ 12.30-3.30pm & 7.30-10.30pm) and **King's Cliff** (mains Rs 80-200; ⊗ noon-10pm) have atmospheric restaurants with log fires and quality food.

QUICK EATS

There are plenty of basic veg places on Commercial and Main Bazaar Rds and you can get a spicy biryani for Rs 10 at street stalls near the bus stand. Ooty is famous for its delicious homemade chocolates. Kings is the original chocolate maker, but shops all over town display homemade varieties for around Rs 50 per 100g.

Hot Breads (Charing Cross; ⊗ 8am-10pm) This popular bakery turns out a huge range of breads, pastries, pies and sweets, including éclairs, croissants and strudel – go early for the fresh stuff.

Shopping

Ooty can be a fun place to shop, but don't expect anything out of the ordinary. The main places to shop are along Commercial Rd where you'll find Kashmiri shops as well as government outlets for Poompuhar, Kairali and Khadi Gramodyog Bhavan.

There's no need to lug warm clothes up to Ooty – you can pick up jackets from Rs 100 and hats and gloves from Rs 10 at shops along Commercial Rd (near the bus stand) or at the **Tibetan market** (9am-8pm) almost opposite the entrance to the Botanical Gardens

Getting There & Away

Without doubt the most romantic way to arrive in Ooty is aboard the miniature train but you'll need to book ahead in the high season. Buses also run regularly up and down the mountain, both from other parts of Tamil Nadu and from Mysore in Karnataka.

BUS

The state bus companies all have **reservation offices** (⊗ 9am-5.30pm) at the busy bus station. There are two routes to Karnataka – the main bus route via Gudalur and the shorter, more arduous route via Masinagudi. The latter is tackled only by minibuses and winds through 36 hairpin bends! There are government buses to Bangalore (Rs 155, eight hours, seven daily) and Mysore (Rs 69, four hours, 11 daily). There are also two private buses a day to Bangalore (Rs 250) and Mysore (Rs 100).

To Coimbatore there are buses every 20 minutes (Rs 37, three hours) via Mettupalayam (Rs 17, two hours), both of which will get you to a train for Chennai or Kochi (Kerala). There are direct overnight bus services to Chennai (Rs 228, 15 hours, two daily).

To get to Mudumalai National Park (Rs 23, 2½ hours, 12 daily), take one of the Mysore buses or one of the small buses that go via the narrow and twisting Sighur Ghat road. Some of these rolling wrecks travel only as far as Masinagudi (Rs 10, 1½ hours), from where there are buses every two hours to Theppakadu (at Mudumalai).

Local buses leave every 30 minutes for Kotagiri (Rs 10, two hours) and every 10 minutes to Coonoor (Rs 6.50, one hour).

TRAIN

The miniature train is the best way to get here with fine views of forest, waterfalls and tea plantations along the way, especially from the front first-class carriage. Since the steam engine pushes, rather than pulls, the train up the hill, the front carriage leads the way. Departures and arrivals at Mettupalayam connect with those of the *Nilgiri Express,* which runs between Mettupalayam and Chennai. The miniature train departs Mettupalayam for Ooty at 7.20am daily (Rs 117/12 in 1st/2nd class; five hours, 46km). If you want a seat in either direction, be at least 45 minutes early or make a reservation (Rs 15) at least 24 hours in advance.

From Ooty the train leaves at 3pm and takes about 3½ hours. There are also three daily passenger trains between Ooty and Coonoor.

Getting Around

Plenty of autorickshaws hang around the bus station – a ride from the train station or bus stand to Charing Cross should cost about Rs 25. Taxis cluster opposite the bus stand and at the top end of Commercial Rd.

There are fixed fares to most destinations including to Kotagiri (Rs 400), Coonoor (Rs 300), Gudalur (Rs 600), Mudumalai National Park (Rs 600) and Coimbatore (Rs 600).

You can hire a bicycle at the bazaar but many of the roads are steep so you'll end up pushing it uphill (great on the way down though!). Motorcycles can be hired from **Classic Rentals** (☎ 2448695; Ettines Rd; ☼ 9am-6pm) at RCM Tours & Travels. A Kinetic Honda or TVS scooter costs Rs 300 for 24 hours (or Rs 50 per hour) and a 100cc Yamaha is Rs 350. A deposit of Rs 500 is usually required.

MUDUMALAI NATIONAL PARK
☎ 0423

In the foothills of the Nilgiris, this 321 sq km **park** (admission Rs 30) and the surrounding forest is the best place in Tamil Nadu for wildlife viewing. Part of the Nilgiri Biosphere Reserve (3000 sq km), the reserve's vegetation ranges from grasslands to semievergreen forests which is home to chital (spotted deer), gaur, tiger, panther, wild boar and sloth bear. Otter and crocodile inhabit the Moyar River. The park's wild elephant population supposedly numbers about 600; however, you're more likely to see their domesticated cousins carrying out logging duties.

The best time to visit Mudumalai is between December and June although the park may be closed during the dry season, February to March. Heavy rain is common in October and November.

Orientation & Information
The main service area in Mudumalai is Theppakadu, on the main road between Ooty and Mysore. Here you'll find the park's **reception centre** (☎ 526235; ☼ 6.30-9am & 3-6pm). There is some very basic accommodation and an elephant camp here.

The closest village is Masinagudi, 7km from Theppakadu.

Wildlife Tours
It's not possible to hike in the park and tours are limited to the sanctuary's mini-buses and elephants. Private vehicles are not allowed. Minibus tours (Rs 35 per person, 45 mins) run from 7am to 9am and 3pm to 6pm and go about 15km around

the outskirts of the park. The one-hour elephant rides (Rs 460 for four people) can be booked in advance at the WWO in Ooty or at the Theppakadu reception centre, although you may be lucky if you just turn up. At the time of research these rides were suspended, due to the poor health of the elephants.

Guides can be hired for trekking outside the park boundaries. There are agencies in Masanagudi and all the resorts have their own guides. **Nature Safari Tours & Treks** (treks per hr Rs 50) is a recommended place in Masanagudi. Some travellers have also recommended Kumar at **Wilderness Eco Tours** (☎ 2526351; www.wilderness-eco-tours.com; treks per hr from Rs 75). He can also be found at the Green Park Resort (see below).

Sleeping & Eating
All budgets are catered for – there are cheap bungalows inside the park at Theppakadu; budget and midrange hotels in Masinagudi and upmarket jungle resorts in Bokkapuram (4km south of Masinagudi).

IN THE PARK
For accommodation in the park, book in advance with the WWO in Ooty (see p386).

Morgan Dormitory (r per person Rs 35) This place is clean and has two four-bed rooms. Each room has a private bathroom with cold water only.

Theppakadu Log House (d/q Rs 330/560) Next to Sylvan Lodge, this is the pick of the places in the park. Overlooking the river, it's comfortable, well maintained and good value. There's a small restaurant.

MASINAGUDI
There are several lodges on the main road in Masinagudi as well as the odd place for a meal. A jeep ride from Masinagudi to the park costs around Rs 70, or wait for one of the buses passing through between Ooty and Theppakadu.

Kongu Lodge (☎ 526131; 8/38 Main Rd; s/d Rs 150/162) On the main road in Masinagudi, this hotel has simple rooms with private bathroom and hot water. There's also a restaurant and bar.

Green Park Resorts (☎ 2526351; Singara Rd; d Rs 400-550, tree house Rs 750, 8-bed cottage Rs 1600) Green Park, 2km west of Masinagudi, is the best midrange option here but it's nowhere near the standard of the resorts in Bokkapuram. It's set in a pleasant garden of palms and pines and surrounded by forest. The garden restaurant and bar is a good spot for post-trek socialising. There are nondescript double rooms and overpriced cottages.

BOKKAPURAM

This area south of Masanagudi is home to a gaggle of fine forest resorts. Most listings here are family-run businesses with a warm, homely atmosphere, high standards and breathtaking views. The attraction here is wildlife – trekking in the jungle, jeep safaris, night safaris and bird-watching. Many resorts provide a pick-up service from nearby towns (starting from Rs 500), otherwise hire any jeep in Masinagudi. It's best to book rooms in advance, particularly in season. Each resort offers a range of services including visits to Mudumalai National Park with an elephant ride, hikes with a guide, fishing and horse riding, all of which cost extra. All places have their own restaurants but costs shown here are for accommodation only. Meals are extra and usually start at around Rs 100.

Jungle Retreat (☎ 2526470; www.jungleretreat.com; tree house or bamboo huts Rs 1200, cottage Rs 1200-2000, camping Rs 200; 🏊) Jungle Retreat is one of the most stylish resorts in the area, with lovingly built stone cottages decked out with classic furniture, sturdy, ecofriendly bamboo huts with private bathroom, and a couple of tree houses, all spread out to give a feeling of seclusion. It's also possible to camp and there's a dormitory for groups. The bar, restaurant and common area is a great place to meet fellow travellers and the owners are knowledgeable and friendly with a large area of private forest at their disposal.

Wild Canopy (☎ 2526660; tree house or cottage Rs 5000) Stunning is one way to describe this up-

market new jungle hideaway. Set on 350 acres of private forest, there's a man-made waterhole to attract wildlife and two tree houses perched 15m high above the jungle canopy. Reached by a staircase, the luxury tree houses have running hot and cold water and room service! If you suffer from vertigo, there are two luxury ground level stone cottages with outdoor Jacuzzi on the veranda. For a secluded jungle experience, it's worth the price.

Forest Hills Guest House (☎ 2526216; forest hills@softhome.net; s/d/tr from Rs 750/995/1200, huts Rs 995) Forest Hills is a small, intimate guesthouse (10 rooms on 12 acres) with a couple of cute bamboo huts with private bath and spacious rooms. There's a slight colonial air here with a gazebo-style bar, games rooms and barbecue pit.

Jungle Hut Nature Resort (☎ 2526240; www .junglehut.net; d/tr Rs 1000/1400; 🏊) Built around its own waterhole, Jungle Hut has clean and comfortable cottages and a pleasant, grassy setting. There's a small playground and resident farm animals, making it a good place for families.

Getting There & Away

Buses from Ooty to Mysore and Bangalore (in Karnataka) stop at Theppakadu (Rs 23, 2½ hours, 11 daily). Bus services run every two hours between Theppakadu and Masinagudi.

The longer route to or from Ooty is via Gudalur (67km). The direct route to Masinagudi; however, is an interesting 'short cut' (Rs 10, 1½ hours, 36km) which involves taking one of the small government buses that make the trip up (or down) the tortuous Sighur Ghat road. The bends are so tight and the gradient so steep that large buses simply can't use it. Private minibuses heading to Mysore also use this route but if you want to get off at Masinagudi, you'll have to pay the full fare (Rs 125).

Andaman & Nicobar Islands

Andaman & Nicobar Islands

Once known as Kalapani (Black Waters) for its role as a feared penal settlement, the Andaman and Nicobar Islands are now a relaxed tropical island outpost – belonging to India but geographically closer to Southeast Asia. The islands' location is close to the epicentre of the undersea earthquake that caused the 2004 Boxing Day tsunami, which in turn led to devastating loss of life and homes on the southerly Nicobar Islands and Little Andaman. Apart from flooding on low-lying areas of South Andaman Island and damage to the reefs near Wandoor, the main Andaman island group escaped major damage.

Superb, near-deserted beaches, incredible corals and marine life, an intriguing colonial past and the remnants of a stone-age culture lure travellers to these mysterious islands, 1000km off the east coast of India in the Bay of Bengal. The territory comprises 572 tropical islands (of which 36 are inhabited), with unique fauna and lush forests, although the Nicobar Islands are off-limits to tourists.

Until the beginnings of colonial rule, the islands were populated mainly by indigenous peoples, but today the majority of the Andamans' population are mainland settlers or their descendants who live in and around Port Blair, the capital, on South Andaman. Notwithstanding the tsunami aftermath, the Andamans have been changing fast in recent years. Tourist infrastructure is developing and charter flights to the islands are planned from Southeast Asia. Although it's remote, and with visitor restrictions discouraging mass tourism, now is a good time to visit these beautiful islands.

HIGHLIGHTS

- Take a full-day snorkelling trip or cruise through mangrove swamps on **Havelock Island** (p404)
- Scuba dive or snorkel around the islands of the sublime **Mahatma Gandhi Marine National Park** (p404)
- Spend a few hours exploring the ghosts of the past on **Ross Island** (p403) – the former 'Paris of the East'
- Laze on the idyllic beaches of Havelock Island, especially **Radha Nagar** (p404)
- Take a road trip through the heart of the Andamans to **Diglipur** (p407)
- Relive the horror of Port Blair's colonial past at the **Cellular Jail** (p400)

★ Diglipur

★ Havelock Island

Port Blair ★★ Ross Island

Mahatma Gandhi
Marine National Park ★

History

It's not known when the first inhabitants arrived on the Andaman and Nicobar Islands but their presence was documented in the 2nd century by Ptolemy, and later in the 7th century by Xuan Zang.

In the late 17th century, the islands were annexed by the Marathas, whose empire consumed vast areas of India. Two centuries later the British found a use for them as a penal colony, initially to detain 'regular criminals' from mainland India and later to incarcerate political dissidents – the freedom fighters for independence. During WWII, the islands were occupied by the Japanese, who were regarded with ambivalence by the islanders. Some initiated guerrilla activities against them, while others regarded them as liberators from British colonialism.

Following Independence in 1947, the islands were incorporated into the Indian Union. Since then, massive migration from the mainland has inflated the island population from a few thousand to more than 350,000. With this influx, tribal land rights and environmental protection have at times been disregarded.

Climate

Sea breezes keep temperatures within the 23°C to 31°C range and the humidity at around 80% all year. The southwest monsoons come to the islands between mid-May and June, and the northeast monsoons between November and December. The best time to visit is between December and early April, when the days are warm, but not oppressive, and the nights pleasant.

FAST FACTS

- Population: 356,265
- Area: 8248 sq km
- Capital: Port Blair
- Main languages: Hindi, Bengali, Tamil and tribal languages
- Telephone area code: ☎ 03192
- When to go: December to April

Geography & Environment

The islands form the peaks of a vast submerged mountain range that extends for almost 1000km between Myanmar (Burma) and Sumatra. The majority of the land area is taken up by the Andamans at 6408 sq km. The Nicobar Islands begin 50km south of Little Andaman.

The isolation of the Andaman and Nicobar Islands has led to many endemic species of both flora and fauna. Of 62 identified mammals, 32 are unique to the islands. Among these are the Andaman wild pig, the crab-eating macaque, the masked palm civet and, species of tree shrews and bats. Almost 50% of the islands' 250 bird species are endemic. Eagles, megapodes, swiftlets, doves, teals and hornbills inhabit the islands. The isolated beaches provide excellent breeding grounds for turtles. While dolphins are frequently sighted, the once abundant dugongs have all but vanished.

Mangroves are an important aspect of the flora, offering a natural protective barrier to both land and sea. Further inland the evergreen and moist deciduous forests contain many important tree species, including the renowned padauk – a hardwood with light and dark colours occurring in the same tree.

Information

For contact details of shipping companies, see p395. Even though they're 1000km east of the mainland, the Andamans still run on Indian time. This means that it can be dark by 5pm and light by 4am. The high season is December and January.

ACCOMMODATION

Accommodation choices and standards are on the way up in the Andamans. Just

---

FESTIVALS IN THE ANDAMAN ISLANDS

The 10-day **Island Tourism Festival** is held in Port Blair, usually in January. Dance groups come from surrounding islands and the mainland, and various cultural performances are held at the Exhibition Complex. One of the festival's more bizarre aspects is the Andaman dog show, but there's also a flower show, a baby show and a fancy-dress competition! For information, check the website of **A&N Tourism** (www.and.nic.in).

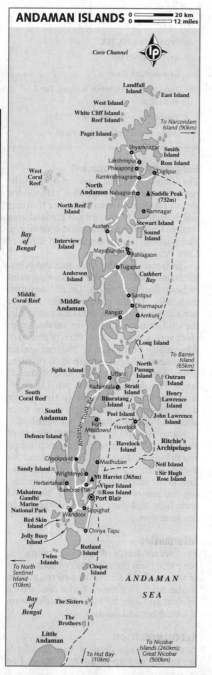

ANDAMAN ISLANDS
0 ——— 20 km
0 ——— 12 miles

Coco Channel

Landfall Island
East Island
West Island
White Cliff Island
Reef Island
To Narcondam Island (90km)
Paget Island
Shyamnagar
Smith Island
Lakshmipur
Phaiapong
Ross Island
Ramkrishnagram
Diglipur
West Coral Reef
North Andaman
Nabagram
Saddle Peak (732m)
North Reef Island
Ramnagar
Austen
Stewart Island
Bay of Bengal
Interview Island
Sound Island
Mayabunder
Pahlagaon
Anderson Island
Tugapur
Cuthbert Bay
Middle Coral Reef
Middle Andaman
Santipur
Rangat
Dharmapur
Amkunj
Long Island
To Barren Island (65km)
Spike Island
North Passage Island
Uttara
Outram Island
South Coral Reef
Kadamtala
Strait Island
Bharatang Island
Henry Lawrence Island
South Andaman
Peel Island
John Lawrence Island
Port Meadows
Havelock
Defence Island
Havelock Island
Ritchie's Archipelago
Checkpoint
Madhuban
Neil Island
Sandy Island
Wrightmyo
Mt Harriet (365m)
Sir Hugh Rose Island
Herbertabad
Mahatma Gandhi Marine National Park
Bamboo Flat
Viper Island
Ross Island
Port Blair
Sippighat
Wandoor
Red Skin Island
Chirya Tapu
Jolly Buoy Island
Rutland Island
Twins Islands
To North Sentinel Island (10km)
Cinque Island
ANDAMAN SEA
Bay of Bengal
The Sisters
The Brothers
Little Andaman
To Hut Bay (10km)
To Nicobar Islands (260km); Great Nicobar (500km)
Andaman Trunk Rd

a few years ago the only places to stay outside Port Blair were tatty government guesthouses and basic forest rest houses. These days you can stay in cheap bamboo huts or a handful of romantic upmarket resorts on Havelock and Neil Islands. Although taxes are low, accommodation is expensive by Indian standards – some of the midrange and top-end places in Port Blair are grossly overpriced – but budget travellers can find a cheap lodge in Port Blair or a simple hut by the beach on Havelock for less than Rs 150.

Prices can shoot up in the peak season (15 December to 15 January). Prices given in this chapter are for midseason.

Rules on camping are a bit hazy but you currently can't pitch a tent on beaches or forest reserve areas, which pretty much rules out wild camping altogether. Check with the Andaman & Nicobar (A&N) Tourism office (see p396) or the office of the Chief Wildlife Warden in Port Blair (see opposite).

PERMITS

The Nicobar Islands are off limits to all except Indian nationals engaged in research, government business or trade. All foreigners need a permit to visit the Andaman Islands, but there's no need to arrange it in advance – the permit is issued on arrival. The 30-day maximum permit (which can be extended to 45 days), allows foreigners to stay in Port Blair, with overnight stays also permitted on South and Middle Andaman (excluding tribal areas), North Andaman (Diglipur), Long Island, North Passage, Little Andaman (excluding tribal areas), Havelock and Neil Islands.

The permit also allows day trips to Jolly Buoy, South Cinque, Red Skin, Ross, Narcondam, Interview and Rutland Islands, as well as The Brothers and The Sisters. Boat trips to Barren Island are allowed, although you are not allowed to disembark.

To obtain the (free) permit, air travellers simply present their passport and fill out a form on arrival at the immigration hall at Port Blair airport. Permits are usually issued for as long as you ask (up to 30 days) on the application form, so even if you intend to stay only a week, it's best to ask for the whole 30 days.

Boat passengers will probably be met by an immigration official on arrival, but if not you should seek out the immigration office at Haddo Jetty immediately – you won't be able to travel around without the permit (police will frequently ask to see it, especially when disembarking on another island). Rules change periodically, so it's worth checking with the relevant authorities before purchasing your ticket:

A&N Tourism office (Map p399; ☎ 232747; fax 230933; www.and.nic.in; Port Blair; ☉ 8.30am-1pm & 2-5pm Mon-Fri, 8.30am-noon Sat)

Foreigners' Registration Office Chennai (Madras; ☎ 044-28278210); Kolkata (Calcutta; ☎ 033-22473300)

Shipping Corporation of India (SCI; www.shipindia .com) Chennai (☎ 044-25231401; fax 25231218; Rajaji Salai); Kolkata (☎ /fax 033-22482354; 1st fl, 13 Strand Rd); Port Blair (Map p399; ☎ 233347; Aberdeen Bazaar)

As well as visitor permits, additional permits are required to visit some other islands, national parks and sanctuaries. To obtain permits for areas *not* covered by the permit issued on arrival, visit the **Chief Wildlife Warden** (CWW; Map p399; ☎ 03192-33549; Haddo Rd, Haddo, Port Blair). You will need to make an application, which consists of a letter stating your case, the name of the boat and the dates involved. The permit should be issued within the hour. If you intend to visit islands south of Mayabunder, you must then present your permit to the **District Conservator of Forests** (DCF; Map p399; ☎ 03192-33321; WL-I, Haddo Rd, Haddo, Port Blair), next door to the CWW. Visitors to islands north of Mayabunder should present their permit to the **DCF** (WL-II, Mayabunder) on arrival. How to go about getting the permit, how much it costs and whether it is in fact possible to get one (it's not always) should be explained at the CWW when you make your application. These offices open from 8.30am to noon and 1pm to 4pm Monday to Friday. Most permits cost Rs 20 per person per day.

National Parks & Sanctuaries

Special day permits are required to visit national parks and sanctuaries on the islands, and in this case it's not the hassle of getting the permit but the cost that hurts. For national parks (such as the Mahatma Gandhi Marine National Park or Saddle

---

EARTHQUAKES & AFTERSHOCKS

The Andaman and Nicobar Island chain is no stranger to earthquakes and tremors. In 1941 an earthquake measuring 7.7 on the Richter scale rocked South and Middle Andaman, destroying many buildings and causing the British administrative centre on Ross Island to be abandoned. A resulting tsunami wave of about 1m reportedly reached the east coast of India, and more than a dozen earthquakes and aftershocks were felt over the next six months on the islands.

It was a far more devastating event at 7.58am on 24 December 2004, when an undersea earthquake measuring 9.0 occurred off the northeastern tip of Sumatra (Indonesia). It was not the tremors that caused the most damage, but the powerful tsunami that swept across the Bay of Bengal and Andaman Sea, devastating parts of Indonesia, Sri Lanka, India, the Maldives, Thailand and the Nicobar Islands. Soon after, a massive aftershock occurred beneath the Andaman and Nicobar Islands, causing more damage and 'uplifting' several islands along the west coast of the Andaman chain (including Sentinel and Interview) by as much as 2m. The tsunami's effect on the low-lying Nicobar Islands was severe. When the tidal wave hit the islands, including Great Nicobar, Car Nicobar, Little Andaman, Nancowrie, Katchal and many smaller islands, thousands were caught in its wake. Official figures show 6100 confirmed dead, many more missing and thousands left homeless, evacuated to relief camps in Port Blair. Initial access to some islands proved difficult, so many people were left stranded for days, without food or water, waiting for help.

Fortunately the more northerly Andaman Island chain was spared the carnage – low-lying parts of South Andaman were flooded, leaving many homeless, and water surged into shore areas of Port Blair and islands such as Havelock, but with little lasting damage. Still, geologists estimate as many as 10,000 aftershocks in the three months following the tsunami, some measuring up to 6.5. British geologist Dr Mike Searle says some 1300km of the plate boundary, between the Indian plate to the west and the Burma–Andaman–Sumatra plate to the east, was ruptured, while the Indian plate is presently underthrusting to the east. While he says such a catastrophe may never again be seen in this lifetime, these remote islands are clearly a seismic hotspot.

Peak National Park) the permits costs Rs 50/500 for Indians/foreigners. For sanctuaries, such as Ross and Smith Islands, near Diglipur, the cost is Rs 25/250.

Students with valid ID can avoid this and pay only Rs 5, but you must go to the Chief Wildlife Warden in Port Blair (see p395) and get a letter authorising the discount.

TOURISM OFFICES

Andaman & Nicobar Tourism (A&N Tourism; Map p399; ☎ 232747; fax 230933; www.and.nic.in; Port Blair; ☽ 8.30am-1pm & 2-5pm Mon-Fri, 8.30am-noon Sat) is the main tourism body for the islands.

Activities

DIVING

The crystal-clear waters, superb coral, kaleidoscopic marine life and some virtually undiscovered sites make the Andamans a world-class diving destination.

The downside is that in recent years there has been little stability in the diving industry and dive operators have come and gone. The main problem seems to be an over-regulation of the industry and the fact that foreign instructors can't get the necessary permits to work here.

Dive Operators

There are currently three professional dive outfits on Havelock Island and another due to open at Wandoor. The dive season is usually from December to April. The centres offer fully equipped boat dives, Discover Scuba Diving courses, open water and advanced courses, as well as Divemaster training. Prices may vary depending on the location, number of participants and duration of the course, but diving in the Andamans is not cheap (compared with Southeast Asia) at around US$50/80 for a single/double boat dive. In national parks there's an additional cost of Rs 1000 per person per day payable directly to the park.

Andaman Dive Club (Map p405; ☎ 282002; www .andamandiveclub.com) Based at No 1 Village on Havelock, this outfit charges US$80 to US$100 for two boat dives and US$340/225 for PADI open water/advanced courses. Also offers multiday packages and expedition dives.

Barefoot Scuba (Map p405; in Port Blair ☎ 237656; www.barefootindia.com) Based at Barefoot Jungle Resort in Havelock, with another outfit due to open at Wandoor, Barefoot offers two boat dives for US$80 and open water courses for Rs 15,000.

Dive India (Map p405; ☎ 282472; www.diveindia.com) This dive outfit is based at the Wild Orchid on Havelock Island. The cost is Rs 2000/3000/4000 for one/two/three boat dives. A Discover Scuba Diving course is Rs 3000; a PADI open water course is Rs 15,500 and the advanced open water course is Rs 10,500 (Rs 21,000 for both combined).

Dive Sites

Recommended dive sites include **Cinque Island** (p404; North Point, Southeast Reef), **North Passage Island** (Fish Rock), **Little Andaman** (p408; Bala Reef), **Wandoor** (p403), **Rutland Island** (Corruption Rock) and **Snake Island**. The greatest range of options is off **Havelock Island** (p404) where sites include Mac Point, Aquarium, Barracuda City, Turtle Bay, Seduction Point, Lighthouse, The Wall, Pilot Reef and Minerva Lodge.

SNORKELLING

Much easier and cheaper to arrange than diving, snorkelling can be a highly rewarding excursion. Good snorkelling gear is rarely available at the sites themselves, so make arrangements before setting out from Port Blair, or better still bring your own gear from home or buy it on the Indian mainland where it's cheaper. **Havelock Island** (p404) is one of the best places for snorkelling as many accommodation places will organise boat trips out to otherwise inaccessible coral reefs and islands.

The closest place to Port Blair for snorkelling is North Bay. Other popular sites include Wandoor, Jolly Buoy, Red Skin, Cinque, Neil and Little Andaman Islands.

SURFING

Intrepid surfing travellers have been whispering about **Little Andaman** (p408) since it first opened up to foreigners about seven years ago. Although the island is still quite remote, surfers continue to drift down there for the reliable waves off the east coast. Several companies, including **SEAL** (http://seal-asia .com), offer liveaboard surfing charters, usually sailing from Thailand or Myanmar.

Getting There & Away

Getting to the Andamans can be an adventure in itself if you take the boat from Chennai or Kolkata. It's a long journey and you'll need to plan ahead as there's usually only one or two sailings a fortnight from each mainland city. Flying is quick and easy but you'll need to book ahead to ensure a seat in the high season.

AIR
Indian Airlines (in Port Blair Map p399; ☎ 233108; ◷ 9am-1pm & 2-4pm Mon-Sat; in Chennai ☎ 044-28555201; in Kolkata ☎ 033-22110730) flies daily

to Port Blair from Chennai (US$230, two hours) at 6.15am, and 11 times a week from Kolkata (US$245). **Jet Airways** (in Port Blair ☎ 236922; in Chennai ☎ 044-28414141) flies daily from Chennai (US$235) at 9.50am.

Weekly charter flights were scheduled to begin operating from Bangkok (Thailand) to Port Blair in 2005 but were shelved after

ISLAND INDIGENES

The Andaman and Nicobar Islands' indigenous peoples constitute just 12% of the population and, in most cases, their numbers are decreasing.

Onge

Two-thirds of Little Andaman's Onge Island was taken over by the Forest Department and 'settled' in 1977. The 100 or so remaining members of the Onge tribe are confined to a 25-sq-km reserve covering Dugong Creek and South Bay. Anthropological studies suggest that the Onge population has declined due to demoralisation through loss of territory. Most of the island population was evacuated to Port Blair following the tsunami.

Sentinelese

The Sentinelese, unlike the other tribes in these islands, have consistently repulsed outside contact. Every few years, contact parties arrive on the beaches of North Sentinel Island, the last redoubt of the Sentinelese, with gifts of coconuts, bananas, pigs and red plastic buckets, only to be showered with arrows, although in recent years encounters have been a little less hostile. About 250 Sentinelese remain.

Andamanese

Numbering only about 40, it seems impossible that the Andamanese can escape extinction. There were almost 5000 Andamanese in the mid-19th century. Their friendliness to the colonisers was their undoing, and by the beginning of the 20th century most of the population had been swept away by measles, syphilis and influenza epidemics. They've been resettled on tiny Strait Island.

Jarawa

The 350 remaining Jarawa occupy the 639-sq-km reserve on South and Middle Andaman Islands. Their territory has been disrupted by the Andaman Trunk Rd, forest clearance and settler and tourist encroachment. In 1953 the chief commissioner requested an armed sea plane bomb Jarawa settlements. Today, it is tourists that bombard the Jarawas.

Shompen

Only about 250 Shompen remain in the forests on Great Nicobar. Hunter-gatherers who live along the riverbanks, they have resisted integration and shy away from areas occupied by Indian immigrants.

Nicobarese

The 30,000 Nicobarese are the only indigenous people whose numbers are not decreasing. The majority have converted to Christianity and have been partly assimilated into contemporary Indian society. Living in village units led by a head man, they farm pigs and cultivate coconuts, yams and bananas. The Nicobarese, who probably descended from people of Malaysia and Myanmar, inhabit a number of islands in the Nicobar group, centred on Car Nicobar, the region worst affected by the tsunami.

the tsunami. They may now start in 2006 and will run from January to April (US$400 return). To use the service you must book a package and return to Bangkok on a charter flight – the service can't be used as a stepping stone between the Indian mainland and Thailand. The charter company is Thai-based **PB Air** (www.pbair.com) and you can book through **A&N Islands Tours & Travels** (☎ 245068; www.anislands.com; 20/4 AIR Rd) in Port Blair.

BOAT

There are usually four to six sailings a month between Port Blair and the Indian mainland – fortnightly to/from Kolkata (56 hours) and weekly (in high season) to/from Chennai (60 hours) on four vessels operated by **SCI** (Map p399; ☎ 233347; fax 33778; www .shipindia.com; Aberdeen Bazaar, Port Blair). The schedule is erratic, so check with the SCI in advance or see the **A&N Tourism** (www.and.nic.in) website, which usually posts an up-to-date schedule. Also, take the sailing times with a large grain of salt – travellers have reported sitting on the boat at Kolkata harbour for up to 12 hours, or waiting to dock near Port Blair for several hours, so with holdups and depending on the weather and sea conditions, the trip can take three full days or more. The service from Chennai goes via Cap Nicobar once a month, taking an extra two days, but only residents may disembark. Less frequent services operate from Visakhapatnam in Andhra Pradesh (see p425 for more details).

If you're buying your return ticket in Port Blair, go to the 1st floor of the A&N Tourism office (see p396) where they can reserve you a berth under the tourist-quota system. If you can, it's best to arrange return tickets on the mainland when purchasing your outward ticket.

Ships currently in use are the MV *Nancowry* and MV *Swarajdweep* from Chennai, the MV *Nicobar* and MV *Akbar* from Kolkata, and MV *Harshavardan* from both ports.

Classes vary slightly between the boats, but the cheapest class of accommodation is bunk (Rs 1510), which can be difficult to get. Next up is 2nd or B class (Rs 3870, 16 berths), 1st or A class (Rs 4860, four to six berths) and deluxe cabin (Rs 5880). Food (tiffin for breakfast, thalis for lunch

and dinner) costs around Rs 150 per day. Almost everyone complains; bring something (fruit in particular) to supplement your diet. Some bedding is supplied, but if you're travelling bunk class, bring a sleeping sheet. Many travellers take a hammock to string up on deck.

See p394 for other SCI office addresses.

Getting Around

All roads – and ferries – lead to Port Blair, but getting around the islands can be a slow process, particularly to outlying islands. The main island group – South, Middle and North Andaman – is connected by road and bridges. Buses run from Port Blair to Wandoor and north to Bharatang, Rangat, Mayabunder and finally to Diglipur, 325km north of the capital. Don't expect to cover any more than 30km per hour, even in a taxi.

Of course, a boat is the only way to reach most islands and the romance of ferry travel is alive and well here – you'll often see flying fish and even dolphins from crowded decks. It's relatively quick and easy to get to Havelock and Neil Islands, and there are regular ferries to Long Island, Little Andaman, plus longer-haul trips to Rangat, Mayabunder and Diglipur among others. The best source of information about interisland ferry schedules is in the numerous newssheets that are widely available in Port Blair. The daily *Andaman Herald*, and the *Daily Telegrams* list sailing times a week in advance.

A subsidised inter-island helicopter service was launched in 2003, but its future remains uncertain because of the high cost and relatively low demand. At the time of writing most flights were to the Nicobar Island group.

PORT BLAIR

☎ 03192 / pop 100,186

The capital sprawls around a harbour on the east coast of South Andaman and is undoubtedly the administrative nerve centre of these islands. It's not a particularly attractive town, with only one half-decent beach, but there's plenty to see relating to the islands' colonial past, and this is the only place to change money, access the Internet and book onward transport, so most travellers will spend at least a few days here. If

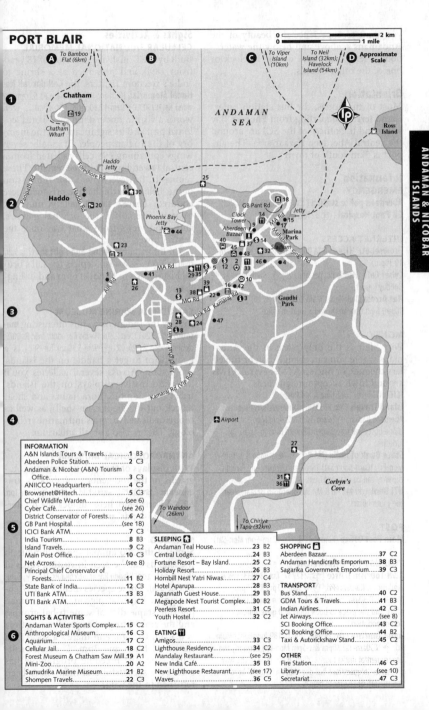

PORT BLAIR

INFORMATION
A&N Islands Tours & Travels..............1 B3
Abedeen Police Station......................2 C3
Andaman & Nicobar (A&N) Tourism
Office...3 C3
ANIICCO Headquarters.......................4 C3
Browsenet@Hitech.............................5 C3
Chief Wildlife Warden.....................(see 6)
Cyber Café.....................................(see 26)
District Conservator of Forests..........6 A2
GB Pant Hospital..........................(see 18)
ICICI Bank ATM..................................7 C3
India Tourism......................................8 B3
Island Travels......................................9 C2
Main Post Office................................10 C3
Net Across....................................(see 8)
Principal Chief Conservator of
Forests..11 B2
State Bank of India............................12 C3
UTI Bank ATM...................................13 B3
UTI Bank ATM...................................14 C2

SIGHTS & ACTIVITIES
Andaman Water Sports Complex.....15 C2
Anthropological Museum..................16 C3
Aquarium...17 C2
Cellular Jail..18 C2
Forest Museum & Chatham Saw Mill.19 A1
Mini-Zoo...20 A2
Samudrika Marine Museum...............21 B2
Shompen Travels...............................22 C3

SLEEPING
Andaman Teal House.........................23 B2
Central Lodge....................................24 B3
Fortune Resort – Bay Island.............25 C2
Holiday Resort...................................26 B3
Hornbill Nest Yatri Niwas.................27 C4
Hotel Aparupa...................................28 B3
Jagannath Guest House......................29 B3
Megapode Nest Tourist Complex......30 B2
Peerless Resort..................................31 C5
Youth Hostel......................................32 C2

EATING
Amigos...33 C3
Lighthouse Residency.........................34 C2
Mandalay Restaurant.....................(see 25)
New India Café...................................35 B3
New Lighthouse Restaurant............(see 17)
Waves..36 C5

SHOPPING
Aberdeen Bazaar...............................37 C2
Andaman Handicrafts Emporium.....38 B3
Sagarika Government Emporium.....39 C3

TRANSPORT
Bus Stand...40 C2
GDM Tours & Travels........................41 B3
Indian Airlines....................................42 C3
Jet Airways.....................................(see 8)
SCI Booking Office.............................43 C3
SCI Booking Office.............................44 B2
Taxi & Autorickshaw Stand...............45 C2

OTHER
Fire Station..46 C3
Library..(see 10)
Secretariat...47 C3

you want to experience the beauty of the Andamans – above and below the water – book a ferry and move on to Havelock or one of the other islands.

Orientation

Most of the hotels, the bus station, inter-island ferries (departing from Phoenix Bay Jetty) and the offices of the SCI are around the central Aberdeen Bazaar area. The airport is 5km south of town.

Information

EMERGENCY

Aberdeen police station (☎ 33077, 32100; MG Rd)
GB Pant Hospital (☎ 32102; GB Pant Rd)

INTERNET ACCESS

Browsenet@Hitech (MA Rd; per hr Rs 30; 🕑 8.30am-10.30pm)
Cyber Café (Haddo Rd; per hr Rs 20; 🕑 9am-9pm) At Holiday Resort.
Net Across (Junglighat Main Rd; per hr Rs 20; 🕑 9am-10pm) Next door to the India Tourism office.

MONEY

Port Blair is the only place in the Andamans where you can change cash or travellers cheques, or find an ATM. Several ATMs around town accept foreign cards.

ICICI ATM (cnr Foreshore & MA Rds)
Island Travels (☎ 233358; islandtravels@yahoo.com; Aberdeen Bazaar; 🕑 9am-1pm & 2-4pm Mon-Sat) This is one of several travel agencies with foreign-exchange facilities.
State Bank of India (MA Rd; 🕑 9am-noon & 1-3pm Mon-Fri, 10am-noon Sat) Travellers cheques and foreign currency can be changed here.
UTI Bank (cnr MG Rd & MA Rd, Aberdeen Bazaar) Near the youth hostel.

POST

Main Post Office (Kamaraj Rd; 🕑 10am-5pm Mon-Sat)

TOURIST INFORMATION

A&N Tourism Office (☎ 232747; fax 230933; www.and.nic.in; Kamaraj Rd; 🕑 8.30am-1pm & 2-5pm Mon-Fri, 8.30am-noon Sat) This is the main island tourist office and the place to book tours and government accommodation.
India Tourism (☎ 233006; 2nd fl, 189 Junglighat Main Rd; 🕑 8.30am-12.30pm & 1-5pm Mon-Fri) Formerly the Government of India tourist office, it has little in the way of answers to questions but does have a range of brochures and its staff are eager to help.

Sights & Activities

CELLULAR JAIL NATIONAL MEMORIAL

Built by the British over a period of 18 years from 1890, and preserved as a shrine to India's freedom fighters, the **Cellular Jail National Memorial** (GB Pant Rd; admission Rs 5, camera/video Rs 10/50; 🕑 9am-12.30pm & 1.30-5pm) is well worth a visit to understand the islands' colonial past and its significance in the memory of the Indian people. Originally seven wings containing 698 cells radiated from a central tower, but only three remain. These remnants, however, give a fair impression of the 'hell on earth' that the prisoners here endured. There's an art gallery, museum, martyrs' memorial, the original gallows, and good views from what was once the central tower.

An informative **sound-and-light show** (adult/child Rs 20/10; 🕑 Mon-Sat) depicts the jail's brutal history. It's in Hindi at 6pm and in English at 7.15pm.

SAMUDRIKA MARINE MUSEUM

Run by the Indian navy, this interesting **museum** (☎ 32012, ext 2214; Haddo Rd; adult/child Rs 10/5, camera/video Rs 20/40; 🕑 9am-5.30pm Tue-Sun) is a good place to get a handle on the islands' eco-system. Across several galleries you'll find informative displays on the islands' tribal communities, flora, fauna and shells (check out the giant clam shell), as well as rooms dedicated to corals and marine archaeology. There's also a small aquarium.

ANTHROPOLOGICAL MUSEUM

With displays of tools, clothing and photographs of the indigenous inhabitants, this **museum** (☎ 232291; adult/child Rs 10/5; 🕑 9am-1pm & 1.30-4.30pm Fri-Wed) helps unlock the mysteries of the islands' tribal cultures.

MINI-ZOO

Some of the 200 animal species unique to the islands can be seen in rusting cages at the small **zoo** (Haddo Rd; adult/child Rs 2/1; 🕑 8am-5pm Tue-Sun). These species include the Nicobar green imperial pigeon, the Andaman pig (the staple diet of some tribal groups) and the crab-eating macaque. Feeding time is 8.30am to 9am, and there's a short film shown at 10am and 3pm. The zoo's salt-water crocodile breeding programme has been very successful and many have been returned to the wild.

FOREST MUSEUM & CHATHAM SAW MILL
On Chatham Island (which is reached by a road bridge), the **saw mill** (admission Rs 2; ☟ 8.30am-2.30pm) was set up by the British in 1836 and is one of the largest wood processors in Asia. Inside is the forest museum, which displays locally grown woods, including the padauk, and has displays on the history of timber milling on the island. It may not be to everyone's taste – especially to that of environmentalists – but the mill provides a bit of perspective on the islands' colonial history and economy.

AQUARIUM & MARINA PARK
The **aquarium** (Mahabir Singh Rd; adult/child Rs 5/3; ☟ 9am-1pm & 2-4.45pm Thu-Tue, closed 2nd Sat of month) displays some of the 350 species found in the Andaman Sea, as well as some interesting live specimens in the tanks, including puffer fish, batfish and tiger fish. The adjacent **Marina Park** (Mahabir Singh Rd) is a thin strip of rusting kids' rides and there's also a miniature train here. Both were damaged by the tsunami but they should be open by now.

ANDAMAN WATER SPORTS COMPLEX
At the **water sports complex** (☟ 9am-5pm) you can rent rowboats, windsurfing equipment and sailing dinghies. Water skiing costs Rs 300 for 15 minutes; jet skis are Rs 250 for 15 minutes; windsurfing is Rs 50 for 30 minutes; a glass-bottomed boat is Rs 120 per hour; and parasailing is Rs 600 for once circuit with the speed boat (approximately five minutes). To rent a mask and snorkel costs Rs 100 per day.

CORBYN'S COVE
Corbyn's Cove, 4km east of the airport and 7km south of the town, is the nearest beach to Port Blair – a small curve of sand backed by palms and the Peerless Resort. It's popular for swimming, sunset-viewing and lazing around.

Tours
Possible day tours include Port Blair city tours (adult/child Rs 52/26), Wandoor Beach (Rs 104/52), Mt Harriet (Rs 156/78), and, less often, Cinque Island or Little Andaman. Most tours will operate only with a minimum number of bookings. Travel agencies:

A&N Islands Tours & Travels (☎ 245068; www .anislands.com; 20/4 AIR Rd)
Andaman Teal House (☎ 232642; Haddo Rd)
Island Travels (☎ 233034; islandtravels@yahoo.com; Aberdeen Bazaar) Opposite Sampat Lodge.
Shompen Travels (☎ 233028; Kamaraj Rd)

Sleeping
Accommodation is quite scattered in Port Blair, but the cheapest places are within a few kilometres of each other around MA Rd and Aberdeen Bazaar. Checkout is usually 8am but can be as early as 7am to get rooms ready for new arrivals – pack the night before!

BUDGET
Youth Hostel (☎ 232459; dm/d Rs 50/100) This hostel, opposite the stadium, is a rare Indian YHA, although the only discount is for students (Rs 30). It's still the cheapest place around but in high season it's often filled with groups.

Central Lodge (☎ 233632; Link Rd; s/d with shared bathroom Rs 70/100, d with private bathroom Rs 120) This is a basic wooden building set back from the road. Small rooms are a bit grim but it's a popular cheapie – a throwback to simple lodgings on the backpacker trail of old, but without the banana pancakes.

Jagannath Guest House (☎ 232148; 72 MA Rd; s/d/tr Rs 200/300/450) This is a reasonably good budget choice, not least because the management is accustomed to travellers. Rooms are simple but relatively clean and most come with a small balcony.

Holiday Resort (☎ 30516; info@aboutandamans .com; Prem Nagar; s/d Rs 350/500, s/d with AC Rs 600/800; ☒ ▣) Don't be fooled by the name – this isn't a resort or much of a place for a holiday, but it's central, clean and straddles budget and midrange mainly because there are AC rooms and TVs.

MIDRANGE
Megapode Nest Tourist Complex (☎ 232207; aniid co@vsnl.com; off Haddo Rd; s/d from Rs 1000/1400, cottages Rs 2000; ☒) At Haddo, on the hill above the bay, the Megapode Nest is good value in the upper midrange. Many of the rooms have harbour views and there are large AC doubles and generous yurt-style AC cottages. Prices include breakfast, and it's always pleasant to sit in the garden and sip a cold beer.

Hornbill Nest Yatri Niwas (☎ 46042; hornbill resort@rediffmail.com; d from Rs 800, s/d with AC Rs 950/1250; 🗐 🖳) Perched on a hill about 1km north of Corbyn's Cove, this place has a potentially good location but the coastal outlook is largely wasted. Rooms are nothing special for the price. There's a semi open-air restaurant and bar.

Andaman Teal House (☎ 234060; Haddo Rd; d without/with AC Rs 400/800; 🗐) Run by A&N Tourism (bookings must be made through the tourist office; see p396), this is reasonably central and has a range of ageing rooms spilling down the hillside. The AC rooms at the top are definitely the best (with TV, carpet and furniture) – the others are bare and musty.

Hotel Aparupa (☎ 246582; hotelaparupa@yahoo .com; Link Rd; s/d Rs 900/1200; 🗐) This smart new hotel has 26 smallish but immaculate rooms with tile floors, TV and central AC. There's a good little restaurant with a view of sorts and a bar.

TOP END

Major credit cards are accepted at the following hotels and prices include breakfast.

Fortune Resort – Bay Island (☎ 234101; sripad sudhir@yahoo.com; Marine Hill; s/d Rs US$66/99, ste s/d US$132/165; 🗐 🖳) Port Blair's top hotel also boasts the best location, perched above the ocean with fine sea views from its terraced garden and balcony restaurant. The rooms, while comfortable with polished floors, balconies, neat furnishings and TV, are a bit on the snug side and way overpriced – get your money's worth and ask for a sea-facing room. There's an excellent sea-water swimming pool and a good restaurant and bar.

Peerless Resort (☎ 229263; pblbeachinn@sancharnet .in; s/d Rs 2250/3650, cottage d Rs 4500; 🗐) The location is the main plus for Peerless Resort – just back from Corbyn's Cove Beach. Otherwise, the rooms are ageing, undersized and overpriced, although most have a balcony. The manicured gardens are pleasant, and there's a tennis court, Ayurvedic centre, beachfront bar and restaurant.

Eating

Port Blair has an eclectic range of restaurants – from cheap Indian thali places around the bazaar to upmarket hotel restaurants. Good seafood is available at a few places.

Amigos (mains Rs 37-70; ⏱ 7am-10pm) This spotless veg restaurant, just south of Aberdeen Bazaar, whips up good veg pizzas, burgers and sandwiches.

New Lighthouse Restaurant (Marina Park; mains Rs 25-75, seafood Rs 150-350; ⏱ 8am-11pm) This decaying structure next to the aquarium has a breezy semi open-air section with a view over the water. Fresh seafood – including whole fish, crab and lobster (prices depend on weight and season) – is the main attraction here, but it's also a good place for breakfast or an evening beer.

Lighthouse Residency (MA Rd, Aberdeen Bazaar; mains Rs 45-110; ⏱ 11am-11pm) Modern and euro-chic, this restaurant and cocktail bar is bright, white and spotless almost to the point of sterility. The speciality is Thai and Chinese, but Indian and Continental features on the menu, including fresh seafood.

Mandalay Restaurant (Marine Hill; ⏱ 7-10.30am, 12.30-2.30pm & 7-10.30pm) The open-deck restaurant at Fortune Resort – Bay Island (see left) is worth a splurge for the views alone, and you can fill up on the daily buffets (breakfast Rs 180, lunch and dinner buffet Rs 350).

Waves (mains Rs 30-95; ⏱ 10am-11pm) This breezy open-air restaurant fronts Corbyn's Cove Beach, so it's a good spot for lunch or an evening meal beneath the palms. Seafood is available (Malai prawns Rs 75, crab and lobster by weight), along with Thai and Indian dishes. Next door, Corbyn Cove Hut is good for snacks and cold beer (Rs 65).

New India Café (MA Rd) For cheap eats, try this place at Hotel Jai Matha.

Shopping

Aberdeen Bazaar is typically Indian – lined with stalls selling cheap clothing and household goods. Island crafts such as fine wood carvings, shell jewellery, bamboo and cane furniture, are available from a handful of emporiums and speciality shops. Most of the shells on sale are collected legally – a good emporium can show proof of this.

Andaman Handicrafts Emporium (☎ 240141; MG Rd, Middle Point)

Sagarika Government Emporium (MG Rd, Middle Point; ⏱ 9am-7pm Mon-Sat, 9am-noon & 3-7pm Sun)

Getting There & Away

See p396 for details on transport to and from the Andaman Islands.

BOAT

From Chatham Wharf there are several daily passenger ferries to Bamboo Flat (Rs 3, 15 minutes), but most island ferries depart from Phoenix Bay Jetty. Advance tickets for boats can be purchased from the ticket counters between 9am and 11am here between 9am and 11am the day before travel. On some boats, such as the Neil and Havelock Island ferries, tickets can be purchased on the boat but in high season you risk missing out.

BUS

From the bus stand in Port Blair there are buses to Wandoor (Rs 8, 1½ hours, eight daily) and Chiriya Tapu (Rs 9, two hours, four daily). There's a daily bus at 4.30am to Diglipur (Rs 120, 12 hours) via Mayabunder, a direct bus at 5am to Mayabunder (Rs 95, nine hours) and a 5.45am bus to Rangat (Rs 65, six hours).

Getting Around

The central area is easy enough to get around on foot, but if you want to get out to Corbyn's Cove, Haddo or Chatham Island, you'll need some form of transport. A taxi or autorickshaw from the airport to Aberdeen Bazaar costs around Rs 35. From Aberdeen Bazaar to Phoenix Bay Jetty is about Rs 25 and to Haddo Jetty it's around Rs 35.

The best way to explore the island south of Port Blair is on a moped or motorbike. They can be hired through **GDM Tours & Travels** (☎ 232999; MA Rd) for Rs 150 per day for a gearless scooter or Rs 200 per day for a 125cc motorbike. A Rs 1000 deposit is required and helmets are supplied. Jagannath Guest House (see p401) also has a few mopeds (from Rs 150 per day).

Bicycles are good for getting around the town and the immediate Port Blair area. They can be hired from stalls in Aberdeen Bazaar for Rs 40 per day.

AROUND PORT BLAIR & SOUTH ANDAMAN
Ross Island

An essential half-day trip from Port Blair, this eerie place was once the administrative headquarters for the British. **Ross Island** (admission Rs 20) is where all the action was in those heady colonial days and newspapers

of the day fondly called it the 'Paris of the East'. However, the manicured gardens and grand ballrooms were destroyed by an earthquake in 1941. Six months later, after the Japanese entered WWII, the British transferred their headquarters to Port Blair. The island was again damaged by the tsunami in 2004.

Many of the buildings still stand as evocative ruined shells slowly being consumed by the trees of the island. Landscaped paths cross the island and all of the buildings are labelled. There's a small museum with historical displays and some photos of Ross Island in its heyday.

Ferries to Ross Island (Rs 16, 20 minutes) depart from the Water Sports Complex Jetty in Port Blair at 8.30am, 10.30am, 12.30pm and 2pm Thursday to Tuesday; check current times when you buy your ticket, as times can be affected by tides. Ross Island is controlled by the navy and visitors must sign in on arrival and pay the entry fee.

Viper Island

The afternoon boat trip to **Viper Island** (admission Rs 5) is worthwhile to see the sobering remains of the ochre-coloured brick jail and the gallows built by the British in 1867. Viper is named after a 19th-century British trading ship that was wrecked nearby.

A harbour cruise to Viper Island leaves from the Water Sports Complex Jetty daily at 3pm (Rs 65, 45 minutes each way), stopping at the island for about 20 minutes. On Wednesdays (when no boats are going to Ross Island), there are more frequent ferries.

Mt Harriet

Mt Harriet (365m) is across the inlet, north of Port Blair. There's a nature trail up to the top with good views. To reach Mt Harriet, take the Bamboo Flat passenger ferry (Rs 3, 15 minutes), which leaves regularly from Chatham Jetty, or the vehicle ferry (Rs 3, 30 minutes), which leaves every two hours from Phoenix Bay Jetty. From Bamboo Flat a road runs 7km along the coast and up to Mt Harriet. Taxis will do the trip for Rs 250.

Wandoor

Wandoor, a tiny speck of a village 29km southwest of Port Blair, is the jumping-off point for the superb **Mahatma Gandhi Marine National Park** (Indian/foreigner Rs 50/500), which covers 280 sq km and comprises 15 islands. The diverse scenery includes mangrove creeks, tropical rainforest and reefs supporting 50 types of coral. Unfortunately, the marine park and Jolly Buoy and Red Skin Islands were closed to visitors due to reef damage following the tsunami. If they reopen, boats usually leave from Wandoor village jetty for visits to **Jolly Buoy Island** (adult/child Rs 125/60; ☻ Thu-Tue) or **Red Skin Island** (adult/child Rs 90/45; ☻ Sat-Thu). Since this is a national park, you must first obtain a permit from the Wildlife Warden Office in Port Blair (see p395), or from the office next to the Wandoor Jetty.

Buses run from Port Blair to Wandoor (Rs 8, 1½ hours). About 2km beyond the Wandoor Jetty are a number of quiet, sandy **beaches** with some excellent snorkelling.

Mangrove Bay Hotel (☎ 280088; d Rs 250-300) is in the village close to the jetty but the rooms are utterly basic for this price. A new eco-retreat back from Wandoor beach was closed after the tsunami but may re-open – check with the tourist office.

Chiriya Tapu

Chiriya Tapu, 30km south of Port Blair, is a tiny fishing village with beaches and mangroves. There's a beach about 2km south of Chiriya Tapu that has some of the best snorkelling in the area. There are seven buses a day to the village from Port Blair (Rs 8, 1½ hours) and it's possible to arrange boats from here to Cinque Island.

Cinque Island

The uninhabited islands of North and South Cinque, connected by a sandbar, are part of the wildlife sanctuary south of Wandoor, just off Rutland Island. The islands are surrounded by coral reefs, and are among the most beautiful in the Andamans. Visiting boats usually anchor off South Cinque and passengers transfer via dinghy to the beach.

Only day visits are allowed and unless you're on one of the day trips occasionally organised by travel agencies, you need to get permission from the Chief Wildlife Warden (p395). The islands are two hours by boat from Chiriya Tapu or 3½ hours from Wandoor.

HAVELOCK ISLAND

With one of the Andaman's most dazzling beaches and plenty of cheap bamboo hut accommodation, Havelock is the island of choice for travellers wanting to kick back and enjoy the slow (but not comatose) pace of island life. It's easily accessible from Port Blair, and offers excellent snorkelling and scuba-diving opportunities. Although it's the most developed of the islands, it's still very low-key and simple – a world away from the beach resorts of mainland India or Southeast Asia.

Inhabited by Bengali settlers, Havelock is about 54km northeast of Port Blair and covers 100 sq km. Only the northern third of the island is settled, and each village is referred to by a number. Boats dock at the jetty at No 1 Village; the main bazaar is 2km south at No 3 Village; and most of the accommodation is strung along the east coast between Nos 2 and 5.

Sights & Activities

Radha Nagar Beach (also called No 7), on the northwestern side of the island about 12km from the jetty, is a gorgeous stretch of squeaky white sand and crystal-clear water backed by native forest. Don't miss a sunset here. You can take a short **elephant ride** (adult/child Rs 20/10; ☻ 2-4pm) through the shady forest.

Secluded **Elephant Beach** is further north and reached by a 40-minute walk through a muddy elephant logging trail and swamp, but the beach itself has virtually disappeared after the tsunami and at tide it's impossible to reach – ask locally.

A highlight of Havelock is **snorkelling** or **fishing**, and the best way to do either is on a boat trip organised by one of the accommodation places. Trips cost from Rs 300 to 1000, depending on the number of people and the distance. Wild Orchid (see the boxed text, p406) organises full-day trips (per couple from Rs 2000) that take you through a mangrove swamp and to some great snorkelling sites. Havelock is the premier spot for **scuba diving** on the Andamans and there are three dive outfits here (see p396 for more information).

Sleeping

Heading south along the coast from the jetty there's a string of simple hut resorts and a few romantic, upmarket places at No 5 Village or west to No 7 Village.

Pristine Beach Resort (☎ 282344; huts Rs 100-150; cottages with private bathroom Rs 250-300) Cute huts, a nice bit of beach, fine restaurant and a licence to serve alcohol make this a cut above most places.

Emerald Gecko (small huts Rs 200-300, large huts Rs 800-1000) A short walk south of the Dolphin Beach Resort, this is a step up in quality from the other hut resorts. There are two superb double-storey huts, with open-roofed bathroom, lovingly constructed from bamboo rafts that have drifted ashore from Myanmar. There are also some budget huts, a restaurant and bar. Book through the Wild Orchid (see the boxed text, p406).

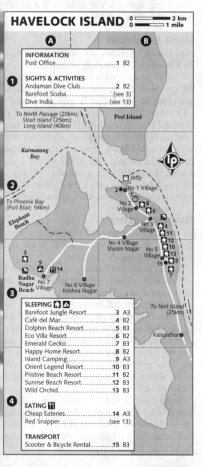

HAVELOCK ISLAND

0 ─── 2 km
0 ─── 1 mile

INFORMATION
Post Office...............................1 B2

SIGHTS & ACTIVITIES
Andaman Dive Club...................2 B2
Barefoot Scuba.........................(see 3)
Dive India................................(see 13)

To North Passage (20km);
Strait Island (25km);
Long Island (40km)

Peel Island

Karmatang Bay

To Phoenix Bay
(Port Blair; 54km)

Elephant Beach

🕀 Jetty
No 1 Village
No 2 Village
No 3 Village
No 4 Village
Shyam Nagar No 5 Village
Radha Nagar Beach No 7 Village No 6 Village
Krishna Nagar

To Neil Island
(25km)

Kalapathar

SLEEPING
Barefoot Jungle Resort...............3 A3
Café del Mar.............................4 B2
Dolphin Beach Resort.................5 B3
Eco Villa Resort........................6 B2
Emerald Gecko.........................7 B3
Happy Home Resort...................8 B2
Island Camping.........................9 A3
Orient Legend Resort.................10 B3
Pristine Beach Resort.................11 B2
Sunrise Beach Resort..................12 B3
Wild Orchid.............................13 B3

EATING
Cheap Eateries.........................14 A3
Red Snapper............................(see 13)

TRANSPORT
Scooter & Bicycle Rental............15 B3

Island Camping (tents Rs 150-500) Island Camping offers tented accommodation in an enviable location, nestled among the palms at the end of the road to Radha Nagar Beach. All tents have solid floors, raised camp beds and mosquito nets. It's open from November to March; book through A&N Tourism in Port Blair (see p396).

Barefoot Jungle Resort (☎ 282151, in Port Blair ☎ 237656; www.barefootindia.com; cottages Rs 3600-5300; 🔲) For the location alone – ensconced in the forest just back from Radha Nagar Beach – this is one of the Andamans best eco-friendly hang-outs. Accommodation is in beautifully designed, relatively luxurious timber and bamboo-thatched cottages with four-poster beds, stylish bathrooms are verandas. The newest cottages are superb, with AC, hot water, teak furniture and large picture windows. Rates include tastefully prepared meals, and there's a bar. There's also an Iyengar yoga centre in a secluded forest location here, and the owners are planning to build some budget cottages.

Dolphin Beach Resort (☎ 282411; d Rs 500, with AC Rs 1500-2000; 🔲) Run by A&N Tourism (p396), this is Havelock's original resort with beachfront accommodation in tired-looking but comfortable hexagonal cottages with TV and bathroom. The service here is indifferent at best.

Numerous small places have set up under the palm trees, with accommodation in sturdy bamboo huts with lights and fan for around Rs 100 to 300, and all have their own restaurants. Good places:
Café del Mar (☎ 282343; huts Rs 200, with private bathroom Rs 500)
Eco Villa (☎ 282072; huts Rs 75-100)
Happy Resort (☎ 282061; Govind Nagar Beach)
Orient Legend Resort (☎ 282389; huts Rs 150-250)
Sunrise Beach Resort (huts Rs 100-250)

Eating

Just about all places to stay have their own open-sided restaurants, with the standard fare of breakfast (omelettes, toast, coffee etc) and simple Indian and Chinese dishes.

Red Snapper (mains Rs 75-250) At the Wild Orchid (see the boxed text, p406), this is one of the few genuinely good places to eat on the island. Lovingly prepared fresh fish and seafood is usually available (often caught by the owner or guests!) and the menu includes Thai, Chinese, Indian and

Continental dishes, such as coconut prawn curry (Rs 125) and *bebinca* (layered coconut pancakes; Rs 65) for dessert. There's also a bar.

There are also cheap eateries serving thalis and fish dishes in No 5 Village and on the road leading to No 7 beach.

Getting There & Away

Ferries sail to Havelock from Phoenix Jetty in Port Blair twice a day (Rs 65, Rs 130 for AC seat, 2½ to three hours). The morning ferry (departing 7am from Port Blair) usually goes direct to Havelock, and returns at 10am. The afternoon ferry (1.30pm from Port Blair) goes via Neil Island and returns from Havelock to Port Blair at 5pm. Check times in the newspaper or at the jetty. The ferry from Neil Island to Havelock (Rs 23, one hour) picks up at 4pm. Occasional ferries to Long Island also call in at Havelock. Following the tsunami, ferries schedules were slightly reduced – check in advance.

Getting Around

A local bus connects the jetty and villages on an hourly circuit, but having your own transport is useful on Havelock. You can rent mopeds or motorbikes (Rs 150 per day) from the shop outside the entrance to Dolphin Beach Resort, or ask at your hotel. Bicycles (Rs 40 per day) can be found at the

---

SOMETHING SPECIAL

Wild Orchid (☎ 282472; www.wildorchidanda man.com; d cottages without/with AC Rs 1800/2200; 🗶) This is a wonderfully romantic place to stay. Set back from a secluded beach, it's a mellow, friendly place with tastefully furnished rooms in cottages designed in traditional Andamanese style. Modern bathrooms, four-poster beds and private verandas add to the comfort factor. The hosts, Benny and Lynda, are a mine of information and are almost always up for an evening drink and chat with guests. There's also an Ayurvedic centre in season here and a fine restaurant (p405) and bar. Bookings can be made through **Island Travels** (☎ 233358; islandtravels@yahoo.com) in Port Blair. Rates rise by 50% between 15 December and 15 January.

---

same shop, in No 3 Village or accommodation places.

An autorickshaw from the jetty to No 3 Village is Rs 30, to No 5 is Rs 50 and to No 7 it's Rs 200.

NEIL ISLAND

If you're looking for peace, isolation and near-deserted beaches without being a castaway, Neil Island, 40km northeast of Port Blair, is a good place to get off the ferry. Much quieter than nearby Havelock Island, Neil is populated by Bengali settlers involved in agriculture and fishing, and has several accommodation options, with more likely to pop up in the future. The main activities here are lying on the beach, snorkelling, or cycling through the island's flat paddy fields and farms.

Sights & Activities

Neil Island's beaches are numbered 1 to 5. **No 1 Beach** is the prettiest and most accessible, a 40-minute walk west of the jetty and village. Most of the accommodation places are close to No 1 Beach and the island's best snorkelling is around the coral reef at the far (western) end of this beach. At low tide it's difficult getting over the coral into the water. **No 5 Beach**, reached via the village road to the eastern side of the island, is an enclosed stretch with a bit of swell. It's a pleasant bike ride out here (about 10km from the village) – ask directions locally.

Sleeping & Eating

In the village, a few hundred metres from the jetty, there's a market, a few shops and a couple of basic restaurants.

West of the jetty along No 1 Beach are several 'eco-friendly' resorts with basic huts and more comfortable cottages.

Cocon Huts (☎ 282528; huts Rs 50, cottages Rs 350-400) The first place you come to along the beach, and accessible along the road about 500m from the village market (behind the playing fields), this a friendly place with simple huts and a few excellent bamboo cottages with tiled floor and spotless private bathrooms.

Tango Beach Resort (☎ 282583; huts Rs 50, cottages Rs 500) Further west, this is a similar set up, though the cottages aren't quite as good as Cocon Huts. However, it's closer to the better part of No 1 Beach.

Pearl Park Resort (☎ 282510; huts Rs 100, cottages & rooms Rs 800-1000) Pearl Park is the island's most upmarket place but it's still very earthy and set in a beautiful garden of palms and flowering plants. As well as very basic thatch huts, there are two romantic, stilted Nicobarese-style circular cottages and a couple of concrete hotel-style rooms.

Getting There & Away

A daily fast ferry leaves from Phoenix Bay Jetty in Port Blair at 1.30pm, stopping at Neil Island (Rs 65, 1½ hours). The same ferry then goes to Havelock Island (Rs 23, 1½ hours) at 3pm, though it's often late. Another ferry arrives from Havelock daily at around 8am, continuing on to Port Blair.

LONG ISLAND

This secluded little island, off the south-east coast of Middle Andaman about 80km north of Port Blair, has one small village and several sandy beaches at Lalaji Bay. The only accommodation is the Forest Rest House. The official position on whether you can camp changes regularly, but at the time of writing, camping was not permitted on beaches or forest areas, so check the situation with the A&N Tourist Office (see p400) in Port Blair.

The ferry from Port Blair to Rangat (via Neil and Havelock Islands) calls at Long Island (Rs 43, eight hours) five times a week. Bicycles are the main form of transport on the island.

MIDDLE ANDAMAN

The Andaman Grand Trunk Rd runs north from Port Blair to Bharatang Island and Middle Andaman, which are linked by bridges. This road runs beside Jarawa reserves on the west coasts of South and Middle Andaman. Motorcycles are forbidden beyond the checkpoint, 40km outside of Port Blair.

You can get to **Rangat** daily from Port Blair via the Havelock, Neil or Long Island ferries (Rs 80, nine hours) or by bus (Rs 65, six hours).

A bus runs to Cuthbert Bay for A&N Tourism's **Hawksbill Nest** (☎ 279022; 4-bed dm Rs 500, d with/without AC Rs 600/400; ❄). Bookings must be made at A&N Tourism in Port Blair (see p396).

Mayabunder, 71km north of Rangat, is linked by the daily bus from Port Blair (Rs 90, nine hours) and also by occasional ferries. A short private boat ride from Mayabunder Jetty takes you to tiny Avis Island, where you'll find beaches and **Sea'n'Sand** (☎ 273454), with four bamboo cottages that have private bathroom.

Swiftlet Nest (dm Rs 125, d with/without AC Rs 600/400; ❄) is at Karmatang Bay, 13km northeast of Mayabunder.

NORTH ANDAMAN

Diglipur, the main town of North Andaman, is as far north as you can get in the island chain and the only place on North Andaman where foreigners can stay.

Ferries arrive at the Aerial Bay Jetty and from there it's 11km southwest to Diglipur village – where you'll find the bus stand, basic restaurants, a market and a couple of lodges – and 9km southeast along the coast to accommodation places at Kalipur.

Sights & Activities

The twin islands of **Smith** and **Ross**, connected by a narrow sand bar, are accessible by boat and here you can walk through forest, or swim and snorkel in the shallow waters. Since this is designated as a marine sanctuary, you must get a permit (Indian/foreigner Rs 25/250) from the **Forest Office** (⏰ 6am-2pm) opposite the Aerial Bay Jetty. A local ferry calls at the islands twice a day, dropping at one end and picking up from the other. Check times – you may feel more comfortable chartering a fishing boat for the day for around Rs 500.

At 732m, **Saddle Peak** is the highest point in the Andamans. You can trek through subtropical forest to the top and back from Kalipur in about six hours. Again a permit is required from the Forest Office (Indian/foreigner Rs 50/500) and a local guide will make sure you don't get lost – ask at Pristine Beach Resort (see p408).

Leatherback turtles nest (December to February) at a number of locations along this coastline.

Sleeping & Eating

There are two places to stay opposite each other at Kalipur, 9km south of the Aerial Bay Jetty. Buses run along this route (Rs 8); an autorickshaw costs about Rs 100.

Pristine Beach Resort (☎ 201837; huts Rs 200-350)
Huddled among the palms between paddy
fields and the beach, Pristine is a lovely
place with bamboo huts on stilts, a restaurant and friendly owners.

Turtle Resort (☎ 272553; s/d Rs 150/400, d with AC
Rs 600, 4-bed dm Rs 500; ⌘) On a small hill with
some reasonable views, this A&N Tour-
ism hotel provides some level of comfort,
though it's a little run down and has a forlorn feel. Book ahead through A&N Tourism (see p396) in Port Blair.

Getting There & Away
There are daily buses to/from Port Blair
(Rs 120, 12 hours), as well as buses to Mayabunder (Rs 30, 2½ hours) and Rangat (Rs
50, 4½ hours).

There are usually three overnight ferries
from Phoenix Bay Jetty per week to Diglipur (seat Rs 81, berth Rs 150, 10 hours).

LITTLE ANDAMAN
Although earmarked for tourist development, Little Andaman is still an outpost and
one of the more remote inhabited islands
in the group at 120km south of Port Blair.
The populated east coast was badly affected
by the tsunami, so check the situation with
accommodation and facilities here before
setting out. The big attractions here for
travellers are pristine beaches, forests and
surfing.

Little Andaman is home to members of
the Onge tribe, who were relocated to a
tribal reserve in 1977 when the government
began developing the island for agriculture
and logging of forest timber. One such
development is a 1500-hectare **red oil palm
plantation** about 11km from Hut Bay. Settlement and opening up of the island has

had a serious impact on the Onge through
loss of environment and hunting grounds –
only 100 or so remain. The tribal reserve is
out of bounds for tourists.

Ferries land at the Hut Bay Jetty on the
east coast and from there most of the accessible beaches and attractions are to the
north.

About 11km north of Hut Bay, **Netaji
Nagar Beach** is an idyllic white-sand beach
backed by forest.

A further 3km north is another excellent
beach at **Butler Bay**. The beach is good for
swimming and surfing, but not for snorkelling. Elephant rides into the forest can be
organised here.

Sleeping & Eating
Little Andaman is one island where new
accommodation places are likely to appear
in the future, but there are currently two
basic options for travellers – both damaged
by the tsunami.

ANIFPDCL Guest House (☎ 744207, in Port Blair
232866; pblvanvikas@sancharnet.com; per person Rs 150,
with AC Rs 240; ⌘) At Hut Bay, this guesthouse
the has no-frills rooms.

Butler Bay Beach Resort (cottages Rs 100-300) At
Butler Bay, this place has beautifully located
beachfront cottages, also run by the ANI-
FPDCL (Andaman & Nicobar Islands Forest Plantation Development Corporation),
and there's a basic restaurant here.

Getting There & Away
Boats sail from Port Blair to Hut Bay (Rs 19/
49/57 indeck/chair/bunk class, eight hours)
five or six times a week. At the time of writing there was one weekly helicopter flight
from Port Blair to Hut Bay on Saturday
(Rs 1488, 35 minutes).

Andhra Pradesh

Aside from tens of millions of pilgrims, not many people make the trip to Andhra Pradesh. But Andhra's a place with subtle charms, quiet traditions and a long history of spiritual scholarship. The state is 95% Hindu, but you wouldn't know it in the capital's Old Town, where Islamic monuments and the call of the muezzin are more ubiquitous than the garlanded, twinkling tableaux of Ganesh. The city's rich Islamic history announces itself in Hyderabad's huge, lavish mosques and the stately Qutb Shahi tombs – but also, more softly, in the tiny mosque in the Charminar and in the sounds of Urdu floating through the air.

Meanwhile, in the city's north, a 17.5m-high statue of the Buddha announces another Andhran history: the region was an international centre of Buddhist thought for several hundred years from the 3rd century BC. Today, ruins of stupas and monasteries defy impermanence around the country, especially at Amaravathi and Nagarjunakonda.

Travelling here is like a treasure hunt: the jewels have to be earned. The stunning Eastern Ghats near Visakhapatnam only emerge after hours on a broad-gauge line. A family workshop filled with exquisite traditional paintings appears after a meander through Sri Kalahasti. And the most famous wait of all, through a long, holy maze filled with pilgrims at Tirumala, is rewarded with a glimpse of Lord Venkateshwara, who, if you're lucky, will grant you a wish.

HIGHLIGHTS

- Buy an old drum and more bangles than you need while soaking up centuries-old ambience at Hyderabad's colourful **Laad Bazaar** (p415)
- Receive loving kindness from the many Buddha statues, from **Hyderabad** (p416) to **Nagarjunakonda** (p422) and **Amaravathi** (p426)
- Get hypnotised by the lush intricacy and rich colours of *kalamkari* paintings in the little village of **Sri Kalahasti** (p429)
- Ascend the ancient spiral steps of the **Charminar** (p415) for a breathtaking view of Hyderabad
- Enjoy the beauty of the spectacular Eastern Ghats as your passenger train chugs through the mountains to the **Araku Valley** (p425)
- Find devotion you didn't know you had for Lord Venkateshwara and mingle with the pilgrims at **Tirumala** (p427) as they shed their hair for their deity
- Picnic atop the ruins of the 16th-century **Golconda Fort** (p415) and then wander in and out of the various **royal tombs of the Qutb Shahi kings** (p416)

★ Araku Valley

★ Hyderabad

★ Amaravathi

★ Nagarjunakonda

★ Tirumala ★ Sri Kalahasti

History

By the 1st century AD the Satavahana dynasty reigned throughout the Deccan plateau. It evolved from the Andhra people, whose presence in southern India may date back to 1000 BC. Buddhist thought may have caught on here as early as the time of the Buddha, and in the 3rd century BC the Andhras embraced Buddhism, building huge edifices in its honour. In the coming century, the Andhras would develop a flourishing civilisation that extended from the west to the east coasts of South India.

From the 7th to the 10th century, the Chalukyas ruled the area, establishing their Dravidian style of architecture, especially along the coast. The Chalukya and Chola dynasties

merged in the 11th century to be overthrown by the Kakatiyas, who introduced pillared temples into South Indian religious architecture. Following the Kakatiya rule, the Vijayanagars rose to become one of the most powerful empires in India.

FESTIVALS IN ANDHRA PRADESH

Festivals in this boxed text are marked on Map p411.

Sankranti (Jan; statewide) This important Telugu festival marks the end of harvest season. Kite-flying competitions are held, women decorate their doorsteps with colourful *kolams* (or *rangolis* – rice-flour designs) and men decorate cattle with bells and fresh horn paint.

Industrial Exhibition (❶; Jan/Feb; Hyderabad, opposite) A huge exhibition with traders from around India displaying their wares, accompanied by a colourful, bustling fair.

Deccan Festival (❷; Feb; Hyderabad, opposite) Pays tribute to Deccan culture. Urdu *mushairas* (poetry readings) are held, along with Qawwali (Sufi devotional music) and other local music and dance performances.

Shivaratri (Feb/Mar; statewide) During a blue moon, this festival celebrates Shiva with all-night chanting, prayers and fasting. It's especially big in Sri Kalahasti, where hordes of pilgrims descend on the Sri Kalahasteeswara Temple. Devotees also visit the important Shiva shrine at Amaravathi.

Muharram (❸; Feb/Mar; Hyderabad, opposite) The Muslim period of Muharram, commemorating the martyrdom of Mohammed's grandson, lasts 14 days in Hyderabad. Shiites wear black in mourning, and throngs gather at Mecca Masjid.

Ugadi (Mar; statewide) Telugu new year is celebrated with *pujas* (offerings or prayers), mango-leaf *toranas* (architraves) over doorways, and sweets and special foods.

Mahankali Jatra (Jun/Jul; statewide) A festival honouring Kali, with colourful processions in which devotees convey *bonalu* (pots of food offerings) to the deity. Secunderabad's Mahankali Temple goes wild.

Mrigasira (❹; Jun/Jul; Hyderabad, opposite) Also known as Mrugam, this event marks the start of the monsoon with a feast of local fish. A fascinating aspect of this festival is the medical treatment administered to thousands of asthma sufferers. The treatment, more than 150 years old, involves swallowing live fish that have consumed a herbal remedy. It's believed that the remedy was revealed by a sage to the ancestors of the physicians who now dispense it.

Batakamma (❺; Sep/Oct; Hyderabad, opposite, & Warangal, p423) Women and girls in the north of the state participate in this celebration of womanhood. It involves dancing and feasting, and the goddess Batakamma is worshipped in the form of elaborate flower arrangements that women make and set to drift on rivers.

Brahmotsavam (❻; Sep/Oct; Tirumala, p427) Initiated by Brahma himself, the nine-day festival sees the Venkateshwara temple adorned in decorations. Special *pujas* and colourful chariot processions are a feature of the festivities, and it's considered an auspicious time for *darshan* (deity viewing).

Pandit Motiram–Maniram Sangeet Samaroh (❼; Nov; Hyderabad, opposite) This four-day music festival, named for two renowned classical musicians, celebrates Hindustani music.

Lumbini Festival (❽; 2nd Fri in Dec; Hyderabad, opposite, & Nagarjunakonda, p422) The three-day Lumbini Festival honours Andhra's Buddhist heritage.

Visakha Utsav (❾; Dec/Jan; Visakhapatnam, p424) A general celebration of all things Visakhapatnam, with classical and folk dance and music performances; some of the events are staged on the beach.

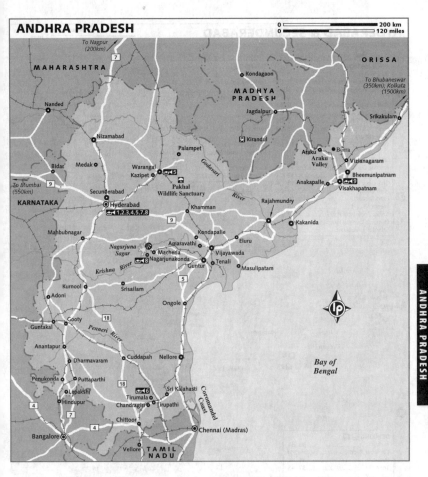

ANDHRA PRADESH

By the 16th century the Islamic Qutb Shahi dynasty was established in the city of Hyderabad but was to fall in 1687 to the Mughal emperor Aurangzeb. In the 18th century, the post-Mughal rulers in Hyderabad, known as nizams, retained relative control as the British and French vied for trade, though their power gradually weakened. The region became part of independent India in 1947, and in 1956 the state of Andhra Pradesh, an amalgamation of Telugu-speaking areas, was created.

Geography

Most of Andhra Pradesh is situated on the Deccan (south) plateau – one of the oldest geological formations in India. The Godavari and Krishna Rivers cut their way through the plateau, forming large deltas before entering the Bay of Bengal.

HYDERABAD & SECUNDERABAD

☎ 040 / pop 5.5 million / elev 600m

Hyderabad and Secunderabad, City of Pearls, was once the seat of the mighty Vijayanagar empire. Today, the west side of Andhra Pradesh's capital is, with Bangalore, the seat of India's mighty software empire; it goes by the name 'Cyberabad' and generates jobs, wealth and posh lounges with abandon.

Across town from all this sheen is the old Muslim quarter, with centuries-old Islamic monuments and even older charms.

ANDHRA PRADESH

HYDERABAD & SECUNDERABAD

0 —————— 2 km
0 —————— 1 mile

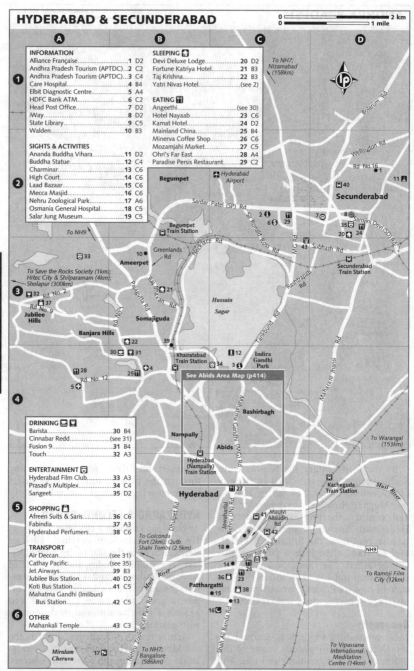

INFORMATION
Alliance Française...........................1 D2
Andhra Pradesh Tourism (APTDC)..2 C2
Andhra Pradesh Tourism (APTDC)..3 C4
Care Hospital...................................4 B4
Elbit Diagnostic Centre..................5 A4
HDFC Bank ATM.............................6 C2
Head Post Office.............................7 D2
iWay...8 D2
State Library...................................9 C5
Walden..10 B3

SIGHTS & ACTIVITIES
Ananda Buddha Vihara..................11 D2
Buddha Statue...............................12 C4
Charminar......................................13 C6
High Court.....................................14 C6
Laad Bazaar..................................15 C6
Mecca Masjid................................16 C6
Nehru Zoological Park...................17 A6
Osmania General Hospital.............18 C5
Salar Jung Museum........................19 C5

SLEEPING
Devi Deluxe Lodge.........................20 D2
Fortune Katriya Hotel....................21 B3
Taj Krishna....................................22 B3
Yatri Nivas Hotel.......................(see 2)

EATING
Angeethi...................................(see 30)
Hotel Nayaab.................................23 C6
Kamat Hotel..................................24 D2
Mainland China.............................25 B4
Minerva Coffee Shop.....................26 C6
Mozamjahi Market.........................27 C5
Ohri's Far East...............................28 A4
Paradise Persis Restaurant............29 C2

DRINKING
Barista..30 B4
Cinnabar Redd...........................(see 31)
Fusion 9...31 B4
Touch...32 A3

ENTERTAINMENT
Hyderabad Film Club......................33 A3
Prasad's Multiplex..........................34 C4
Sangeet..35 D2

SHOPPING
Afreen Suits & Saris........................36 C6
Fabindia...37 A3
Hyderabad Perfumers.....................38 C6

TRANSPORT
Air Deccan.................................(see 31)
Cathay Pacific...........................(see 35)
Jet Airways.....................................39 B3
Jubilee Bus Station.........................40 D2
Koti Bus Station.............................41 C5
Mahatma Gandhi (Imlibun)
  Bus Station..................................42 C5

OTHER
Mahankali Temple..........................43 C3

To NH7; Nizamabad (158km)

Bolarum Rd

Wellington Rd

Rd No.16

Secunderabad

Begumpet

Hyderabad Airport

Sardar Patel (SP) Rd

St Ronald Ross Rd

Sarojini Devi (SD) Rd

To NH9

Begumpet Train Station

Necklace Rd

Subhash Rd

Secunderabad Train Station

To Save the Rocks Society (1km);
Hitec City & Shilparamam (4km);
Sholapur (300km)

Greenlands Rd

Ameerpet

Rd No. 2

Raj Bhavan Rd

Panjagutta Rd

Hussain Sagar

Jubilee Hills

Rd No. 9

Banjara Hills

Somajiguda

Khairatabad Train Station

Indira Gandhi Park

Rd No. 12

Mahatma Gandhi (MG) Rd

See Abids Area Map (p414)

Bashirbagh

Nampally

Abids

Hyderabad (Nampally) Train Station

To Warangal (153km)

Jawaharlal Nehru (NJ) Rd

Kacheguda Train Station

Musi River

Hyderabad

To Golconda Fort (2km); Qutb Shahi Tombs (2.5km)

Dhulpet Rd

Maulvi Alauddin Rd

NH9

To Ramoji Film City (12km)

Salar Jung Marg

Musi River

Nehru Zoological Park Rd

To NH7; Bangalore (586km)

Shah Ali Banda Rd

Patthargatti

Miralam Cheruvu

To Vipassana International Meditation Centre (14km)

An important centre of Islamic culture, Hyderabad is southern India's counterpart to the Mughal splendour of Delhi, Agra and Fatehpur Sikri, and a sizeable percentage of Hyderabad's population is Muslim. The city gracefully combines Hindu and Islamic traditions – while a strategically placed 17.5m-high Buddha looks on.

You're likely to be taken aback by the chilled-out kindness of Hyderabadis, and many find the city delightful: lots to see and do with almost none of the hassle found in other parts.

History

Hyderabad owes its existence to a water shortage. Towards the end of the 16th century, the banks of the Musi River proved to be a preferable location for Mohammed Quli, of the Qutb Shahi dynasty. The royal family abandoned Golconda Fort and established the new city of Hyderabad there. In 1687 it was overrun by the Mughal emperor Aurangzeb. Subsequent rulers of Hyderabad were viceroys, installed by the Mughal administration in Delhi.

In 1724 the Hyderabad viceroy, Asaf Jah, took advantage of waning Mughal power and declared Hyderabad an independent state with himself as leader. The dynasty of the nizams of Hyderabad began, and the traditions of Islam flourished. Hyderabad became a focus for arts, culture and learning and the centre of Islamic India. Its abundance of rare gems and minerals – the world-famous Kohinoor diamond is from here – furnished the nizams with enormous wealth.

In the early 19th century the British established a military barracks at Secunderabad, named after the nizam at the time, Sikander Jah. When Independence came in 1947, the then nizam of Hyderabad, Osman Ali Khan, considered amalgamation with Pakistan, but tensions between Muslims and Hindus increased. Military intervention saw Hyderabad join the Indian union.

Orientation

Hyderabad has three distinct areas. The Old Town by the Musi River has bustling bazaars and important landmarks, including the Charminar. North of the river is Mahatma Gandhi (Imlibun) bus station,

Hyderabad (Nampally) station and the main post office. Mahatma Gandhi Rd (MG Rd, also known as Abids Rd) runs through the Abids district, which is a good budget-accommodation area.

Further north again, beyond the artificial lake, the Hussain Sagar, lies Secunderabad, with its Jubilee bus station and huge railway station, the start and end point for many major trains to the region.

Jubilee Hills and Banjara Hills, west of Hussain Sagar, are where the well-heeled – and their restaurants, shops and lounges – reside. Further west is Cyberabad's capital, Hitec (Hyderabad Information Technology Engineering Consulting) City, with its landmark Cybertowers housing numerous software-development corporations.

Information

BOOKSHOPS

On Sunday, secondhand books are sold on MG Rd in Abids; a few gems nestle among the computer books.

AA Hussain & Co (Map p414; MG Rd; ⏱ 10.30am-8.30pm Mon-Sat) Tonnes of Indian and foreign authors.

MR Book Stall (Map p414; MG Rd; ⏱ 10.30am-9pm) New and secondhand novels.

Walden (Map p412; ☎ 23413434; Greenlands Rd, Begumpet; ⏱ 9am-8.30pm) Megastore with books, magazines and stationery.

CULTURAL CENTRES & LIBRARIES

Alliance Française (Map p412; ☎ 27700734; www.afindia.org; Rd No 16, West Marredpally, Secunderabad; ⏱ 9am-1pm & 2-6pm Mon-Fri, 9am-1pm Sat)

British Library (Map p414; ☎ 23230774; www.britishcouncilonline.org; Secretariat Rd; ⏱ 11am-7pm Tue-Sun) British newspapers and a library for books, CDs and videos. Annual membership costs Rs 800.

State Library (Map p412; ☎ 24600107; Maulvi Allaudin Rd; ⏱ 8am-8pm Fri-Wed) Has more than three million books, including some rare and precious manuscripts.

INTERNET ACCESS

iWay (Map p412; Taj Tristar Hotel Bldg, SD Rd, Secunderabad; per hr Rs 30; ⏱ 8am-midnight)

Reliance Web World (Map p414; MPM Mall, Abids Circle; per hr Rs 30; ⏱ 9.30am-11pm)

LEFT LUGGAGE

The Hyderabad and Secunderabad train stations, as well as Mahatma Gandhi bus station, have left-luggage facilities, charging Rs 10 per bag per day.

MEDIA

Channel 6 and **Wow! Hyderabad** (www.wowhydera bad.com) are good 'what's on' guides, available at newsstands and bookshops (Rs 15).

MEDICAL SERVICES

Apollo Pharmacy (Map p414; ☎ 23431707; Hyderguda Main Rd; ☉ 24hr) Can sometimes deliver.

Care Hospital Banjara Hills (Map p412; ☎ 55668888; Rd No 1); Nampally (Map p414; ☎ 55517777; Mukarramjahi Rd) Reputable hospital with 24-hour pharmacy.

MONEY

The banks offer the best currency-exchange rates here. American Express (Amex) and Thomas Cook change currency and trav-

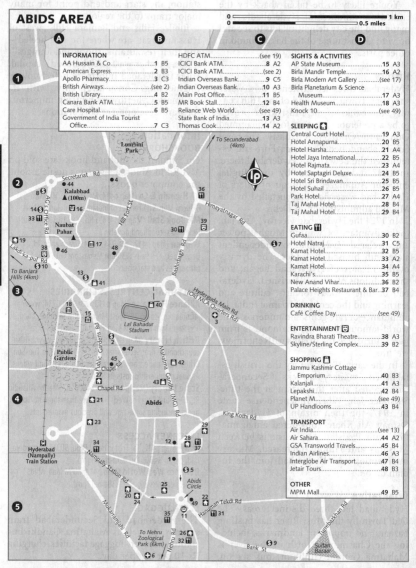

ABIDS AREA

0 —————— 1 km
0 —————— 0.5 miles

INFORMATION		
AA Hussain & Co....................**1** B5	HDFC ATM.......................(see 19)	SIGHTS & ACTIVITIES
American Express...................**2** B3	ICICI Bank ATM...................**8** A2	AP State Museum.................**15** A3
Apollo Pharmacy...................**3** C3	ICICI Bank ATM...................(see 2)	Birla Mandir Temple.............**16** A3
British Airways.....................(see 2)	Indian Overseas Bank...........**9** C5	Birla Modern Art Gallery ....(see 17)
British Library......................**4** B2	Indian Overseas Bank..........**10** A3	Birla Planetarium & Science
Canara Bank ATM...................**5** B5	Main Post Office..................**11** B5	Museum........................**17** A3
Care Hospital.......................**6** B5	MR Book Stall.....................**12** B4	Health Museum..................**18** A3
Government of India Tourist	Reliance Web World..............(see 49)	Knock 10.........................(see 49)
Office...........................**7** C3	State Bank of India..............**13** A3	
	Thomas Cook....................**14** A2	SLEEPING 🛏
		Central Court Hotel..............**19** A3
		Hotel Annapurna..................**20** B5
		Hotel Harsha......................**21** A4
		Hotel Jaya International...........**22** B5
		Hotel Rajmata....................**23** A4
		Hotel Saptagiri Deluxe............**24** B5
		Hotel Sri Brindavan...............**25** B5
		Hotel Suhail......................**26** B5
		Park Hotel.........................**27** A4
		Taj Mahal Hotel...................**28** B4
		Taj Mahal Hotel...................**29** B4
		EATING 🍴
		Gufaa.............................**30** B2
		Hotel Natraj......................**31** C5
		Kamat Hotel......................**32** B5
		Kamat Hotel......................**33** A2
		Kamat Hotel......................**34** A4
		Karachi's..........................**35** B4
		New Anand Vihar.................**36** B2
		Palace Heights Restaurant & Bar..**37** B4
		DRINKING
		Café Coffee Day..................(see 49)
		ENTERTAINMENT 🎭
		Ravindra Bharati Theatre.........**38** A3
		Skyline/Sterling Complex.........**39** B2
		SHOPPING 🛍
		Jammu Kashmir Cottage
		Emporium.....................**40** B3
		Kalanjali.........................**41** A3
		Lepakshi..........................**42** B4
		Planet M.........................(see 49)
		UP Handlooms...................**43** B4
		TRANSPORT
		Air India..........................(see 13)
		Air Sahara........................**44** A2
		GSA Transworld Travels..........**45** B4
		Indian Airlines....................**46** A3
		Interglobe Air Transport..........**47** B4
		Jetair Tours......................**48** B3
		OTHER
		MPM Mall........................**49** B5

Map labels: To Secunderabad (4km); Lumbini Park; Secretariat Rd; Kalabhad ▲(100m); Naubat Pahar ▲; Himayatnagar Rd; Hill Fort St; AG's Office Rd; Lakdi-ka-pul Rd; To Banjara Hills (4km); Bashirbagh Rd; Hyderguda Main Rd (Old MLA Quarters Rd); Lal Bahadur Stadium; Public Gardens Rd; Public Gardens; Chapel Rd; Mahatma Gandhi (MG) Rd; Abids; King Kothi Rd; Hyderabad (Nampally) Train Station; Nampally Station Rd; Abids Circle; Mukarramjahi Rd; Hanuman Tekdi Rd; To Nehru Zoological Park (6km); Nehru Rd; Bank St; Turrebazkhan Rd; Sultan Bazaar

ANDHRA PRADESH

ellers cheques with no commission. ATMs accepting international cards and Visa are scattered around town; HDFC Bank and ICICI have several.

American Express (Map p414; ☎ 23231613; Chapel Rd; ✆ 9.30am-6.30pm Mon-Fri, to 2.30pm Sat)

Indian Overseas Bank (Map p414; ☎ 24756655; Bank St; ✆ 10.30am-3pm Mon-Fri)

State Bank of India (Map p414; ☎ 23210301; HACA Bhavan, AG's Office Rd; ✆ 10.30am-4pm Mon-Fri)

Thomas Cook (Map p414; ☎ 23296521; Nasir Arcade, AG's Office Rd; ✆ 9.30am-6pm Mon-Fri, to 5pm Sat)

POST

Head post office (Map p412; Rashtrapati Rd, Secunderabad) Keeps the same hours as the main post office.

Main post office (Map p414; Abids Circle; ✆ 8am-8.30pm Mon-Sat, 10am-6pm Sun, poste restante 10am-noon Mon-Sat) Doubles as the local landmark.

TOURIST INFORMATION

Andhra Pradesh Tourism (APTDC) Hyderabad (Map p412; ☎ 23453036; www.aptourism.com; Tankbund Rd; ✆ 8am-8pm); Secunderabad (Map p412; ☎ 27893100; Yatri Nivas Hotel, SP Rd; ✆ 7am-7.30pm) Organises tours.

Government of India Tourist Office (Map p414; hotline ☎ 1363, office ☎ 23261360; Netaji Bhavan, Himayatnagar Rd; ✆ 9.30am-6pm Mon-Fri, to 2pm Sat)

Sights

CHARMINAR & BAZAARS

Hyderabad's principal landmark, the **Charminar** (Four Towers; Map p412; admission Rs 5; ✆ 9am-5.30pm) was built by Mohammed Quli Qutb Shah in 1591 to commemorate the end of a devastating epidemic. Standing 56m high and 30m wide, this four-columned structure creates four arches facing the cardinal points. There's a minaret sitting atop each column.

The small mosque on the 2nd floor is the oldest in Hyderabad. It has spiral staircases that lead up the columns, where there are views of the city. With luck, the man with the key will let you in for Rs 100. The structure is illuminated from 7pm to 9pm daily.

West of the Charminar, the famous **Laad Bazaar** (Map p412) has everything from the finest perfumes, fabrics and jewels to musical instruments and kitchen implements. You can see artists creating their works of fine *bidri* (inlaid silverware), large pots and musical instruments. The lanes around the Charminar form the centre of India's pearl

trade. Some great deals can be had – if you know your stuff.

MECCA MASJID

Adjacent to the Charminar is the **Mecca Masjid** (Map p412; Patthargatti; ✆ 8am-noon & 3-8pm), one of the world's largest mosques, with space for 10,000 worshippers. Construction began in 1614, during Mohammed Quli Qutb Shah's reign, but the mosque wasn't finished until 1687, by which time the Mughal emperor Aurangzeb had annexed the Golconda kingdom. The minarets were originally intended to be much higher but, as he did with the Bibi-qa-Maqbara in Aurangabad, Aurangzeb sacrificed aesthetics for economics.

Several bricks embedded above the gate are made with soil from Mecca – hence the name. The colonnades and door arches, with their inscriptions from the Quran, are made from single slabs of granite that were quarried 11km away and dragged here by a team of 1400 bullocks.

To the left of the mosque, an enclosure contains the tombs of Nizam Ali Khan and his successors. Guides here offer tours for around Rs 50.

SALAR JUNG MUSEUM

The huge collection of the **Salar Jung Museum** (Map p412; ☎ 24523211; Salar Jung Marg; Indian/foreigner Rs 10/150; ✆ 10am-5pm Sat-Thu), dating back to the 1st century, was put together by Mir Yusaf Ali Khan (Salar Jung III), the grand vizier of the seventh nizam, Osman Ali Khan. The 35,000 exhibits from every corner of the world include sculptures, wood carvings, devotional objects, Persian miniature paintings, illuminated manuscripts, weaponry and more than 50,000 books.

Avoid visiting the museum on Sunday when it's bedlam. From any of the bus stands in the Abids area, take bus No 7, which stops at the nearby Musi River bridge.

Not far west of the bridge, facing each other across the river, are the spectacular **High Court** (Map p412) and **Osmania General Hospital** (Map p412) buildings, built in the Indo-Saracenic style.

GOLCONDA FORT

Although the bulk of this 16th-century **fortress** (Map p416; Indian/foreigner Rs 5/100; ✆ 8am-6.30pm Tue-Sun) dates from the time of the Qutb

Shah kings, its origins, as a mud fort, have been traced to the earlier reigns of the Yadavas and Kakatiyas.

Golconda had been the capital of the independent state of Telangana for nearly 80 years when Sultan Quli Qutb Shah abandoned the fort in 1590 and moved to the new city of Hyderabad.

In the 17th century, Mughal armies from Delhi were sent to the Golconda kingdom to enforce payment of tribute. Abul Hasan, last of the Qutb Shahi kings, held out at Golconda for eight months against Emperor Aurangzeb's massive army. The emperor finally succeeded with the aid of a treacherous insider.

It's easy to see how the Mughal army was nearly defeated. The citadel is built on a granite hill 120m high and surrounded by crenellated ramparts constructed from large masonry blocks. Outside the citadel there stands another crenellated rampart, with a perimeter of 11km, and yet another wall beyond this. The massive gates were studded with iron spikes to obstruct war elephants.

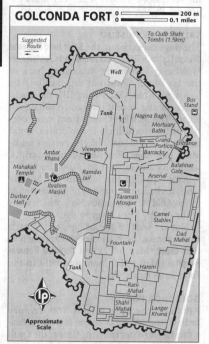

GOLCONDA FORT

Survival within the fort was also attributable to water and sound. A series of concealed glazed earthen pipes ensured a reliable water supply, while the acoustics guaranteed that even the smallest sound from the Grand Portico would echo across the fort complex.

Knowledgeable guides around the entrance will ask Rs 250 for a 1½-hour tour and lose interest in any offer below Rs 150. You can usually find the *Guide to Golconda Fort & Qutb Shahi Tombs* (Rs 10) on sale here.

An autorickshaw from Abids costs around Rs 150 return, including waiting time. Early morning is best for peace and quiet.

A trippy **sound-and-light show** (admission Rs 25; English version ⏲ 6.30pm Nov-Feb, 7pm Mar-Oct) is also held here.

TOMBS OF QUTB SHAHI KINGS

These graceful domed **tombs** (Off Map p416; admission Rs 10, camera/video Rs 20/100; ⏲ 9.30am-5.30pm) sit serenely in landscaped gardens about 1.5km northwest of Golconda Fort's Balahisar Gate. You could easily spend half a day here taking photos and wandering in and out of the mausoleums and various other structures. The upper level of Mohammed Quli's tomb, reached via a narrow staircase, has good views of the area. *The Qutb Shahi Tombs* (Rs 20) is sold at the ticket counter.

The tombs are an easy walk from the fort, but an autorickshaw ride shouldn't be more than Rs 15, or you could hop on bus No 80S, which stops right outside.

BUDDHA STATUE & HUSSAIN SAGAR

Hyderabad boasts one of the world's largest freestanding stone **Buddha statues** (Map p412). After five years of work on the project, it was completed in 1990. However, when the 17.5m-high, 350-tonne monolith was being ferried to its place in the **Hussain Sagar** (Map p412), the barge sank, taking eight people with it. The statue languished underwater until a Goan salvage company raised it – undamaged – in 1992. It's now on a plinth in the middle of the lake.

Frequent **boats** (Rs 25; ⏲ 9am-9pm) make a 30-minute return trip to the statue from **Lumbini Park** (Map p414; admission Rs 2; ⏲ 9am-9pm Tue-Sun), a pleasant place to enjoy Hyderabad's spectacular sunsets and the popular musical fountain. If you prefer to see Buddha from the air, five-minute **parasailing rides** (Rs 300; 9am-9pm) are sometimes available.

The Tankbund Rd promenade, which skirts the eastern shore of Hussain Sagar, has great views of the Buddha statue.

AP STATE & HEALTH MUSEUMS

The **AP State Museum** (Map p414; ☎ 23232267; Public Gardens Rd, Nampally; admission Rs 10; 10.30am-5pm Sat-Thu) hosts a small collection of important archaeological finds from the area, as well as a small but fascinating exhibition of photographs and letters of Mahatma Gandhi. The museum is floodlit at night.

Well worth a visit is the nearby **Health Museum** (admission free; 10.30am-1.30pm & 2-5pm Mon-Sat), where you'll see a bizarre collection of medical and public-health paraphernalia.

BIRLA MANDIR TEMPLE & PLANETARIUM

The **Birla Mandir Temple** (Map p414; 7am-noon & 2-9pm), constructed of white Rajasthani marble in 1976, graces Kalabahad (Black Mountain), one of two rocky hills overlooking the southern end of Hussain Sagar. Dedicated to Lord Venkateshwara, the temple is a popular Hindu pilgrimage centre and affords excellent views over the city, especially at sunset.

The **Birla Planetarium & Science Museum** (Map p414; ☎ 23235081; planetarium Rs 15, museum Rs 13; museum 10.30am-8pm, till 3pm Fri, closed last Thu of month) is on Naubat Pahar (Drum Rock), the hill adjacent to the Birla Mandir Temple. The planetarium has daily sessions in English at 11.30am, 4pm and 6pm. The museum has exhibits on science through the ages, as well as some excellent art and archaeological exhibitions. The small **Birla Modern Art Gallery** (Map p414; admission Rs 10; 10.30am-6pm), next door, is worth a browse.

INDIRA GANDHI PARK

Crammed full of big old palm trees, this spacious **park** (Map p412; admission Rs 5; 8am-7pm), just east of Tankbund Rd, is a welcome retreat from the heat and bustle of the city. It has a playground and a small artificial lake where you can rent boats, but the best thing to do is pull up a shady piece of grass and chill out for a while.

RAMOJI FILM CITY

Connoisseurs of Bollywood kitsch cannot afford to miss the four-hour tour of **Ramoji Film City** (Off Map p412; ☎ 23235678; www.ramojifilmcity.com; admission Rs 200; 9am-6pm), an 800-hectare movie-making complex. This place has everything – dance routines, gaudy fountains, flimsy film sets – and the whole thing wraps up with a Wild West song-and-dance number. The 'Royal Package' (Rs 700) gets you AC transport and lunch at a five-star hotel. Bus No 205, 206 or 207 from the Women's College, 100m northeast of Koti bus station, takes about an hour to get here.

NEHRU ZOOLOGICAL PARK

One of India's largest zoos, the **Nehru Zoological Park** (Zoo Park; Map p412; ☎ 24477355; Nehru Zoological Park Rd; admission Rs 10, camera Rs 10; 9am-5pm Tue-Sun) spreads over 1.2 sq km of landscaped gardens. Its 3000 animals live in large, open enclosures. It's certainly less depressing than the average Asian zoo. Lion 'safaris' (Rs 15) run throughout the day.

Activities

The Theravada **Ananda Buddha Vihara** (Map p412; ☎ 27732421; www.buddhavihara.com; Mahendra Hills; 5.30am-12.30pm & 4-8.30pm) will eventually include a museum of Buddhist art and a library of Buddhist literature. At the time of writing, only the temple – on a hill with incredible views – was complete. Meditation sessions and discourses are held Sundays 5pm to 7pm and on full-moon days from 11am; instruction is provided.

An autorickshaw from Abids will cost around Rs 40.

Courses

The **Vipassana International Meditation Centre** (Dhamma Khetta; Off Map p412; ☎ 24240290; www.dhamma.org; Nagarjuna Sagar Rd, Kusumnagar) offers intensive 10-day meditation courses at its lush, peaceful grounds 20km outside the city. Courses are given free of charge; apply by email or at the Hyderabad **office** (☎ 24732569). A shuttle runs to/from Hyderabad on the first and last day of courses.

Tours

APTDC (see p415) conducts numerous tours, including full-day city (Rs 190), Ramoji Film City (Rs 375), Nagarjuna Sagar (Rs 310) and Tirupathi (Rs 1725, three days) tours. The evening city tour (Rs 140) takes in Hitec City, the botanic gardens and Golconda Fort's sound-and-light show.

The **Save the Rocks Society** (Off Map p412; ☎ 23 552923; www.hyderabadgreens.org; 1236 Rd No 60, Jubilee Hills) organises monthly walks through the Andhran landscape to raise awareness of the damage done by intensive quarrying.

Sleeping

Most hotels charge a 5% 'luxury' tax, which is not included in the prices quoted here. Rooms tend to fill up so call ahead.

BUDGET

The best cheap hotels are in the Abids area between Abids Circle and Hyderabad train station. All hotels listed below have 24-hour checkout.

Hotel Sri Brindavan (Map p414; ☎ 23203970; fax 232 00204; Nampally Station Rd; s/d from Rs 315/400; ※) The curved balcony and fresh lemon-yellow paint give this well-ordered place a slight Art Deco feel. Rooms are tidy and compact, and those in the back are surprisingly peaceful.

Hotel Suhail (Map p414; ☎ 24610299; Troop Bazaar; s/d from Rs 160/250) Tucked away behind the main post office and the Grand Hotel, the Suhail is an excellent deal. Rooms are large and quiet and have balcony and constant hot water.

Hotel Saptagiri Deluxe (Map p414; ☎ 24603601; www.hotelsaptagirindeluxe.com; Nampally Station Rd; r from Rs 400; ※) It doesn't give the warmest welcome in town, but rooms, though small, are clean and newish.

Park Hotel (Map p414; ☎ 55789125; Public Gardens Rd; s/d from Rs 325/435; ※) The rooms here are small and the paint's chipped, but they're very clean and have balcony.

Hotel Annapurna (Map p414; ☎ 24732616; Nampally Station Rd; s/d from Rs 175/275) It's very run-down but has a certain *je ne sais quoi*. Rooms are arranged in a circle like pie pieces, there's kitschy mirror art in the lobby and the staff are vaguely professional.

If you arrive late at Secunderabad train station, try the clean but noisy **retiring rooms** (☎ 27786802; dm from Rs 50, s/d from Rs 150/250; ※) or nearby **Devi Deluxe Lodge** (Map p412; ☎ 27713913; Rezimental Bazaar; s/d from Rs 300/350; ※).

MIDRANGE

APTDC's paying-guest programme (☎ 23450444; reservations 24hr) can find you rooms in private homes for around Rs 500 to 600.

The following all have 24-hour checkout.

Hotel Jaya International (Map p414; ☎ 24752929; hoteljaya@sancharnet.in; Hanuman Tekdi Rd; s/d from Rs 400/495; ※) Sunny, central, well run – and often full so book ahead. The Rs 25 buffet breakfast is a bargain.

Hotel Rajmata (Map p414; ☎ 55665555; fax 2320 4133; Public Gardens Rd; s/d Rs 590/690) Rooms here vary; the better ones are big and bright. It's a little overpriced, but the place is professionally run and has a helpful travel desk.

Taj Mahal Hotel (Map p414; ☎ 30622256; sundar taj@satyam.net.in; cnr MG & King Kothi Rds; s/d incl breakfast from Rs 700/1050; ※) This rambling heritage building has plants peppered about, old-fashioned window frames and antique furniture in some of the rooms. Some are better than others so ask to see a few.

Taj Mahal Hotel (Map p414; ☎ 24758221; King Kothi Rd; s/d from Rs 450/700; ※) The copycat Taj, just east of the original, is nice in a different way, with spacious rooms set back from the road. All have balconies and good bathrooms with constant hot water.

Hotel Harsha (Map p414; ☎ 23201188; www.hotel harsha.net; Public Gardens Rd; s/d from Rs 690/825; ※) The recently renovated Harsha has bright rooms with big windows. New bathrooms have gleaming tiles, constant hot water and postmodern toilets.

Yatri Nivas Hotel (Map p412; ☎ 27816881; SP Rd, Secunderabad; s/d Rs 800/900) Retro, with large, clean rooms with constant hot water, as well as two decent restaurants and a passable bar.

TOP END

Central Court Hotel (Map p414; ☎ 23232323; www .thecentralcourt.com; Lakdi-ka-pul; s/d incl breakfast from Rs 1795/2695; ※ 🖳) Central, spotless and very efficiently run, with free airport drop off. Staff are happy and eager to please.

Fortune Katriya Hotel (Map p412; ☎ 23325678; www.fortunekatriya.com; Raj Bhavan Rd, Somajiguda; s/d incl breakfast from US$70/85; ※ 🖳) The Katriya, relatively new on the scene, is good value for the money; rooms are simple but classy, with all the mod cons (except carpeting).

Taj Krishna (Map p412; ☎ 55662323; www.tajhotels .com; Rd No 1 Banjara Hills; s/d from US$200/225; ※ 🖳) The sort of opulence you expect for the price: a lobby resembling a *mahal* (palace), marble-inlaid hallway floors and rooms with elegant furniture and piles of taffeta pillows.

Eating

Andhra Pradesh's cuisine has two major influences. The Mughals brought tasty biryanis, *haleen* (pounded, spiced wheat with mutton – see the boxed text, p420) and kebabs. The Andhra style is vegetarian and famous for its spiciness.

CITY CENTRE
Mozamjahi Market (Map p412; cnr Mukarramjahi & Jawaharlal Nehru Rds; 6am-6pm) A great place to buy fruit and veggies (or ice cream), while enjoying the alluring architecture.

Kamat Hotel (Map p412; SD Rd, Secunderabad; meals Rs 20-70; 7am-10pm;) Each Kamat (other branches are located on AG's Office Rd, Nampally Station Rd and Troop Bazaar – see map p414) is slightly different, but they're all cheap and good. The thalis (Rs 25 to 37) are reliably delish.

Hotel Natraj (Map p414; Hanuman Tekdi Rd; meals Rs 18; 6.30am-11pm) A simple place serving up excellent thalis and tiffins (snacks).

Hotel Nayaab (Map p412; Patthargatti; mains Rs 30-80; 4am-midnight) This Old Town restaurant/bakery does mutton, chicken, kebabs and biryani and has the best ceiling in town.

New Anand Vihar (Map p414; cnr Himayatnagar & Bashirbagh Rds; snacks Rs 8-35; 8.30am-10.30pm) Excellent *pav bhaji* (vegetable curry sandwiches), samosa *chaat* (snacks with a variety of flavours) and other snacks.

Minerva Coffee Shop (Map p412; Salar Jung Marg; mains Rs 60-85; 7.30am-10.30pm;) The North Indian thali (Rs 85) in this old-school coffee shop is a delight – five delicious curries, topped off with fruit salad and ice cream. All with a river view.

Paradise Persis Restaurant (Map p412; cnr SP & MG Rds, Secunderabad; meals Rs 50-150; 11.30am-11.30pm) This place has a range of eating options, from footpath kebab joints to fancy rooftop dining. It's known for its biryanis.

SOMETHING SPECIAL

Gufaa (Map p414; Ohri's Cuisine Court, Bashirbagh Rd; mains Rs 115-195; 11.30am-3.30pm & 7pm-midnight;) The most eccentric member of Hyderabad's theme-restaurant family has faux-rock walls with African masks, leopard-print upholstery, twinkling stars on the ceiling and red roses on the tables. And, it serves Peshawari food. But somehow it works, and even 'dhal with roti' (black dhal stewed with fresh cream and tomatoes, and roti made with chillies) becomes something extraordinary here.

Palace Heights Restaurant & Bar (Map p414; 8th fl, Triveni Complex; mains Rs 90-170; noon-11pm;) This pearl in the dirty shell of an old city-centre building has incredible views. The service is excellent, the wine list reasonable (Rs 500 a bottle) and the menu extensive.

Karachi's (Map p414; Jawaharlal Nehru Rd, Abids; meals Rs 15-35; 10.30am-10.30pm Tue-Sun;) A tacky, fun fast-food joint with good *chaat* (snacks), pizza and the enigmatic 'Chinese dosa'.

BANJARA HILLS
Mainland China (Map p412; GS Plaza, Rd No 1; mains Rs 110-225; 12.30-3.30pm & 7.30-11.30pm;) Fabulous Chinese food in a soothing setting. Subtle flavours include sliced fish with Shaoxiang wine and wood ear mushrooms.

Ohri's Far East (Map p412; Rd No 12; mains Rs 100-220; noon-midnight;) The pan-Asian menu here includes some exquisite dishes – try the Malay fried bean sprouts with grated coconut (Rs 130). Tadka, a good North Indian restaurant, is just downstairs.

Angeethi (Map p412; 7th fl, Reliance Classic Bldg, Rd No 1; mains Rs 90-150; 12.30-3.30pm & 7-11.30pm;) The setting, designed to resemble an old Punjabi *dhaba* (snack bar), is over the top. But Angeethi does truly outstanding North Indian and Punjabi dishes, such as corn *methi malai* (sweet-corn stew with fenugreek leaves).

Drinking
CAFÉS
Hyderabad's wired, after all, so of course there's:

Barista (Map p412; Reliance Classic Bldg, Rd No 1; coffees Rs 20-45; 8am-11.30pm;)

Café Coffee Day (Map p414; MPM Mall; coffees Rs 15-40; 8am-11.30pm;)

BARS
Begumpet has some OK bars, but otherwise, the only respectable places to drink are Banjara Hills' atmospheric and expensive lounges. The following all serve lunch and dinner, but lounging runs from around 6pm to midnight. Beer starts at Rs 120, cocktails at Rs 250.

Touch (Map p412; Trendset Towers, Rd No 2, Banjara Hills; per couple Sat Rs 1000;) Sporting a sort of feminine *Star Wars* look, with futuristic white furniture and chiffon screens, Touch is all about image. It's a stylish, comfy place to watch the beautiful people.

ANDHRA PRADESH

BEATING THE BHATTIS

If you're travelling around Andhra Pradesh during Ramadan (known locally as Rama-zan), look out for the clay ovens called *bhattis*. You'll probably hear them before you see them. Men gather around, taking turns to vigorously pound *haleen* (a mixture of meat and wheat) inside purpose-built structures. Come nightfall, the serious business of eating begins. The taste is worth the wait.

Fusion 9 (Map p414; 1st Ave, Rd No 1, Banjara Hills; 🍴) Soft lighting and cosy décor are a nice backdrop to live jazz on Fridays. The food here (mains Rs 140 to 215) is also good.

Cinnabar Redd (Map p412; 1st Ave, Rd No 1, Banjara Hills; 🍴) In the same building as Fusion 9, Cinnabar Redd is draped in red velvet and candlelight. There's a DJ on weekends, and ladies get a free drink on Tuesdays.

Entertainment

Knock 10 (Map p414; ☎ 55250055; MPM Mall; Rs 75-90; 🕙 9.30am-midnight) Bowling, bumper cars and Skee-ball.

Ravindra Bharati Theatre (Map p414; ☎ 2323 3672; www.artistap.com; Public Gardens Rd) This theatre has regular performances of music, dance and drama. Check local papers for details.

Hyderabad Film Club (Map p412; ☎ 23730265; Ameerpet) The film club shows foreign films, sometimes in conjunction with the Alliance Française.

Some cinemas showing English-language movies:

Prasad's Multiplex (Map p412; ☎ 23448989; NTR Marg) A monstrous IMAX theatre.

Sangeet (Map p412; ☎ 27703864; SD Rd, Secunderabad) Specialises in Hollywood blockbusters.

Skyline/Sterling Complex (Map p414; ☎ 23222633; Bashirbagh) Similar to Sangeet.

Shopping

The bazaars near the Charminar (see p415) are the most exciting places to shop. Here you'll find exquisite pearls, silks, gold and fabrics alongside billions of bangles.

Hyderabad Perfumers (Map p412; Patthargatti; 🕙 10am-8.30pm Mon-Sat) The family-run Hyderabad Perfumers, which has been in business for four generations, can whip something up for you on the spot.

Afreen Suits & Saris (Map p412; Patthargatti; 🕙 11am-11pm) Has a wide range of silks and fabrics at fixed prices and accepts credit cards.

Fabindia (Map p412; Rd No 9, Banjara Hills; 🕙 10am-7.30pm Tue-Sun) The fabulous Fabindia has ready-made traditional men's and women's clothes in stunning fabrics at good prices.

Planet M (Map p414; MPM Mall; 🕙 11am-9pm) This is the place to get your English-subtitled Bollywood DVDs.

Kalanjali (Map p414; Public Gardens Rd; 🕙 9.30am-8.30pm Mon-Sat) With a huge range of arts, crafts, fabrics and clothing, Kalanjali is a good place to prepare for the bazaar: the prices are higher, but you'll get a feel for what things are worth in a relaxed environment.

These are some of Hyderabad's many state outlets:

Jammu Kashmir Cottage Emporium (Map p414; Babukhan Estate, Bashirbagh Rd; 🕙 9.30am-9pm Mon-Sat)

Lepakshi (Map p414; Gunfoundry; 🕙 10am-8pm Mon-Sat) Andhra crafts.

UP Handlooms (Map p414; MG Rd; 🕙 10am-8.30pm Mon-Sat) Crafts and furniture from Uttar Pradesh.

Getting There & Away

Hyderabad has air, road and rail links to most major Indian cities. Most international flights go via Mumbai (Bombay).

AIR

Airline offices are generally open 10am to 5.30pm Monday to Friday, with a break for lunch, and 10am to 1pm Saturday.

Indian Airlines (Map p414; ☎ 23299333; AG's Office Rd) has flights to Tirupathi (US$95, four weekly), Bangalore (US$125, twice daily), Visakhapatnam (US$120, one daily), Chennai (Madras; US$125, three daily), Mumbai (US$130, three daily), Kolkata (Calcutta; US$230, one daily), and Delhi (US$230, two daily).

Jet Airways (Map p412; ☎ 23401222; Nav Bharat Chambers, Raj Bhavan Rd, Somajiguda), with similar prices to Indian Airlines, flies daily to Bangalore, Chennai, Delhi, Kolkata and Mumbai. **Air Sahara** (Map p414; ☎ 23212237; Secretariat Rd) has daily flights to Bangalore, Delhi, Kolkata and Pune. **Air Deccan** (Map p412; ☎ 30902527, call centre ☎ 9845777008; 1st Ave, Rd No 1, Banjara Hills) flies daily to Bangalore, Chennai, Delhi, Tirupathi, Vijayawada and Visakhapatnam for about half the price of the others.

Some of Hyderabad's international airline offices:

Air India (Map p414; ☎ 23389711; HACA Bhavan, AG's Office Rd)

British Airways (Map p414; ☎ 23241661; Chapel Rd)

Cathay Pacific (Map p412; ☎ 27702234; 44 SD Rd, Secunderabad)

GSA Transworld Travels (Map p414; ☎ 23210947; Chapel Rd) For Qantas.

Interglobe Air Transport (Map p414; ☎ 23233590; Chapel Rd) For Air New Zealand, Delta, South African, United and Virgin Atlantic.

Jetair Tours (Map p414; ☎ 23230947; 1st fl, Summit House, Hill Fort Rd) For Air France, American and Gulf Air.

BUS

Hyderabad's long-distance bus stations are mind-bogglingly efficient. **Mahatma Gandhi bus station** (Imlibun; Map p412; ☎ 24601126) serves all parts of the state and interstate (see the table, below), and has a **computerised advance booking office** (🕐 8am-9pm). Secunderabad's **Jubilee bus station** (Map p412; ☎ 27802203) operates buses to Bidar (Rs 56, four hours, four daily) and Bangalore (Rs 325 deluxe, 12 hours, five daily), as well as a daily Volvo AC super-deluxe bus to both Bangalore (Rs 555, 10 hours) and Chennai (Rs 600, 12 hours).

Private bus companies with super-deluxe services to Bangalore, Mumbai, Chennai, Nagpur and Tirupathi have offices on Nampally High Rd, near the station entrance.

Buses from Mahatma Gandhi bus station:

Destination	Fare (Rs)	Duration (hr)	Departures
Bangalore	310 (D)/550 (V)/570 (A)	12/10/10	15 daily
Bijapur	148 (O)/ 212 (D)	10	2 daily
Chennai	600 (V)	12	1 daily
Hospet	380 (D)	12	2 daily
Mumbai	380 (D)/ 700 (V)	16/12	1 daily
Nagarjunakonda	62 (O)	3	hourly
Tirupathi	293 (D)/ 500 (V)	12/10	10 daily
Vijayawada	140 (O)	6	half-hourly
Warangal	55 (O)/78 (D)	3	hourly

(O) – ordinary, (D) – semideluxe, (A) – AC sleeper, (V) –Volvo AC

TRAIN

Secunderabad (Map p412), Hyderabad (Map p412) – also known as Nampally – and Kacheguda (Map p412) are the three major train stations. Most through trains (not originating in Hyderabad) leave from Secunderabad and stop at Kacheguda, a convenient set-down for Abids. See the boxed text, p422, for key routes. Bookings can be made at Hyderabad and Secunderabad stations from 8am to 8pm Monday to Saturday (to 2pm Sunday). Both stations have a tourist counter. For general inquiries, phone ☎ 131; for reservations, ☎ 135.

Getting Around
TO/FROM THE AIRPORT

Hyderabad Airport (Map p412) is in Begumpet, 8km north of Abids. Take an autorickshaw from Abids (Rs 30 to 40) or a taxi (Rs 120). A prepaid autorickshaw from the airport costs Rs 75.

AUTORICKSHAW

Drivers are generally willing to use their meters. Flag fall is Rs 8 for the first kilometre, then Rs 4 for each additional kilometre. Between 10pm and 5am a 50% surcharge applies.

BUS

Lots of useful local buses originate at Koti bus station (Map p412), so if you come here you might get a seat. The 'travel as you like' ticket (Rs 30), available from bus conductors, permits unlimited travel anywhere within the city on the day of purchase.

Useful local bus routes:

Bus No	Route
20D	Jubilee station–Charminar
1P	Secunderabad station–Jubilee station
2, 8A, 2U, 2V, 8U	Charminar–Secunderabad station
1K, 40, 1B, 3SS	Secunderabad station–Koti station
20P, 20V, 49, 49P	Secunderabad station–Nampally
65G, 66G	Charminar–Golconda
7Z	Secunderabad station–Zoo Park
87	Charminar–Nampally
1190R, 142M	Nampally–Golconda
142K	Koti–Golconda

CAR

There are places around Nampally station where you can rent a car and driver; **City Cabs**

(☎ 27760000; Begumpet) is reliable for local taxis. For longer trips, try **Banjara Travels** (☎ 23394368; Rd No 12, Banjara Hills) or **Ravi's Tours & Travels** (☎ 55768462; DK Rd, Ameerpet).

NAGARJUNAKONDA
☎ 08680

The ancient remains at this site, 150km southeast of Hyderabad, were discovered in 1926 by archaeologist AR Saraswathi. Two major excavations were carried out before 1953, when it became known that the area would be flooded by the **Nagarjuna Sagar**, the reservoir to be created by a massive hydro-electric project in 1960. A major six-year excavation was undertaken to unearth the area's many Buddhist ruins: stupas, *viharas* (monastery complexes), *chaityas* (temples) and *mandapams* (pillared pavilions), as well as some outstanding examples of white-marble depictions of the Buddha's life. The finds were reassembled on Nagarjuna-konda, an island in the middle of the dam.

Prehistoric remnants suggest human activity began here around 200,000 years ago. From the 2nd century BC until the early 3rd century AD, Nagarjunakonda and nearby Amaravathi became the sites of powerful Hindu and Buddhist empires.

Nagarjunakonda may be named after Nagarjuna, the revered Buddhist monk who governed the sangha (community of Bud-dhist priests) for nearly 60 years in the 2nd century AD. He founded the Madhyamika school, which studied and developed the teachings of Mahayana Buddhism.

Sights
NAGARJUNAKONDA MUSEUM

This thoughtfully laid-out **museum** (Indian/foreigner Rs 2/US$2; ⏱ 9.30am-3.45pm Sat-Thu) has Stone Age picks, hoes and spears on exhibit, but more impressive are its Buddha statues and the carved stone slabs that once adorned stupas. Most of them are from the 3rd century AD and depict scenes from the Buddha's life, interspersed with *mithuna* (pairs of men and women) figures languorously looking on.

Launches (Rs 45, one hour) depart for the island from Vijayapuri, on the banks of Nagarjuna Sagar, at 8.30am and 1.30pm daily.

The launch stays at the island for 30 minutes. To do the place justice, take the morning launch out and the afternoon one back. Weekends and holidays are crowded, so extra express launches may run for Rs 60. Bring food and water with you.

Sleeping & Eating

Nagarjunakonda is popular, and accommodation can be tight during May school holidays.

MAJOR TRAINS FROM HYDERABAD & SECUNDERABAD

Destination	Train no & name	Fare (Rs)	Duration (hr)	Departures
Bangalore	2430 *Rajdhani*	1065/1625	12	7.25pm S (Mon, Tue, Fri & Sat)
	7085 *Secunderabad-Bangalore Exp*	268/762/1118	12	6.40pm S, 7pm K
Chennai	7054 *Hyderabad-Chennai Exp*	281/762/1118	13	3.45pm H, 4.20pm S
	2760 *Charminar Exp*	319/837/1260	14	8.10pm H, 8.40pm S
Delhi	2723 *Andhra Pradesh Exp*	473/1275/1991	22	6.40am H, 7.10am S
	2429/2437 *Rajdhani*	1750/2520	22	6.55am S (Mon-Fri)
Kolkata	2704 *Falaknuma Exp*	434/1078/1873	27	5.40pm S
	7046 *East Coast Exp*	454/1088/1883	31½	6.50am H, 7.10am S
Mumbai	7002 *Hussain-Sagar Exp*	297/762/1118	15	2.20pm H
	7032 *Hyderabad-Mumbai Exp*	297/762/1118	16	8.40pm H
Tirupathi	7424 *Narayanadri Exp*	268/762/1118	14	6pm S
	7497 *Venkatadri Exp*	268/762/1118	12	8pm K

S – Secunderabad, H – Hyderabad, K – Kacheguda. Rajdhani fares are 3AC/2AC; express (Exp) fares are sleeper/3AC/2AC.

Nagarjuna Resort (☎ 08642-242471; r from Rs 370; ✷) The most convenient place to stay, right across the road from the boat launch, has spacious rooms with geysers. Those in front have good views, and there's a multi-cuisine restaurant.

Project House (Punnami; ☎ 276540; r from Rs 200; ✷) This place is 5km from the jetty, opposite the main bus stand in Hill Colony. Rooms are basic but clean enough, and the veg restaurant is OK.

Vijay Vihar Complex (☎ 277362; r from Rs 450; ✷) A further 2km up the hill, this fancy place sits above the lake. Rooms in the Samagamam building (Rs 650) have balconies with excellent views. The restaurant has a range of veg and nonveg meals (Rs 40 to 60).

Getting There & Away
The easiest way to visit Nagarjunakonda is with **APTDC** (☎ 040-27893100; tours Rs 310). Tours depart Hyderabad daily (subject to demand) at 7am from Yatri Nivas Hotel (see p418), returning at 9.30pm.

If you'd rather make your own way there, regular buses link Hyderabad and Vijayawada with Nagarjuna Sagar. The nearest train station is 22km away at Macherla, from where buses leave regularly for Nagarjuna Sagar.

WARANGAL
☎ 0870 / pop 528,570
Warangal was the capital of the Kakatiya kingdom, which covered the greater part of present-day Andhra Pradesh from the late 12th to early 14th centuries until it was conquered by the Tughlaqs of Delhi. The Hindu Kakatiyas were great builders and patrons of the arts, and it was during their reign that the Chalukyan style of temple architecture reached its pinnacle.

If you're interested in Hindu temple development, then it's worth the trip to Warangal, which is also a friendly city, and Palampet (see p424). It's possible – but not leisurely – to visit both places on a long day trip from Hyderabad, 157km away.

Warangal is a cotton market town, and there's a colourful wool market around the bus-stand area in the cooler months.

Orientation & Information
The Warangal train station and bus stand are opposite each other. The post office and police station are on Station Rd, to the left as you leave the train station. Main Rd connects Warangal and Hanamkonda.

There are some **Internet cafés** (MG Rd; per hr around Rs 40) near Hotel Ratna. Bank services in Warangal are limited to the ATM (Visa and Plus) at the **State Bank of Hyderabad** (Station Rd).

Sights
FORT
Warangal's **fort** (Indian/foreigner Rs 5/US$2) was a massive construction with three distinct circular strongholds surrounded by a moat. Four paths with decorative gateways, set according to the cardinal points, led to a huge central Shiva temple. The gateways are still obvious, but much of the fort is in ruins.

The fort is easily reached from Warangal by bus, bike or autorickshaw (Rs 50 return, including waiting time).

HANAMKONDA
Built in 1163, the **1000-Pillared Temple** (☺ 6am-6pm) on the slopes of Hanamkonda Hill, 400m from the Hanamkonda crossroads, is a fine example of Chalukyan architecture in a peaceful, leafy setting. Dedicated to three deities – Shiva, Vishnu and Surya – it has been carefully restored with intricately carved pillars and a central, very impressive Nandi.

Down the hill and 3km to the right is the small **Siddheshwara Temple**. The **Bhadrakali Temple**, featuring a stone statue of Kali, seated with a weapon in each of her eight hands, is high on a hill between Hanamkonda and Warangal.

Sleeping
Warangal has a range of good budget hotels. The train station has two **retiring rooms** (r without/with AC Rs 100/200; ✷). All those listed have 24-hour checkout.

Hotel Surya (☎ 2441834; fax 2441836; Station Rd; s/d incl breakfast from Rs 350/400; ✷) Near the stations, this modern and extremely well-run hotel has smart rooms with constant hot water and a good restaurant downstairs.

Vijaya Lodge (☎ 2501222; fax 2446864; Station Rd; s/d from Rs 120/155) About 100m up the road, the Vijaya is a great deal, with tidy, compact, lemon-yellow rooms.

Hotel Ratna (☎ 2500645; fax 2500096; MG Rd; s/d from Rs 200/299; ✷) The Ratna has shiny floors and professional staff, and it accepts MasterCard and Visa. Its veg restaurant, Kavya, gets good reviews (mains Rs 40 to 75).

Hotel Ashoka (☎ 2578491; fax 2579260; Main Rd, Hanamkonda; s/d from Rs 295/425; ❄) Not as good as the Ratna, the Ashoka is still an OK option. The compound includes a veg and nonveg restaurant, a bar/restaurant and a pub.

Eating

Warangal has several 'meals' places, some of which have seen better days. The hotel restaurants are good bets.

Sri Raghavendra Bhavan (Station Rd; meals Rs 20; ❄ 7am-10pm) Best 'meals' in Warangal. It's close to Hotel Surya.

Ruchi Tiffins (Main Rd; meals Rs 17; ❄ 7.30am-11pm) Best 'meals' in Hanamkonda.

Surabhi (Station Rd; mains Rs 40-75; ❄ 7am-11pm; ❄) Surprisingly good food in somewhat elegant surroundings. The menu includes such wonders as the 'Surabhi special dosa', stuffed with carrots, *paneer* (unfermented cheese), onions and ghee (Rs 30).

Getting There & Away

Bus services run to Vijayawada (Rs 105, seven hours, seven daily) from Warangal. Frequent buses to Hyderabad (Rs 74, 3½ hours) depart from Hanamkonda bus station, a Rs 4 bus ride away.

Warangal is a major rail junction. Trains go regularly to Hyderabad (Rs 49/209 2nd class/chair, three hours), Vijayawada (Rs 71/282 2nd class/chair, four hours) and Chennai (Rs 281/735/1126 sleeper/3AC/2AC, 10 hours). Three trains go to Delhi daily, and one train heads each day to Ahmedabad, Jaipur and Varanasi.

Getting Around

Bus No 28 goes to the fort at Mantukonda and regular buses go to all the other sites. You can rent bicycles at **Ramesh Kumar Cycle Taxi** (Station Rd; per hr Rs 2; ❄ 8am-10.15pm). A shared autorickshaw ride costs Rs 5.

AROUND WARANGAL
Palampet

About 60km northeast of Warangal, the stunning **Ramappa Temple** (❄ 6am-6.30pm), built in 1234, is an attractive example of Kakatiya architecture, although it was clearly influenced by Chalukya and Hoysala styles. Its pillars are ornately carved and its eaves shelter fine statues of female forms.

Just 1km south, the Kakatiyas constructed **Ramappa Cheruvu** to serve as temple tank. The artificial lake now assumes a natural presence in the landscape.

The best way to get here is by private car. Frequent buses run from Hanamkonda to Mulugu (Rs 22), but you may or may not get a bus from here to Palampet.

VISAKHAPATNAM
☎ 0891 / pop 1.3 million

Visakhapatnam – also known as Vizag (*vie-zag*) – is Andhra Pradesh's second-largest city, though it feels more like an aging beach-resort town. These days, it's more famous for its shipbuilding and steel industries than for its beaches, but the run-down boardwalk along Ramakrishna Beach has spunk and the beach at nearby Rushikonda is one of Andhra's best. Vizag is also a good base from which to visit the Araku Valley (see opposite).

Orientation

Vizag's train station sits in a hubbub of shops and hotels not far from the port; Waltair and its Ramakrishna Beach are 2km southeast of this, and the bus station, also known as RTC Complex, is about 1.5km northwest.

Information

ATMs are all around, including a State Bank of India ATM at the train station and an Andhra Bank ATM in the Dwarkanigar Complex near the bus station. Both take Visa.

For Internet access try **iWay** (CMR Complex, Daba Gardens, Main Rd; per hr Rs 25; ❄ 9am-9pm).

Sights & Activities

The long beaches of **Waltair** overlook the Bay of Bengal, with its mammoth ships and brightly painted fishing boats. Visible nearby is the **Dolphin's Nose**, a rocky promontory jutting into the harbour.

The best beaches for swimming are at **Rushikonda**, 8km north. On the way, **Kailasagiri Hill** has gardens, playgrounds and a gargantuan Shiva and Parvati. The views from the hill and from the **Kailasagiri Passenger Ropeway** (☎ 2551334; admission Rs 35; ❄ 11am-1pm & 3-8.30pm Nov-May, 3-6.30pm Jun-Oct) are awesome.

At Simhachalam Hill, 10km northwest of town, is a fine 11th-century **Vishnu Temple** (❄ 6-10am & 4-6pm) in Orissan style. You can give *puja* (Rs 10 to 100) to the deity, who's covered with sandalwood paste. Bus No 6 A/H goes here.

Tours

APTDC (train station ☎ 2587067, bus stand ☎ 2746446) operates full-day city tours that include Vishnu Temple (Rs 280) and day tours to the Araku Valley and Borra Caves (see right; Rs 375).

Sleeping & Eating

VISAKHAPATNAM

Budget and midrange hotels huddle around the train station, which has **railway retiring rooms** (r from Rs 200; ❄). At night, guys barbecue fish (Rs 80) along Ramakrishna Beach.

Sree Kanya Lodge (☎ 2564881; fax 2554184; Bowdara Rd; s/d from Rs 200/350; ❄) Near the train station, Sree Kanya is a clean, straightforward place with 24-hour checkout and hot water.

Park (☎ 2754488; www.theparkhotels.com; Beach Rd; s/d from Rs 2600/3000; ❄ ☐ ☎) The Park is right on the beach front, and all rooms have sea views. It's a classy place, but could use a little touch-up.

Masala (Signature Towers, Dwarakanagar; mains Rs 40-95; ☐ 11.30am-3pm & 7.30-11pm; ❄) Near Sampath Vinayaka Temple, Masala does out-of-this-world Andhra, tandoori and Chinese. Try the *royyala pulusu* (Andhrastyle prawns; Rs 85).

New Andhra Hotel (Sree Kanya Lodge, Bowdara Rd; mains Rs 25-75; ☐ 11.30am-3.30pm & 7-11.30pm; ❄) A modest little place with great, damn-hot Andhra dishes.

RUSHIKONDA

Sai Priya Resort (☎ 2790333; www.saipriya.com; cottages/r from Rs 500/800; ❄ ☎) This tranquil place on the shore has elegant rooms and cool cottages of bamboo and cane. Checkout is a rather rude 8am, though, and the service charge is a whopping 10%.

Punnami Beach Resort (☎ 2790733; r Rs 950; ❄) Set on a cliff top five minutes' walk from the beach, the Punnami has spacious rooms with bay views. The restaurant serves good, cheap food.

Getting There & Away

AIR

Vizag's **airport** (☎ 2572020) is 13km west of town. An autorickshaw should cost Rs 150. Bus No 38 will take you there for Rs 6.

Indian Airlines (☎ 2746501, 2572020; LIC Bldg) flies to Chennai (US$130, daily), Hyderabad (US$120, daily), Kolkata (US$155, three weekly) via Bhubaneswar (US$130), and Delhi (US$295, four weekly).

Air Deccan (☎ 9849677008) has daily flights to Hyderabad for around Rs 2500.

BOAT

Boats depart every now and then for Port Blair in the Andaman Islands (see p398). If you want to try your luck, bookings for the 56-hour journey can be made at the **Shipping Office** (☎ 2565597; Av Bhanoji Row; ☐ 8am-5pm) in the port complex.

BUS

You'll probably take the train to/from Vizag, but its **bus stand** (☎ 2746400) is well organised, with frequent services to Vijayawada (Rs 193 deluxe, nine hours).

TRAIN

Visakhapatnam Junction station is on the Kolkata–Chennai line. The overnight *Coromandel Express* (Rs 338/900/1385 sleeper/3AC/2AC, 15 hours) is the fastest of the six daily trains running to Kolkata. Heading south, it goes to Vijayawada (Rs 192/485/795 sleeper/3AC/2AC, 5½ hours) and Chennai (Rs 320/835/1320 sleeper/3AC/2AC, 13 hours). Seven other trains head to Vijayawada daily; four others go to Chennai.

AROUND VISAKHAPATNAM

Andhra's best train ride is through the magnificent Eastern Ghats to the **Araku Valley**, 120km north of Vizag. The area is home to isolated tribal communities, and the tiny **Museum of Habitat** (admission Rs 5; ☐ 9am-12.30pm & 1.30-5.30pm) has fascinating exhibits of

---

SOMETHING SPECIAL

Yes, it hurts to say the name, but the little forest retreat of **Jungle Bells** (Tyda; cottages from Rs 400; ❄), 45km from Araku, is the best way to immerse yourself in the mountains. Wooden cottages – including the revolutionary 'igloo hut' – are tucked away in lush woods, and light trekking is possible. Book at the offices of the **APTDC** (bus stand ☎ 2746446, train station ☎ 2587067) in Vizag.

indigenous life. APTDC (see p425) runs a tour from Vizag, which takes in the million-year-old limestone **Borra Caves** 30km away, filled with stalagmites and stalactites.

The **Mayuri Hill Resort** (cottages from Rs 300; 🔆), near the museum, has cottages with good views.

A daily train leaves Vizag at 7.45am (Rs 24, five hours) and Araku (Rs 24, five hours) at 3pm. It's a slow, spectacular ride on a broad-gauge line; sit on the right-hand side coming out of Vizag for the best views. For Jungle Bells (see the boxed text, p425), get off at Tyda station, 500m from the resort.

VIJAYAWADA
☎ 0866 / pop 1 million

Vijayawada, at the head of the delta of the mighty Krishna River, is considered by many to be the heart of Andhra culture and language. The main attractions here are temples, including ancient rock-cave temples, and the Buddhist ruins at Amaravathi. Surrounded by hills and intersected by canals, it's an appealing place, as well as an important port and a bustling town.

Every 12 years millions of pilgrims descend on Vijayawada for Krishna Pushkaram, when Lord Pushkara is believed to reside in the River Krishna.

Orientation

Vijayawada is sprawling, with the Krishna River cutting across the southern end of the city. The train station is in the centre of town, near the Governorpet neighbourhood, which has lots of hotels. The main bus station is south of here. Most autorickshaws around town cost Rs 15.

Information

Apollo Pharmacy (☎ 2432333; Vijaya Talkies Junction, Karl Marx Rd; 🕐 24hr)

APTDC booth (train station) Pretty useless.

APTDC office (☎ 2571393; MG Rd; 🕐 9.30am-5.30pm Mon-Sat) In the south of town, across from the PWD Grounds. Also not very helpful.

HDFC Bank ATM (Mahalakshmi Towers, Raja Gopala Archari St) West of Hotel Grand Residency; takes Visa.

ICICI Bank ATM (MG Rd) By the tourist office; takes Visa.

Main bus station cloakroom (per day Rs 10) Leave your luggage here.

State Bank of Hyderabad (☎ 2572912; Governorpet; 🕐 10.30am-2.30pm Mon-Fri) Changes currency and travellers cheques. It's down the street from Vijayawada.net.

Vijayawada.net (Governorpet; per hr Rs 20; 🕐 9.30am-11pm) Off Prakasam Rd, towards Apsara Theatre.

Sights
KANAKA DURGA TEMPLE

This **temple** (Indrakila Hill) is dedicated to Kanaka Durga, the goddess and protector of the city. Legend has it that she eradicated powerful demons from the area. She now receives continual gratitude from her followers, who credit her with Vijayawada's prosperity.

CAVE TEMPLES

Eight kilometres west of Vijayawada, the striking 7th-century **Undavalli cave temples** (Indian/foreigner Rs 5/US$2; 🕐 8am-6pm) house a huge statue of the reclining Vishnu. Other shrines are dedicated to the Trimurti (the triad – Brahma, Vishnu and Shiva). The caves are well worth a visit. Bus No 301 goes here.

AMARAVATHI

Amaravathi, 60km west of Vijayawada, was once the Andhran capital and a significant Buddhist centre. The Mahayana monk Nagarjuna constructed India's biggest **stupa** here 2000 years ago. All that remains are a mound and some stones, but the nearby **museum** (Indian/foreigner Rs 5/US$2; 🕐 10am-5pm Sat-Thu) has a small replica of the stupa, with its intricately carved pillars, marble-surfaced dome and carvings of the life of the Buddha. If you're into Buddhist history, you'll no doubt want to visit Amaravathi, but its best sculptures are now in Chennai's Government Museum (p320).

Buses run from Vijayawada to Amaravathi (via Guntur) every hour from 6am to 9pm (Rs 20). APTDC organises tours for Rs 60, subject to demand.

Punnami Hotel (☎ 08645-255332; dm/d Rs 75/275) has basic rooms. There's not much in the way of eating options in Amaravathi; you may want to bring your own food.

Sleeping & Eating

The train station's clean and spacious **retiring rooms** (s/d from Rs 100/200; 🔆) are a great option, even if you're not travelling the next morning.

All of the following places have 24-hour checkout.

Sree Lakshmi Vilas Modern Cafe (☎ 2572525; Besant Rd, Governorpet; s with shared bathroom Rs 90,

s/d with private bathroom from Rs 150/280; meals Rs 20)
With black-and-white check floors and
thick wooden banisters, this place has a
heavy 1940's vibe. It's super clean, and the
veg restaurant is excellent, with fresh juices
(Rs 20) and mismatched wooden chairs.

Hotel Santhi (☎ 2577351; santhihotel@rediffmail
.com; Apsara Theatre Junction, Governorpet; s/d from Rs
350/450; ✸) The Santhi is newish and well
organised and has spotless pink rooms with
new bathrooms.

Hotel Grand Residency (☎ 2668505; grandvja@sify
.com; Prakasam Rd; s/d Rs 750/850; ✸) Light, airy
rooms that aren't huge but very smart, with
some style, eg lacquered furniture.

Orchids (mains Rs 40-125; ☺ 7am-11pm) Downstairs from the Grand Residency, Orchids
is a classy place with great veg and nonveg
Indian food. The hotel also has a bar.

Getting There & Away
The enormous bus stand is 1.5km from the
train station and has a helpful **inquiry desk**
(☎ 2522200). Frequent services run to Hyderabad (Rs 140 deluxe, six hours), Amaravathi (Rs 20, two hours), Warangal (Rs
115 deluxe, six hours) and Visakhapatnam
(Rs 197 deluxe, 10 hours).

Vijayawada is on the main Chennai–
Kolkata and Chennai–Delhi railway lines.
All express trains stop here. The daily
Coromandel Express runs to Chennai (Rs
227/553/843 sleeper/3AC/2AC, seven
hours) and, the other way, to Kolkata (Rs
401/1073/1667 sleeper/3AC/2AC, 20
hours). Speedy *Rajdhani* (Thursday and
Saturday) and *Jan Shatabdi* (daily except
Tuesday) trains also ply the Chennai–
Vijayawada route.

Plenty of trains run to Hyderabad (Rs
182/484/723 sleeper/3AC/2AC, 6½ hours),
Tirupathi (Rs 191/480 sleeper/3AC, seven
hours) and Puri (Rs 303/795/1238 sleeper/
3AC/2AC, 17 hours).

The **computerised advance booking office**
(☎ 133) is in the station basement.

TIRUMALA & TIRUPATHI
☎ 0877 / pop 302,000
The 'holy hill' of Tirumala is one of the
most important pilgrimage centres in
India – and indeed the world: it's said
that Venkateshwara Temple eclipses Jeru-
salem, Rome and Mecca for sheer numbers
of pilgrims.

There are never fewer than 5000 pilgrims
here at any one time – in a single day, the
total often reaches 100,000 – and *darshan*
(deity viewing) runs around the clock.
Temple staff alone number 18,000, and
the efficient **Tirumala Tirupathi Devasthanams**
(TTD; www.tirumala.org) administers the crowds.
It also runs *choultries* (guesthouses) for
pilgrims in Tirumala and Tirupathi, the
service town at the bottom of the hill. The
private hotels and lodges are in Tirupathi,
so a fleet of buses constantly ferries the pilgrims the 18km up and down the hill from
well before sunrise until well after sunset.

Tirumala is an engrossing place, but receives few non-Hindu visitors. The crowds
can certainly be overwhelming, but Tirumala somehow has a sense of serenity and
ease about it and is worth a visit, even if
you're not a pilgrim.

Information
You'll find most of your worldly needs in
Tirupathi. Both the main bus station and
the train station have 24-hour cloakrooms
(per day Rs 10).

Apollo Pharmacy (☎ 2252314; G Car St; ☺ 24hr)

APTDC office (☎ 2255385; TA Area; ☺ 9am-6pm)
Extremely helpful folks near the train station.

Om Internet (Sri Vijay Plaza; per hr Rs 30; ☺ 8am-
11pm) Across from the bus stand.

State Bank of Hyderabad ATM (Railway Station Rd)
To your left as you leave the train station. It takes Visa
and Plus.

Sights
VENKATESHWARA TEMPLE
Devotees flock to Tirumala to see Venkateshwara, an avatar of Vishnu. Among the
many powers attributed to him is the grant-
ing of any wish made before the idol at Tirumala. Many pilgrims also donate their hair to
the deity, an act symbolic of renouncing the
ego, so hundreds of barbers attend to devotees, and Tirumala and Tirupathi are filled
with bald men, women and children.

The hill itself and the surrounding area
have religious significance, and the temple's history may date back 2000 years. The
main **temple** is a beautiful and atmospheric
place, bathed in soft light and flower garlands. As you approach the inner sanctum,
the passageway grows dark and begins to
smell of incense and resonate with chanting. Then, finally, there's Venkateshwara,

sitting gloriously on his throne and inspiring bliss and love among his visitors. You'll have a moment to make a wish and then you'll be out again.

'Ordinary *darshan*' requires a wait of several hours in the claustrophobic metal cages ringing the temple. 'Special *darshan*' tickets (Rs 50) can be purchased a day in advance in Tirupathi. These come with a *darshan* time and are supposed to get you through the queue in two hours. In practice, it can take up to five. Really, the only hassle-free way to do this is to have either crack-of-dawn *darshan* or VIP 'cellar' *darshan*, both of which involve minimal waiting. For the latter, bring your passport and Rs 100 to room 17 of the Vaikuntam 'Q' Complex at Tirumala. You'll have to sign a declaration of faith in Lord Venkateshwara.

Tours

If you're pressed for time, **APTDC** (Rs 1725) runs two-day tours to Tirumala from Hyderabad. They leave at 1.30pm, returning at 6pm on the third day, and include accommodation and 'special *darshan*'. **KSTDC** (Rs 875) runs one-day tours from Bangalore, too. For more information on tours from Chennai, see p323.

Sleeping & Eating

Most non-Hindu visitors stay in Tirupathi, which has a range of good accommodation.

TIRUMALA

Vast **dormitories** (beds free) surround the temple on Tirumala Hill, but these are intended for pilgrims. Rooms for pilgrims in **guesthouses** (Rs 100-750) are also available. If you want to stay, check in at the Central Reception Office, near the Tirumala bus stand, or reserve online at www.ttdsevaonline.com (reservations not accepted for festivals). On weekends the place becomes outrageously crowded.

Huge **dining halls** (meals free) in Tirumala serve thousands of meals daily to pilgrims. There are also numerous little veg restaurants serving 'meals' for Rs 10.

TIRUPATHI

Hotels are clustered around the main bus stand, 500m from the centre of town, and around the train station, which has **retiring rooms** (r Rs 100-250; ✷).

Hotel Woodside (☎ 2284464; 15 G Car St; s/d incl breakfast from Rs 250/299; ✷) The best deal in town is cheerful and relatively new, with royal-blue walls, plaid curtains and gleaming bathrooms. The restaurant downstairs isn't bad, either.

Hotel Mamata Lodge (☎ 2225873; fax 2225797; 1st fl, 170 TP Area; s/d/tr/q Rs 150/250/300/350) A decent cheapie across from the main bus stand. Don't go to the downstairs lodge of the same name – things get pretty grim down there.

Hotel Sri Padmavathi Srinivasa (☎ 5569204; s/d Rs 150/250) Rooms are small and some have no windows, but somehow they work. It's a clean place with a warm welcome, just off G Car St.

Bhimas Deluxe (☎ 2225521; www.bhimasdeluxe .com; 34-38 G Car St; r from Rs 650; ✷) Light-wood furniture and fancy towel racks set this place apart from the rest, though it could use a lick of paint.

Hotel Sindhuri Park (☎ 2256430; www.hotel sindhuri.com; 119 TP Area; s/d from Rs 700/900; ✷ ▯) Rooms at the professional Sindhuri Park are well appointed and have central AC; some have views of the Pushkarna Tank out front.

Punjabi Dhaba (G Car St; mains Rs 30-60; ✷ 7am-11pm) North Indian stand-bys and the delicious Special Punjabi Thali (Rs 60).

Lakshmi Narayana Bhavan (TP Area; mains Rs 20-50; ✷ 5am-11pm; ✷) This joint serving veggie meals is opposite the main bus stand and directly next to Hotel Mayura (beware of imposters!).

Hotel Vaikuntan (49 G Car St; mains Rs 20-60; ✷ 5.30am-midnight) A bustling 'meals' spot.

Getting There & Away

It's possible (but not advisable) to visit Tirupathi on a long day trip from Chennai. If travelling by bus or train, you can buy 'link tickets', which include the transport from Tirupathi to Tirumala. These can save time and confusion on arrival.

AIR

Indian Airlines (☎ 2233992; Tirumala Bypass Rd), 2km outside of town, has flights to Hyderabad (US$90, one hour, four weekly). **Air Deccan** (☎ 2285471) plies the same route daily for Rs 2200. The easiest way to book either of these is with **Mitson Travels** (☎ 2225981; 192 Railway Station Rd; ✷ 9am-8pm Mon-Sat, to 1pm Sun), across from the train station's 'parcel office'.

BUS

Tirupathi's mega **bus station** (☎ 2225333) has frequent buses to Chennai (Rs 51, four hours) and Hyderabad (Rs 500 in Volvo AC deluxe, 11 hours). Tonnes of APSRTC and KSTDC buses go to Bangalore (deluxe/Volvo AC deluxe Rs 206/250, 5½ hours), and two direct, overnight buses head to Puttaparthi daily (Rs 143, eight hours).

TRAIN

Tirupathi station (☎ 2251131) is well served by express trains.

Destination	Fare (Rs)	Duration (hr)	Departures
Bangalore	* Rs 87/176/437/681	7	2 daily
Chennai	** Rs 49/20	3	3 daily
Madurai	# Rs 268/726/1131	12	1 daily
Mumbai	Rs 365/998/1565	24	1 daily
Secunderabad	Rs 268/726/1131	13	4 daily
Vijayawada	## Rs 97/181/480/744	8	5 daily

* 2nd class/sleeper/3AC/2AC ; ** 2nd class/chair ;
# sleeper/3AC/2AC;
##2nd class/sleeper/3AC/2AC

Getting Around

BUS

Tirumala Link buses run out of two bus stands in Tirupathi: next to the main bus stand and near the train station. The sce-nic 18km trip to Tirumala takes one hour (Rs 44 return).

If there's a big crowd, and you have to wait to get on a bus in either Tirumala or Tirupathi, then there'll be enough people around to share a taxi (Rs 250).

WALKING

TTD has constructed probably the best footpath in India for pilgrims to walk up to Tirumala. It's about 15km and takes four to six hours. Leave your luggage at the toll gate at Alipiri near the Hanuman statue. It will be transported free to the reception centre. It's best to walk in the cool of the evening, but there are shady rest points along the way, and even a canteen.

AROUND TIRUPATHI

Chandragiri Fort

Only a couple of buildings remain from this 15th-century **fort** (☎ 2276246; Indian/foreigner Rs 5/US$2; 8am-6.30pm Sat-Thu), 14km west of Tirupathi. Both the Rani Mahal and the Raja Mahal, which houses a small **museum** (10am-5pm Sat-Thu), were constructed under Vijayanagar rule and resemble structures in Hampi's Royal Centre. There's a nightly **sound-and-light show** (admission Rs 30; English version 8pm Mar-Oct, 7.30pm Nov-Feb), narrated by Bollywood stars. Buses for Chandragiri leave from the front of Tirupathi train station every 15 minutes.

Sri Kalahasti

Around 36km east of Tirupathi, Sri Kalahasti is known for its **Sri Kalahasteeswara**

ANDHRA PRADESH

ANCIENT DESIGNS REVISITED

The ancient tradition of *kalamkari* was practiced for centuries in South India to create artwork for temples and royalty. The richly patterned paintings depict plants, birds and animals with elaborate black outlines and deep colours. The art form derives its name from the *kalam* (pen) used to create the intricate designs.

The fabric, usually cotton, is primed by immersing it in a compound of *myrabalam* (resin) and cow's milk for one hour. The figures are drawn with a pointed bamboo stick that's been dipped in a mixture of fermented jaggery and water, and vegetable dyes are then applied; different effects are achieved with cow dung, ground seeds, plants and flowers.

Kalamkari was revived in the late 1950s when a training centre was established in Sri Kalahasti. Here, the artists usually represent stories from the Mahabharata and the Ramayana, and while some places have adopted chemical dyes, the Sri Kalahasti artists retain the ancient methods and natural ingredients.

You can meet the artists and see them at work at the home of **G Krishna Reddy** (☎ 08578-230576; Agraharam) or next door at Sri Vijayalakshmi Fine Kalamkari Arts.

Temple and as a centre for *kalamkari* art (see p429). The temple has particular significance for Shaivites as it's linked to four other temples that each honour Shiva as one of the elements; here the element is air. The temple derives its name from the legend of three animals that worshipped Shiva: a snake (*sri*), a spider (*kala*) and an elephant (*hasti*).

Buses leave Tirupathi for Sri Kalahasti every 10 minutes (Rs 16, 45 minutes). The *kalamkari* artists are in the Agraharam neighbourhood, 2.5km from the bus stand.

PUTTAPARTHI
☎ 08555

Prasanthi Nilayam (Abode of Highest Peace), in the southwestern corner of Andhra Pradesh at Puttaparthi, is the main ashram of Sri Sathya Sai Baba, who has a huge following in India and around the globe. He set up this ashram 40 years ago, and spends most of the year here, but sometimes moves to Whitefields Ashram near Bangalore, or to Kodaikanal in Tamil Nadu in the hot season.

Sleeping & Eating

Most people stay at the **Ashram** (☎ 287164; www.sathyasai.org), a small village with all amenities. Accommodation and food are cheap but very basic. Advance bookings aren't taken. The chief area for accommodation outside the ashram is Main Rd.

Sri Sai Sadan (☎ 287507; Hanuman Temple Main Rd; r from Rs 420; 🔀) Spacious rooms have constant hot water and balconies with good

views. There's a good roof-garden restaurant, too.

Hotel Chaithanya (☎ 287265; Main Rd; hotelchaith anyaintl@yahoo.com; r from Rs 700; 🔀) This modern hotel (think tiles and sunset paintings) is set around a quiet courtyard at the top end of town. Rooms have constant hot water.

World Peace Café (Main Rd; mains Rs 25-70; 🕑 7am-10pm) Has been known to lure the odd devotee away from the ashram dining hall. The breezy rooftop place opposite the ashram serves a wide range of herbal teas, pastries, health foods and good filter coffee.

Bamboo Nest (Chitravathi Rd; mains Rs 40-80; 🕑 7.30am-10.30pm) This Tibetan place does good *momos* (dumplings), noodles and juices (Rs 25).

Sri Krishna Bhavan (Main Rd; meals Rs 22; 🕑 7am-11pm) Uphill from the ashram, this place is popular with the locals for thali and tiffin.

Getting There & Away

Puttaparthi is most easily reached from Bangalore; eight buses (Rs 100, four hours) and four trains (Rs 146/559 sleeper/2AC, three hours) head here daily. You can also take a taxi (Rs 1000 to 1200).

Buses run to/from Tirupathi (Rs 143, eight hours, two daily) and Chennai (Rs 242 deluxe, 12 hours, three daily), but for most other destinations, the train's the way to go.

The station has a computerised advance train reservation office. For Hyderabad, an overnight train goes daily to Kacheguda (Rs 238/640 sleeper/3AC, 11 hours), and a *Rajdhani* express goes to Secunderabad four

---

THE GOD OF BIG THINGS

Many times a year, the population of Puttaparthi swells to more than 50,000. The drawcard, of course, is Sai Baba. Puttaparthi is his birthplace and where he established his main ashram, Prasanthi Nilayam.

It's difficult to overestimate the pulling power of this man who, aged 14, declared himself to be the reincarnation of Sai Baba, a saintly figure who died in 1918.

In November 2000 an estimated one million people gathered at the ashram to celebrate Sai Baba's 75th year. The massive gig resembled an Olympics opening ceremony. Sai Baba's elaborately adorned elephant, Sai Gita, led a procession of bands, dancing troupes and flag bearers from 165 countries. Many devotees regard Sai Baba as a true avatar.

Everything about Sai Baba is big: the Afro hairdo; the big name–devotees, including film stars, politicians and cricket superstar Sachin Tendulkar; and the money (millions of dollars) pumped into the nearby hospital, schools and university. And there's the big controversy. Serious allegations of sexual misconduct and molestation have led some devotees to lose faith. Others, however, regard such controversy as simply another terrestrial test for their avatar.

days a week. An overnight train also runs to Visakhapatnam (Rs 335/913/1429 sleeper/3AC/2AC, 20½ hours), stopping at Vijaya-wada on the way. One service, at 11.20pm, heads to Mumbai (Rs 335/913/1429 sleeper/3AC/2AC, 20½ hours).

Indian Airlines flies regularly from Bangalore (US$50) and Mumbai (US$150).

Getting Around

For such a small place there are a lot of autorickshaws around. No trip in town should cost more than Rs 10. The large bus station has regular buses to surrounding areas.

LEPAKSHI

An hour down the road from Puttaparthi is Lepakshi, site of the impressive **Veerbhadra Temple**. Look out for the monolithic Nandi bull at the town's entrance. The temple is currently being restored, but still holds many well-preserved carvings. Visitors can enter the inner sanctum and should bring plenty of small change to pay for the various blessings they will receive inside. A knowledgeable English-speaking guide is well equipped to answer questions and has no aversion to throwing in the odd tall story to keep things interesting.

ANDHRA PRADESH

Orissa

Some states induce tourist frenzy, but not laid-back Orissa where once you hit the beach your plans could be in jeopardy. Be lucky with your timing and you can see two events of a lifetime. One is spiritual: thousands swarm into Puri for the annual festival when the god Jagannath, with brother and sister, is pulled on mighty chariots between temples. The second is natural: the nesting and hatching of endangered olive ridley turtles.

Orissa has always been a cultured state. Witness the mighty Sun Temple of Konark, a dream of genius carved out of stone and adorned with a storyboard of Orissan life. Modern artistry exists with astonishingly high quality painting, silverwork and textiles. Many of Orissa's interesting sites are clustered together along the coast; inland is a different India, a tribal India where diverse groups, despite living a precarious existence on the edge of mainstream society, have managed to retain their strong social structures and a vibrant culture that's expressed in their clothing, music and dance.

And there's an Orissa where the wild beasts stir. Chilika Lake and its rare dolphins, Debrigarh Wildlife Sanctuary and Badrama National Park; Similipal National Park, where wild elephants tootle into Chahala salt lick; or Bhitarkanika Wildlife Sanctuary, where monster crocs lurk in muddy mangroves.

Puri is also for weary travellers who have endured the rough and tumble of Indian travel and an endless rice'n'curry diet. Visitors come to kick back, gorge on backpacker fare and swap travelling tales. The beach scene is no Kerala or Goa but it's still happy 'sand, waves and sea' and, of course, seafood. Orissans claim they eat a lot and there's no reason not to join them with scrumptious fish, prawn and crab dishes.

HIGHLIGHTS

- Poke around the myriad **Hindu temples** (p437) in old Bhubaneswar
- Get caught up in the **Rath Yatra** (p444) hullabaloo, one of India's most spectacular festivals in Puri
- Dose up on amazement at the majestic **Sun Temple** (p447) in Konark
- Spot elephants and maybe an elusive carnivore in the forests of **Similipal National Park** (p454)
- Say hi to big crocs, lizards, flashy kingfishers and herons as your boat chugs through **Bhitarkanika** (p456)
- Recuperate from hard travelling and eat too much seafood in **Puri** (p441)
- Tour Orissa's **tribal areas** (p452) and wonder how long such distinctive cultures can survive in modern India

Similipal National Park ★
Bhitarkanika ★
Bhubaneswar ★
★ ★ Konark
Puri
★ Tribal Areas
★ Tribal Areas

ORISSA

History

Despite having been a formidable maritime empire, with trading routes down into Indonesia, the history of Orissa (formerly 'Kalinga') is hazy until the demise of the Kalinga dynasty in 260 BC at the hands of the great emperor Ashoka. Appalled at the carnage he had caused, Ashoka forswore violence and converted to Buddhism.

Around the 1st century BC Buddhism declined and Jainism was restored as the faith of the people. During this period the monastery caves of Udayagiri and Khandagiri (p438) were excavated as important Jain centres.

By the 7th century AD, Hinduism had supplanted Jainism. Under the Kesari and Ganga kings, trade and commerce increased and Orissan culture flourished – countless temples from that classical period still stand. The Orissans defied the Muslim rulers in Delhi until finally falling to the Mughals during the 16th century, when many of Bhubaneswar's temples were destroyed.

Until Independence, Orissa was ruled by Afghans, Marathas and the British.

At the end of the 1990s a Hindu fundamentalist group, Bajrang Dal, undertook a violent campaign against Christians in Orissa in response to missionary activity. Squeezed in the middle are the tribal people, targeted because they are 'easy souls', without power, and illiterate. Matters came to a tragic head in 1999 when an Australian missionary and his two sons were burnt alive sleeping in their car. Since then violence has died down.

In the same year a devastating cyclone lashed the coast. Officially, 9524 people died (the unofficial estimate is at least 50,000); about one million were left homeless.

The creation of the neighbouring states of Jharkhand and Chhattisgarh has prompted calls for the formation of a separate, tribal-oriented state, Koshal, in the northwest of Orissa, with Sambalpur as the capital.

FESTIVALS IN ORISSA

Festivals in this boxed text are marked on the Map p434.

Makar Mela (**1**; 2nd week of Jan; Kalijai island, Chilika Lake, p449) Celebrates the point when the sun enters the orbit of Capricorn. Surya, the sun god, is the attention of special worship.

Adivasi Mela (**2**; 26-31 Jan; Bhubaneswar, p435) Features the world of art, dance and handicrafts, as practised by Orissa's tribal groups.

Magha Mela (**3**; Jan/Feb; Konark, p447) Sun festival, with pilgrims bathing en masse at the beach before sunrise before worshipping at the temple.

Maha Shivaratri (**4**; Feb/Mar; Bhubaneswar, p435) Devotees fast and perform pujas throughout the night ready to witness the priest climbing to the top of Lingaraj Mandir to place a sacred lamp.

Ashokastami (**5**; Apr/May; Bhubaneswar, p435) The idol of Lord Lingaraj is taken by chariot to Bindu Sagar for ritual bathing and then to Rameswaram Temple for a four-day stay.

Rath Yatra (**6**; Jun/Jul; Puri, p441) Immense chariots containing Lord Jagannath, brother Balbhadra and sister Subhadra are hauled from Jagannath Temple to Gundicha Mandir.

Beach Festival (**7**; Nov; Puri, p441) Song, dance and cultural activities, including sand artists, on the beach.

Tribal Festival (16-18 Nov; location varies) An exposition of Orissan tribal dances and music. Contact Orissa Tourism as the location changes yearly.

Baliyatra (**8**; Nov/Dec; Cuttack, p455) Four days commemorate past trading links with Indonesia. People go to the Mahanadi River, bathe and sail tiny boats made of pitch and paper. A huge fair is held on the river bank.

Konark Festival (**9**; 1-5 Dec; Konark, p447) Features enchanting music and traditional Odissi dance, a seductive temple ritual with origins in medieval Tantra. Festivities are in the open-air auditorium, with the Sun Temple specially lit in the background.

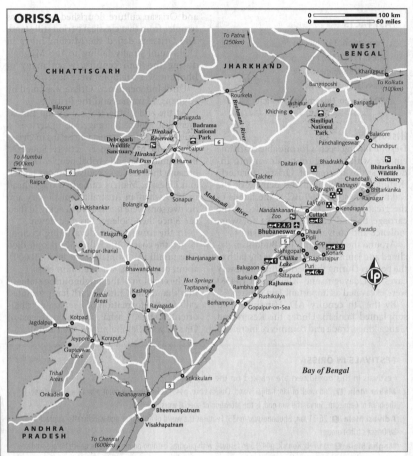

ORISSA

Climate

Orissa has some considerable extremes, with summer temperatures ranging from 27° to 49°C, with quite high humidity along the coast. Inland temperatures are several degrees cooler. Winter temperatures range from 5° to 16°C, while some high inland areas can receive frost. Monsoon time is July to October, when cyclones are likely.

Information

Orissa Tourism Development Corporation (OTDC), the commercial arm of Orissa Tourism, runs tours and hotels throughout the state. **Orissa Tourism** (www.orissatourism.gov .in) has a presence in cities and most towns where the office is a one-stop shop for both information and tour/hotel booking. It also maintains a list of approved guides for tribal-area visits.

ACCOMMODATION

All places listed in this chapter, unless otherwise mentioned, come with private bathrooms and sit-down flush toilets. During festivals and holidays, coastal Orissa becomes bunged up with Bengali holiday-makers so replan your visit or book accommodation and transport well in advance.

PERMITS

While no permits are needed, there are tribal areas in central and western Orissa

where foreigners have to register their details with the police. This is all done for
you if you are on a tour but independent
visitors should check their plans with the
police in the nearest city.

Dangers & Annoyances
Mosquitoes here have a record of being malaria carriers. Load yourself up with pills
(see p505), repellents and bring a mosquito
net in case your hotel doesn't provide one.

Getting There & Away
Major road and rail routes between Kolkata (Calcutta) and Chennai pass through
coastal Orissa and Bhubaneswar with spur
connections to Puri. Road and rail connect
Sambalpur with Chhattisgarh and Madhya
Pradesh. Air routes connect Bhubaneswar
to Delhi, Mumbai (Bombay), Chennai (Madras) and Kolkata.

Unless otherwise mentioned, train fares in
this chapter are non-AC sleeper/3AC sleeper/
2AC sleeper.

Getting Around
Public transport in the coastal region is
good with long-distance buses and some
train routes serving the west. Lack of suitable transport makes hiring a car for touring around the interior the only feasible
option.

BHUBANESWAR
☎ 0674 / pop 647,310
Bhubaneswar's modern expansion has
tacked concrete blocks onto its historic old
city, a placid tangle of streets to the south.
First glances suggest another congested Indian city but wide streets have reduced that
sense of claustrophobia.

The old city's spiritual centre is around
Bindu Sagar; in this hub of religious bustle
50-odd temples remain from thousands that
once stood here, representing a flowering of
Orissan medieval temple architecture.

The city is also a base for day trips to
Dhauli (p441), Konark (p447), Nandankanan
Zoo (p441) and Cuttack (p455).

Orientation
Most lodgings, restaurants, banks and transport are within an area bounded by Cuttack
Rd, Rajpath, Sachivajaya Marg and the train
station.

Information
BOOKSHOPS
Modern Book Depot (modbooks@cal2.vsnl.net.in;
Station Sq; ⊙ 9.30am-2pm & 4.30-9pm) Maps, English-
language novels, coffee-table books and books on Orissa.

INTERNET ACCESS
Cyber Vision (cnr Cuttack Rd & Rajpath; per hr Rs 15;
⊙ 7am-11.30pm)
Info Matrix (74-P Ashok Nagar, Janpath; per hr Rs 15;
⊙ 9am-10pm)

LEFT LUGGAGE
Train station (per piece per day Rs 10; ⊙ 24hr)

MEDICAL SERVICES
Capital Hospital (☎ 2401983; Sachivajaya Marg) 24-hour
pharmacy on site.

MONEY
Centurion Bank (Janpath) MasterCard and Visa ATM.
State Bank of India (☎ 2533671; Rajpath;
⊙ 9.30am-4pm Mon-Fri, 9am-12.30pm Sat, closed
2nd Sat in month) Cashes travellers cheques and foreign
currency.

PHOTOGRAPHY
Neel Kamal (29 Western Market Bldg, Rajpath; ⊙ 8.30am-
8.30pm) Photographic supplies and film printing.

POST
Post office main office (☎ 2402132; cnr Mahatma
Gandhi & Sachivajaya Margs; ⊙ 9am-7pm Mon-Sat);
Market Bldg (Rajpath; ⊙ 9am-5pm Mon-Sat)

TOURIST INFORMATION
Government of India tourist office (☎ /fax
2432203; BJB Nagar; ⊙ 9am-6pm Mon-Fri, 9am-1pm
Sat) India-wide information.
Orissa Tourism main office (☎ 2431299; www.orissa
tourism.gov.in; behind Panthanivas Tourist Bungalow, Lewis
Rd; ⊙ 10am-5pm Mon-Sat, closed 2nd Sat in month);
airport (☎ 2534006); train station (☎ 2530715; ⊙ 24hr)
Tourist information, maps and lists of recommended guides.
Orissa Tourism Development Corporation (OTDC;
☎ 2432382; behind Panthanivas Hotel, Lewis Rd;
⊙ 10am-5pm Mon-Sat) Commercial arm of Orissa
Tourism. Books sightseeing tours, hotels and Indian
Airlines tickets.

Sights
BINDU SAGAR
Also known as Ocean Drop Tank, **Bindu Sagar**
reputedly contains water from every holy
stream, pool and tank in India – obviously

BHUBANESWAR

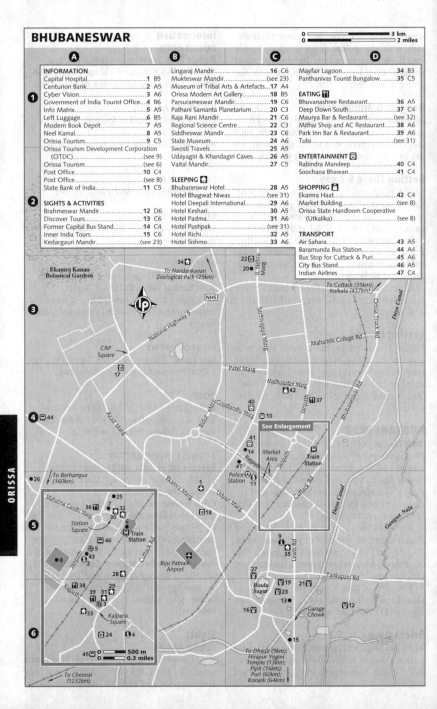

0	3 km
0	2 miles

Ⓐ   **Ⓑ**   **Ⓒ**   **Ⓓ**

INFORMATION
Capital Hospital...................................1 B5
Centurion Bank....................................2 A5
Cyber Vision..3 A6
Government of India Tourist Office....4 B6
Info Matrix..5 B5
Left Luggage.......................................6 B5
Modern Book Depot.............................7 A5
Neel Kamal...8 A5
Orissa Tourism....................................9 C5
Orissa Tourism Development Corporation
(OTDC)..(see 9)
Orissa Tourism..............................(see 6)
Post Office..10 C4
Post Office.......................................(see 8)
State Bank of India...........................11 C5

SIGHTS & ACTIVITIES
Brahmeswar Mandir..........................12 D6
Discover Tours...................................13 C6
Former Capital Bus Stand..................14 C4
Inner India Tours...............................15 C6
Kedargauri Mandir.......................(see 23)

Lingaraj Mandir.................................16 C6
Mukteswar Mandir.......................(see 23)
Museum of Tribal Arts & Artefacts...17 A4
Orissa Modern Art Gallery.................18 B5
Parsurameswar Mandir......................19 C6
Pathani Samanta Planetarium...........20 C3
Raja Rani Mandir...............................21 C6
Regional Science Centre....................22 C3
Siddheswar Mandir............................23 C6
State Museum....................................24 A6
Swosti Travels....................................25 A5
Udayagiri & Khandagiri Caves...........26 A5
Vaital Mandir.....................................27 C5

SLEEPING
Bhubaneswar Hotel............................28 A5
Hotel Bhagwat Niwas...................(see 31)
Hotel Deepali International.................29 A6
Hotel Keshari.....................................30 A5
Hotel Padma......................................31 A6
Hotel Pushpak...............................(see 31)
Hotel Richi...32 A5
Hotel Sishmo.....................................33 A6

Mayfair Lagoon.................................34 B3
Panthanivas Tourist Bungalow...........35 C5

EATING
Bhuvanashree Restaurant..................36 A5
Deep Down South..............................37 C4
Maurya Bar & Restaurant.............(see 32)
Mithai Shop and AC Restaurant........38 A6
Park Inn Bar & Restaurant.................39 A6
Tulsi...(see 31)

ENTERTAINMENT
Rabindra Mandeep.............................40 C4
Soochana Bhawan..............................41 C4

SHOPPING
Ekamra Haat......................................42 C4
Market Building..............................(see 8)
Orissa State Handloom Cooperative
(Utkalika)....................................(see 8)

TRANSPORT
Air Sahara...43 A5
Baramunda Bus Station......................44 A6
Bus Stop for Cuttack & Puri...............45 A6
City Bus Stand...................................46 A5
Indian Airlines...................................47 C4

Ekamra Kanan
Botanical Gardens

NH5

To Nandankanan
Zoological Park (25km)

To Cuttack (35km);
Kolkata (437km)

National Highway 5

CRP
Square

Patel Marg

Madhusudan Marg

Maharishi College Rd

Gopabandhu Marg

To Berhampur
(160km)

Azad Marg

Ekamra Marg

Udyan Marg

See Enlargement

Market
Area

Train
Station

Police
Station

Cuttack Rd

Mahatma Gandhi Marg

Station
Square

Train
Station

Janpath

Rajpath

Biju Patnaik
Airport

Kalpana
Square

Bindu
Sagar

Lewis Rd

Tankapani Rd

Garage
Chowk

Gangua Nala

500 m
0.3 miles

To Chennai
(1232km)

To Dhauli (5km);
Hirapur Yogini
Temple (13km);
Pipli (16km);
Puri (60km);
Konark (64km)

ORISSA

a good place to wash away sin. During the Ashokastami festival (p433), the Lingaraj Mandir's deity is brought here for ritual bathing.

TEMPLES
Lingaraj Mandir and the other temples dotted around Bindu Sagar may suffice, but for more, amble along to the cluster of temples by Lewis Rd. For the works, charter an autorickshaw for two to three hours (about Rs 200).

Lingaraj Mandir excludes non-Hindus and Raja Rani charges an entrance fee. Priests expect a donation as they're not salaried; Rs 10 is reasonable and you'll be expected to enter the amount in a visitors' book. Consider it a guiding fee as undoubtedly the priest will reveal something about his temple.

Lingaraj Mandir
This 54m-high **temple**, dedicated to Tribhuvaneswar (Lord of Three Worlds) and surrounded by more than 50 smaller temples and shrines, dates from 1090 to 1104, although parts are over 1400 years old. The granite block, representing Tribhuvaneswar, is bathed daily with water, milk and bhang (marijuana). In the northeastern corner, there's an attractive temple to Parvati and a chamber where 51 beggars and 51 priests eat daily food offerings, purportedly consumed by Parvati. The main gate, guarded by two moustachioed yellow lions, is a spectacle in itself as lines of pilgrims approach, *prasad* (temple-blessed food offering) in hand.

Because the temple is surrounded by a wall, and closed to non-Hindus, (Indira Gandhi wasn't allowed in, as her husband was a Parsi), foreigners can see it only from a viewing platform. Face the main entrance, walk around to the right and find the viewing platform down a short laneway to the left. You might be asked for a 'donation'; again, Rs 10 is enough. On the way you should see a couple of gigantic wheels used in the Ashokastami festival.

Vaital Mandir
This 8th-century **temple**, with a double-storey 'wagon roof' influenced by Buddhist cave architecture, was a centre of Tantric worship, eroticism and bloody sacrifice. Look closely, you'll see some very early

erotic carvings on the walls. The grotesque Chamunda (Kali) can be seen in the dingy interior, although her necklace of skulls and her bed of corpses are usually hidden beneath her temple robes.

Parsurameswar Mandir
Just west of Lewis Rd lies a cluster of about 20 smaller but important temples. Best preserved is **Parsurameswar Mandir**, a small but ornate Shiva temple built around AD 650. It has lively bas-reliefs of jolly elephant and horse processions, and Shiva images.

Mukteswar, Siddheswar & Kedargauri Mandirs
Not far from Parsurameswar is the small, 10th-century **Mukteswar Mandir**, one of the most ornate temples in Bhubaneswar. Intricate carvings show a mixture of Buddhist, Jain and Hindu styles. The ceiling carvings and stone arch are particularly striking but the beautiful arched *torana* (architrave) in front, clearly showing Buddhist influence, takes the prize.

Siddheswar Mandir, in the same compound, is a later but plainer temple but has a fine red-painted Ganesh.

Over the road is **Kedargauri Mandir**, one of the oldest temples in Bhubaneswar, although it has been substantially rebuilt.

Raja Rani Mandir
This **temple** (admission Indian/foreigner Rs 5/100, video Rs 25; ☼ sunrise-sunset) is an ASI monument, hence the admission fee. Built around 1100 and surrounded by relaxing gardens, it's famous for its ornate *deul* (temple sanctuary) and tower. Around the compass points are pairs of statues representing eight *dikpalas* (guardians) who protect the temple. Between them, nymphs, embracing couples, elephants and lions languish in niches and decorate the pillars.

Brahmeswar Mandir
Standing in well-kept parkland, flanked on its plinth by four smaller structures, this 9th-century **temple** is a smaller version of Lingaraj Mandir. It's notable for its finely detailed sculptures with erotic elements.

REGIONAL SCIENCE CENTRE
Dinosaur-infatuated kiddies will love this parkland **museum** (☎ 2542795; JL Nehru Marg;

admission Rs 7; ☺ 10.30am-5.30pm) with its versions of prehistoric beasties. Other treats are hands-on demonstrations of the laws of physics and displays on astronomy and insects.

STATE MUSEUM
This **museum** (☎ 2431797; Lewis Rd; admission Rs 1; ☺ 10am-4pm Tue-Sun, ticket office closed 1-2pm) boasts Orissa's best collection of rare palm-leaf manuscripts, traditional and folk musical instruments, Bronze Age tools, an armoury and a fascinating display of Orissan tribal anthropology.

The magnificent collection of Buddhist and Jain sculptures, which is displayed in chronological order, constitutes the most important antiquities in the museum.

MUSEUM OF TRIBAL ARTS & ARTEFACTS
For anyone considering a visit to the tribal areas, this **museum** (☎ 2563649; admission free; ☺ 10am-5pm, closed 2nd Sat in month), off NH5, is a must. Dress, ornaments, weapons (some dangerous-looking 'blow up in your hands' home-made guns), household implements and musical instruments are on display in well-lit and captioned galleries.

PATHANI SAMANTA PLANETARIUM
This interesting **planetarium** (☎ 2581613; JL Nehru Marg; admission Rs 12; ☺ 2-6pm Tue-Sun, in English 4pm) features hour-long 'out-of-this-world' shows.

ORISSA MODERN ART GALLERY
Housing a high standard of contemporary art by local artists, this small **gallery** (☎ 9861093875; 132 Forest Park; admission free; ☺ 11am-1.30pm & 4-8pm Mon-Sat, 4-8pm Sun) also has prints and originals for sale.

UDAYAGIRI & KHANDAGIRI CAVES
Six kilometres west of the city centre are two hills riddled with **rock-cut shelters** (admission to both sites Indian/foreigner Rs 55/100, video Rs 25, guides one side/both sides Rs 150/250; ☺ sunrise-sunset). Many are ornately carved and thought to have been chiselled out for Jain ascetics in the 1st century BC.

There seems to be a deal between the site's monkeys and the banana and peanut sellers by the gates. Be aware that you will have to present any hand-held bags for the monkeys to inspect and any food will be confiscated. We actually saw it happen.

Udayagiri (Sunrise Hill) on the northern side has the more interesting caves.

Ascend the ramp, noting **Swargapuri** (Cave 9) to the right with its devotional figures. **Hathi Gumpha** (Cave 14) at the top is plain, but a 117-line inscription relates the exploits of its builder, King Kharaveli of Kalinga, who ruled from 168 to 153 BC.

Clamber up around to the left where you'll see **Bagh Gumpha** (Tiger Cave; Cave 12), with its entrance carved as a tiger mouth. Nearby are **Pavana Gumpha** (Cave of Purification) and small **Sarpa Gumpha** (Serpent Cave), where the tiny door is surmounted by a three-headed cobra. On the summit are the remains of a defensive position. As you descend around to the southeast you'll come to the single-storey elephant-guarded **Ganesh Gumpha** (Cave 10), almost directly above the two-storey **Rani ka Naur** (Queen's Palace Cave; Cave 1). This is the largest and most interesting of the caves and is carved with Jain symbols and battle scenes.

Continue back to the entrance via **Chota Hathi Gumpha** (Cave 3), with its carvings of elephants, and the double-storey **Jaya Vijaya Cave** (Cave 5) with a bodhi tree carved in the central compartment.

Across the road, Khandagiri offers fine views over Bhubaneswar from its summit. The steep path splits about one-third of the way up the hill. The right path goes to **Ananta Cave** (Cave 3), with its carved figures of athletes, women, elephants and geese carrying flowers. Further along is a series of **Jain temples**; at the top is another (18th-century) Jain temple.

Buses don't go to the caves, but plenty pass nearby on National Hwy 5, or take an autorickshaw (about Rs 50 one way).

Tours
Orissa Tourism (☎ 2431299; www.orissatourism.gov.in; behind Panthanivas Tourist Bungalow, Lewis Rd; ☺ 10am-5pm Mon-Sat, closed 2nd Sat in month) offers a free guided tour of Bhubaneswar's temples at 8am on the last Sunday of the month. The tour, starting and finishing points are different each time, so contact Orissa Tourism for details.

A city tour offered by **OTDC** (☎ 2432382; behind Panthanivas Hotel, Lewis Rd; city tour Rs 130, out of city Rs 150; ☺ 10am-5pm Mon-Sat), covers the Nandankanan Zoo, Dhauli, Lingaraj and Mukteswar temples, the State Museum and Udayagiri and

Khandagiri Caves. Another tour goes to Pipli, Konark and Puri. Both tours require a minimum of five people and leave from the Panthanivas Tourist Bungalow.

The tour operators below organise customised tours into Orissa's tribal areas; these can also include visits to handicraft villages, and Similipal and Bhitarkanika National Parks. Prices are based on a minimum of two people depending on transport (non-AC/AC) and hotel standards. Tribal tours usually start on a Sunday or Monday to fit in with village markets.

Discover Tours (☎ 2430477; www.orissadiscover.com; 463 Lewis Rd; 7-day tribal tour US$35-50, 3-day Similipal tour US$45-50; ☒ 8am-7.30pm Mon-Sat) Specialises in tribal and textile village tours and Similipal National Park.

Inner India Tours (☎ 2341115; www.innerindia.com; plot 494/3 Gangotri Nagar Rd; tours per day from US$80; ☒ 10am-7pm Mon-Sat) The owner, a former guide, organises tours into tribal areas that can also include Chhattisgarh. Similipal tours cost from US$90 per day.

Swosti Travels (☎ 2535773; www.swosti.com; Hotel Swosti complex, Janpath; per day around US$100; ☒ 8am-8pm) Apart from hotel bookings and car rental, it runs tours to the tribal areas and national parks.

Sleeping

Bhubaneswar is well equipped with accommodation, but no great traveller dens – you might want to pay a little more than base rate to avoid that boxed-in feeling.

BUDGET

Hotel Pushpak (☎ 2310185; Kalpana Sq; d from Rs 250, s/d with AC Rs 750/1000; ☒) A worn but cared-for hotel with cleaner-than-most sheets. The cheaper rooms are fairly bare but the recently renovated AC rooms are good. Checkout is 24 hours; there's a restaurant and bar.

Hotel Padma (☎ 2313330; fax 2310904; Kalpana Sq; s with shared bathroom Rs 70, d Rs 200-250) Padma's two very cheap rooms masquerade as prison cells but with early release each morning. Comfort comes with paying more: an extra Rs 50 brings a TV and phone. Car rental and ticketing can be organised here.

Hotel Bhagwat Niwas (☎ 2313708; Kalpana Sq; s Rs 160-220, d Rs 250-450, d with AC Rs 750-900; ☒) Hiding behind the Padma and signed down a small lane, the Bhagwat has rooms around a courtyard, some with a balcony. Room 36 is the best of the AC lot.

Bhubaneswar Hotel (☎ /fax 2313245; Cuttack Rd; s/d from Rs 150/225, s/d with AC Rs 500/600; ☒) The

hierarchy of room rates is determined by your TV choice. Non-TV viewers will be quite happy in cheaper rooms, which are the better option. Checkout is 24 hours.

Hotel Deepali International (☎ 2310270; 54 Buddhanagar, Kalpana Sq; s/d Rs 275/350, with AC Rs 600/650; ☒) Probably the best hotel on Cuttack Rd, it's partially hidden behind a rank of small stalls. A tidy and well-cared-for hotel with plenty of potted plants, it's got a choice of toilets types; checkout is 24 hours.

MIDRANGE & TOP END

Hotel Richi (☎ 2534619; fax 2539418; 122A Station Sq; s/d from Rs 250/375, r with AC from Rs 700; ☒) Proximity to the train station makes this a haven for railway-weary travellers. Rates include breakfast, there's 24-hour checkout and a 24-hour coffee shop to while away ungodly hours.

Hotel Keshari (☎ 2534994; 113 Station Sq; s/d from Rs 675/775; ☒) Five minutes from the train station, Keshari has a restaurant and a noon checkout; some cheap rooms are to be avoided but the AC rooms are OK. The hotel assumes you carry dollars but you can argue to pay in rupees.

Panthanivas Tourist Bungalow (☎ 2432314; Lewis Rd; r Rs 480, with AC Rs 600; ☒) Despite a lost glory and needing renovation, the Panthanivas is well located, quiet and the closest hotel to the temples. Checkout is 8am.

Hotel Sishmo (☎ 2433600; www.hotelsishmo.com; 86/A-1 Rajpath; s/d Rs 2200/2900; ☒ ☒ ☒) A luxurious place with friendly staff and some pleasant rooms; the better ones have pool

(Rs 125 for nonguests) and distant temple views. There's a commodious bar and good restaurant. Discounts are a possibility.

Eating & Drinking

Mithai Shop & AC Restaurant (Rajpath; meals Rs 15-75) Cyclone-force fans make it difficult to hold the menu but are most refreshing when the heat strikes. This place is Jagannath's gift to thali lovers and connoisseurs of Indian sweets and ice cream.

Maurya Bar & Restaurant (Hotel Richi, Station Sq; dishes Rs 20-60; 🕑) Nearest to the train station, so suitable for pre- or post-travel drinks. Bar and restaurant sit side by side but if you want a beer with your meal you have to eat (same menu) in the bar.

Deep Down South (New Marrion Hotel complex, Janpath; dishes Rs 20-50) First have a lassi, then go for the *masala dosa* (curried veggies in a crisp pancake) special, which has to be the world's largest, measuring at least 1m by 1.5cm, backed with an all-you-can-eat sambar. Room left over? There's also a sweet shop.

Park Inn Bar & Restaurant (Rajpath; meals Rs 40-85; 🕑 10am-11pm) A cinema-dark bar with attentive waiters always ready to suggest another cold beer. Lots of nice cooking smells from the kitchen make you hungry for chicken, fish or prawn dishes.

Bhuvanashree Restaurant (cnr Janpath & Mahatma Gandhi Marg; thalis Rs 31-45) Bustling waiters, chattering customers, a stream of food, and simple, subtle tastes. You'll leave feeling it was money well spent.

Tulsi (Pushpak Hotel, Kalpana Sq; dishes Rs 25-60) A pure veg restaurant specialising in thalis and fruit juices. The interior is interestingly painted with tribal art.

Entertainment

Rabindra Mandeep (☎ 2417677; Sachivajaya Marg) and **Soochana Bhawan** (☎ 2530794; Sachivajaya Marg) are concert venues periodically used for music or dance performances. There's no easy way to find out what's coming up, bar telephoning the venues.

Shopping

A wide-ranging exposition of Orissan handicrafts can be found at **Ekamra Haat** (☎ 2403169; Madhusudan Marg; 🕑 10am-9pm), a permanent market with 42 shops in a large garden space.

Orissan textiles, including appliqué and *ikat* (fabric made with thread that's tie-

dyed before weaving) work, can be bought around **Market Building** (Rajpath) or the **Orissa State Handloom Cooperative** (Utkalika; Eastern Tower, Market Bldg; 🕑 10am-1.30pm & 4.30-9pm Mon-Sat).

Both sides of Rajpath, between Janpath and Sachivajaya Marg, are given over to day and night sell-almost-anything markets. You'll be able to buy a mozzie net here for a visit to the coast.

Getting There & Away

AIR

Indian Airlines (☎ 2530544; Rajpath; 🕑 10am-5pm Mon-Sat) fly to Delhi (US$225, 2.15pm) and Mumbai (US$260, 1.45pm). Alliance Air, a subsidiary of Indian Airlines, flies to Chennai (US$210, 2pm Tuesday, Thursday, Saturday) and Kolkata (US$95, 10.50am Monday, Wednesday, Friday, Sunday, 11.45am Tuesday, Thursday, Saturday).

Air Sahara (☎ 2535007; airport 2535748; 1st fl, 57 Janpath; 🕑 10am-5.30pm) flies to Mumbai (US$280, 1pm) and Kolkata (US$95, 10.10am).

BUS

Baramunda bus station (☎ 2400540; NH5) has frequent buses to Cuttack (Rs 13, one hour), Puri (Rs 20, 1¼ hours) and Konark (Rs 18, two hours), and hourly buses to Berhampur (Rs 50, five hours).

Several services go to Kolkata (Rs 180, 12 hours, 4pm to 7pm), Sambalpur (Rs 155, nine hours, 7.30pm to 10pm) and infrequent services to Baripada (Rs 120, seven hours).

Cuttack buses go from the City bus stand, just off Station Sq, and the bus stop at the top end of Lewis Rd, from where buses also go to Puri.

TRAINS

The *Coromandal Express* travels daily to Chennai (Rs 341/958/1532, 20 hours, 9.35pm). The *Purushotlam Express* goes to Delhi (Rs 425/1194/1910, 30½ hours, 10.37pm) and the *Konark Express* to Mumbai (Rs 398/1093/1748, 37 hours, 3pm). Howrah is connected to Bhubaneswar by the *Jan Shatabdi* (Rs 147/485 in 2nd class/chair car, 7¾ hours, 5.45am) and the *Sri Jagannath Express* (Rs 167/468/748, 8¾ hours, 11.45pm).

Getting Around

There are ever-willing cycle- and autorickshaws to take you around. No buses go to the airport; a taxi costs about Rs 100 from the centre. An autorickshaw to the airport costs about Rs 50 but you'll have to walk the last 500m from the airport entrance. Prepaid taxis from the airport to central Bhubaneswar cost Rs 90, and Puri or Konark Rs 550.

AROUND BHUBANESWAR
Nandankanan Zoological Park

Famous for its white tigers, the **zoo** (☎ 246 6075; admission Indian/foreigner Rs 5/40, car Rs 35, optional guide Rs 45, camera/video Rs 5/500; ☉ 8am-5pm Tue-Sun) also boasts rare Asiatic lions, rhinoceroses, copious reptiles, monkeys and deer. Just inside the gate, the small Nature Interpretation Centre has some displays about Orissa's major national parks.

Other attractions include a **toy train** (Rs 10) and **boat rides** (per person for 30 min Rs 15-40). A swooping **cable car** (Rs 25; ☉ 8am-4pm) crosses a lake, allowing passengers to get off halfway and walk down (300m) to the **State Botanical Garden**. Highlight for many is the **lion and tiger safari** (Rs 30) which leaves on the hour from 10am-noon & 2-4pm) in an 'armoured' electric bus.

OTDC has a **café** (meals Rs 25; ☉ 8am-4.30pm) selling basic food.

OTDC tours stop here for only an (insufficient) hour or so. From Bhubaneswar, frequent public buses (Rs 6, one hour) leave from Kalpana Sq (near Padma Hotel) and outside the former Capital bus stand for Nandankanan village, about 400m from the entrance to the zoo. They may state 'Nandankanan' or 'Patia' as their destination.

Dhauli

After slaughtering members of his family to gain power, and then hundreds of thousands of people on the battlefield, Ashoka penitently converted to Buddhism. In about 260 BC one of his famous edicts was carved onto a large rock at Dhauli, 8km south of Bhubaneswar. The rock is now protected by a grill-fronted building and above, on top of a hillock is a carved elephant. His edicts are detailed on several noticeboards at the base.

On a nearby hill is the huge, white and lovely **Shanti Stupa** (Peace Pagoda), built by the Japanese in 1972. Older Buddhist reliefs are set into the modern structure.

The turn-off to Dhauli is along the Bhubaneswar–Puri road, accessible by any Puri or Konark bus (Rs 6). From the turn-off,

it's a flat 3km walk to the rock, and then a short, steep walk to the stupa. By autorickshaw, a one-way trip costs about Rs 90.

Hirapur

Among iridescent-green paddies, 15km from Bhubaneswar, is a small village with an important **Yogini Temple**, one of only four in India. The low, circular structure, open to the sky, has 64 niches within, each with a black chlorite goddess. Getting here requires hired transport or coming on OTDC's tours.

Pipli

This town, 16km southeast of Bhubaneswar, is notable for its brilliant appliqué craft, door and wall hangings and the more traditional canopies hung over Jagannath and family during festival time. Hung outside the shops, they turn the main road into an avenue of rainbow colours. Pipli is easily accessible by any bus between Bhubaneswar and Puri or Konark.

SOUTHEASTERN ORISSA

PURI

☎ 06752 / pop 157,610

Attracted by spiritual or earthly pleasures, three types of visitors come to Puri – Hindu pilgrims, Indian holiday-makers and foreign travellers – set up camp in different parts of town and rarely mix. For Hindus, Puri is one of the holiest pilgrimage places in India, with religious life revolving around the great Jagannath Mandir and its famous Rath Yatra (Car Festival). Unfortunately, all Hindu temples are closed to non-Hindus.

Puri's other attraction is its long, sandy beach and esplanade – an Indian version of an English seaside. Backing this, in Marine Pde, is a long ribbon of old hotels, flashy resorts and company holiday homes that become instantly full when Kolkata rejoices in a holiday.

In the 1970s Puri became a scene on the hippie trail wending its way through Southeast Asia, attracted here by the sea and bhang, legal in Shiva's Puri. That scene fizzled out like a smoked roach. Travellers now come just to hang out together, gorge on good food, recharge their backpacking spirit and plan what to do next.

PURI

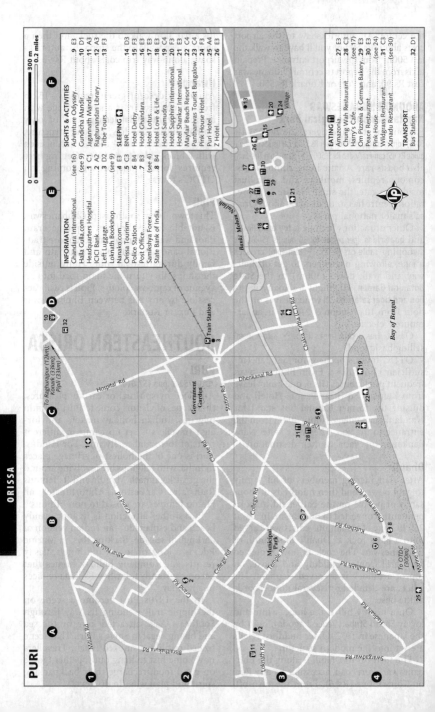

INFORMATION
Chandara International	(see 16)
Halla Gulla.com	(see 9)
Headquarters Hospital	1 C1
ICICI Bank	2 A2
Left Luggage	3 D2
Loknath Bookshop	(see 9)
Nanako.com	4 E3
Orissa Tourism	5 C3
Police Station	6 B4
Post Office	7 B3
Samikshya Forex	(see 4)
State Bank of India	8 B4

SIGHTS & ACTIVITIES
Adventure Odyssey	9 E3
Gundicha Mandir	10 D1
Jagannath Mandir	11 A3
Raghunandan Library	12 A3
Tribe Tours	13 F3

SLEEPING
BNR	14 D3
Hotel Derby	15 F3
Hotel Ghandara	16 E3
Hotel Lotus	17 E3
Hotel Love & Life	18 E3
Hotel Samudra	19 C4
Hotel Sapphire International	20 F3
Hotel Shankar International	21 C4
Mayfair Beach Resort	22 C4
Panthanivas Tourist Bungalow	23 F3
Pink House Hotel	24 F3
Puri Hotel	25 A4
Z Hotel	26 E3

EATING
Amazonia	27 E3
Chung Wah Restaurant	28 C3
Harry's Cafe	(see 17)
Om Pizzeria & German Bakery	29 E3
Peace Restaurant	30 E3
Pink House	(see 24)
Wildgrass Restaurant	31 C3
Xanadu Restaurant	(see 30)

TRANSPORT
Bus Station	32 D1

Orientation

The action is along a few kilometres of coast, with the laid-back traveller village clustered around Chakra Tirtha (CT) Rd to the east, busy Marine Pde to the west and resorts in the middle. A few blocks inland is the holy quarter's chaotic jumble of streets. Buses and trains arrive in the centre of town.

Information

BOOKSHOPS

Loknath Bookshop (CT Rd; ☼ 9am-noon & 3-9pm) Sells and exchanges second-hand books.

INTERNET ACCESS

Halla Gulla.com (CT Rd; per hr Rs 30; ☼ 8am-10pm) Also CD burning from digital camera Rs 40 to 55 per CD.
Nanako.com (CT Rd; per hr Rs 30; ☼ 7.30am-11pm)

LEFT LUGGAGE

Train station (per piece per day Rs 10; ☼ 24hr)

MEDICAL SERVICES

Headquarters Hospital (☎ 223742; Grand Rd)

MONEY

ICICI Bank (1 Naya Plaza, Grand Rd) MasterCard and Visa ATM.
Samikshya Forex (☎ 2225369; CT Rd; ☼ 6am-10pm) Cashes travellers cheques and foreign currencies; changes torn rupee notes.
State Bank of India (☎ 223682; CT Rd; ☼ 10.30am-4pm Mon-Fri, 10.30am-1pm Sat) Slowly cashes travellers cheques and foreign currency.

POST

Post office (☎ 222051; cnr Kutchery & Temple Rds; ☼ 10.30am-5.30pm)

TOURIST INFORMATION

Orissa Tourism (☎ 222664; CT Rd; ☼ 10am-5pm Mon-Sat); train station (☎ 223536; ☼ 7am-9pm) Tourist information, hotel, vehicle and tour booking.
OTDC (☎ 223526; Marine Pde; ☼ 6am-10pm) Booking office and start/finish point for day tours.

TRAVEL AGENCIES

Gandhara International (☎ 2224623; www.hotelgandhara.com; Hotel Gandhara, CT Rd) Air ticketing, and car hire from Rs 4 per kilometre.
Samikshya Forex (☎ 2225369; CT Rd; ☼ 6am-10pm) Ticketing.

Dangers & Annoyances

Ocean currents can be treacherous in Puri, so don't venture out of your depth. Watch the locals or ask one of the curiously out-fitted *nolias* (lifeguards), with their white-painted, cone-shaped wicker hats and short dapper lungis, for the best spots.

Muggings and attacks on women have been reported along isolated stretches of beach, even during the day, so take care.

Sights

JAGANNATH MANDIR

This mighty **temple** belongs to Jagannath, Lord of the Universe and incarnation of Vishnu. The jet-black deity with large, round, white eyes is hugely popular across Orissa. Built in its present form in 1198, the temple is surrounded by two walls; its 58m-high *sikhara* (spire) is topped by the flag and wheel of Vishnu.

Guarded by two stone lions and a pillar crowned by the Garuda that once stood at the Sun Temple at Konark, the eastern entrance, or Lion Gate, is the passageway for the chariot procession of Rath Yatra. The southern, western and northern gates are guarded by statues of men on horseback, tigers and elephants, respectively.

Jagannath, brother Balbhadra and sister Subhadra reside supreme in the central *jagamohan* (assembly hall). The brothers have arms but no hands, while smaller Subhadra, sitting in between, has neither. Priests continually garland and dress the three throughout the day for different ceremonies. Incredibly, the temple employs about 6000 men to perform the complicated rituals involved in caring for the gods. An estimated 20,000 people – divided into 36 orders and 97 classes – are dependent on Jagannath for their livelihood. The kitchen, with 400 cooks, is reportedly the largest in the world.

Non-Hindus can spy from the roof of **Raghunandan Library** (☼ 9am-1pm & 4-7pm) opposite. Ask permission; a 'donation' is compulsory (about Rs 10) and your amount is entered in a book.

BEACH

Puri is no palm-shaded paradise – the **beach** is wide, shelves quickly, is shadeless but is the seaside. To the east it's a public toilet for the fishing village. Between Pink House Hotel and Hotel Shankar International, the beach improves but keep away from the fetid drain oozing into the sea.

ORISSA

By Marine Pde the beach is healthier and often crowded with energetic holiday-makers, especially at night. Look out for artists constructing sand sculptures, a local art form.

It's worth getting up before sunrise to watch the fishermen head out through the surf and, for a little financial motivation, they might take you along.

Tours

OTDC (☎ 223526; Marine Pde; tour No 1 Rs 130, tour No 2 Rs 110) runs day trips. Tour No 1 skips through Konark, Dhauli, Bhubaneswar's temples, Udayagiri and Khandagiri Caves plus Nandankanan Zoo. Tour No 2 goes for a boat jaunt on Chilika Lake.

Several tour operators organise custom tours into Orissa's tribal areas that can include visits to handicraft villages plus Similipal and Bhitarkanika National Parks. For more details see p438 and the boxed text, p452.

Adventure Odyssey (☎ 2226642; travelpack_orissa@ hotmail.com; CT Rd) Runs a seven-day/six-night tour from €60 per day. A Similipal four-day/three-night trip costs €370; adding Bhitarkanika is an extra €200. A Chilika Lake tour with a night camp on Rajhansa Beach costs €80 for two people.

Gandhara International (☎ 2224623; www.hotel gandhara.com; Gandhara Hotel CT Rd; 2 people US$420) Organises a three-day/four-night tribal tour.

Tribe Tours (☎ /fax 2224323; CT Rd; ⏰ 7.30am-9pm) Runs a six-day/seven-night tour from €60 per day. A three-day/two-night Similipal tour costs from €250.

Festivals

One of India's greatest annual events, **Rath Yatra**, takes place each June or July (second day of the bright half of Asadha month) in Puri and across Orissa, when a fantastic procession spills forth from Jagannath Mandir. Rath Yatra commemorates Krishna's journey from Gokul to Mathura. Jagannath, brother Balbhadra and sister Subhadra are dragged along Grand Rd in three huge 'cars', known as *ratha*, to Gundicha Mandir.

The main car of Jagannath (origin of 'juggernaut') stands 14m high. It rides on 16 wheels, each over 2m in diameter – in centuries past, devotees threw themselves beneath the wheels to die gloriously within the god's sight. Four thousand professional temple employees haul the cars, which take enormous effort to pull and are virtually impossible to turn or stop. In Baripada a woman-only team

pulls Subhadra. Hundreds of thousands of pilgrims (and tourists) swarm to witness this stupendous scene, which can take place in temperatures in the 40s.

The gods take a week-long 'summer break' at Gundicha Mandir before being hauled back to Jagannath Mandir, in a repeat of the previous procession. After the festival, the cars are broken up and used for firewood in the temple's communal kitchens, or for funeral-pyre fuel. New cars are constructed each year.

Periodically, according to astrological dictates, the gods themselves are disposed of and new images made. The old ones are buried in a graveyard inside of the northern gate of Jagannath Mandir.

Orissa Tourism's leaflets *Rites and Rituals of Lord Jagannath* and *Rath Yatra* reveal the secrets of a god's life.

Sleeping

Puri gets booked solid for any Kolkata holidays. For Rath Yatra, Durga Puja (Dussehra), Diwali and the end of December and New Year, book well in advance. You may have more luck with Z Hotel and Hotel Ghandara, which only take foreign tourists.

Prices below are for October to February. Healthy discounts can be negotiated during monsoon; prices can triple during a festival. Annoyingly, many hotels have early checkout times due to early morning arrivals of overnight trains bringing fresh holiday-makers.

BUDGET

These places are all in a strip along the eastern end of CT Rd. The Z and Ghandara are suitable for solo women travellers.

Z Hotel (☎ 222554; www.zhotelindia.com; dm women only Rs 60, r with shared bathroom Rs 300, d with private bathroom Rs 600) Z is a travellers' favourite and rightly so. Formerly the home of a maharaja, it has huge, spotless, airy rooms, many of them facing the sea. There are great common areas, a good garden and roof terrace plus a restaurant. The two doubles with an enclosed balcony are well worth the splurge.

Hotel Ghandara (☎ 224117; www.hotelgandhara .com; dm Rs 40, dm women only Rs 50, s/d with shared bathroom Rs 110/150, s/d from Rs 350/450, with AC Rs 550/750; 🅿 🖳) Arrayed around a tree-shaded garden, Ghandara has a wide range of rooms for different budgets. The rear five-storey block has some fine rooftop AC rooms catching breezes and views; other rooms have balconies. A nice touch is a daily newspaper to your room. There's a garden and rooftop restaurant, and a travel agency on site.

Pink House Hotel (☎ 222253; d with shared bathroom Rs 100-250) Off CT Rd, and closest to the beach with sand drifting to your front door, these simple rooms come either on the beach side with little verandas, or round at the back.

Hotel Derby (☎ 223961; Off CT Rd; r Rs 300-350) This is one of the older hotels, with small, neat rooms cheerfully set in a garden close to the beach. Mozzie nets are provided.

Hotel Lotus (☎ 2227033; r from Rs 100) The owners of Harry's Cafe downstairs have gone into the hotel trade with some sparkling rooms. There's a choice of toilets, some rooms have a balcony and all are fan-cooled.

Hotel Love & Life (☎ 224433; fax 226093; dm Rs 30, s/d with shared bathroom Rs 80/100, s/d from Rs 125/250, cottages Rs 250, with AC Rs 750; 🖳) Basic dorms, acceptable rooms in a three-storey building, and some cottages at the rear. Management is friendly and helpful and the place has a relaxed atmosphere.

MIDRANGE & TOP END
Hotel Shankar International (☎ 222696; r from Rs 300, AC cottages Rs 750; 🖳) Off CT Rd, with rooms in three places. Nicest are the more expensive cottages, which have swinging seats on the veranda and the nearby whisper of the ocean. Opposite is a three-storey block with unexciting rooms sharing a common veranda. Between these two places are some cosy, cheap rooms facing the sea.

BNR (☎ 222063; fax 223005; CT Rd; s/d from Rs 400/650, with AC Rs 650/900; 🖳) BNR stands for Bengal National Railways, which explains the steam locomotive parked in the front garden. A huge heritage building, an ossified remnant of the British Raj, has stately rooms, liveried staff and a library with old books. Damn decent place, old chap!

Panthanivas Tourist Bungalow (☎ 222740; r Rs 400-650, with AC Rs 850; 🖳) Off CT Rd, the new block gazes right onto the sea; best rooms and views are on the 1st floor. The old block is rather barrackslike, but the whole place has an air of friendly nonchalance.

Hotel Sapphire International (☎ 226488; r in old block Rs 200-600, new block Rs 850-1850; 🖳) Crowding behind Pink House this hotel consists of two largish blocks catering for Kolkata's salary earners whose dearness allowances

(extra salary paid to compensate for living in an expensive city) permit such holidays. Some rooms have sea views and most share a common veranda.

Puri Hotel (☎ 222114; www.purihotelindia.com; Marine Pde; d from Rs 250, with AC from Rs 800; 🖳) A Bengali holiday institution and the place to bring the whole family. Room sizes go all the way to sleeping 10, and the quasi-British kitsch rooms (hotel built 1947) are quite acceptable. Children under six stay free.

Mayfair Beach Resort (☎ 227800; www.mayfair hotels.com; r with cable TV & breakfast from Rs 3300; 🖳 🖳) The benchmark for Puri luxury, with small hideaway units nestled into lovely gardens dotted with tasteful (imitation) temple statues. The swimming pool (guests only) comes with a swim-up bar and the hotel has a semiprivate beach.

Hotel Samudra (☎ 222705; fax 228654; r Rs 550-750, with AC from Rs 900; 🖳) Backing onto the beach, off CT Rd, this hotel is classy and most rooms have balconies facing the sea and are luxurious; avoid rooms at the front with the smell wafting in from the creek. Room 318 has been recommended.

Eating & Drinking
Puri is a refuge from standard Indian fare. Seafood is the pig-out item and in CT Rd there's the muesli, filter coffee, pancakes and puddings you've been craving. Most places serve beer.

Peace Restaurant (CT Rd; dishes Rs 20-120; 🕑 6am-11pm) 'Peace Restaurant world famous in Puri but never heard of anywhere else'. So reads the menu, which features curries, macaroni and tasty fish dishes. This restaurant, with a delightful garden, is deservedly popular.

Xanadu Restaurant (CT Rd; dishes Rs 30-95; 🕑 6.30am-11pm) One for the early riser, choose a breakfast fry-up or muesli under the shade of palm, banana, papaya and acacia trees. In the evening, over a cold beer and some crunchy pappadum, you can choose between prawns (best in town) or a down-to-earth cauliflower cheese; or maybe both together.

Om Pizzeria & German Bakery (CT Rd; items Rs 10-35; 🕑 7.30am-8pm) This well-known chain (Rishikesh, Manali, Leh, Kathmandu etc) again brings you superb coffee, delectable cinnamon rolls and marvellous muesli, fruit, honey and curd.

Amazonia (CT Rd; dishes Rs 20-55) Another garden restaurant, with lilting background sounds of alternative Indian music. Decide between fish, prawns or a veg curry.

Pink House (mains Rs 60) On the beach edge next to the Pink House Hotel, Pink House is an open-air restaurant that does all the things a traveller would want: muesli or pancakes for breakfast, both if you're hungry; and lots of fish and prawns for every other meal.

Chung Wah Restaurant (VIP Rd; dishes Rs 60-110; 🔀) Chinese food in India is often a disaster, a Chindian mix losing all the attributes of both cuisines and gaining nothing. The Chung Wah serves the real thing; oh the subtleties of a good sweet and sour!

Wildgrass Restaurant (VIP Rd; mains Rs 50-100; 🕒7am-midnight) Wildgrass is a garden gone wild with trees and shrubs. There's only room left over for a small restaurant and little hideaway cubbies under thatched canopies. The fairly regular menu is enlivened with fish dishes and 'lob star' at Rs 120 (order in advance).

Harry's Cafe (CT Rd; dishes Rs 20-55) Harry's serves up strictly vegetarian food without onions or garlic; the food is tasty and the staff are friendly. It's open early for breakfast.

Shopping

Shops along Marine Pde sell crafts, fabric, beads, shells and bamboo work. Stalls at the eastern end of town, nearer the village, sell Kashmiri and Tibetan souvenirs.

Near Jagannath Mandir, many places sell palm-leaf paintings, handicrafts and Orissan hand-woven *ikat* (fabric), which you can buy in lengths or as ready-made garments. Popular souvenirs include cheap, silk-screen-printed postcards and Jagannath images – carved, sculpted or painted.

Getting There & Away

BUS

From the sprawling **bus station** (☎ 224461) near Gundicha Mandir, frequent buses serve Konark (Rs 15, 30 minutes), Satapada (Rs 19, three hours) and Bhubaneswar (Rs 24, two hours). For Pipli and Raghurajpur, take the Bhubaneswar bus. For other destinations change at Bhubaneswar.

TRAIN

Book well ahead on the **train reservation line** (☎ 131; 🕒 8am-8pm Mon-Sat, 8am-2pm Sun) if travelling during holiday and festival times. CT Rd agencies will book tickets for a small fee.

The *Purushottam Express* travels to Delhi (Rs 433/1216/1946, 32 hours, 9.05pm), while Howrah can be reached on both the *Puri-Howrah Express* (Rs 157/442/707, 10¼ hours, 7pm) and the *Jaganath Express* (Rs 157/442/707, 10½ hours, 10pm). The *Tapaswini Express* runs to Sambalpur (Rs 158/442/706, eight hours, 10.40pm), and the *Neelachal Express* goes to Varanasi (Rs 313/879/1406, 22¼ hours, 9.30am), continuing to Delhi on Tuesday, Friday and Sunday.

Getting Around

Several places along CT Rd hire out bicycles for around Rs 15 per day and mopeds/motorcycles for Rs 150/250.

RAGHURAJPUR

The artists' village of **Raghurajpur**, 14km north of Puri, is two streets of thatched brick houses, adorned with mural paintings of geometric patterns and mythological scenes – a traditional art form that has almost died out in Orissa.

SHOPPING IN ORISSA

Ancient Orissa's diverse guilds of *shilpins* (artisans) grew rich on Puri's pilgrimage status and are still in business today. The appliqué work of Pipli (near Bhubaneswar) features brightly coloured patches of fabric, and Cuttack is known for its *tarakasi* (silver-filigree ornaments). Raghurajpur (near Puri) is famous for its *pattachitra* (paintings on specially prepared cloth) and intricate images from the Kamasutra, painstakingly inscribed onto palm leaves *(chitra pothi)*.

Many Orissans work as handloom weavers, producing numerous types of unique silk and cotton fabrics. The Sambalpur region specialises in *ikat* fabrics, a technique involving tie-dyeing the thread before it's woven.

The best places to pick up these items are where they are produced, more specifically from the artists or workers themselves. Ekamra Haat (p440) in Bhubaneswar is the best place to shop for all of Orissa's crafts.

The village is also famous for its *pattachitra* work using a cotton cloth coated with a mixture of gum and chalk and then polished. With eye-aching attention and a very fine brush, artists mark out animals, flowers, gods and demons, which are then illuminated with bright colours.

Another craft *(chitra pothi)* is etching images onto dried palm-leaf sections with a fine stylus, after which the incisions are dyed with a wash of colour.

Take the Bhubaneswar bus and look for the 'Orissa Tourism Craft Village' signpost 11km north of Puri, then walk or take an autorickshaw for the last 1km.

KONARK
☎ 06758 / pop 15,020

The majestic Sun Temple at Konark – a Unesco World Heritage site – is, like the Taj Mahal, one of India's signature buildings and Konark exists purely for it. Most visitors are day-trippers from Bhubaneswar or Puri.

Originally nearer the coast (the sea has receded 3km), Konark was visible from far out at sea and known as the 'Black Pagoda' by sailors, in contrast to the whitewashed Jagannath of Puri.

Orientation & Information

The main Bhubaneswar–Puri road swings around the temple and past a couple of hotels and a splash of eateries. Behind, and to the east, is the **post office** (☉ 10am-5pm Mon-Sat) and back streets of souvenir stands. There is also a **tourist office** (☎ 236821; Yatri Nivas hotel; ☉ 10am-5pm Mon-Sat).

Sights
SUN TEMPLE

Sublimely beautiful, the **Sun Temple** (admission Indian/foreigner Rs 10/250, video Rs 25, guides per hr Rs 100; ☉ sunrise-sunset) was constructed in mid-13th century, probably by Orissan king Narashimhadev I to celebrate his military victory over the Muslims. In use for maybe only three centuries, the first blow occurred in the late 16th century when marauding Mughals removed the copper over the cupola. This vandalism may have dislodged the loadstone leading to the partial collapse

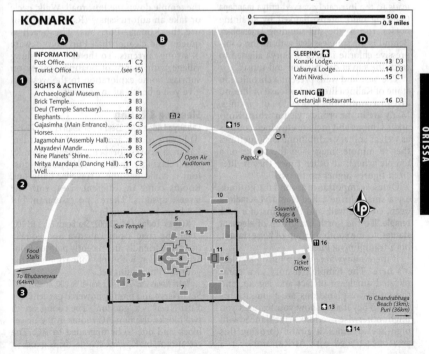

KONARK

0 — 500 m
0 — 0.3 miles

INFORMATION
Post Office.................................1 C2
Tourist Office.........................(see 15)

SIGHTS & ACTIVITIES
Archaeological Museum..............2 B1
Brick Temple................................3 B3
Deul (Temple Sanctuary)...........4 B3
Elephants....................................5 B2
Gajasimha (Main Entrance)........6 C3
Horses...7 B3
Jagamohan (Assembly Hall)........8 B3
Mayadevi Mandir.......................9 B3
Nine Planets' Shrine..................10 C2
Nritya Mandapa (Dancing Hall)...11 C3
Well...12 B2

SLEEPING
Konark Lodge............................13 D3
Labanya Lodge..........................14 D3
Yatri Nivas................................15 C1

EATING
Geetanjali Restaurant...............16 D3

Open Air Auditorium

Pagoda

Souvenir Shops & Food Stalls

Sun Temple

Food Stalls

To Bhubaneswar (64km)

Ticket Office

To Chandrabhaga Beach (3km); Puri (36km)

ORISSA

of the 40m-high *sikhara*; subsequent cyclones probably compounded the damage.

As late as 1837 one half of the *sikhara* was still standing but collapsed completely in 1869. (An illustration in the Yatri Nivas foyer pictures the Sun Temple with still half a *sikhara* and gives an idea of its splendour.) Gradually, shifting sands covered the site, with only the *deul* and *jagamohan* rising proud of its burial mound. Excavation and restoration began in 1901; the *jagamohan* was closed off and filled with rocks and sand to prevent it from collapsing inwards.

The entire temple was conceived as the cosmic chariot of the sun god, Surya. Seven mighty prancing horses (representing the days of the week) rear at the strain of moving this leviathan of stone on 24 stone cartwheels (representing the hours of the day) positioned around the temple base. The temple was positioned so that dawn light would illuminate the *deul* interior and the presiding deity, which may have been moved to Jagannath Mandir in Puri in the 17th century.

The **gajasimha** (main entrance) is guarded by two stone lions crushing elephants and leads to the intricately carved **nritya mandapa** (dancing hall). Steps, flanked by straining horses, rise to the still-standing **jagamohan**. Behind is the spireless **deul** with its three impressive chlorite images of Surya aligned to catch the sun at dawn, noon and sunset.

The base and walls present a chronicle in stone of Kalinga life, a storyboard of life and love in a continuous procession of carvings. Many are in the erotic style for which Konark is famous and include entwined couples as well as solitary exhibitionists. Sometimes they're minute images on the spoke of a temple wheel; at other times they're life-sized figures higher up the walls.

Of lesser importance around the grounds are a small shrine called **Mayadevi Mandir**; a deep, covered **well**; and the ruins of a **brick temple**. To the north is a group of **elephant statues**, to the south a group of **horse statues**, both trampling soldiers.

If there's anywhere worth hiring a guide, it's here. The temple's history is a complicated amalgam of fact and legend, and the guides' explanations are thought-provoking. They'll also show you features you might otherwise overlook – the dancer with high-heeled shoes, a giraffe (proving this area once traded with Africa) and even a man treating himself for venereal disease! Be sure your guide is registered. There are only 29 registered guides in Konark and the name board by the entrance has still to be updated. Unlicensed (and maybe unreliable) guides will dog your steps from arrival.

NINE PLANETS' SHRINE

This 6m-chlorite **slab**, once the architrave above the *jagamohan*, is now the centrepiece of a small shrine just outside the temple walls. Carved seated figures represent the Hindu nine planets – Surya (the sun), Chandra (moon), Mars, Mercury, Jupiter, Venus, Saturn, Rahu and Ketu.

ARCHAEOLOGICAL MUSEUM

This largish **museum** (☎ 236822; admission Rs 5; ☻ 10am-5pm Sat-Thu), next to Yatri Nivas, contains many sculptures and carvings found during excavations of the Sun Temple. Some smaller pieces (eg the statue of Agni, the fire god) are particularly impressive.

CHANDRABHAGA BEACH

The local beach at **Chandrabhaga** is 3km from the temple down the Puri road. Walk, cycle or take an autorickshaw (Rs 50 return) or use the Konark–Puri bus. The beach is quieter and cleaner than Puri's but beware of strong currents. To the east is a fishing village with plenty of boating activity on sunrise. Some exploration to the west can give you a beach all to yourself.

Sleeping & Eating

Labanya Lodge (☎ 236824; Sea Beach Rd; r Rs 75-150; ▣) With rooms around a central garden, Labanya scores for being cheap, friendly and relaxingly quiet. With enough custom it could become a traveller hang-out. Rooms come in different sizes, with the largest upstairs. There's no restaurant but food can be ordered in.

Konark Lodge (☎ 236502; Sea Beach Rd; r Rs 100) Over the road from Labanya and equally quiet, the friendly and recently painted Konark is smaller, with only four rooms. Bring your own mosquito net.

Yatri Nivas (☎ 236820; r non-AC Rs 200, AC 400; ▣) Set in large and prettily flowered gardens, the Yatri Nivas is a 'goodun'. The rooms are in two blocks; the non-AC rooms in the newer block and due to be upgraded to AC. The restaurant, by Konark standards, is good.

Geetanjali Restaurant (dishes Rs 25-55) Caters mostly to day-trippers who just stagger from the temple entrance opposite desperate for refreshments. Cleaner and much nicer than other eating places in Konark, it has the best food in town.

Getting There & Away

Overcrowded minibuses run along the pretty coastal road between Puri and Konark (Rs 13, one hour, hourly until about 5pm). There are also regular departures to Bhubaneswar (Rs 18, two hours). Konark is included in OTDC tours from Bhubaneswar (p438) and Puri (p444). Because the Puri–Konark road is flat, some diehards even cycle the 36km from Puri.

CHILIKA LAKE

Chilika Lake is Asia's largest brackish lagoon. Swelling from 600 sq km in April/May to 1100 sq km in the monsoon, the shallow lake is separated from the Bay of Bengal by a 60km-long sand bar called Rajhansa. Due to silting, a new mouth was dredged in 2000.

The lake is noted for the million-plus migratory birds – including osprey, grey-legged geese, herons, cranes and flamingos – that flock here in winter (from November to mid-January) from as far away as Siberia and Iran. Possibly the largest congregation of aquatic birds on the subcontinent, they concentrate in a 3-sq-km area within the bird sanctuary on Nalabana Island. Changes in salinity have caused some birds to move to Mangaljodi near the northern shore. Problems such as silting and commercial prawn farming are also threatening this important wetland area and the livelihood of local fishers.

Other attractions are rare Irrawady dolphins near Satapada, the pristine beach along Rajhansa and Kalijai temple where Hindu pilgrims flock for the Makar Mela festival (p433) in January.

Satapada

☎ 06752

This small village, on a headland jutting southwestwards into the lake, is the starting point for most boat trips. There's an **Orissa Tourism office** (☎ 262077; Yatri Nivas; 24hr) here.

SIGHTS & ACTIVITIES

Boat trips from Satapada usually cruise to the new sea mouth for a tuck-in of fresh prawns, a paddle in the sea and some dolphin and bird spotting en route.

OTDC (☎ 262077; Yatri Nivas hotel; 6-7/8-10/20/34 seater per hr Rs 410/460/630/790) has boat hire or a three-hour tour (per person Rs 80) at 10.30am.

Dolphin Motor Boat Association (☎ 262038; Satapada jetty; 1-8hr trips per boat Rs 300-1000), a co-operative of local boat owners, has set-price trips mixing in dolphin sightseeing, a sea-mouth visit, Nalabana bird sanctuary and Kalijai Island temple.

A regular ferry (Rs 18, four hours, departs noon, returns 6am next day) plies between Satapada and Barkul.

The **Chilika Lake Wetland Centre** (☎ 262013; admission Rs 10; 10am-5pm) is a professionally collated exhibition on the lake, wildlife and human inhabitants. The centre has an upstairs observatory with a telescope and bird identification charts.

SLEEPING & EATING

Yatri Nivas (☎ 262077; d Rs 150) A good option with balconies (some with lake views) and clean beds. The restaurant is good.

Several shops and food stalls line the road to the jetty. Don't forget to take water on your boat trip.

Barkul

☎ 06756

On the northern shore of Chilika, Barkul is just a splatter of houses and food stalls on a lane off the national highway. **Orissa Tourism** (☎ 220855; 10am-5pm Mon-Sat closed 2nd Sat in month) has a presence here.

Boats go to Nalabana and Kalijai Island. Nalabana is best visited in early morning and late afternoon, November to late February. Video cameras require permission from the **Forest Department** (☎ 220434) in Balugaon.

OTDC runs a boat trip (Rs 400) to the sea mouth with some dolphin spotting. With a minimum of 14 people OTDC runs tours to Kalijia (Rs 50), and Nalabana and Kalijai (Rs 150). Otherwise, a boat with a noiseless engine (doesn't scare birds) can be hired for Nalabana (Rs 900, two hours) or an ordinary boat for Kalijai (Rs 450, 2½ hours). Private operators charge around Rs 350 an hour.

At **Panthanivas Hotel** (☎ 220488; r Rs 490, with AC Rs 850;), a beautiful garden slopes down to the lake, giving agreeable views to all the very pleasant rooms.

ORISSA

Frequent buses dash along the national highway between Bhubaneswar and Berhampur. You can get off anywhere on route.

A ferry goes to Satapada (p449).

Rambha

The small town of Rambha is the nearest place to stay for turtle watching on Rushikulya beach. Boat hire costs Rs 410 for a three-hour trip around the lake.

Rambha Panthanivas (☎ 06810-278346; dm Rs 50, d Rs 350, with AC Rs 600; 🔀), about 200m off the main road, and 1km west of Rambha centre, has reasonable rooms with balconies overlooking the lake. The restaurant is surprisingly good. Order crab masala; messy but oh so yummy.

Buses and five trains connect with Bhubaneswar or Berhampur.

Rushikulya

The nesting beach for olive ridley turtles is on the northern side of Rushikulya River, near the villages of Purunabandh and Gokharkuda. The nearest accommodation is in Rambha (above), 20km away.

During nesting and hatching there'll be conservationists on the beaches and activity takes place throughout the night. Don't use lights during hatching as they distract the turtles away from the sea.

GOPALPUR-ON-SEA
☎ 0680 / pop 6660

Gopalpur-on-Sea is a seaside town the British left to slide into history until Bengali holiday-makers discovered its attractions in the 1980s. Prior to this, it had a noble history as a seaport with connections to Southeast Asia.

It's no paradise beach but its quiet and peaceful, relatively clean, blue-water beach is the big draw. Mooch about, inspect the fishing community and old port, and relax for a while.

Orientation & Information

The main road from the national highway rushes straight through town and fizzles into a big space in front of the sea. Around here are most of the town's hotels and restaurants. There's a PCO (Public Call Office) by Krishna's restaurant; the bus stand is 500m before the beach.

Sights

Peering over the town is the **lighthouse** (admission Rs 5; 🕒 3.30-5.30pm) with its immaculate gardens and petite staff cottages. It's a late-afternoon draw card and after puffing up a never-ending spiral staircase you're rewarded with views, welcome cooling breezes and mobile-phone reception.

ORISSA'S ENDANGERED TURTLES

Critically endangered olive ridley turtles swim up from deeper waters beyond Sri Lanka to mate and lay their eggs on Orissa's beaches. The main nesting sites are Gahirmatha within the Bhitarkanika National Park, Devi near Konark and Rushikulya.

Turtle deaths (an estimated 100,000 in the last 10 years) come from illegal fishing (within 10km of the coast), mechanised fishing with fine-meshed nets, and not using required turtle exclusion devices (TEDs), which are gateways to freedom that allow trapped air-breathing turtles to escape. About 5% of fish also escape but fishermen disagree with this figure and want government compensation before they use TEDs. Another threat has been afforestation of the Devi beach-nesting site with casuarina trees. While preserving the beaches, they take up soft sand necessary for a turtle hatchery. Now a further threat is intended oil exploration off Gahirmatha during turtle-massing times.

Turtles mass at sea between late October and early December. Then in January they congregate near nesting beaches and, if conditions are right, they come ashore over four to five days. If conditions aren't right, they reabsorb their eggs, as happened in 1997 and 1998.

Hatching takes place 50 to 55 days later. Hatchlings are guided to the sea by the luminescence of the ocean and can be easily distracted by bright lights; unfortunately the national highway runs within 2km of Rushikulya beach, so many turtles paddle the wrong way. However, villagers in the Sea Turtle Protection Committee gather up errant turtles and take them to the sea.

The best place to see nesting and hatching is at Rushikulya (above).

Dangers & Annoyances

Foreigners, especially women, are always an attraction for the curious, particularly men hoping to see a little flesh. It can be incredibly annoying. One option is to walk well away from the centre of things, best with fellow-traveller company, or to plonk yourself near an Indian family and bask under their general protection.

Swimming off Gopalpur is an untested activity; most domestic visitors are content with a paddle and there may well be undercurrents to contend with.

Sleeping & Eating

Gopalpur can be booked out during holiday and festival time. Prices below are for the high season (November to January); discounts are available at other times.

Hotel Sea Pearl (☎ 2242556; d with side view Rs 600-700, with sea view Rs 750, with AC Rs 850-1000; 🕸) Any nearer the sea and it'd be in it; Sea Pearl has some great rooms, especially the upper-storey, front-facing, non-AC rooms. Rooms 203 and 204 have balconies and view.

Lobo's Lodge (☎ 2242068; Main Rd; d Rs 400) A former home of a British memsahib, Lobo's has eight big comfortable doubles with homely comforts surrounded by a secluded garden. Food is available.

Hotel Green Park (☎ 2242016; greenpark016@ yahoo.com; d Rs 200-400, with AC & view Rs 600; 🕸) One street back from the beach, Green Park is a clean and friendly option. Some rooms have front-facing balconies and there's a 24-hour checkout.

Hotel Rosalin (☎ 2242071; r with shared or private bathroom Rs 150) A small, single-storey house, opposite Sea Shell, with small rooms around a garden. It's for those who are over budget.

Hotel Holiday Home (☎ 2242049; Main Rd; d from Rs 250) Facing the beach at the end of Main Rd, this pre-Independence building is popular with families because some of its rooms have five beds. A large communal terrace provides sea views; food can be arranged.

Sea Shell (dishes Rs 15-45; ⏰ 8am-11pm) Jostling the beach, thatch-roofed and with open sides for your views and sea breezes, Sea Shell is an ideal place to while away the day with a good book, some snacks and a resuscitating beer at night. The fish is marvellous.

Krishna's (dishes Rs 25-60) This is a cheerful, bustling place, highly rated by the locals,

which does some decent fish, Indian and Chinese food.

Getting There & Away

Frequent, crowded minibuses travel to Berhampur (Rs 6, one hour), where you can catch onward transport. Alternatively, an autorickshaw costs Rs 150.

WESTERN ORISSA

TAPTAPANI

Apart from the small **hot springs** in this peaceful village in the Eastern Ghats hills, there's not much else to see.

For a great winter treat (December nights plunge to zero) book one of the two rooms at **Panthanivas Tourist Bungalow** (☎ 06816-255031; s/d Rs 450/600, with hot bath Rs 800). Hot spring water is channelled directly to vast tubs in its Roman-style bathrooms. Rooms can be rented for the day at half-price.

Buses go regularly to Berhampur (Rs 25, two hours).

JEYPORE

☎ 06854 / pop 77,000

Visitors will most likely stay here while exploring local tribal areas. There's a **State Bank of India ATM** (Bazaar branch, Main Rd).

Hotel Madhumati (☎ 241377; NKT Rd; s/d Rs 175/250, with aircooler Rs 200/300, with AC Rs 225/550; 🕸) is in a quiet neighbourhood, surrounded by lawns, and well kept by genial staff. Cheaper rooms have fans and squat toilets. **Hello Jeypore** (☎ 231127; pankajagrawal@flashmail.com; s/d from Rs 595/695; 🕸) is more upmarket with clean, fairly modern, well-equipped rooms.

The **bus station** (☎ 233181; Main Rd) has local and distance services by ordinary or deluxe bus. Frequent buses go to Koraput (Rs 8, one hour). Others go to Berhampur (Rs 130 to 165, 12 hours, depart hourly from noon to 8pm), Bhubaneswar (Rs 250, 16 hours, seven buses from 12.30pm to 6pm) and Sambalpur (Rs 160 to 200, 12 hours, depart 12.30pm, 1.30pm, 3pm and 5.30pm).

Jeypore is on the scenic Jagdalpur–Visakhapatnam railway line.

Train No 1VK connects Jeypore with Jagdalpur (sleeper Rs 31, 1¾ hours, 3.40pm), and 2VK connects Jeypore with Visakhapatnam (sleeper Rs 61, nine hours, 11.25am), calling at Koraput (sleeper Rs 31, 1¾ hours).

ORISSA

ORISSA'S INDIGENOUS TRIBES

Sixty two tribal groups (Adivasi) live in Orissa in an area that also encompasses Chhattisgarh and Andhra Pradesh. In Orissa they account for one quarter of the state's population and mostly inhabit the jungles and hilly regions of the centre and southwest. Regardless of their economic poverty, they have highly developed social organisations and distinctive cultures expressed in music, dance and arts.

Tribal influence on Indian culture is little recognised, but it is claimed that early Buddhist sanghas were modelled on tribal equality, lack of caste and respect for all life. Many of the Hindu gods, including Shiva and Kali, have roots in tribal deities. Later, many Adivasis became integrated into Hindu society as menials, while others retreated into hilly or forested areas.

Most Adivasis were originally animists but have been the attention of soul-seeking missionaries Christian missionaries over the last 30 years. In reaction, extreme Hindu groups have been aggressively converting the Adivasis to Hinduism. Naxalites have also exploited Adivasi powerlessness by using them as foot soldiers, all the while claiming to defend them.

The tribes have become something of a tourist attraction with visits possible to some villages and *haats* (village markets) that Adivasis attend on a weekly basis. There are arguments regarding the morality of visiting Adivasi areas, as tourism at present brings very little income to the tribes.

Of the more populous tribes, the Kondh, number about one million and are based in the southwest, around Koraput, and near Sambalpur in the northwest. The Santal, with a population above 500,000, live around Baripada and Khiching in the far north. The 300,000 Saura live near Bolangir in the west. The Bonda, known as the 'Naked People' for wearing minimal clothing, have a population of about 5000 and live in the hills near Koraput.

It is important to visit these areas on an organised tour for the following reasons:

■ Some areas are prohibited and others require permits, which are much more easily obtained by a tour operator.

■ Some tribal areas are hard to find and often not accessible by public transport.

■ Adivasis often speak little Hindi or Oriya, and usually no English.

■ Some tribes can get angry, even violent, if foreigners visit their villages uninvited and without official permission.

■ Some people do not allow themselves to be photographed.

Most tours start from Bhubaneswar (see p438) or Puri (see p444), take in the more accessible areas in the southwest and can then go on to visit Similipal National Park. Options can include jungle trekking, staying at a village (tents and cooking supplied by the tour operator) and visiting one or more of the *haats*.

AROUND JEYPORE
Koraput
☎ 06852

The **tourist office** (☎ 250318; Raipur-Visakhapatnam Rd; ☼ 10am-5pm Mon-Sat, closed 2nd Sat in month) has information and can arrange car hire.

The **Tribal Museum** (admission free; ☼ 3-5pm Mon, Tue & Thu-Sat, 10am-4pm Sun) was under renovation at the time of research but will be an important place to visit for an understanding of Orissa's tribes.

For non-Hindus unable to visit Puri's Jagannath Mandir there's the opportunity to visit a **Jagannath temple** here that comes with an exhibition of gods of the different states of India. Another display has examples of traditional murals with information about them. At the back of the temple is a series of apses containing statuettes of Jagannath in his various guises and costumes.

Onkadelli

This small village, 65km from Jeypore, has a **haat** (☼ Thu, best time 11am-2pm) that throngs with Bonda, Gadaba and Didai people. Photography should only be done with the acceptance of the subject, and visitors should not photograph the Bonda.

Gupteswar Cave

Located 64km west of Jeypore, **Gupteswar Cave** is a cave temple dedicated to Shiva on account of a handily shaped stalagmite serving as a lingam. Take a torch, as there are a few passages and chambers to explore alongside the lingam's grotto.

JEYPORE TO SAMBALPUR

The road between Jeypore and Sambalpur passes through a region rich in handicrafts. Many master craftspeople here have been recognised nationally and internationally.

Down the back lanes of **Kotpad**, 40km north of Jeypore, is a thriving home-based fabric-dyeing industry. Along the lanes you'll see ropes of thread in a rich range of colours from reds and burgundies to browns laid out to dry.

The Costa Pada area in **Baripalli** is where to discover how tie-dye *ikat* textiles are created. Skeins of threads separated into cords are wrapped around frames. Painstakingly, these cords are then tied in red cotton to mark out the dyeing pattern. Strips of rubber are then wound around to protect the undyed areas. Dyed and dried, the threads are then woven on the many looms you can see through open doorways. There's also a thriving terracotta industry here.

SAMBALPUR

☎ 0663 / pop 154,170

Sambalpur is the centre for the textile industry spread over western Orissa. If you haven't already bought examples of *ikat* or *sambalpuri* weaving, Gole Bazaar is the place to look. The town is important as a base for nearby Badrama National Park, and Debrigarh Wildlife Sanctuary on the edge of Hirakud Dam. There are no money-changing facilities.

Orientation & Information

National Highway 6 passes through Sambalpur to become VSS Marg.

Orissa Tourism (☎ 2411118; Panthanivas Tourist Bungalow, Brooks Hill; ☉ 10am-5pm Mon-Sat, closed 2nd Sat in month) Can arrange tours to Debrigarh and Badrama.

State Bank of India (VSS Marg) MasterCard and Visa ATM next to Sheela Towers hotel.

Sleeping & Eating

The following places can be found bunched together along VSS Marg.

Rani Lodge (☎ 2522173; s/d Rs 90/150) A cheap but clean and well-cared-for hotel that provides mosquito nets. It's just the place for an early morning departure, with the muezzin at the mosque opposite providing an early wake-up call.

Hotel Sujata (☎ 2400403; s Rs 150, d Rs 250-350, s/d with AC Rs 450/550; ✵) An ordinary, run-of-the-mill hotel for business wallahs and does well at it. Rooms are clean, bathrooms good and the staff helpful.

Sheela Towers (☎ 2403111; www.sheelatowers.com; s/d Rs 390/450, with AC Rs 650/750; ✵) Sambalpur's top-notch hotel, with a range of well-equipped and maintained rooms; non-AC rooms are particularly good value. Check-out is 24 hours. The very fine restaurant provides a buffet breakfast and there's a relaxing **bar** (☉ 10.30am-10.30pm; ✵).

Hong Kong Restaurant (dishes Rs 40-90; ☉ 11am-3pm, 6-10.30pm Tue-Sun) A rarity, an authentic Chinese restaurant run by Chinese, so expect the real thing, even takeaway.

Bombay Sweets (snacks Rs 5-20; ☉ 7am-10.30pm) This small café-cum–sweet shop serves up cheap snacks and some absolutely gorgeous Indian sweets.

Getting There & Away

The **government bus stand** (Laxmi Talkies) has buses running to Jeypore (Rs 155/200 in standard/deluxe, 14 hours, five daily) and Berhampur (Rs 166, 12 hours, 6pm and 9pm). Adjacent travel agencies book buses leaving from the **private bus station** (☎ 2540601), 2km from city centre. Several buses go to Bhubaneswar (Rs 160, eight hours), Raipur (Rs 130, eight hours) and Jashipur for Similipal (Rs 180, 10 hours, 5pm, 9pm and 9.45pm).

Train No 8451 *Tapaswini Express* goes to Puri (Rs 148/416/666, nine hours, 11.15pm) via Bhubaneswar (Rs 130/365/584, seven hours). Other trains go to Howrah and Delhi.

AROUND SAMBALPUR
Debrigarh Wildlife Sanctuary

The 347-sq-km **Debrigarh Wildlife Sanctuary** (☎ 0663-2402741; admission Rs 10, camera Rs 2, car Rs 5; ☉ 8am-5pm 1 Oct-30 Jun), 40km from Sambalpur, is an easy day out. Mainly dry deciduous forest blankets the Barapahad Hills down to the shores of the vast Hirakud reservoir, a home for migratory birds in winter. Major wildlife here includes deer,

ORISSA

antelopes, sloth bears, langur monkeys and the ever-elusive tigers and leopards. Access requires a 4WD, which can be arranged through Orissa Tourism or your hotel for about Rs 800 for a half day.

Badrama National Park

This **park** (Ushakothi; admission Rs 5, camera Rs 5, vehicle entry Rs 5; ☉ 1 Nov–mid-Jun) shelters elephants, tigers, panthers and bears. Unusually for a wildlife area, night visits are possible and best done in a 4WD. A guide isn't necessary but can be provided.

Huma

The leaning **Vimaleswar temple** at Huma, 32km south of Sambalpur, is a small Shiva temple where the *deul* slants considerably in two directions. The puzzle is that the porch of the temple appears square and there are no apparent filled-in gaps between the porch and *deul*. Was it built that way?

Khiching

On the way east to Similipal (north of the highway), about 50km west of Jashipur, is the 10th-century **Maa Kichakeswari temple** (☉ 8am-noon & 3-8pm), reconstructed in 1934. Another of Shiva's avatars, Kichakeswari, is resident in this single-room temple. Outside are several bands of sculptures with lions crushing elephants, Durga killing a buffalo demon, Ganesh, *apsaras* (heavenly nymphs) and some head-on erotica, including a shield-your-eyes fellatio scene.

NORTHEASTERN ORISSA

SIMILIPAL NATIONAL PARK

☎ 06792

The 2750-sq-km **Similipal National Park** (admission Indian/foreigner Rs 10/100, camera Indian/foreigner Rs 20/30, video by special permission, vehicle Rs 100; ☉ 6am-noon day visitor, entry by 2pm with accommodation reservation 1 Nov-15 Jun) is Orissa's prime wildlife sanctuary.

The scenery is remarkable: a massif of prominent hills creased by valleys and gorges, and made dramatic by plunging waterfalls, including the spectacular 400m-high **Barheipani Waterfall** and the hanging 150m-high **Joranda Waterfall**. The jungle is an atmospheric mix of dense sal forest and rolling open savanna. The core area is only 850 sq km and much of the southern part is closed to visitors.

The wildlife list is impressive: 29 reptile species, 214 birds and 42 mammals, including 2500 deer and 7000 sambar providing enough takeaway for 100 leopards and 97 tigers. The tigers aren't tracked; the best chance to spot them will be at the **Joranda salt lick**. What you may well see is your first wild elephant (there are 432 in the park), most probably at the **Chahala salt lick**.

Orientation & Information

There are two entrances, **Tulsibani**, 15km from Jashipur, on the northwestern side, and **Pithabata**, near Lulung, 25km west of Baripada. Options are a day visit or an overnight stay within the park.

Entry permits can be obtained in advance from the **assistant conservator of forests** (☎ 06797-232474; National Park, Jashipur, Mayurbhanj District, 757091), or the **field director, Similipal Tiger Reserve Project** (☎ 06792-252593; Bhanjpur, Baripada, Mayurbhanj District, 757002). Alternatively a day permit can be purchased from either gate.

Visitors either come on an organised tour or charter a vehicle (Rs 1200 to 2000 per day for 4WD); hiring a guide (around Rs 400) is advisable.

If you want to avoid the hassles of arranging permits, transport, food and accommodation, an organised tour is the answer; see p438, p444 and opposite for details.

Sleeping & Eating

Most accommodation is at 700m above sea level; in winter (November–February) overnight temperatures can plummet to zero.

Forest Department (d Indian/foreigner from Rs 440/880) Seven sets of forest bungalows with Chahala, Joranda and Newana being best for animal spotting and Barheipani for views. The very basic accommodation has to be booked well in advance (30 days) with the field director at Baripada – see above. You have to bring your own food and water.

Aranya Nivas Tourist Lodge (dm Rs 100, d with fan Rs 600) This lodge, 5km inside the Pithabata gate, is run by OTDC; book with Orissa Tourism in Baripada (opposite).

JASHIPUR

☎ 06797

This slip of a town is an entry point for Similipal Park and a place to collect an entry permit and organise a guide and transport. Accommodation is limited and eating places few.

SOMETHING SPECIAL

Dhaba (🕒 24hr) Throughout India there are unnamed *dhabas* (snack bars) serving some of the best food here, like this one on the Tulsibani side of Jashipur. The menu's very basic, dhal and rice or chapati, maybe *rajma* (kidney beans) or a *channa masala* with as many cups of 'ready-made' (chai) as you can stomach. The décor could leave something to be desired but you'll be joined by those connoisseurs of *dhaba* food – truck drivers. Look for a pile of trucks outside a *dhaba* and you'll know you've got a goodie. Many customers means the food's always fresh, always hot and very tasty.

The **youth hostel** (☎ 232633; dm Rs 50, d Rs 100) off Main Rd is bare-bones accommodation with no food available. For more comfort, **Sai Ram Hotel** (☎ 232827; Main Rd; s Rs 70, d non-AC/AC Rs 200/500; 🍴), a comparatively new hotel, has small singles, good non-AC rooms and bigger AC rooms. The owner can arrange Similipal trips.

BARIPADA
☎ 06792

With the very helpful **Orissa Tourism** (☎ 252 710; Baghra Rd; 🕒 10am-5pm Mon-Sat, closed 2nd Sat in month), this town is the better place to organise a Similipal visit.

Places to stay include **Hotel Durga** (☎ 253438; r Rs 160, with AC from Rs 500; 🍴), with good-value, fan-cooled cheaper rooms, restaurant and bar. **Hotel Ambika** (☎ 252557; bid_ambica@sancharnet .in; 🍴) is a large rambling hotel set in some pleasant gardens. The rooms are fine and there's a good bar and restaurant. It can organise Similipal trips.

Buses go to Kolkata (Rs 100, three hours, seven buses between 5am and 11.15am) and frequently to Bhubaneswar (Rs 130, five hours) and Balasore (Rs 30, one hour).

CUTTACK
☎ 0671 / pop 535,140

Cuttack, one of Orissa's oldest cities, was the state capital until 1950; today it's a chaotic jumble of colourful bazaars. The **tourist office** (☎ 2612225; Link Rd; 🕒 10am-5pm Mon-Sat, closed 2nd Sat in month) is along the Bhubaneswar road. Shopping is great: saris, horn and brassware are manufactured here, along with the famed, lacelike, silver filigree work

(tarakasi). The best jewellers are on **Naya Sarak** and **Chowdary Bazaar**, while you can see pieces being crafted in **Mohammedia Bazaar**.

The 14th-century **Barabati Fort**, about 3km north of the city centre, once boasted nine storeys, but only some foundations and moat remain. The 18th-century **Qadam-i-Rasool** shrine, in the city centre, is sacred to Hindus as well as Muslims (who believe it contains footprints of the Prophet Mohammed).

Bhubaneswar and its better range of accommodation is less than an hour away and Cuttack can easily be covered in a day trip. Express buses to Bhubaneswar leave every 10 minutes (Rs 14, 30 to 45 minutes).

BALASORE
Balasore, the first major town in northern Orissa, was once an important trading centre with Dutch, Danish, English and French warehouses. Now it's a staging post for Chandipur or Similipal National Park. **Orissa Tourism** (☎ 262048; 1st fl, TP Bldg, Station Sq; 🕒 10am-5pm Mon-Sat, closed 2nd Sat in month) is 500m from the train station.

Several buses leave from Remuna Golai at around 10pm for Kolkata (Rs 160, seven to eight hours) and frequently for Bhubaneswar (Rs 75, five hours). Infrequent buses to Chandipur mean an autorickshaw (Rs 100) is a better option.

CHANDIPUR
☎ 06782

Quieter than Puri, more refined and interesting than Gopalpur-on-Sea, this delightful seaside village ambles down to the ocean through a short avenue of casuarina and palm trees. The place amounts to a couple of hotels, snack places and some souvenir shops. Chandipur has a huge beach at low tide when the sea is some 5km away; it'll be safe to swim here when there's enough water.

A bustling fishing village, the home of refugee Bangladeshis, is 2km further up the coast at a river mouth. In the early morning, walk up and watch the boats unloading unusual fish and huge trays of prawns.

Panthanivas Tourist Bungalow (☎ 272251; dm Rs 80, d non-AC/AC Rs 360/700; 🍴) has the best location, overlooking the beach. Of the two blocks choose the one with sea views for a dramatic sunrise. Alternatively, there's the **Hotel Chandipur** (☎ 270030; d non-AC/AC from Rs 200/650; 🍴), a three-sided, three-storey

ORISSA

hotel around a courtyard with a fountain and fragrant frangipani trees.

BHITARKANIKA WILDLIFE SANCTUARY
☎ 06729

Three rivers flow out to sea south of Chandipur, forming a delta crisscrossed by a tidal maze of muddy creeks. An ecologically important mangrove forest, it contains 63 of the world's 75 mangrove varieties. Hundreds of estuarine crocodiles, some 6m-plus monsters, bask on mud flats waiting for the next meal to float by; Dangmar Island contains a successful breeding and conservation programme for these crocodiles. Less dangerous creatures are pythons, water monitors, wild boar and timid deer.

The flash of bright colour will be a kingfisher; there are eight species, plus 190 other bird species. A large heronry on Bagagaham Island is home for birds arriving in early June to nest up to November.

The sanctuary also protects the Gahirmatha nesting beach of the endangered olive ridley turtles (see the boxed text, p450). Gahirmatha is out of bounds due to a missile-testing site on one of the nearby Wheeler Islands. Rushikulya (p450) is a more accessible nesting beach.

Orientation & Information

Some of this 672-sq-km delta forms **Bhitarkanika Wildlife Sanctuary** (☎ 272460; permit Indian/foreigner Rs 1/10, camera Indian/foreigner Rs 25/50, video Indian/foreigner Rs 500/1000, boat Rs 10, overnight boat parking Rs 100). Get a permit at the Chamdbali **jetty** (🕐 6am-6pm), from where boats can be hired (Rs 1600) to travel into the sanctuary.

Sights

First stop is a permit check at Khola jetty before chugging on to **Dangmar Island** for the crocodile conservation programme and an interesting **interpretive centre** (admission free; 🕐 8am-5pm) about the sanctuary. Binoculars can be useful to scan trees for birds, mud banks for crocs and lizards and the undergrowth for boar and deer.

The **heronry** at Bagagaham Island is reached by a wonky boardwalk leading to a watchtower, where the height allows you to spy on a solid mass of herons nesting in the treetops.

Back at Khola, a 2km walk leads to Rigagada with an interesting 18th-century **Jag-**

annath temple built with some passionate erotica in Kalinga style. While there, take an amble through this typical Orissan village and guess which century you're in.

Sleeping & Eating

Aranya Nivas (☎ 220397; Chandbali; dm Rs 50, d Rs 150) Set in a pleasant garden within 50m of the Chandbali jetty. Accommodation is surprisingly good value and the restaurant serves up some scrumptious food.

Forest Rest Houses (dm Indian/foreigner Rs 40/80, d from Rs 150/300) Basic dorms and rooms at Dangmal and Ekakula with solar light, mosquito nets and shared bathrooms. You need to bring your own drinking water and food, which staff will cook for you. The haphazard **divisional forest officer** (☎ 272460; Rajnagar; 🕐 10am-5pm Mon-Sat, closed 2nd Sat in month) processes the bookings, which must be paid well in advance. These difficulties make going through a travel agent more desirable.

LALITGIRI, UDAYAGIRI & RATNAGIRI

These Buddhist ruins are on hilltops about 60km northeast of Cuttack. No local accommodation and inadequate transport means that the only feasible way to visit is by hired car.

Ratnagiri

Ratnagiri has the most interesting and extensive **ruins** (admission Indian/foreigner Rs 5/100, video Rs 25; 🕐 sunrise-sunset). Two large monasteries flourished here from the 6th to 12th centuries and noteworthy is an exquisitely carved gateway and remains of a 10m-high stupa. The **museum** (admission Rs 2; 🕐 10am-5pm Sat-Thu) contains sculptures from the three sites.

Udayagiri

Another **monastery complex** is being excavated here. At present there's a large pyramidal brick stupa with a seated Buddha and some beautiful doorjamb carvings. Expect an entry fee soon.

Lalitgiri

Several **monastery ruins** (admission Indian/foreigner Rs 5/100, video Rs 25; 🕐 sunrise-sunset) are scattered up a hillside leading to a small museum and a hillock crowned with a shallow stupa. During excavations of the stupa in the 1970s, a casket containing gold and silver relics was found.

Directory

CONTENTS

Accommodation	457
Activities	459
Business Hours	461
Children	462
Climate Charts	462
Courses	463
Customs	464
Dangers & Annoyances	465
Disabled Travellers	467
Discount Cards	467
Embassies & High Commissions	467
Festivals & Events	468
Food	470
Gay & Lesbian Travellers	470
Holidays	471
Insurance	471
Internet Access	471
Laundry	472
Legal Matters	472
Maps	472
Money	473
Photography	475
Post	475
Shopping	476
Solo Travellers	480
Telephone	480
Time	481
Toilets	481
Tourist Information	481
Travel Permits	482
Visas	482
Volunteer Work	483
Women Travellers	485

ACCOMMODATION

Accommodation in South India ranges from incredibly cheap fleapit hotels to expensive five-star offerings.

Accommodation listings in this book appear under a Sleeping heading, and may be divided into budget, midrange and top-end categories. Recommendations in these listings are in descending order of preference. Prices in this book are full price in high season and include bathroom. Exceptions are noted in specific listings throughout.

Hotel tariffs vary regionally – see individual chapters to gauge accommodation costs in the area(s) you intend visiting. Note that the tariffs in this book are based on a hotel's cheapest room rates and don't include taxes unless otherwise indicated.

Many hotels operate on a 24-hour checkout system (ie your time starts when you check in), while others, especially tourist hotels in resort areas like Goa and the Andamans, have fixed (often early morning) check-out times – it pays to ask.

Credit cards are accepted at most top-end hotels and many midrange ones; however, few budget places will take them.

Be aware that in tourist hot spots (eg beach resorts of Goa or Kerala) fledgling hotels may 'borrow' the name of a thriving competitor to confuse travellers. To avoid landing at an inferior copycat hotel, ensure that you know the *exact* name of your preferred hotel, and before paying your driver double check that you have in fact been taken to it, as some cheeky chaps will hastily try to offload you at hotels where they receive commissions. Sound pollution can be bothersome (especially in urban centres), so pack good-quality earplugs and request a quiet room.

Accommodation Options
BUDGET & MIDRANGE HOTELS

Many a traveller to India has a story about staying in a squalid dive for Rs 20, and while there are plenty of stained, cockroach-infested rooms, you don't need to sink that low to find cheap, good-value accommodation. Budget hotels cost around Rs 100 to 400 a double, and all but the cheapest have a private bathroom. Shoestring travellers may like to consider bringing their own sleeping sheets and pillowcases, as some of the cheaper places have bed linen that even the most enthusiastic dhobi-wallah (washerperson) couldn't whiten, and more than a few travellers have encountered bed bugs.

It's rare to find hostel-style dormitory beds geared at travellers (as opposed to itinerant truck drivers) in South India, except at railway retiring rooms (p458) and the Salvation Army youth hostels in Mumbai (Bombay) and Chennai (Madras).

Some of the best budget accommodation can be found at backpacker-friendly places, such as the beach resorts of Goa and Kerala – where you can sleep in a bamboo-and-thatch hut for about Rs 100 – and Hampi and Mamallapuram.

Midrange hotels range from Rs 500 to 1000. In this category most hotels come with ceiling fans or air-conditioning, private bathroom and usually satellite TV. They offer more comfort than their budget brothers, but can be a mixed bag: some have dreary, boxlike rooms while others ooze with character.

CAMPING

There are few camping sites around India, but travellers with their own vehicles can usually find hotels with gardens where they can park and camp for a nominal charge that includes communal bathroom facilities.

GOVERNMENT ACCOMMODATION & TOURIST BUNGALOWS

During the Raj era, a string of government-run accommodation units were established with labels like Rest Houses, Dak Bungalows, Circuit Houses, PWD (Public Works Department) Bungalows and Forest Rest Houses. Most of these are reserved for government officials, although some may open to tourists (inquire in advance). In national parks and forest reserves they may be the only accommodation available. They invariably have to be booked in advance through the relevant government organisation.

'Tourist Bungalows' are usually run by the state government; their facilities and service vary enormously. Some offer cheap dorm beds as well as private rooms. The local branch of the state government tourist office may be found on the premises of these Tourist Bungalows.

RAILWAY RETIRING ROOMS

These are located at train stations, and you can technically only stay here if you have an ongoing train ticket or Indrail Pass. The rooms, which are usually plain but clean, are handy if you have an early morning train departure, although they can be noisy and the private rooms often cost more than a midrange hotel. Most are let on a 24-hour basis, and offer dormitories and private rooms.

TEMPLES & RESTHOUSES

Accommodation (for a donation) is available at some gurdwaras (Sikh temples) and *dharamsalas* (pilgrims' resthouses). These simple lodgings are essentially for pilgrims, so please exercise judgment about the appropriateness of staying. Always abide by any protocols.

TOP-END HOTELS

In the bigger cities or tourist resorts, top-end hotels range from swanky five-star chains, such as the Oberoi, Taj, Hyatt and Welcomgroup (affiliated to Sheraton), to less glamorous four-star properties. These will usually have a swimming pool, opulent lobbies, fancy restaurants and 24-hour room service.

SLEEPING IN STYLE

We've included some stand-out accommodation options throughout this book under the heading 'Something Special'. Try these places for a splurge…

- Costa Malabari (p307), near Kannur, Kerala – a delightful guesthouse in the heart of Theyyam territory
- Fernhills Palace (p388), Ooty, Tamil Nadu – kingly living in the former summer residence of the Maharaja of Mysore
- Rainforest Retreat (p231), near Madikeri, Karnataka – forest-chic cottages on an organic plantation
- Siolim House (p191), Siolim, Goa – beautifully restored colonial mansion
- Taj Mahal Palace & Tower (p109), Mumbai – plush palace rooms in Mumbai's premier hotel
- Verandah in the Forest (p145), Matheran, Maharashtra – elegant gem of a Raj-era hotel
- Wild Orchid (p406), Havelock Island, Andamans – mellow, tastefully furnished Andamanese-style cottages by the beach

---

GET TO KNOW YOUR BATHROOM

Certain terminology is commonly used in the Sleeping sections throughout this book; mostly 'private bathroom' and 'shared bathroom'. However, several other terms may be used throughout the country. 'Common bath', 'without bath' or 'shared bath' mean communal bathroom facilities. 'Attached bath', 'private bath' or 'with bath' indicates that the room has its very own bathroom. Only the very cheapest accommodation has shared bathrooms, so unless otherwise stated, places to stay listed in this book have private bathrooms.

'Running' or 'constant' water indicates that there is water available around the clock (although it's not always the case in reality). 'Bucket water' means that water is, as the name suggests, available in buckets. Many hotels only have running cold water in bathrooms, but can provide hot water in buckets (sometimes only between certain hours and often for a small charge).

Hotels that advertise 'room with shower' can sometimes be misleading. Even if a bathroom does have a shower, it's a good idea to check that it actually works before accepting the room. Some hotels surreptitiously disconnect showers to save costs, while the showers at other places render a mere trickle of water.

A geyser is a small hot-water tank, usually found in cheaper hotels. Some geysers need to be switched on an hour or so before use.

Regarding toilets, unless squat toilets are specifically mentioned in this book, bathrooms have sit-down flush toilets. In South India, squat toilets may be referred to as 'Indian' or 'floor' toilets, while the sit-down variety is known as 'Western' or 'commode'. Many hotels have rooms with both styles, so if you prefer a sit-down toilet, ask for it.

Note that US dollar rates usually apply to foreigners. Top-end hotel prices cost around US$60 to US$200 for a double room.

While the luxury business hotels are all pretty predictable, there are some places worth seeking out, such as the heritage hotels in Pondicherry, resort hotels of Goa and Kerala, the Raj-era mansions of Udhagamandalam (Ooty) and the Taj Mahal Palace in Mumbai.

Additional Costs
SEASONAL VARIATIONS

In popular tourist hangouts (hill stations, beaches, place of pilgrimage etc) most hoteliers crank up their high-season prices (see regional chapters for details).

The definition of the high and low seasons varies depending on location. For beaches like Goa and Kerala it's basically a month before and two months after Christmas. In the hill stations it's usually from April to July when domestic tourists flock to the hills for a cool change. Some hotels charge higher rates for the Christmas and New Year period, or over major religions festivals, such as Diwali. Conversely, in the low season, prices at even normally expensive hotels can be surprisingly affordable. It's always worth asking for a better rate if the hotel doesn't seem busy.

TAXES & SERVICE CHARGES

Most state governments slap a variety of taxes on hotel accommodation. At most rock-bottom places (usually under Rs 200) you won't have to pay any taxes, but the level of tax increases with the cost of the room. Once you get into the top end of budget places, and certainly in midrange and top-end accommodation, you'll have to pay the curious 'luxury' tax; these vary from state to state and are detailed in the regional chapters.

On top of taxes, many midrange and top-end hotels have a 'service charge' (usually around 10%). This may be restricted to room service and telephone use, or may be levied on the total bill. Rates quoted in this book's regional chapters exclude taxes unless otherwise indicated.

ACTIVITIES

From trekking in the hills to scuba diving or snorkelling, South India has a wide range of activities – those listed here represent just some possibilities.

Ensure you have adequate insurance; many travel insurance policies won't cover dangerous activities, including trekking!

Ayurveda

Ayurveda clinics, resorts and colleges, where you can get individual massages or full treatment courses, are especially plentiful in Kerala, Karnataka and Goa – see those chapters for details. For further information see the boxed text, p271.

Bird-Watching

India has some of the world's major bird breeding and feeding grounds. The following are some of South India's prime bird-watching sites:

Calimere Wildlife & Bird Sanctuary (p356) In Tamil Nadu, noted for its flocks of migratory waterfowl.

Chilika Lake (p449) In Orissa, possibly India's largest congregation of aquatic birds.

Karanji Lake Nature Park (p222) Many species of aquatic birds, in Mysore, Karnataka.

Kumarakom Bird Sanctuary (p284) In Kerala, variety of domestic and migratory birds.

Thattekkad Bird Sanctuary (p289) In Kerala, over 270 bird species, including rarer ones, such as the Sri Lankan frogmouth.

Vedantangal Bird Sanctuary (p337) In Tamil Nadu, important breeding ground for waterbirds from October to March.

Boating

Scenic lake or river trips, sometimes geared towards wildlife spotting, are possible at the following places:

Bhitarkanika Wildlife Sanctuary (p456) In Orissa, crocodile and other wildlife spotting.

Chilika Lake (p449) In Orissa, dolphin- and bird-spotting tours.

Kerala backwaters (p278) Boat tours on a 900km network of waterways.

Periyar Wildlife Sanctuary (p286) In Kerala, tours in South India's most popular wildlife park.

Cycling & Motorcycling

There are some great organised bicycle or motorcycle tours available, or you can arrange your own rental (details provided in some regional chapters). For recommended organised motorcycle tours see p496.

Goa is probably the best place in India to hire a motorcycle or moped and go cruising through the backroads. It's also perfect for cycle touring.

Diving, Snorkelling & Water Sports

There are PADI-affiliated dive schools in Goa, Lakshadweep and the Andaman Islands. Of these, Havelock Island in the Andamans is probably the best place in India for scuba diving. In Goa, several beach operators offer water sports, such as waterskiing, parasailing, windsurfing and jet-skiing – see the Goa chapter (p162) for details.

Before plunging into the ocean, read the boxed text, below. Areas outside Goa offering diving opportunities:

Andaman Islands (p396) World-class dive destination. Season from December to March/April.

Lacadives (Lakshadweep; p311) Various dive sites. Season from October to mid-May.

Hangliding & Paragliding

Goa is a popular place for paragliding, or try the hills between Mumbai and Pune. Options:

RESPONSIBLE DIVING

To help preserve the ecology and beauty of reefs, adopt the following guidelines when diving:

- Never use anchors on the reef, and take care not to ground boats on coral.

- Avoid touching or disturbing living marine organisms – they can be damaged by even the gentlest contact. If you must hold on to the reef, only touch exposed rock or dead coral.

- Be conscious of your fins. Even without contact, the surge from fin strokes near the reef can damage delicate organisms. Take care not to kick up clouds of sand, which can smother organisms.

- Practise and maintain proper buoyancy control. Major damage can be done by divers descending too fast and colliding with the reef.

- Don't collect or buy corals or shells.

- Ensure that you take home all your rubbish and any litter you may find. Plastics in particular are a serious threat to marine life. Do not feed fish.

- Choose a dive company with appropriate environmental policies and practices.

PRACTICALITIES

- Electricity is 230V to 240V, 50 Hz AC and sockets are the three round-pin variety. Blackouts are more common during the hotter months.

- Officially India is metric. Terms you're likely to hear are: lakhs (one lakh = 100,000) and crores (one crore = 10 million).

- Major English-language dailies include the *Hindustan Times, Times of India, Indian Express, Hindu* and *Economic Times*. Regional English-language and local-vernacular publications are found nationwide and include *Mid-Day*, the *Herald* and the *Deccan Herald*.

- Incisive current-affair reports are printed in *Frontline, India Today*, the *Week, Sunday* and *Outlook*. For India-related travel articles get *Outlook Traveller*.

- The national (government) TV broadcaster is Doordarshan. More widely watched are satellite and cable TV; channels include BBC, CNN, Discovery, Star Movies, HBO and MTV. TV (and radio) programme/frequency details appear in most major English-language dailies.

- Government-controlled All India Radio (AIR) nationally transmits local and international news. There are also private channels broadcasting news, music, current affairs, talkback and more.

Arambol Paragliding (p191), in Goa.
Lonavla Mumbai-based Nirvana Adventure (p147) offers paragliding in Maharashtra.

Kayaking & River Rafting

South India doesn't have the wild river rafting opportunities found in the Himalaya, but there are a few possibilities for rafting:
Bangalore getoff ur ass (p210) offers rafting and kayaking trips in western Karnataka.
Goa Day Tripper (p183), in Calangute, offers rafting on the Kali River.
Karjat Mumbai-based Outbound Adventure (p105) offers rafting trips in Maharashtra from June to September.
Mumbai H2O Water Sports Complex (p105) hires kayaks.

Trekking

The best trekking in India is in the north, but the Western and Eastern Ghats also provide some great forest treks. Trekking in national parks or reserves must usually be done with a guide. Some of the best areas for treks include the Kodagu Hills around Madikeri in Karnataka, the Nilgiri Hills around Ooty in Tamil Nadu and the Travancore range around Munnar in Kerala. Try the following operators for guided treks.
Karnataka Several organisations offer treks in the region, including Bangalore-based getoff ur ass (p210). In Madikeri organised one- to 10-day treks explore 1700m peaks.
Mudumalai National Park Guided treks (p390) outside the park in Tamil Nadu.
Ooty In Tamil Nadu, hill and jungle treks (p386).
Periyar Wildlife Sanctuary In Kerala, two- or three-day 'tiger trail' treks (p286).

Wayanad Wildlife Sanctuary (p306) Rainforest treks in Kerala.

Wildlife Safaris

You can organise jeep and/or elephant safaris through operators at several wildlife sanctuaries in South India:
Badrama National Park (p454) Jeep safaris in Sambalpur, Orissa.
Debrigarh Wildlife Sanctuary (p453) Jeep safaris in Sambalpur, Orissa.
Mudumalai National Park (p390) Organised elephant and minibus tours in Tamil Nadu.
Similipal National Park (p454) Organised tours or self-drive in Orissa.
Southern Karnataka Jungle Lodges & Resorts (p210) in Bangalore offers safaris in Nagarhole National Park and several other reserves.
Wayanad Wildlife Sanctuary (p306) Jeep safaris in Kerala.

BUSINESS HOURS

Official business hours are 9.30am to 5.30pm Monday to Friday. Unofficially business tend to be open 10am to 5pm.

Most banks are open from 10am to 2pm (some 9am to 1pm and 1.30pm to 4pm) on Monday to Friday, and 10am to noon on Saturday – there are often variations, so it pays to check. In big cities and tourist centres there are invariably foreign-exchange offices open longer, usually till 9pm.

In most cities, the main post office is open from around 10am to 5pm on Monday to Friday (some close for lunch anytime

DIRECTORY

between 1pm and 2pm) and on Saturday until noon (occasionally Sunday). Some stay open longer (see regional chapters for details).

Shop hours vary regionally, but most tend to open from around 10am to 6pm and close once a week (often Sunday).

Restaurant opening hours vary from region to region and, unless otherwise mentioned in the regional chapters' individual restaurant reviews, are from around 8am to 10pm. However, some restaurants close between breakfast, lunch and dinner – see the Eating sections of regional chapters for details.

CHILDREN

Being a family-oriented society, India is a very child-friendly destination. Despite the wonderful acceptance of children, travelling with kids in India can be hard work, requiring constant vigilance – be especially cautious near roads, as traffic can be erratic to say the least. Any long-distance road travel should include adequate stops, as rough roads can make travel more draining than usual. Train is usually the most comfortable mode of travel, especially for long trips. Always carry sufficient clean drinking water.

Health risks, such as diarrhoea, can be much more of a threat to children than adults – for information see p506. If your child takes special medication, bring along an adequate stock in case it's not easily found locally.

For helpful hints, see Lonely Planet's *Travel with Children,* and the Lonely Planet website (www.lonelyplanet.com), which has a subdirectory on travelling with children, as well as the Thorn Tree travel forum, which can connect you with people who have travelled with young ones.

Practicalities

Many hotels have 'family rooms' or will happily provide an extra bed, and the more upmarket hotels may offer baby-sitting facilities and/or kid's activity programs – inquire in advance. The more upmarket hotels have cable TV, which has children's channels, such as the Cartoon Network.

Standard baby products, such as nappies (diapers), are available in most of the larger cities, where nappies start at Rs 63 (pack of

10) and baby milk powder is Rs 140 (500g); these can be considerably more expensive beyond big cities.

Breast-feeding in public is generally not condoned by Indian society.

Sights & Activities

Allow several days for your child to acclimatise to the explosion of sights, smells, tastes and sounds in India. Start with short outings and make sure to include child-friendly attractions (these are generally more prevalent in the bigger cities), such as the Nehru Planetarium (p104) in Mumbai, theme parks, such as Kanyakumari (p374), or national parks, such as Sanjay Gandhi National Park (p121). Zoos, including those of Kerala (p264) and Hyderabad and Secunderabad (p417) should also win a warm response.

Beaches make great family outings. Some of India's best include those of Goa (see the boxed text, p168), Kerala (p258), Pondicherry (p347) and Gokarna (p240).

Hill stations, apart from offering cool retreats, have forested swathes that make for picturesque picnic spots. As most are geared to family tourism, they also offer child-oriented 'perks', from paddle boats to pony rides. Ooty (p387) is especially well set-up for families, with Jolly World, a children's theme park.

India's bounty of festivals may also capture your child's imagination, although you should be aware that these can attract suffocating crowds. For festival details see p468 and the boxed texts Festivals In... at the start of regional chapters.

Travelling off-the-beaten track can be a mixed blessing – you won't find the facilities and comforts of the cities, but you'll find less traffic, both human and mechanical, and with that, more peace.

For further destination-specific sights and activities that may appeal to your children, read the regional chapters.

CLIMATE CHARTS

South India has a largely tropical climate that can be roughly divided into two distinct seasons – the wet (monsoon) and the dry. It's hot year-round – except in the elevated hills – but May to September are the warmest months. For comprehensive details, see p19.

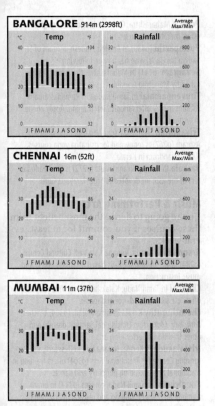

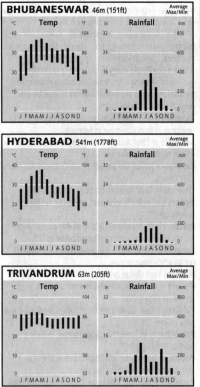

COURSES

To find out about courses that may be available, inquire at tourist offices, ask fellow travellers, and peruse newspapers and magazines. As well as the various courses listed here, there are cooking courses (p80). Some recommended courses are listed here.

Ayurveda & Naturopathy

If you're interested in learning about naturopathy or the ancient science of Ayurveda, try these places:

Bangalore Naturopathy and Ayurveda therapies (p212). In Karnataka.

Mysore Ayurveda courses (p222). In Karnataka.

Languages

To get any real benefit from studying a language you should be prepared to make a long-term commitment (especially beginners). Some courses enforce minimum durations. These places offer courses:

Chennai All levels of Hindi, plus Tamil courses (p323). In Tamil Nadu.

Kerala Vijnana Kala Vedi Cultural Centre (p284) offers Malayalam, Hindi and Sanskrit classes.

Mumbai Beginners Hindi and Marathi classes (p106).

Meditation & Yoga

Many places in India offer a combination of yoga and meditation classes. Some only accept students prepared to commit to a certain period of time. You should also be aware that some meditation courses require students to abide by a vow of 'noble silence' – no talking, reading or writing for a certain number of days. Inquire in advance.

With so many meditation and yoga courses available in India these days, some outfits are more reputable than others (especially in tourist traps). Seek advice from tourist offices and other travellers, and visit several to find out which best suits your needs before committing. Many of the ashrams (spiritual communities) offer yoga and meditation courses; see below.

The following represent some of the many possibilities; for those that impose no fees, donations are appreciated:

Anjuna Goa Purple Valley Yoga Centre (p187) offers *ashtanga* (following eight 'limbs', including postures and meditation), hatha and pranayama (traditional breath control) yoga, and meditation.

Arambol In Goa, Himalayan Iyengar Yoga Centre (p191) runs courses from November to February.

Auroville In Tamil Nadu, site of the Matrimandir (p351), a unique meditation chamber.

Calangute In Goa, the Natural Health Centre (p183) offers yoga classes.

Chennai In Tamil Nadu, Hatha yoga classes (p323).

Hyderabad In Andhra Pradesh, *vipassana* meditation courses (p417).

Igatpuri In Maharashtra, 10- and 45-day courses at the world's largest *vipassana* meditation centre (p127).

Lonavla In Maharashtra, Kaivalyadhama Yoga Hospital (p146) offers yogic healing.

Mumbai Yoga classes (p106).

Mysore In Karnataka, world-renowned *ashtanga* yoga, and hatha yoga (p223).

Palolem In Goa, Bhakti Kutir (p201) offers meditation and yoga courses.

Pondicherry In Tamil Nadu, yoga courses, including teacher-training (p347).

Poondi In Tamil Nadu, Isha Yoga Centre (p379) is an ashram offering meditation and yoga.

Pune In Maharashtra, Ramamani Iyengar Memorial Yoga Institute (p152) runs Iyengar yoga courses (five-years' experience required).

Thiruvananthapuram (Trivandrum) Sivananda Yoga Vedanta Dhanwantari Ashram (p267) is renowned for its hatha yoga courses. Near Trivandrum in Kerala.

ASHRAMS

Ashrams are places of communal living established around the philosophies of a particular guru (spiritual guide). Codes of conduct vary from ashram to ashram, so make sure you're willing to abide by these before committing. Also read the boxed text, p465. Ashrams in South India:

Amrithapuri In Kerala, Matha Amrithanandamayi Mission (p278) is a large ashram with the female guru Amma (mother) – 'The Hugging Mother'.

Paunar In Maharashtra, Brahmavidya Mandir Ashram (p141) was established by Gandhi's disciple Vinoba Bhave.

Pondicherry In Tamil Nadu, Sri Aurobino Ashram (p345) offers yoga instruction.

Poondi In Tamil Nadu, Isha Yoga Centre (p379) is an ashram offering meditation and yoga.

Pune In Maharashtra, Osho Meditation Resort (p151) offers meditation courses.

Puttaparthi (p430) In Andhra Pradesh, ashram of Sri Sathya Sai Baba, who has a huge following.

Sevagram (p141) In Maharashtra, the ashram established by Mahatma Gandhi.

Tiruvannamalai In Tamil Nadu, Sri Ramanasramam Ashram (p343) offers meditation training. Apply ahead in writing.

Trivandrum Sivananda Yoga Vedanta Dhanwantari Ashram (p267) is renowned for its hatha yoga courses. Near Trivandrum in Kerala.

Varkala In Kerala, Sivagiri Mutt (p272) is the headquarters of the ashram devoted to Sree Narayana Guru.

Music & Performing Arts

You're going to derive the most benefit from these courses if you commit for at least several weeks.

Aranmula In Kerala, Vijnana Kala Vedi Cultural Centre (p284) offers *kathakali* (plays based on Hindu epics) and music instruction.

Chennai In Tamil Nadu, Kalakshetra Arts Village (p326) offers classical Tamil dance and music.

Cheruthuruthy Kerala Kalamandalam (p304) teaches *kathakali, kootiattam* (traditional Sanskrit drama) and other traditional performing arts.

Irinjalakuda In Kerala, Natana Kairali Research and Performing Centre for Traditional Arts (p304) offers training in traditional arts, including puppetry and dance.

Pondicherry In Tamil Nadu, courses (p347) in *bharathanatiyam* (dance), singing and musical instruments, including veena and tabla.

Trivandrum In Kerala, courses (p264) on *kathakali* and *kootiattam*.

Other Courses

These are a couple of other course possibilities:

Kumarakom Vijnana Kala Vedi Cultural Centre (p284) offers *kalarippayat* (Tamil martial art) classes. In Kerala.

Trivandrum CVN Kalari Sangham (p263) offers *kalarippayat* classes. In Kerala.

CUSTOMS

The usual duty-free regulations apply for India; that is, 1L of alcohol and 200 cigarettes or 50 cigars or 250g of tobacco.

You are allowed to bring in expensive items, such as video cameras and laptop computers . However these items may have to be entered on a 'Tourist Baggage Reexport' form to ensure you take them out with you when you leave (although this isn't always policed).

ASHRAMS & GURUS

Many people visit India especially to spend time at an ashram and to receive *darshan* (literally, a glimpse of God) through an audience with a guru, who is a spiritual guide. The word guru traditionally means either 'the dispeller of darkness' or 'heavy with wisdom'.

Most gurus live in an ashram ('place of striving'). An ashram is established when a guru stays in one place and disciples congregate. Many ashrams are the legacies of gurus who have since died. The ashrams of living gurus reflect the disposition of the founder and their perception of the needs of their disciples. For example, at one ashram you may be expected to contribute by working either towards the ashram's upkeep or on one of its charitable projects, whereas at another you may be expected to practise meditation for a certain amount of time each day.

It's important to realise that ashram life isn't for everyone. Many ashrams have codes of conduct, including a dress code. The diet is almost always vegetarian, and you may also be asked to abstain from eggs, tobacco, alcohol, garlic and onions.

Many ashrams have programs that include meditation, philosophical discourse and yoga. In addition to being a spiritual retreat, a genuine ashram also plays a role in contributing to society. Their welfare programs may include free health care, education and food distribution. While many larger ashrams even run their own hospitals, clinics and schools. The money for such programs is raised through donations and, according to tradition, ashrams can only accept money by 'donation' (which often includes accommodation – please don't neglect to give something).

Most ashrams don't require notice of your arrival but, if you're unsure, check in advance. Gurus sometimes move around without much notice, so it's best to check in advance.

The atmosphere surrounding an ashram can have a profound and deeply moving effect on visitors; however, you are urged to use common sense and discernment, as regrettably not all ashrams (or gurus) are as sincere in their motives as others. Talk to locals and fellow travellers to see which ashram or guru might best suit you.

South India's most high-profile guru is Sai Baba, whose main ashram is at Puttaparthi in Andhra Pradesh, where people gather in their thousands to catch a glimpse of him. Recently his ashrams have received bad press for alleged sexual assaults and a pervading authoritarian atmosphere.

Lesser known, but nevertheless someone who has attracted a large following in the foreign community, is Matha Amrithanandamayi in Kerala (p278). Her ashram is at Amrithapuri, and *darshan* here is quite unlike anything you might have experienced before. Matha Amrithanandamayi hugs each and every devotee in turn, and the devotees number many thousands.

The famous Osho Meditation Resort (p151) in Pune, founded by the late Bhagwan Rajneesh, still attracts Western devotees in their hundreds.

The Sri Aurobindo Ashram (p345) in Pondicherry is also popular among Westerners, and its spiritual tenets represent a synthesis of yoga and modern science. The Sri Ramanasramam Ashram (p343), at the foot of Annamalai in Tamil Nadu, still draws devotees of Sri Ramana Maharshi, who died in 1950.

Technically you are supposed to declare any amount of cash or travellers cheques over US$10,000 on arrival in India. Regarding Indian currency, officially you are not supposed to take any into or out of India. Some travellers, however, have been told that they can import a maximum of Rs 5000.

If you're entering India from Nepal you are not entitled to import anything free of duty.

There are certain restrictions about what you can take out of India – see the boxed text, p476.

DANGERS & ANNOYANCES

In India, as in any place in the world, common sense and caution are your best weapons against theft or worse. Chat with other travellers and tourism officials about any latest potential hazards. See the India branch of Lonely Planet's **Thorn Tree forum** (www.lonelyplanet.com), where travellers often post warnings about problems. Women travellers should see p485.

Contaminated Food & Drink

In past years some private medical clinics have provided patients with more treatment than is necessary in order to procure larger medical insurance claims – get several opinions where possible. This scam has thankfully been quashed, but there's always the chance it could reappear.

Water can also be a potential problem. Always ensure the seal is intact on bought mineral water and check that the bottom of the bottle hasn't been tampered with. Crush plastic bottles after use to prevent them being misused later. Better still, bring along water-purification tablets to avoid adding to India's plastic waste problem.

Festivals

Be extra careful if you're travelling by train during major festivals, as there have been cases of people being crushed to death at stations when boarding trains.

Care is needed during the Holi festival (p470). Although it is mostly good fun, there have been incidences of people being doused with toxic substances mixed in water, sometimes leaving them scarred. During Holi, there's also a tradition of guzzling alcohol and consuming cannabis-derived bhang in the form of lassis, pakoras and cookies. Female travellers have been groped by spaced-out blokes – particularly in touristy areas. Officials advise women to avoid venturing onto the streets alone during Holi.

Scams

A scam is any form of deception – subtle or otherwise – designed to fleece money from unsuspecting tourists. In India there are people constantly cooking up new and more elaborate scams, though in the south you won't find as much of the gem and carpet too-good-to-be-true scams. The main places to be wary are big cities, such as Mumbai and Chennai, and at tourist centres, such as Goa and parts of Kerala. Anything that seems a bit suspicious probably is, but there's no need to descend into paranoia about every offer you get.

Things to look out for include anybody offering to change money. There's absolutely nothing to be gained by changing money on the street, and the guys that do it are often expert con men with a bag of sleight-of-hand tricks. Even if you get offered a good rate and count your money carefully you may lose out. One scam is switching foreign currency. You proffer a US$50, which the

moneychanger takes, but he then asks if you have a US$100 instead. Before handing back the US$50 he exchanges it for a US$1. If you don't notice until later, he's made US$49.

Minor scams in Mumbai include the young girl carrying a baby and speaking impeccable English. She doesn't want money, but could you buy some milk powder for the baby? She takes you to a shop where you pay an inflated price and later sells it to the vendor for a nice profit. A similar trick is the shoeshine boy who claims he's the only kid on the block without a proper box. You buy it, he sells it back and makes more money than a shoeshine boy could make in a month. These are pretty harmless scams that tug at the heart strings, but no-one likes to feel like they are being tricked.

Swimming

Beaches can have dangerous rips and currents, and there are usually drownings each year. Always check locally before swimming anywhere in the sea.

Theft & Druggings

Never leave important valuables (passport, tickets, money) in your room (see p474) and always keep luggage securely locked. On trains, keep your gear near you; padlock bags to the luggage rack or loops found under some train seats. Thieves tend to target popular tourist train routes, such as Mumbai to Goa. There have been reports of backpacks being slashed. Be extra alert during train departure times, when the confusion and crowds are at their worst. Airports are another place to exercise caution, as after a long flight you're unlikely to be at your most alert.

Occasionally tourists (especially those travelling solo) are drugged and robbed during train or bus journeys, although reports of this are relatively rare in South India. Unwary travellers are befriended, offered a spiked drink (to send them to sleep) and their valuables are then stolen. It's wise to politely decline drinks or food offered by relative strangers (use your instincts), particularly if you're alone.

A good travel-insurance policy is essential (see p471). Travellers cheques can be replaced if you have records; see p474.

Make sure you keep a photocopy or two of your passport, including the visa page (keep this separately from your passport), as well as a copy of your plane ticket. Some travellers scan copies of important documents to keep on the Internet as back up.

Touts & Commission Agents

India's tourist centres are a magnet for touts, all vying for your cash. They're particularly prevalent at airport terminals and bus or train stations, waiting to snare the fresh (most vulnerable) arrivals. Often they're rickshaw or taxi-wallahs. Some try to gauge your vulnerability by inquiring whether it's your first trip to India – say it isn't. Their goal is to divert you to a hotel where they earn the highest commission. Some hotels refuse to pay touts, and you'll more often than not hear stories about those places being 'full', 'under renovation', 'closed' or whatever. Nine times out of 10 they'll be just that – stories.

Commission agents also receive a fee for carting you to certain dealers, often with spiels about 'my brother's shop' and 'special deal at my friend's place'. If you are taken to a hotel, shop or even restaurant, the price you pay will be inflated by up to 50% (sometimes more), so try to visit these places independently.

On the flip side, touts can be beneficial if you arrive in a town without a hotel reservation when some big festival is on, or during the peak season – they'll know which places have beds.

Women

Women have reported being molested by masseurs and other therapists. No matter where you are, try to check the reputation of any teacher or therapist before going to a solo session. If at any time you feel uneasy, leave.

DISABLED TRAVELLERS

India's crowded public transport, crush of people in urban areas and variable infrastructure can test even the hardiest traveller. If you're physically handicapped or visually impaired, these pose even more of a challenge. However, seeing the way mobility-impaired locals whiz through city traffic in modified bicycles proves that nothing is impossible.

India has limited wheelchair-friendly hotels (mostly top end), restaurants and of-fices. Staircases are often steep. Footpaths, where they exist, are often riddled with holes, littered with debris and packed with pedestrians, severely hindering movement.

If your mobility is considerably restricted, you could consider travelling with an able-bodied companion. Additionally, hiring a car with a driver will make moving around a whole lot easier (see p495).

Organisations that may offer further advice include **The Royal Association for Disability and Rehabilitation** (RADAR; ☎ 020-7250 3222; www .radar.org.uk; 12 City Forum, 250 City Rd, London EC1V 8AF, UK) and **Mobility International USA** (MIUSA; ☎ 541-3431284; www.miusa.org; PO Box 10767, Eugene, OR 97440, USA).

DISCOUNT CARDS
Senior Cards

For those aged over 65, Sahara Airlines offers a 50% discount on domestic air travel, while Jet Airways offers 25% off. Discounts on other air carriers may emerge as competition among domestic airlines increases (ask travel agents). If you're over 60, you're entitled to a 30% discount on train travel.

Bring your passport as proof of age.

Student & Youth Cards

Student cards are of limited use – many student concessions have either been eliminated or replaced by 'youth fares' or other age concessions. Hostels run by the Indian Youth Hostels Association are part of the Hostelling International (HI) network; an HI card entitles you to standard discount rates. YMCA/YWCA members are also entitled to standard discounts on accommodation.

Foreigners aged below 30 receive a 25% discount on domestic air tickets.

EMBASSIES & HIGH COMMISSIONS
Indian Embassies & High Commissions

The following represent just some of India's missions worldwide. For comprehensive contact details, see www.meaindia.nic .in (click on the 'Missions & Posts Abroad' link).

Apart from the main mission, many countries also have consulates – inquire locally for these (as well as for relevant fax/email details).

Australia (☎ 02-6273 3999; 3-5 Moonah Place, Yarralumla, ACT 2600)

Bangladesh (☎ 02-9889339; House 2, Rd 142, Gulshan I, Dhaka)

Canada (☎ 613-744 3751; 10 Springfield Rd, Ottawa, Ontario K1M 1C9)

France (☎ 01 40 50 70 70; 15 Rue Alfred Dehodencq, 75016 Paris)

Germany (☎ 00 49-30-257950; Tiergartenstrasse 17, 10785, Berlin)

Ireland (☎ 01-497 0843; 6 Leeson Park, Dublin 6)

Israel (☎ 03-529 1999; 140 Hayarkon St, Tel Aviv, 61033)

Italy (☎ 064 88 46 42; Via XX Settembre 5, 00187 Rome)

Japan (☎ 0332-622 391; 2-2-11 Kudan Minami, Chiyoda-ku, Tokyo 1020074)

Nepal (☎ 014-410900; 336 Kapurdhara Marg, Kathmandu)

The Netherlands (☎ 0703-46 97 71; Buitenrustweg 2, 2517 KD, The Hague)

New Zealand (☎ 04-473 6390; 180 Molesworth St, Wellington)

Pakistan (☎ 0512-206950; G5, Diplomatic Enclave, Islamabad)

Sri Lanka (☎ 012-421605; 36-38 Galle Rd, Colombo 3)

Thailand (☎ 0 2258 0300; 46 Soi Prasarnmitr, Soi 23, Sukhumvit Rd, Bangkok 10110)

UK (☎ 020-7836 8484; India House, Aldwych, London WC2B 4NA)

USA (☎ 202-939 9806; 2536 Massachusetts Ave NW, Washington DC 20008)

Embassies & High Commissions in South India

Most diplomatic missions are based in the nation's capital, Delhi, but there are consulates in Mumbai and Chennai. Most missions operate from 9am to 5pm Monday to Friday (some close between 1pm and 2pm).

If your country's mission is not listed here, that doesn't necessarily mean it's not represented in India – see the local phone directory or call one of the listed missions for relevant contact details.

Australia (☎ 011-51399900; www.ausgovindia.com; 36 Maker Chambers VI, Nariman Point, Mumbai)

Austria (☎ 022-22874758; www.bmaa.gv.at; 26 Maker Chambers VI, Nariman Point, Mumbai)

Canada (☎ 022-22876027; www.dfait-maeci.gc.ca/new-delhi; 4th fl, 41/42 Maker Chambers VI, Nariman Point, Mumbai)

France Mumbai (☎ 022-56694000; www.consulfrance-bombay.org; 7th fl, Hoechst House, Vinayak K Shah Rd, Nariman Point); Pondicherry (☎ 0413-2339534; 10 Marine St)

Germany Mumbai (☎ 022-22832422; www.german consulatemumbai.org; 10th fl, Hoechst House, Vinayak K Shah Rd, Nariman Point); Chennai (☎ 044-28210810; www.chennai.diplio.de; 49 Ethiraj Rd, Egmore)

Israel (☎ 022-22819993; 16th fl, Ernest House, Nariman Point, Mumbai)

Italy (☎ 022-23804071; www.italianconsulatemumbai .com; 72 G Deshmukh Marg, Mumbai)

Japan (☎ 022-23517101; www.in.emb-japan.go.jp; ML Dahanukar Marg, Cumbala Hill, Mumbai)

Malaysia (☎ 044-24342049; mwmadras@vsnl.com; 6 Sriram Nagar, North St, Alwarpet, Chennai)

The Netherlands (☎ 022-22016750; Forbes Bldg, Charanjit Rai Marg, Mumbai)

New Zealand (☎ 044-28112472; www.hollandinindia .org; 132 Cathedral Rd, Chennai)

Singapore (☎ 044-28158207; www.mfa.gov.sg/chennai/; 17a North Boag Rd, Chennai)

Sri Lanka Mumbai (☎ 022-22045861; 34 Homi Modi St); Chennai (☎ 044-24987896; 196 TTK Rd, Alwarpet)

Switzerland Mumbai (☎ 022-22884563; 102 Maker Chambers IV, Nariman Point); Chennai (☎ 044-24353886; 224 TTK Rd, Alwarpet)

Thailand (☎ 022-23631404; www.thaiemb.org.in; 4th fl, 33 Dr Purandare Marg, Mumbai)

UK (☎ 022-56502222; Maker Chambers IV, Nariman Point, Mumbai)

USA (☎ 022-23633611; http://mumbai.usconsulate.gov; Lincoln House, 78 Bhulabhai Desai Rd, Mumbai)

FESTIVALS & EVENTS

Most holidays and festivals follow either the Indian lunar calendar (a complex system determined chiefly by astrologers) or the Islamic calendar (which falls about 11 days earlier each year; 12 days earlier in leap years), and therefore changes from year to year relative to the Gregorian calendar. The Indiawide holidays and festivals listed here are arranged according to the Indian lunar (and Gregorian) calendar, which starts in Chaitra (March or April) – contact local tourist offices for exact festival dates, as many are variable.

Many festivals in India occur during *purnima* (full moon), which is traditionally auspicious.

The 'wedding season' generally occurs between the cooler months of November and March (wedding dates revolve around auspicious timings set by astrologers). During this period you're likely to see at least one wedding procession on the street – a merry mix of singing, dancing and a loud brass band.

The following represent major national festivals – for details about regional ones see the Festivals In… boxed texts at the beginning of regional chapters.

Chaitra (March/April)
Mahavir Jayanti This Jain festival commemorates the birth of Mahavira, the founder of Jainism.
Ramanavami Hindu temples all over India celebrate the birth of Rama. In the week leading up to Ramanavami, the Ramayana is widely read and performed.
Easter This Christian holiday marks the crucifixion and Resurrection of Christ.

Vaisakha (April/May)
Buddha Jayanti This 'triple-blessed festival' falls on the full moon (usually in May, sometimes in late April or early June), and celebrates the Buddha's birth, enlightenment and attainment of nirvana.
Eid-Milad-un-Nabi This Islamic festival celebrates the birth of the Prophet Mohammed.

Jyaistha (May/June)
No major festivals currently fall during this period.

Asadha (June/July)
Rath Yatra (Car Festival) Lord Jagannath's great temple chariot makes its stately journey from his temple in Puri (p441) during this Hindu festival. Similar festivals take place in other locations.

Sravana (July/August)
Naag Panchami This Hindu festival is dedicated to Ananta, the serpent upon whose coils Vishnu rested between universes. Snake charmers do a roaring trade, despite protests by animal-rights activists. Snakes are believed to have power over the monsoon rainfall and keep evil away from homes.
Raksha Bandhan (Narial Purnima) On the full-moon day girls fix amulets known as *rakhis* to the wrists of their (not necessarily blood-related) brothers to protect them in the coming year. The brothers reciprocate with gifts. Some people also worship the Vedic sea god Varuna.

Bhadra (August/September)
Independence Day This public holiday on 15 August marks the anniversary of India's Independence in 1947.
Drukpa Teshi This festival celebrates the first teaching given by the Buddha.
Ganesh Chaturthi This joyful festival celebrates the birth of the popular elephant-headed god, Ganesh, and has particular verve in Mumbai. On the last day of the festival clay idols of Ganesh, the god of good fortune, are paraded through the streets before being ceremoniously immersed in a river, sea or water tank.
Janmastami The anniversary of Krishna's birth is celebrated with happy abandon — in tune with Krishna's own mischievous moods. Devotees fast all day until midnight, and in Mathura (Krishna's birthplace) the festivities last longer.

Shravan Purnima
On this day of fasting, high-caste Hindus replace the sacred thread looped over the left shoulder.
Pateti Parsis celebrate their new year at this time.

Asvina (September/October)
Navratri (Festival of Nine Nights) This Hindu festival leading up to Dussehra is dedicated to the goddess Durga who beheaded a demon. Goddesses Lakshmi and Saraswati, of wealth and learning respectively, also get special praise. Hindus take part in rituals, fasting and prayer; then after sundown there's often *dandiya raas,* folk dancing with sticks. Some regions also have nightly *garbas* (folk dances without the sticks). Festivities are particularly vibrant in Gujarat and Maharashtra.
Dussehra (Durga Puja) This festival celebrates Durga's victory over the buffalo-headed demon Mahishasura and often ends with the burning of images of the demon king Ravana. It's also known as Ram Lila (Life Story of Rama), with fireworks and re-enactments of the Ramayana.
Gandhi Jayanti This public holiday is a solemn celebration of Mohandas Gandhi's birth anniversary on October, at many places associated with his life, including the Gandhi National Memorial (p152) in Pune and the Sevagram Ashram (p141) in northern Maharashtra.

Kartika (October/November)
Diwali (Deepavaali) For this happiest festival of the Hindu calendar (on the 15th day of Kartika), oil lamps are lit to show Rama the way home from exile, sweets are given and firework displays let off. The festival lasts for five days. On the first day, doorsteps are decorated with *rangolis/kolams* (chalk/rice-flour designs); day two celebrates Krishna's victory over the tyrant Narakasura; day three is spent worshipping Lakshmi; day four commemorates the visit of the friendly demon Bali; and on the fifth day men receive an auspicious tikka (forehead mark) from their sisters.
Govardhana Puja This Hindu festival is dedicated to the holy cow.
Ramadan (Ramazan) This 30-day dawn-to-dusk fast marks the ninth month of the Islamic calendar, the month during which the Prophet Mohammed had the Quran revealed to him in Mecca. This festival moves forward 11 days each year and is due to begin in late September in 2006.
Eid al-Fitr This feast celebrates the end of Ramadan; festivities continue for three days. In 2006 it's scheduled to fall in October.

Aghan (November/December)
Nanak Jayanti The birthday of Guru Nanak, the founder of Sikhism, is celebrated with prayer readings and processions.

Pausa (December/January)
Christmas Day Christians celebrate the anniversary of the birth of Christ on 25 December.

Eid al-Adha This Islamic occasion commemorates the Prophet Ibrahim's readiness to obey God even to the point of sacrificing his son.

Losar Tibetan New Year is a splendid time to be in McLeod Ganj (Himachal Pradesh) – the Dalai Lama often holds teaching sessions here. Some regions celebrate this festival in February or March.

Magha (January/February)

Republic Day This public holiday on 26 January celebrates the anniversary of India's establishment as a republic in 1950; there are activities in all state capitals but most spectacularly in Delhi, where there's a military parade along Rajpath.

Pongal This four-day festival marks the end of the harvest season. It's observed on the first day of the Tamil month of Thai, which is in the middle of January. Festivities include the boiling-over of a pot of *pongal* (a mixture of rice, sugar, dhal and milk), symbolic of prosperity and abundance. On the third day, cattle are decorated and fed the *pongal*.

Vasant Panchami It's traditional to dress in yellow to celebrate this Hindu festival, held on the 5th day of Magha. In some places Saraswati, the goddess of learning, is honoured. Books, musical instruments and other related objects are placed in front of the goddess to receive her blessing.

Phalguna (February/March)

Holi This is one of the most exuberant Hindu festivals, when people celebrate the beginning of spring by throwing coloured water and *gulal* (powder) at one another. Don't wear good clothes and be ready to duck. Women see also p485. On the night before Holi, bonfires are built to symbolise the destruction of the evil demon Holika. It's mainly a northern festival, as there's no real winter to end in the south.

Muharram An Islamic festival commemorating the martyrdom of the Prophet Mohammed's grandson, Imam.

Shivaratri This day of Hindu fasting is dedicated to Shiva, who danced the *tandava* (cosmic dance) on this day. Temple processions are followed by the chanting of mantras and anointing of linga (phallic symbols).

FOOD

Sampling the local cuisine is undoubtedly one of the highlights of a visit to South India. To get a taste of what's on offer, see the Eating sections in the regional chapters. In some of these sections, eateries are listed under 'Restaurants' and 'Quick Eats' subheadings: Quick Eats includes street stalls, market vendors, takeaway counters, sweet shops and the like; they're open from early morning (or lunchtime) to late at night. Restaurants cover pretty much everything else.

For comprehensive coverage of South India's culinary scene, including information on cooking courses, see p80.

GAY & LESBIAN TRAVELLERS

In India, homosexual relations for men are illegal and the penalties for transgression can theoretically be up to life imprisonment. There's no law against lesbian sexual relations.

Like heterosexual Western couples travelling in India, both married and unmarried, gay and lesbian travellers should exercise discretion and refrain from displaying overt affection towards each other in public.

Many foreigners make the assumption that Indian men holding hands are gay; however, this is actually a common and accepted expression of nonsexual friendship.

Publications & Websites

The Mumbai publication, *Bombay Dost*, is a gay and lesbian magazine available from

---

KUMBH MELA

According to Hindu creation myths, the gods and demons once fought a great battle for a *kumbh* (pitcher) containing the nectar of immortality. Vishnu got hold of the container and spirited it away, but in flight four drops of nectar spilt on the earth – at Allahabad, Haridwar, Nasik and Ujjain. Every three years, one of the four sites chosen by the holy drops takes its turn throwing the fantastical event known as (Maha) Kumbh Mela.

The Kumbh Mela attracts tens of millions of Hindu pilgrims who flock here for the largest religious congregation on earth. It draws masses of Hindu holy men, especially the Nagas (naked sadhus) of militant Hindu monastic orders. Kumbh Mela doesn't belong to any caste or creed, and perhaps more than any single event captures the huge mix of religious and cultural backgrounds that swarm together to form the fabric of Indian society. During the event, a sea of tents is set up to house the flood of pilgrims. Astrologers carefully pinpoint the auspicious time to take a holy dip and, at this time, the first to do so are the Nagas.

The next Kumbh Mela is scheduled to take place in 2007 at Nasik.

105 Veena-Beena Shopping Centre, Bandra West, Mumbai, as well as at a limited number of bookshops and newsstands in various Indian cities.

For further information about India's gay scene, there are some excellent websites, including **Bombay Dost** (www.bombay-dost.com), **Gay Bombay** (www.gaybombay.com), **Humrahi** (www.geocities.com/WestHollywood/Heights/7258) and **Humsafar** (www.humsafar.org).

Support Groups

Several organisations in Bangalore offer support to the gay and lesbian community. A weekly support group for gay, lesbian, bisexual and transgender people is run by **Good As You** (☎ 080-22230959; sahayabangalore@hotmail.com; Bangalore). The NGO **Swabhava** (☎ 080-22124441; http://swabhava_trust.tripod.com; 54 Manjappa Rd, Shanthinagar, Bangalore 560027) works directly with issues affecting lesbians, gays and transsexuals. This organisation operates a helpline and conducts various research projects for which volunteers may be needed.

Sangama (☎ 080-22868680; www.sangama.org; Flat 13, Royal Park Apartments, 34 Park Rd, Tasker Town, Bangalore 560051) deals with crisis intervention and community outreach predominantly for gay and bi men and women, transgenders and *hijra*s (transvestites and eunuchs). It has walk-in services, runs advocacy programmes and provides research resources, including newspaper documentation and a small library. It may also offer volunteering possibilities (phone directly for details).

Sahodaran (☎ 044-8252869; www.sahodaran.faith-web.com; 1st fl, 127 Sterling Rd, Nungambakkam, Chennai) is a support group for gay men, and holds social group meetings (in English) every Thursday evening.

HOLIDAYS

In India there are officially three national public holidays: Republic Day (26 January), Independence Day (15 August) and Gandhi Jayanti (2 October). However, various states may have their own designated holidays. There are also holidays during major festivals (often only followed by certain religions), which include Diwali, Dussehra and Holi (all three are Hindu festivals), Nanak Jayanti (Sikh), Eid al-Fitr (Islamic), Mahavir Jayanti (Jain), Buddha Jayanti (Buddhist), and Easter and Christmas (Christian). For festival dates, see p468.

Most businesses (offices, shops etc) close on public holidays. Accommodation at festival destinations can be difficult to find and the room rates often skyrocket due to heightened demand. It's wise to make reservations well in advance if you intend visiting during major festivals.

INSURANCE

A travel insurance policy to cover theft, loss and medical problems is wise. Be aware that some policies specifically exclude dangerous activities, which can include scuba diving, motorcycling and even trekking. There is a wide variety of policies available, so check the small print carefully.

You might prefer a policy that pays doctors or hospitals directly rather than you having to pay on the spot and claim later (although this may not always be possible in India). If you have to claim later, ensure you keep all documentation. Check that the policy covers an emergency flight home, and that it adequately covers India and adjacent countries (if you intend travelling on).

If you have something stolen, immediately report it to the police. Ensure you get a statement proving you have done so – this is essential if you want to make an insurance claim. Note that it's crucial to get a police report in India if you've had anything stolen, as insurance companies may refuse to reimburse you without one.

INTERNET ACCESS

Internet outlets are widespread in South India, especially in cities and tourist areas. Even small towns will have at least one place where you can get online, but don't expect to find anything in the rural backblocks.

In cities you'll find fast ADSL connections, but smaller places may be excruciatingly slow. Good Internet places also offer printing, backup onto CDs (for digital photos) and cheap international phone calls. As power cuts in South India are not unusual, it's a good idea to save a long email as a text document first.

Internet charges vary (see the Internet Access sections in the regional chapters for exact costs), but fall anywhere between Rs 10 and 60 per hour. Some places enforce a minimum time of 15 minutes.

Most travellers make use of India's widespread (and cheap) Internet cafés and free

DIRECTORY

Web-based email, such as **Yahoo** (www.yahoo.com) or **Hotmail** (www.hotmail.com). However, if you want to hook up to the Internet on your own machine, you'll need to join a local ISP (unless you have an ISP that supports global roaming Internet connections, giving you local phone numbers that connect to your own provider).

If you're thinking of travelling with a notebook or hand-held computer, be aware that your modem may not work in India. The safest option is to buy a reputable 'global' modem before you leave home, or buy a local PC-card modem if you're spending an extended time away. Also, you won't be able to plug into telephone connectors anywhere except in business hotels that offer this facility. A better option is to use an infra-red or Blue-Tooth connection via a mobile phone (preferably with a local prepaid card). A useful investment is a universal AC adaptor, which will enable you to plug in without frying the innards of your machine. You'll also need a plug adaptor for India. For more information on travelling with a portable computer, see www.teleadapt.com.

For information on Internet resources see p23.

LAUNDRY

Unless a hotel has its own in-house laundry your clothes will be washed by a dhobi-wallah. If you don't think your gear will stand up to being beaten clean, hand wash them yourself or give them to a drycleaner (where available). Washing powder can be bought cheaply virtually everywhere in India.

At budget and midrange hotels clothes are usually washed by a dhobi. You simply hand over your dirty clothes in the morning, and you'll usually get them back washed and pressed that same evening for a minimal cost (around Rs 5 to 10 per item).

Most, if not all, upmarket hotels have an in-house laundry with upmarket charges to match. Many crank up the price for same-day service.

LEGAL MATTERS

If you're in a sticky legal situation, immediately contact your embassy (p467). You should be aware that foreign travellers are subject to Indian laws, and in the Indian justice system it can often seem that the burden of proof is on the accused.

You should carry your passport at all times, and the less you have to do with the local police (unless getting a written statement from them if you've had anything stolen; essential for your insurance claims) the better.

Drugs

India has long been known for its smorgasbord of illegal drugs (mostly marijuana and its derivative hashish), but would-be users should be aware of the very severe risks. Apart from opening yourself up to being taken advantage of, if convicted on a drugs-related charge, sentences are for a *minimum* of 10 years and there is no remission or parole. Cases can take several years to appear before a court while the accused waits, locked up. In addition, there's usually a hefty monetary fine. In Goa the police have been getting quite tough on drugs-related issues involving foreigners, so you should take the risk very seriously. Claims of foreigners having drugs planted on them, or being extorted on 'suspicion' of possessing drugs, are not unknown.

Smoking

The Indian government has banned smoking in public places and prohibited all forms of tobacco advertising. The ban includes all government buildings and public transport, although does not cover snuff and chewing tobacco, which account for the bulk of tobacco consumption in India. Transgressors face a mere Rs 100 fine, which probably accounts for the limited success of the ban.

MAPS

There's a dearth of high-quality maps in India. Some of the better possibilities include TTK's Discover India series, which has a number of state, regional and city maps. Eicher produces excellent street atlases for Bangalore, Mumbai and Chennai, as well as useful foldaway city maps. The Survey of India publishes decent city, state and country maps, while the Indian Map Service has a series of handy state road atlases (based on Survey of India maps). These maps are available at good bookshops.

Throughout India, state government tourist offices stock local maps, which are often dated and lacking in essential detail, but still reasonably useful for general orientation.

MONEY

The rupee (Rs) is divided into 100 paise (p). There are coins of five, 10, 20, 25 and 50 paise and Rs 1, 2 and 5, and notes of Rs 10, 20, 50, 100 and 500. There is a Rs 1000 note, but this is not always easy to get.

Twenty-four hour ATMs linked to international networks are common in most parts of India. This means that travellers can now rely on debit cards as a primary cash source. A cash or travellers cheque backup (preferably US dollars) is recommended in case you lose or break your card, or if ATMs are temporarily out of order. See the Money sections of this book's regional chapters for details about what's accepted where.

Remember, you must present your passport whenever changing currency and travellers cheques.

For information about costs read p20. See the inside front cover for exchange rates.

ATMs

All big Indian cities and an ever-growing number of smaller towns have 24-hour ATMs that accept Cirrus, Maestro, MasterCard, Plus and Visa cards. Banks in South India that currently accept foreign cards include Citibank, HDFC, ICICI, UTI, HSBC and some State Bank of India ATMs.

Don't rely on ATMs as your sole source of cash if you're planning to travel beyond the larger towns or away from tourist centres, as they either won't be available at all, or may not accept foreign cards. Alternatively, ensure you withdraw adequate cash from ATMs in big cities before venturing off.

Be aware that your bank may impose higher charges on international transactions, so once in India it's generally more economical to withdraw big amounts of money at once rather than making lots of small transactions. Check in advance with your home bank whether your card can access banking networks in India and, if so, what the charge (if any) per transaction is and if they have schemes to minimise these.

Note that several travellers have reported ATMs snatching back money if you don't remove it within around 30 seconds. Conversely, some people have said that ATMs can take more than 30 seconds to actually release cash, so don't hastily abandon the ATM assuming something has gone wrong.

The ATMs listed in this book's regional chapters all accept foreign cards (but not necessarily all types of cards).

Cash

It's no problem changing money in the bigger cities and towns or at tourist hotbeds. However, it's advisable to have some US dollars or UK pounds sterling (the most widely accepted currencies) in cash in case you're unable to change travellers cheques or use a credit card, especially in smaller towns. Many off-the-beaten-track places may not offer any moneychanging facilities at all, so take along an adequate stock of rupees.

Whenever you change money, make sure to take your time and check each note. Some bills look quite similar, so check them very carefully. Don't accept any filthy, ripped or disintegrating notes, as you'll have difficulty getting people to accept these (you can change them at the Reserve Bank of India as a last resort).

It can be difficult to use large denomination notes because of a seemingly perpetual lack of change in shops, taxis etc, so it's a good idea to maintain a constant stock of smaller currency.

Credit Cards

Most major cities and tourist centres accept credit cards, with MasterCard and Visa being the most widely accepted. Cash advances on major credit cards can be made at various banks (although not always in smaller towns). Credit cards are accepted at almost all top-end hotels and at many midrange ones; however, only a handful of budget hotels/restaurants/shops accept them. Major travel agents, airlines and some rail booking centres (such as in Mumbai or Chennai) accept credit cards.

Encashment Certificates

By law, all foreign currency must be changed at official moneychangers or banks, which will give you an encashment certificate (these money-exchange receipts are valid for three months). The certificates are required to re-exchange rupees exceeding Rs 10,000 into foreign currency when departing India (see Cash section, above). You'll need to have encashment certificates totalling the amount of rupees you intend changing back to foreign currency. Some shipping agents may request them as well.

Cash withdrawals from ATMs don't provide encashment certificates – most banks and moneychangers won't change rupees back into foreign currency for plastic transactions; however, most international airports will (on presentation of your ATM slip).

Note that money-exchange receipts are required when paying for tourist quota train tickets in rupees.

Encashment certificates are also needed for tax clearance certificates. See the Visas section (p482) for more details.

International Transfers

Naturally it's preferable not to run out of money, but if you do, you can have money transferred in no time at all (at a charge, of course) via Thomas Cook's Moneygram service or at Western Union, which both have branches throughout India. To collect cash, you need to bring along your passport and the name and reference number of the person who sent the funds.

Moneychangers

Usually open for longer hours than the banks, private moneychangers are a convenient option, and are located virtually everywhere in cities and tourist areas. However, it pays to compare the rates with those at the bank, and as with anywhere, check you are given the correct amount.

Security

The safest place for your money and your passport is next to your skin, either in a moneybelt around your waist or in a secure pouch under your shirt. Never, ever carry these things in your luggage. You're also asking for trouble if you walk around with your valuables in a shoulder bag. Bum bags (thankfully a dying tourist trend) are not recommended, as they virtually advertise that you have a stash of goodies and are easy pickings for thieves. Never leave your valuable documents and travellers cheques in your hotel room (including under your mattress). If the hotel is a reputable one, you should be able to use the hotel safe.

It's wise to peel off at least US$100 and keep it stashed away separately from your main horde, just in case. Finally, try to sepa-

rate your big notes from your small ones so you don't publicly display large wads of cash when paying for minor services, such as shoe polishing and tipping.

Tipping, Baksheesh & Bargaining

In tourist restaurants or hotels, where a service fee is usually already added on to your bill, tipping is optional. In smaller places, where there is no service fee, a tip is appreciated. Hotel and train porters expect around Rs 10 to carry bags, and hotel staff also expect around the same to provide services above and beyond the call of duty. It's not mandatory to tip taxi or autorickshaw drivers.

Baksheesh can be defined as a 'tip' and it also refers to giving alms to beggars. Many Indians implore tourists not to hand out sweets, pens or money to children, as it is positive reinforcement to beg. Instead you may like to donate to a school or charitable organisation (see p483).

Apart from at fixed-price shops, bargaining in South India is the norm – see the boxed text, p479.

Travellers Cheques

All major brands are accepted in India, with American Express (Amex) and Thomas Cook being the most widely traded. Pounds sterling and US dollars are the safest bet, especially beyond the major cities. Not all places take all brands – which means it pays to carry more than one flavour. Charges for changing travellers cheques vary from place to place and bank to bank.

Always keep an emergency cash stash in case you lose your travellers cheques, and in that same place (ie separate from your travellers cheques) keep a record of the cheques' serial numbers, proof of purchase slips, encashment vouchers and your photocopied passport details (data and visa pages). If you do lose your cheques, contact the Amex or Thomas Cook office in the closest capital city – to find out branches nationwide contact their offices in Delhi.

American Express (☎ 23719506; A-Block, Connaught Pl; ⊗ 9.30am-6.30pm Mon-Fri, 9.30am-2.30pm Sat) Also has an Amex-only ATM.

Thomas Cook International airport (☎ 25653439; ⊗ 24hr); Janpath (☎ 23342171; Imperial hotel; ⊗ 9.30am-7.30pm Mon-Fri, 9am-6pm Sat & Sun); New Delhi train station (☎ 23211819; ⊗ 24hr)

To rapidly replace lost travellers cheques you need the proof-of-purchase slip and the numbers of the missing cheques (some places require a photocopy of the police report and a passport photo). If you don't have the numbers of your missing cheques, Amex (or whichever company has issued them) will contact the place where you bought them.

PHOTOGRAPHY

For useful tips and techniques on travel photography, read Lonely Planet's *Travel Photography* guide.

Digital

Modern digital processing and memory cards are currently only available from photographic shops in the larger cities; however, the availability of digital services and products is set to escalate over the coming years. More widespread are shops/Internet centres that will download images onto CD (from Rs 50 to 110). Many travellers use this system, keeping CDs as backup or for emailing shots home. For digital processing at photo shops, the charge is roughly Rs 6 per print plus Rs 15 for developing. A 128mb Sony memory stick is Rs 2800.

Print & Slide

Colour print film-processing facilities are readily available in most South Indian cities. Film is relatively cheap and the quality is usually good. You'll only find colour slide film in the major cities and tourist traps. On average, to develop regular-sized colour prints costs around Rs 6 per print plus Rs 15 for processing. Passport photos are good value at about Rs 60/100 for four/10 shots (ready in around 10 minutes).

Always check the use-by date on local film and slide stock. Be wary of street hawkers who have been known to load old or damaged film into new-looking canisters. The hapless tourist only discovers this when the film is developed. It's best to only buy film from reputable stores – and preferably film that's been refrigerated.

Restrictions

India is touchy about photos being taken of places of military importance – this can include train stations, bridges, airports, military installations and border regions.

Places of worship (temples and mosques) may prohibit photography – if in doubt, ask. See p52 for etiquette about photographing people.

POST

Postal and poste restante services are generally good, although mail posted from India can sometimes take up to three weeks to arrive at its destination. Although the Indian postal system is usually reliable, it's safer to use courier services (such as DHL) to send and receive items of value. These services, available in some cities, can reliably arrange speedy air freight around the world; from Delhi to the UK or France DHL charges Rs 2299/2656 for 500g/1kg and to Australia it's Rs 2224/2643 for 500g/1kg.

Sending Mail

Posting aerogrammes and postcards overseas costs Rs 8.50 and Rs 8 respectively, and airmail letters are Rs 15. For postcards, it's not a bad idea to stick on the stamps *before* writing on them. This is because post offices don't always have Rs 8 stamps and can give you as many as four stamps per card – a real nuisance if you've already written on it and have only left space for one stamp! To eliminate the risk of stamp theft, request stamps to be franked in front of you.

Posting parcels is quite straightforward and prices vary depending on the weight. In the main cities, there's usually a person at or near the post office who sews parcels up in cheap linen. The post office will have the necessary customs declaration forms. To avoid paying duty at the delivery end, specify that the contents are a 'gift' under the value of Rs 1000.

Books or printed matter can go by bookpost (maximum 5kg), which is considerably cheaper than parcel post, but the package must be wrapped a certain way: make sure that the package can be opened for inspection along the way, or that it's wrapped with the two ends exposed so that the contents are visible. A customs declaration form is usually not necessary. Overseas bookpost rates vary depending on the weight; Rs 127/260/478/940 for 500g/1kg/2kg/4kg.

Express post has a maximum of 35kg. Charges to various destinations:

Australia 1st kilogram Rs 700, each additional kilogram Rs 300.

Europe & UK 1st kilogram Rs 950, each additional kilogram Rs 300.

USA 1st kilogram Rs 775, each additional kilogram Rs 400.

Receiving Mail

To receive mail in India, request that senders address letters to you with your surname in capital letters and underlined, followed by poste restante, GPO (main post office), and the city or town in question. Many 'lost' letters are simply misfiled under given (first) names, so always check under both. Ask senders to provide a return address in case you don't collect your mail. Letters sent via poste restante are held for one month before being returned. To claim mail, you'll need to show your passport. It's best to have parcels sent to you by registered post.

SHOPPING

You'll find a treasure trove of things to buy in South India, from exquisite textiles and carpets to beautiful jewellery and handicrafts. Specialities from all over the country can be found. Rajasthani crafts, such as sequinned and mirrored embroidery or colourful saris, and Kashmiri shawls, carpets and carvings, can be found everywhere, especially at tourist-oriented markets (such as the Anjuna flea market) and city shopping centres. Kashmiris especially are among India's most ubiquitous traders!

Be very cautious when buying items that include delivery to your country of residence. You may be told that the price includes home delivery and all customs and handling charges, but this is not always the case. For other important warnings read Scams (p466) and Touts & Commission Agents (p467).

Unless you're at fixed-price shops (such as cooperatives and government emporiums), you'll invariably have to bargain – see the boxed text, p479.

RESPONSIBLE SHOPPING

Tourists can put their money to excellent use by shopping at cooperatives. These have been set up to protect and promote the income of day labourers and handicraft producers at the grassroots level. For the customer, the quality of products is generally superior to other shops and the prices are fixed, so you don't have to haggle.

India has a plethora of impressive cooperatives. Those described here represent just some of these, so during your travels keep your eyes peeled for others.

The Kanhirode Weavers Co-operative (20km northeast of Kannur in Kerala) is a handloom factory that produces high-quality furnishing fabrics, saris, dhotis (like long loincloths) and silks; they'll give you a quick tour and you can buy items directly from the factory.

Over in Chennai, SIPA's Craftlink (p327) supports local artists and craftspeople. Also helping people at the grassroots level are the Khadi & Village Industries, which are found nationwide.

On a general note, as large-scale production of machine-printed material threatens artisans' livelihoods, buy genuine handblock-printed material products (the handmade ones will have block marks and messy edges on the reverse side), which are nicer in any case.

Keep in mind that *shahtoosh* shawls (manufactured in Jammu & Kashmir) have been officially banned, as the wool comes from the endangered Tibetan antelope. If you're offered one of these shawls, don't buy it and inform the police. Also resist the temptation to buy authentic furniture and fittings from traditional (eg Ladakhi) houses and *havelis* (traditional, often ornately decorated residences in places like Rajasthan and Gujarat), as it robs India of its cultural heritage – look for quality reproductions instead.

Finally, always encourage all vendors to wrap your purchases in paper, not plastic bags.

Antiques & Wildlife Restrictions

The export of objects more than 100 years old is prohibited, making the required export clearance certificate difficult to obtain. If in doubt, contact Delhi's **Archaeological Survey of India** (☎ 011-23010822; Janpath; ◷ 9.30am-1.30pm & 2-6pm Mon-Fri) next to the National Museum.

The Indian Wildlife Protection Act bans any form of wildlife trade. Don't buy any products that further endanger threatened species and habitats – doing so can result in heavy fines and even imprisonment.

Carpets

Almost all the carpets you'll see for sale in South India come from Kashmir, Rajasthan or Uttar Pradesh. Kashmiri rugs are either made of pure wool, wool with a small percentage of silk to give them a sheen (known as 'silk touch') or pure silk. The latter are more for decoration. Kashmiri carpets can cost anywhere from Rs 200 to 8000 per square foot, with wool being cheaper than silk. The number of knots per square inch (from 200 to 1800) also affects the price.

In Kashmir and Rajasthan, coarsely woven woollen *numdas* (also spelt *namdas*) are produced and can also make nice wall-hangings. These are more primitive and folksy, and are consequently cheaper than the fine carpets. These types of carpets are also found for sale in South India.

Jewellery

South India's most important jewellery-making centres are Hyderabad, Bangalore, Mysore, Ooty and Thanjavur. Cuttack (p455) in Orissa is a centre for delicate silver filigree jewellery and ornaments. South Indian jewellery is generally distinguished from that made in the north by its use of motifs inspired by nature – lotus buds, flowers, grass stalks and, in Kerala, birds. Throughout South India you can find finely crafted gold and silver rings, anklets, earrings, toe-rings, necklaces and bangles. Pieces can often be crafted to order.

Virtually every town in South India has at least one basic bangle shop. These sell an extraordinary variety at just Rs 20 to 200 for a set of 12 (made from materials like plastic, glass, brass and wood).

If you feel like being creative and making your own necklace, loose beads of agate, turquoise, carnelian and silver can be found for sale. Buddhist meditation beads made of gems, wood or inlaid bone make nifty souvenirs; prices cost around Rs 25 for wooden beads to 500 for an amber string.

Pearls are produced by most seaside states (they're a speciality of Hyderabad) and crafted into jewellery in many other Indian states – you'll find them at most state emporiums. Prices vary depending on the colour and shape – you pay more for pure white pearls or rare colours, like black and red, and perfectly round pearls are more expensive than misshapen or elongated pearls. However, the quirky shapes of Indian pearls are actually often more alluring than the perfect round balls. A single strand of seeded pearls can cost as little as Rs 200, but better-quality pearls start at Rs 600.

Leatherwork

As the cow is sacred in India, leatherwork here is made from buffalo, camel, goat or some other substitute. Chappals, wonderful leather sandals found all over India, are a popular traveller's purchase. In Maharashtra, the town of Kolhapur (p159) is especially famous for its chappals, and they are also good in Pune (p149) and Matheran (p144), with prices generally starting at around Rs 150.

Rajasthan (especially Jaipur) is famed for its *jootis* (traditional pointy-toed shoes); those for men often have curled-up toes. Punjab also produces good jootis. Jootis are available in South India from markets and city shopping centres.

In the larger cities, such as Chennai (p327) and Mumbai (p115), you'll find well-made, moderately priced leather handbags and other leather accessories.

Metalwork & Bronze Figures

Bidriware is a craft named after the town of Bidri in northern Karnataka where silver is inlaid into gunmetal. Hookah pipes, lamp bases and jewellery boxes are made in this manner. Bidri employs the technique of sand-casting – artisans make a mould from sand, resin and oil.

Small bronze figures of various deities are available in Tamil Nadu, especially in and around major temple towns. The bronze makers (called shilpis) still employ the centuries' old lost-wax method of casting, a legacy of the Chola period when bronze sculpture reached its apogee in skill and artistry. A wax figure is made, a mould is formed around it and the wax is melted and poured out. The molten metal is poured in and when it's solidified the mould is broken open. Figures of Shiva as Lord of the Dance, Nataraja, are among the most popular. Small copper bowls, cigarette boxes and paan containers are still handmade in Hyderabad (p411). Bell metal lamps are a good buy in Thrissur (Trichur; p301). Cuttack (p455) in Orissa has a tradition of brassware.

DIRECTORY

Paintings

Reproductions of old miniatures are widely available, but are of variable quality (the cheaper ones have less detail and usually use inferior materials). Beware of paintings purported to be antique – it's highly unlikely and in any case items over 100 years old can't be exported from India.

In Kerala and to a lesser extent Tamil Nadu, you'll come across miniature paintings on leaf skeletons enclosed on a printed card depicting domestic and rural scenes, as well as deities. In Andhra Pradesh you can buy paintings on cloth called *kalamkari*.

The village of Raghurajpur (p446), 14km from Puri, is an artists' colony. They make *patta chitra* painting, which involves preparing cotton cloth with a mixture of gum and chalk that is then polished to make it tough. Outlines of characters from India's mythologies, and deities are drawn with exceedingly fine paintbrushes and then coloured in. Another craft practised in the same village is carving onto dried palm leaf sections with a fine stylus after which the incisions are dyed with a wash of colour. There's another artists' colony at Cholamandal (p330) south of Chennai in Tamil Nadu.

Shawls, Silk & Saris

When it comes to shawls, the highest prices are generally for those that are finely embroidered, such as the traditional winter shawls from Kullu in Himachal Pradesh. Be aware that although some shopkeepers may insist they're genuine, many so-called pashmina shawls are actually made from a mixture of yarns. For the real thing, you can easily pay at least Rs 6000 for the authentic 'slides through a wedding ring' article.

Aurangabad (p131) is the traditional centre for the production of *himroo* shawls, sheets and saris. Made from a blend of cotton, silk and silver thread, these garments cost from about Rs 500 and are often decorated with motifs from the Ajanta Cave paintings. The exquisite silk and gold-thread saris produced at Paithan (p131) are more exclusive – they range from around Rs 6000 to a mind-blowing Rs 300,000.

The 'silk capital' of India is Kanchipuram in Tamil Nadu, where some of the most prized wedding saris are produced, but you can also pick up inexpensive silk scarves and ties (see the boxed text, p339). When shopping for silk, remember it will only become soft after you wash it.

Stone Carvings

In Mamallapuram (Mahabalipuram; p336) craftsmen have revived the ancient works of Pallava sculptors; these can be bought from around Rs 300 (for a small piece) to 400,000 for a massive Ganesh. Also good in South India are bronze and carvings from Thanjavur (p359) and Trichy (p363).

Textiles

Textile production is India's major industry and around 40% of the total production is at the village level, where it is known as *khadi*. There are government *khadi* emporiums (known as Khadi Gramodyog) around the country, and here you can buy handmade items of home-spun cloth, including the popular 'Nehru jackets' and kurta pyjama.

Appliqué in India involves sewing and embroidering cut out figures of bright cloth onto a contrasting or complementary colour cloth to produce bed linen, bags, tablecloths and lamp shades. Sometimes small circles of mirror glass are also embroidered in.

Orissa has a reputation for bright appliqué and handmade silk and cotton fabrics, with Sambalpur (p453) specialising in *ikat* (a southeast-Asian technique that involves tie-dying the thread before it's woven). The Orissan town of Pipli (p441), between Bhubaneswar and Puri, produces some particularly vivid appliqué work.

Batik can be found through India, but is particularly good in the larger cities, such as Mumbai. Fabulous batik work can be seen on saris and *salwar kameez* in trendy city boutiques. *Kalamkari* cloth from Andhra Pradesh is an associated but far older craft. It traditionally emerged around South India's temples – the designs reflect elements of temple murals, and are largely used as decorative cloths during devotional ceremonies and festivals.

Big Indian cities, such as Mumbai and Chennai, are great places to pick up *haute couture* (high fashion) by talented Indian designers, as well as more moderately priced western fashions.

Woodcarving

Mysore (p218) is known as South India's main centre of sandalwood carving, and

THE ART OF HAGGLING

Haggling is a must in most parts of India. Shopkeepers in tourist hubs are accustomed to travellers who have lots of money and little time to spend it. It's not unusual to be charged at least double, or even triple the 'real' price.

So how do you know if you're being overcharged and need to strike back with some serious haggling? Well, you're safe in government emporiums, cooperatives and modern shopping complexes, where the prices are usually fixed. But in most other shops that cater primarily to tourists, be prepared to don your haggling hat. The kind of places that usually fall into this category include handicraft, carpet, painting, souvenir and clothing shops.

The first 'rule' to haggling is never show too much interest in the item you want to buy. Secondly, don't buy the first item that takes your fancy. Wander around and price things, but don't make it obvious, otherwise if you return to the first shop the vendor will know it's because they are the cheapest.

Decide how much you would be happy paying and then express a casual interest in buying. If you have absolutely no idea of what something should really cost, start by slashing the price by half (even more in touristy spots). This is usually completely unacceptable to the vendor, but it works as a good starting point to haggle for a happy compromise. You'll find that many shopkeepers lower their so-called 'final price' if you proceed to head out of the shop saying you'll 'think about it'.

Haggling is a way of life in India, but it should never turn ugly. Keep in mind exactly how much a rupee is worth in your home currency so you don't lose perspective, and if a vendor seems to be charging an unreasonably high price and is unwilling to negotiate, simply look elsewhere.

while sandalwood was once reserved for carving deities, nowadays all manner of things are made, from solid pieces of furniture to keyrings and delicate fans. Rosewood is used for making furniture, and carving animals and elephants is a speciality of Kerala.

Kerala, along with coastal Karnataka, is a centre for marquetry, which uses woods of various hues (including rosewood) and, in Mysore, ivory substitutes. Carved wooden furniture and other household items, either in natural finish or lacquered, are also made in various locations. Woodcarvers' skills are very much in evidence in the major temple towns of Tamil Nadu.

Wooden boxes and chests, once major dowry items, are available in the antique shops of Fort Cochin (p291) in Kerala. Although they are still made by local artisans, metal cupboards and trunks are replacing the wooden versions and they are becoming rarer. Dowry boxes are usually made from the wood of the jackfruit tree (sometimes rosewood), and are reinforced with brass hinges and brackets.

Wooden toys are also made in many regions of South India. Brightly painted buses and trucks are made in Trivandrum (p261) and in Balasore (p455).

Other Buys

Attar (essential oil) shops can be widely found throughout India. Mysore is especially famous for its sandalwood oil – read the boxed text, p221.

In Tamil Nadu's Ooty (p384) and Kodaikanal (p375), look out for the aromatic and medicinal oils made from herbs, flowers and eucalyptus.

Indian incense is exported worldwide, with Bangalore and Mysore being major producers. Incense from Auroville (p351), an ashram near Pondicherry, is of high quality. Nag Champa is another popular incense brand and is produced by devotees of Sai Baba (see the boxed text, p430). It has a sandalwood base, yet has a distinctive fragrant scent drawing from a variety of sources.

Specialities of Goa include cashew and coconut *feni*. This head-spinning spirit often comes in decorative souvenir bottles, costs from around Rs 30 to more than Rs 1000. Traditional clay pipe chillums and hookah pipes (smoking and possessing drugs is illegal but buying the paraphernalia is not!) are also popular. The Wednesday flea market at Anjuna is the place to shop for crafts and souvenirs from all over India.

Cuttack (p455) in Orissa is famed for its lacelike, silver filigree work known as *tarakasi*. A silver framework is made and then filled in with delicate curls and ribbons of thin silver.

Pondicherry (p344) is especially known for its fine handmade paper, batiks and *kalamkari* (similar to batik) drawings.

Throughout India you can find a phenomenal range of well-priced books – see the Bookshops sections of individual regional chapters. Also good value are music CDs featuring Indian artists – for instance, *bhajans* (devotional songs) CDs start at just Rs 90. CDs featuring Western artists tend to fall in the Rs 295 to 600 range. Music shops often also sell DVDs; English DVDs range from around Rs 199 to 1199, while Hindi DVDs from Rs 149 to 349.

SOLO TRAVELLERS

Perhaps the most significant issue facing solo travellers is cost. Single-room rates at guesthouses and hotels are sometimes not that much lower than rates for a double; some midrange and top-end places don't even offer a single tariff, instead charge a flat double rate (try to bargain this down on the basis that you're by yourself).

In terms of transport, you'll save money if you find others to share taxis and autorickshaws. This is also advisable if you intend on hiring a car with driver.

Although most solo travellers experience no major problems in India, remember that some less honourable souls (locals and travellers alike) may view lone tourists as an easy target for theft. Don't be paranoid, but, like anywhere else in the world, it's wise to stay on your toes in unfamiliar surroundings. In tourist areas, you shouldn't have any trouble finding other travellers to hook up with.

For important information specific to women, see p485.

TELEPHONE

Even in the smallest towns you'll find private PCO/STD/ISD call booths with local, interstate and international dialling; these are invariably cheaper than calls made from hotel rooms. Many booths are open 24 hours and a digital meter means you can see what the call is costing. It also gives you a print-out when the call is finished. Faxes can usually also be sent from these booths.

Throughout most of India, interstate calls from booths charge the full rate from around 9am to 8pm. After 8pm the cost slides, with the cheapest time to call being between 11pm and 6am.

Direct international calls from call booths cost an average of Rs 22 to 40 per minute depending on the country you are calling. The cheapest international calls can be made through Internet cafés using Net2phone or a similar service. Calls cost from as little as Rs 5 per minute to the USA, Rs 7 to Australia and Rs 10 to Europe.

India has both **White Pages** (www.indiawhite pages.com) and **Yellow Pages** (www.indiayellowpages .com) online.

Mobile Phones

The advantages of bringing your own mobile phone to India are that local networks are reasonably cheap to use, getting hooked up to the mobile phone network is pretty straightforward, and you can conveniently keep in touch with home or other travellers. On top of that, calls (even international) are cheap by world standards.

In most towns you simply buy a prepaid mobile-phone kit (SIM card and phone number) from any phone shop or other outlets, such as PCO/STD/ISD booths, Internet cafés and grocery stores. The most popular (and reliable) companies are Airtel, Hutch (Orange in some states), BPL and Idea.

The SIM card itself costs only about Rs 100, but you usually pay for an additional amount of credit to get started. You then buy recharge cards (top-ups) from any phone shop from Rs 100 to 3400. Usually credit must be used (or topped up) within a fixed period (ie 15 to 60 days) and the amount you pay for a credit top-up is not the amount you get on your phone – state taxes and service charges come off first, so for a Rs 500 top-up you'll get around Rs 375 worth of calls. Note that with some networks, recharge cards are being replaced by direct credit, where you pay the vendor and the credit is deposited straight to your phone – ask which system is in use before you buy.

Calls made within the state or city you bought the SIM card are cheap – less than Rs 1 per minute – and you can call internationally for less than Rs 25 per minute. SMS messaging is even cheaper. The more credit you have on your phone, the cheaper the call rate.

However, some travellers have reported having difficulty using their mobile phone (either no coverage at all or frequent cut offs). International texting can be reliable on some days and not on others – you can normally receive text messages but sometimes can't send any replies for days at a time.

The downside to travelling interstate with a mobile phone is that the prepaid system in India is not a truly national system – major cities and all states have their own mobile phone networks. If you move outside the network area in which you purchased the phone or SIM card, you'll have to ensure the phone company has roaming capabilities – the major companies, such as Airtel, have more-or-less Indiawide roaming. Away from the state in which you bought the SIM card, call rates are usually a little higher and you will be charged for incoming calls as well as outgoing calls. Although in some cases the incoming charges are higher than the outgoing, so receiving a lengthy call from home will really chew through your credit! Otherwise – and notwithstanding local technology glitches – the roaming system seems to work fine. However, check with the vendor before you buy the mobile-phone kit to make sure it meets all your requirements.

As the mobile-phone industry is an evolving one, mobile-phone rates, suppliers and coverage are all likely to develop over the life of this book.

Phone Codes

To make a call *to* India from overseas, dial the international access code of the country you're in, then 91 (international country code for India), then the area code (drop the initial 0; this zero only applies for calls made within India) and then the local number. See the regional chapters for area codes.

To make an international call *from* India, dial 00 (international access code from India) then the country code (of the country you are calling) then the area code and finally the local number.

Also available is the Home Country Direct service, which gives you access to the international operator in your home country. For the price of a local call, you can then make reverse-charge (collect) or

phonecard calls. Some countries and their numbers:

Country	Number
Australia	☎ 0006117
Canada	☎ 00016788
Germany	☎ 0004917
Japan	☎ 0008117
The Netherlands	☎ 0003117
Singapore	☎ 0006517
Spain	☎ 0003417
UK	☎ 0004417
USA	☎ 000117

TIME

India is 5½ hours ahead of GMT/UTC, 4½ hours behind Australian Eastern Standard Time (EST) and 10½ hours ahead of American EST. The local standard time is known as Indian Standard Time (IST), although many affectionately dub it 'Indian Stretchable Time'.

See the World Time Zones Map, p527.

TOILETS

Public toilets are generally confined to the major cities and at tourist sites (eg museums), upmarket shopping complexes and cinemas, but they can be few and far between. Not all have toilet paper and the cleanliness is variable to say the least.

When it comes to effluent etiquette, it's customary to use your left hand and water, not toilet paper. A strategically placed tap, usually with a plastic jug nearby, is available in most bathrooms. If you can't get used to the Indian method, bring your own paper (widely available in cities and towns). However, stuffing paper, sanitary napkins and tampons down the toilet is going to further clog an already overloaded sewerage system. Often a bin is provided for disposing of used toilet paper and other items – please use it.

TOURIST INFORMATION
Local Tourist Offices

In addition to the national (Government of India) tourist office, each state maintains its own tourist office. The state offices vary widely in their efficiency and usefulness. Some are run by enthusiastic souls; others have grumpy or disinterested staff who can be abrupt to the point of rudeness. At some offices you'll be lucky to get more than yes or no responses – just politely persist. Apart from

DIRECTORY

dispensing verbal information, most tourist offices have a healthy stock of brochures (free) and often a free local map. Many state governments also operate a chain of tourist bungalows (accommodation), a number of which house state tourism offices.

For details about specific tourist offices, see the Information sections of this book's regional chapters.

Tourist Offices Abroad

The **Government of India** (Ministry of Tourism; www .incredibleindia.org) provides general tourist-related information about the country. Its website provides information in English, French, German and Spanish.

To access Indian regional office links click on www.tourismofindia.com/foot/links.htm.

The Government of India operates tourist offices abroad, which include the following:

Australia (☎ 02-9264 4855; goitosyd@nextcentury.com .au; Level 2, Piccadilly, 210 Pitt St, Sydney, NSW 2000)

Canada (☎ 416-962 3787; indiatourism@bellnet.ca; 60 Bloor St, West Ste 1003, Toronto, Ontario, M4W 3B8)

France (☎ 01 45 23 30 45; intourpar@aol.com; 11-13 Blvd Haussmann, F-75009, Paris)

Germany (☎ 069-242 94 90; info@india-tourism.com; Basolar Strasse 48, D-60329, Frankfurt am-Main 1)

Italy (☎ 028 05 35 06; info@indiatourismmilan.com; Via-Albricci 9, Milan 20122)

The Netherlands (☎ 0206 20 89 91; info.nl@india -tourism.com; Rokin 9/15, 1012 KK Amsterdam)

UK (☎ 020-7437 3677; info@indiatouristoffice.org; 7 Cork St, London W1S 3LH)

USA Los Angeles (☎ 213-380 8855; goitola@aol.com; Room 204, 3550 Wiltshire Blvd, Los Angeles, CA 900102485); New York (☎ 212-586 4901' ny@itonyc.com; Ste 1808, 1270 Ave of the Americas, NY 100201700)

TRAVEL PERMITS

Even with a visa, you're not permitted to travel everywhere in South India. Some national parks and forest reserves require a permit if you intend to go trekking, and a permit (issued free) is required to visit the Andaman Islands (p394) and another to visit Lakshadweep (p309).

VISAS

You must get a visa *before* arriving in India. Six-month multiple-entry visas (valid from the date of issue) are issued to nationals of most countries (check visa options with the Indian embassy in your country) regardless of whether you intend staying that long or

re-entering the country. Visas cost A$75 (an extra A$15 service fee applies to consulates) for Australians, US$60 for US citizens and UK£30 for Britons.

You may not be issued a visa to enter India unless you hold an onward ticket, which is taken as sufficient evidence that you intend to leave the country.

Extended visas (up to five years) are possible for people of Indian descent (excluding those in Pakistan and Bangladesh) who hold a non-Indian passport and live abroad. A special People of Indian Origin (PIO) card is also possible (valid for 15 years). Contact your embassy for more details.

For visas beyond six months, you technically need to register at the Foreigners' Regional Registration Office (FRRO; see below) within 14 days of arriving in India and get a tax clearance certificate before departure. For the certificate, go to the Foreign Section of the **Income Tax Office** (☎ 011-23379161; Indra-prastha Estate; ☽ 10am-1.30pm & 2.30-6pm Mon-Fri). This certificate supposedly proves that your time in India was financed with your own money. You'll need to show your passport, visa extension form, any other appropriate paperwork, and a bunch of bank encashment certificates and/or ATM slips.

Visa Extensions

Fourteen-day extensions are possible under exceptional circumstances from the Foreigners' Regional Registration Office (FRRO), found in some main Indian cities (see the Information sections of regional chapters); however, many may direct travellers to Delhi for extensions. Travellers have been known to have success getting extensions in Mumbai with a bit of persistence, but don't count on it. You can only get another six-month tourist visa by leaving the country – many travellers skip over to Sri Lanka, Nepal or on a cheap flight to Bangkok, but be aware that some travellers report difficulties getting another visa in Kathmandu.

In Delhi, the **Foreigners' Regional Registration Office** (☎ 011-26711443; fax 26711348; Level 2, East Block 8, Sector 1, RK Puram, Delhi; ☽ 9.30am-1.30pm & 2-3pm Mon-Fri) is located behind the Hyatt Regency hotel. Come here for replacement visas (if you've had your lost/stolen passport replaced) as well as visa extensions.

For those with a good reason, the FRRO issues 14-day visa extensions, free for nationals of all countries, except Japan (Rs 390), Sri Lanka (Rs 235), Russia (Rs 1860) and Romania (Rs 500). Bring your confirmed air ticket, one passport photo and a photocopy of your passport (information and visa pages). For 14-day extensions you only need to visit the FRRO; however, applying for a (maximum) one-month extension (all nationalities Rs 1860) on a six-month visa entails shuttling between the FRRO and the Foreigner's Division of the **Ministry of Home Affairs (Foreigners Division)** (☎ 011-23385748; 26 Jaisalmer House, Man Singh Rd, Delhi; ☷ 10am-noon Mon-Fri). For this longer extension, first you need an exceptionally good reason, then you must collect the long-term visa extension form from the Ministry of Home Affairs. Be prepared to wait. Then take the form and three passport photos to the FRRO. If the extension is authorised, the authorisation has to be taken *back* to the Ministry of Home Affairs, where the actual visa extension is issued.

VOLUNTEER WORK

Numerous charities and international aid agencies have branches in South India and, although they're generally staffed by locals, there are opportunities for foreigners. You are more use to the charity concerned if you write in advance and, if you're needed, stay for long enough to be of help. A week on a hospital ward may go a little way towards salving your own conscience, but you may actually do little more than get in the way of the people who work there long term.

Flexibility in what you are prepared to do is also vital. Some charities are inundated with foreign volunteers to help babies in an orphanage for instance, but few are willing to work with adults with physical or intellectual disabilities.

If you're a Bollywood fan there may be opportunities for working as an extra (see the boxed text, p104). For details about Chennai's film industry (and the possibility of being an extra), see p321.

Aid Programmes in India

Following are some of the programmes operating in South India that may have opportunities for volunteers. You should contact them in advance, rather than just turning up on their doorstep expecting to be automatically offered a position. Donations of

money or clothing from travellers may also be warmly welcomed. Some NGOs may also offer volunteer work – for details go to www.indianngos.com.

Note that unless otherwise indicated, volunteers are expected to cover their own costs (accommodation, food, transport etc).

For information about current volunteer possibilities at the places we've listed, contact each directly.

ANDHRA PRADESH

The **Confederation of Voluntary Associations** (COVA; ☎ 040-24572984; www.covanetwork.org; 20-4-10, Charminar, Hyderabad) is an umbrella organisation for around 800 NGOs based in Andhra Pradesh. The organisations deal with a wide range of issues, from civil liberties to sustainable agriculture, but the majority focus on women and children. Volunteer work is broad, extending from youth development to community-health programmes.

With an animal hospital and sanctuary for disabled donkeys, **Karuna Society for Animals and Nature** (☎ 08555-287214; www.karunasociety .org; 2/138/C Karuna Nilayam, Prasanthi Nilayam Post; Anantapur 515134) is doing heart-warming work to rescue sick and mistreated animals.

GOA

Goa's paramount environmental group is the **Goa Foundation** (☎ 0832-2263305; www.olb.com; c/o Other India Bookstore, Mapusa, Goa 403507), which also runs some voluntary programmes, such as clean-ups.

KARNATAKA

Volunteer opportunities in Bangalore may also be possible at the gay and lesbian support groups Sangama (p471) and Swabhava (p471).

The **Ashoka Trust for Research in Ecology and the Environment** (Atree; ☎ 080-3530069; www.atree .org; 659 5th A Main Rd, Hebbal, Bangalore 560024) is committed to sustainable development issues related to conservation and biodiversity. It takes volunteers with experience or an interest in conservation or environmental issues.

Equations (☎ 080-25244988; www.equitabletourism .org; 23-25 8th Cross, Vignan Nagar, New Thippasandra Post, Bangalore 560075) works to promote 'holistic tourism', and protect local communities from exploitative tourism through lobbying, local training programmes and research publications.

MAHARASHTRA

An NGO that melds science, technology and spiritual philosophies with research and development projects, **Nimbkar Agricultural Research Institute** (☎ 02166-222396; http://nariphaltan .virtualave.net/; Phaltan-Lonand Rd, Tambmal, PO Box 44, Phaltan, Maharashtra) has a focus on sustainable development, animal husbandry and renewable energy. One-year internships are available for assistance in energy and agriculture research. Shorter-term researchers are also needed, and there are also opportunities for fundraisers.

Located 30km from Pune is **Sadhana Village** (☎ 020-25380792; pusadhana@vsnl.com; Priyankit, 1 Lokmanya Colony, Opp.Vanaz Paud Rd, Pune 411038), a residential care centre for intellectually disabled adults. Volunteers (who receive accommodation and meals; donations appreciated) assist in coordinating workshops and cultural activities. The centre also runs community-development programmes focusing on women and children.

MUMBAI

Independent trust **Child Relief and You** (CRY; ☎ 022-23096845; www.cry.org; 189A Anand Estate, Sane Guruji Marg, Mumbai 400011) organises fundraising for more than 300 projects Indiawide, including a dozen projects in Mumbai helping deprived children. The **Vatsalya Foundation** (☎ 022-24962115; Anand Niketan, King George V Memorial, Dr E Moses Rd, Mahalaxmi, Mumbai 400011) works with Mumbai's street children, focusing on rehabilitation and reintroducing them to mainstream society. It can also be contacted through the Concern India Foundation (described next).

The charitable trust **Concern India Foundation** (☎ 022-22880129; www.concernindia.org; 3rd fl, Ador House, 6 K Dubash Marg, Mumbai 400001) supports development-oriented organisations working with vulnerable members of the community. It doesn't engage in fieldwork; its speciality is networking. The foundation is happy to field requests from travellers who wish to offer their time, and will try to match your skills or interests with particular projects. Volunteers should be prepared to commit for at least six months and preferably speak Hindi. Volunteering possibilities may also be possible in other major Indian cities.

Saathi (☎ 022-23520053; www.saathi.org; Agripada Municipal School, Farooque Umarbhouy Lane, Mumbai, 400011) works primarily with youths living on the streets and runaway adolescent girls. It also has a project in Ahmedabad (Gujarat) for children affected by communal violence, as well as an ecoproject in Kerala.

ORISSA

The **Wildlife Society of Orissa** (☎ 0671-2311513; A-320, Sahid Nagar, Bhubaneswar 751007) works to save endangered species in Orissa, especially the olive ridley turtle (see the boxed text, p450).

TAMIL NADU

In Chennai, volunteers may be needed at the **GoS Bala Vihar** (☎ 044-28228054; 10 Halls Rd, Kilpauk, Chennai), a home for children who require special care; **Missionaries of Charity** (☎ 044-25953078; 71 Main Rd, Royapuram, Chennai), part of Mother Teresa's Kolkata-based operation, helping the socially disadvantaged; or **Sneha** (☎ 044-28115050; 4 Lloyd's Lane, Royapettah, Chennai), a telephone helpline for lonely, depressed and suicidal people (volunteers must first complete a four-day training course).

The NGO **Rural Institute for Development Organisation** (RIDE; ☎ 04112-268393; www.charityfocus .org/India/host/RIDE; 46 Periyar Nagar, Little Kanchipuram) works with around 200 villages in Kanchipuram to remove children from forced labour and into transition schools. Volunteers can contribute in teaching, administrative and support roles. See the boxed text, p51 for more on child labour.

The **Society for Education, Village Action & Improvement** (SEVAI; ☎ 0431-2685227; www.sevai.org; 133 Karur Main Rd, Allur) works with rural poor in the villages of central Tamil Nadu, helping with education, housing construction, drinking water and hygiene.

Overseas Volunteer Placement Agencies

For long-term posts, the following organisations may be able to offer advice:

Action Without Borders (☎ 212-843 3973; www .idealist.org; Ste 1510, 360 West 31st St, New York, NY 10001, USA)

AidCamps International (☎ 020-8291 6181; www .aidcamps.org; 5 Simone Ct, Dartmouth Rd, London SE26 4RP, UK)

Australian Volunteers International (☎ 03-9279 1788; www.ozvol.org.au; PO Box 350, Fitzroy VIC 3065, Australia)

Co-ordinating Committee for International Voluntary Service (☎ 01 45 68 49 36; www.unesco.org/ccivs; Unesco House, 31 Rue Francois Bonvin, 75732 Paris Cedex 15, France)

Global Volunteers (☎ 651-407 6100; www.global volunteers.org; 375 East Little Canada Rd, St Paul, MN 55117-1628, USA)

Voluntary Service Overseas (VSO; ☎ 020-8780 7200; www.vso.org.uk; 317 Putney Bridge Rd, London SW15 2PN, UK)

Working Abroad (☎ /fax France office only 04-68 26 41 79; www.workingabroad.com; PO Box 454, Flat 1, Brighton, BN1 3ZS, East Sussex, UK)

Other useful sites:
- www.volunteerabroad.com
- www.studyabroad.com
- www.responsibletravel.com

WOMEN TRAVELLERS

Solo women travellers will most likely receive some form of unwanted attention while in India, whether it's constant staring or groping on public transport. South India may be safer in this respect than the north, but it's also more conservative in places, and the way you dress and act in public may have an impact on how you're treated. Even on the beach resorts of Goa and Kerala – where locals have become accustomed to the sight of westerners wearing little more than a G-string and a smile – local sensibilities have to be respected. In some cases the behaviour of scantily clad westerners has even become a perverse 'attraction' with young Indian men cruising Goa to ogle foreign women. Regrettably, the skimpy clothing and culturally inappropriate behaviour of a minority of foreign women seems to have had a ripple effect on the perception of foreign women in general. An increasing number of female travellers have reported some form of sexual harassment (mainly lewd comments and groping) despite making an effort to act and dress conservatively.

Most cases are reported in prominent tourist destinations. While there's no need to be concerned to the point of paranoia, you should be aware that your behaviour and dress code is under scrutiny. Although sexual harassment (sometimes locally referred to as 'Eve-teasing') has risen over recent years, India still has less reported sex crimes than most Western nations.

Getting stared at is, unfortunately, something you'll have to get used to. Just be thick-skinned and don't allow it to get the better of you. It's best to refrain from returning stares, as this may be considered a come-on;

dark glasses can help. A good way to block out stares in restaurants is to take a book or postcards to write home. Other harassments encountered include: provocative gestures, jeering, getting 'accidentally' bumped into on the street and being followed. Exuberant special events (such as the Holi festival) can be notorious for this (see p466).

Based on feedback we've received, women travelling with a male partner are less likely to be harassed. However, a foreign woman of Indian descent travelling with a non-Indian male may cop disapproving stares; having a non-Indian partner is still not condoned in parts of India.

Ultimately, there are no sure-fire ways of shielding yourself from sexual harassment, even for those who do everything 'right'. You're essentially going to have to use your own judgement and instincts as there isn't a blanket rule that applies to every case. If the warnings in this section make travel in India seem a little daunting, remember that most men are not out to bother you, and the problems mentioned here are just things to be aware of.

What to Wear

Warding off sexual harassment is often a matter of common sense and appropriate behaviour. What you wear can help enormously. Steer clear of sleeveless tops, shorts, miniskirts (ankle-length skirts are recommended), skimpy, see-through or tight clothing. Baggy clothing that hides the contours of your body is the way to go.

In some areas, such as Goa and Mumbai, there's generally a more liberal attitude towards dress (eg you're not expected to be covered from head to toe at nightclubs or on beaches), but this doesn't give you the green light to roam around half-dressed wherever you go.

Many Indian women wear saris or *salwar kameez* whenever swimming in public (except at pools). When swimming at beaches/rivers/lakes off-the-tourist-track, foreign women are going to be better received by also covering up (eg wearing knee-length shorts and T-shirts, or a sarong).

Wearing Indian dress, when done properly, makes a positive impression and, although we've had a few reports of women still being groped, most were pleasantly surprised by the effect it had in curtailing harassment. The *salwar kameez* (traditional dresslike tunic and trouser combination), widely worn by Indian women, is regarded as respectable attire and wearing it will reflect your veneration for local dress etiquette. It's practical, comfortable, attractive, and comes in a range of designs and prices. A cotton *salwar kameez* is also surprisingly cool in the hot weather. The *dupatta* (long scarf) that is worn with this outfit is handy if you visit a shrine that requires your head to be covered.

Wearing a *choli* (small tight blouse worn underneath a sari) or a sari petticoat (which many foreign women mistake for a skirt) in public is rather like strutting around half-dressed – don't do it.

Read personal experiences proffered by fellow women travellers at www.journeywoman.com, which has a section devoted to dress (follow the prompts to India).

Staying Safe

Women have reported being molested by masseurs and other therapists. No matter where you are, try to check the reputation of any teacher or therapist before going to a solo session. If at any time you feel uneasy, leave. For gynaecological health issues, seek out a female doctor.

To keep conversations with men short, get to the point as quickly and politely as possible. Getting involved in inane conversations with men can be misinterpreted as a sign of sexual interest. Questions such as 'do you have a boyfriend?' or 'you are looking very beautiful' are indicators that the conversation may be taking a steamy tangent. Some women prepare in advance by wearing a pseudo wedding ring, or by announcing early on that they are married or engaged (regardless of whether they are or not). For many, this has proved effective in keeping interactions 'lust-free'. If, despite your efforts, you still get the uncomfortable feeling that your space is being encroached upon, the chances are that it is. A firm request to keep away is usually enough to take control of the situation, especially if it's loud enough to draw attention from passers-by. Alternatively, the silent treatment can be a remarkably good way of getting rid of unwanted male company.

When interacting with men on a day-to-day basis, adhere to the local practice of not shaking hands. Instead, relay respect and avoid giving men the wrong 'signal' by saying 'namaste' – the traditional, respectful Hindu greeting, often accompanied by a small bow with the hands brought together at the chest or head level.

Female film-goers will probably feel more comfortable (and decrease the chances of potential harassment) by going to the cinema with a companion, as it's uncommon for women to see a movie alone.

Lastly, it's wise to arrive in towns before dark and, of course, always avoid walking alone at night, especially in isolated areas. Unlit back lanes in Goa should be avoided at night – several sexual assaults have been reported in recent years.

Taxis & Public Transport

Officials recommend that solo women pre-arrange an airport pick-up from their hotel if their flight is scheduled to arrive late at night. If that's not possible, catch a prepaid taxi, and make a point of (in front of the driver) writing down the car registration and driver's name and giving it to one of the airport police.

Whenever you catch a taxi, avoid doing so late at night (when many roads are deserted) and never agree to having more than one man (the driver) in the car. The driver will invariably try to convince you that it's 'just his brother' or 'for more protection' etc – but authorities warn against it, so it pays to heed their advice. Women are also advised against wearing expensive-looking jewellery, as it can make them a target.

On extended train and bus travel, being a woman has some glowing advantages. Women can queue-jump without consequence and on trains where there are special ladies-only carriages. Women have reported less hassle by opting for the more expensive classes on trains, especially for overnight trips. If you're travelling overnight in a three-tier carriage, try to get the uppermost berth, which will give you more privacy (and distance from potential gropers).

On public transport, don't hesitate to return any errant limbs and put some item of luggage in between you. If all else fails, find a new spot. You're also within your rights to tell such a nuisance to shove off – loudly enough to garner public attention, which should shame them into leaving you alone.

Transport

CONTENTS

Getting There & Away 487
Entering The Country 487
Air 487
Land 490
Sea 491
Getting Around 492
Air 492
Bicycle 493
Boat 494
Bus 494
Car 495
Hitching 495
Motorcycle 496
Local Transport 496
Tours 498
Train 498

GETTING THERE & AWAY

South India can be reached directly by air – into the major international airports located at Mumbai (Bombay) or Chennai (Madras) or on a charter flight to Goa – or overland from elsewhere in India. Delhi in North India is a major hub and domestic flights from there will take you to most cities in South India.

ENTERING THE COUNTRY

Everyone needs a valid passport and visa to enter India (p482). If you're flying into one of the major airports, entry formalities are straightforward, although security checks are understandably tight. You can also enter India overland at border crossings from Pakistan and Nepal.

Passport

To enter India you must have a valid passport, visa (see p482) and onward/return ticket. Once in India, if your passport is lost or stolen, immediately contact your country's representative, for details see p468. It's wise to keep photocopies of your passport and airline ticket.

THINGS CHANGE...

The information in this chapter is particularly vulnerable to change. Check directly with the airline or a travel agent to make sure you understand how a fare (and ticket you may buy) works and be aware of the security requirements for international travel. Shop carefully. The details given in this chapter should be regarded as pointers and are not a substitute for your own careful, up-to-date research.

AIR
Airports & Airlines

The main international airports in South India are Mumbai's **Chhatrapati Shivaji International Airport** (BOM; ☎ 022-28636767; www.mumbai airport.com), and Chennai's **Anna International Airport** (MAA; ☎ 044-22560551; www.chennaiairport.com). Another option is to fly direct into Delhi's **Indira Gandhi International Airport** (DEL; ☎ 011-25652011; www.delhiairport.com). See the boxed text, p491 for details of getting to South India from Delhi.

Direct charter flights from the UK and Europe land at Goa's Dabolim airport and, while you can get some cheap deals, you must also return via a charter flight. There are also some charter flights to Thiruvananthapuram (Trivandrum) in Kerala. There are a growing number of alternatives to the two main airports, mostly via the Arab Gulf States or Sri Lanka. Kochi and Kozhikode have connections to the Arab Gulf States, while Thiruvananthapuram also has flights to Sri Lanka and the Maldives.

The only direct international flights from Bangalore are to Muscat (Oman), Sharjah (United Arab Emirates), Bangkok (Thailand) and Singapore.

India's national carrier is **Air India** (www.air india.com), which also carries passengers on some domestic sectors of international routes (see p492). **Indian Airlines** (www.indian-airlines.nic.in), India's major domestic carrier, also flies to 20 neighbouring countries. The safety records of Air India and Indian Airlines can be viewed on www.airsafe.com/index.html. For details about India's domestic airlines see p492.

The following airlines fly to and from South India (see their websites for contact details).

Aeroflot (code SU; www.aeroflot.org) Hub: Sheremetyevo International Airport, Moscow

Air Canada (code AC; www.aircanda.com) Hub: Vancouver Airport

Air France (code AF; www.airfrance.com) Hub: Charles de Gaulle, Paris

Air India (code AI; www.airindia.com) Hub: Indira Gandhi International Airport, Delhi

Alitalia (code AZ; www.alitalia.com) Hub: Fiumicino International Airport, Rome

Biman Bangladesh Airlines (code BG; www.bangladesh online.com/biman/) Hub: Zia International Airport, Dhaka

British Airways (code BA; www.british-airways.com) Hub: Heathrow Airport, London

Cathay Pacific Airways (code CX; www.cathaypacific.com) Hub: Hong Kong International Airport

Emirates (code EK; www.emirates.com) Hub: Dubai International Airport

Gulf Air (code GF; www.gulfairco.com) Hub: Bahrain International Airport

Japan Airlines (code JL; www.jal.com.au) Hub: Narita Airport

KLM – Royal Dutch Airlines (code KL; www.klm.com) Hub: Schiphol Airport, Amsterdam

Kuwait Airways (code KU; www.kuwait-airways.com) Hub: Kuwait International Airport

Lufthansa Airlines (code LH; www.lufthansa.com) Hub: Frankfurt International Airport

Malaysian Airlines (code MH; www.malaysianairlines .com) Hub: Kuala Lumpur International Airport

Qantas Airways (code QF; www.qantas.com.au) Hub: Kingsford Smith Airport, Sydney

Royal Nepal Airlines Corporation (code RA; www.royal nepal.com) Hub: Kathmandu Airport

Singapore Airlines (code SQ; www.singaporeair.com) Hub: Changi Airport, Singapore

Sri Lankan Airlines (code UL; www.srilankan.aero) Hub: Bandaranaike International Airport, Colombo

Swiss International Airlines (code LX; www.swiss.com) Hub: Zurich International Airport

Tickets

As travellers aren't generally issued a tourist visa to India unless they have an onward/return ticket, few visitors buy international tickets in India itself. For those who do need a ticket, international schedules and fares are available from travel agents in India.

International fares to India fluctuate according to low, shoulder and high seasons. The fares we've given represent the average fares of various carriers servicing India.

DEPARTURE TAX

The departure tax of Rs 500 (or Rs 150 for Bangladesh, Bhutan, Nepal, Pakistan, Maldives and Sri Lanka) is included in the price of the airline ticket – check with your travel agent. Sometimes tickets bought in India don't include the 5% government tax or departure tax – in this case you have to pay at the airport, usually when you check in. Try and get a clear assurance that these are included in the ticket price when you buy it.

Individual carriers haven't been specifically mentioned as their routes and fares are subject to change over the life of this book. Contact a travel agent or surf the Net to get up-to-the-minute fares and schedules.

The departure tax of Rs 500 (Rs 150 for most South and Southeast Asian countries) is included in the price of 99% of all tickets to India.

Online ticket sales are handy for straightforward trips with few or no connecting flights. However, travel agencies are recommended for special deals, sorting out tricky connections, and organising insurance and Indian visas.

Africa

There are plenty of flights between East Africa and Mumbai due to the large Indian population in Kenya. Typical one-way fares from Nairobi to Mumbai US$400 and from Johannesburg US$500. **Rennies Travel** (www .renniestravel.com) and **STA Travel** (www.statravel.co.za) have offices throughout southern Africa. Check their websites for branch locations.

Asia

Offices for **STA Travel** (Bangkok ☎ 02-236 0262; www.statravel.co.th; Hong Kong ☎ 852-27361618; www .statravel.com.hk; Japan ☎ 0353-912 922; www.statravel .co.jp; Singapore ☎ 6737 7188; www.statravel.com.sg) are widely found throughout Asia. Another resource in Japan is **No 1 Travel** (☎ 0332-056 073; www.no1-travel.com); in Hong Kong try **Four Seas Tours** (☎ 22007760; www.fourseastravel.com/english).

BANGLADESH

Indian Airlines and Biman Bangladesh Airlines fly between Mumbai via Kolkata and Dhaka for US$250.

MALAYSIA
The return fare from Kuala Lumpur to Chennai costs from US$330.

MYANMAR
Indian Airlines flies from Yangon to Kolkata for US$180 one way.

NEPAL
Indian Airlines and Royal Nepal Airlines Corporation (RNAC) share routes between India and Kathmandu. There are flights from Kathmandu to Mumbai for around US$190. Druk Air (Royal Bhutan Airlines) also has flights.

SINGAPORE
Return fares from Singapore to Mumbai or Chennai are available for about US$530 with Air India; you'll pay more with Singapore Airlines or Thai Airways International.

SRI LANKA
There are flights between Colombo and Mumbai, Chennai, Tiruchirappalli and Thiruvananthapuram. The fare from Colombo to Chennai is around US$110.

THAILAND
Bangkok is the most popular departure point from Southeast Asia into India. Return flights are available from Bangkok to Mumbai for US$520.

It's possible to reach Port Blair in the Andaman Islands on a direct charter flight from Bangkok between January and April, but you must return on a prebooked charter flight. See p397 for details.

Australia

Both **STA Travel** (☎ 1300 733 035; www.statravel.com .au) and **Flight Centre** (☎ 133133; www.flightcentre .com.au) have offices throughout Australia. For online bookings, try www.travel.com .au. **Trailfinders** (www.trailfinders.com.au; Melbourne ☎ 03-9600 3022; Sydney ☎ 02-9247 7666) is an excellent discount ticket agency, with offices in Sydney, Melbourne, Perth, Brisbane and Cairns.

Qantas is the only airline with direct, nonstop flights, flying to Mumbai from Sydney or Melbourne for around A$1800. Malaysian Airlines, Singapore Airlines, Sri Lankan Airlines and Gulf Air all have return fares from A$1400 to Mumbai and

Chennai, with at least one Southeast Asian stopover. Sri Lankan Airlines is worth checking out for cheap fares, including from the east coast.

Canada

Fares from Canada are similar to those from the USA. **Travel Cuts** (☎ 800-667-2887; www.travel cuts.com) is Canada's national student travel agency. For online bookings try www.expe dia.ca and www.travelocity.ca.

From Canada most flights to India are via Europe, but there are options for travel via the USA or Asia. Low-season return fares from Vancouver to Mumbai start from around C$3000, flying with Air Canada, Northwest Airlines or KLM. Return fares from Montreal or Toronto to Mumbai in the low season start at C$1700 with Air France or Air Canada. From Chennai to Toronto, return fares cost around C$2200.

Continental Europe

FRANCE
Recommended travel agencies include **Anyway** (☎ 0892 893 892; www.anyway.fr); **Lastminute** (☎ 0892 705 000; www.lastminute.fr); **Nouvelles Frontières** (☎ 0825 000 747; www.nouvelles-frontieres .fr); **OTU Voyages** (www.otu.fr) and **Voyageurs du Monde** (☎ 01 40 15 11 15; www.vdm.com). Paris to Mumbai return costs around €650 with Air France or Lufthansa.

GERMANY
Some recommended travel agencies in Germany include **Just Travel** (☎ 089 747 3330; www .justtravel.de); **Lastminute** (☎ 01805 284 366; www.last minute.de) and **STA Travel** (☎ 01805 456 422; www.sta travel.de) for travellers under the age of 26. **Usit Campus** (Call Centre ☎ 01805 788336, Cologne ☎ 0221 923990; www.usitcampus.de) has several offices in Germany. A return flight from Frankfurt to Mumbai costs from €600.

THE NETHERLANDS
Recommended agencies include **Airfair** (☎ 0206-20 51 21; www.airfair.nl); **NBBS Reizen** (☎ 0206-20 50 71; www.nbbs.nl); and **Budget Air** (☎ 0206-27 12 51; www.nbbs.nl). Return fares from Amsterdam to Mumbai are around €600.

SPAIN
Recommended agencies include **Barcelo Viajes** (☎ 902 11 62 26; www.barceloviajes.com) and **Nouvelles Frontières** (☎ 902 17 09 79; www.nouvelles-frontieres.es).

New Zealand

Both **Flight Centre** (☎ 0800 243 544; www.flight centre.co.nz) and **STA Travel** (☎ 0508 782 872; www .statravel.co.nz) have branches throughout the country. The site www.travel.co.nz is recommended for online bookings.

There are no direct flights between India and New Zealand, so airlines offer stopovers in Asia. Low-season return fares to Mumbai or Chennai from Auckland start from NZ$1400 with Singapore Airlines, Malaysia Airlines and Air New Zealand via Kuala Lumpur.

UK

Discount air travel is big business in London. Advertisements for many travel agencies appear in the travel pages of weekend broadsheet newspapers, in *Time Out*, the *Evening Standard* and in the free magazine *TNT*.

From London to Mumbai or Chennai you can pick up return flights from £300 to £500. The number of airlines flying these routes are too numerous to mention, but Middle Eastern airlines, such as Emirates, Gulf Air, Qatar Airways, Kuwait Airways and Syrian Arab Airlines, are good value, and you can always pick up a cheap, if nerve-wracking, flight with Aeroflot (actually they've improved in recent years) or with the Central Asian airlines, like Turkmenistan Airways and Uzbekistan Airways.

Some companies offer cheap charter flights to Goa and Kerala, but by law you must also return on a charter flight, which doesn't make for a flexible trip.

Recommended travel agencies:

Bridge the World (☎ 0870 444 7474; www.b-t-w.co.uk)
Flightbookers (☎ 0870 010 7000; www.ebookers.com)
Flight Centre (☎ 0870 890 8099; flightcentre.co.uk)
North-South Travel (☎ 01245 608 291; www.north southtravel.co.uk) North-South Travel donates part of its profit to projects in the developing world.
Quest Travel (☎ 0870 442 3542; www.questtravel.com)
STA Travel (☎ 0870 160 0599; www.statravel.co.uk) For travellers under 26 years.
Trailfinders (www.trailfinders.co.uk)
Travel Bag (☎ 0870 890 1456; www.travelbag.co.uk)

USA

Discount travel agents in the USA are known as consolidators (although you won't see a sign on the door saying 'Consolidator'). San Francisco is the ticket consolidator capital of America, although some good deals can be found in Los Angeles, New York and other big cities.

Council Travel (www.ciee.org), America's largest student travel organisation, has around 60 offices in the USA. **STA Travel** (www.statravel .com) has offices in Boston, Chicago, Miami, New York, Philadelphia, San Francisco and other major cities.

From the east coast most flights to India are via Europe. Low-season return fares from New York to Mumbai or Chennai start from around US$1100.

From the west coast, say Los Angeles to Mumbai or Chennai, you can pick up return flights from US$1300 if you're willing to make a few stopovers.

For online bookings try:

CheapTickets www.cheaptickets.com
Expedia www.expedia.com
American Express Travel www.itn.net
Lowestfare.com www.lowestfare.com
Orbitz www.orbitz.com
STA Travel www.sta.com
Travelocity www.travelocity.com

LAND

It's possible, of course, to get to South India overland via the long haul through North India. The classic hippie route from Europe to Goa involves travelling via Turkey, Iran and Pakistan. Other overland options are via Bangladesh or Nepal. There are no open borders between Myanmar (Burma) and India or Bangladesh.

Via Pakistan, there's currently only one border crossing open – at Wagah (Attari on the Indian side) just east of Lahore – and although tensions between India and Pakistan are still high, the crossing presents no problem to travellers provided your paperwork is in order. There is a direct Lahore–Delhi bus on Tuesday, Wednesday, Friday and Saturday for Rs 1250, but it's just as easy and more fun to organise your own road and rail transport.

There are three main land entry points into Nepal: at Sunauli/Bhairawa (south of Pokhara); Raxaul Bazaar/Birganj (south of Kathmandu); and Kakarbhitta (near Siliguri in the far east). Travelling to or from Delhi, the route through Sunauli/Bhairawa via Varanasi is the most popular and convenient.

From Bangladesh, the direct bus service between Dhaka and Kolkata is the most convenient option.

GETTING TO SOUTH INDIA FROM DELHI

Delhi is the capital of India, and its major international and domestic transport hub. When flying from some parts of the world it may work out cheaper and more convenient to fly to Delhi and to head south from there. Because of the distances involved in getting to the southern states from Delhi, your best options are to fly or to take a train.

Air

The domestic terminals (Terminals IA and IB of the Indira Gandhi International Airport) are 15km from the city centre, and the international terminal (Terminal II) is a further 5km. There's a free Indian Airlines-Air India (IAAI) bus between the two terminals, or you can use the Ex-Service-men's Air Link Transport Service (EATS). There are 24-hour State Bank of India and Thomas Cook foreign-exchange counters in the arrivals hall, after customs and immigration. Once you've left the arrivals hall you won't be allowed back in.

All the domestic airlines have frequent flights from Delhi to the big South Indian cities, but Indian Airlines is the only option for smaller destinations. Budget carrier Air Deccan flies from Delhi to Chennai (Madras), Mumbai (Bombay), Bangalore and Hyderabad at discount fares. Whoever you fly with, the trick is to book a connecting domestic flight in advance (unless, of course, you want to spend some time in Delhi). Do it over the Internet well in advance – you may be lucky and only have a few hours layover or you might have to stay overnight. Of course, we'd take a prepaid taxi to the city, stay overnight and probably head down to Agra to see the Taj Mahal before continuing on to South India, but that's another story. You can buy tickets to South India from any of the many travel agencies, or you can buy them from the following airline offices:

Indian Airlines (☎ 3310517) F Block (☎ 141; Connaught Place, Delhi; ⏱ 24hr); Sardarjung airfield (Aurobindo Marg, Delhi)

Jet Airways (☎ 6853700; N40 Connaught Circus, Delhi)

Sahara Airlines (☎ 3326851; Ambadeep Bldg, Kasturba Gandhi Marg, Delhi)

Train

It's a long way by train from Delhi to the south in a single journey. Consider taking an air-con sleeper (either two-tier or three-tier). In Delhi, trains to South Indian destinations leave from New Delhi train station. Visit the **International Tourist Bureau** (☎ 23405156; 1st floor, New Delhi train station; ⏱ 8am-8pm Mon-Sat, 8am-2pm Sun), which is the place to go if you want a tourist-quota allocation, you're the holder of an Indrail Pass or want to buy an Indrail Pass. It gets very busy, and it can take up to an hour to get served. If you make bookings here, tickets must be paid for with rupees backed up by bank exchange certificates, or in US dollars and pounds sterling with any change given in rupees.

The **main ticket office** (⏱ 7.45am-9pm Mon-Sat, 7.45am-1.50pm Sun) is on Chelmsford Rd, between New Delhi train station and Connaught Place. It's well organised, but can get chaotic. Take a numbered ticket as you enter the building and then wait at the allotted window. It can take up to an hour to get served.

There are direct trains from Delhi to Mumbai (Rs 365/1025; 23 to 28 hours; seven daily); Chennai (Rs 477/1340; 34 to 37 hours; three daily); Bangalore (Rs 501/1408; 42 hours; two daily); Hyderabad (Rs 409/1149; 22 to 26 hours; three daily); and Bhubaneswar (Rs 341/958; 29 to 33 hours; four daily). All prices are given for sleeper and three-tier AC tickets. Fares are approximate since some trains take different routes. Contact **Indian Railways** (www.indianrail.gov.in) for full details.

SEA

There are currently no international passenger boat services to or from South India. For a number of years a ferry link between Sri Lanka and South India has been rumoured, proposed and rejected. Due to ongoing unrest in northern Sri Lanka and the inability of either government to come to an agreement, it doesn't look like such a service will start up any time soon. A proposed service between Tuticorin (Tamil Nadu) and Colombo was on the drawing board in 2003, but it was opposed by the Tamil Nadu state government. Another suggestion has been the longer Colombo–Kochi (Kerala) route, but that also failed to get off the ground. It's likely that a ferry service will start up eventually – for progress updates, inquire locally.

GETTING AROUND

AIR

South India is well covered by three main domestic airlines, plus the first of the no-frills budget airlines, Air Deccan. Flights aren't particularly cheap – Indian Airlines and Jet Airways charge foreigners in US dollars at a considerably higher fare than Indians. The busiest airports in the region are Mumbai, Chennai, Bangalore and Hyderabad, but dozens of smaller cities also have airports.

Airlines in South India

India's main domestic carriers, Indian Airlines and Jet Airways, cover extensive routes in South India. Jet Airways has proven to be India's best airline since it first hit the skies in 1993, with efficient staff, good inflight service and a near perfect safety record. Indian Airlines, and its subsidiary Alliance Air, used to be notorious for cancelled flights and the odd crash, but competition has certainly led to an improvement. Both airlines offer computerised booking, including Internet booking with electronic ticketing, and both have almost identical fares, charged to foreigners in US dollars.

Another well-established carrier is the Hyderabad-based Air Sahara, with flights from Hyderabad, Bhubaneshwar, Bangalore, Mumbai, Goa, Kolkata, Chennai, Pune and numerous other places. It has an excellent safety record, high standard of service and online booking. Fares are similar to the main carriers, although Air Sahara is moving towards cutting fares.

The new kid on the block is Bangalore-based Air Deccan, a 'no-frills', low-fare airline, flying out of Bangalore, Mumbai, Chennai, Goa, Madurai, Kolkata, Coimbatore, Hyderabad, Mangalore, and Delhi, among other places. Air Deccan doesn't have a dual-pricing policy – everyone pays in rupees – and if you get in early you can get some very cheap deals. For example, Mumbai–Chennai costs Rs 1800 (compared with US\$170, or around Rs 7500 with the major carriers), or Goa–Bangalore for Rs 1400. Although you can make phone reservations, Air Deccan is geared towards online booking and e-ticketing, so the easiest way to get information is on the Internet. Being a fledgling airline with a small fleet, there's likely to be teething problems – some travellers have complained that there are no allocated seats, so it's a bit like boarding an Indian bus – but it certainly deserves support.

From around mid-2005 there are expected to be at least three new low-cost domestic airlines in India, one of which is Kingfisher Airlines. The introduction of these new carriers is set to spark (long overdue) price wars in India's airline industry – hopefully the fares quoted in the regional chapters of this book will be lower by now. However, there's always the possibility of low-cost airlines going broke within months of operation. To stay abreast of the latest situation consult travel agents and browse the Internet.

A nifty booklet containing domestic air schedules and fares is *Excel's Timetable of Air Services Within India* (Rs 40; published monthly). It's available at city newsstands and bookshops. At the time of writing, the airlines listed here offered domestic services to various Indian destinations (see websites for these). These airlines have offices in major Indian cities – for contact details see the websites and the Getting There & Away sections of some regional chapters:

Air Deccan (www.airdeccan.net) Offers very competitive fares. It services a limited number of destinations, but these are expected to increase in coming years.

Air India (www.airindia.com) The national carrier also flies on a few domestic sectors of international routes. Note that most of these flights leave from international terminals (check in advance).

Indian Airlines (www.indian-airlines.nic.in) India's major domestic carrier, and its subsidiary Alliance Air, offer flights to 57 destinations within India and to 20 neighbouring countries. Its service gets mixed reports and its safety record is not as good as other domestic carriers.

Jagson Airlines (www.jagsonairline.com)

Jet Airways (www.jetairways.com) Rated by many as India's best airline, with efficient staff and a modern fleet.

Sahara Airlines (www.airsahara.net)

Air Passes

Air passes don't represent great value if you're only travelling around South India. The best one on offer is Jet Airways' Visit India fare, which costs US$320/630/895 for 7/15/21 days (50% less for children under 12). It allows unlimited travel within a specific region (North, South, East or West) with one restriction – you can't go to the same place twice unless you take a connecting flight. The South India region includes Bangalore, Calicut, Chennai, Cochin, Coimbatore, Hyderabad, Madurai, Mangalore and Trivandrum, but not Port Blair. The West region includes Aurangabad, Goa, Mumbai, Nagpur and Pune. If you're planning a whirlwind trip of three or four cities (or more), it could be good value, but splitting the country into regions makes the pass restrictive and you can probably find better deals with Air Deccan on the main routes.

Indian Airlines' Discover India pass costs US$400/630/895 for 7/15/21 days, while its India Wonder fare costs US$300 for one week's unlimited travel within any of four regions, two of which use Mumbai and Chennai as hubs. There are no discounts for Indian Airlines passes, and nor do they include Port Blair or Agatti on Lakshadweep.

Reservations

The main airlines have computerised booking. Phone numbers for offices are given in the regional chapters. Reconfirmation is not necessary for domestic airlines, but it pays to check. Some dishonest travel agents in India sell tickets without confirmed status, so you turn up at the airport and find you're waitlisted. Check if it reads 'OK' in the status column on the ticket, and there should be a confirmation code on the ticket.

Tickets can be paid for with rupees, foreign currency and in most cases with credit cards. A lost ticket is bad news – airlines may issue a replacement ticket at their discretion, but a refund is almost impossible.

Indian Airlines and Jet Airways offer a 25% discount to anyone aged between 12 and 30.

The easiest way to make a booking is online. You can look up seat availability, check fares and reserve a seat in minutes. You'll need an email address, and it helps to have a printer handy so you can print the reservation form that will serve as your ticket.

BICYCLE

South India offers plenty of variety for the cyclist. There are (relatively) smooth-surfaced highways, rocky dirt tracks, coastal routes through coconut groves, winding country roads through spice plantations and more demanding routes in the Western Ghats.

Nevertheless, long-distance cycling is not for the faint of heart or weak of knee. You'll need physical endurance to cope with the roads, traffic and the climate. The distance you cycle can be dictated by available accommodation as not all villages have a place to stay. If you're cycling in a hot climate, try to get your cycling done by noon as the sun may be too strong in the afternoon. Hotels also fill up in the afternoon and it's usually dark by 6pm, so these are additional reasons to get an early start.

There's no restriction in bringing a bicycle into India. Although most travellers prefer to hire or buy a bike in India, by all means consider bringing your own. Mountain bikes are especially suited to India's terrain. Inquire in your home country about air transport and customs formalities.

Try to read some books on bicycle touring, such as the Sierra Club's *The Bike Touring Manual* by Rob van de Plas (Bicycle Books, 1993). Cycling magazines provide useful information and their classifieds sections are good places to look for a riding companion. Also have a look at the **Cyclists Touring Club** (www.ctc.org.uk) and the **International Bicycle Fund** (www.ibike.org). Your local cycling club may also be a handy information source.

If you're a serious cyclist or amateur racer and wish to get in touch with counterparts while in India, there's the **Cycle Federation of India** (☎ /fax 011-23392578; Yamuna Velodrome, IGI Sports Complex, New Delhi; ☒ 10am-5pm Mon-Fri, 10am-2pm Sat).

Hire

Even in the smallest towns there is usually at least one outlet that rents bikes, but these are invariably old Indian rattlers that are only suitable for short distances. In Andhra Pradesh and Tamil Nadu, hourly rates for bicycle hire begin at Rs 2, and daily rates start from Rs 15 to 20. In touristy areas (such as Goa and parts of Kerala) expect to pay more – Rs 40 per day in Goa and Rs 30 per day in Hampi in Karnataka.

TRANSPORT

On the Road

Although road rules are virtually nonexistent, India has some truly stunning cycling possibilities from high-altitude passes to lush coastal routes.

For an eight-hour pedal an experienced cyclist averages 70km to 100km a day on undulating plains, or 50km to 70km in mountainous areas on sealed roads; cut this by at least one-third for unsealed roads. If you've never cycled long distances, start with 20km to 40km a day.

It's obviously more pleasurable to ride on quieter roads, but 'quiet' is relative. Any road that links two reasonable-sized towns will have trucks, cars, taxis, motorcycles and buses travelling at unsafe speeds and overtaking blindly with horns blaring. Might is right and as a cyclist you don't get much of a say. Stick to the edges and be prepared to get off the road! Avoid big cities where the chaotic traffic can be a hazard. Having said that, there are plenty of breezy backlanes, especially in rural Goa and Kerala. One thing you can be sure of is that you'll be the focus of attention wherever you go, especially in rural areas. Be warned that asking directions can send you on a wild goose chase – get as many opinions as possible!

Roads don't often have paved shoulders and are very dusty, so keep your chain lubricated and bring a spare.

Always make inquiries before venturing off road. Avoid leaving anything on your bike that can be easily removed when it's unattended. You may like to bring along a padlock and chain. However, don't be paranoid – your bike is probably safer in India than in many Western cities.

Purchase

There are many brands of Indian clunkers, including Hero, Atlas, BSA and Raleigh. Raleigh is considered the best, followed by BSA, which has an extensive line of models including some sporty jobs. Hero mountain-style bicycles are on sale in the larger towns, from simple five-speed versions to those with full suspension and 15 gears for around Rs 4000.

Reselling a bicycle is usually a breeze. Count on getting about 60% to 70% of what you paid if it was a new bike. A local rental shop will probably be interested, or simply ask around to find potential buyers.

BOAT

Apart from backwater trips through Kerala, river crossings in Goa and a few lake cruises, there's not much call for boat travel in South India. The exception is the passenger ferries from Chennai and Kolkata to the Andaman Islands (see p396), and the MV *Sultan,* which cruises around Lakshadweep (see p310).

BUS

The bus system in South India is comprehensive and can certainly fill in the gaps not served by trains. In most towns, at virtually any time of day, there will be a bus heading in the direction you want to go. One advantage to the bus is that they are usually very frequent. On popular city to city routes you'll find a bus leaving every half-hour (or even every few minutes), so you can simply turn up at the station and jump on the next available service. The downside is that buses tend to be crowded, slow and uncomfortable, especially if you need more legroom than the average Indian does.

Signs at bus stands and on the buses themselves are often in the local script, but bus conductors almost always speak some English, and if you just say your destination it shouldn't take long before someone points you in the right direction.

The most hair-raising aspects of bus travel are the poor quality of the roads and the speed at which the buses travel. For trips of more than a couple of hours it's better to take a train if possible. In the interior of Orissa, you don't have much choice apart from clapped-out buses and bone-jarring roads.

From cities such as Mumbai, Chennai, Bangalore and Trivandrum, there are agents and touts selling tickets for 'luxury' private buses that go to major long-haul destinations. These usually have reclining seats, videos blaring out Hindi music from Bollywood films (usually all night on overnight trips) and reserved seating.

Classes

In some states there is a choice of buses on major routes: ordinary, superfast (which really translates as superslow), express, superexpress, semiluxe, deluxe and deluxe air-con. The most common bus classes are described here.

ORDINARY
These generally have five seats across – three on one side of the aisle, two on the other – although if there are only five people sitting in them consider yourself lucky! Aisles are often crammed with baggage and in some more remote places there will be people travelling 'upper class' (ie on the roof). Ordinary buses tend to be frustratingly slow, are usually in an advanced state of decrepitude and make frequent stops.

EXPRESS
These are a big improvement on 'ordinary' buses in that they stop far less often. They're still crowded, but at least you feel like you're getting somewhere. The fare is usually a few rupees more than on an ordinary bus.

SEMILUXE, DELUXE & DELUXE AIR-CON
These also have five seats across, but the seats have more padding, as well as 'luxuries' like tinted windows, and the buses stop infrequently. The fare is about 20% more than the ordinary fare. The big difference between deluxe and semiluxe is that deluxe buses have only four seats across and these will usually recline.

Reservations
Major city bus stations and some private operators have computerised advance booking. It's rarely necessary to make a reservation for a bus, unless you desperately need to be on a particular long-distance deluxe service.

CAR
Hiring a Car & Driver
Long-distance car hire with a driver is an increasingly popular way to get around parts of India. It's not overly expensive and you have the flexibility to go where you want when you want. You can also get to off-the-beaten-track places a lot quicker than you could with bus connections.

Almost any local taxi will quite happily set off on a long-distance trip in India – inquiring at a taxi rank is the easiest way to find a car. You can also ask your hotel or any travel agent to book one for you. Although this will usually cost more, you have someone to contact should things go wrong. Most trips are officially based on a minimum of 250km per day (200km per day in Kerala) and cost from

about Rs 4.5 per km for a sturdy Hindustan Ambassador sedan up to Rs 8 for an air-con vehicle. But if you're hiring for at least several days, try to negotiate a daily rate (from Rs 800 per day), as this works out cheaper. Generally you pay half the money in advance to cover fuel costs, plus the driver's expenses (known as *batta* and usually amounting to around Rs 100 per day). You'll have to pay any road toll fees (levied on certain highways), and remember you will always have to pay the return fare whether or not you are making the return trip.

A few tips. If you're hiring for more than a day, try to get a driver who speaks at least some English (the more the better) and has knowledge of the region. Always agree on the terms beforehand so that the driver isn't dictating where and when you stop, or demanding extra money for his food and lodging that may have been covered in the initial fee. If you're happy with the service at the end of the trip, a tip (say Rs 50 a day) is the best way to show your appreciation.

Self-Drive Hire
Self-drive car rental in South India is possible but not common, and considering it's generally cheaper to hire a car *and* driver, it makes little sense to get behind the wheel on India's hair-raising roads. If you're still interested in self-drive, Budget, Euro Car, Hertz and several other companies maintain offices in the major cities and in Goa. Expect to pay Rs 800 to 1500 per day (with a two-day minimum). You officially need either a valid International Driving Permit or a valid driving licence from your home country.

Driving in India is legally (but often only theoretically) on the left side of the road, in right-hand drive vehicles.

HITCHING
Hitching is never entirely safe in any country in the world, and we don't recommend it. Travellers who decide to hitch should understand that they are taking a small but potentially serious risk.

Hitching is not much of an option in South India anyway, because the concept of a 'free ride' may not be understood. There are many more trucks on long-distance routes than private cars. You are then stuck with the old quandaries of: 'Do they understand what I am doing?', 'Will the driver expect to be paid?', 'Will they be unhappy if I don't offer to pay?', 'Will they be unhappy if I offer' or 'Will they simply want too much?'.

Women are strongly advised against hitching alone.

MOTORCYCLE

Motorcycle touring has long been popular with foreign visitors to India, and for many riders the classic Indian-made Enfield Bullet is the only way to go. Motorcycle riding is an exhilarating way to see the countryside, and offers the freedom to go when and where you like. If you plan to do a lot of touring, it pays to be an experienced rider. India is no place to learn how to ride a motorcycle – roads are often in poor condition, truck and bus drivers are certifiably nuts, and you'll inevitably have to negotiate the crowded, confusing streets of a city like Mumbai or Chennai.

Hazards range from goats crossing the road to abandoned trucks in the middle of the road. And, of course, there are the perpetual potholes and unmarked speed humps to contend with. Rural roads sometimes have various crops laid out on roads to be threshed by passing vehicles – it can be a real hazard for bikers. Avoid covering too much territory in one day. As so much energy is spent simply concentrating on the road, long days are exhausting and potentially dangerous. On busy national highways expect to average 50km/h without stops; on smaller roads, where driving conditions are worse, 10km/h is not an unrealistic average. On the whole, on good roads you can easily expect to cover a minimum of 100km a day (up to 300km with minimal stops).

You'll need a valid International Driving Permit to motorcycle in India.

Motorcycle tours are a superb (no hassles) way of seeing India. They usually operate with a minimum number of people and some can even be tailor-made. In South India try **Classic Bike Adventure** (☎ 0832-262076; fax 276124, 277343; Casa Tres Amigos, Socol Vado No 425, Assagao, Bardez, Goa), a German company offering motorcycle tours to various destinations lasting several weeks.

Hire

If you are planning an independent trip, bikes can be rented in South India. In Mumbai you can purchase a motorcycle on

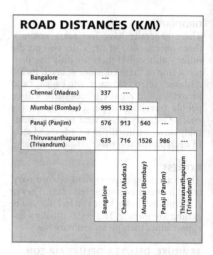

ROAD DISTANCES (KM)

	Bangalore	Chennai (Madras)	Mumbai (Bombay)	Panaji (Panjim)	Thiruvananthapuram (Trivandrum)
Bangalore	---				
Chennai (Madras)	337	---			
Mumbai (Bombay)	995	1332	---		
Panaji (Panjim)	576	913	540	---	
Thiruvananthapuram (Trivandrum)	635	716	1526	986	---

a guaranteed buy-back scheme (p120), starting from around Rs 20,000. Goa, however, is the place you're most likely to rent a bike. You can easily find bikes available for rent from a gearless Honda scooter at around Rs 700 per week to a 500cc Enfield for about Rs 2000 to 3000 a week. See the Goa chapter for more details (p167). You may be asked to leave a cash deposit or some form of ID.

Purchase

For serious long-distance touring, purchasing a second-hand machine is the way to go, and it's simply a matter of asking around. Check English-language newspapers and ask at mechanics. Real enthusiasts should check out the Enfield factory in Chennai (p323). Because of the number of bikes and the fact that locals are accustomed to foreigners, Goa is probably the best place in South India to start your search.

To buy a new bike, you officially have to have a local address and be a resident foreign national. When buying second-hand, all you need to do is give an address. Second-hand bikes (two to three years old) cost about US$1000 for a 500cc. Transferring ownership costs Rs 1000 to 1500.

When the time comes to sell the bike, try not to appear too anxious to get rid of it. If you get a reasonable offer, grab it.

LOCAL TRANSPORT

Although there are comprehensive (and cheap) local bus networks in most major towns and cities, unless you have time to familiarise yourself with the routes it's quicker and easier to use taxis, autorickshaws or cycle-rickshaws.

A basic ground rule applies to any form of transport where the fare isn't ticketed or fixed (unlike a bus or train), or calculated by a meter – agree on the fare beforehand. If you don't, you can expect arguments and hassles when you get to your destination. If you have baggage, make sure there are no extra charges, or you may be asked for more at the end of the trip. If a driver refuses to use the meter (almost always), or insists on an extortionate rate (guaranteed), bargain hard or simply walk away – if he really wants the job the price will drop. If you can't agree on a reasonable fare, go and find another driver. One of your abiding memories of India will be haggling with autorickshaw drivers, but as with any form of negotiation, remain calm and keep it friendly.

When catching taxis or rickshaws always make sure you have enough small change, as drivers rarely do. If you are staying or dining at a top-end venue and you need to catch a rickshaw, try walking a few hundred metres down the road to avoid the drivers who hang outside assuming you're a cash cow. It's also a good idea to carry around a business card of the hotel in which you are staying, as your pronunciation of streets, hotel names etc may be incomprehensible to drivers.

Fares are often steeper at night (as much as double the day fare) and some drivers charge a few rupees extra for luggage.

In some small country towns and hill stations, horse-drawn carriages, such as tongas (two-wheelers) and victorias (four-wheelers), still run. Small trucks are sometimes used on country routes – climb up into the back of the truck and hang on as best you can.

Autorickshaw

Few vehicles define urban India like the autorickshaw – the noisy, smoke-belching, three-wheel contraption powered by a two-stroke motorcycle engine with a driver up front and seats for two passengers behind. Also known as autos or scooters, they buzz around just about every Indian city or town, polluting the air and scanning the crowds for passengers. South Mumbai is an exception – autorickshaws are banned from the central city area.

They're generally about half the price of a taxi, rarely have working meters, and follow the same ground rules of bargaining and agreeing on fares as taxis. Getting a fair price from autorickshaw driver's is generally possible, getting the *local* price is not. Because of their size, autorickshaws are often faster than taxis for short trips and their drivers are decidedly nuttier – hair-raising near misses and glancing-blow collisions are not infrequent; thrillseekers will love it!

Drivers will very often wait if you are making a return journey (as opposed to a 'drop only'). Generally the 'waiting' fee will be about Rs 50 for one hour; Rs 10 to 15 for a quick stop. Drivers vary widely in their knowledge of their cities. If you are going to a fairly obscure destination, it helps to have it written down in the local dialect to show the driver.

Cycle-rickshaws

Cycle-rickshaws are becoming scarce in South India these days but you'll still find them in Chennai and Pondicherry. This is effectively a three-wheeler bicycle with a seat for two passengers behind the rider. Generally, prices are a lot lower than autorickshaws, they're obviously a lot slower and the drivers really work for their money!

Motorcycles

Goa is the only place in India where motorcycles are a licensed form of transport. They take one person on the back and are a quick, inexpensive way to cover short distances.

Taxi

There are taxis in most towns in India, and most of them (certainly in the major cities) are metered. Getting a metered fare, however, is rather a different situation, except in Mumbai where most drivers will happily use the meter. Even if you convince a driver to use the meter, it will almost certainly be out of date. Fares are adjusted upwards so much faster and more frequently than meters are recalibrated that drivers almost always have 'fare adjustment cards' indicating what you should pay compared with what the meter indicates. This is, of course, wide open to abuse. You have no idea if you're being shown the right card, or if the taxi's meter has actually been recalibrated and you're being shown the card anyway.

The only answer to all this is to try to get an idea of what the fare should be before departure (ask information desks at the airport or at your hotel). You'll soon begin to develop a feel for what the meter says, what the cards say and what the two together should indicate.

To/From the Airport

Official airport buses are becoming a thing of the past in India, so your best bet is a taxi or autorickshaw. It's possible at, say Mumbai or Chennai, to catch a local bus or train from a station near the airport, but when you're weighed down with baggage it's often more trouble than it's worth.

When arriving at an airport in South India, the first thing to do is find out if there's a prepaid taxi booth inside the arrival hall, such as those at Mumbai and Chennai. If there is, pay for a taxi there. If you don't do this and simply walk outside to negotiate your own price, you'll probably pay as much and also have to go through the hassle of negotiating. Autorickshaws are marginally cheaper, so are useful if there's only one or two of you.

TOURS

Within India there are tours operated either by the Government of India tourist office, the state tourist office or the local transport company – sometimes all three. There's also a plethora of private operators. Tours are generally good value, particularly in places where the sights are spread out. However, a drawback is that many cram too much into a short period.

Organised Tours

Many international companies offer tours to India that range from destination-specific packages to activity-based or other speciality options. To find tours that best fit your needs, quiz travel agents and surf the Net. Some interesting possibilities:

Essential India (www.essential-india.co.uk) Various tailor-made and special-interest tours, including those with a focus on crafts, photography, cooking, pottery and even writing.

Exodus (www.exodustravels.co.uk) A wide array of specialist options, including 'Yoga in the Himalayas', 'Spice Trails of Kerala' and 'Lost Kingdoms of Central India'.

India Profile (www.indiaprofile.com) Offers theme-based options, including Ayurvedic, meditation, yoga, fishing, golf, cooking and tribal tours.

Indian Encounters (www.indianencounters.com) Tailor-made and special-interest tours, including wildlife, painting, cooking, bird-watching and architecture-appreciation components, as well as horse-riding, walking and jeep safaris.

India Wildlife Tours (www.india-wildlife-tours.com) Apart from wildlife tours, possibilities include fishing, golf, river-rafting, architecture-appreciation, ethnic textiles, rejuvenation, nature and beach tours.

Intrepid Travellers (www.intrepidtravel.com) A range of choices that intertwines various special-interest aspects (eg culinary, mountain walks) with standard tours.

Peregrine Adventures (www.peregrine.net.au) Offers some interesting trekking and safari tours.

Sacred India Tours (www.sacredindia.com) Has a focus on sacred sites and events. Also offers yoga, meditation and Ayurvedic tours.

TRAIN

A trip to India wouldn't be the same without riding the rails. A train trip here is more than just a journey, it's a cultural experience,

---

TOP FIVE TRAIN JOURNEYS

If you love rail travel, don't miss these...

- Blue Mountain Railway – the miniature steam train from Mettupalayam to Ooty climbs up through the stunning Nilgiri Hills (p389)

- Konkan Railway – the trip from Mumbai to Goa on India's newest stretch of rail line passes between the scenic coast and the Western Ghats (p117)

- Matheran Toy Train – miniature diesel train running from Neral (north of Mumbai) to the hill station of Matheran (p146)

- Rajdhani Express from Trivandrum – from the Keralan capital to Goa, this 16-hour journey takes you up the coast in style (p266)

- Visakhapatnam-Araku Valley through Eastern Ghats – a superb 120km ride from the coast through the rugged Eastern Ghats to the tribal communities in Araku Valley (p425) a vast melting pot of sights and smells, chai-wallahs, impossibly crowded stations and scenic window-gazing. India has the world's biggest train network under single management, and with over 60,000km of track and 1.6 million staff, **Indian Railways** (www.indianrail .gov.in) is the world's biggest employer. At first the railways can seem as complicated as India itself, yet it's simple enough once you get used to it. While sometimes slower than buses, train journeys are more relaxing and even a little romantic. And for overnight journeys, trains are far preferable to buses. Life on board is quite communal. You not only share a compartment, but food, water and conversation.

There are tourist quotas for many express trains, and special offices or counters for foreigners in major cities and destinations (for these tickets you must bring an encashment certificate or ATM receipt to back up rupees). We've listed important trains throughout this guide but there are many, many more. The national timetable *Trains at a Glance* (Rs 25) has 200 pages of train schedules and gives train names, numbers and fare lists – it's available at bookshops in major train stations and is essential if you plan to do a lot of train travel. There are also regional guides (such as *Southern Railway* and *South Central Railway*), which cover every passenger train travelling obscure branch lines.

Classes

The most basic class on an express train is 2nd-class seat, which is also the only class available on local passenger trains. There are no reservations, so it can be a crowded free-for-all on hard bench seats. Next up is sleeper class, which is an open non-AC carriage. During the day seating is unreserved,

but after 9pm you must have a sleeping berth (the seats fold up to three tiers of bunks) and anyone without a reservation gets kicked out. This is a cheap option for overnight travel at Rs 91 for 200km, but it can be hot, noisy and no bedding is supplied. Other classes are three-tier AC (3A) and two-tier AC (2A) which, as the names suggest, have two and three tiers of bunks respectively in air-con carriages. Two-tier is roughly twice the price of three-tier. Overnight trips on these classes come with pillows, sheets and blankets. There's also a 1st-class AC class (1A), which few trains have these days, and chair class (CC), which is an air-con seating-only carriage on day trains.

Finally there are special trains, such as the *Shatabdi* express trains, which are fast same-day services between major and regional cities of between three and eight hours. These are the fastest and most expensive trains, with only two classes – AC executive chair and AC chair.

Rajdhani express trains are long-distance services, and offer 1st class (1A); two-tier AC (2A); three-tier AC (3A); and 2nd class (P for passenger is the designation on train timetables).

Costs

Fares are calculated by distance, so you can work out the fare for a given journey in any class using the distance and fare table in *Trains at a Glance*. As a guide, a 300km express train trip in 2nd class costs Rs 78; in sleeper class it's Rs 124, and in three-tier AC it's Rs 356 and in two-tier AC it's Rs 570. The trip from Mumbai to Goa (765km, 12 hours) costs Rs 253/711/1137 in sleeper/three-tier AC/two-tier AC. There's an extra charge of around Rs 25 for reservations.

EXPRESS TRAIN FARES IN RUPEES

Distance (km)	1AC	2AC	3AC	Chair car (CC)	Sleeper (SL)	Second (II)
100	542	322	158	122	56	35
200	794	430	256	199	91	57
300	1081	556	348	271	124	78
400	1347	693	433	337	154	97
500	1613	830	519	404	185	116
1000	2628	1352	845	657	301	188
1500	3328	1712	1070	832	381	238
2000	4028	2072	1295	1007	461	288

Tickets are refundable, but fees apply. When refunding your ticket you officially have a magic pass to go to the front of the queue, as the next person might require the spot you're surrendering. We've never seen if this actually works.

Left Luggage

Most stations will have left-luggage rooms, which cost a couple of rupees per day for one bag. They're useful if you want to visit but not stay in a town, or to hunt for accommodation unencumbered.

Reservations

Once upon a time, making a reservation at a station was a nightmare, with the potential to consume half a day. Things are a lot easier these days with computerised booking systems and even online booking. To make a reservation at a station you must fill out a form showing which class you need and the train's name and number (this is where *Trains at a Glance* comes in handy). For overnight journeys it's best to reserve your place a couple of days in advance, particularly if it's a holiday period. If there is no special foreign tourist quota counter at the station, you have to adopt local queuing practices. These range from reasonably orderly lines to mosh pits. There are sometimes separate Ladies' Queues, but usually the same window handles men and women each at a time. This means that women can go to the front of the queue, next to the first man at the window, and get served almost immediately. Also check if there is a credit-card counter (Mumbai and Chennai station have them) – not only can you pay by credit card, but there are rarely any queues.

If this all sounds too much, many travel agencies and hotels are in the business of purchasing train tickets for a small commission. But watch out for small-fry travel agents who promise express train tickets and deliver tickets for obscure mail or passenger trains. Only leave a small deposit, if any, and check the tickets before paying.

Reserved train tickets will show your berth and carriage number. A list of names and berths are posted on the end of each reserved carriage.

If you can't buy a reserved seat, you can ask if there is a waiting list, or try your luck by getting on with an open (unreserved) ticket, which you can buy at any counter one hour before departure. Unless it's a popular express train or a busy holiday, this usually works. Find a reserved-class carriage and a spare seat, and wait for the conductor (officially the Travelling Ticket Examiner or TTE) to find you. Explain you could only buy an unreserved ticket and ask (begging sometimes helps) about vacancies. There's almost always a spare berth somewhere and the conductor will be happy to oblige. You pay the difference between the ordinary fare and the fare of the class you're in.

Finally, you can reserve tickets up to 60 days in advance on the Internet using the **Indian Railways** (www.indianrail.gov.in) website. The site gives timetables, seat availability and fare information, and allows you to make reservations if you register with a user name and password. The downside is that tickets are couriered to your specified address, which can be a problem if you're on the move in India. Check if it's possible to collect tickets from the station.

Train Passes

Indrail passes permit unlimited travel for the period of their validity, but the consensus is that they aren't good value, and more importantly they don't get you to the front of the queue. To get full value out of them you'd need to travel about 300km every single day. However, some people find them useful for journeys soon after they arrive in South India. Most Western countries have travel agencies that arrange or sell Indrail passes, and they're sold at nine major train stations in South India, including the four main cities, Mumbai, Chennai, Bangalore and Hyderabad-Secunderabad and also at Vasco da Gama/Margao, Trivandrum, Aurangabad, Vijayawada and Puttaparthi.

The cost obviously varies depending on the class and period of validity. A seven-day pass in sleeper class costs US$80; the same pass in AC classes (2A, 3A and chair class) is US$135. Children between five and 12 years pay half-fare. There is no refund for lost or partially used tickets.

Health

CONTENTS

Before You Go   **501**
Insurance   501
Vaccinations   501
Internet Resources   503
Further Reading   503
In Transit   **503**
Deep Vein Thrombosis (DVT)   503
Jet Lag & Motion Sickness   503
In India   **504**
Availability of Healthcare   504
Infectious Diseases   504
Traveller's Diarrhoea   506
Environmental Hazards   506
Women's Health   508

While the potential dangers of travelling in India can seem quite ominous, in reality few travellers experience anything more than an upset stomach. Hygiene is generally poor throughout the country, so food- and water-borne illnesses are common. Travellers tend to worry about contracting infectious diseases, but infections are a rare cause of *serious* illness or death in travellers. Pre-existing medical conditions, such as heart disease, and accidental injury (especially traffic accidents) account for most life-threatening problems.

Fortunately most travellers' illnesses can either be prevented with some common-sense behaviour or be treated easily with a well-stocked traveller's medical kit. The following advice is a general guide only and does not replace the advice of a doctor trained in travel medicine.

BEFORE YOU GO

Pack medications in their original, clearly labelled containers. A signed and dated letter from your physician describing your medical conditions and medications, including generic names, is very useful. If carrying syringes or needles, be sure to have a physician's letter documenting their medical necessity. If you have a heart condition, bring a copy of your ECG taken just prior to travelling.

If you take any regular medication, bring double your needs in case of loss or theft. You'll be able to buy many medications over the counter in India without a doctor's prescription, but it can be difficult to find some of the newer drugs, particularly the latest antidepressant drugs, blood pressure medications and contraceptive pills.

INSURANCE

Even if you are fit and healthy, don't travel without health insurance – accidents do happen. Declare any existing medical conditions you have – the insurance company will check if your problem is pre-existing and will not cover you if it is undeclared. You may require extra cover for adventure activities such as rock climbing and scuba diving. If your health insurance doesn't cover you for medical expenses abroad, consider getting extra insurance. If you're uninsured, emergency evacuation is expensive; bills of over US$100,000 are not uncommon.

Find out in advance if your insurance plan will make payments directly to providers or reimburse you later for overseas health expenditures. (In many countries doctors expect payment in cash.) Some policies offer lower and higher medical-expense options; the higher ones are chiefly for countries that have extremely high medical costs, such as the USA. You may prefer a policy that pays doctors or hospitals directly rather than you having to pay on the spot and claim later. If you have to claim later, make sure you keep all documentation. Some policies ask you to call back (reverse charges) to a centre in your home country where an immediate assessment of your problem is made.

VACCINATIONS

Specialised travel-medicine clinics are your best source of information; they stock all available vaccines and will be able to give specific recommendations for you and your trip. The doctors will take into account factors such as past vaccination history, the length of your trip, activities you may be undertaking and underlying medical conditions, such as pregnancy.

Most vaccines don't give immunity until at least two weeks after they have been given, so visit a doctor four to eight weeks before departure. Ask your doctor for an International Certificate of Vaccination (otherwise known as the 'yellow booklet'), which will list all the vaccinations you've received.

Recommended Vaccinations

The World Health Organization (WHO) recommends the following vaccinations for travellers to India (as well as up to date measles, mumps and rubella vaccinations):

Adult diphtheria and tetanus Single booster recommended if none in the previous 10 years. Side effects include sore arm and fever.

Hepatitis A Provides almost 100% protection for up to a year; a booster after 12 months provides at least another 20 years' protection. Mild side effects, such as headache and sore arm, occur in 5% to 10% of people.

Hepatitis B Now considered routine for most travellers. Given as three shots over six months. A rapid schedule is also available, as is a combined vaccination with Hepatitis A. Side effects are mild and uncommon, usually headache and sore arm. In 95% of people lifetime protection results.

Polio In 2004 polio was still present in India. Only one booster is required as an adult for lifetime protection. Inactivated polio vaccine is safe during pregnancy.

Typhoid Recommended for all travellers to India, even if you only visit urban areas. The vaccine offers around 70% protection, lasts for two to three years and comes as a single shot. Tablets are also available; however, the injection is usually recommended as it has fewer side effects. Sore arm and fever may occur.

Varicella If you haven't had chickenpox, discuss this vaccination with your doctor.

The immunisations below are recommended for long-term travellers (more than one month) or those at special risk:

Japanese B Encephalitis Three injections in all. Booster recommended after two years. Sore arm and headache are the most common side effects. Rarely, an allergic reaction comprising hives and swelling can occur up to 10 days after any of the three doses.

Meningitis Single injection. There are two types of vaccination: the quadravalent vaccine gives two to three years' protection; meningitis group C vaccine gives around 10 years'

MEDICAL CHECKLIST

Recommended items for a personal medical kit:

- Antifungal cream, eg Clotrimazole
- Antibacterial cream, eg Muciprocin
- Antibiotics for skin infections, eg Amoxicillin/Clavulanate or Cephalexin
- Antihistamine – there are many options, eg Cetrizine for daytime and Promethazine for night
- Antiseptic, eg Betadine
- Antispasmodic for stomach cramps, eg Buscopam
- Contraceptive method
- Decongestant, eg Pseudoephedrine
- DEET-based insect repellent
- Diarrhoea medication – consider packing an oral rehydration solution (eg Gastrolyte), diarrhoea 'stopper' (eg Loperamide) and antinausea medication (eg Prochlorperazine). Antibiotics for diarrhoea include Norfloxacin or Ciprofloxacin; for bacterial diarrhoea Azithromycin; for Giardia or amoebic dysentery Tinidazole.

- First-aid items such as scissors, elastoplasts, bandages, gauze, thermometer (but not mercury), sterile needles and syringes, safety pins and tweezers
- Ibuprofen or another anti-inflammatory
- Indigestion medication, eg Quick Eze or Mylanta
- Iodine tablets (unless you are pregnant or have a thyroid problem) to purify water
- Laxative, eg Coloxyl
- Migraine medication if you suffer from them
- Paracetamol
- Pyrethrin to impregnate clothing and mosquito nets
- Steroid cream for allergic/itchy rashes, eg 1% to 2% hydrocortisone
- Sunscreen and hat
- Throat lozenges
- Thrush (vaginal yeast infection) treatment, eg Clotrimazole pessaries or Diflucan tablet
- Ural or equivalent treatment if prone to urine infections

HEALTH

protection. Recommended for long-term backpackers aged under 25.

Rabies Three injections in all. A booster after one year will then provide 10 years' protection. Side effects are rare – occasionally headache and sore arm.

Tuberculosis (TB) A complex issue. Adult long-term travellers are usually recommended to have a TB skin test before and after travel, rather than vaccination. Only one vaccine given in a lifetime.

Required Vaccinations

The only vaccine required by international regulations is yellow fever. Proof of vaccination will only be required if you have visited a country in the yellow fever zone within the six days prior to entering India. If you are travelling to India from Africa or South America, you should check to see if you require proof of vaccination.

INTERNET RESOURCES

There is a wealth of travel health advice on the Internet. **LonelyPlanet.com** (www.lonelyplanet .com) is a good place to start. Some other suggestions:

Centers for Disease Control and Prevention (CDC; www.cdc.gov) Good general information.

MD Travel Health (www.mdtravelhealth.com) Provides complete travel health recommendations for every country, updated daily.

World Health Organization (WHO; www.who.int/ith/) Its superb book *International Travel & Health* is revised annually and available online.

FURTHER READING

Lonely Planet's *Healthy Travel – Asia & India* is a handy pocket size and packed with useful information, including pretrip planning, emergency first aid, immunisation and disease information, and what to do if you get sick on the road. Other recommended references include *Traveller's Health* by Dr Richard Dawood and *Travelling Well* by Dr Deborah Mills – check out the website of **Travelling Well** (www.travellingwell.com.au).

IN TRANSIT

DEEP VEIN THROMBOSIS (DVT)

Deep vein thrombosis (DVT) occurs when blood clots form in the legs during flights, chiefly because of prolonged immobility. The longer the flight, the greater the risk. Though most clots are reabsorbed unevent-

---

fully, some may break off and travel through the blood vessels to the lungs, where they may cause life-threatening complications.

The chief symptom of DVT is swelling or pain of the foot, ankle, or calf, usually but not always on just one side. When a blood clot travels to the lungs, it may cause chest pain and difficulty in breathing. Travellers with any of these symptoms should immediately seek medical attention.

To prevent the development of DVT on long flights you should walk about the cabin, perform isometric compressions of the leg muscles (ie contract the leg muscles while sitting), drink plenty of fluids, and avoid alcohol and tobacco.

JET LAG & MOTION SICKNESS

Jet lag is common when crossing more than five time zones; it results in insomnia, fatigue, malaise or nausea. To avoid jet lag drink plenty of nonalcoholic fluids and eat light meals. Upon arrival, seek exposure to natural sunlight and readjust your schedule (for meals, sleep etc) as soon as possible.

Antihistamines, such as dimenhydrinate (Dramamine), promethazine (Phenergan) and meclizine (Antivert, Bonine), are usually the first choice for treating motion sickness. Their main side effect is drowsiness. An herbal alternative is ginger, which works like a charm for some people.

IN INDIA

AVAILABILITY OF HEALTHCARE

Medical care is hugely variable in India. Some cities now have clinics catering specifically to travellers and expats. These clinics are usually more expensive than local medical facilities, but are worth utilising, as they will offer a superior standard of care. Additionally, they understand the local system, and are aware of the safest local hospitals and best specialists. They can also liaise with insurance companies should you require evacuation. Recommended clinics are listed under Information in individual chapters in this book. It is difficult to find reliable medical care in rural areas.

Self-treatment may be appropriate if your problem is minor (eg traveller's diarrhoea), you are carrying the relevant medication and you cannot attend a recommended clinic. If you think you may have a serious disease, especially malaria, do not waste time; travel to the nearest quality facility to receive attention. It is always better to be assessed by a doctor than to rely on self-treatment.

Before buying medication over the counter, always check the use-by date and ensure the packet is sealed. Don't accept items that have been poorly stored (eg lying in a glass cabinet exposed to the sun).

INFECTIOUS DISEASES
Coughs, Colds & Chest Infections
Around 25% of travellers to India will develop a respiratory infection. This usually starts as a virus and is exacerbated by environmental conditions, such as pollution in the cities, or cold and altitude in the mountains. Commonly a secondary bacterial infection will intervene which is marked by fever, chest pain and coughing up discoloured or blood-tinged sputum. If you have the symptoms of an infection, seek medical advice or commence a general antibiotic.

Dengue Fever
This mosquito-borne disease is becomingly increasingly problematic in the tropical world, especially in the cities. As there is no vaccine available it can only be prevented by avoiding mosquito bites. The mosquitoes that carry dengue bites day and night, so use insect avoidance measures at all times. Symptoms of dengue fever include high fever, severe headache and body ache (dengue was previously known as 'breakbone fever'). Some people develop a rash and experience diarrhoea. There is no specific treatment, just rest and paracetamol. Do not take aspirin as it increases the likelihood of haemorrhaging. See a doctor to be diagnosed and monitored.

Hepatitis A
A problem throughout the region, this food- and water-borne virus infects the liver, causing jaundice (yellow skin and eyes), nausea and also lethargy. There is no specific treatment for hepatitis A, you just need to allow time for the liver to heal. All travellers to India should be vaccinated against hepatitis A.

Hepatitis B
The only sexually transmitted disease that can be prevented by vaccination, hepatitis B is spread by body fluids. The long-term effects can include liver cancer and cirrhosis.

Hepatitis E
Hepatitis E is transmitted through contaminated food and water, and has similar symptoms to hepatitis A but is far less common. It is a severe problem in pregnant women, and can result in the death of both mother and baby. There is currently no vaccine, and prevention is by following safe eating and drinking guidelines.

HIV
HIV is spread via contaminated body fluids. Make sure to avoid unsafe sex, unsterile needles (including in medical facilities) and procedures, such as tattoos. The growth rate of HIV in India is one of the highest in the world.

Influenza
Present year-round in the tropics, influenza (flu) symptoms include high fever, aches, runny nose, cough and sore throat. It can be severe in people over the age of 65 or in those with underlying medical conditions, such as heart disease or diabetes – vaccination is recommended. There is no specific treatment, just rest and paracetamol.

Japanese B Encephalitis
This viral disease is transmitted by mosquitoes and is rare in travellers. Like most mosquito-borne diseases, it is becoming a more common problem in affected countries. Most cases occur in rural areas, and vaccination is recommended for travellers spending more than one month outside of cities. There is no treatment, and a third of infected people will die, while another third will suffer permanent brain damage.

Malaria

For such a serious and potentially deadly disease, there is an enormous amount of misinformation concerning malaria. You must get expert advice as to whether your trip actually puts you at risk. For most rural areas, the risk of contracting malaria far outweighs the risk of any tablet side effects. Before you travel, seek medical advice on the right medication and dosage for you.

Malaria is caused by a parasite transmitted by the bite of an infected mosquito. The most important symptom of malaria is fever, but general symptoms, such as headache, diarrhoea, cough or chills, may also occur. Diagnosis can only be made by taking a blood sample.

Two strategies should be combined to prevent malaria – mosquito avoidance and antimalaria medications. Most people who catch malaria are taking inadequate or no antimalarial medication.

Travellers are advised to prevent mosquito bites by taking these steps:

- Use a DEET-containing insect repellent on exposed skin. Wash this off at night, as long as you are sleeping under a mosquito net. Natural repellents, such as citronella, can be effective, but must be applied more frequently than products containing DEET.
- Sleep under a mosquito net impregnated with permethrin
- Choose accommodation with screens and fans (if not air-conditioned)
- Impregnate clothing with permethrin in high-risk areas
- Wear long sleeves and trousers in light colours
- Use mosquito coils
- Spray your room with insect repellent before going out for your evening meal

There is a wide variety of medication available.

The effectiveness of the **Chloroquine and Paludrine** combination is now limited in many parts of South Asia. Common side effects include nausea (40% of people) and mouth ulcers.

The daily tablet **Doxycycline** is a broad-spectrum antibiotic that has the added benefit of helping to prevent a variety of tropical diseases, including leptospirosis, tick-borne disease and typhus. The potential side ef-

fects include photosensitivity (a tendency to sunburn), thrush (in women), indigestion, heartburn, nausea and interference with the contraceptive pill. More serious side effects include ulceration of the oesophagus – you can help prevent this by taking your tablet with a meal and a large glass of water, and never lying down within half an hour of taking it. It must be taken for four weeks after leaving the risk area.

Lariam (Mefloquine) has received much bad press, some of it justified, some not. This weekly tablet suits many people. Serious side effects are rare but include depression, anxiety, psychosis and having fits. Anyone with a history of depression, anxiety, other psychological disorder or epilepsy should not take Lariam. It is considered safe in the second and third trimesters of pregnancy. Tablets must be taken for four weeks after leaving the risk area.

The new drug **Malarone** is a combination of Atovaquone and Proguanil. Side effects are uncommon and mild, most commonly nausea and headache. It is the best tablet for scuba divers and for those on short trips to high-risk areas. It must be taken for one week after leaving the risk area.

Rabies

Around 30,000 people die in India each year from rabies. This uniformly fatal disease is spread by the bite or lick of an infected animal – most commonly a dog or monkey. You should seek medical advice immediately after any animal bite and commence postexposure treatment. Having a pretravel vaccination means the postbite treatment is greatly simplified. If an animal bites you, gently wash the wound with soap and water, and apply iodine-based antiseptic. If you are not prevaccinated, you will need to receive rabies immunoglobulin as soon as possible, and this is almost impossible to obtain in much of India.

STDs

Common sexually transmitted diseases in India include herpes, warts, syphilis, gonorrhoea and chlamydia. People carrying these diseases often have no signs of infection. Condoms will prevent gonorrhoea and chlamydia but not warts or herpes. If after a sexual encounter you develop a rash, lumps, discharge or pain when passing urine, seek immediate medical attention. If you have been sexually active during your travels, have an STD check on your return home.

Tuberculosis

While TB is rare in travellers, those who have significant contact with the local population (such as medical and aid workers and long-term travellers) should take precautions. Vaccination is usually only given to children under the age of five, but adults at risk are recommended pre- and post-travel TB testing. The main symptoms are fever, cough, weight loss, night sweats and tiredness.

Typhoid

This serious bacterial infection is also spread via food and water. It gives a high and slowly progressive fever, headache, and may be accompanied by a dry cough and stomach pain. It is diagnosed by blood tests and treated with antibiotics. Vaccination is recommended for all travellers spending more than a week in India. Be aware that vaccination is not 100% effective, so you must still be careful with what you eat and drink.

TRAVELLER'S DIARRHOEA

Traveller's diarrhoea is by far the most common problem affecting travellers – between 30% and 70% of people will suffer from it within two weeks of starting their trip. In over 80% of cases, traveller's diarrhoea is caused by a bacteria (there are numerous potential culprits), and therefore responds promptly to treatment with antibiotics. Treatment with antibiotics will depend on your situation – how sick you are, how quickly you need to get better, where you are etc.

Traveller's diarrhoea is defined as the passage of more than three watery bowel actions within 24 hours, plus at least one other symptom, such as fever, cramps, nausea, vomiting or feeling generally unwell.

Treatment consists of staying well hydrated; rehydration solutions like Gastrolyte are the best for this. Antibiotics, such as Norfloxacin, Ciprofloxacin or Azithromycin, will kill the bacteria quickly. Loperamide is just a 'stopper' and doesn't get to the cause of the problem, though it can be helpful (eg if you have to go on a long bus ride). Don't take Loperamide if you have a fever, or blood in your stools. Seek medical attention quickly if you do not respond to an appropriate antibiotic.

Amoebic Dysentery

Amoebic dysentery is very rare in travellers, but is often misdiagnosed by poor-quality labs. Symptoms are similar to bacterial diarrhoea, ie fever, bloody diarrhoea and generally feeling unwell. You should always seek reliable medical care if you have blood in your diarrhoea. Treatment involves two drugs: Tinidazole or Metronidazole to kill the parasite in your gut and then a second drug to kill the cysts. If left untreated, complications such as liver or gut abscesses can occur.

Giardiasis

Giardia is a parasite that is quite common in travellers. Symptoms include nausea, bloating, excess gas, fatigue and intermittent diarrhoea. The parasite will go away if left untreated, but this can take months. The treatment of choice is Tinidazole, with Metronidazole being a second-line option.

ENVIRONMENTAL HAZARDS
Air Pollution

Air pollution, particularly vehicle pollution, is an increasing problem in most of India's major cities. If you have severe respiratory problems, speak with your doctor before travelling to any heavily polluted urban centres. This pollution also causes minor respiratory problems, such as sinusitis, dry throat and irritated eyes. If troubled by the pollution, leave the city for a few days and get some fresh air.

Diving & Surfing

Divers and surfers should seek specialised advice before they travel to ensure their medical kit contains treatment for coral and reef cuts and tropical ear infections, as well as the standard problems. Divers should ensure their insurance covers them for decompression illness – get specialised dive insurance through an organisation, such as **Divers Alert Network** (DAN; www.danseap.org). Have a dive medical before you leave your home country – there are certain medical conditions that are incompatible with diving.

Food

Eating in restaurants is the biggest risk for contracting travellers' diarrhoea. Ways to avoid it include eating only freshly cooked food, and avoiding shellfish and food that has been sitting in buffets. Peel all fruit, cook vegetables and soak salads in iodine water for at least 20 minutes. Eat in busy restaurants with a high turnover of customers.

Heat

South India can be hot and humid through the year. It can take at least two weeks to adapt to the hot climate. Swelling of the feet and ankles is common, as are cramps caused by excessive sweating. Prevent these by avoiding dehydration and excessive activity in the heat. Take it easy when you first arrive. Don't eat salt tablets (they aggravate the gut); rehydration solution or salty food helps. Treat cramps by stopping activity, resting, rehydrating with double-strength rehydration solution and gently stretching.

Dehydration is a contributor to heat exhaustion. Symptoms include feeling weak, headache, irritability, nausea or vomiting, sweaty skin, a fast, weak pulse, and a normal or slightly elevated body temperature. Treatment involves getting out of the heat and/or sun, fanning the sufferer and applying cool wet cloths to the skin, laying the sufferer flat with their legs raised and rehydrating with water containing ¼ teaspoon of salt per litre. Recovery is rapid and it is common to feel weak for some days afterwards.

Heat stroke is a serious medical emergency. Symptoms come on suddenly and include weakness, nausea, a hot dry body with a body temperature of over 41°C, dizziness, confusion, loss of coordination, fits, and eventually collapse and loss of consciousness. Seek medical help and commence cooling by getting the person out of the heat, removing their clothes, fanning them, and applying cool wet cloths or ice to their body, especially to the groin and armpits.

Prickly heat is a common skin rash in the tropics, caused by sweat being trapped under the skin. The result is an itchy rash of tiny lumps. Treat it by moving out of the heat and into an air-conditioned area for a few hours and by having cool showers. Creams and ointments clog the skin so they should be avoided. Locally bought prickly-heat powder can be helpful.

DRINKING WATER

- Never drink tap water
- Bottled water is generally safe – check the seal is intact at purchase
- Avoid ice
- Avoid fresh juices – they may have been watered down
- Boiling water is the most efficient method of purifying it
- The best chemical purifier is iodine. It should not be used by pregnant women or those with thyroid problems.
- Water filters should also filter out viruses. Ensure your filter has a chemical barrier, such as iodine, and a small pore size, eg less than four microns.

Tropical fatigue is common for long-term expats based in the tropics. It's rarely due to disease, and is caused by the climate, inadequate mental rest, excessive alcohol intake and the demands of daily work in a different culture.

Insect Bites & Stings

Bedbugs don't carry disease but their bites are itchy. They live in the cracks of furniture and walls, and then migrate to the bed at night to feed on you. You can treat the itch with an antihistamine. Lice inhabit various parts of your body but most commonly your head and pubic area. Transmission is via close contact with an infected person. They can be difficult to treat and you may need numerous applications of an antilice shampoo, such as permethrin. Pubic lice are usually contracted from sexual contact.

Ticks are contracted in rural areas. Ticks are commonly found behind the ears, on the belly and in armpits. If you have had a tick bite and experience symptoms, such as a rash at the site of the bite or elsewhere, fever or muscle aches, you should see a doctor. Doxycycline prevents tick-borne diseases.

Leeches are found in humid rainforest areas. They do not transmit any disease, but their bites are often intensely itchy for weeks afterwards and can easily become infected. Apply an iodine-based antiseptic to any leech bite to help prevent infection.

Bee and wasp stings mainly cause problems for people who are allergic to them. Anyone with a serious bee or wasp allergy should carry an injection of adrenaline (eg an Epipen) for emergency treatment. For others pain is the main problem – apply ice to the sting and take painkillers.

Skin Problems

Fungal rashes are common in humid climates. There are two common fungal rashes. The first occurs in moist areas that get less air, such as the groin, armpits and between the toes. It starts as a red patch that slowly spreads and is itchy. Treatment involves keeping the skin dry, avoiding chafing and using an antifungal cream, such as Clotrimazole or Lamisil. *Tinea versicolor* is quite common – this fungus causes small, light-coloured patches, most commonly on the back, chest and shoulders. Consult a doctor.

Cuts and scratches become easily infected in humid climates. Take meticulous care of any cuts and scratches to prevent complications, such as abscesses. Immediately wash all wounds in clean water and apply antiseptic. If you develop signs of infection (increasing pain and redness), see a doctor. Divers and surfers should be particularly careful with coral cuts, as they easily become infected.

Sunburn

Even on a cloudy day sunburn can occur rapidly. Always use a strong sunscreen (at least factor 30), making sure to reapply after a swim, and always wear a wide-brimmed hat and sunglasses outdoors. Avoid lying in the sun during the hottest part of the day (10am to 2pm). If you become sunburnt, stay out of the sun until you have recovered, apply cool compresses and take painkillers for the discomfort. One percent

hydrocortisone cream applied twice daily is also helpful.

WOMEN'S HEALTH

Pregnant women should ensure they receive specialised advice before travelling. The ideal time to travel is in the second trimester (between 16 and 28 weeks), when the risk of pregnancy-related problems is at its lowest and pregnant women generally feel at their best. Always carry a list of quality medical facilities available at your destination and ensure you continue your standard antenatal care at these facilities. Avoid travel in some rural areas with poor transportation and medical facilities. Most of all, ensure travel insurance covers all pregnancy-related possibilities, including premature labour.

Malaria is a high-risk disease in pregnancy. WHO recommends that pregnant women do *not* travel to areas with Chloroquine-resistant malaria. None of the more effective antimalaria drugs are completely safe in pregnancy.

Traveller's diarrhoea can quickly lead to dehydration and result in inadequate blood flow to the placenta. Many of the drugs used to treat various diarrhoea bugs are not recommended in pregnancy. Azithromycin is considered safe.

In most places, supplies of sanitary products (pads, rarely tampons) are readily available. Birth control options may be limited, so bring adequate supplies of your own form of contraception. Heat, humidity and antibiotics can all contribute to thrush. Treatment is with antifungal creams and pessaries, such as Clotrimazole. A practical alternative is a single tablet of Fluconazole (Diflucan). Urinary tract infections can be precipitated by dehydration or long bus journeys without toilet stops; bring suitable antibiotics.

Language

CONTENTS

Tamil	509
Kannada	511
Konkani	512
Malayalam	512
Marathi	513
Telugu	514

There is no one 'Indian' language as such. The constitution recognises 18 official languages, including English. The non-English varieties fall roughly into two main groups: Indic (or Indo-Aryan) and Dravidian. There were also over 1600 minor languages and dialects.

The native languages of the regions covered in this book are Tamil, Kannada, Konkani, Malayalam, Marathi, Oriya, and Telugu. They mostly belong to the Dravidian language family, although these have been influenced to varying degrees during their development by Hindi and Sanskrit. As the predominant languages in specific geographic areas they have in effect been used to determine the regional boundaries for the southern states.

Major efforts have been made to promote Hindi as the 'official' language of India, and to gradually phase out English. While Hindi is the predominant language of the north, it bears little relation to the Dravidian languages of the south; subsequently very few people in the south speak Hindi. Resistance to change has been strongest in the state of Tamil Nadu, and as a result, Tamil is still very much the predominant language of South India. English is also widely spoken.

TAMIL

Tamil is the official language in the South Indian state of Tamil Nadu and the Union Territory of Pondicherry.

Tamil is classed as a South Dravidian language, and is one of the major Dravidian languages of South India. The exact origins of the Dravidian family are unknown, but it is believed to have arrived in India's north west around 4000 BC, gradually splitting into four branches with the passage of time. Tamil became isolated to India's south as the Indo-Aryan language varieties such as Hindi became more dominant in the north.

Along with Sanskrit, Tamil is recognised as one of the two classical languages of India. It has a very rich historical tradition dating back more than 2000 years. Since then three forms have been distinguished: Old Tamil (200 BC to AD 700), Middle Tamil (AD 700 to AD 1600) and Modern Tamil (AD 1600 to the present).

Modern Tamil is diglossic in nature, meaning that it has two distinct forms: literary or classical (used mainly in writing and formal speech), and spoken (used in everyday conversation). The spoken form has a wide range of dialects, varying in social, cultural and regional dimensions. Irrespective of the differences, a common variety called Standard Spoken Tamil is widely used in mass media and by all Tamils in their day-to-day life.

Tamil has its own alphabetic script, which isn't used in this language guide. Our transliteration system is intended as a simplified method of representing the sounds of Tamil using the Roman alphabet. As with all such systems it's not exact and should be seen only as an approximate guide to the pronunciation of the language.

PRONUNCIATION
Vowels
a	as the 'u' in 'run'
aa	as in 'rather'
e	as in 'met'
i	as in 'bit'
ee	as in 'meet'
o	as in 'hot'
oo	as in 'boot'
u	as in 'put'

Vowel Combinations
ai	as in 'aisle'
au	as the 'ow' in 'how'

Consonants

g	as in 'go'
k	as in 'kit'
ñ	as the 'ni' in the word 'onion'; as in the Spanish *señor*
s	as in 'sit'
zh	as the 's' in 'pleasure'

Retroflex Consonants

Some consonants in Tamil and the other languages of India are a little more complicated because they represent sounds not found in English. The most common variants are called 'retroflex' consonants, where the tongue is curled upwards and backwards so that the underside of the tip makes contact with the alveolar ridge (the ridge of tissue on the roof of the mouth a little behind the teeth). Retroflex consonants are represented in this guide by a dot below the letter (in Tamil, these are ḷ, ṇ and ṭ). If the lingual gymnastics prove too much you'll find that you can still make yourself understood by ignoring the dot and pronouncing the letter as you would in English.

ACCOMMODATION

hotel	hotal/vituti
guesthouse	viruntinar vituti
youth hostel	ilaiñar vituti
camping ground	tangumitam

Do you have any rooms available?	araikal kitaikkumaa?
for one/two people	oruvar/iruvarukku
for one/two nights	oru/irantu iravukal
How much is it per night/per person?	oru iravukku/oru nabarukku evallavu?
Is breakfast included?	kaalai sirruṇṭiyuṭan serttaa?

CONVERSATION & ESSENTIALS

Hello.	vaṇakkam
Goodbye.	poyiṭṭu varukiren
Yes/No.	aam/illai
Please.	tayavu ceytu
Thank you.	nanri
That's fine, you're welcome.	nallatu varuka
Excuse me.	mannikkavum
Sorry/Pardon.	mannikkavum
Do you speak English?	neenkal aankilam pesuveerkalaa?
How much is it?	atu evvalavu?
What's your name?	unkal peyar enna?
My name is ...	en peyar ...

NUMBERS

0	boojyam
1	onru
2	irantu
3	moonru
4	naanku
5	aintu
6	aaru
7	ezhu
8	ettu
9	onpatu
10	pattu
100	nooru
1000	aayiram
2000	irantaayiram
100,000	latsam (written 1,00,000)
1,000,000	pattu latsam (written 10,00,000)
10,000,000	koti (written 1,00,00,000)

SHOPPING & SERVICES

bank	vangi
chemist/pharmacy	aruntukkataikkaarar/ maruntakam
... embassy	... tootarakam
market	maarkkeṭ
medicine	maruntu
newsagent	niyoos ejensi
post office	tabaal nilayam
public telephone	potu tolaipesi
stationers	elutuporul vanikar
tourist office	surrulaa seyti totarpu aluvalakam
What time does it open/close?	tirakkum/mootum neram enna?
big	periya
small	siriya

TIMES & DAYS

What time is it?	mani ettanai?
day	pakal
night	iravu
week	vaaram
month	maatam
year	varutam
today	inru
tomorrow	naalai

yesterday	nerru
morning	kaalai
afternoon	matiyam
Monday	tinkal
Tuesday	sevvaay
Wednesday	putan
Thursday	viyaazhan
Friday	velli
Saturday	sani
Sunday	ñaayiru

TRANSPORT

Where is a/the ...?	... enke irukkiratu?
Go straight ahead.	neraaka sellavum
Turn left/right.	valatu/itatu pakkam tirumbavum
near	arukil
far	tooram
What time does the	eppozhutu atutta ...
next ... leave/arrive?	sellum/varum?
boat	paṭaku
bus (city)	peruntu (nakaram/ulloor)
bus (intercity)	peruntu (veliyoor)
tram	traam
train	rayil
I'd like a ... ticket.	enakku oru ... ṭikkeṭ veṇum
one-way	vazhi
return	iru vazhi
1st class	mutalaam vakuppu
2nd class	irantaam vakuppu

SIGNS – TAMIL

வழி உள்ளே	Entrance
வழி வெளியே	Exit
திறந்துள்ளது	Open
அடைக்கப்பட்டுள்ளது	Closed
தகவல்	Information
அனுமதி இல்லை	Prohibited
காவல் நிலையம்	Police Station
மலசலகூடம்	Toilets
ஆண்	Men
பெண்	Women

---

left luggage	tavara vitta saamaan
timetable	kaala attavanai
bus stop	peruntu nilayam
train station	rayil nilayam
I'd like to hire a ...	enakku ... vaatakaikku venum
car	kaara
bicycle	saikkil

KANNADA

Kannada (also known as Kanarese) is also a Dravidian language and it is the official language of the state of Karnataka in India's south west. After Telugu and Tamil it's the third most common Dravidian language of South India.

The earliest known example of Kannada literature is Kavirajamarga, which dates back to the 9th century AD, and today the modern language is represented by a thriving tradition covering all literary genres.

See the pronunciation guide in the Tamil section of this chapter for an explanation of the retroflex consonants (ḍ, ḷ, ṇ, ṣ and ṭ).

CONVERSATION & ESSENTIALS

Hello.	namaste or namaskaara
Excuse me.	kṣamisi
Please.	dayaviṭṭu
Thank you.	vandanegaḷu
Yes/No.	havdu/illa
How are you?	hege ideeri?
Very well, thank you.	bahaḷa oḷḷeyadu vandanegaḷu
What's your name?	nimma hesaru enu?
My name is ...	nanna hesaru ...
Do you speak English?	neevu ingliṣ mataaḍteeraa?
I don't understand.	nanage artha aagalla
Where is the hotel?	hoṭel ellide?
How far is ...?	... eṣtu doora?
How do I get to ...?	naanu allige hogodu hege?
How much?	eṣtu?
This is expensive.	idu dubaari
What is the time?	gaṇṭe eṣtu?
medicine	auṣadhi
big	dodda
small	cikka
today	ivattu
day	hagalu
night	raatri
week	vaara
month	tingaḷu
year	varṣa

NUMBERS

1	ondu
2	eradu
3	mooru
4	naalku
5	aydu
6	aaru
7	elu

8	*entu*
9	*ombhattu*
10	*hattu*
100	*nooru*
1000	*ondu saavira*
2000	*radu saavira*
100,000	*lakṣa* (written 1,00,000)
1,000,000	*hattu lakṣa* (written 10,00,000)
10,000,000	*koti* (written 1,00,00,000)

KONKANI

After a long and hard-fought battle Konkani was finally recognised in 1992 as the official language of the small state of Goa on India's southwest coast. Until then, argument had raged that Konkani was actually no more than a dialect of Marathi, the official language of the much larger neighbouring state of Maharashtra.

Even though Konkani is virtually the only universally understood language of Goa, centuries of colonial rule, significant dialectal variation and as many as five different scripts meant that defining it as an official language would always be problematic. The issue was further complicated by the varying loyalties of Goa's population: the high caste and predominantly Catholic and Hindu Brahmin families who spoke Portuguese, English and Konkani, and the lower caste, mainly Hindu families who tended to speak Marathi as a first language and some Konkani as a second language. Despite these obstacles Konkani went on to be added to the Indian Constitution as the country's 18th national language.

CONVERSATION & ESSENTIALS

Hello.	*paypadta*
Excuse me.	*upkar korxi*
Please.	*upkar kor*
Thank you.	*dev borem korum*
Yes/No.	*oi/naah*
How are you?	*kosso assa?* (m)
	kossem assa? (f)
Very well, thank you.	*bhore jaung*
What's your name?	*tuje naav kide?*
Do you speak English?	*to English hulonk jhana?*
I don't understand.	*mhaka kay samzona na*
Where is a hotel?	*hotel khoy aasa?*
How far is ...?	*anig kitya phoode ...?*
How do I get to ...?	*maka kashe ... meltole?*
How much?	*kitke poishe laqthele?*

This is expensive.	*chod marog*
What's the time?	*vurra kitki jali?*
medicine	*vokot*
big	*hodlo*
small	*dhakto*
today	*aaj*
day	*dees*
night	*racho*
week	*athovda*
month	*mohino*
year	*voros*

NUMBERS

1	*ek*
2	*don*
3	*tin*
4	*char*
5	*panch*
6	*sou*
7	*sat*
8	*att*
9	*nov*
10	*dha*
20	*vis*
30	*tis*
40	*chalis*
50	*ponnas*
60	*saatt*
70	*sottor*
80	*oixim*
90	*novodh*
100	*xembor*
200	*donshe*
1000	*ek hazaar*
2000	*don hazaar*
100,000	*lakh* (written 1,00,000)
10,000,000	*crore* (written 1,00,00,000)

MALAYALAM

Like Tamil, Malayalam belongs to the Dravidian language family. Though there are obvious lexical links between the two languages, with many words sharing common roots, Malayalam includes a far greater number of borrowings from ancient Indian Sanskrit. Its divergence from Tamil began some time after the 10th century AD, with the first official literary record of it dating back to Ramacharitam, a 'pattu' poem written in the late 12th century. The modern form of the Malayalam script developed from the 16th century literary works of Tuñcatt Ezuttacchan.

Malayalam is the official language of the state of Kerala on India's far southwestern coast.

See the pronunciation guide in the Tamil section of this chapter for an explanation of the retroflex consonants (ḍ, ḷ, ṇ, ṛ, ṣ and ṭ).

CONVERSATION & ESSENTIALS

Hello.	namaste
Excuse me.	ksamikkoo
Please.	dayavucheytu
Thank you.	nanni
Yes/No.	aanaate/alla
How are you?	sukhamaaṇo?
Very well, thank you.	sukham tanne
What's your name?	ninnaluṭe pera entaaṇu?
My name is ...	ente peru ...
Do you speak English?	ninnaḷ ingleeṣa samsaarikkumo?
I don't understand.	enikka aṛiyilla
Where is the hotel?	hottal eviṭeyaaṇa?
How far is ...?	... vetra dooramaaṇa?
How do I get to ...?	... aviṭe ennane pokaṇam?
How much?	eṭra?
This is expensive.	vila kootutal aaṇa
What's the time?	mani eṭrayeyi?

medicine	marunnu
big	valiya
small	cheriya
today	inna
day	divasam
night	raaṭri
week	aalca
month	maasam
year	varsam

NUMBERS

1	onna
2	raṇḍa
3	moonna
4	naala
5	ancha
6	aaṛa
7	ela
8	eṭṭa
9	ombata
10	patta
100	nooṛa
1000	aayiram
2000	raṇḍaayiram
100,000	lakṣam (written 1,00,000)
1,000,000	patta lakam (written 10,00,000)
10,000,000	koṭi (written 1,00,00,000)

MARATHI

Marathi is the official language of the state of Maharashtra and is one of India's national languages. Like its close linguistic relative, Konkani (the official language of Goa), it belongs to the Indo-Aryan language family. As a result of linguistic influences from neighbouring regions you may notice considerable dialectal variation in Marathi as you move around Maharashtra.

CONVERSATION & ESSENTIALS

Hello/Goodbye.	namaskar
Excuse me.	maaf kara
Please.	krupaya
Yes.	ho
No.	nahi
How are you?	tumhi kase aahat?
Very well, thank you.	mee thik aahe, dhanyawad
What's your name?	aapla nav kai aahe?
Do you speak English?	tumhala english yeta ka?
I don't understand.	mala samjat nahi
Where is a hotel?	hotel kuthe aahe?
How do I get to ...?	... kasa jaycha mhanje sapdel?
How much?	kevdhyala?/kai kimmat?
This is expensive.	khup mahag aahe
What's the time?	kiti vajle?

medicine	aushadh
big	motha/mothi (m/f)
small	lahan
today	aaj
day	divas
night	ratra
week	aathavda
month	mahina
year	varsha

NUMBERS

1	ek
2	don
3	tin
4	char
5	pach
6	saha
7	sat
8	aath
9	nou
10	daha
100	shambhar
200	donshe
1000	ek hazar

LANGUAGE

2000	don hazar
100,000	ek lakh (written 1,00,000)
10,000,000	daha koti (written 1,00,00,000)

TELUGU

Telugu is a Southeast Dravidian language spoken mainly in the state of Andhra Pradesh on India's east coast; it became the state's official language in the mid-1960s. With around 70 million speakers it is the most predominant of South India's four major Dravidian languages. Its literary history dates back to the 11th century AD when the poet Nannaya produced a translation of parts of the Mahabharata. While Sanskrit has played a major role in Telugu literature over the centuries, there is an increasing tendency for written works to reflect the more colloquial variety of Modern Standard Telugu. See the pronunciation guide in the Tamil section of this chapter for an explanation of the retroflex consonants (ḍ, ḷ, ṇ and ṭ).

CONVERSATION & ESSENTIALS

Hello.	namaste/namaskaaram
Excuse me.	ksamiñchaṇḍi
Please.	dayatsesi
Thank you.	dhanyawaadaalu
Yes.	awunu
No.	kaadu
How are you?	elaa unnaaru?/
	elaa baagunnaaraa?
Very well, thank you.	baagunnaanu dhanyawaadaalu
What's your name?	mee peru emiṭi?/nee peru emiṭi?
My name is ...	naa peru ...

Do you speak	meeku anglam waccha?
English?	
I don't understand.	naaku artham kaawaṭamledu
Where is the hotel?	hoṭal ekkada undi?
How far is ...?	... enta dooram?
How do I get to ...?	... nenu akkaḍiki weḷḷaṭam elaa?
How much?	enta?
This is expensive.	idi chaalaa ekkuwa
What's the time?	gaṇṭa enta?/ṭaym enta?

medicine	awsadham/mandu
big	pedda
small	tsinna
today	eeroju/eenaaḍu/neḍu
day	pagalu
night	raatri
week	waaram
month	nela/maasam
year	eḍu/samwatsaram

NUMBERS

1	okaṭi
2	reṇḍu
3	mooḍu
4	naalugu
5	aydu/ayidu
6	aaru
7	eḍu
8	enimidi
9	tommidi
10	padi
100	nooru/wanda
1000	weyyi/weyi
2000	reṇḍuwelu
100,000	laksa (written 1,00,000)
1,000,000	padilaksalu (written 10,00,000)
10,000,000	koṭi (written 1,00,00,000)

Glossary

Here, with definitions, are some unfamiliar words and abbreviations you might meet in this book. For definitions of food and drink, see the Food & Drink chapter (p88).

abbi – waterfall
Abhimani – eldest son of Brahma
Abhimanyu – son of Arjuna
acha – 'OK' or 'I understand'
acharya – revered teacher; spiritual guide
Adivasi – tribal person
agarbathi – incense
Agasti – legendary Hindu sage, revered in the south, as he is credited with introducing Hinduism and developing the Tamil language
Agni – major deity in the Vedas; mediator between men and the gods; also fire
ahimsa – discipline of nonviolence
AIR – All India Radio, the national broadcaster
air-cooled room – room in guesthouse, hotel or home, generally with a big, noisy water-filled fan built into the wall
amir – Muslim nobleman
amrita – immortality
Ananda – Buddha's cousin and personal attendant
Ananta – snake on which Vishnu reclined
Andhaka – 1000-headed demon, killed by Shiva
angrezi – foreigner
anikut – dam
anna – 16th of a rupee; no longer legal tender
Annapurna – form of Durga; worshipped for her power to provide food
apsara – heavenly nymph
Aranyani – Hindu goddess of forests
Ardhanari – Shiva's half-male, half-female form
Arishta – *daitya* who, having taken the form of a bull, attacked Krishna and was killed by him
Arjuna – Mahabharata hero and military commander who married Subhadra, took up arms and overcame many demons. He had the Bhagavad Gita related to him by Krishna, led Krishna's funeral ceremony and finally retired to the Himalaya.
Aryan – Sanskrit for 'noble'; those who migrated from Persia and settled in northern India
Ashoka – ruler in the 3rd century BC; responsible for spreading Buddhism into South India
ashram – spiritual community or retreat
ashrama – Hindu system; there are three stages in life recognised by this system: *brahmachari, grihastha* and *sanyasin* but this kind of merit is only available to the upper three castes

ASI – Abbreviation for the Archaeological Survey of India; an organisation involved in monument preservation
atman – soul
attar – essential oil; used as a base for perfumes
autorickshaw – noisy, three-wheeled, motorised contraption for transporting passengers, livestock etc for short distances; found throughout the country, they are cheaper than taxis
Avalokiteshvara – in Mahayana Buddhism, the bodhisattva of compassion
avatar – incarnation of a deity, usually Vishnu
ayah – children's nurse or nanny
Ayurveda – the ancient and complex science of Indian herbal medicine and healing
azad – free (Urdu), as in Azad Jammu & Kashmir
azan – Muslim call to prayer

baba – religious master or father; term of respect
bagh – garden
bahadur – brave or chivalrous; an honorific title
baksheesh – tip, donation (alms) or bribe
Balarama – brother of Krishna
bandar – monkey
bandh – general strike
bandhani – tie-dye
banian – T-shirt or undervest
baniya – moneylender
banyan – Indian fig tree
bazaar – market area; a market town is also called a bazaar
bearer – rather like a butler
beedi – small, hand-rolled cigarette; really just a rolled-up leaf
begum – Muslim princess or woman of high rank
Bhagavad Gita – Hindu Song of the Divine One; Krishna's lessons to Arjuna, the main thrust of which was to emphasise the philosophy of *bhakti*; it is part of the Mahabharata
Bhairava – the Terrible; refers to the eighth incarnation of Shiva in his demonic form
bhajan – devotional song
bhakti – surrendering to the gods; faith
bhang – dried leaves and flowering shoots of the marijuana plant; legal in some holy towns such as Puri
bhangra – rhythmic Punjabi music/dance
Bharat – Hindi for India
Bharata – half-brother of Rama; ruled while Rama was in exile
Bharata Natyam – classical dance of Tamil Nadu
bhavan – house, building; also spelt *bhawan*

bheesti – see *bhisti*

Bhima – Mahabharata hero; he is the brother of Hanuman and renowned for his great strength

bhisti – water carrier

bhoga-mandapa – Orissan hall of offering

bhojanalya – see *dhaba*

bidi – see *beedi*

bindi – forehead mark (often dot-shaped) worn by women

BJP – Bharatiya Janata Party

Bodhi Tree – tree under which the Buddha sat when he attained enlightenment

bodhisattva – literally 'one whose essence is perfected wisdom'. In Early Buddhism, bodhisattva refers only to the Buddha during the period between his conceiving the intention to strive for Buddhahood and the moment he attained it; in Mahayana Buddhism, one who renounces nirvana in order to help others attain it.

Bollywood – India's answer to Hollywood; the film industry of Mumbai (Bombay)

Brahma – Hindu god; worshipped as the creator in the Trimurti

brahmachari – chaste student stage of the *ashrama* system

Brahmanism – early form of Hinduism which evolved from Vedism (see *Vedas*); named after Brahmin priests and Brahma

Brahmin – member of the priest/scholar caste, the highest Hindu caste

Buddha – Awakened One; the originator of Buddhism; also regarded by Hindus as the ninth incarnation of Vishnu

Buddhism – see *Early Buddhism*

bugyal – high-altitude meadow

bund – embankment or dyke

bunder – shipping wharf

burka – one-piece garment used by conservative Muslim women to cover themselves from head to toe

bustee – slum

cantonment – administrative and military area of a Raj-era town

caravanserai – traditional accommodation for camel caravans

Carnatic music – classical music of South India

caste – a Hindu's hereditary station (social standing) in life; there are four castes: the Brahmins, the Kshatriyas, the Vaishyas and the Shudras

cenotaph – a monument honouring a dead person whose body is somewhere else

chaitya – Sanskrit form of 'cetiya', meaning shrine or object of worship; has come to mean temple, and more specifically, a hall divided into a central nave and two side aisles by a line of columns, with a votive stupa at the end

chakra – focus of one's spiritual power; disclike weapon of Vishnu

chalo – colloquial term for 'let's go' (Hindi)

Chamunda – form of Durga; a real terror, armed with a scimitar, noose and mace, and clothed in elephant hide, her mission was to kill the demons Chanda and Munda

chandra – moon, or the moon as a god

Chandragupta – Indian ruler, 3rd century BC

chappals – sandals or fancy leather thonglike footwear; flip-flops

charas – resin of the marijuana plant; also referred to as 'hashish'

charbagh – formal Persian garden, divided into quarters (literally 'four gardens')

charpoy – simple bed made of ropes knotted together on a wooden frame

chedi – see *chaitya*

chela – pupil or follower, as George Harrison was to Ravi Shankar

chhatri – cenotaph (literally 'umbrella'); small domed Mughal kiosk

chillum – pipe of a hookah; commonly used to describe the pipes used for smoking *ganja*

chinkara – gazelle

chital – spotted deer

chogyal – king

choli – sari blouse

choultry – pilgrim's rest house; also called 'dharamsala'

chowk – town square, intersection or marketplace

chowkidar – night watchman, caretaker

Cong (I) – Congress Party of India; also known as Congress (I)

coolie – labourer or porter

CPI – Communist Party of India

CPI (M) – Communist Party of India (Marxist)

crore – 10 million

dacoit – bandit (particularly armed bandit), outlaw

dagoba – see *stupa*

daitya – demon or giant who fought against the gods

dak – staging post, government-run accommodation

Dalit – preferred term for India's Untouchable caste; see also *Harijan*

Damodara – another name for Krishna

dargah – shrine or place of burial of a Muslim saint

darshan – offering or audience with someone; viewing of a deity

darwaza – gateway or door

Dasaratha – father of Rama in the Ramayana

Dattatreya – Brahmin saint who embodied the Trimurti

Deccan – meaning 'South', this refers to the central South Indian plateau

deul – temple sanctuary

devadasi – temple dancer

Devi – Shiva's wife; goddess

dhaba – basic restaurant or snack bar

dham – holiest pilgrimage places of India

dharamsala – pilgrim's rest house

dharma – the word used by both Hindus and Buddhists to refer to their respective moral codes of behaviour

dharna – nonviolent protest

dhobi – person who washes clothes; commonly referred to as *dhobi-wallah*

dhobi ghat – place where clothes are washed

dhol – traditional, large, two-sided Punjabi drum

dholi – man-carried portable 'chairs'; people are carried in them to hill-top temples etc

dhoti – like a lungi, but the ankle-length cloth is then pulled up between the legs; worn by men

dhurrie – cotton rug

Digambara – 'Sky-Clad'; Jain group that demonstrates disdain for worldly goods by going naked

dikpala – temple guardian

Din-i-Ilahi – Akbar's philosophy asserting the common truth in all religions

diwali – the festival of lights; one of the major festivals of the Hindu calendar

dowry – money and goods given by a bride's parents to their son-in-law's family; it's illegal but still widely exists with some arranged marriages

Draupadi – wife of the five Pandava princes in the Mahabharata

Dravidian – general term for the cultures and languages of the deep south of India, including Tamil, Malayalam, Telugu and Kannada

dun – valley

dupatta – long scarf for women often worn with the *salwar kameez*

durbar – royal court; also a government

Durga – the Inaccessible; a form of Shiva's wife, Devi, a beautiful, fierce woman riding a tiger; a major goddess of the Shakti sect

dwarpal – doorkeeper; sculpture beside the doorways to Hindu or Buddhist shrines

Early Buddhism – any of the schools of Buddhism established directly after Buddha's death and before the advent of Mahayana. A modern form is the Theravada (Teaching of the Elders) practised in Sri Lanka and Southeast Asia. Early Buddhism differed from the Mahayana in that it did not teach the bodhisattva ideal.

elatalam – small hand-held cymbals

election symbols – identifying symbols for the various political parties, used to canvas illiterate voters

Emergency – period in the 1970s during which Indira Gandhi suspended many political rights

Eve-teasing – sexual harassment

export guru – guru whose followers are mainly Westerners

fakir – Muslim who has taken a vow of poverty; may also apply to *sadhus* and other Hindu ascetics

filmi – slang describing anything to do with Indian movies

firman – royal order or grant

gaddi – throne of a Hindu prince

Ganesh – Hindu god of good fortune; popular elephant-headed son of Shiva and Parvati, he is also known as Ganpati and his vehicle is a ratlike creature

Ganga – Hindu goddess representing the sacred Ganges River; said to flow from Vishnu's toe

ganga aarti – river worship ceremony

ganj – market

ganja – dried flowering tips of marijuana plant

gaon – village

garbha griha – the inner, or 'womb' chamber of a Hindu temple

garh – fort

gari – vehicle; 'motor gari' is a car and 'rail gari' is a train

Garuda – man-bird vehicle of Vishnu

gaur – Indian bison

Gayatri – sacred verse of Rig-Veda repeated mentally by Brahmins twice a day

geyser – hot-water unit found in some bathrooms

ghat – steps or landing on a river, range of hills, or road up hills

ghazal – Urdu song derived from poetry; sad love theme

gherao – industrial action where the workers lock in their employers

giri – hill

Gita Govinda – erotic poem by Jayadeva relating Krishna's early life as Govinda

Goan trance – style of electronic dance music originating from Goa

godmen – commercially minded gurus; see also *export guru*

godown – warehouse

goonda – ruffian or tough; political parties have been known to employ them in gangs

Gopala – see Govinda

gopi – milkmaid; Krishna was fond of them

gopuram – soaring pyramidal gateway tower of Dravidian temples

Govinda – Krishna as a cowherd; also just cowherd

grihastha – householder stage of the *ashrama* system; followers discharge their duty to ancestors by having sons and making sacrifices to the gods

gufa – cave

gulli – lane or alleyway

gumbad – dome on an Islamic tomb or mosque

gurdwara – Sikh temple

guru – holy teacher; in Sanskrit literally *'goe'* (darkness) and *'roe'* (to dispel)

Guru Granth Sahib – Sikh holy book

haat – village market

haj – Muslim pilgrimage to Mecca

haji – Muslim who has made the *haj*

hammam – Turkish bath; public bathhouse

Hanuman – Hindu monkey god, prominent in the Ramayana, and a follower of Rama

Hara – one of Shiva's names

Hari – another name for Vishnu

Harijan – name (no longer considered acceptable) given by Gandhi to India's Untouchables, meaning 'children of god'

hartal – strike

hashish – see *charas*

hathi – elephant

haveli – traditional, often ornately decorated, residences, particularly those found in Rajasthan and Gujarat

havildar – army officer

hijab – headscarf used by Muslim women

hijra – eunuch

Hinayana – see *Early Buddhism*

hindola – swing

Hiranyakasipu – *daitya* king killed by Narasimha

Holi – exuberant Hindu festival marking the end of winter

hookah – water pipe used for smoking ganja or strong tobacco

hotel – a place to eat, and sometimes a place to stay as well

howdah – seat for carrying people on an elephant's back

hu-tu-tu – see *kabaddi*

iftar – breaking of the Ramadan fast at sunset

ikat – fabric made with thread which is tie-dyed before weaving

imam – Muslim religious leader

imambara – tomb dedicated to a Shiite Muslim holy man

Indo-Saracenic – style of colonial architecture that integrated Western designs with Islamic, Hindu and Jain influences

Indra – significant and prestigious Vedic god; god of rain, thunder, lightning and war

Indrail pass – allows unlimited travel on Indian railways for the period of its validity

Ishwara – another name given to Shiva; lord

Jagadhatri – Mother of the World; another name for Devi

jagamohan – assembly hall

Jagannath – Lord of the Universe; a form of Krishna

jali – carved lattice (often marble) screen, also used to refer to the holes or spaces produced through carving timber or stone

Janaka – father of Sita

jataka – tale from Buddha's various lives

jawan – policeman or soldier

jheel – swampy area

jhuggi – shanty settlement; also called *bustee*

jhula – bridge

ji – honorific that can be added to the end of almost anything as a form of respect; thus 'Babaji', 'Gandhiji'

jooti – traditional pointy-toed shoe of Rajasthan; also found elsewhere in India

juggernaut – huge, extravagantly decorated temple 'car' dragged through the streets during Hindu festivals

jumkahs – earrings

jyoti linga – most important shrines to Shiva, of which there are 12

kabaddi – traditional game (similar to tag)

Kailasa – sacred Himalayan mountain; home of Shiva

kalamkari – designs painted on cloth using vegetable dyes

Kali – the Black; terrible form of Devi commonly depicted with black skin, dripping with blood, and wearing a necklace of skulls

Kalki – White Horse; future (10th) incarnation of Vishnu which will appear at the end of Kali-Yug, when the world ceases to be; has been compared to Maitreya in Buddhist cosmology

Kama – Hindu god of love

kameez – woman's shirtlike tunic

Kanishka – important king of the Kushana empire who reigned in the early Christian era

Kannada – state language of Karnataka

Kanyakumari – Virgin Maiden; another name for Durga

kapali – sacred bowl made from a human skull

karma – Hindu, Buddhist and Sikh principle of retributive justice for past deeds

karmachario – workers

Karmasutra – erotic Sanskrit text giving rules for love and sexual pleasure

Kartikiya – Hindu god of war, Shiva's son

Kathakali – traditional dance form of Kerala

kathputli – puppeteer; also known as *putli*-wallah

Kedarnath – name of Shiva and one of the 12 *jyoti linga*

khadi – homespun cloth; Mahatma Gandhi encouraged people to spin this rather than buy English cloth

Khalistan – former Sikh secessionists' proposed name for an independent Punjab

Khalsa – Sikh brotherhood

Khan – Muslim honorific title

kho-kho – traditional game (similar to tag)

khol – black eyeliner

khur – Asiatic wild ass

kiang – wild ass found in Ladakh

kirtan – Sikh hymn-singing

koil – Hindu temple

kolam – also known as *rangoli*; traditional chalk design drawn over the threshhold of a home or temple to bring good fortune and ward off bad luck

kompu – C-shaped, metal trumpet

Konkani – state language of Goa

kos minar – milestone

kot – fort

kothi – residence, house or mansion

kotwali – police station

Krishna – Vishnu's eighth incarnation, often coloured blue; he revealed the Bhagavad Gita to Arjuna

Kshatriya – Hindu caste of soldiers or administrators; second in the caste hierarchy

Kuchipudi – classical dance form of Andhra Pradesh

kund – lake or tank; Toda village

kurta – long shirt with either short collar or no collar

Kusa – one of Rama's twin sons

lakh – 100,000

Lakshmana – half-brother and aide of Rama in the Ramayana

Lakshmi – Vishnu's consort, Hindu goddess of wealth; she sprang forth from the ocean holding a lotus

lathi – heavy stick used by police, especially for crowd control

lehanga – very full skirt with a waist cord

lingam – phallic symbol; symbol of Shiva; plural 'linga'

lok – people

Lok Sabha – lower house in the Indian parliament (House of the People)

loka – realm

lungi – worn by men, this loose, coloured garment (similar to a sarong) is pleated by the wearer at the waist to fit snugly

machaan – observation tower

madrasa – Islamic seminary

maha – prefix meaning 'great'

Mahabharata – Great Hindu Vedic epic poem of the Bharata dynasty; containing approximately 10,000 verses describing the battle between the Pandavas and the Kauravas

Mahabodhi Society – founded in 1891 to encourage Buddhist studies

Mahadeva – Great God; Shiva

Mahadevi – Great Goddess; Devi

Mahakala – Great Time; Shiva and one of 12 *jyoti linga*

mahal – house or palace

maharaja – literally 'great king'; princely ruler

maharana – see *maharaja*

maharao – see *maharaja*

maharawal – see *maharaja*

maharani – wife of a princely ruler or a ruler in her own right

mahatma – literally 'great soul'

Mahavir – last *tirthankar*

Mahayana – the 'greater-vehicle' of Buddhism; a later adaptation of the teaching which lays emphasis on the bodhisattva ideal, teaching the renunciation of *nirvana* (ultimate peace and cessation of rebirth) in order to help other beings along the way to enlightenment

Mahayogi – Great Ascetic; Shiva

Maheshwara – Great Lord; Shiva

Mahisa – Hindu demon

mahout – elephant rider or master

Mahratta – see *Maratha*

maidan – open (often grassed) area; parade ground

Maitreya – future Buddha

Makara – mythical sea creature and Varuna's vehicle; crocodile

Malayalam – state language of Kerala

mandal – shrine

mandala – circle; symbol used in Hindu and Buddhist art to symbolise the universe

mandapa – pillared pavilion a temple forechamber

mandi – market

mandir – temple

mantra – sacred word or syllable used by Buddhists and Hindus to aid concentration; metrical psalms of praise found in the Vedas

Mara – Buddhist personification of that which obstructs the cultivation of virtue, often depicted with hundreds of arms; also the god of death

Maratha – central Indian people who controlled much of India at various times and fought the Mughals and Rajputs

Marathi – lanuage of Maharashtra

marg – road

Maruts – Hindu storm gods

masjid – mosque

mata – mother

math – monastery

maund – unit of weight now superseded (about 20kg)

mehndi – henna; ornate henna designs on women's hands (and often feet) for certain festivals and ceremonies (eg marriage)

mela – fair or festival

memsahib – Madam; respectful way of addressing women

Meru – mythical mountain found in the centre of the earth; on it is Swarga

mihrab – mosque 'prayer niche' that faces Mecca

mithuna – pairs of men and women; often seen in temple sculpture

Mohini – Vishnu in his female incarnation

moksha – liberation from *samsara*

monsoon – rainy season

morcha – mob march or protest

mudra – ritual hand movements used in Hindu religious dancing; gesture of Buddha figure

muezzin – one who calls Muslims to prayer, traditionally from the minaret of a mosque

Mughal – Muslim dynasty of subcontinental emperors from Babur to Aurangzeb

mujtahid – divine

mullah – Muslim scholar or religious leader

mund – village

nadi – river

Naga – mythical serpentlike beings capable of changing into human form

namaste – traditional Hindu greeting (hello or goodbye), often accompanied by a small bow with the hands brought together at the chest or head level, as a sign of respect; also known as *namaskar*

namaz – Muslim prayers

namkin – prepackaged spicy nibbles

Nanda – cowherd who raised Krishna

Nandi – bull, vehicle of Shiva

Narasimha – man-lion incarnation of Vishnu

Narayan – incarnation of Vishnu the creator

Narsingh – see *Narasimha*

natamandir – dancing hall

Nataraja – Shiva as the cosmic dancer

nawab – Muslim ruling prince or powerful landowner

Nilakantha – form of Shiva; his blue throat is a result of swallowing poison that would have destroyed the world

nilgai – antelope

nirvana – this is the ultimate aim of Buddhists and the final release from the cycle of existence

niwas – house, building

nizam – hereditary title of the rulers of Hyderabad

noth – the Lord (Jain)

NRI – Non-Resident Indian; of economic significance to modern India

nullah – ditch or small stream

Om – sacred invocation representing the absolute essence of the divine principle; for Buddhists, if repeated often enough with complete concentration, it leads to a state of emptiness

Oriya – state language of Orissa

Osho – the late Bhagwan Shree Rajneesh, a popular, controversial guru

padma – lotus; another name for the Hindu goddess Lakshmi

padyatra – 'foot journey' made by politicians to raise support at village level

paise – the Indian rupee is divided into 100 paise

palanquin – boxlike enclosure carried on poles on four men's shoulders; the occupant sits inside on a seat

Pali – the language, related to Sanskrit, in which the Buddhist scriptures were recorded; scholars still refer to the original Pali texts

palia – memorial stone

palli – village

Panchatantra – series of traditional Hindu stories about the natural world, human behaviour and survival

panchayat – village council

pandal – marquee

pandit – expert or wise person; sometimes used to mean a bookworm

Parasurama – Rama with the axe; sixth incarnation of Vishnu

Parsi – adherent of the Zoroastrian faith

Partition – formal division of British India into two separate countries, India and Pakistan, in 1947

Parvati – another form of Devi

patachitra – Orissan cloth painting

PCO – Public Call Office from where you can usually make interstate and international phone calls

peepul – fig tree, especially a bo tree

peon – lowest grade clerical worker

pinjrapol – animal hospital run by Jains

pir – Muslim holy man; title of a Sufi saint

Pongal – Tamil harvest festival

pradesh – state

pranayama – study of breath control

prasad – temple-blessed food offering

puja – literally 'respect'; offering or prayers

pukka – proper; a Raj-era term

pukka sahib – proper gentleman

punka – cloth fan, swung by pulling a cord

Puranas – set of 18 encyclopaedic Sanskrit stories, written in verse, relating to the three gods, dating from the 5th century AD

purdah – custom among some conservative Muslims (also adopted by some Hindus, especially the Rajputs) of keeping women in seclusion; veiled

Purnima – full moon; considered to be an auspicious time

putli-wallah – puppeteer; also known as *'kathputli'*

qila – fort

Quran – the holy book of Islam, also spelt Koran

Radha – favourite mistress of Krishna when he lived as a cowherd

raga – any of several conventional patterns of melody and rhythm that form the basis for freely interpreted compositions

railhead – station or town at the end of a railway line; termination point

raj – rule or sovereignty; British Raj (sometimes just Raj) refers to British rule

raja, rana – king

rajkumar – prince

Rajput – Hindu warrior caste, former rulers of north-western India

Rajya Sabha – upper house in the Indian parliament (Council of States)

rakhi – amulet

Rama – seventh incarnation of Vishnu

Ramadan – the Islamic holy month of sunrise-to-sunset fasting (no eating, drinking or smoking); also referred to as Ramazan

Ramayana – the story of Rama and Sita and their conflict with Ravana is one of India's best-known epics

rangoli – elaborate chalk, rice-paste or coloured powder design; also known as *kolam*

rani – female ruler or wife of a king

ranns – deserts

rasta roko – roadblock set up for protest purposes

rath – temple chariot or car used in religious festivals

rathas – rock-cut Dravidian temples

Ravana – demon king of Lanka who abducted Sita; the titanic battle between him and Rama is told in the Ramayana

rawal – nobleman

rickshaw – small, two- or three-wheeled passenger vehicle

Rig-Veda – original and longest of the four main Vedas, or holy Sanskrit texts

rishi – any poet, philosopher, saint or sage; originally a sage to whom the hymns of the Vedas were revealed

rudraksh mala – strings of beads used in *puja*

Rukmani – wife of Krishna; died on his funeral pyre

sadhu – ascetic, holy person, one who is trying to achieve enlightenment; often addressed as *'swamiji'* or *'babaji'*

sagar – lake, reservoir

sahib – respectful title applied to a gentleman

salai – road

salwar – trousers usually worn with a *kameez*

salwar kameez – traditional dresslike tunic and trouser combination for women

samadhi – in Hinduism, ecstatic state, sometimes defined as 'ecstasy, trance, communion with God'; in Buddhism, concentration; also a place where a holy man has been cremated/buried, usually venerated as a shrine

sambalpuri – Orissan fabric

sambar – deer

samsara – Buddhists, Hindus and Sikhs believe earthly life is cyclical; you are born again and again, the quality of these rebirths being dependent upon your karma in previous lives

Sangam – ancient academy of Tamil literature; means literally 'the meeting of two hearts'

sangha – community or order of Buddhist priests

Sankara – Shiva as the creator

sanyasin – like a *sadhu;* a wandering ascetic who has renounced all worldly things as part of the *ashrama* system

Saraswati – wife of Brahma, goddess of learning; sits on a white swan, holding a *veena*

Sati – wife of Shiva; became a *sati* ('honourable woman') by immolating herself; although banned more than a century ago, the act of *sati* is still occasionally performed

satra – Hindu Vaishnavaite monastery and centre for art

satsang – discourse by a swami or guru

satyagraha – nonviolent protest involving a hunger strike, popularised by Mahatma Gandhi; from Sanskrit, literally meaning 'insistence on truth'

Schedule Tribes – official term for Adivasis or tribal people

Scheduled Castes – official term used for the Untouchables or Dalits

sepoy – formerly an Indian solider in British service

serai – accommodation for travellers

shahada – Muslim declaration of faith ('There is no God but Allah; Mohammed is his prophet'); one of the five pillars of wisdom

Shaivism – worship of Shiva

Shaivite – follower of Shiva

shakti – creative energies perceived as female deities; devotees follow Shaktism

shikhar – hunting expedition

shirting – material from which shirts are made

Shiv Sena – Hindu nationalist party, influential in Maharashtra

Shiva – Destroyer; also the Creator, in which form he is worshipped as a lingam

Shivaji – great Maratha leader of the 17th century

shola – virgin forest

shree – see *shri*

shri, shree – honorific; these days the Indian equivalent of Mr or Mrs, also spelt sri or sree

shruti – heard

Shudra – caste of labourers

sikhara – towering roof of a Hindu temple, often pyramidal in South India

Singh – literally 'lion'; a surname adopted by Rajputs and Sikhs

sirdar – leader or commander

Sita – the Hindu goddess of agriculture; more commonly associated with the Ramayana

sitar – Indian stringed instrument

Siva – see *Shiva*

Sivaganga – water tank in temple dedicated to Shiva

Skanda – another name for Kartikiya

sonam – karma accumulated in successive reincarnations

sri – see *shri*

stupa – Buddhist religious monument composed of a solid hemisphere topped by a spire, containing relics of the Buddha; also known as a 'dagoba' or 'pagoda'

Subhadra – Krishna's incestuous sister

Subrahmanya – another name for Kartikiya

Sufi – Muslim mystic

Sufism – Islamic mysticism

suiting – material from which suits are made

Surya – the sun; a major deity in the Vedas

sutra – string; list of rules expressed in verse

swami – title of respect meaning 'lord of the self'; given to initiated Hindu monks

swaraj – independence

Swarga – heaven of Indra

sweeper – lowest caste servant, performs the most menial of tasks

tabla – twin drums

tal – lake

taluk – district

Tamil – language of Tamil Nadu; people of Dravidian origin

tandava – Shiva's cosmic victory dance

tank – reservoir

tantric Buddhism – Tibetan Buddhism with strong sexual and occult overtones

tatty – woven grass screen soaked in water and hung outside windows to cool the air

tempo – noisy three-wheeler public transport vehicle; bigger than an autorickshaw

thakur – nobleman

thangka – Tibetan cloth painting

theertham – temple tank

Theravada – orthodox form of Buddhism practiced in Sri Lanka and Southeast Asia which is characterised by its adherence to the Pali canon; literally, 'dwelling'

thiru – holy

tikka – a mark Hindus put on their foreheads

tilak – forehead mark of devout Hindu men

tirthankars – the 24 great Jain teachers

tonga – two-wheeled horse or pony carriage

topi – pith helmet; used during the Raj era; cap

torana – architrave over a temple entrance

toy train – narrow-gauge train; mini-train

Trimurti – triple form; the Hindu triad of Brahma, Shiva and Vishnu

Tripitaka – classic Buddhist scriptures, divided into three categories, hence the name 'Three Baskets'

tripolia – triple gateway

Uma – Shiva's consort; light

Untouchable – lowest caste or 'casteless', for whom the most menial tasks are reserved; the name derives from the belief that higher castes risk defilement if they touch one; formerly known as Harijan, now Dalit

Upanishads – esoteric doctrine; ancient texts forming part of the Vedas; delving into weighty matters such as the nature of the universe and soul

urs – death anniversary of a revered Muslim; festival in memory of a Muslim saint

Vaishya – member of the Hindu caste of merchants

Valmiki – author of the Ramayana

Vamana – fifth incarnation of Vishnu, as the dwarf

varku – sacred flute made from a thigh bone

varna – concept of caste

Varuna – supreme Vedic god

Vedas – Hindu sacred books; collection of hymns composed in preclassical Sanskrit during the second millen-

nium BC and divided into four books: Rig-Veda, Yajur-Veda, Sama-Veda and Atharva-Veda

veena – stringed instrument

vihara – Buddhist monastery, generally with central court or hall off which open residential cells, usually with a Buddha shrine at one end

Vijayanagar empire – one of South India's greatest empires, lasted from the 14th to 17th centuries AD; the Vijayanagar capital was in Hampi in Karnataka

vikram – another name for a tempo or a larger version of the standard tempo

vimana – principal part of Hindu temple

vipassana – the insight meditation technique of Theravada Buddhism in which mind and body are closely examined as changing phenomena

Vishnu – part of the Trimurti; Vishnu is the Preserver and Restorer who so far has nine avatars: the fish Matsya; the tortoise Kurma; the wild boar Naraha; Narasimha; Vamana; Parasurama; Rama; Krishna; and Buddha

wadi – hamlet

wallah – man; added onto almost anything, eg *dhobi*-wallah, *chai*-wallah, taxi-wallah

wazir – title of chief minister used in some former Muslim princely states

yagna – self-mortification

yakshi – maiden

yali – mythical lion creature

yantra – geometric plan said to create energy

yatra – pilgrimage

yatri – pilgrim

yogini – female goddess attendants

yoni – female fertility symbol

zakat – tax in the form of a charitable donation, one of the five 'Pillars of Islam'

zamindar – landowner

zazen – deep meditation

zenana – area in an upper-class home where women are secluded; still partly operates in some Indian palaces

Behind the Scenes

THIS BOOK

The 1st edition of *South India* was coordinated by Christine Niven, and the 2nd by Richard Plunkett. This 3rd edition was coordinated by Paul Harding, who also wrote the Tamil Nadu and Andaman Islands chapters. Other regional chapters were written by Janine Eberle (Kerala), Patrick Horton (Orissa), Amy Karafin (Andhra Pradesh and Karnataka) and Simon Richmond (Mumbai, Maharashtra and Goa). Dr Trish Batchelor wrote the Health chapter, and some material from the Food & Drink chapter is from *World Food India* by Martin Hughes. Thanks to Sarina Singh for help with Indiawide background and practical information.

THANKS from the Authors

Paul Harding Thanks to all those travellers, officials and everyday locals who offered advice, conversation and information on this trip, especially the NGOs and relief workers I spoke to after the tsunami. Big thanks to Hannah for all the phone calls, to Janine for some downtime on the road, to Benny and Lynda, Vinod Kumar, Shanthi Krishnan, Rachel for saving my notebook, and the lovely people who helped me get into the test match. Big thanks to Sarina in Melbourne for encouragement and debriefs, and also to the editing and mapping team at LP Melbourne.

Janine Eberle In Kerala, big thanks to some very helpful people: Hilda Pereira in Trivandrum, Usha Tytus in Kollam, Vinu and Anoop in Alleppey, PG Varghese in Kochi, Suresh Kumar in Kumily and PS Kurian in Kannur, and also to Rich Freeman for sharing his knowledge. Thanks to Sarina Singh for her invaluable support and very useful tips about being tough and tenacious ('like a soldier'), and to Paul Harding for supplying most of the 10% of fun. At Lonely Planet, thanks to the production team for their assistance and understanding, and to the other CEs for their support (and for covering for me).

Patrick Horton Thanks to Madhya Pradesh Tourism, especially Veena Raman and Vishnu Devi, numero uno Ambassador driver and Hindi language coach; well done *chota bhai*. Also thanks to RK Rai of MP Tourism, who unexpectedly kept popping up along my MP path. In Chhattisgarh, thanks to

knowledgeable Jaspreet Singh of the Chhattisgarh Tourism Board, who revealed the state's secrets, and also to his wife and his mother, who almost burst my stomach with too many delightful *parathas*. The indefatigable and enigmatic Sasanka Rath of Orissa Tourism revealed parts of his state little known to visitors. A big thanks as usual to Amar, PD and Viney at Uni-Crystal for their advice and lunchtime thalis. Lastly and without peer, friends Avenish and Ushe who always provide my Delhi home.

Amy Karafin My sincere thanks go to the people of Karnataka and Andhra Pradesh, who on so many occasions were a source of great inspiration to me. Thanks also to Sathya Babu, Ram Manchi, Mahesh Narasimhan, Arun Netravali, Dilip Patel, Ashok Phansalkar and CS Rao for their help in getting things off the ground, and to Mom and Dad for all the help Stateside. To Malini and Hariharan in Bombay for absorbing me into their home, and to Jayasree Anand for making Hyderabad a happy place, thank you. In Bylakuppe, I am grateful to Wangden Tsering and Prem Singh, mostly for their radiance, which stayed with me long after I left. Special thanks go also to Eva Wutschka for crossing my path; Benjamine and Bhushan Oberoi for the many Bangalore leads; Raghu Raman in Mysore for the Dussehra that never was; Janine Eberle, Shahara Ahmed and Sarina Singh for the great guidance; the readers who wrote in with suggestions; Erik Vickstrom, my reader; et Maïmouna Ciss – *dieureudieuf*. Last and most, my deepest gratitude goes to SN Goenka and everyone at Dhamma Giri, Dhamma Khetta and Dhamma Nagajjuna for their *dana* and *metta*. *Bhavatu sabba mangalam*.

Simon Richmond Extra special thanks go to the wonderful Deborah, Kanwalinder, family and staff (Rita and Brian in particular) for their unstinting hospitality and insights into living in Mumbai, and Kamleish Amin who was a great guide to the city. Many thanks to Mathili Ahluwalia for her shopping tips, and to Homi for the drive up to Matheran and Lonavla. In Goa, Ajit and Jack Sukhija were splendid company and an enormous help. Thanks to John for organising the trip to Chandor and to Charles Beek for his genial company in Anjuna.

CREDITS

Commissioning Editor Janine Eberle
Coordinating Editor Kate McLeod
Coordinating Cartographers Sarah Sloane, Jimi Ellis
Coordinating Layout Designer Jim Hsu
Managing Cartographer Shahara Ahmed
Managing Editor Brigitte Ellemor
Assisting editors Sarah Bailey, Emma Koch, Kate Majic, Kristin Odijk
Cover Designer Pepi Bluck
Indexers Kate McLeod, Andrea Dobbin
Project Manager Celia Wood
Language Content Coordinator Quentin Frayne
Thanks to Adriana Mammarella, Kate McDonald, Sally Darmody, Rebecca Lalor, Nick Stebbing, Yvonne Bischofberger and Suzannah Shwer

THANKS from Lonely Planet

Many thanks to the hundreds of travellers who used the last edition and wrote to us with helpful hints, useful advice and interesting anecdotes:

A Phillip Adams, Jacqueline Afum, Husain Akbar, Dennis Akkerman, Mike & Hildy Albin, G W Albury, Martin Allenbach, Lawrence Alpren, Ms Amrah, Anil Amrit, Ravi Ananthanarayanan, Nicholas Anchen, Alex Andrews, Sofie Andries, Sam Anthonysz, Joe Ardy, Manju Arif, Andrew Armstrong, Hazel Armstrong, Jennifer Atkinson, James Auld **B** Tania Babic, Frank Bacon, Katie Baddeley, Lindsay Baker, Omer Baki, Roman Bansen, Stephen Barber, Stefi Barna, Stephanie Barnes, Bryan Barragan, David Barrett, Rainer Barthels, Urs Bartholet, Jenny & Guido Battig, Mat Beesley, Barbara Benham, Svein Arne Berg, Phillipp Berger, Ajay Bhargov, Rajiv Bhatia, Majlin Bienz, Gideon Bierer, Fran Bigman, Mark Binnenpoorte, Kaspar Binz, Jack Birch, Matthew Bird, Philip Birzulis, Henrik Bjerreso, Neil Bjorkman, Helen Black, Dennis Blackmore, Margaret Blake, David Bloch, Frank Blom, Christina Boeryd, Jonathan Boom, Mauro Borneo, Sarah Bothwell, Cliff Bott, Graham Boulding, Steve Braithwaite, Ramon Bramona, Anna Bromley, Mary Brosnan, Eric Brouwer, Margriet Brouwer, Roel Brouwer, Lorelei Broxson, Andreas Buettner, Garth Burgoine, Rowland Burley **C** Andrew Cadotte, Davide Calamia, Barbara Callaghan, Linda & John Campbell, Suzanne Campbell, Linda Cane,

Alan & Clare Cannon, Claire Carvello, Paola Casanova, Chris Castagnera, Ian Catanach, Marta Ceriani, M Chandran, Karine Chapelle, Anubha Charan, Cecilia Chaudhary, Oga Cho, John Christiensen, Yesudas Chungath, Frederik Claeye, Vinnie Clark, Debi Clarke, V F Clasby, Stephen Clendinnen, Mireille Colahan, Dany Cote, Ranald Coyne, Mel Crowe, Debra Cruz, Noel Cudden, Nicky Cussons, Richard Cutler **D** Melanie Da Costa, Ketan Dalal, Petra Damm, Thomas Danielsen, Bracali Dario, Sheila Darzi, Simon & Cathlyn Davidson, Emma Dawson, Nicky Dawson, Stephan D'Costa, Alfonso de Melo, Alann de Vuyst, Steve Deadman, Chantal Demaire, Catherine Diggle, Raphael Dischl, Chris & Sally Drysdale, Christopher Dunn, Stuart Dutson **E** Aimee Eden, Loretta Egan, Niels Langager Ellegaard, Lenzinger Emanuel, Robert Erenstein, Chris & Helen Evans, Ruth Evans **F** Steven Faulkner, Deirdre Feddes, Iain Felstead, Anna Fernandes, Bernd Filsinger, Amanda Fisher, Gaynor Fitzgibbon, Sylvia Florin, Signe Foersom, Andrew Forde-Johnston, David Fordham, Kate Foster, Allyson Fox, Clive France, Daniel Frankl, Waltraud Frauenhuber, Robert Froeschl, Anne Froger **G** Danie Gagne, Elisabeth Gardner, Paul Garenfeld, Shayne Gary, Michael Gascoigne, John Germinario, Frederike Gerstner, Christina & Scott Gifford, Dev Gopalasamy, Theresa Grebin, Clinton Green, Eric Green, Mike & Christabel Grimmer, Ewoud Groenendijk, Shirley Gutwerg **H** Olli Halikka, Timothy Hallam, Mario Hammer, Nada Hankin, Lincoln Harris, Edith Hartmann, Pierre Haski, Jennifer Hayes, Paul Haywood, Alexander Heitkamp, Oliver Helmreich, Andrea Henrie, Nicki Hepstonstall, Michael Herger, Felix Heubaum, Eva Heywood, Alexander Hillebrand, Helena Hillila-Lund, Erin Hird, Keith Hobbs, Bertil Holstensson, Richard Hooper, Christoffer Hornborg, Stacy Horne, Brigitte Horrenberger, Cat Horswill, Clecie Hunter, Anthony Hurley, Vicky Hurley, Mark Huys **I** Rachel & Martin Ive, R S Iyer **J** Shirley Jackson, Anjana Jacob, Fiona Jeffrey, Holly Jenkins, Peter Jensen, Lee Jhonson, Ulric Johannesen, Mathew John, Claire Jolly, Chris Jones, Sue & Ray Jones, Bo Jonsson, William Jope, Meredith Josey, Janina Juchnowicz, Frank Juhas **K** Haemish Kane, Anand Kaper, Sebastian Kastner, Shannon Katary, John Kavanagh, Yorgos Kechagioglou, Stephen King, Juergen Kirst, Juha Klaavu, Dietmar Klaus, Manuel Klauser, Anne-Marie Kleijberg, Monique Kleinendorst, Jacco Kleingeld, Iris Knauer, Elinor Komissar, Evan Konecky, Jeroen Kortenhorst, Gandhi, Gauri & Sanjay Kothari, Denis Krahn, Clare Krebsbach, Katja Kremendahl, Tordis Kremendahl, Soren Kristensen,

THE LONELY PLANET STORY

The story begins with a classic travel adventure: Tony and Maureen Wheeler's 1972 journey across Europe and Asia to Australia. There was no useful information about the overland trail then, so Tony and Maureen published the first Lonely Planet guidebook to meet a growing need.

From a kitchen table, Lonely Planet has grown to become the largest independent travel publisher in the world, with offices in Melbourne (Australia), Oakland (USA) and London (UK). Today Lonely Planet guidebooks cover the globe. There is an ever-growing list of books and information in a variety of media. Some things haven't changed. The main aim is still to make it possible for adventurous travellers to get out there – to explore and better understand the world.

At Lonely Planet we believe travellers can make a positive contribution to the countries they visit – if they respect their host communities and spend their money wisely. Every year 5% of company profit is donated to charities around the world.

Nancy Krudsen **L** Simone Laarmans, Alessandra l'Abate, Mark Langley, John LaPlante, Charlotte Larson, Jules Lasson, Helen Lauritzen, Ceri Lawley, Barbara Lawrence, P N Lawrence, Anthony Lawton, Darren Lee, Michele Lefranc, Karen Lepere, Vicky Levine, Noah Levinson, Michael Lewis, Kyrre Lind, Morten Lindgren, Jonas Lindholm, Jette Lindstrom, Steven Lipari, Samson Litwak, Sarah Livermore, N Logan, Lene Lomholt, Hazel & Roger Lowther **M** Thijs Maas, John MacNamara, Paola Maggiani, Elena Magni, Sahag Mahrejian, Suresh Kumar Mahto, Eric Maier, Patricia Maier, Silvia Maier, Simon Maier, Hitesh Makwana, Andrea Malcouronne, Sonja Marish, Elizabeth Markevitch, Alvin Marks, Robert Marsh, Margeaux Marshall, Roger Martin, Iris Mascarenhas, Toni Maslen, Barry Masters, Janet & Seth Maybin, Claudine Maynard, Wendy McCarty, Laura Mcclelland, Catherine McCormick, Kamran Kingwell McGee, Meridyth McIntosh, Marcus & Emina McPorsche, Vandana Mehta, Max Menendez, Verena Mett, Irmgard Meyer, Neal Michael, Inez Michiels, Liore Milgrom-Elcott, Kerstin Mischke, Bernhard Mittenhuber, Monica Mody, Aymeric Moizard, Shamim Moledina, Francesca Molendini, Daniele Monnier, Nicolas Moroz, Llinos Morris, Claire Morrison, James Morrison, Thomas Mueller, Sandip Mukherjee, Carlos Mundy **N** Ahana Nagda, Sumeer Nagpaul, Bob Naik, Satoshi Nakano, Aravind Narasipur, Sonia Narayanan, Pete Nelson, Willy Nelson, Penny Nettelfield, Ruth Neumeister, Henry Newman, James Newman, P Nielsen, Ted Nobbs, SH Nolte, Lisa Norris **O** Thomas Obitz, Alice O'Connor, Altaire O'Driscoll, Lisa O'Farrell, Kate Olding, Christel Olijslager, David Oliver **P** Peter Padam, Chris Paget, Ned Pakenham, Carmen Palma, Aurojit Panda, Marlis Pantal, Gavin Pardoe, Kajal Parikh, Aristea Parissi, Sally & Alistair Parker, John Pascoe, Mukesh Patel, Jim Peacock, Tara Pearman, Anna-Maria Peeters, Diki Perrottet, Peggy Pfeiffer, Marie-Christine Pic, Barry Pittard, Wilfried Poelmans, Martin Potter, Ben Presnell, Ansula Press, Jay Priebe, Rod Priest, Stanley Proud **Q** John Quinn **R** Anne-Gaelle Rabaud, Raja Raghunath, Susan Rakoczy, Arul Ramiah, Sabin Ranabhat, Eleanor Ransom, Vijayendra Rao, Vinita Rashinkar, Clothilde Regnier, Greg Reigstad, Janet Reigstad, Heidi Reyntjens, Pat Ribbans, Hannah Richardson, Arianna Rinaldo, Mike Rinker, Ben Robson, John Rose, John Rosling, Geoffrey Roth, Sushanta Roy-Choudhury, Catherine Ryan **S** Madhu Sagar, Sheela Sahtoe, K R Sajeev, Daniel Salton, Dusan Samudovsky, Ben Sand, Joachim Sandstrom, Nantha Satgunasingam, Christian

Schafer, Harry Schiechel, E Schillinger, Nicolai Schirawski, Bruno Schmitz, Karin & Manuel Schneider-Gujer, Katrin Schnellmann, Brigitte Schoebi, Sabine Schoska, Kees & Ineke Schouten, Willem-Peter Schouten, Walter Schultz, Ronald Schuurhuizen, Edwin Schuurman, Daniel Schwetka, Rudi Scobie, Mark Scott, Joel Segre, Berenike Sehorst, Gertrud Servo, Martina Sester, Pratish Sharma, Anurag Shekhar, Jeannie Sheppard, Tegan Shohet, Amelia Shoreland, Robert Shroyer, Lena Sieber, Lincoln Siliakus, Nolan Simmons, Gurfateh Phil Singh, E Sivakumar, Karen Slevin, Analisa Smith, Angela Smith, George Smith, Melanie Smith, Will Snell, Peter Snoeckx, Jonas Soderlund, Christian Spanner, Richard Sparks, Melissa Spectre, Fred Spengler, Michael Spice, Jakob Sprickerhof, Keith Springford, V Sreekrishnan, Jonathon Steele, Alexander Stein, Rob Steinbusch, Marsha Stewart, Aviad Stier, David Stillitz, Bob Stirling, James Stone, Balz Strasser, Francoise Strauss, Iselin Aasedotter Stroenen, Wendy Sunney, S Swaminathan, Suzanna Szabo **T** Anna Tapp, Kelly Tarbuck, Robert Tattersall, Dominique Taxi, Sandra Taylor, Robert Temel, Ben Tettlebaum, Mathias Thalmann, Christina Themar, Derek Thompson, Malcolm Thornton, Amelia Tienghi, Dudley Tolkien, Rachael Trainor, Trang Tu, Fredrik Tukk **U** Ejji Umamahesh, Andreas Unterkircher **V** Juha Valimaki, Erwin van Asbeck, Katrien van Damme, Chris Vaughan, Margit Veldhuyzen, Ireen Verdegaal, Jeroen Vermeer, Clem Vetters, Anne Vial, Sharon Vincin, Karen Vingtans, Joseph Vivera, Tim Vivian, Don Vogelesang, Matthias von Schumacher, Joel Voyer, Martine Vuillard **W** Capt Wadehn, Gail Waldby, Craig Walker, Amy Walshe, I M Waters, Trudy Watson, Fay Watts, Kate Webb, Mark Webb, Peter Wehmeier, Nicole Welt, Romy Wessner, Rob Whadcock, Richard White, Mandy Whitton, Jo Wickens, Mandy Wickham, Stefan Wicki, Bianca Wiedemann, Thorsten Wienhold, Simen Wiig, Paul Williams, Damon Wischik, Emily Wouters, Dave & Hannah Wright, Ian Wright, Linda Wright, Sarah Wright **Y** Karen Yakymishen, Phillip Yearwood **Z** Andreas Zahner, Benjamin Zeitlyn, Tobi Zeyher, Ning Zheng, Nadia Zuodar

ACKNOWLEDGMENTS

Many thanks to the following for the use of their content:
Globe on back cover © Mountain High Maps 1993 Digital Wisdom, Inc.

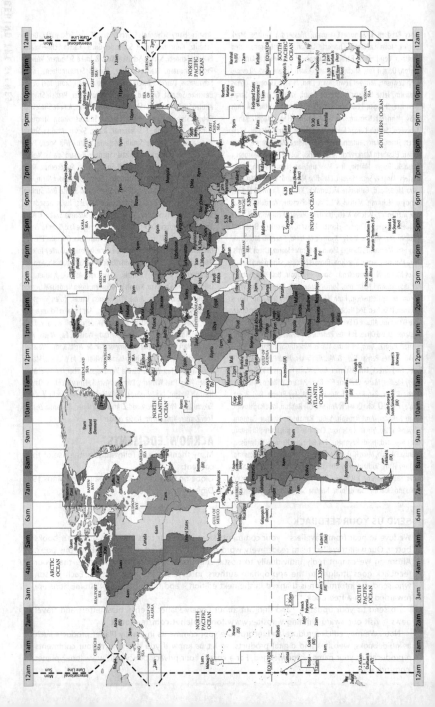

Index

A

accommodation 457-9, *see also individual locations & types of accommodation*
activities 459-61
Adam's Bridge 371
Adivasis 51, 452
Agatti Island 310
Agonda 200
AIDS 51
Aihole 252
air travel 487-90, 492-3
  airline offices 492
  to/from Africa 488
  to/from Asia 488-9
  to/from Australia 489
  to/from Canada 489
  to/from Continental Europe 489
  to/from Delhi 491
  to/from NZ 490
  to/from UK 490
  to/from USA 490
Ajanta 135-8, **136**
Alappuzha, *see* Alleppey
Alleppey 277-82, **281**
Amaravathi 426
Ambedkar, Dr Bhimrao Ramji 140
amphibians 74
Andaman & Nicobar Islands 392-408, **394**
  snorkelling 396
Andamanese people 397
Andhra Pradesh 409-31, **411**
Anegondi 245
animals 69-74, 200 *see also individual species* & national parks & wildlife sanctuaries
  endangered species 70
Anjuna 186-8, **186**
Araku Valley 425-6
Arambol 191-3, **192**
archaeological sites
  Nagarjuna 422-3
architecture 61-3, 196
Arjuna's Penance 334
Arossim 196
arts 59-67, 446-7, *see also individual entries*
  courses 284

A (column 2)

ashrams 464-5
  Brahmavidya Mandir 141-2
  Isha Yoga Center 379-81
  Kaivalyadhama Yoga Hospital 146
  Osho Meditation Resort 151, 465
  Sivananda Yoga Vedanta Dhanwantari 267
  Sri Aurobindo 345, 465
  Sri Ramanasramam 343, 465
Asvem 191
ATMs 473
Aurangabad 128-32, **129**
Auroville 351-2
autorickshaw travel 497
Ayurveda 271, 459-60
  courses 212, 230, 284, 463
  Kochi 293
  Kollam 275
  Madikeri 230
  Mysore 222
  Periyar Wildlife Sanctuary 286
  Trivandrum 264
  Varkala 272-3
Ayyappan 55-6

B

backwater cruises 278-9, 5
Badami 249-52, **250**
Badrama National Park 454
Baga 181-6, **182**
baksheesh 474
Balasore 455
Bandipur National Park 227-8
Bangalore 207-18, **208**, **210**, 6
  accommodation 212-13
  attractions 211-12
  drinking 214-15
  entertainment 215-16
  food 213-14
  shopping 216
  travel to/from 216-18
Bangaram Island 310
bargaining 474
Barheipani Waterfall 454
Baripada 455
Baripalli 453
barking deer 72
Barkul 449-50
bathrooms 459

B (column 3)

Baywatch 374
beach shacks 87
beaches
  Agonda 169, 200
  Anjuna 168
  Arambol 168
  Asvem 168, 191
  Baga 168-9, 181-6, **182**
  Benaulim 169, 196-9
  Bhatya 143
  Bogmalo 169
  Butler Bay 408
  Butterfly 200
  Calangute 168-9, 181-3, **182**
  Candolim 169
  Cavelossim 169, 199-200
  Chandrabhaga 448
  Chapora 188-90, **189**
  Chowpatty 101-2
  Colva 169, 196-9
  Corbyn's Cove 401
  Dhanushkodi 371
  Elephant 404
  Elliot's 321
  Ganpatipule 143
  Goa 168-9
  Gokarna 240-1
  Juhu 105
  Kappil 309
  Kovalam 267-70
  Kudle 241
  Majorda 169
  Mandrem 168
  Marina 321
  Miramar 169, 172
  Morjim 168, 190-1
  Neil Island 406
  Netaji Nagar 408
  Om 241
  Palolem 169, 200-2, 5
  Patnem 169, 200
  Puri 443-4
  Radha Nagar 404
  Rushikonda 424
  Samudra 270-1
  Sinquerim 169, 179
  Tarkarli 143-4
  Vagator 168, 188-90, **189**
  Varca 169, 199-200
  Varkala 272-5

beaches *continued*
Velsao 169
Waltair 424
bears 72
Bekal 309
Belur 233-4
Benaulim 196-9, **197**
berries 156
Betul 200
Bhaja 148
bharata natyam 64
bhattis 420
Bhitarkanika Wildlife Sanctuary 76, 456
Bhubaneswar 435-41, **436**
Bibi-ka-Maqbara 128
bicycle travel, *see* cycling
Bidar 256
Bidri 256
Bijapur 252-6, **253**
bird sanctuaries, *see also* national
parks & wildlife sanctuaries
Calimere Wildlife & Bird Sanctuary
(Kodakarrai) 76, 356
Kumarakom Bird Sanctuary 284
Ranganathittu Bird Sanctuary
77, 227
Thattekkad Bird Sanctuary 289
Vedantangal Bird Sanctuary
77, 337
birds 70-1, 264, 289
bird-watching 460
Mysore 222
blackbucks 72
boat travel 491-2, 494
boat trips 460
Alleppey 278
Candolim Beach 180
Goa 162
Kodai 377
Kollam 275, 278
Panaji 173
Periyar Wildlife Sanctuary 286
Satapada 449
Bogmalo 196
Bollywood 60-1, 104
Bombay, *see* Mumbai
Bondla Wildlife Sanctuary 76, 202
bonnet macaques 73
books 21-2, *see also* literature
animals 70, 71, 73
architecture 62, 63

arts & crafts 66
culture 49, 50, 51, 53, 58, 59, 65
environment 69, 77
history 34, 37, 38, 39, 40, 41, 44,
45, 46
music 61
religion 54, 56, 57
travel 21-2
border crossings 490
Braganza House 195
Brahmins 50
Brihadishwara Temple & Fort
357-8
Brindavan Gardens 227
British East India Company 42-4
Buddha Jayanti 469
Buddha statue 416-17
Buddhism 57
buffalo racing 239
bus travel 494-5
business hours 461-2
Butcher Island 121

C
cafés 87
Calangute 181-3, **182**
Calicut 304-6, **305**
Calimere Wildlife & Bird Sanctuary
(Kodakarrai) 76, 356
camping 458
Candolim 179-81, **180**
Cannanore, *see* Kannur
Cape Comorin, *see* Kanyakumari
car travel 495
hire 495
Cardamom Hills 267
Carnatic 61
carpets 477
cash 473
castes 50-1
Cauvery Delta 356
Cavelossim 199-200
caves
Ajanta 135-8, **136**, 8
Aurangabad 128-9
Badami 249-51
Bhaja 148
Borra 426
Edakal 306
Elephanta Island 120-1
Ellora 133-5, **133**, 8
Gupteswar 453
Kanheri 121
Karla 148
Pandav Leni 127

Udayagiri 438
Viswakarma Cave 133-5, 8
Cellular Jail National Memorial 400
Chandipur 455-6
Chandor 195
Chapora 188-90, **189**
Charminar 415
Chennai 316-30, **318-19**, **322-3**
accommodation 323-5
attractions 320-3
entertainment 326
food 325-6
shopping 327
travel to/from 327-9, 328
travel within 330
Chennamangalam 301
Chhatrapati, Shivaji 41
Chhatrapati Shivaji Terminus 101
Chidambaram 352-4, **353**
child labour 51, 339
children, travel with 462
Chilika Lake 449-50
chinkaras 72
Chinnar Wildlife Sanctuary 289
Chiriya Tapu 404
chitals 72
Chola empire 37-8
Chowara 271-2
chowsinghas 72
Christianity 56-7
Christmas Day 469
churches & cathedrals
Basilica of Bom Jesus 177, 8
Christ Church 288
Church & Convent of St Monica 178
Church of Our Lady of the
Immaculate Conception
(Panaji) 171
Church of Our Lady of the
Immaculate Conception
(Pondicherry) 345
Church of St Augustine 178
Church of St Cajetan 177-8
Convent & Church of St Francis of
Assisi 177
Lourdes Church 362
Notre Dame de Anges 346
Sacred Heart Church 345-6
St Francis Church 292
St John's Church 362
St Stephen's Church 386
St Thomas' Cathedral 101
San Thome Cathedral 321
Se Cathedral 176
cinema 60-1

Cinque Island 404
climate 19-20, 462
clothing 48
Cochin, see Kochi
Coimbatore 379-82, **380**
Colaba **99**
Colva 196-9, **197**
commission agents 467
consulates see high commissions
Coonoor 382-4
costs 20-1
Cotigao Wildlife Sanctuary 200
courses 463-4
    arts & crafts 284
    Ayurveda 212, 230, 284, 463
    cooking 88, 284
    Kalarippayat 464
    language 106, 284, 323, 463
    meditation 417, 463-4
    music 223, 284, 464
    naturopathy 463
    performing arts 264, 347, 464
    yoga 106, 146, 152, 187, 212, 223, 267, 323, 379, 463-4
credit cards 473
cricket 33, 67, 114-15, 216
culture 48-68
customs 88
customs regulations 464-5
Cuttack 455
cycle-rickshaws 497
cycling 460, 493-4

D
Dalits 50
dance 63-6, see also kathakali, theyyam
    bharata natyam 64
    nrityagram 218
    odissi 65
dangers 465-7
Dangmar Island 456
Daulatabad 132-3
Debrigarh Wildlife Sanctuary 76, 453-4
deep vein thrombosis (DVT) 503
deforestation 76
dengue fever 504
departure tax 488
dhabas 86
dhal 81
Dharasuram 355-6
Dharmastala 239
Dhauli 441
dholes 73

Diglipur 407
disabled travellers 467
diving 460
    Andaman & Nicobar Islands 396
    Havelock 404
    health issues related to 507
    Lakshadweep 311
Diwali 469
Dolphin's Nose 382
dolphins 72
dolphin-watching 449
dosas 81
drinks 84-6
    beer 85-6
    nonalcoholic 84-5
    wine 85-6
driving licence 495
drugs 165, 472
Drukpa Teshi 469
Dudhsagar Falls 203
dugongs 72
Dussehra (Durga Puja) 124, 206, 469

E
earthquakes 395
Easter 469
economy 33
Eid al-Adha 470
Eid al-Fitr 469
Eid-Milad-un-Nabi 469
El Shaddai 179
electricity 461
Elephanta Island 120-1
elephants 71
email services 471-2
embassies 467-8
emergencies see inside front cover
Emperor Ashoka 35
encashment certificates 473-4
environmental issues 33, 75-9
Eravikulam National Park 289
Ettumanur 284
exchange rates see inside front cover

F
fax services 480
Fernandes House 195
festivals 20, 22, 468-70
    Andaman & Nicobar Islands 393
    Andhra Pradesh 410
    Buddha Jayanti 469
    Christmas Day 469
    dangers 466
    Diwali 469

Drukpa Teshi 469
Dussehra (Durga Puja) 124, 206, 469
Easter 469
Eid al-Adha 470
Eid al-Fitr 469
Eid-Milad-un-Nabi 469
food 86
Gandhi Jayanti 469
Ganesh Chaturthi 96, 124, 469, 12
Goa 164
Govardhana Puja 469
Holi 164, 470
Independence Day 469
Janmastami 469
Karnataka 206
Kerala 260
Kumbh Mela 470
Losar 470
Maharashtra 124
Mahavir Jayanti 469
Muharram 248, 410, 470
Mumbai 96
Naag Panchami 469
Nanak Jayanti 469
Navratri 469
Orissa 433
Pateti 469
Pongal 470
Raksha Bandhan 469
Ramadan 469
Ramanavami 469
Rath Yatra 433, 444, 469
Republic Day 470
Shivaratri 206, 410, 470
Shravan Purnima 469
Tamil Nadu 315
Thrissur Pooram 303, 12
Vasant Panchami 470
fish 71
fishing 5
    Havelock 404
food 80-4, 470
    contamination 465-6, 507
    courses 88
    etiquette 82, 89
    vegetarian 87
football 67
Fort Aguada 179-81, **180**
forts 62-3
    Aguada 179, **180**
    Barabati 455
    Bekal 309
    Brihadishwara 357-8
    Cabo da Rama 200

forts *continued*
Chandragiri 429
Cochin 291-3, **292**
Danesborg 356
Daulatabad 132-3
Golconda 415-16, **416**
Krishnagiri 343-4
Pratapgad 158
Raigad 158-9
Rajagiri 343-4
St Angelo 308
St George 320
Sindhudurg 144
Terekhol 193
Vellore 340-1
Warangal 423

G
Gandhi, Indira 46
Gandhi Jayanti 469
Gandhi, Mahatma 43, 43-4, 373
Gandhi National Memorial 152
Mani Bhavan 103-4
Sevagram 141
Gandhi, Mohandas, *see* Gandhi, Mahatma
Gandhi National Memorial 152
Ganesh 55-62
Ganesh Chaturthi 96, 124, 206, 469, 12
Gangakondacholapuram 356
Ganpatipule 143
Gateway of India 98-9
gaurs 72
gay travellers 470-1
geography 69
geology 69
Gingee 343-4
Goa 161-203, **163**
Gokarna 240-2, **240**
Golconda Fort 415-16, **416**
Golgumbaz 253-4
Gomateshvara Statue 235
Gopalpur-on-Sea 450-1
Govardhana Puja 469
government accommodation 458
Guindy National Park 321
Gupteswar Cave 453
gurus 465
Guruvayur 304

H
haggling 479
Halebid 233-4
Hampi 242-7, **244**, **245**, 9
hangliding 460-1
Harmal, *see* Arambol
Hassan 232-3, **232**
Havelock Island 404-6, **405**
health 501-8
books 503
deep vein thrombosis (DVT) 503
dengue fever 504
heat stroke 507
hepatitis 504
HIV & AIDs 504
insurance 501
malaria 505
rabies 505-6
traveller's diarrhoea 506
typhoid 506
vaccinations 501-3
websites 503
heat stroke 507
hepatitis 504
high commissions 467-8
hijras 53
hill tribes 383
Hinduism 54-6
Hirapur 441
history 34-47
Aryan tribes 34-5
Bahmani empire 38-9
books 34, 37, 38, 39, 40, 41, 44, 45, 46
British East India Company 42-4
British in India 40, 42-4
Chhatrapati, Shivaji 41
Chola empire 37-8
Dutch in India 40
Gandhi, Indira 46
Gandhi, Mahatma 43-4
Independence 43-6
Liberation Tigers of Tamil Eelam 46
Marathas 41-2
Mauryan empire 35-6
Mughals 41-2
Partition 44
Portuguese in India 39-40, 45
trade 36-7
Veerapan 46
Vijayanagar empire 38-9
hitching 495-6
HIV 51, 504-5
Holi 164, 470
holidays 471

homosexuality 50, *see also* gay travellers, lesbian travellers
horse racing 68
Bangalore 216
Mumbai 115
Ooty 387
horse riding
Kodai 377
Ooty 387
Hospet 247-8
hotels 457-9
houseboats 278-9
Huma 454
Hyderabad 411-22, **412**, **414**
accommodation 418
attractions 415-17
drinking 419-20
entertainment 420
food 418-19
shopping 420
travel to/from 420-2

I
Ibrahim Rouza 254
Igatpuri 127-8
Independence Day 469
Indian foxes 73
Indian wolves 73
Indira Gandhi (Annamalai) Wildlife Sanctuary 76, 379
Injambakkkam 330-1
insect bites 507-8
insurance 471
health 501
Internet access 471-2
Internet resources 23
invertebrates 71-2
Islam 56
IT industry 47
itineraries 16, 24-31
across the Deccan 28, **28**
ashram hopping 30, **30**
beaches & backwaters 25, **25**
coast to coast 26-7, **26**
following the festivals 31, **31**
head for the hills 27, **27**
island hopping 29-30, **29**
South India express 24, **24**
temples & pilgrimages 30, **30**
world heritage sites 31, **31**

J
Jainism 57
Jalgaon 138-9
Janjira 142

Janmastami 469
Japanese B encephalitis 505
Jarawa people 397
Jashipur 454-5
jeep safaris 461
    Wayanad Wildlife Sanctuary 306
jet lag 503-4
jewellery 477
Jeypore 451
Jog Falls 239-40
Jolly World 387
Joranda Waterfall 454
Judaism 57

K
Kadmat Island 311
Kalarippayat 68
    courses 464
kambla 68
Kanchipuram 337, **338**
Kannur 307-9
Kanyakumari 372-5, **373**
Karanji Lake Nature Park 222
Karla 148
Karnataka 204-57, **205**
kathakali 65, 284, 297-9, 298, 304, 12
kayaking 461
Kerala 258-311, **259**
Khandagiri Caves 438
Khiching 454
Khuldabad 133
Knesseth Eliyahod Synagogue 100
Kochi 290-300, **294-5**
    accommodation 293-6
    attractions 291-3
    entertainment 297-9
    food 296-7
    travel to/from 299-300
Kodagu Hills 231-2
Kodai 375-9, **376**
Kodaikanal see Kodai
Kodanad Viewpoint 384
Kodavas 229
kolams 66
Kolhapur 159-60
Kollam 275-7, **276**
Konark 447-9, **447**
Konkan Coast 142-4
Koraput 452
Kotagiri 384
Kotpad 453
Kottayam 282-4, **283**
Kovalam 267-70, **268**
Kozhikode, see Calicut
Kuchipudi 65

Kumarakom Bird Sanctuary 284
Kumbakonam 354-5, **354**
Kumbh Mela 470
Kumily 285-7, **285**

L
Laad Bazaar 415
Lakshadweep 309-11, **310**
Lakshmi 55-62
Lalitgiri 456
Lamb's Rock 382
language 509-14
    courses 106, 284, 323, 463
    food vocabulary 88-90
laughter clubs 106
laundry 472
leatherwork 477
left luggage 500
legal matters 472
leopards 73
Lepakshi 431
lesbian travellers 470-1
Liberation Tigers of Tamil Eelam 46
lions 121
literature 59-60, 75, 114
Little Andaman 408
Lonar Meteorite Crater 139
Lonavla 146-8, **147**
Long Island 407
Losar 470
Loutolim 195-6

M
Madgaon, see Margao
Madikeri 229-31
Madras, see Chennai
Madurai 364-70, **365**
magazines 68, 461
Mahabaleshwar 156-8, **157**
Mahabalipuram, see Mamallapuram
Mahabharata 60
Mahakuta Temple 252
Mahamakham Tank 355
Maharashtra 122-60, **123**
Mahatma Gandhi Marine National
    Park 76, 404
Mahavir Jayanti 469
Mahalaxmi Dhobi 104
malaria 505
Malik-e-Maidan 254
Malvan 143-4
Mamallapuram 331-7, **332**, 9
Mandrem 191
Mandya District 227
Mangalore 235-8, **236**

mangroves 76-7
maps 472
Mapusa 178-9
Marathas 41-2
Margao 193-5, **194**
Mariamman Teppakkulam Tank 367
Matha Amrithanandamayi 465
Matheran 144-6, **145**
Matrimandir 351
Maurya, Chandragupta 35-6
media 68
medical services 503
Mehndi 67
Mehta, Gita 60
Mercara, see Madikeri
metalwork 477
metric conversions see inside front
    cover
Middle Andaman 407
Minicoy Island 311
mining 78
Mistry, Rohinton 59
Mohiniyattam 65
Molem & Bhagwan Mahavir Wildlife
    Sanctuary 76, 202-3
money 20-1, 473-5, see also inside
    front cover
moneychangers 474
monkeys 73
monsoon 20
Morjim 190-1
mosques
    Haji Ali's 104
    Jama Masjid 254
    Mecca Masjid 254, 415
motion sickness 503-4
motorcycle travel 460, 496, 497
Mt Arunachaleswar 342-3
Mt Harriet 403
mouse deer 72
Mudabidri 239
Mudumalai National Park 390-1
Mughals 41-2
Muharram 248, 410, 470
Mumbai 91-121, **92**, **94-5**, **97**,
    102-3, 6
    accommodation 106-10
    activities 105
    attractions 98-105
    courses 106
    drinking 112-13
    entertainment 113-15
    festivals 96
    food 110-12
    Internet access 96

Munbai *continued*
  itineraries 93
  medical services 96
  shopping 115-16
  tourist information 98
  tours 106
  travel to/from 116-19
  travel within 119-20
  walking tour 105-6, **105**
Munnar 287-8, **289**
Murud 142-3
Murugan 55-62
museums & galleries
  Anthropological Museum 400
  AP State Museum 417
  Archaeological Museum (Badami) 251
  Archaeological Museum (Hampi) 245
  Archaeological Museum (Konark) 448
  Archaeological Museum (Old Goa) 177
  Archaeological Museum (Thrissur) 301
  Birla Planetarium & Science Museum 417
  Chandrakant Mandare Museum 159
  Chennai 320-1
  Chhatrapati Shivaji Maharaj Vastu Sangrahalaya 100
  Cubbon Park 211
  Folklore Museum 222
  Forest Museum 401
  Goa State Museum 171
  Godly Museum 221
  Health Museum 417
  Hill Palace Museum 301
  Indira Gandhi Rashtriya Manav Sangrahalaya 222
  Indo-Portuguese Museum 292
  Jayachamarajendra Art Gallery 222
  Jehangir Art Gallery 100
  Kanyakumari 374
  Kochi 293
  Krishnapuram Palace Museum 277
  Madurai 367
  Mani Bhavan 103-4
  Museum of Christian Art 178

  Museum of Tribal Arts & Artefacts 438
  Nagarjunakonda Museum 422
  National Gallery of Modern Art 100
  Orissa Modern Art Gallery 438
  Pondicherry Museum 345
  Puthe Maliga Palace Museum 263
  Raja Dinkar Kelkar Museum 151, 151-2
  Regional Science Centre 437-8
  Salar Jung Museum 415
  Samudrika Marine Museum 400
  Shivaji 130
  Shree Chhatrapati Shahu Museum 159
  State Museum 438
  Tata Tea Museum 287
  Thanjavur 358
  Tribal Cultural Museum 152
  Tribal Museum 452
  Tribal Research Centre 386
  Trivandrum 264
  Vellore 341
  Vivekananda Exhibition 373
  Vivekanandapuram 373
  Wayanad Heritage Museum 306
music 61
  courses 223, 284, 464
Muttukadu 331
Mysore 218-25, **219**, 7
  accommodation 223-4
  activities 222-3
  attractions 220-2
  food 224
  shopping 225
  travel to/from 225

N
Naag Panchami 469
Nagarhole National Park 228
Nagarjuna 422-3
Nagpur 139-41
Namdroling monastery 229
Nanak Jayanti 469
Nandankanan Zoological Park 441
Nandi Hills 218
Narayan, RK 59
Nasik 125-7, **125**
Nataraja 352-3
Natharvala Dargah 362
national parks & wildlife sanctuaries 74-5, 76-7, *see also* bird sanctuaries

  Badrama National Park 454
  Bandipur National Park 77, 227-8
  Bhitarkanika National Park 76, 456
  Bondla Wildlife Sanctuary 76, 202
  Calimere Wildlife & Bird Sanctuary (Kodakarrai) 76, 356
  Chinnar Wildlife Sanctuary 289
  Cotigao Wildlife Sanctuary 200
  Debrigarh Wildlife Sanctuary 76, 453-4
  Eravikulam National Park 289
  Guindy National Park 321
  Indira Gandhi (Annamalai) Wildlife Sanctuary 76, 379
  Mahatma Gandhi National Marine Park 76, 404
  Molem & Bhagwan Mahavir Wildlife Sanctuary 76, 202-3
  Mudumalai National Park 77, 390-1
  Nagarhole National Park 77, 228
  Navagaon National Park 76, 139
  Parambikulam Wildlife Sanctuary 290
  Periyar Wildlife Sanctuary 77, 284-7, **285**
  Sanjay Gandhi National Park 77, 121
  Similipal National Park 77, 454
  Tadoba-Andhari Tiger Reserve 77, 139
  Wayanad Wildlife Sanctuary 77, 306-7
naturopathy
  Bangalore 212
  courses 463
Navagaon National Park 76, 139
Navratri 469
Neil Island 406-7
newspapers 68, 461
Nicobar Islands 392-408, **394**
Nicobarese people 397
nilgai 72
Nilgiri Hills 382-90, **382**
Nilgiri langur 73
Nilgiri tahr 289
Nine Planets' Shrine 448
North Andaman 407

O
odissi 65
Old Goa 176-8, **176**, 8
olive ridley turtles 70, 450
Onge people 397
Onkadelli 452

Ooty 384-90, **385**
organised tours 498
Orissa 432-56, **434**
orphanages 334
Osho Meditation Resort 151, 465

P
paan 88
Padmanabhapuram Palace 272
paintings 478
palaces 62-3
Aga Khan 152
Asar 254
Bangalore 212
Krishnapuram 277
Lotus 244
Maharaja 220, 9
Mattancherry 293
Padmanabhapuram 272
Puthe Maliga 263
Shaniwar Wada 152
Thanjavur 358
Tipu Sultan 211-12
Tirumalai Nayak 366-7
Tranquebar 356
Palampet 424
Palolem 200-2, **201**
Panaji 167-76, **170-1**, 6
accommodation 173-4
attractions 171-2
entertainment 174-5
food 174
travel to/from 175
walking tour 172, **172**
Panchakki 130
Pandav Leni 127
Panjim, see Panaji
paragliding 460-1
Arambol 191
Parambikulam Wildlife Sanctuary 290
Pardesi Synagogue 293
parks & gardens
Botanical Gardens 386
Brindavan Gardens 227
Bryant Park 376-7
Centenary Rose Park 386
Chettiar Park 377
Cubbon Park 211
Empress Botanical Gardens 152
Indira Gandhi Park 417
Karanji Lake Nature Park 222
Lalbagh Botanical Gardens 211
Sim's Park 382
Thread Garden 386
Parsi community 101

Parur 301
Parvati 55-62
passports 487
Pateti 469
Pattadakal 252
Periyar Wildlife Sanctuary 77, 284-7,
285
permits
Andaman & Nicobar Islands 394-6
Lakshadweep 309-10
Tamil Nadu 315
photography 475
etiquette 52
pilgrimages
Sravanabelagola 234-5
Tirumala 427
Pipli 441
planetariums
Birla Planetarium & Science
Museum 417
Nehru 104
Pathani Samanta 438
planning 19-23
plants 74
plastic waste 79
politics 32
pollution 78
air 79, 506-7
Ponda 202
Pondicherry 344-51, **346-7**,
347-8
accommodation 348-9
attractions 345-7
food 349
travel to/from 350
Pongal 470
Ponmudi 267
population 32, 53
Port Blair 398-403, **399**
postal services 475-6
pottery 66
poverty 52-3
Pulinkudi 271-2
Pune 149-56, **150**, 7
accommodation 152-3
attractions 151
food 153-4
travel to/from 154-5
Puri 441-6, **442**
Puttaparthi 430-1

Q
Qadam-i-Rasool shrine 455
Quilon, see Kollam
Qutb Shahi Tambl 416

R
rabies 505-6
radio 461
rafting 461
Raghurajpur 446-7
Raigad Fort 158-9
railway retiring rooms 458
Raksha Bandhan 469
Ramadan 469
Ramanavami 469
Ramayana 60
Rambha 450
Rameswaram 370-2, **370**
Ramkund 126
Ramoji Film City 417
Ramtek 141
Ranganathittu Bird Sanctuary 77, 227
Rath Yatra festival 433, 444, 469
Ratnagiri 143, 456
religion 48, 53-8
etiquette 52
reptiles 74
Republic Day 470
responsible travel 165
diving 460
shopping 476
restaurants 86-7
resthouses 458
Ross Island 403, 407
Roy, Arundhati 59
Rushdie, Salman 60
Rushikulya 450

S
Saddle Peak 407
safaris, see jeep safaris, wildlife safaris
safe travel
druggings 466-7
hitching 495-6
Sai Baba 430, 465
St Francis Xavier 177
Sambalpur 453
sambar 72
Samudra Beach 270
sandalwood 221, 225
Sanjay Gandhi National Park 77, 121
saris 478
Satapada 449
scams 466
sculpture 63
Secunderabad, see Hyderabad
senior travellers 467
Senji, see Gingee
Sentinelese people 397
Sevagram 141

shawls 478
Shiva 55-62
Shivaratri 206, 410, 470
sholas 74
Shompen people 397
shopping 446, 476-80
Shravan Purnima 469
silk 339, 478
Similipal National Park 77, 454
Sinhagad 156
Sivasamudram 227
slender loris 73
Smith Island 407
smoking 472
snorkelling 460, *see also* diving
  Andaman & Nicobar Islands 396
  Havelock 404
soccer, *see* football
Somnathpur 226
spices 80, 202, 286
sport 67-8, 114-15, *see also* individual
  sports
Sravanabelagola 234-5
Sri Aurobindo Ashram 465
Sri Kalahasti 429-30
Sri Ramanasramam Ashram 465
Sringeri 238-9
Srirangapatnam 226-7
STDs 506
stone carvings 478
street food 87
Sun Temple 447-8, 11
sunburn 508
swimming 466, *see also* beaches
  currents 466
  Kochi 293

T
Tadoba-Andhari Tiger Reserve 77, 139
Tamil Nadu 312-91, **314**
Tanjore, *see* Thanjavur
Taptapani 451
taxes 459
taxis 497-8
tea 286
telephone services 480-1
temples 458, *see also* mosques,
  churches & cathedrals
  Airatesvara 355-6
  Arunachaleswar 342
  Babulnath 102

Bhandari Basti 235
Bhavani Mandap 159
Birla 417
Brahmeswar Mandir 437
Brihadishwara 356, 357-8
Bull 211
Chandragupta Basti 235
Chandranatha 239
Chandranatha Basti 235
Channekeshava 233
Cheluvanarayana 227
Devarajaswami 339, 11
Durga 252
Five Rathas 333-4
Ganapati 240
Gandamadana Parvatham 371
Ganesh Ratha 334
Golden 229
Gumpha Panchivati 126
Hanamkonda 423
Hoysaleswara 234
Iskcon 211
Jagannath Mandir 443, 11
Jalakanteshwara 341
Janardhana 272
Kadri Manjunatha 237
Kailasa 134
Kailasanatha 338
Kala Rama 126
Kamakshi Amman 339
Kanaka Durga 426
Kapaleeshwarar 321
Kedargauri 437
Keshava 226
Koorti 240
Kothandaraswamy 371
Krishna 238
Kumari Amman 372-3
Kumbeshwara 354
Lakshminarayana 227
Lingaraj Mandir 437
Maa Kichakeswari 454
Mahabaleshwara 240
Mahakuta 252
Mahalaxmi 104, 159
Mallikarjuna 227
Manjunatha 239
Mukteswar 437
Muktidham 126
Nageshwara 355
Omkareshwara 230
Parsurameswar 437
Pataleshvara 152
Raja Rani 437
Ramakrishna Mutt 321

Ramanathaswamy 371
Ramappa 424
Rock Fort 360-1
Sarangapani 354
Saumyakeshava 227
Shiva 284
Shore 333
Shri Mahalsa 202
Shri Manguesh 202
Shri Shantadurga 202
Siddheswar 437
Sree Vallabha 284
Sri Chamundeswari 221
Sri Ekambaranathar 338-9
Sri Jambukeshwara 361-2
Sri Kalahasteeswara 429-30
Sri Krishna 304
Sri Manakula Vinayagar 346-7
Sri Meenakshi 366, 10
Sri Padmanabhaswamy 263
Sri Ranganathaswamy 361
Sun 447-8, 11
Sundar Narayan 126
Trimbakeshwar 127
Trimurti 334
Undavalli 426
Vadakkunathan Kshetram 301
Vaikunta Perumal 339-42, 10
Vaital 437
Vedagirishvara 337
Veerbhadra 431
Venkateshwara 427-8
Vidyashankar 239
Vimaleswar 454
Virupaksha (Hampi) 243
Virupaksha (Pattadakal) 252
Vittala 243
Walkeshwar 103
Yoganarasimha 227
Yogini 441
Zangdogpalri 229
Terekhol Fort 193
textiles 66-7, 478
thalis 82
Thanjavur 356-60, **357**
Tharangambadi, *see* Tranquebar
Thattekkad Bird Sanctuary 289
theft 466-7
theyyam 65, 308
Thiruvaiyaru 360
Thiruvananthapuram, *see* Trivandrum
Thrissur 301-3, **302**
Thrissur Pooram 303, 12
Tibetan settlements 228-9
tigers 72-3, 121, 454

time 481
tipping 474
Tiracol, *see* Terkhol Fort
Tiruchirappalli, *see* Trichy
Tirukkalikundram 337
Tirumala 427
Tirupathi 427
Tiruvannamalai 342-3
toilets 481, *see also* bathrooms
Torda 178
tourist bungalows 458
tourist information 481-2
tours 498
touts 467
train travel 498-500
    classes 499
    famous routes 498
    fares 499-500
    passes 500
    to/from Delhi 491
Tranquebar 356
travel permits 482
travellers cheques 474-5
traveller's diarrhoea 506
trekking 461
    Kodagu region 230
    Ooty 386
Trichur, *see* Thrissur
Trichy 360-4, **361, 362**
Trimbak 127
Tripunithura 301
Trivandrum 261-7, **262**
    accommodation 264-5
    attractions 263-4
    entertainment 265-6
    food 265
    travel to/from 266-7
tsunami 32, 395
tuberculosis 506
Tughlaq, Muhammed 38
turtles 450
TV 68, 461
typhoid 506

U

Udayagiri 456
Udhagamandalam, *see* Ooty
Udupi 238
Untouchables, *see* Dalits

V

vaccinations 501-3
Vagator 188-90, **189**
Vailankanni 356
Varca 199-200
Varkala 272-5, **273**
Vasant Panchami 470
Vedantangal Bird Sanctuary 77,
    337
Veerapan 46
vegetarian travellers 87
Velanganni, *see* Vailankanni
Vellore 340-2, **341**
Venur 239
Vijayanagar empire 38-9, 242
Vijayawada 426-7
Viper Island 403
Visakhapatnam 424-5
visas 482-3, *see also* passports
Vishnu 54-5
Viswakarma Cave 133-5, **8**
Vivekananda Memorial 374
Vizag, *see* Visakhapatnam
volunteer work 483-5
    Andhra Pradesh 483
    Goa 483
    Karnataka 483
    Maharashtra 484
    Mumbai 484
    Orissa 484
    Tamil Nadu 484

W

walking tours
    Mumbai 105-6, **105**
    Panaji 172, **172**
Wandoor 403-4
Warangal 423-4
water
    conservation 78
    pollution 78
    purification 507
water sports 162, 460, *see*
    also individual sports

Baga 183
Calangute 183
waterfalls
    Catherine Falls 384
    Dudhsagar Falls 203
    Jog Falls 239-40
    Silver Cascade 377
Wayanad Wildlife Sanctuary
    306-7
weaving 308
weights & measures 461, *see also*
    inside front cover
Western Ghats (Kerala) 284-90
Western Ghats (Tamil Nadu)
    375-91
white-water rafting 461
wildlife safaris 461
    Sanjay Gandhi National Park
        121
wine 127
women in South India 58-9
women travellers 467, 485-6
women's health 508
woodcarving 478-9

Y

Yakshagana 65-6
yoga
    Anjuna 187
    Bangalore 212
    Chennai 323
    Coimbatore 379
    courses 463-4
    Lonavla 146
    Mumbai 106
    Mysore 223
    Ponmudi 267
    Pune 152

Z

zoos
    Mysore Zoo 222
    Nandankanan Zoological Park
        441
    Nehru Zoological Park 417
    Port Blair 400
Zoroastrianism 57-8

INDEX

540

MAP LEGEND

ROUTES

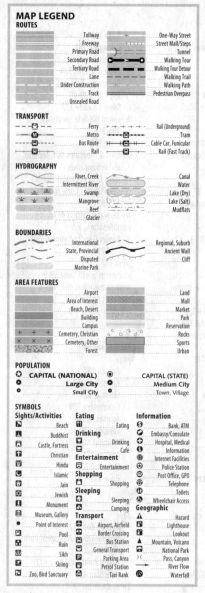

Tollway	One-Way Street
Freeway	Street Mall/Steps
Primary Road	Tunnel
Secondary Road	Walking Tour
Tertiary Road	Walking Tour Detour
Lane	Walking Trail
Under Construction	Walking Path
Track	Pedestrian Overpass
Unsealed Road	

TRANSPORT

Ferry	Rail (Underground)
Metro	Tram
Bus Route	Cable Car, Funicular
Rail	Rail (Fast Track)

HYDROGRAPHY

River, Creek	Canal
Intermittent River	Water
Swamp	Lake (Dry)
Mangrove	Lake (Salt)
Reef	Mudflats
Glacier	

BOUNDARIES

International	Regional, Suburb
State, Provincial	Ancient Wall
Disputed	Cliff
Marine Park	

AREA FEATURES

Airport	Land
Area of Interest	Mall
Beach, Desert	Market
Building	Park
Campus	Reservation
Cemetery, Christian	Rocks
Cemetery, Other	Sports
Forest	Urban

POPULATION

○ CAPITAL (NATIONAL)	◉ CAPITAL (STATE)
● Large City	● Medium City
● Small City	● Town, Village

SYMBOLS

Sights/Activities
- Beach
- Buddhist
- Castle, Fortress
- Christian
- Hindu
- Islamic
- Jain
- Jewish
- Monument
- Museum, Gallery
- Point of Interest
- Pool
- Ruin
- Sikh
- Skiing
- Zoo, Bird Sanctuary

Eating
- Eating

Drinking
- Drinking
- Café

Entertainment
- Entertainment

Shopping
- Shopping

Sleeping
- Sleeping
- Camping

Transport
- Airport, Airfield
- Border Crossing
- Bus Station
- General Transport
- Parking Area
- Petrol Station
- Taxi Rank

Information
- Bank, ATM
- Embassy/Consulate
- Hospital, Medical
- Information
- Internet Facilities
- Police Station
- Post Office, GPO
- Telephone
- Toilets
- Wheelchair Access

Geographic
- Hazard
- Lighthouse
- Lookout
- Mountain, Volcano
- National Park
- Pass, Canyon
- River Flow
- Waterfall

LONELY PLANET OFFICES

Australia
Head Office
Locked Bag 1, Footscray, Victoria 3011
☎ 03 8379 8000, fax 03 8379 8111
talk2us@lonelyplanet.com.au

USA
150 Linden St, Oakland, CA 94607
☎ 510 893 8555, toll free 800 275 8555
fax 510 893 8572, info@lonelyplanet.com

UK
72–82 Rosebery Ave,
Clerkenwell, London EC1R 4RW
☎ 020 7841 9000, fax 020 7841 9001
go@lonelyplanet.co.uk

Published by Lonely Planet Publications Pty Ltd
ABN 36 005 607 983

© Lonely Planet 2005

© photographers as indicated 2005

Cover photographs by Lonely Planet Images: People riding costumed elephants holding unbrellas at Elephant festival in Ernakulam, Eddie Gerald (front); Palolem Beach at sunset, Craig Pershouse (back). Many of the images in this guide are available for licensing from Lonely Planet Images: www.lonelyplanetimages.com

Printed through Colorcraft Ltd, Hong Kong.
Printed in China